AF328435

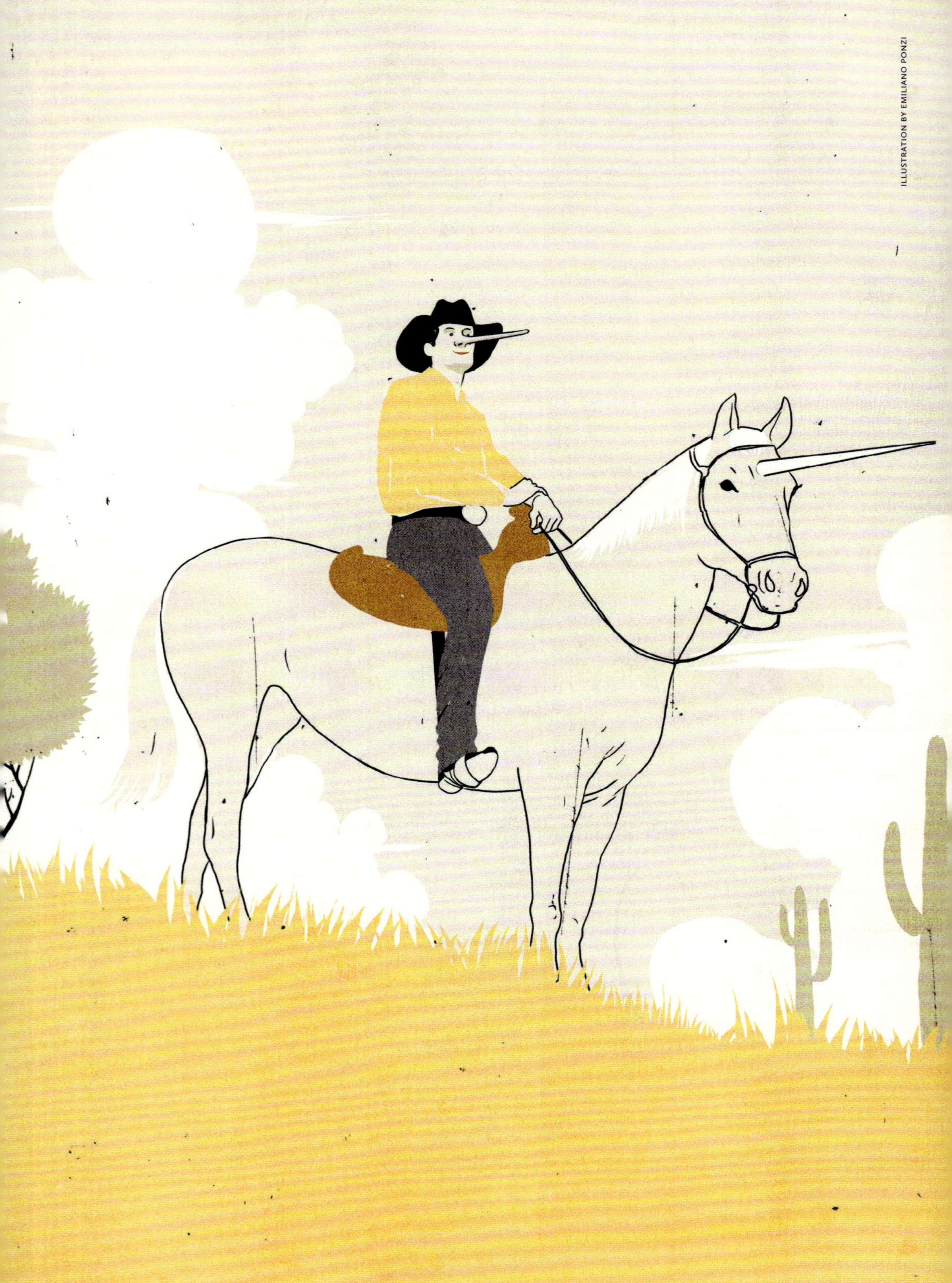

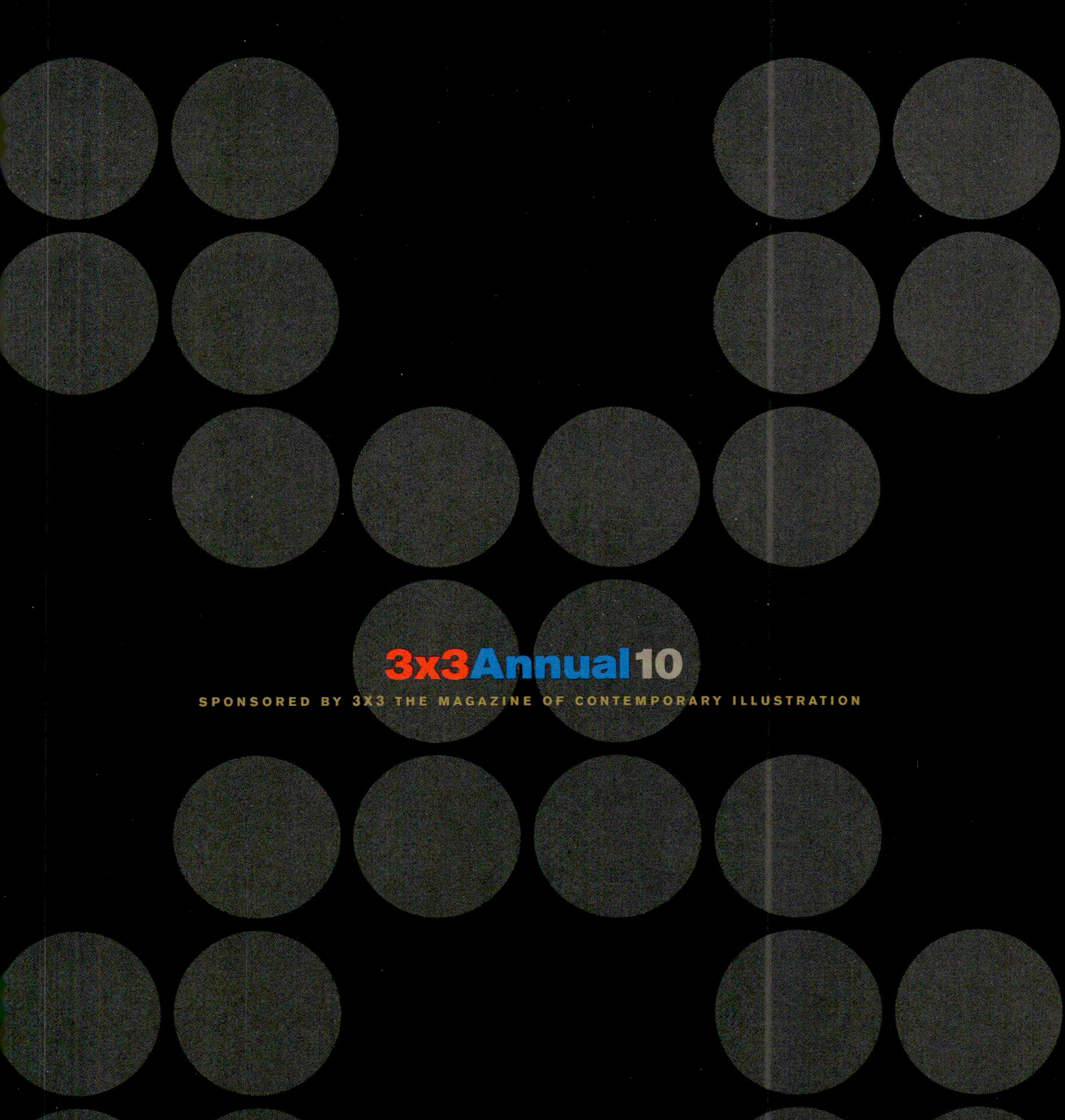
3x3 Annual 10
SPONSORED BY 3X3 THE MAGAZINE OF CONTEMPORARY ILLUSTRATION

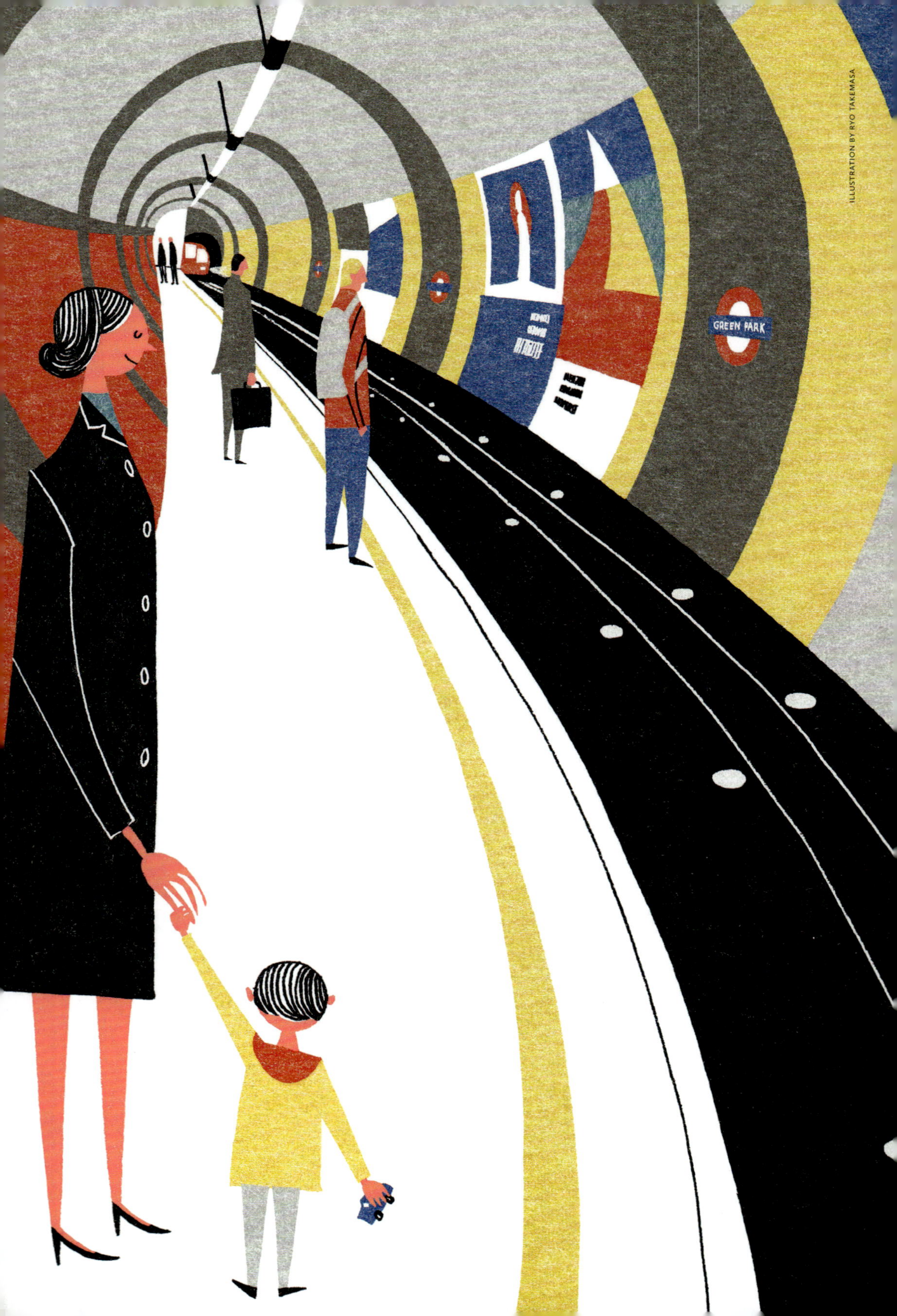

GREEN PARK
ILLUSTRATION BY RYO TAKEMASA

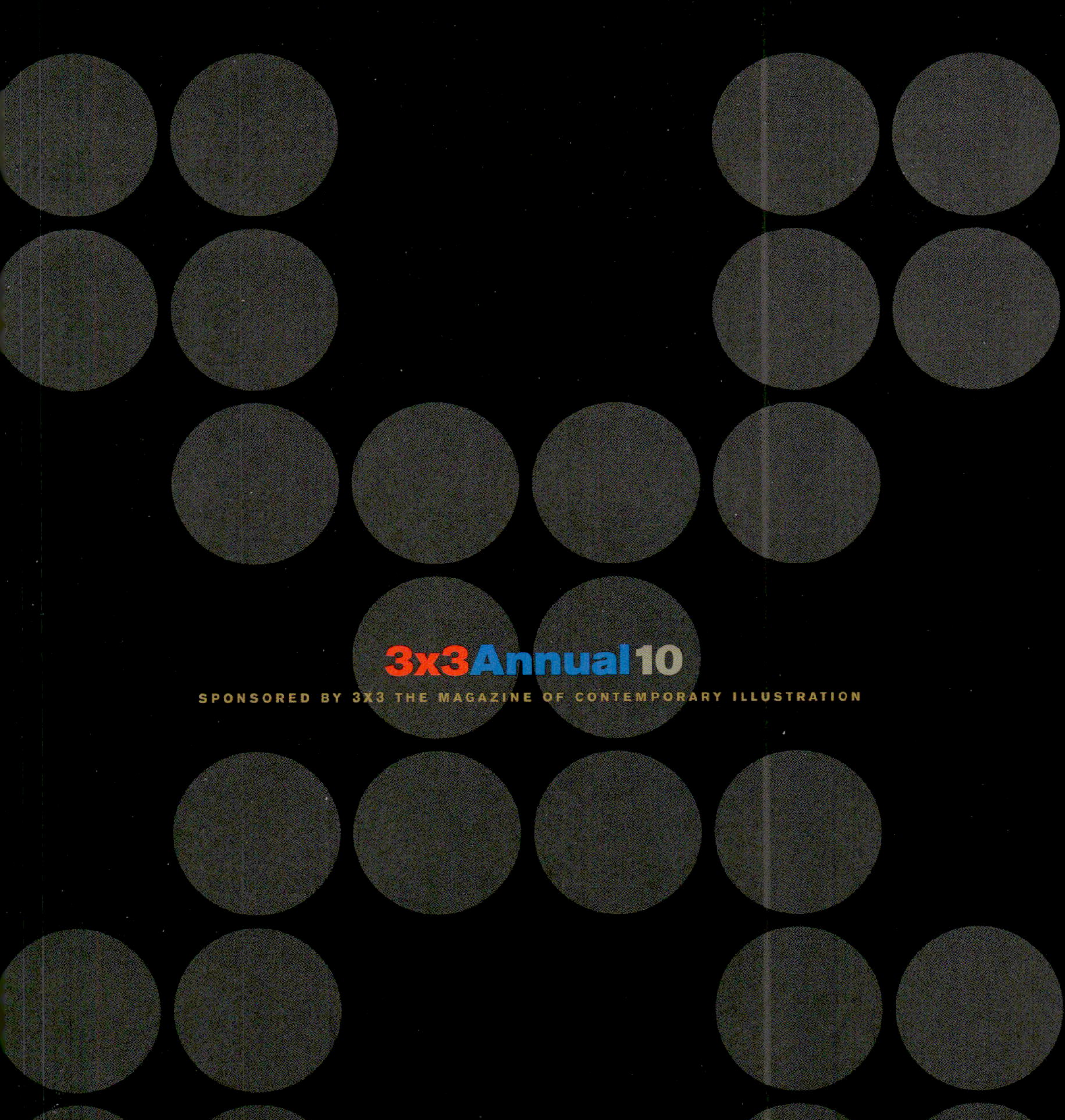
3x3 Annual 10
SPONSORED BY 3X3 THE MAGAZINE OF CONTEMPORARY ILLUSTRATION

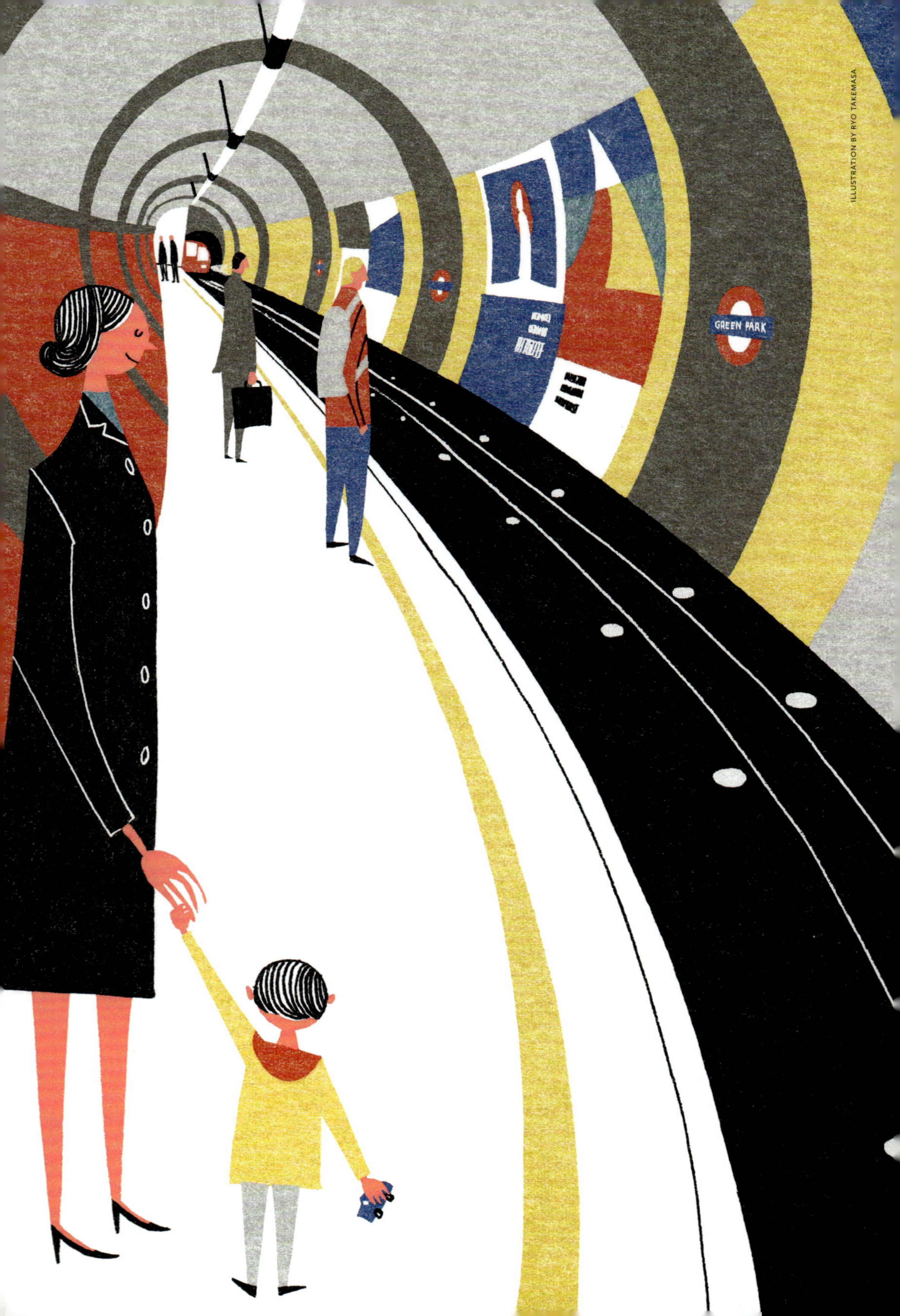

GREEN PARK

CONTENTS

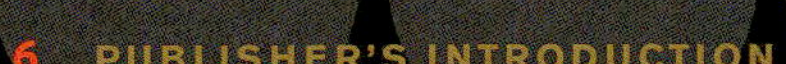

6   PUBLISHER'S INTRODUCTION

7   ILLUSTRATOR : EDUCATOR OF THE YEAR

11   PROFESSIONAL SHOW

293   PICTURE BOOK SHOW

367   STUDENT SHOW

427   INDEX

WELCOME TO THE TENTH ANNUAL COMPILATION OF SOME OF THE BEST ILLUSTRATION DONE IN THE LAST CALENDAR YEAR. WE CAN TRULY SAY THIS IS ONE OF THE FEW IF ONLY ILLUSTRATION ANNUALS WHERE THERE IS A DISTINCT INTERNATIONAL FLAVOR. IT ALL STARTS WITH OUR PANEL OF JUDGES—A SELECT GROUP OF INTERNATIONAL ART DIRECTORS AND DESIGNERS WHO COMMISSION ILLUSTRATION FOR NEWSPAPERS, MAGAZINES, BOOKS, CHILDREN'S BOOKS, ADVERTISING AND A WIDE VARIETY OF ASSIGNMENTS—JOINED BY A EQUALLY DISTINGUISHED GROUP OF ILLUSTRATORS. UNLIKE OTHER SHOWS OUR JUDGES WORK INDEPENDENTLY OVER A TWO-WEEK PERIOD WITHOUT PREJUDICE OR COUNSEL. AND UNLIKE TOO MANY ANNUALS WE HAVE NO QUOTA, NO MAGIC NUMBER WE'RE TRYING TO MATCH TO A SPECIFIC PAGE COUNT. EVERY VOTE MATTERS.

AS WE LOOK BACK OVER OUR TEN YEARS OF COMPETITIONS IT REMAINS CLEAR THAT THE VITALITY OF ILLUSTRATION NEVER CEASES TO AMAZE NOR THE TALENT DIMINISHES IN ITS ABSOLUTE POWER TO PERSUADE. BOUNDARIES DO NOT EXIST WHEN IT COMES TO PRODUCING WORTHY ILLUSTRATIONS; NO ONE COUNTRY MONOPOLIZES THE TALENT OF ARTISTS. IMAGES RING TRUE NO MATTER THE NATIVE LANGUAGE.

NOW MAY WE SUGGEST YOU FIND A COMFORTABLE SEAT AND TAKE YOUR TIME RELISHING THIS YEAR'S WINNING IMAGES. *ENJOY!*   —THE PUBLISHER

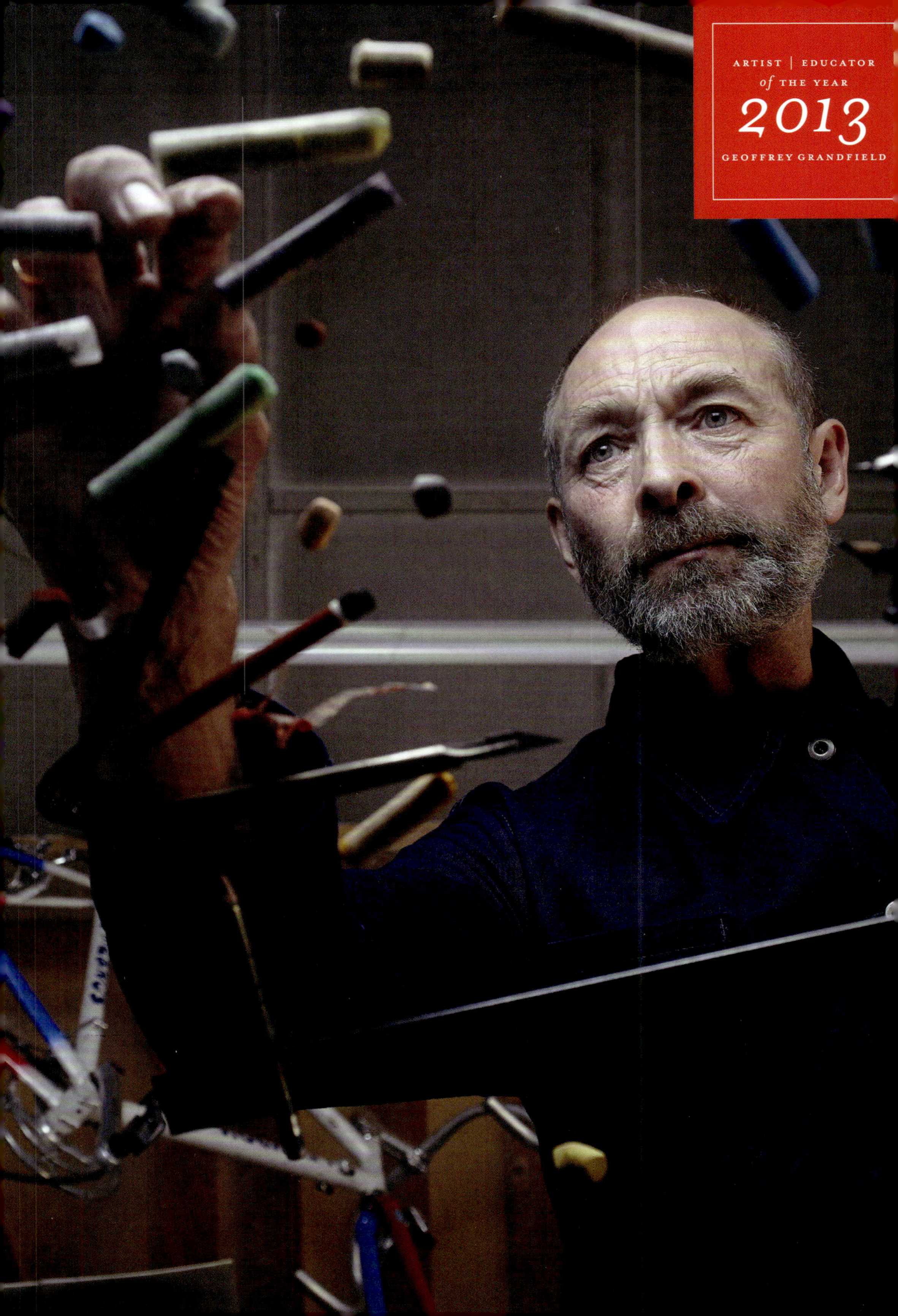

ARTIST | EDUCATOR
of THE YEAR
2013
GEOFFREY GRANDFIELD

GEOFFREY GRANDFIELD loves film noir and it shows. Ask him about influences and he's likely to cite cinematographers, not artists. His path to illustration was pretty much a straight line. Undergrad, graduate school, profession. His approach to subject matter recalls films from the 30s; his choice of perspective and lighting is guided by filmmakers. Something new from something old. Graduating from the Royal College of Art he won the Folio Society first prize for illustration, other awards followed including multiple gold medals from Association of Illustrators, D&AD pencils and Creative Review to name a few. He was listed as one of the top ten illustrators in Great Britain in 2003 by The Independent on Sunday. Principally an editorial illustrator he also counts The Royal Mail, Peguin and Folio Society among his clients. That's when he's not leading the illustration program at Kingston University outside London. With his continued dedication to the field of illustration and his commitment to guiding the next generation of illustrators we are pleased to honor him as our 3x3 Illustrator/Educator of the Year, 2013.

Q Did you always want to be an artist? Do you come from an artistic family?

A I was adopted and had no knowledge of my biological mother and father, so the common question 'where did that talent come from' had a bit more complexity.

I'm not sure I ever consciously intended to be an artist, making work was just a very natural part of what I did with my time and I think perhaps a kind of identity therapy.

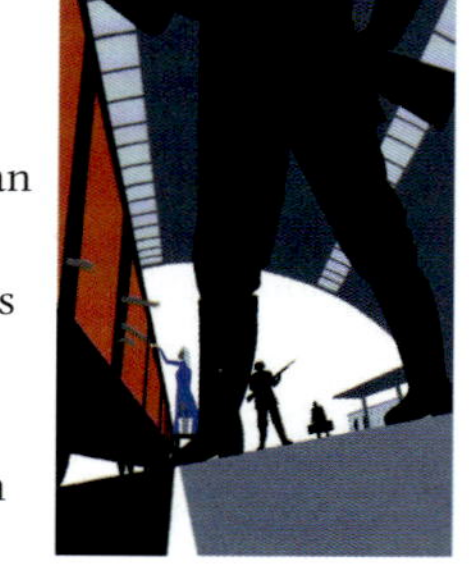

There was a colored pencil drawing of a golden eagle, made when I was five or six that prompted my school teacher to tell my parents that I had 'exceptional talent.' By the time I went to secondary school painting and drawing was very central to who I was and art teachers would single me out to do extra projects, all of which I enjoyed.

I didn't really know anything about art college, no one in my family had been to any form of further education; in 1977 the emphasis was on being lucky enough to get a job. My parents were eventually supportive, though even after graduating from the Royal College of Art (RCA) my mother still suggested that if things don't work out "would I get a job in a bank like the boy next door?"

Q What were some of your early influences?

A If I'm honest I should acknowledge how much I greatly admired the album artwork of Roger Dean, I have no idea why and it's not very cool now.

In 1977 I saw a picture by Russell Mills in a *Sunday Times Magazine* article—it had an odd, disjointed collage composition which I loved, and transpired as an example of the group of Radical illustrators who had emerged from the RCA including Sue Coe and Robert Mason. By that time I was looking at Egon Schiele and Otto Dix and it was apparent to my freshly contextualized eyes how Russell Mills was influenced by Kurt Schwitters and Hannah Höch.

His picture lead me to find out a bit about illustration, where he studied and what an illustrator did. Although Russell evolved in a few years into a more abstract voice, that early body of work remained my key inspiration to become an illustrator.

Mills studied at Maidstone College of Art in Kent and at the Royal College of Art. What I didn't know when I applied at Maidstone was he actually did the graphic design course there and spent most of his time in the refuge of the printmaking area. Maidstone's program was at first a little disappointing, as I thought I was joining 'illustration central' only to find that not everyone there was as obsessive. It wasn't until I started my post-grad at RCA that I really felt illustration could take you anywhere.

Q What led you to a career in illustration?

A I loved the democracy (and still do) of illustration.

For me it is the best communication form, the immediacy of image, visualizing imagination, the inclusivity of representation, the fact it has a job to do and fulfills a need. All these factors were there for me early on and although the style of work certainly modifies through technology and cultural influence they still inspire.

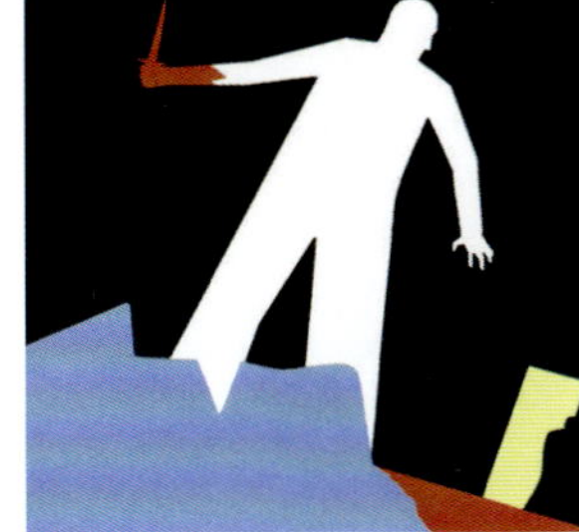

Q What formed your particular vision?

A During the foundation year I discovered 1930s objective photographers like Walker Evans and Bill Brandt and think they influenced my work more than painters or illustrators. Also the imagery of afternoon movies, westerns and crime films were a key visual and narrative inspiration—how black and white could still be vivid in emotional and imaginative terms.

Q How did you get your first big break?

A I was lucky enough to get a Picador cover commission from art director Gary Day-Ellison in my final year at the RCA. And at my post-graduate show I met art director Steve Abbis who commissioned me on the spot for Collins. It all seemed straightforward!

Q Why the choice of editorial illustration?

A Editorial can be uninspiring, but its the mundanity that often kicks start the creative challenge. Editorial often provides a great immediacy and interpretative freedom, it's exciting to start the process against the clock and not know what is going to be the solution. I find it very creatively engaging to illustrate ideas, other peoples and my own, literature, music, especially film; but to render someone elses 'concept' in variations of my 'style' doesn't work for me.

Q How has your work progressed?

A Through deadlines and pressure, I think my visual language has paired down to more essential elements. In terms of the commission process there are advantages in having a kind of genre around

the work. I tend to get material that has doubt, deception, intrigue embedded in it—those themes seem to be quite consistent in society and culture. My interest in the narrative and visual expression found in film noir has proven to be a rich thread of inspiration.

Q How does this interest in film noir translate in your work?

A Perspective and light are often my favorite aspects of creating a response, I aim to use them for expressing content. The central thing is to find a point of view and corresponding light treatment that captures the emotional content. I like the thought that illustration and a film unit camera operator are similar and can bring a consistent visual language to virtually any material.

Q Talk with us a bit about your process.

A As ideas are the motor in what I do, the thinking process is possibly my favorite part. Due to commitments in the day my thinking time is often in the early evening. When I was making a picture each day for a year for *The Times*, I think my process went through a major transformation. Because of print deadlines I would need to respond to a phone call synopsis of an article not yet written and offer a call back solution within 10-minutes each evening, then supply artwork by the next morning, before going to work at Kingston. It meant I would start drawing at 5 or 6am, something I couldn't imagine would be good only to discover that making work before all the complexity of the

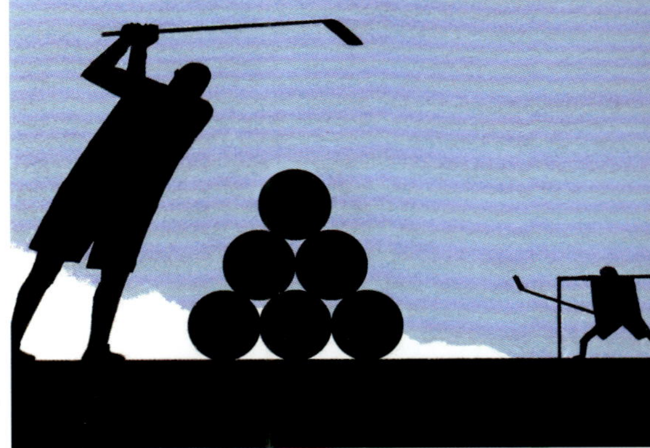

day gets a grip on you is wonderful. It's now my favorite time to draw.

Q And what about the future of illustration?

A Happily there is an old ally: technology. Just as the articulation of the photographic image has been turbocharged by innovation, so the ability

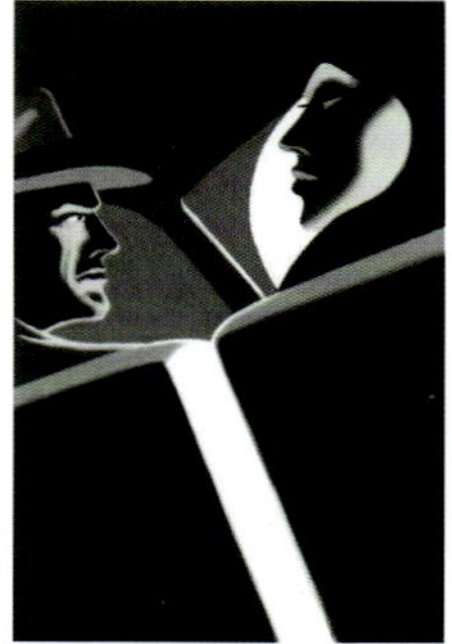
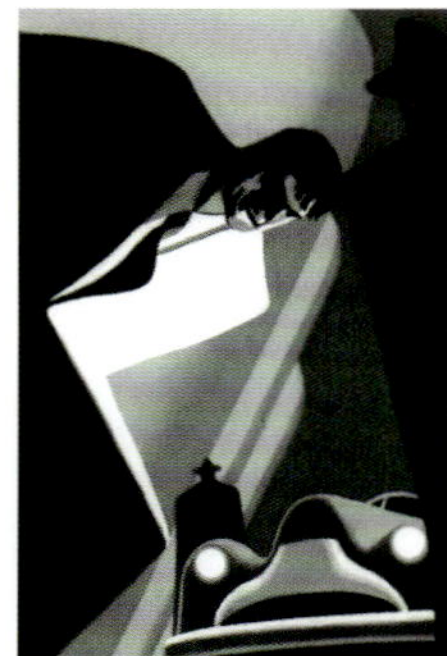

for the constructed image to move from the static base of print to the time base of screen has happened. The possibilities are a new frontier.

Q Let's talk about your experiences as a teacher, what do you feel the role is of an instructor?

A It is a privilege to teach, my approach is to support not instruct! So many students start out with a lack of confidence in their own ideas and look for someone else's. Everyone has ideas, they aren't always great, but I'd rather encourage personal ideas than the rendering of someone else's.

Q Do you feel there is anything missing in today's education of an illustrator?

A As an academic subject it struggles to form a clear and coherent self-image with little theoretical support and a history of being a subset of graphic design 'craft' devoid of original content.

The big enemy though is the commodification of illustration education and the selling of shortcuts, in software and in non-majorshort courses. Plus it can be a popular and apparently cheap subject to run—it is easy to sell the name but leave out the core.

Looking is critical, there is no substitute for analytical and critical looking and making from that base. Like many activities, by putting the hours in an understanding begins to build which is so necessary for original and effective communication. Plus you have to have fun, if you aren't enjoying it, it's unlikely to find an audience.

Q What is your advice to those graduates entering the field today?

A Persevere and follow your instincts. There are many ways to make a living, but to find a creative form where you can make your own individual contribution is rare. Find things that inspire you and articulate them. Lifespans are heading for 100 years, there's time to realize what is important to you and find out if that is also important to others.

communication. Plus you have to have fun, if you aren't enjoying it, it's unlikely to find an audience.

Q What is your advice to those graduates entering the field today?

A Persevere and follow your instincts. There are many ways to make a living, but to find a creative form where you can make your own individual contribution is rare.

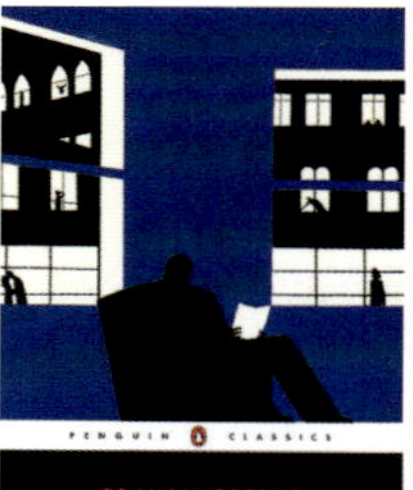

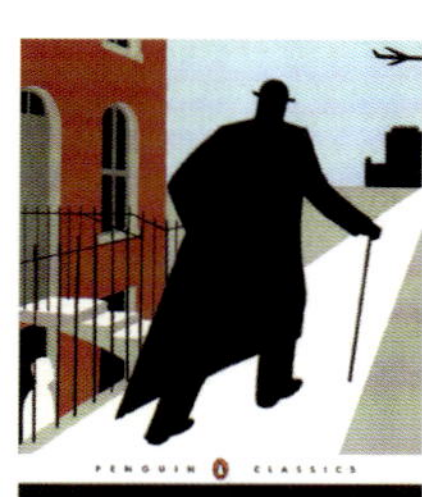

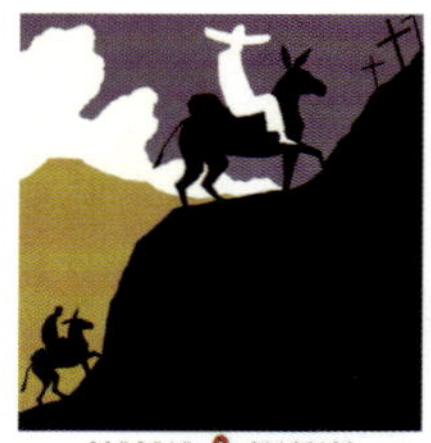

Find things that inspire you and articulate them. Lifespans are heading for 100 years, there's time to realize what is important to you and find out if that is also important to others.

Q Final words to teachers?

A The students create the sense, the institution often makes nonsense

Q And finally, what's in your future?

A I am—as most of the visual world it seems—working on a graphic novel. Come on one of these projects has to succeed, Chris Ware needs some competition!

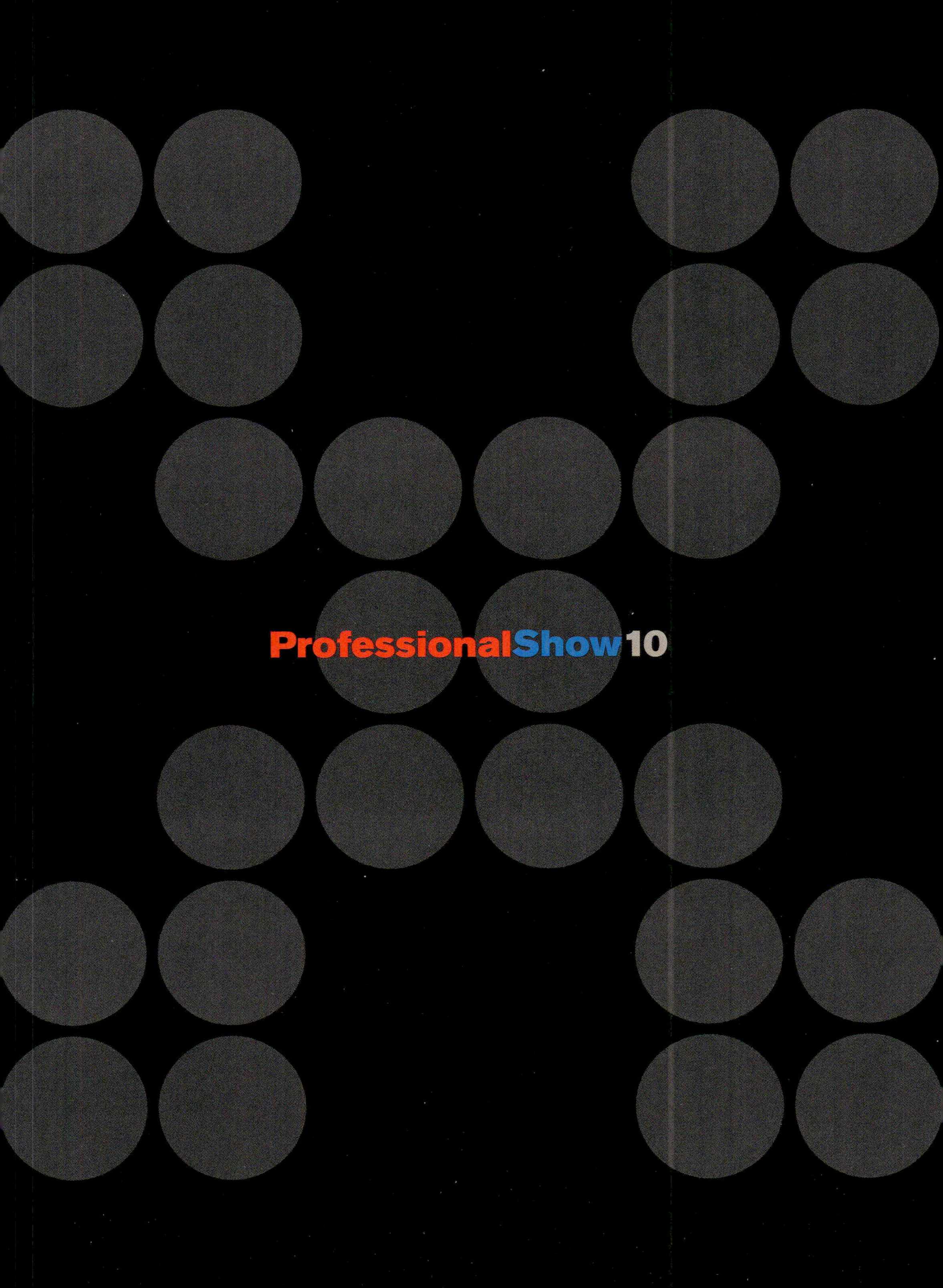
ProfessionalShow10

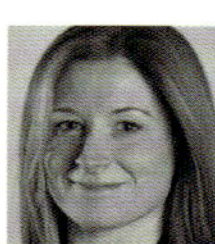 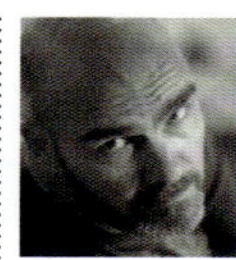 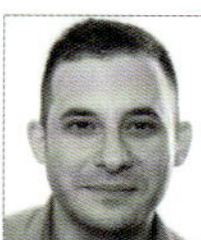 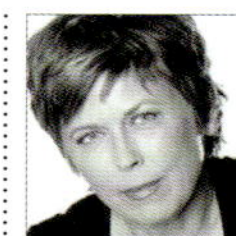 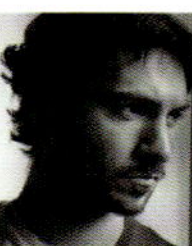 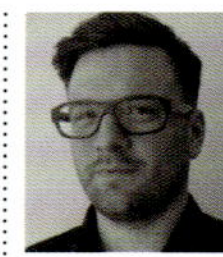 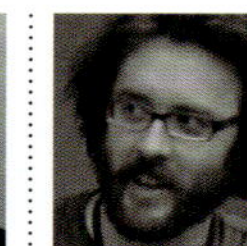 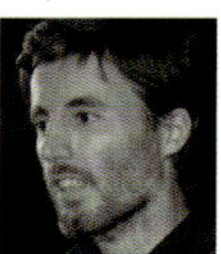

Stephanie Atkinson

Stephnie was appointed art editor of United Kingdom's number-one-selling golf magazine, *Golf Monthly*, in 2010. Over the last ten years she has worked for several magazines across fields as diverse as interiors and the military and has regularly commissioned illustrators from around the globe. Stephanie graduated from the University of Brighton with a BA honors degree in illustration. She lives in London.

Harry Campbell

Harry's distinctive graphic line illustration work can be found in most major publications including *Newsweek,* the *New York Times*, *Time Magzine* and many others. Prior to embarking on his career as a freelance illustrator Harry worked in New York, employed as a designer with companies such as Nickelodeon and Warner Brothers. He has received numerous awards from the Society of Illustrators, *Communication Arts*, and American Illustration. He lives and works in Baltimore, Maryland.

Matt Dorfman

Matt is a New York-based designer, illustrator and art director of the *New York Times'* Op/Ed page. After spending the first decade of the 21st century working for music industry figureheads Island/Def Jam, Republic/Motown Records and the Verve Music Group he traded in music for publishing and counts Penguin, Vintage/Anchor books, *New York Magazine, Vanity Fair, Wired, Pantheon, Bloomberg Business Week*, W.W. Norton and *Time Magazine* among his clients. His work has been recognized by the AIGA, the Art Director's Club, American Illustration, the Society of Illustrators, Society of Publication Designers and the Type Director's Club.

Jocelyne Fournel

Jocelyn has been art director at *L'actualité* for 19 years. She graduated in graphic design at UQAM and begun her magazine adventure with *Montréal ce mois-ci*. A few years and studios later, she left Montréal for London, where she worked for such clients as the World of Interiors and *Sunday Telegraph Magazine*. Back in Montréal, she opened her own studio, working for *MTL Magazine* and Gallimard publishing house. During her career, she has won multiple prizes from the Quebec Association of Magazine Publishers (AQEM) and National Magazine Awards Foundation.

Alessandro Gottardo

Alessandro a.k.a. Shout was born in Pordenone. He studied art in Venice and illustration at the Istituto Europeo del Design in Milan. His client list includes newspapers, magazines, advertising brands, design studios and animation studios. His work has received numerous international awards.

Jakob Hinrichs

Jakob is working from his illustration studio in the heart of Berlin at the Rosenthaler Platz. He is deeply rooted in the city and its creative output. His loud and bold illustrations are influenced by German expressionism and European illustration history. He is known for his strong visual language and background in printmaking—especially woodcut. The work appears in the *New York Times*, the *Guardian*, *American Lawyer* and *Bloomberg Business Week*. He has been recognized by *3x3 Annual*, *Communication Arts* and the Society of Illustrators.

Brian McMullen

Brian is the senior art director at McSweeney's in San Francisco, where he edits and designs the McSweeney's McMullens children's book series. A new picture book he made with Jason Jagel, *Hang Glider & Mud Mask*, can be started from either end and read forever in an infinite loop

Gonçalo Viana

Gonçalo was born in Lisbon, a retro European town famed for its bright light and custard tarts. He studied architecture and moved to London, where he worked at a practice for a few years. Illustration had always been his first love though and back to Lisbon he left architecture and soon started work as a freelance illustrator. Geometry did find a way to seep back in, providing a framework for his smart concepts, strong colors and textures. His conceptual approach has garnered recognition from *Communication Arts*, the *Society for News Design*, *Creative Quarterly*, *3x3 Annual* and *Luerzer's Archive*.

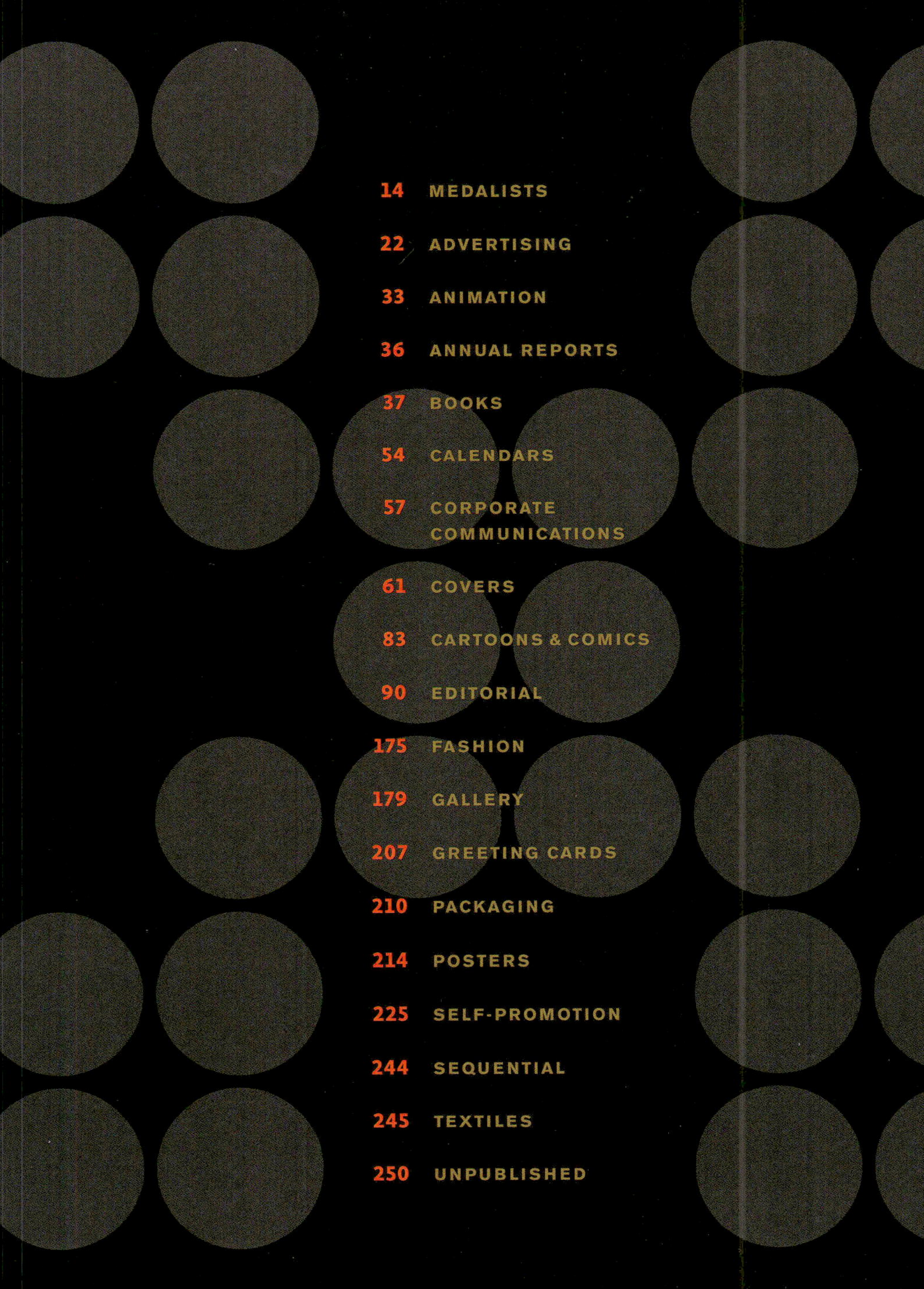

14 MEDALISTS

22 ADVERTISING

33 ANIMATION

36 ANNUAL REPORTS

37 BOOKS

54 CALENDARS

57 CORPORATE COMMUNICATIONS

61 COVERS

83 CARTOONS & COMICS

90 EDITORIAL

175 FASHION

179 GALLERY

207 GREETING CARDS

210 PACKAGING

214 POSTERS

225 SELF-PROMOTION

244 SEQUENTIAL

245 TEXTILES

250 UNPUBLISHED

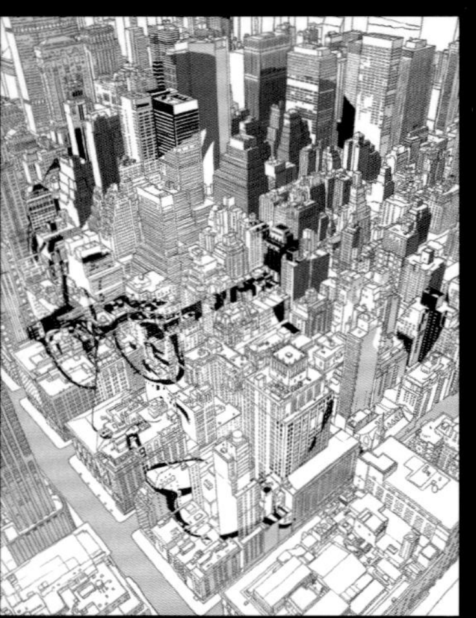
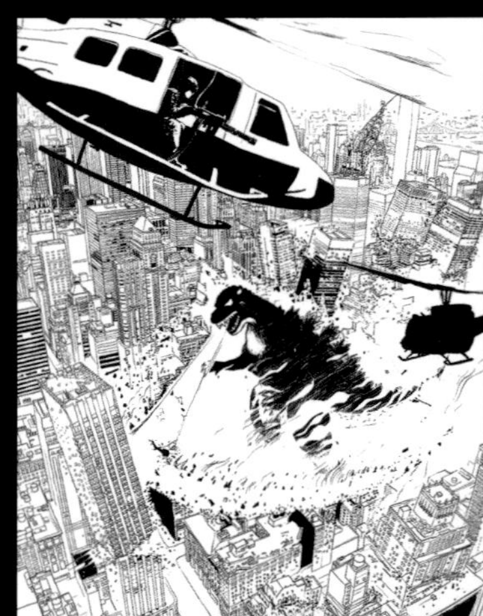
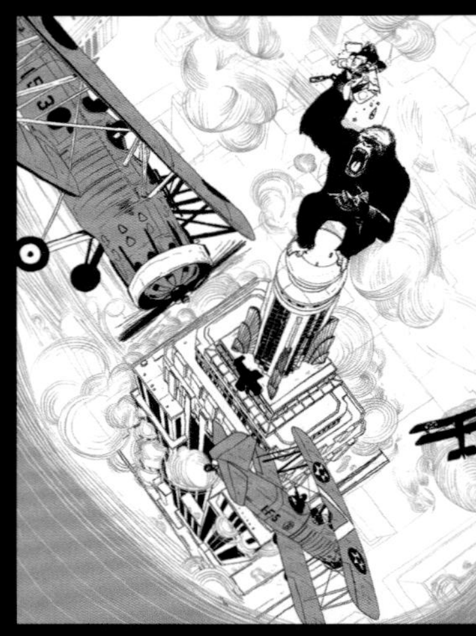
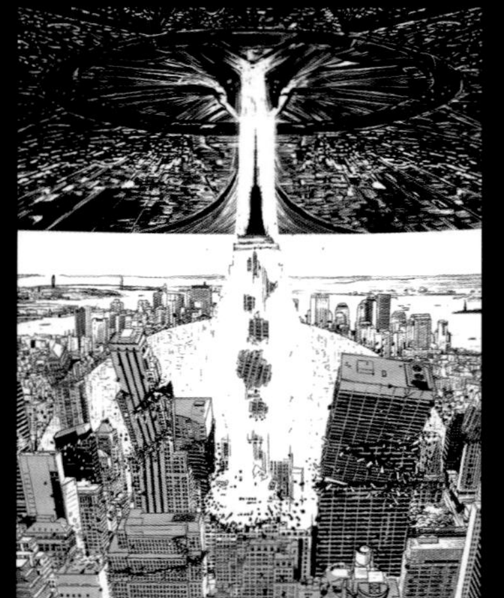
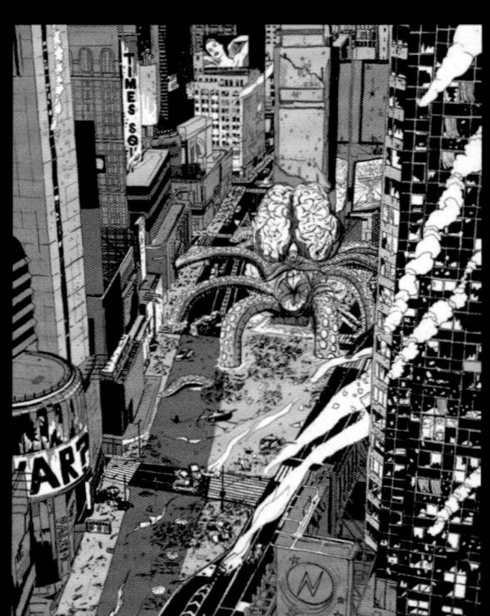

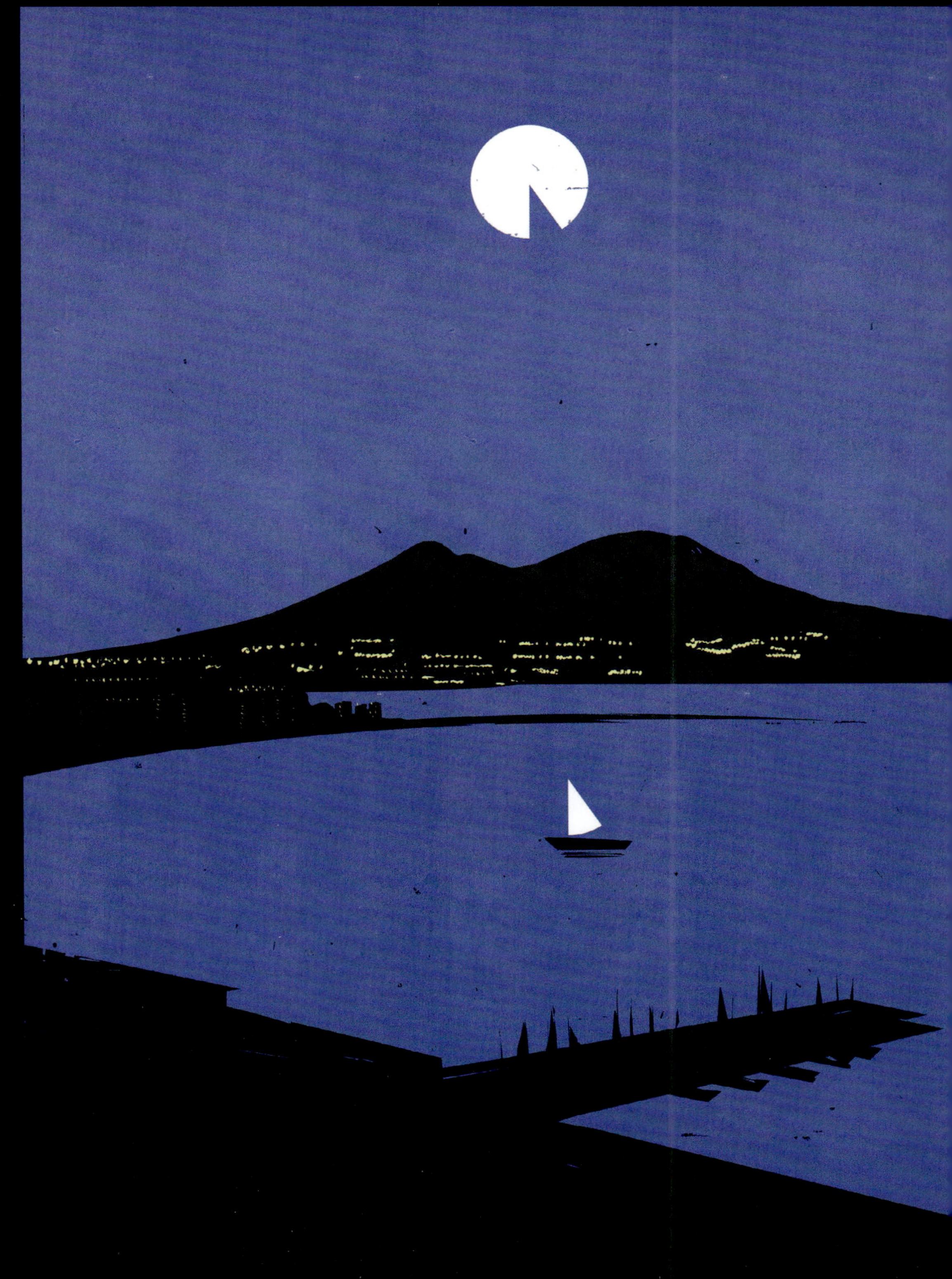

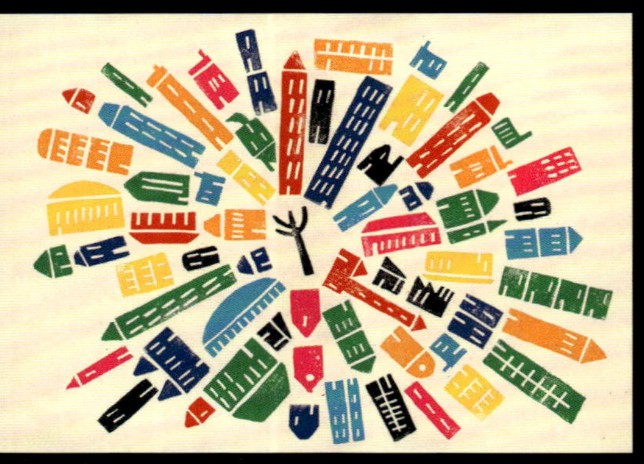
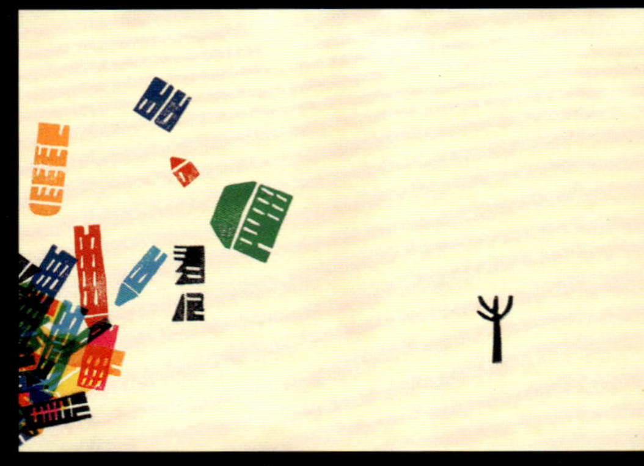
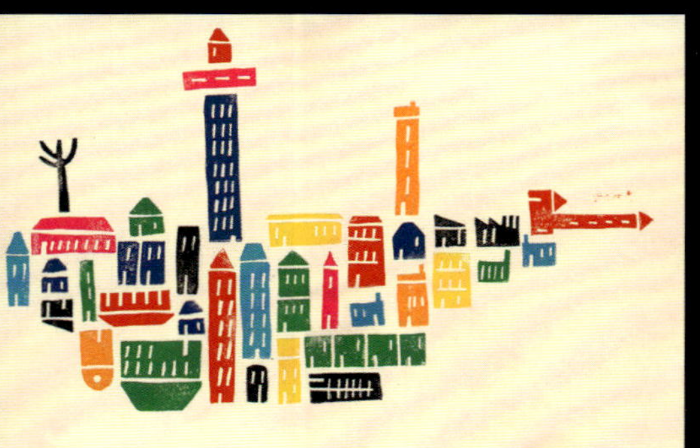
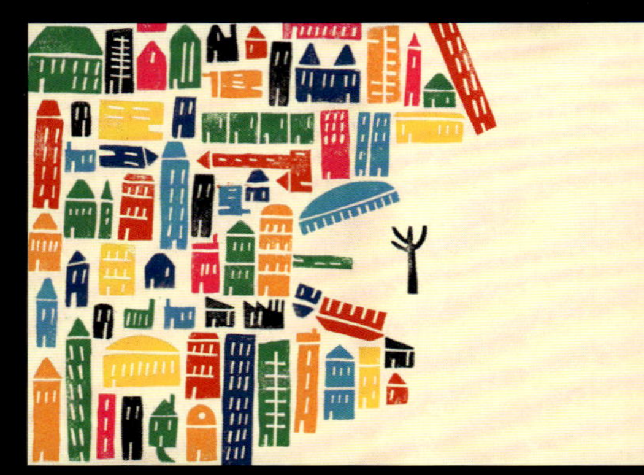
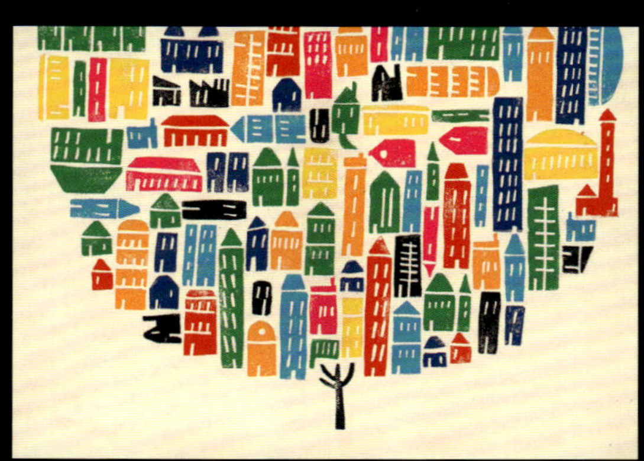

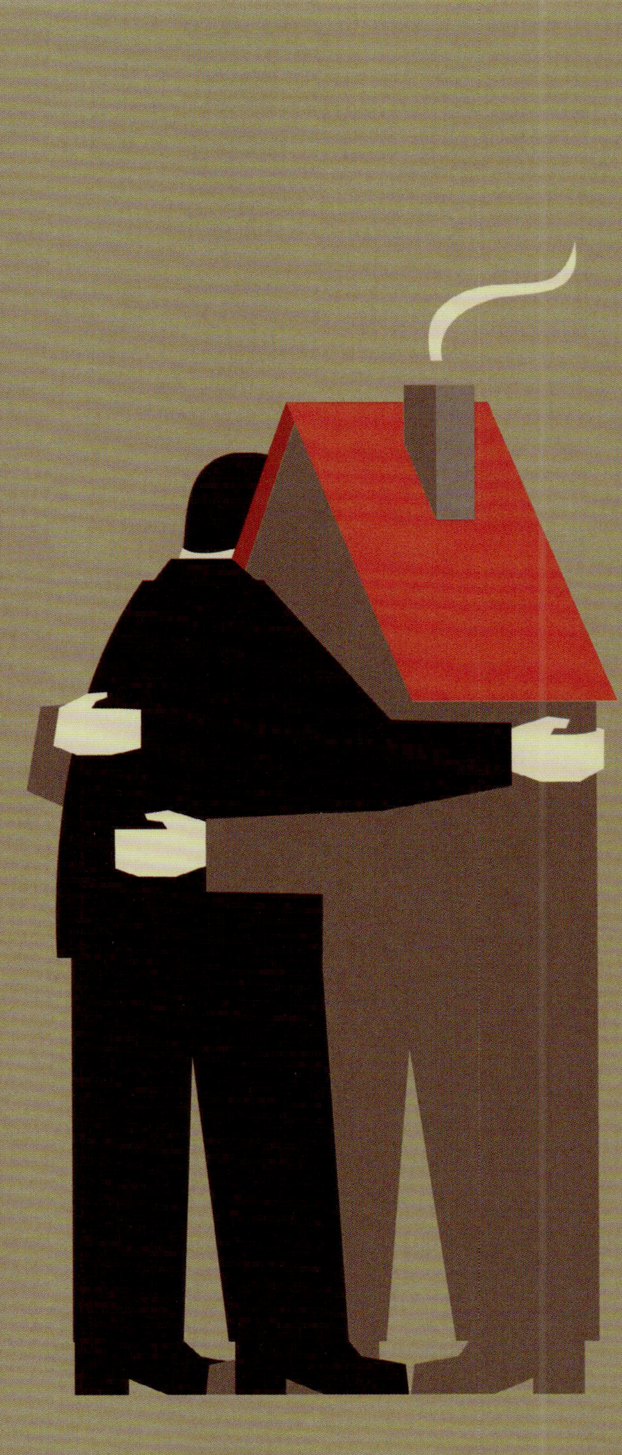

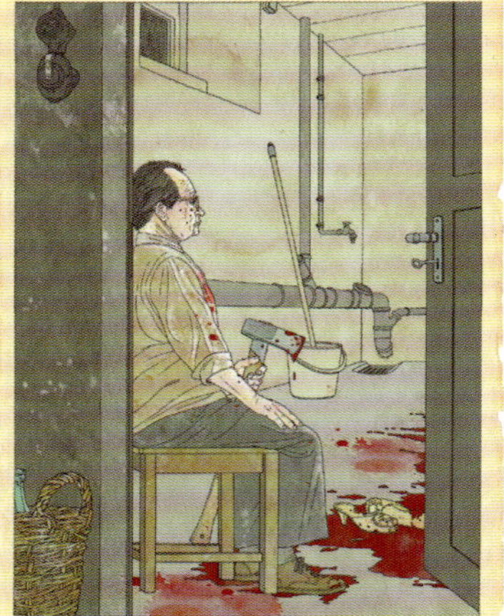

Friedhelm Fähner had spent his whole working life as a GP in Rottweil, 2,800 patients with medical incurance processed every year, doctor's office on the main street, chairman of the Egyptian cultural Association, member of the Lions Club, no criminal offences, nor even minor infringements. Besides his house, he owned two rental properties, a three-year-old E-Class Mercedes with leather upholstery and air conditioning, approximately 750,000 euros in bonds, and a capital sum life insurance policy. Fähner had no children. His only living relative was his sister, six years younger, who lived in Stuttgart with her husband and two sons. Fähner's life wasn't anything that gave rise to stories.

Until the thing with Ingrid.

FROM THE STORY „FÄHNER" BY FERDINAND VON SCHIRACH

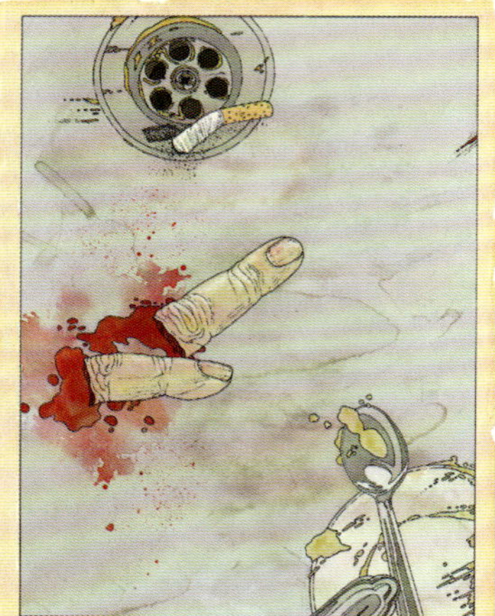

Four hours after the phone call to Tanata, the doorbell rang at Wagners apartment. Wagner opened the door a crack. The gun he stuck into the belt of his pants didn't save him. The first blow to his larynx cut off his breath, and when the garotte ended his life fifteen minutes later, he welcomed his death. Wagner's cleaning lady put down the groceries in the kitchen next morning and saw two severed fingers stuck in the sink. She called the police. Wagner was lying in bed, his thighs clamped together in a vise, two carpenter's nails in the left kneecap and three in the right. There was a garotte around his neck and his tongue hung out of his mouth. Wagner had wet himself before he died, and the investigating officers racked their brains trying to figure out what information he had divulged to the perpetrator.

FROM THE STORY „TANATA'S TEA BOWL" BY FERDINAND VON SCHIRACH

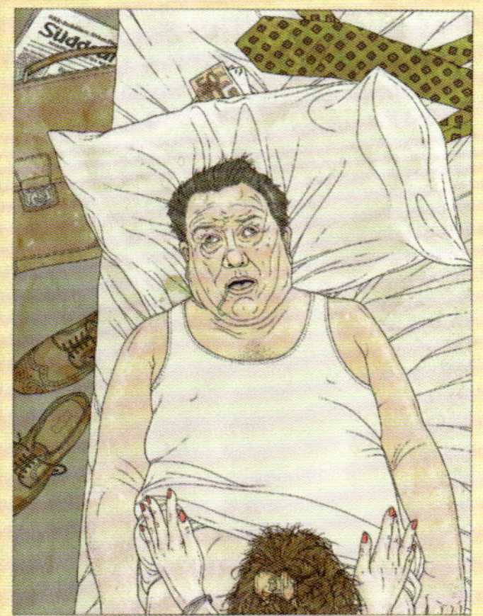

The fat man found the room too small. He was sweating. Today he had to do it in the early morning, he had a meeting at 10:00 a.m. The girl said it was no problem. The bed looked clean, and she was pretty. She couldn't have been older than twenty, beautiful breasts, full mouth, at least five foot ten. Like most girls from Eastern Europe, she wore too much makeup. The fat man liked that. He took seventy euros from his briefcase and sat on the bed. He had laid his rings carefully over the chair; it mattered to him that the creases not be messed up. The girl took off his undershorts. She pushed up the folds of fat in his stomach; all he could now see of her was her hair, and he knew she was going to need quite some time. But that's her job, he thought, and he leaned back. The last thing the fat man felt was a stabbing pain in his chest; he wanted to raise his hands and tell the girl to stop, but all he could do was grunt.
Irina took the grunt to be a sign of assent, and she went on for several minutes before noticing that the man was silent.

FROM THE STORY „BLISS" BY FERDINAND VON SCHIRACH

GOLD *Dietmar Reinhard*

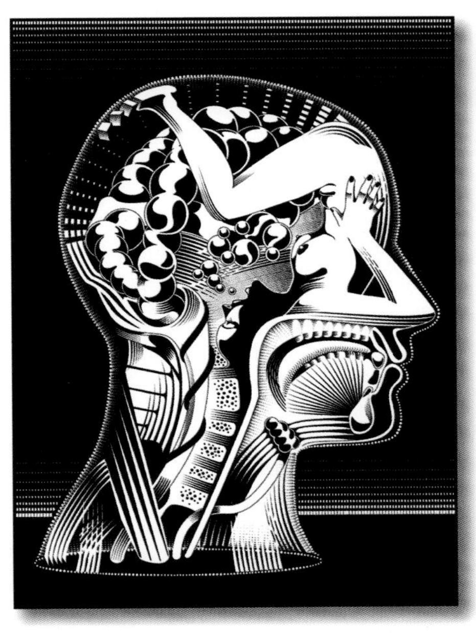

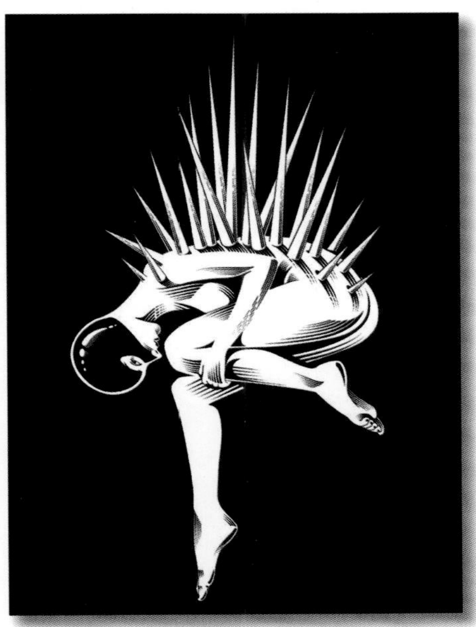

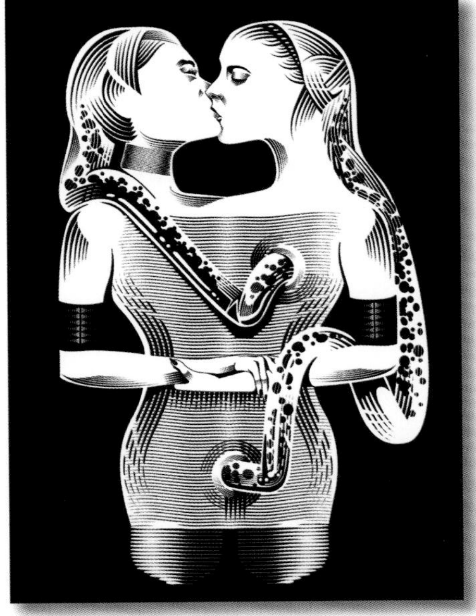

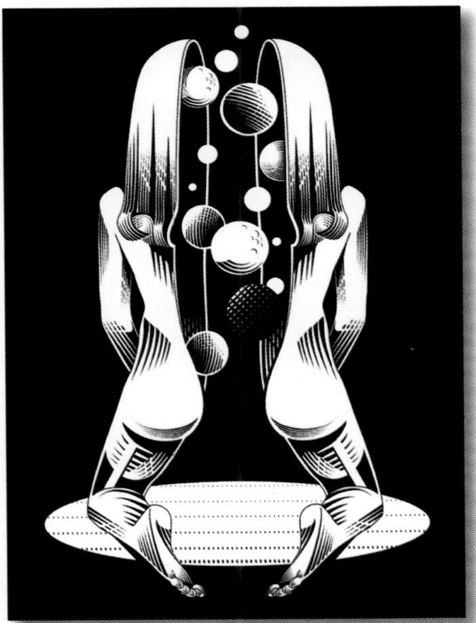

GOLD *Yann Legendre*

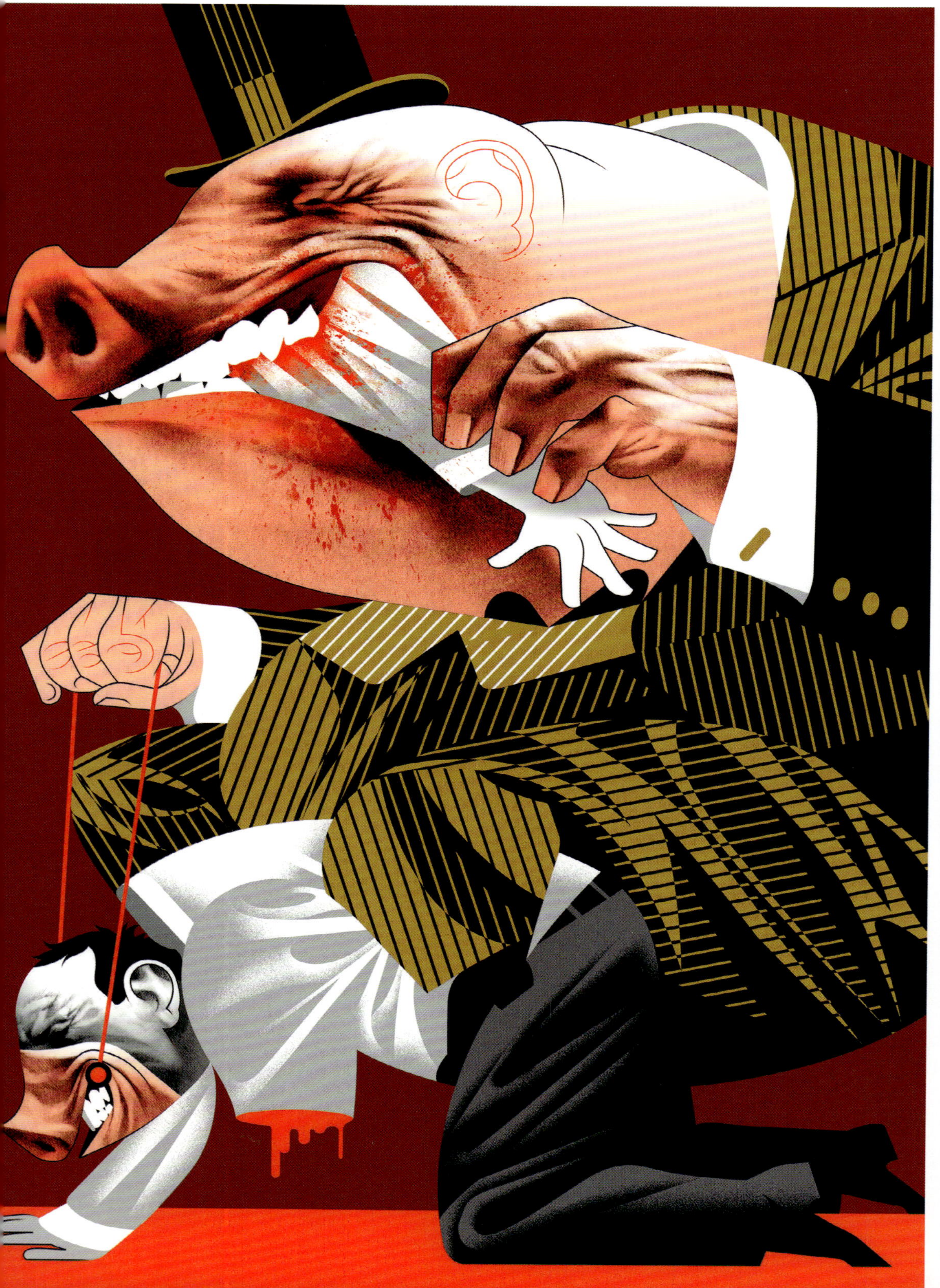

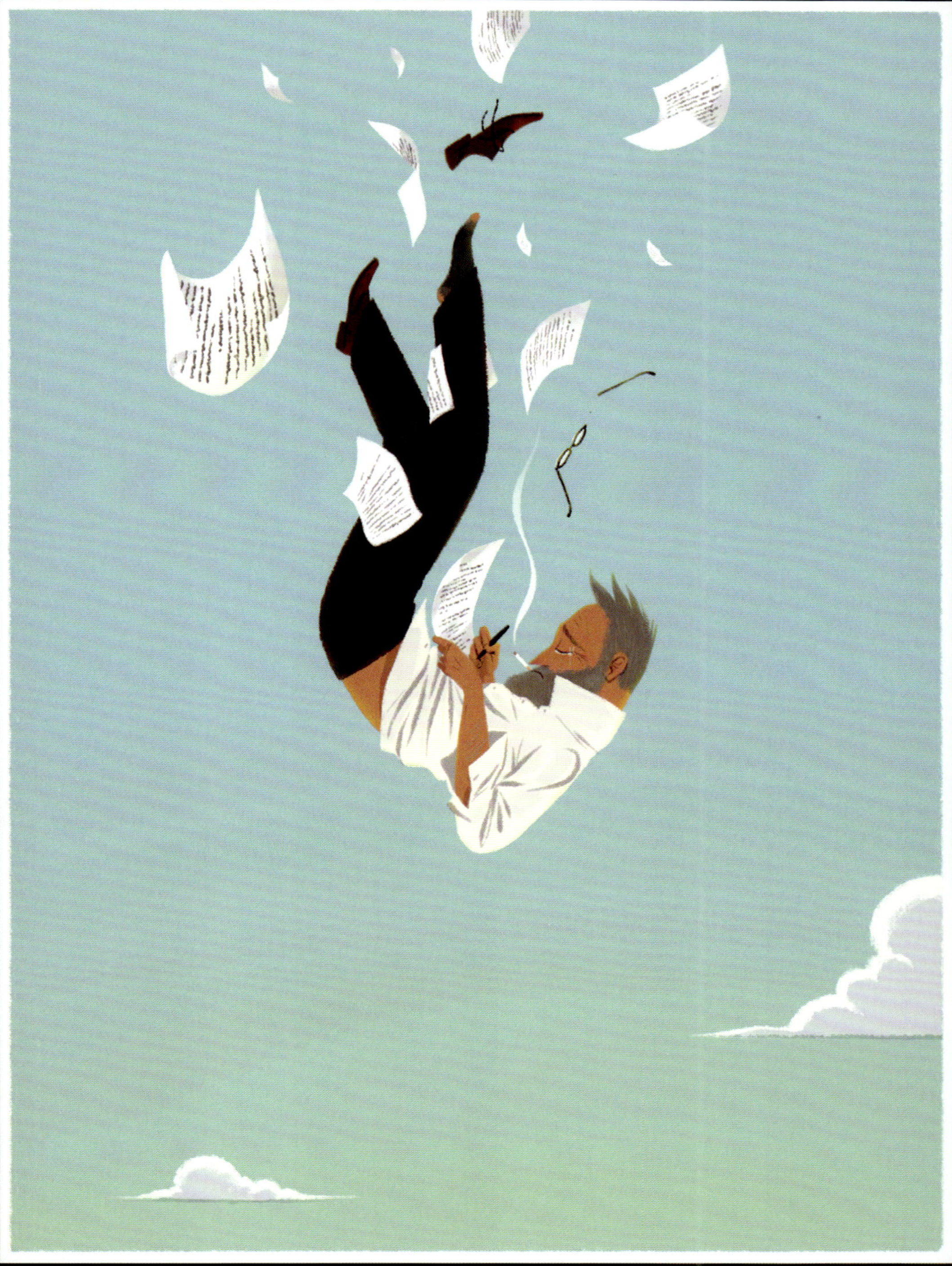

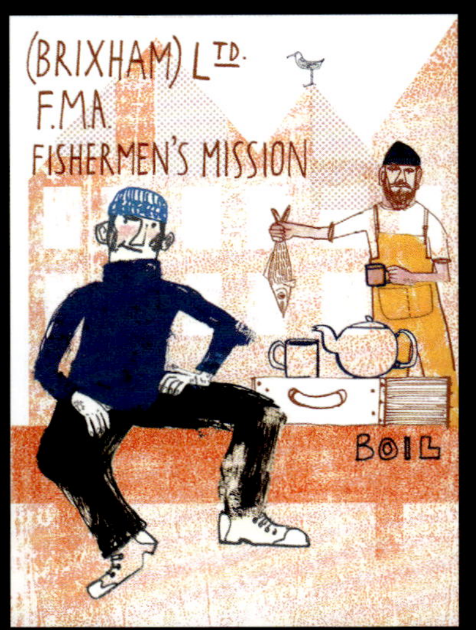

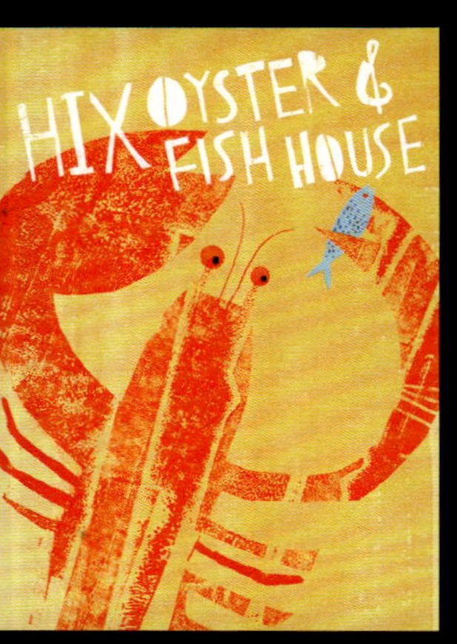

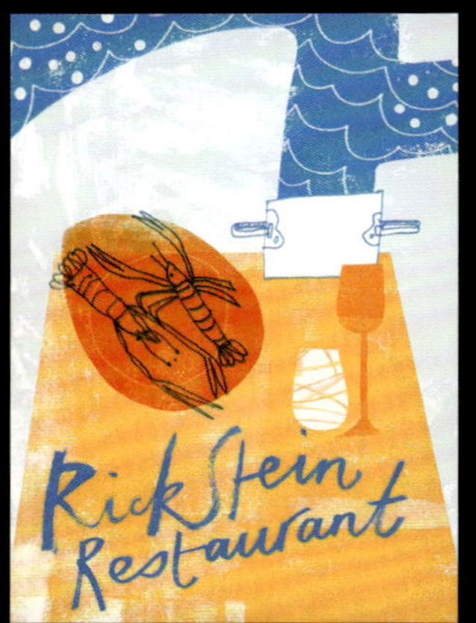

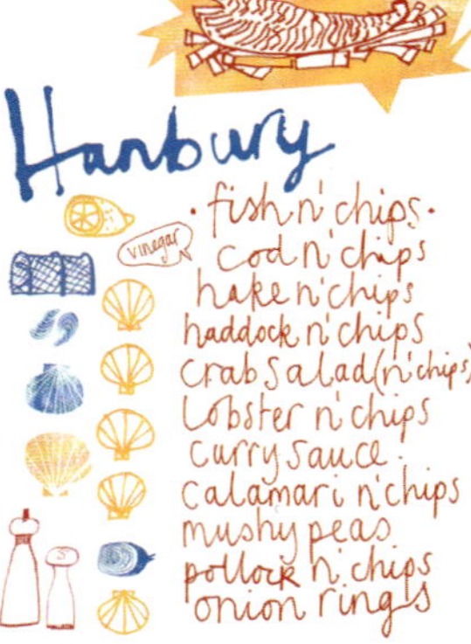

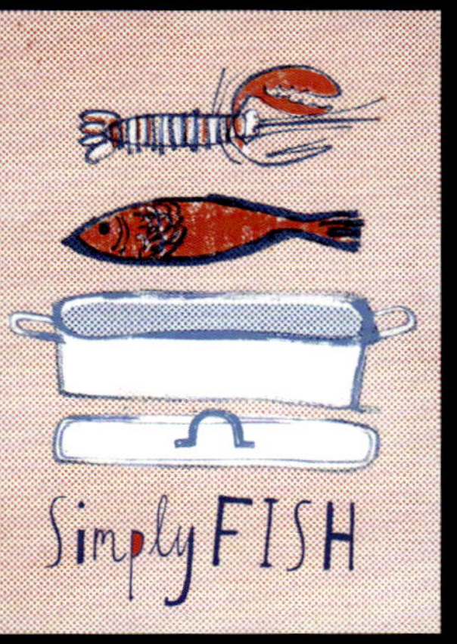

(L) *Jill Calder* (R) *Freddy Boo*

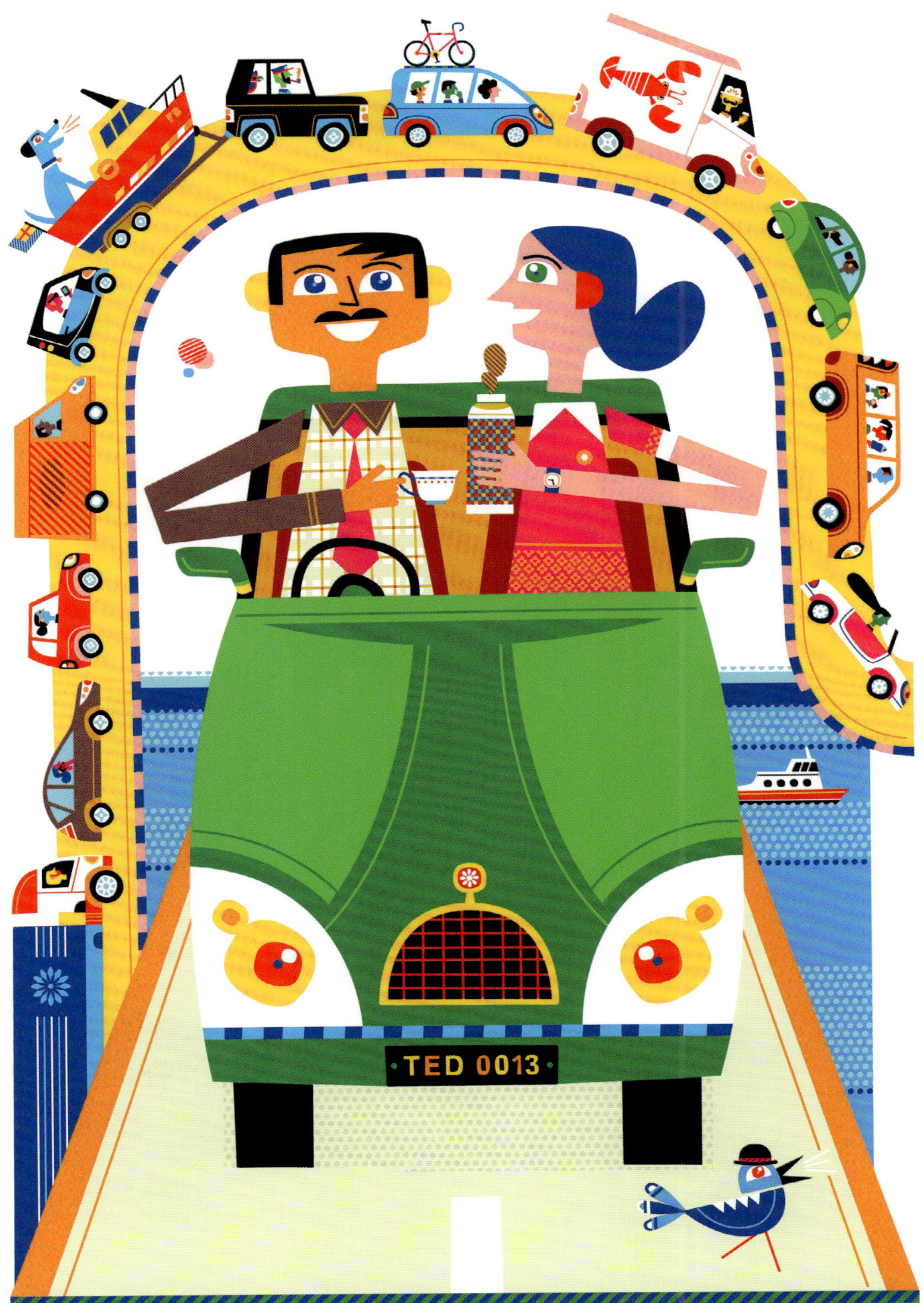
TED 0013

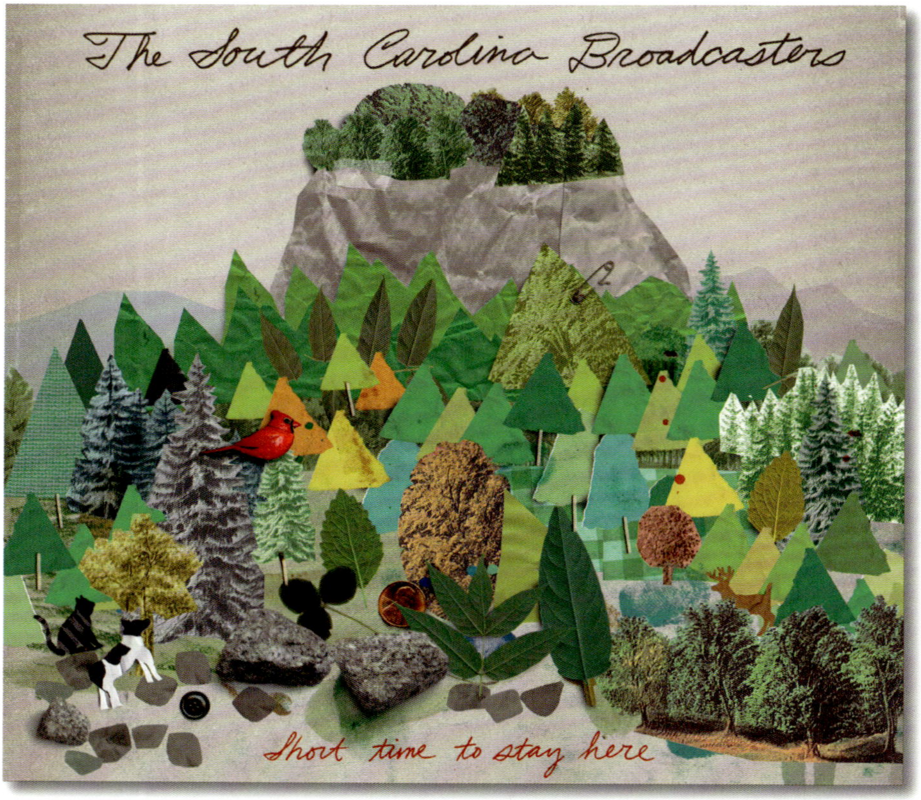

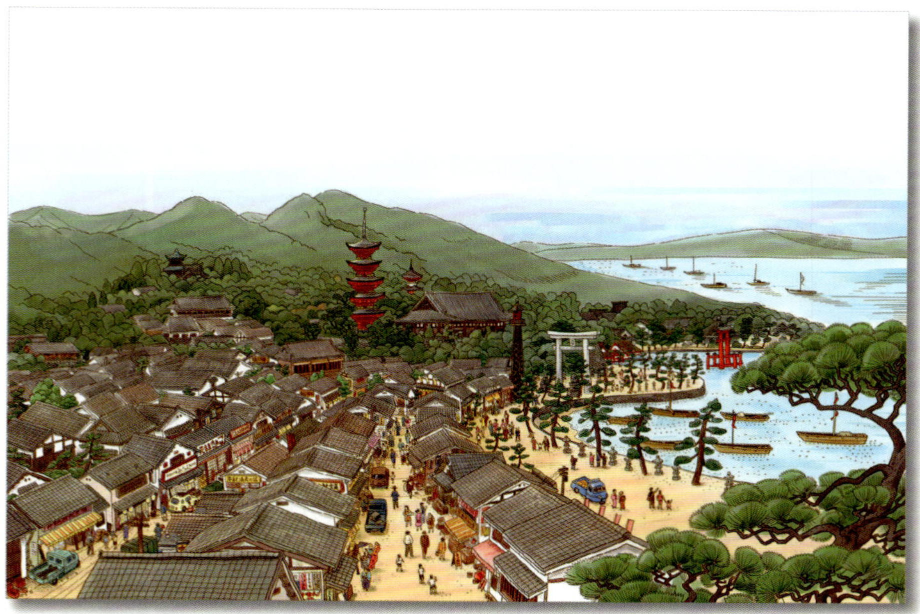

(T) *Doug Chayka* (B) *IC4Design*

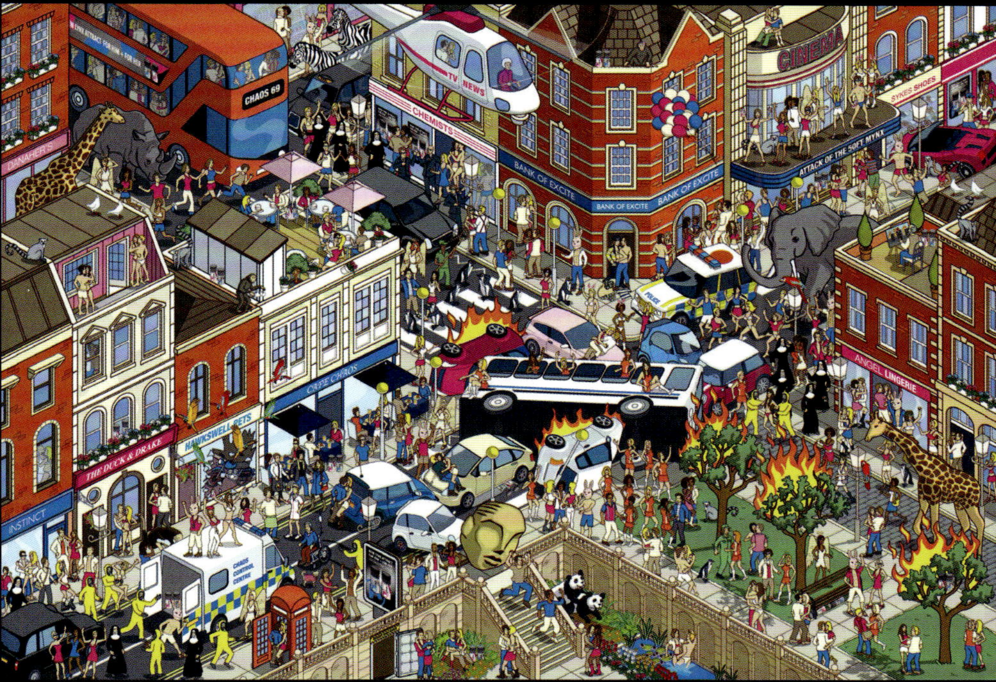

Rod Hunt

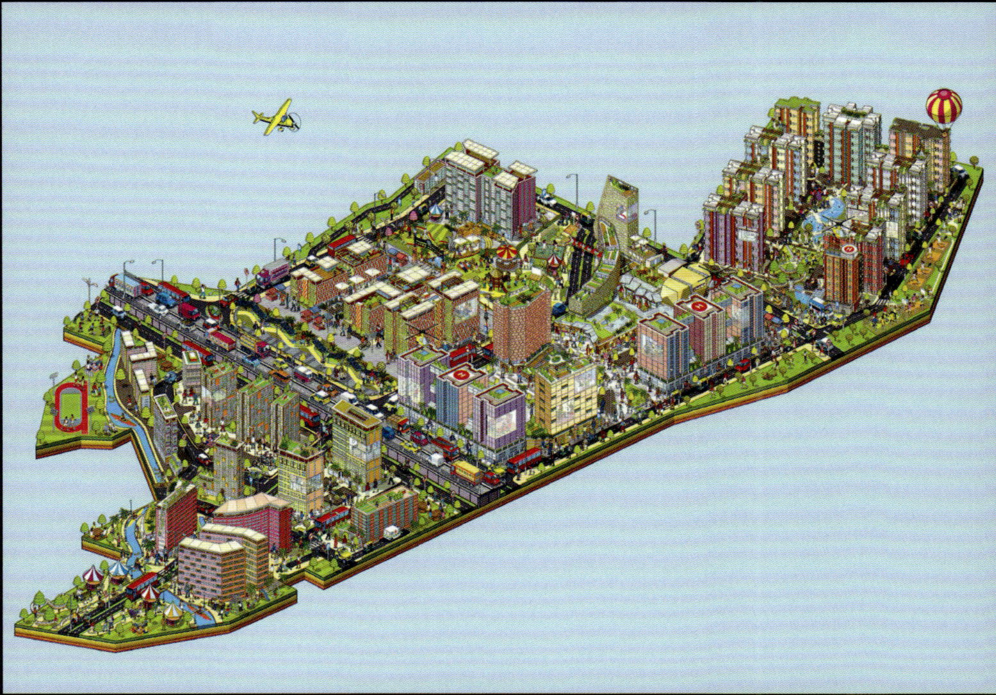

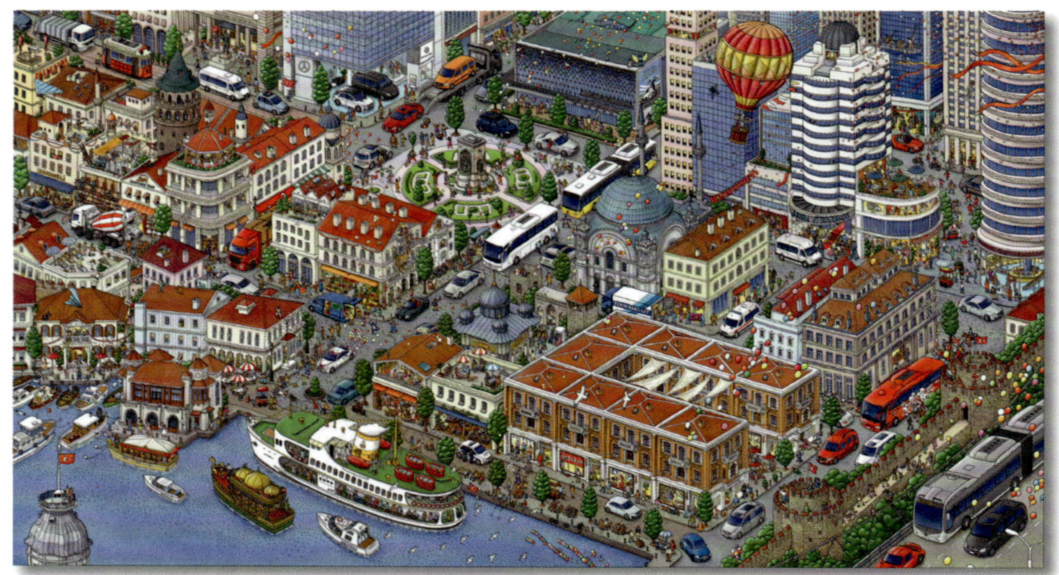

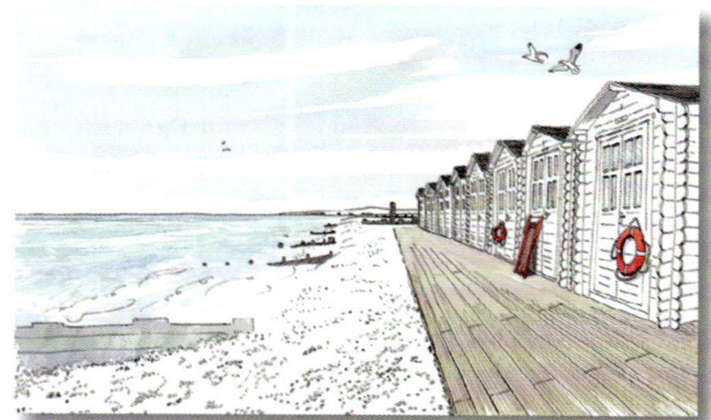

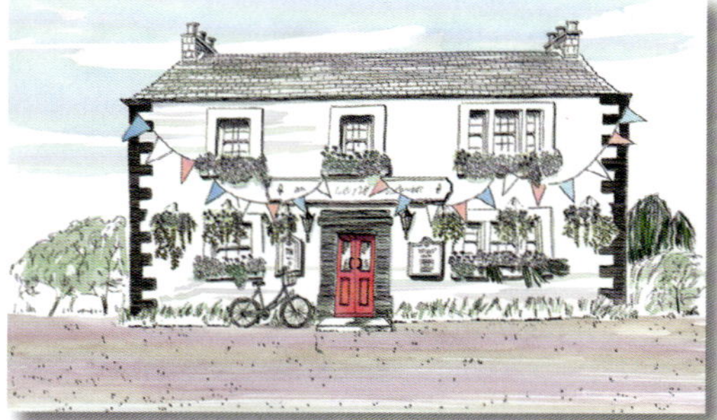

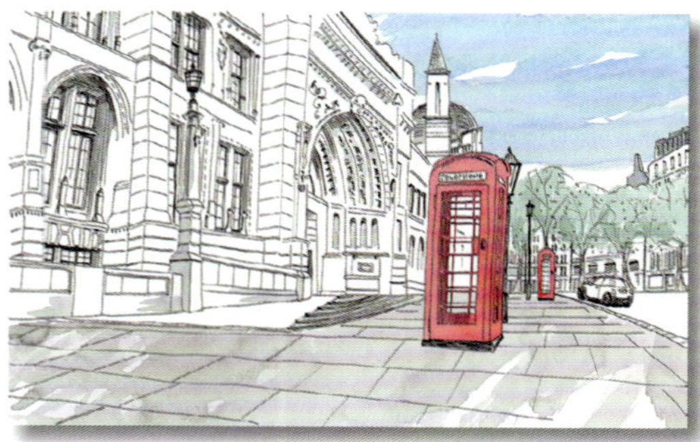

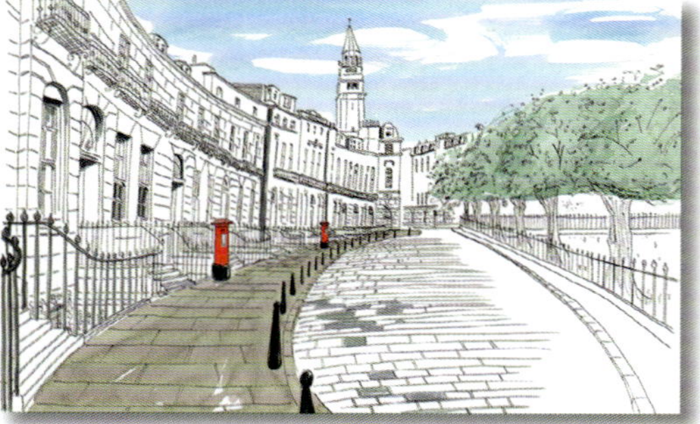

(T) *IC4Design* (B) *Angela McKay* (R) *Jody Hewgill*

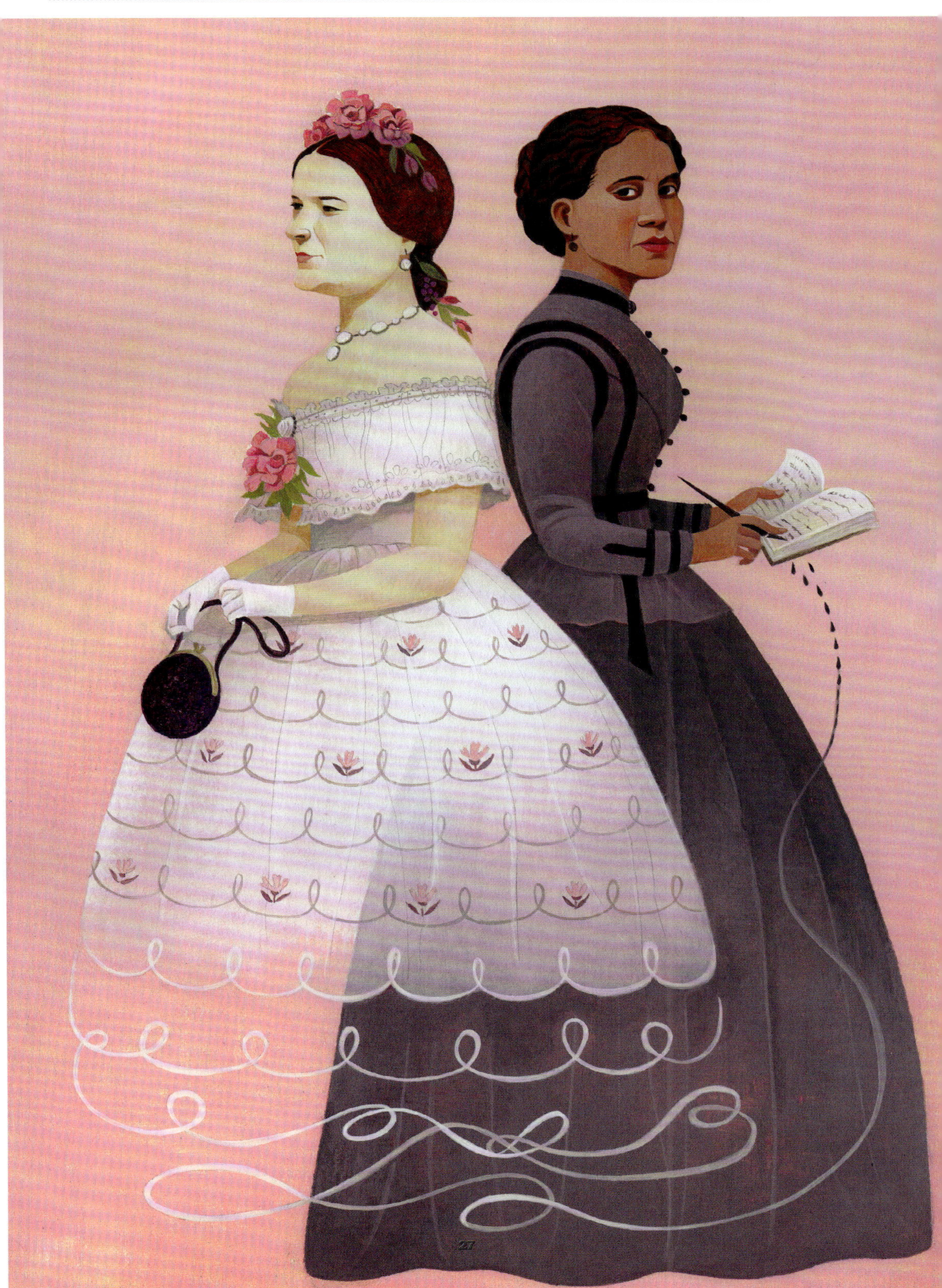

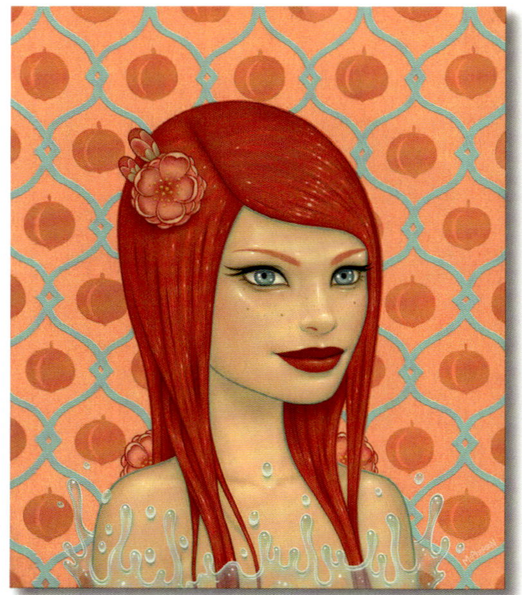 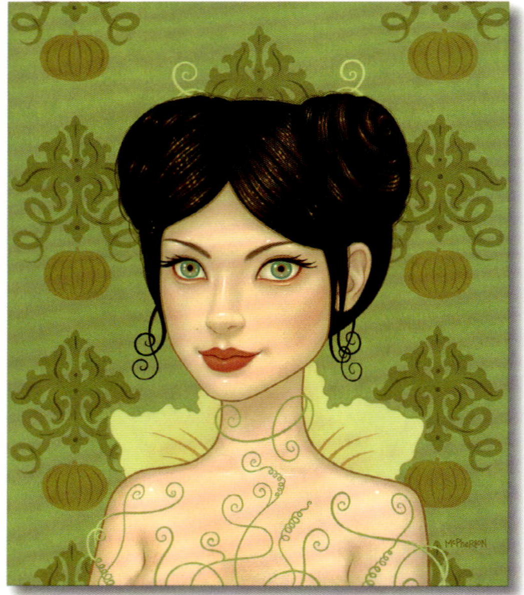
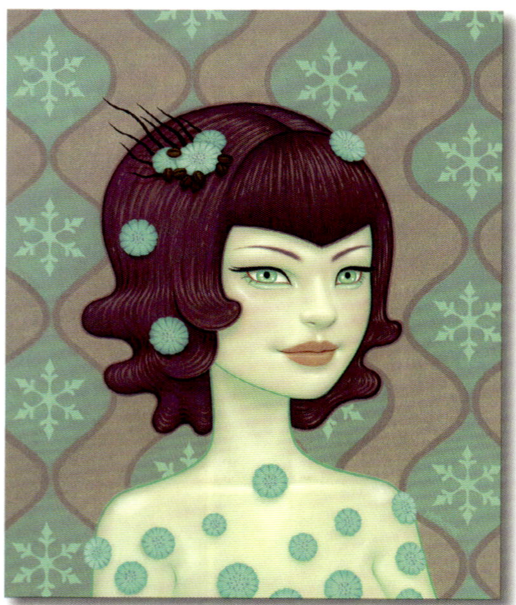 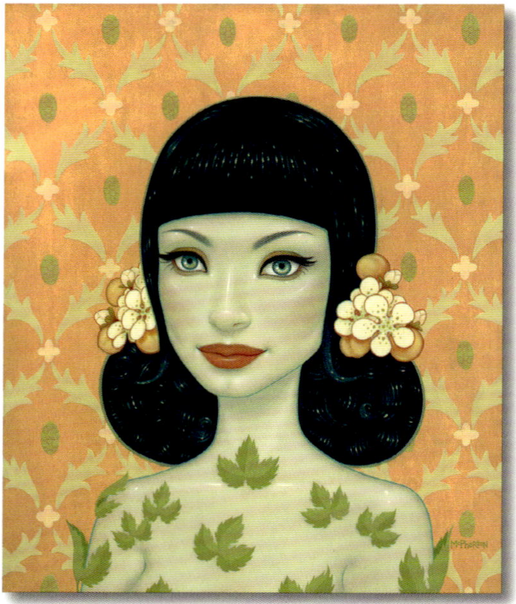

Tara McPherson

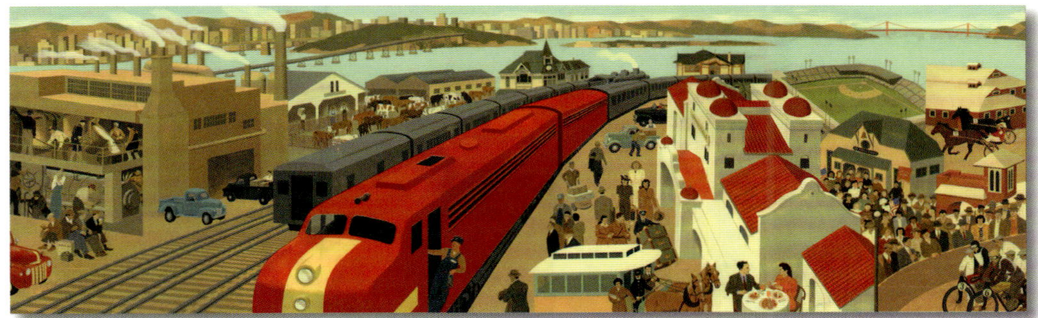

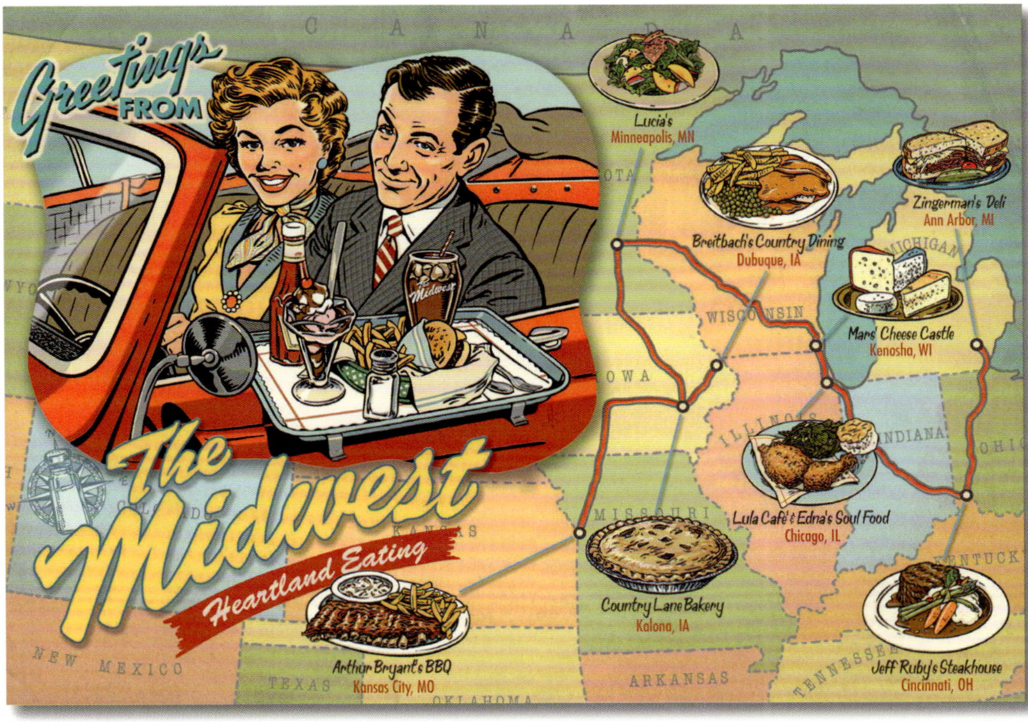

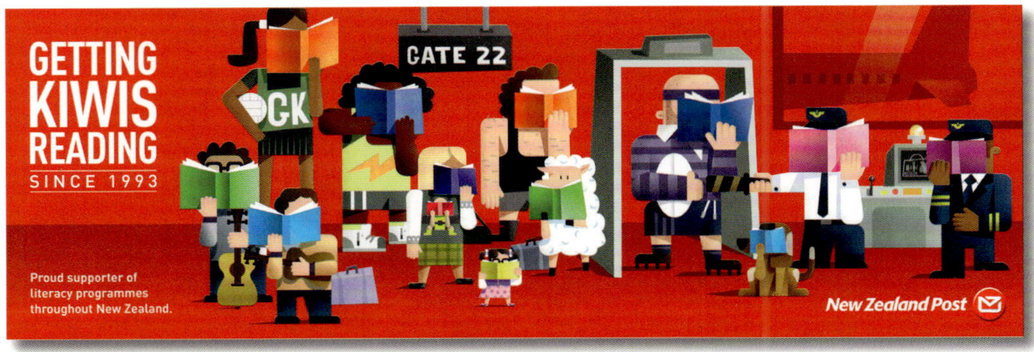

(T) *Curtis Parker* (M) *John Kachik* (B) *Simon Shaw*

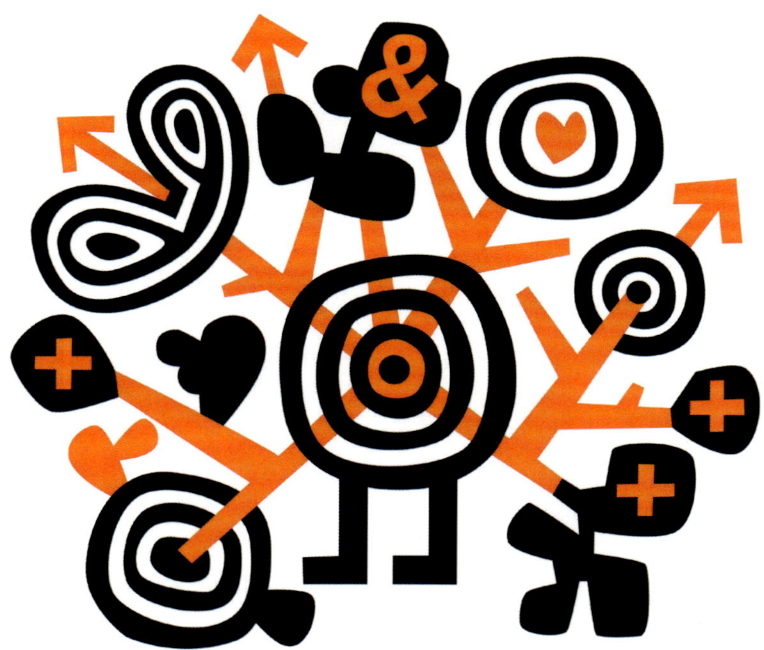

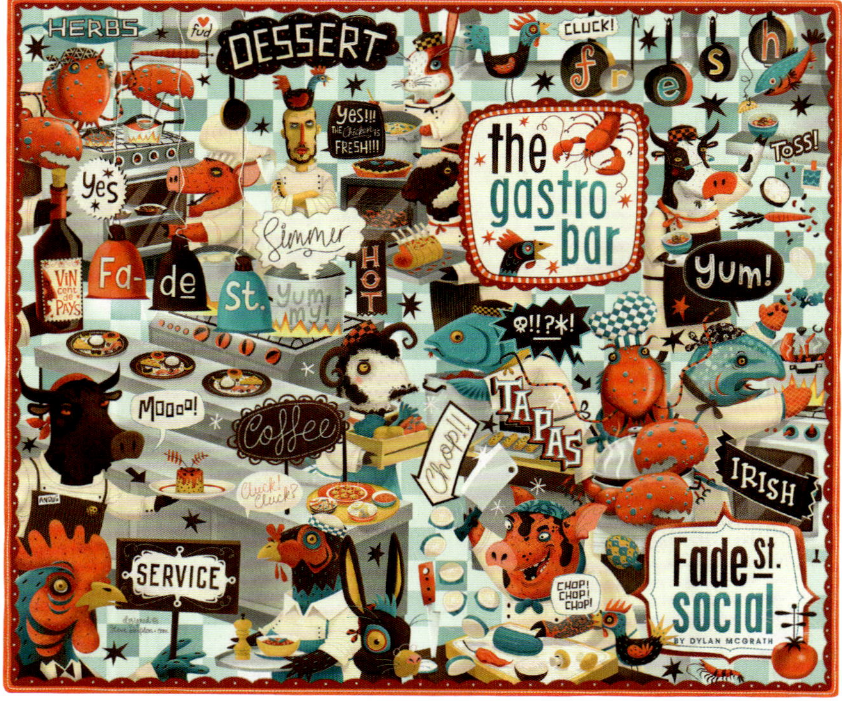

(T) *Lasse Skarbovik* (B) **BRONZE** *Steve Simpson* (R) *Christopher Nielsen*

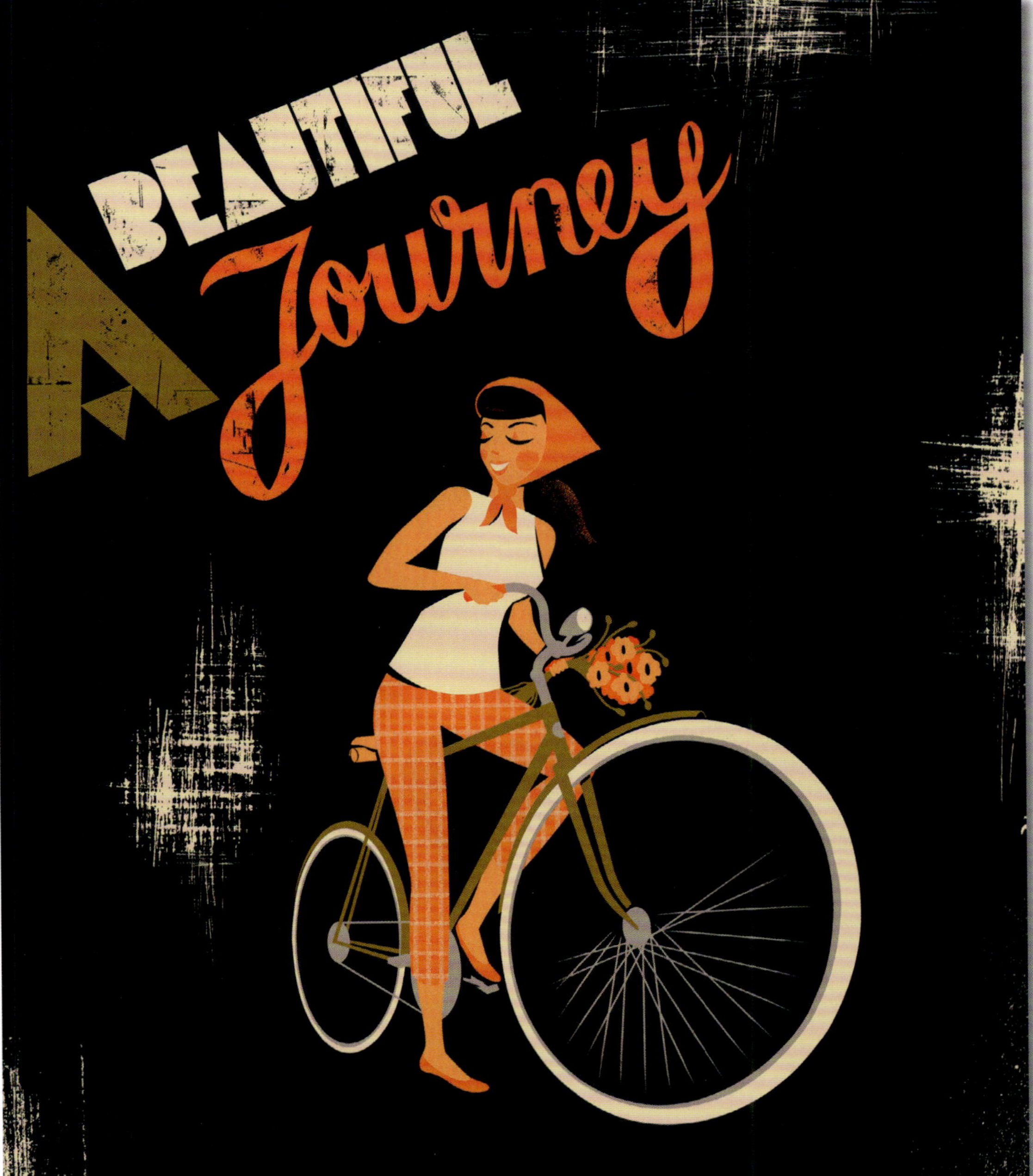
A BEAUTIFUL
Journey
MAINE
RECYCLED

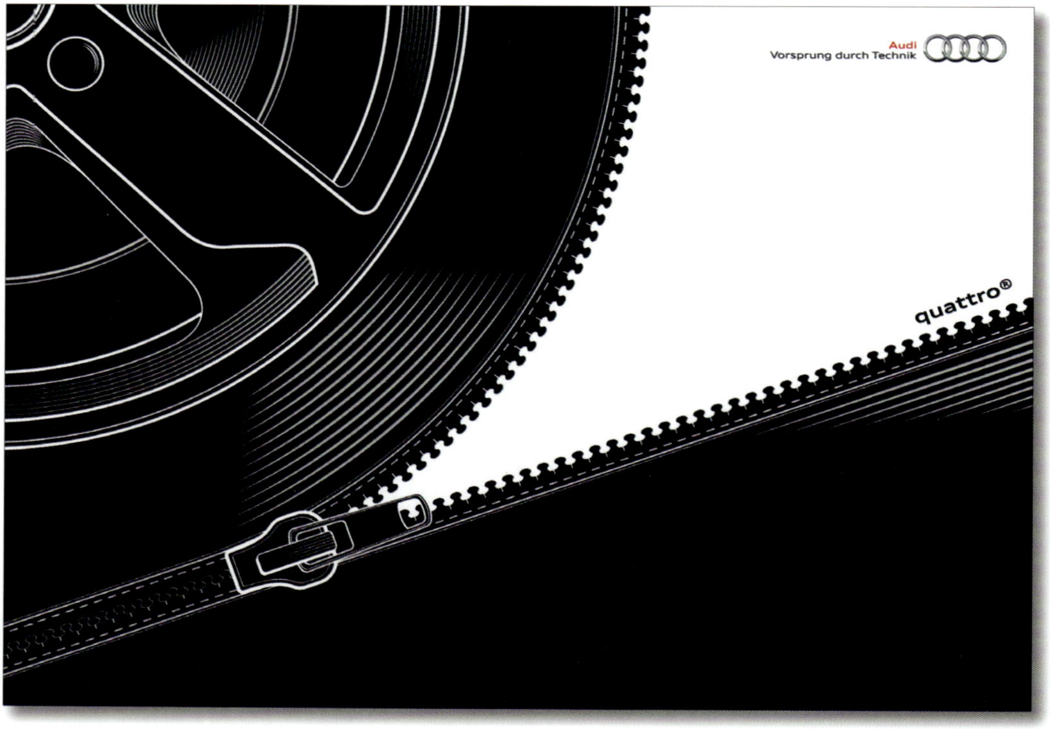

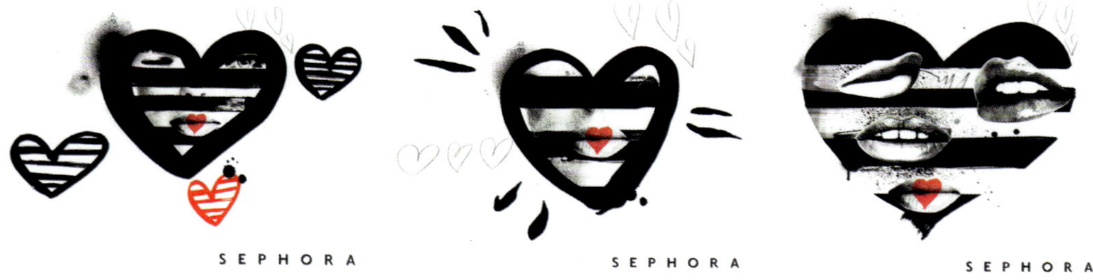

(T) *Steven Bonner* (B) *Caroline Tomlinson*

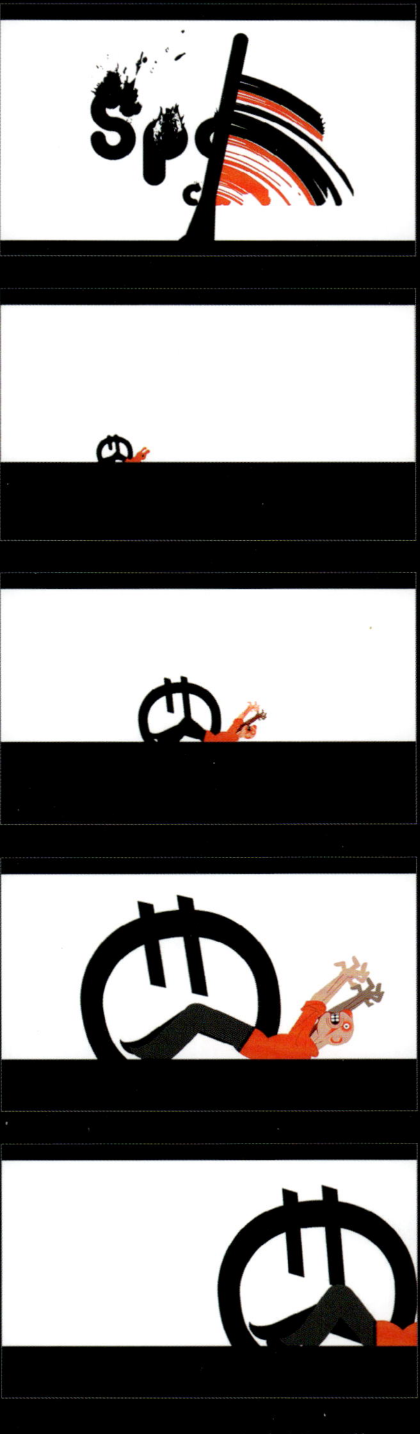

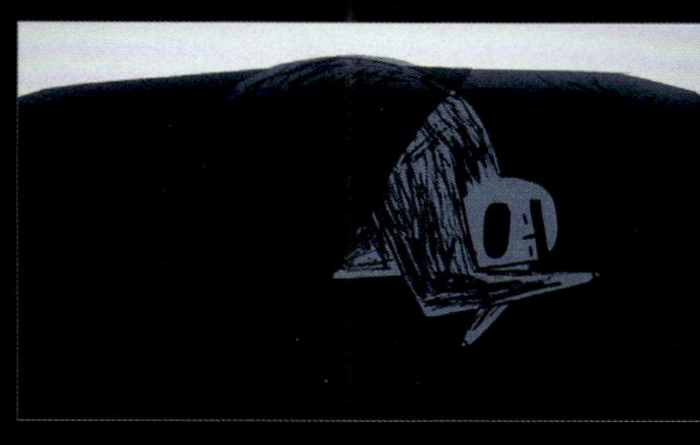
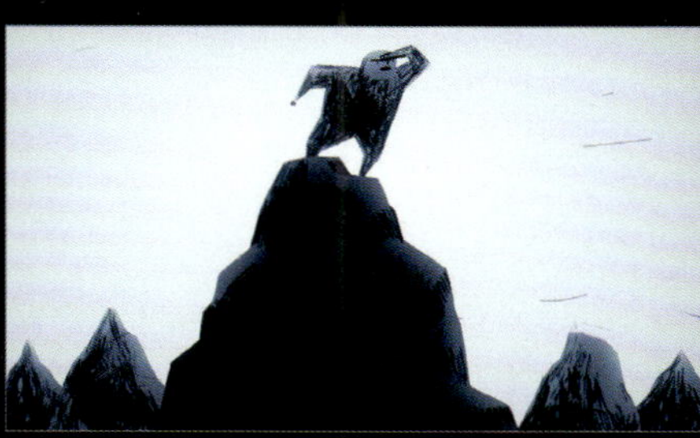
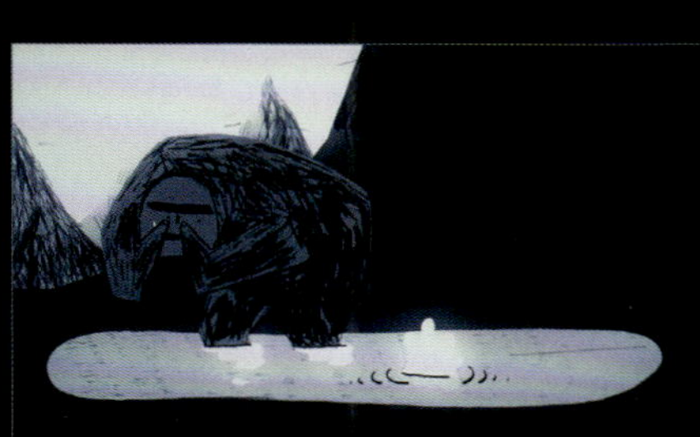
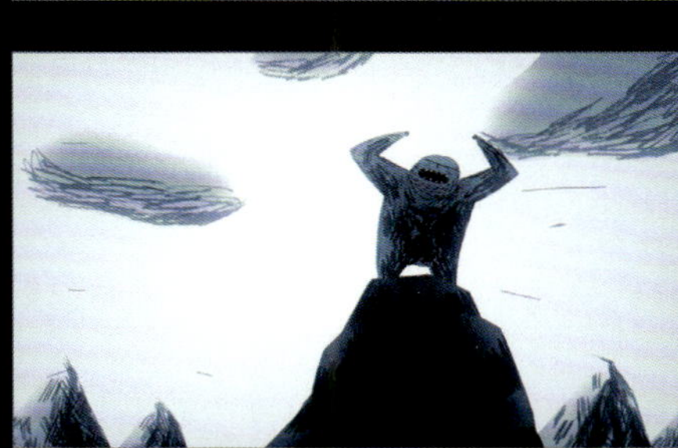
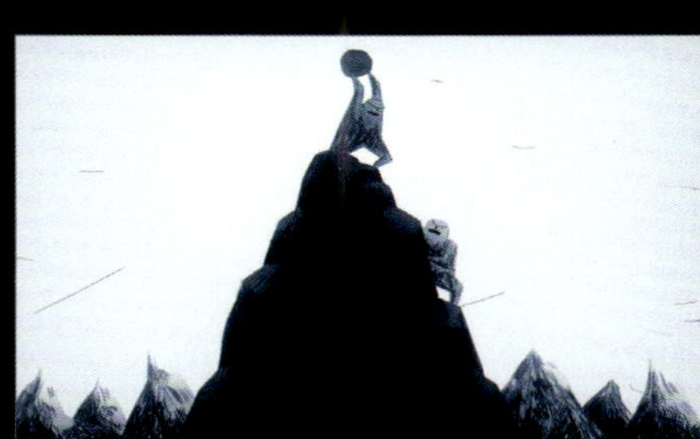

(L) *André Carrilho* (R) DISTINGUISHED MERIT *Patrick Doyon*

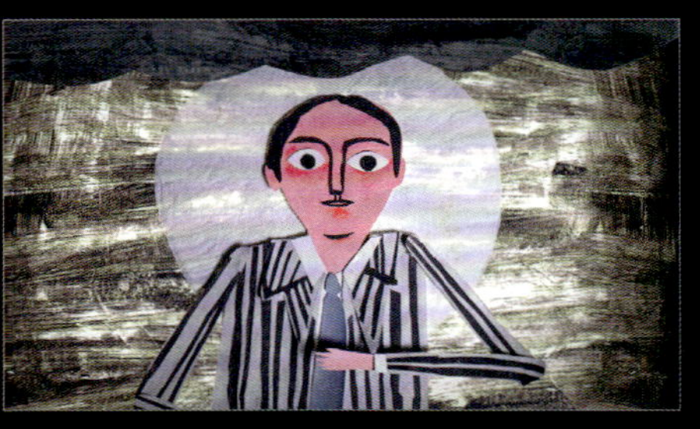
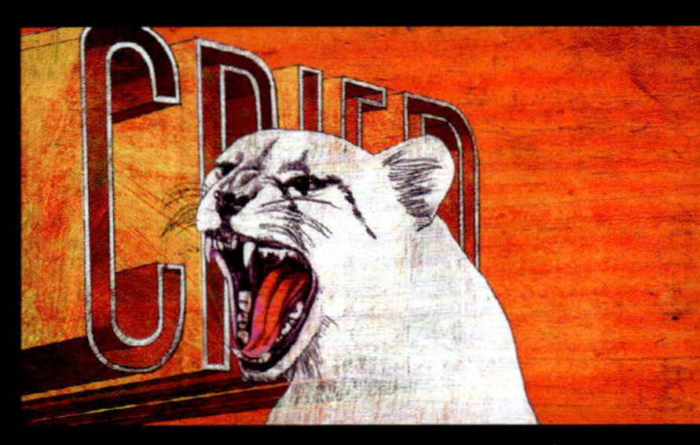
CRIED
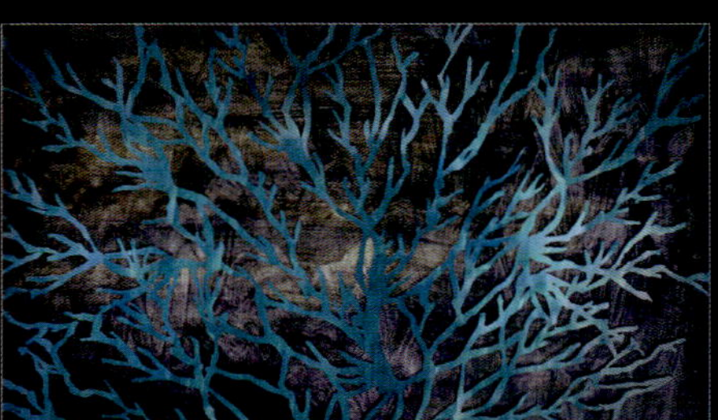
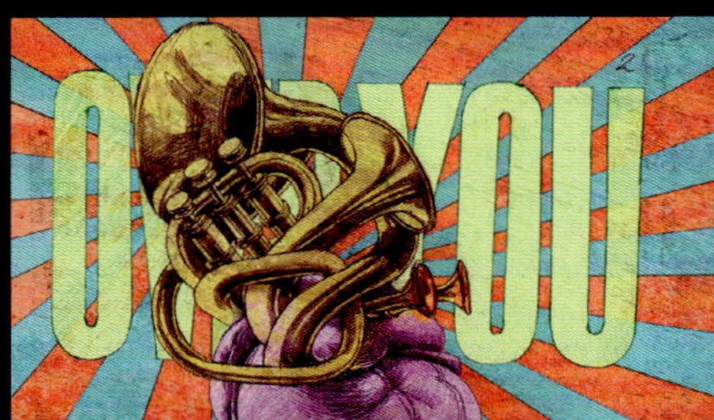
O YOU
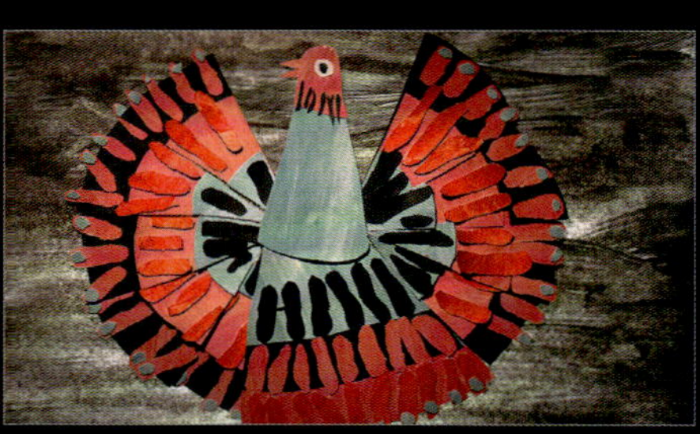
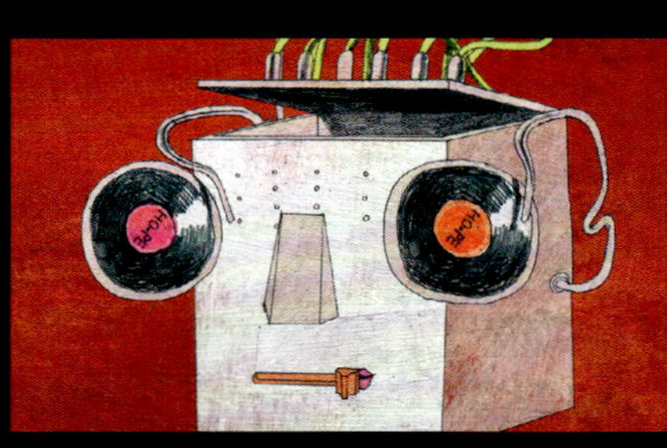
HOPE
HOPE
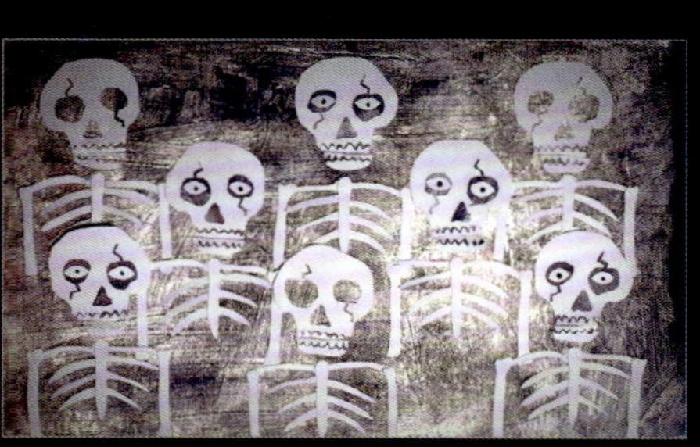
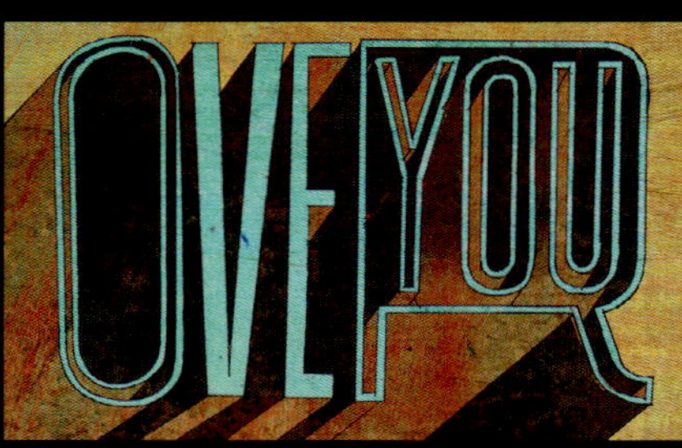
OVE YOU
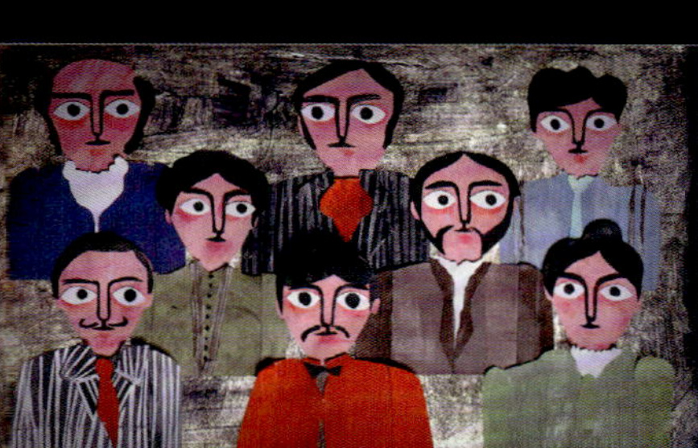
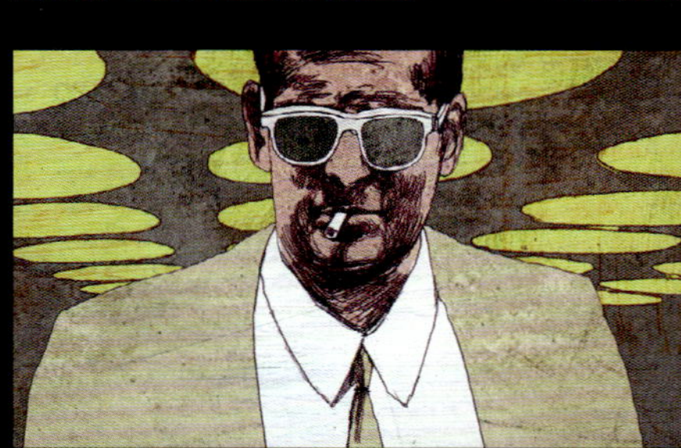

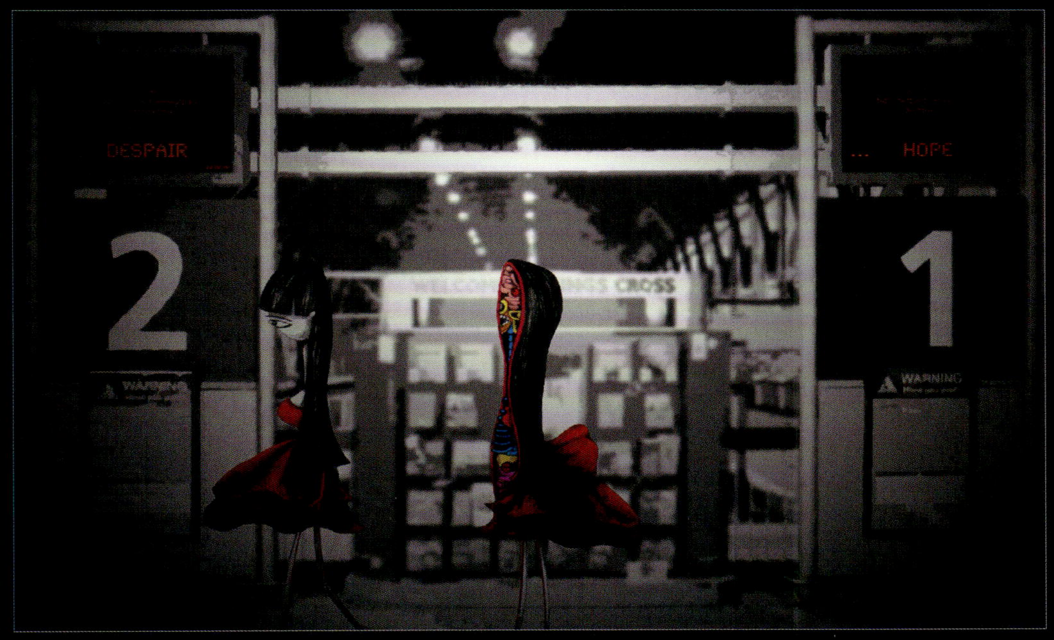

I-Han Chiang

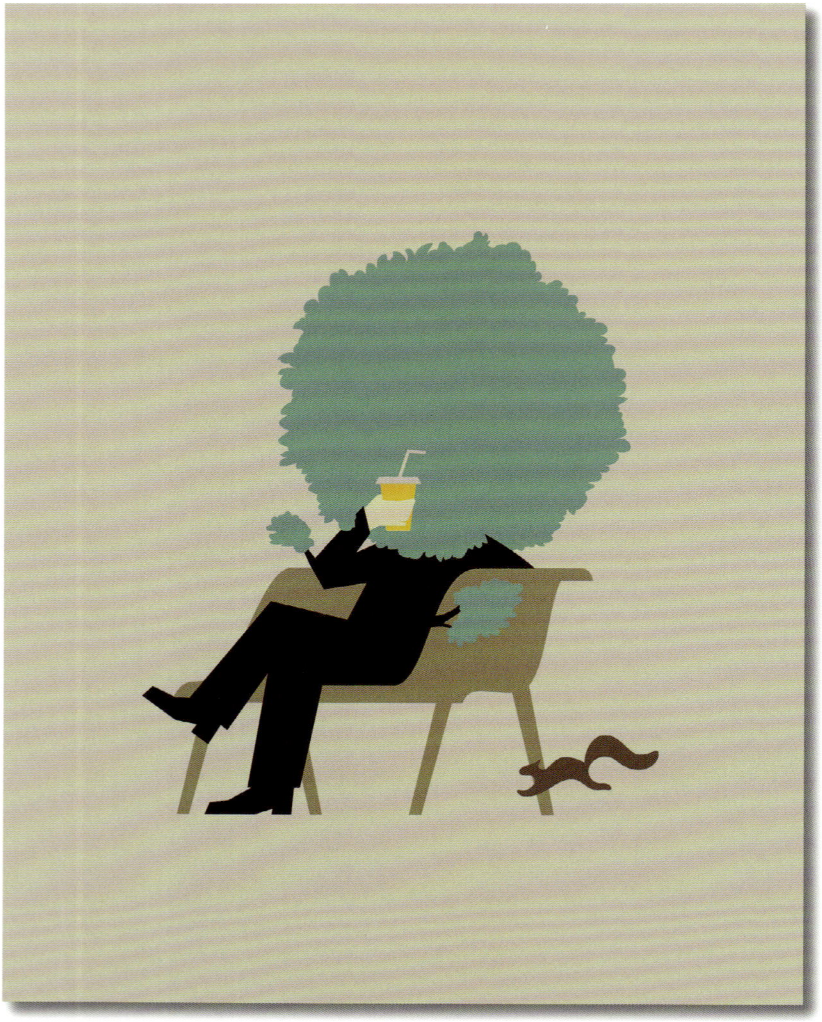

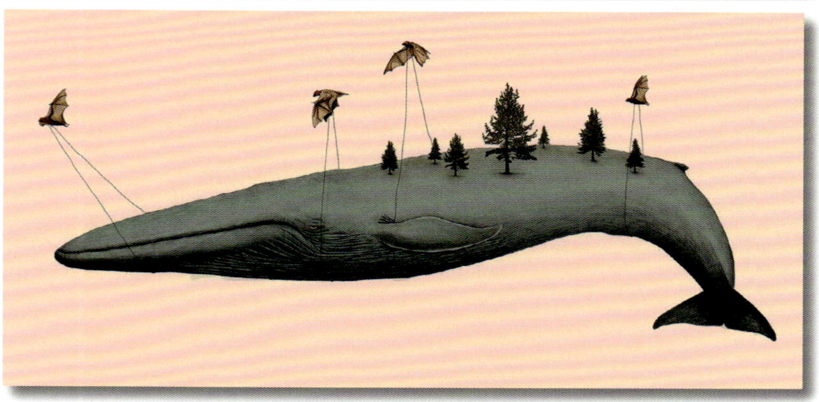

(T) *Aad Goudappel* (B) *Gabriella Barouch*

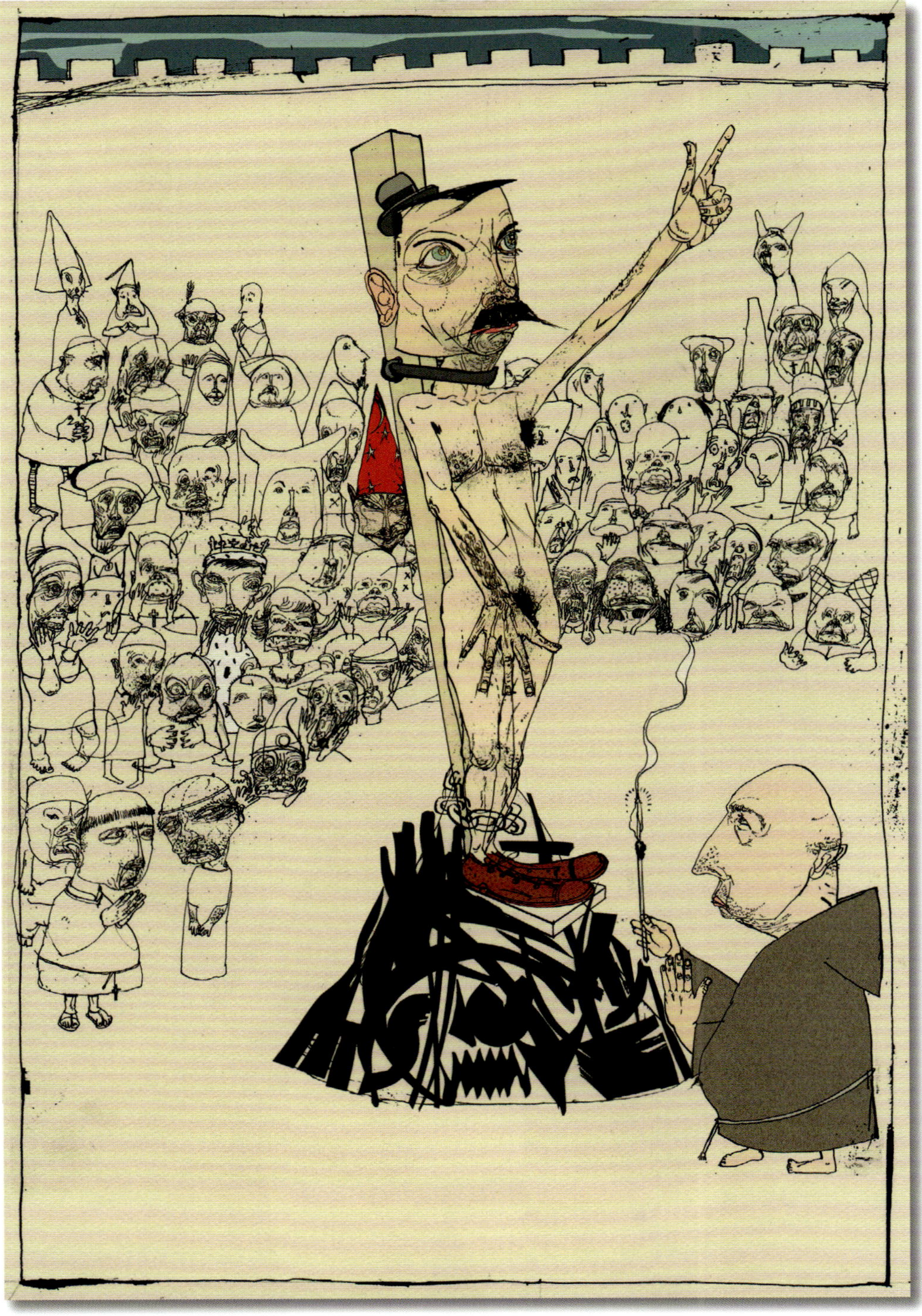

David Hughes

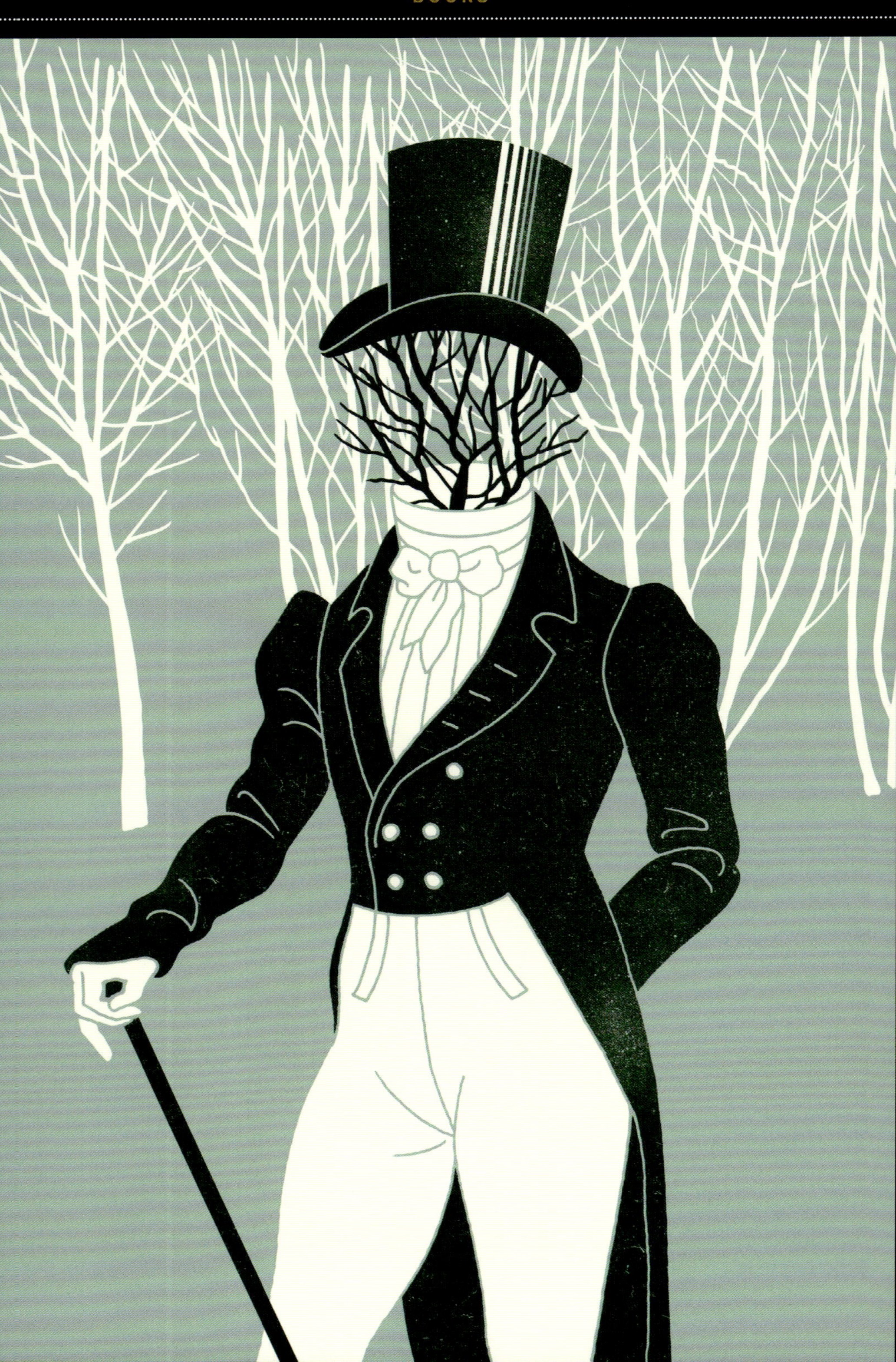

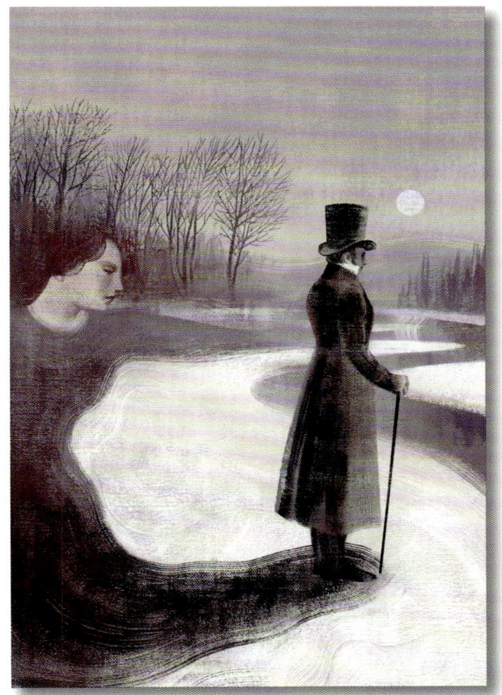
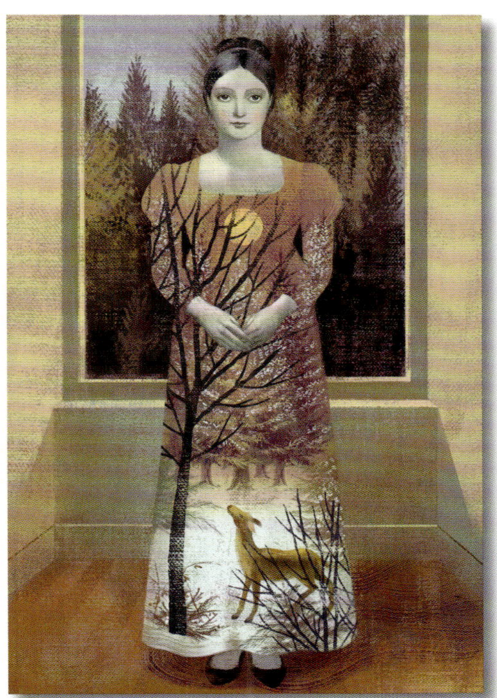
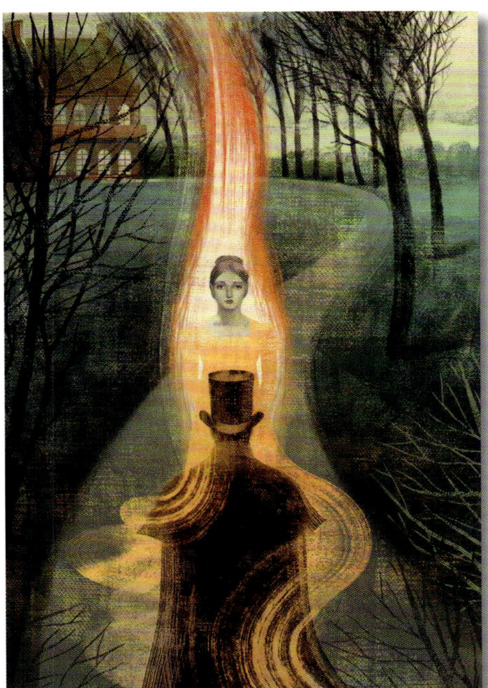
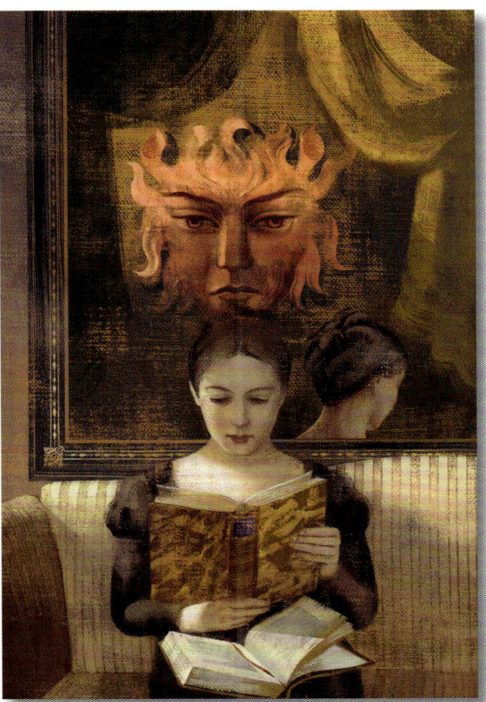

Anna & Elena Balbusso

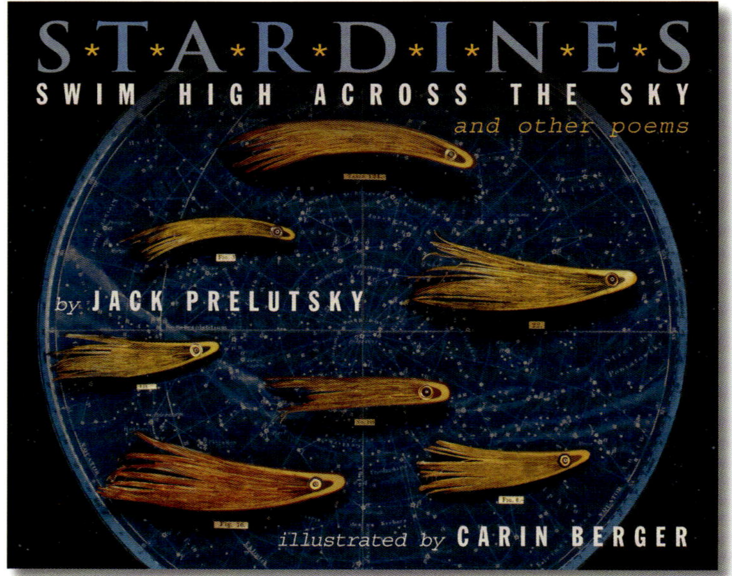
S*TA*R*D*I*N*E*S
SWIM HIGH ACROSS THE SKY
and other poems
by JACK PRELUTSKY
illustrated by CARIN BERGER

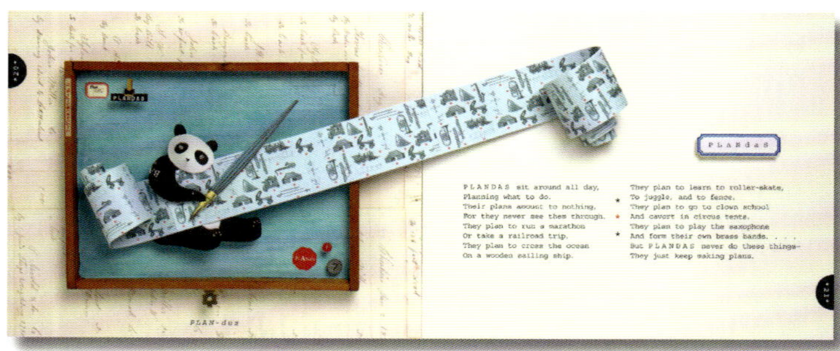
PLANDAS

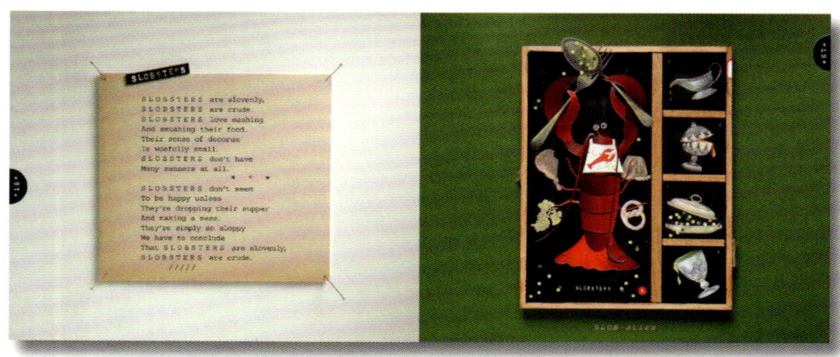

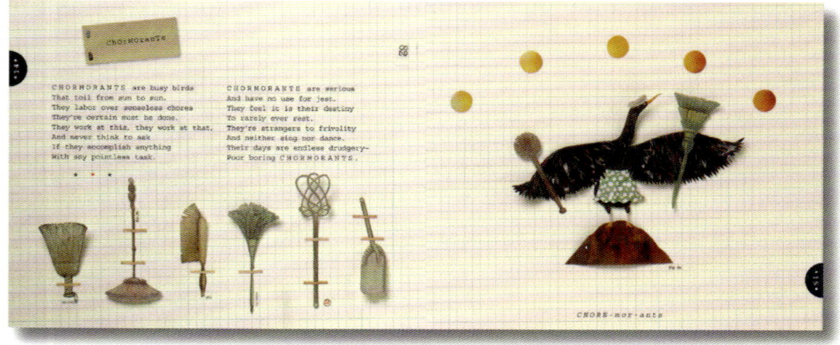

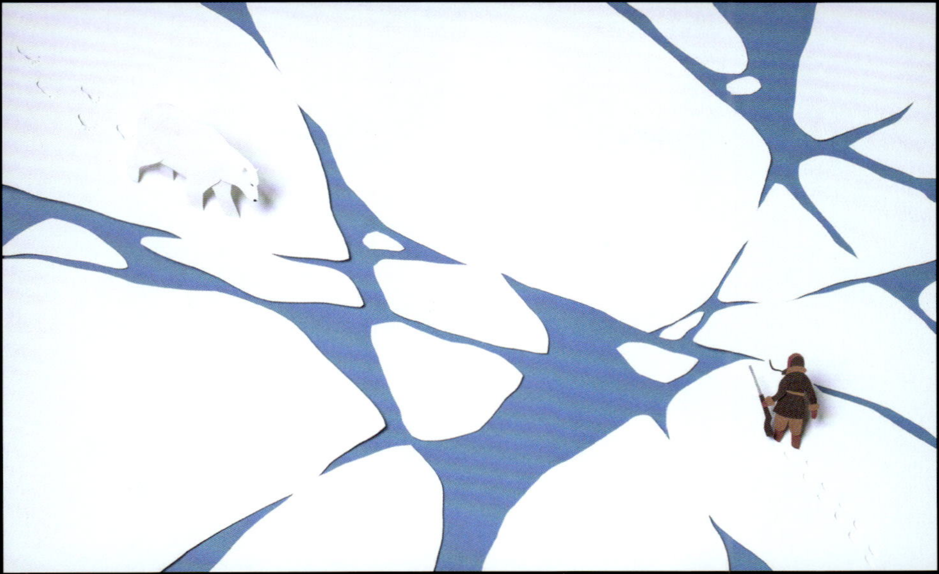

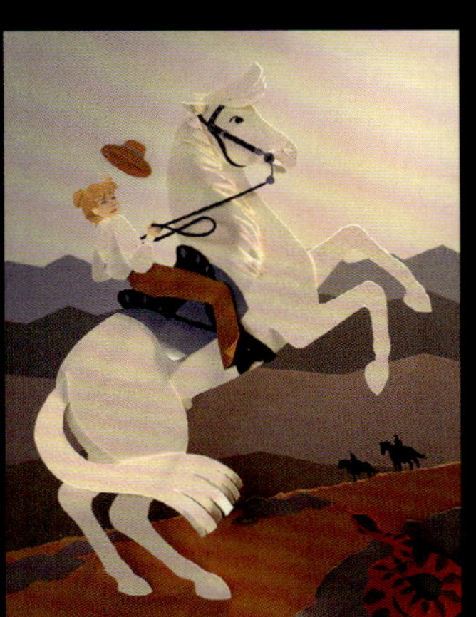

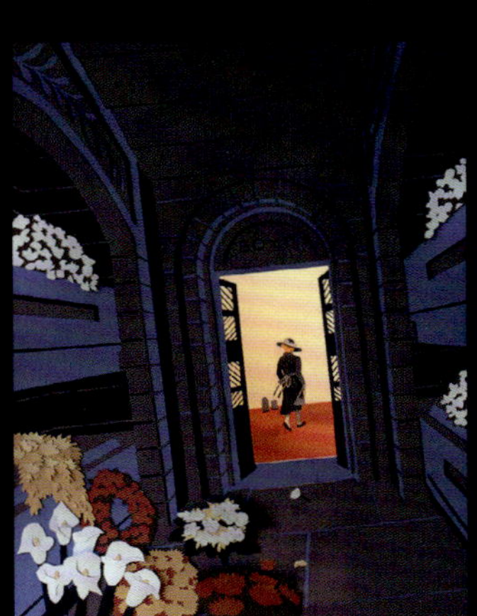

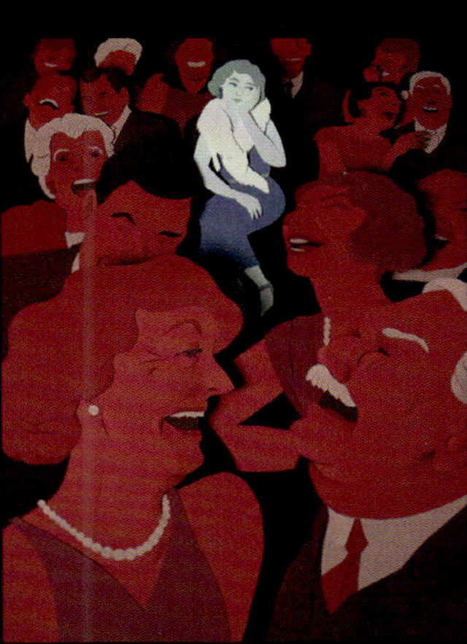

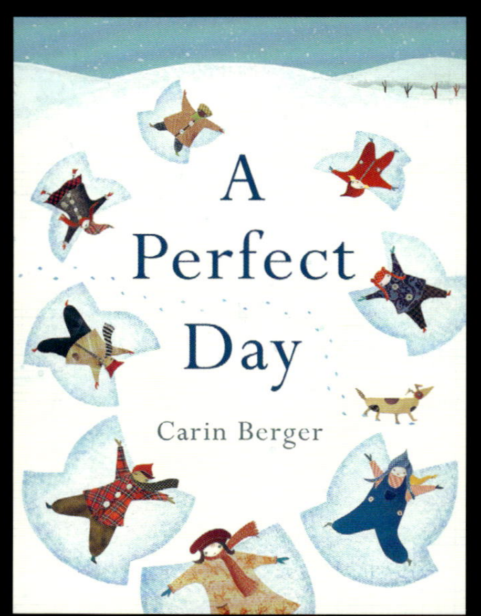

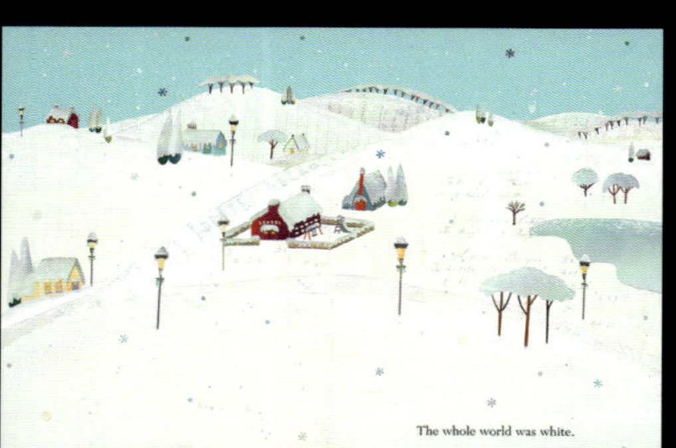

The whole world was white.

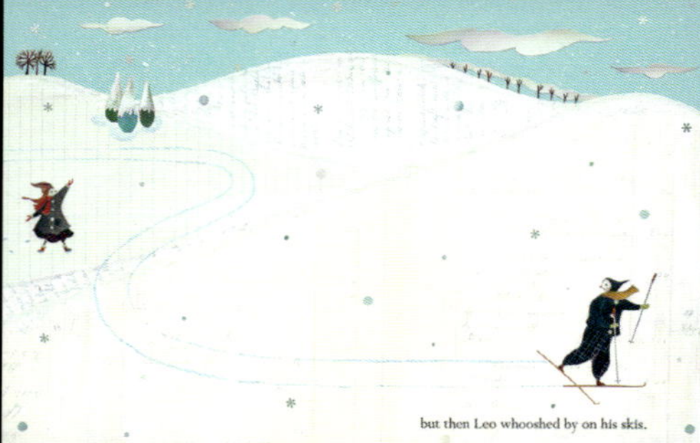

but then Leo whooshed by on his skis.

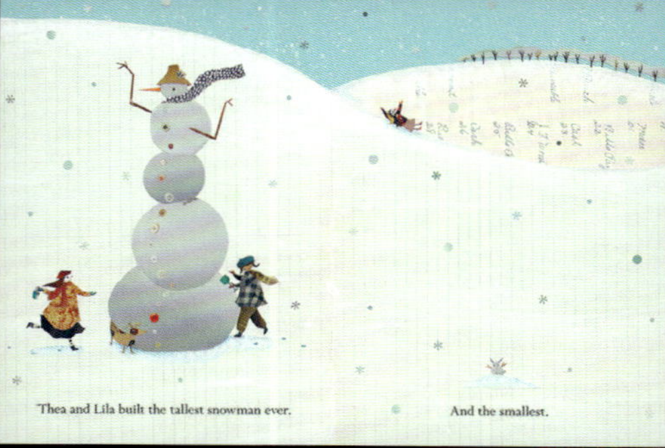

Thea and Lila built the tallest snowman ever.

And the smallest.

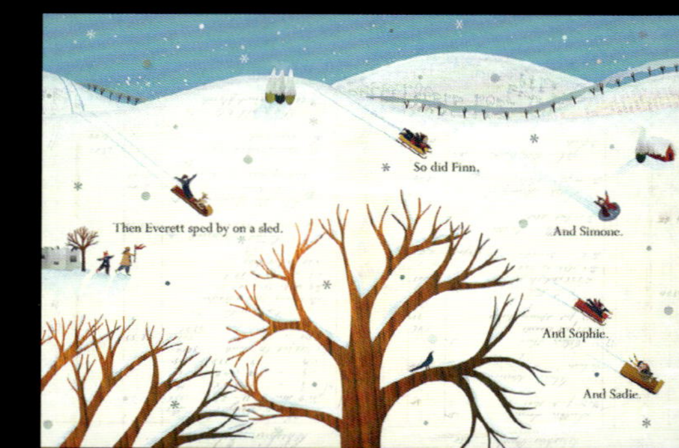

Then Everett sped by on a sled.

So did Finn,

And Simone.

And Sophie.

And Sadie.

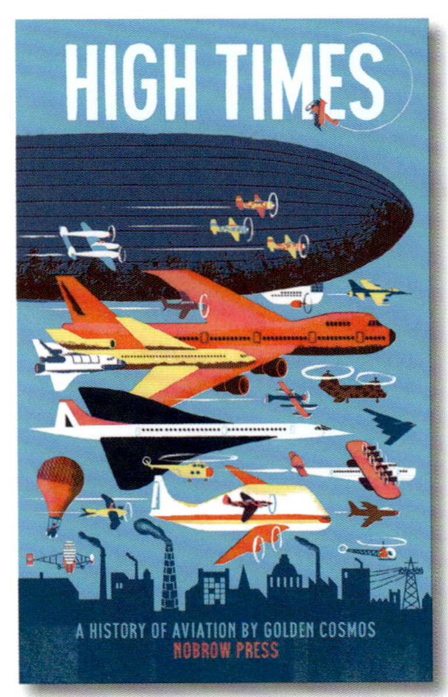

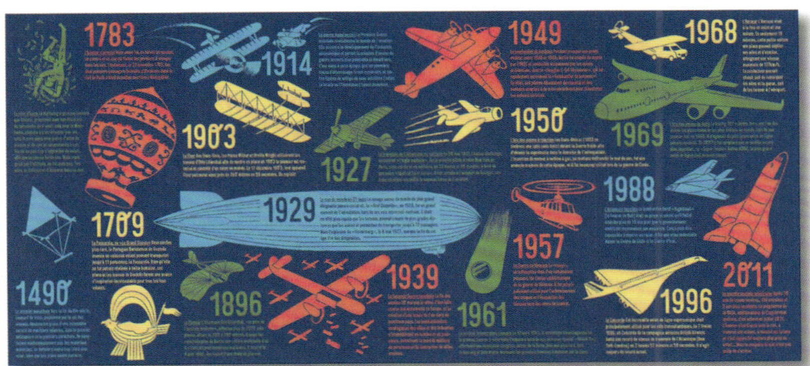

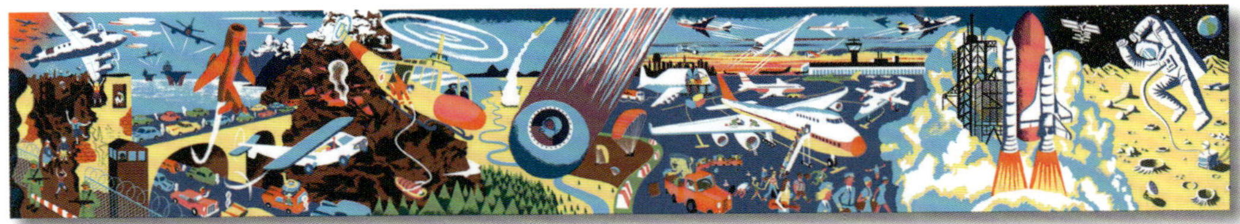

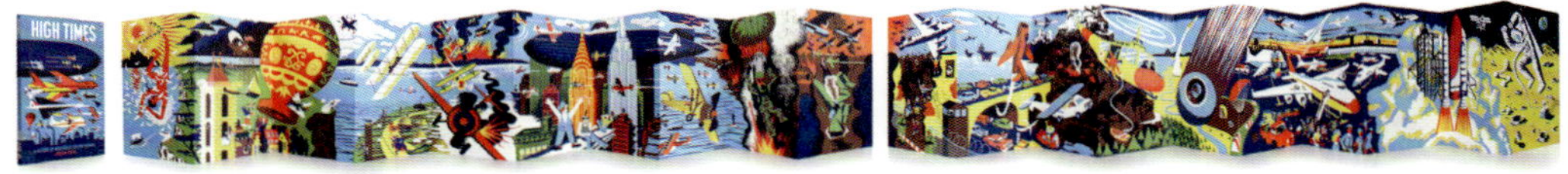

DISTINGUISHED MERIT *Golden Cosmos*

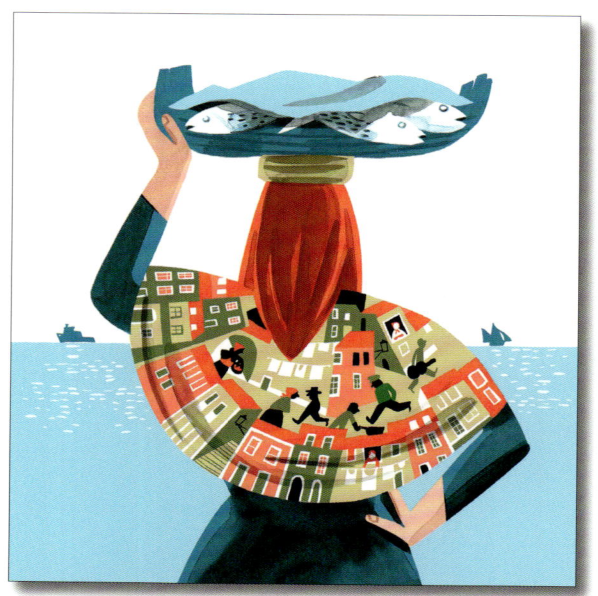

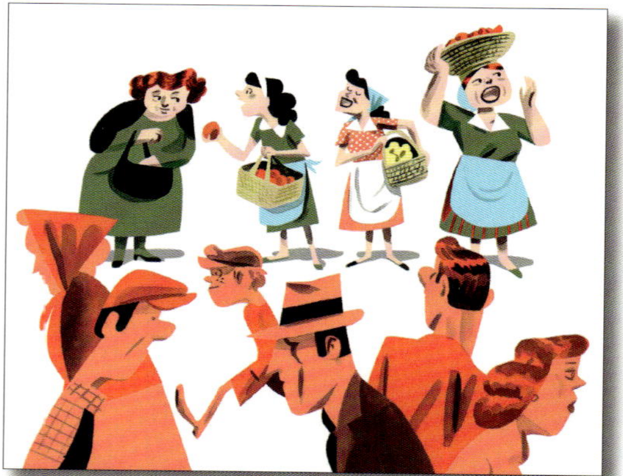

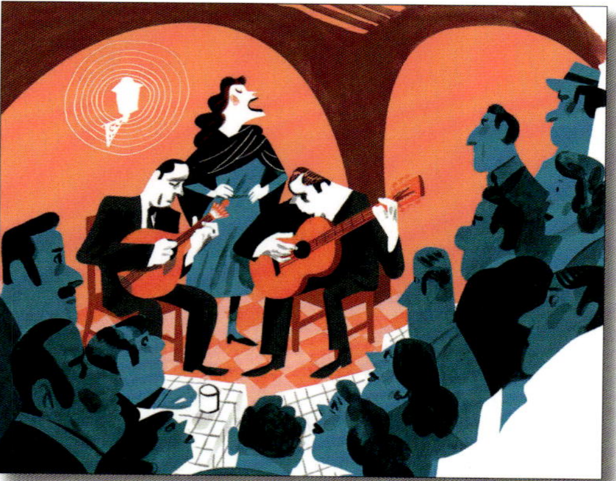

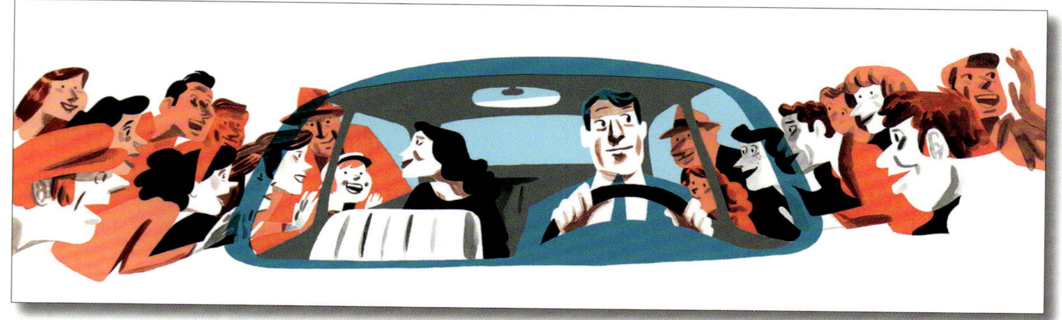

BRONZE *João Fazenda*

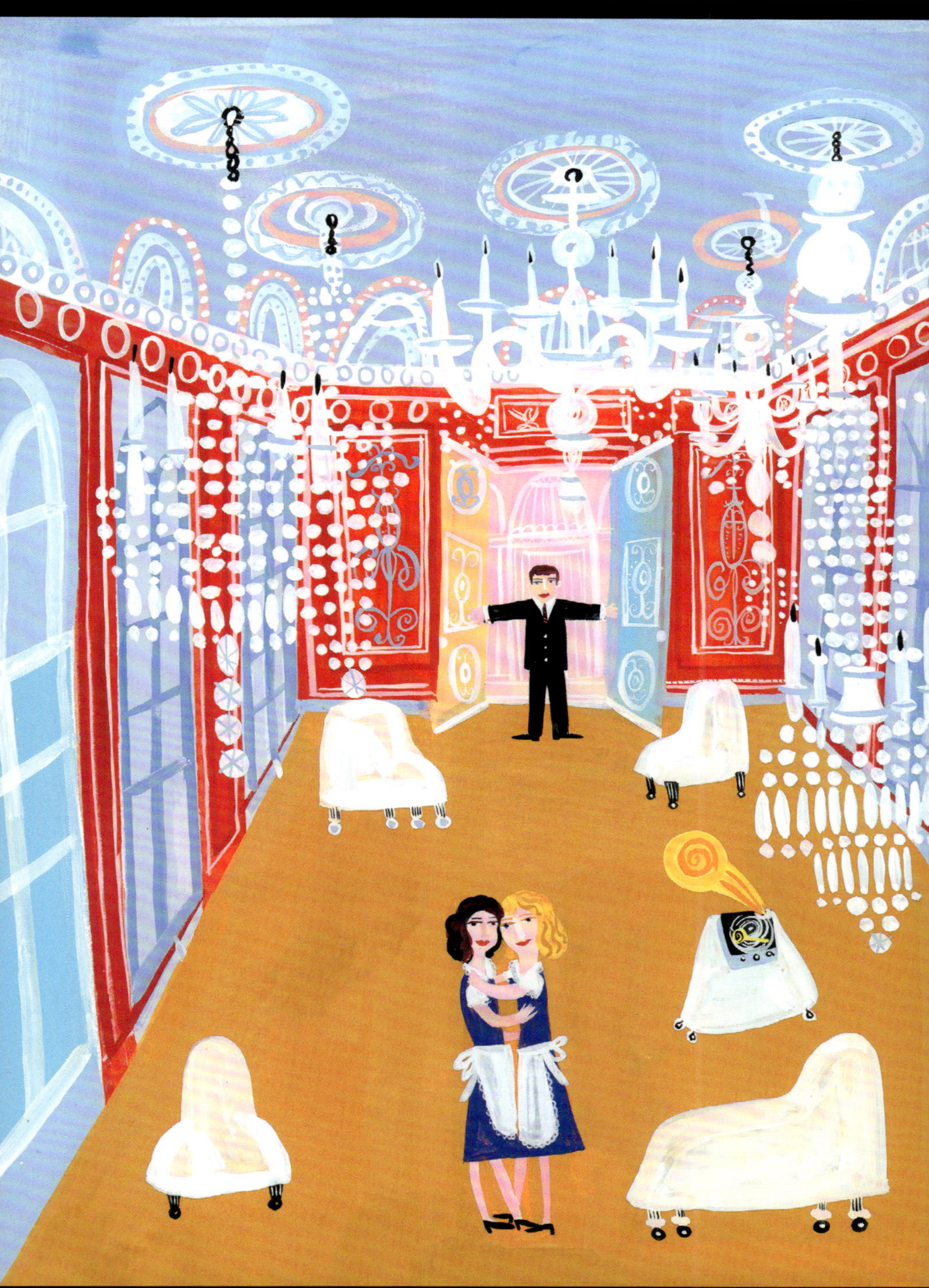

Christopher Corr

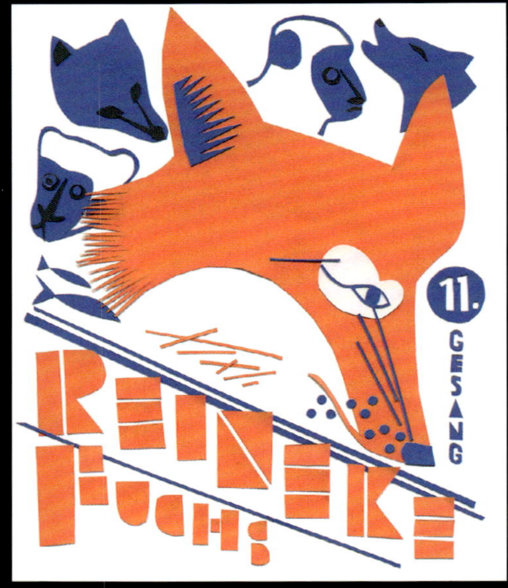

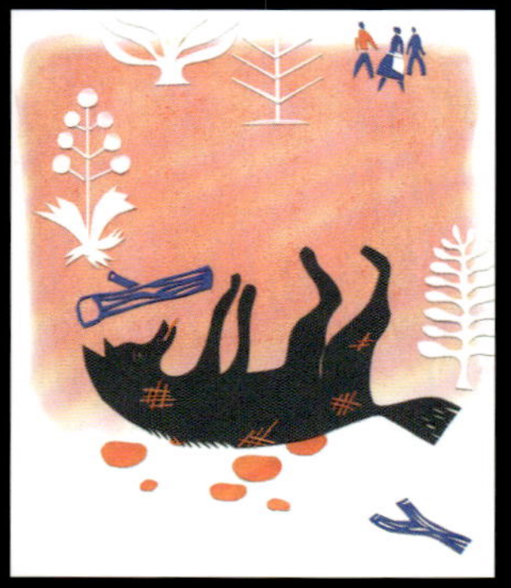

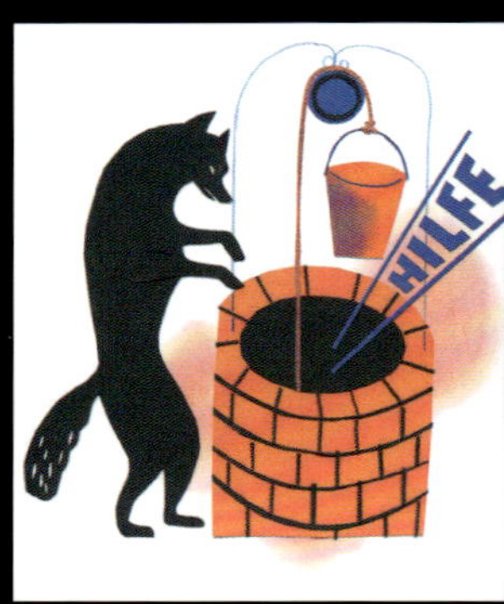

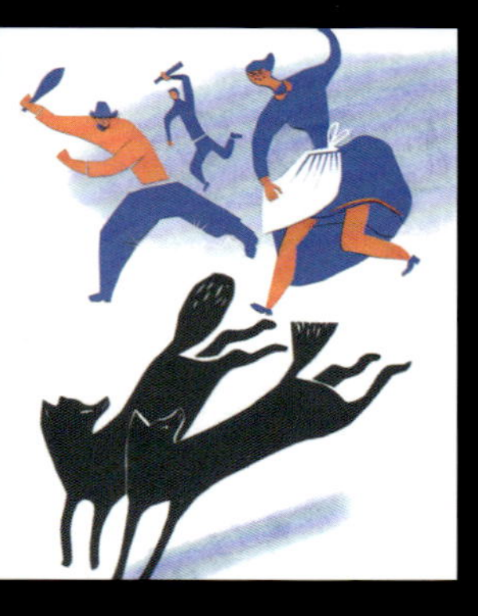

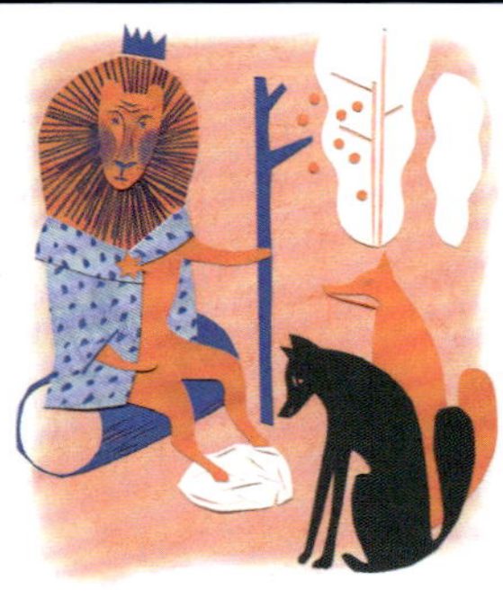

Stephanie Wunderlich

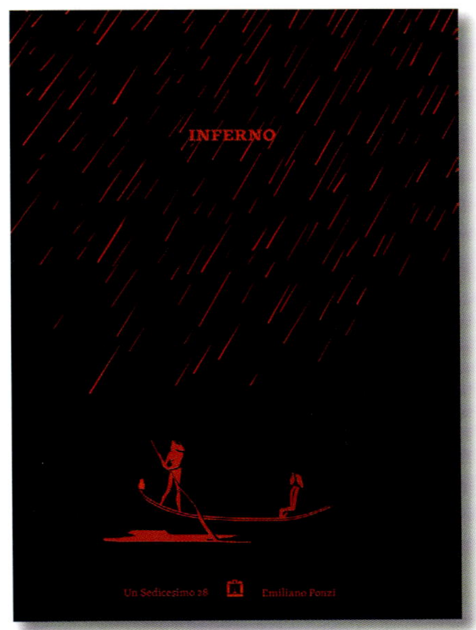

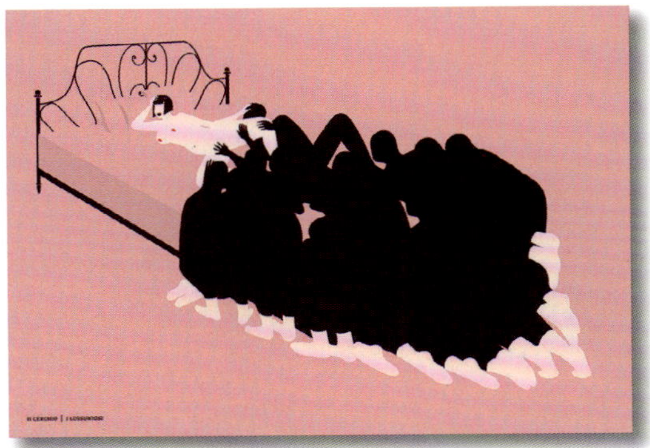

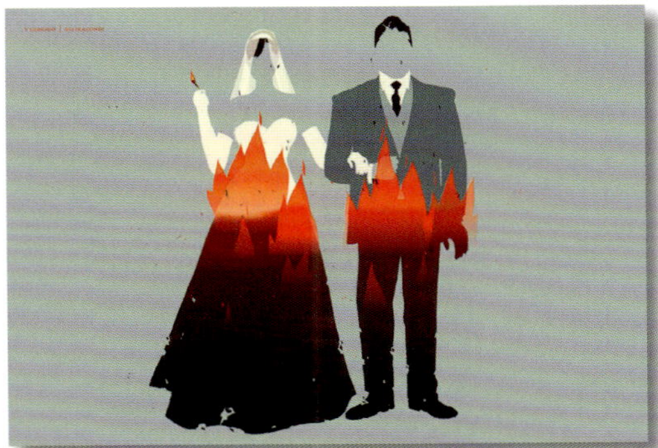

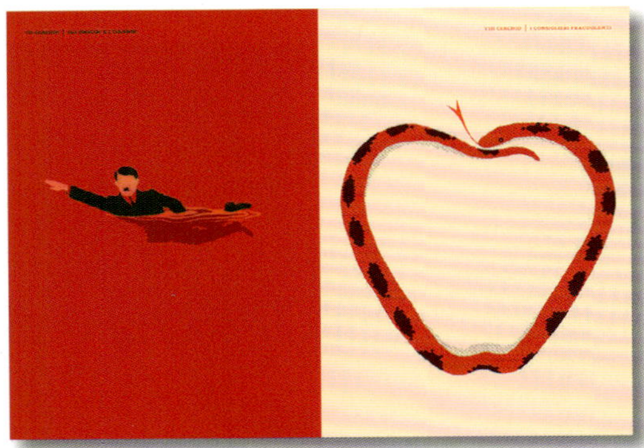

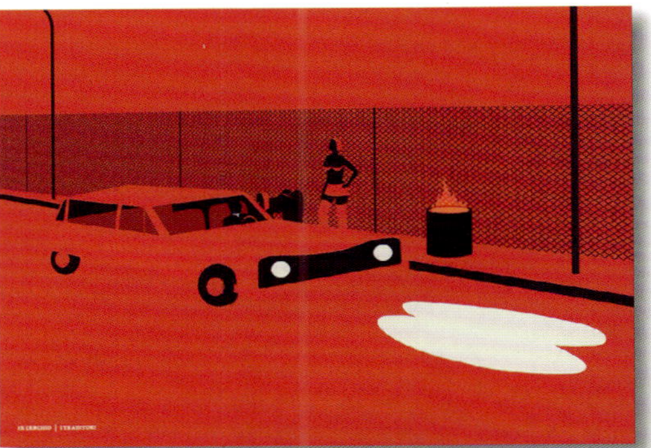

Emiliano Ponzi

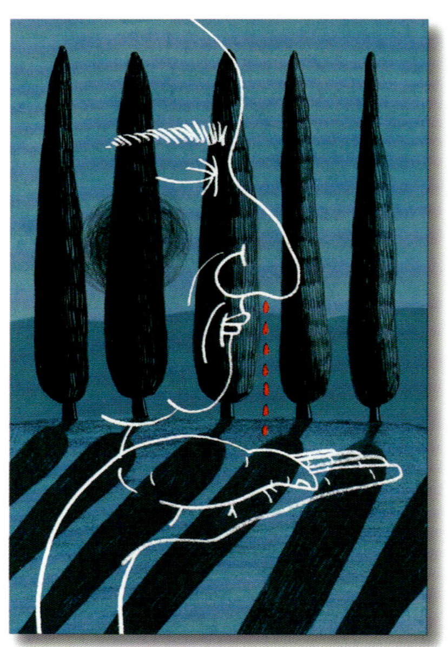

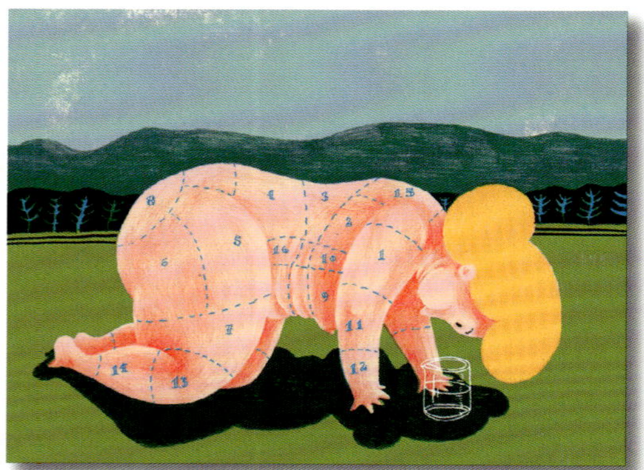

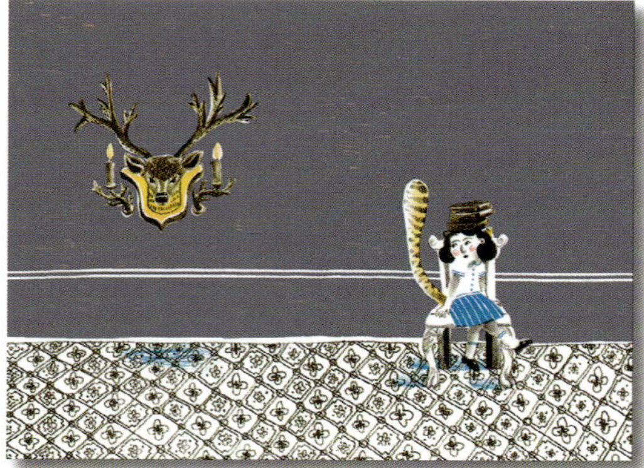

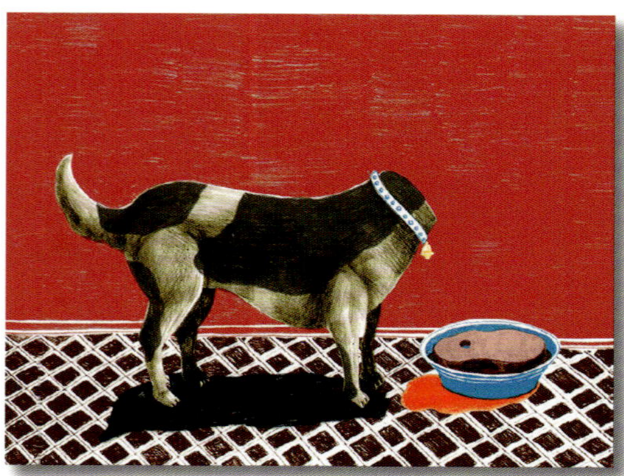

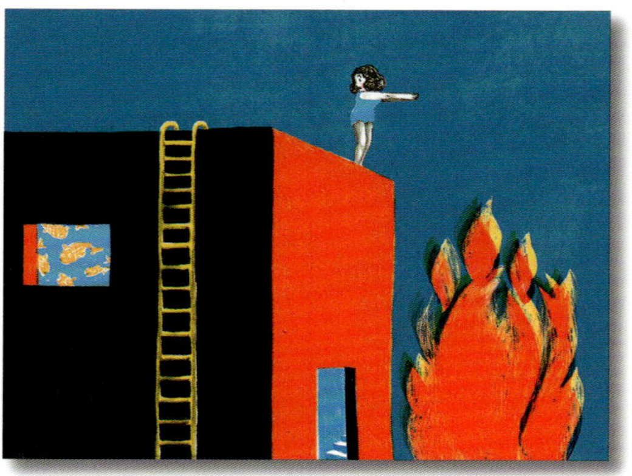

Merav Salomon

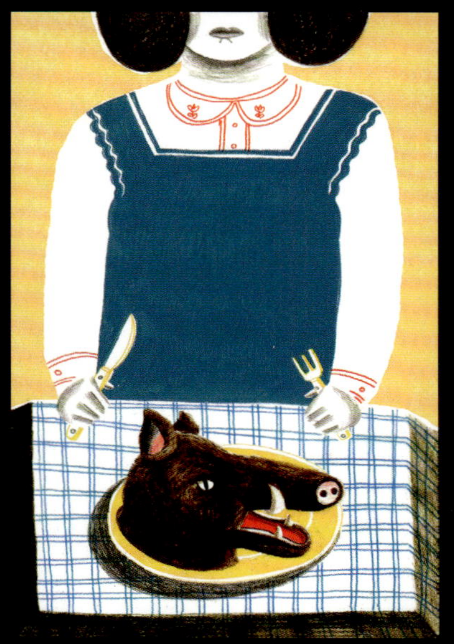

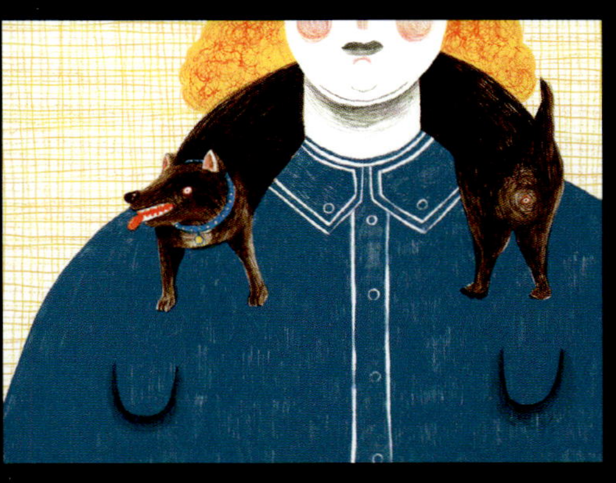

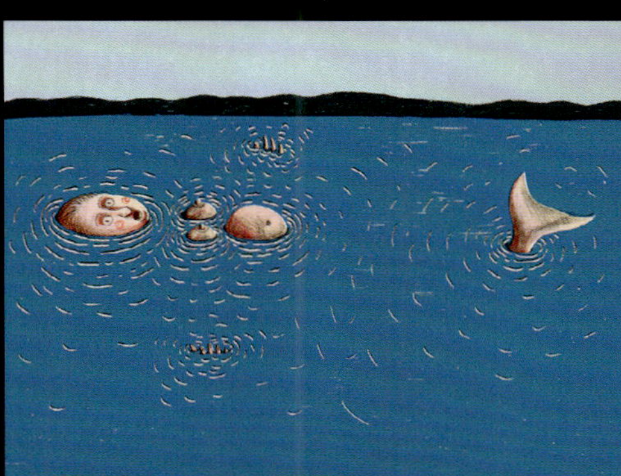

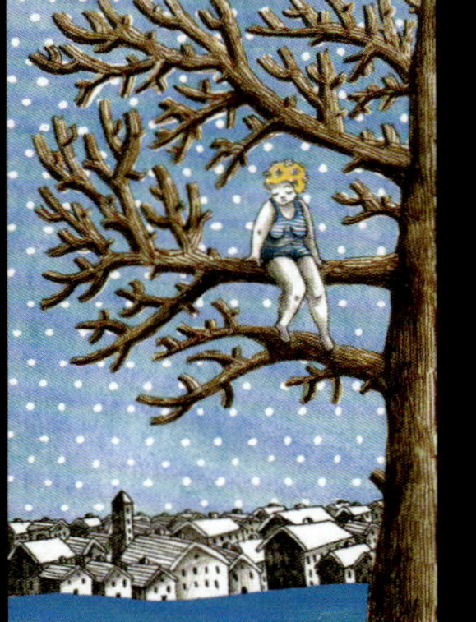

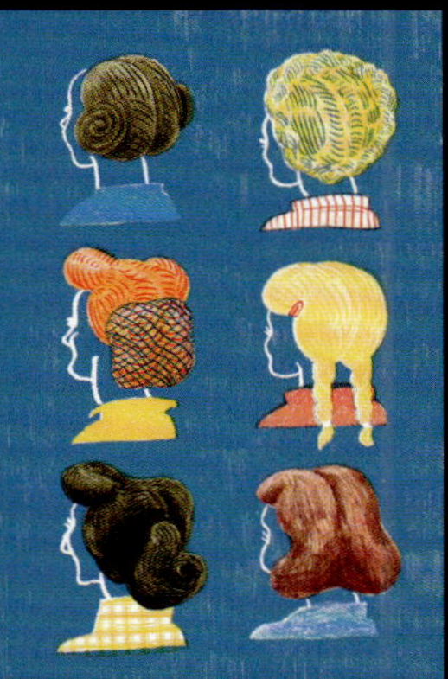

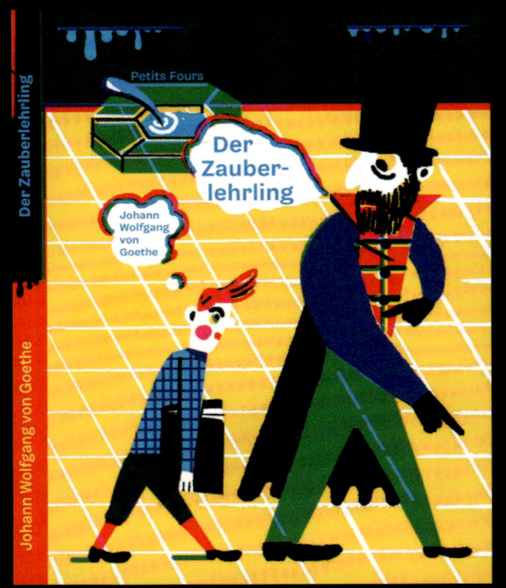
Petits Fours
Der Zauberlehrling
Johann Wolfgang von Goethe
Der Zauberlehrling
Johann Wolfgang von Goethe

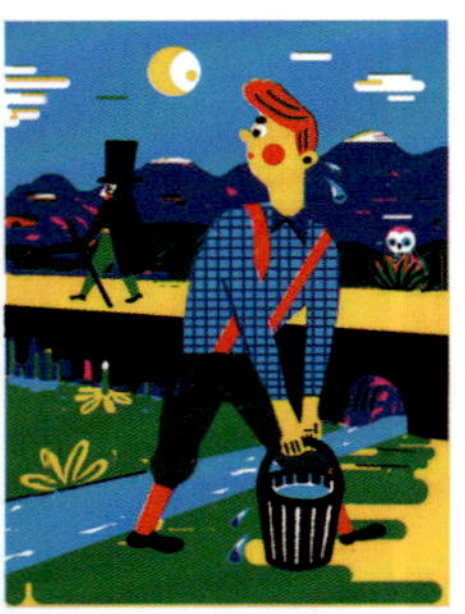

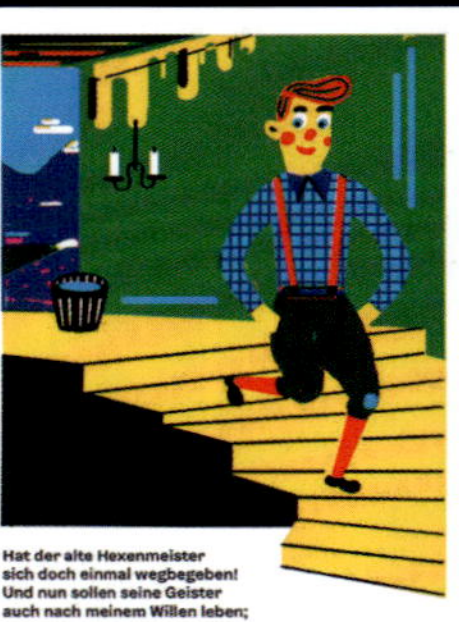
Hat der alte Hexenmeister
sich doch einmal wegbegeben!
Und nun sollen seine Geister
auch nach meinem Willen leben;

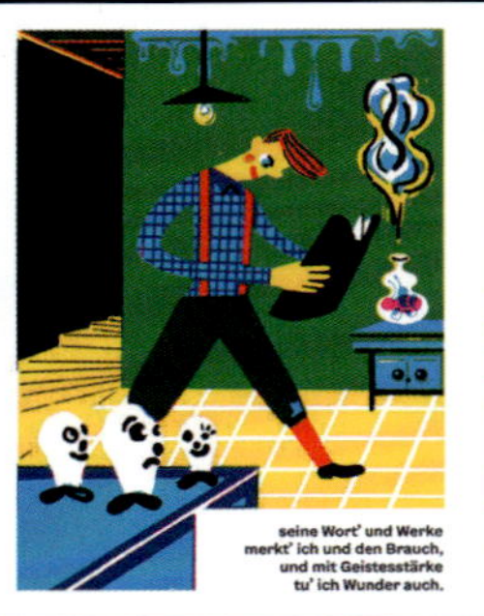
seine Wort' und Werke
merkt' ich und den Brauch,
und mit Geistesstärke
tu' ich Wunder auch.

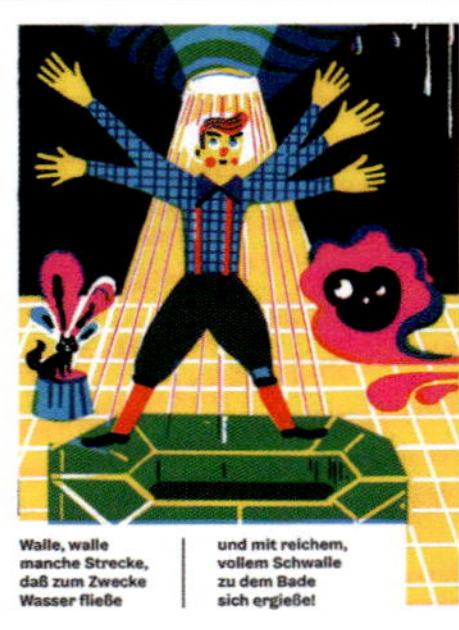
Walle, walle
manche Strecke,
daß zum Zwecke
Wasser fließe

und mit reichem,
vollem Schwalle
zu dem Bade
sich ergieße!

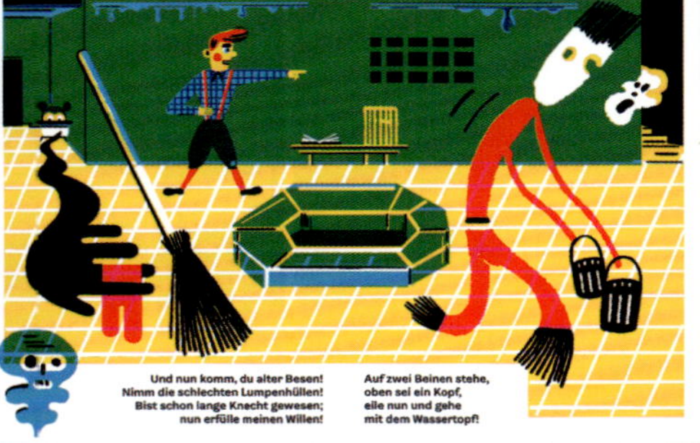
Und nun komm, du alter Besen!
Nimm die schlechten Lumpenhüllen!
Bist schon lange Knecht gewesen;
nun erfülle meinen Willen!

Auf zwei Beinen stehe,
oben sei ein Kopf,
eile nun und gehe
mit dem Wassertopf!

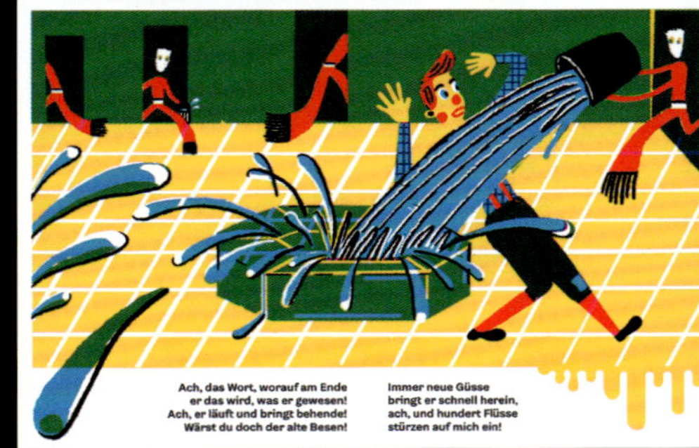
Ach, das Wort, worauf am Ende
er das wird, was er gewesen!
Ach, er läuft und bringt behende!
Wärst du doch der alte Besen!

Immer neue Güsse
bringt er schnell herein,
ach, und hundert Flüsse
stürzen auf mich ein!

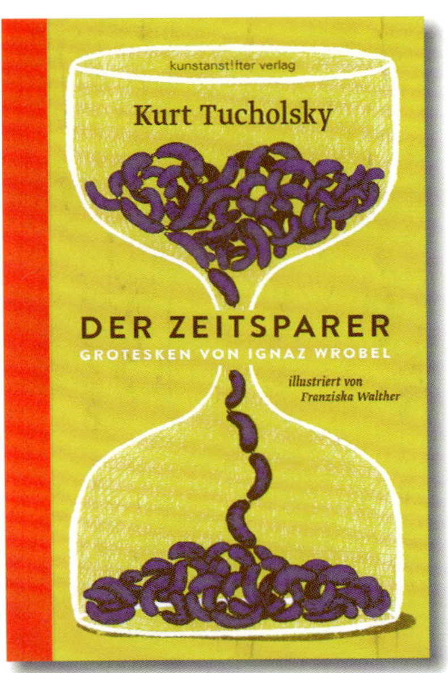

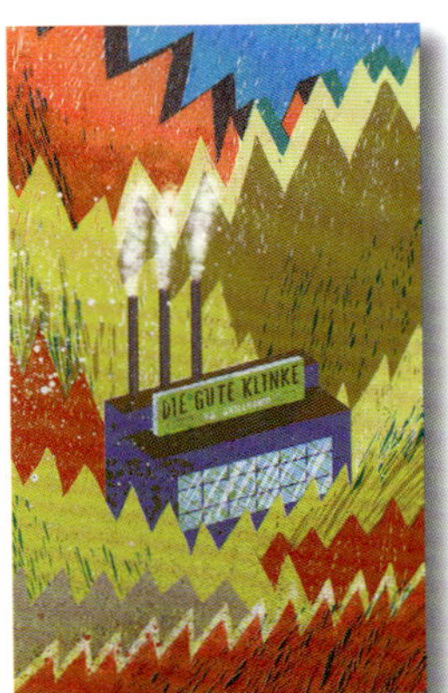

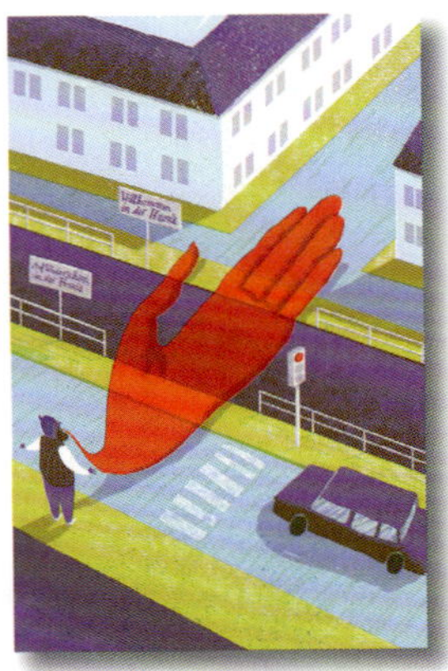

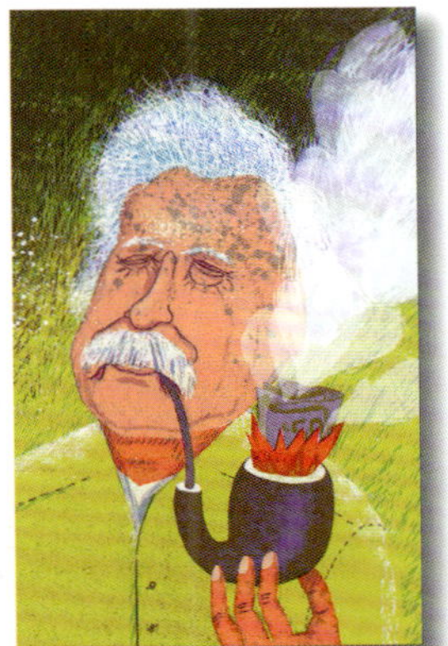

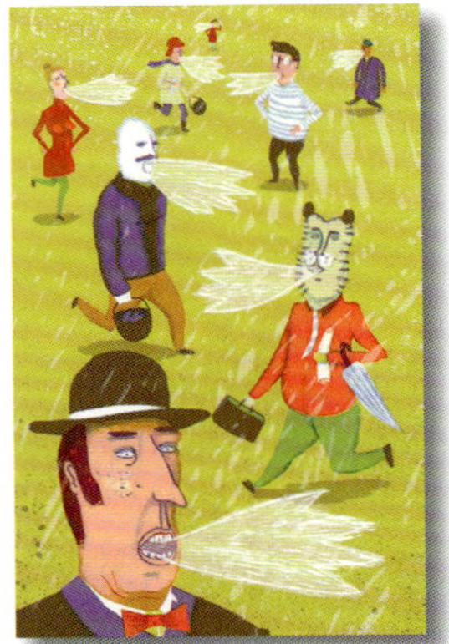

Franziska Walther

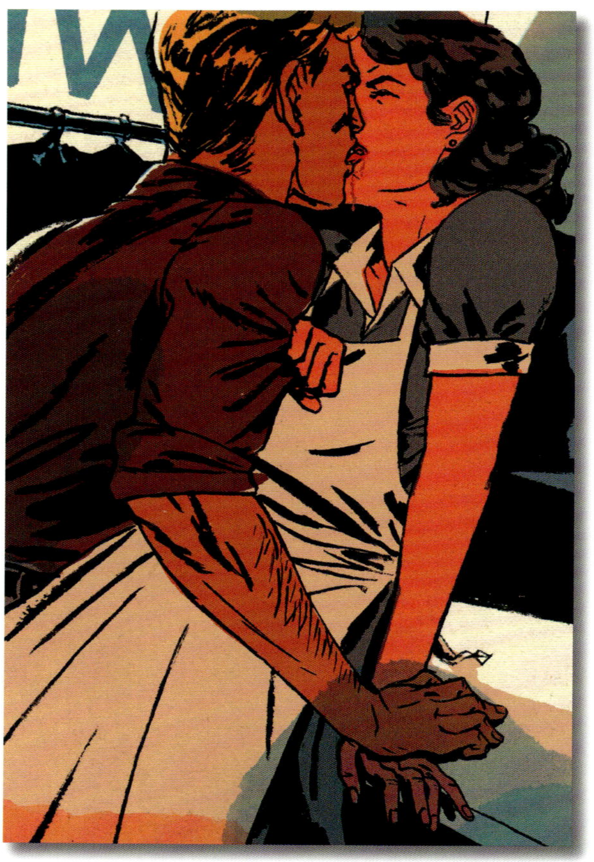

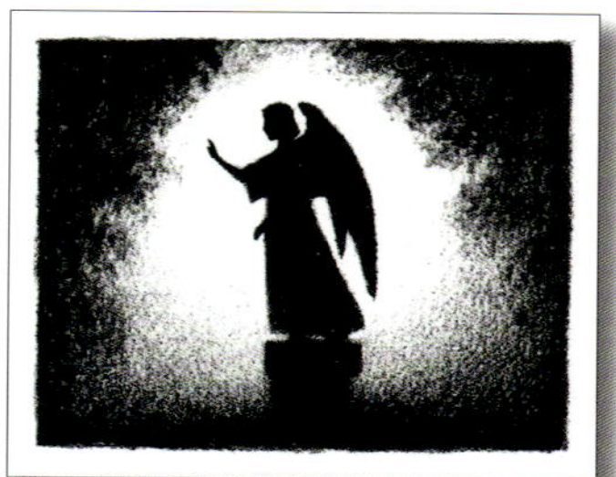

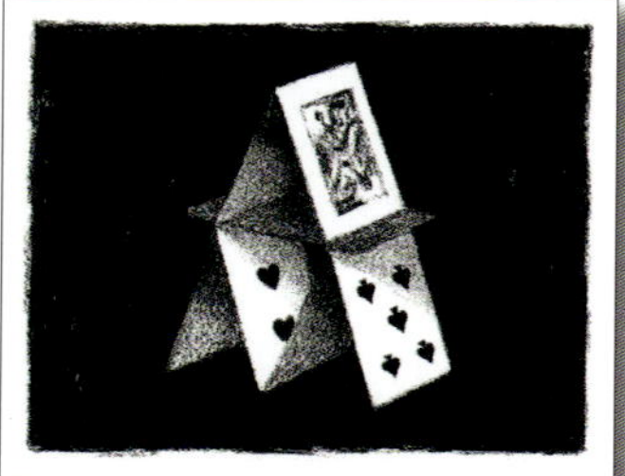

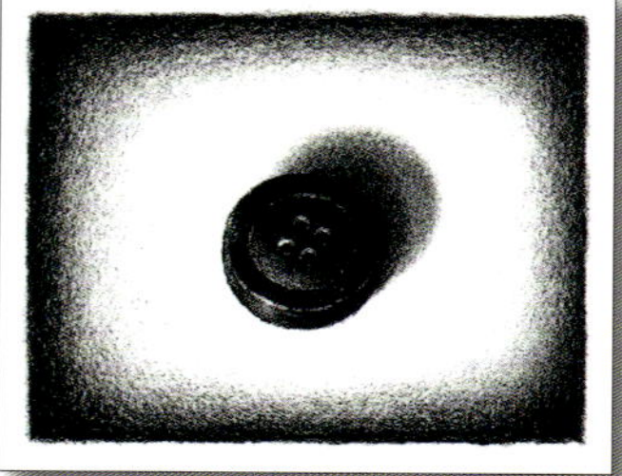

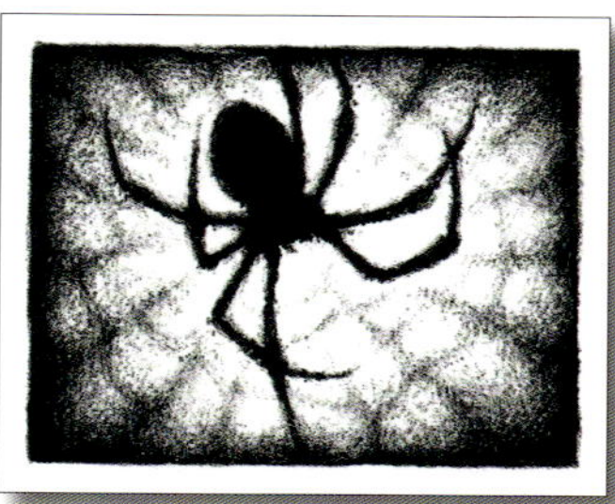

(T) Patrick Leger (B) Houston Trueblood (R) Mari Mitsumi

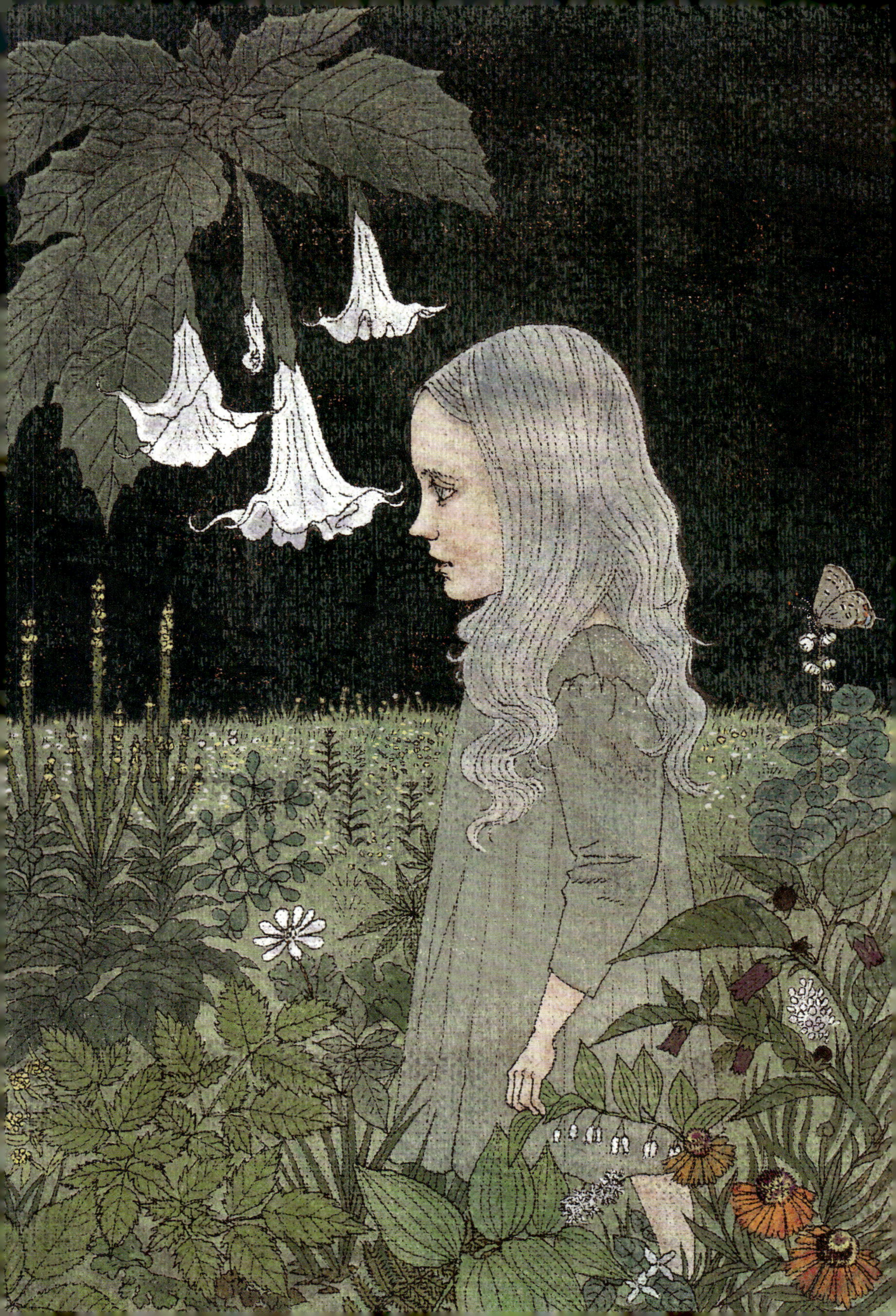

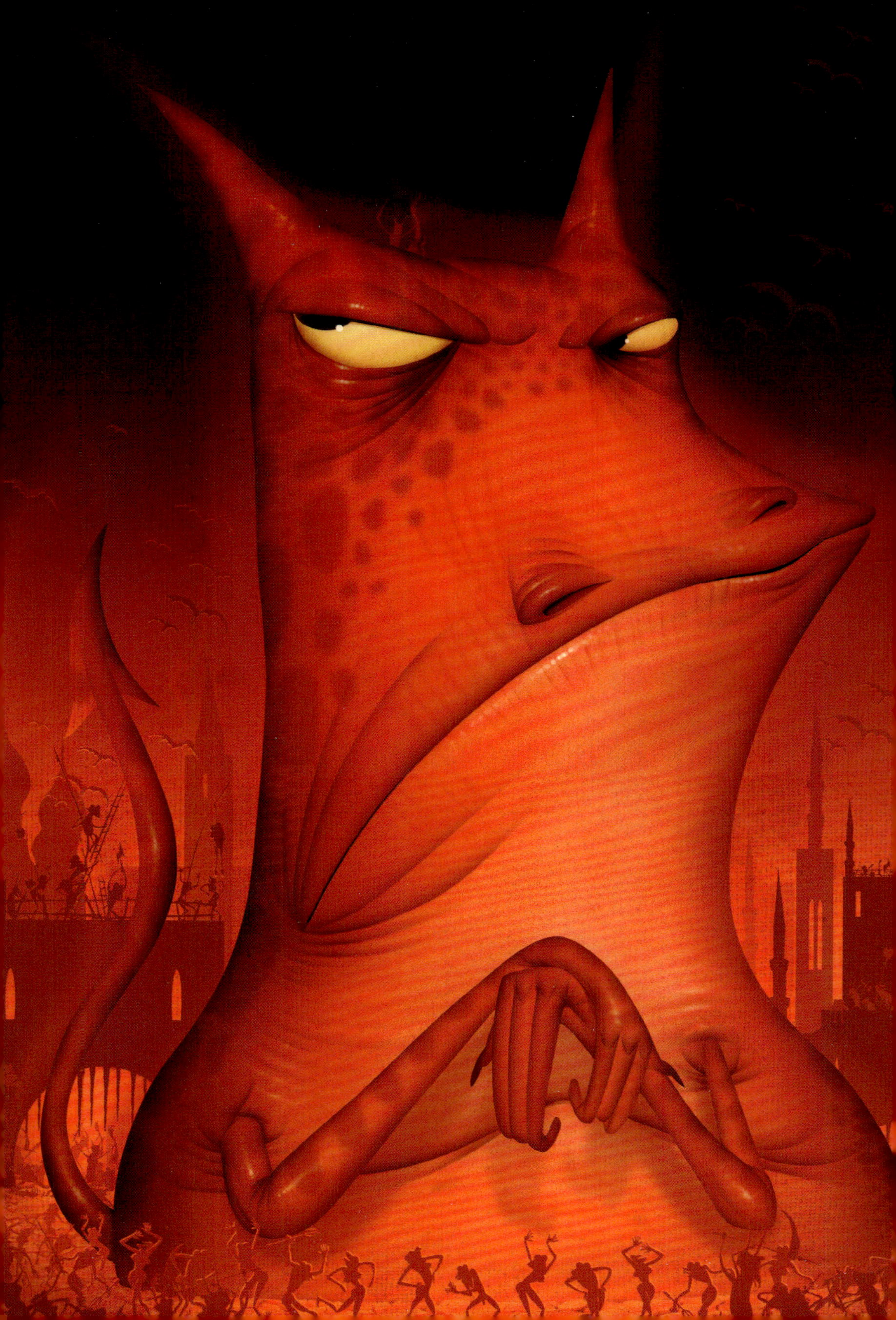

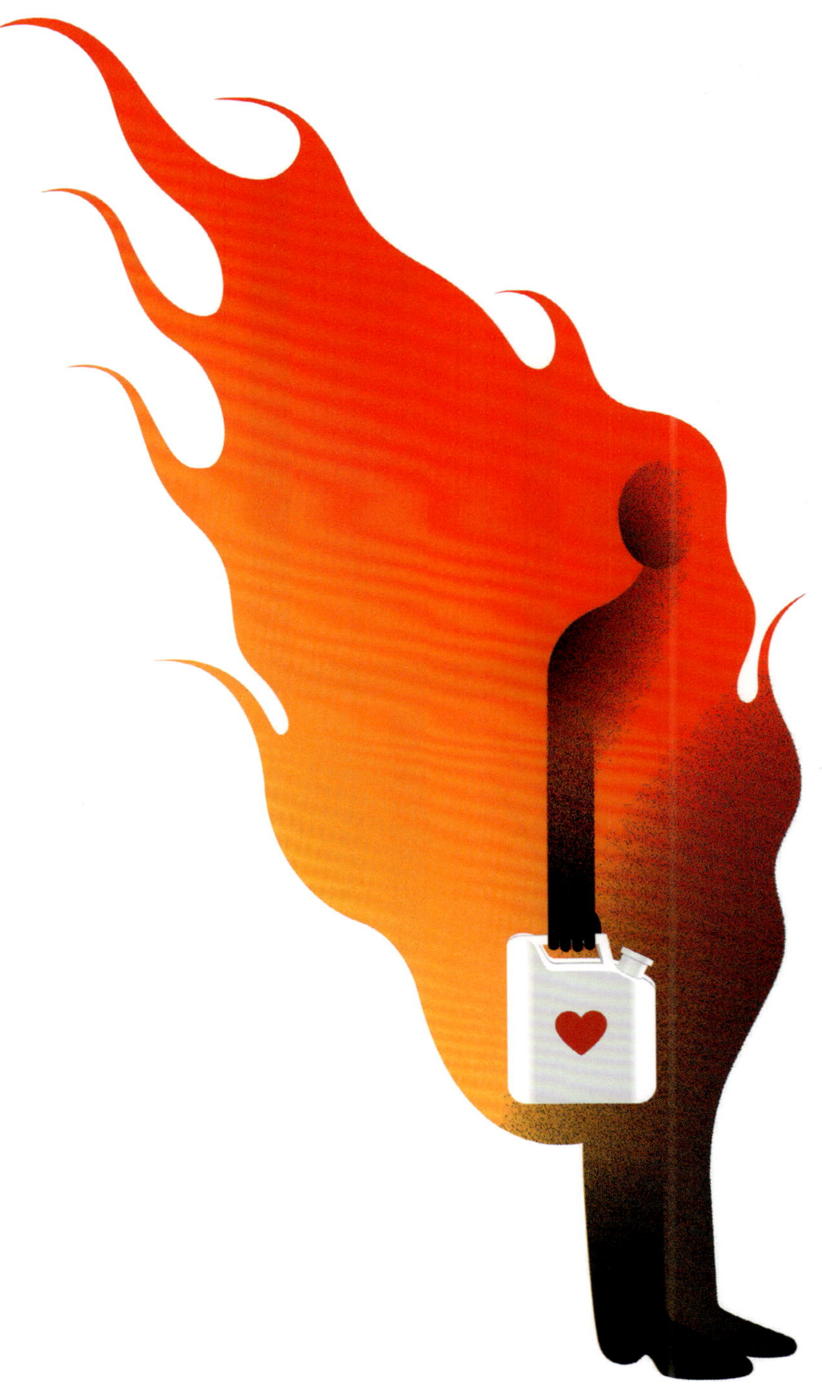

(L) *Bill Mayer* (R) *Mirko Cresta*

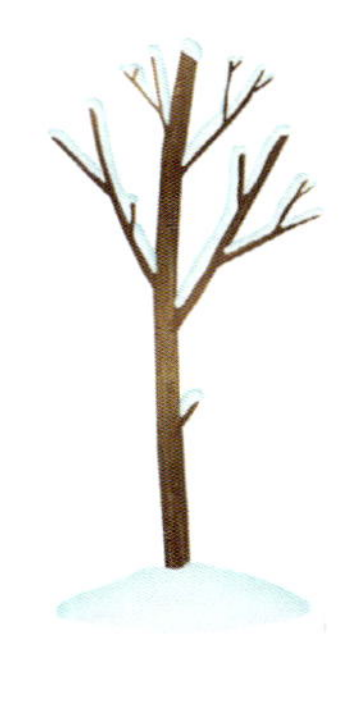

January

S	M	T	W	Th	F	S
		1	2	3	4	5
6	7	8	9	10	11	12
13	14	15	16	17	18	19
20	21	22	23	24	25	26
27	28	29	30	31		

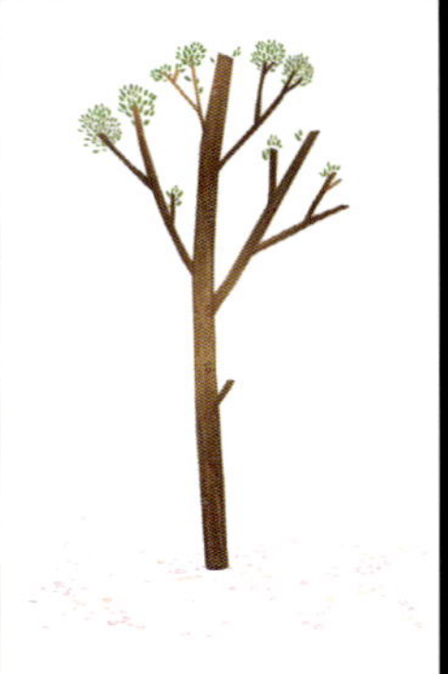

June

S	M	T	W	Th	F	S
						1
2	3	4	5	6	7	8
9	10	11	12	13	14	15
16	17	18	19	20	21	22
23	24	25	26	27	28	29
30						

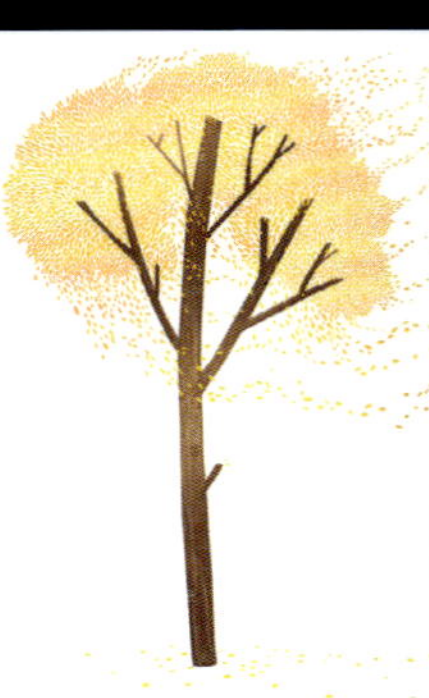

October

S	M	T	W	Th	F	S
		1	2	3	4	5
6	7	8	9	10	11	12
13	14	15	16	17	18	19
20	21	22	23	24	25	26
27	28	29	30	31		

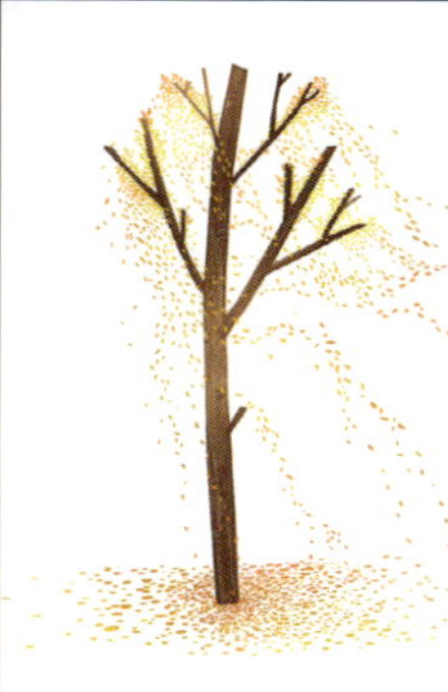

November

S	M	T	W	Th	F	S
					1	2
3	4	5	6	7	8	9
10	11	12	13	14	15	16
17	18	19	20	21	22	23
24	25	26	27	28	29	30

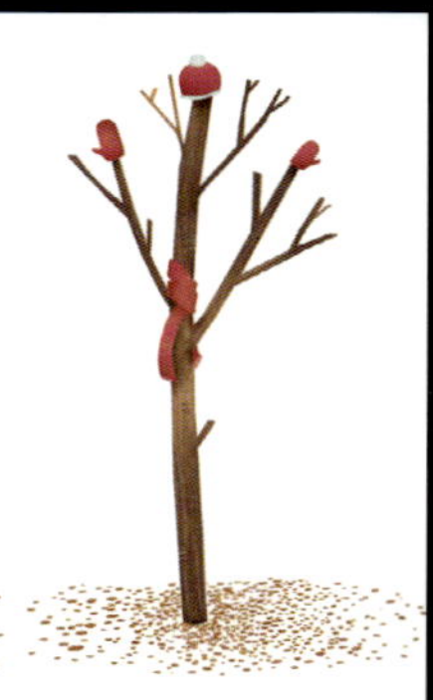

November

S	M	T	W	Th	F	S
					1	2
3	4	5	6	7	8	9
10	11	12	13	14	15	16
17	18	19	20	21	22	23
24	25	26	27	28	29	30

Grace Kim

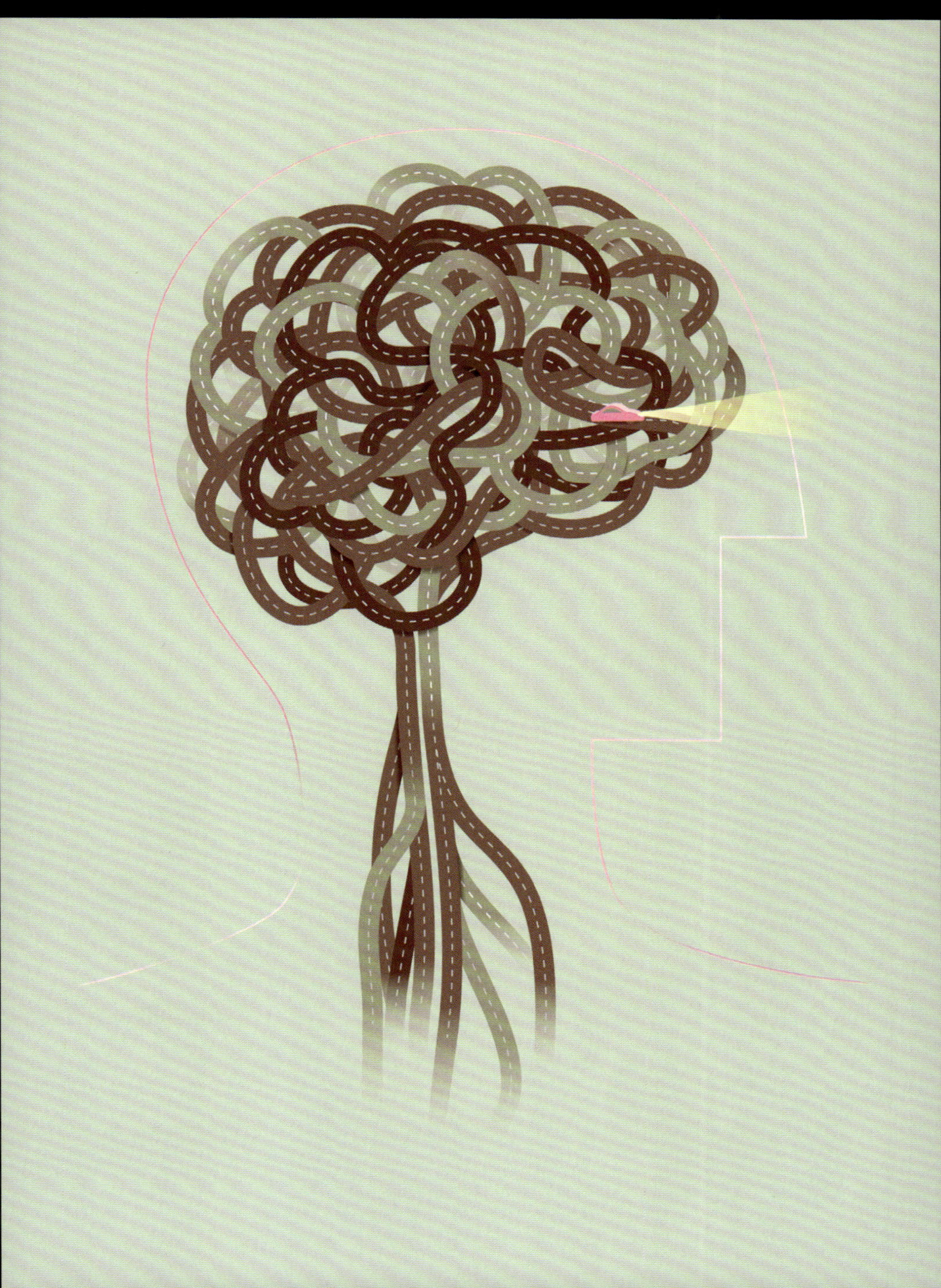

Aad Goudappel

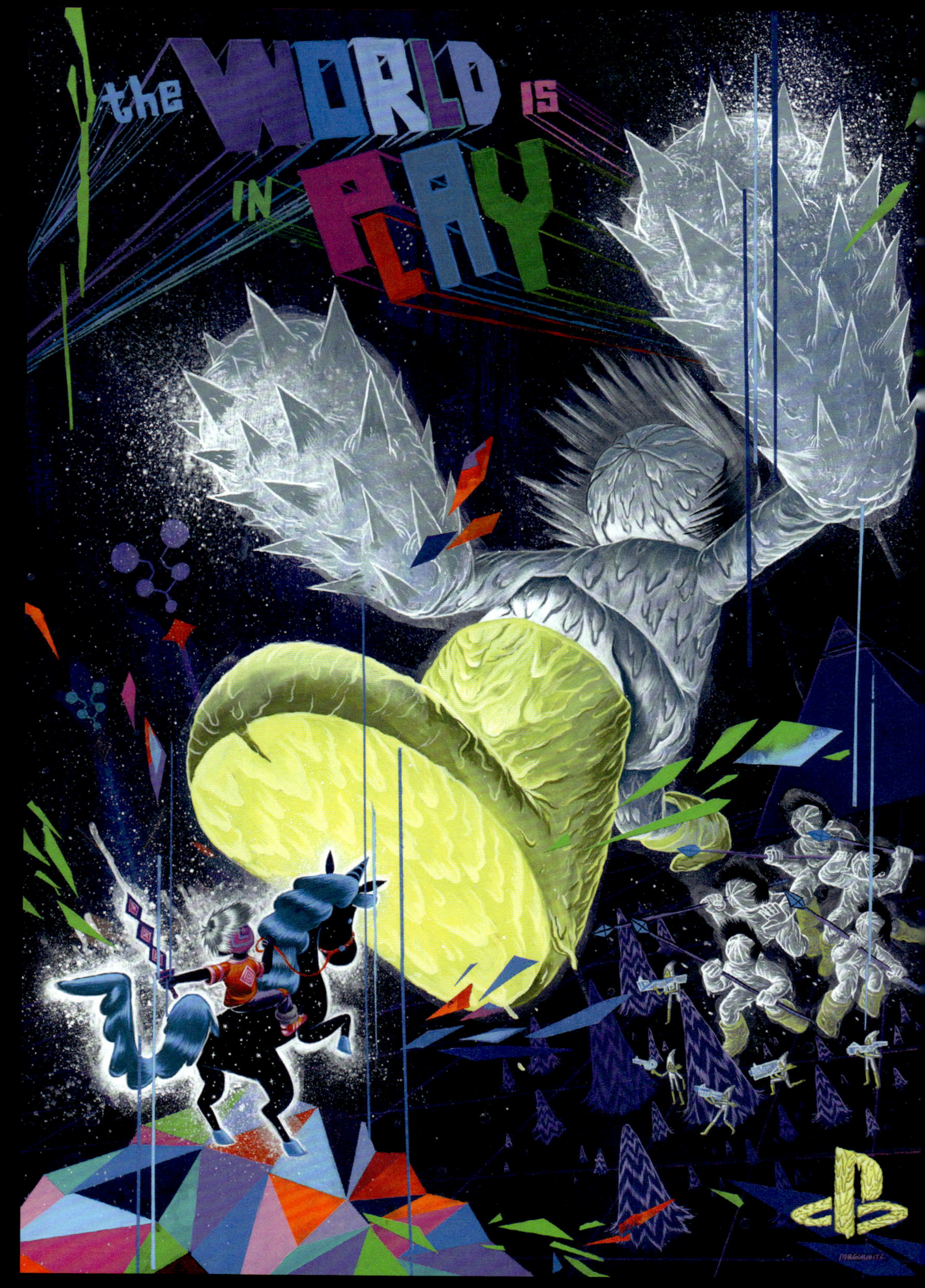
the WORLD IS IN PLAY

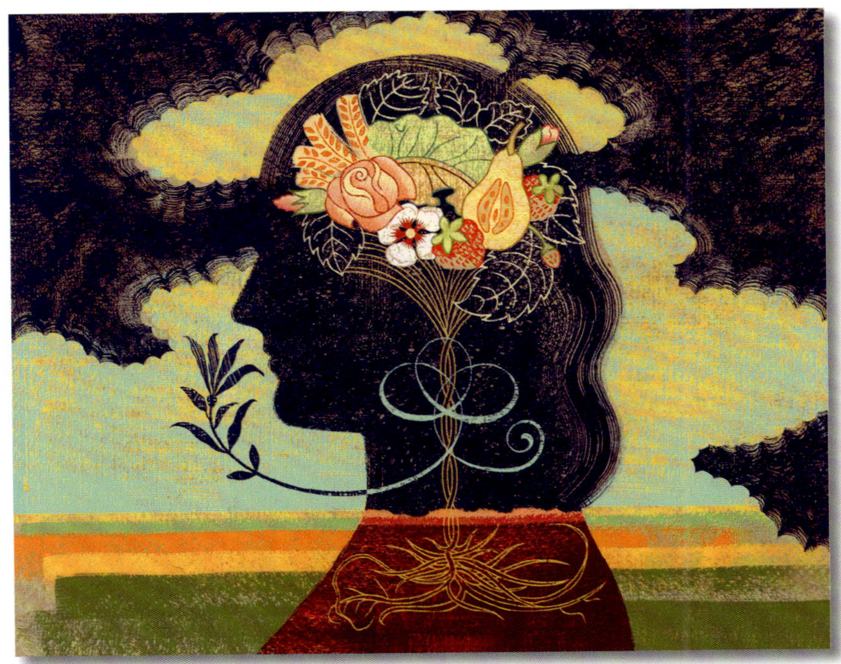

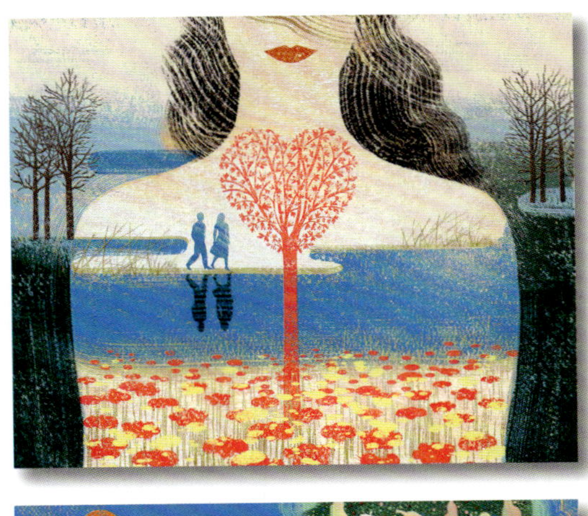

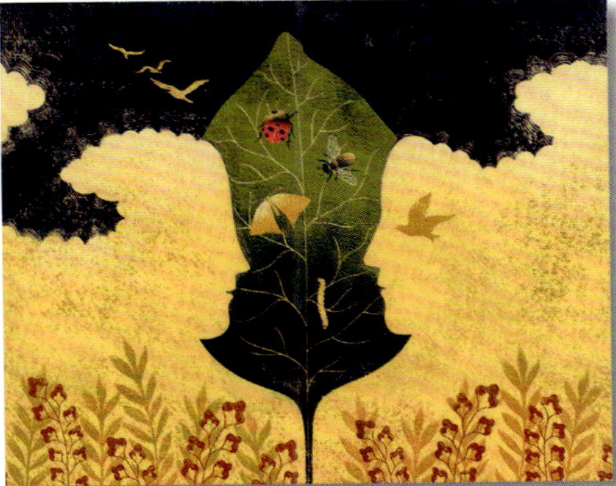

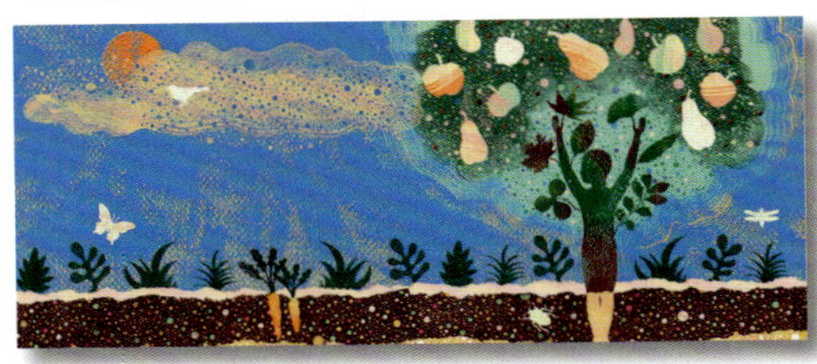

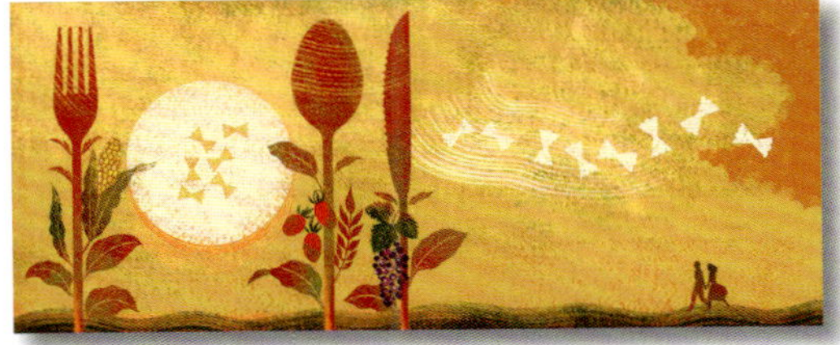

(L) *Charles Glaubitz* (R) *Anna & Elena Balbusso*

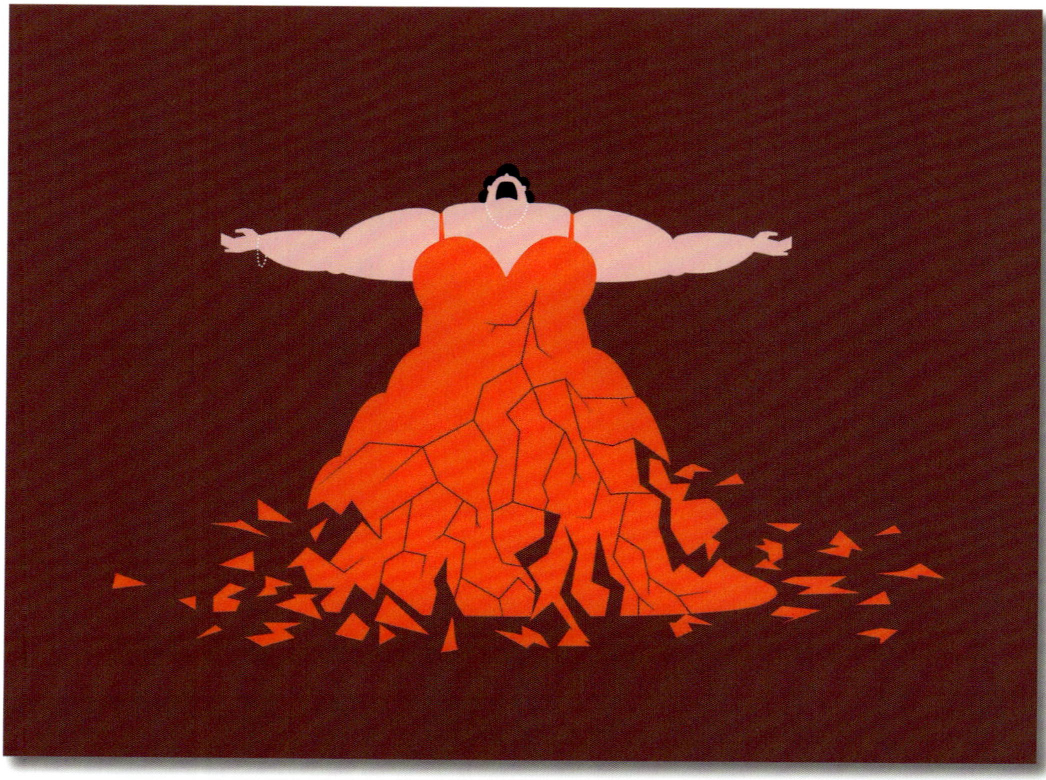

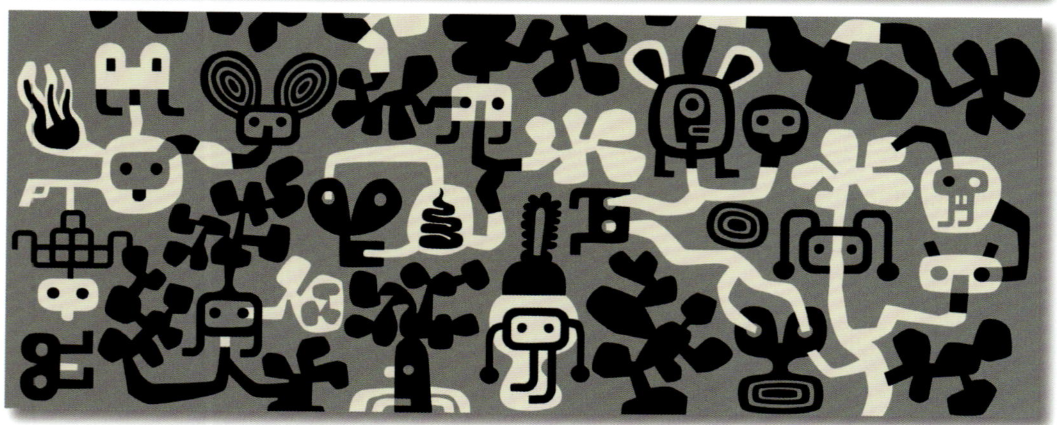

(T) *Aad Goudappel* (B) *Lasse Skarbovik*

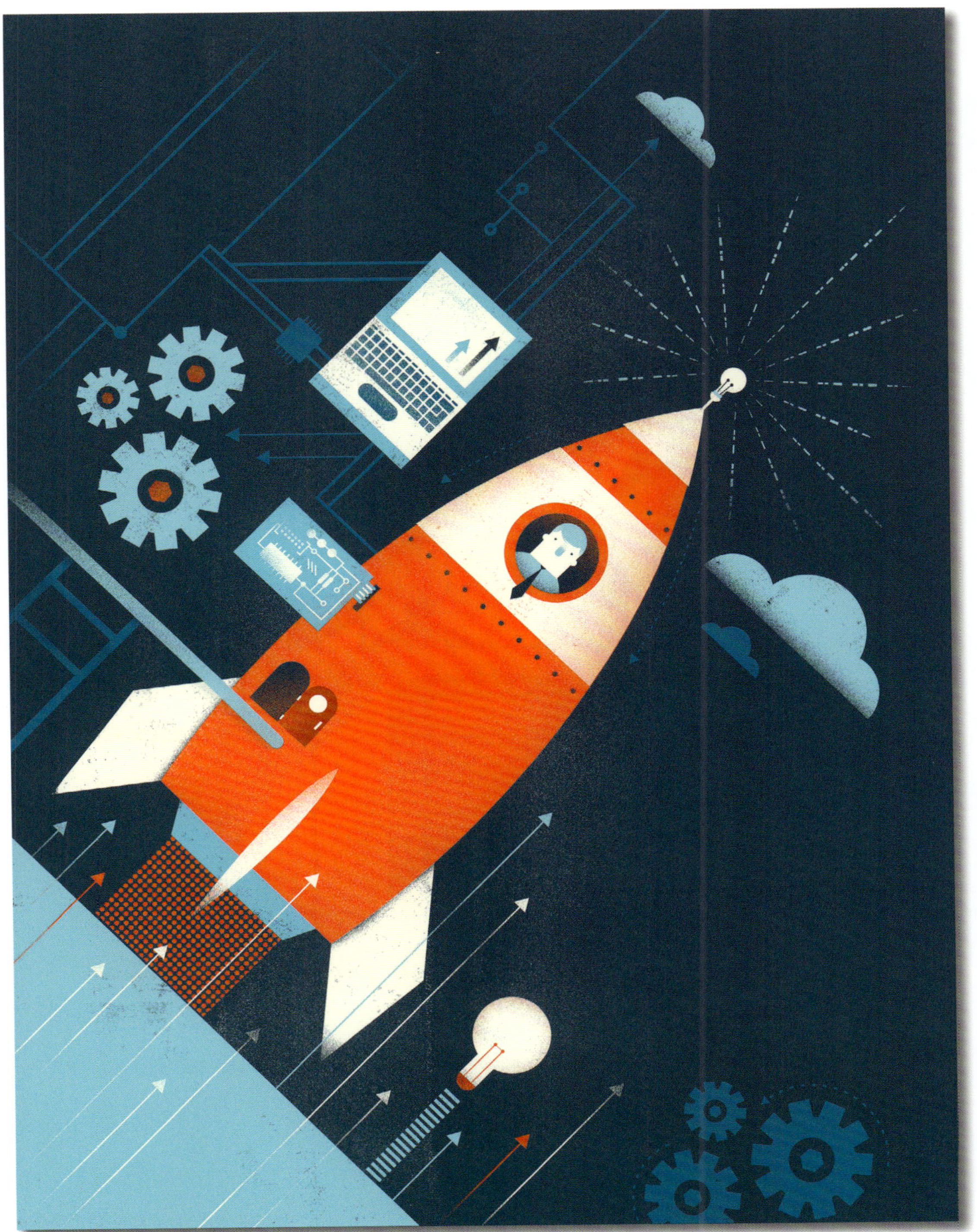

Shaw Nielsen

Marie-Christine Lemieux-Couture

TOUTES MES SOLITUDES!

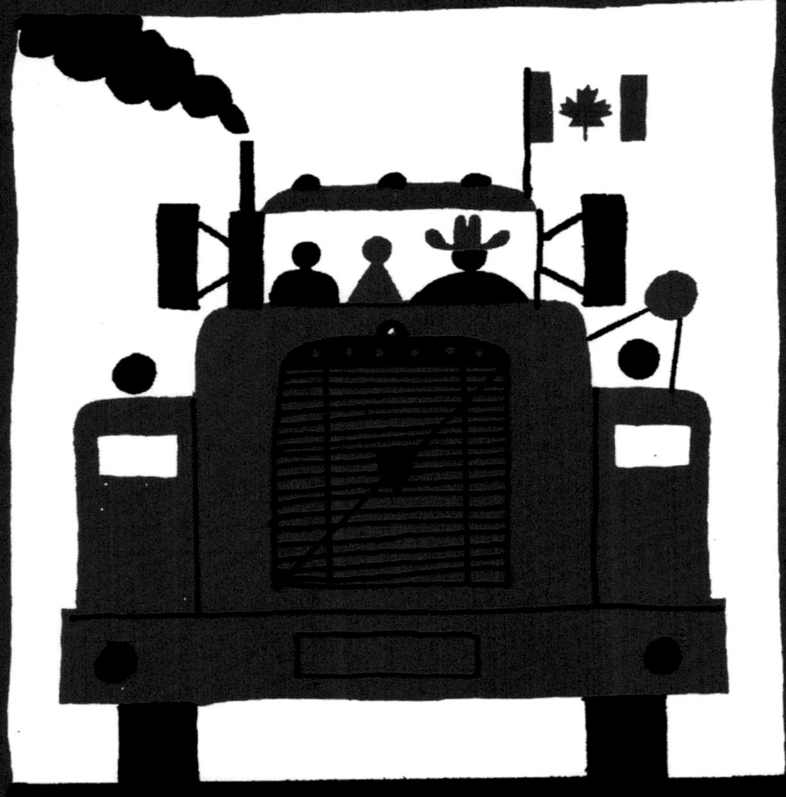

LES ÉDITIONS DE TA MÈRE

Benoit Tardif   Takahisa Hashimoto

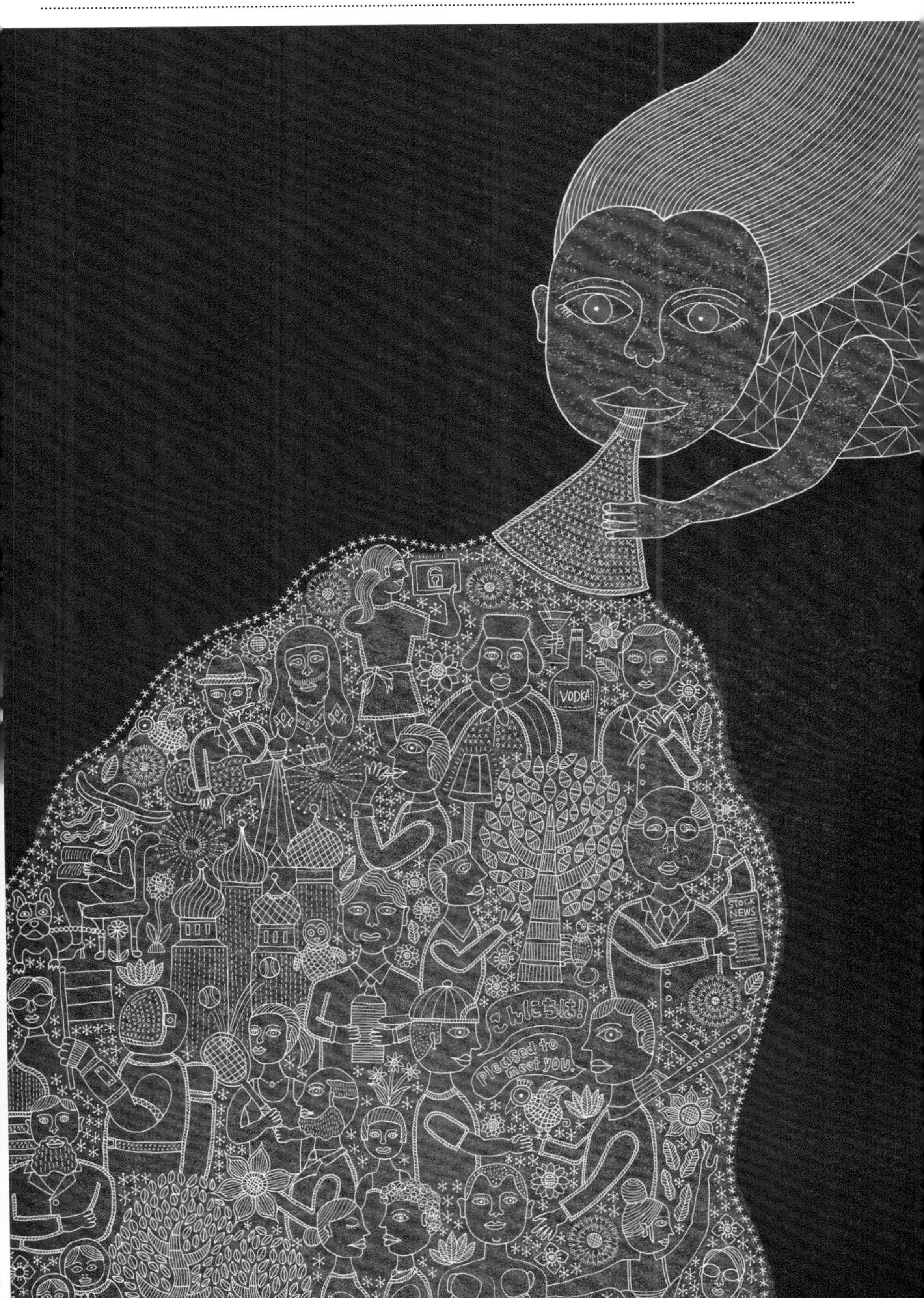
VODKA
STOCK
NEWS
こんにちは!
Pleased to
meet you.

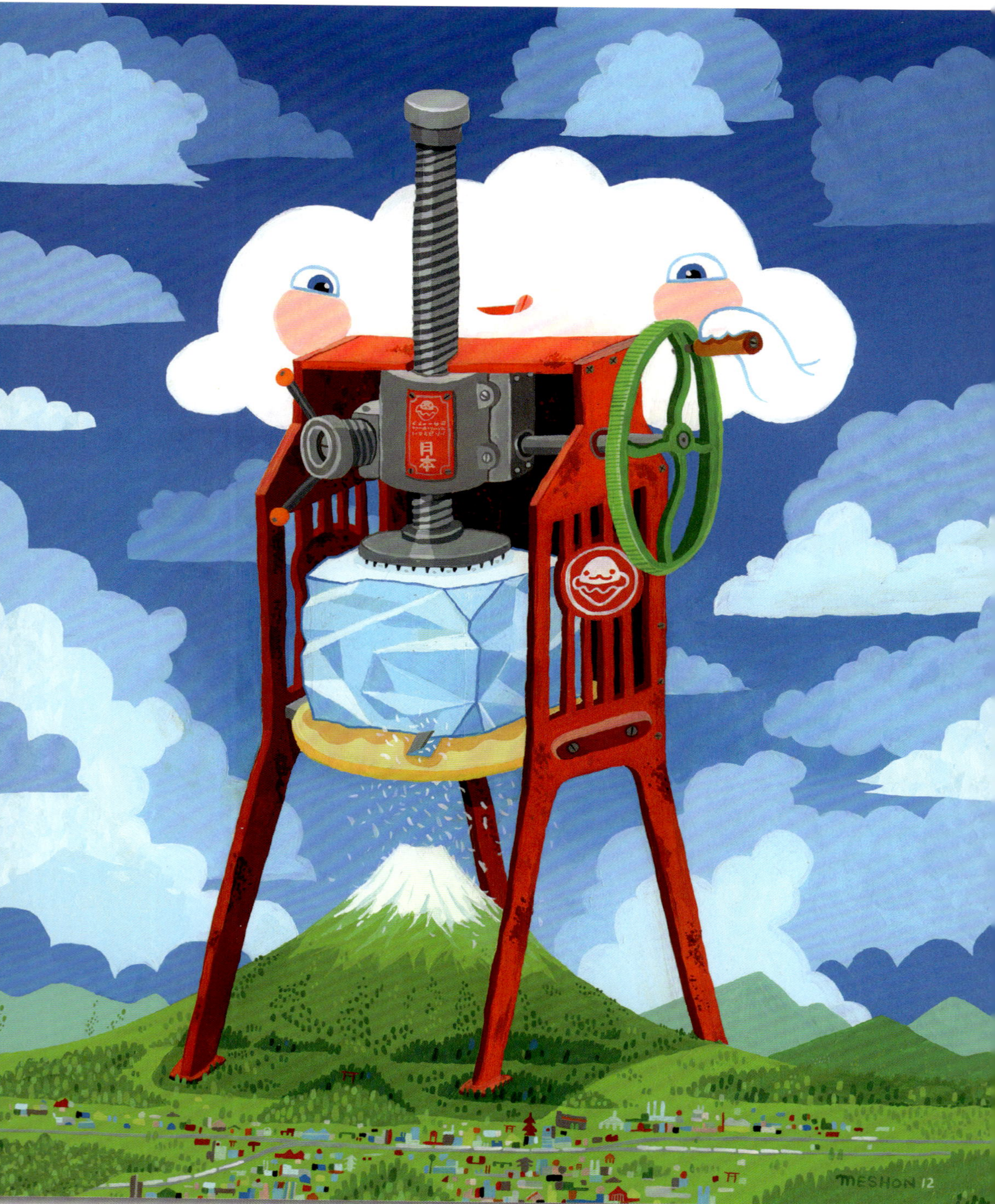

Aaron Meshon

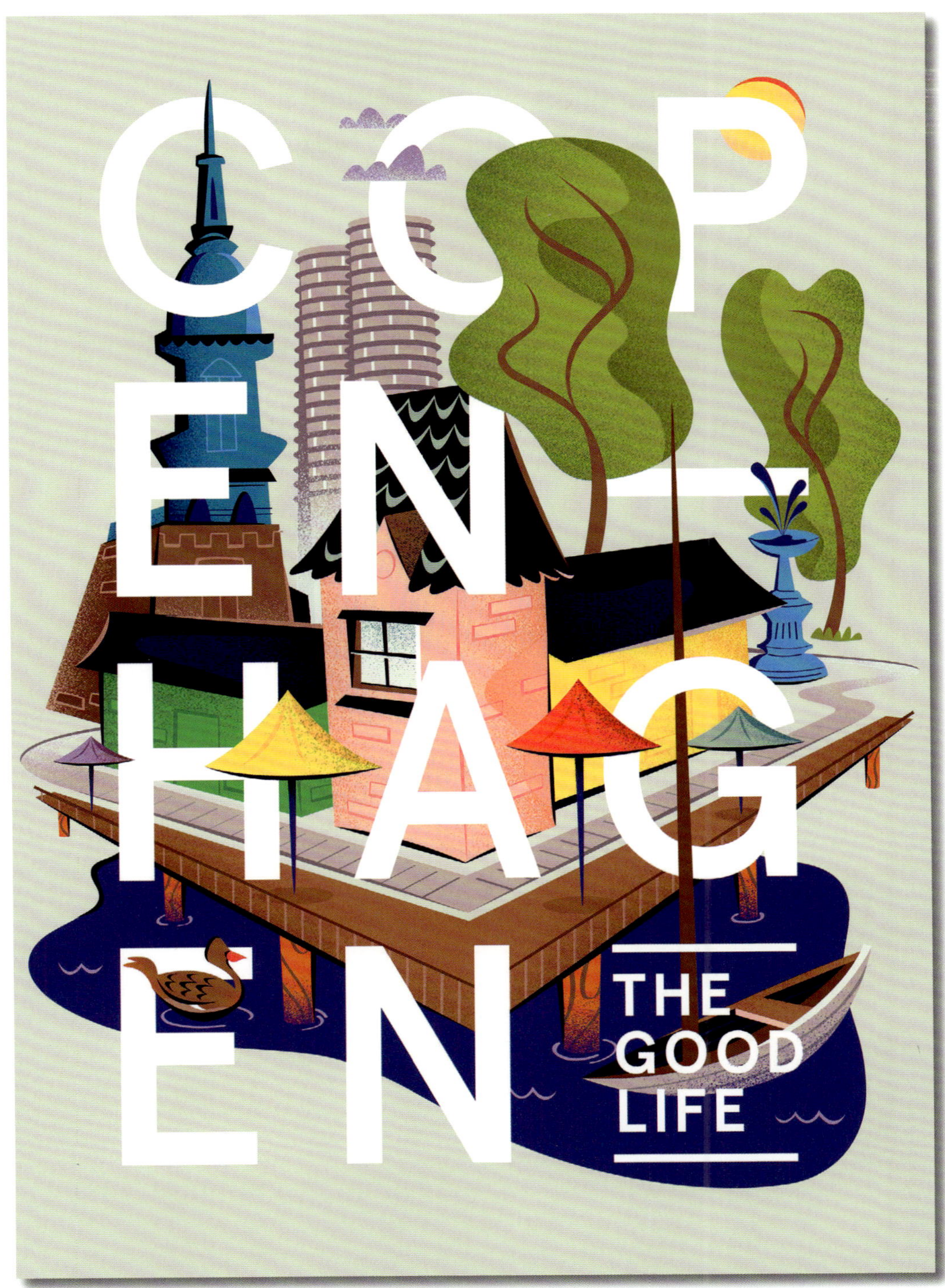

Matthew Chase

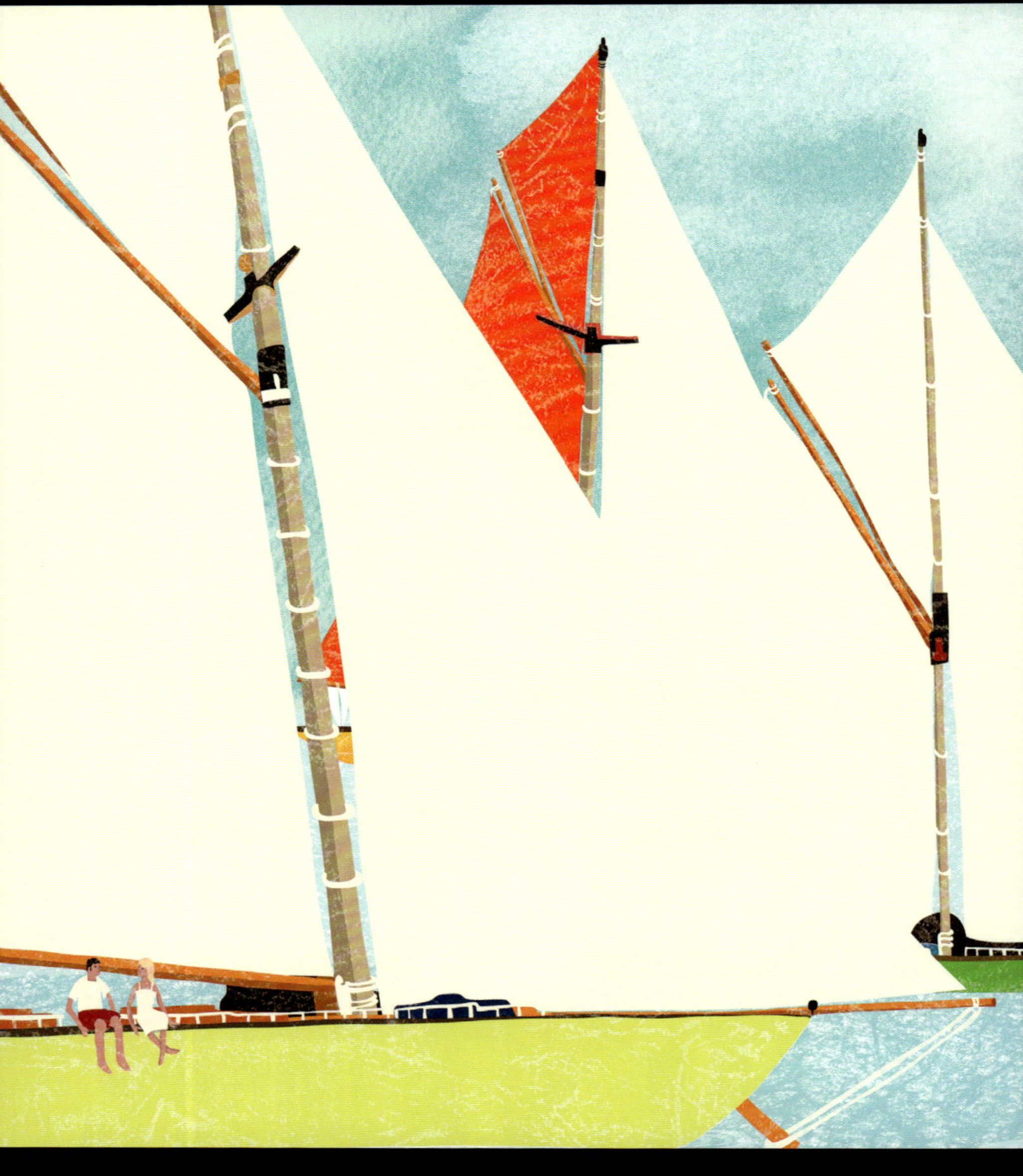

Takayuki Ryujin

ANORAK
THE
HAPPY MAG
FOR KIDS
(AND ANIMALS)
Vol. 26 / RRP £6
www.anorakmagazine.com

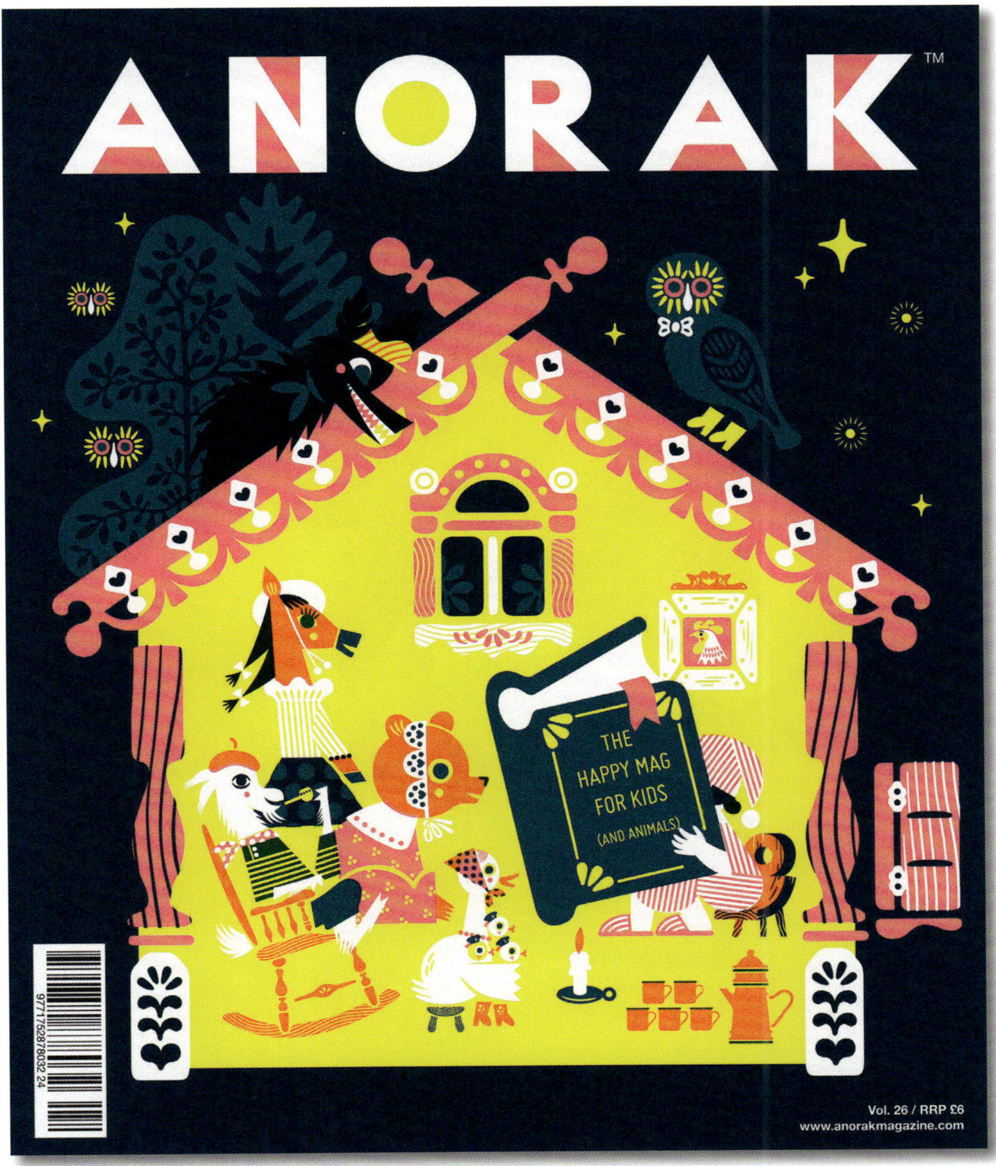

Studio Tipi

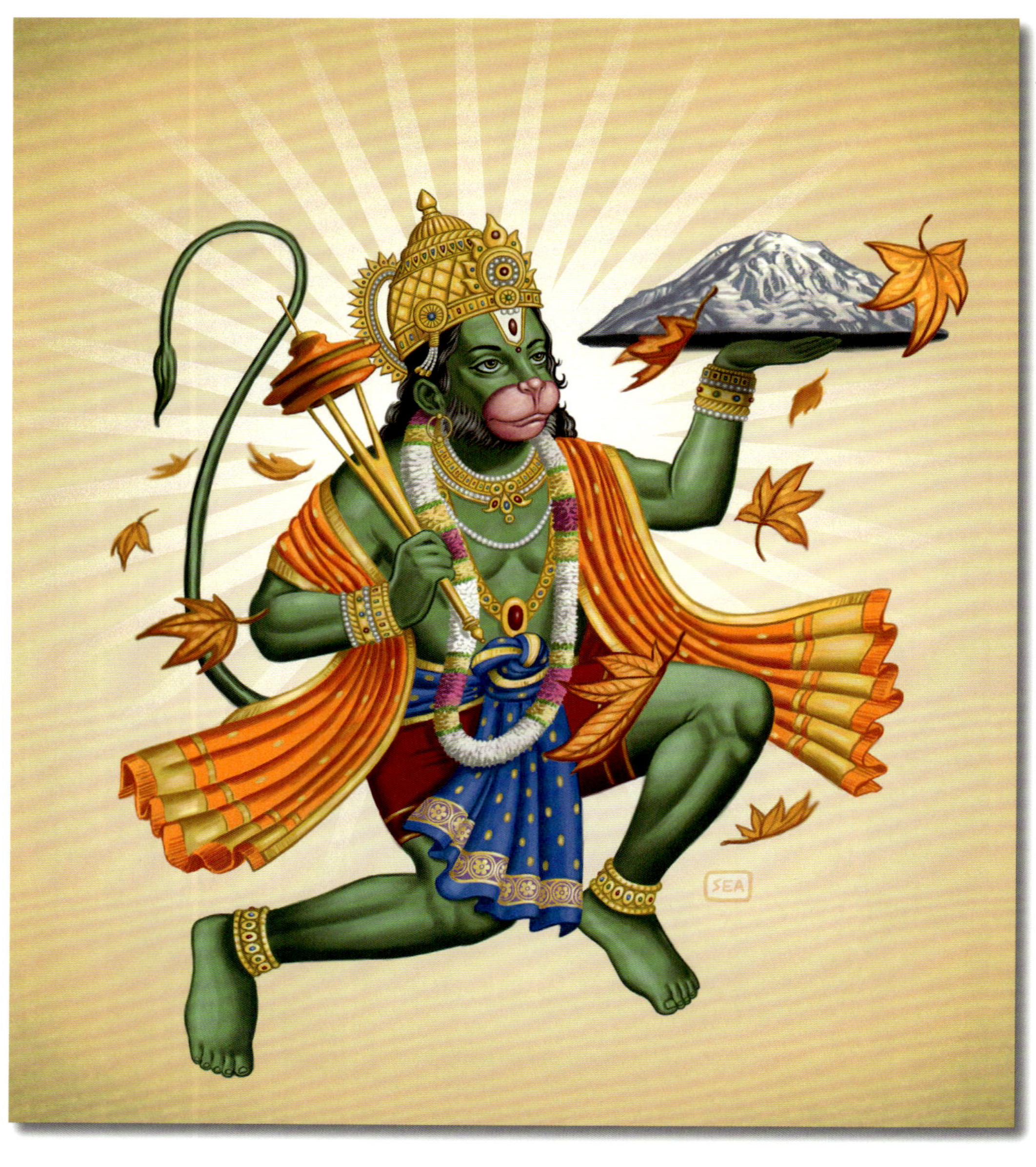

(L) *Scott Anderson* (R) *René Milot*

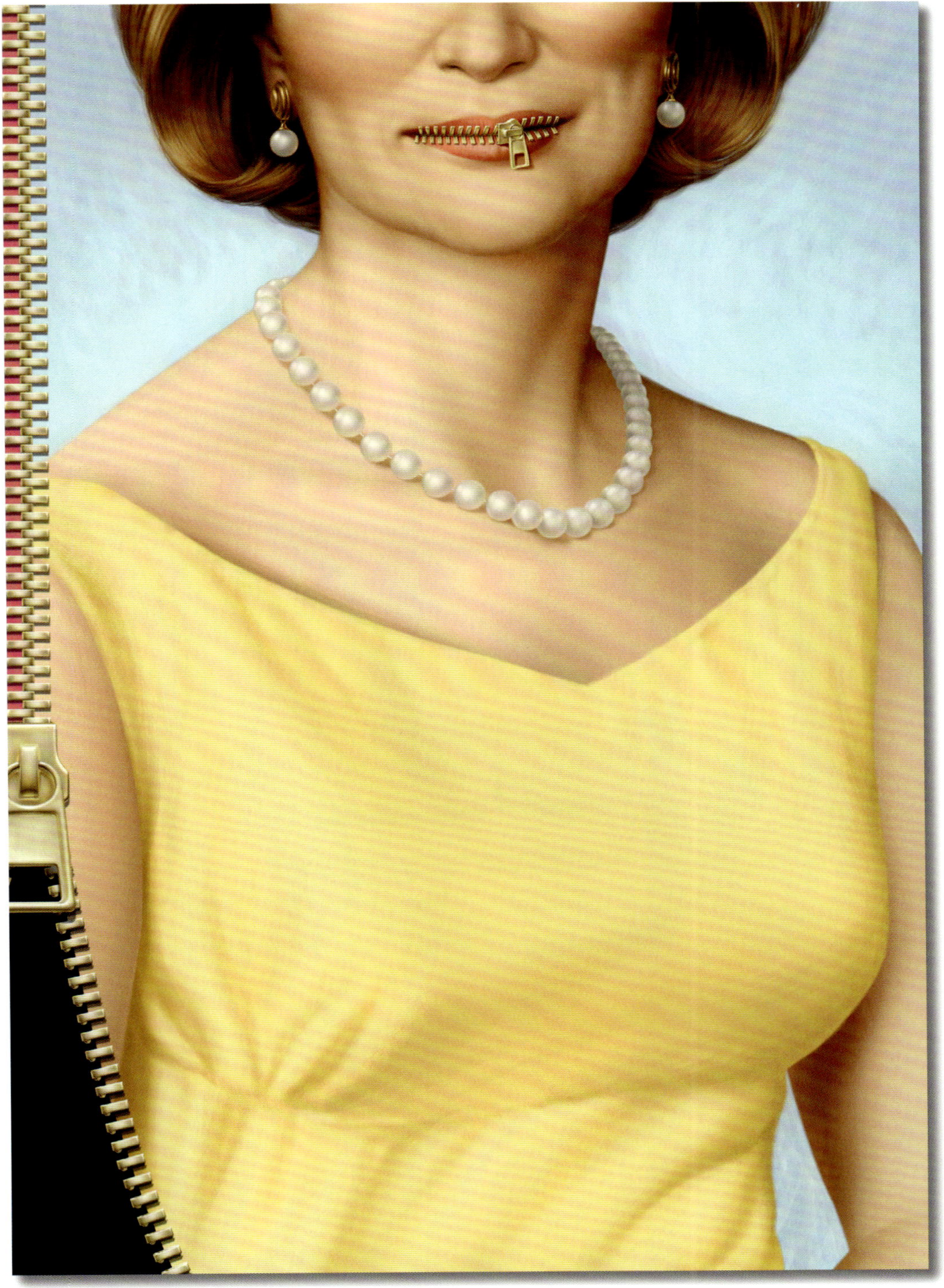

SCBWI
Society of Children's
Book Writers and
Illustrators
HB
0.5
01.23.13
IT'S FREEZING
TODAY!

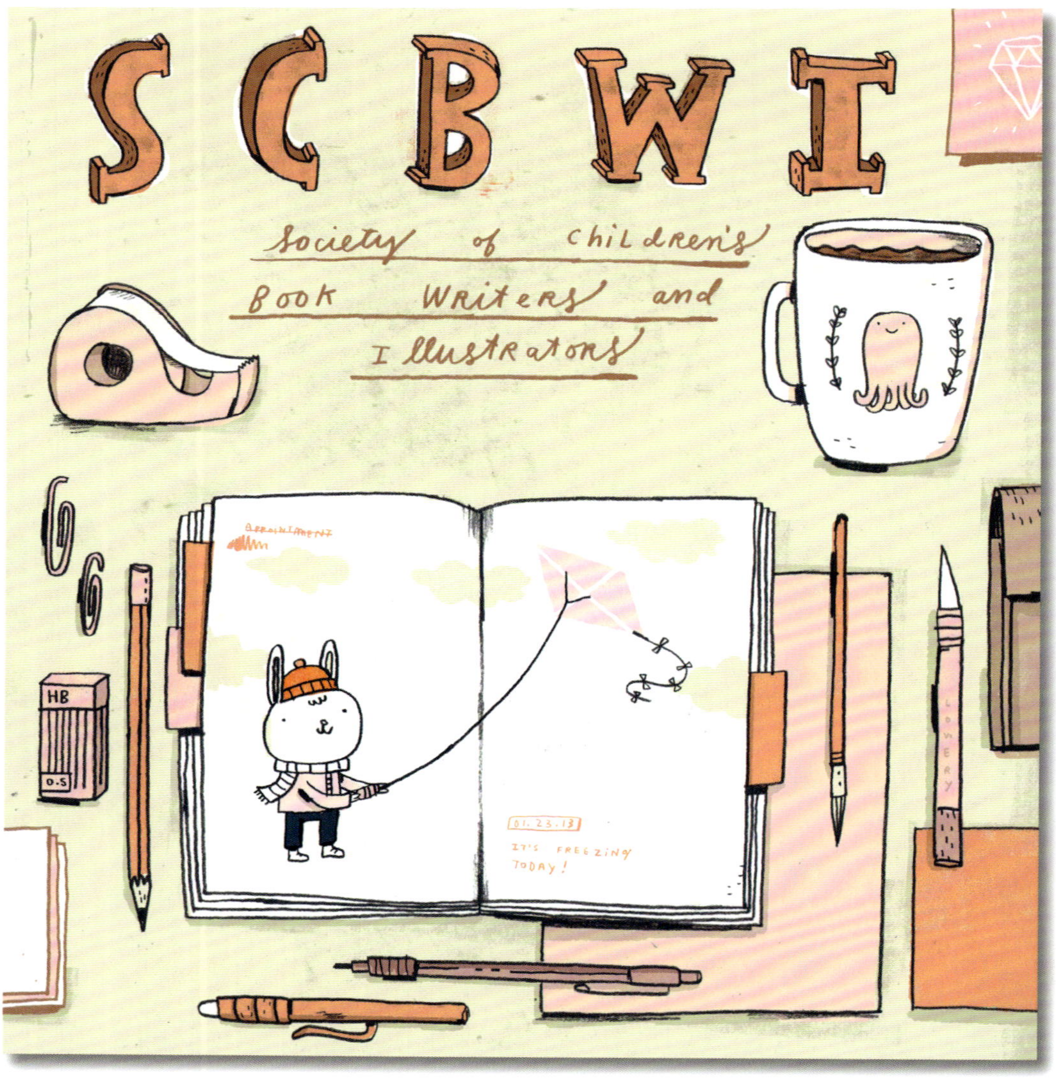

Mike Lowery

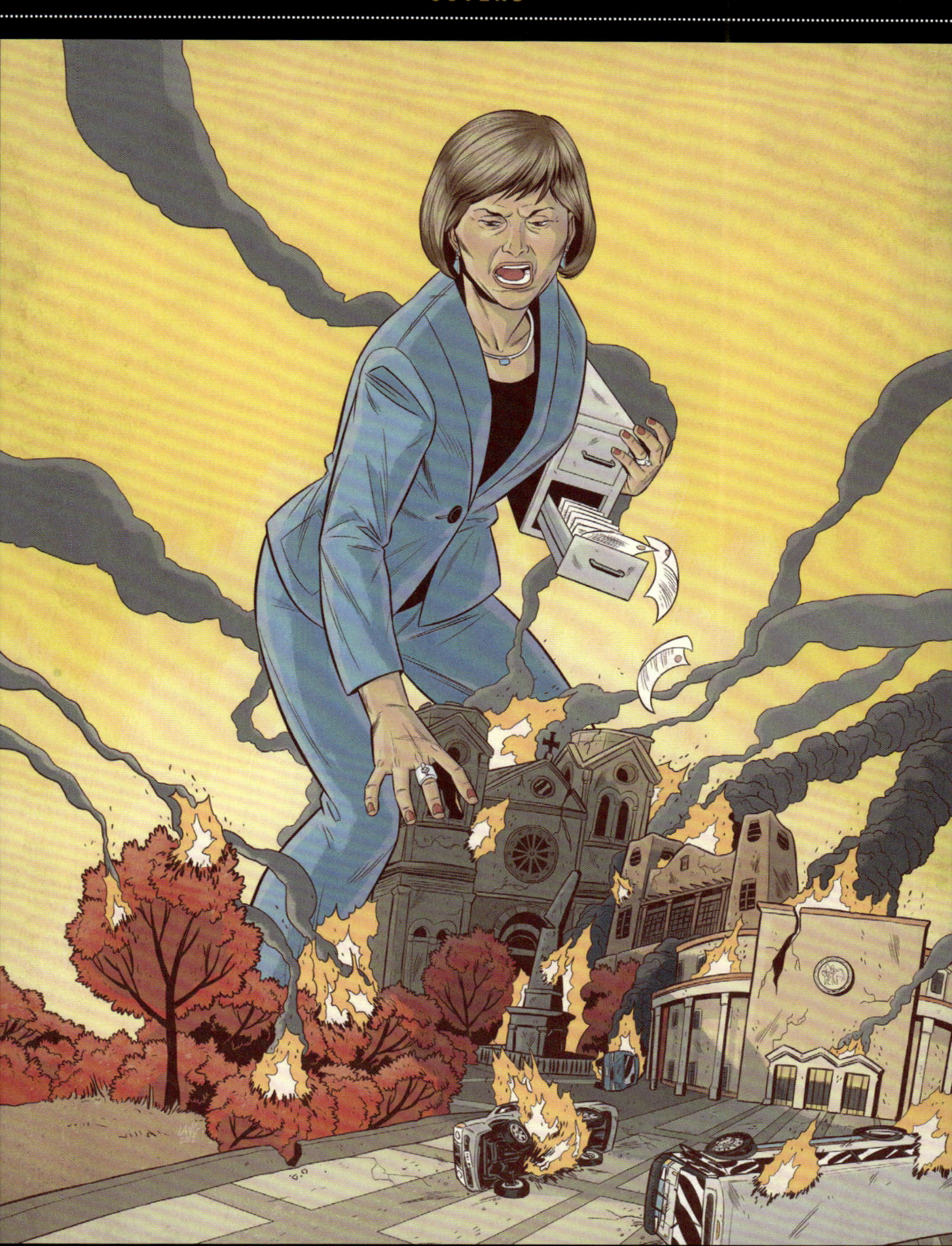

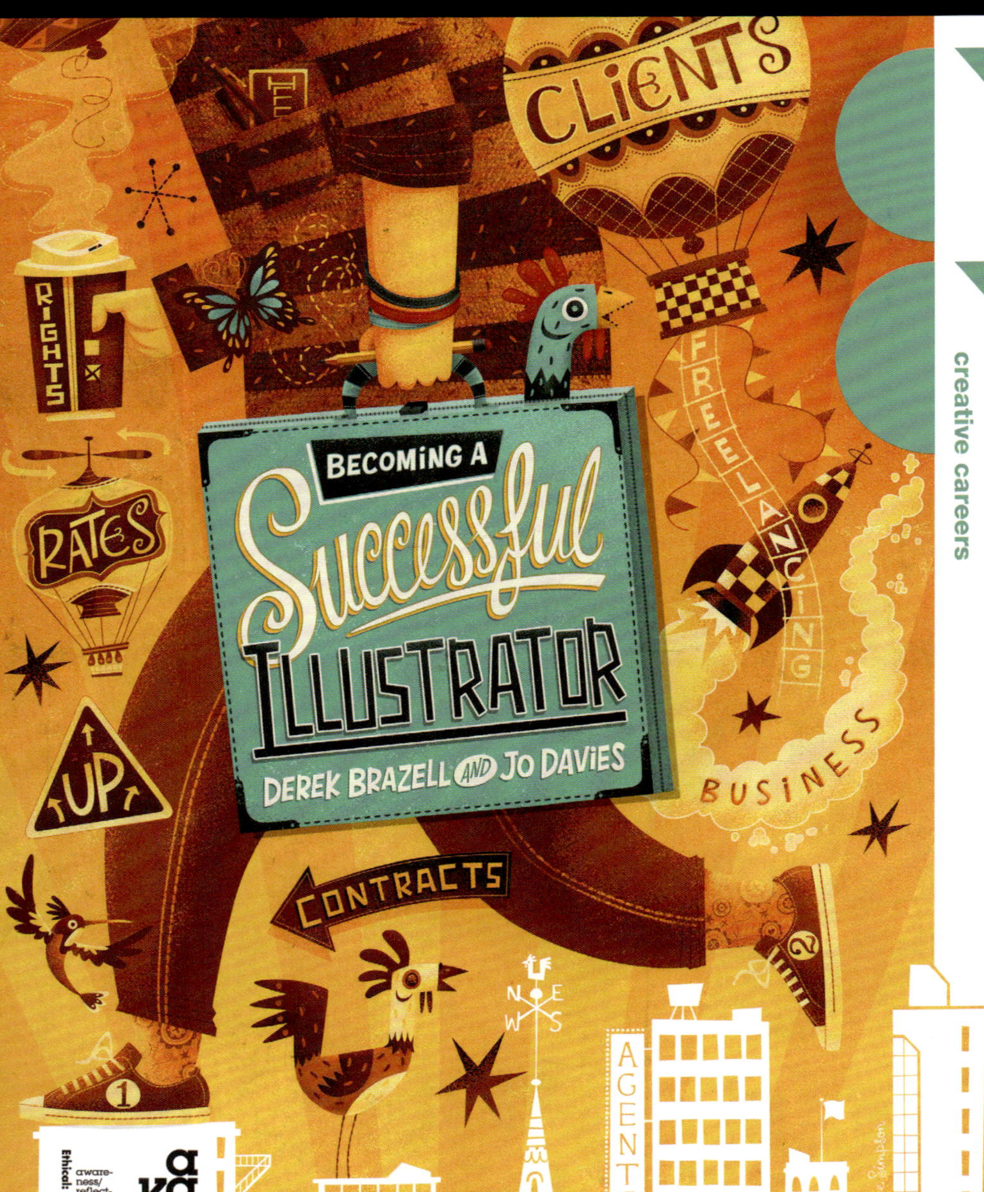
CLIENTS
RIGHTS
RATES
UP
FREELANCING
BUSINESS
BECOMING A
Successful
ILLUSTRATOR
DEREK BRAZELL AND JO DAVIES
CONTRACTS
N E W S
AGENTS
1
2
creative careers
Ethical:
awareness/
reflection/
debate
ava
academia

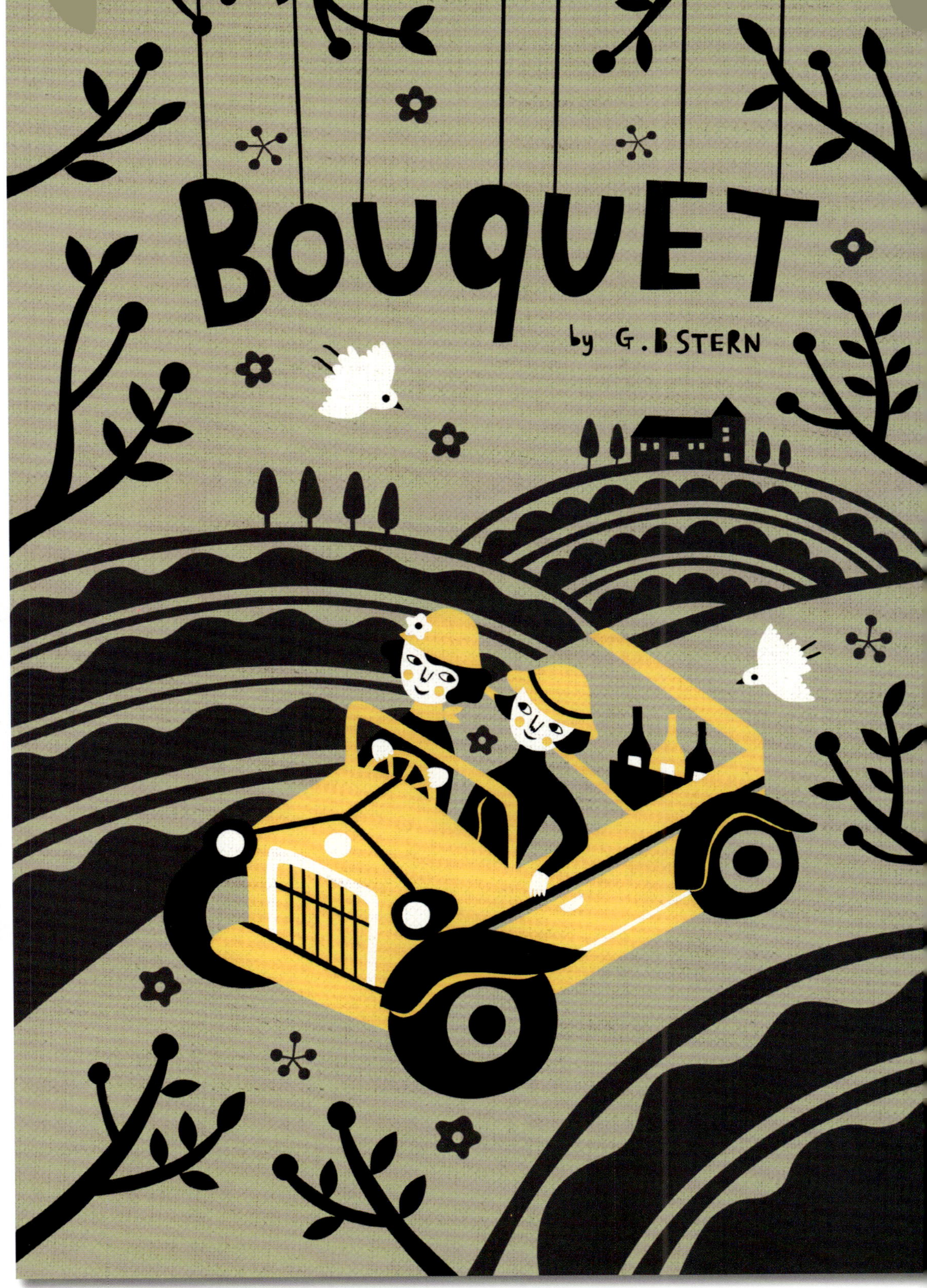

BOUQUET
by G.B STERN

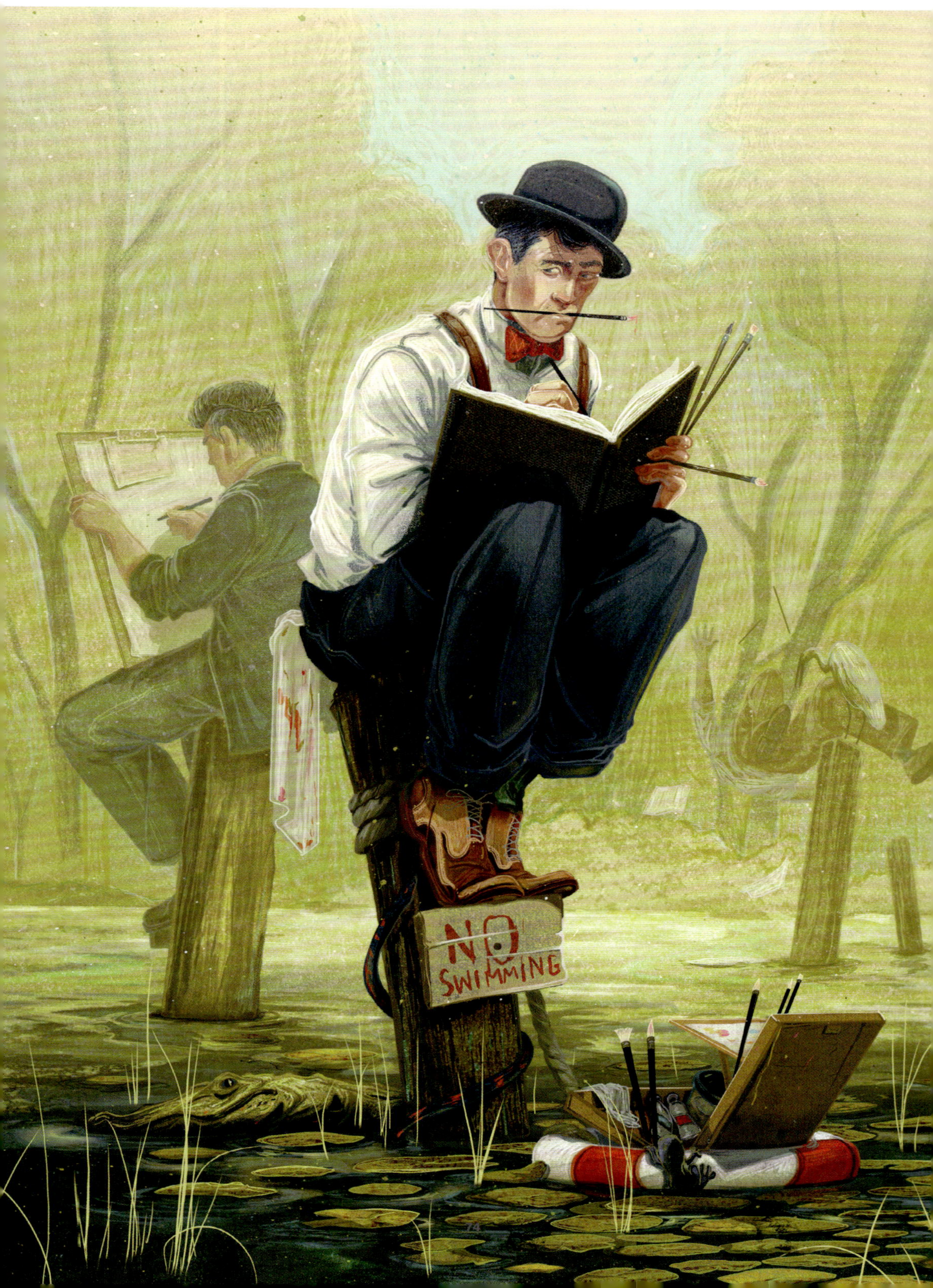

NO
SWIMMING

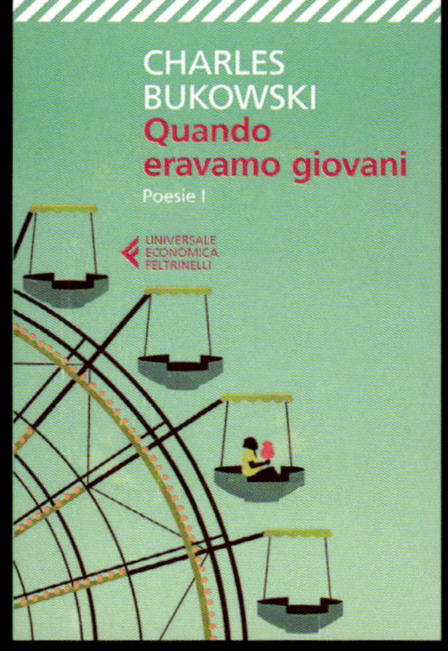
CHARLES
BUKOWSKI
Quando
eravamo giovani
Poesie I
UNIVERSALE
ECONOMICA
FELTRINELLI

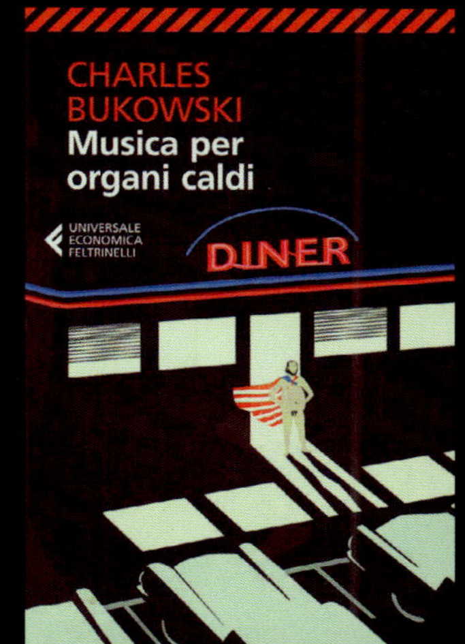
CHARLES
BUKOWSKI
Musica per
organi caldi
UNIVERSALE
ECONOMICA
FELTRINELLI
DINER

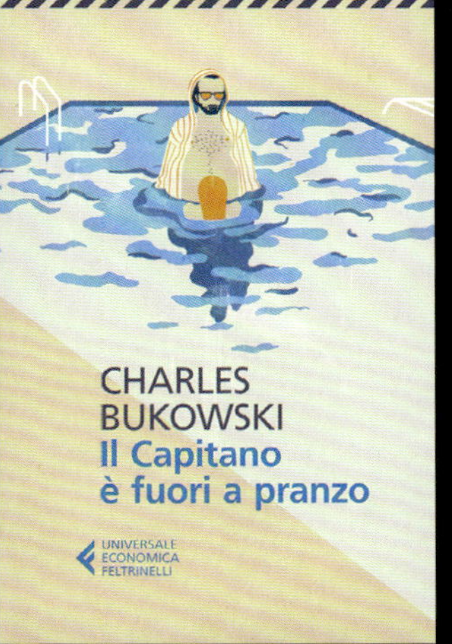
CHARLES
BUKOWSKI
Il Capitano
è fuori a pranzo
UNIVERSALE
ECONOMICA
FELTRINELLI

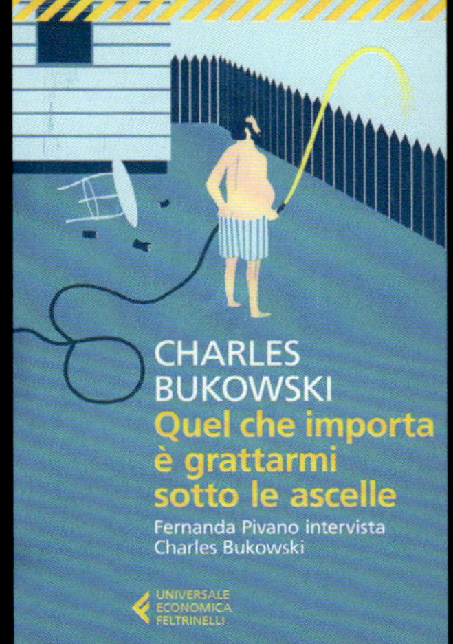
CHARLES
BUKOWSKI
Quel che importa
è grattarmi
sotto le ascelle
Fernanda Pivano intervista
Charles Bukowski
UNIVERSALE
ECONOMICA
FELTRINELLI

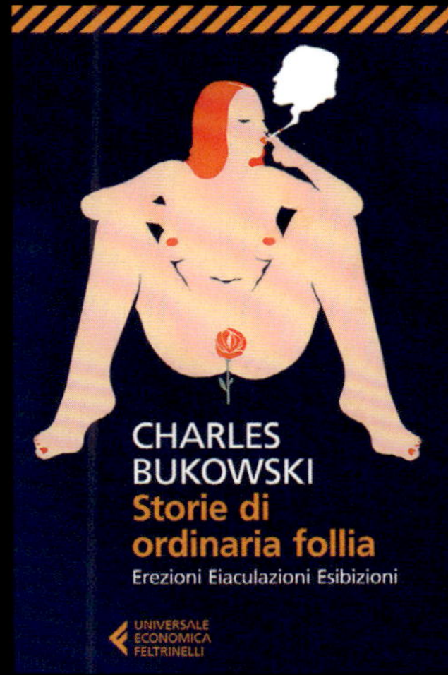
CHARLES
BUKOWSKI
Storie di
ordinaria follia
Erezioni Eiaculazioni Esibizioni
UNIVERSALE
ECONOMICA
FELTRINELLI

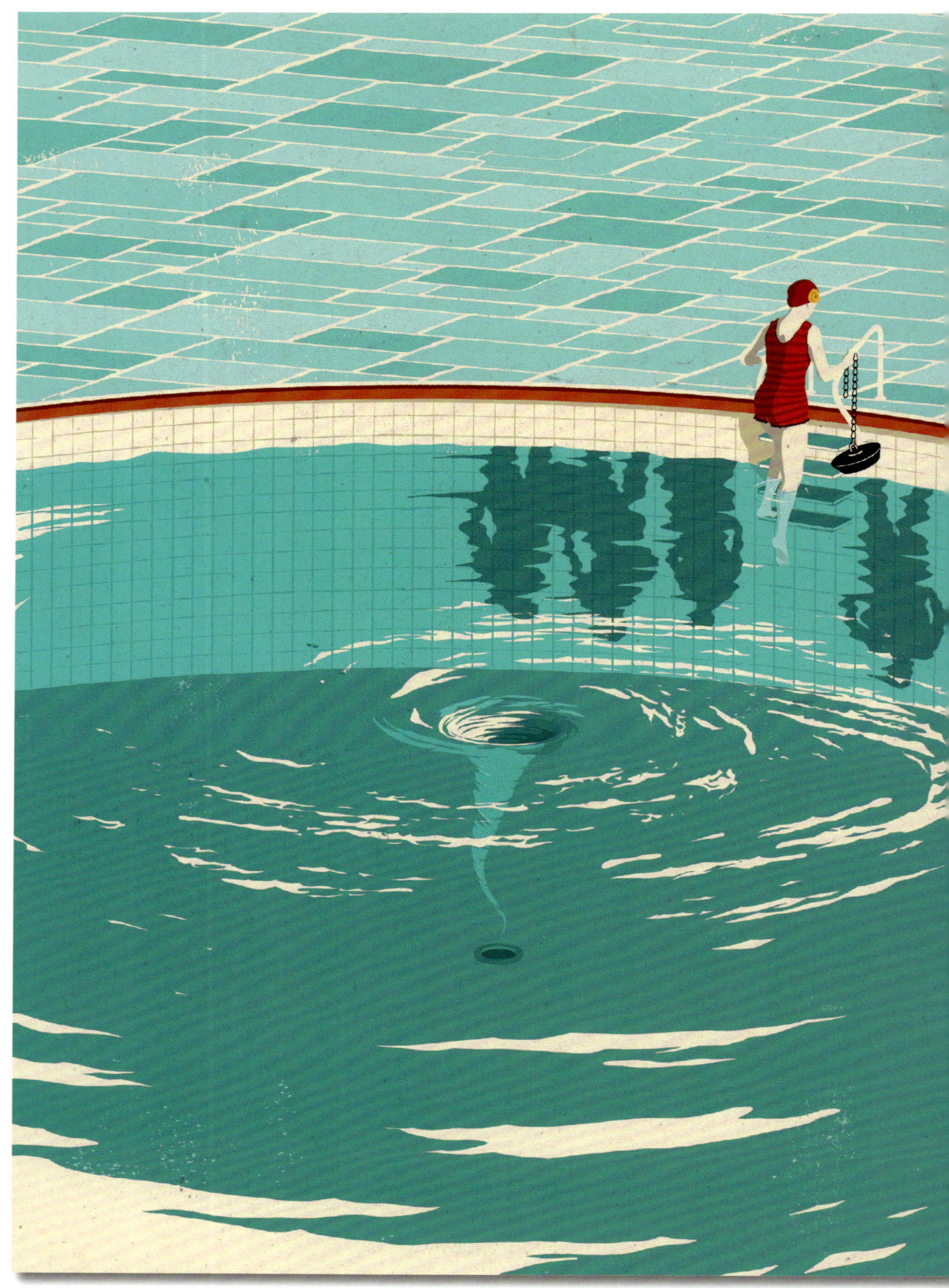

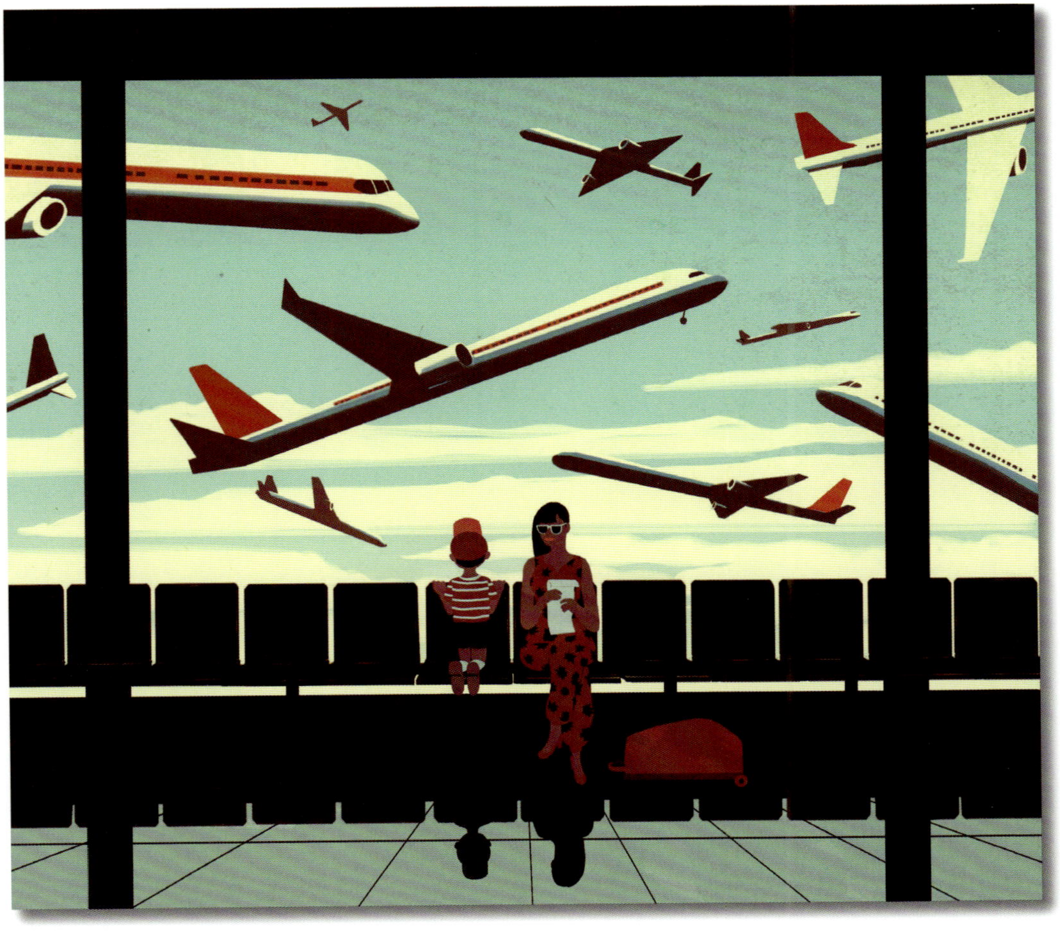

(L) *Mark Smith* (R) SILVER *Emiliano Ponzi*

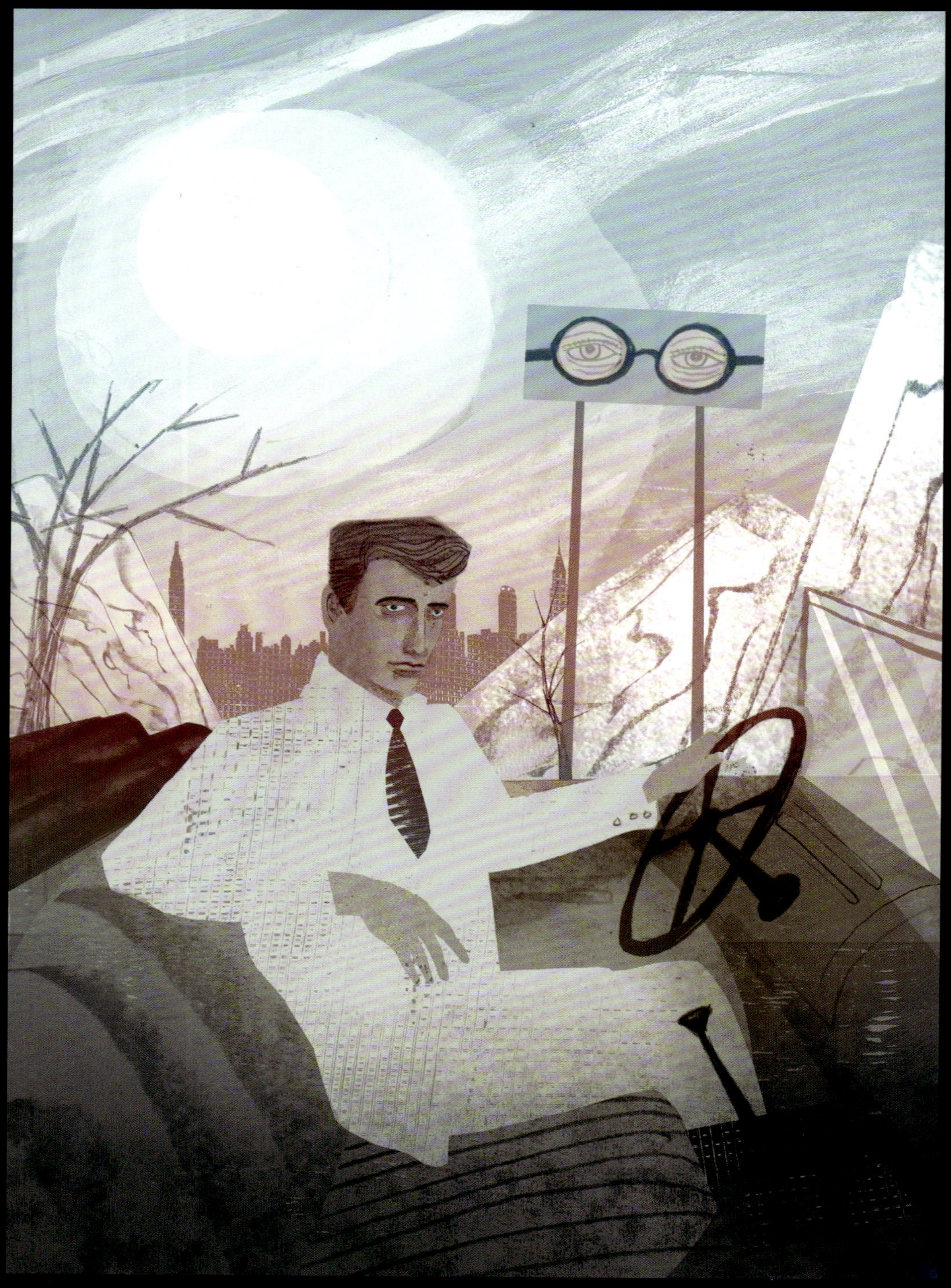

Sam Kalda

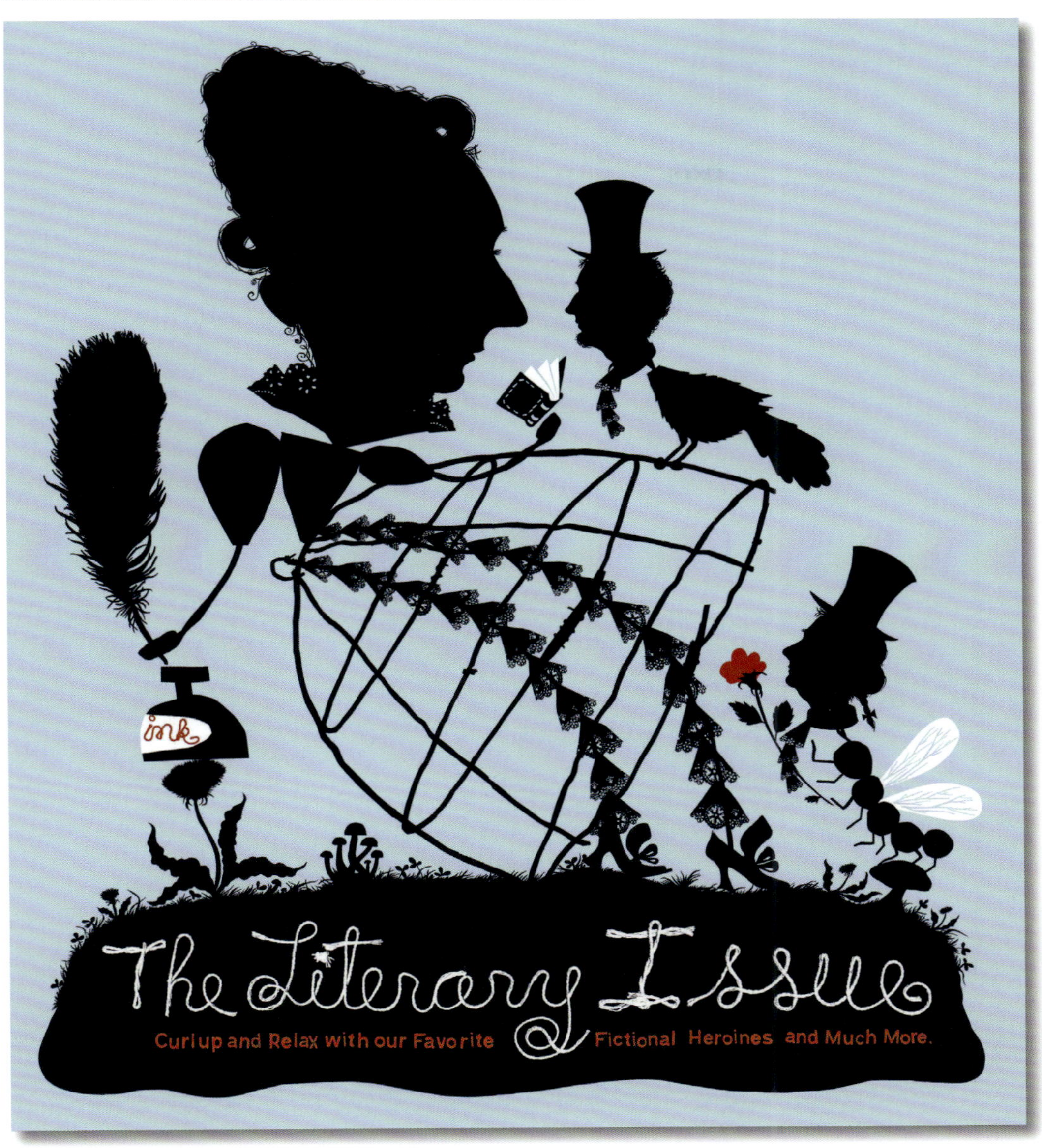

Melinda Beck

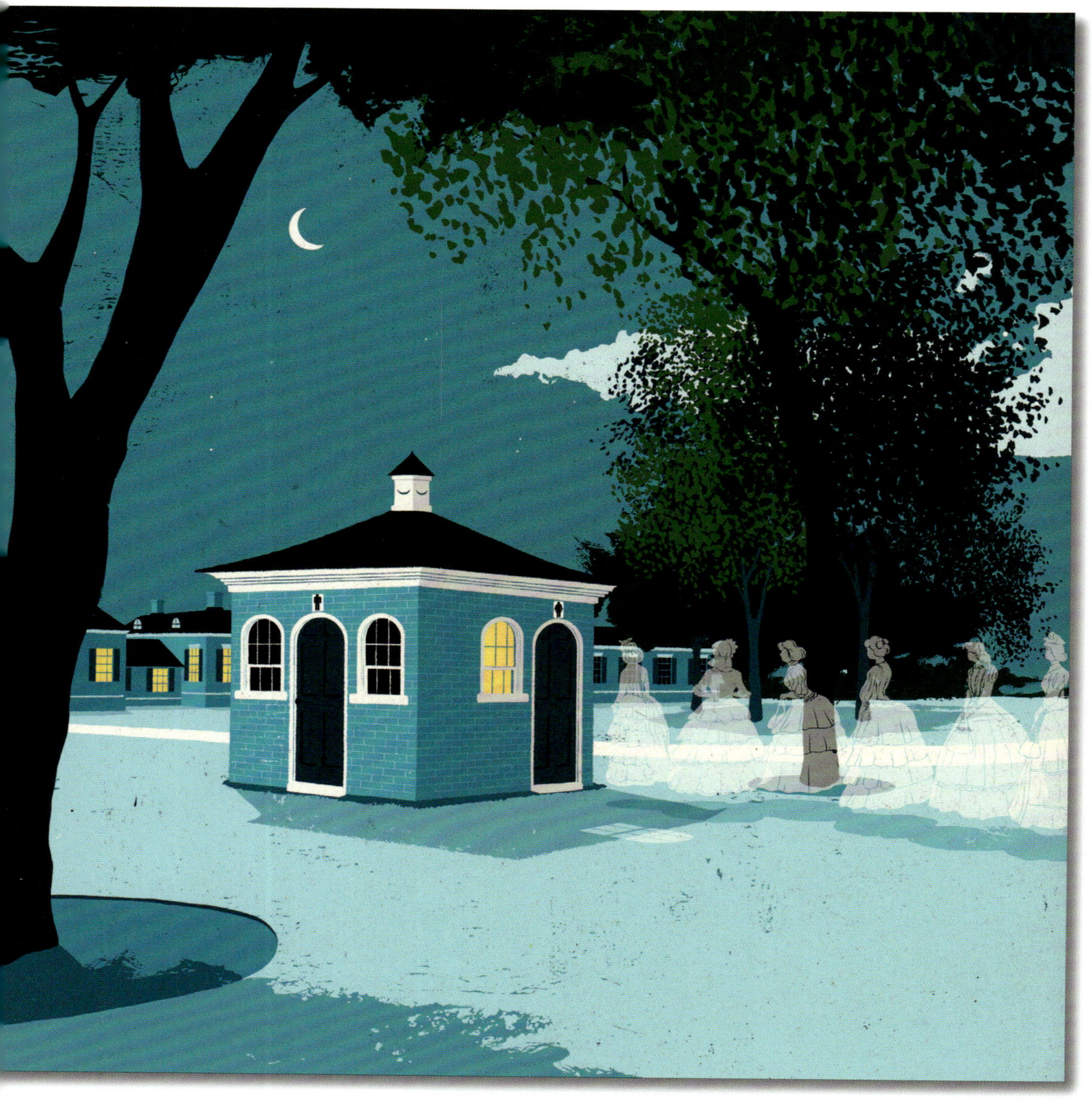

(L) *Mark Smith* *(R)* *Brad Holland*

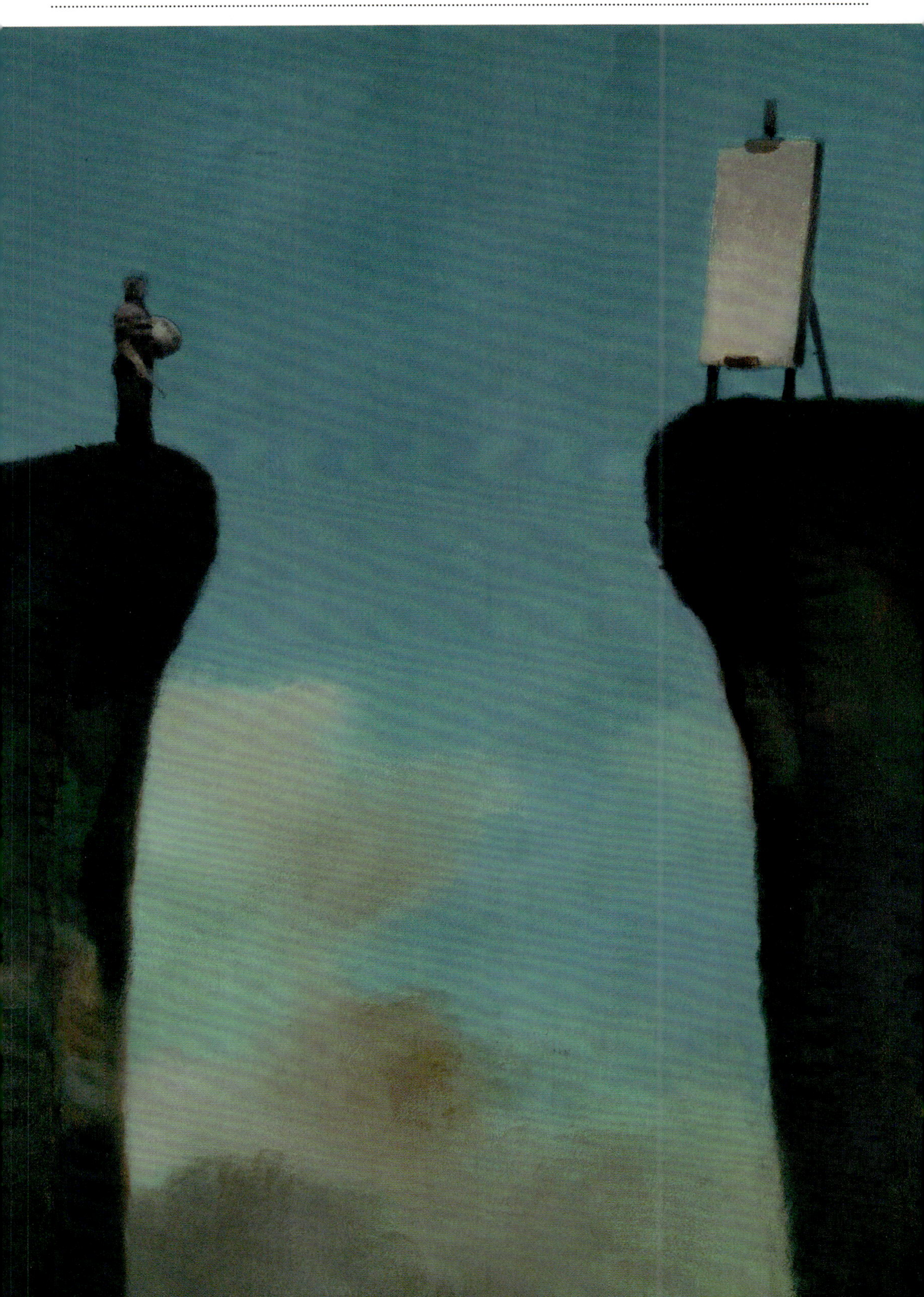

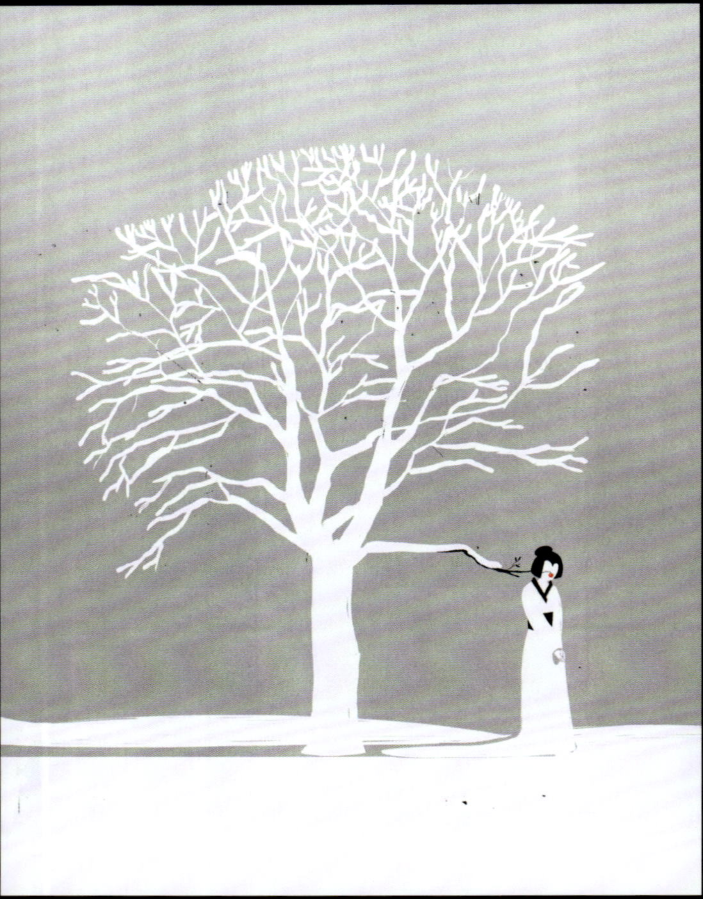

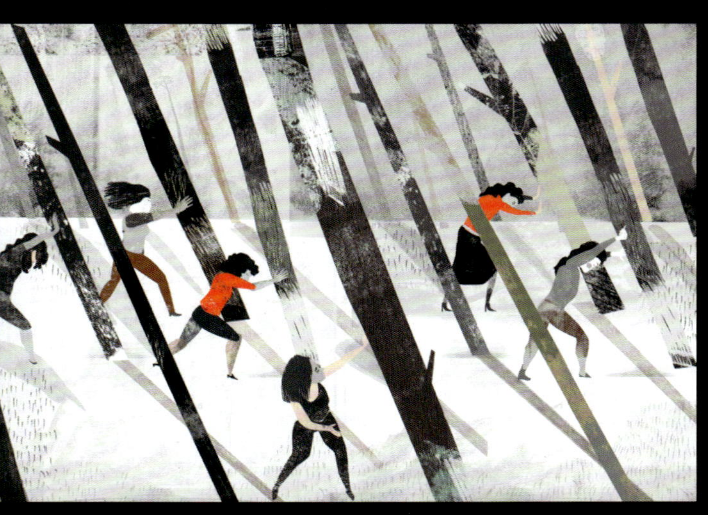

(T) *Alessandro Gottardo* (B) *Masha Manapov*

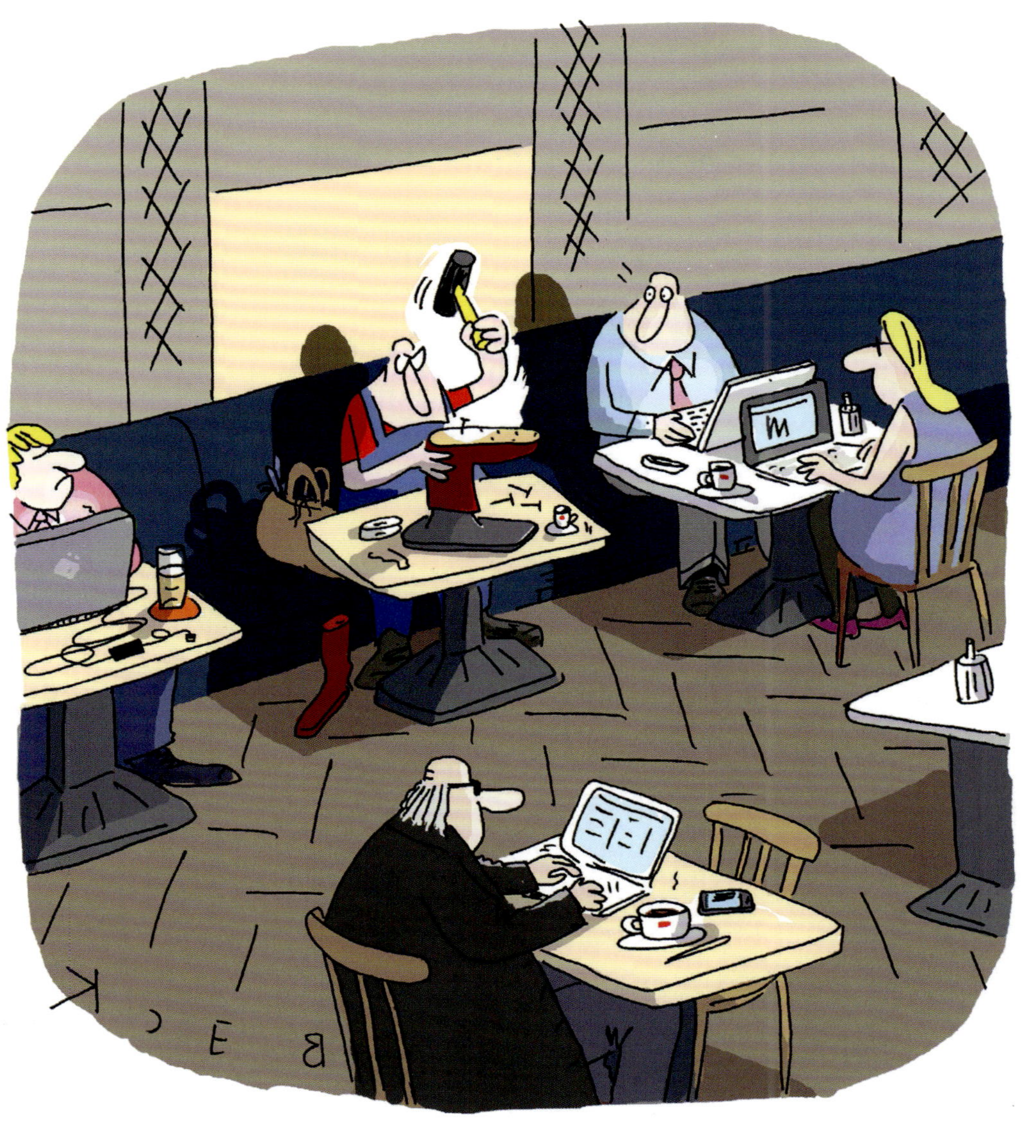

Beck

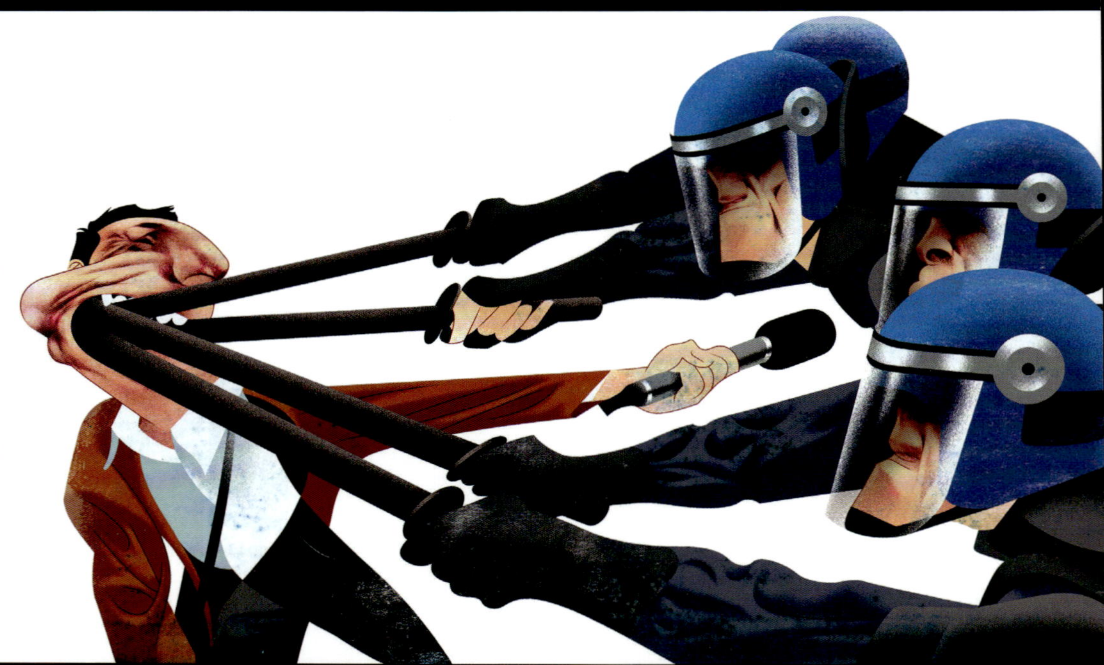

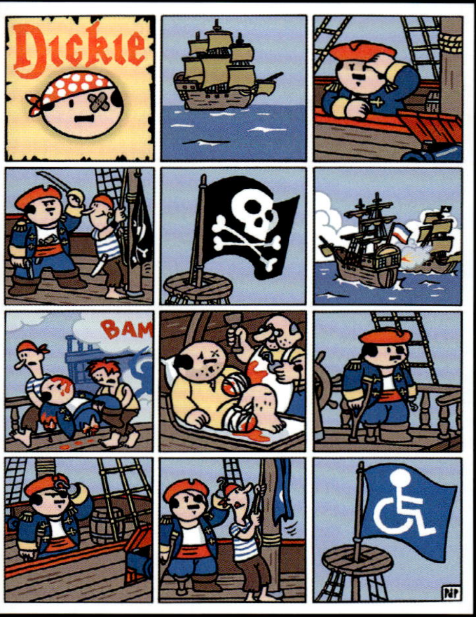

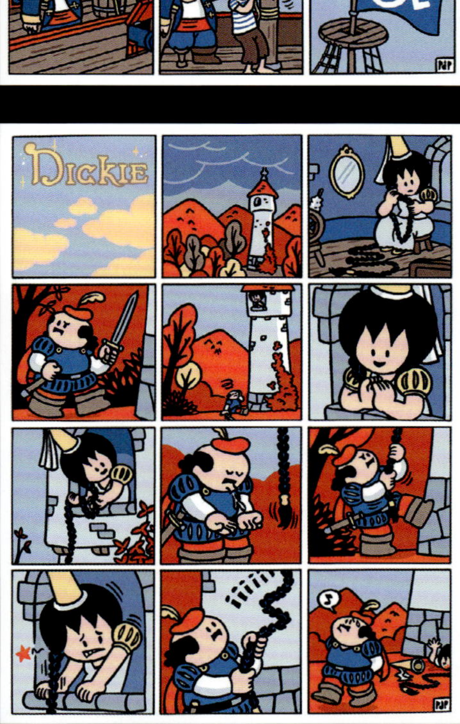
Dickie
BAM
DICKIE
WELKOM

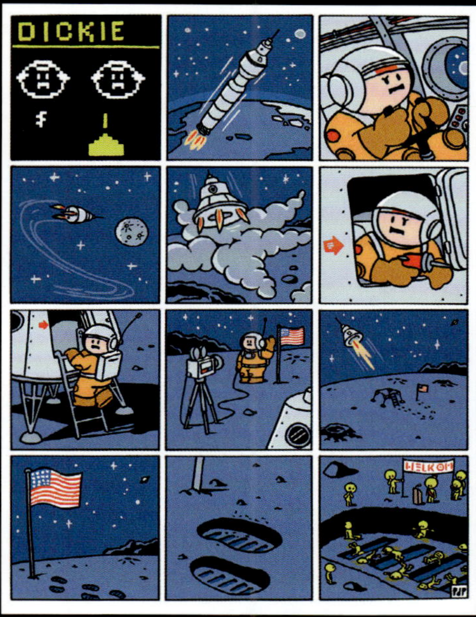

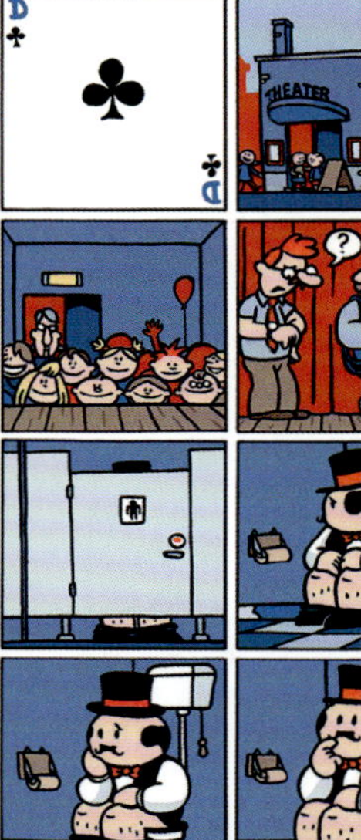
Dickie

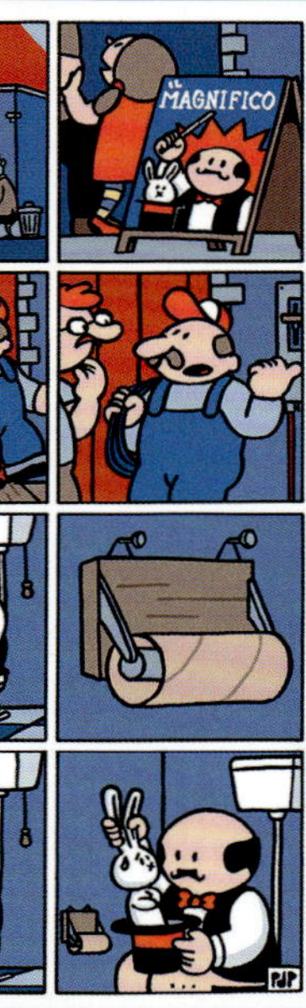
D
THEATER
IL MAGNIFICO

VIRAL

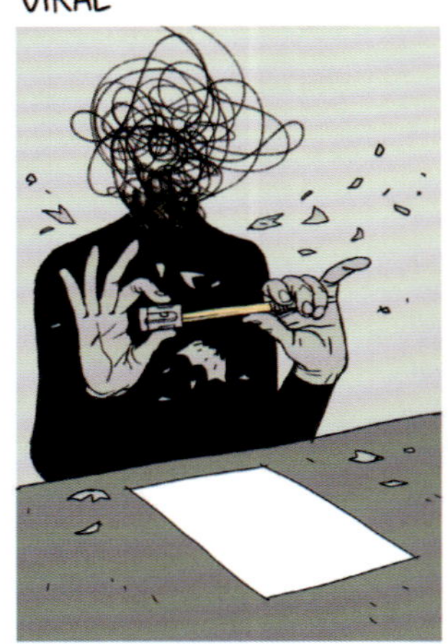
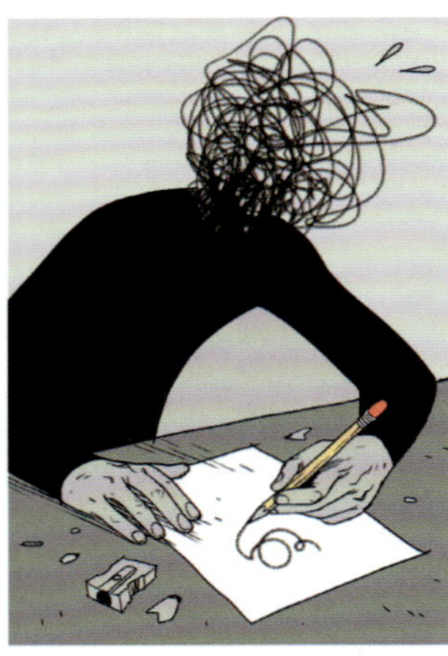
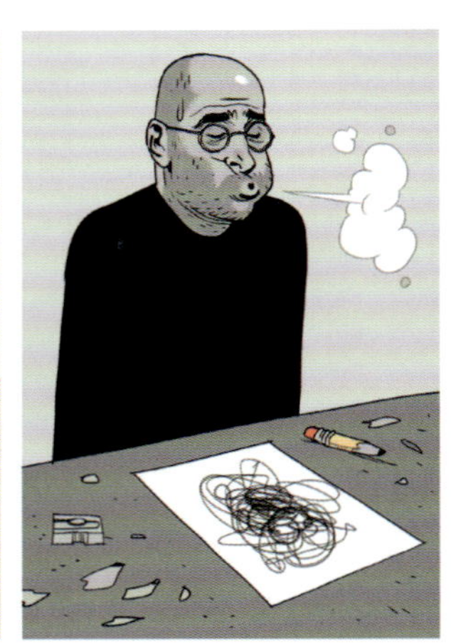
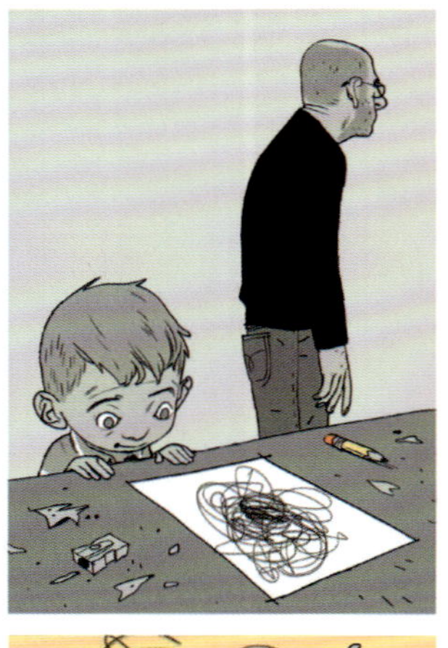
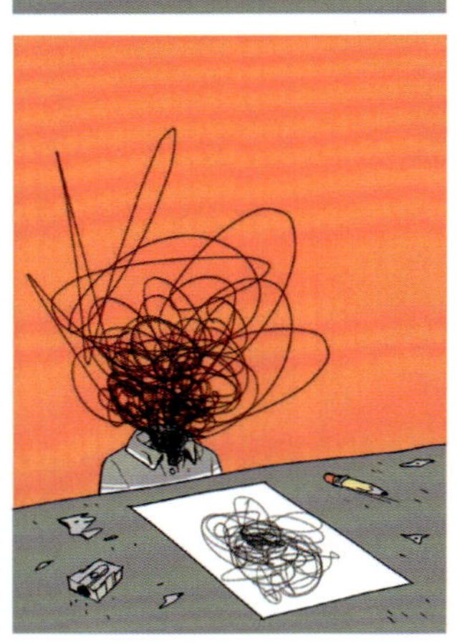
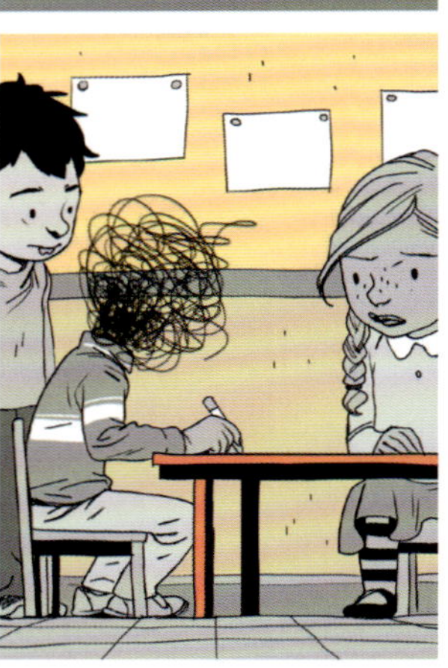
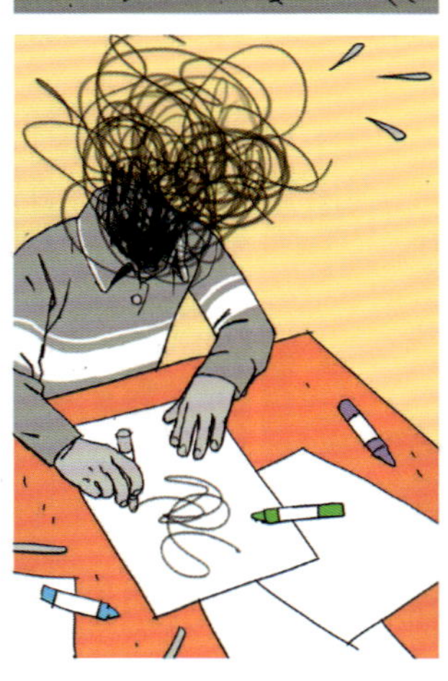
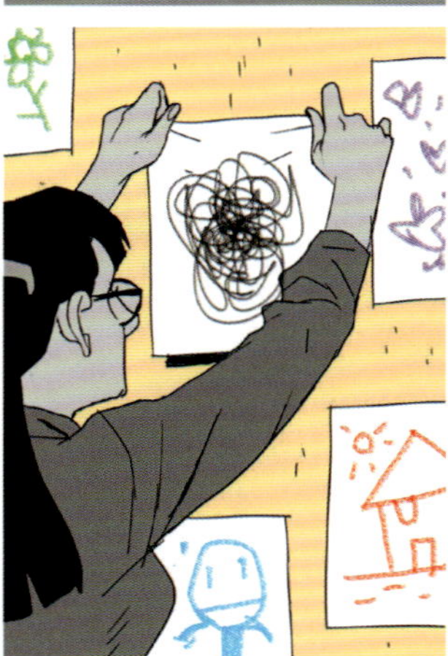
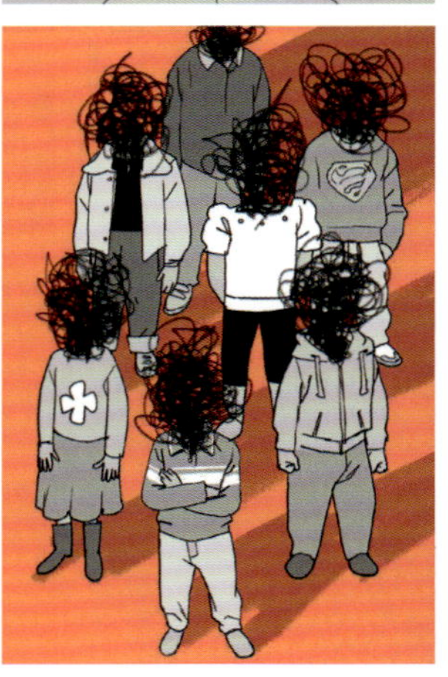

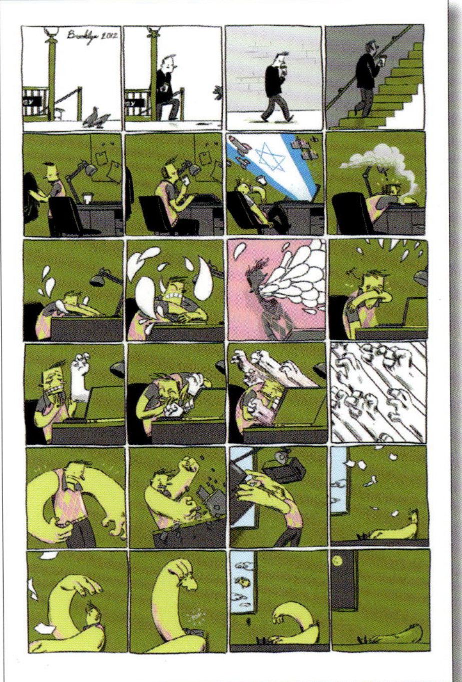

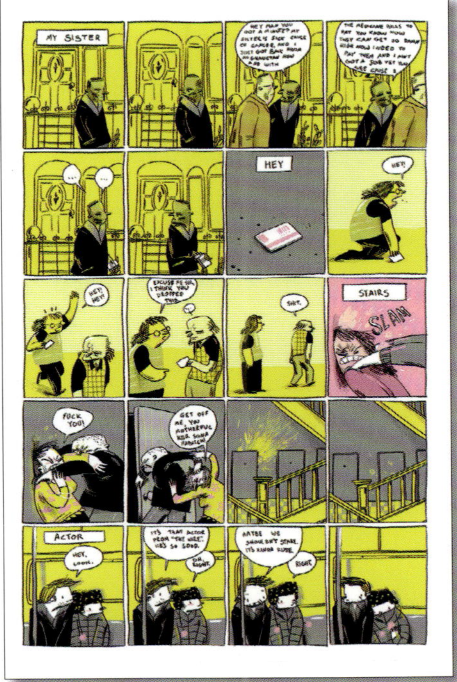

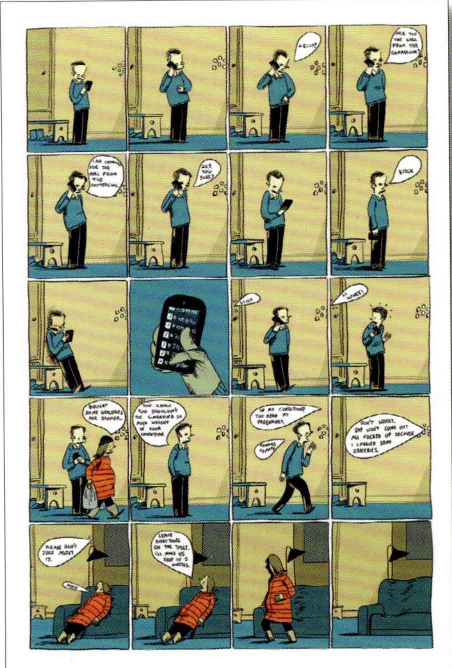

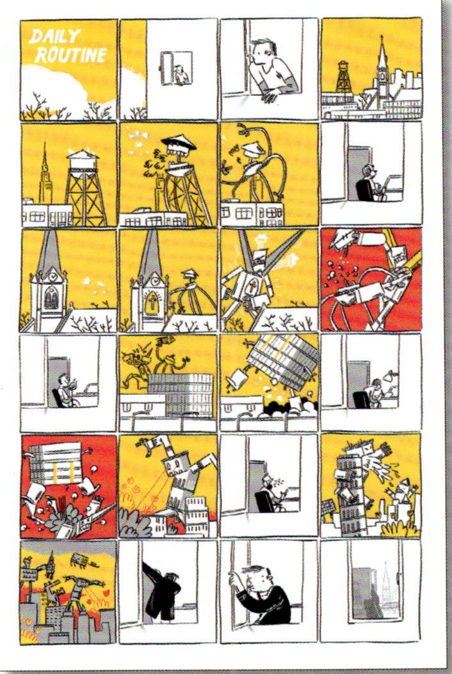

Omer Hoffmann

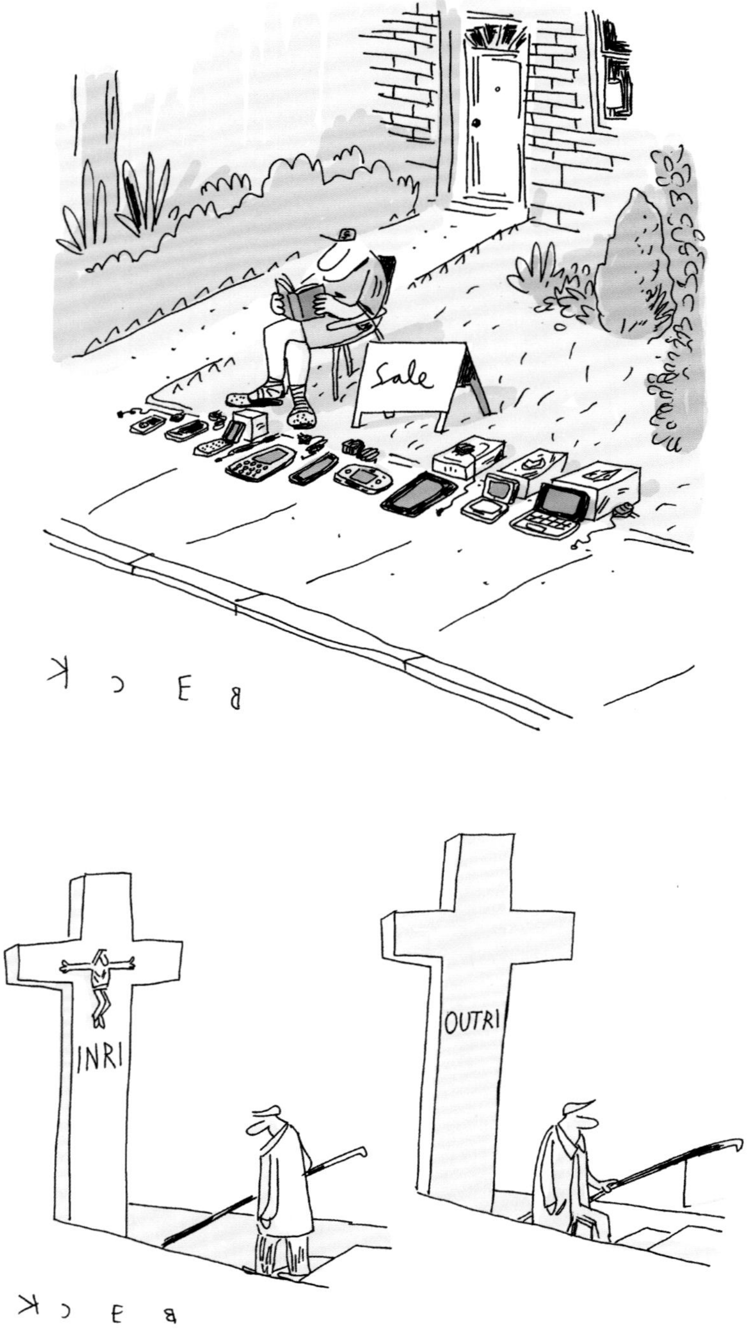

Beck

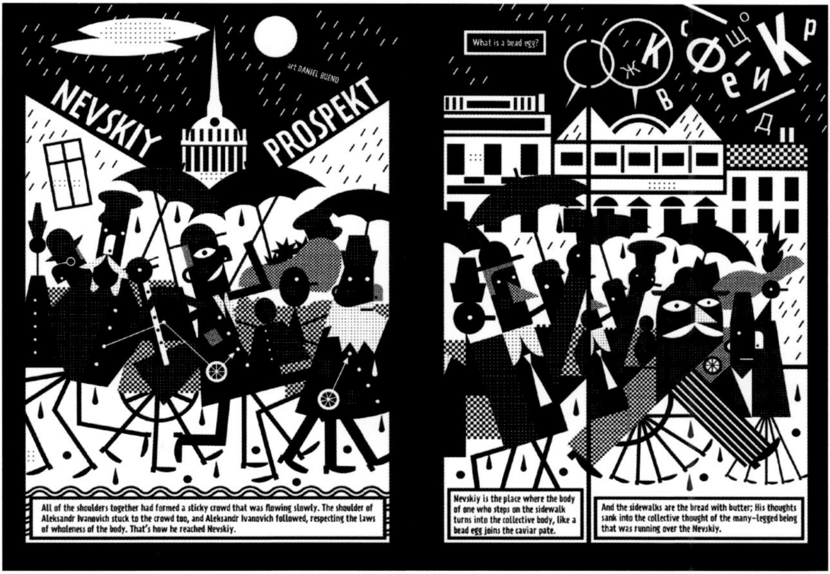

art DANIEL BUEND
NEVSKIY PROSPEKT
All of the shoulders together had formed a sticky crowd that was flowing slowly. The shoulder of Aleksandr Ivanovich stuck to the crowd too, and Aleksandr Ivanovich followed, respecting the laws of wholeness of the body. That's how he reached Nevskiy.
What is a bead egg?
Nevskiy is the place where the body of one who steps on the sidewalk turns into the collective body, like a bead egg joins the caviar pate.
And the sidewalks are the bread with butter; His thoughts sank into the collective thought of the many-legged being that was running over the Nevskiy.
Silently, he focused on those many legs. The Dark Crowd was crawling over the sidewalk. 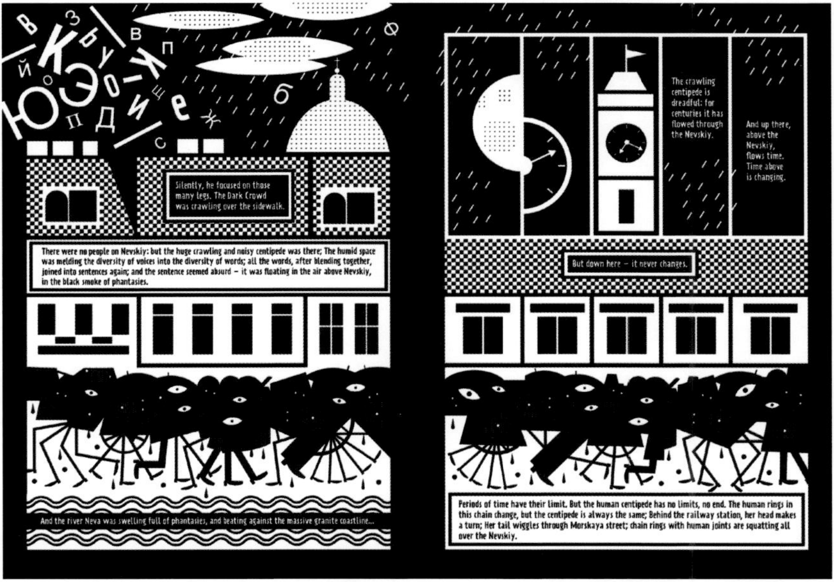
There were no people on Nevskiy: but the huge crawling and noisy centipede was there; The humid space was melding the diversity of voices into the diversity of words; all the words, after blending together, joined into sentences again; and the sentence seemed absurd — it was floating in the air above Nevskiy, in the black smoke of phantasies.
And the river Neva was swelling full of phantasies, and beating against the massive granite coastline...
The crawling centipede is dreadful: for centuries it has flowed through the Nevskiy.
And up there, above the Nevskiy, flows time. Time above is changing.
But down here — it never changes.
Periods of time have their limit. But the human centipede has no limits, no end. The human rings in this chain change, but the centipede is always the same; Behind the railway station, her head makes a turn; Her tail wiggles through Morskaya street; chain rings with human joints are squatting all over the Nevskiy.

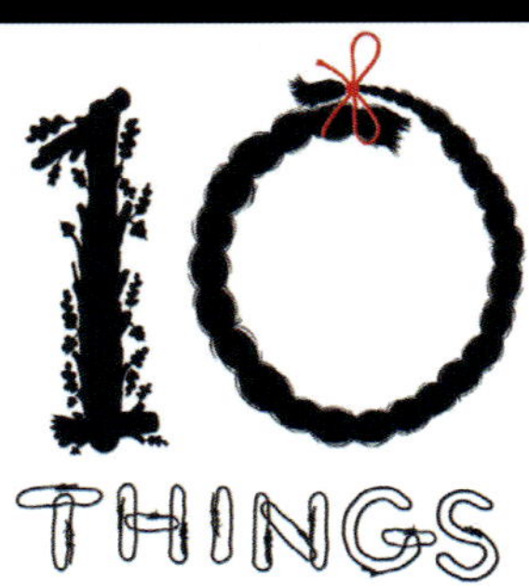

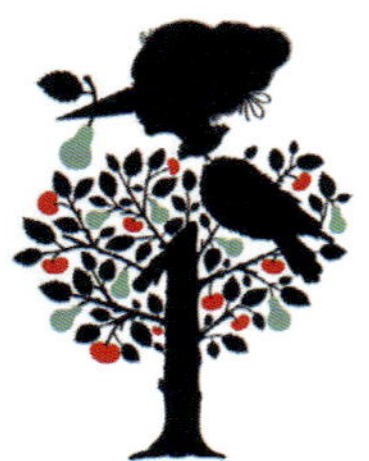

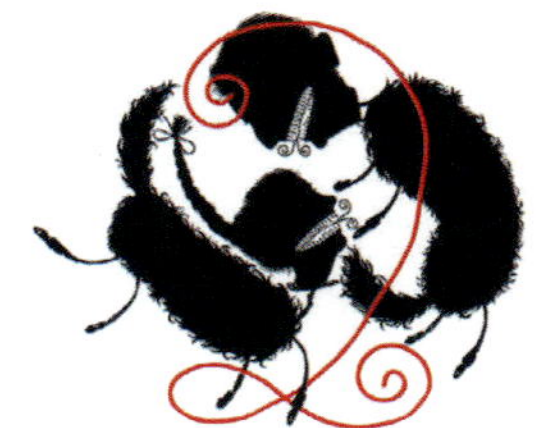

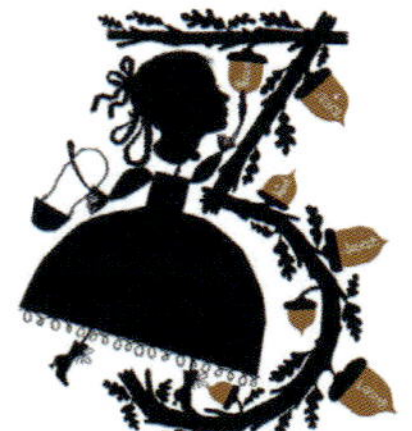

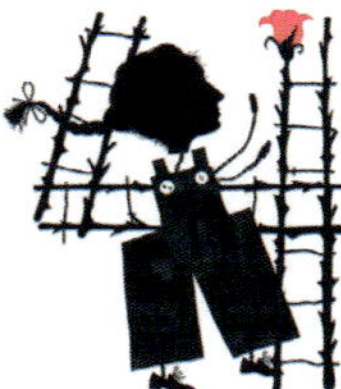

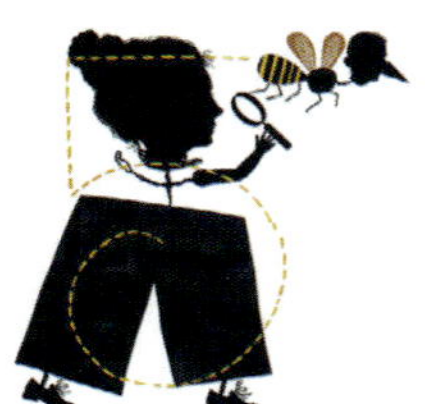

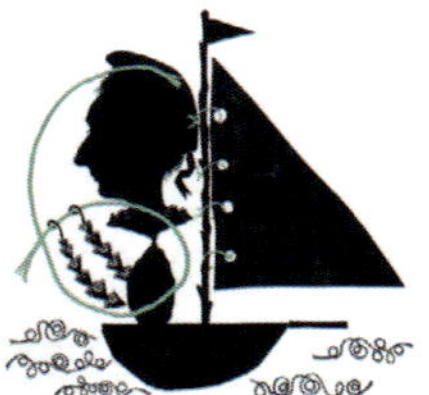

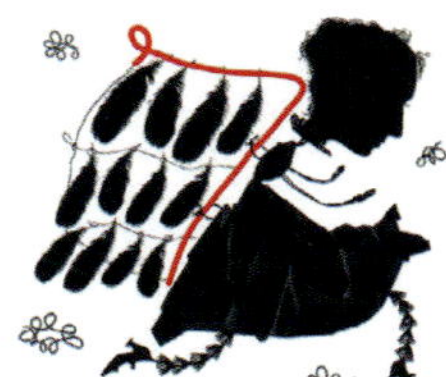

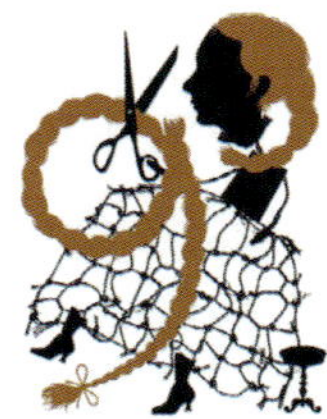

Melinda Beck

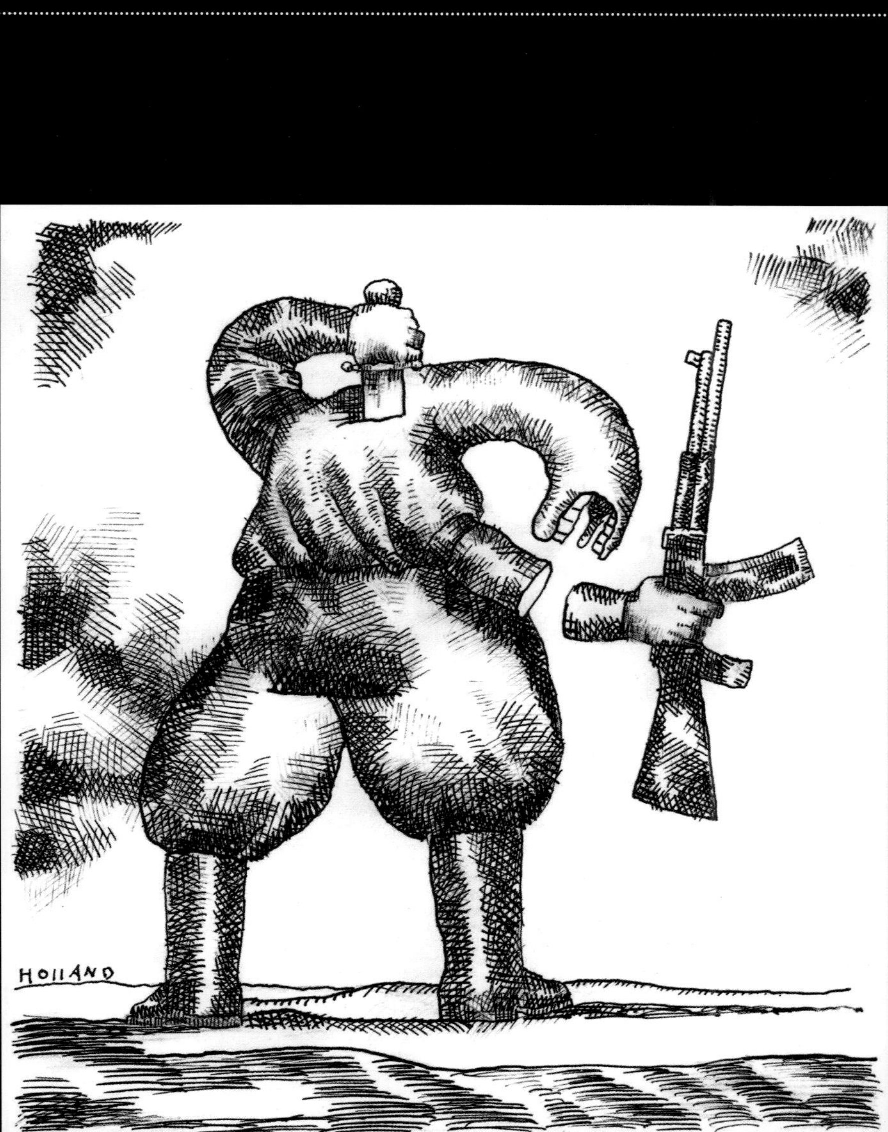
Holland

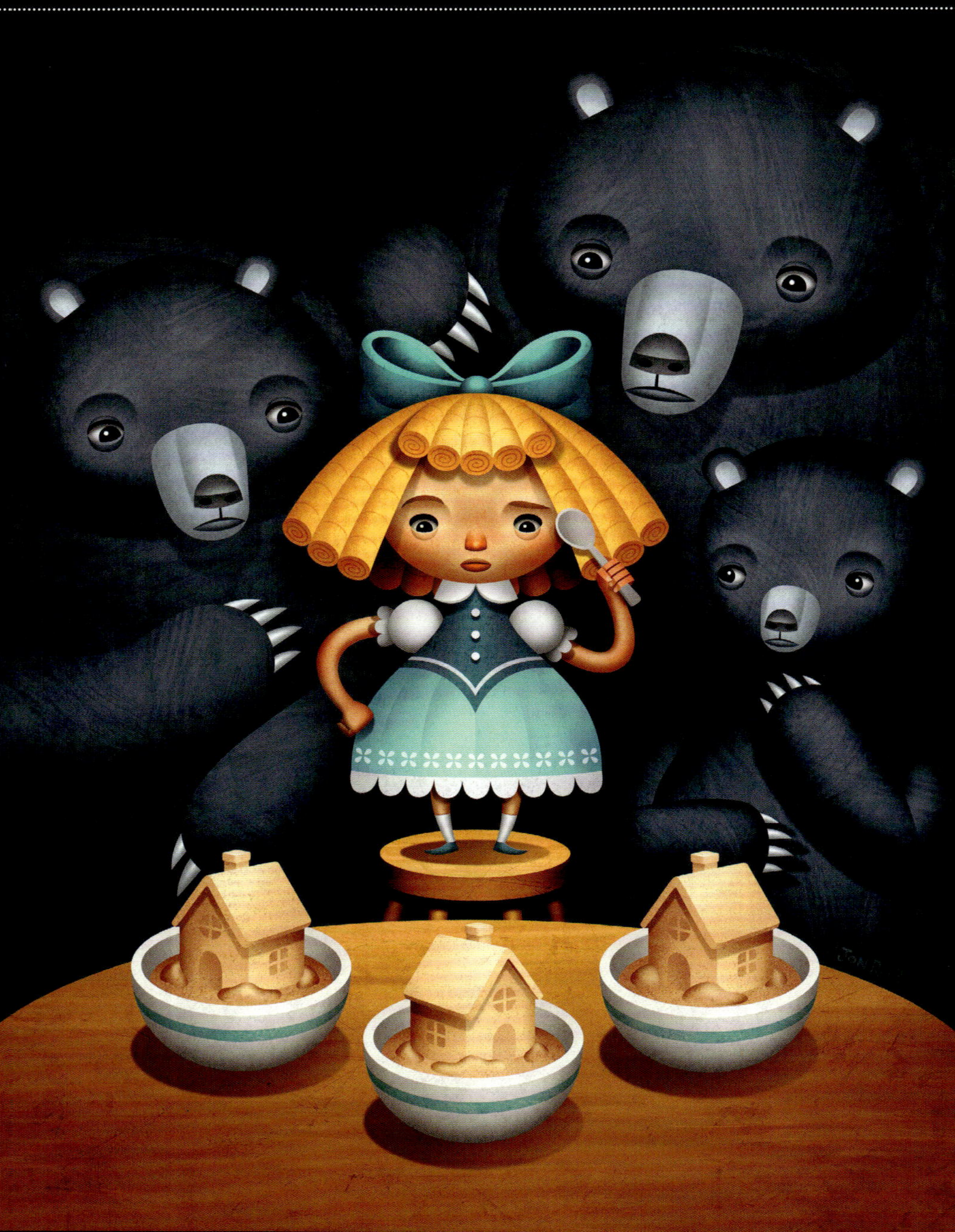

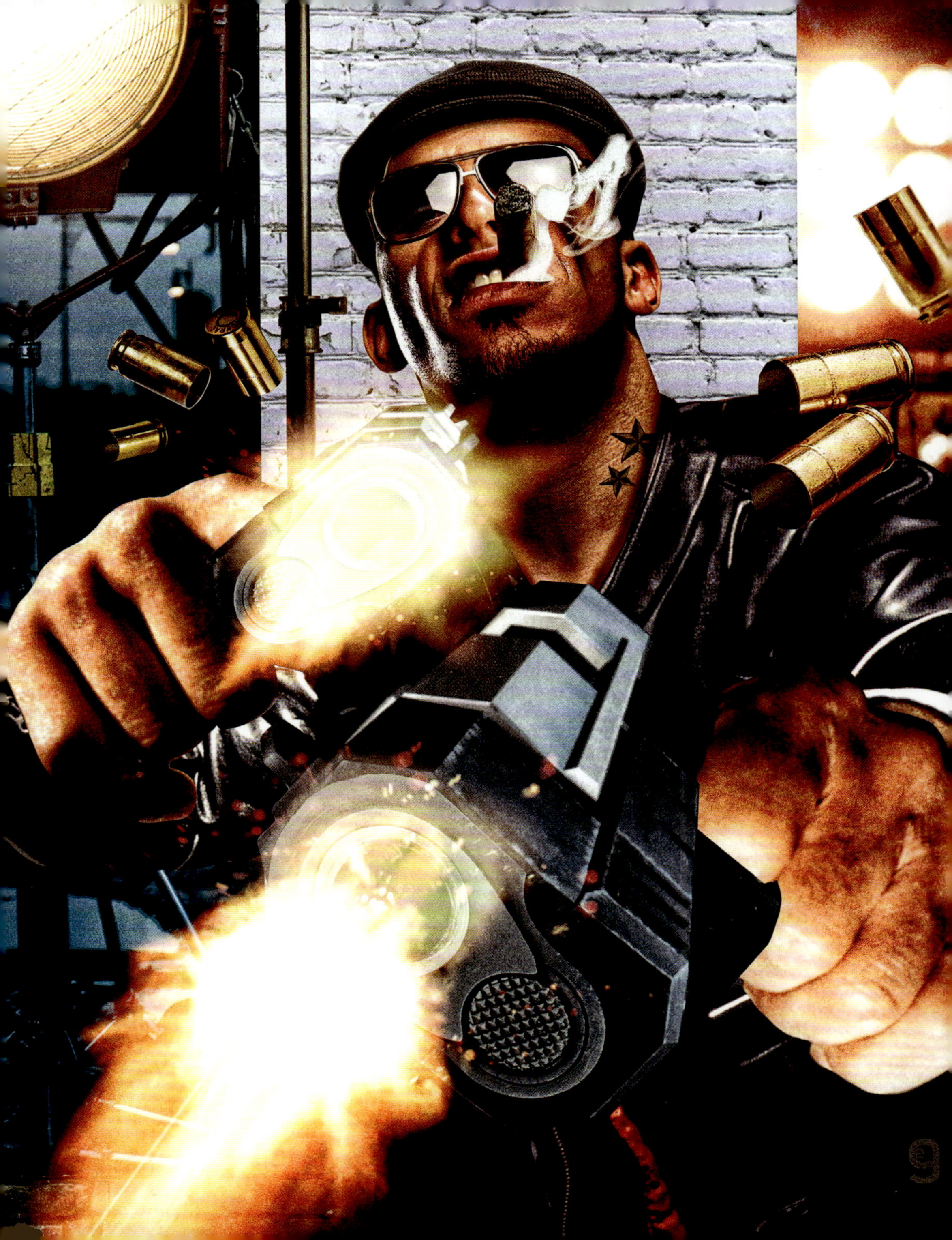

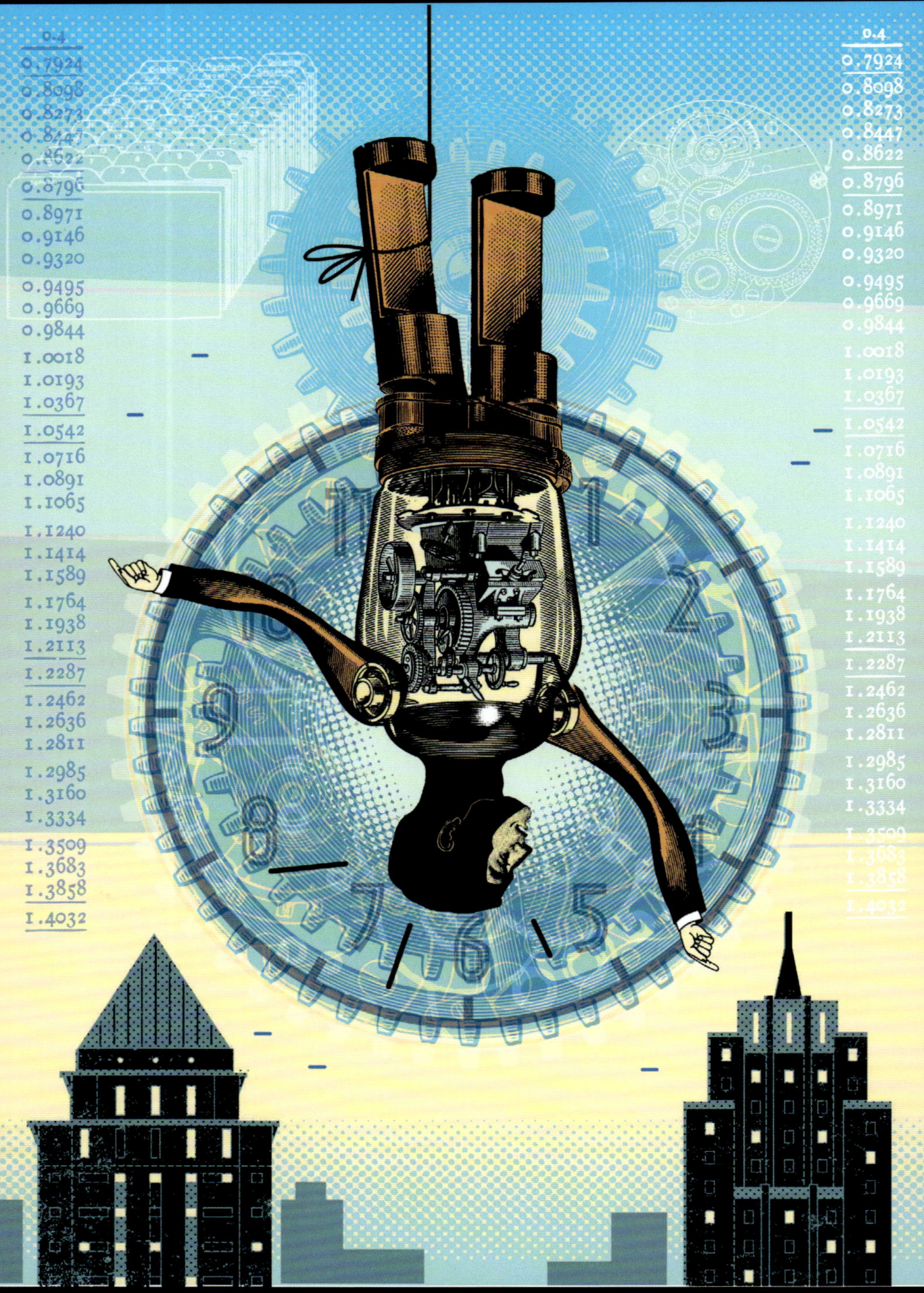

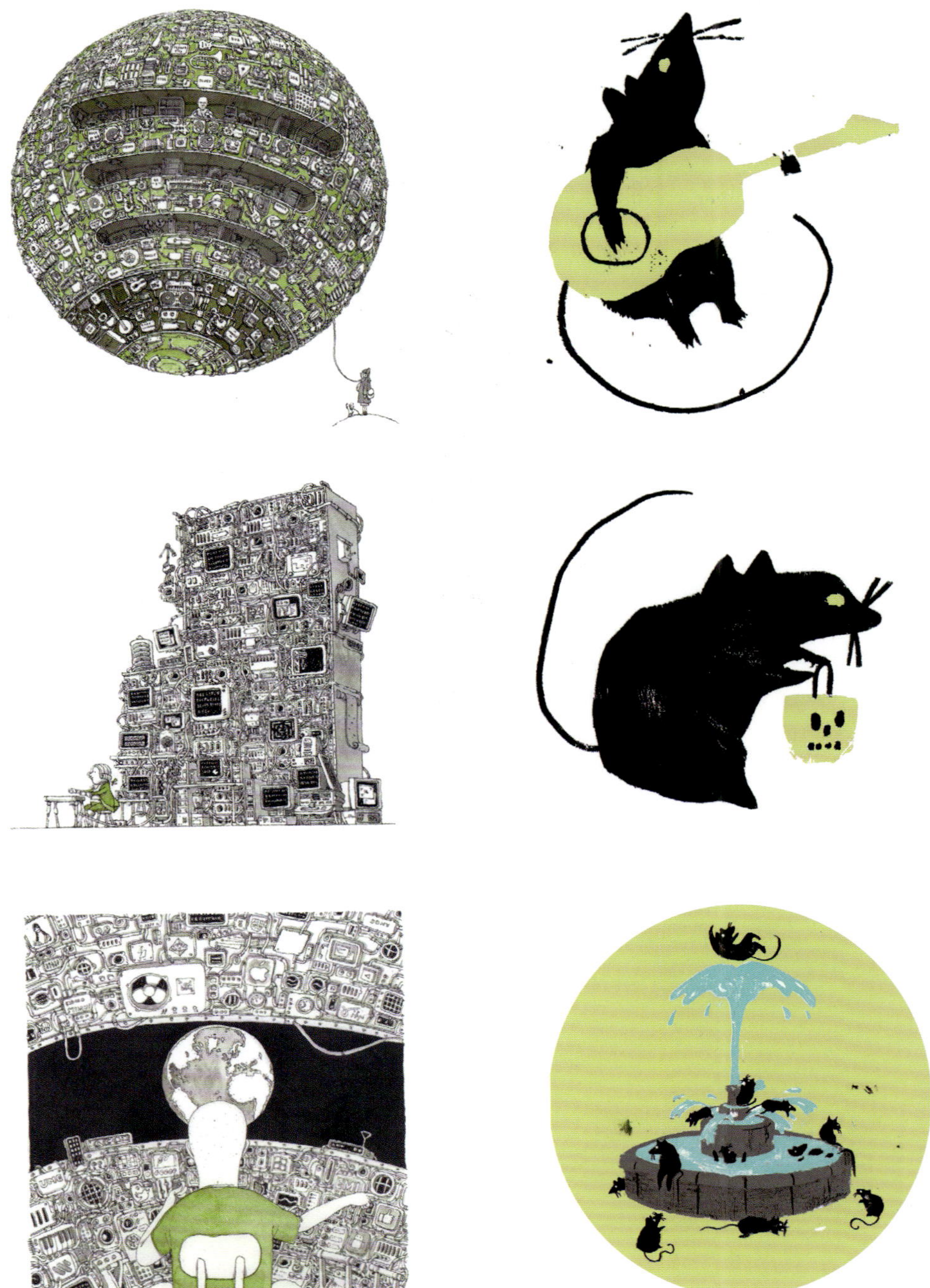

(L) *Mattias Adolfsson* (R) *Daniel Zender*

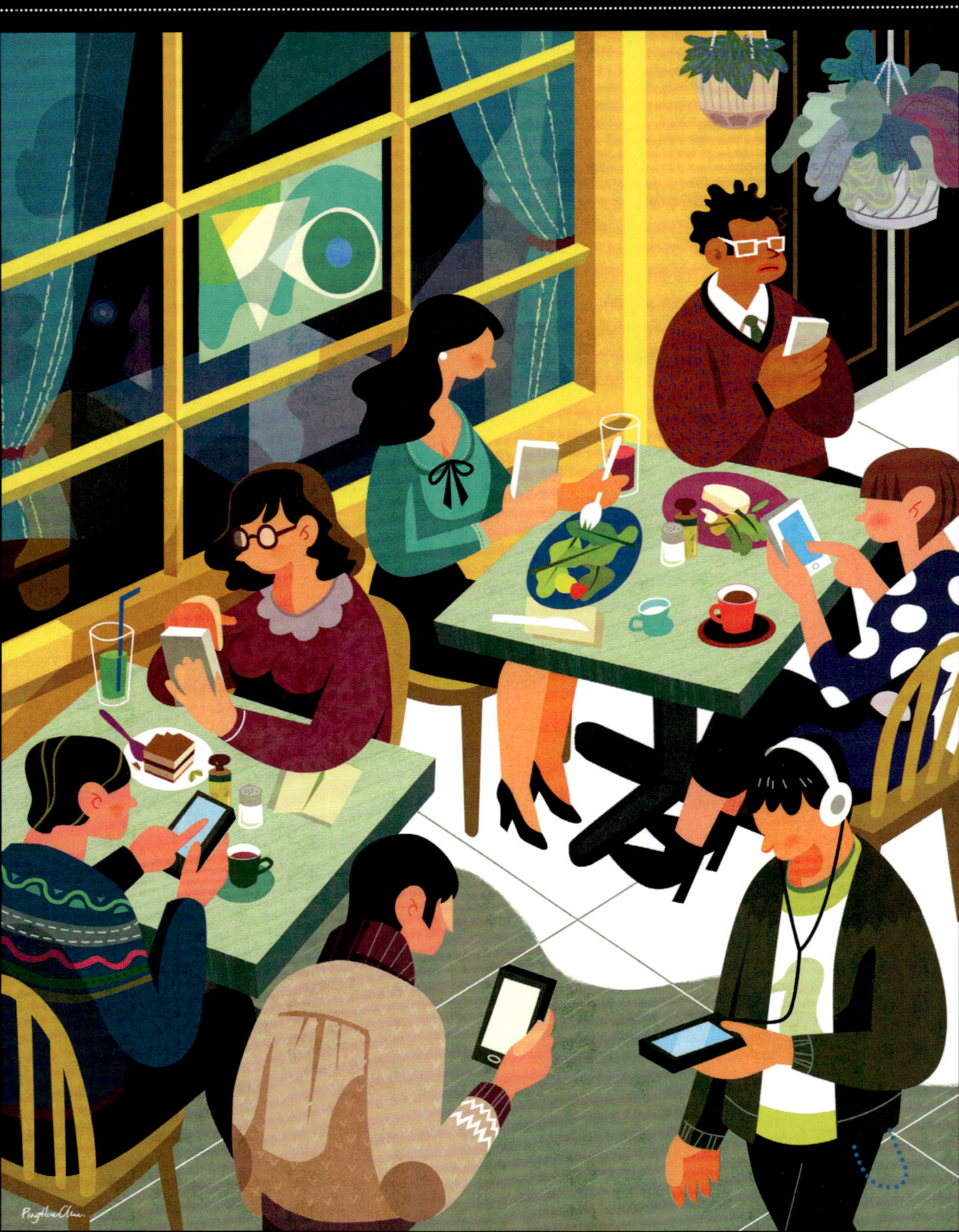

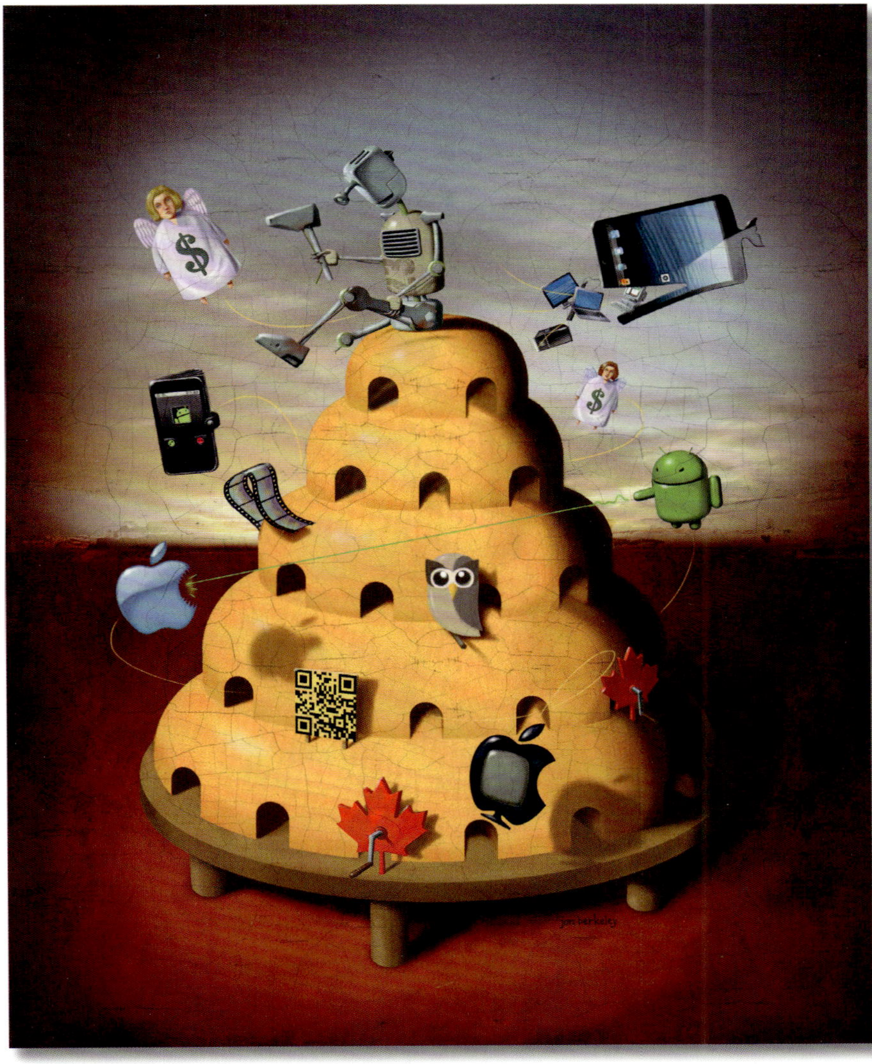

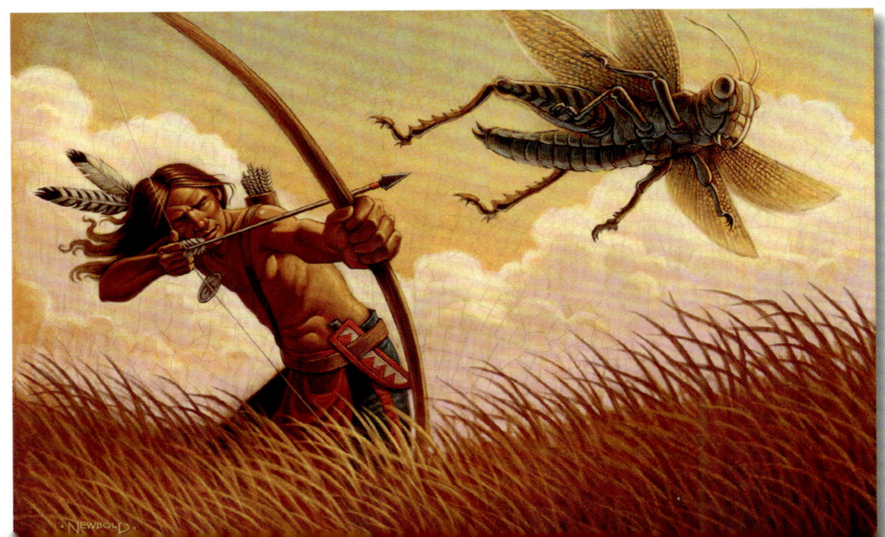

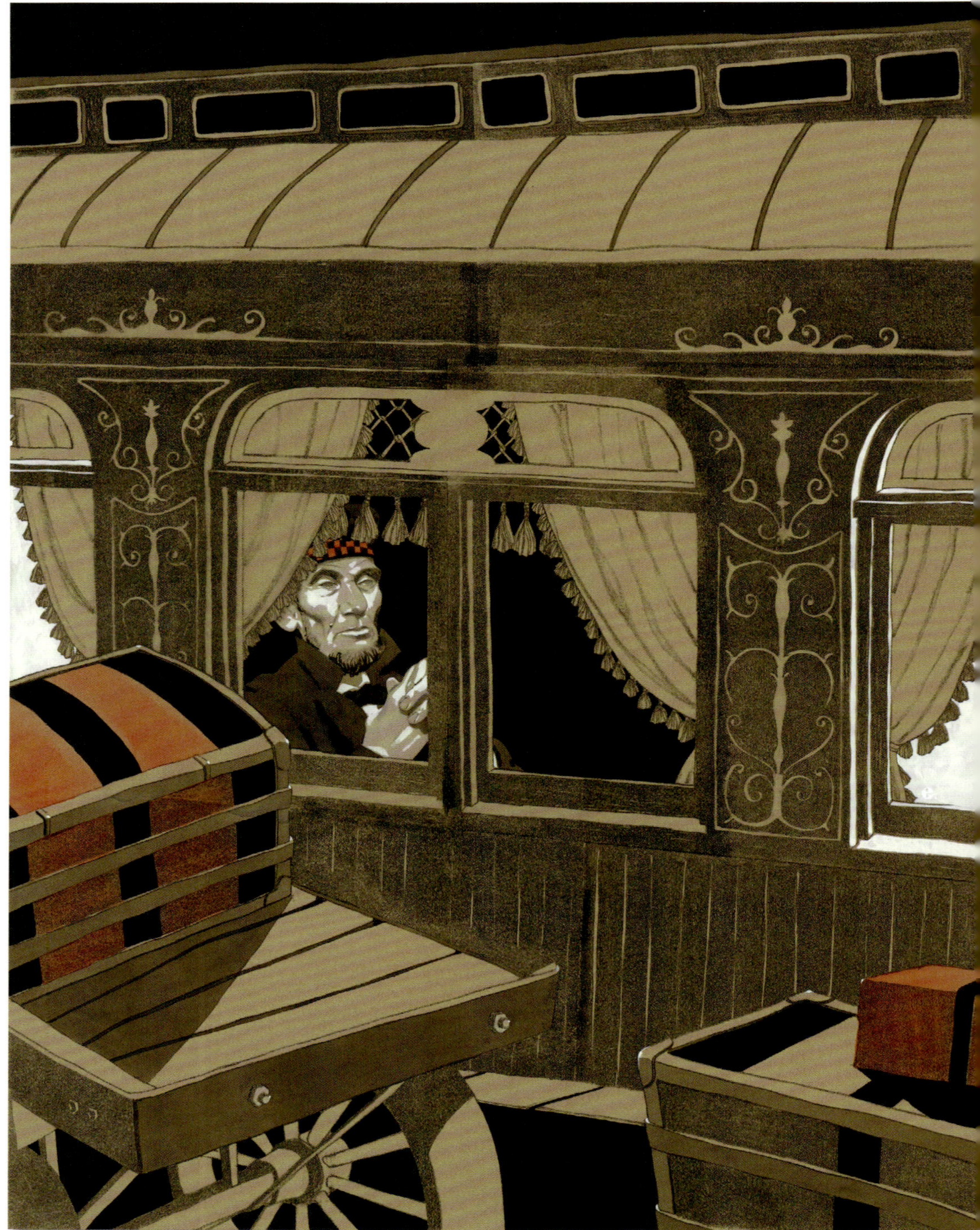

Edward Kinsella III

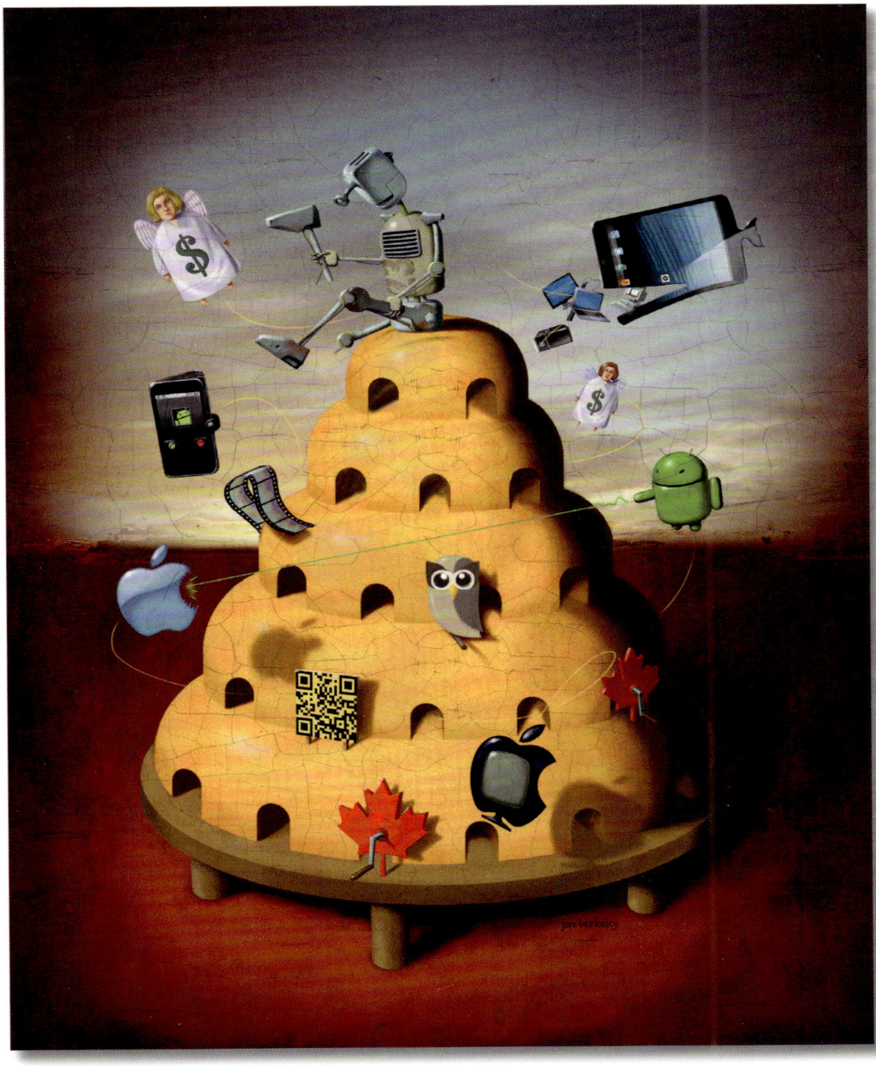

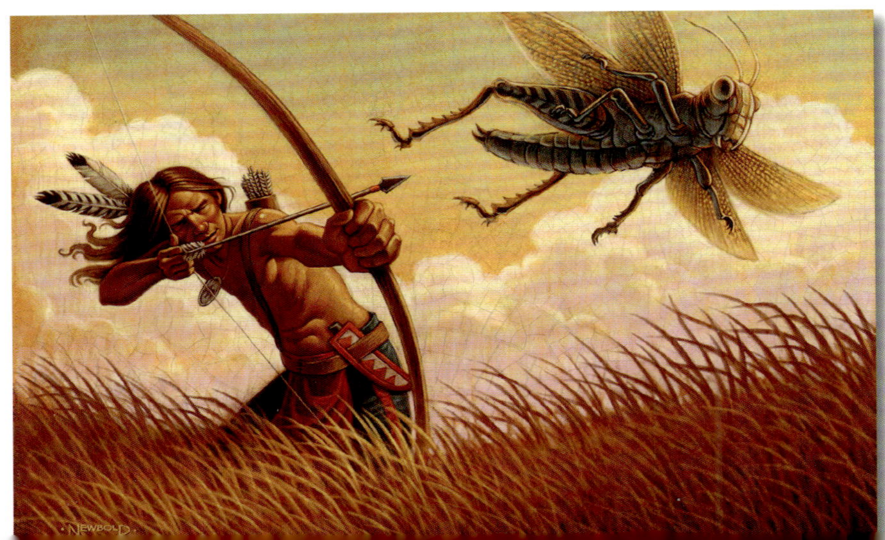

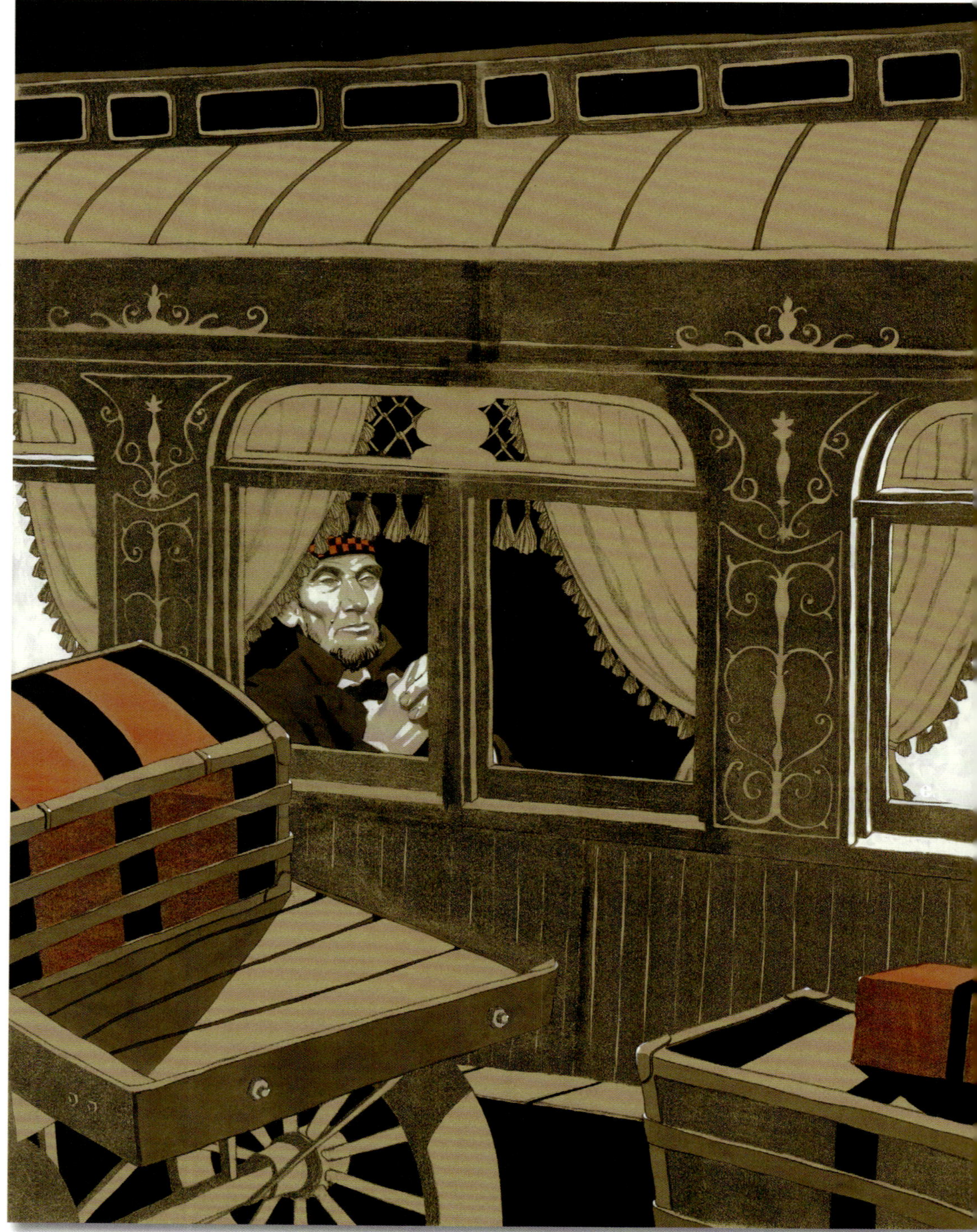

Edward Kinsella III

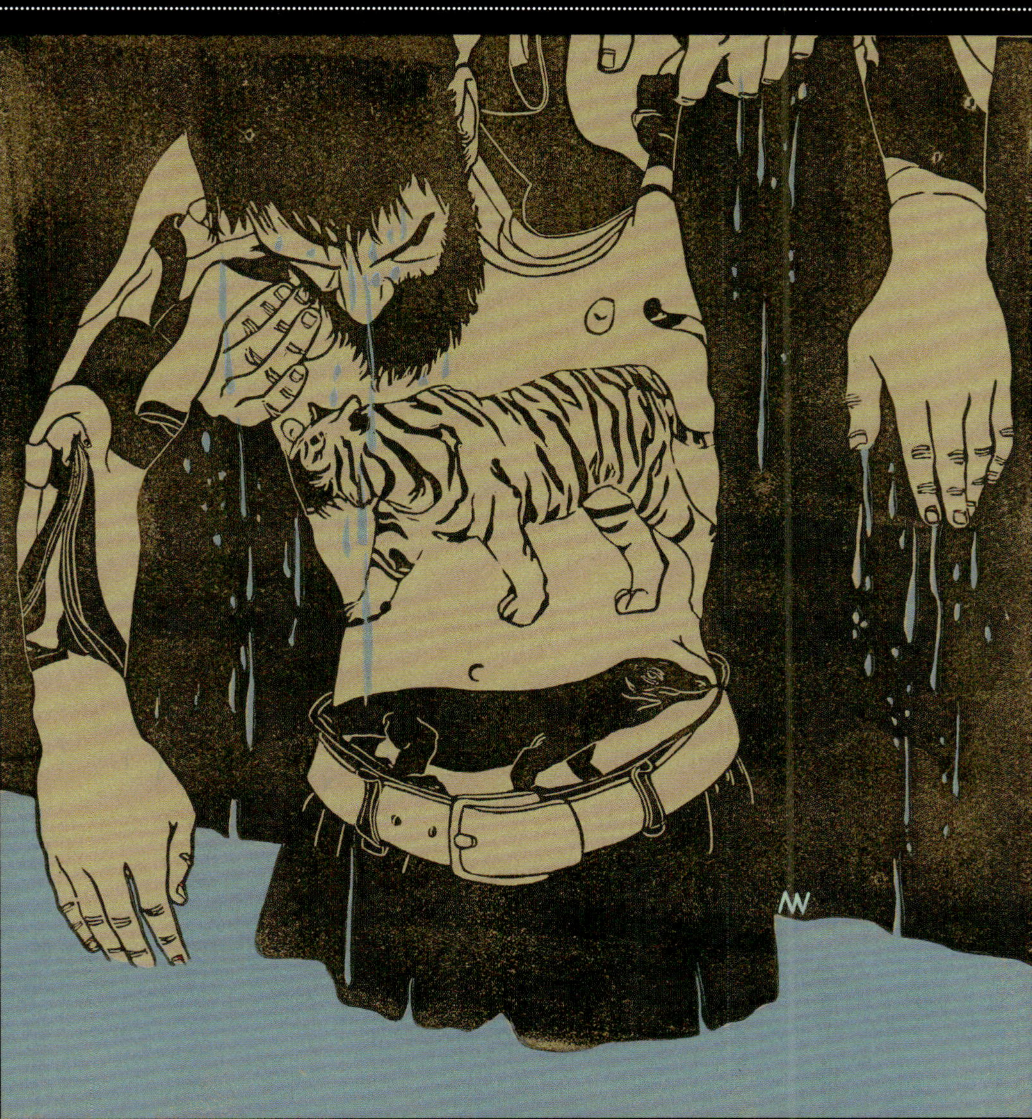

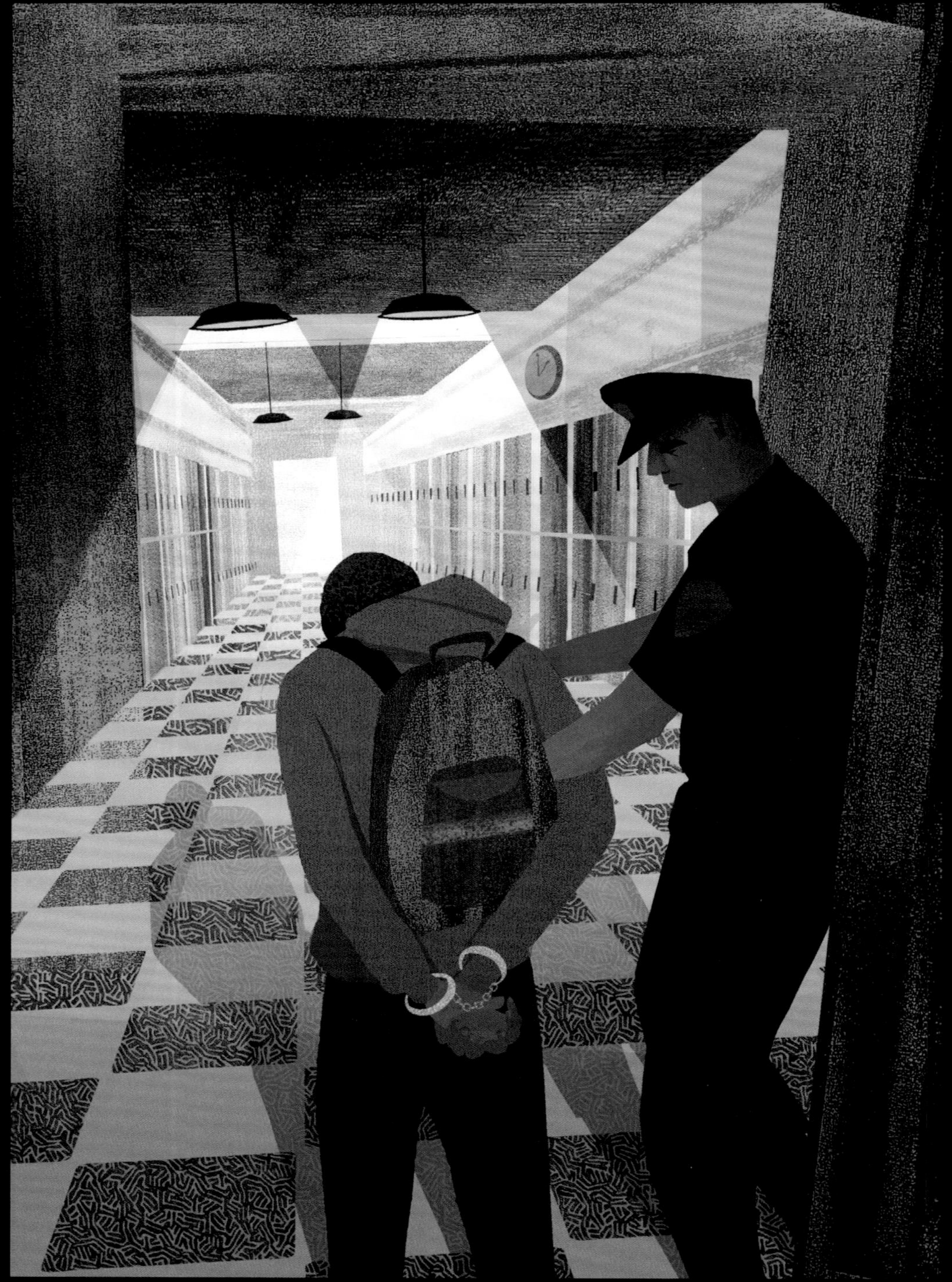

Sam Kalda

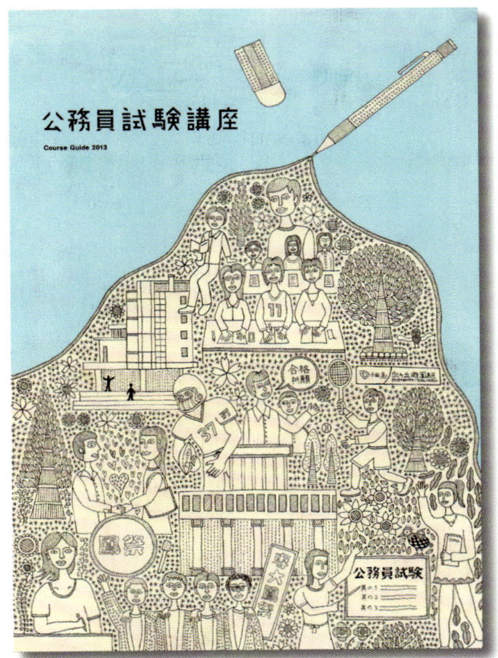

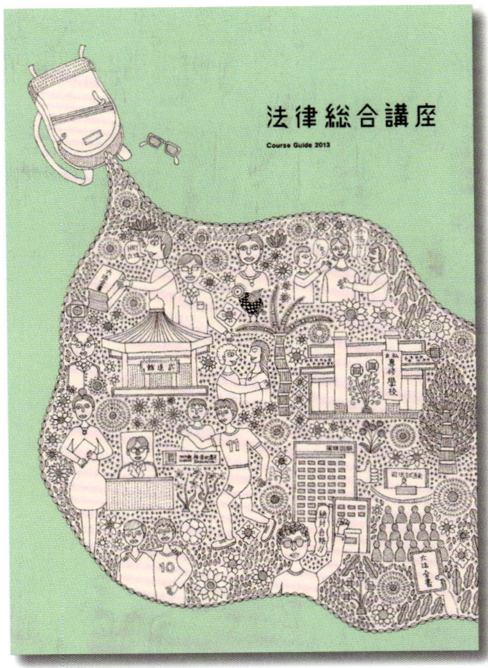

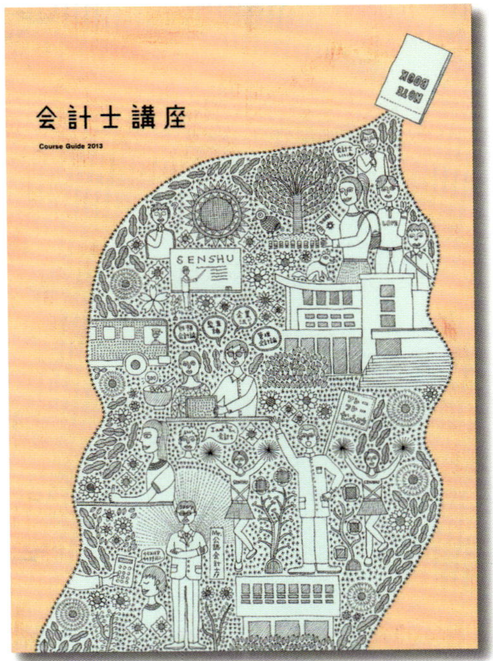

Takahisa Hashimoto

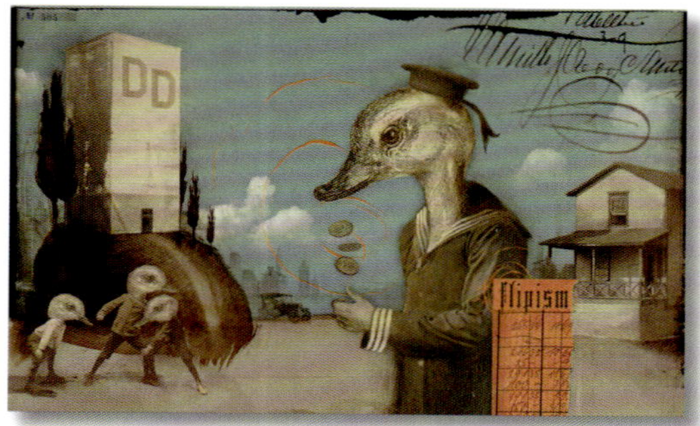

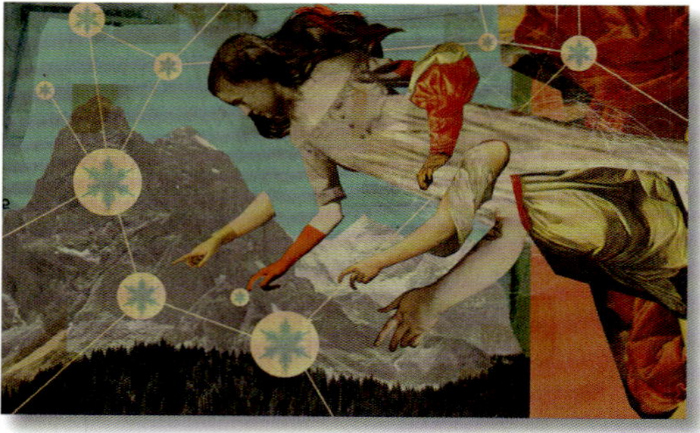

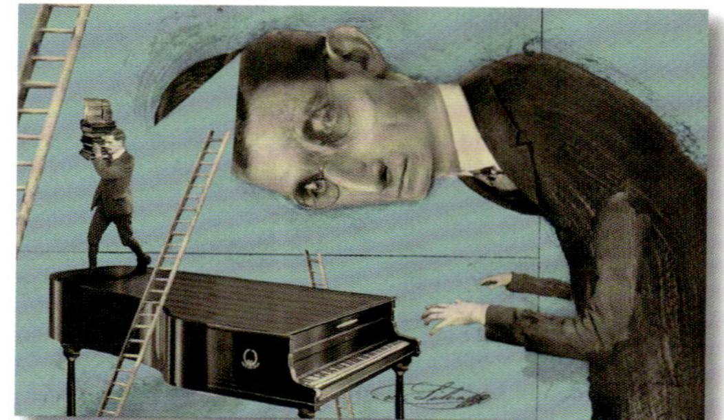

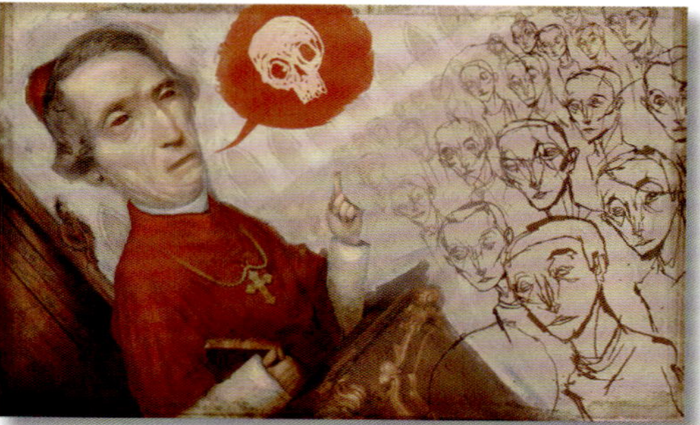

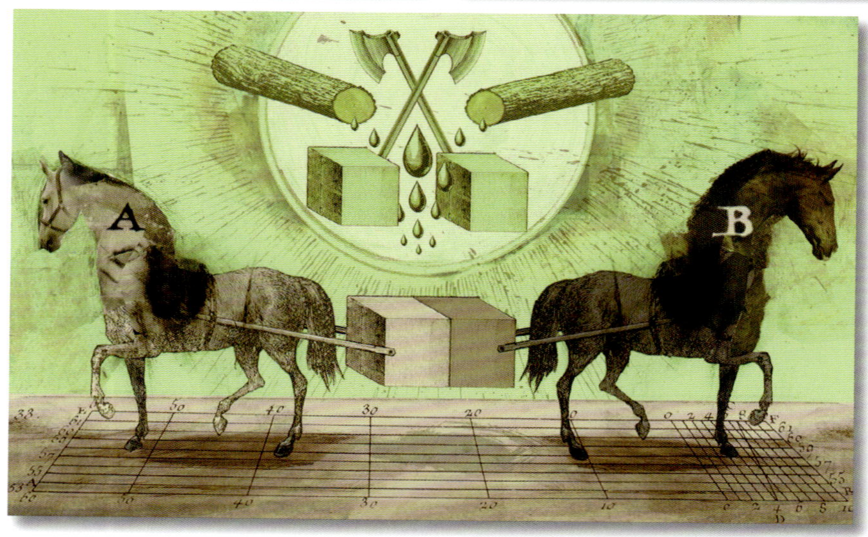

Lars Henkel

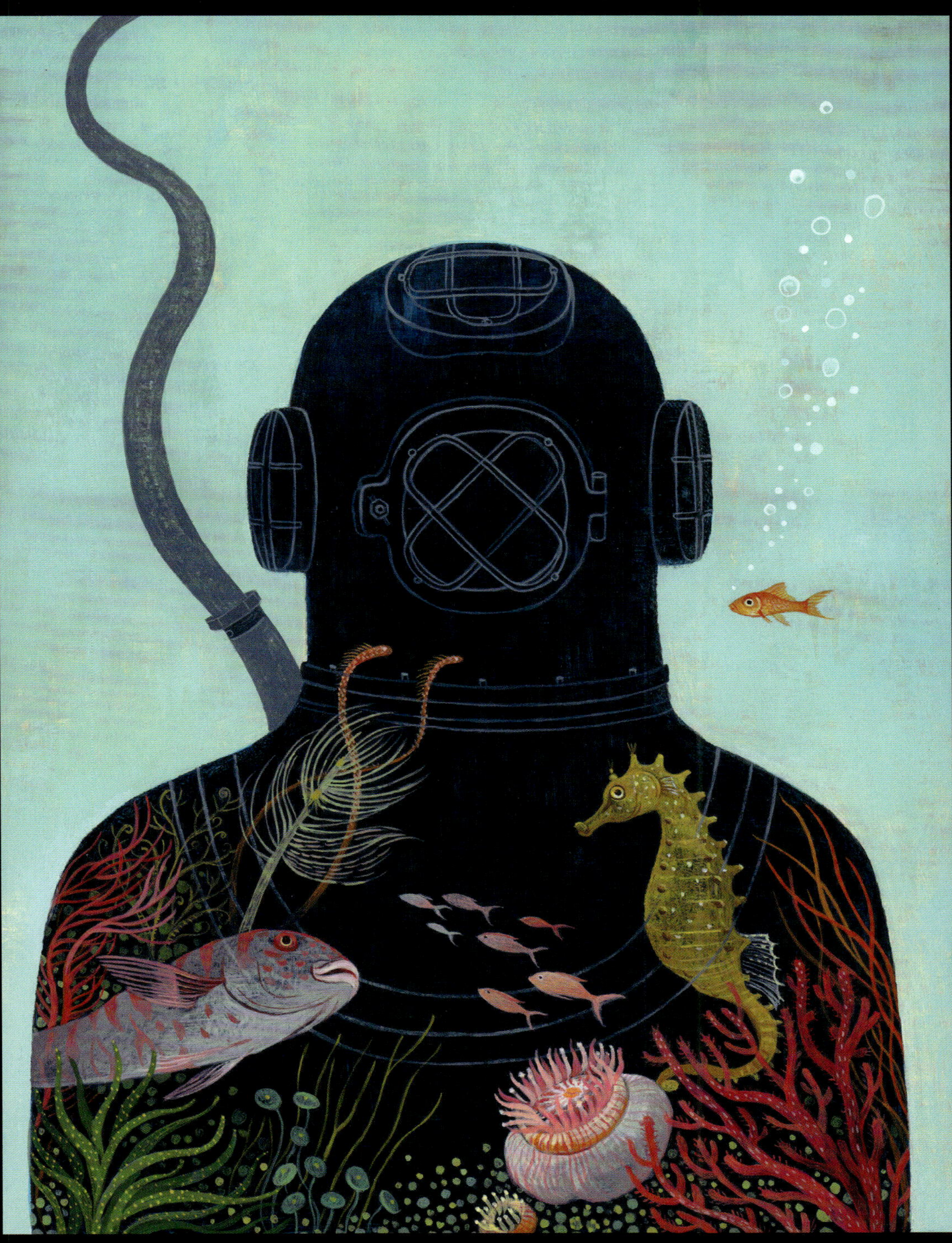

Jody Hewgill

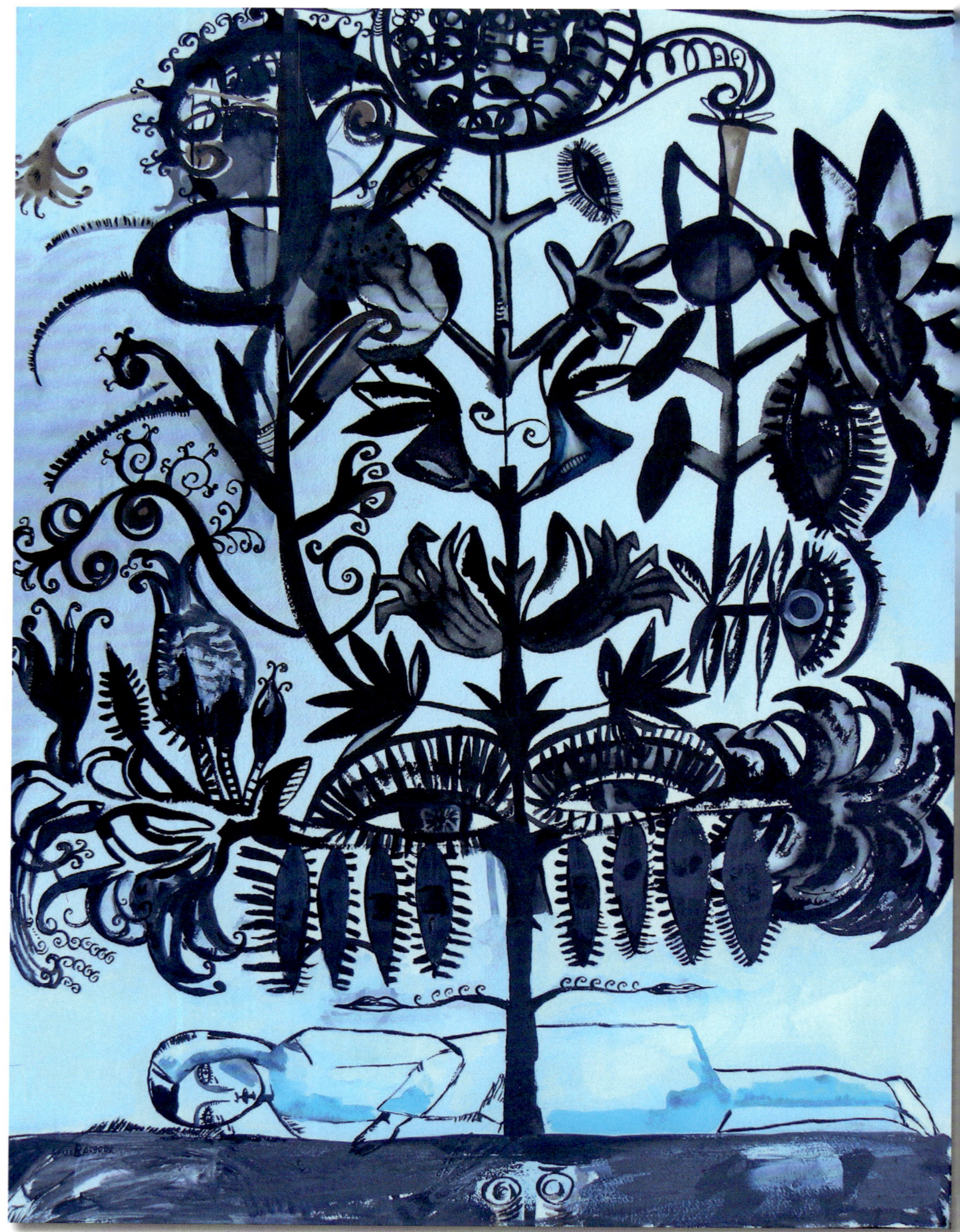

Karen Barbour

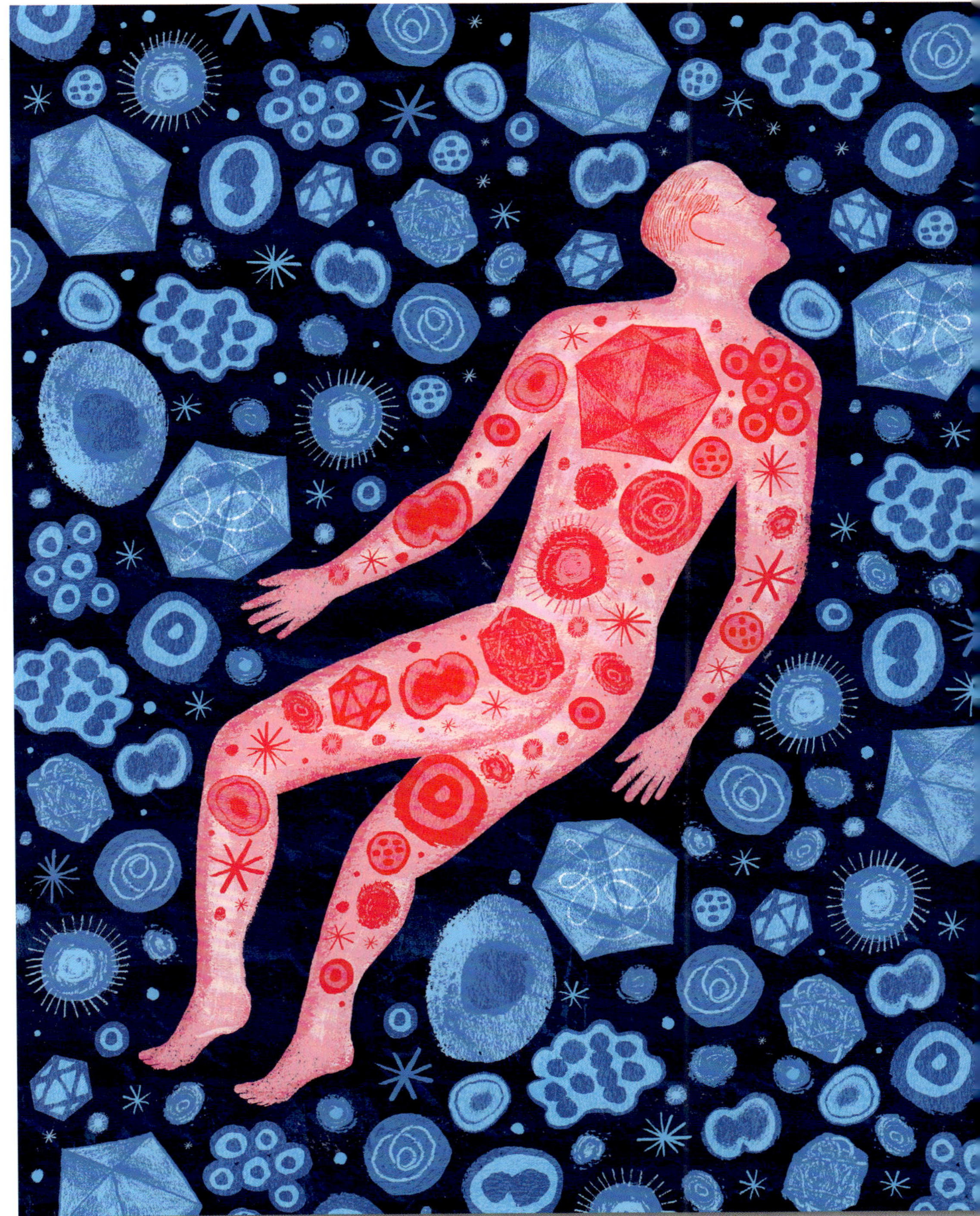

James O'Brien

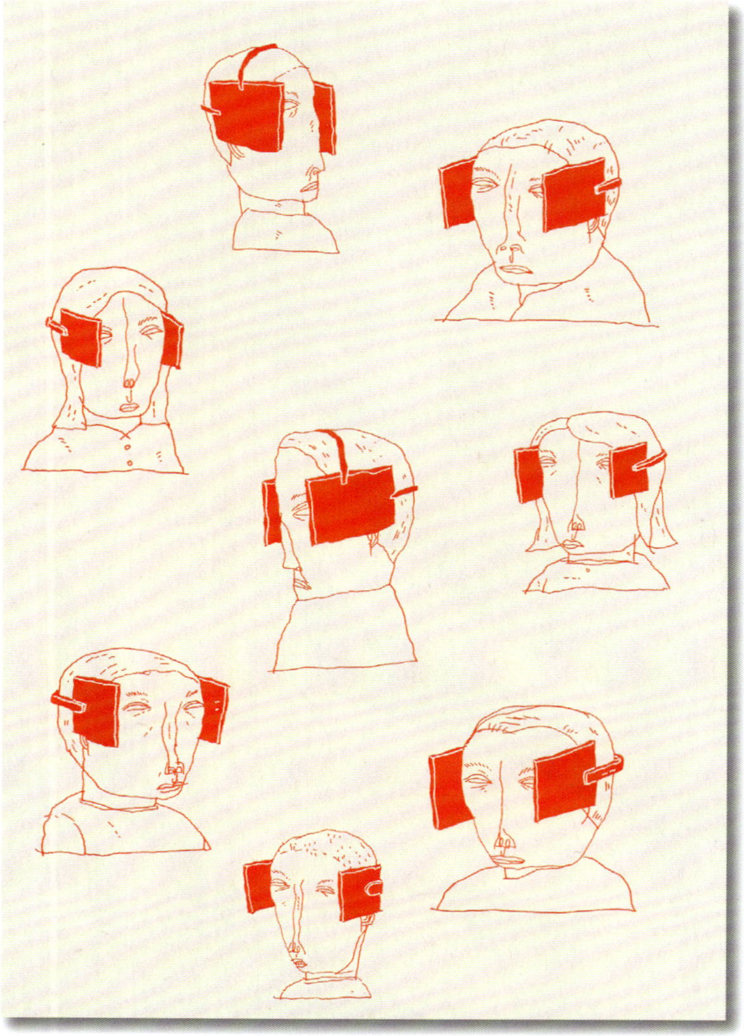

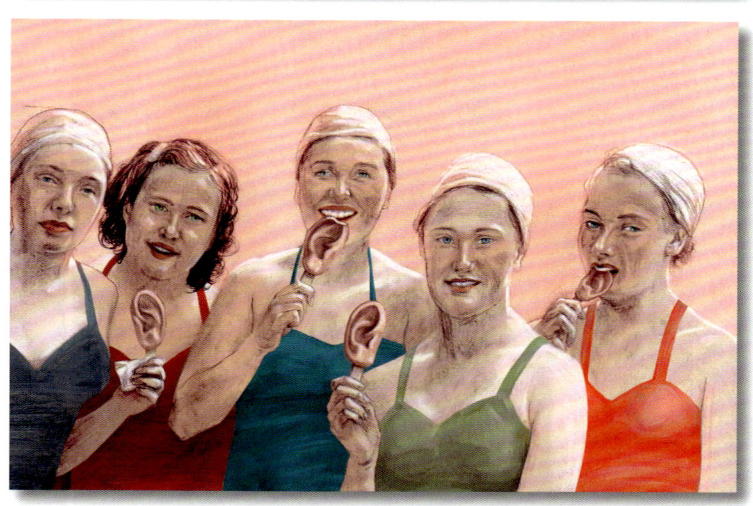

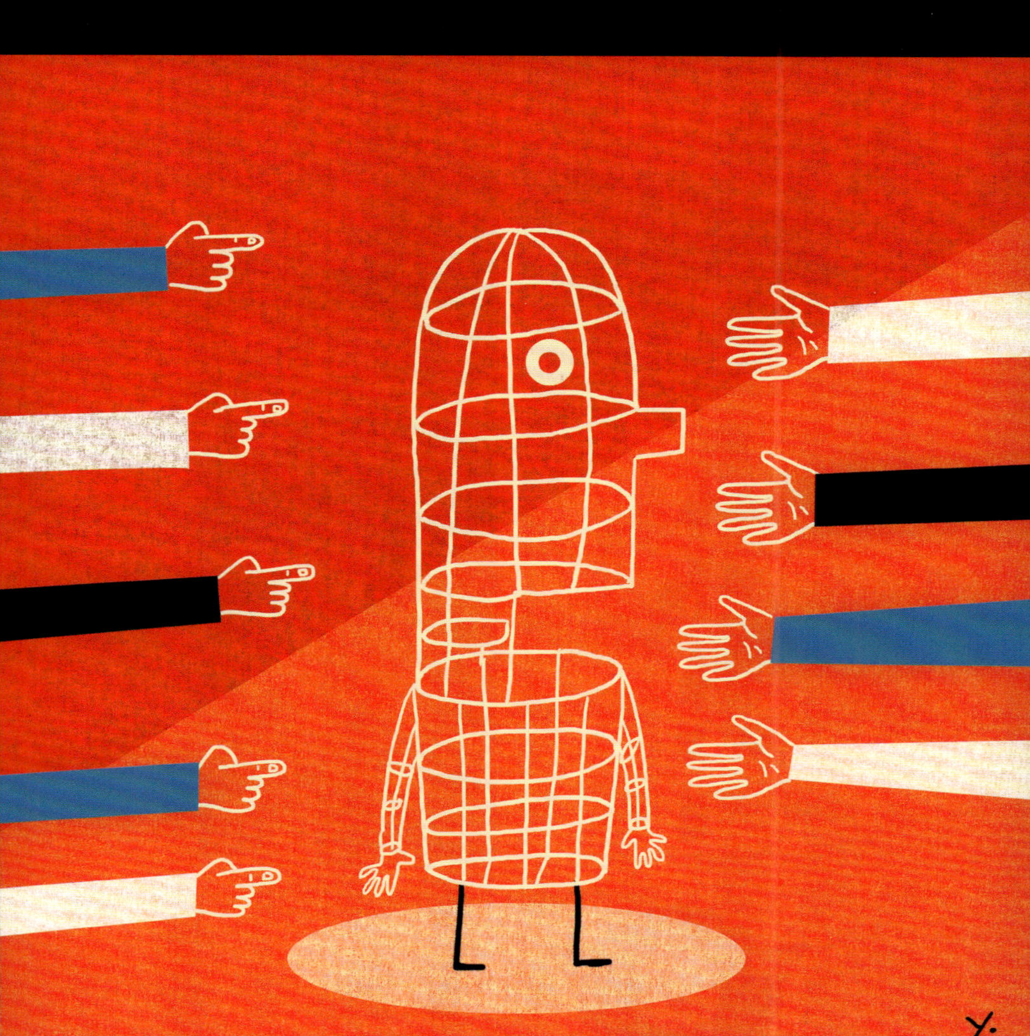

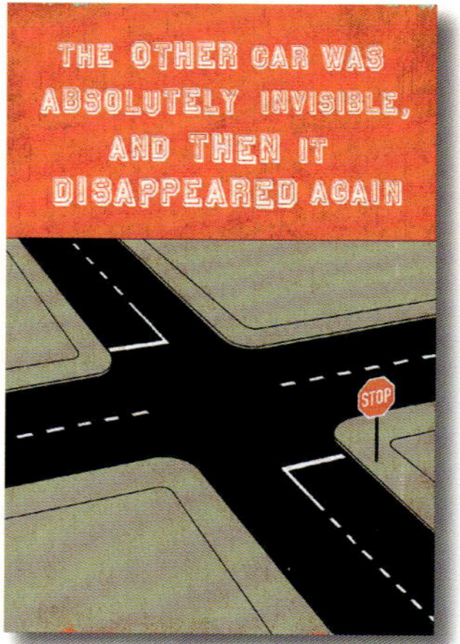

THE OTHER CAR WAS
ABSOLUTELY INVISIBLE,
AND THEN IT
DISAPPEARED AGAIN
STOP

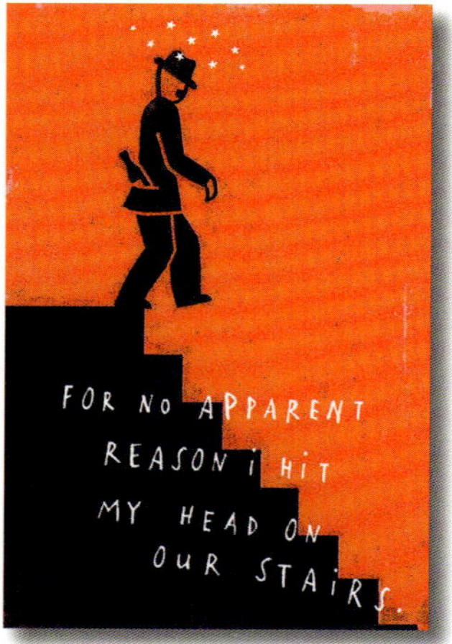

FOR NO APPARENT
REASON I HIT
MY HEAD ON
OUR STAIRS.

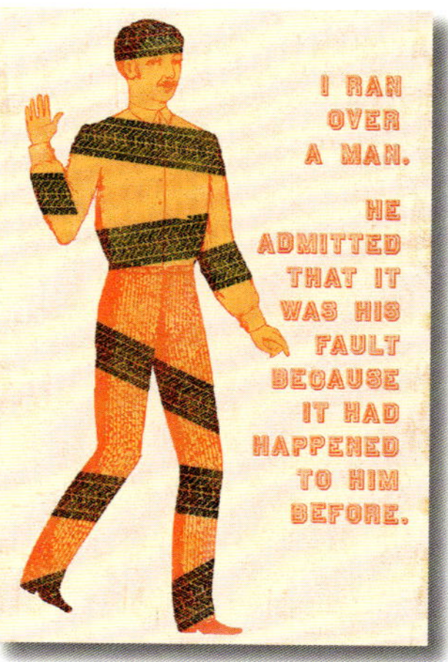

I RAN
OVER
A MAN.

HE
ADMITTED
THAT IT
WAS HIS
FAULT
BECAUSE
IT HAD
HAPPENED
TO HIM
BEFORE.

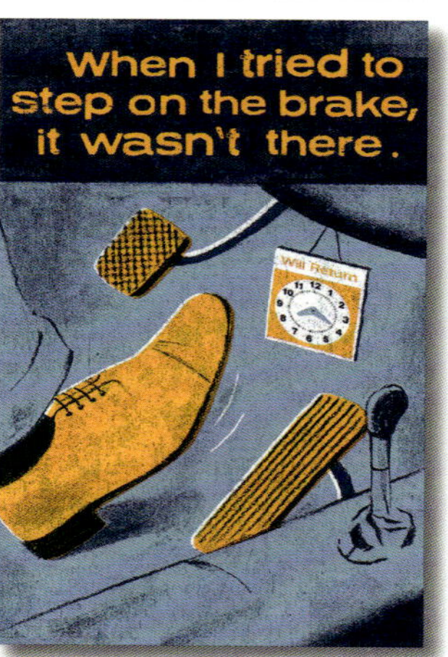

When I tried to
step on the brake,
it wasn't there.
Will Return

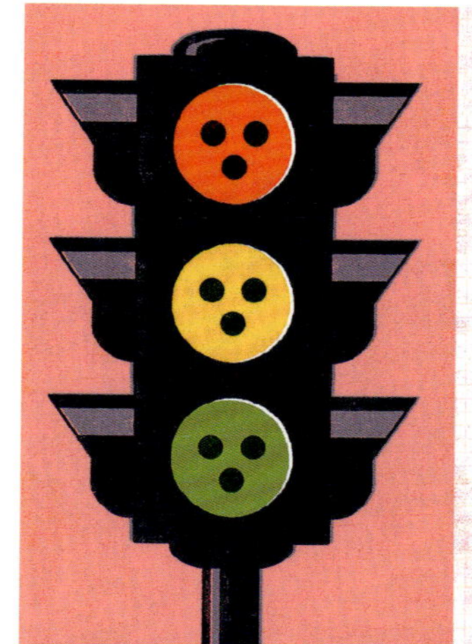

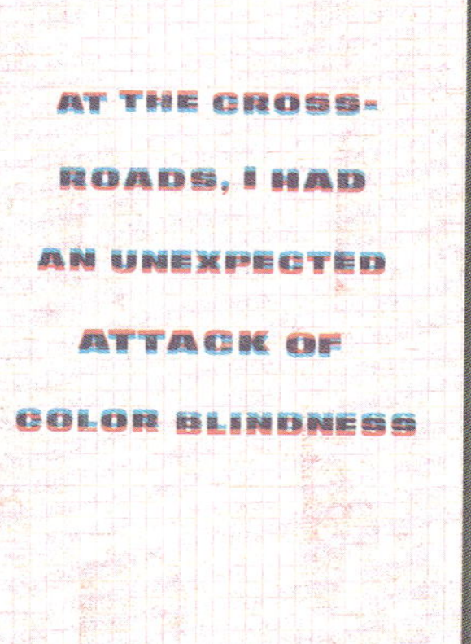

AT THE CROSS-
ROADS, I HAD
AN UNEXPECTED
ATTACK OF
COLOR BLINDNESS

Jens Bonnke

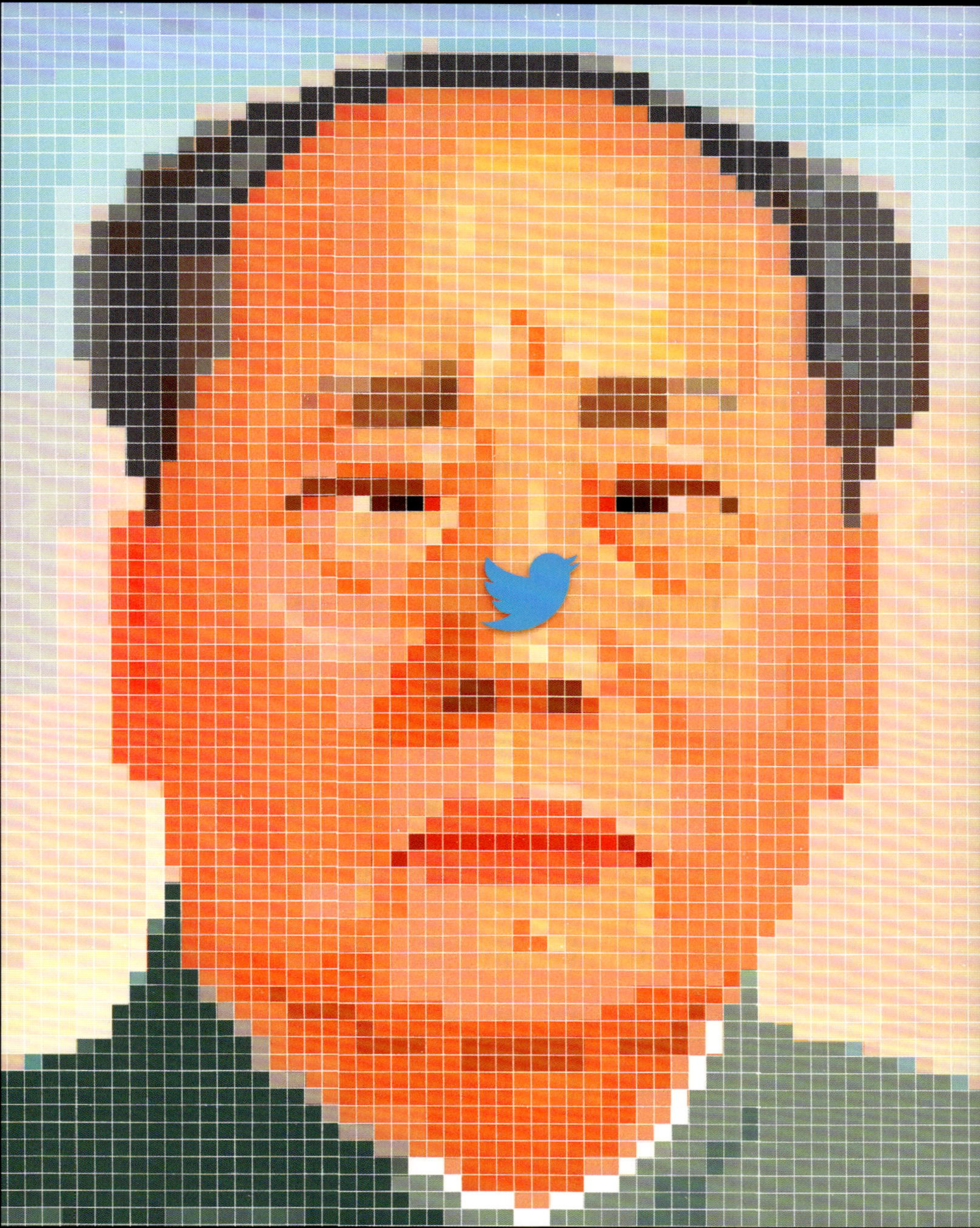

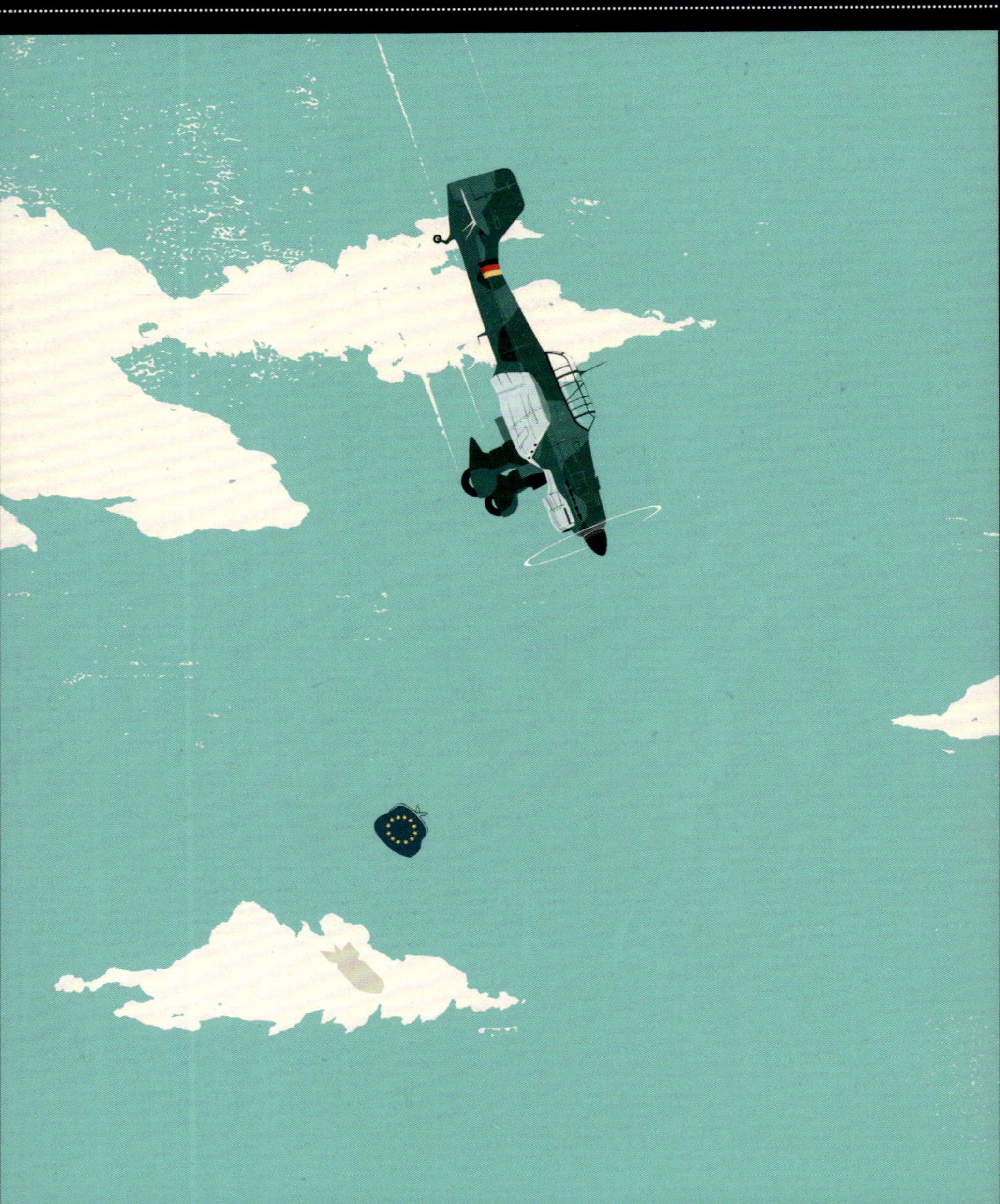

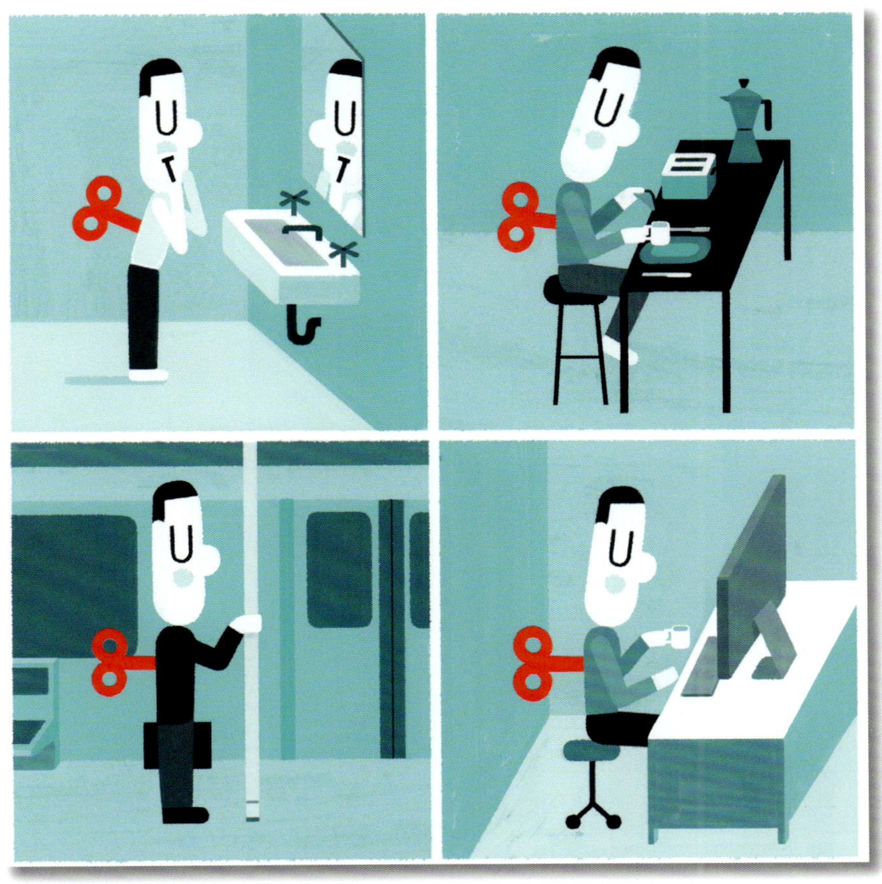

Luc Melanson

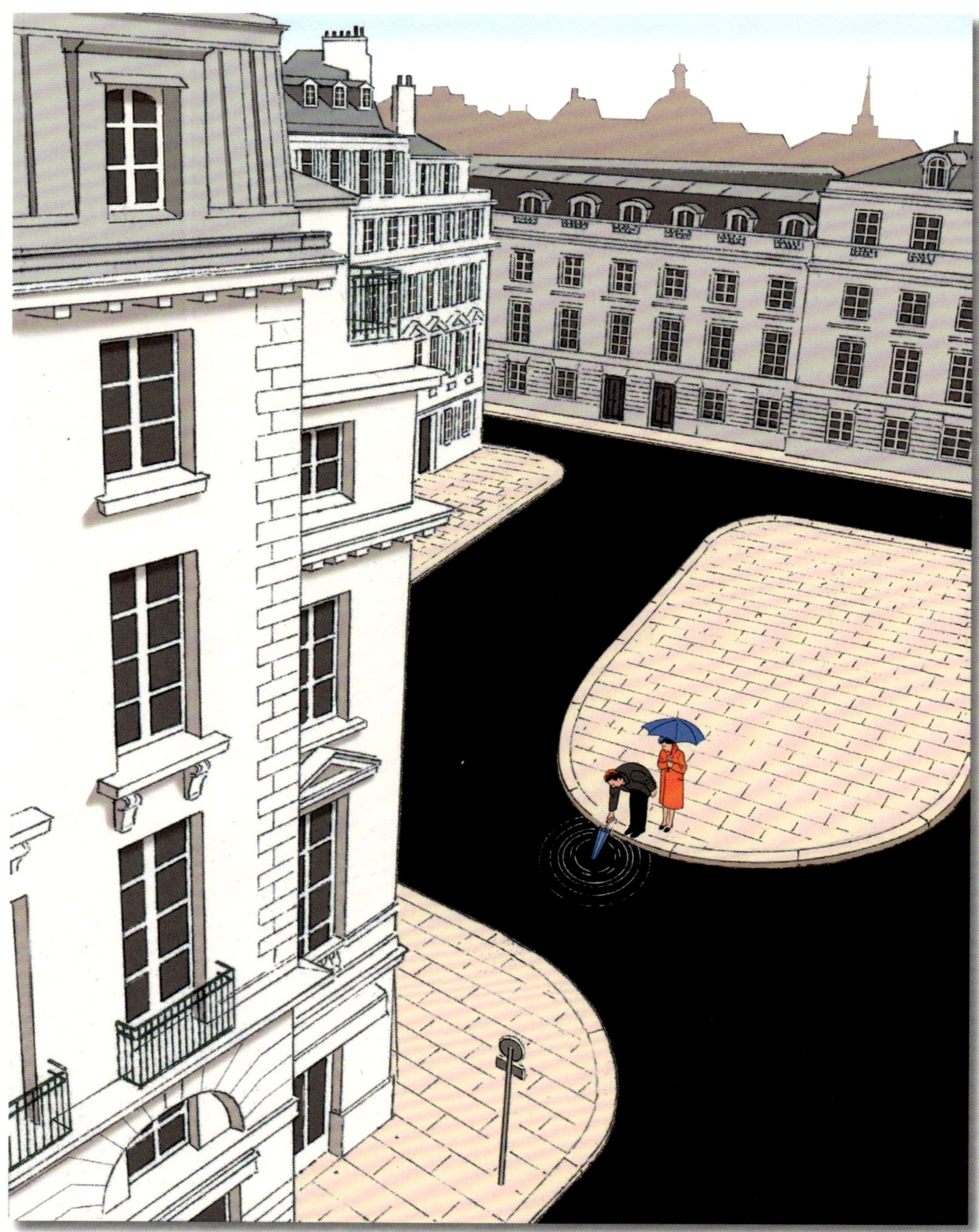

Guy Billout

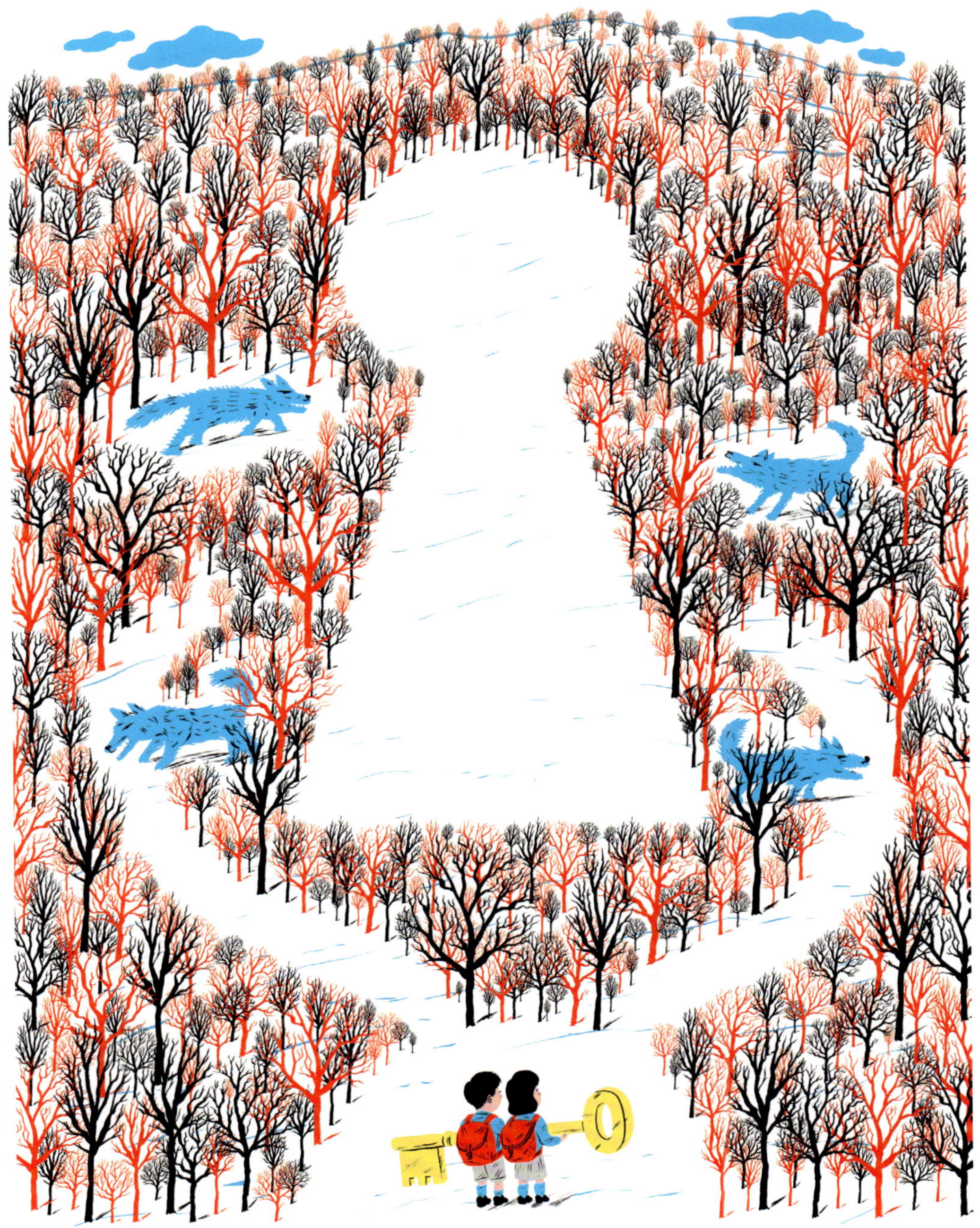

Paul Blow

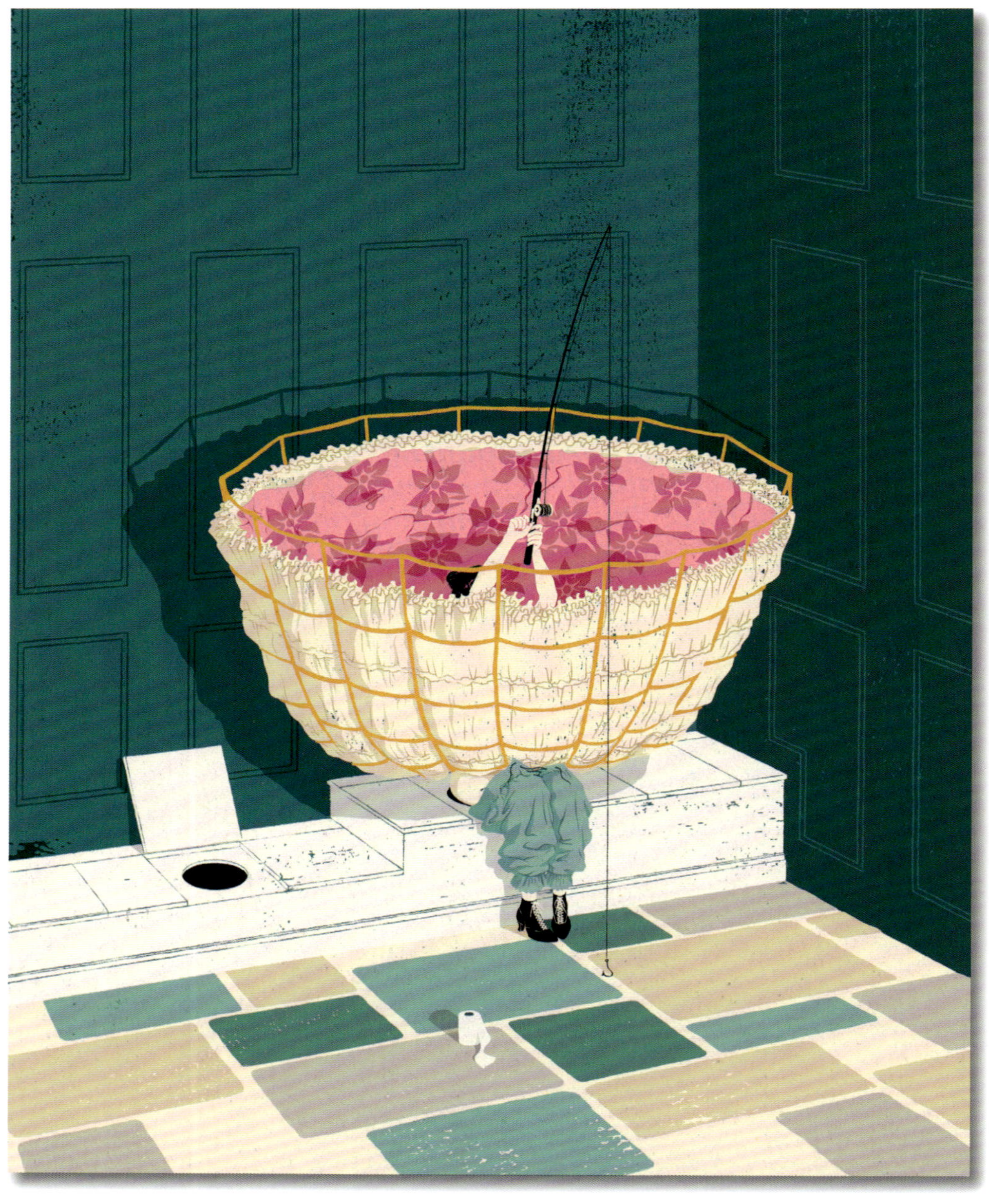

Mark Smith

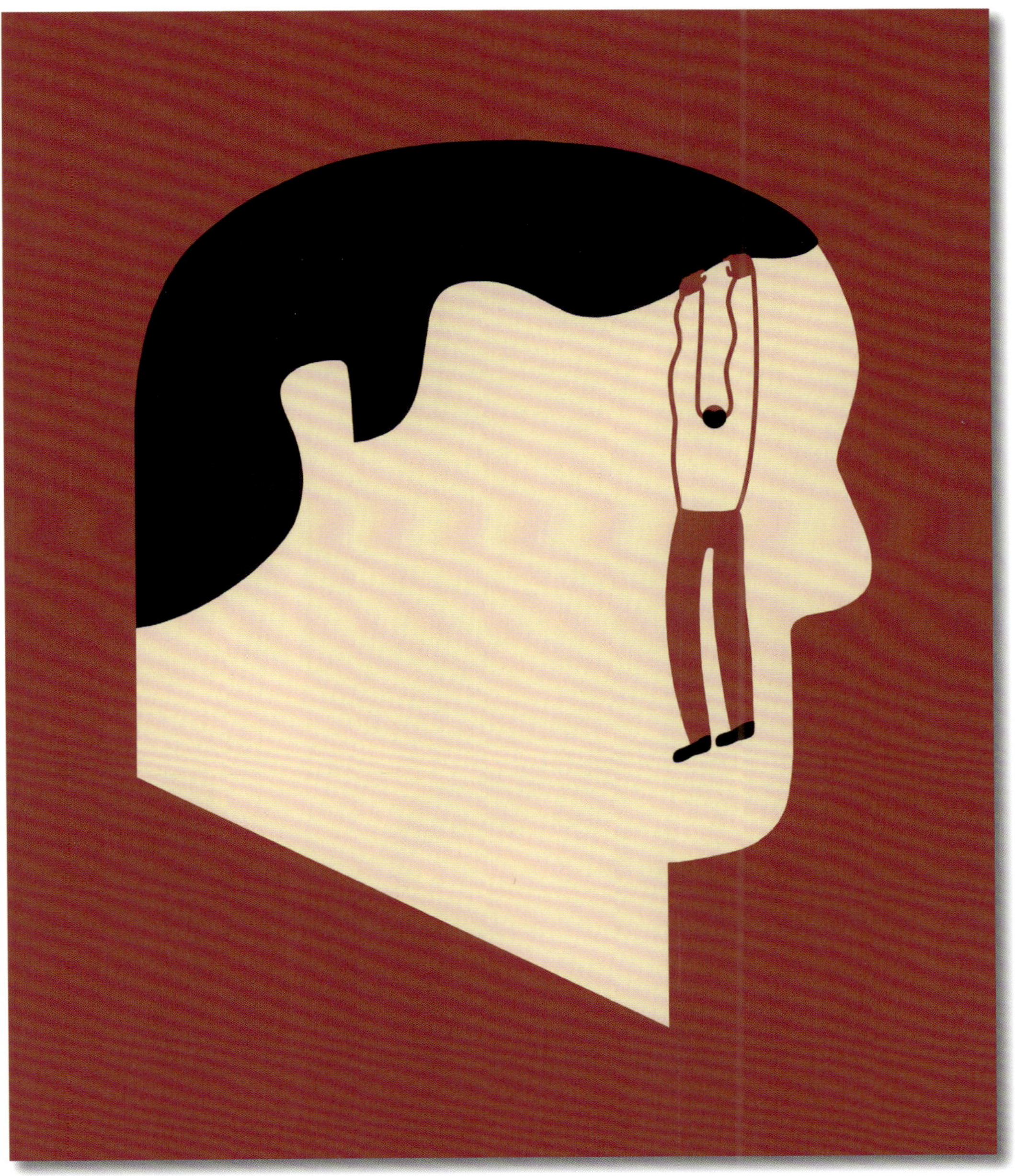

Mágoz

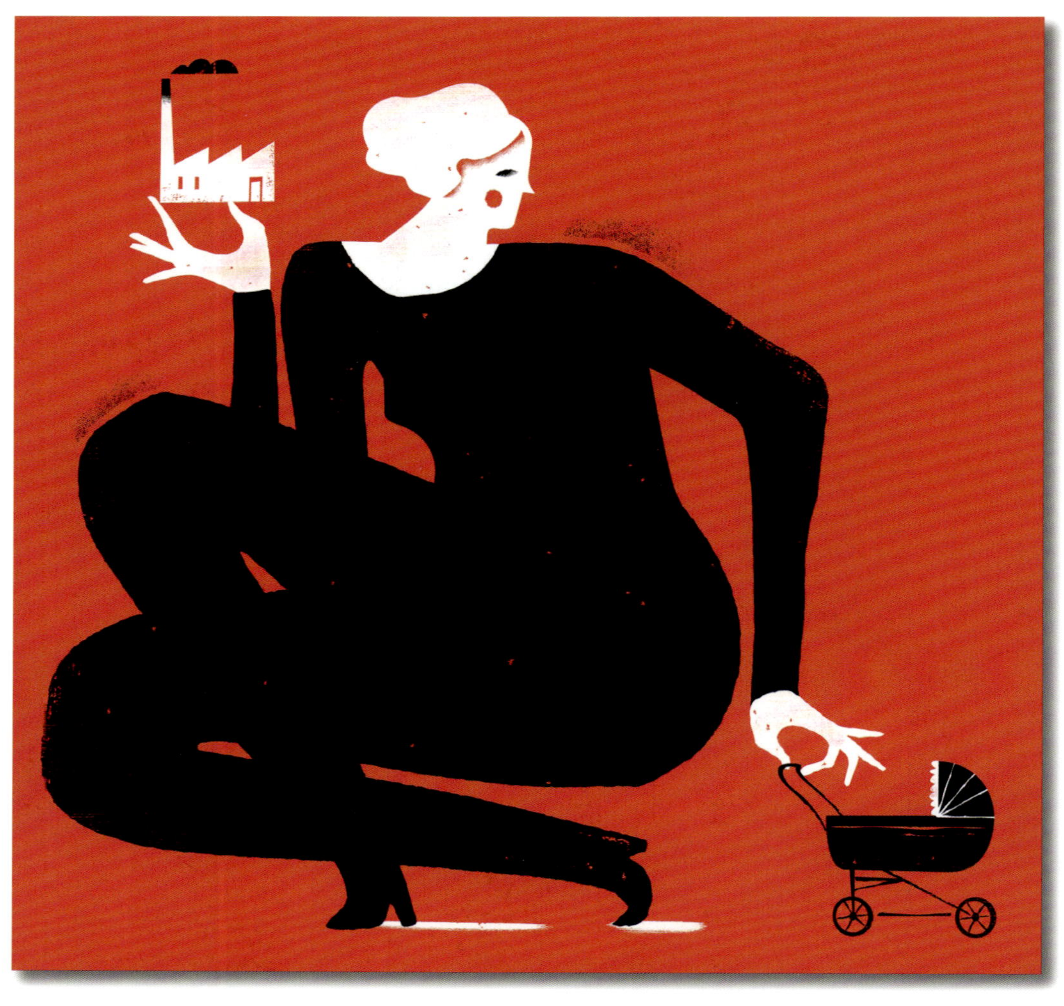

Iker Ayestaran Pradilla

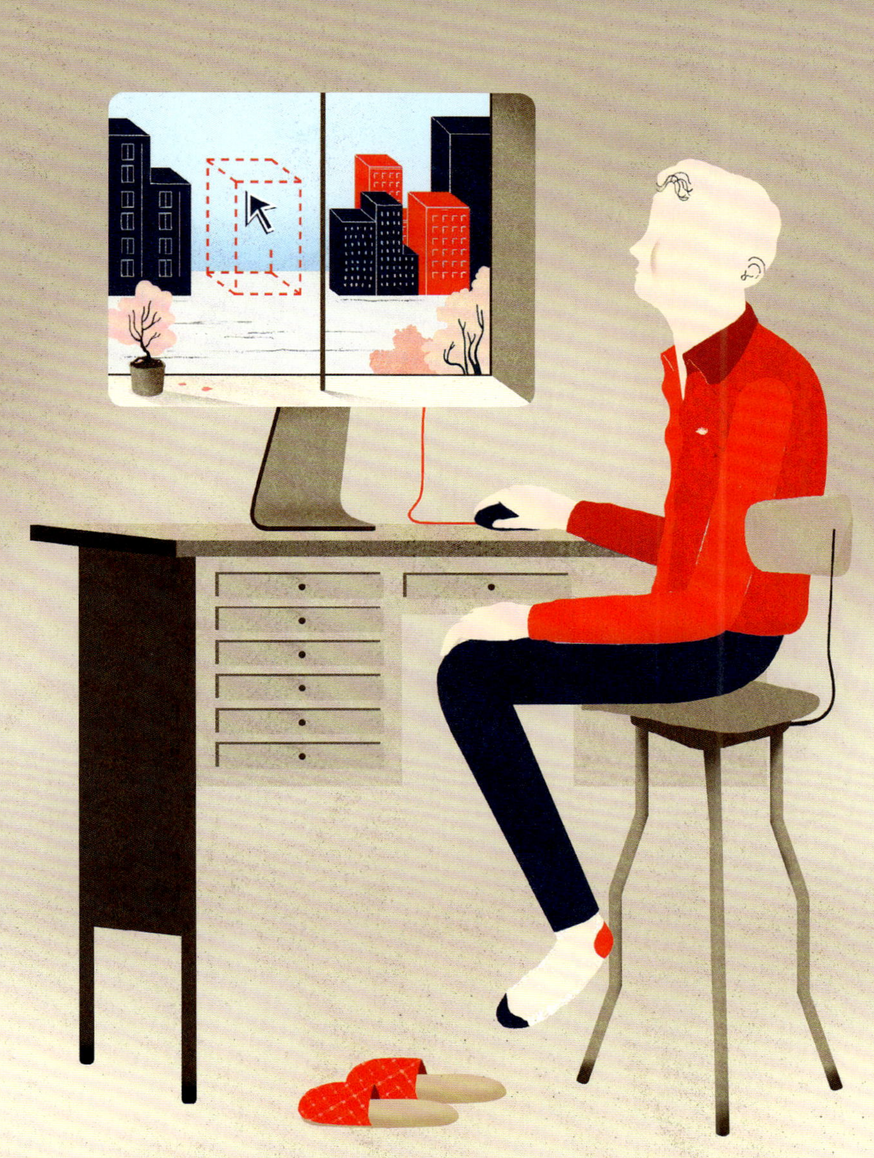

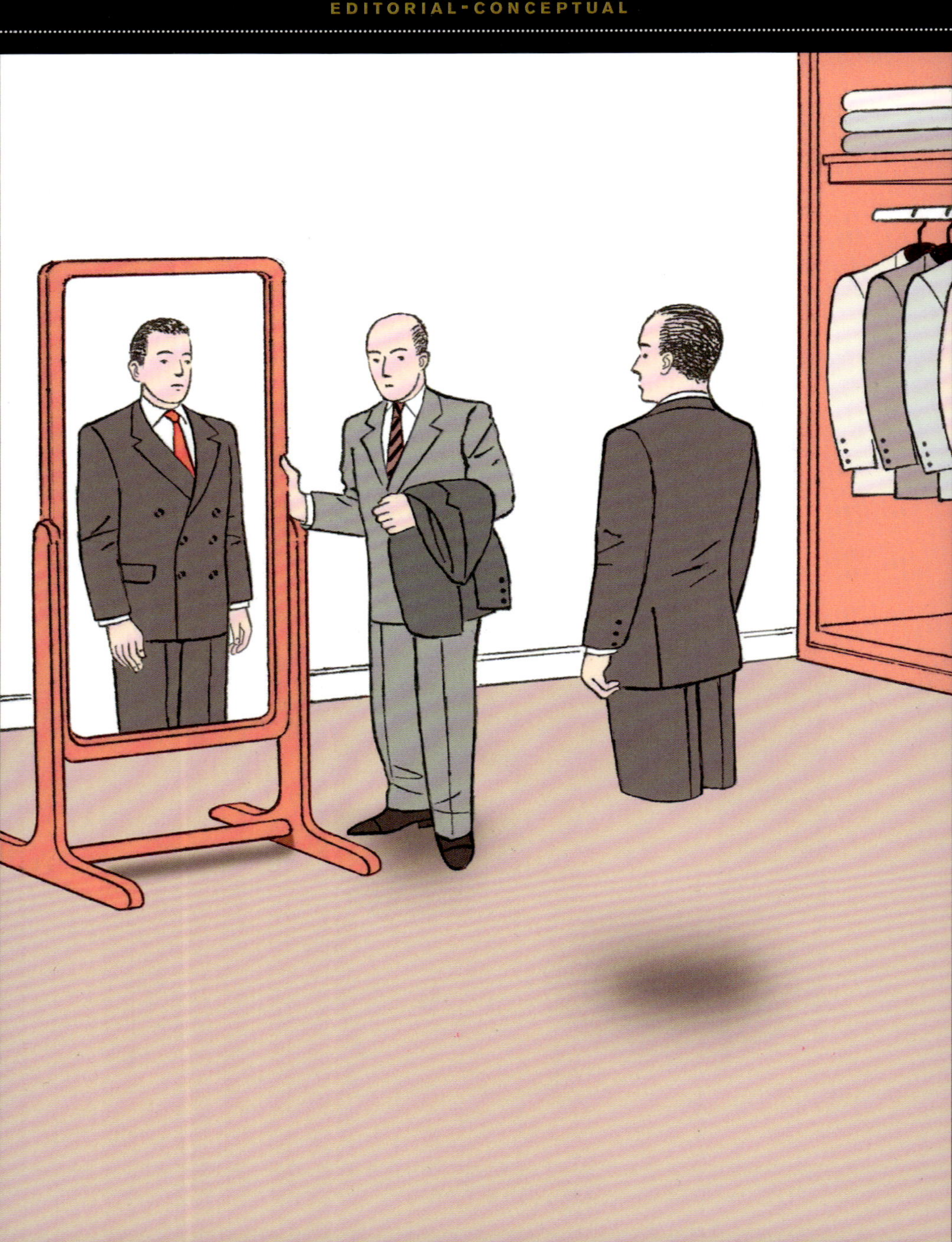

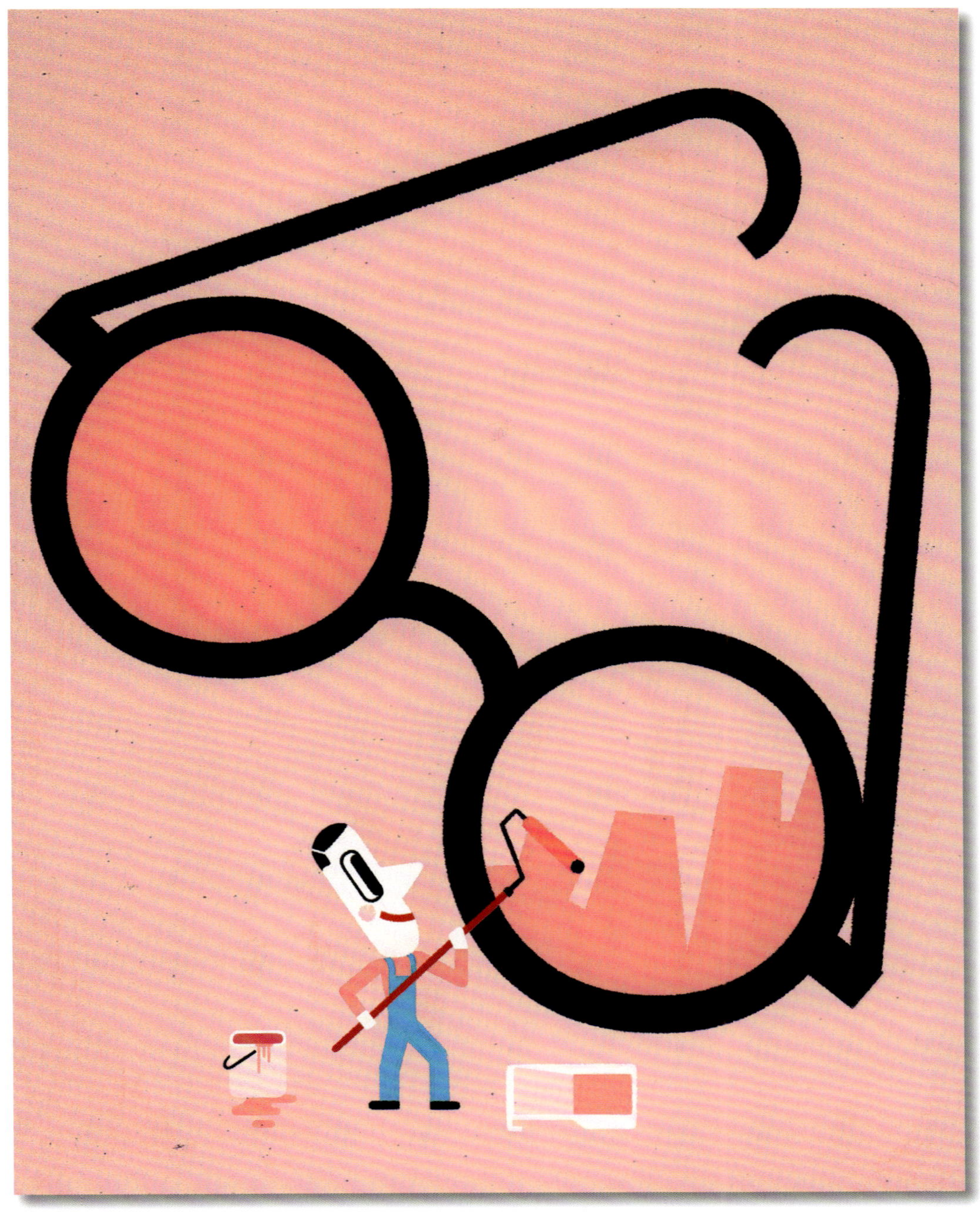

Luc Melanson

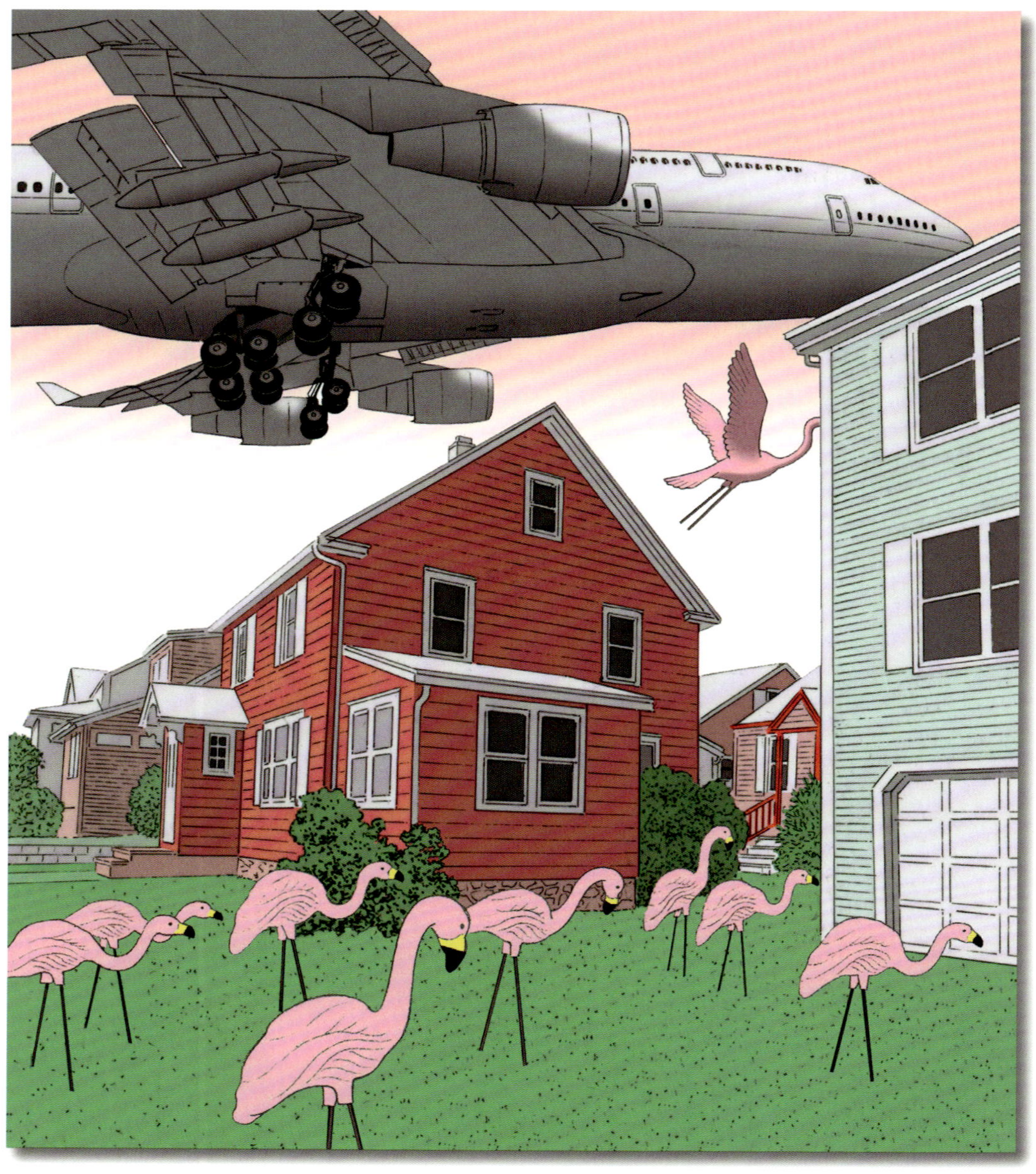

Guy Billout

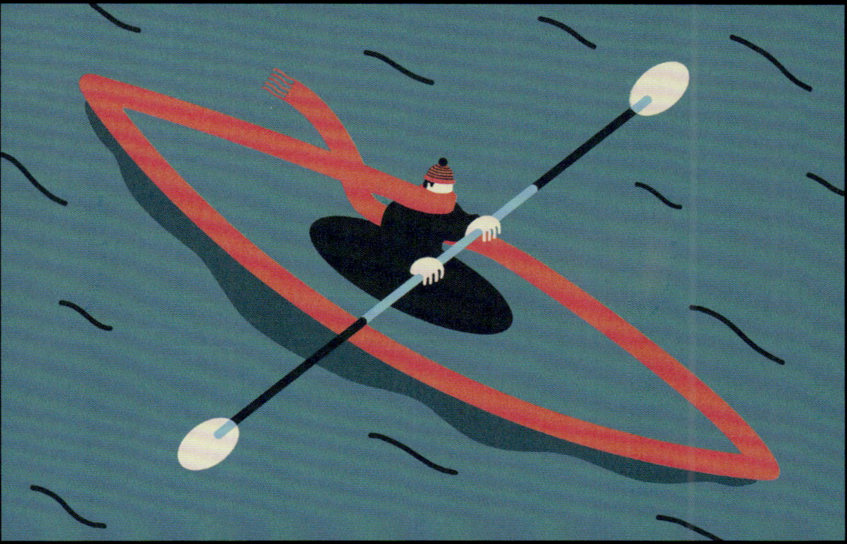

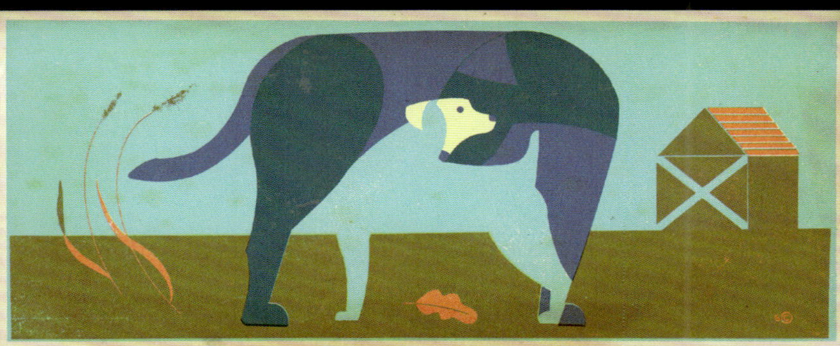

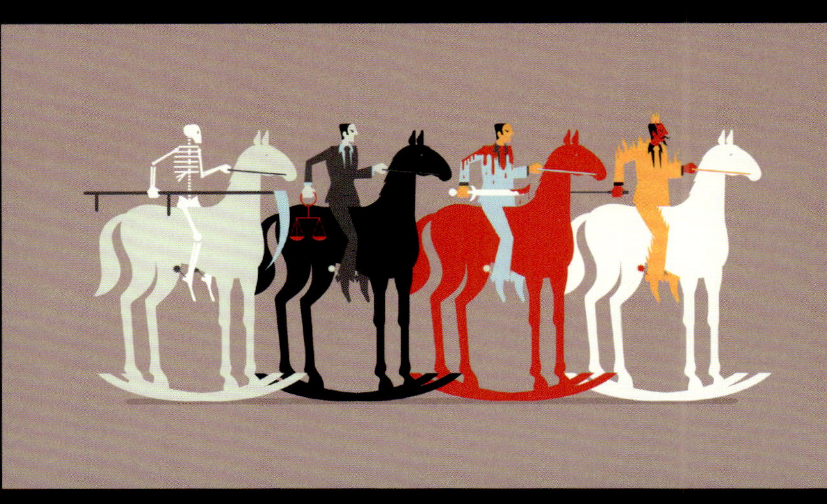

(T) *Mágoz* (M) *Sophie Casson* (B) *Aad Goudappel*

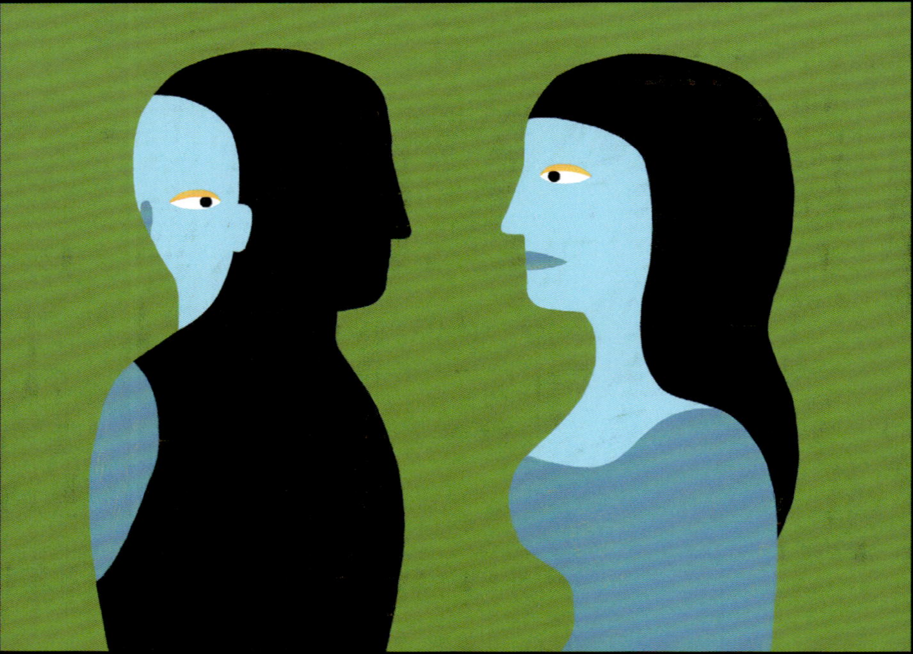

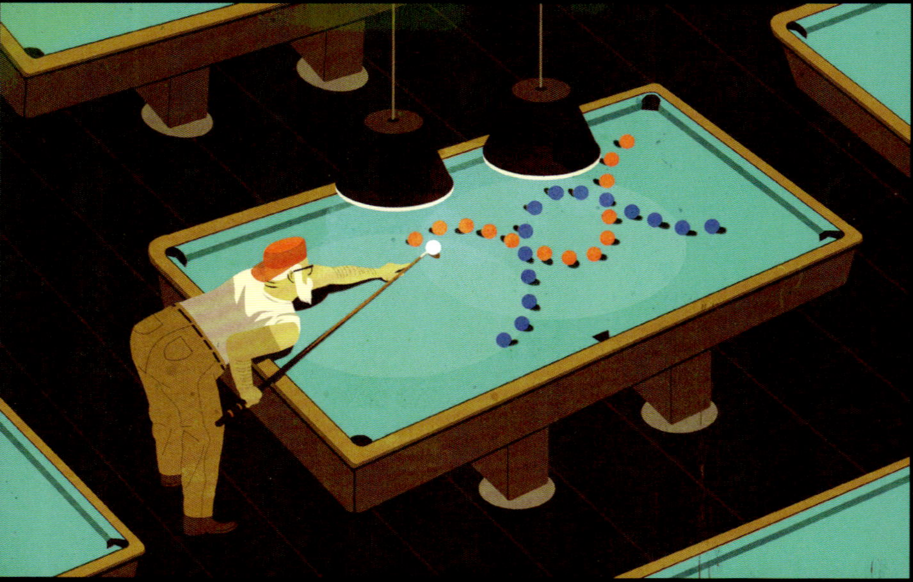

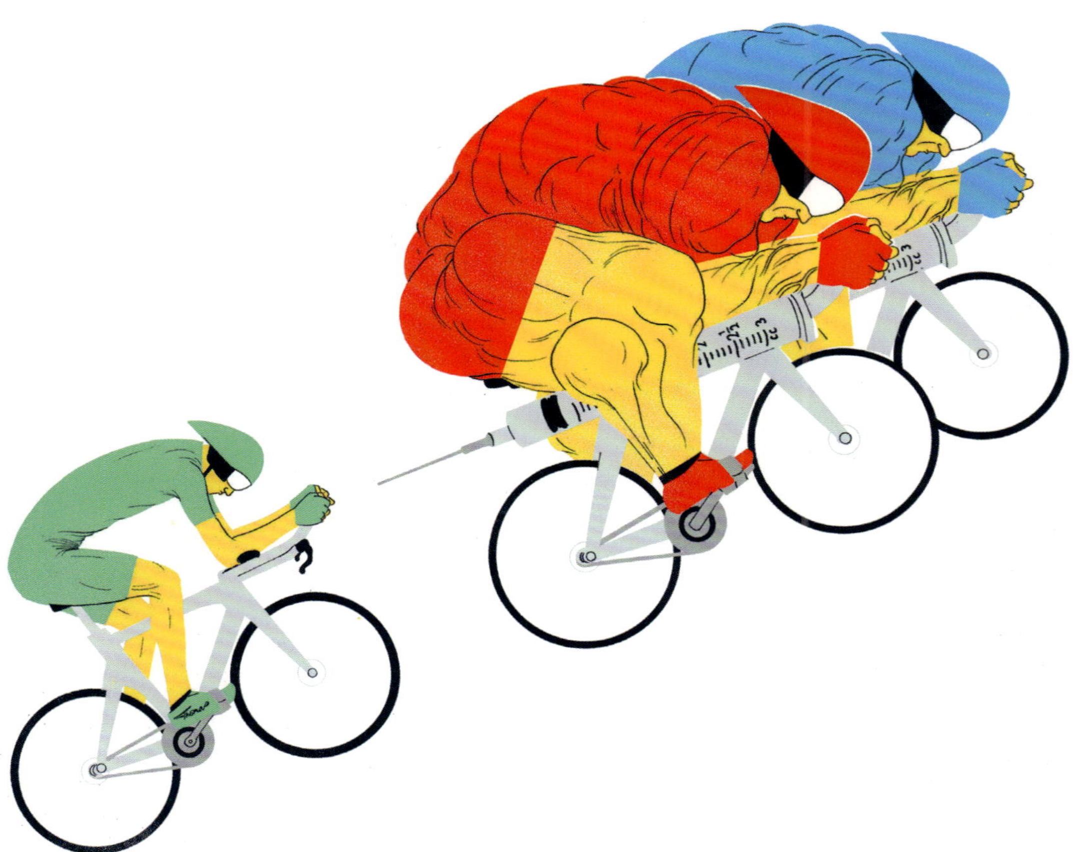

Jacob Thomas

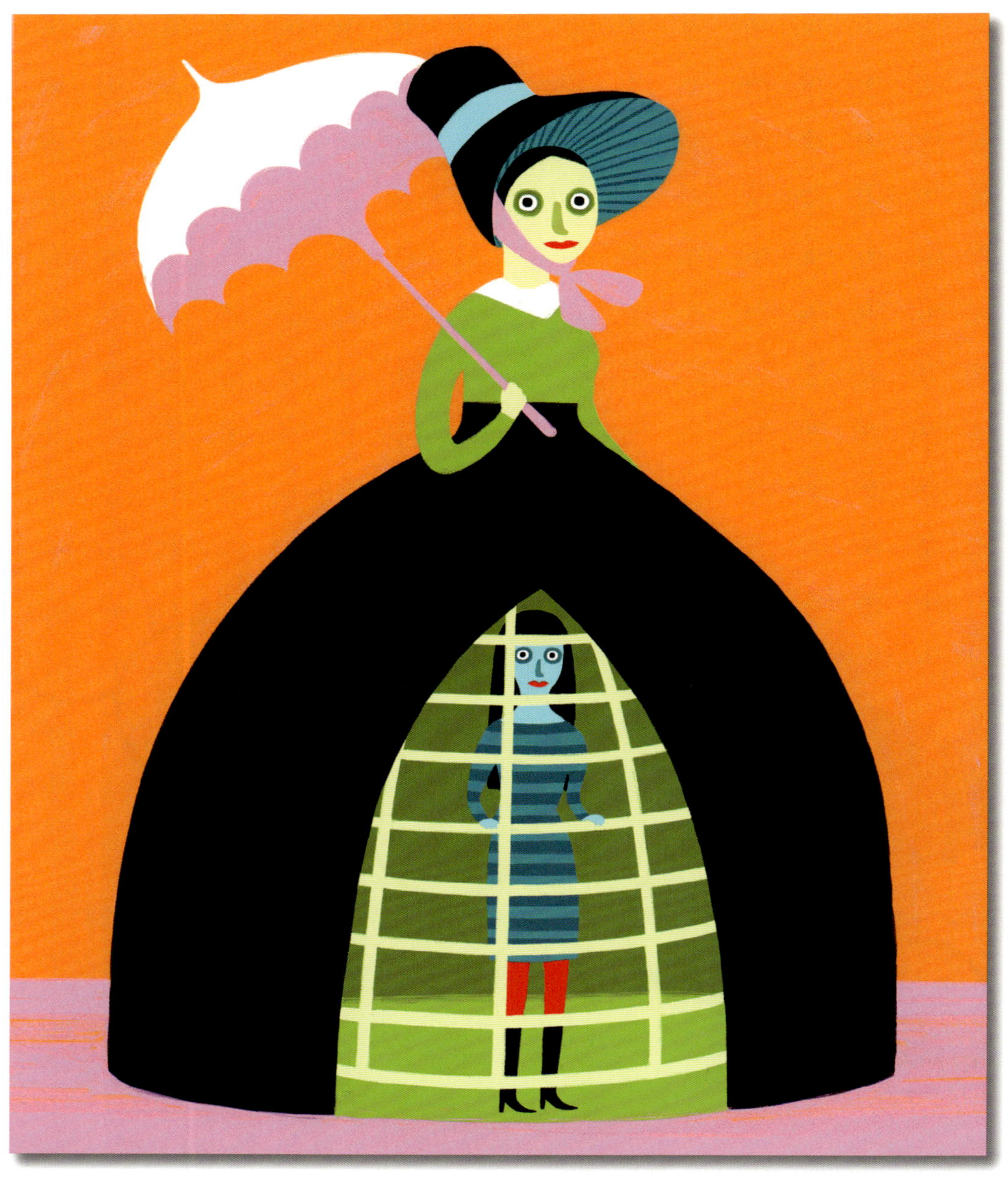

Valeria Petrone

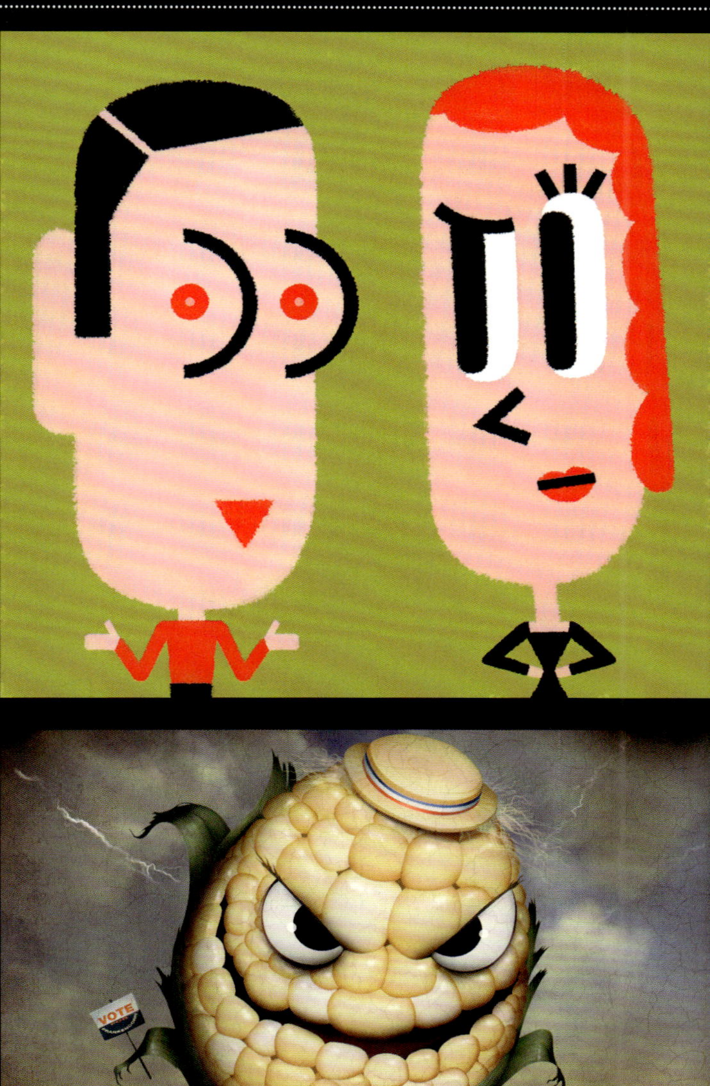
VOTE
VOTE

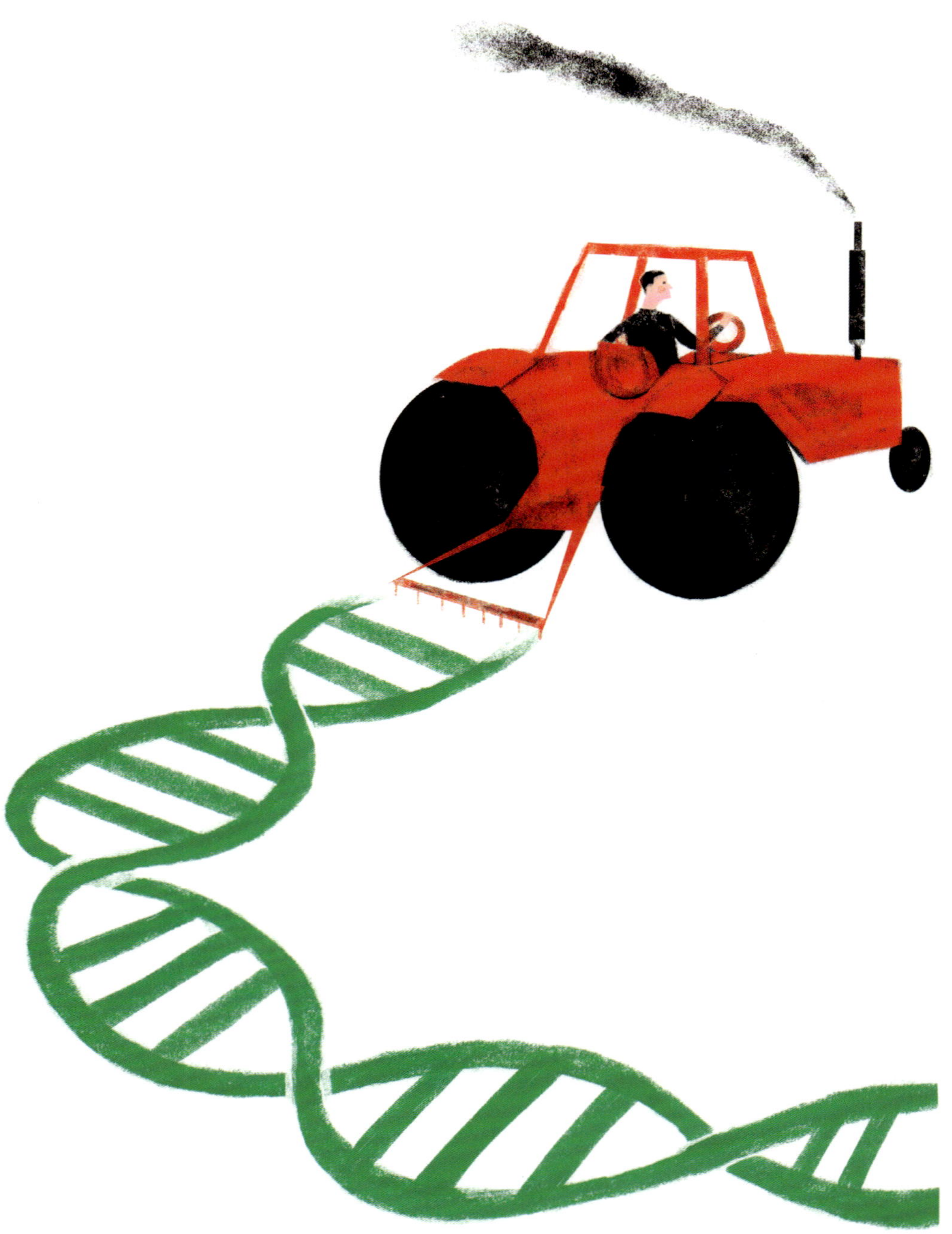

Lorenzo Gritti

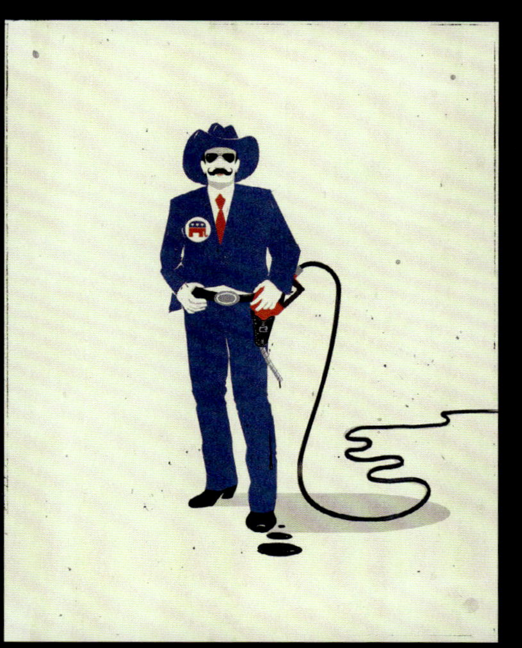

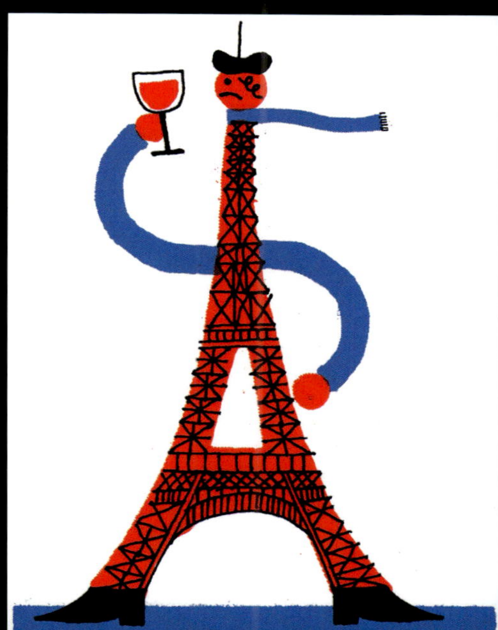

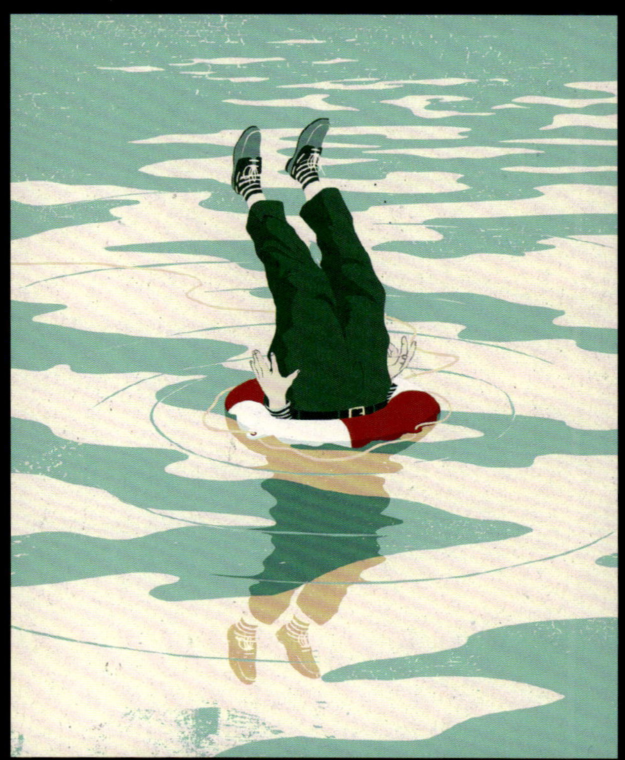

ARCTIC OCEAN
NORTH
SEA
Tropic of Capricorn
PACIFIC OCEAN
ATLANTIC OCEAN
150°
Equator
BLACK
SEA
Tropic of Cancer
INDIAN
OCEAN
MEDIT

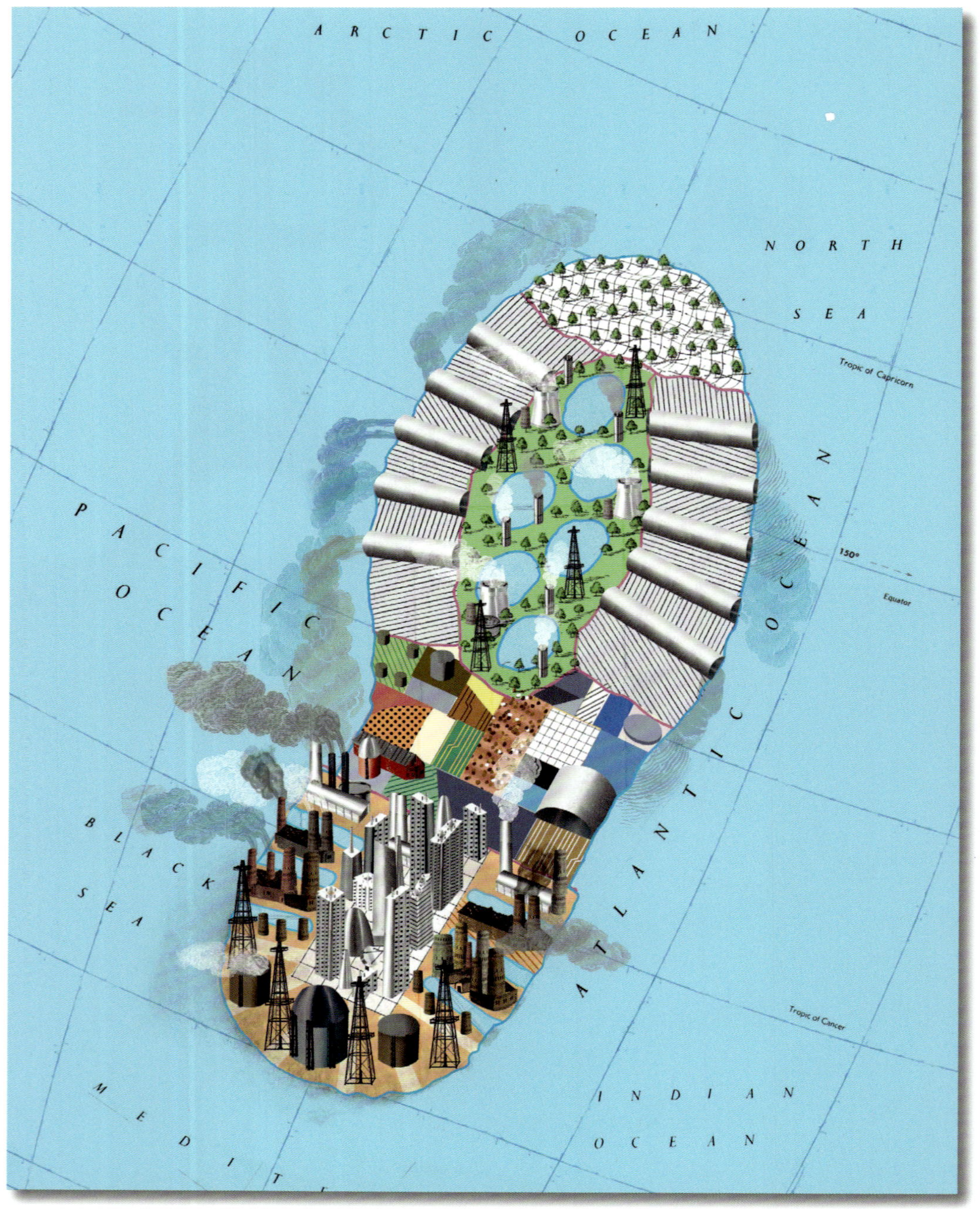

Doug Chayka

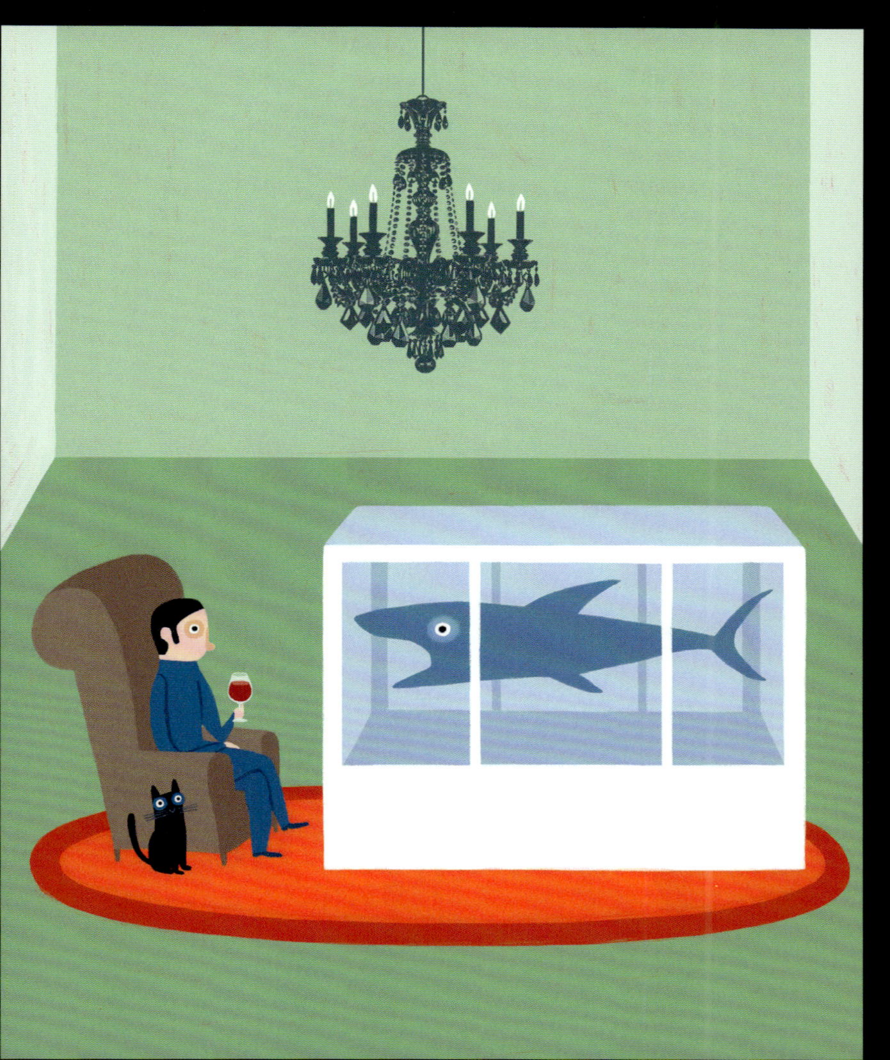

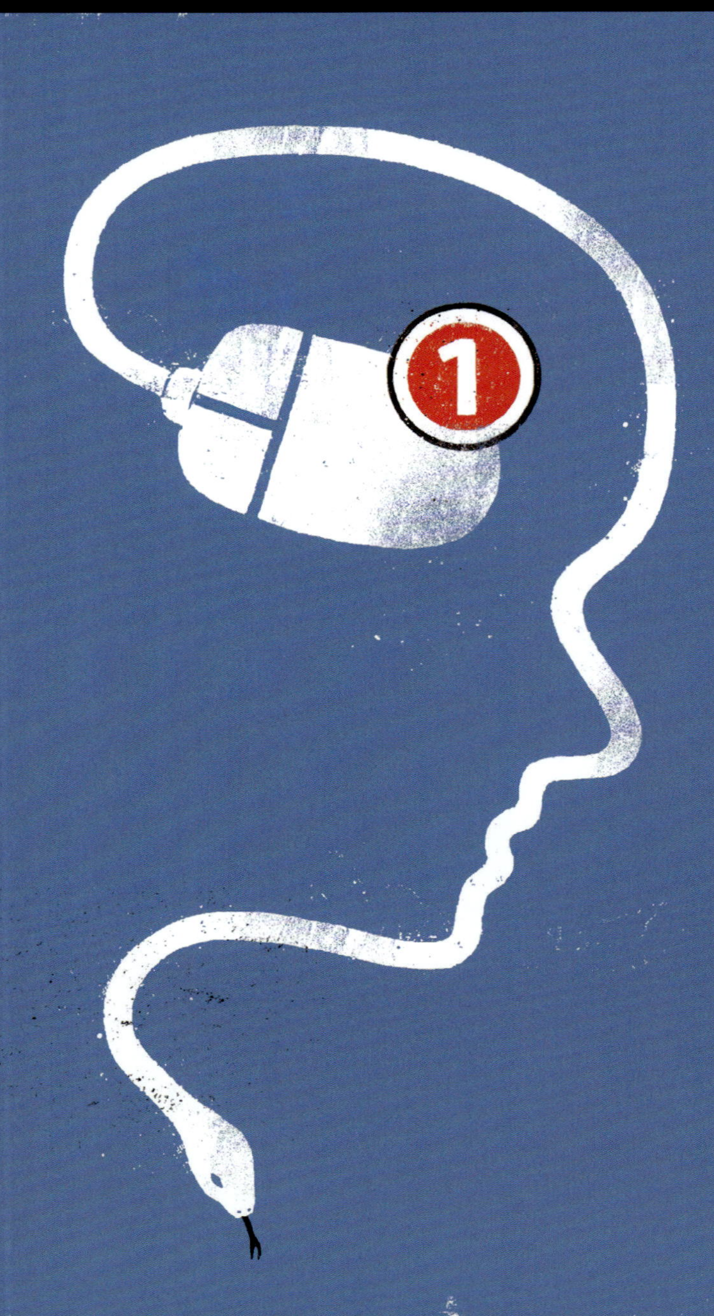

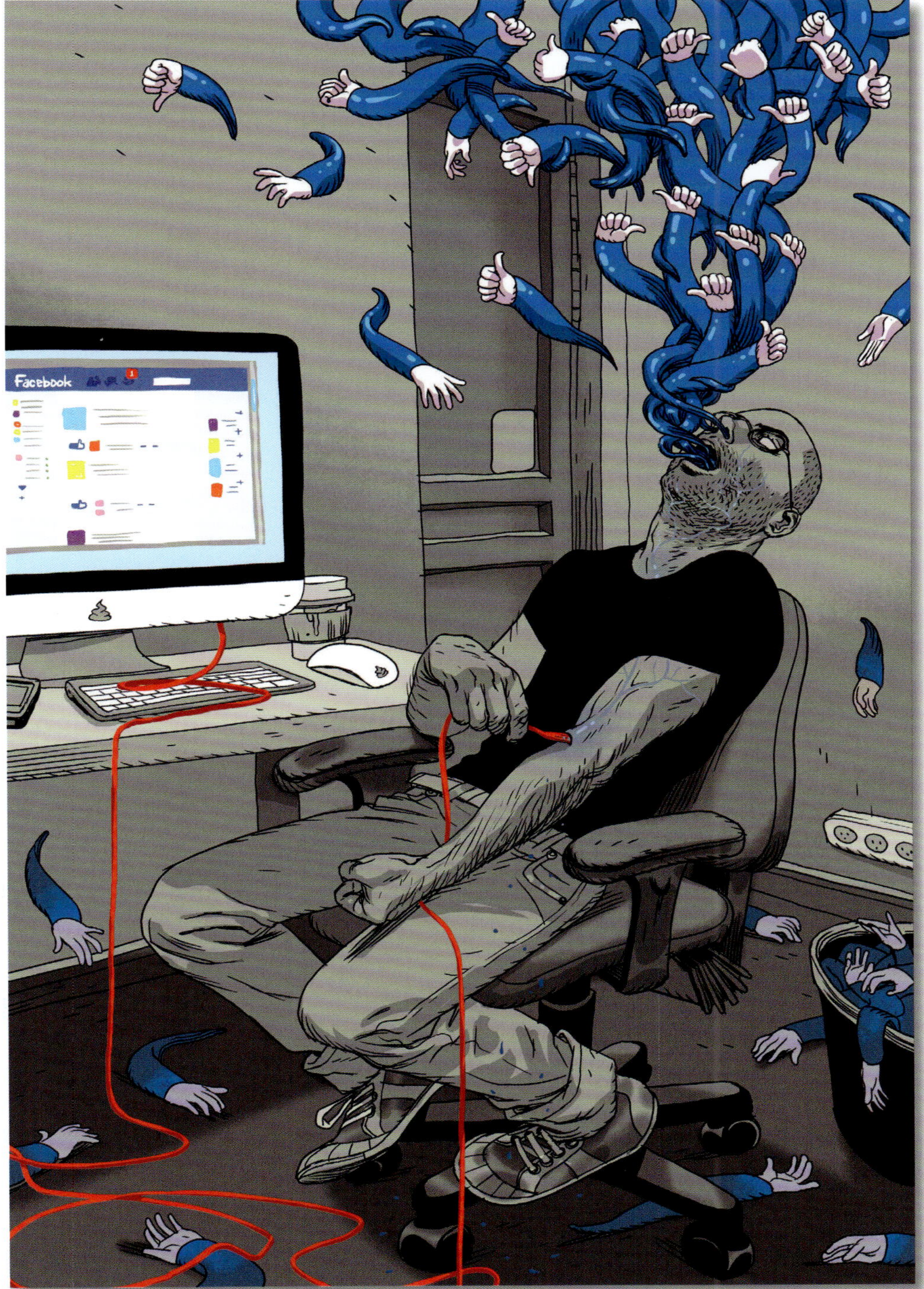

Asaf Hanuka

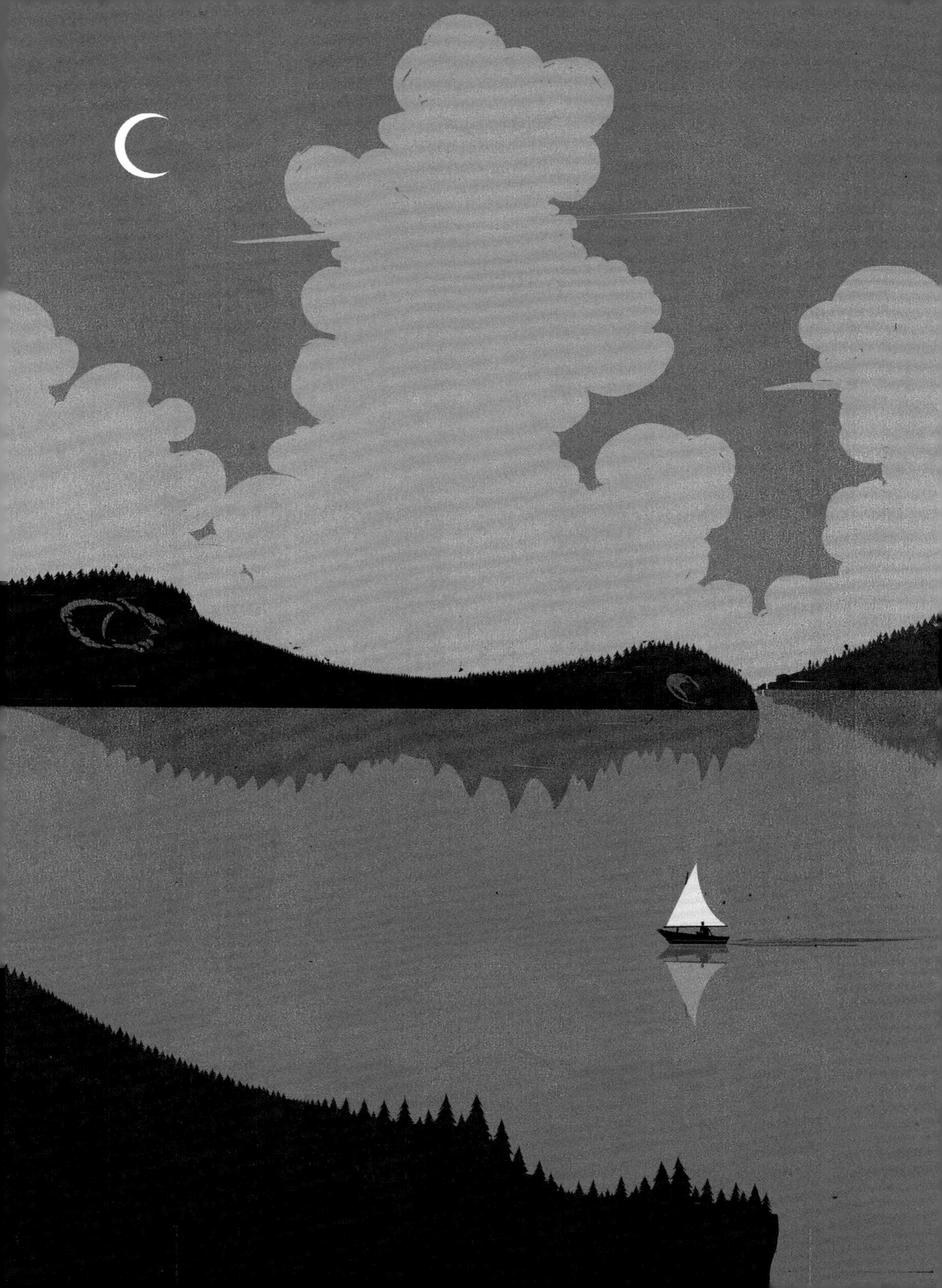

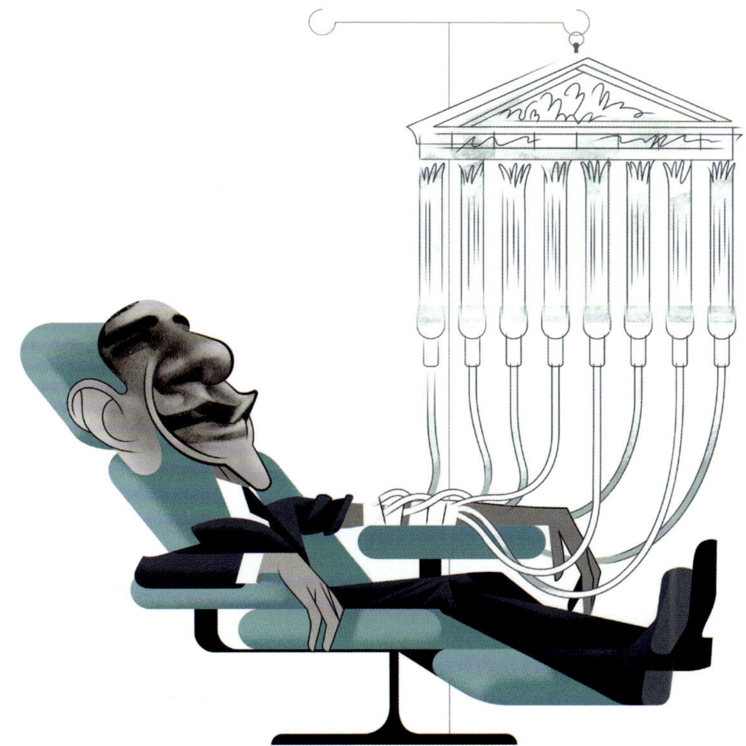

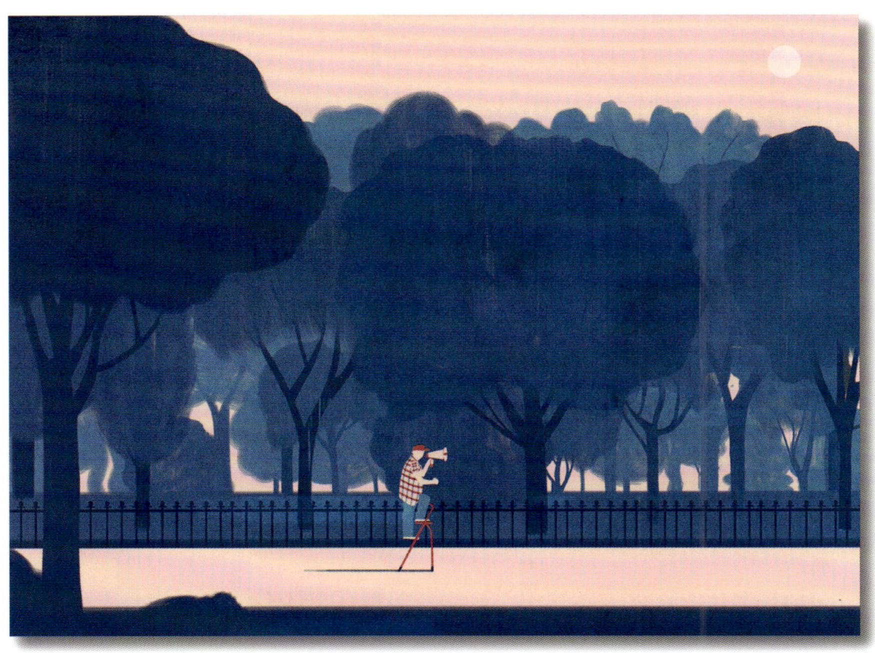

(L) *Alessandro Gottardo* (T) *André Carrilho* (B)) *Emiliano Ponzi*

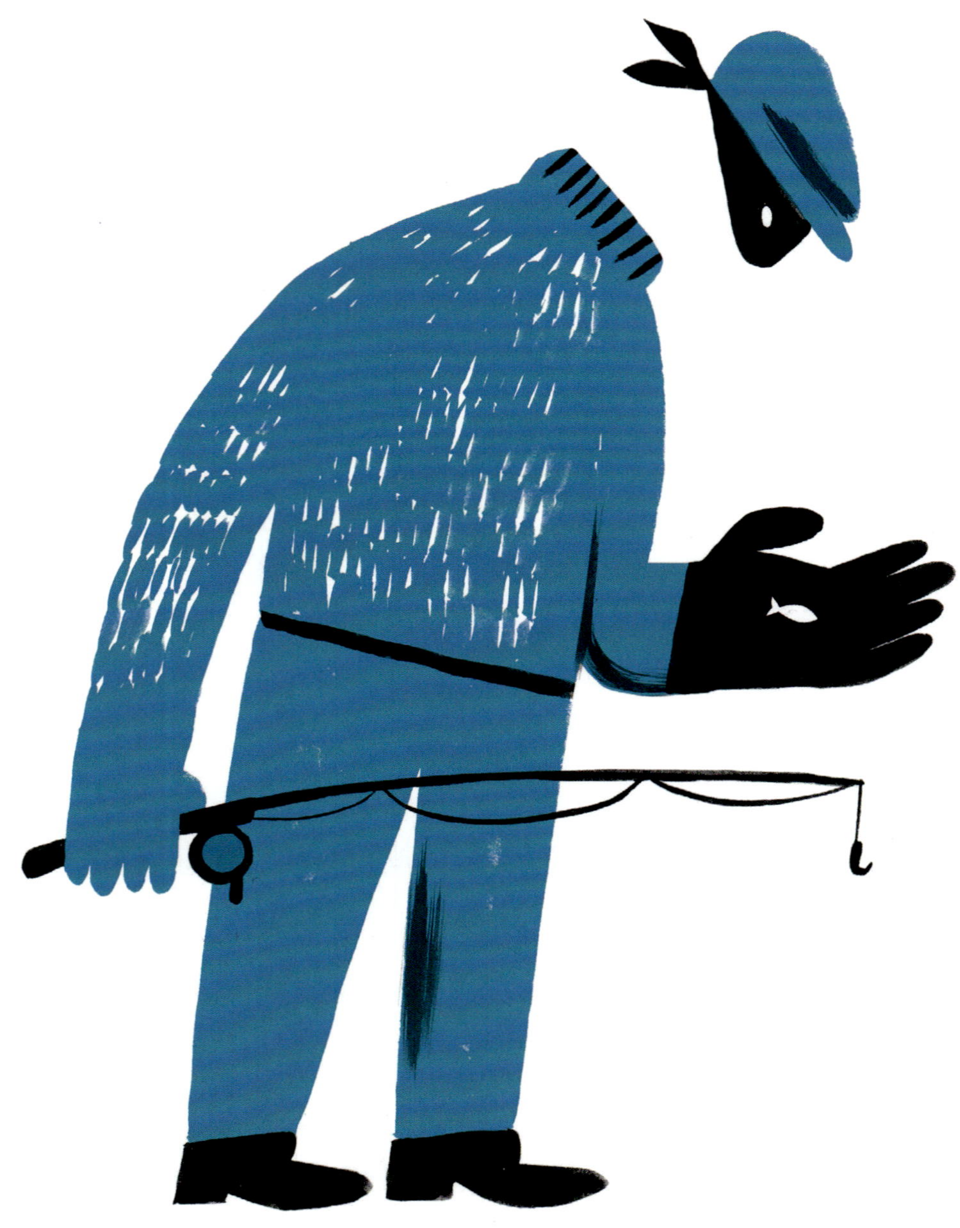

João Fazenda

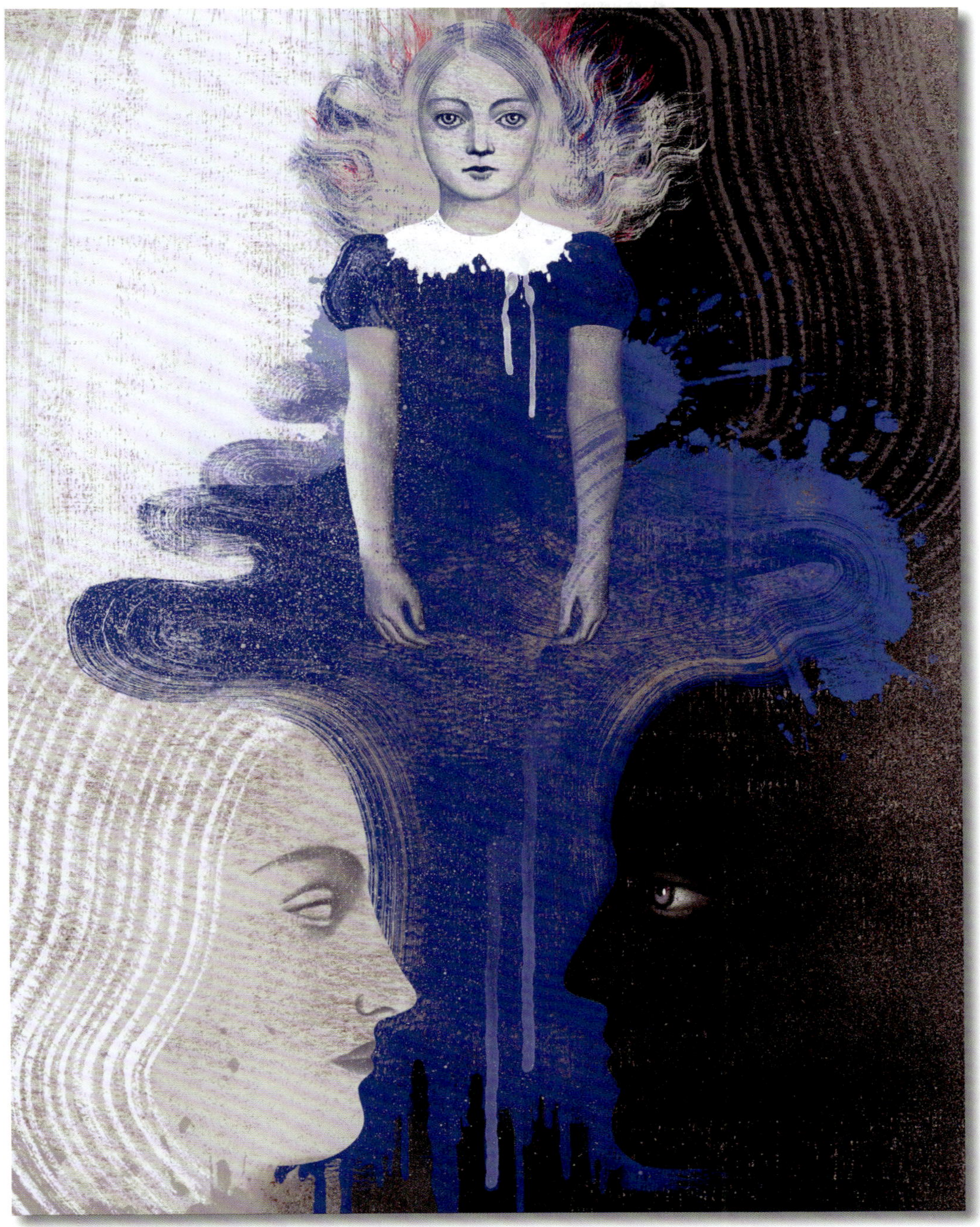

Anna & Elena Balbusso

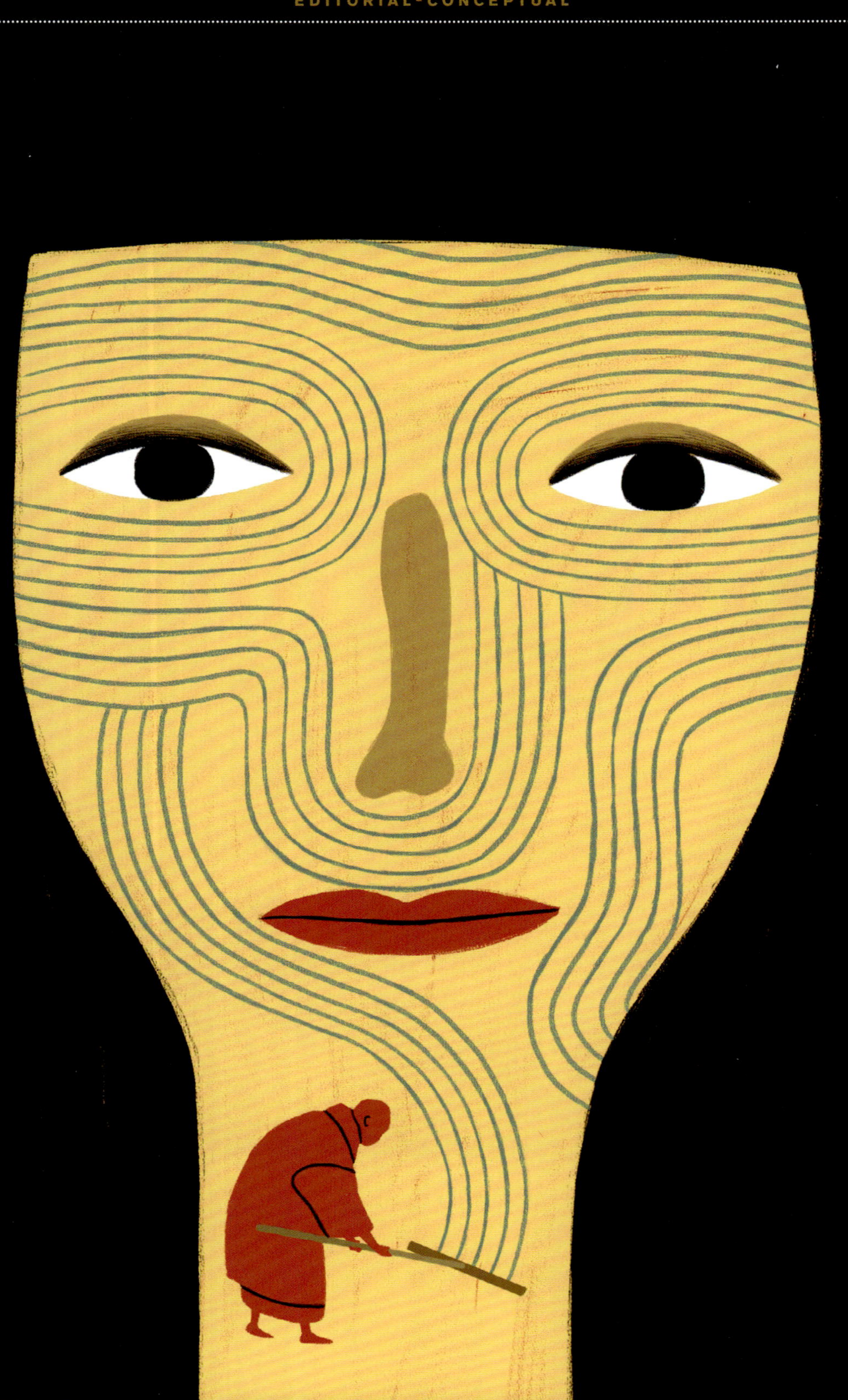

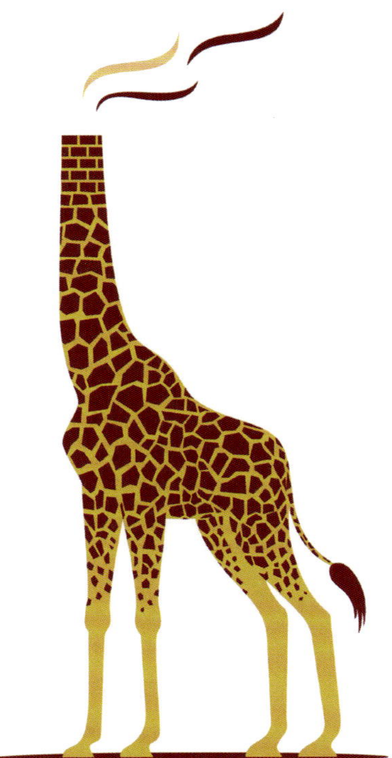

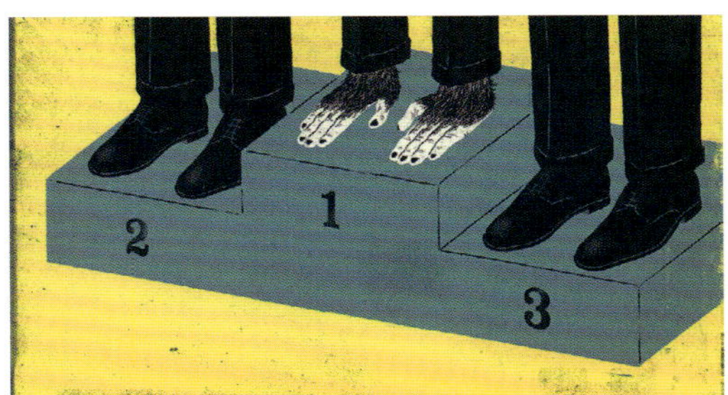

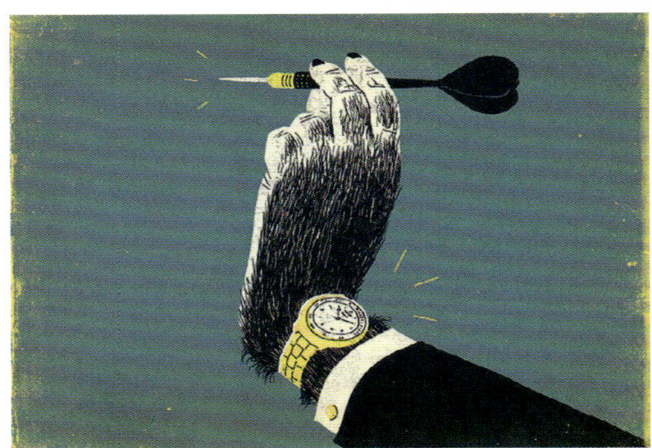

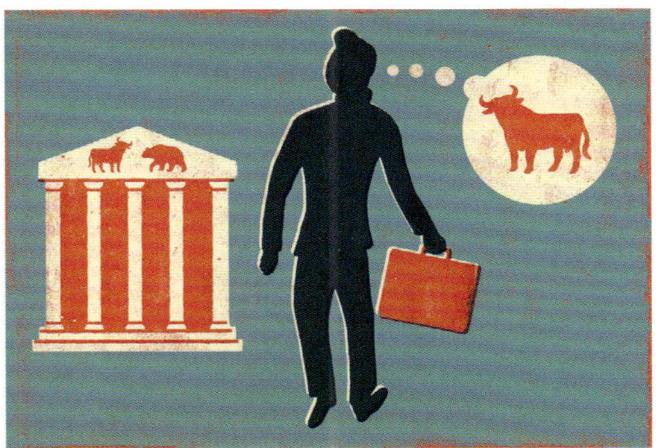

(L) *Valeria Petrone* (T) *Aad Goudappel* (B) *Jens Bonnke*

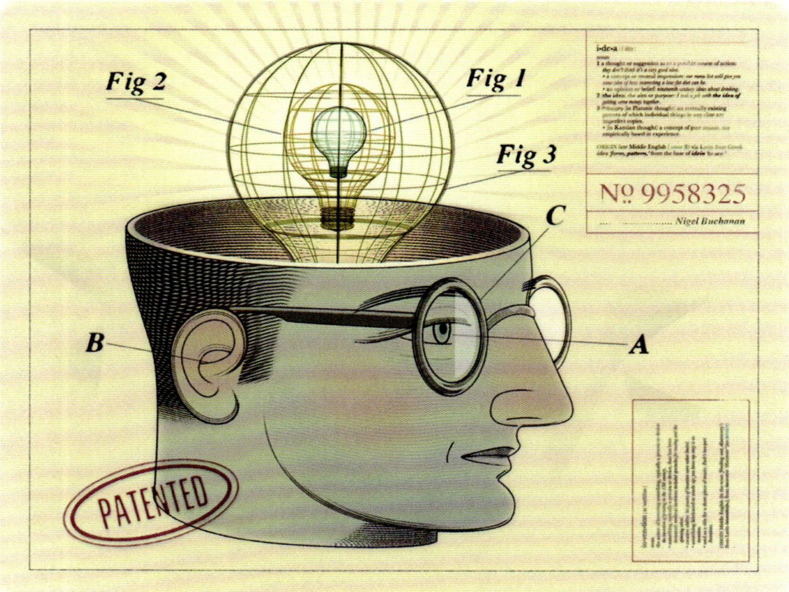

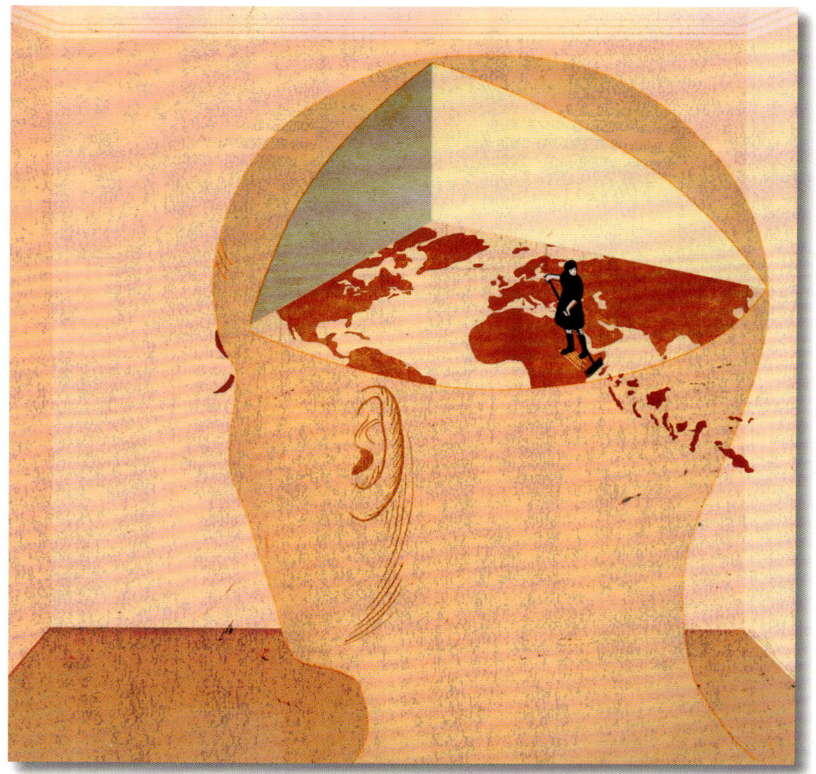

(T) *Nigel Buchanan* (B) *Beppe Giacobbe*

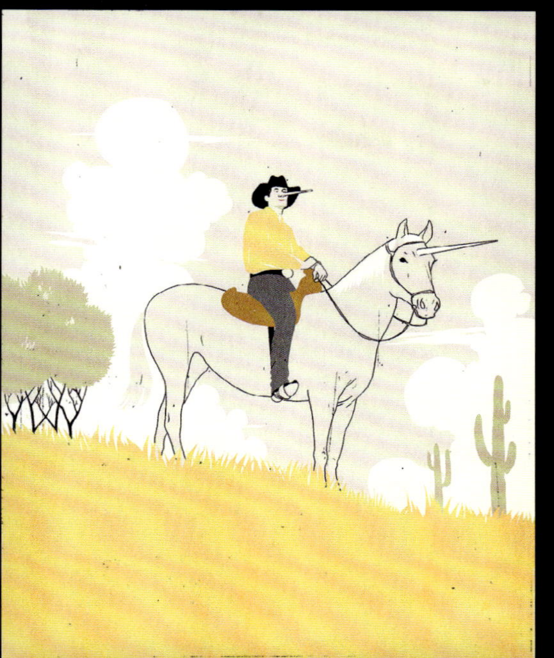

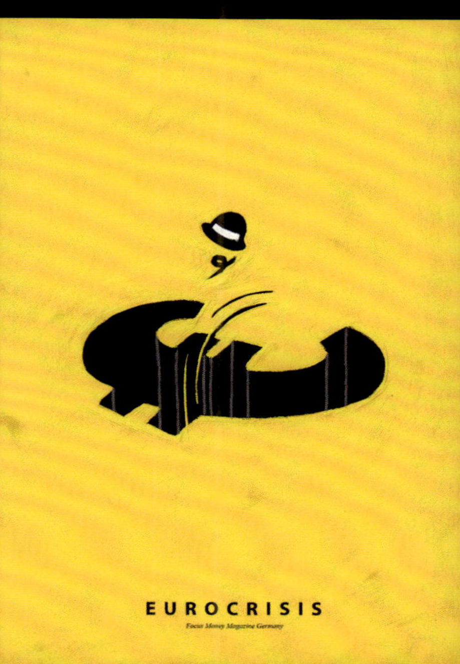

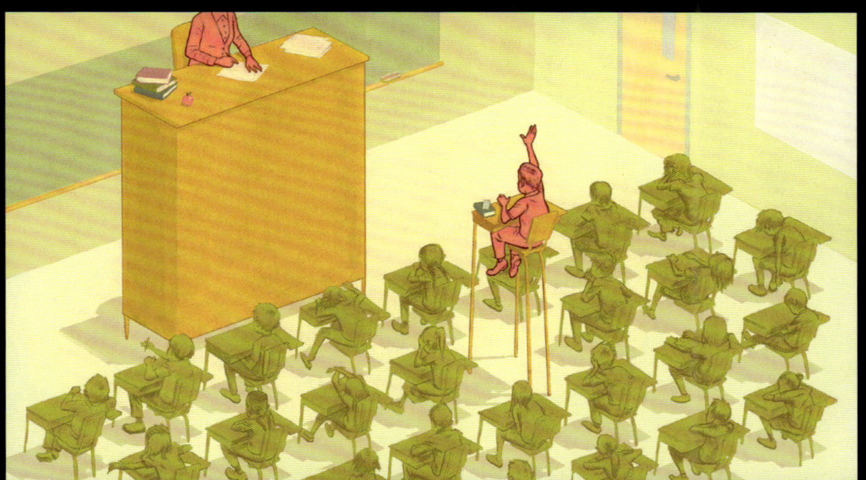

(TL) *Alessandro Gottardo* (TR) *Tim Weiffenbach* (B) *Jori Bolton*

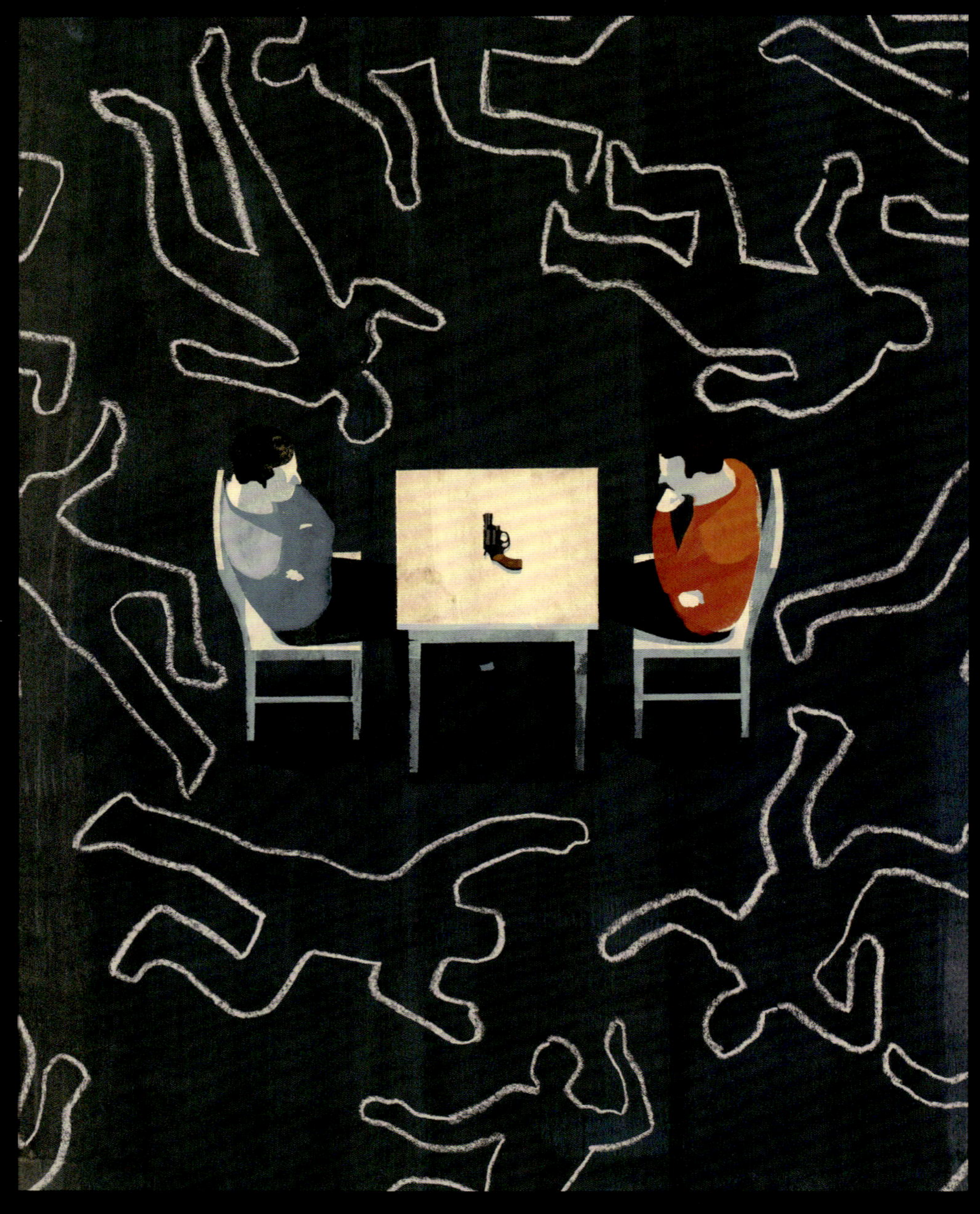

BRONZE *Keith Negley*

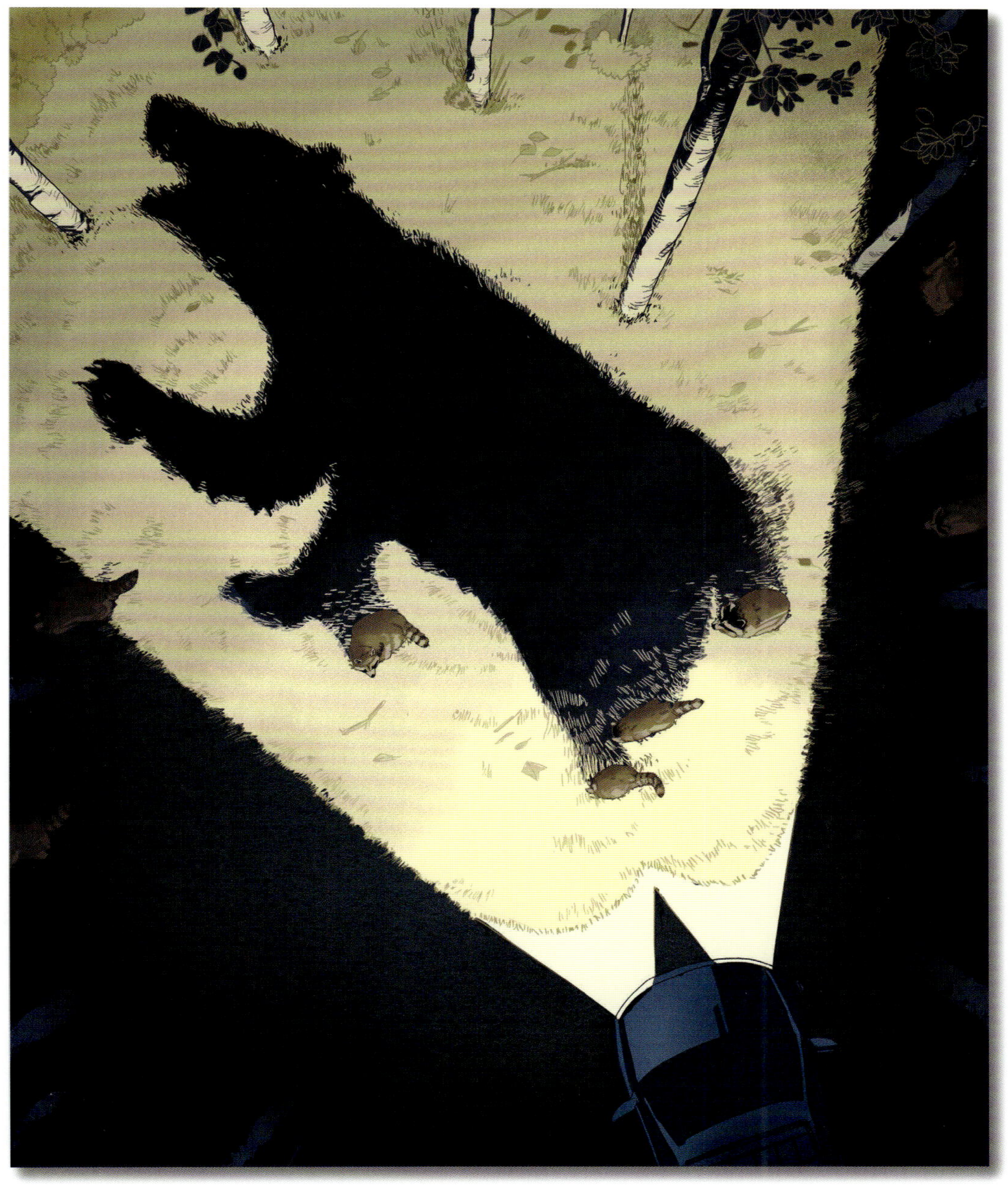

Steven P. Hughes

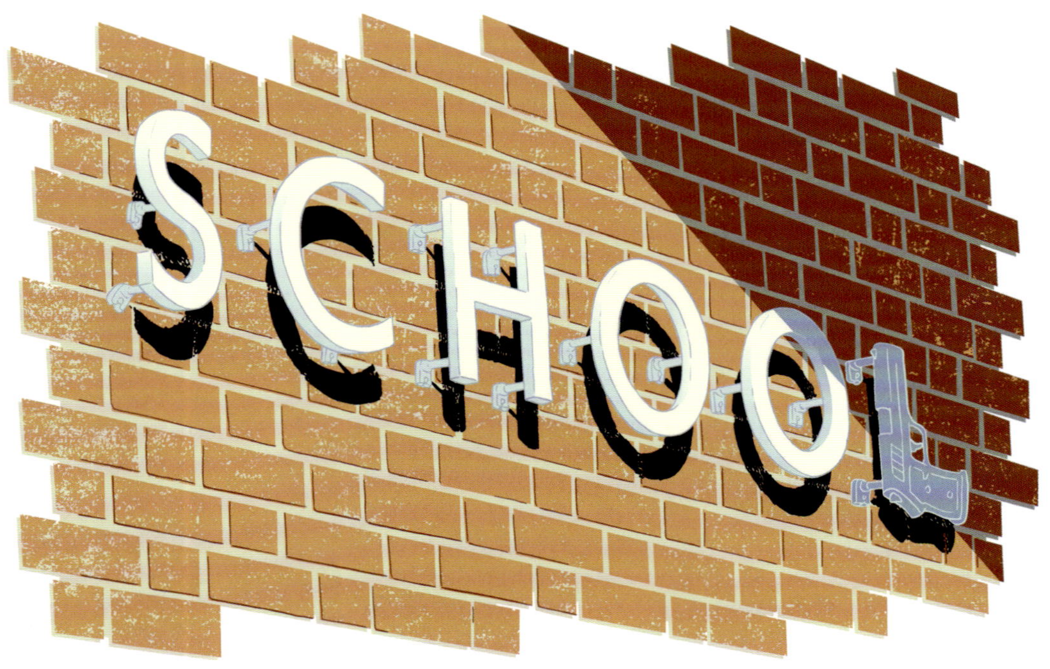

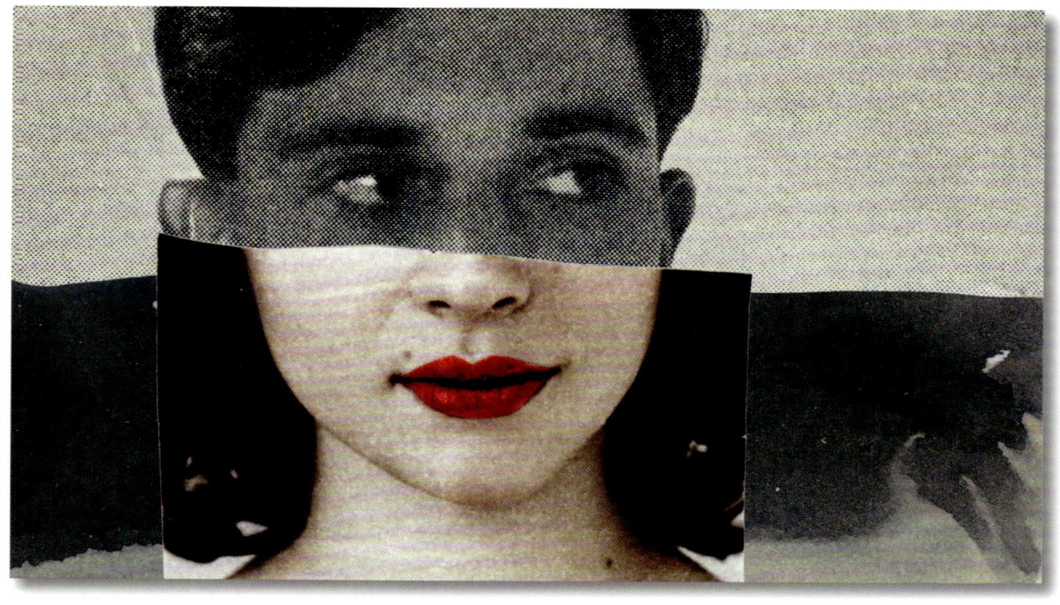

(T) *Carl Wiens* (B) *Michelle Thompson*

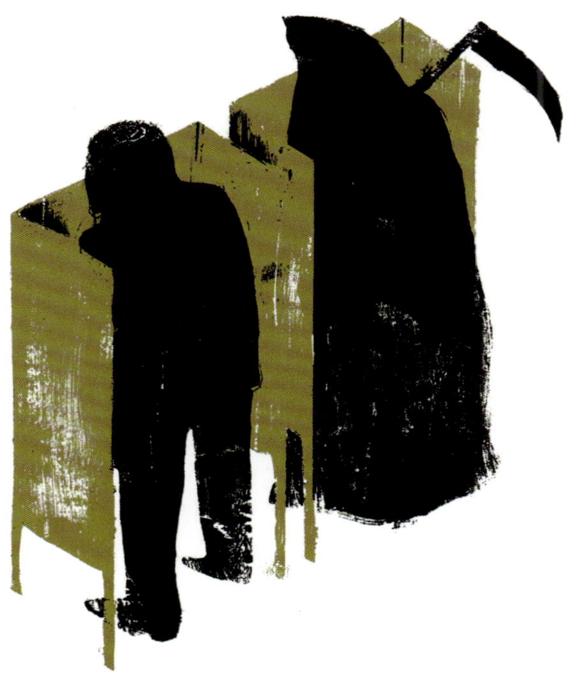

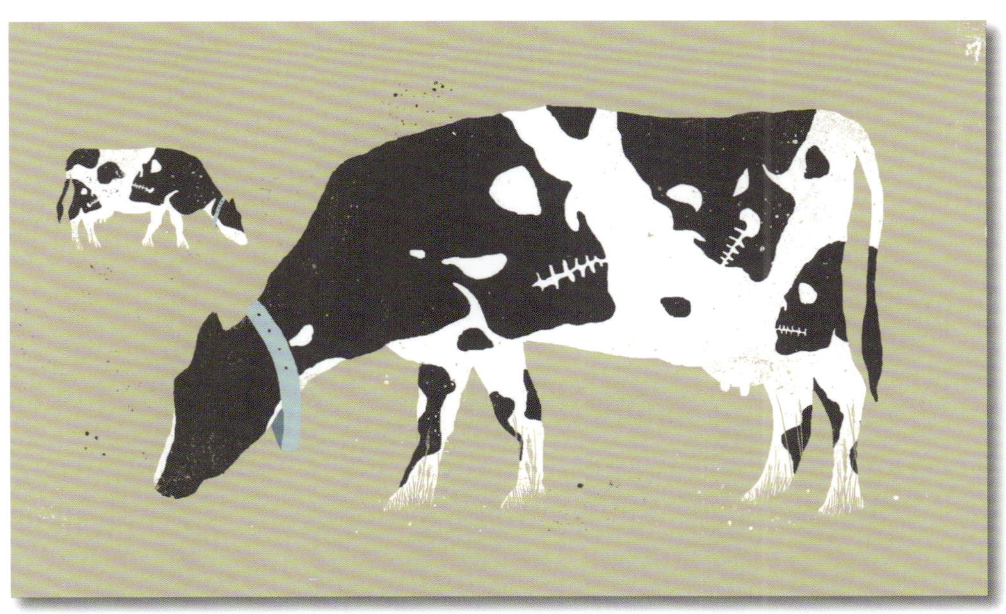

(T) *Daniel Zender* (B) *Sébastien Thibault*

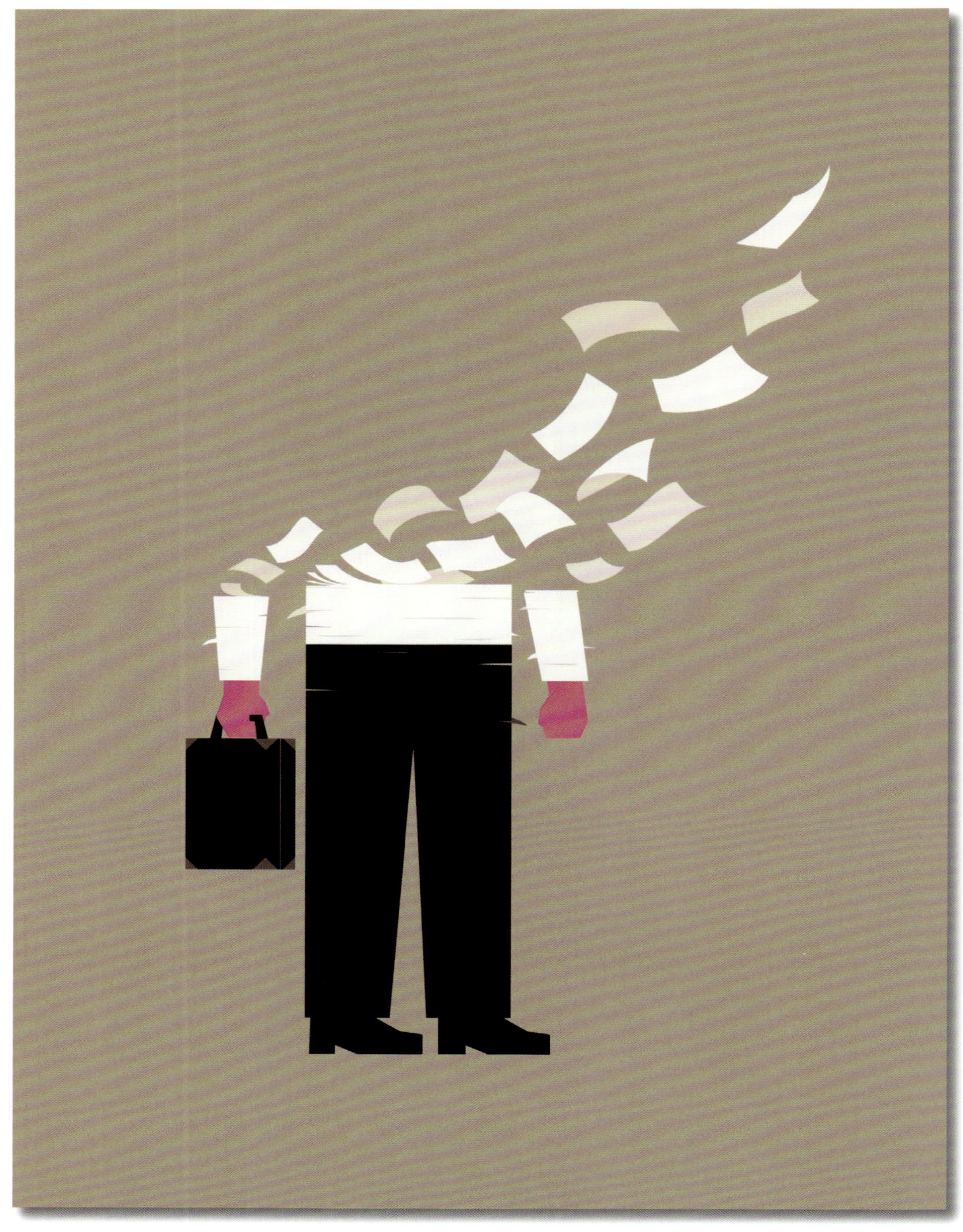

Aad Goudappel

CIUTADELLA
CALA CAVALLERIA BEACH
RESTAURANT
ES CRANC
Talayot
JAIME MASCARÓ
Shoe factory
Monte Toro
CAMI de CAVALLS
BINIBECA
CALA MITJANA BEACH
Cheese factory
HARBOUR of MAHÓN
MENORCA
BINIFADET VINEYARD

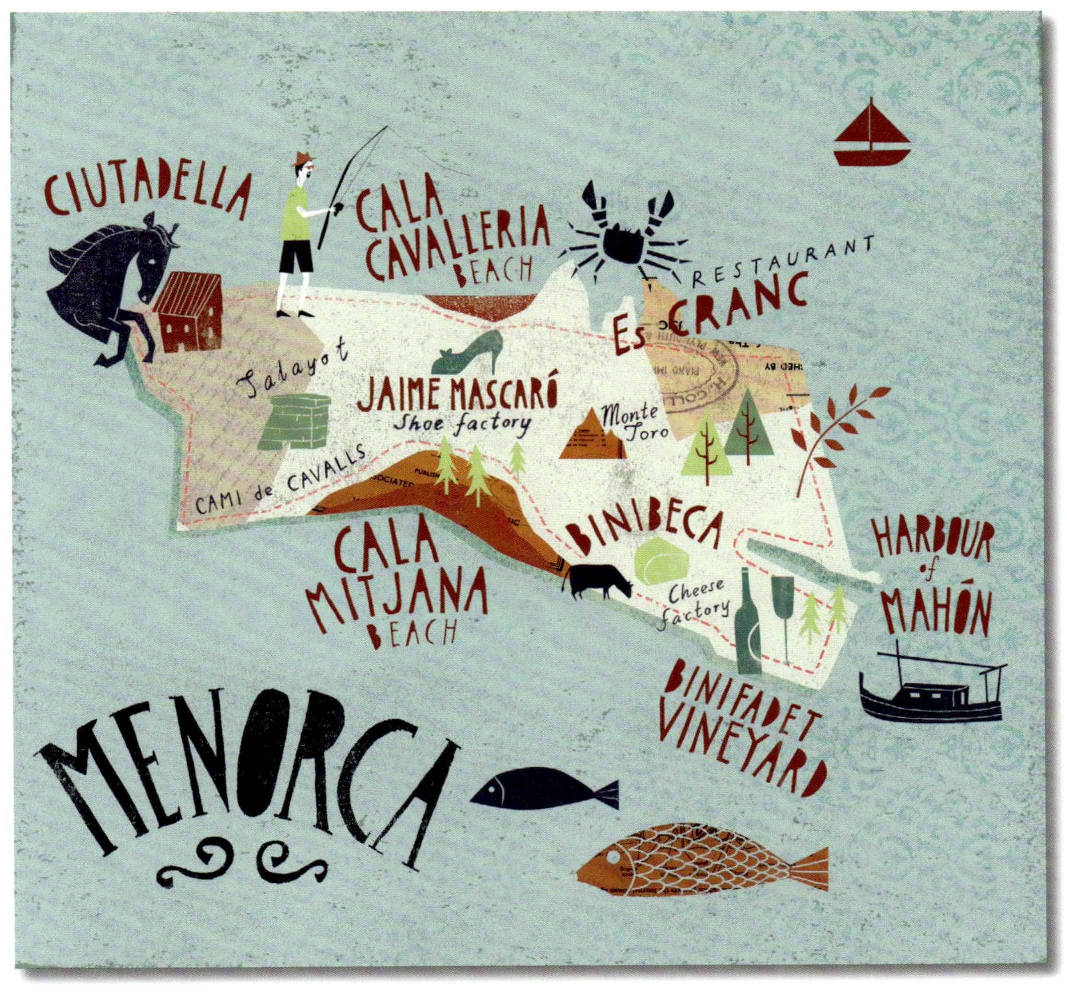

Gary Venn

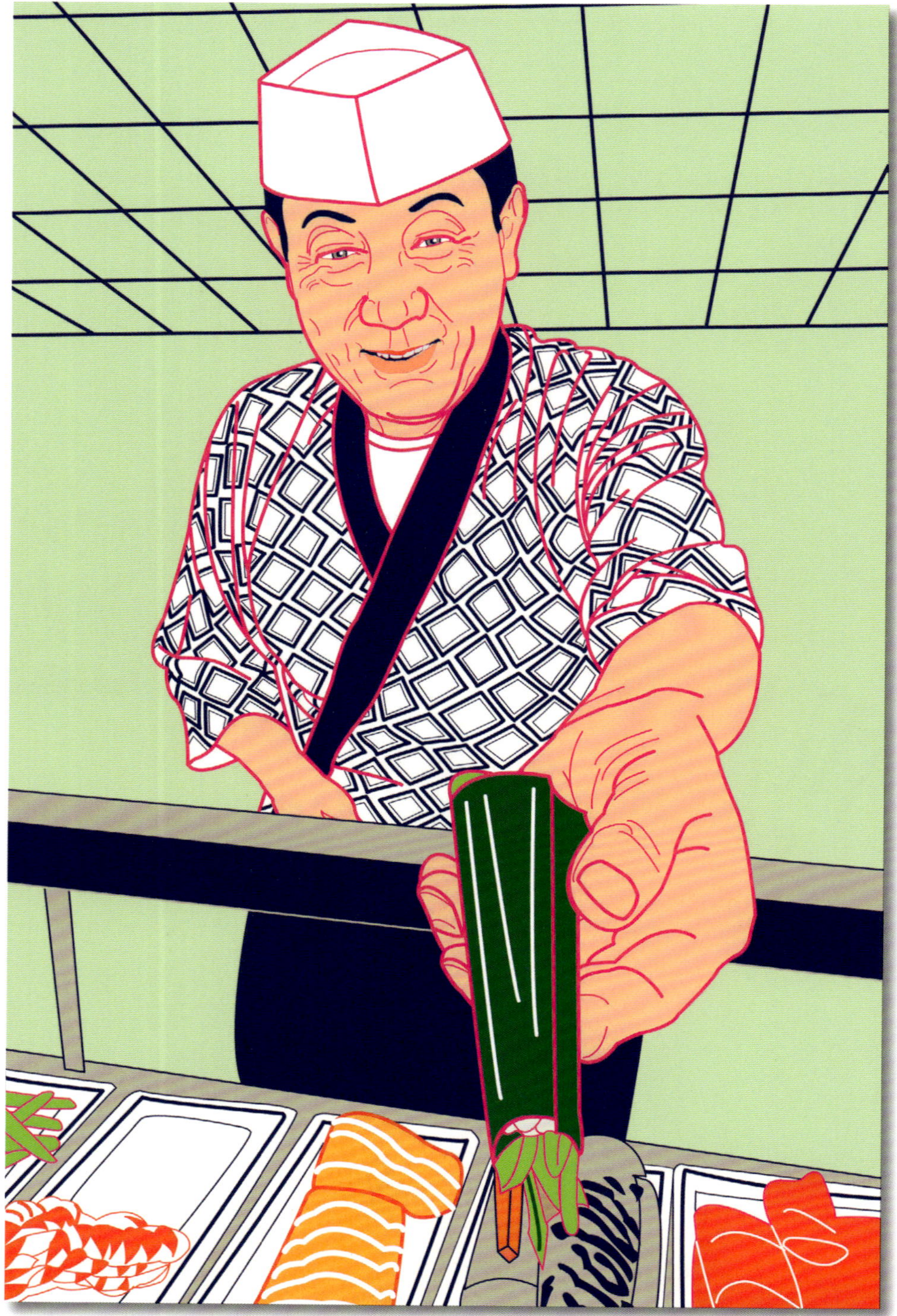

Toni Damkoehler

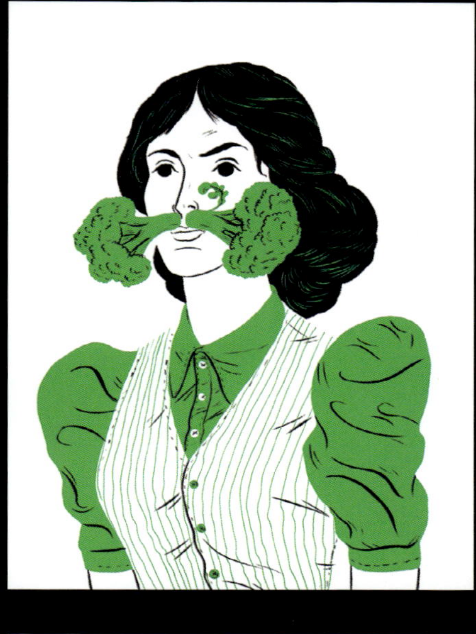

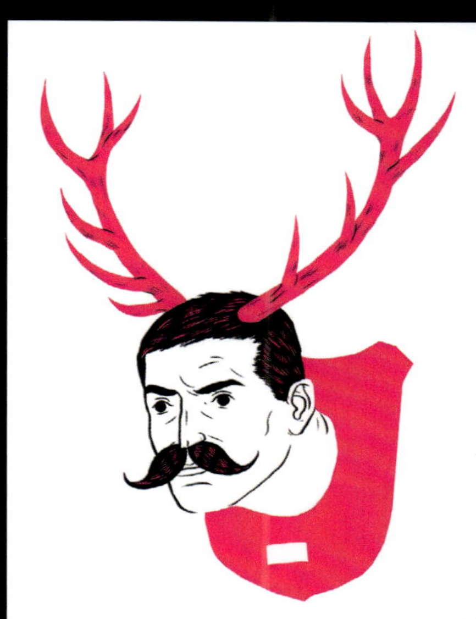

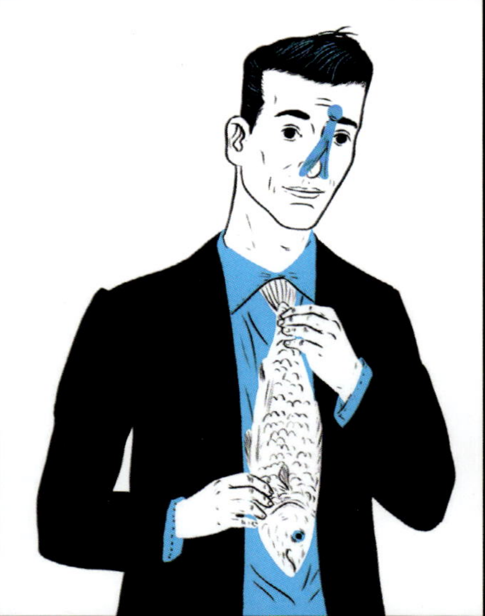

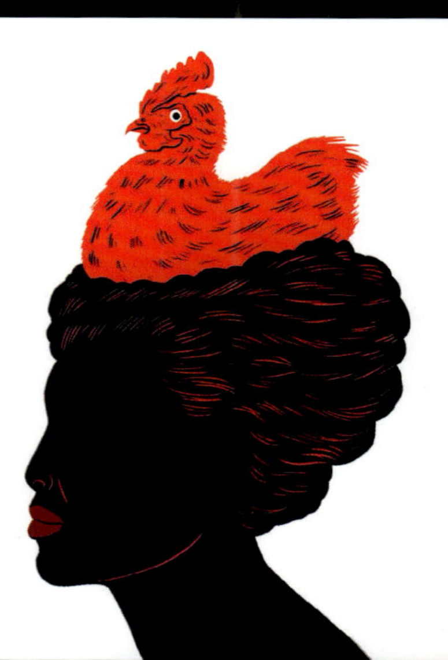

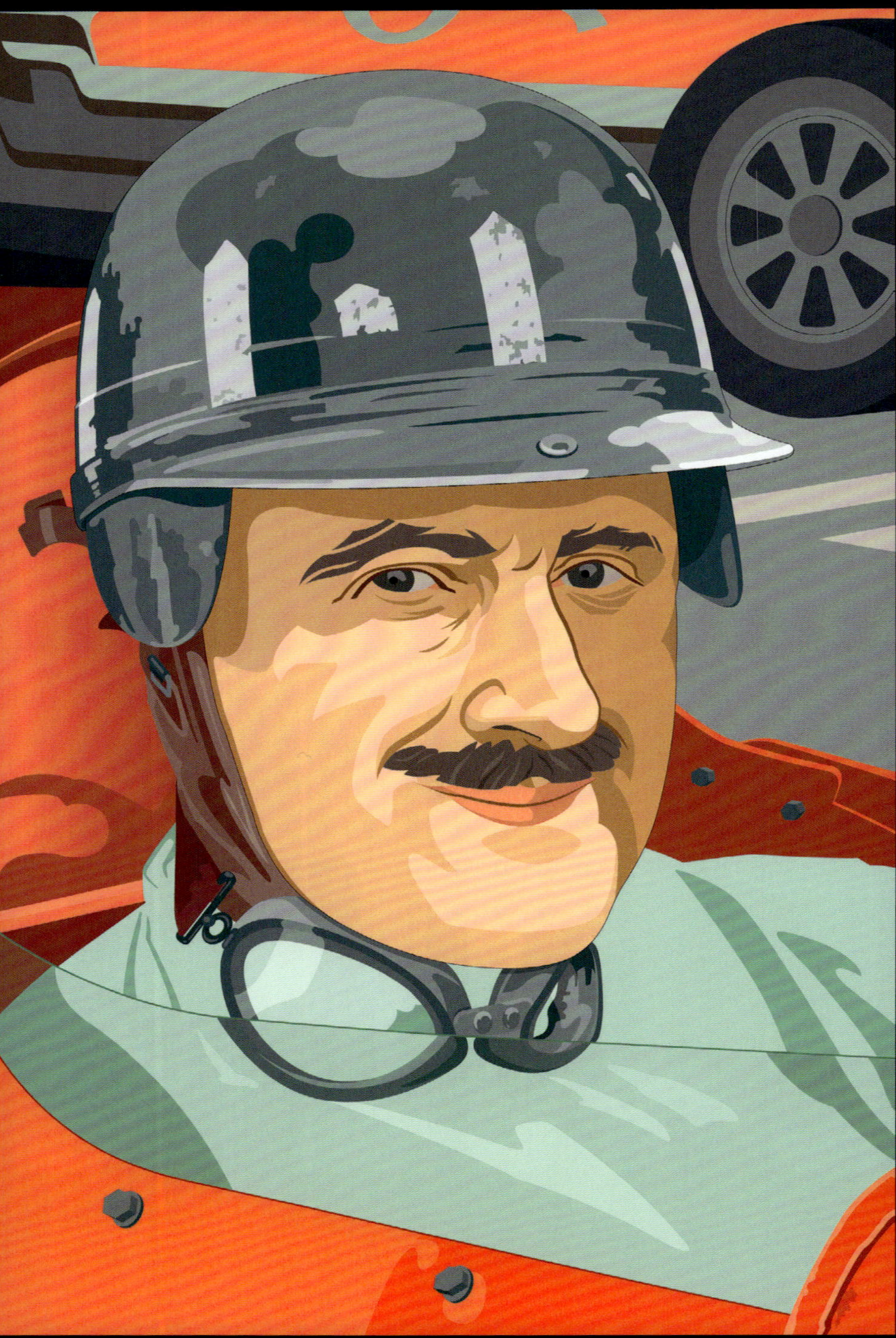

Beugism

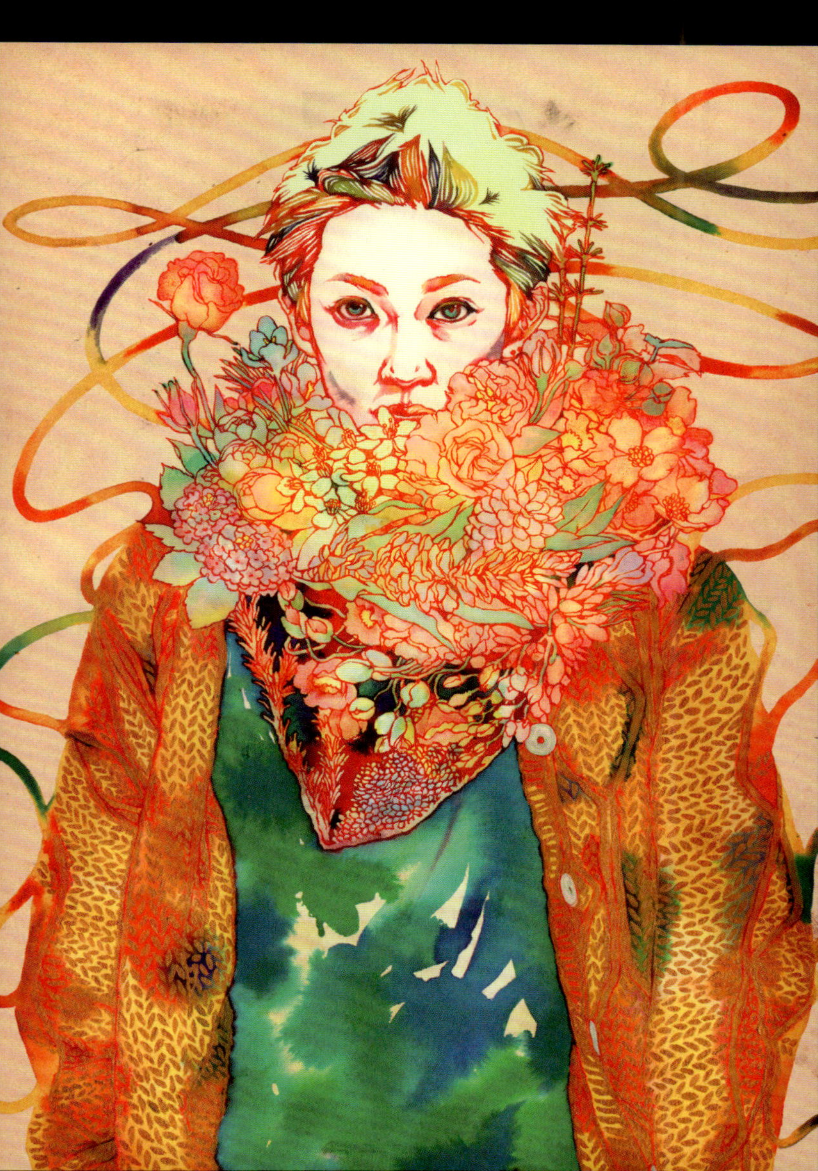

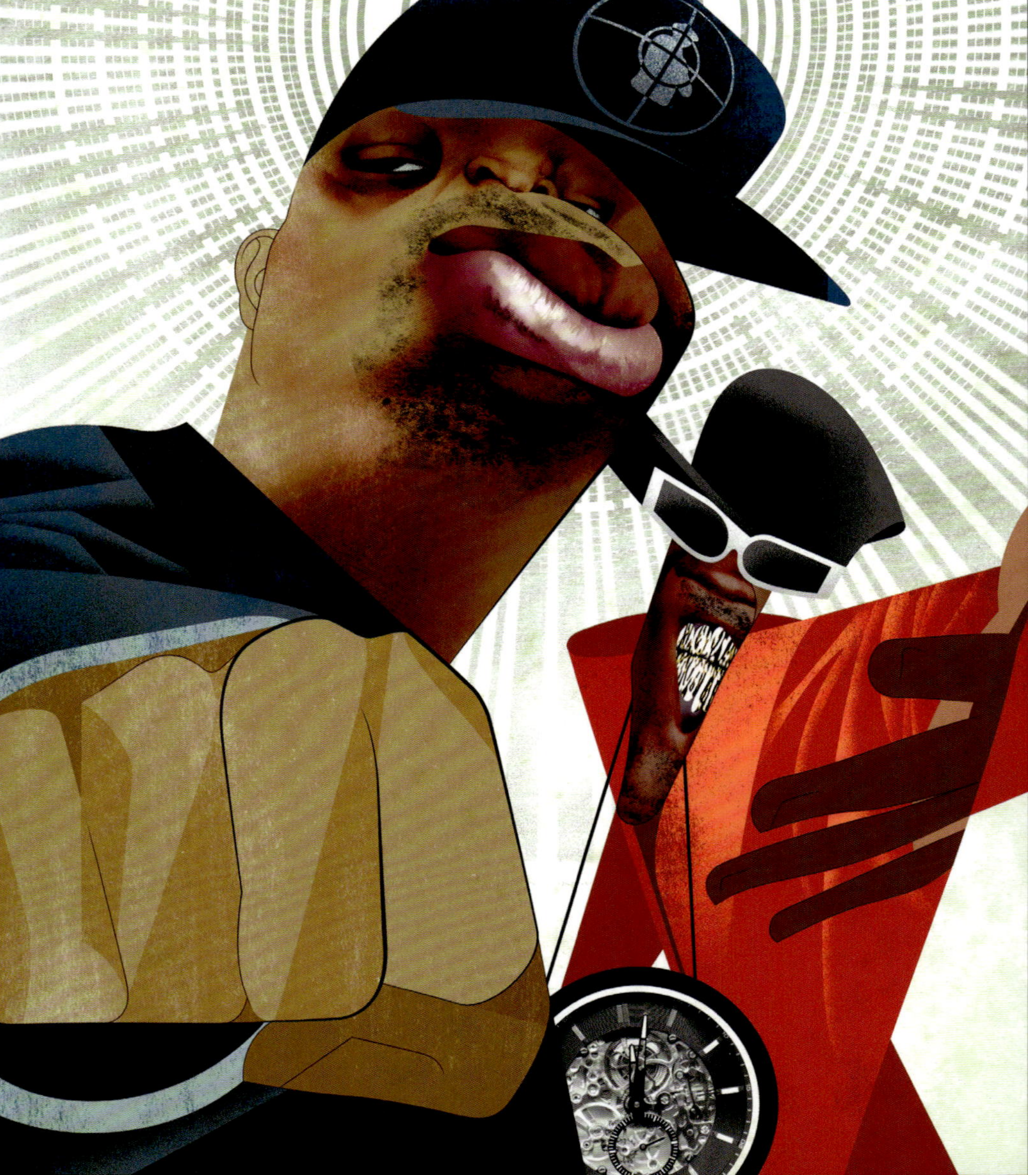

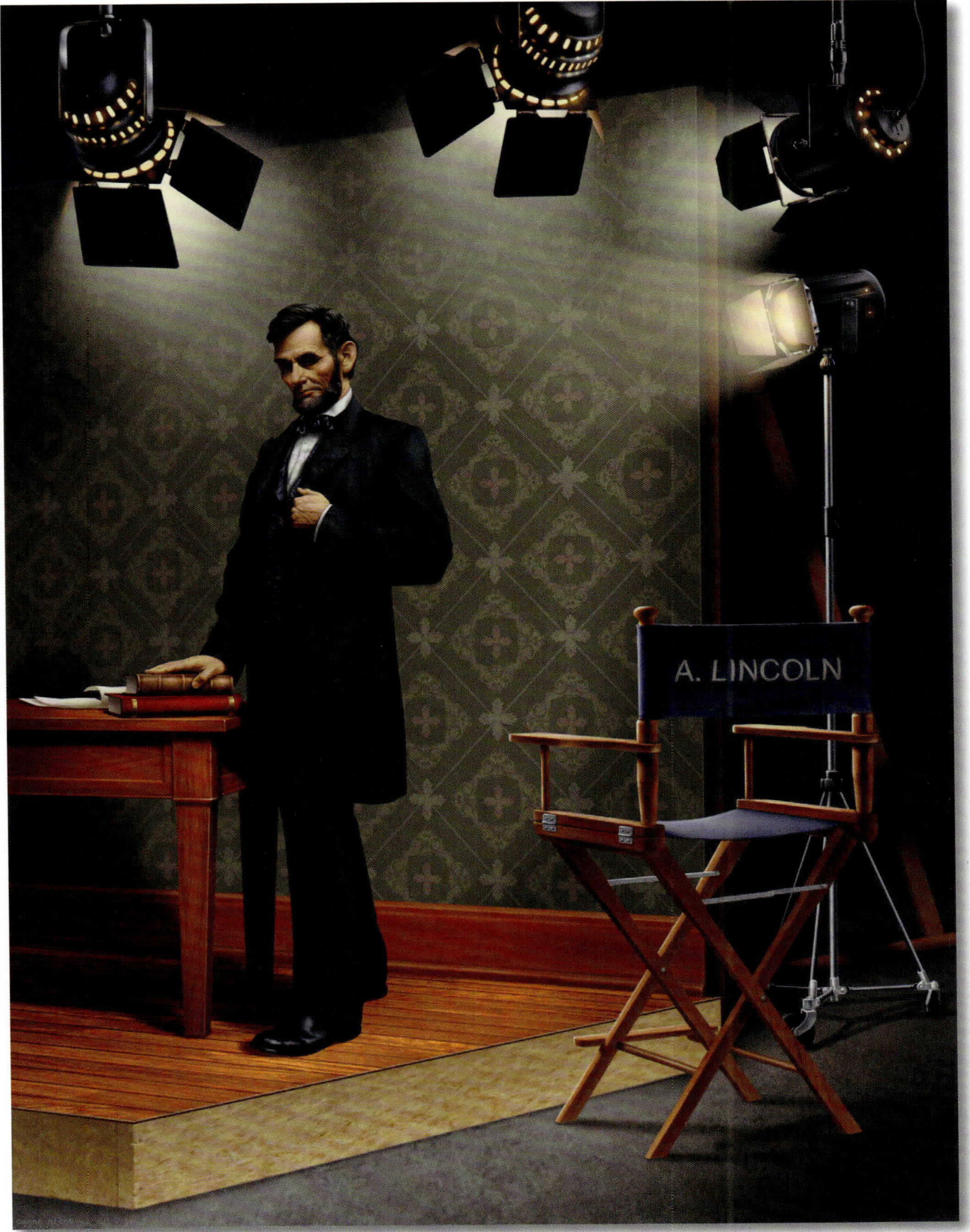

René Milot

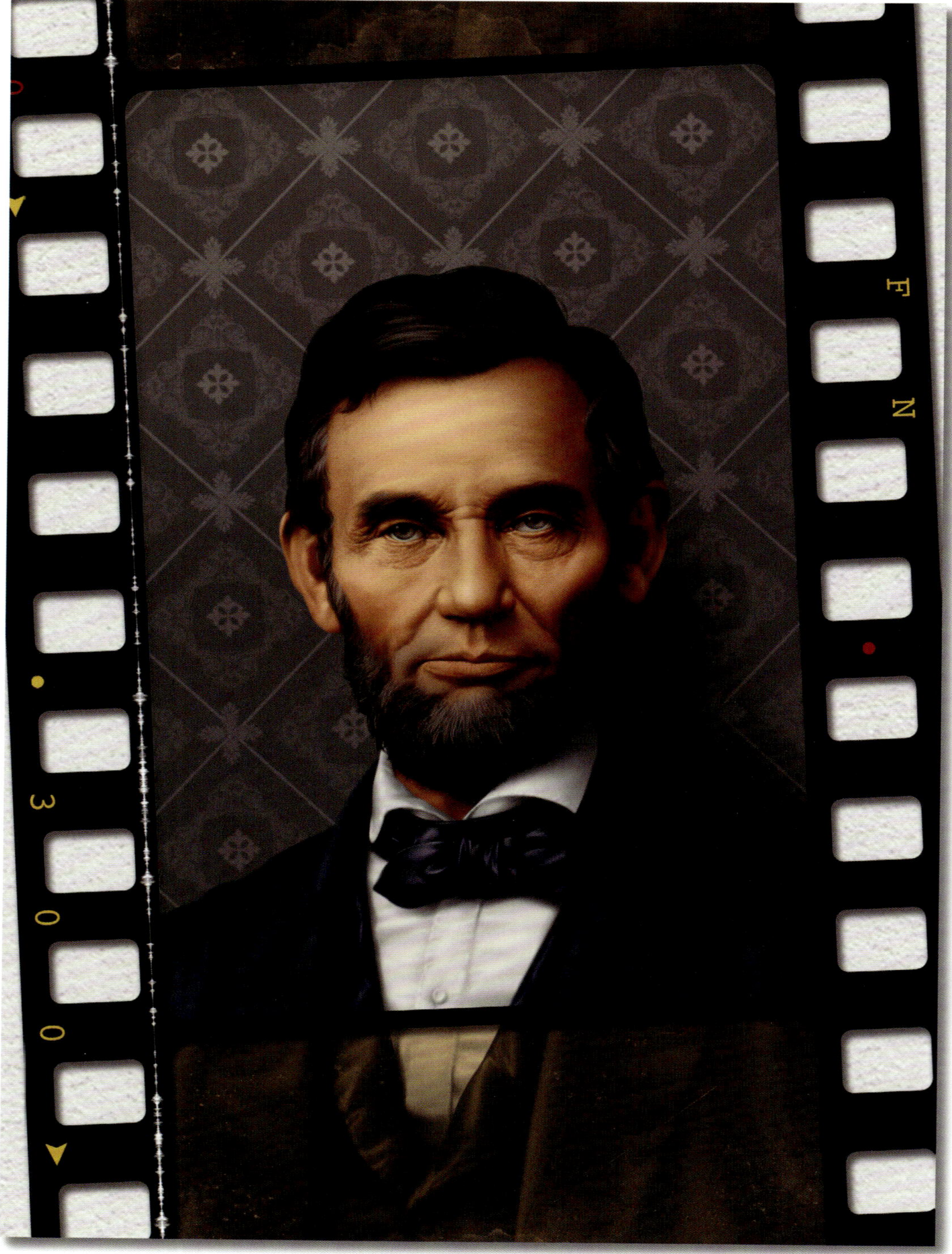

(L) *René Milot* (R) *André Carrilho*

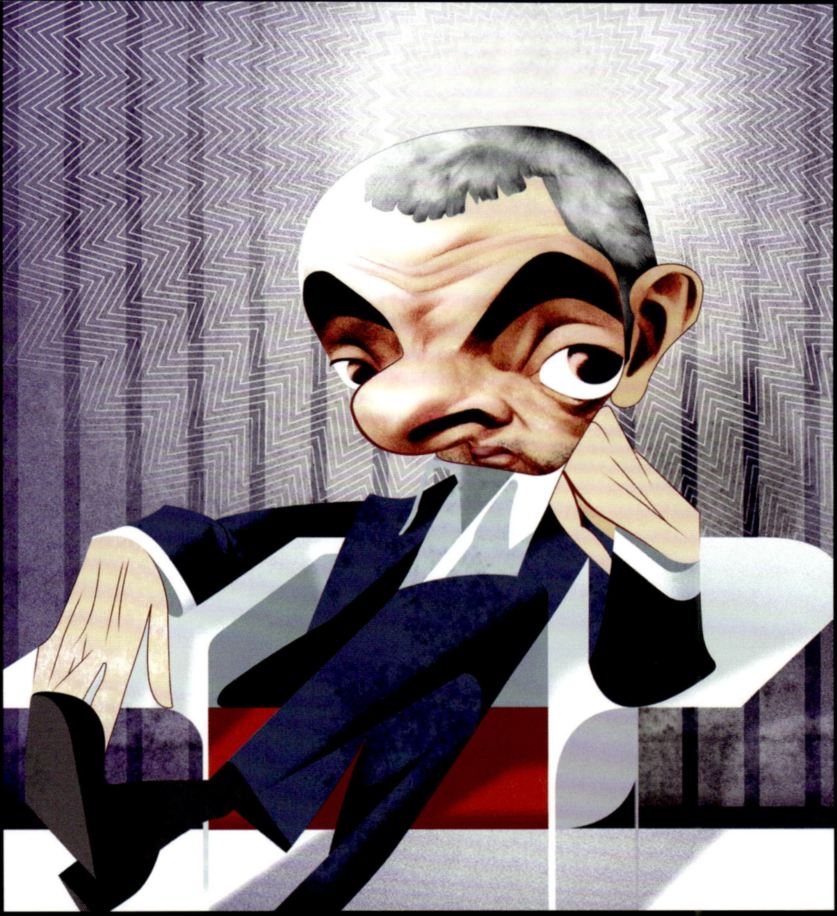

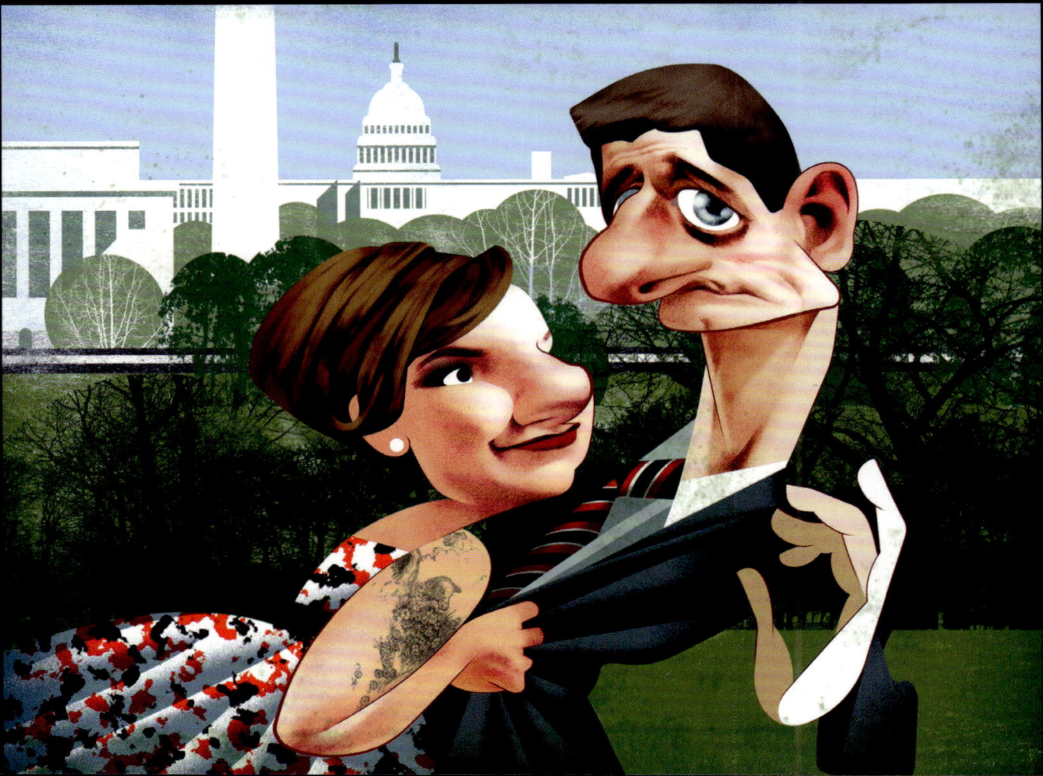

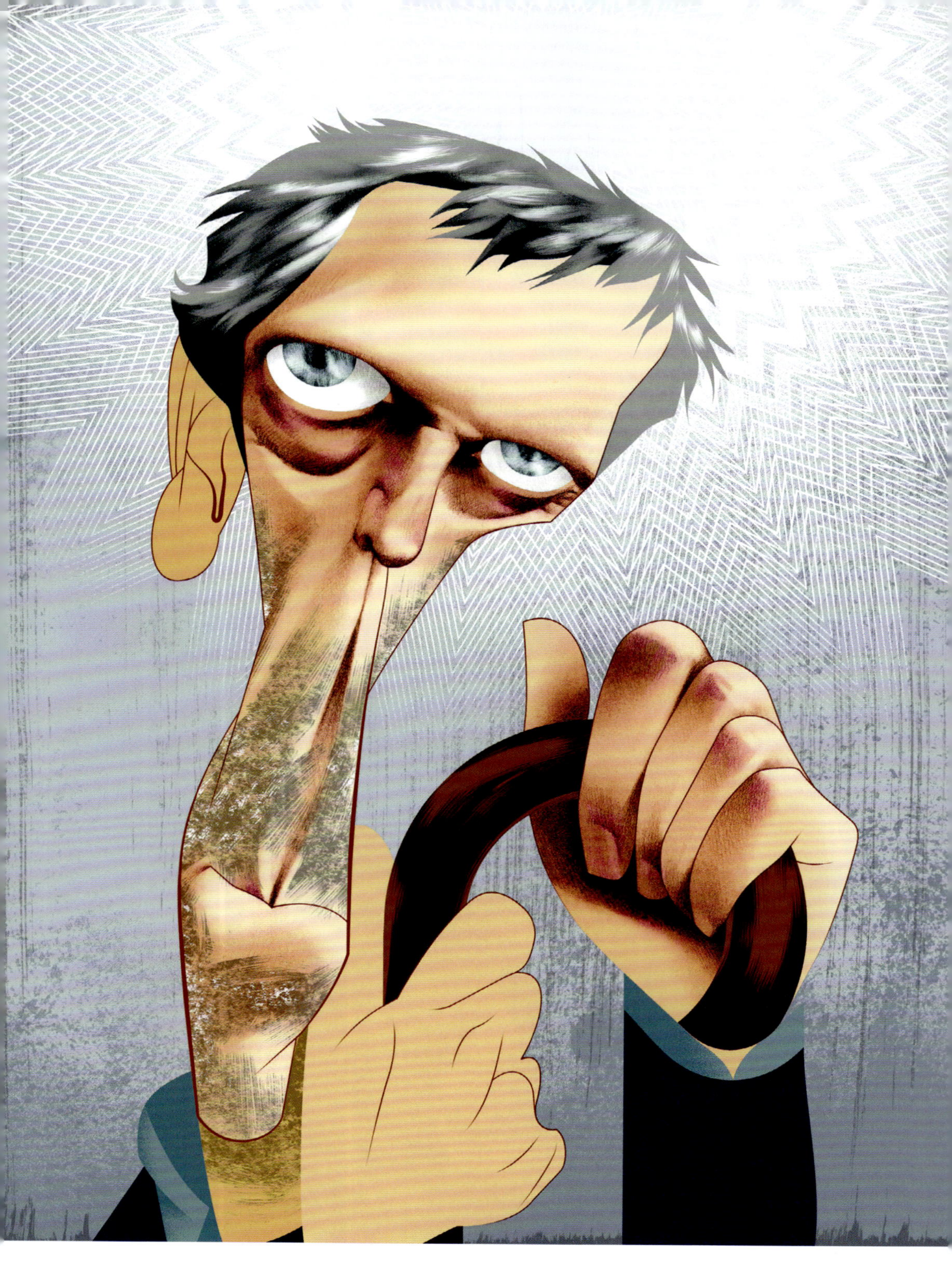

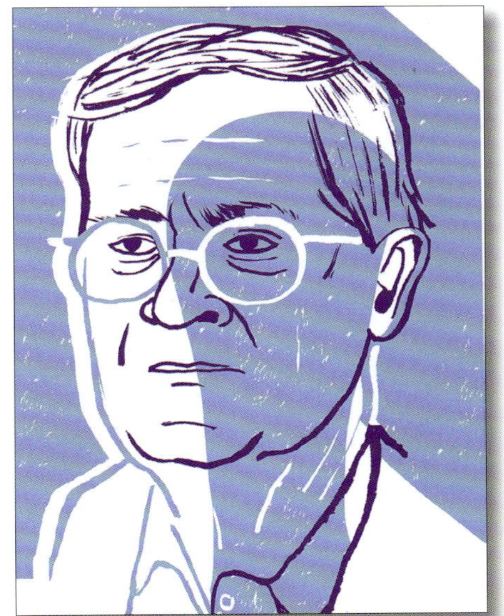
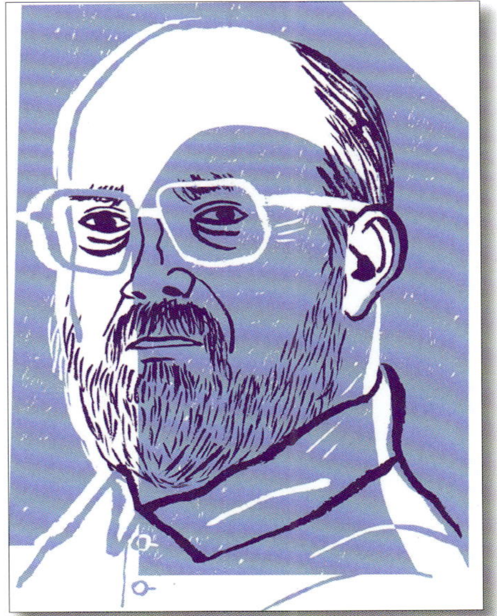
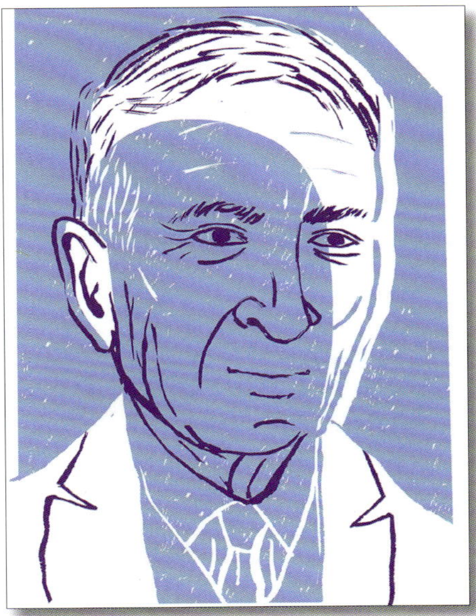
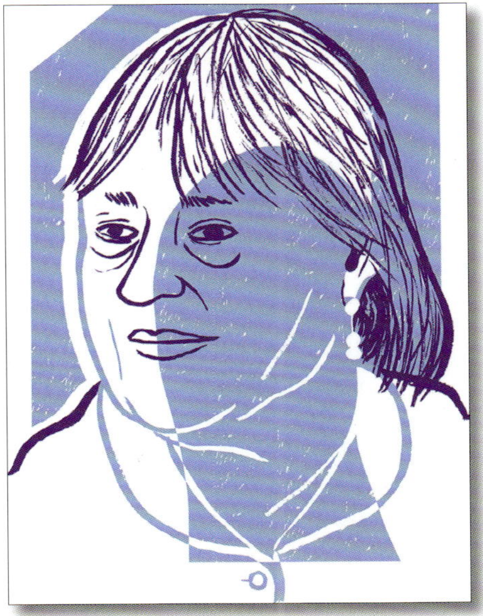

(L) *André Carrilho* (R) *James O'Brien*

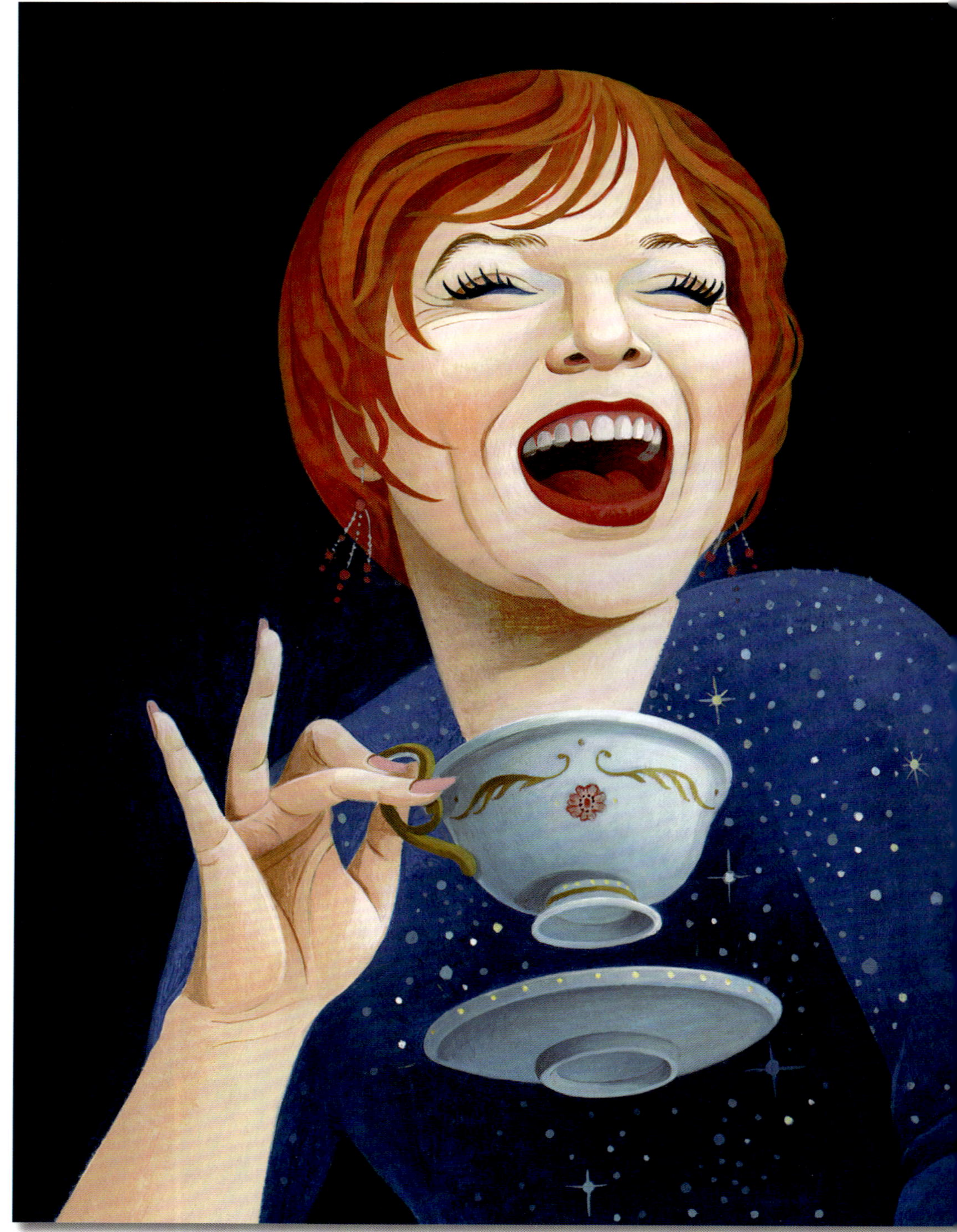

Jody Hewgill

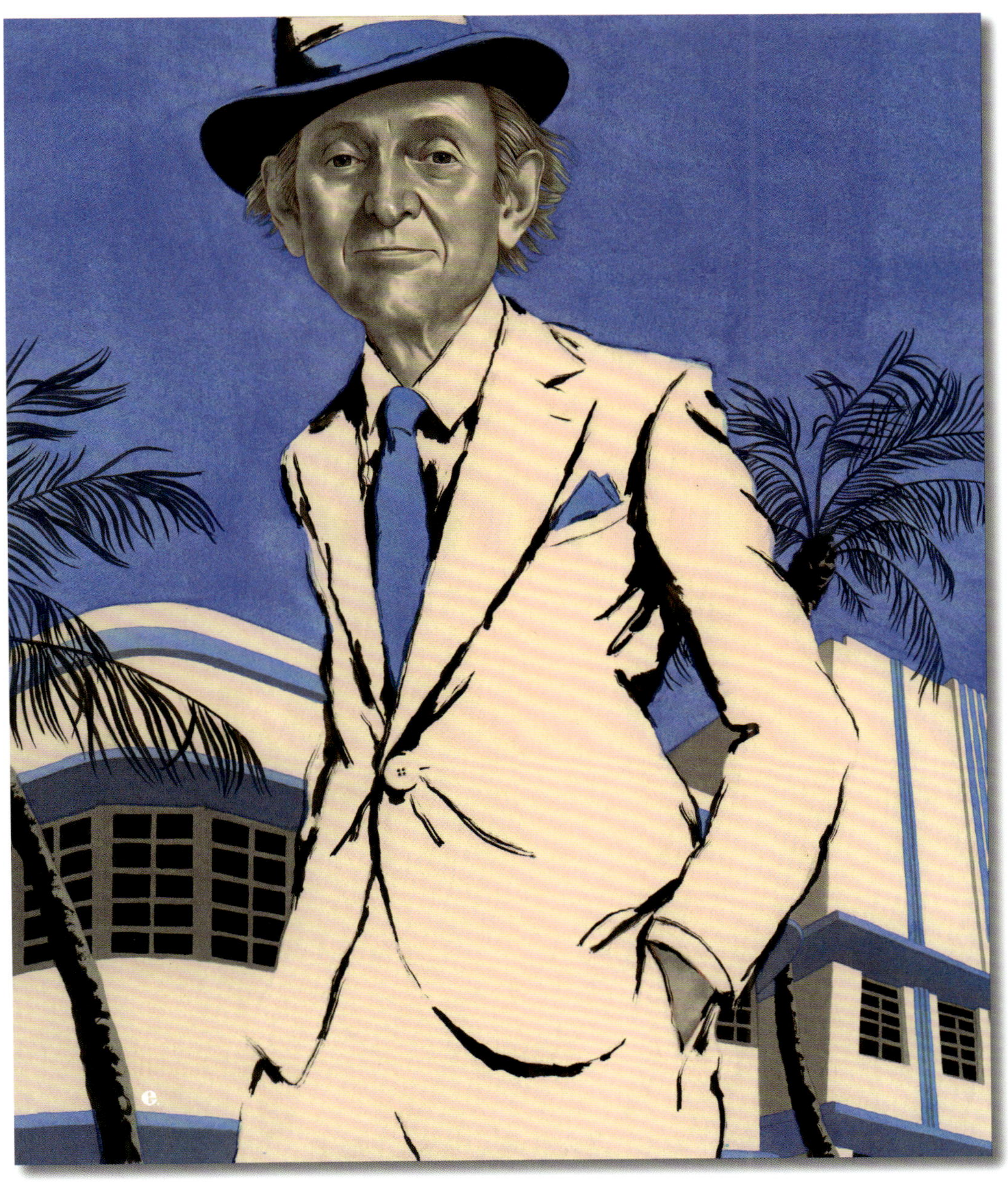

Edward Kinsella III

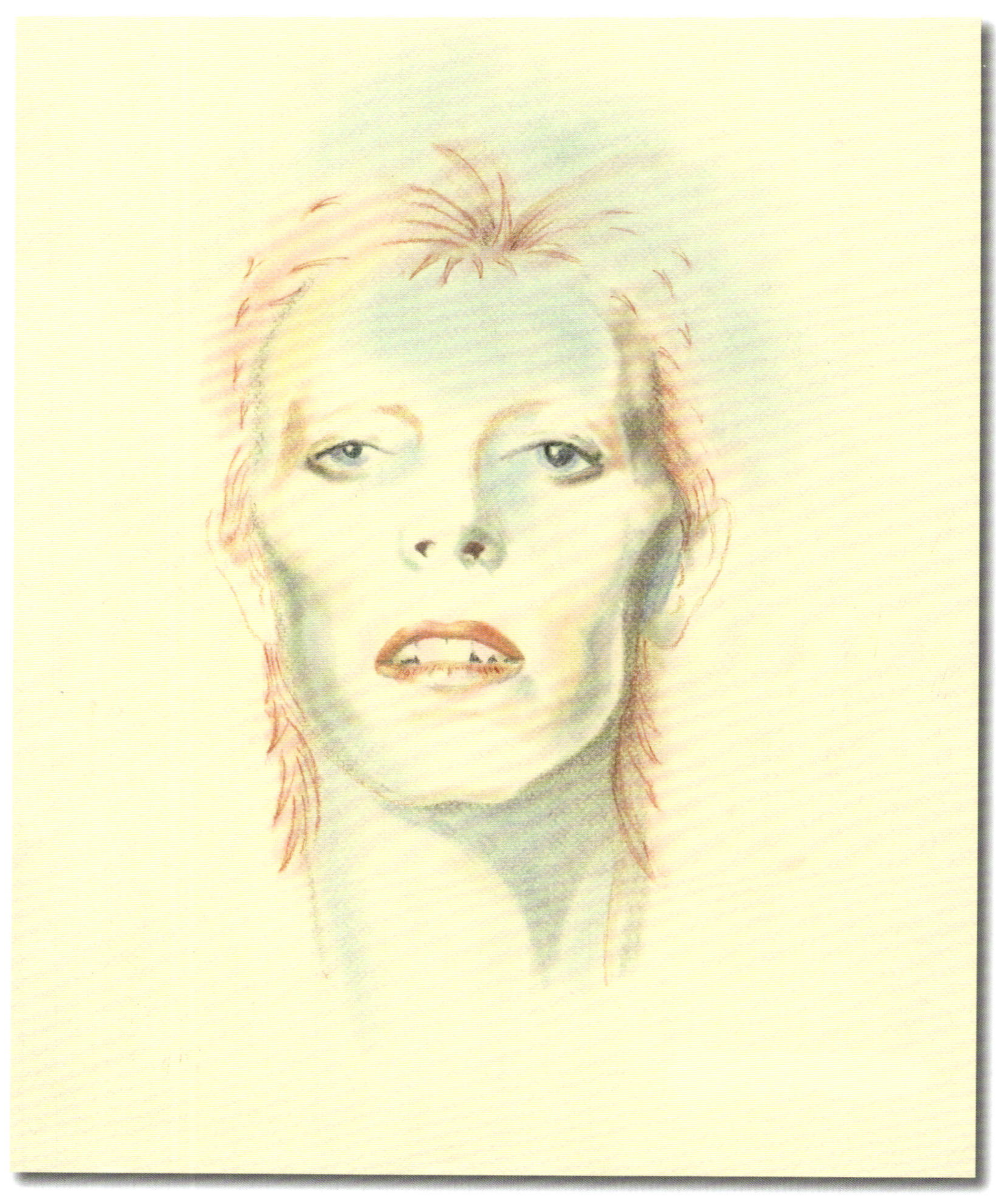

Barbara Nessim

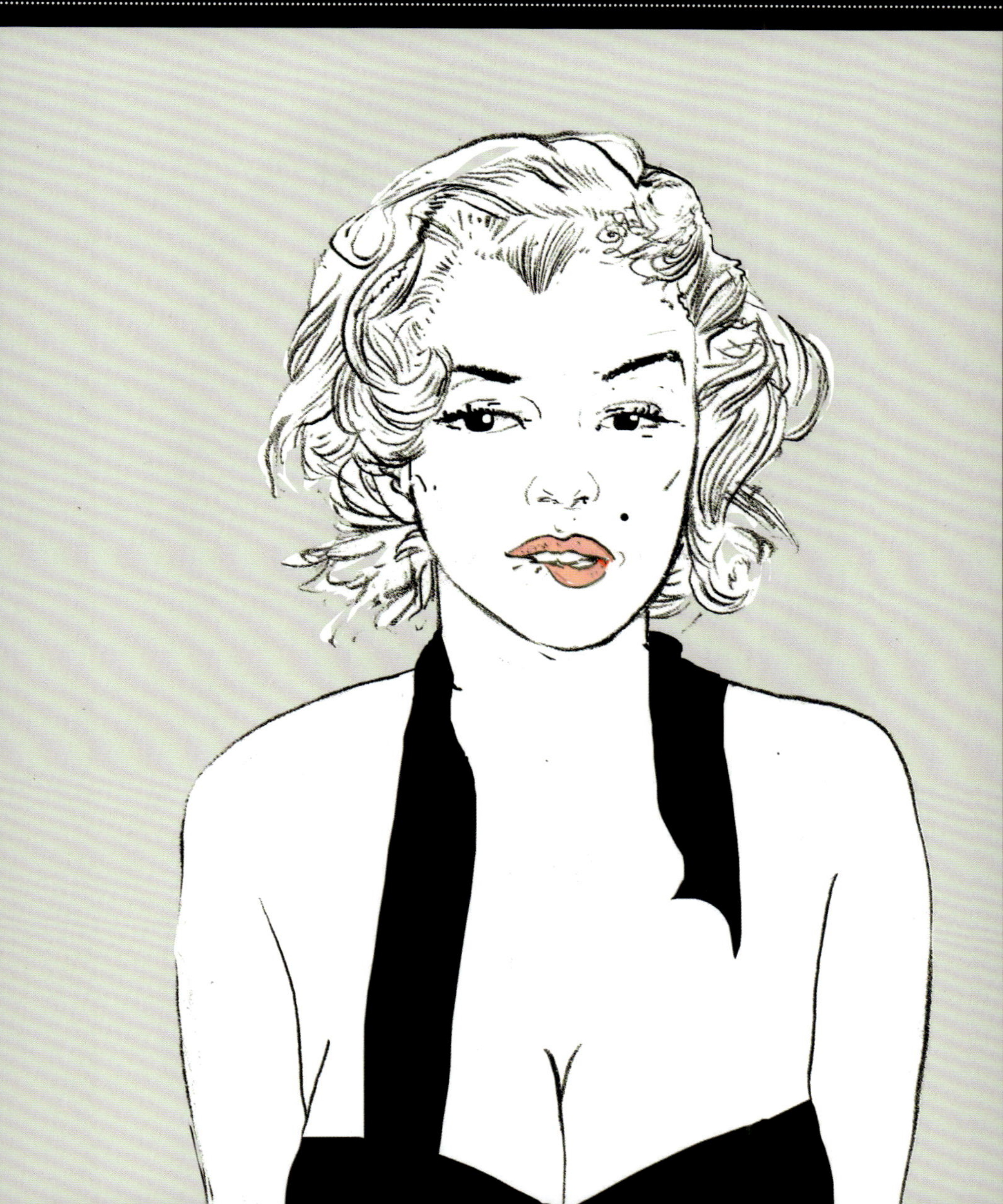

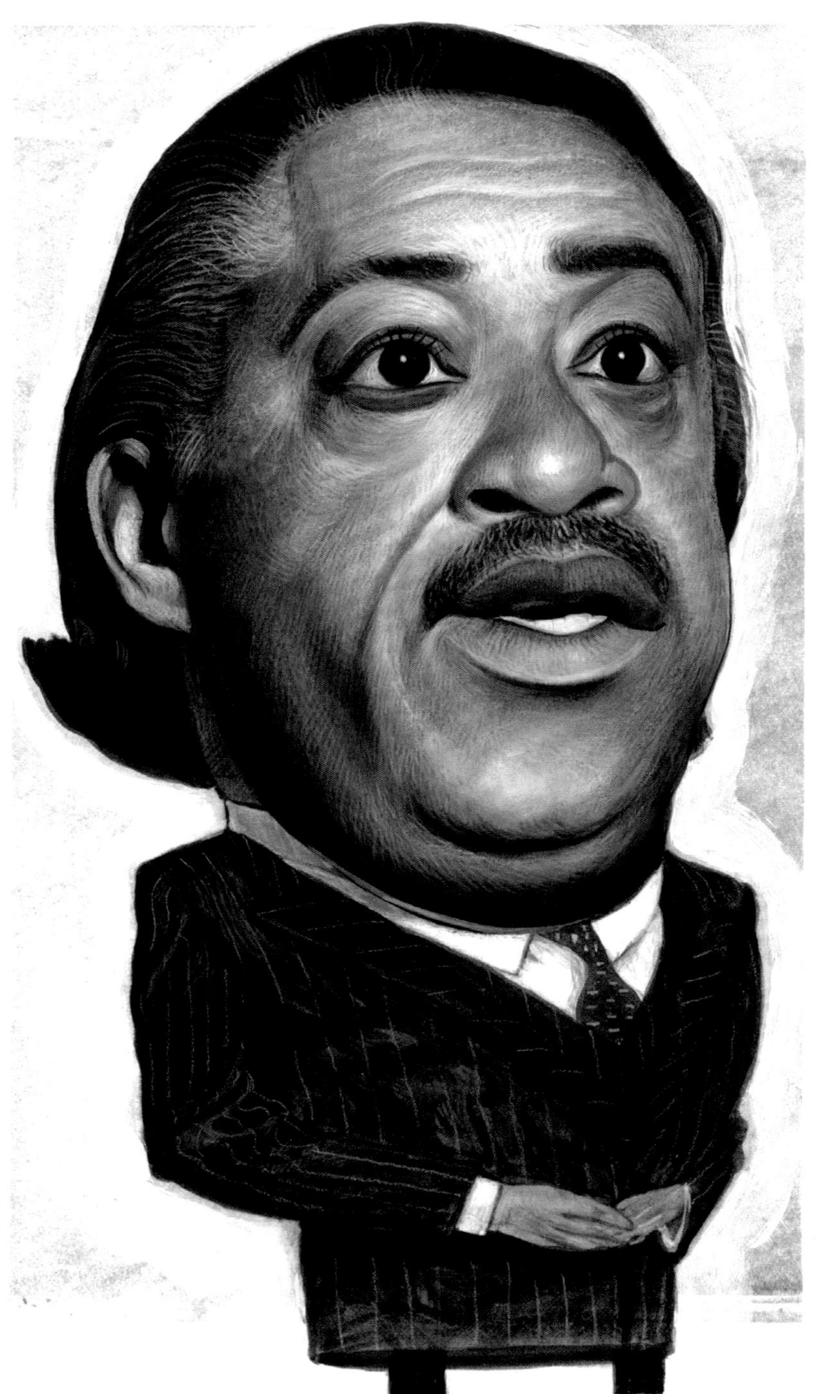

Earl Keleny

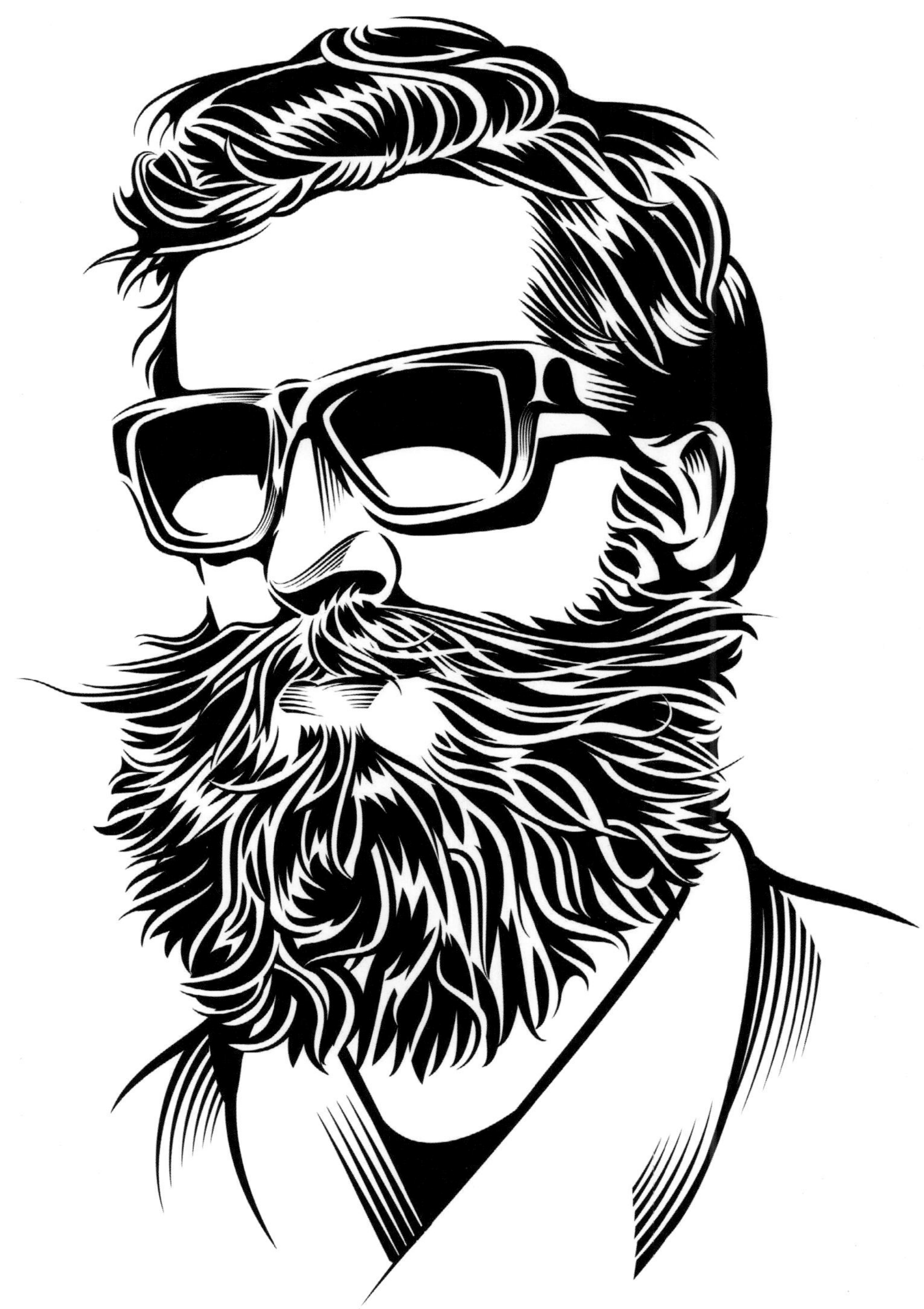

Yann Legendre

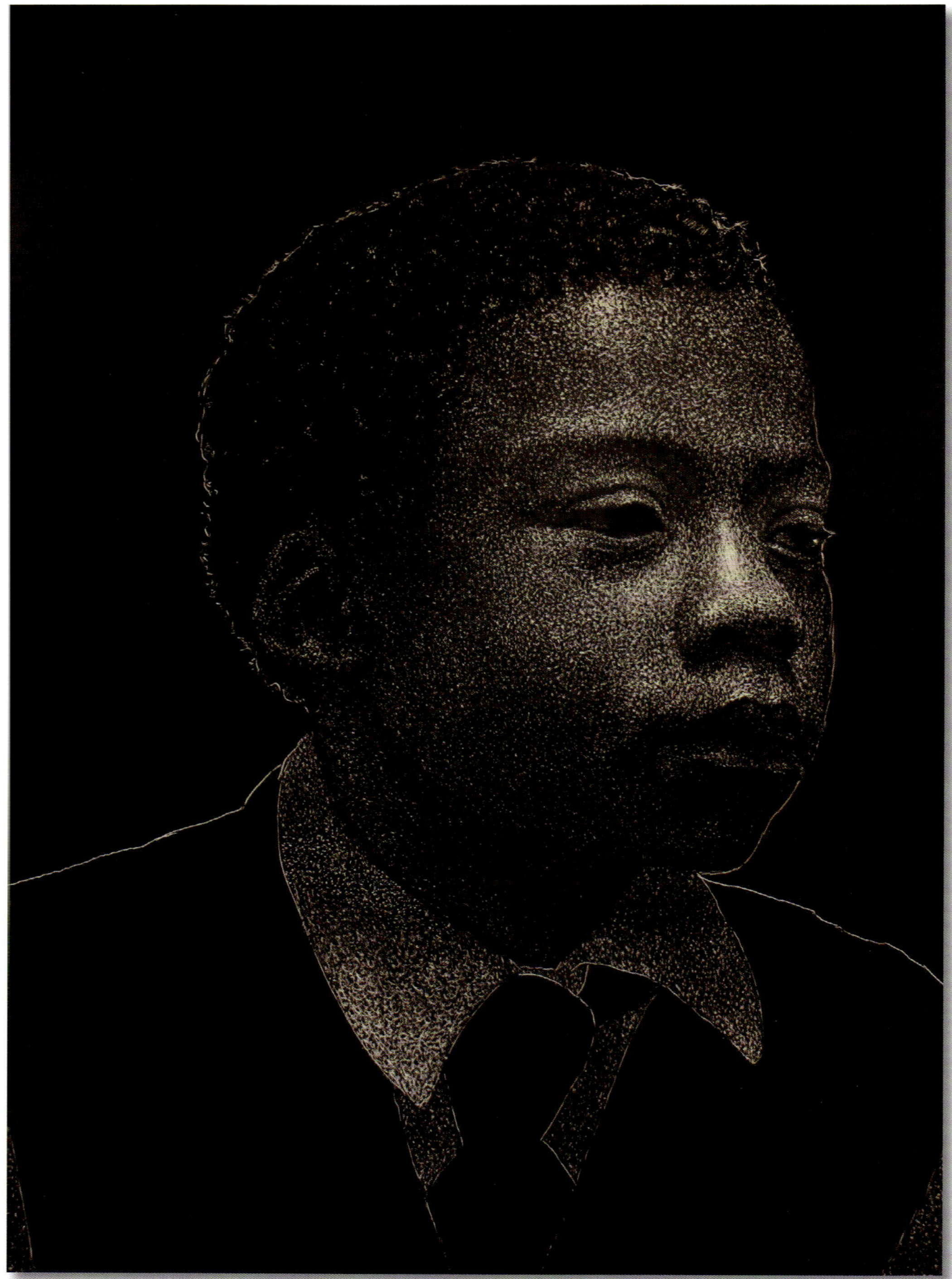

Heather Heckel

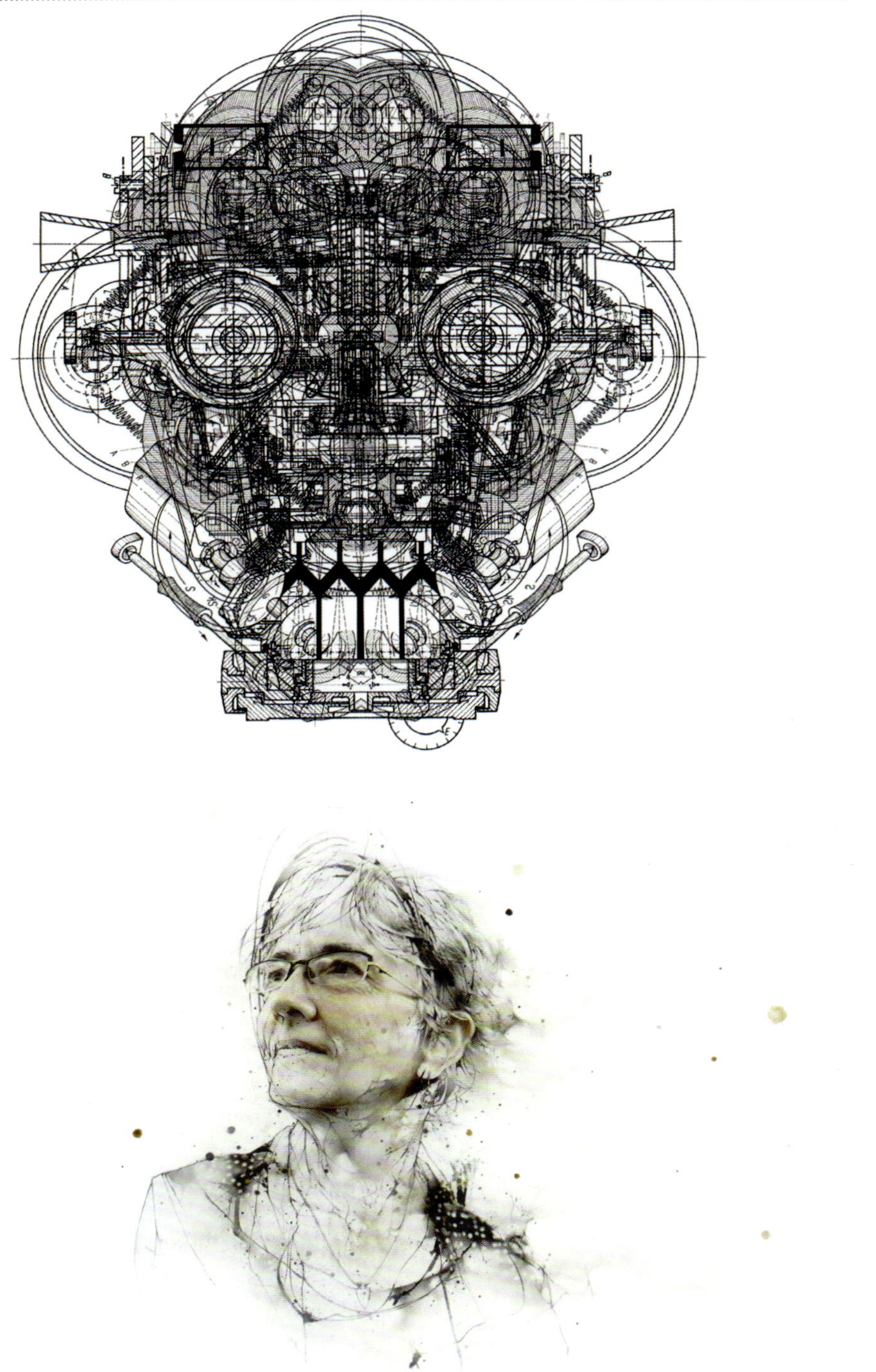

(T) *Christian Gralingen* (B) *Andrew Zbihlyj*

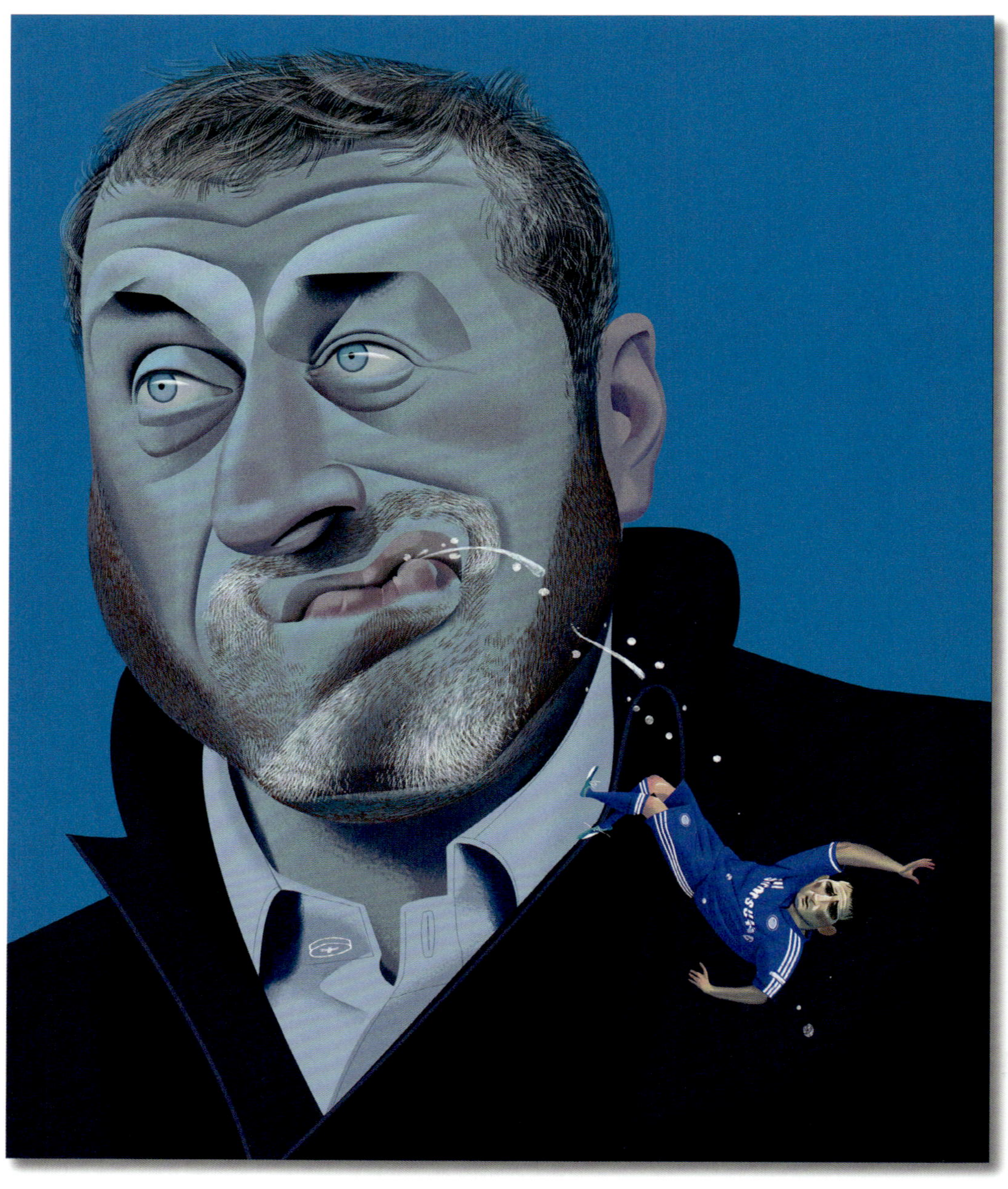

Nigel Buchanan

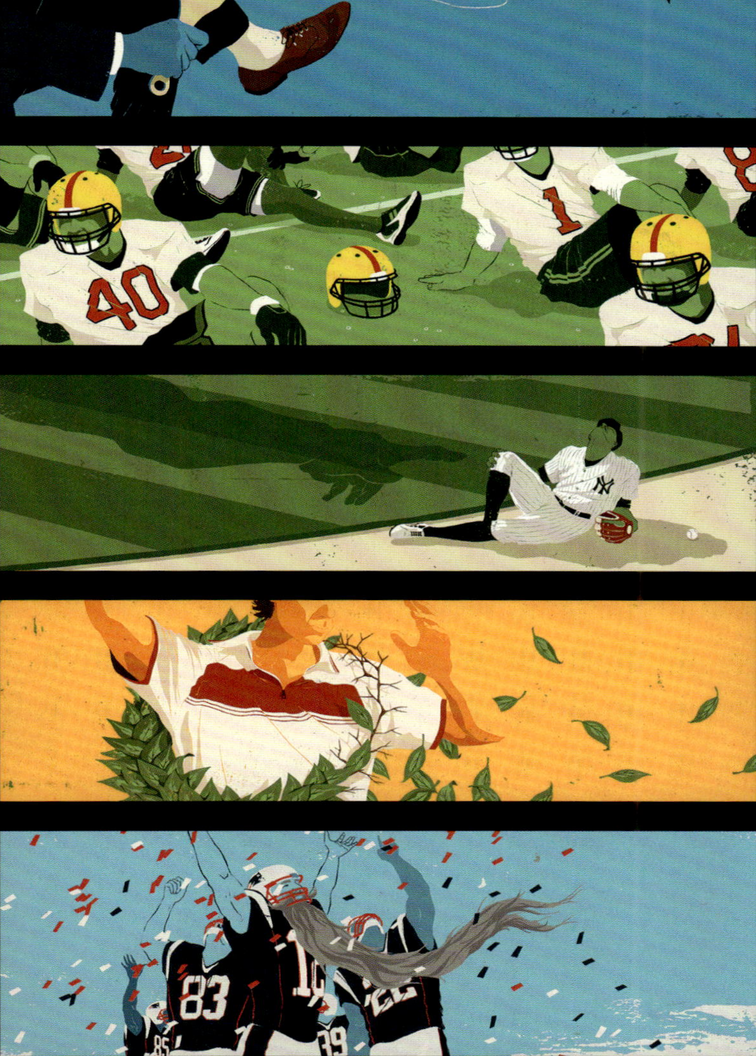

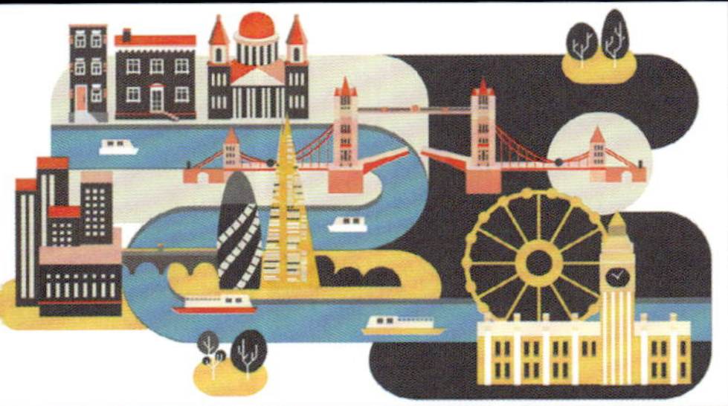

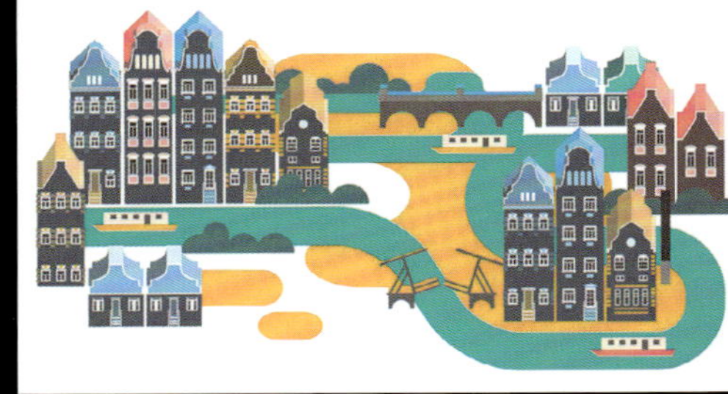

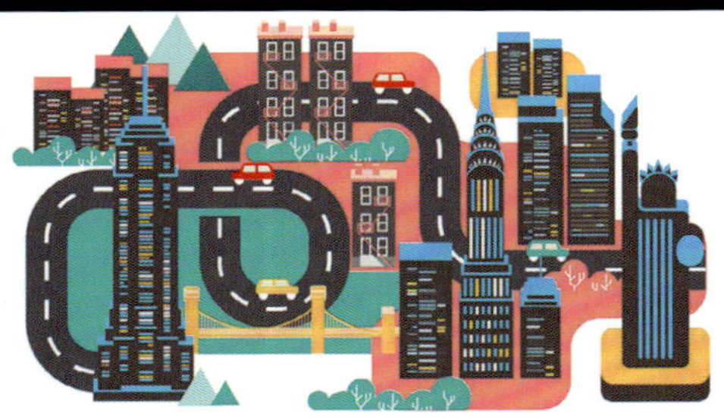

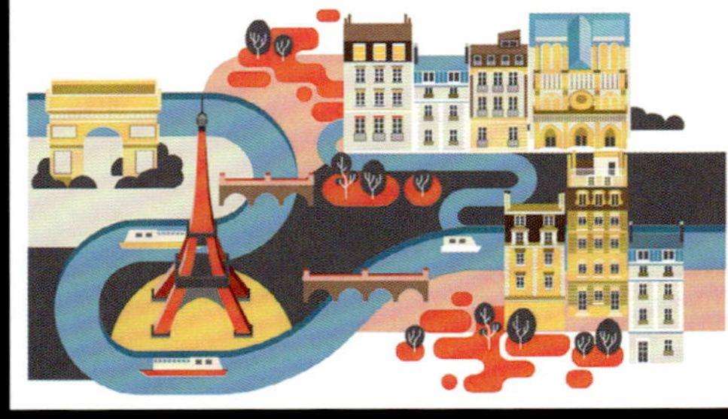

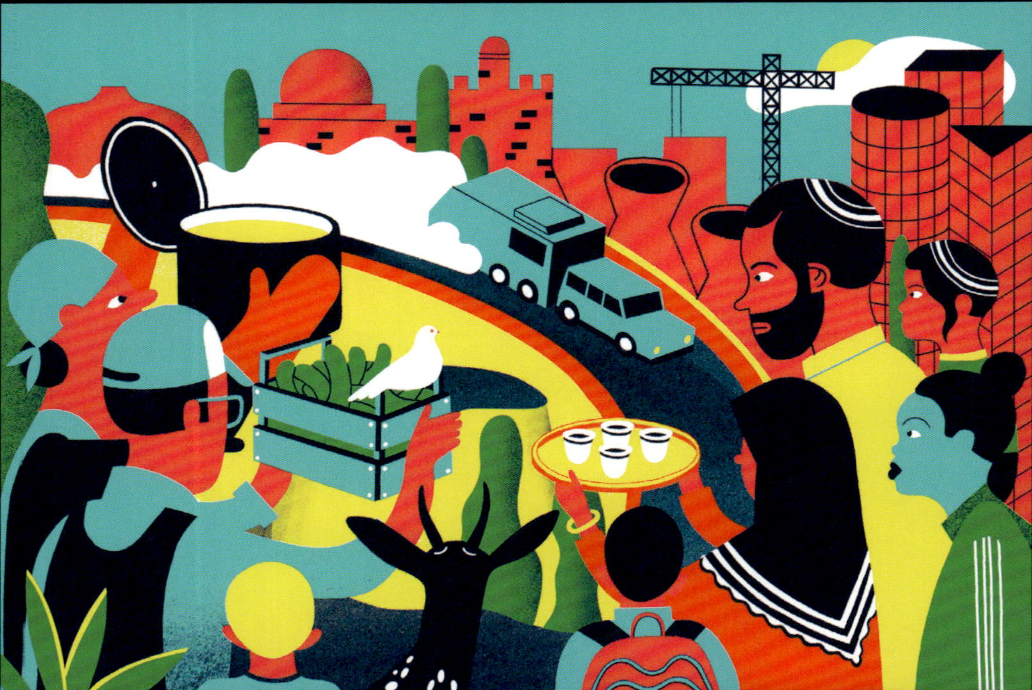

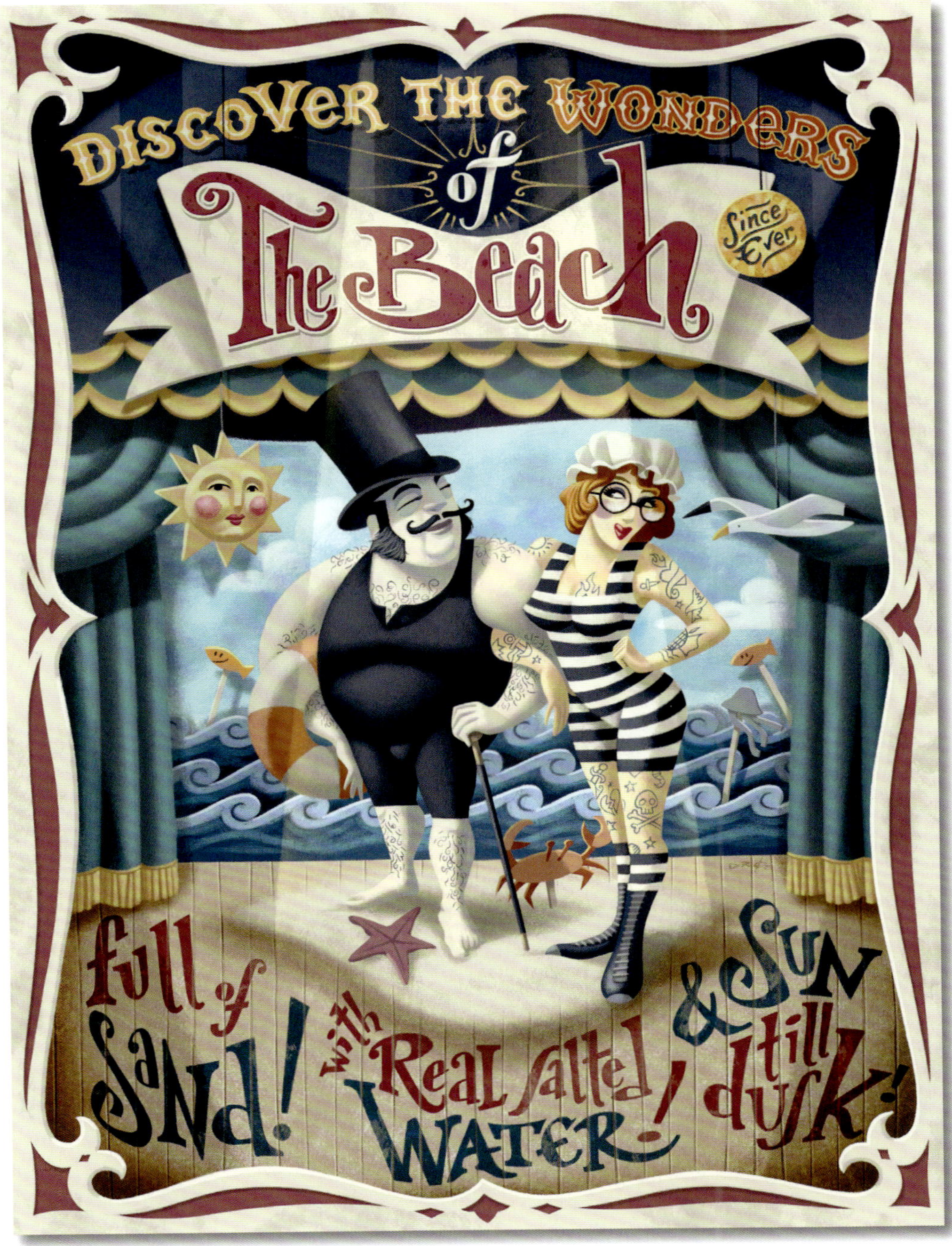

David De Ramón

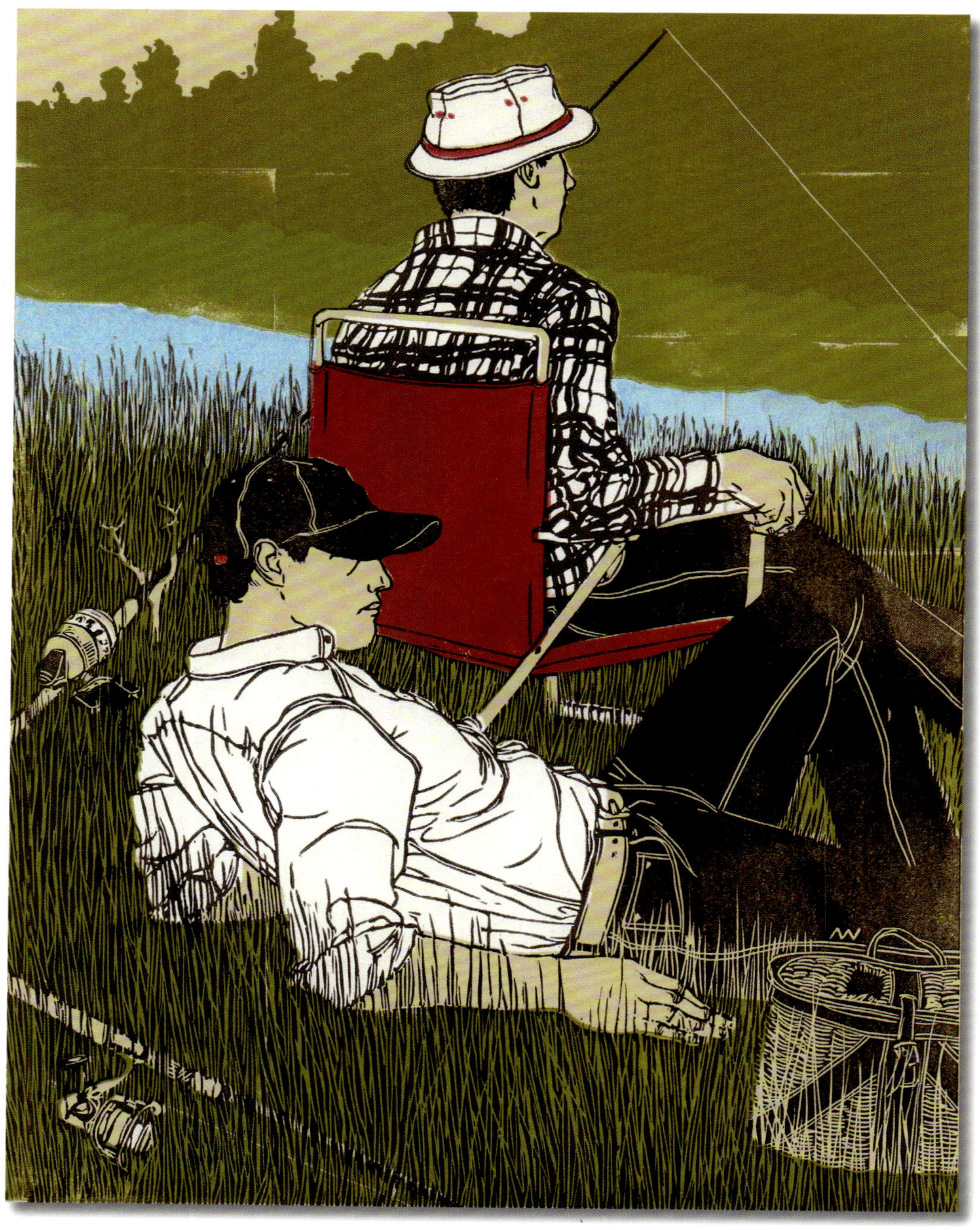

Andrew R. Wright

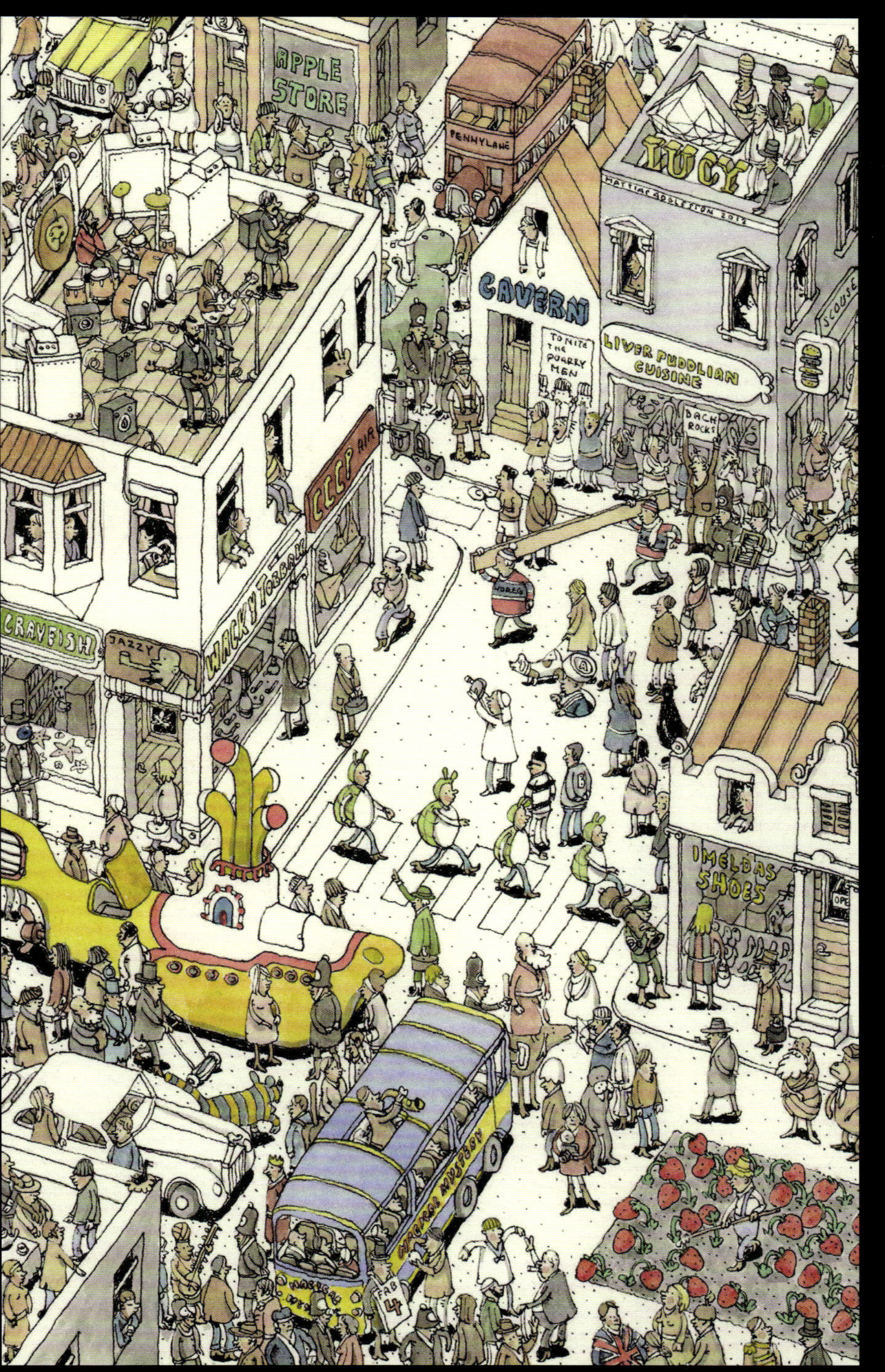

Mattias Adolfsson

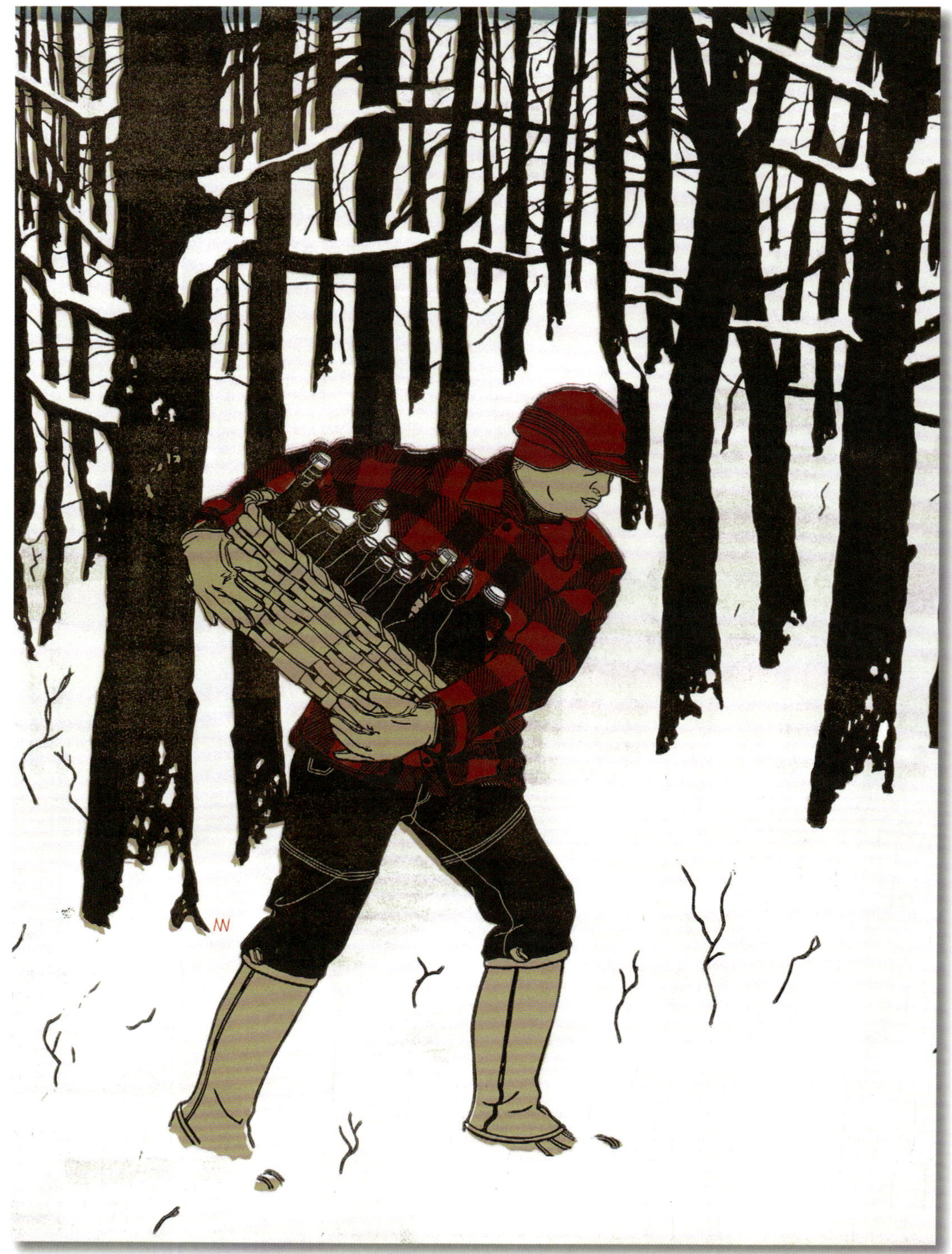

(L) *Andrew R Wright* (R) *Robert Neubecker*

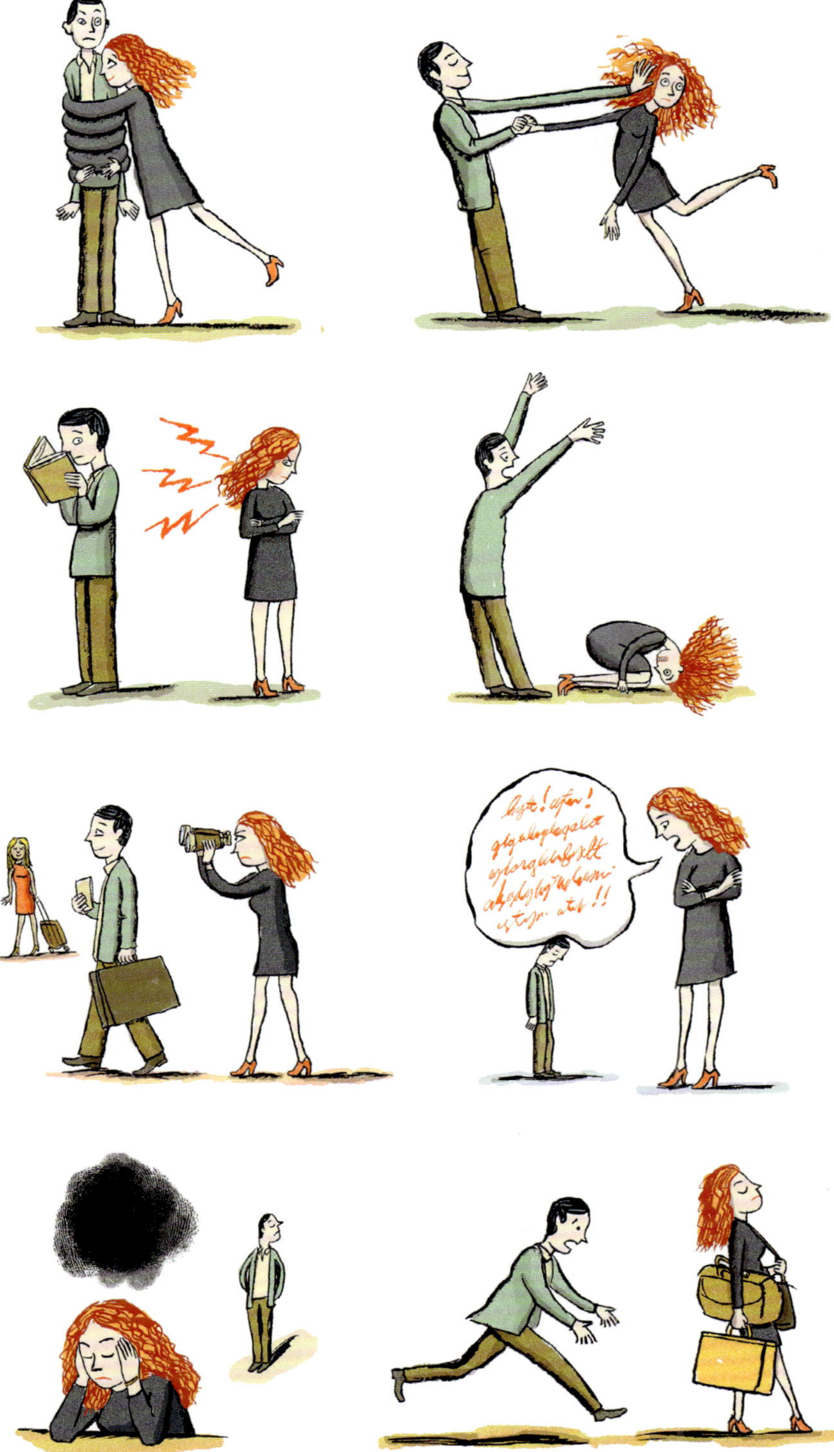

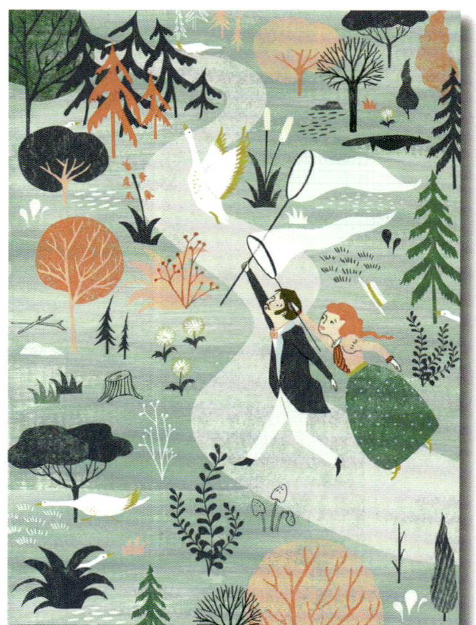

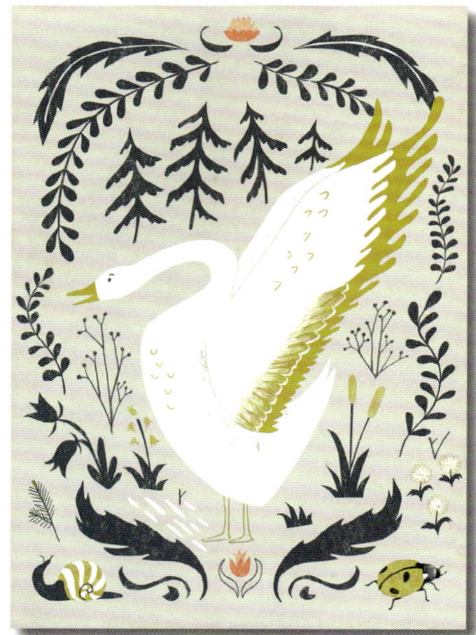

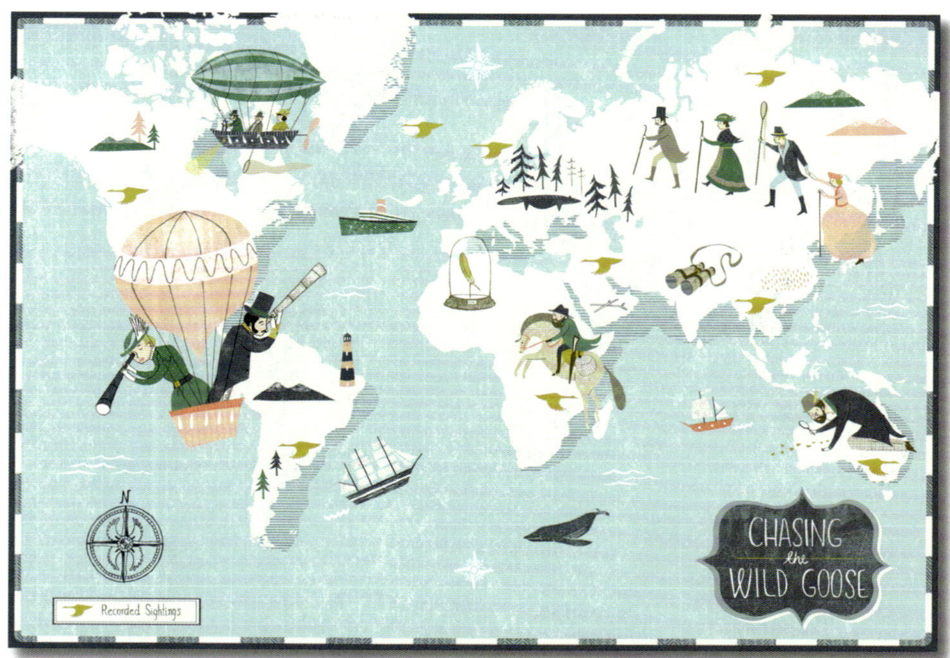

Angela Keoghan

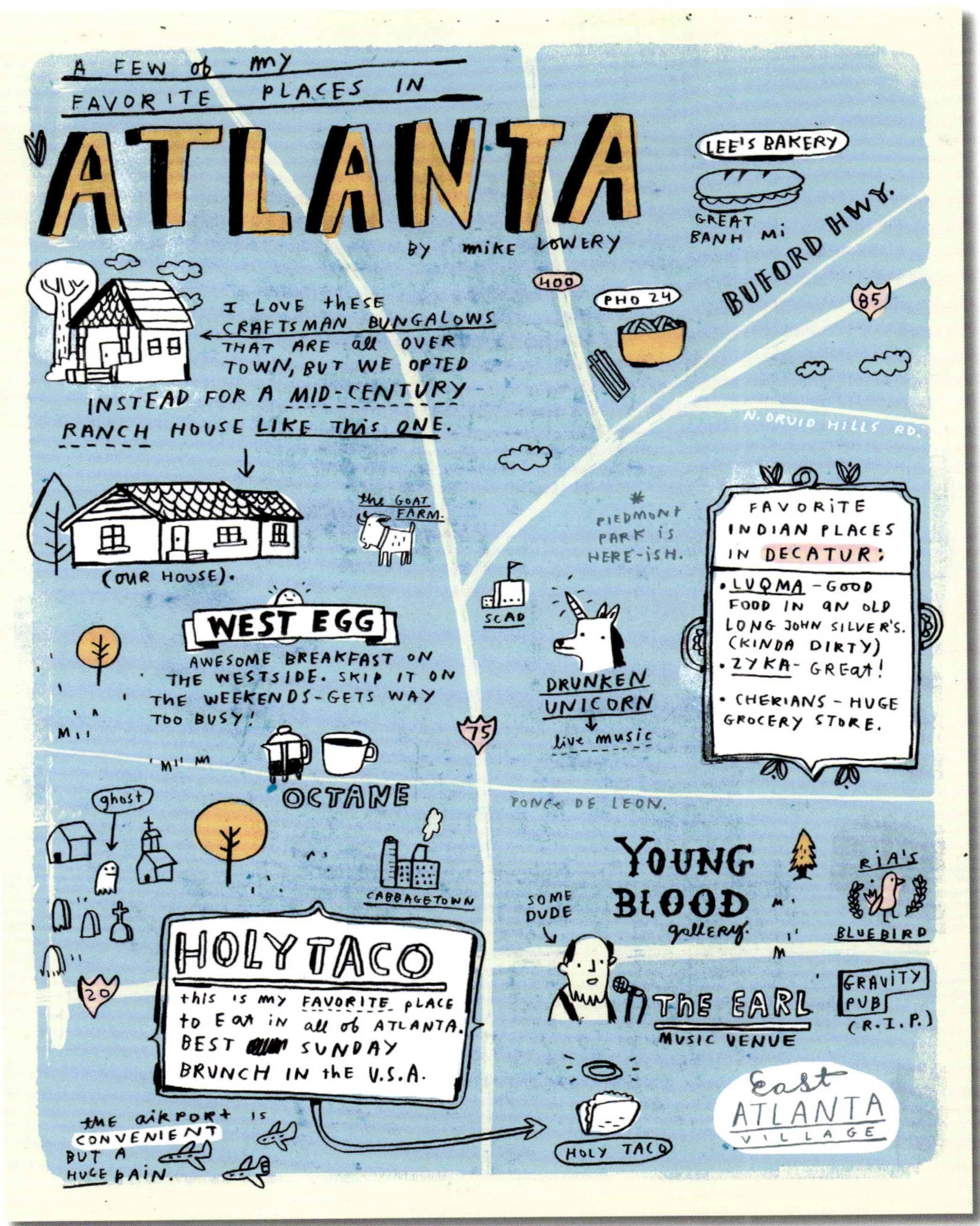
A FEW of my FAVORITE PLACES IN
ATLANTA
BY mike LOWERY
LEE'S BAKERY
GREAT BANH MI
BUFORD HWY.
400
PHO 24
85
I LOVE THESE CRAFTSMAN BUNGALOWS THAT ARE all OVER TOWN, BUT WE OPTED INSTEAD FOR A MID-CENTURY RANCH HOUSE LIKE THIS ONE.
N. DRUID HILLS RD.
(OUR HOUSE).
the GOAT FARM.
PIEDMONT PARK is HERE-ISH.
FAVORITE INDIAN PLACES IN DECATUR:
WEST EGG
AWESOME BREAKFAST ON THE WESTSIDE. SKIP IT ON THE WEEKENDS-GETS WAY TOO BUSY!
SCAD
DRUNKEN UNICORN
live music
• LUQMA - GOOD FOOD IN an OLD LONG JOHN SILVER'S. (KINDA DIRTY)
• ZYKA - GREat!
• CHERIANS - HUGE GROCERY STORE.
75
ghost
OCTANE
PONCE DE LEON.
CABBAGETOWN
YOUNG BLOOD gallery.
RIA'S
BLUEBIRD
20
SOME DUDE
HOLY TACO
this is my FAVORITE place to Eat in all of ATLANTA. BEST SUNDAY BRUNCH IN the U.S.A.
THE EARL
MUSIC VENUE
GRAVITY PUB
(R.I.P.)
the airport is CONVENIENT BUT A HUGE PAIN.
HOLY TACO
East ATLANTA VILLAGE

Mike Lowery

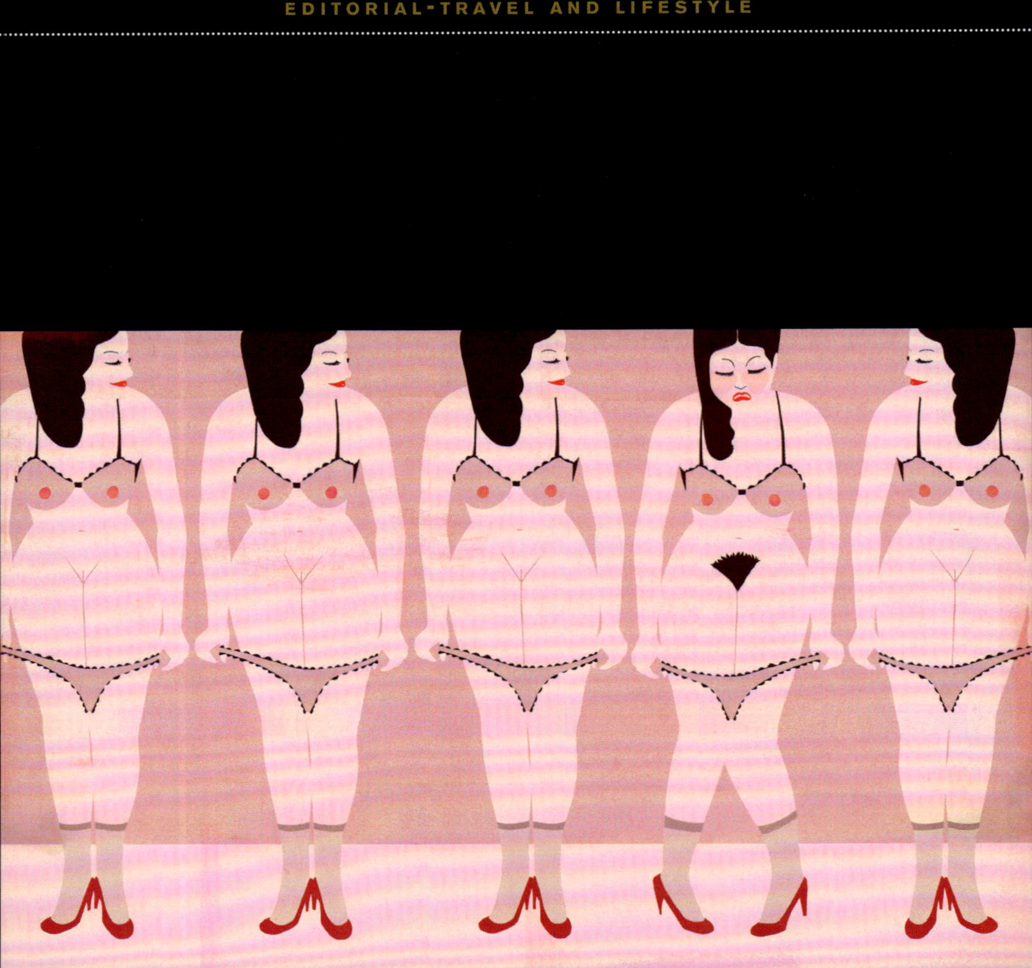

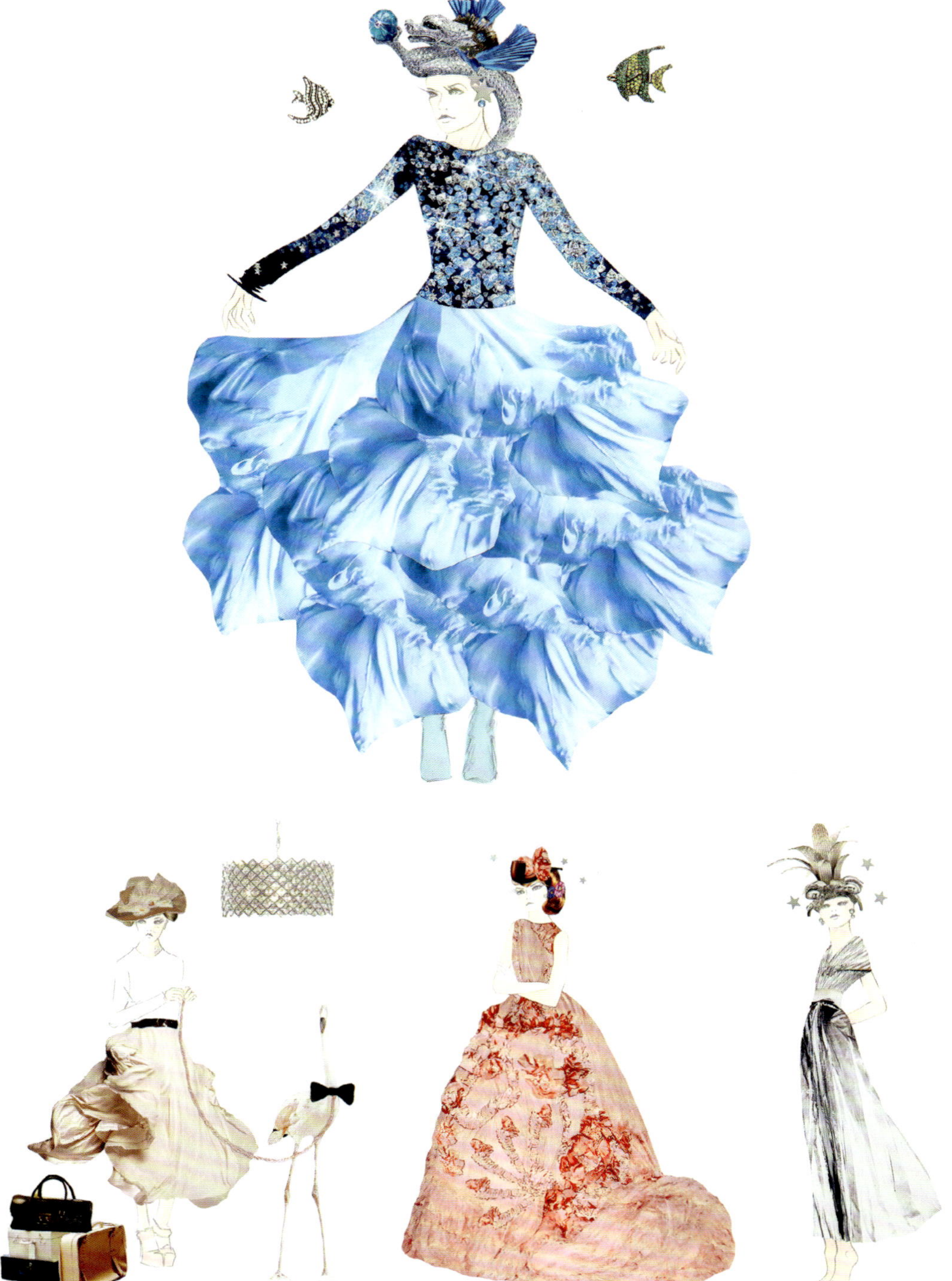

Magpie Belle

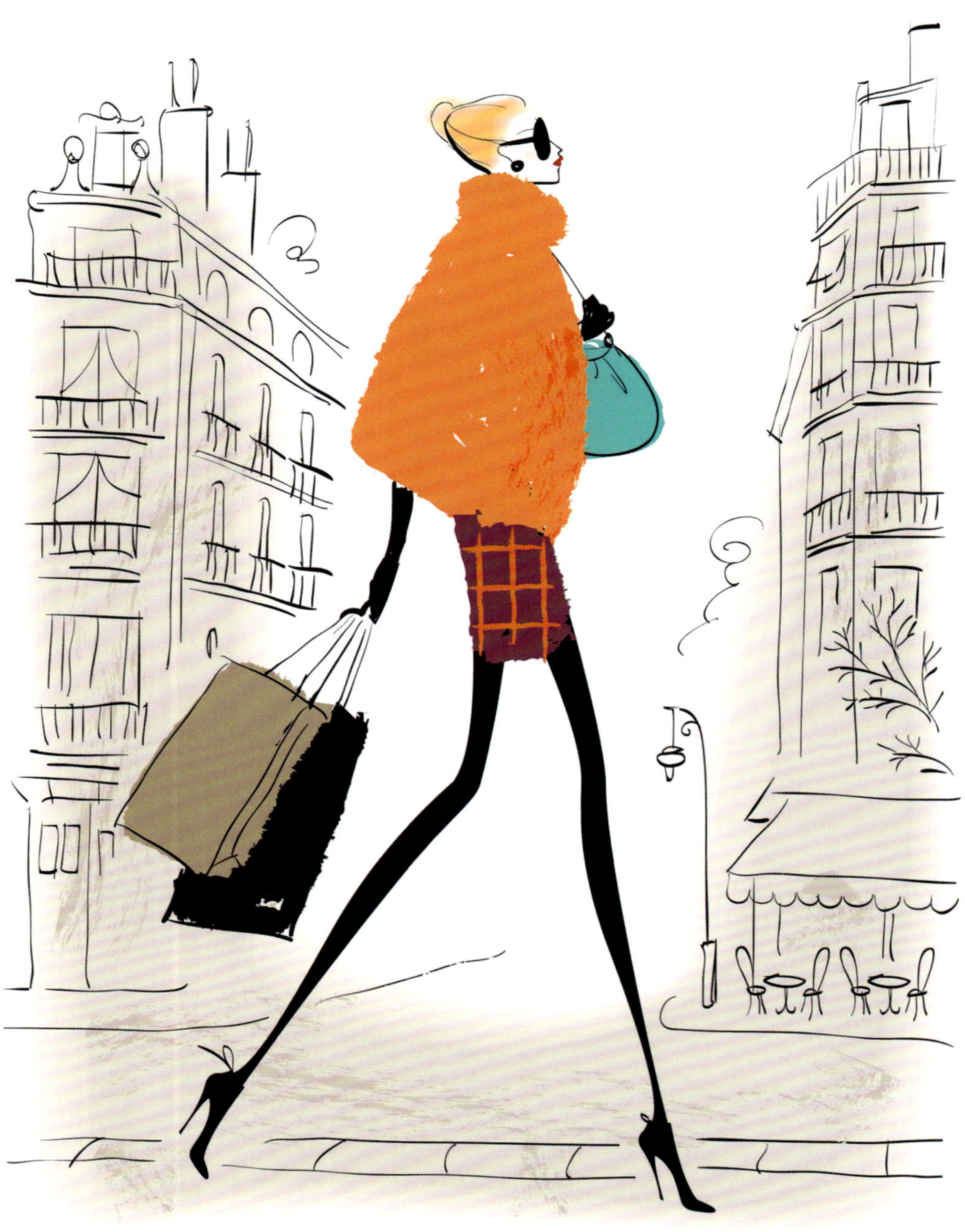

BRONZE *Bojana Dimitrovski*

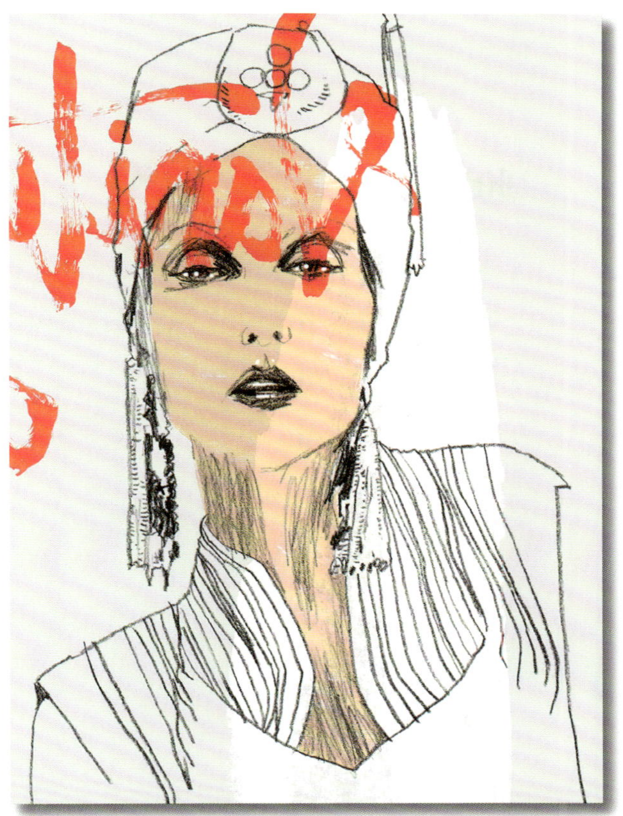

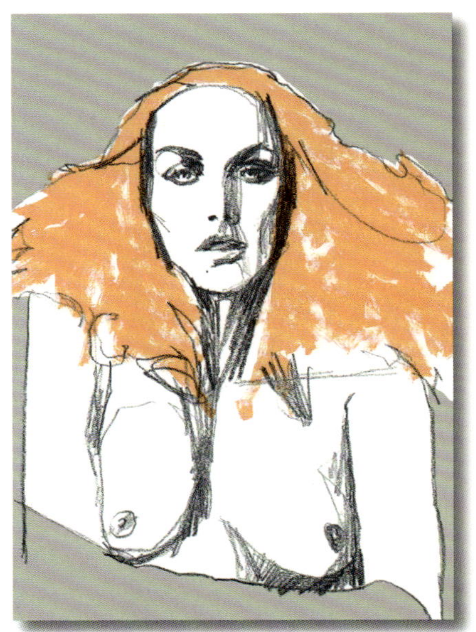

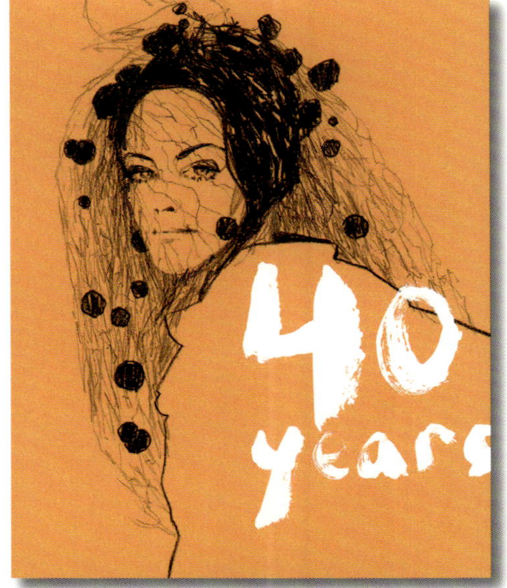

Jonny Ruzzo

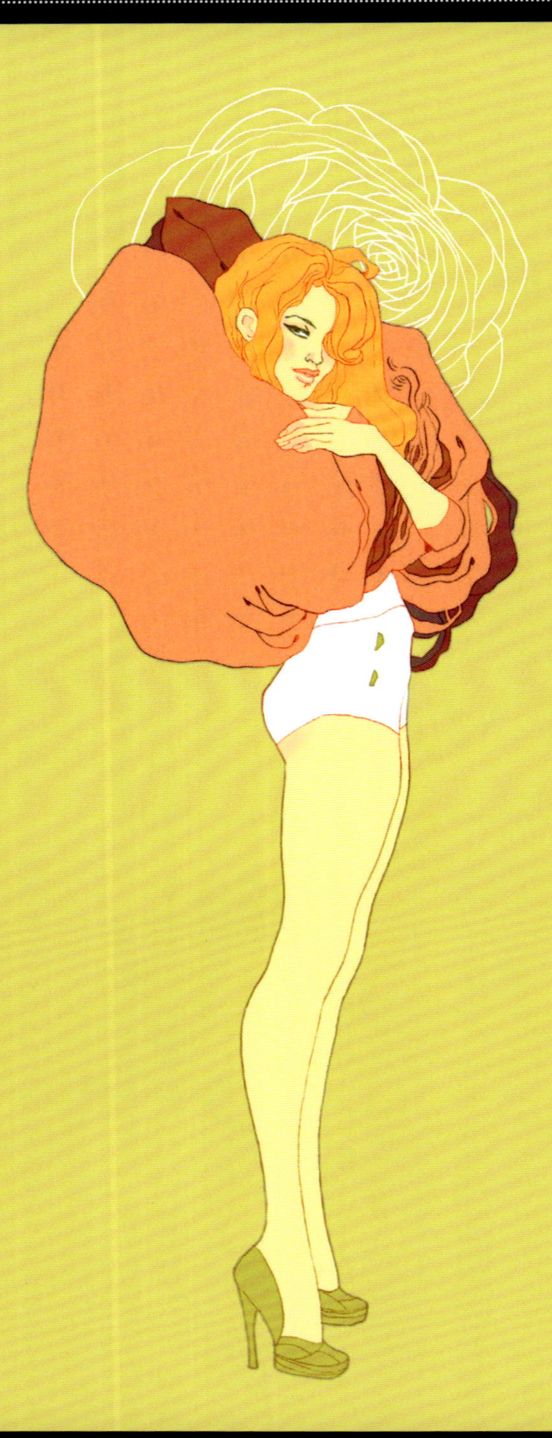

Marguerite Sauvage

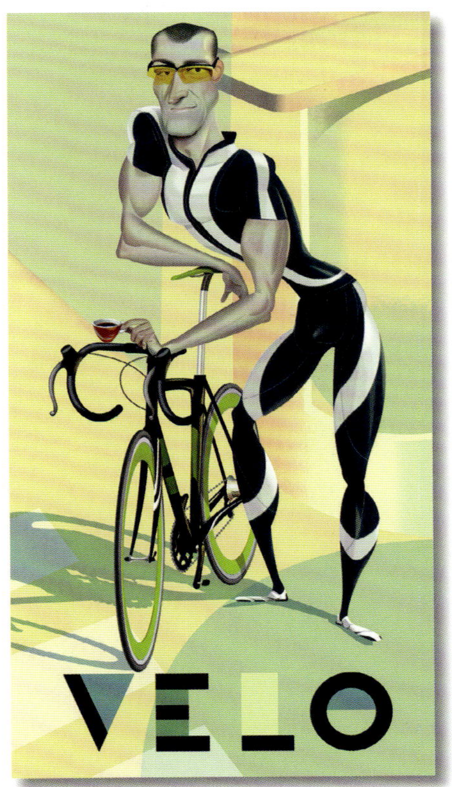

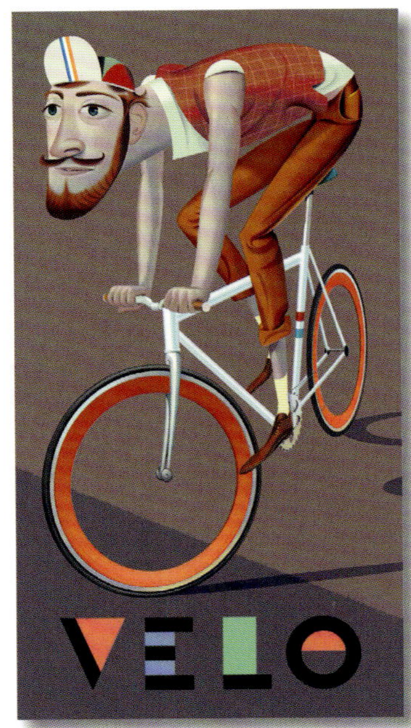

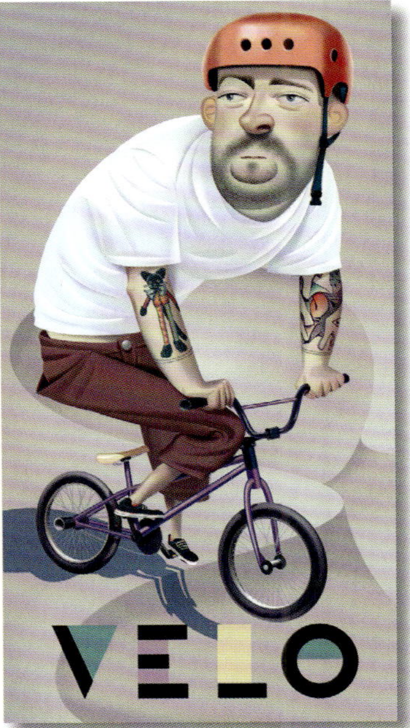

Nigel Buchanan

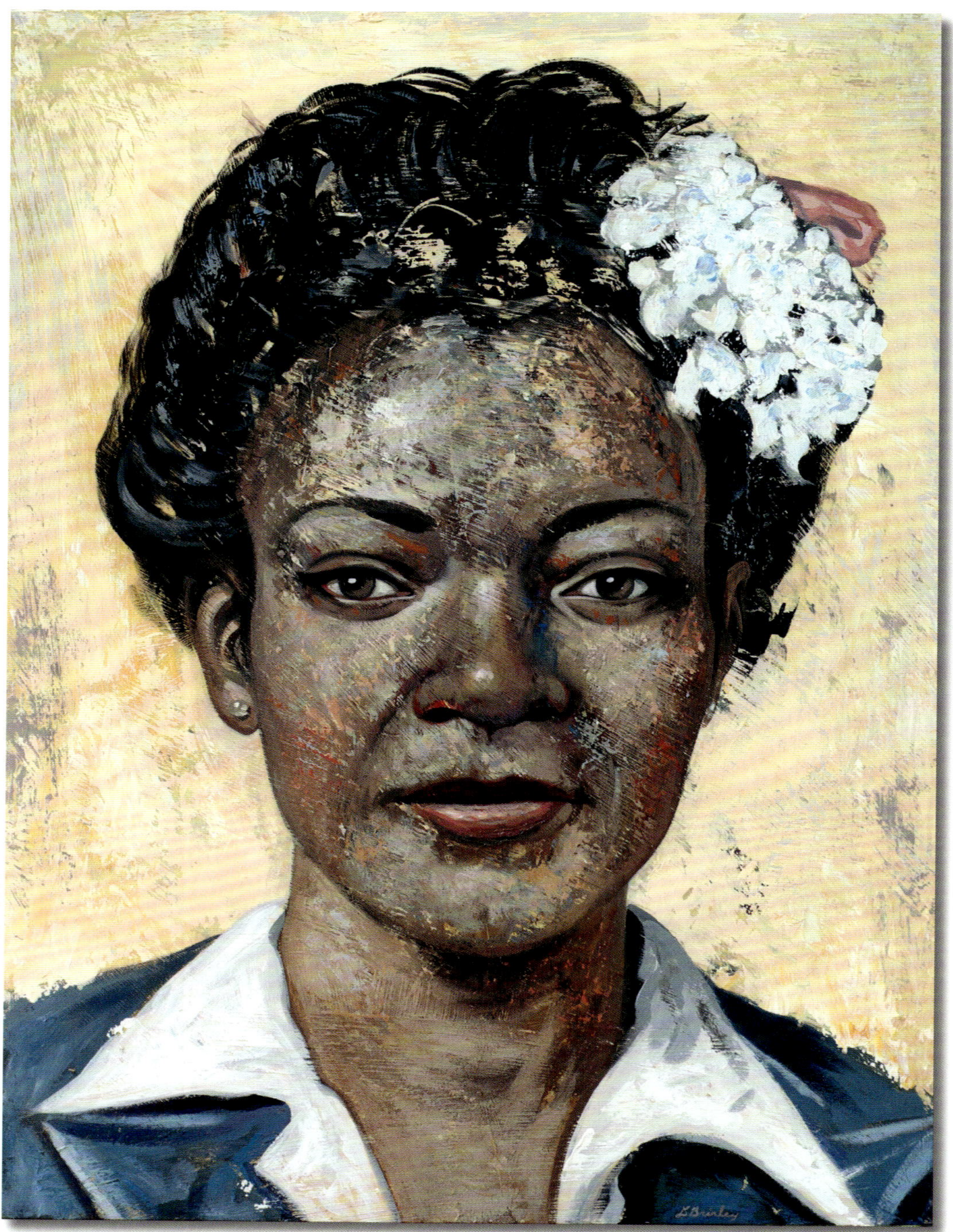

David M. Brinley

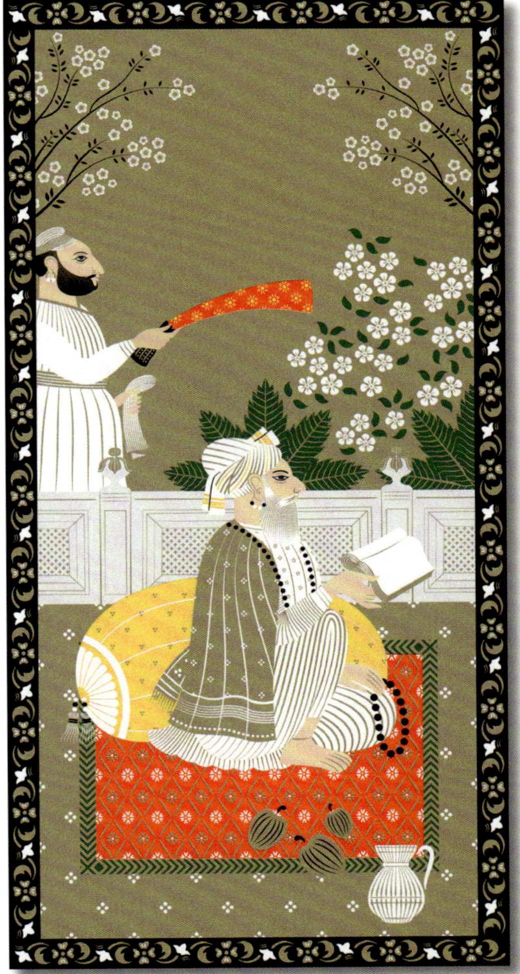

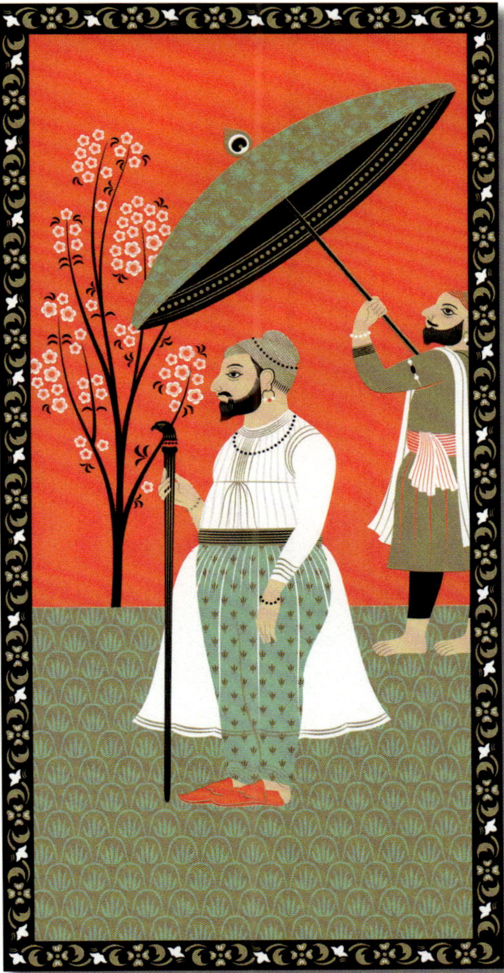

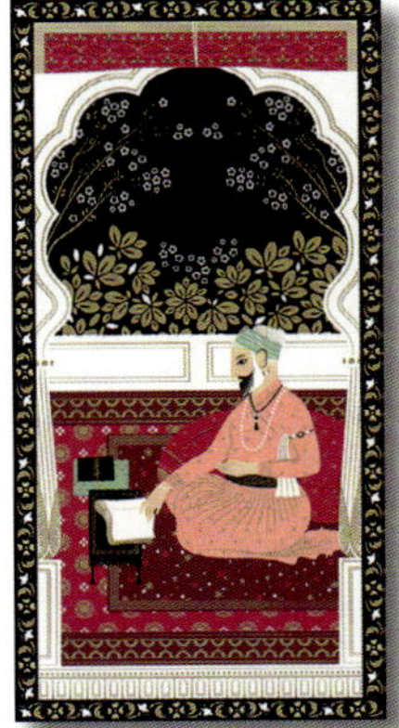

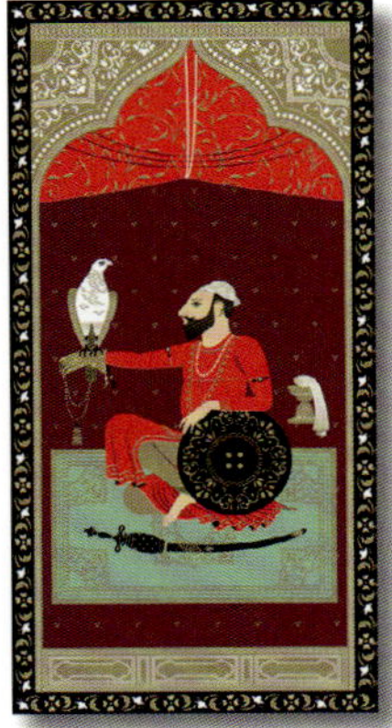

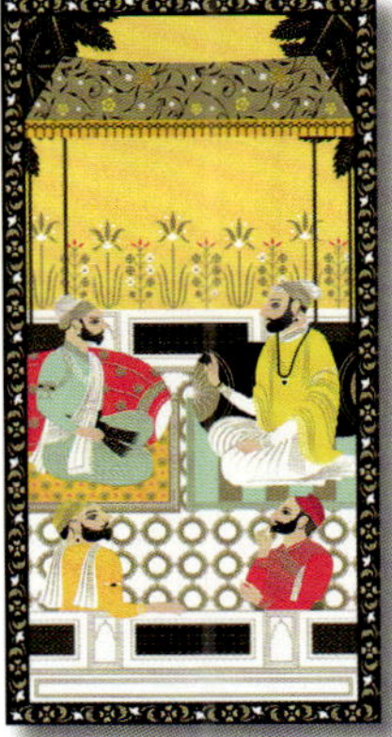

Studio Tipi

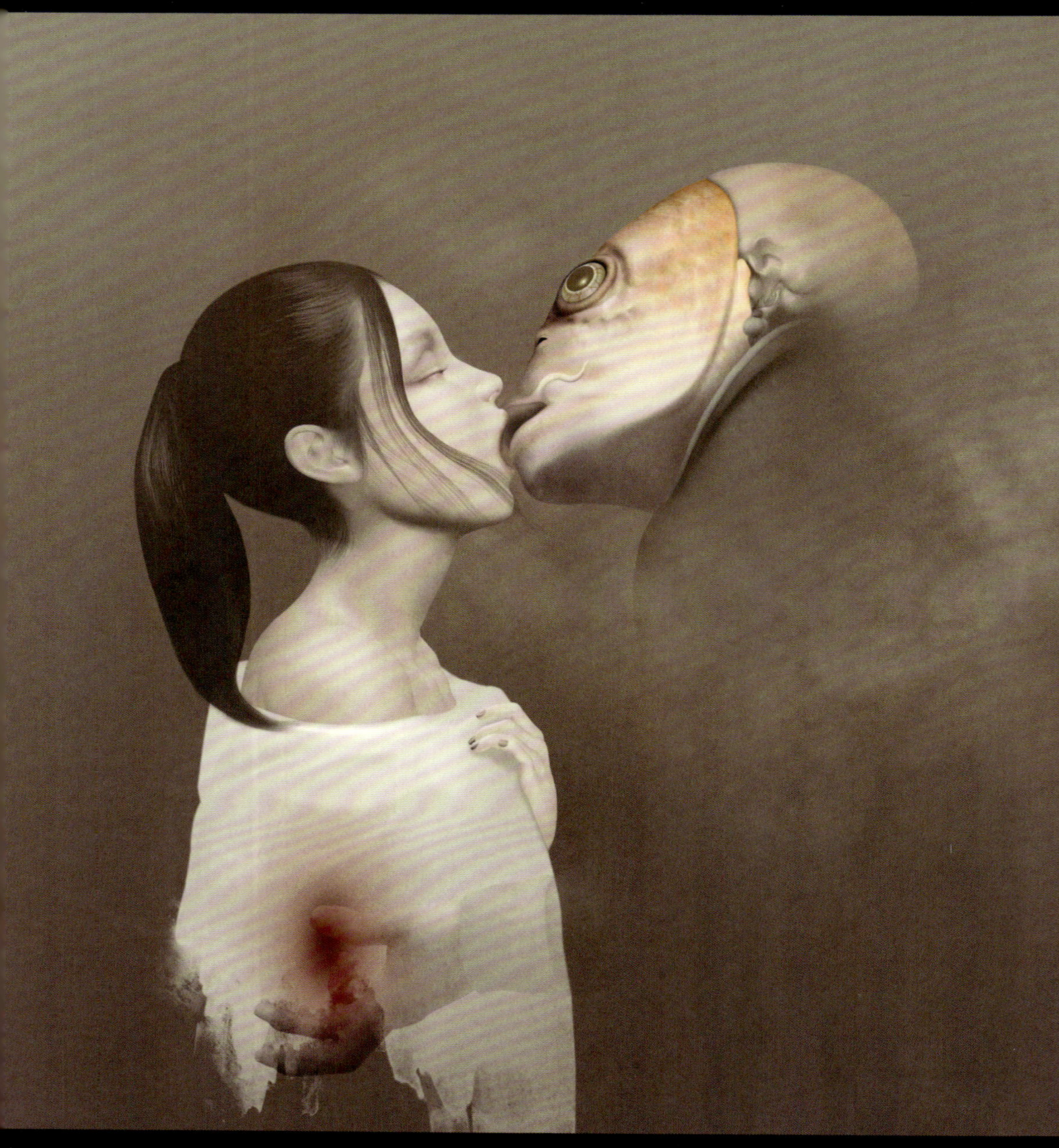

David Ho

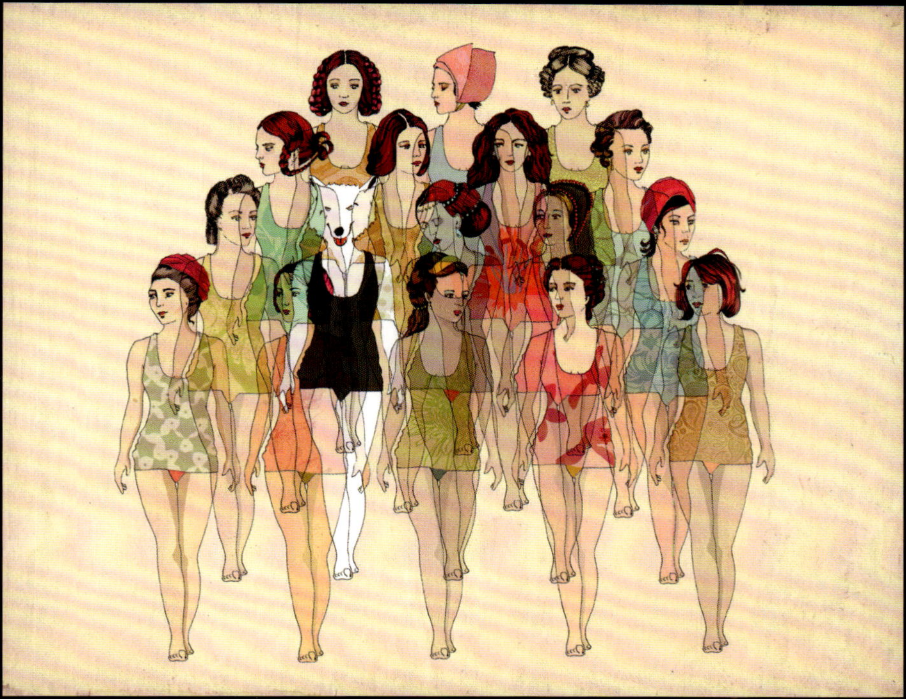

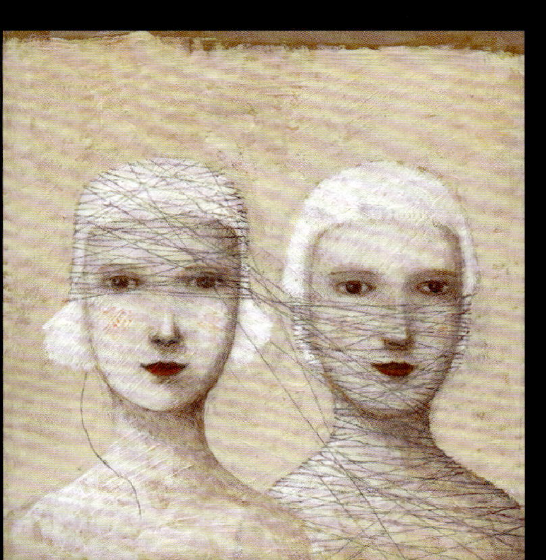

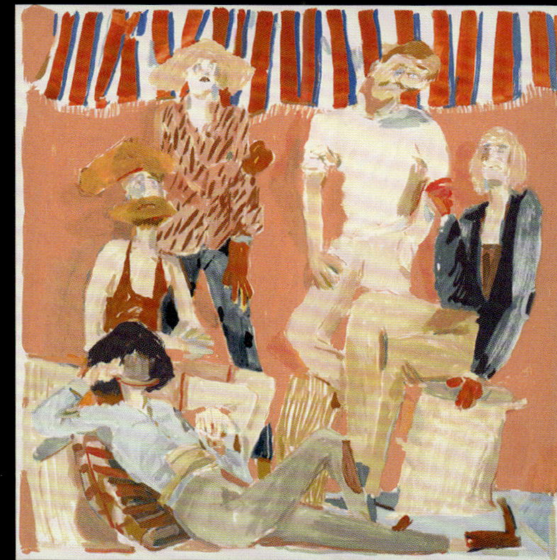

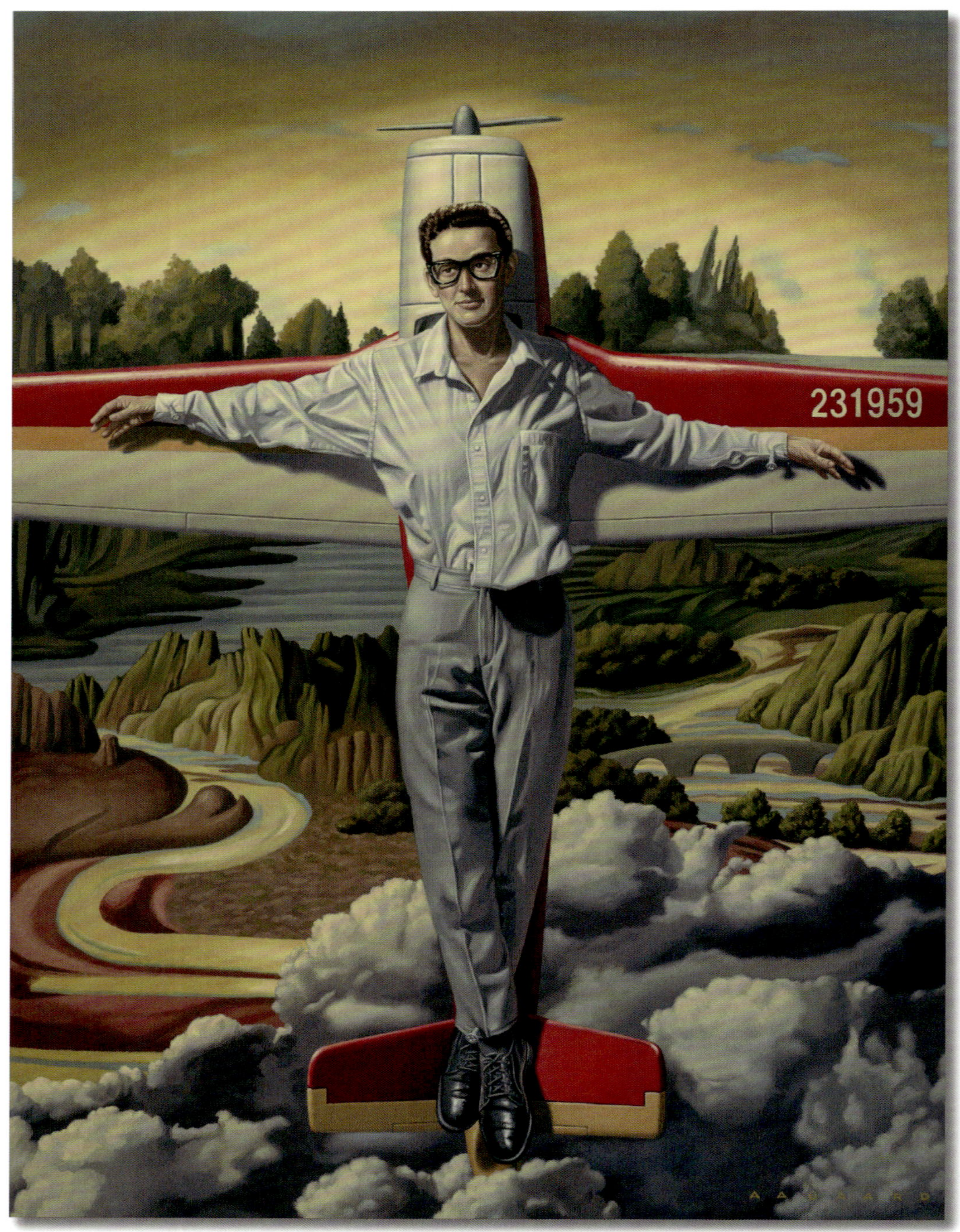

Gary Aagaard

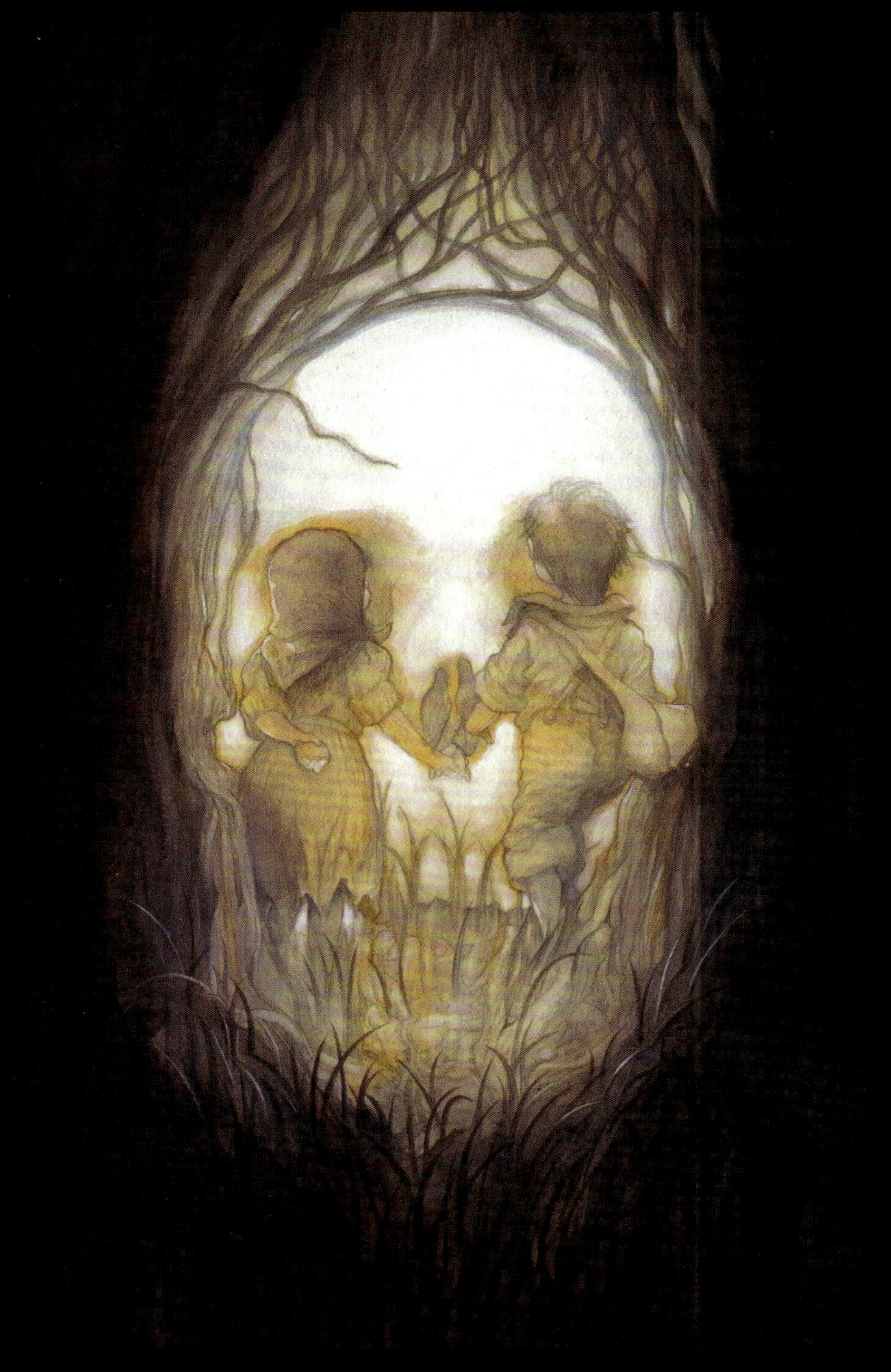

Tohru Patrick Awa

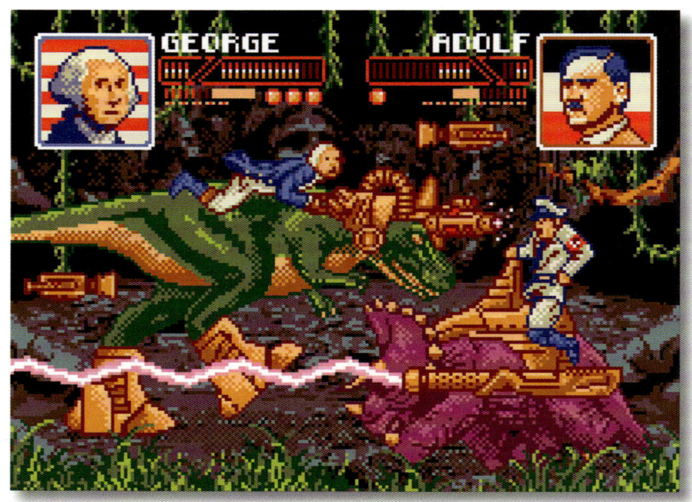

GEORGE
ADOLF

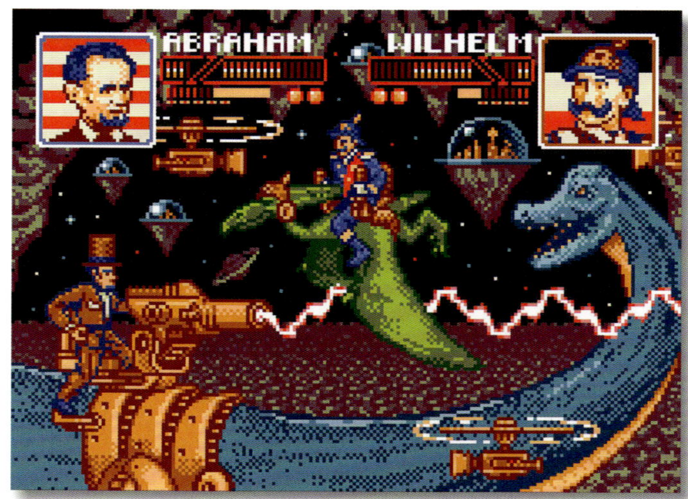

ABRAHAM
WILHELM

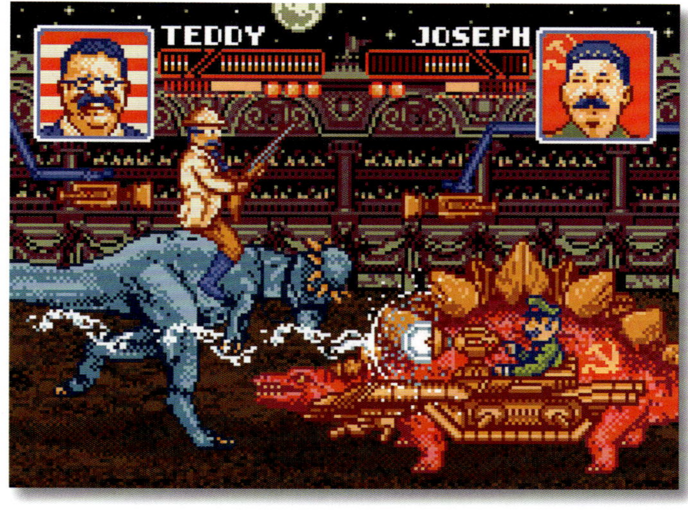

TEDDY
JOSEPH

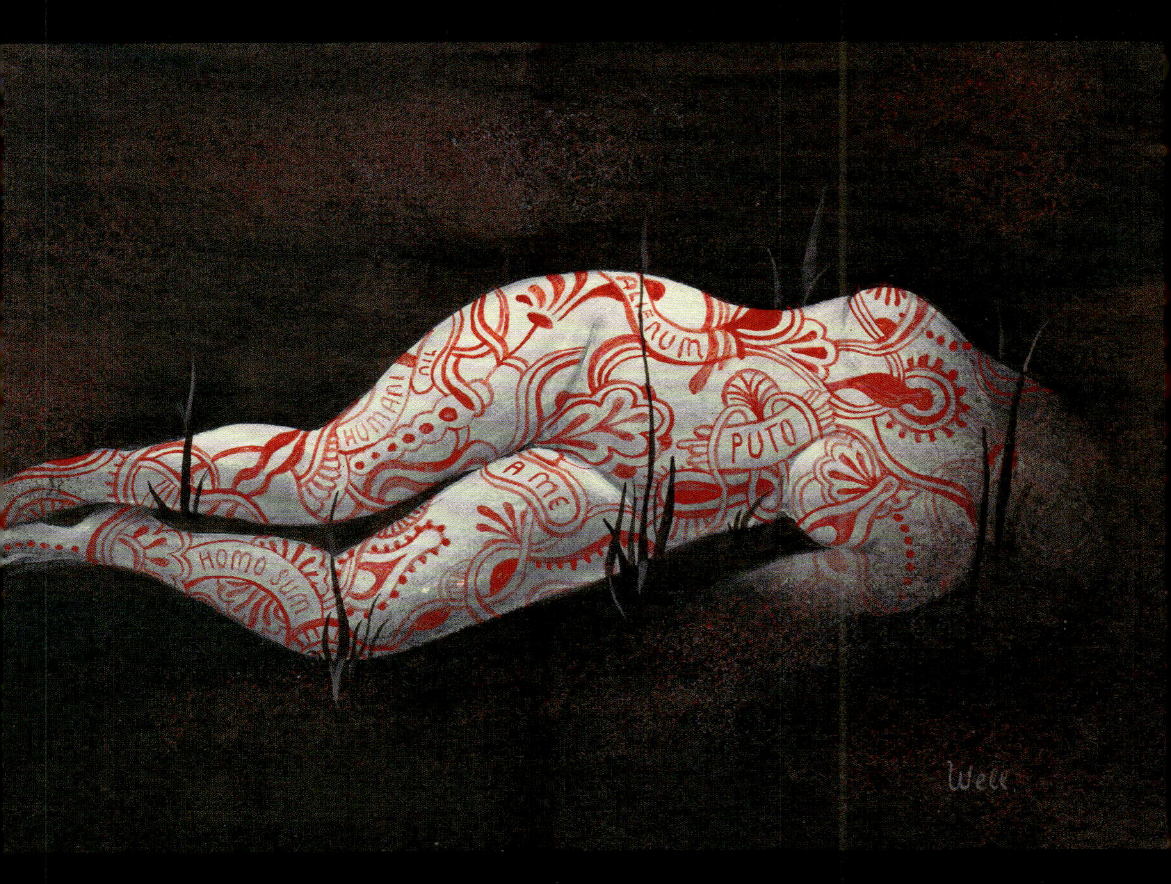

(L) *Jude Buffum* (R) *Alice Wellinger*

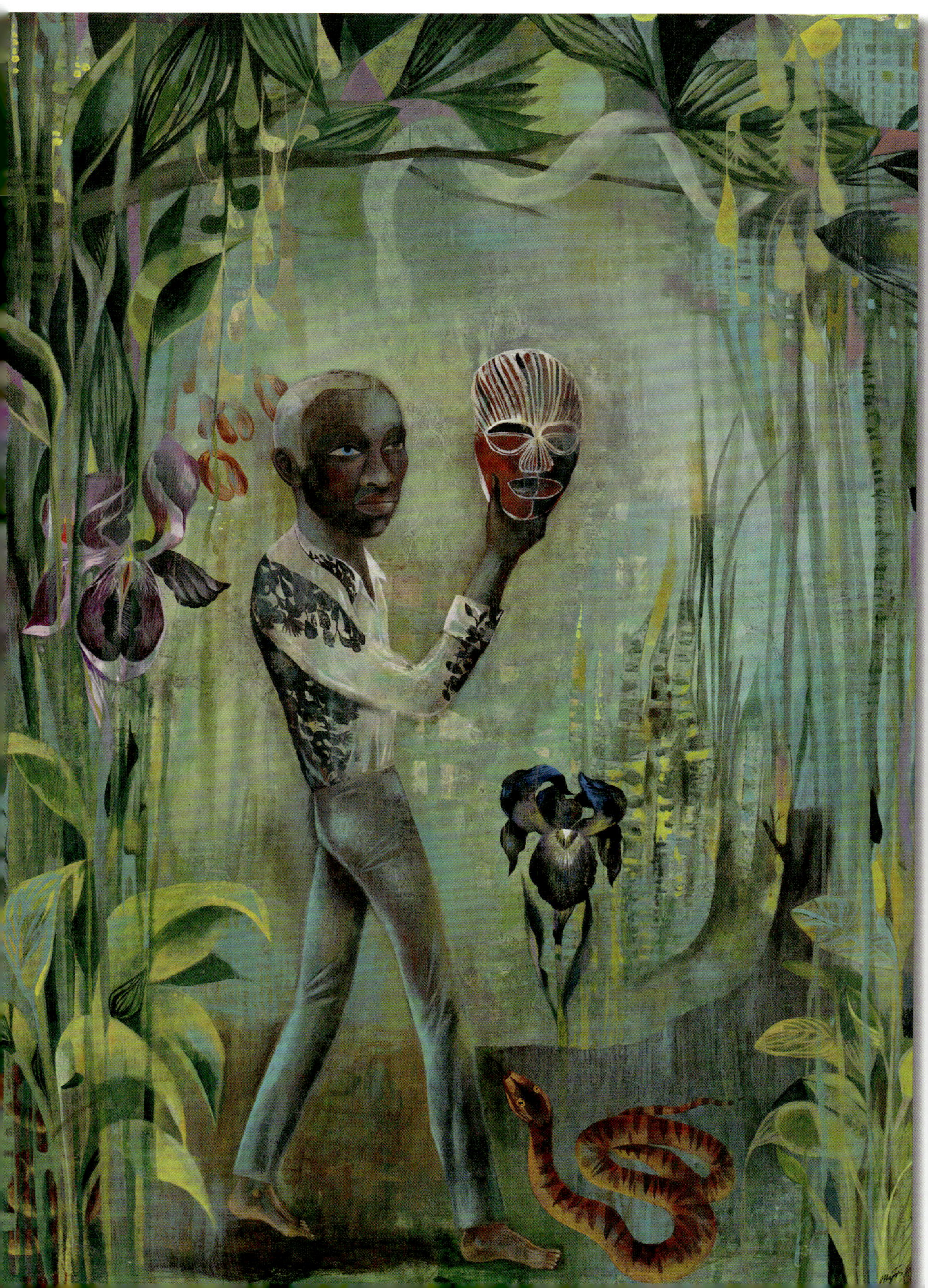

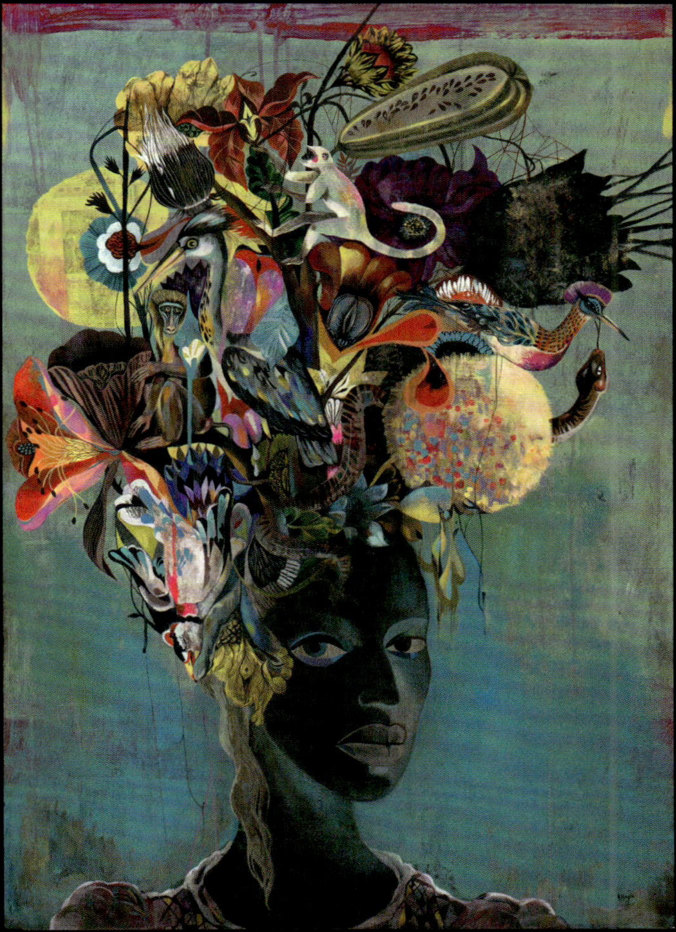

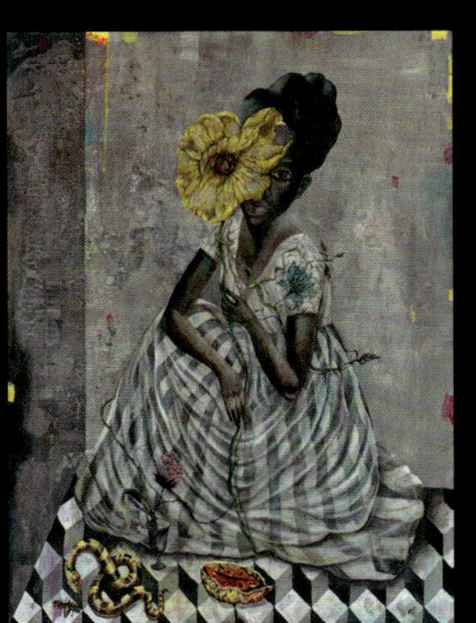

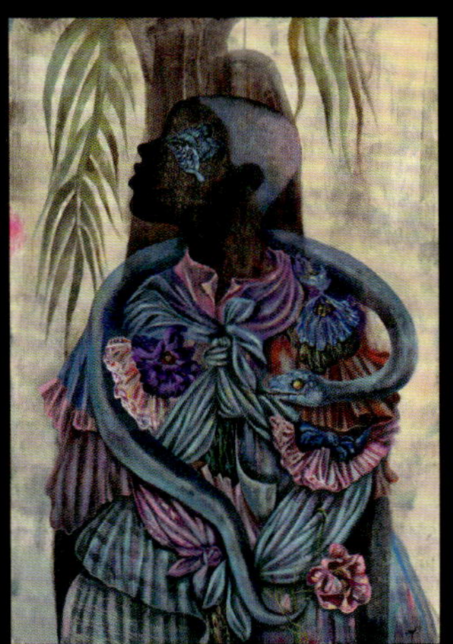

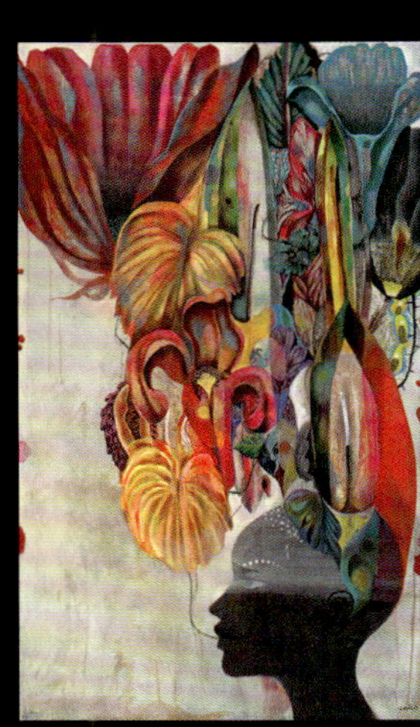

Olaf Hajek

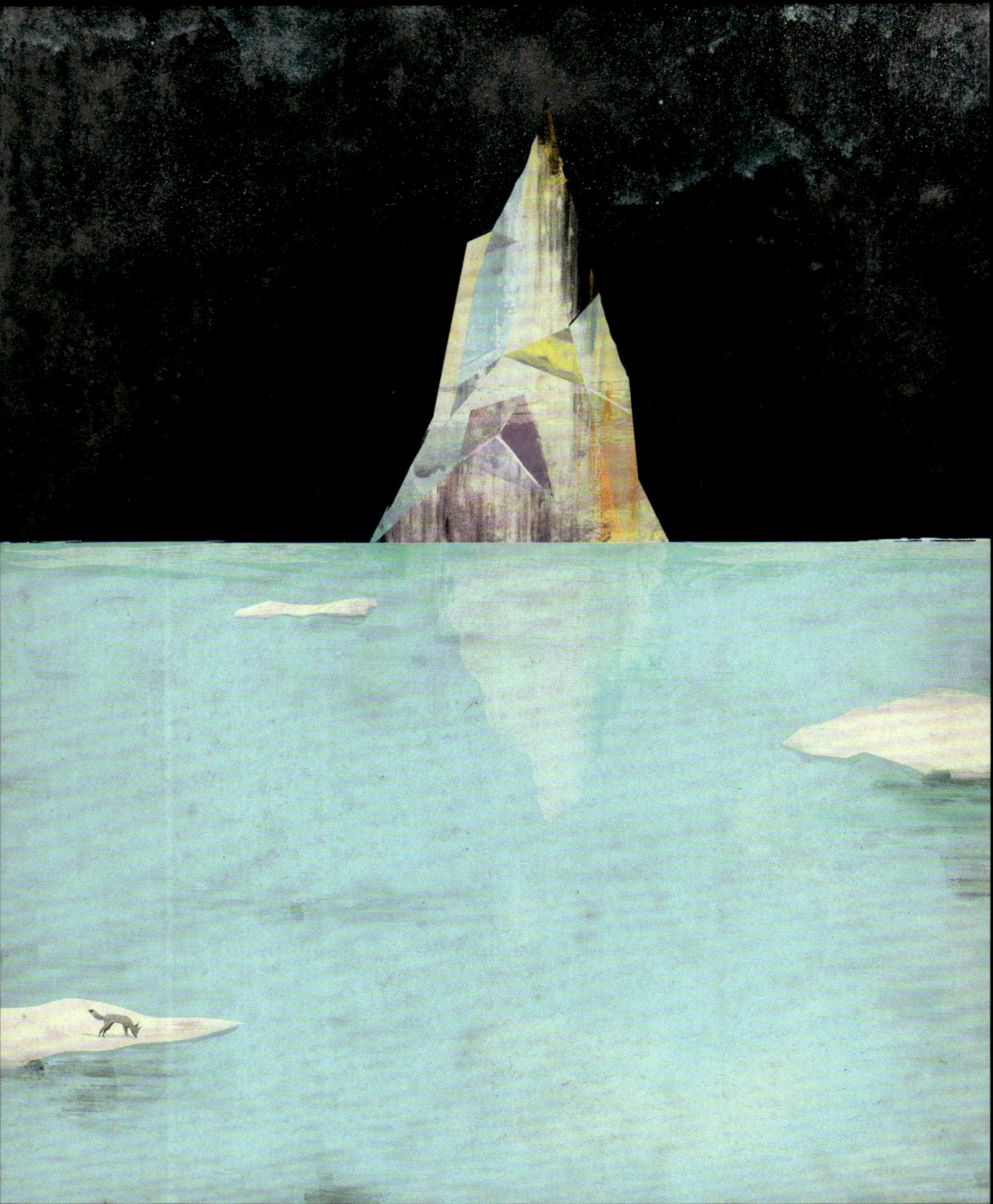

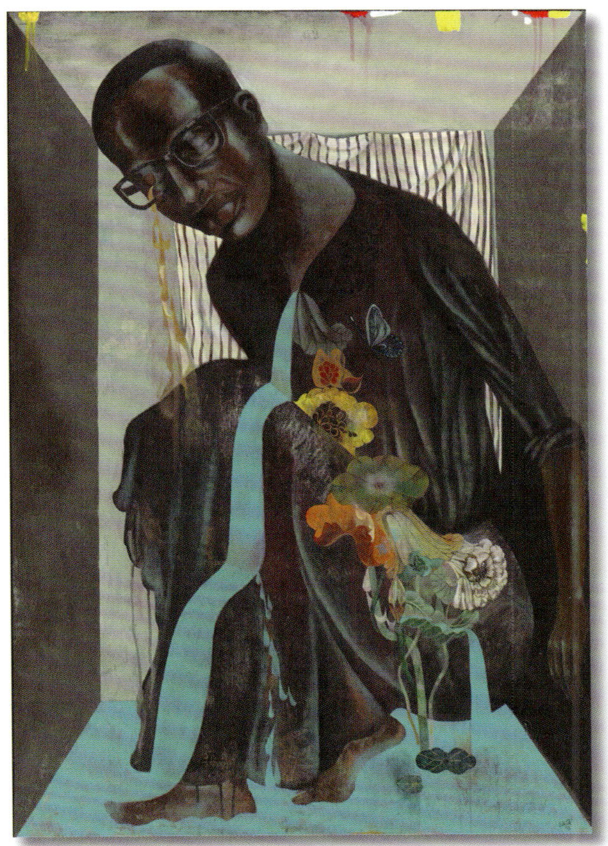

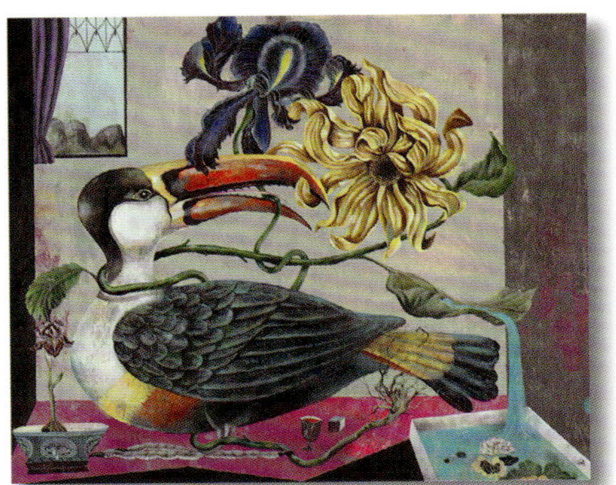

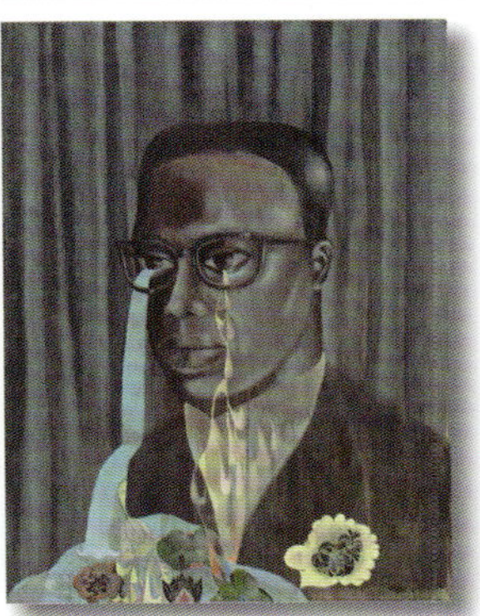

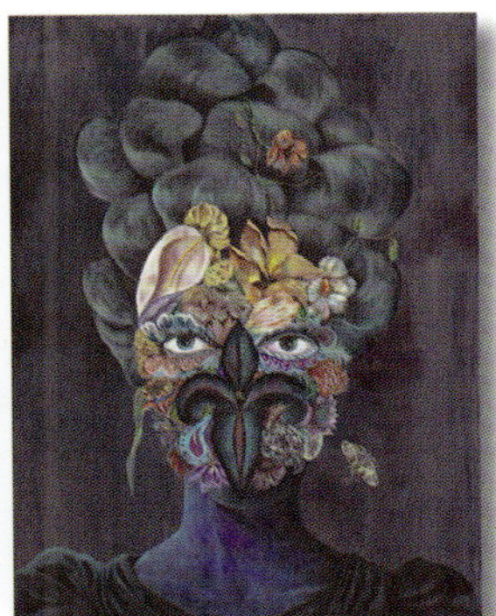

Olaf Hajek

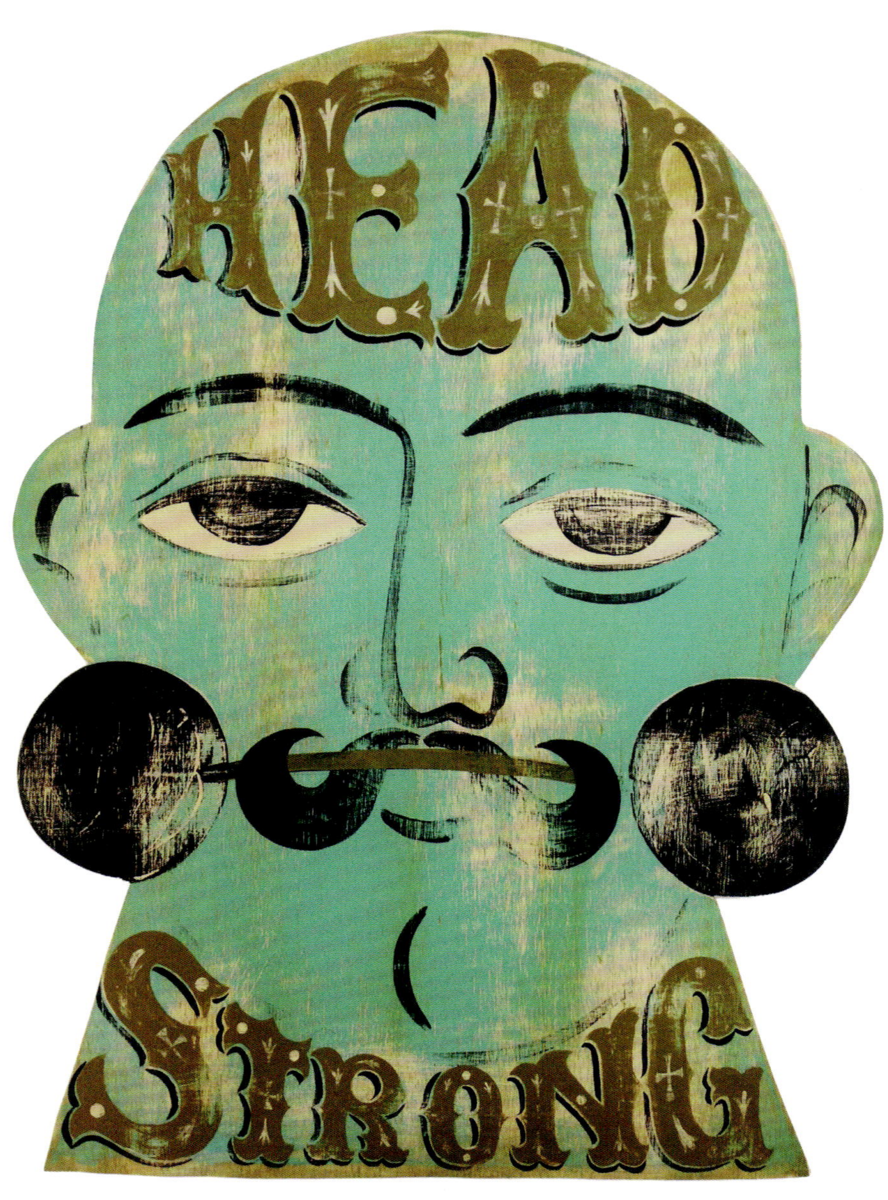

Christopher Nielsen

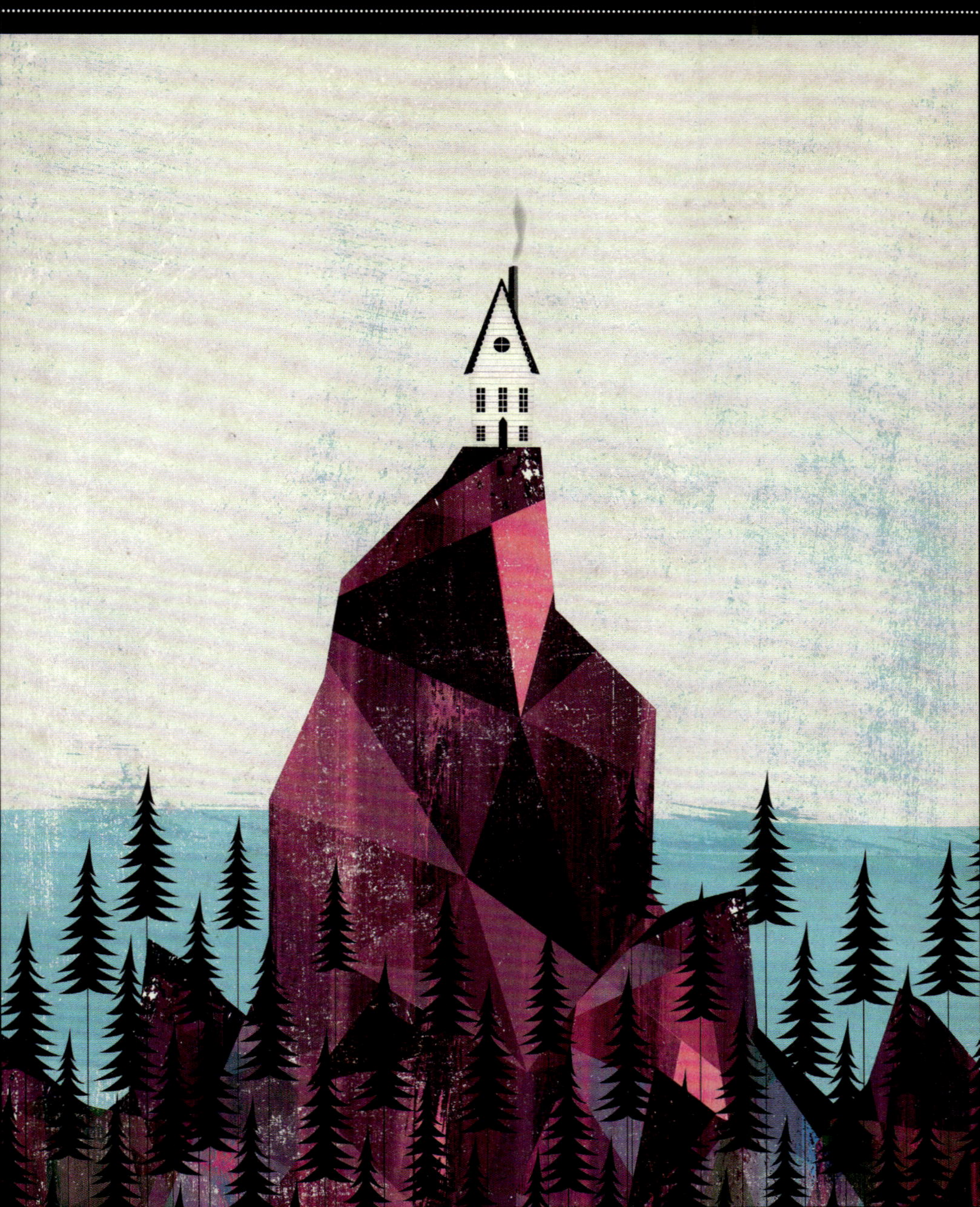

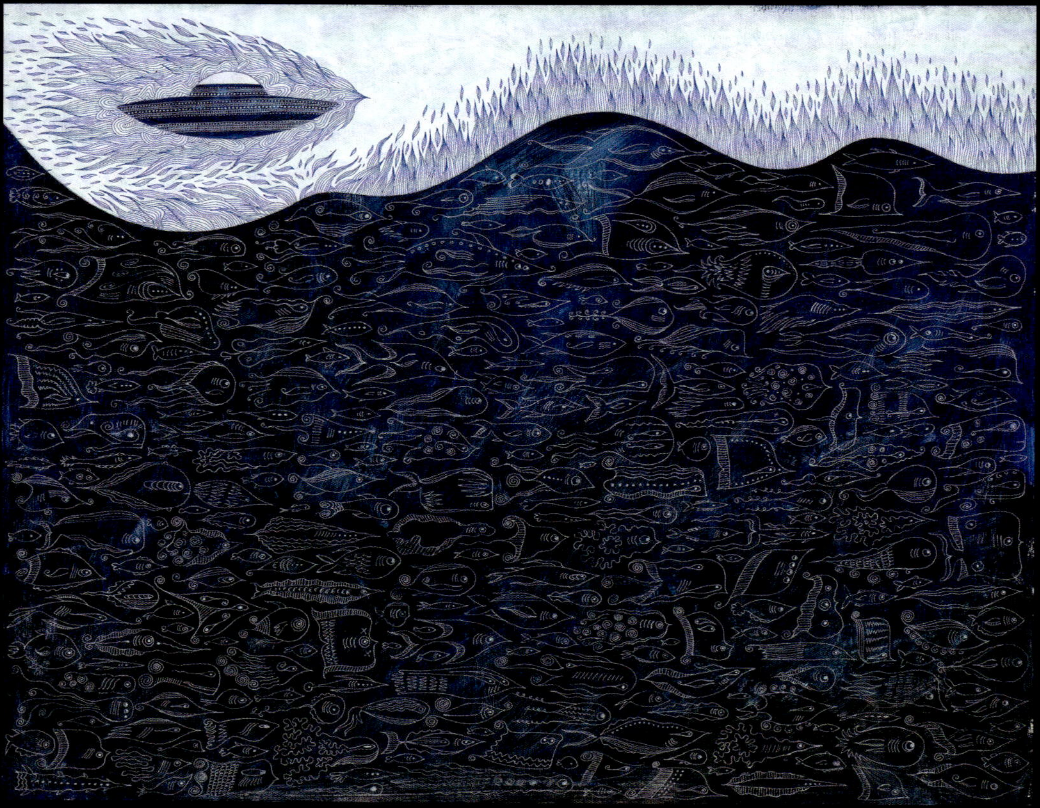

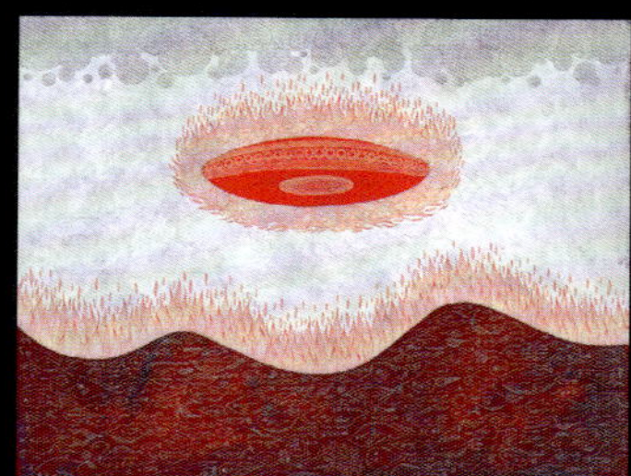

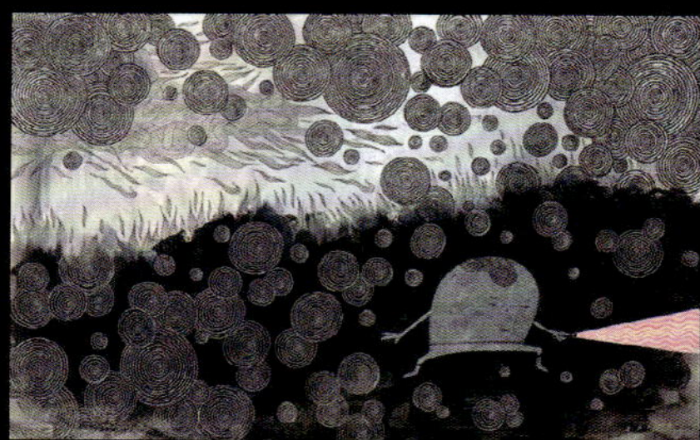

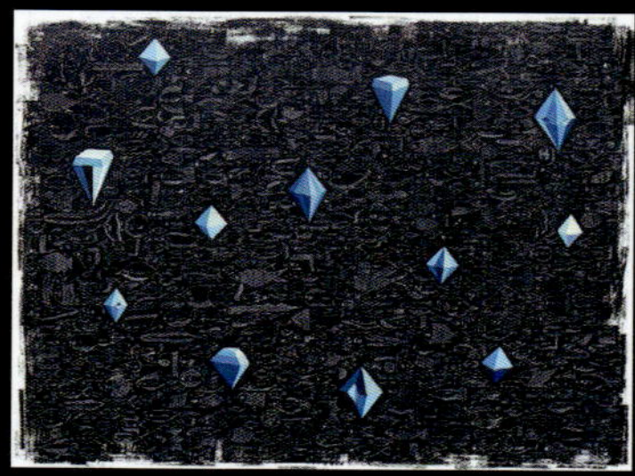

 Scott Bakal *Adam S. Doyle*

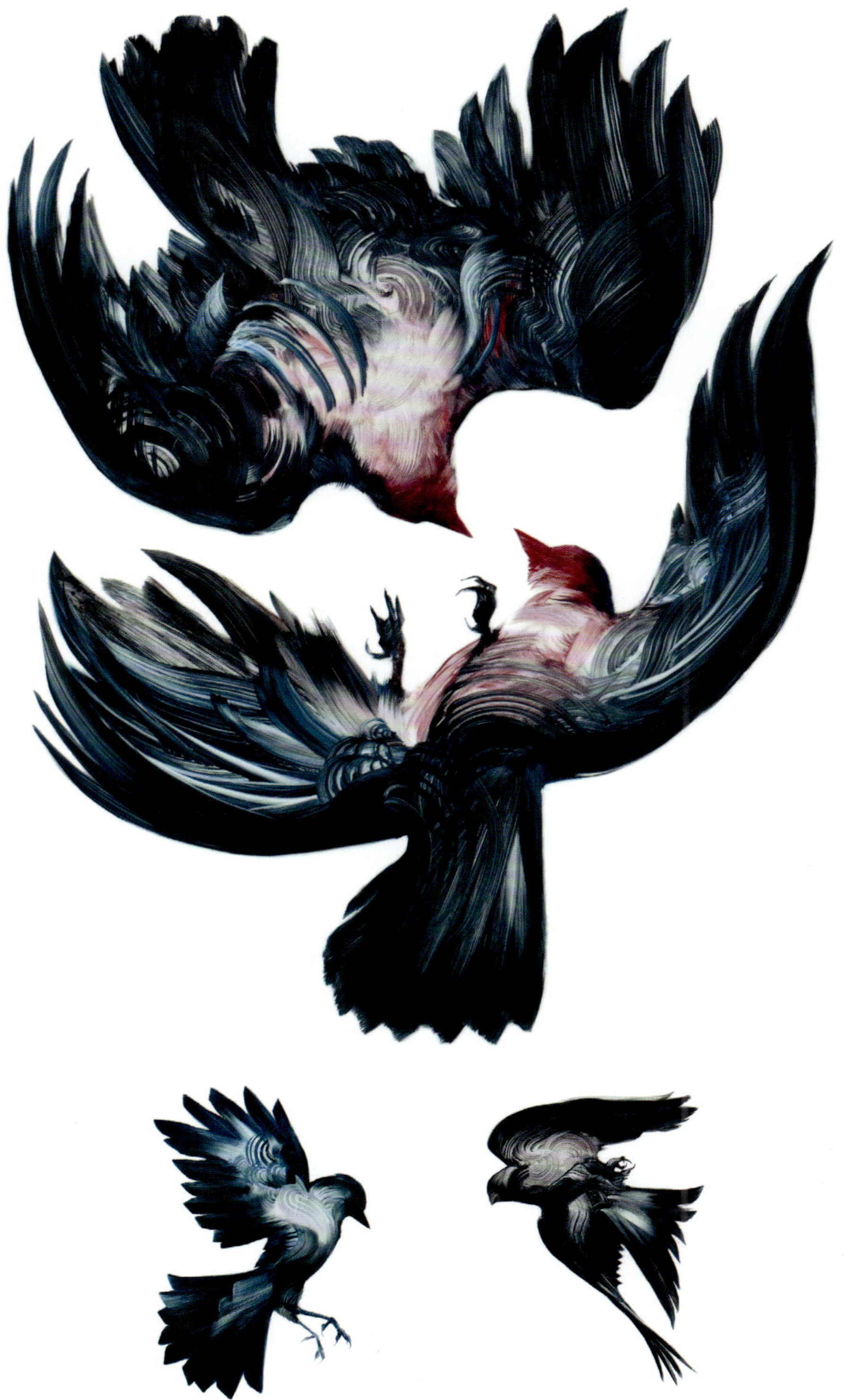

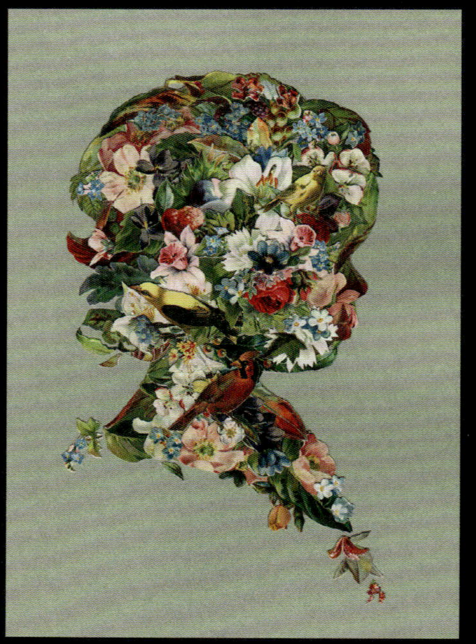

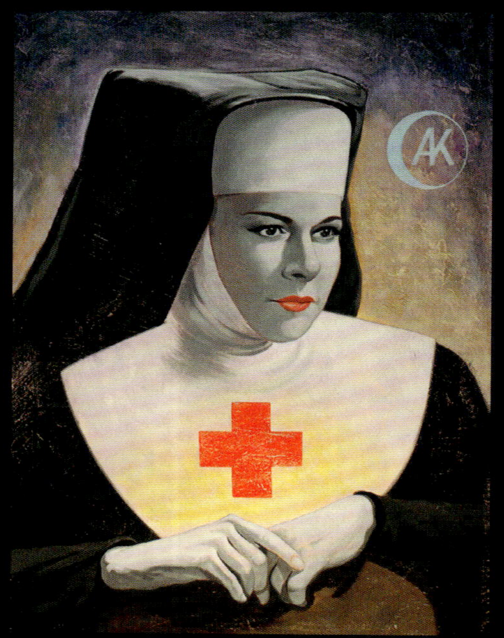

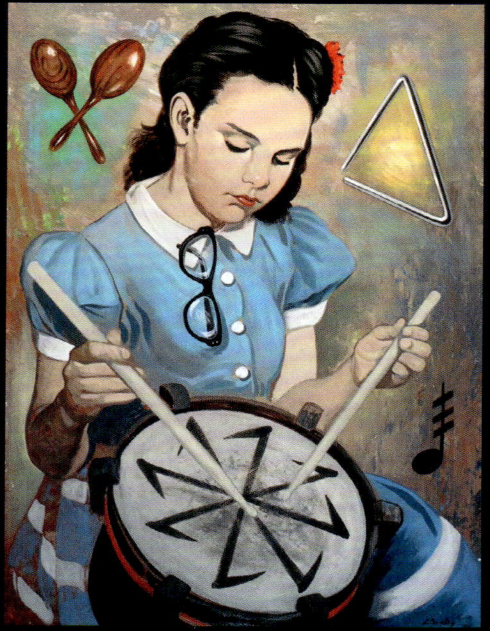

(T) *Billy Renkl* (B) *David M. Brinley*

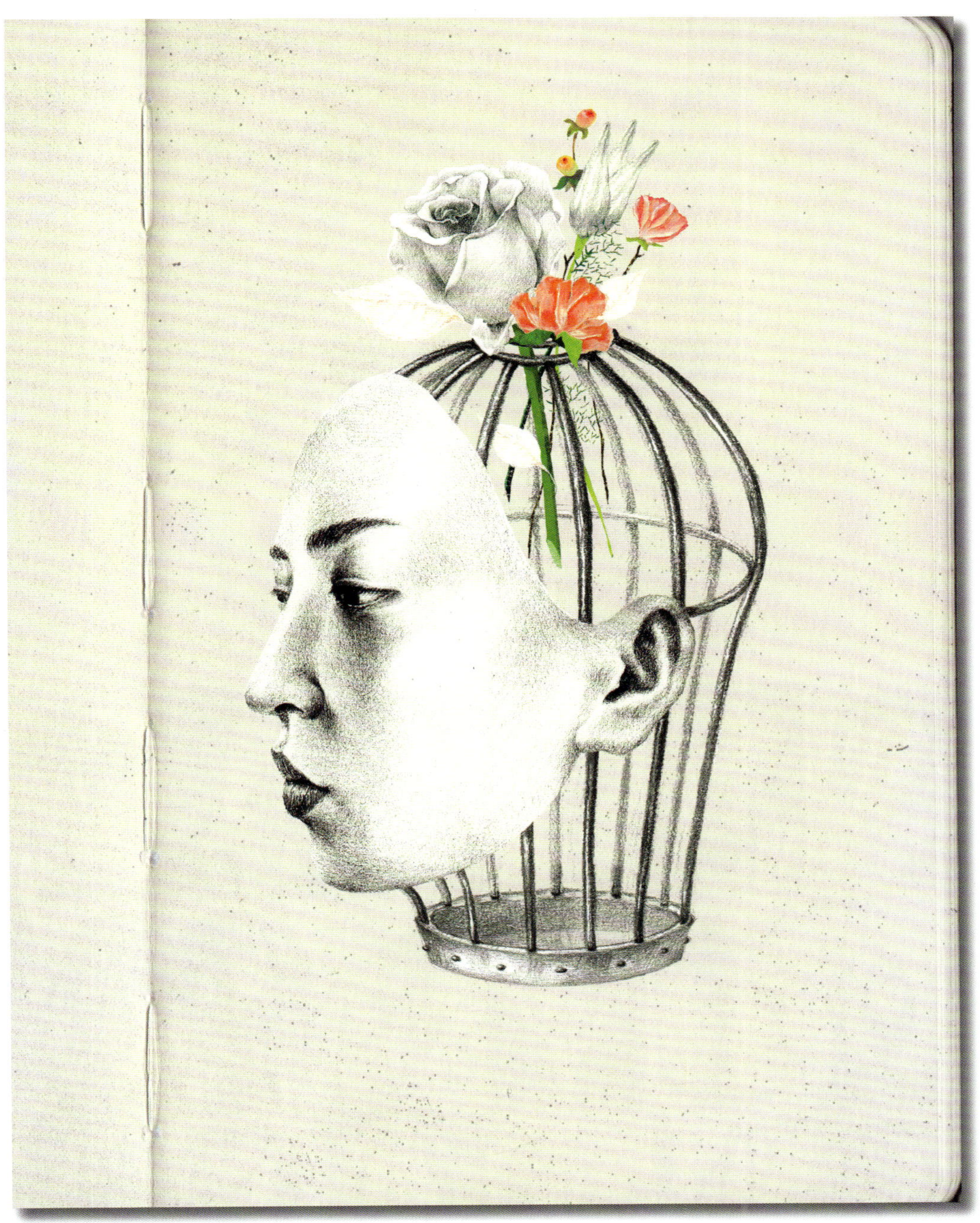

Ahwon Min

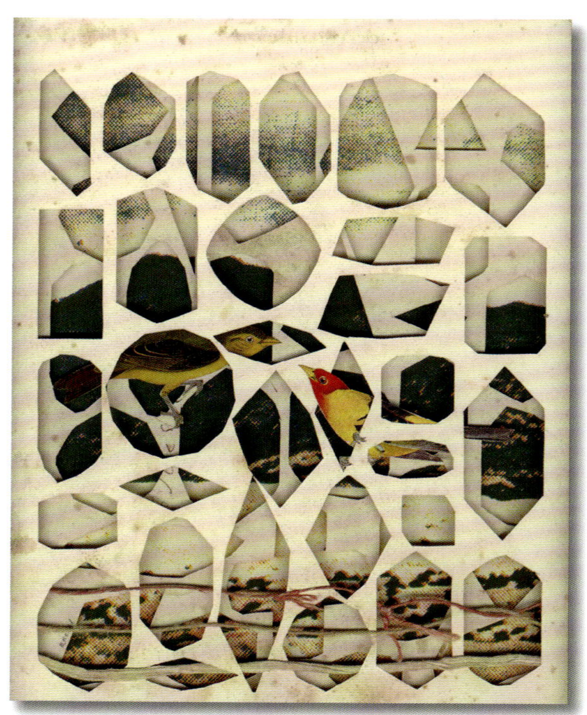

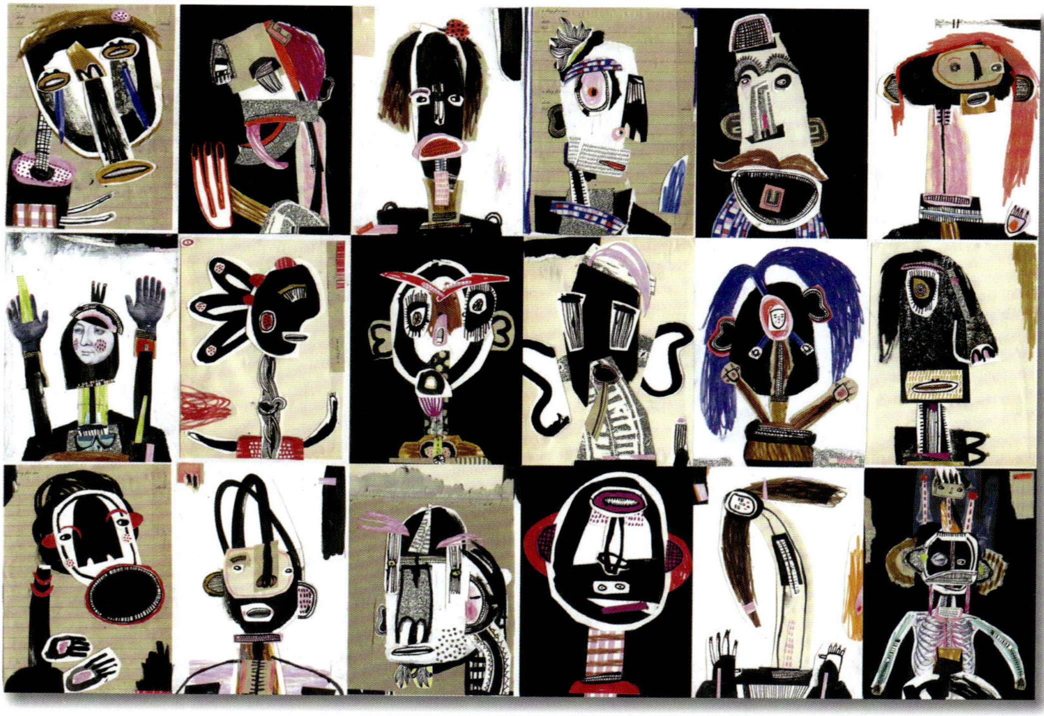

(T) *Billy Renkl* (B) *Dorothea Huber*

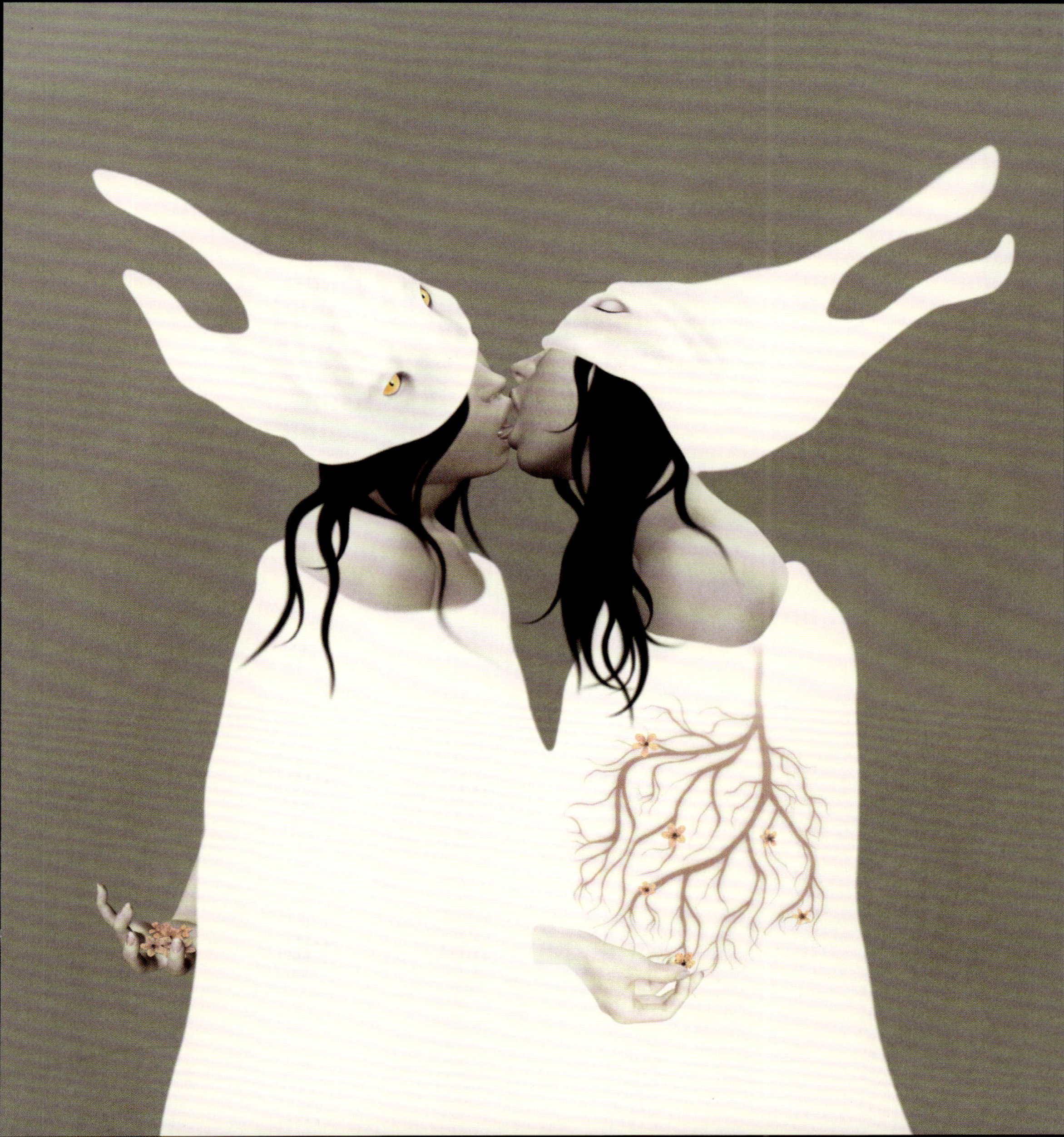

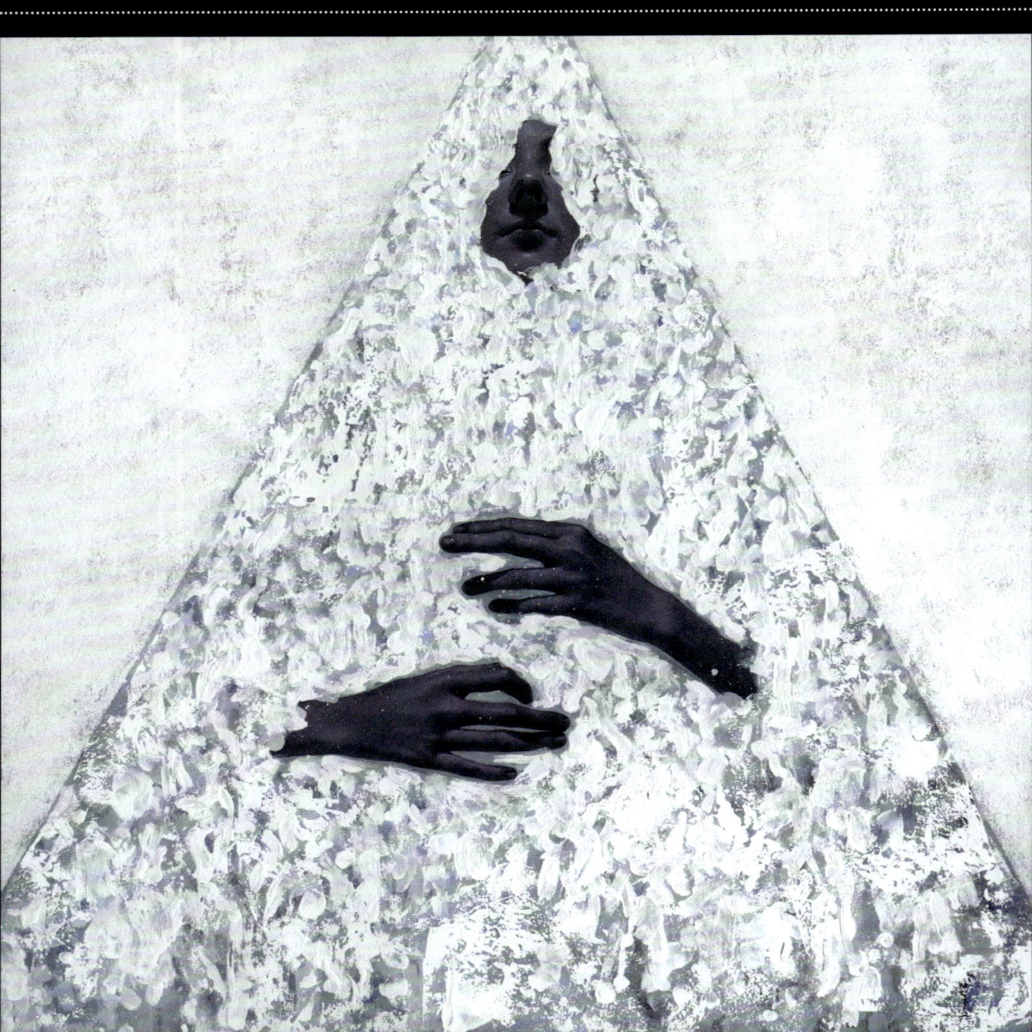

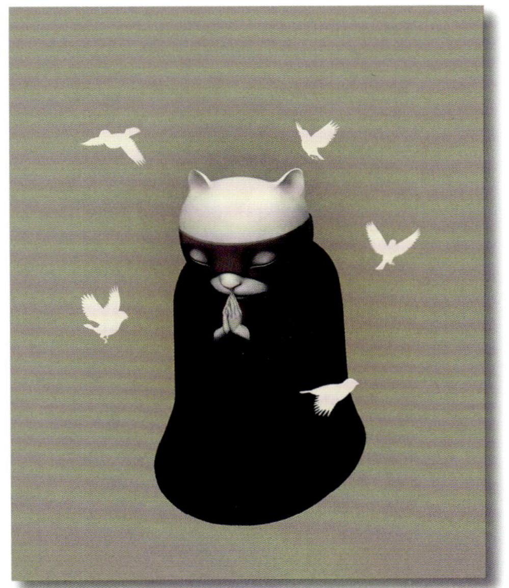

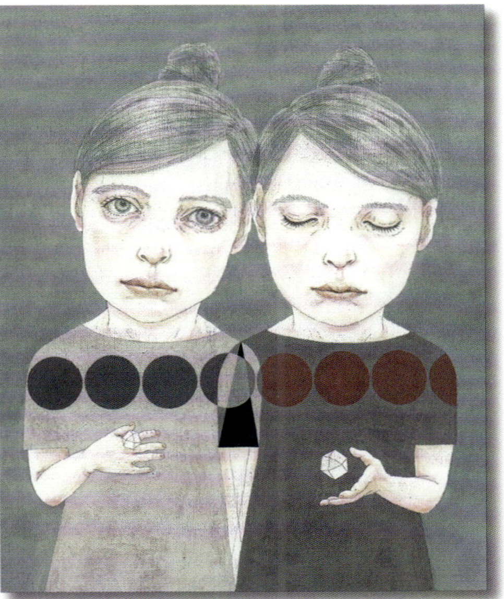

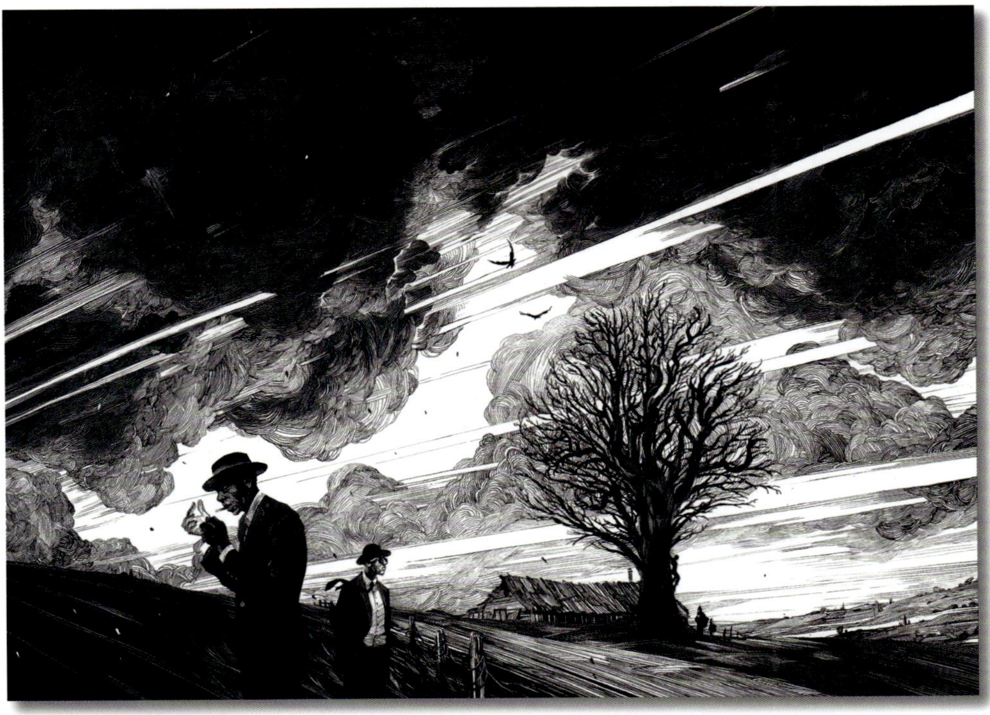

(TL) *David Ho* (TR) *Mari Mitsumi* (B) *Nicolas Delort*

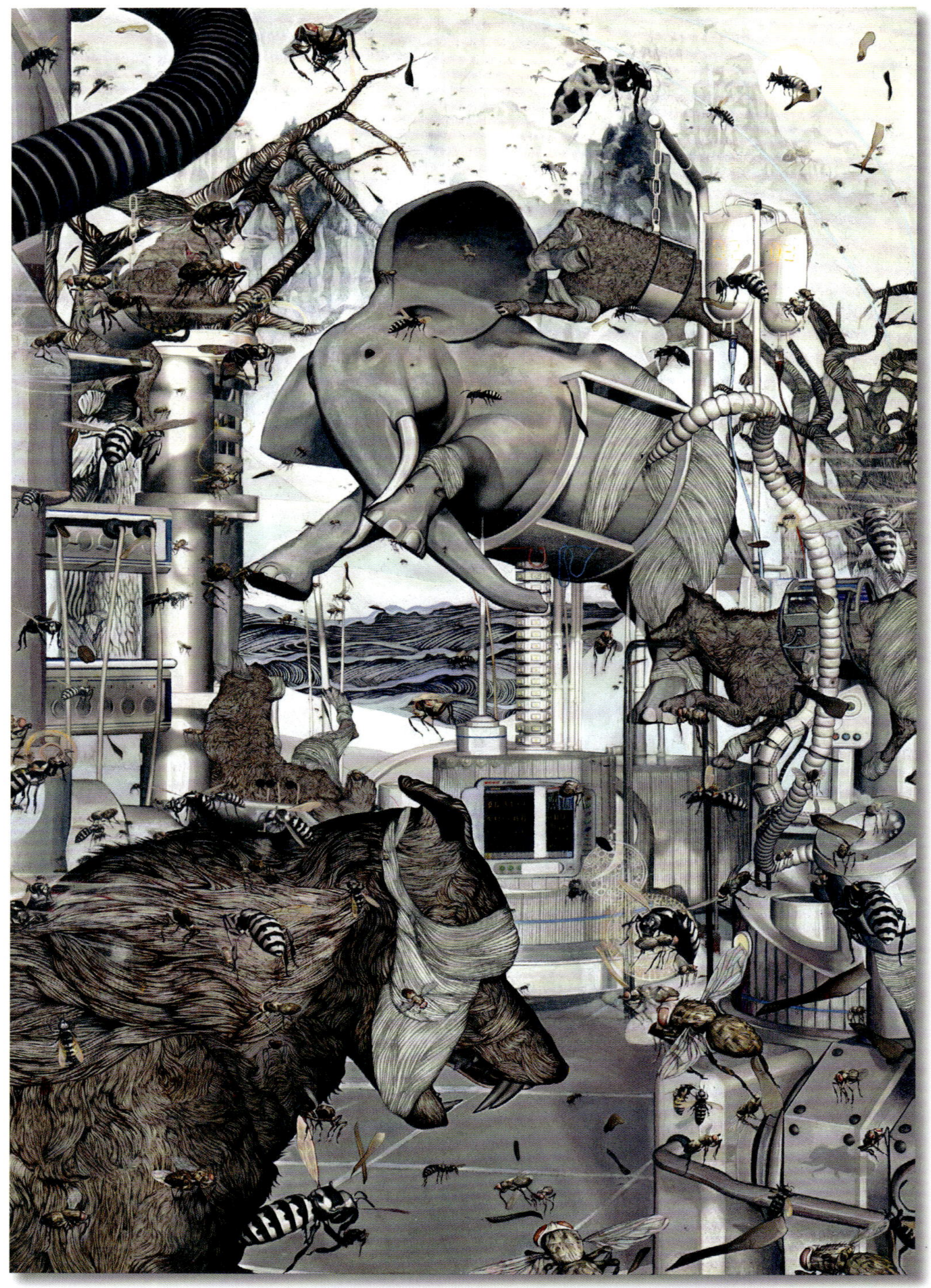

(L) Steven Tabbutt (R) Alice Wellinger

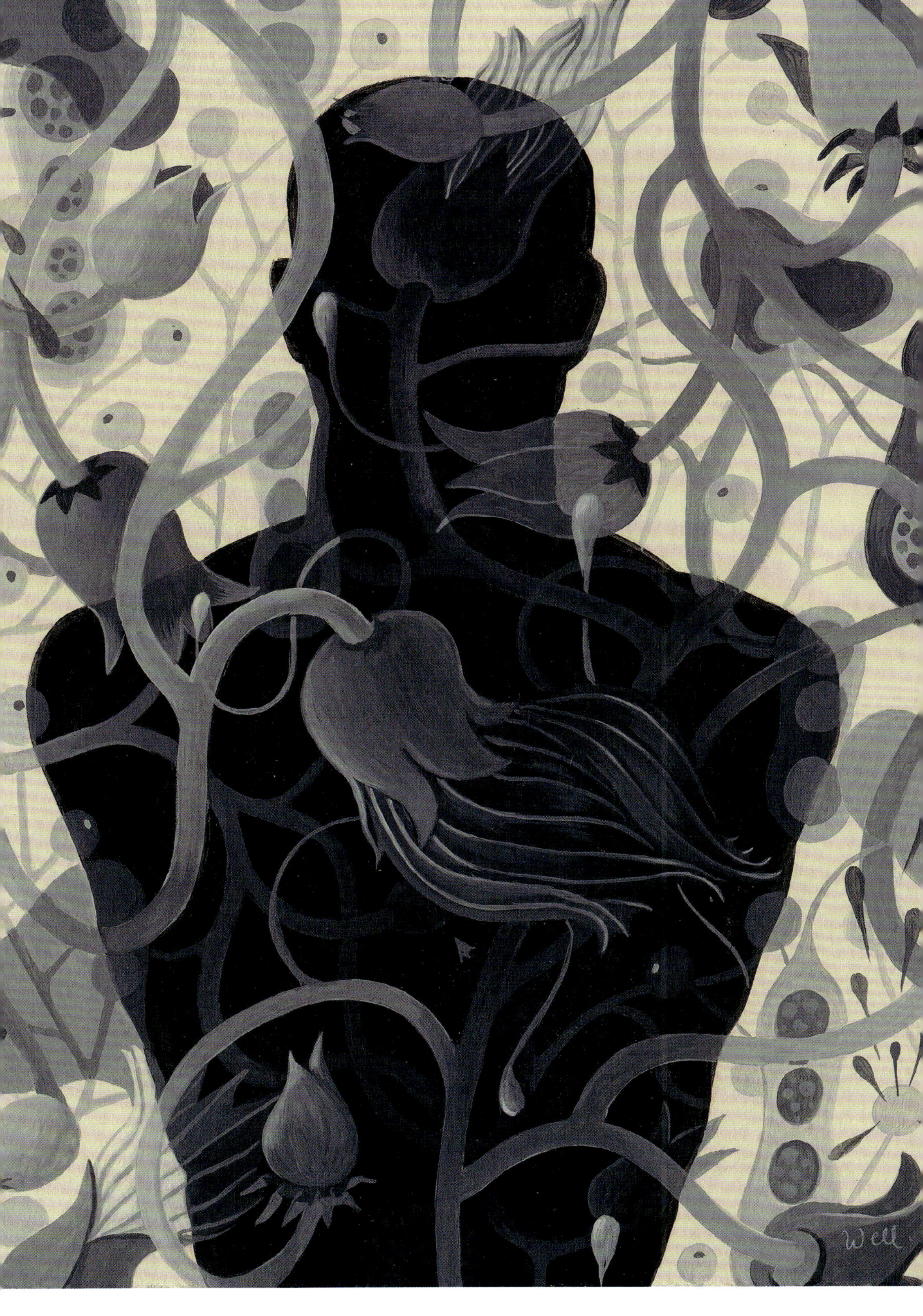

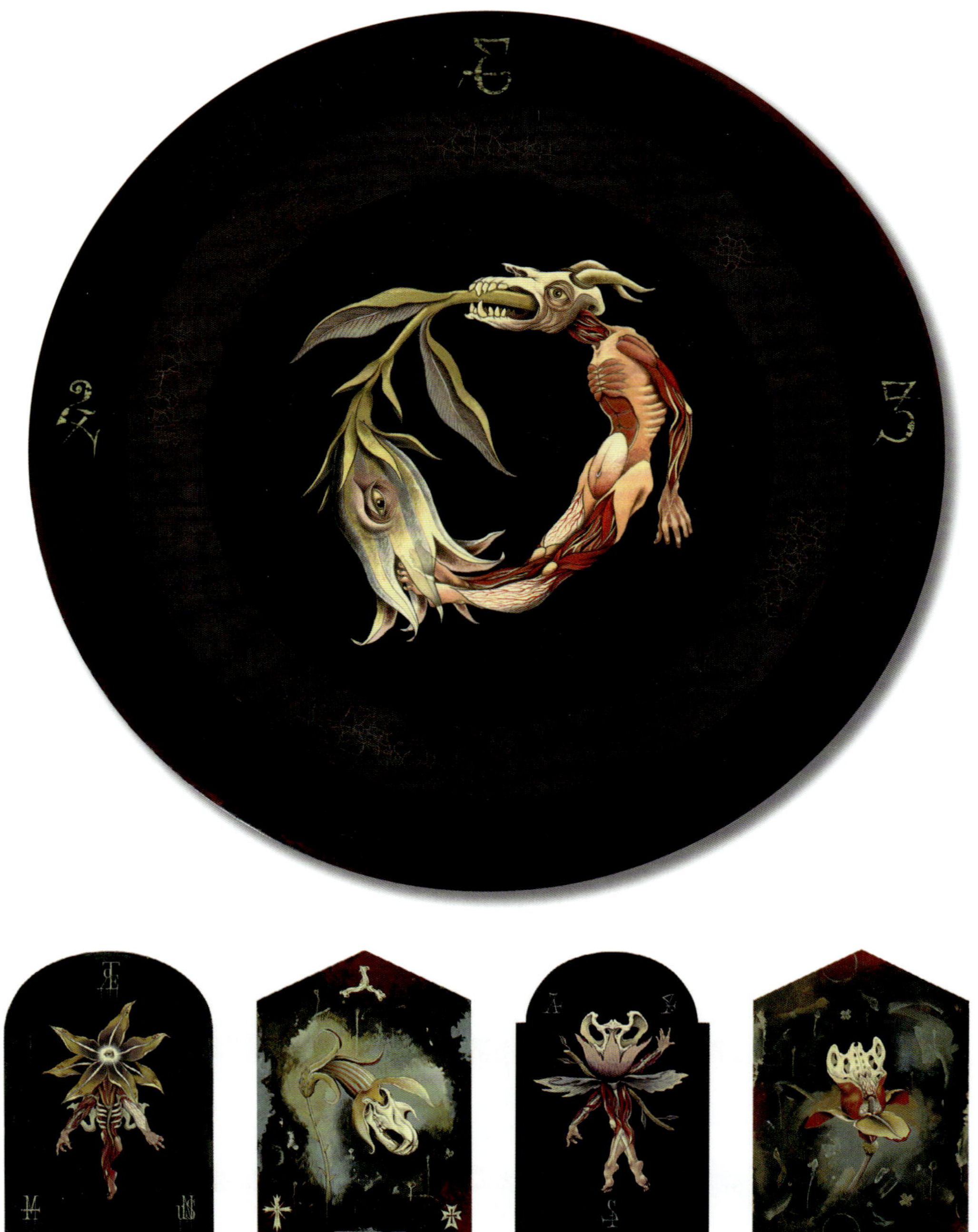

(L) *Pol Turgeon* (R) *Stuart McLachlan*

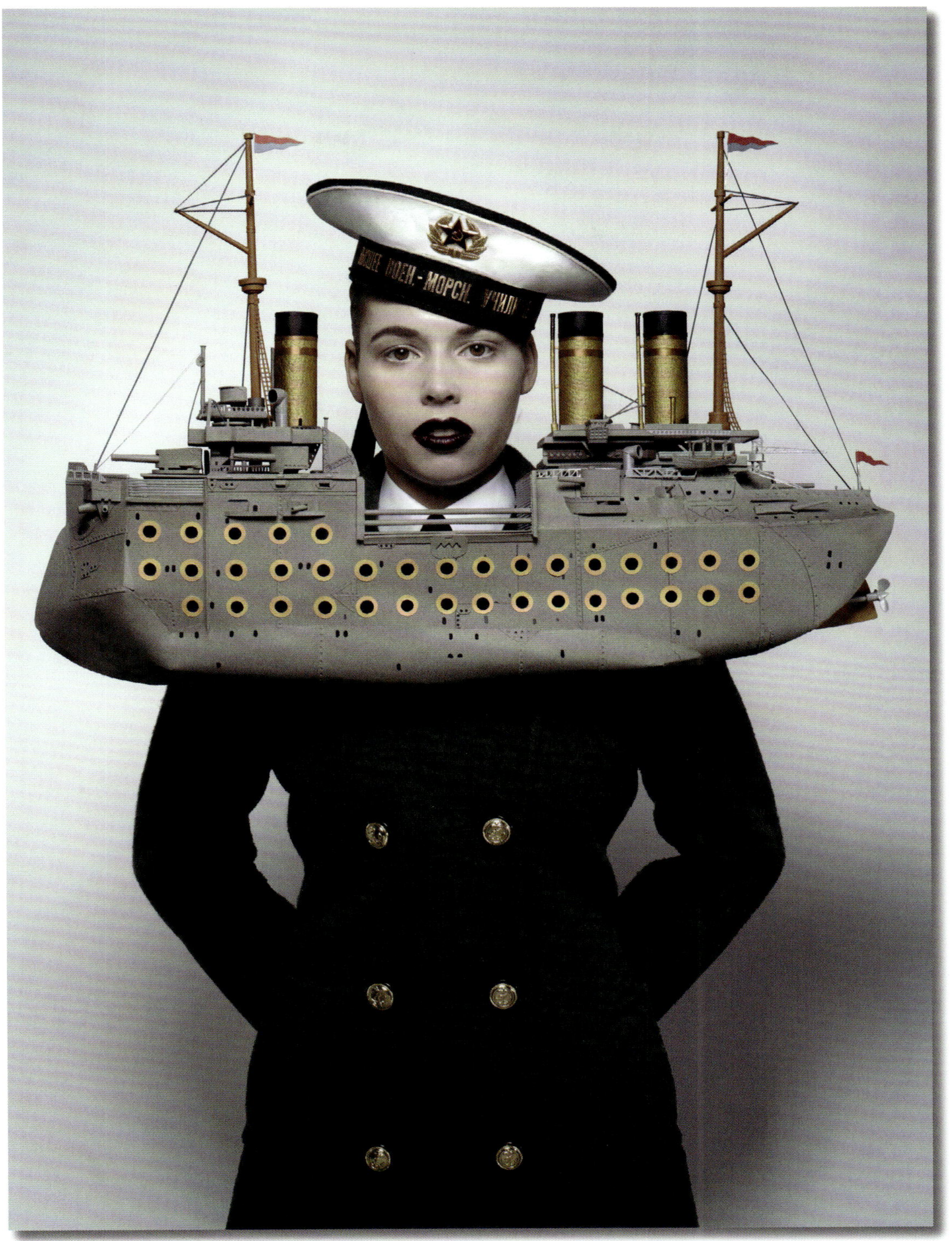
Высшее Воен.-Морск. Училище

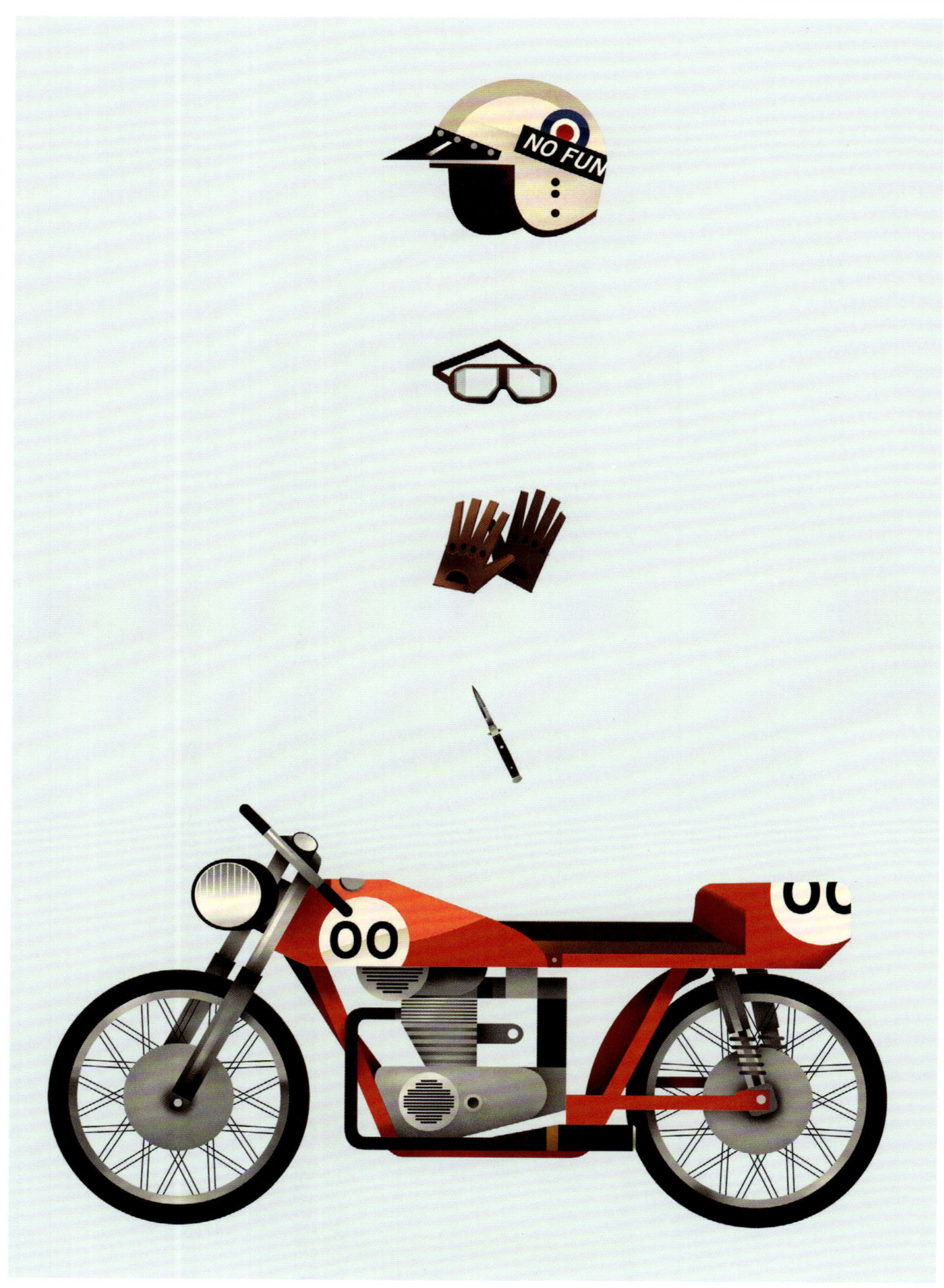

Dave Murray

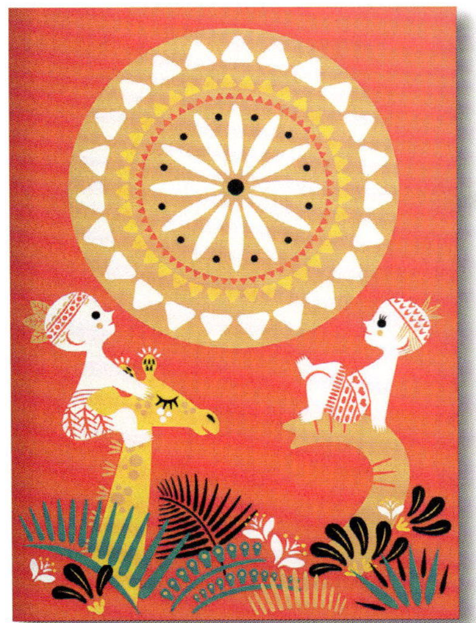

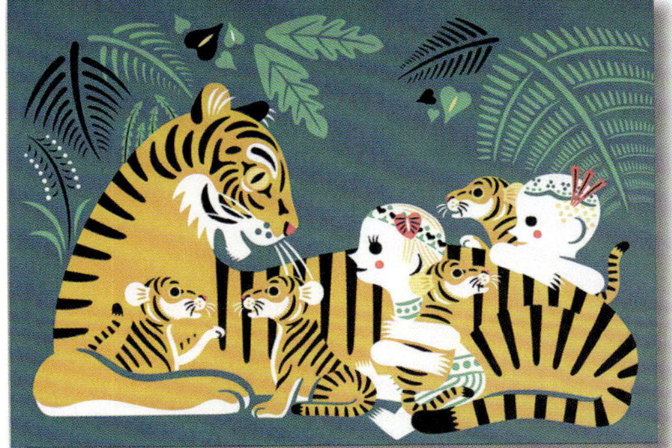

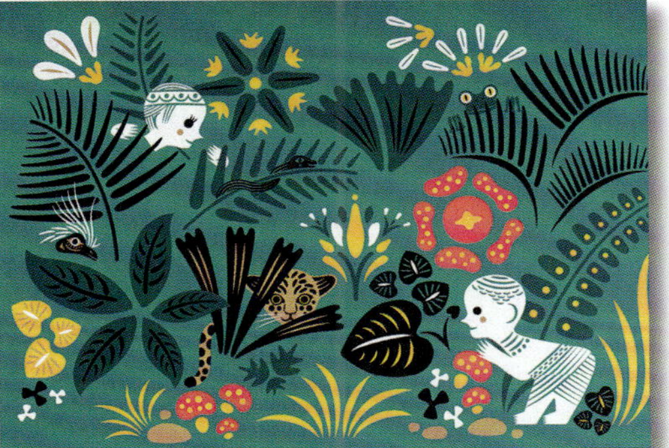

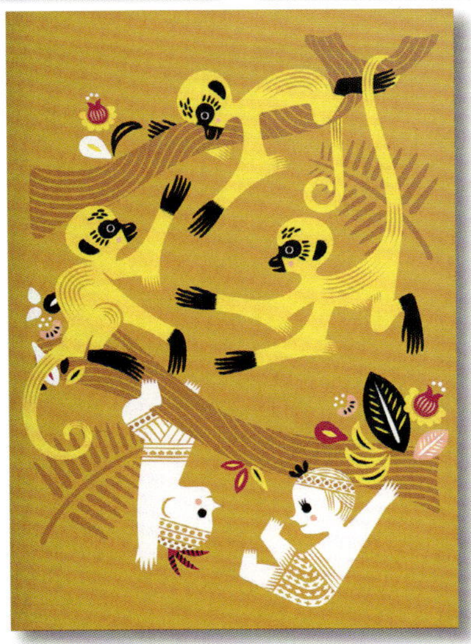

Studio Tipi

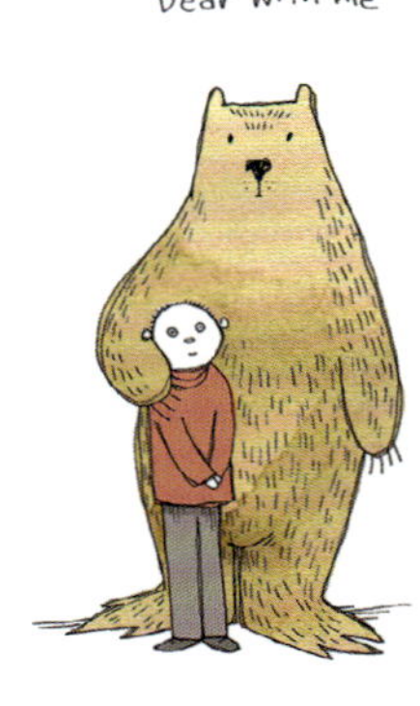
bear with me

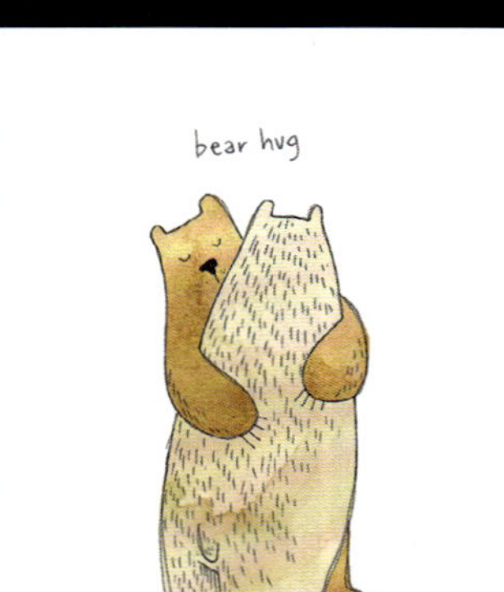
bear hug

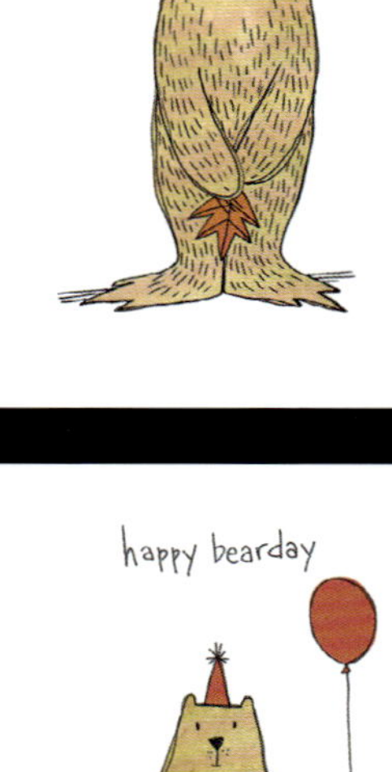
bear naked

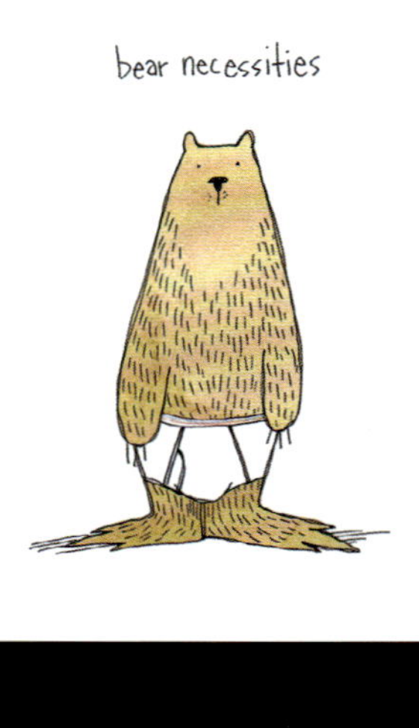
bear necessities

happy bearday

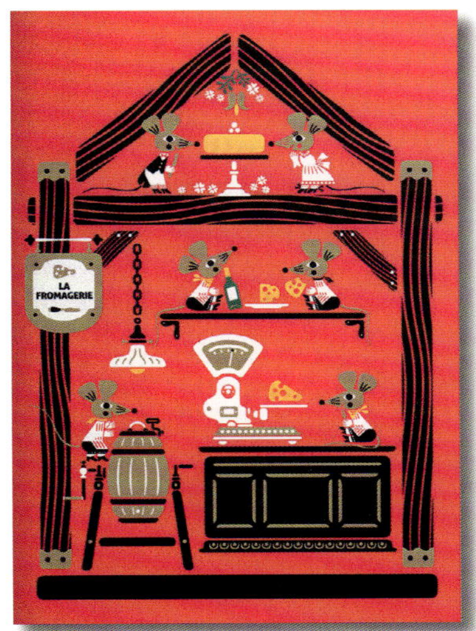

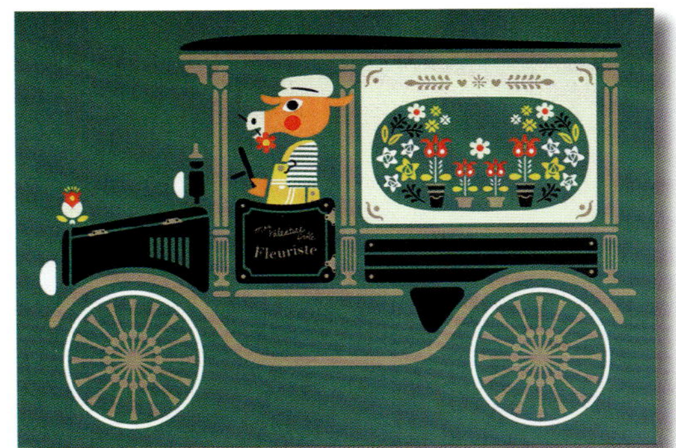

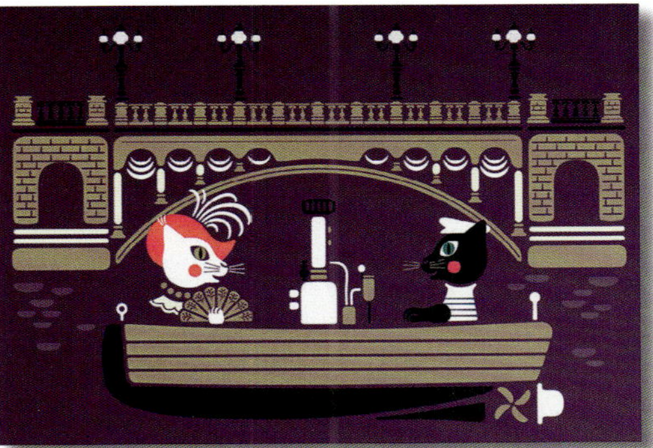

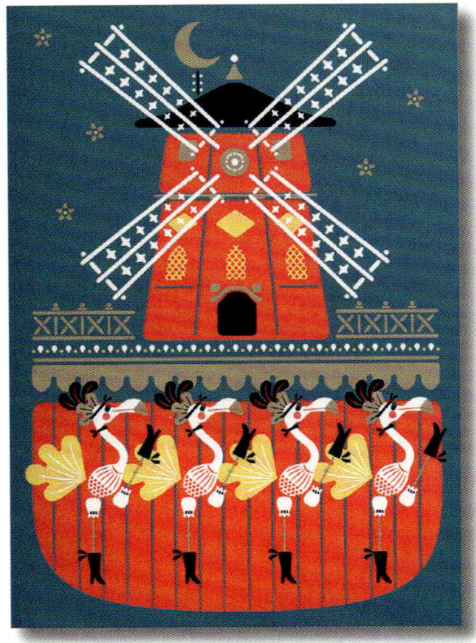

Studio Tipi

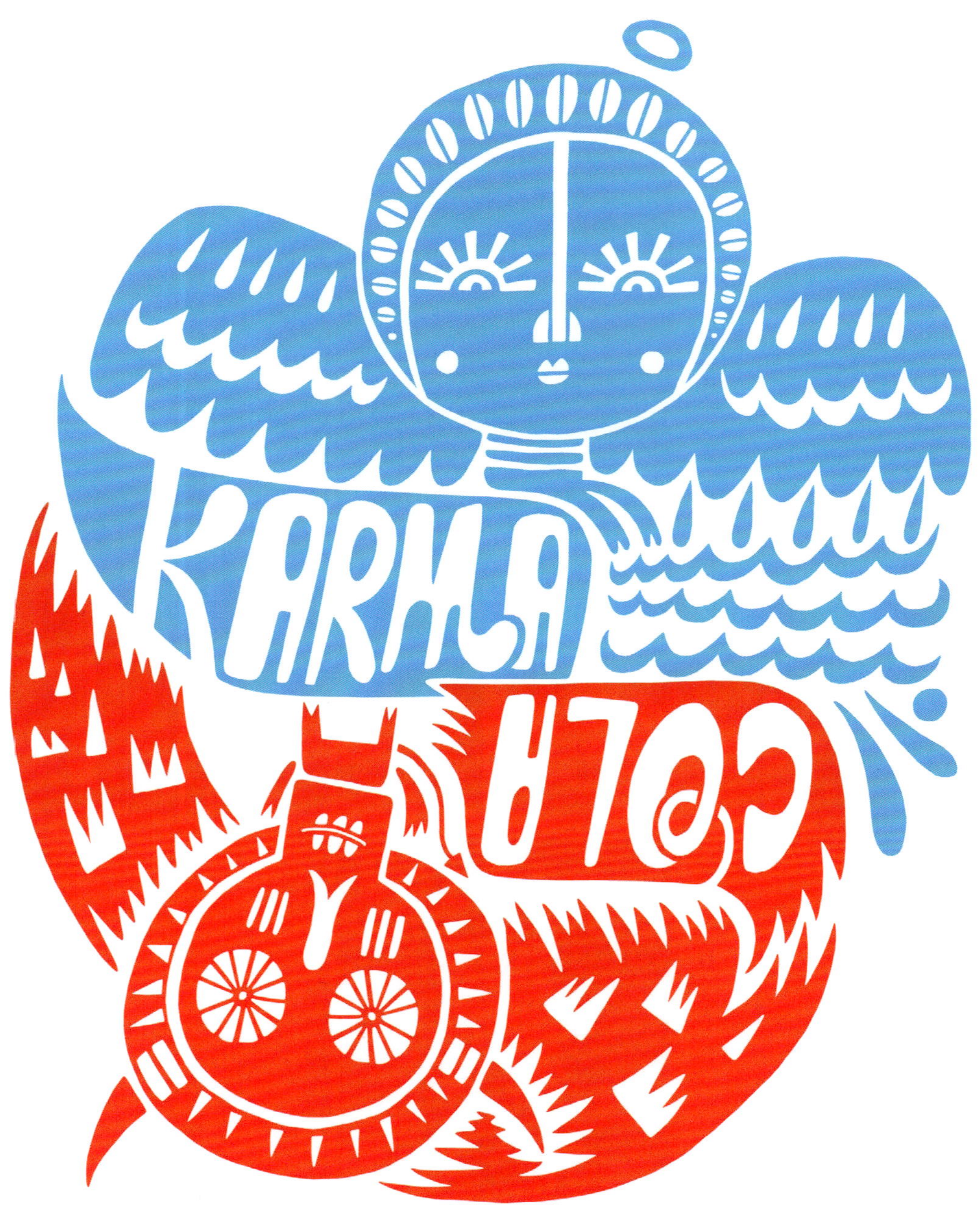

KARMA
COLA

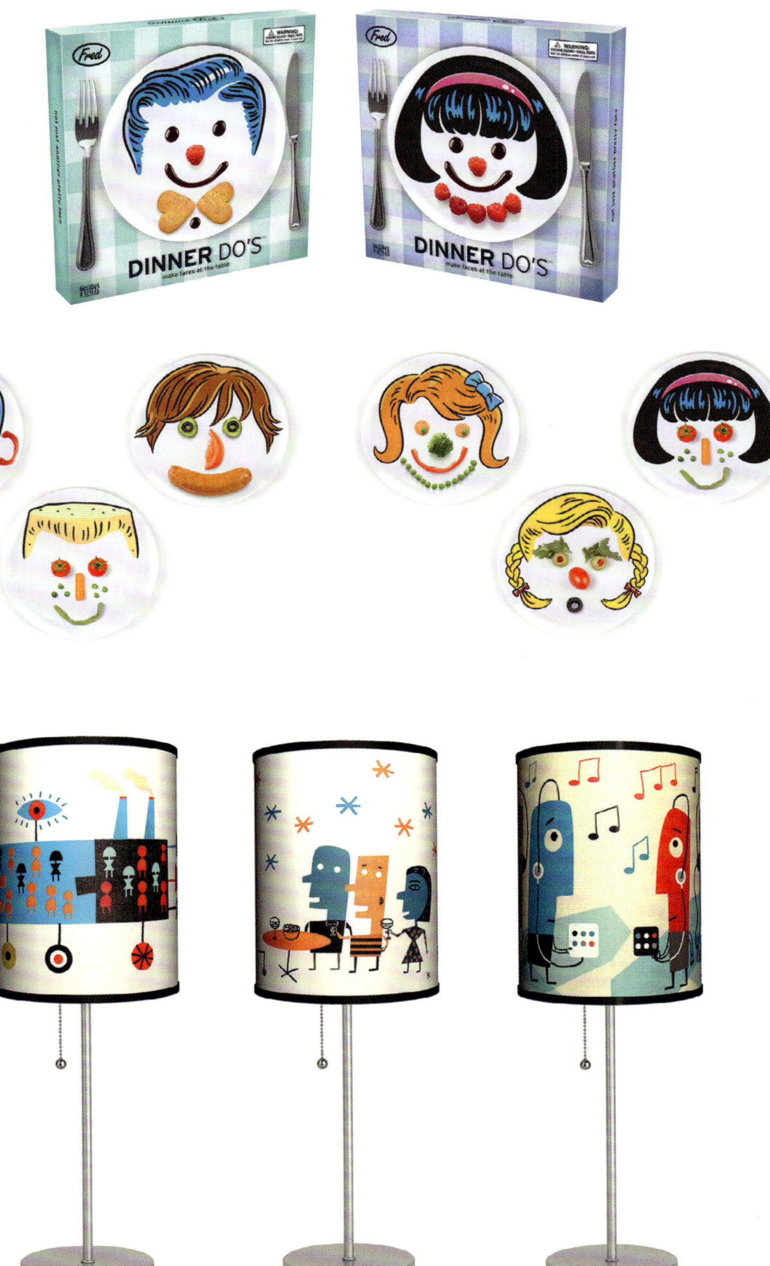

(T) *Chris Gash* (B) *James Yang*

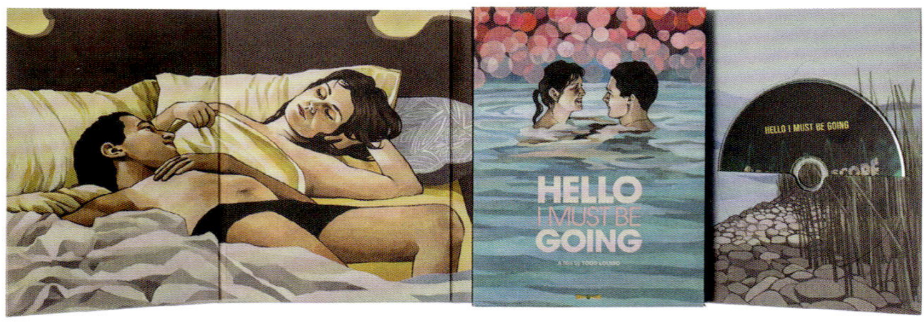

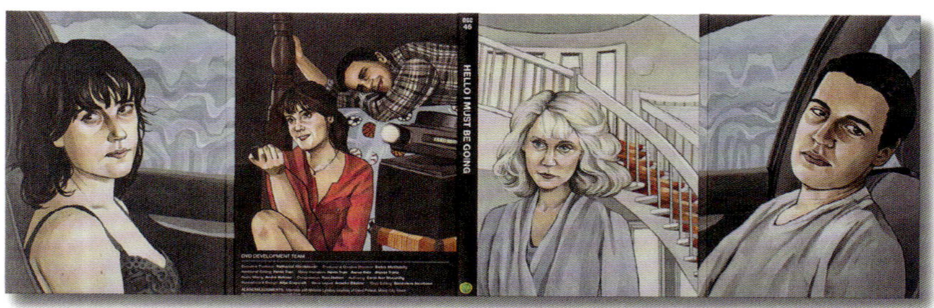

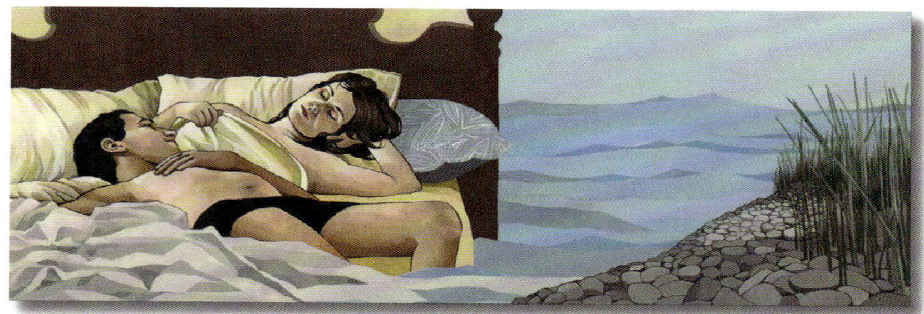

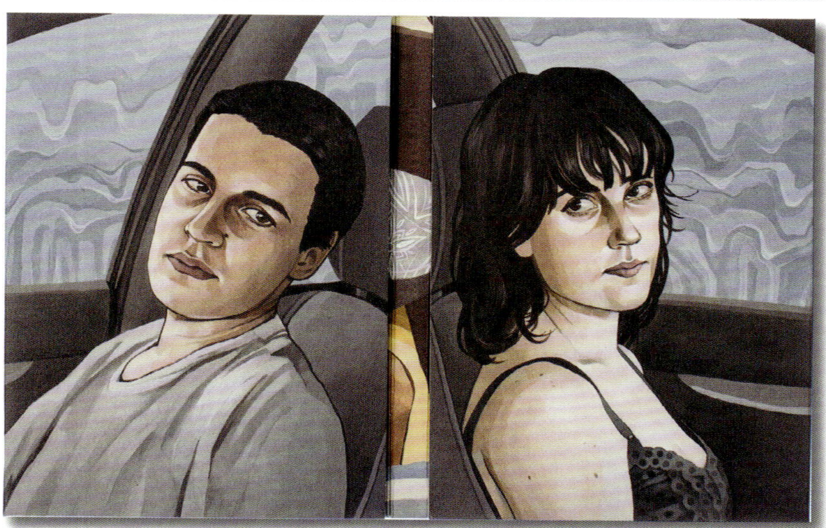

(L) *Alija Craycroft* (RT) *Pol Turgeon* (RB) *Tracy Sabin*

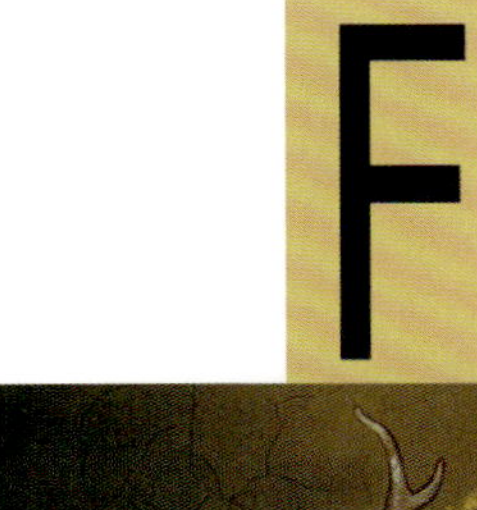

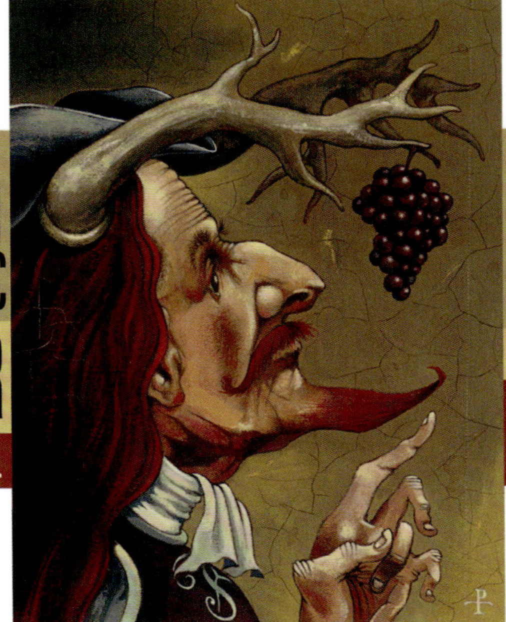
LE
FRON
TENAC
NOIR
2011
DOMAINE
DES
MĒTĒ
ORES
VIN ROUGE
RED WINE
750ml
12% alc./vol.
PRODUIT DU QUÉBEC
PRODUCT OF QUÉBEC

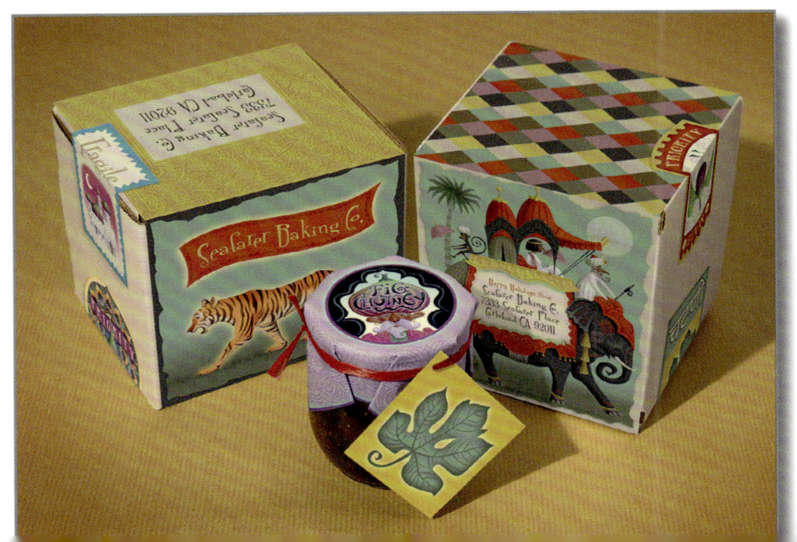
Seafarer Baking Co.
Fig Chutney

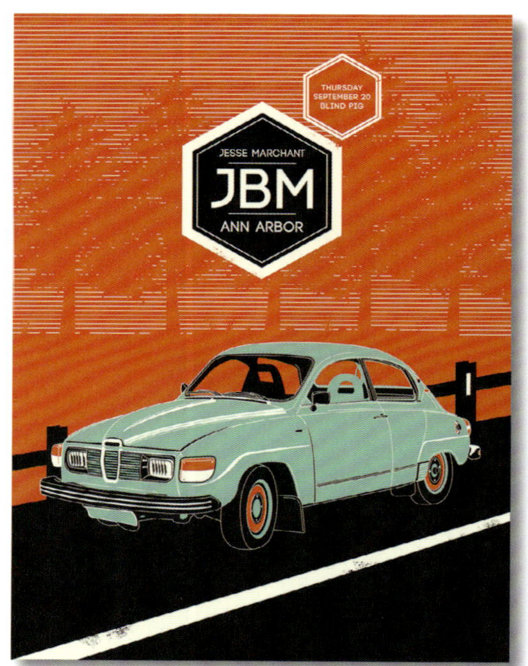
THURSDAY
SEPTEMBER 20
BLIND PIG
JESSE MARCHANT
JBM
ANN ARBOR

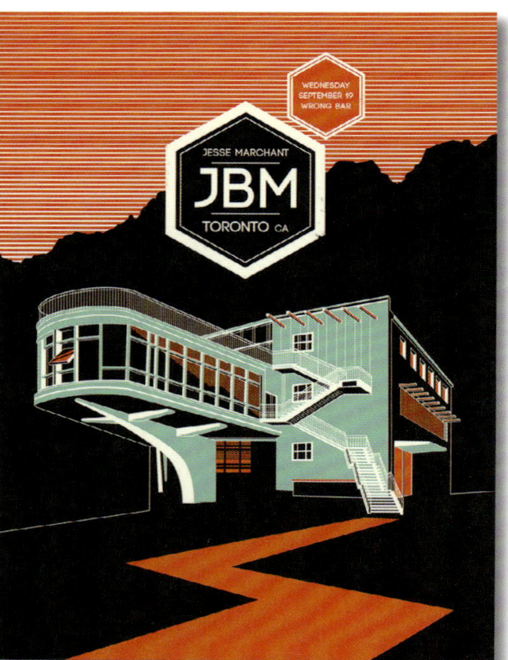
WEDNESDAY
SEPTEMBER 19
WRONG BAR
JESSE MARCHANT
JBM
TORONTO CA

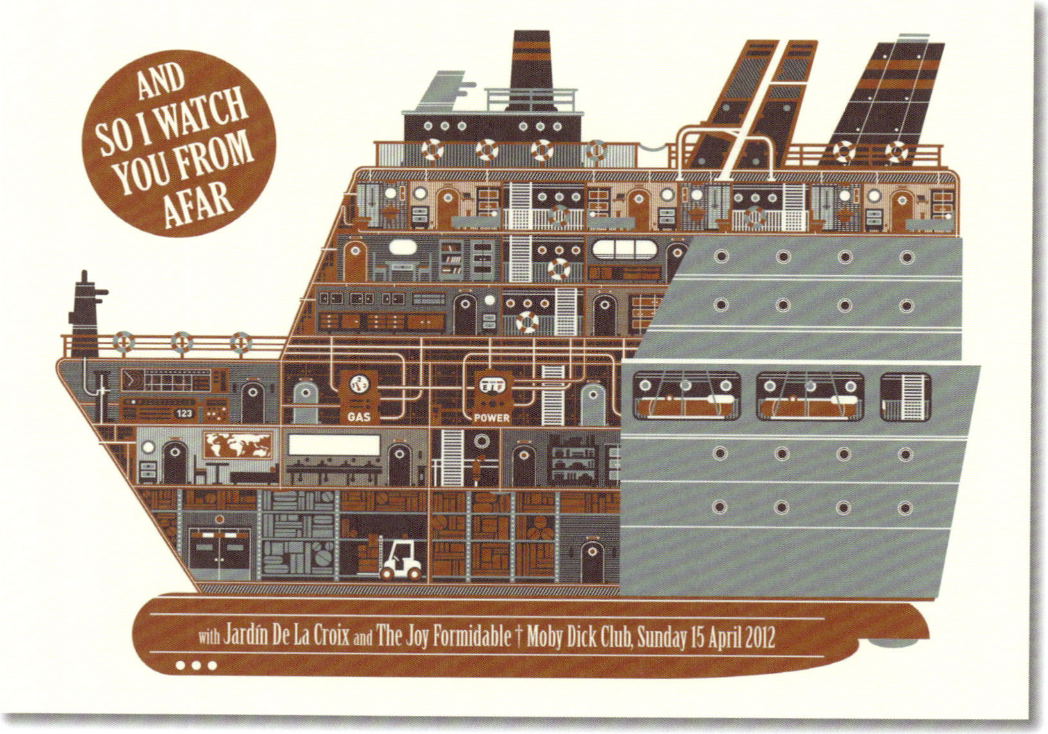

AND
SO I WATCH
YOU FROM
AFAR
GAS
POWER
123
with Jardín De La Croix and The Joy Formidable † Moby Dick Club, Sunday 15 April 2012

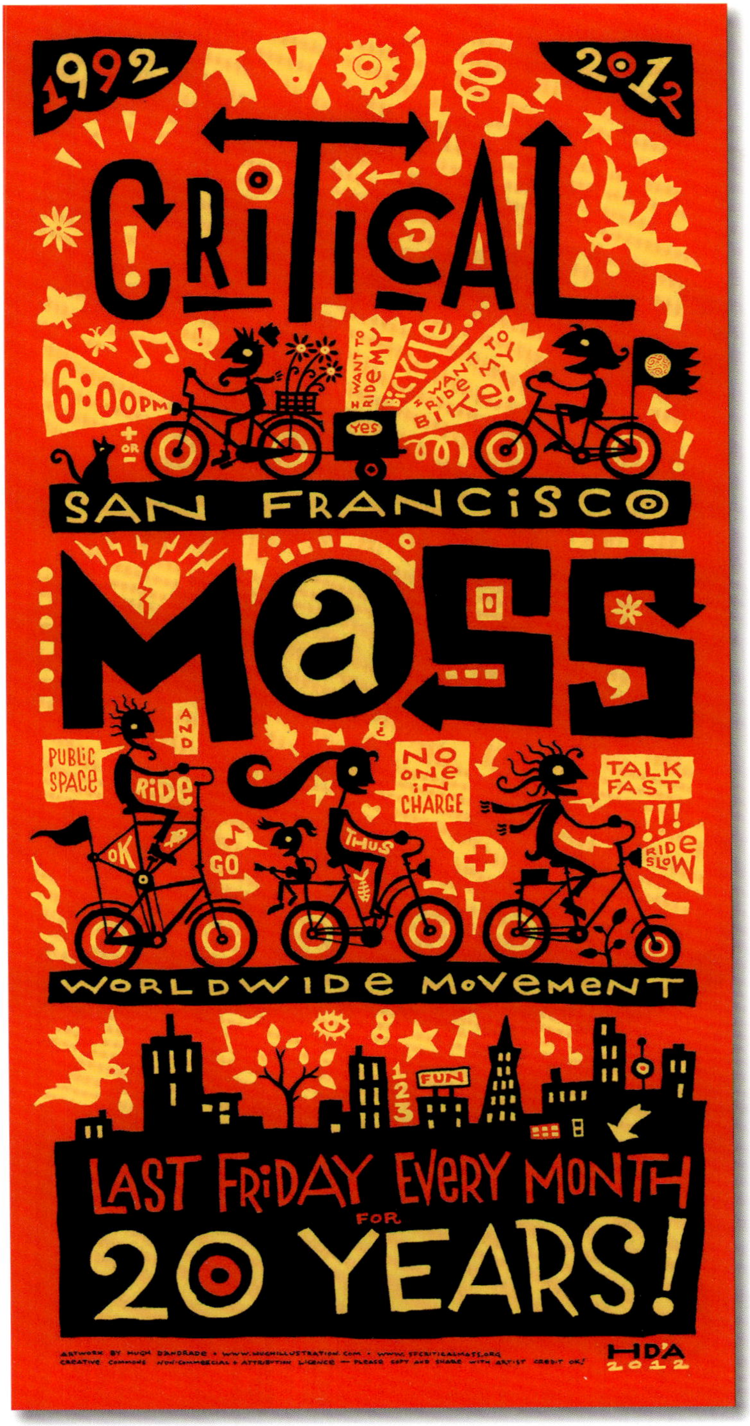

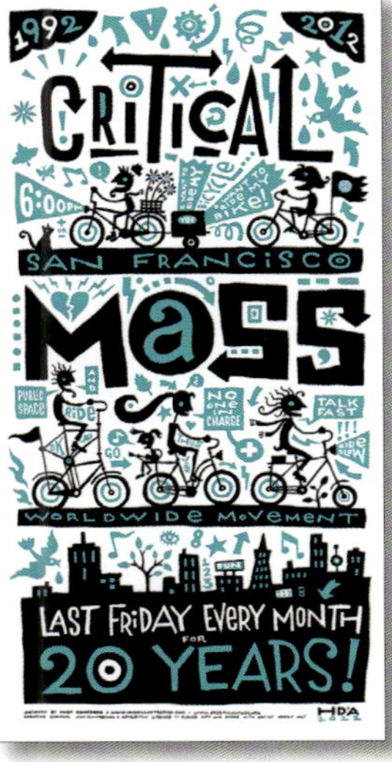

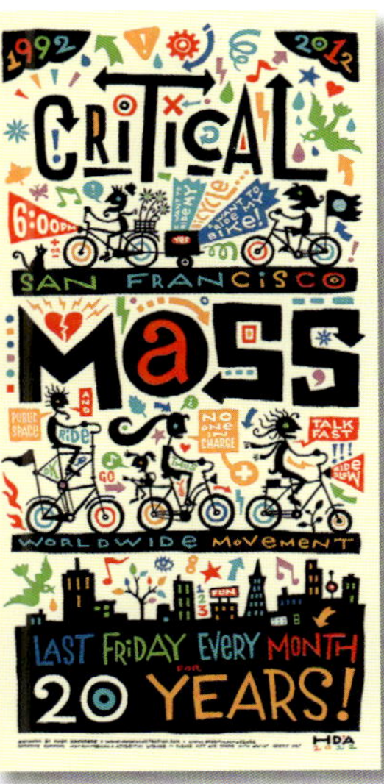

(L) *László Nagy* (R) *Hugh D'Andrade*

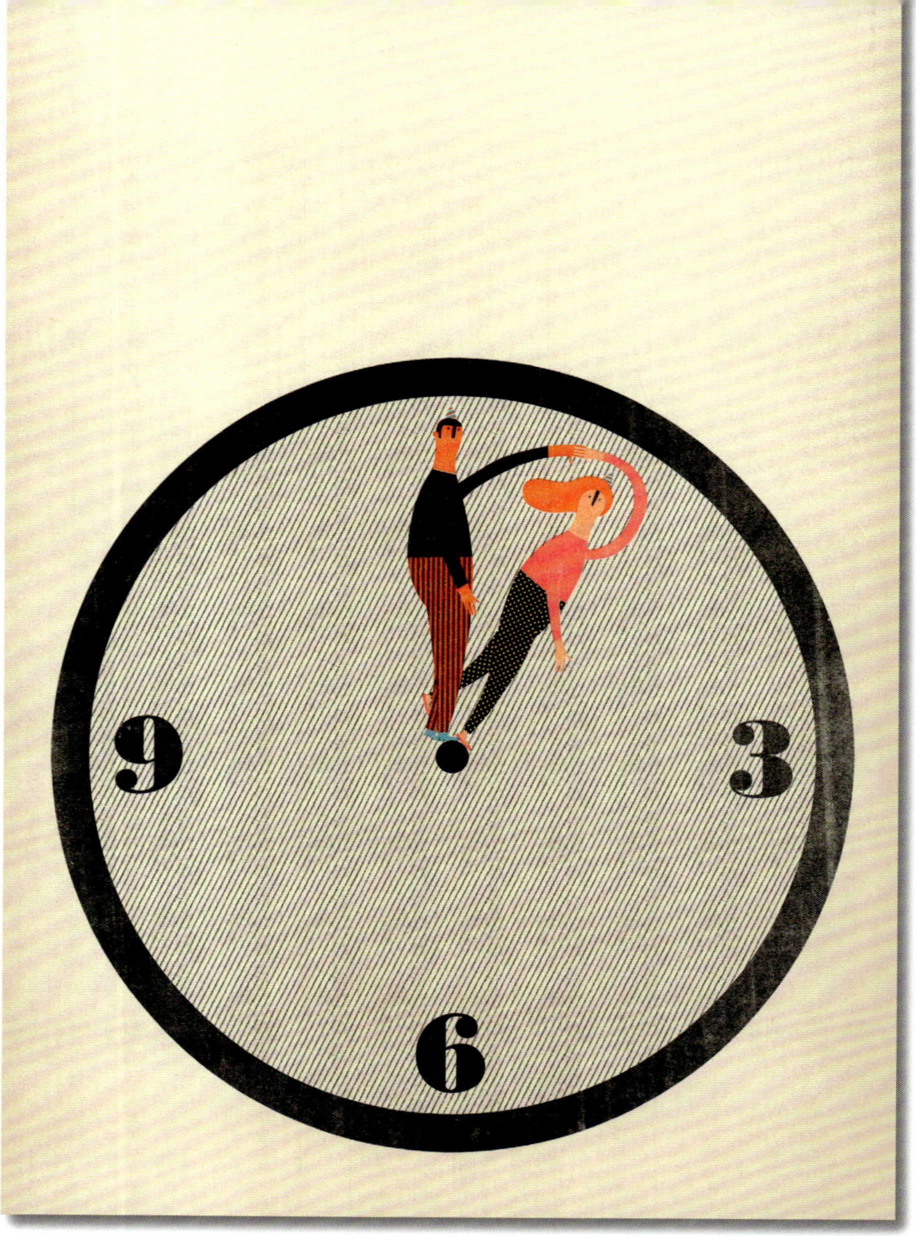

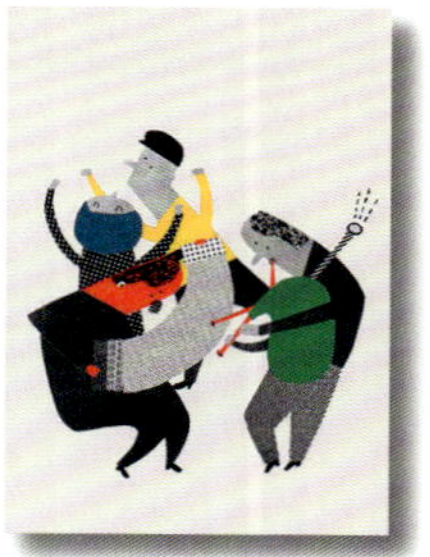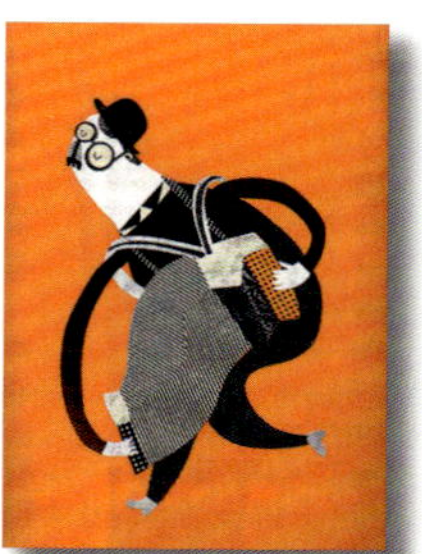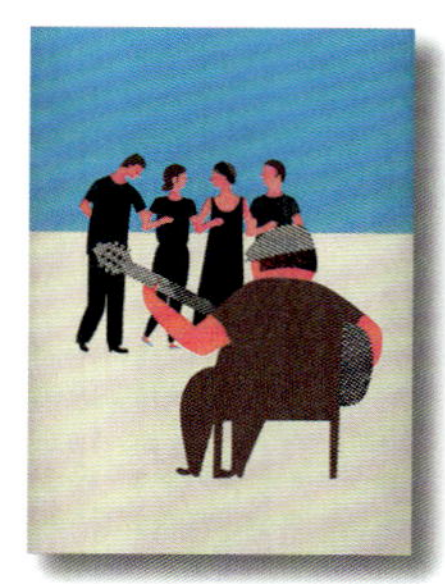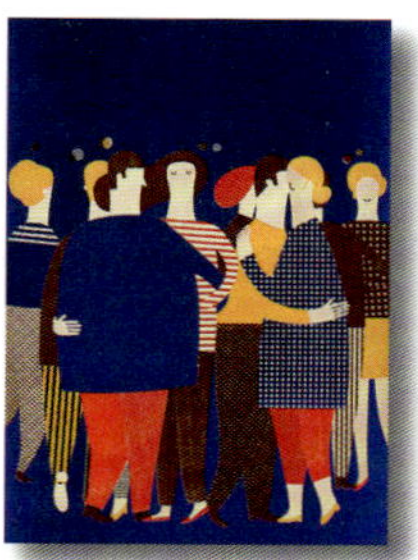

Catarina Sobral

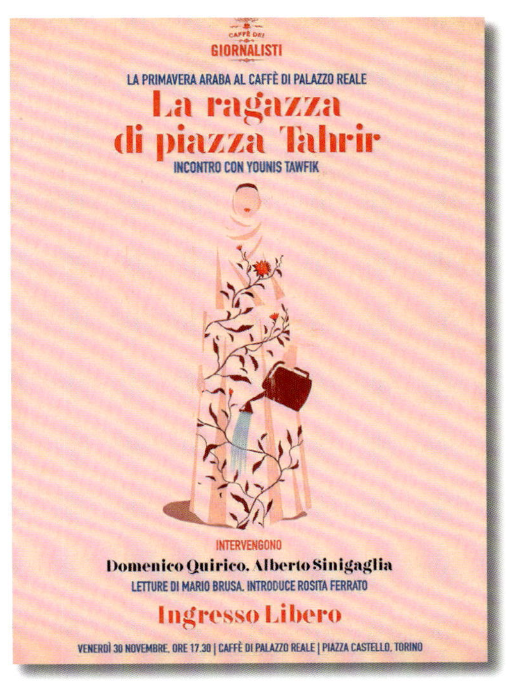

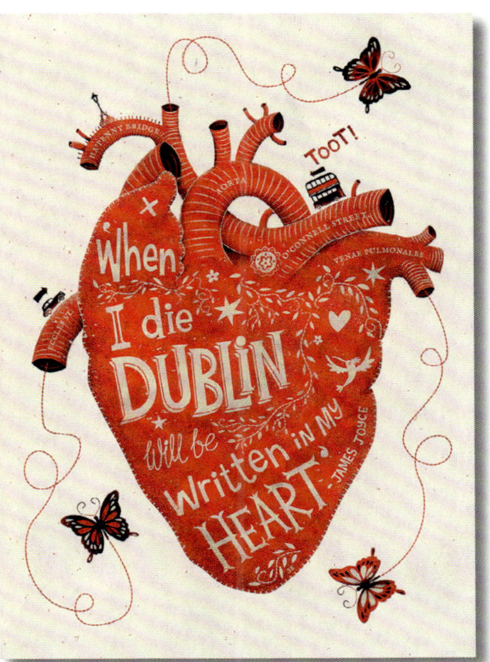

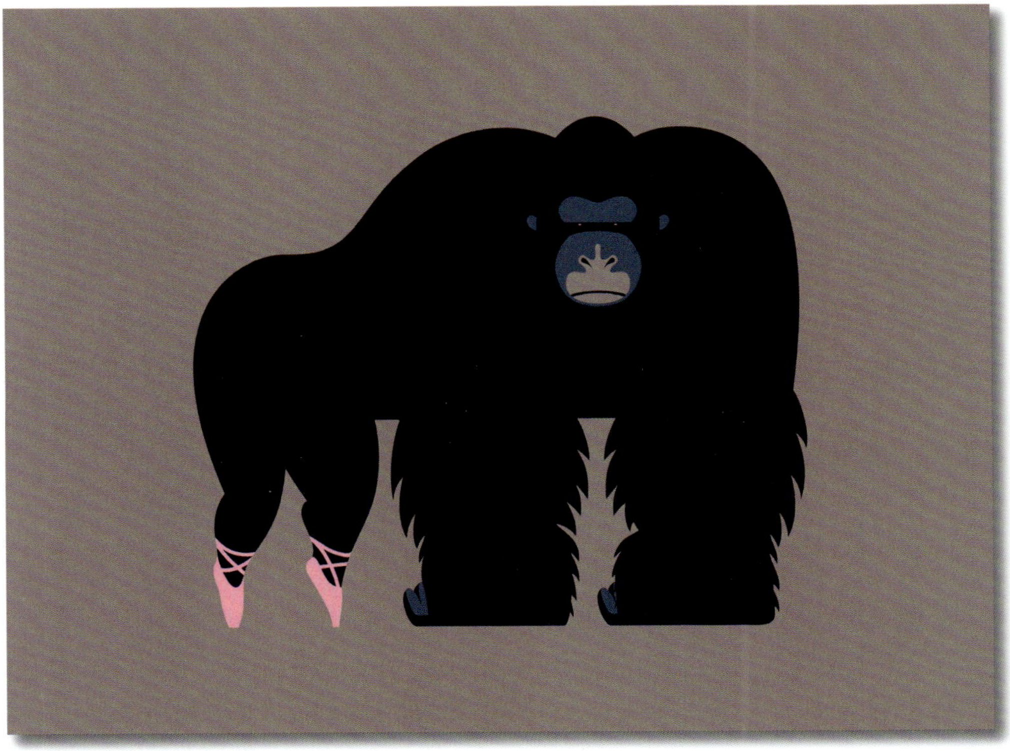

(TL) *Emiliano Ponzi* (TR) *Steve Simpson* (B) BRONZE *Aad Goudappel*

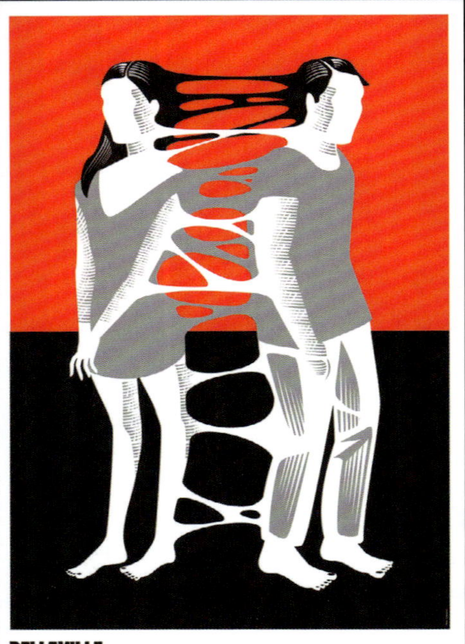

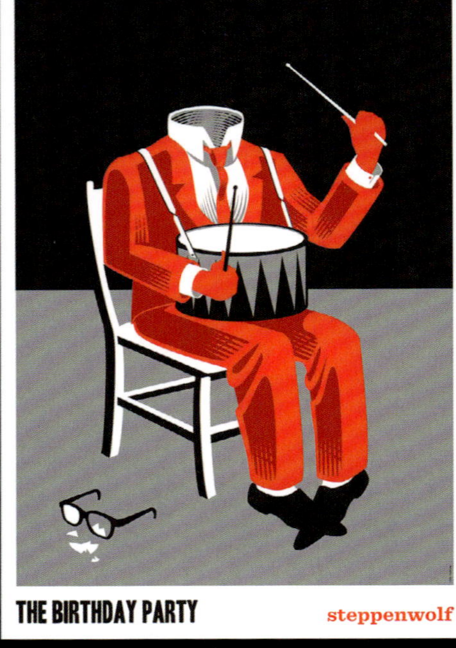

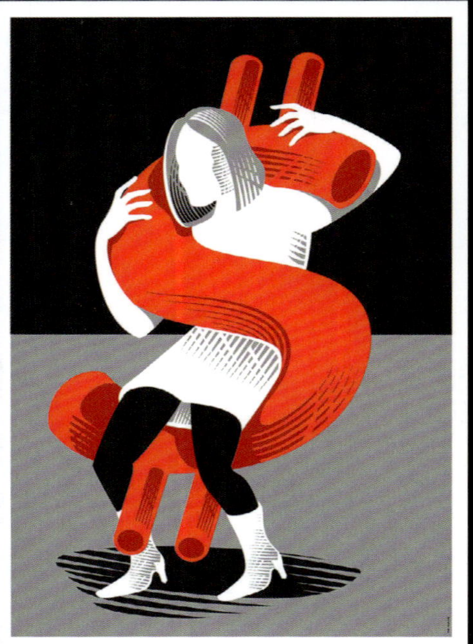

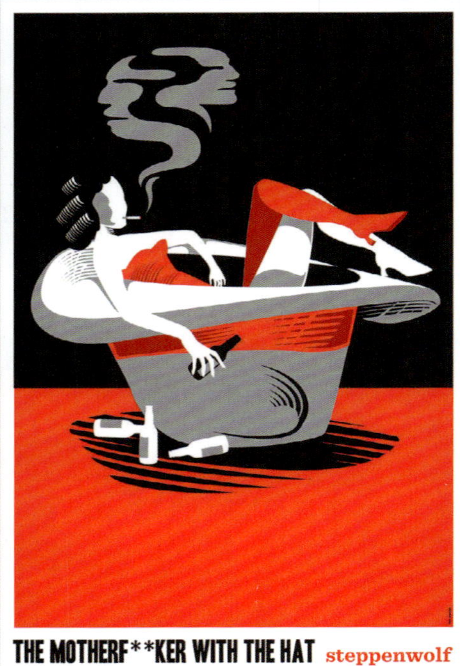

Yann Legendre

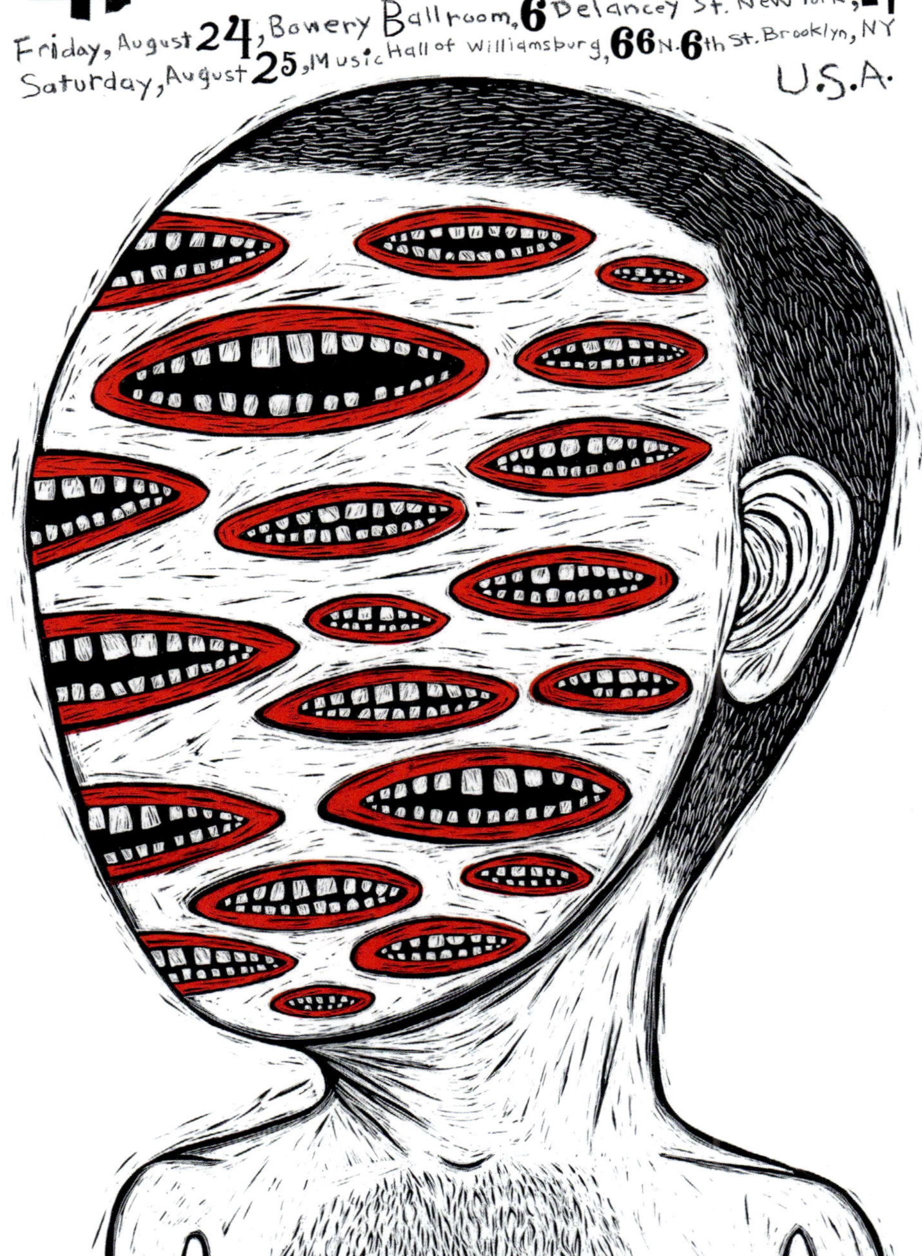

Melinda Beck

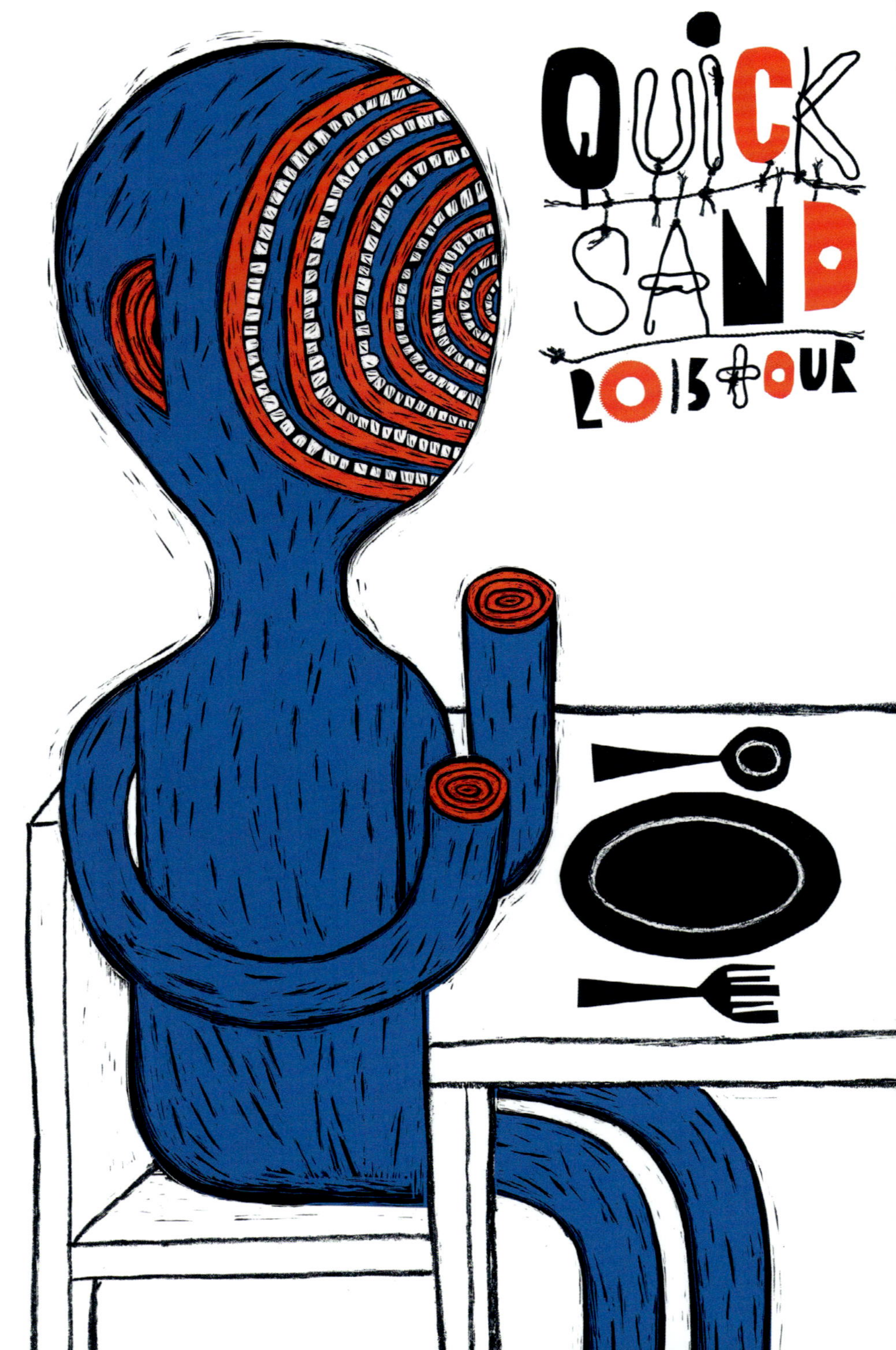

QUICK
SAND
2015 TOUR

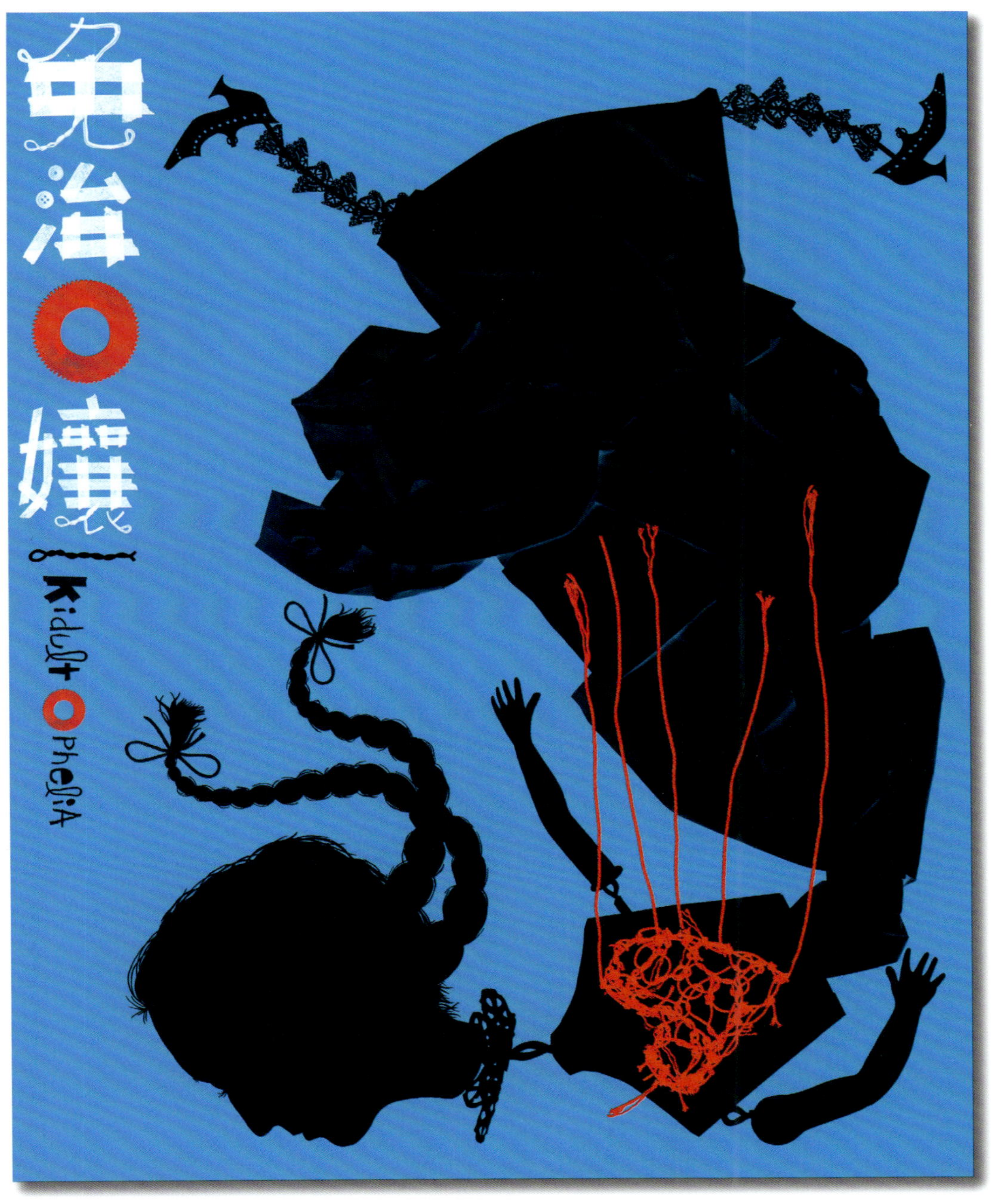

(L) *Melinda Beck* (R) *Melinda Beck*

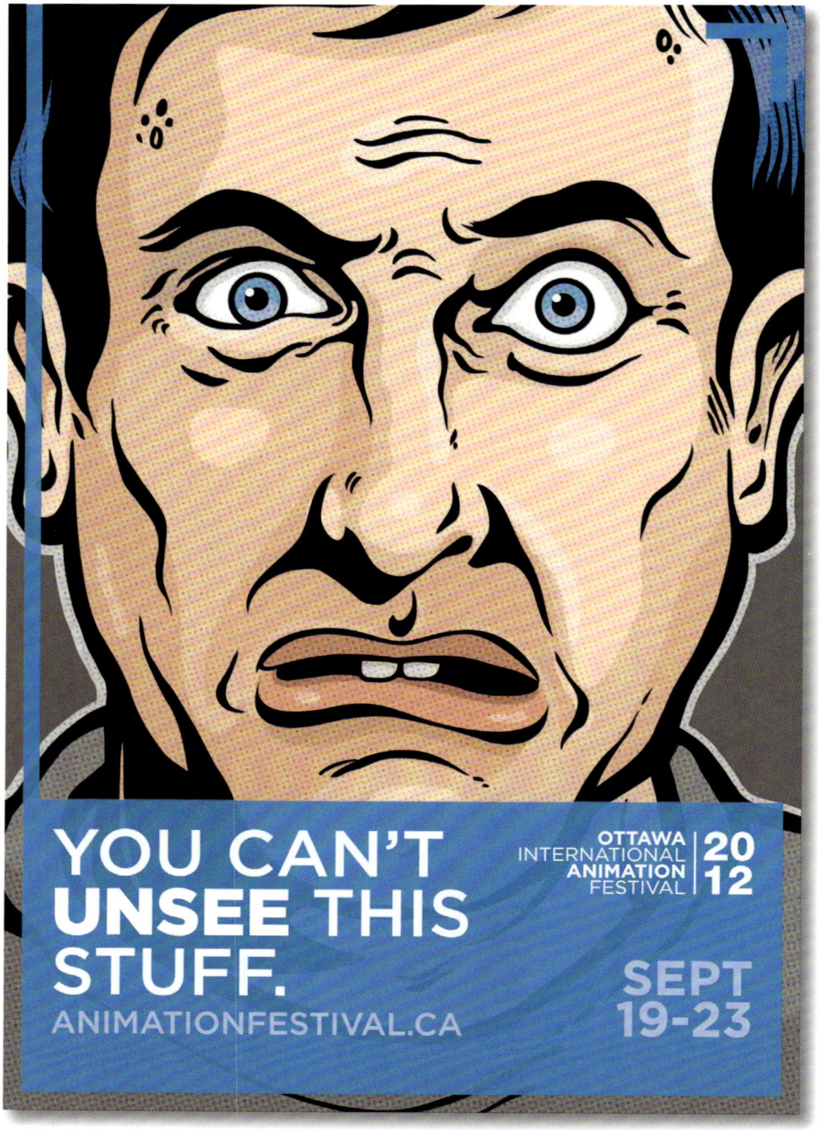

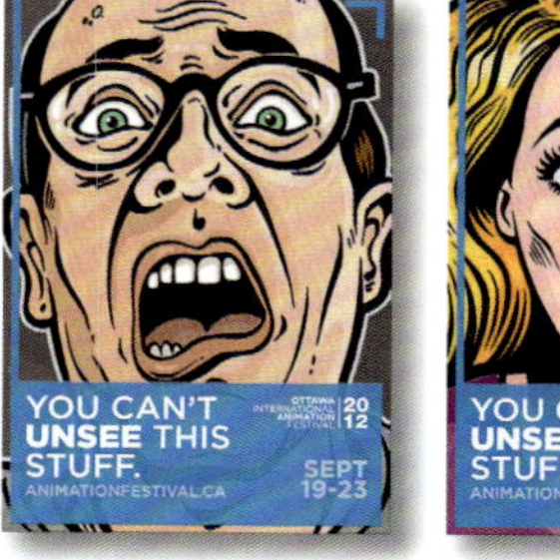

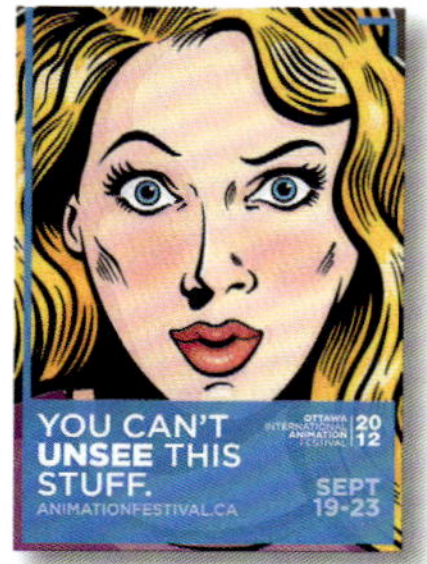

Michael Zavacky

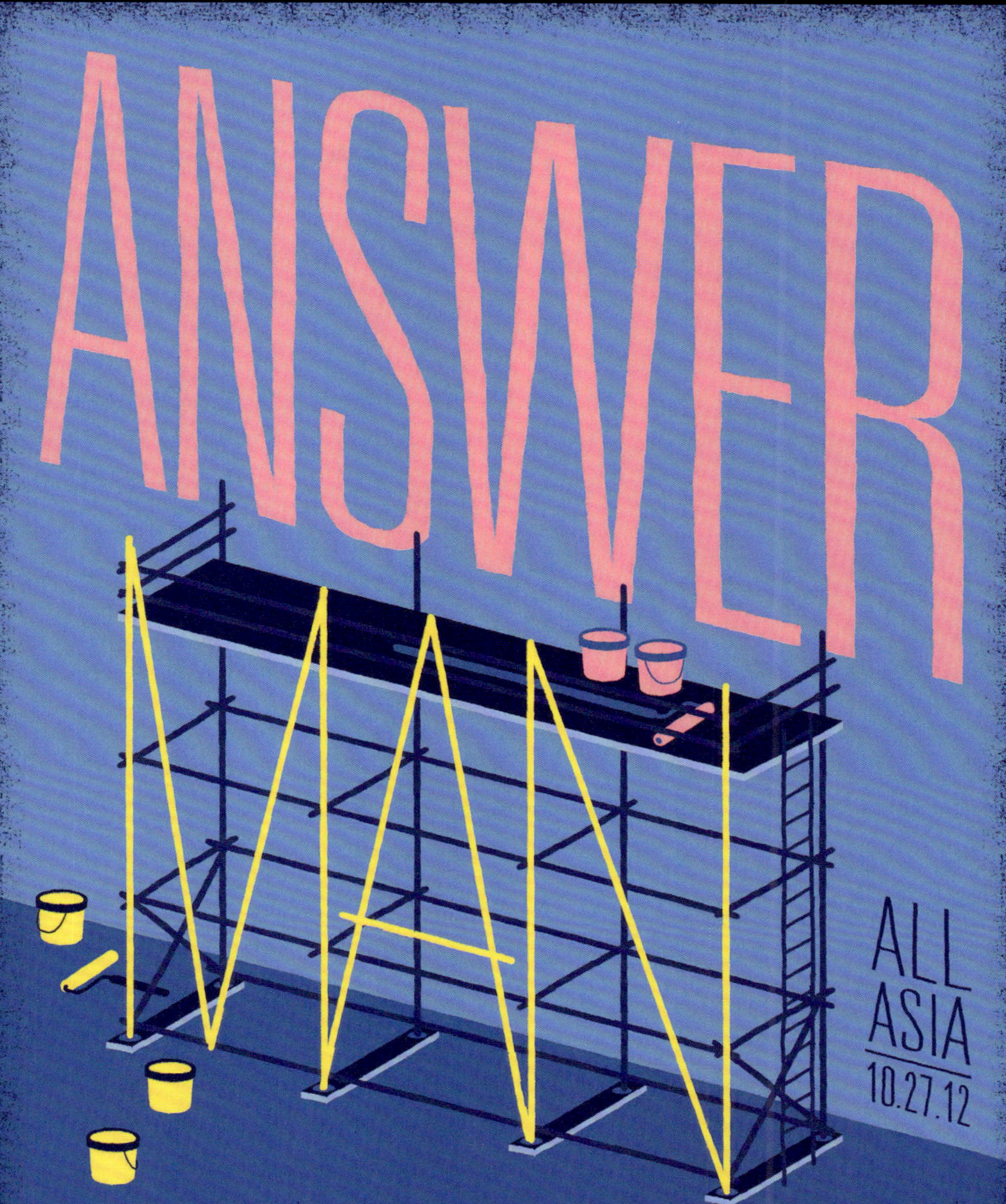

ANSWER
MAN
ALL
ASIA
10.27.12

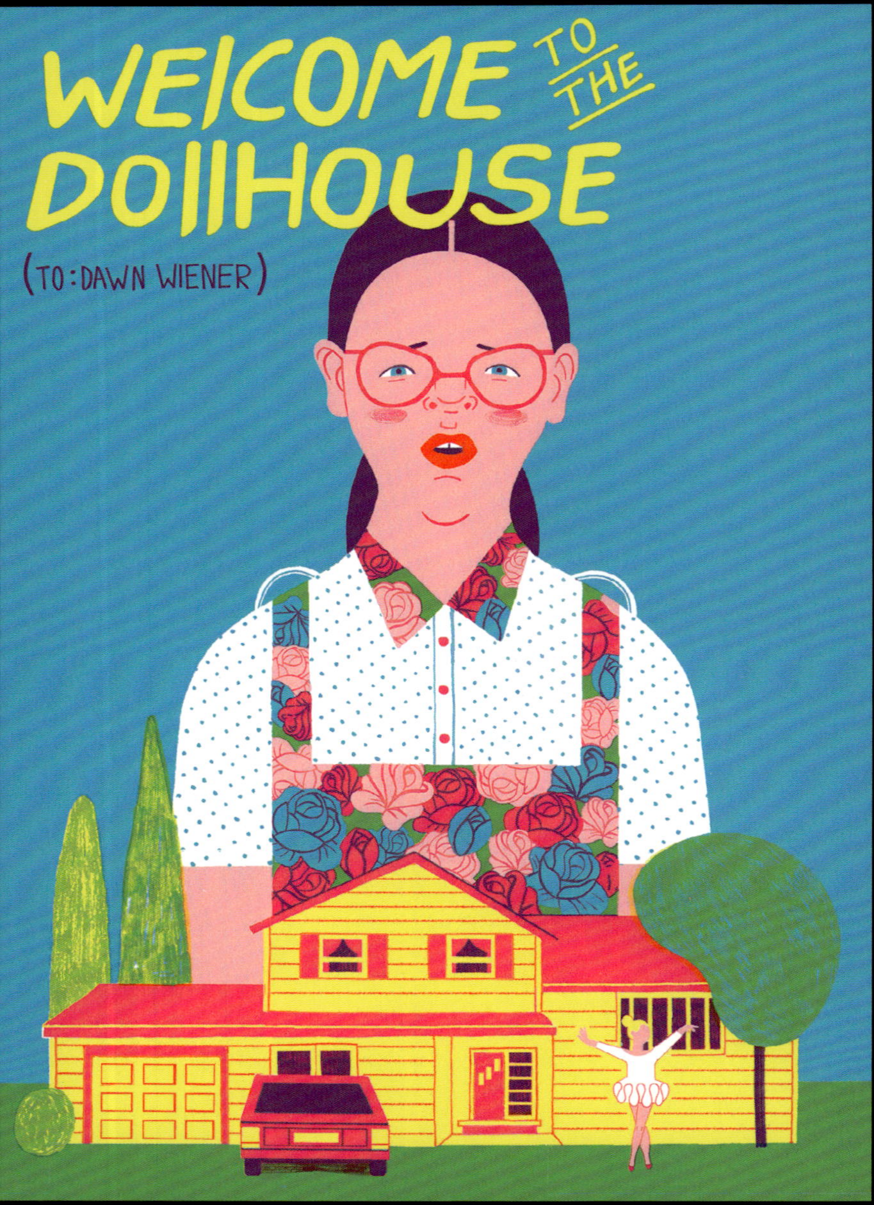

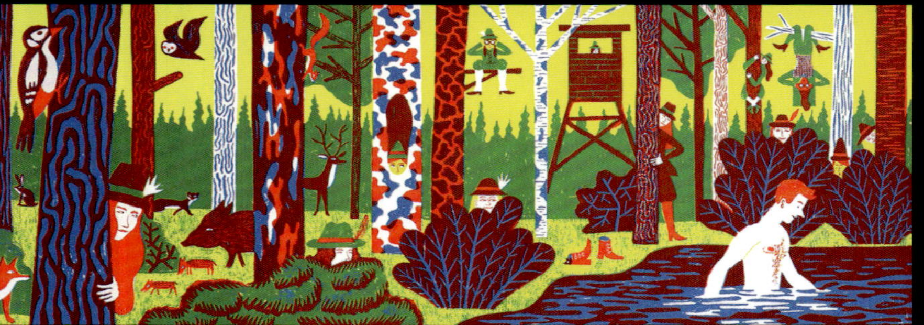
WEICOME TO THE
DOIIHOUSE
(TO:DAWN WIENER)

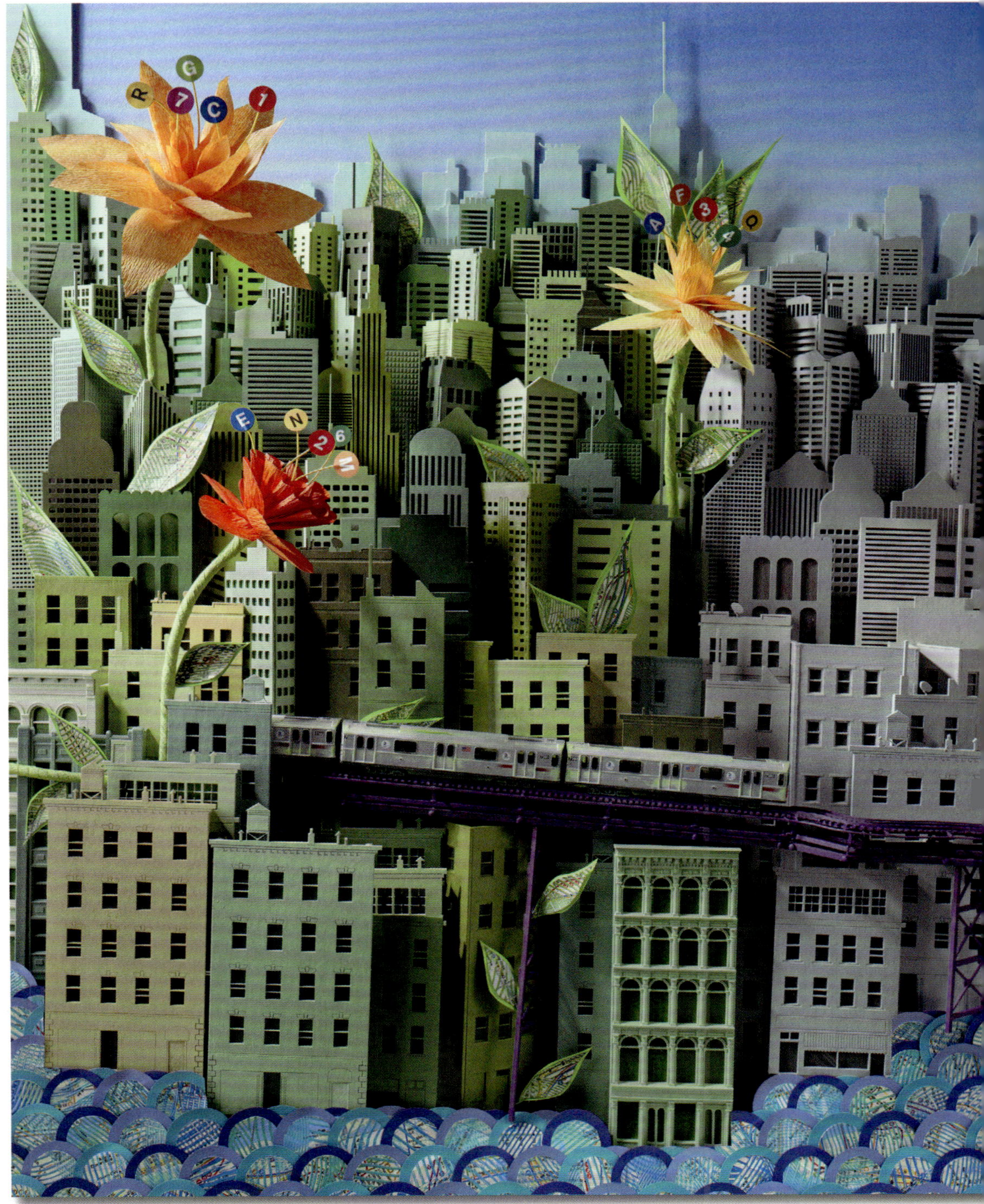

(TL) **SILVER** *Ella Cohen* (BL) *Golden Cosmos* (R) *Pushart*

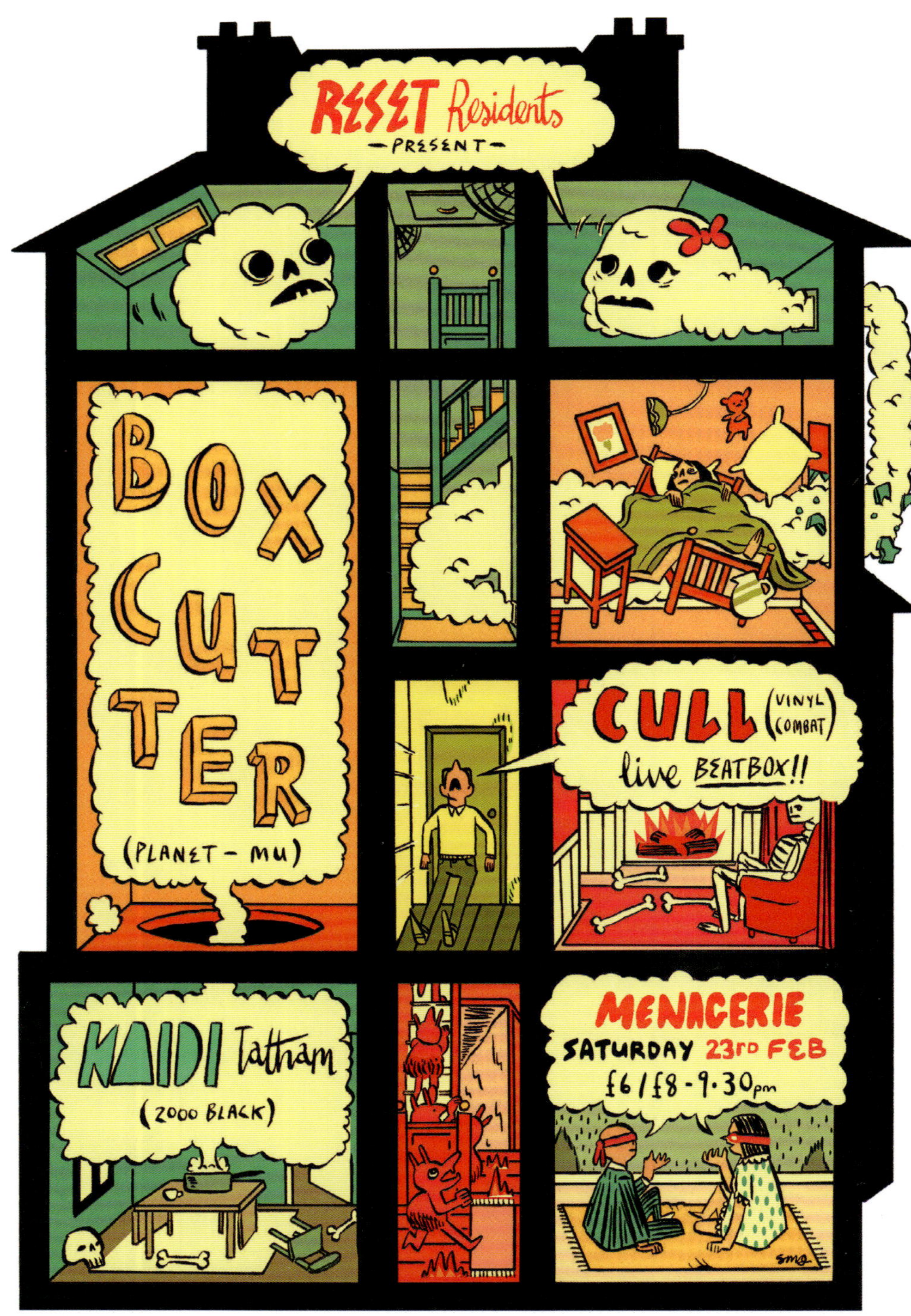

(L) *Stephen Maurice Graham* (R) *Yeji Yun*

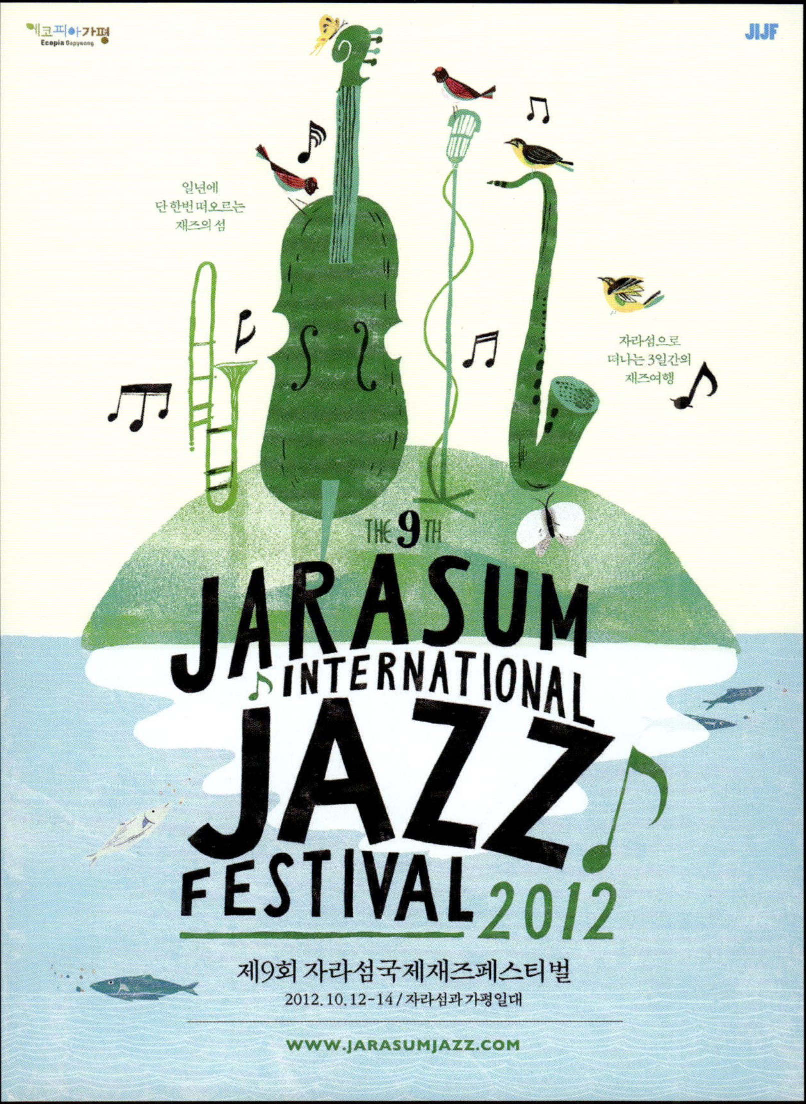

Ecopia Gapyeong
JIJF
일년에
단 한번 떠오르는
재즈의 섬
자라섬으로
떠나는 3일간의
재즈여행
THE 9TH
JARASUM
INTERNATIONAL
JAZZ
FESTIVAL 2012
제9회 자라섬국제재즈페스티벌
2012. 10. 12-14 / 자라섬과 가평일대
WWW.JARASUMJAZZ.COM

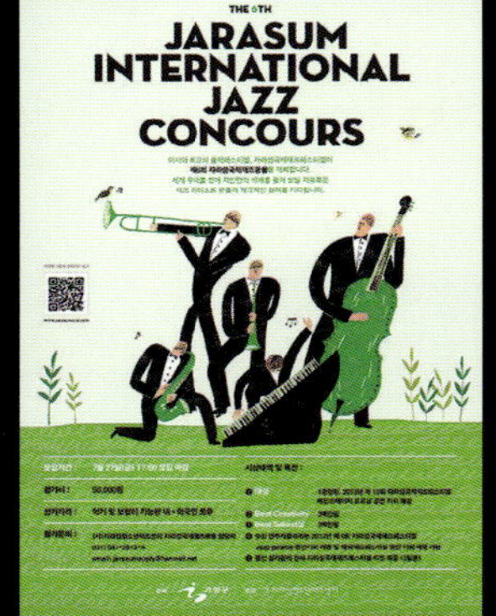

THE 8TH
JARASUM
INTERNATIONAL
JAZZ
CONCOURS

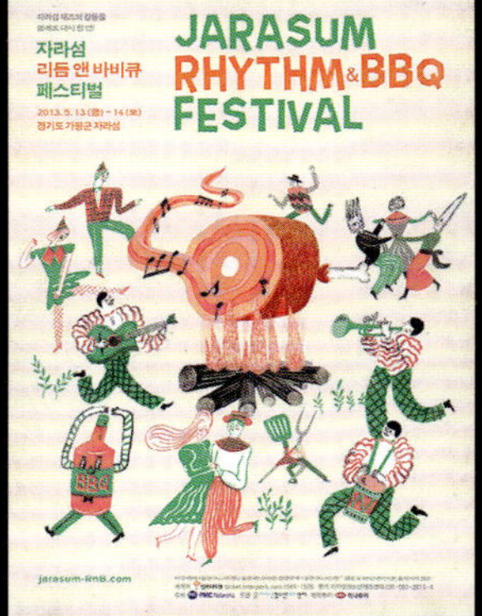

자라섬
리듬 앤 바비큐
페스티벌
2013. 5. 13(월) - 14(토)
경기도 가평군 자라섬
JARASUM
RHYTHM&BBQ
FESTIVAL
jarasum-RnB.com

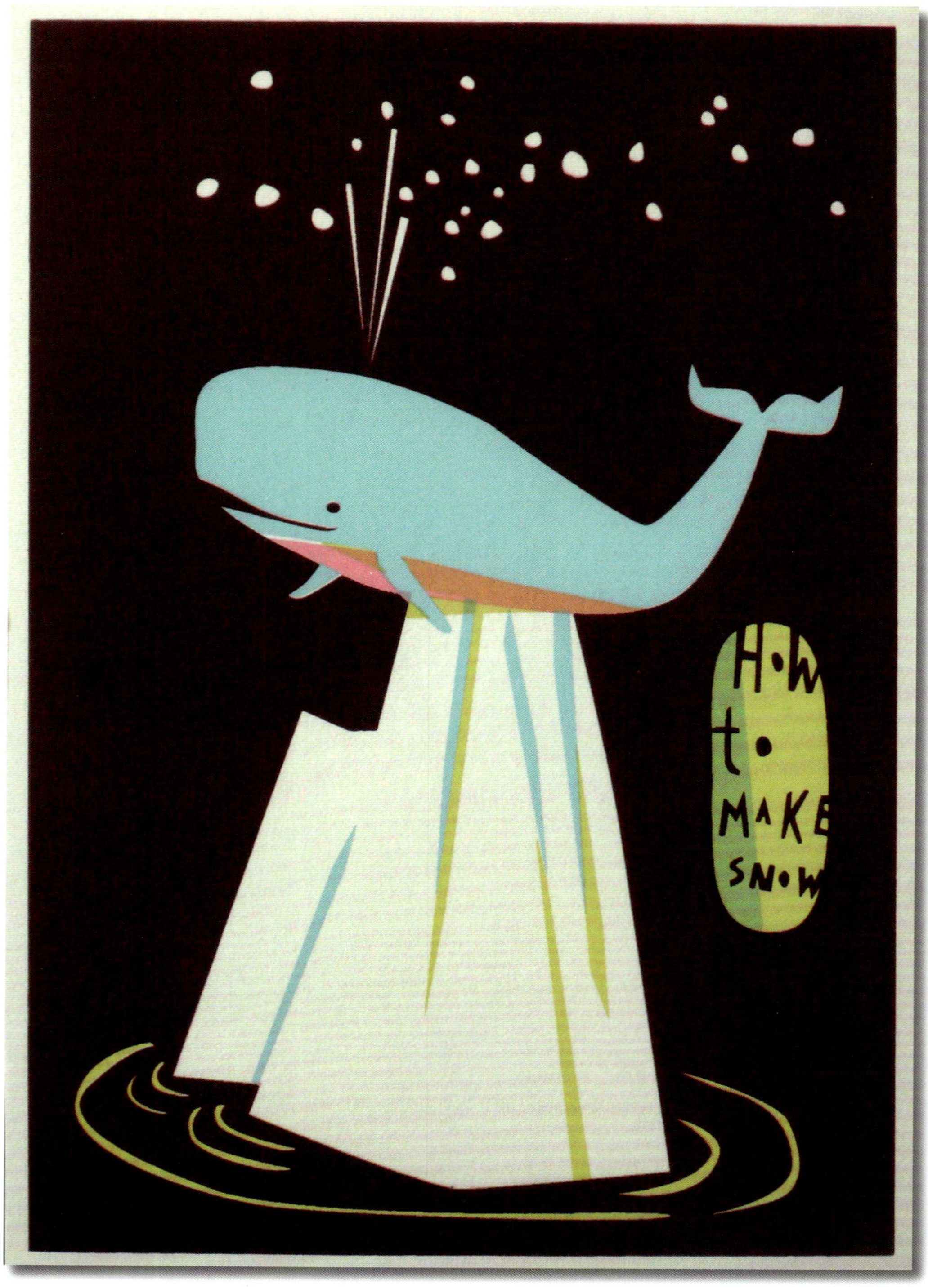

(L) *Monika Aichele* (R) *Zara Picken*

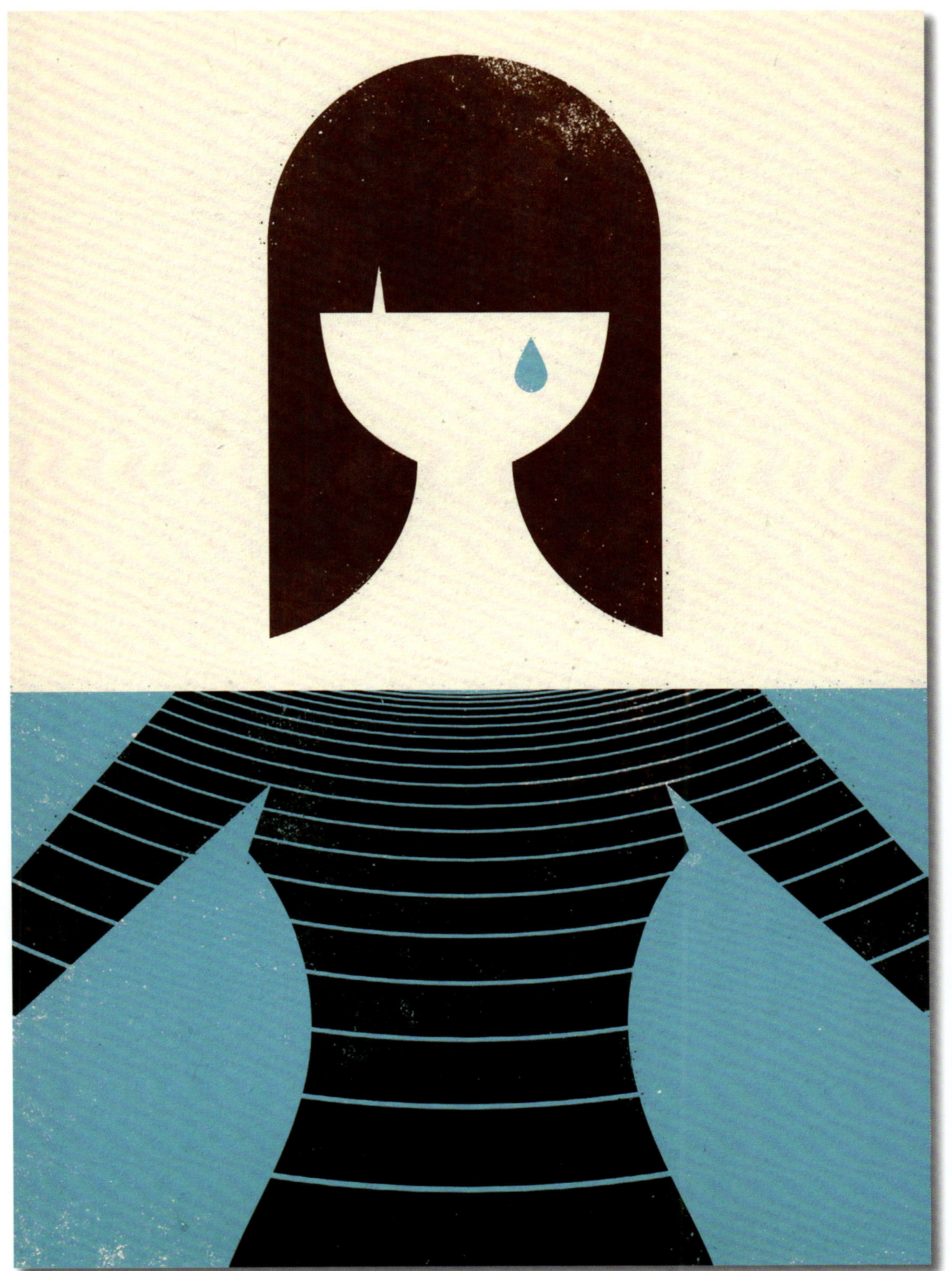

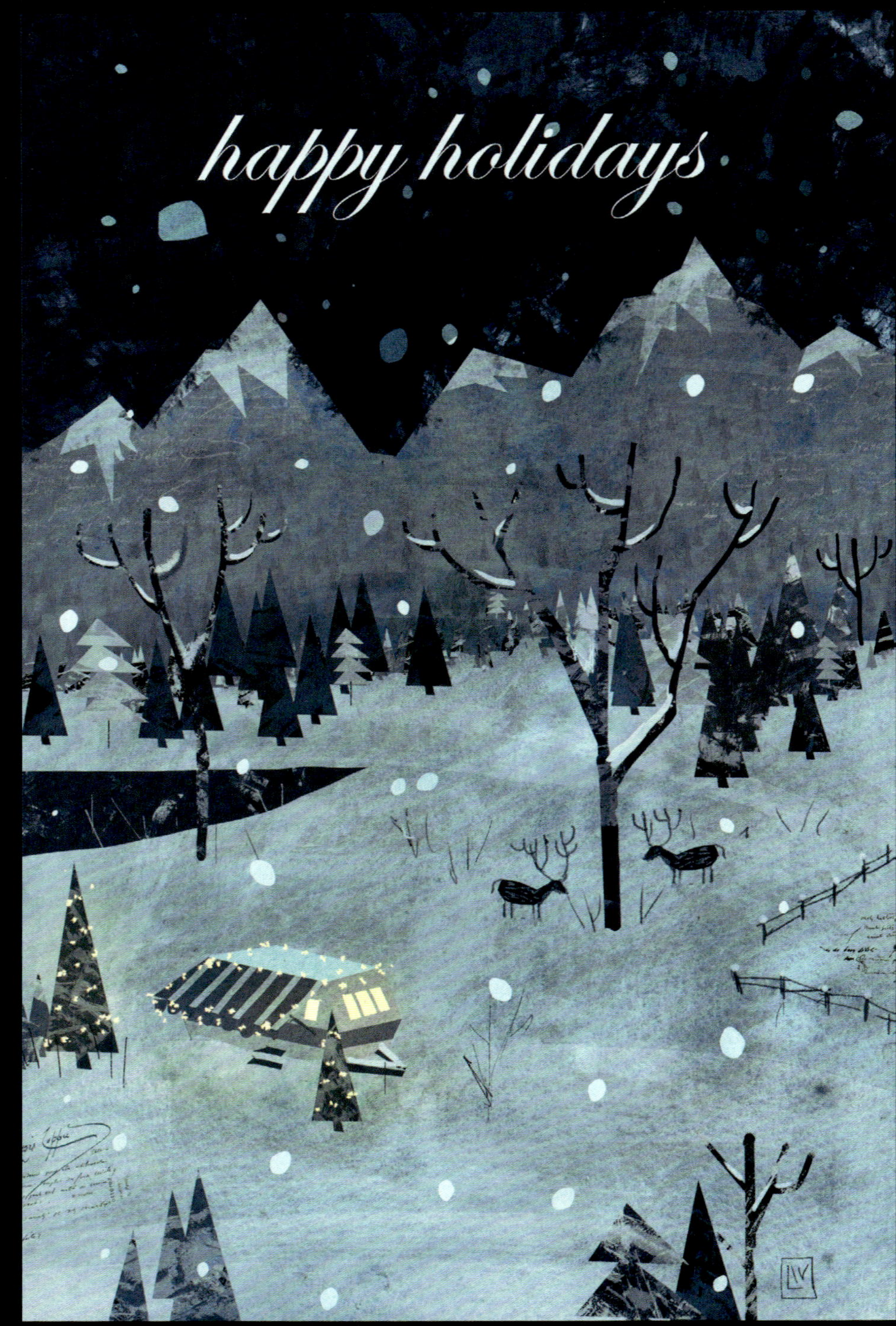
happy holidays

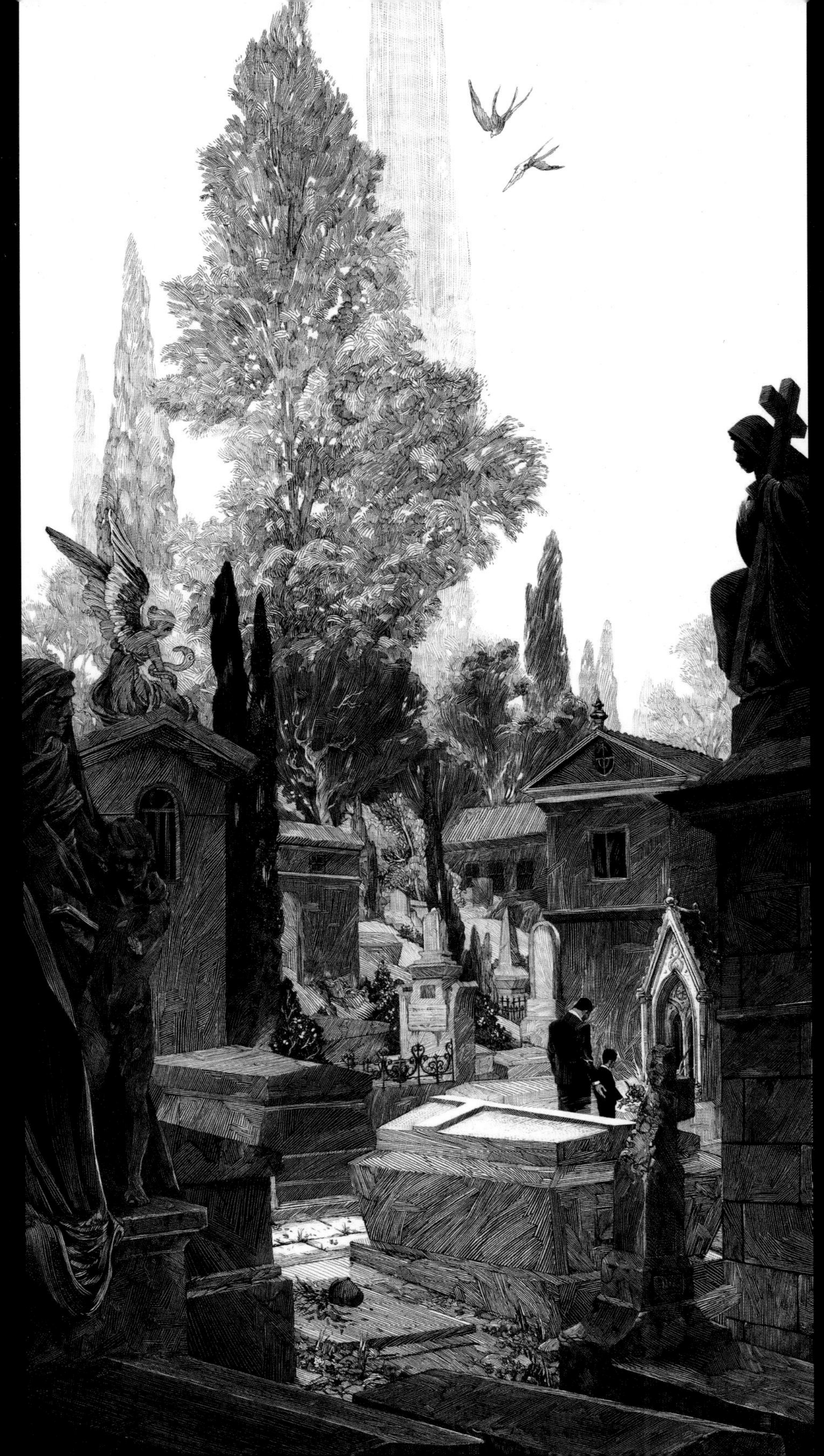

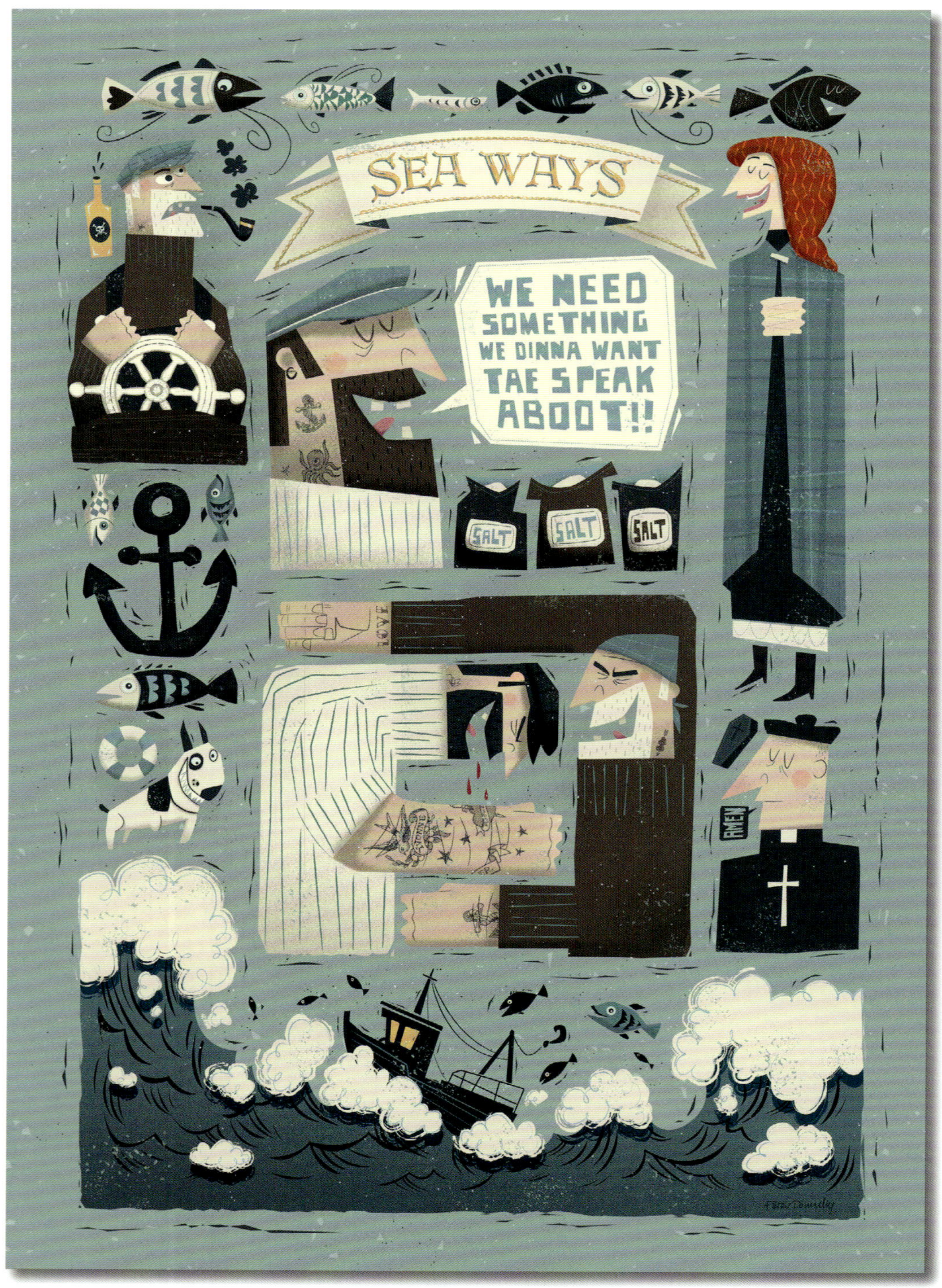

(L) *Peter Donnelly* (TR) *Peter Donnelly* (BR) *Andrew R. Wright*

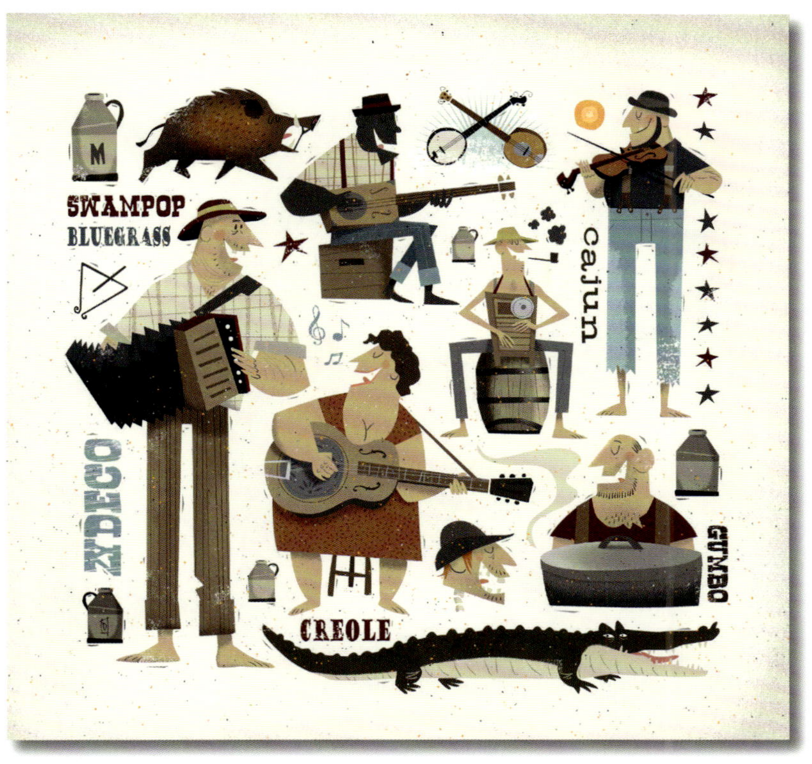

SWAMPOP
BLUEGRASS
cajun
ZYDECO
CREOLE
GUMBO

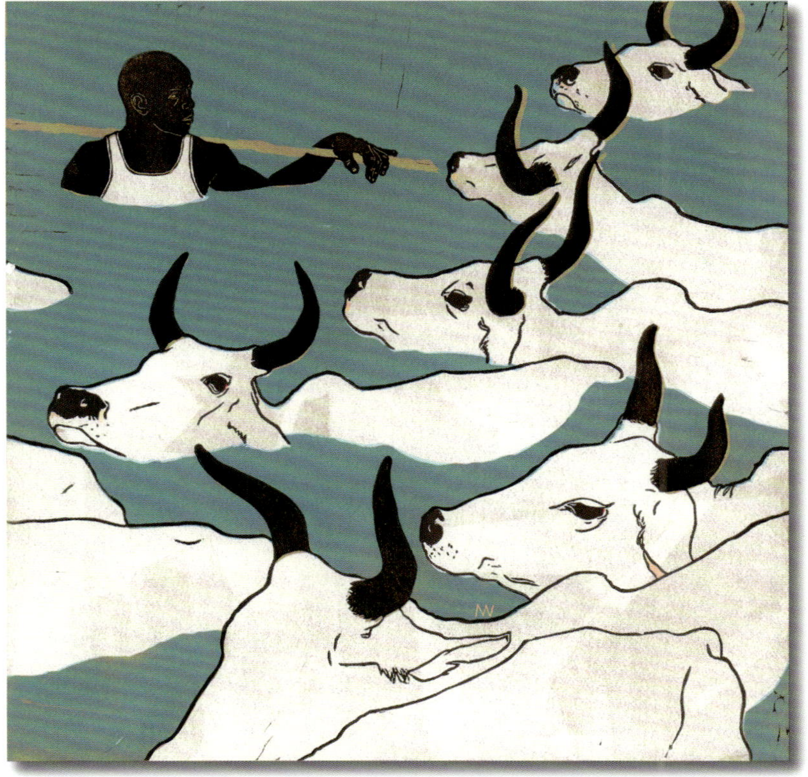

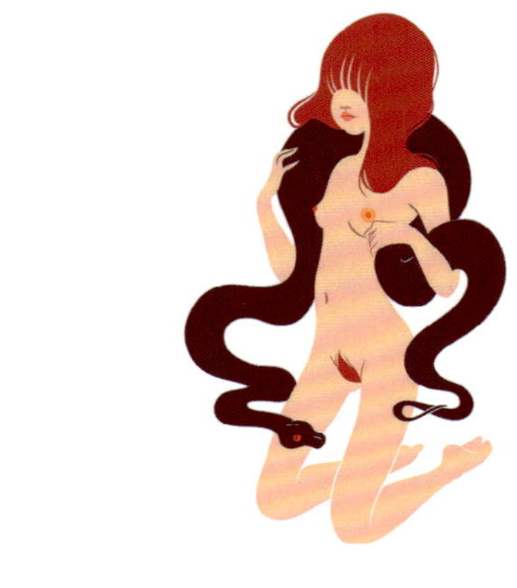
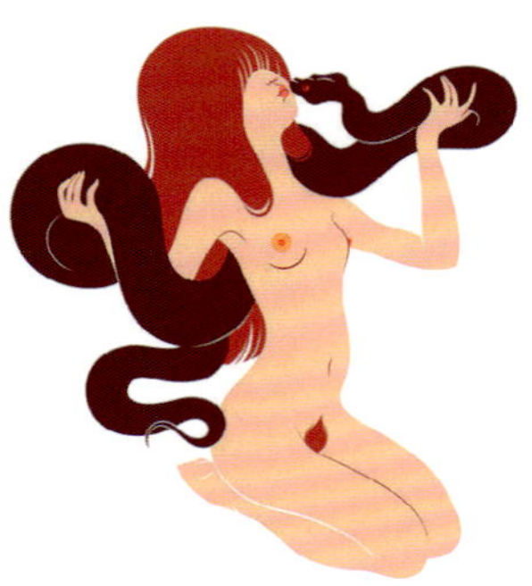
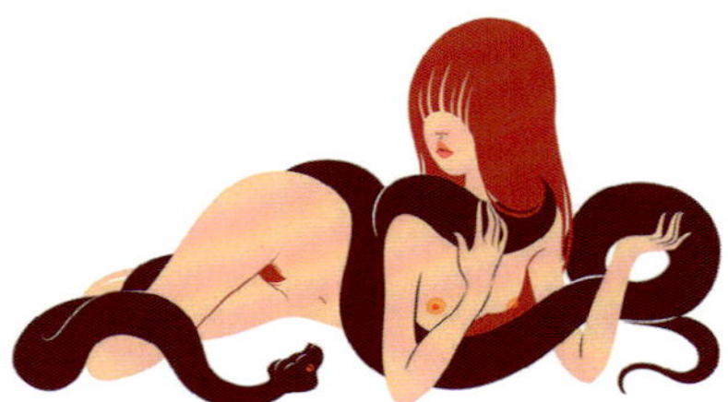
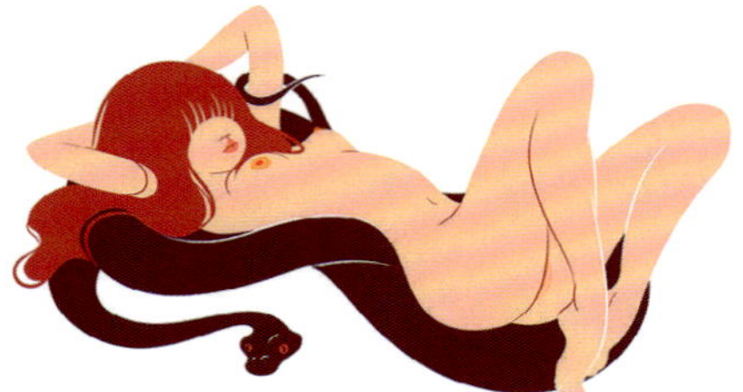
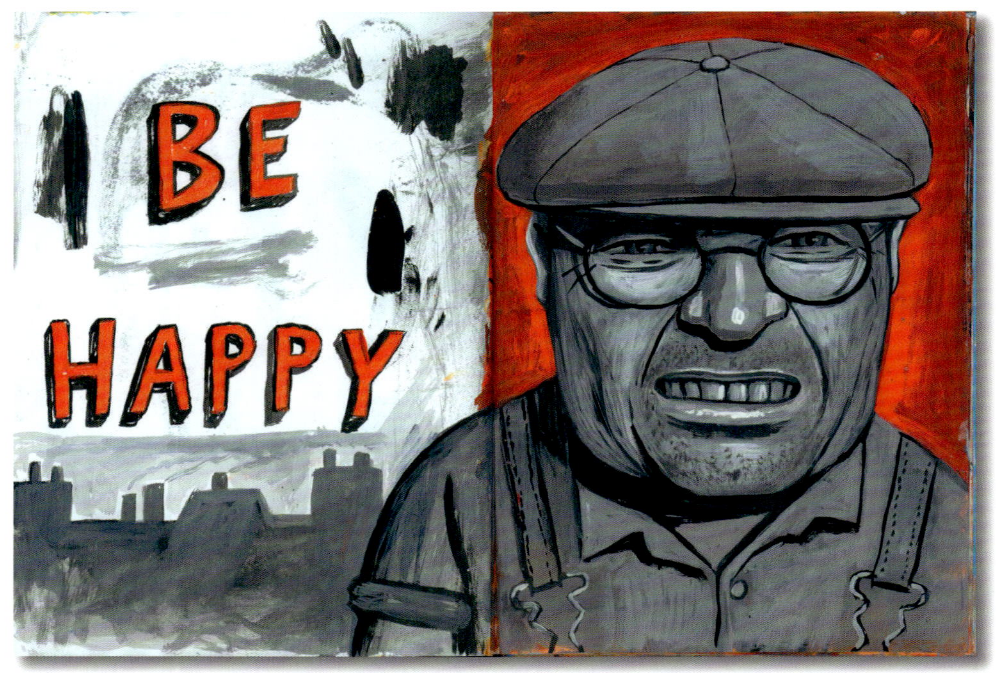

(T) *Gloria Pizzilli* (B) *Charlie Powell* (RT) *Livia Cives* (RB) *Mike Lowery*

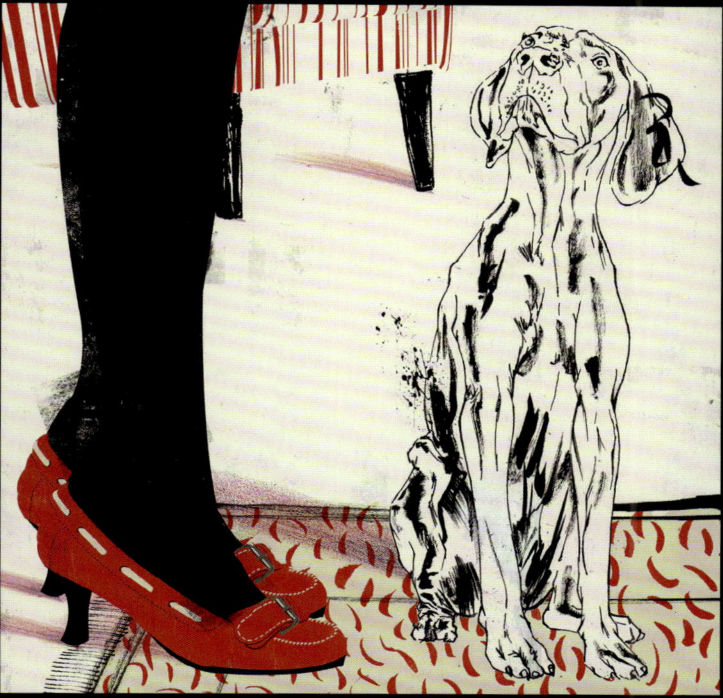

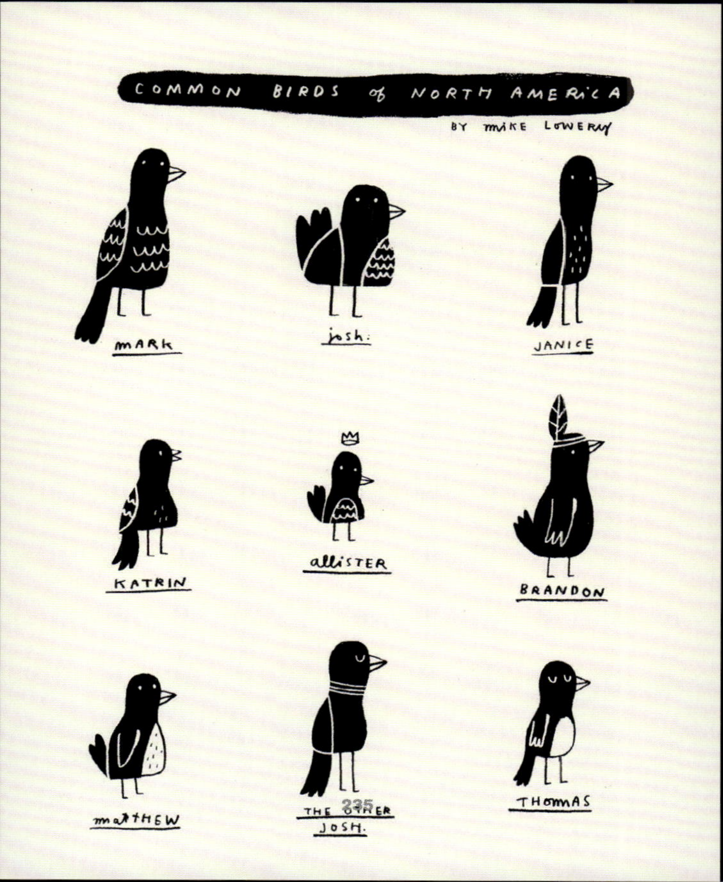

COMMON BIRDS of NORTH AMERICA
BY MiKE LOWERY

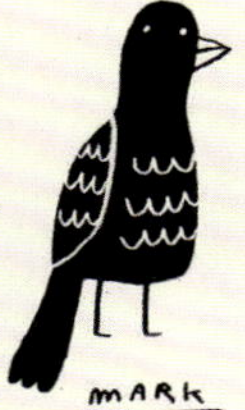

MARK

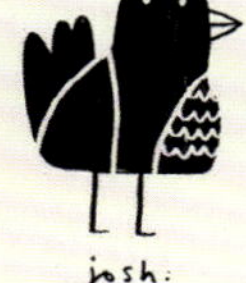

josh.

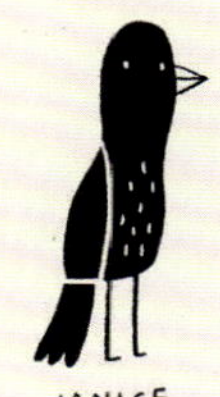

JANICE

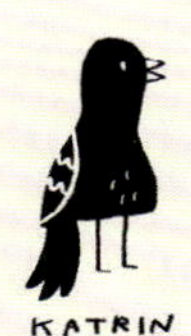

KATRIN

allister

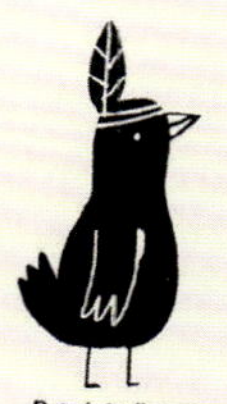

BRANDON

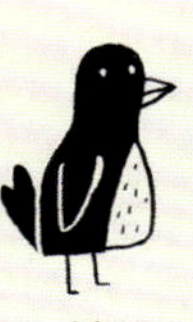

matTHEW

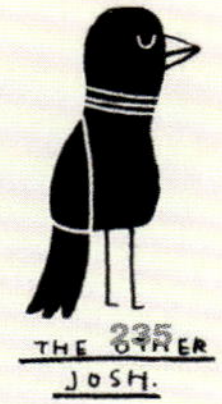

THE OTHER
JOSH.

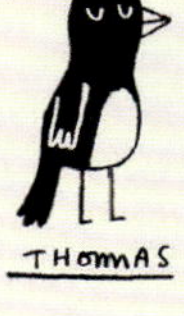

THOMAS

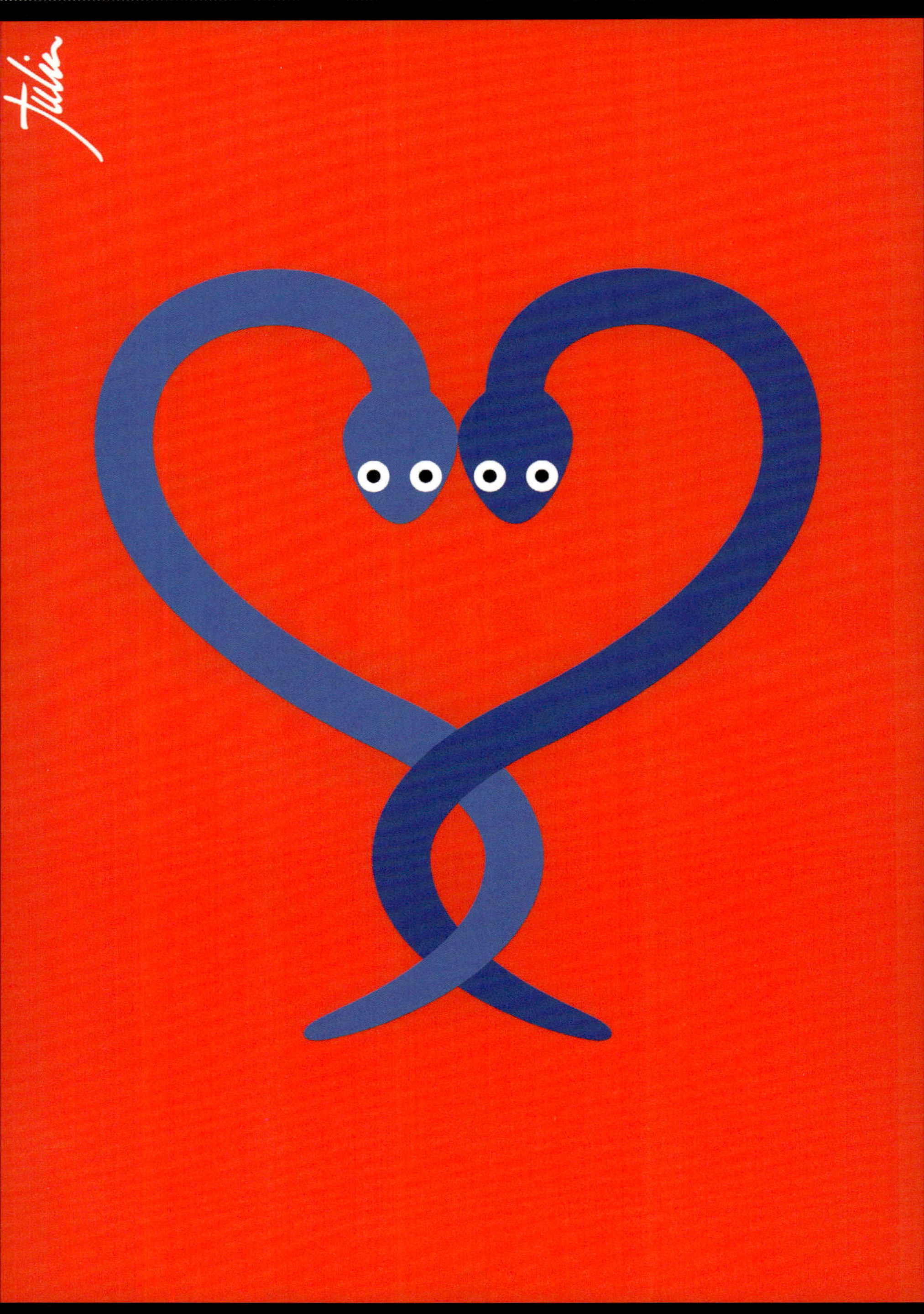

Julien Chung

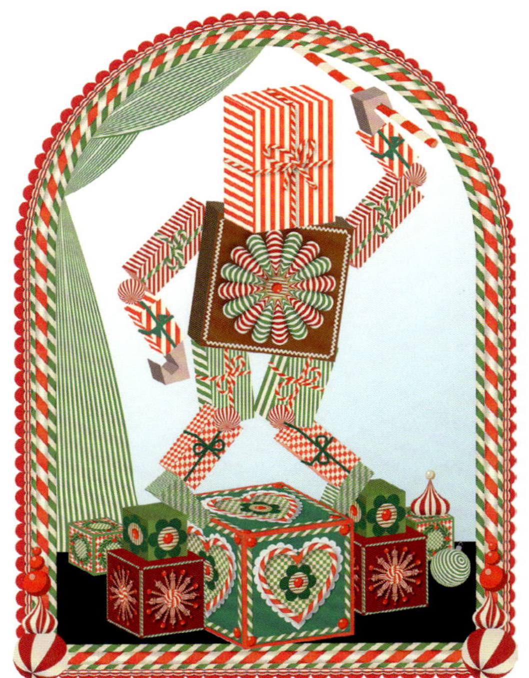
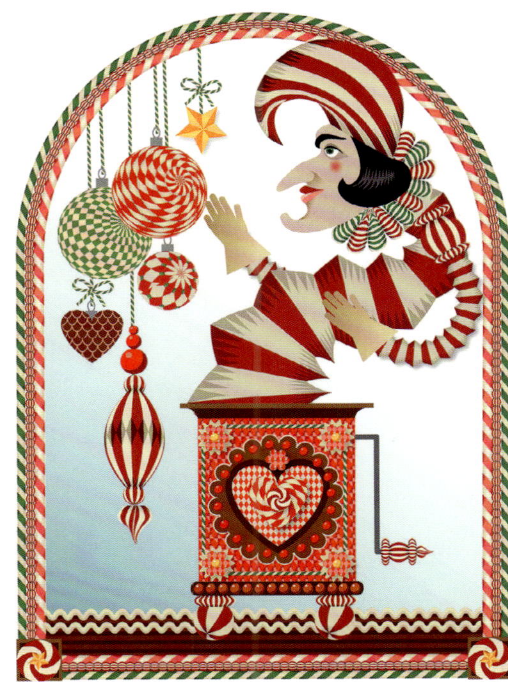
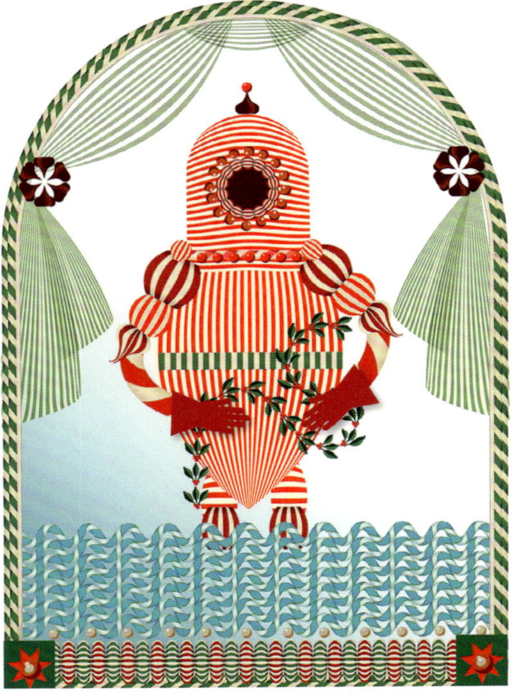
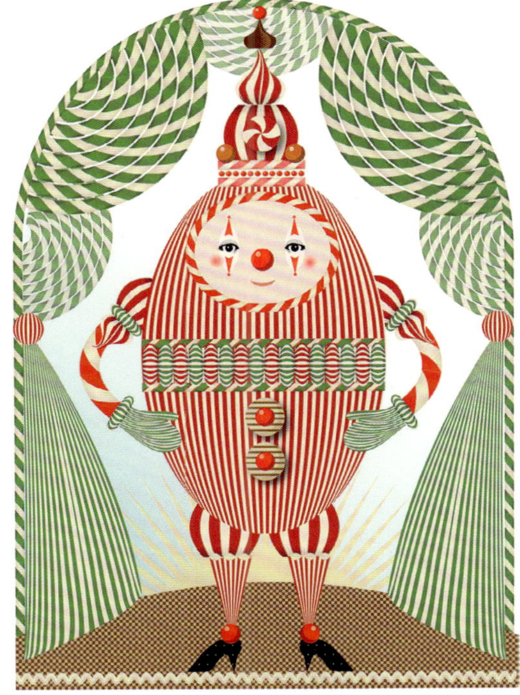

Q. Cassetti

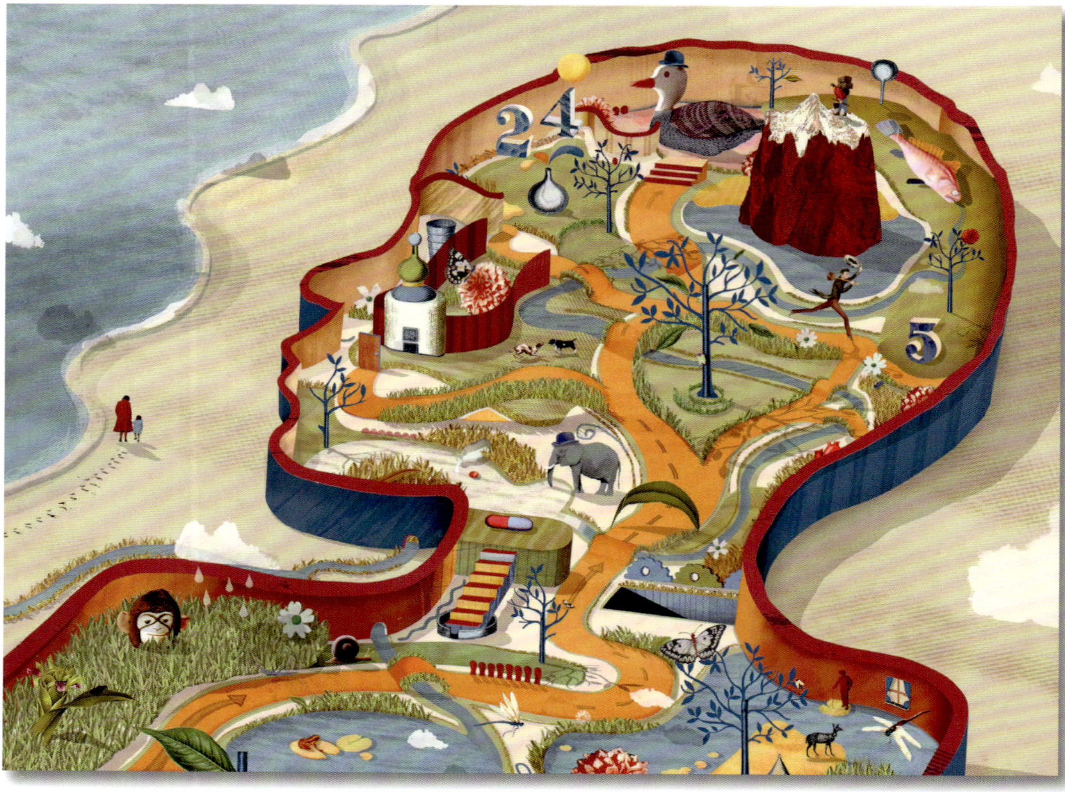

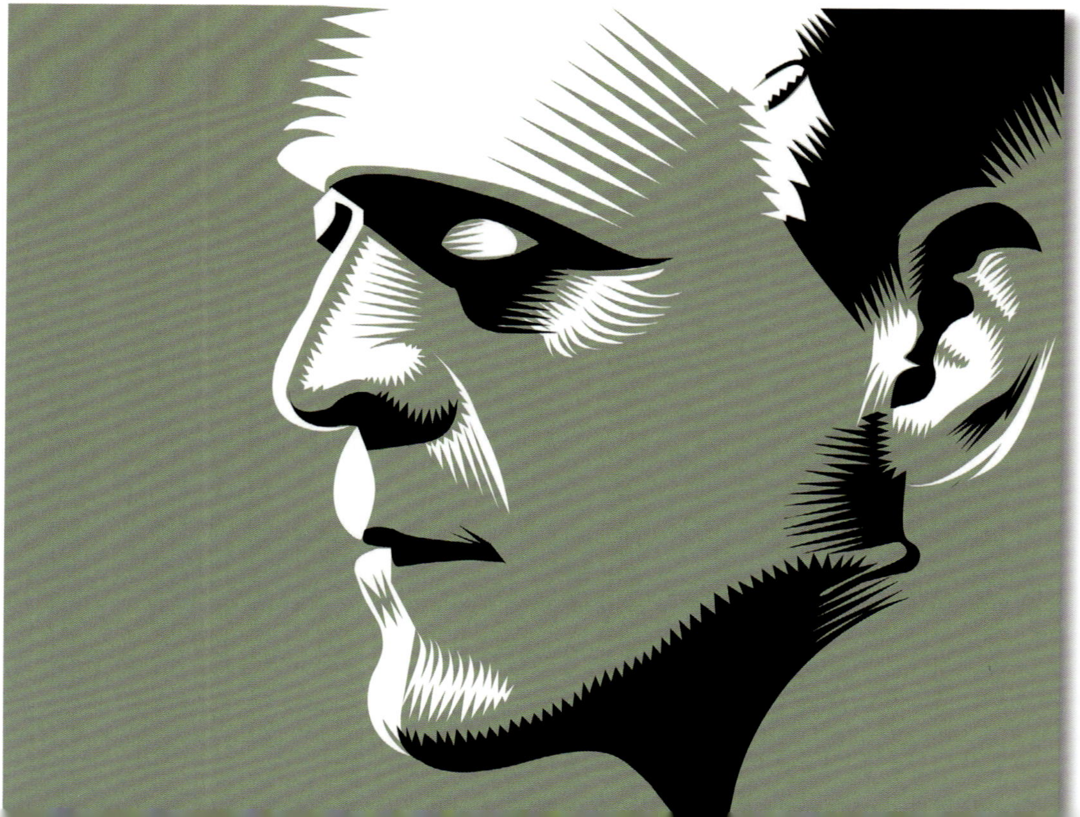

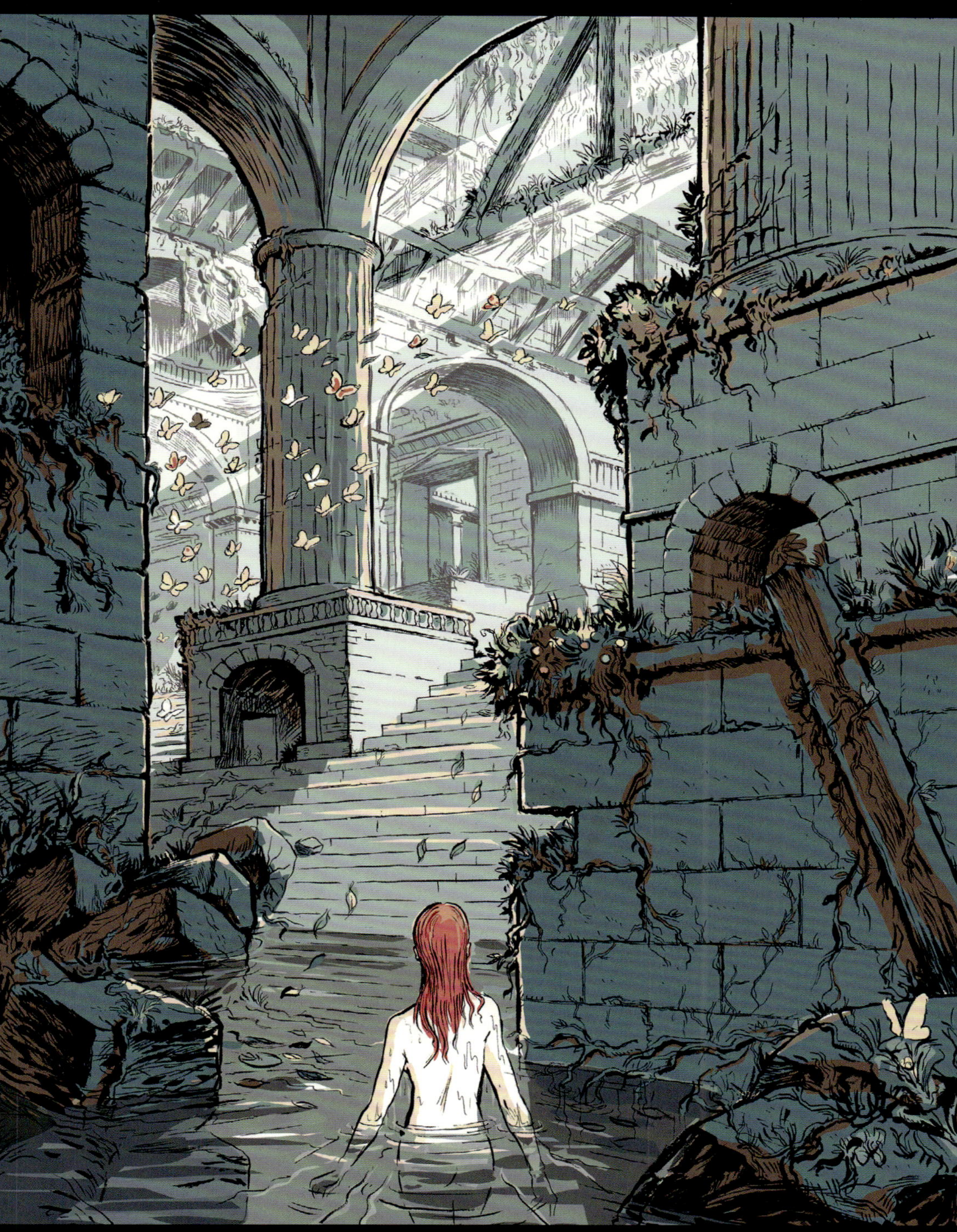

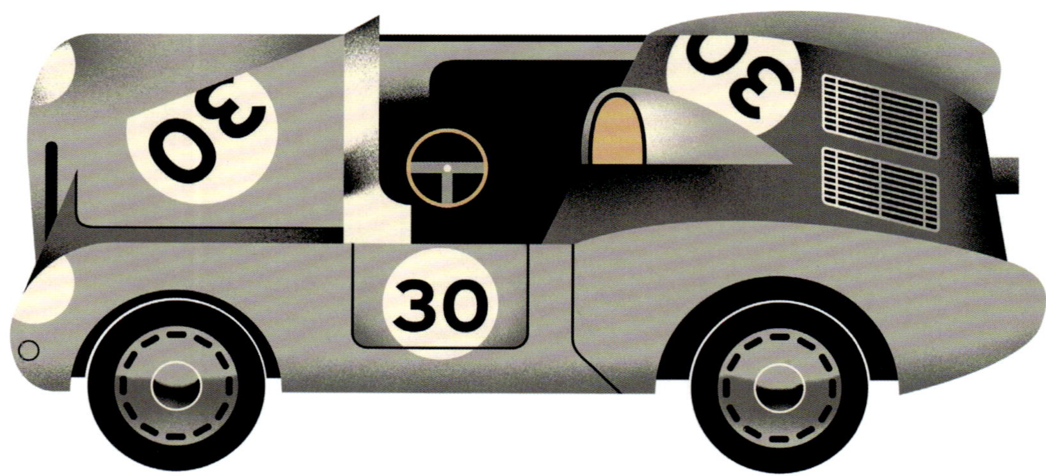

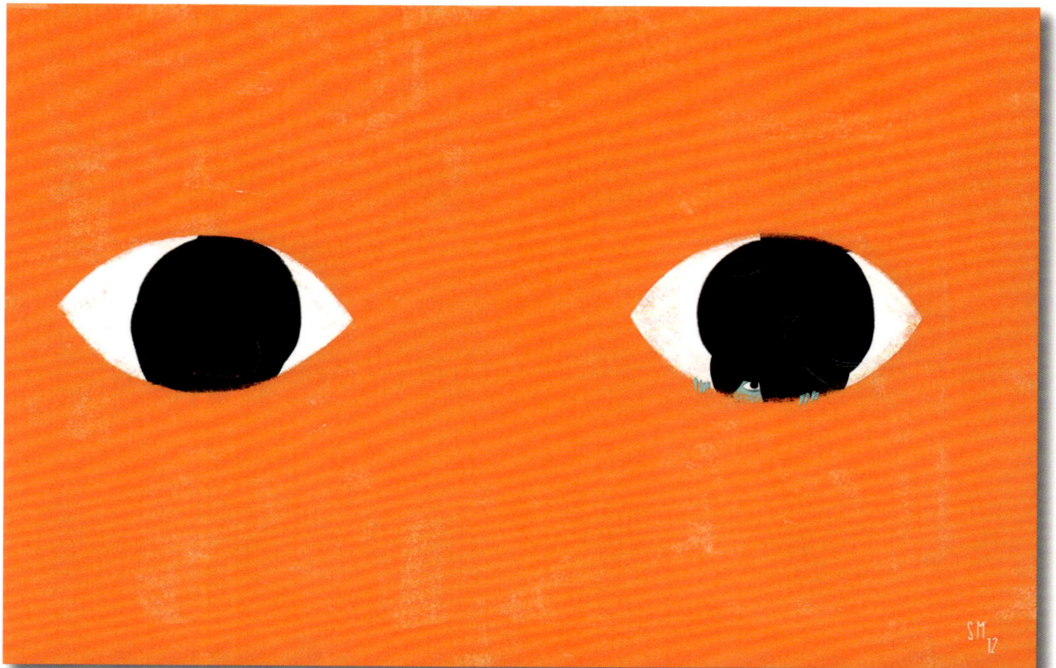

(T) *Dave Murray* (B) *Simone Massoni*

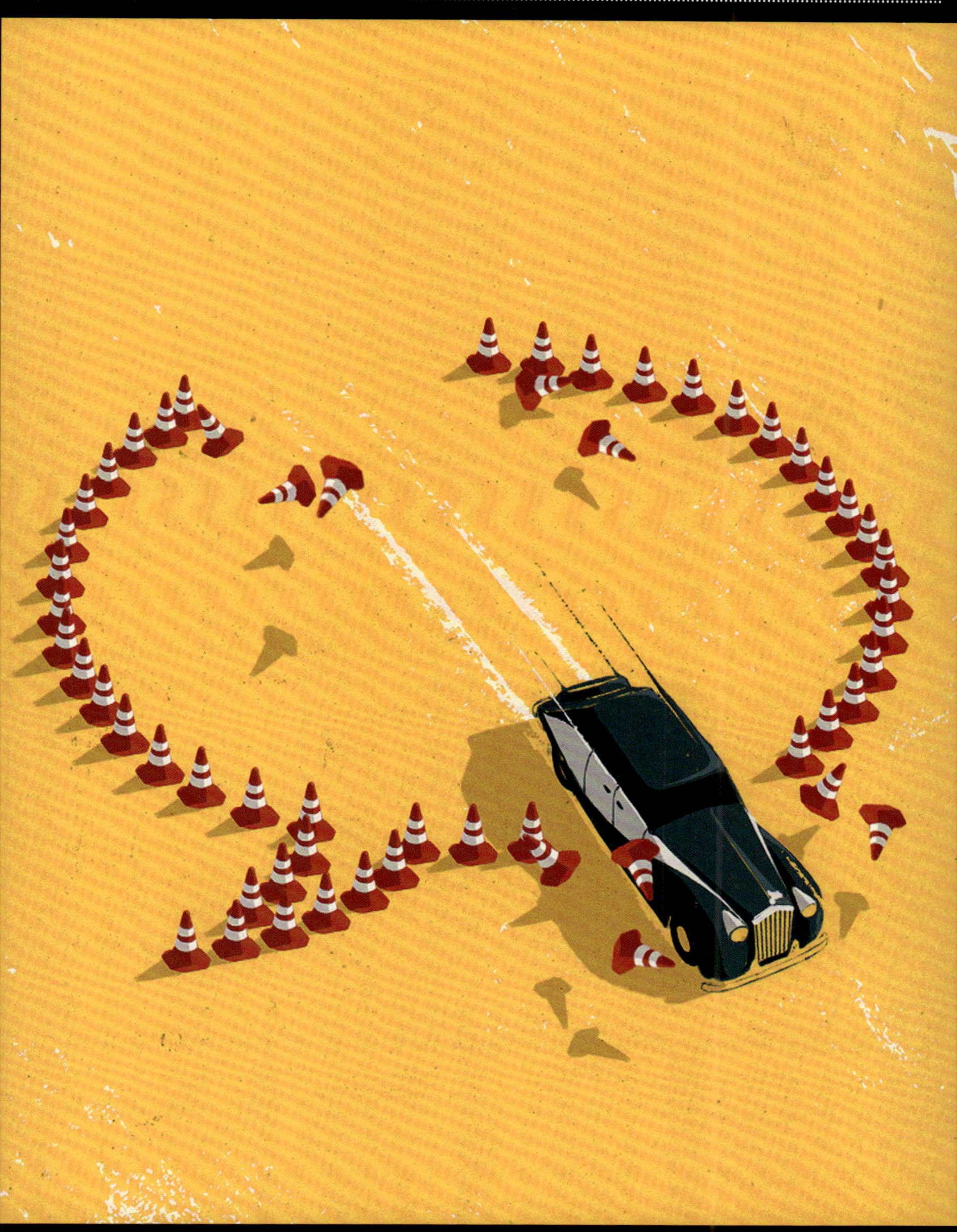

Mark Smith

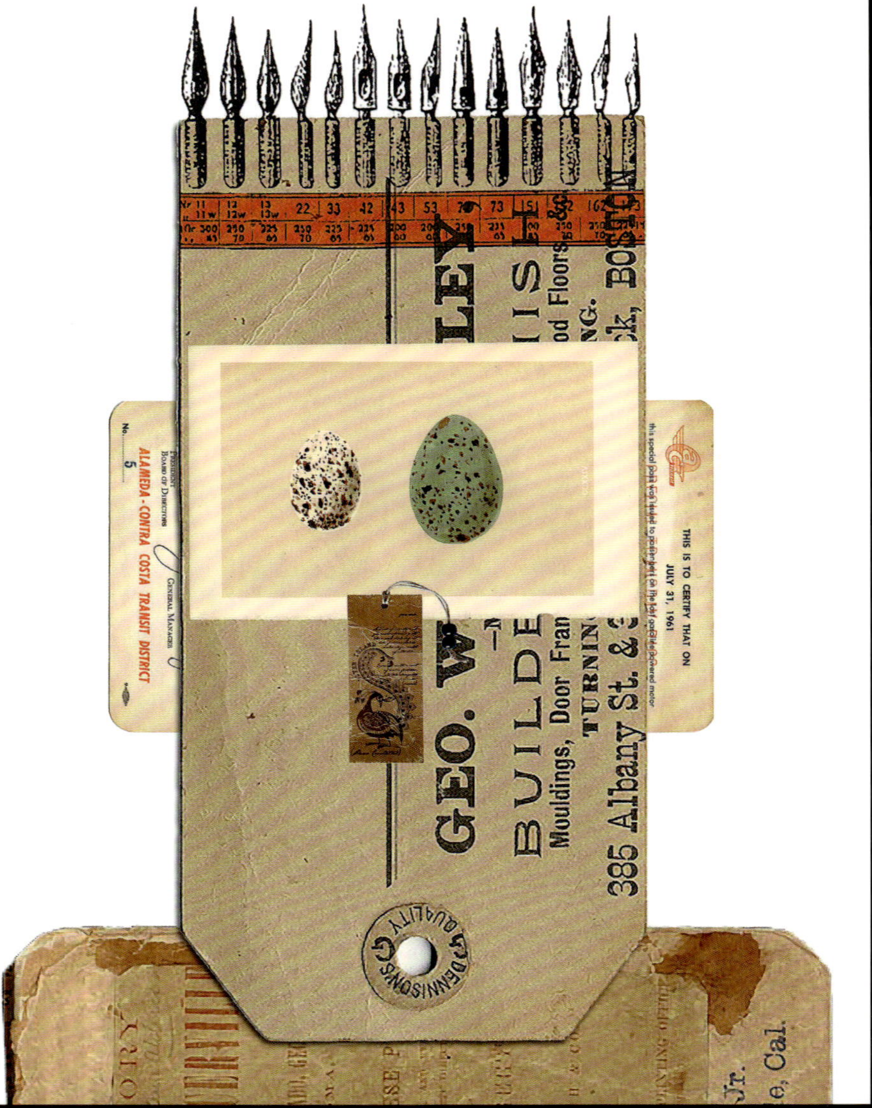

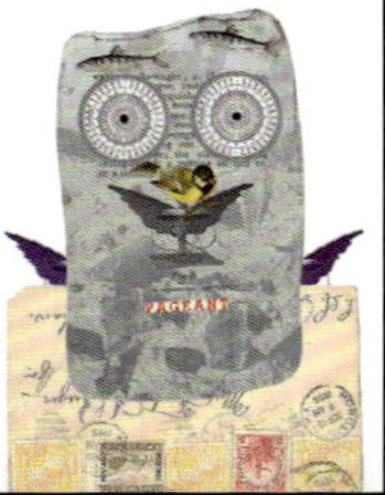
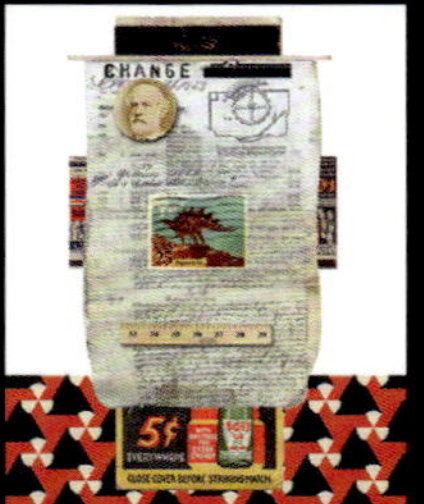
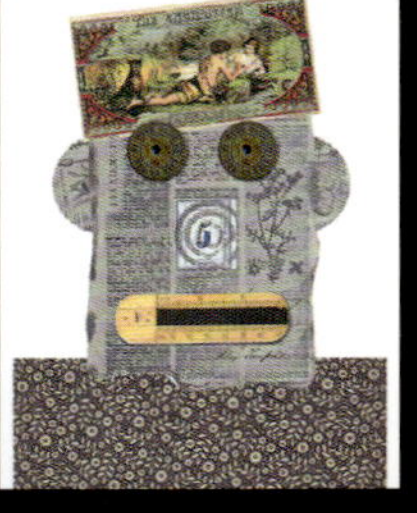
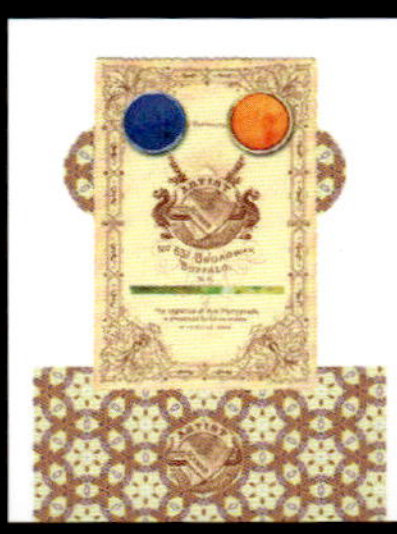

Jim Cohen

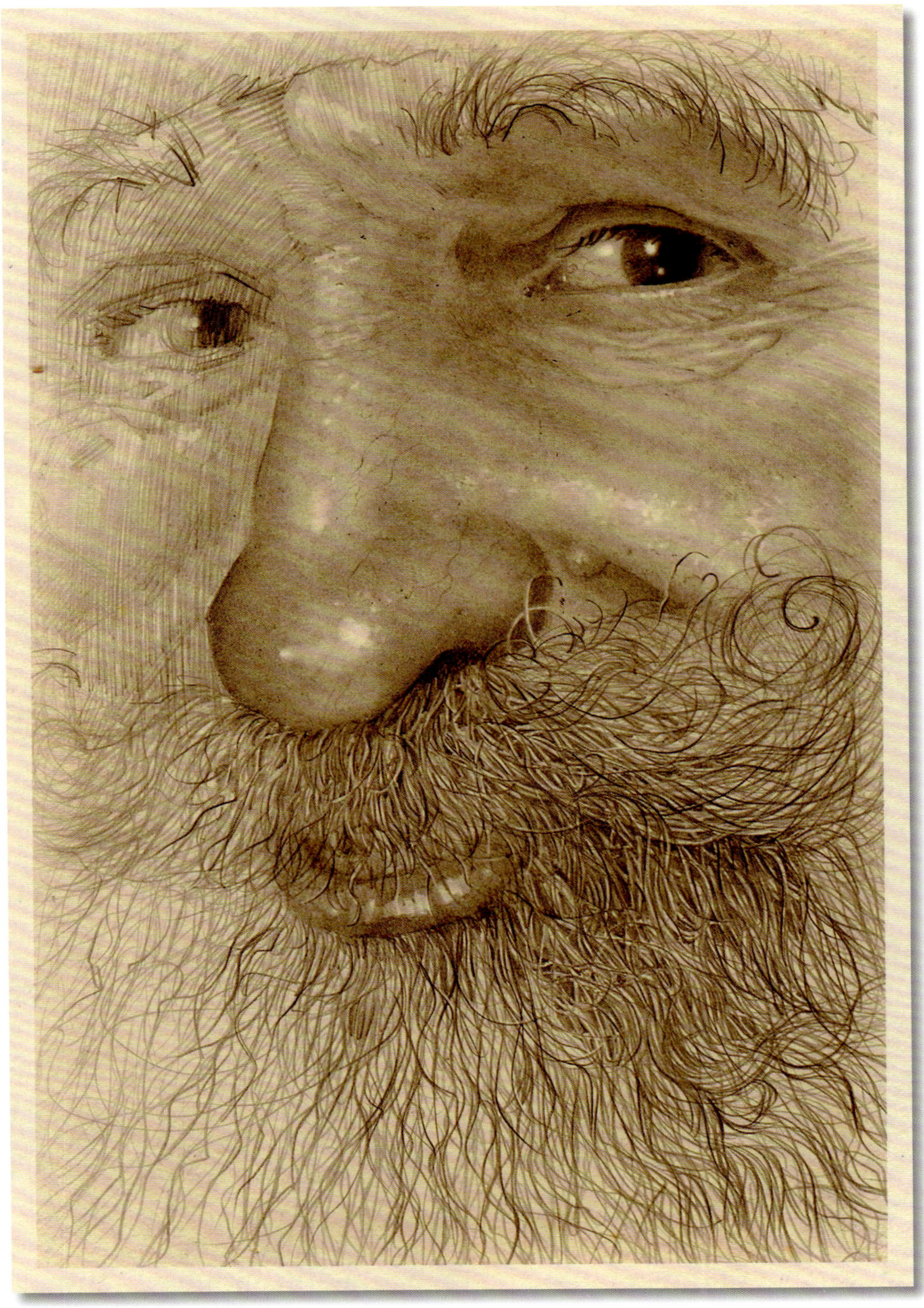

Pawel Zawislak

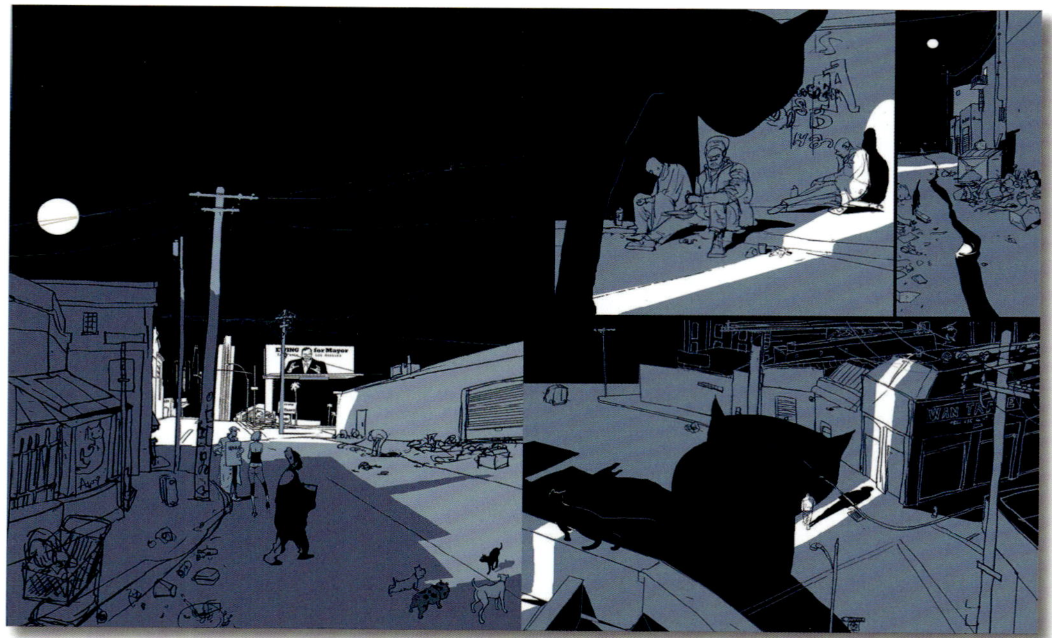
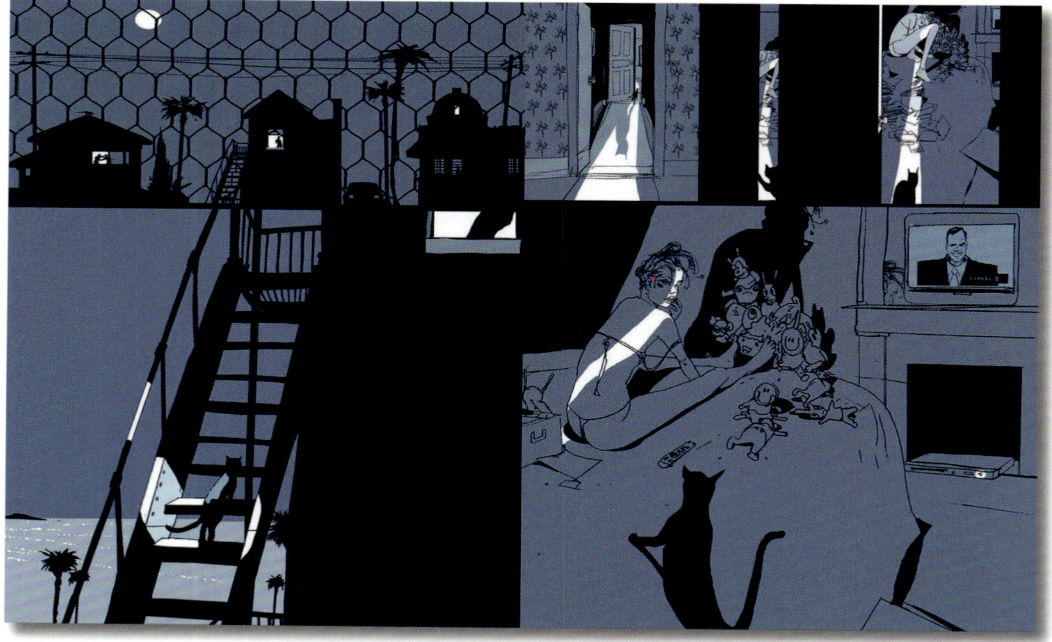

Istvan Banyai

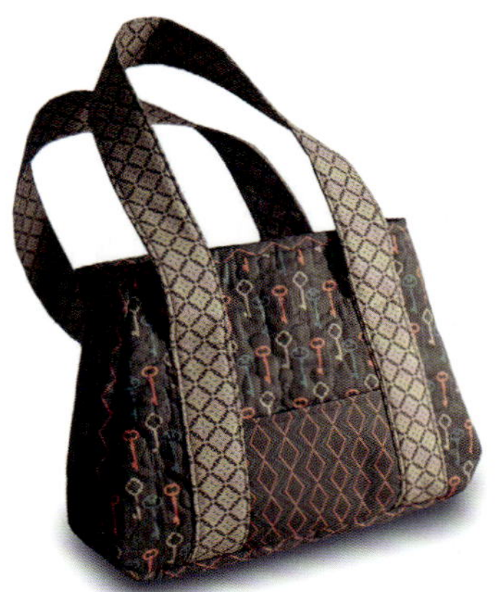

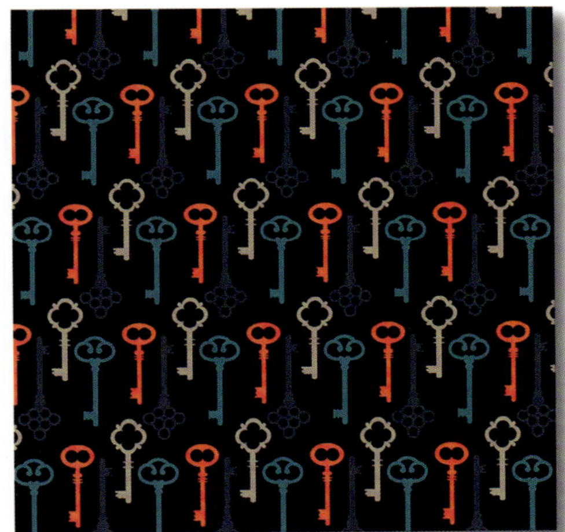

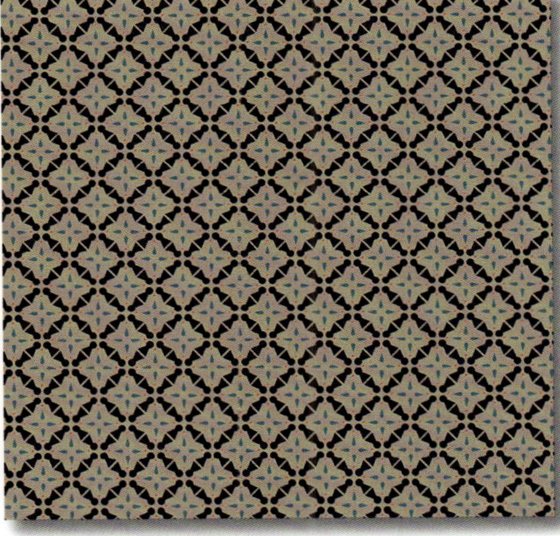

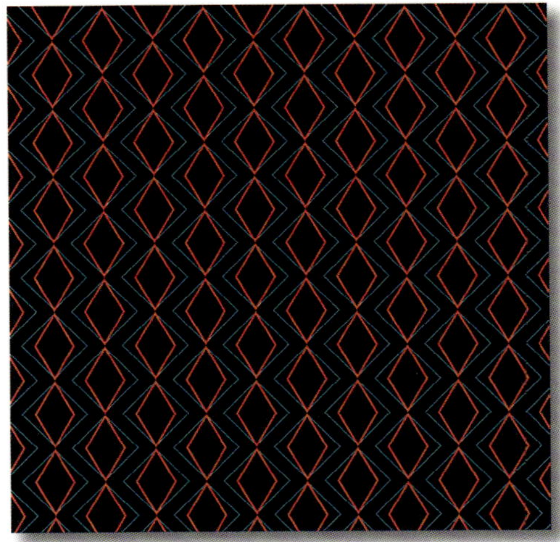

Sherry Saunders

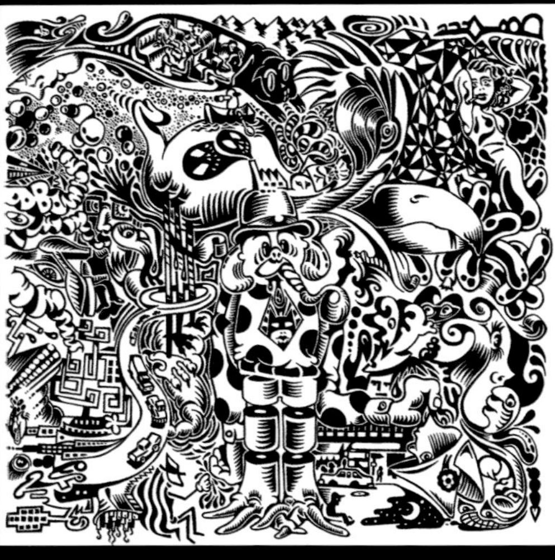

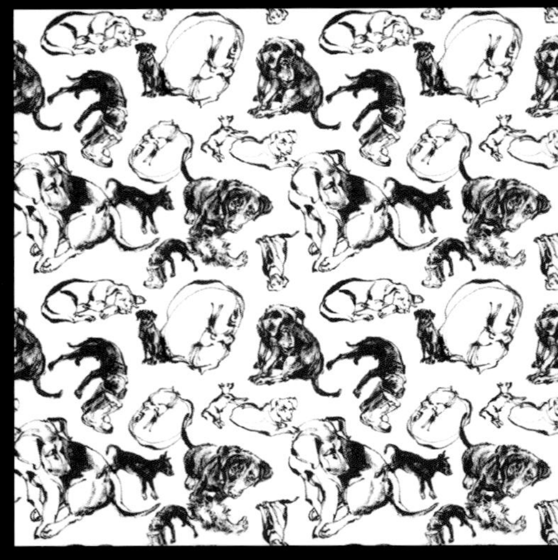

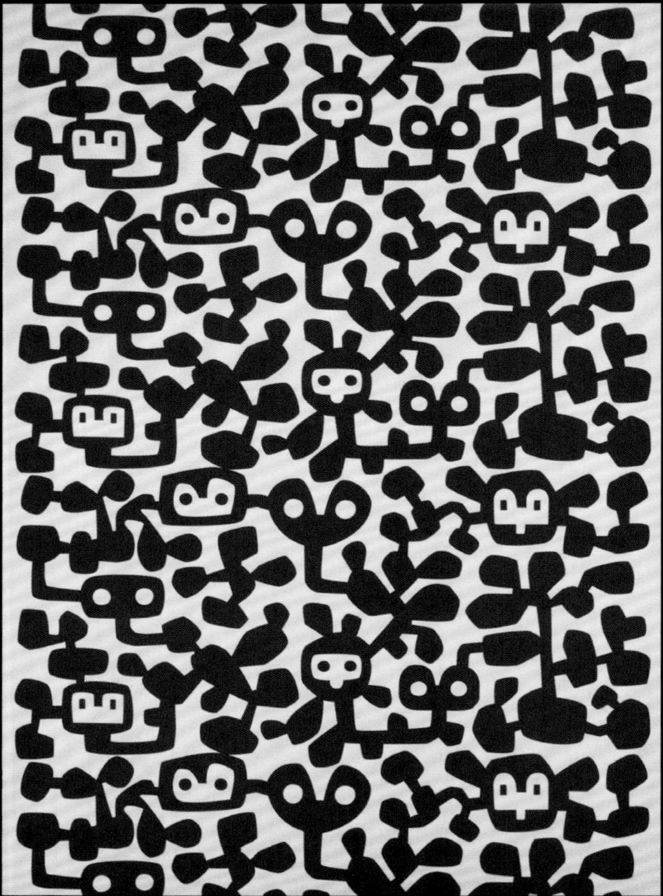

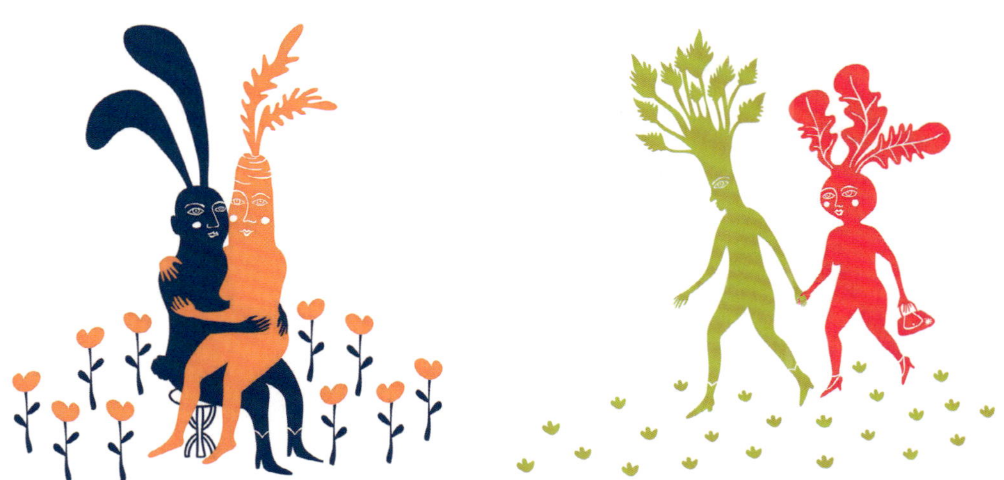

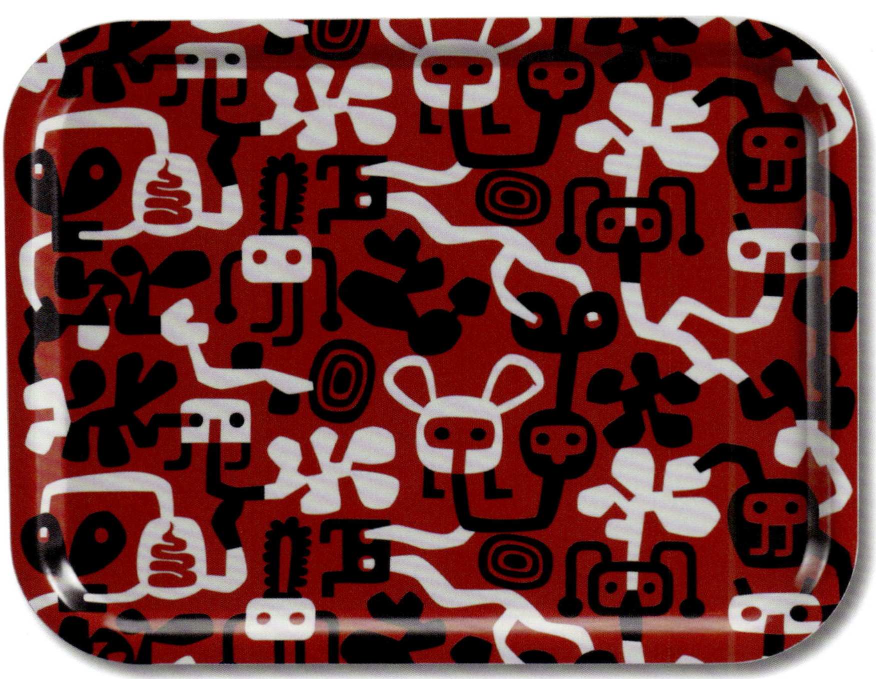

(T) BRONZE *Carla Torres* (B) *Lasse Skarbovik*

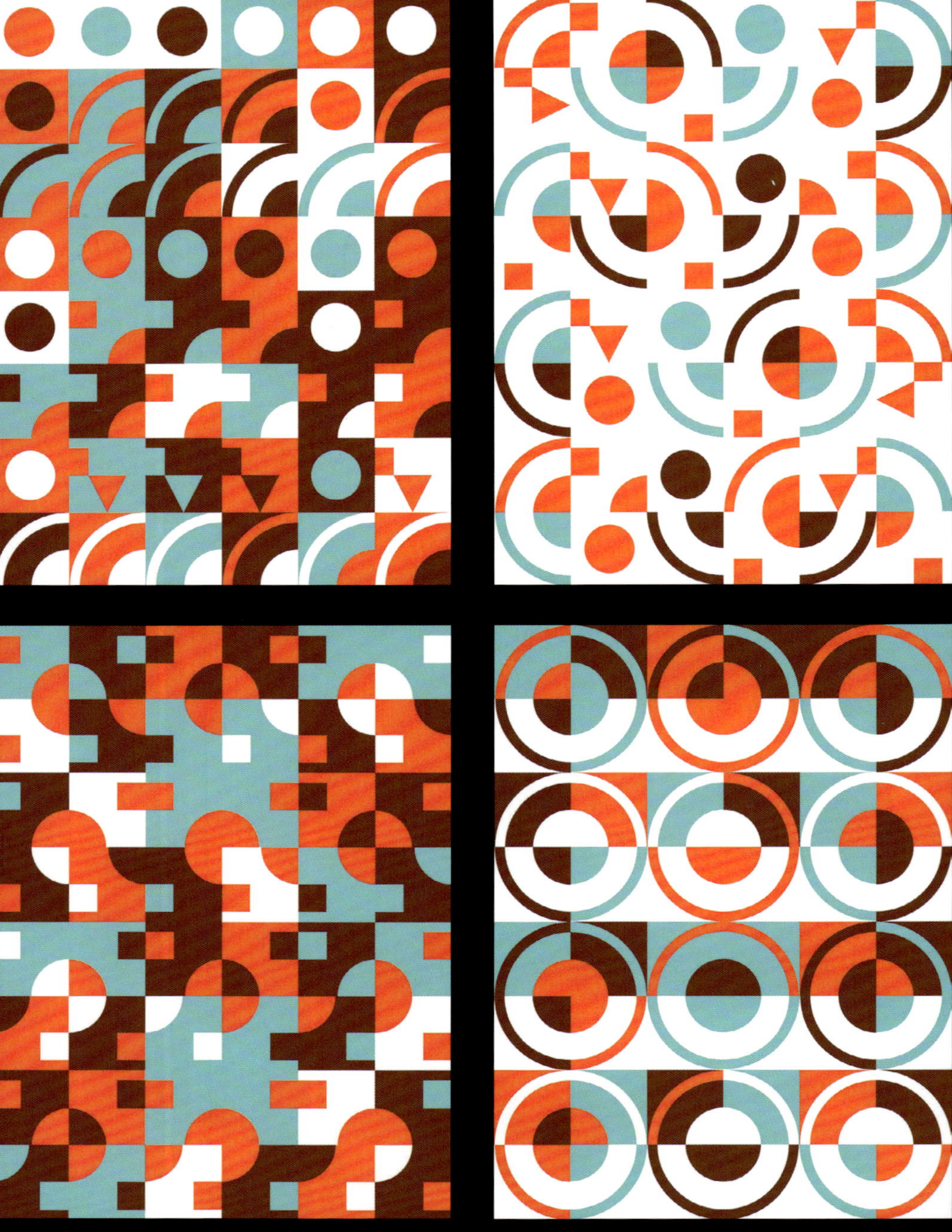

Daniel Bueno

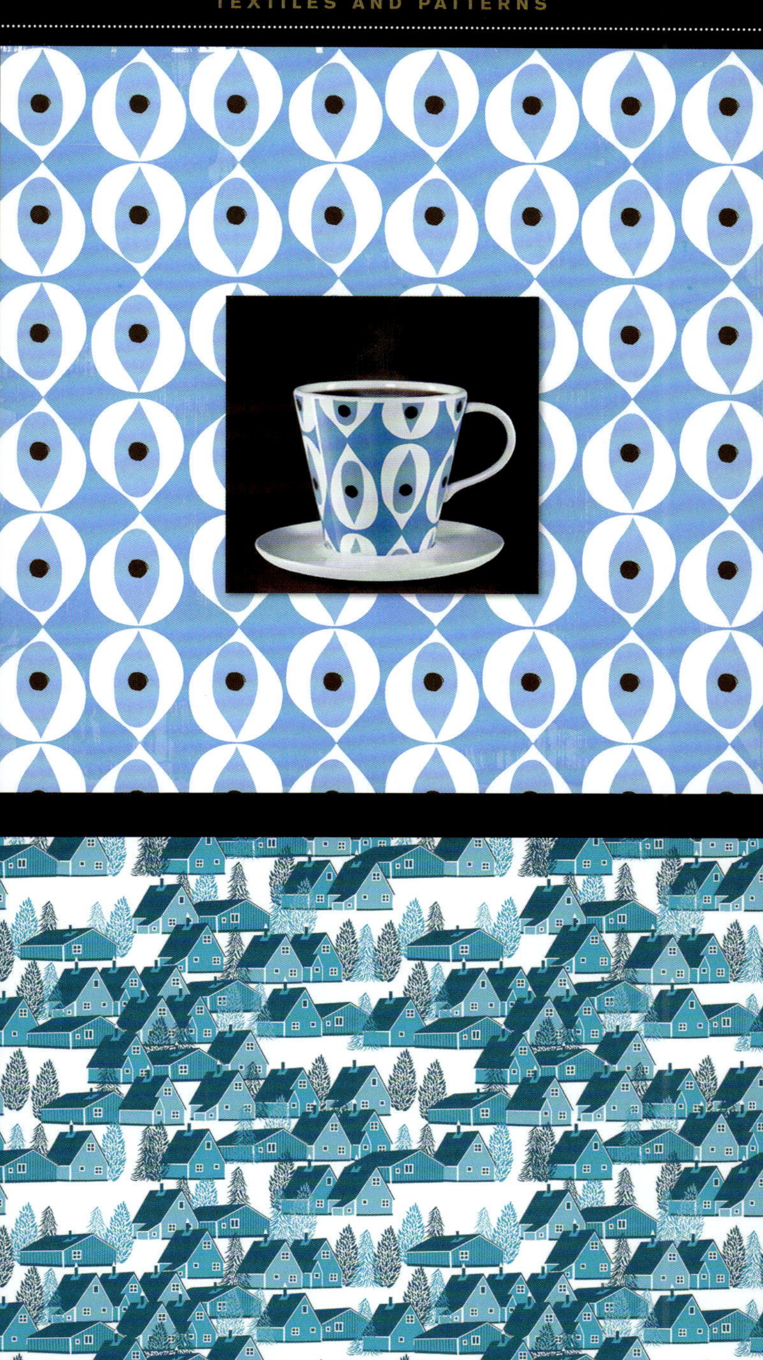

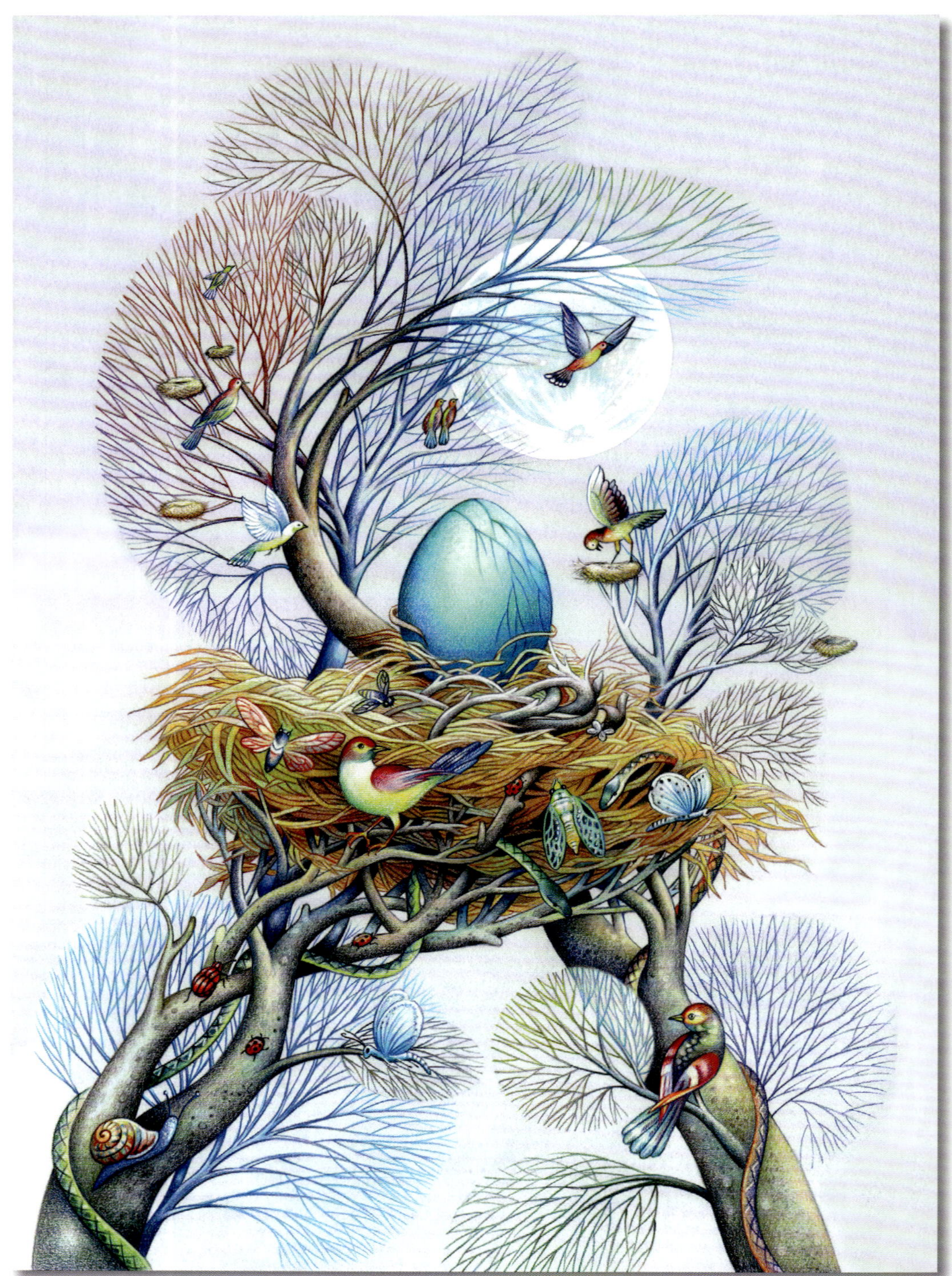

Sylvie Daigneault

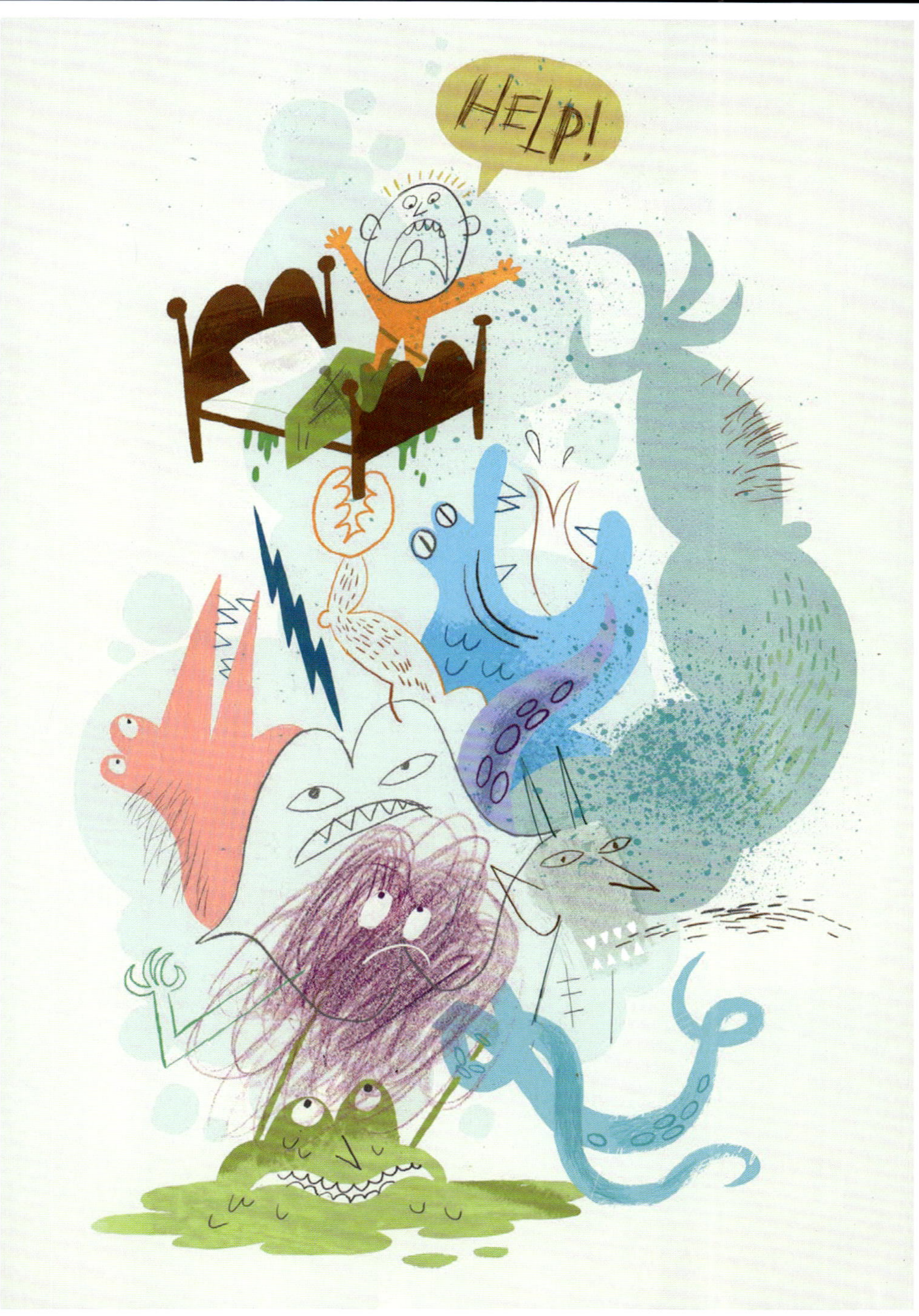

Dan Bob Thompson

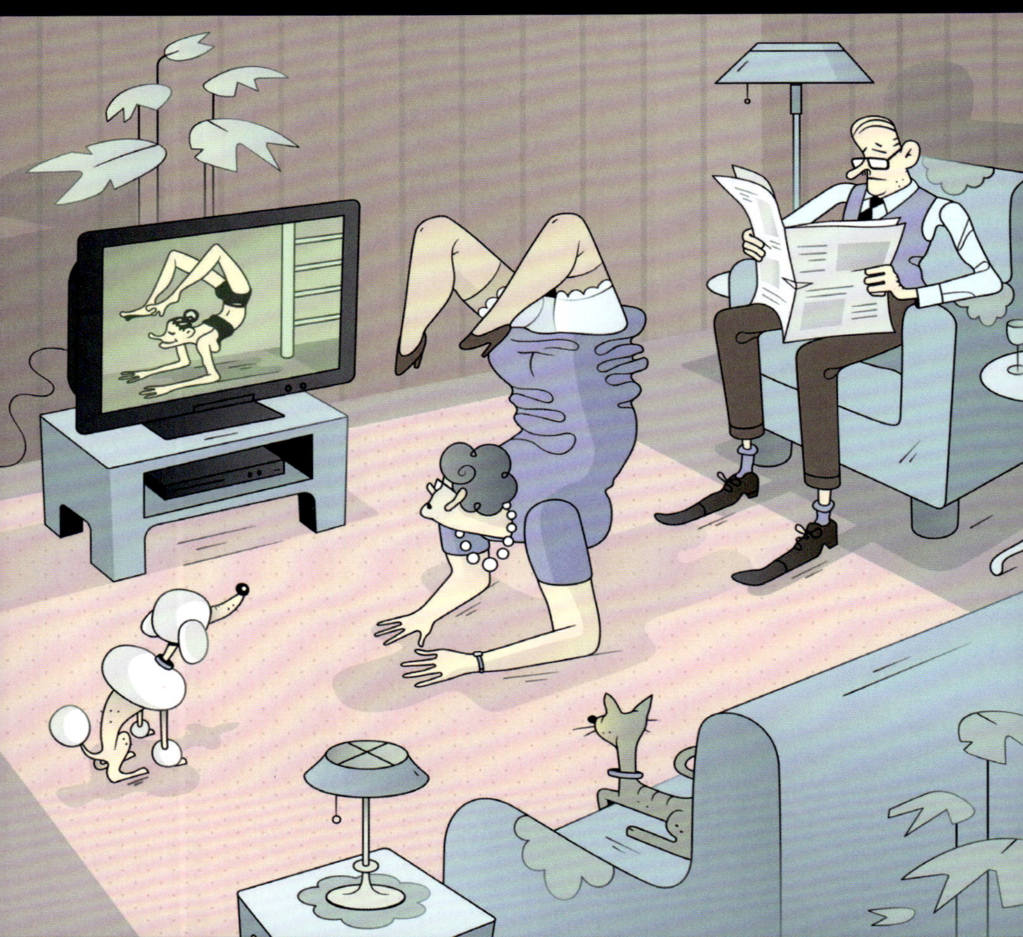

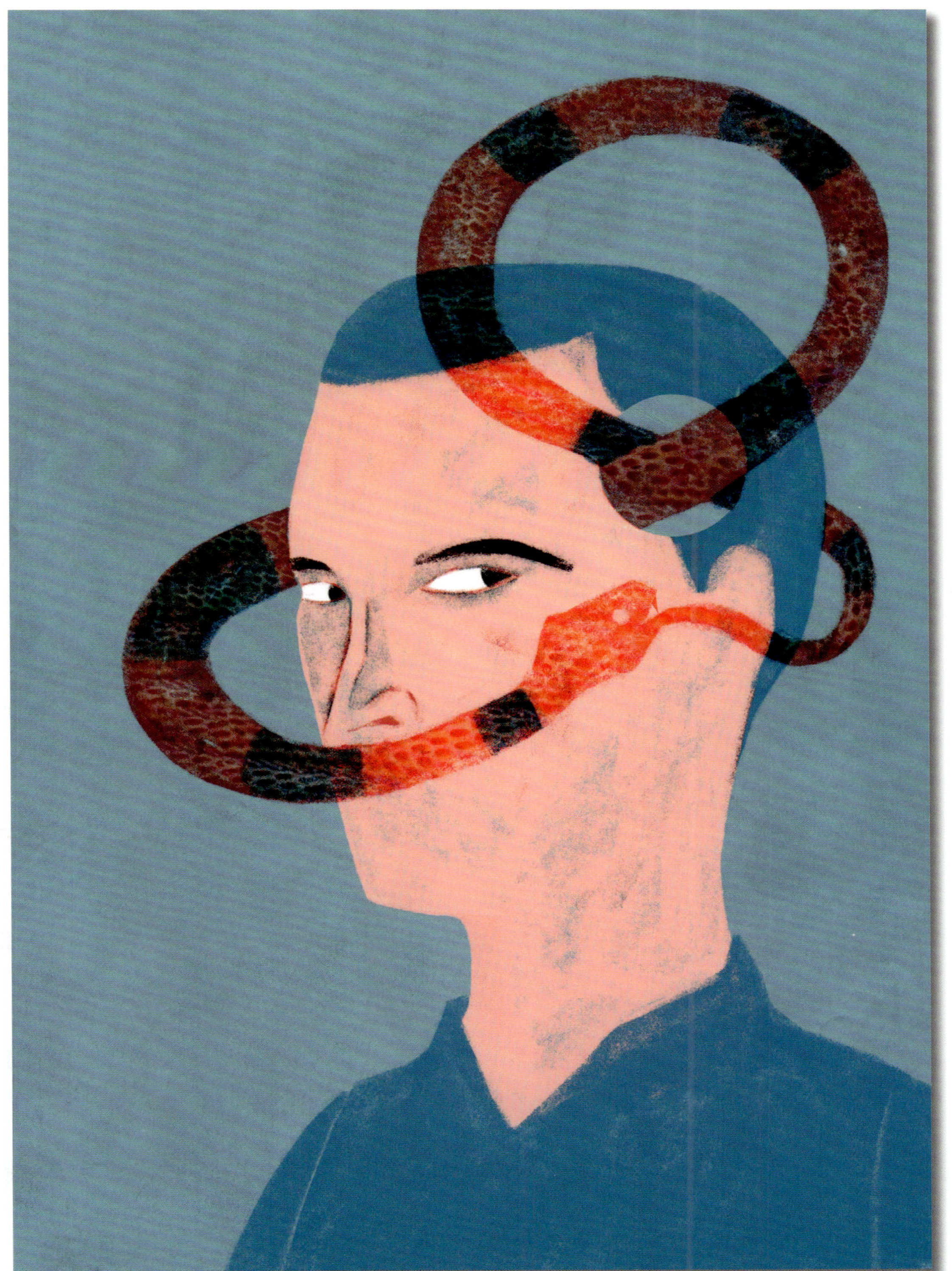

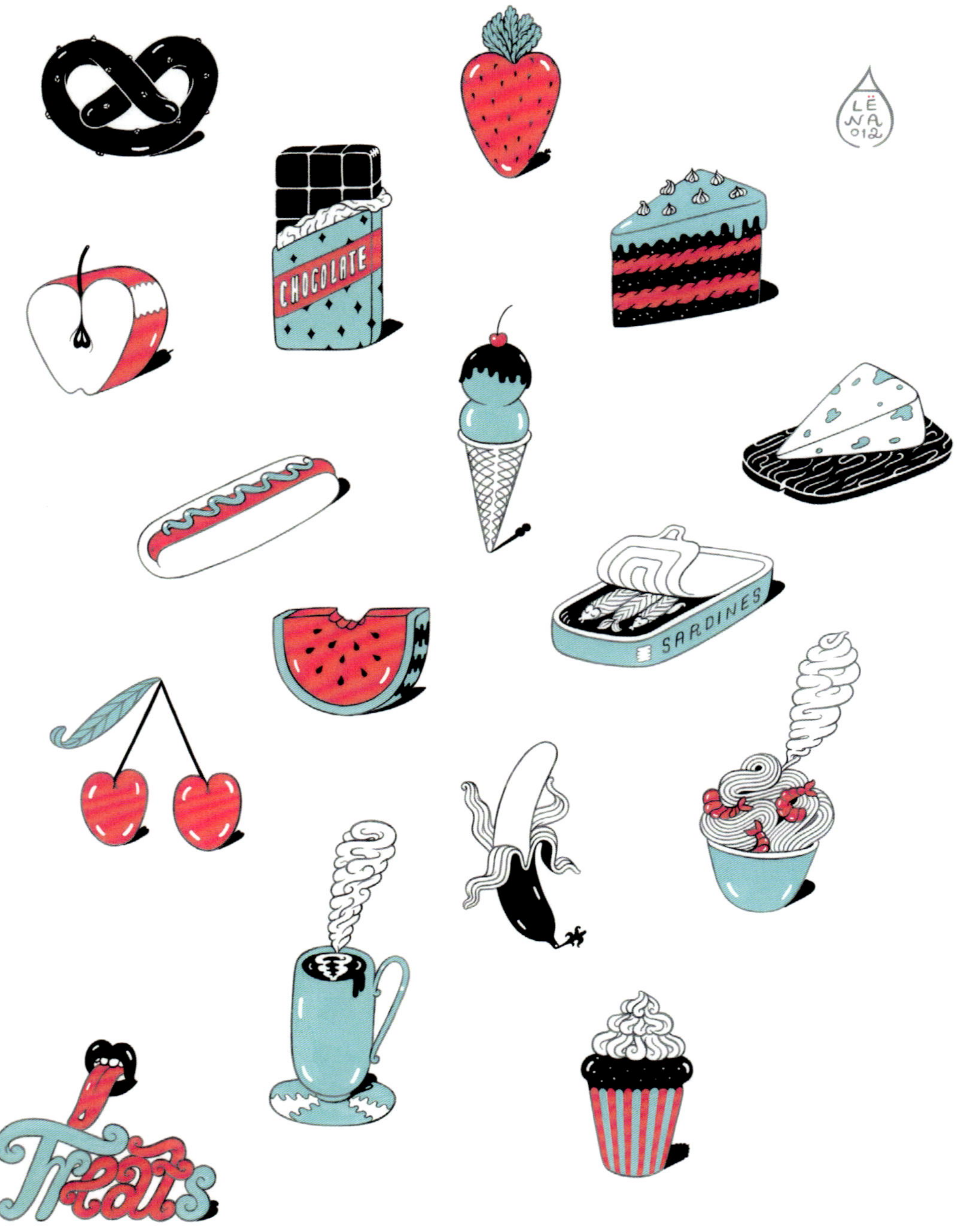

(L) Alena Skarina (R) Benoit Tardif

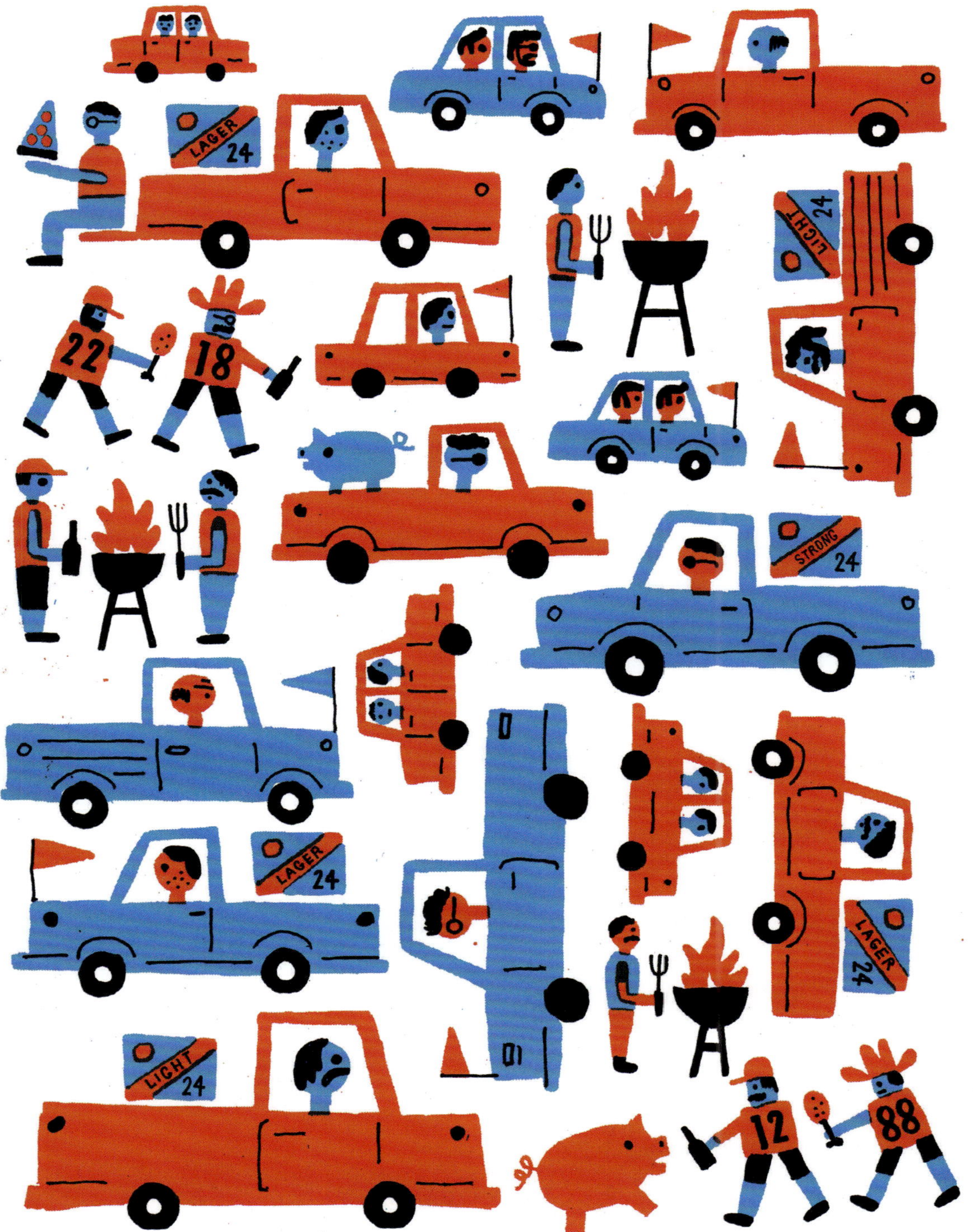
LAGER 24
LIGHT 24
STRONG 24
LAGER 24
LIGHT 24
LAGER 24
22
18
12
88

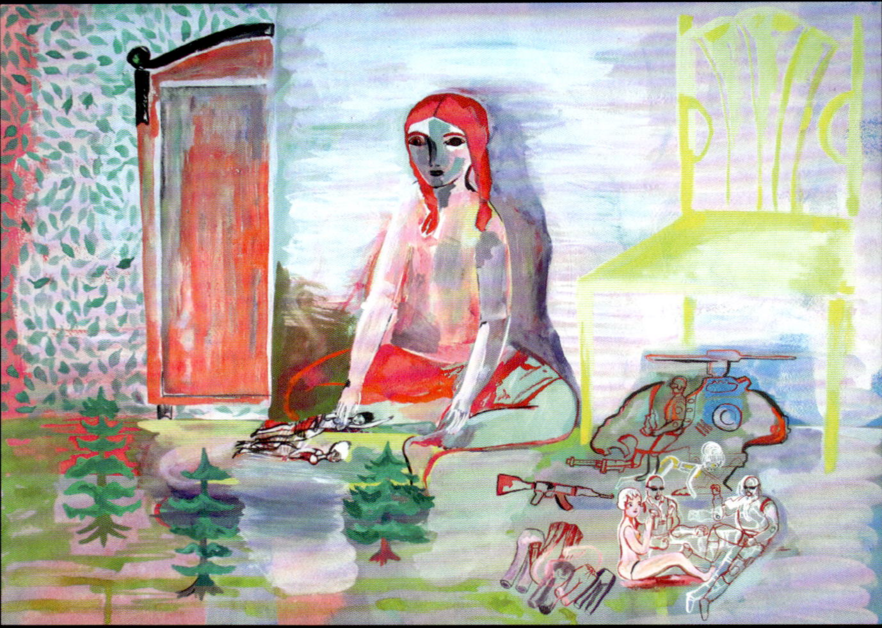

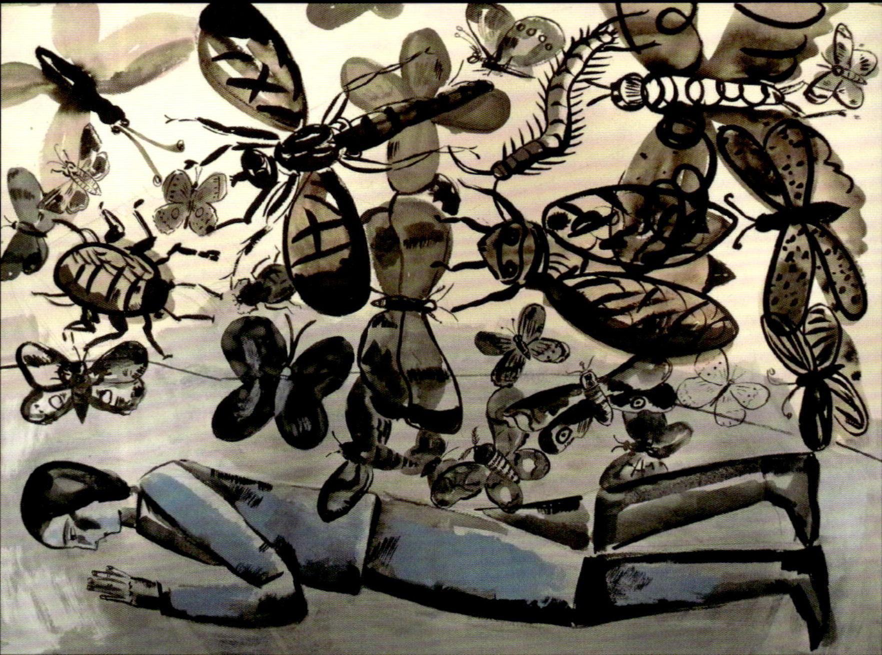

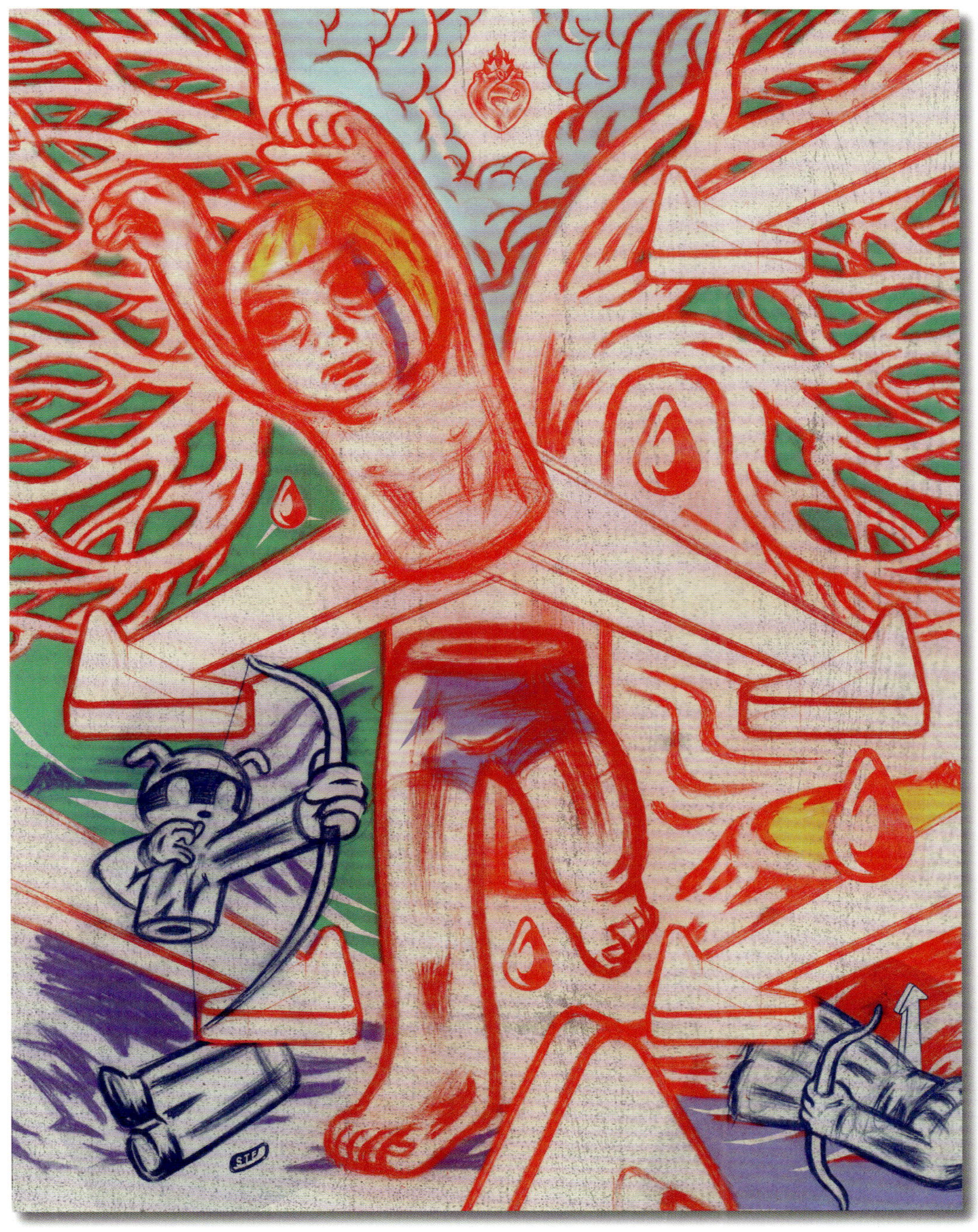

Stephane Defago

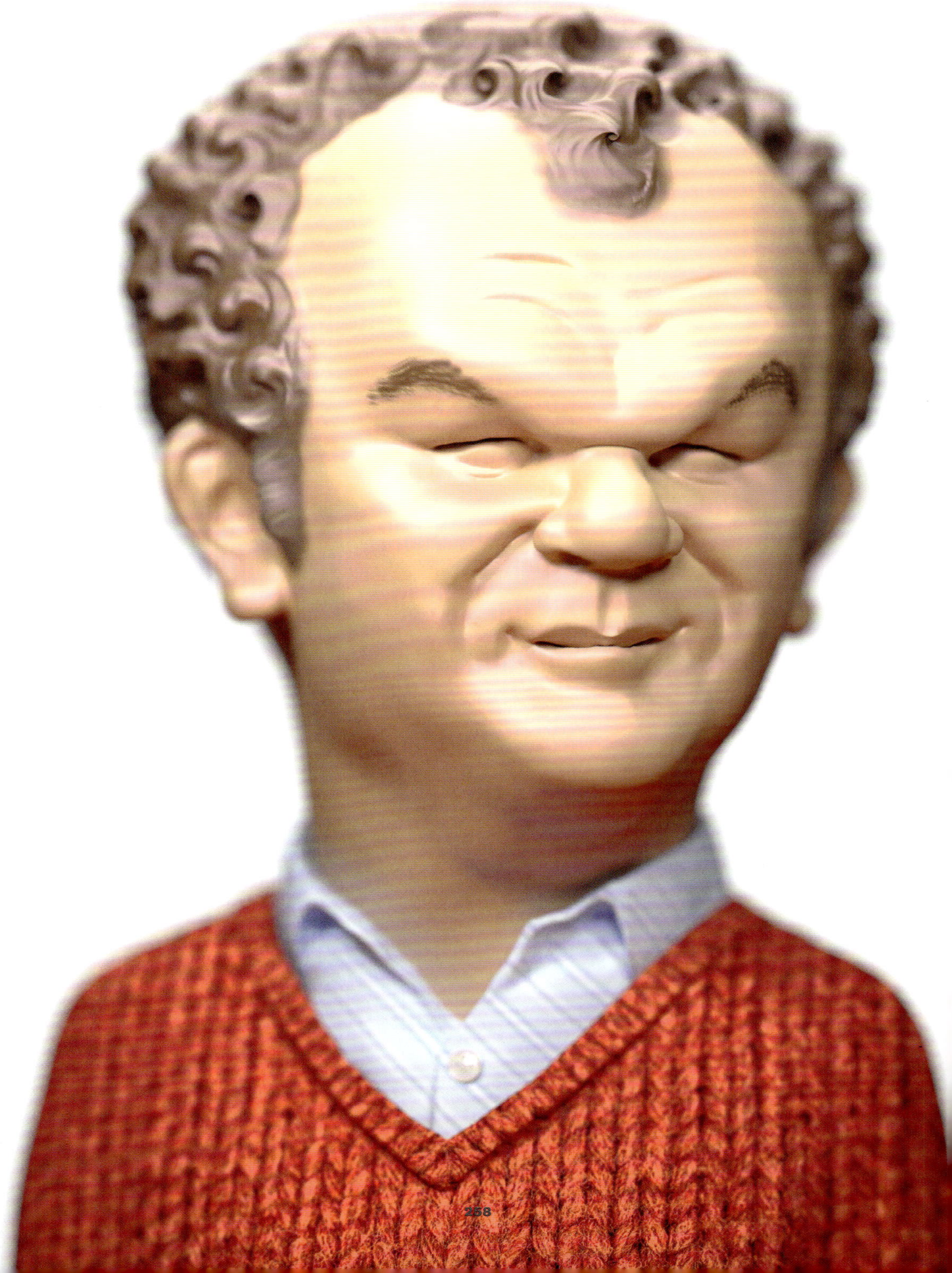

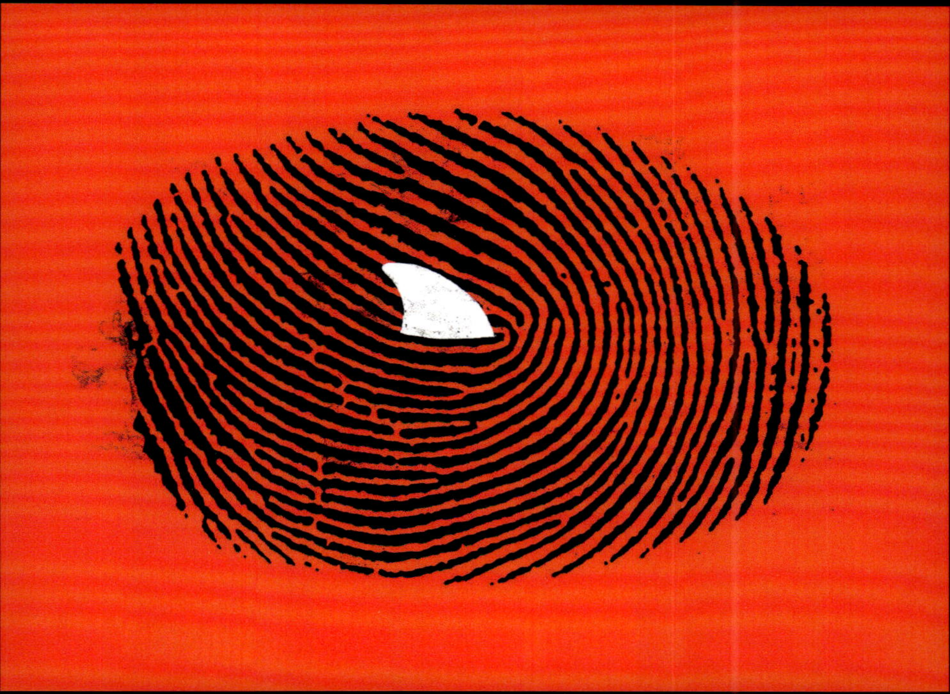

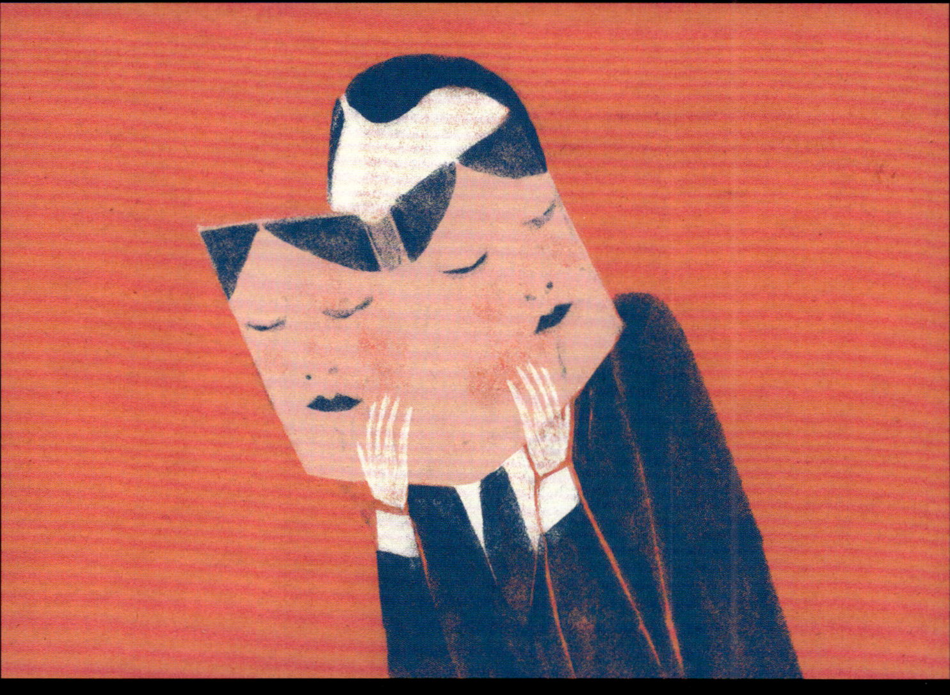

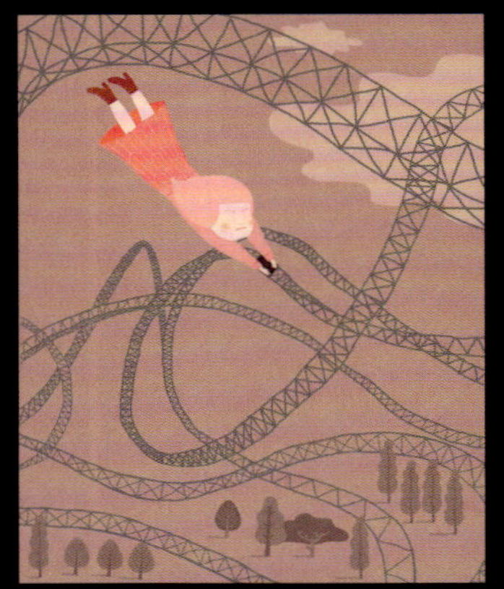
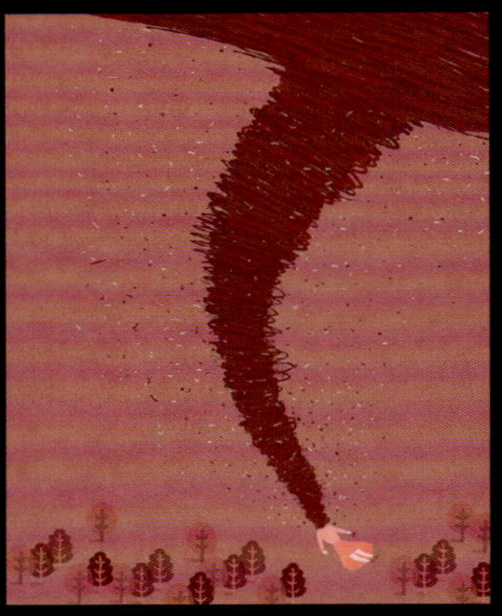
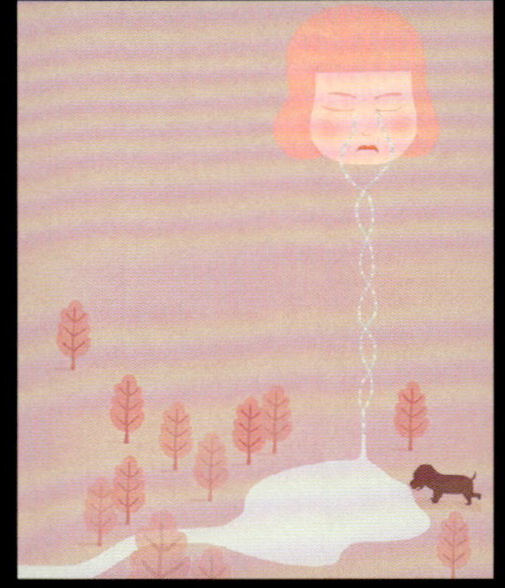
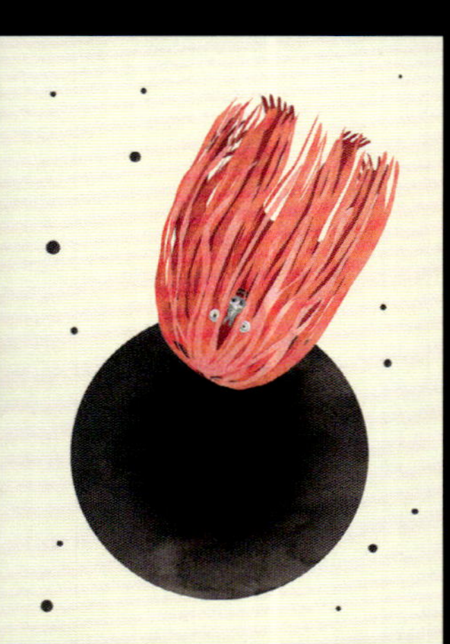
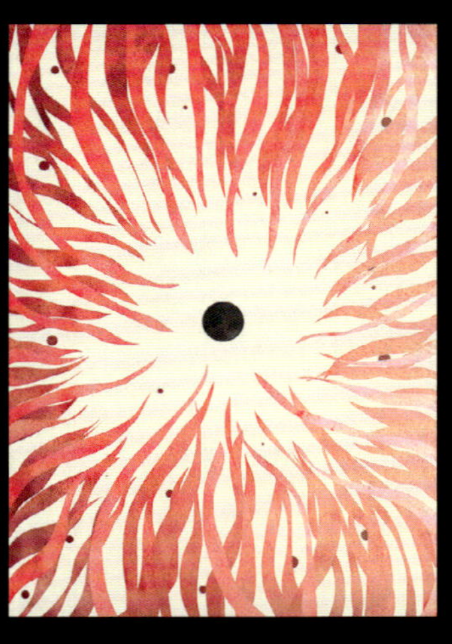
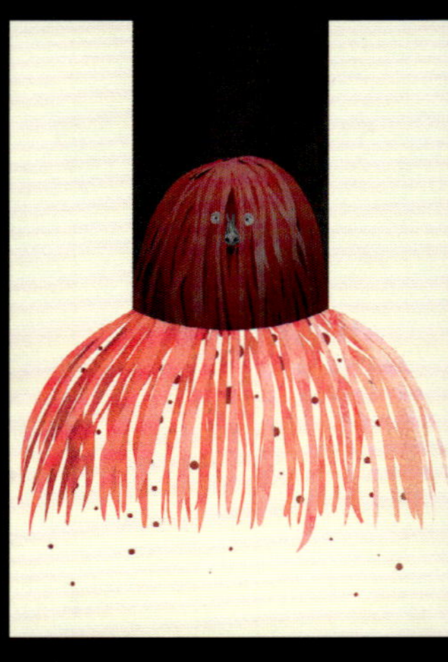

(T) *Meritxell Duran* (B) *Elisa Macellari*

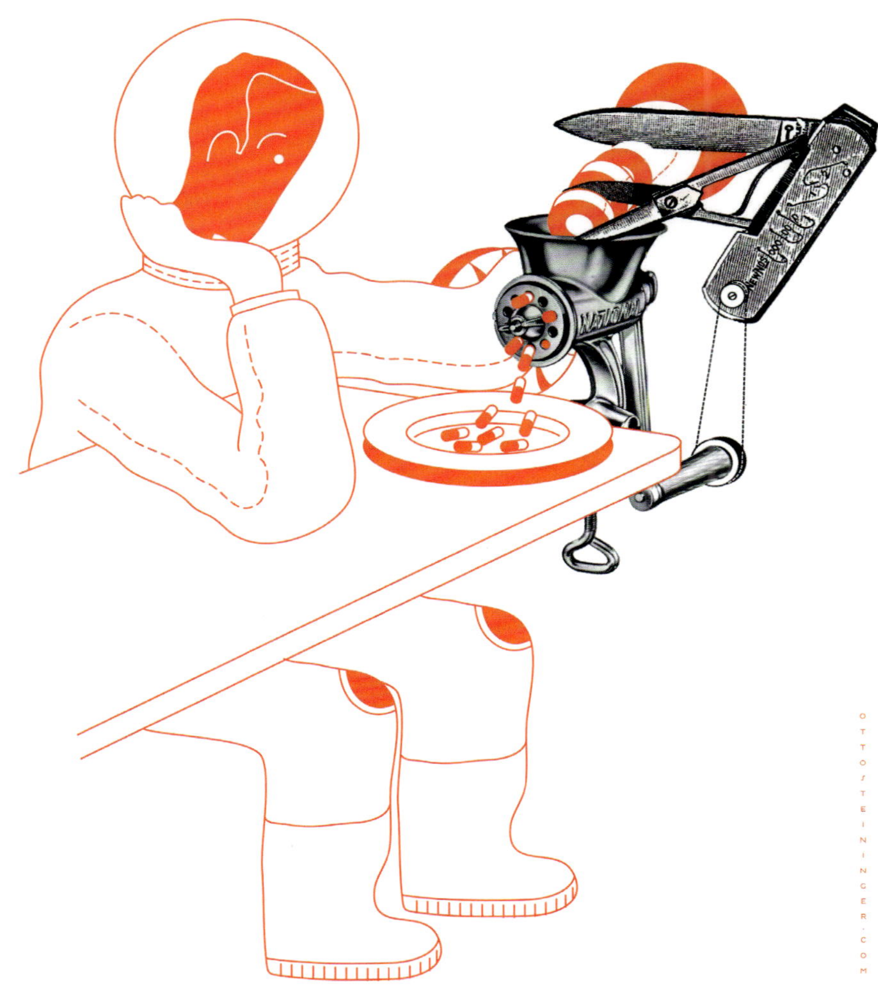

Otto Steininger

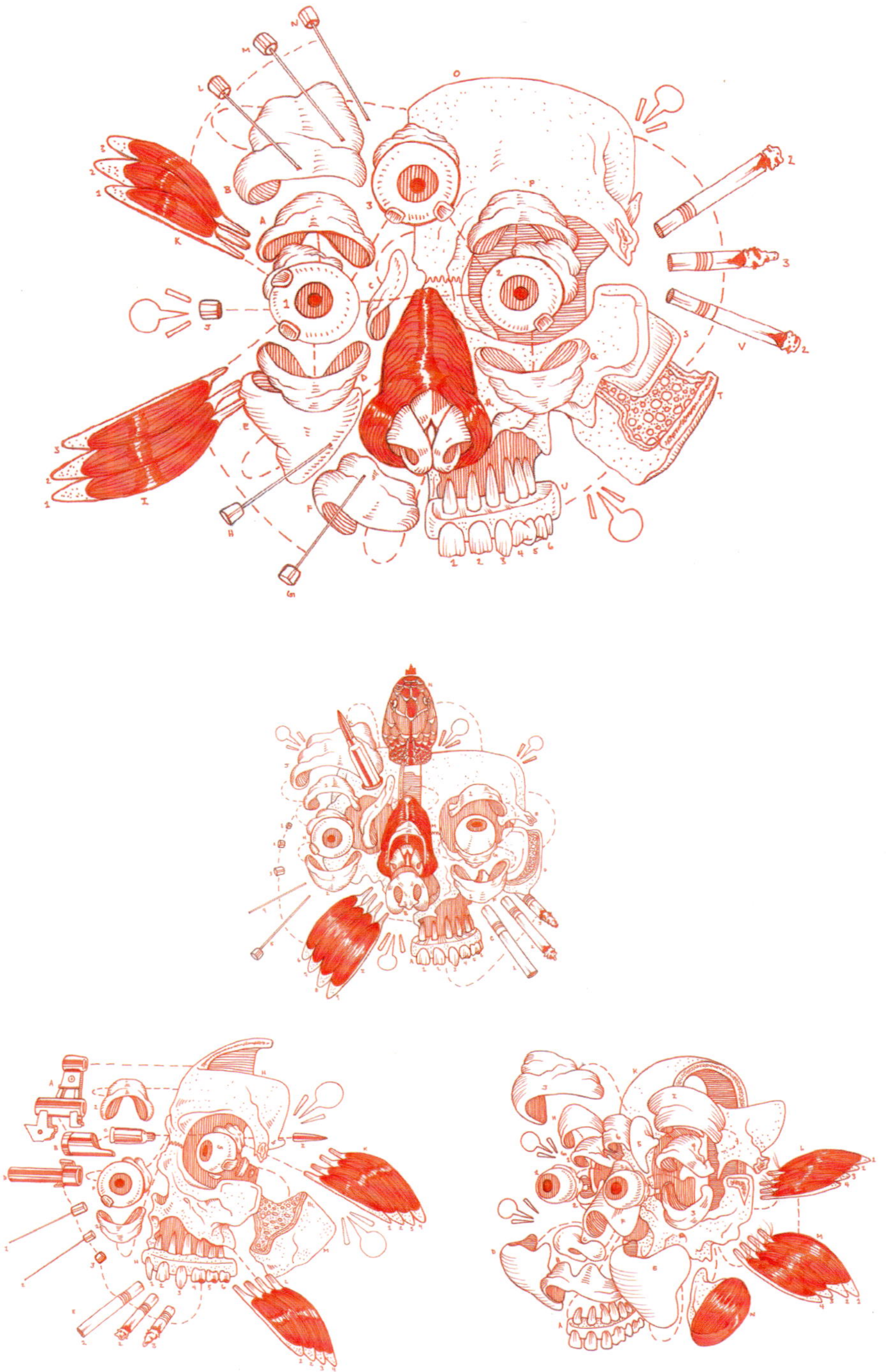

Mike McDonnell

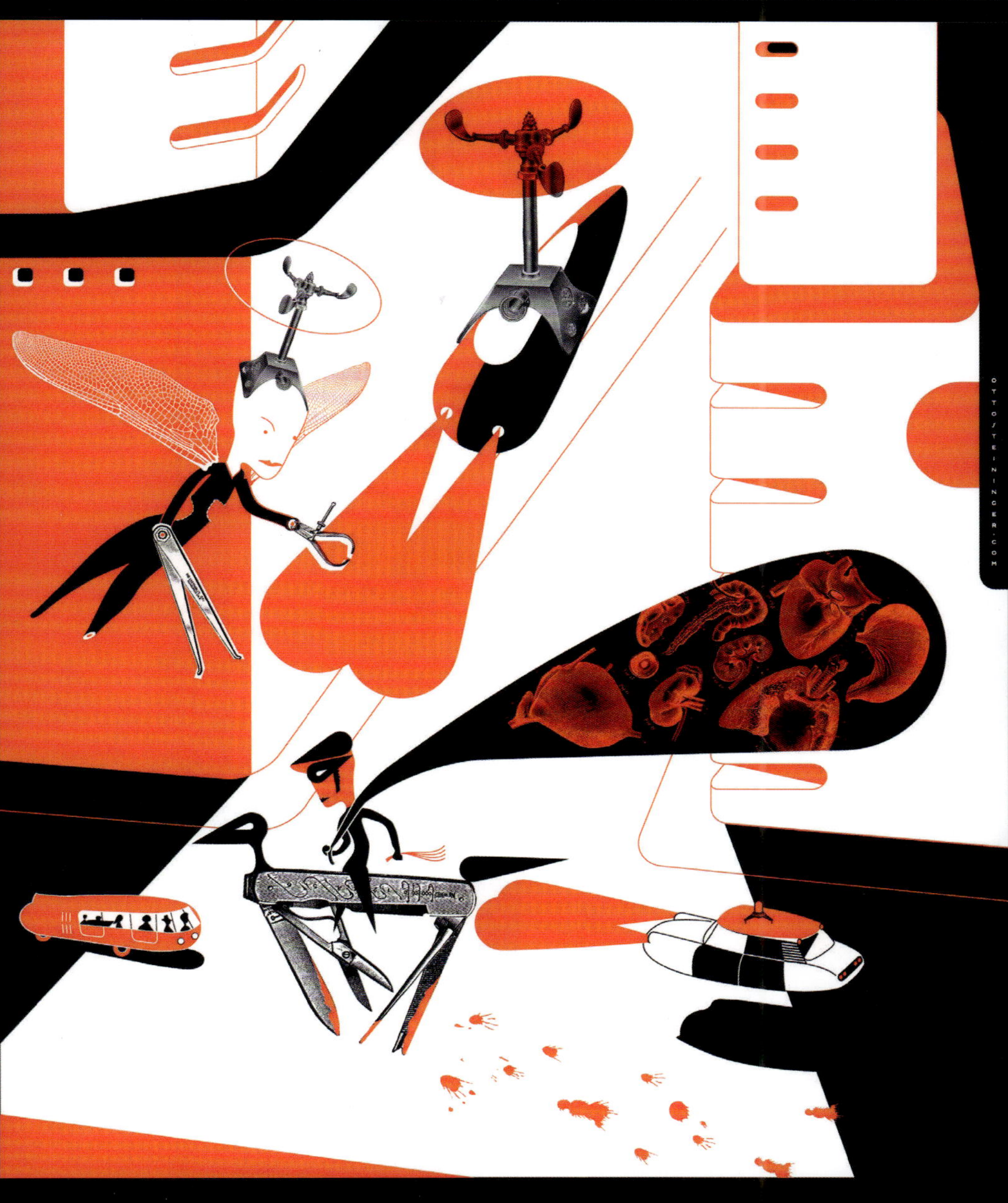

Otto Steininger

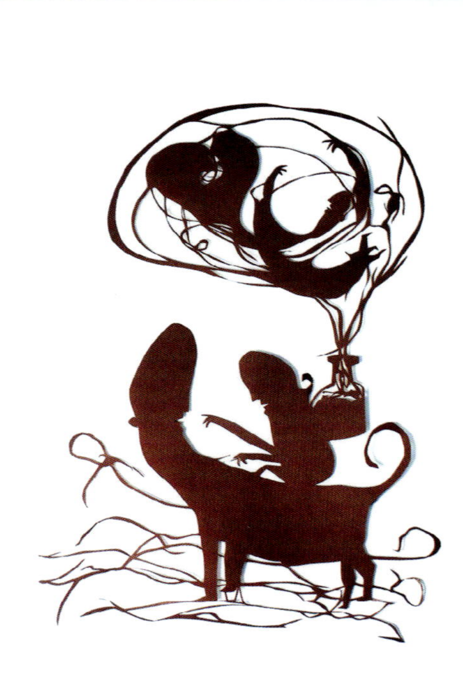

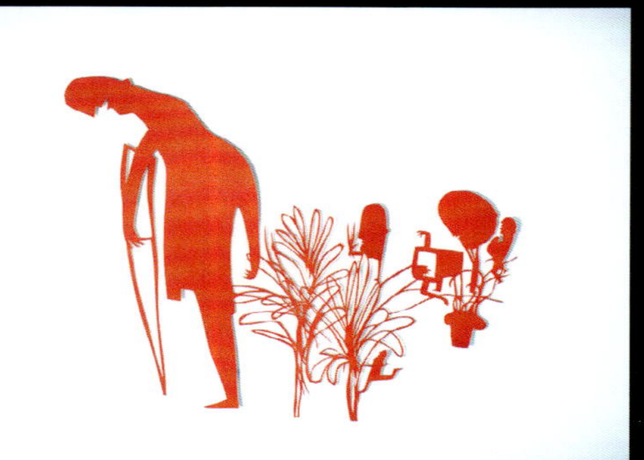

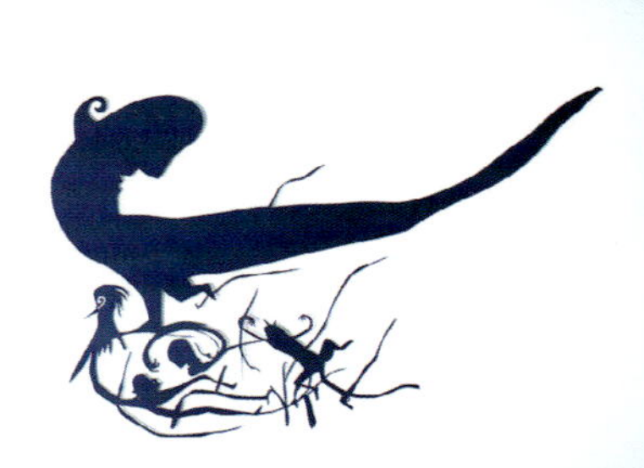

Gémeo Luís

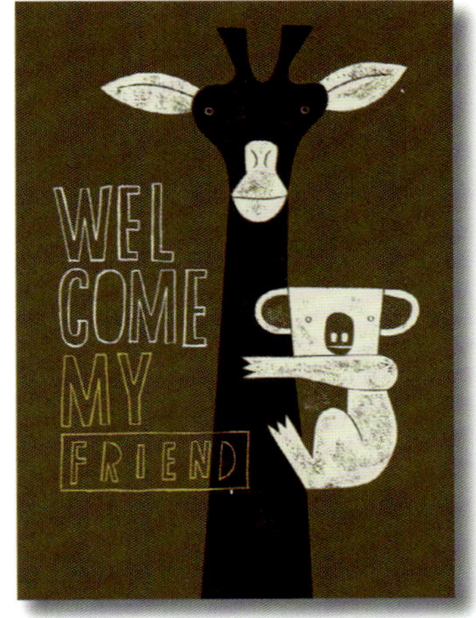

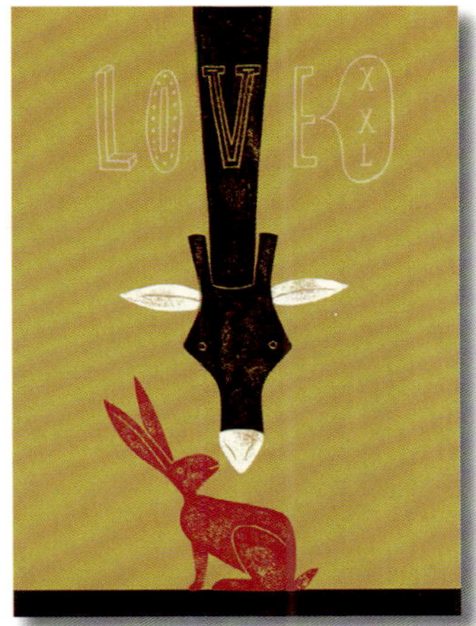

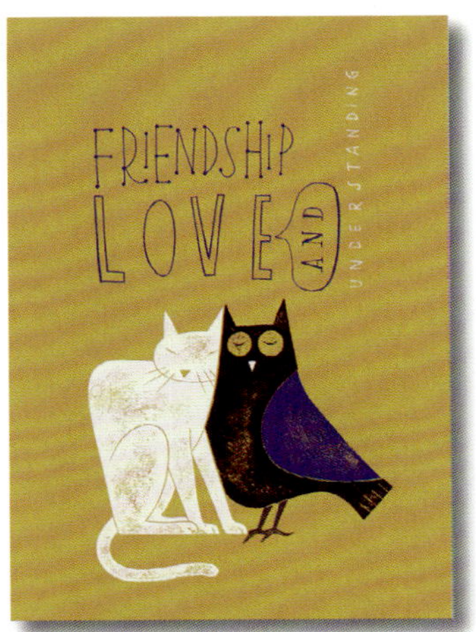

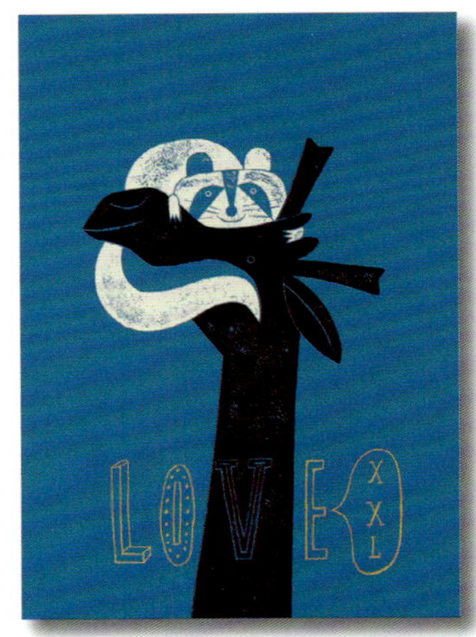

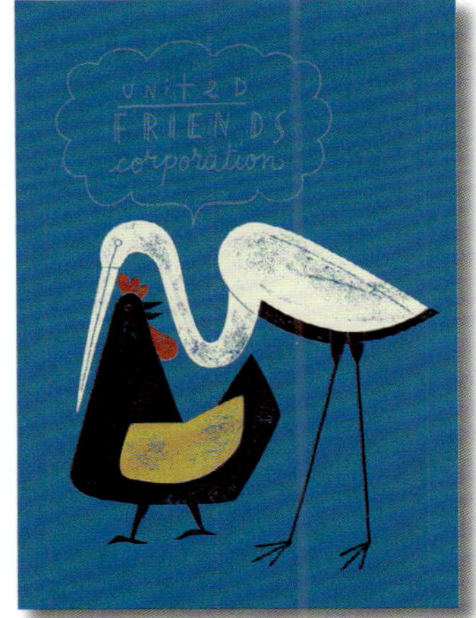

Jean-Manuel Duvivier

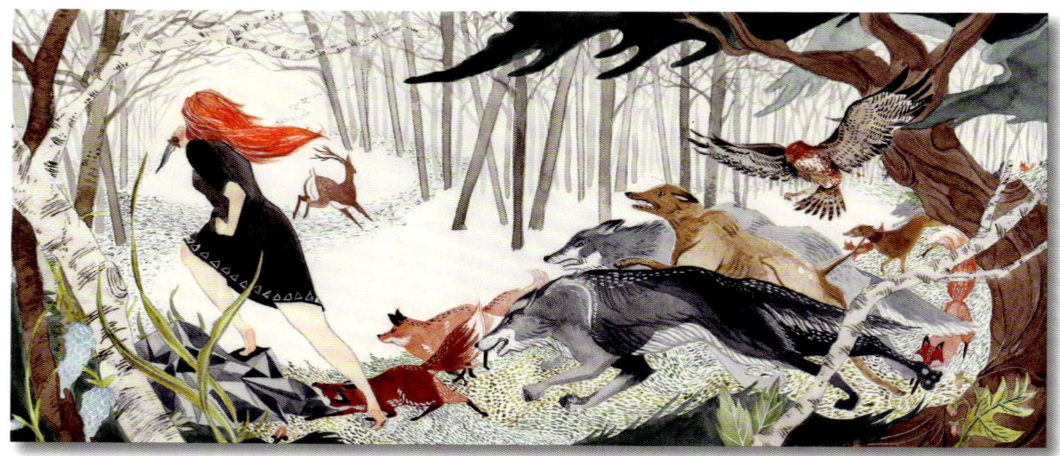

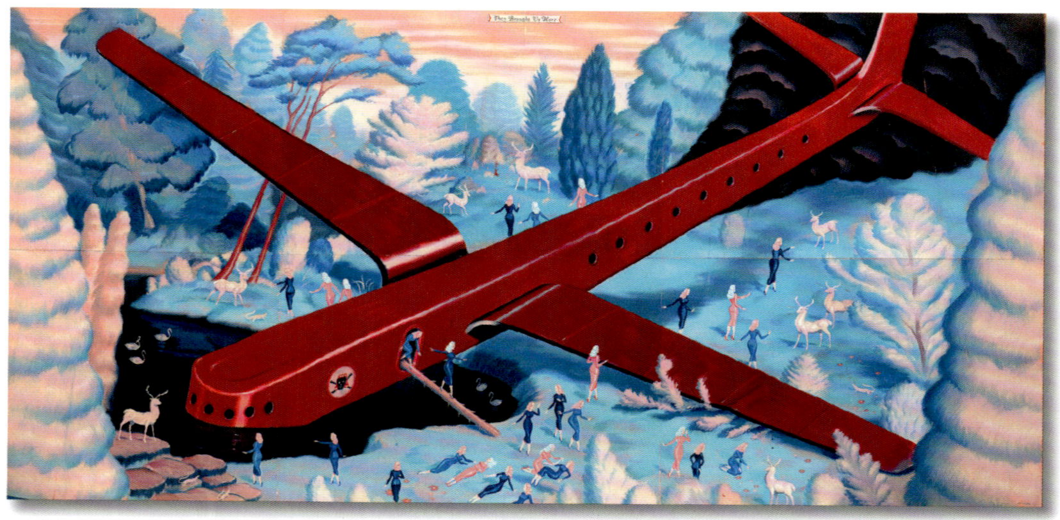

(T) *Jensine Eckwall* (B) *Ryan Heshka* (R) *Wesley Bedrosian*

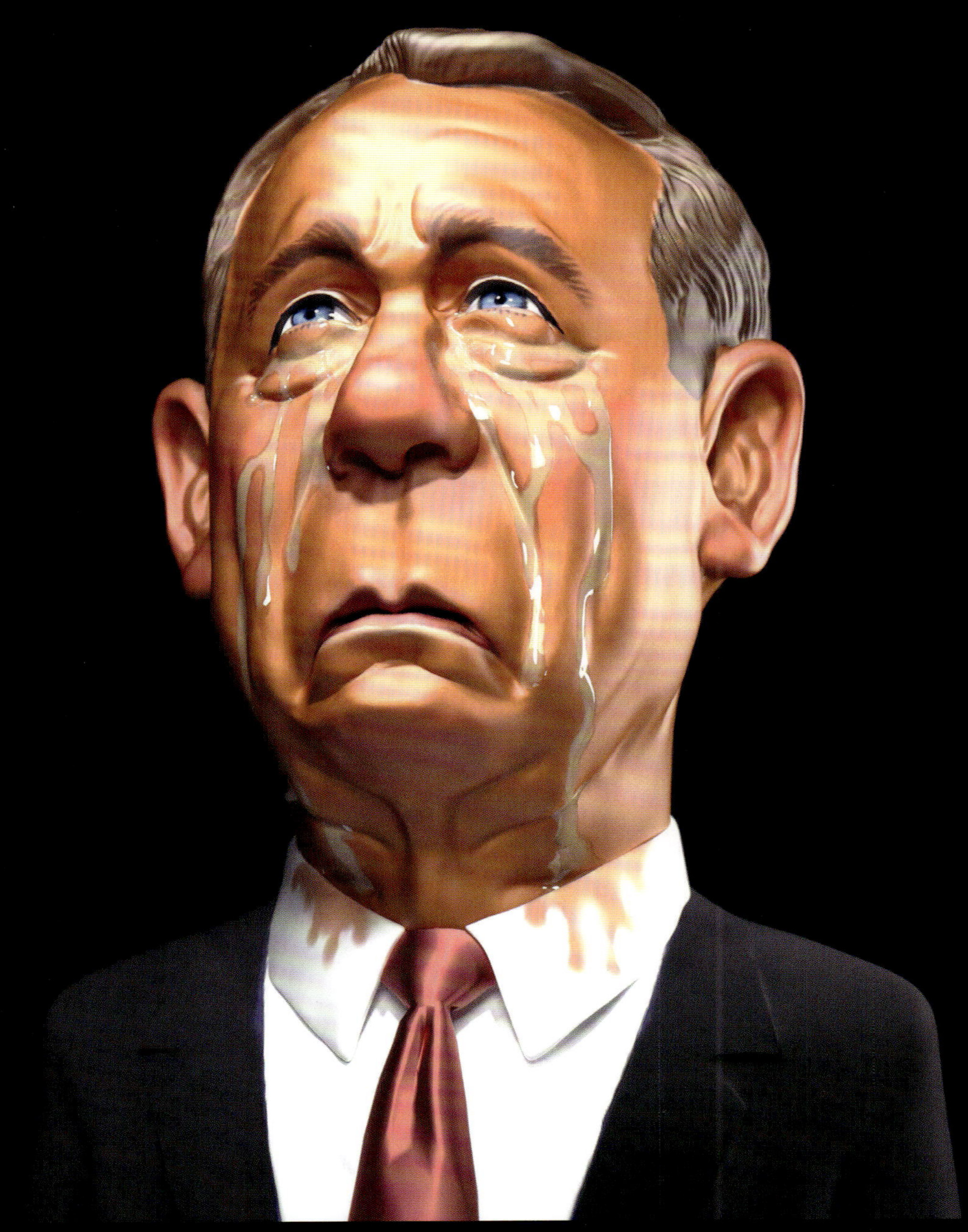

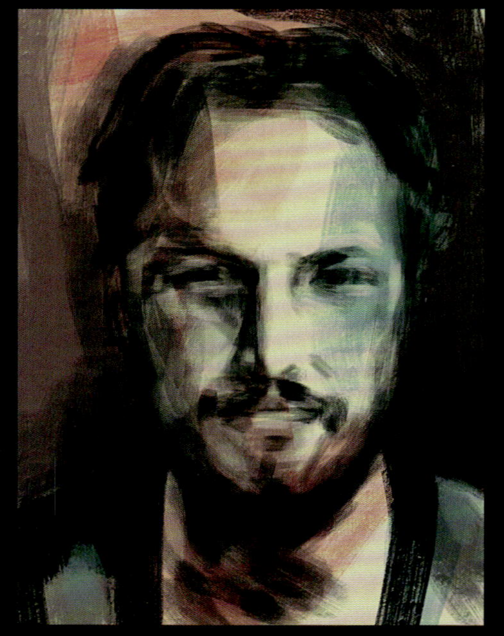

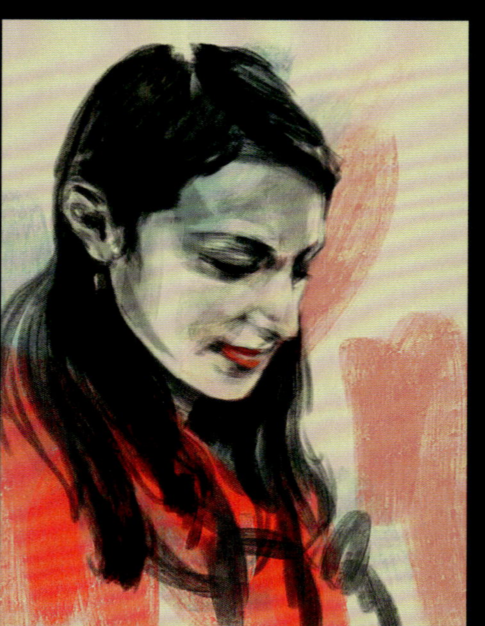

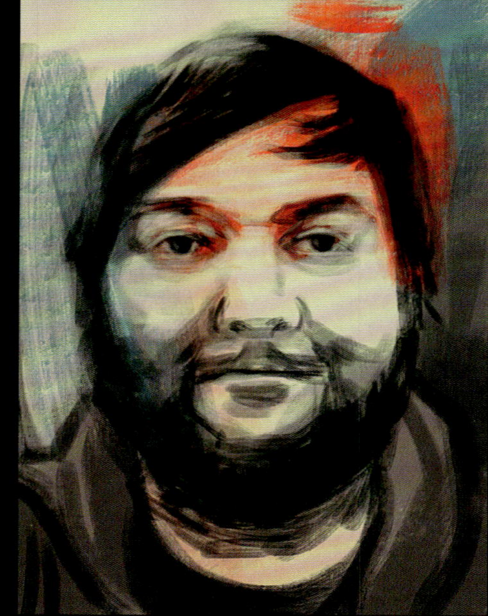

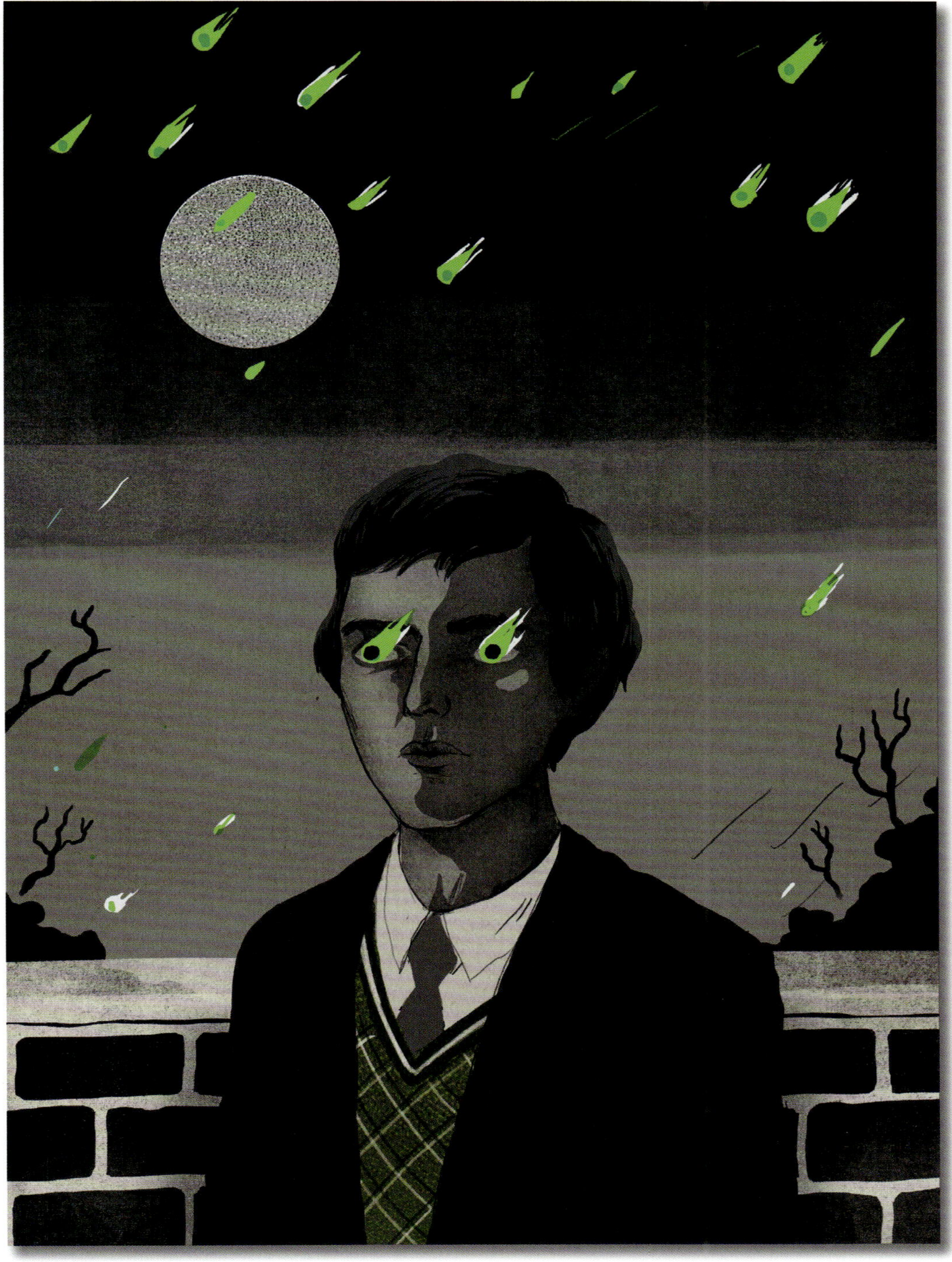

Byron Eggenschwiler

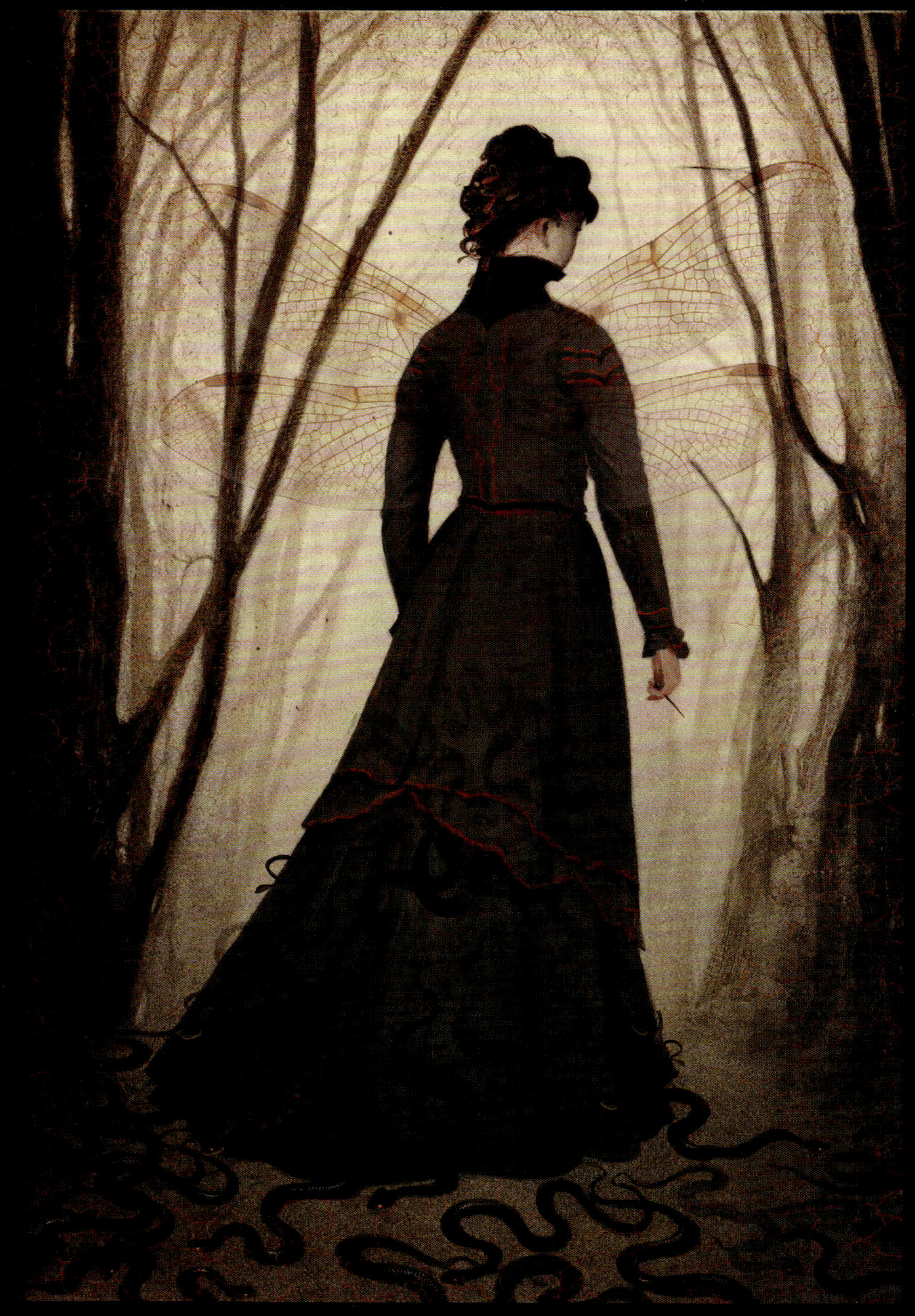

(L) *Bill Mayer* (R) *Giles Mead*

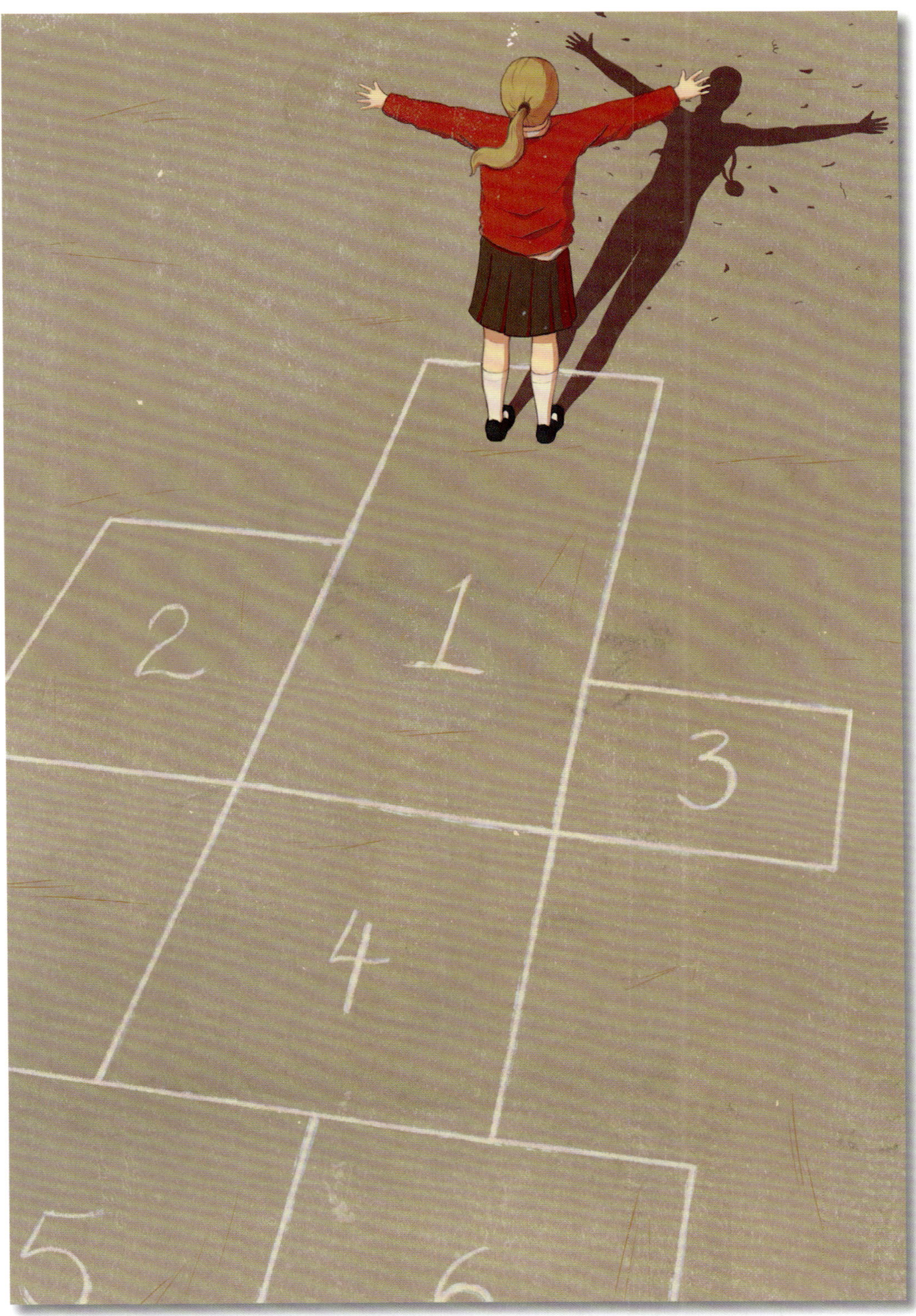

2
1
3
4
5
6

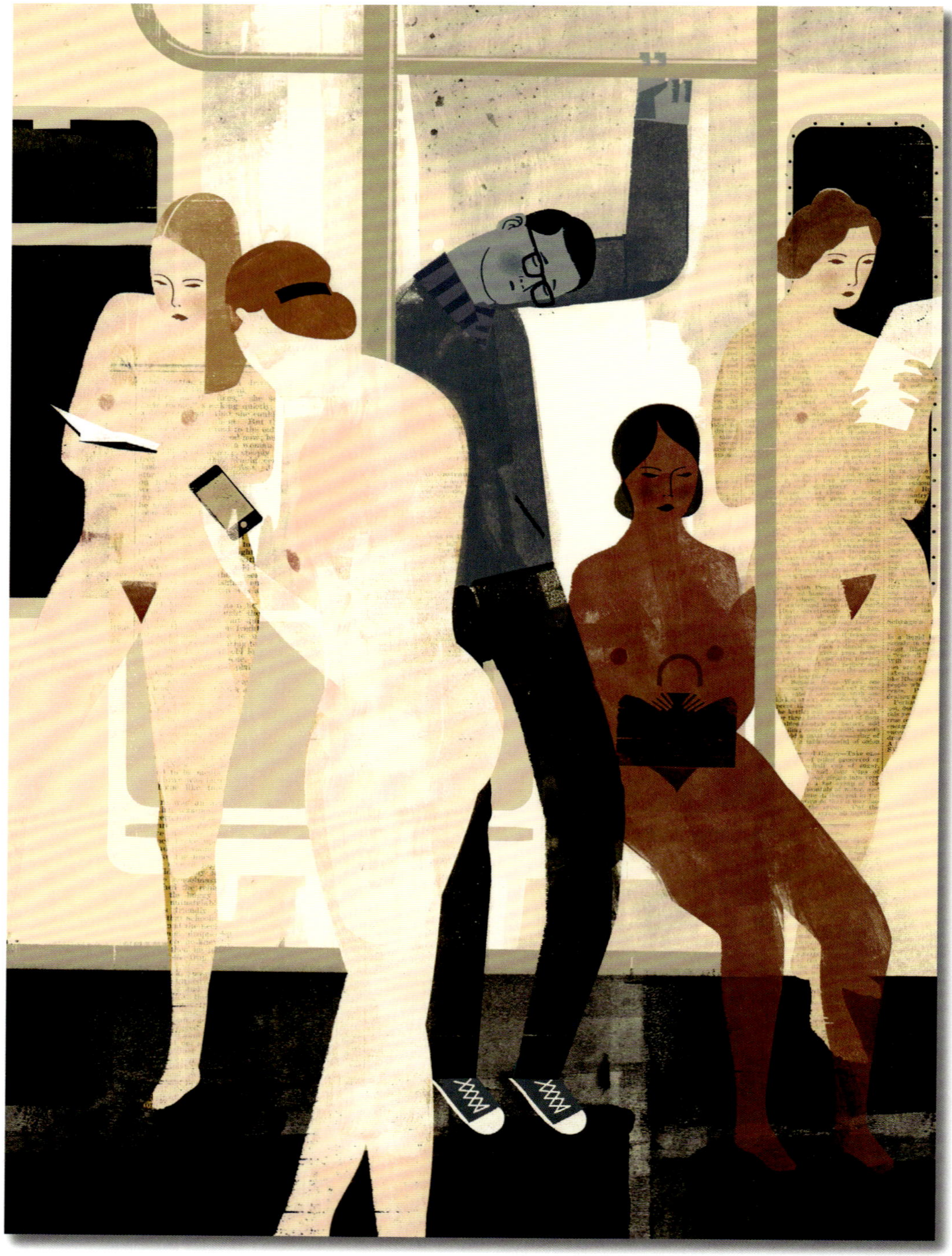

(L) **BRONZE** *Keith Negley* (R) *Peter Diamond*

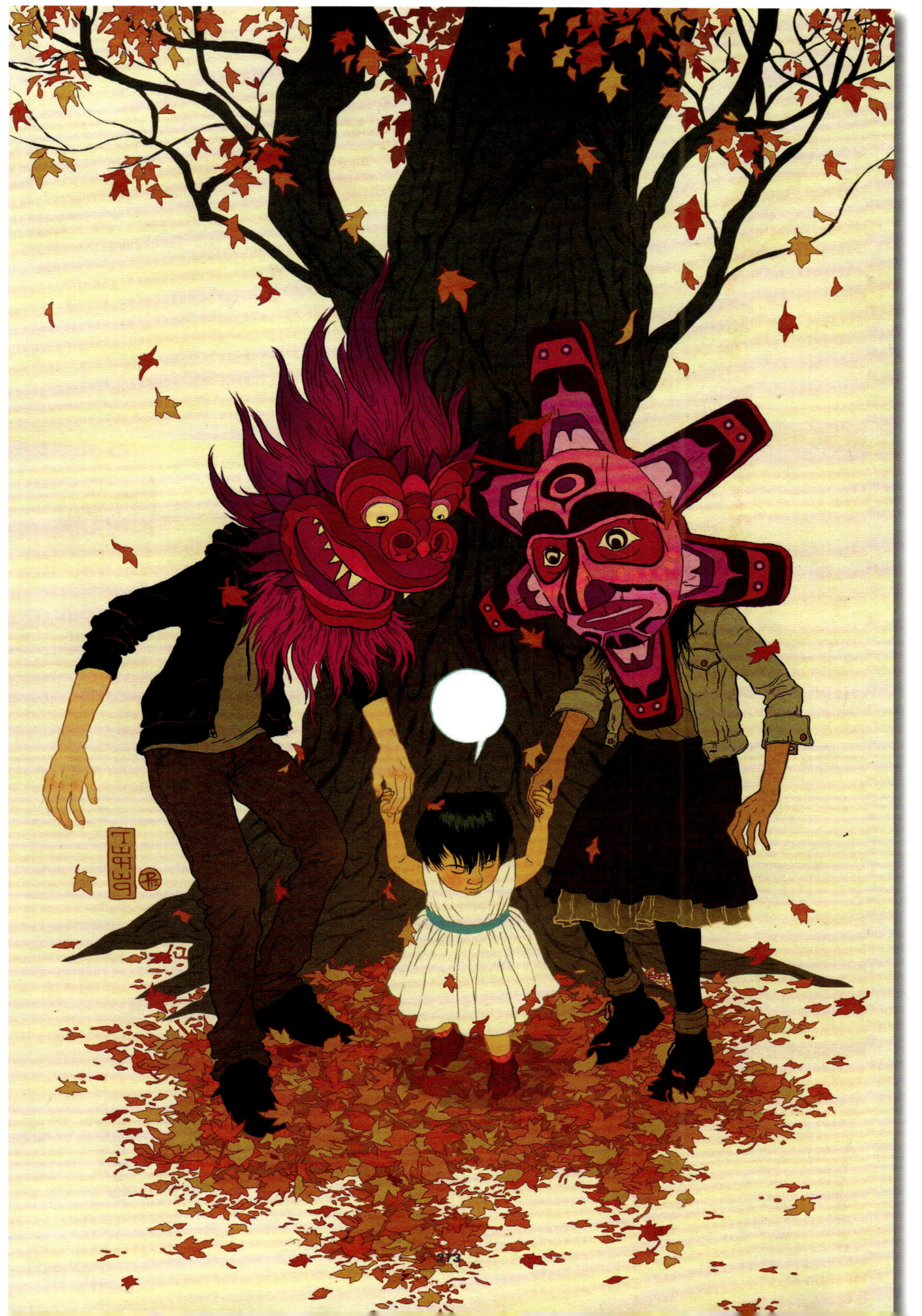

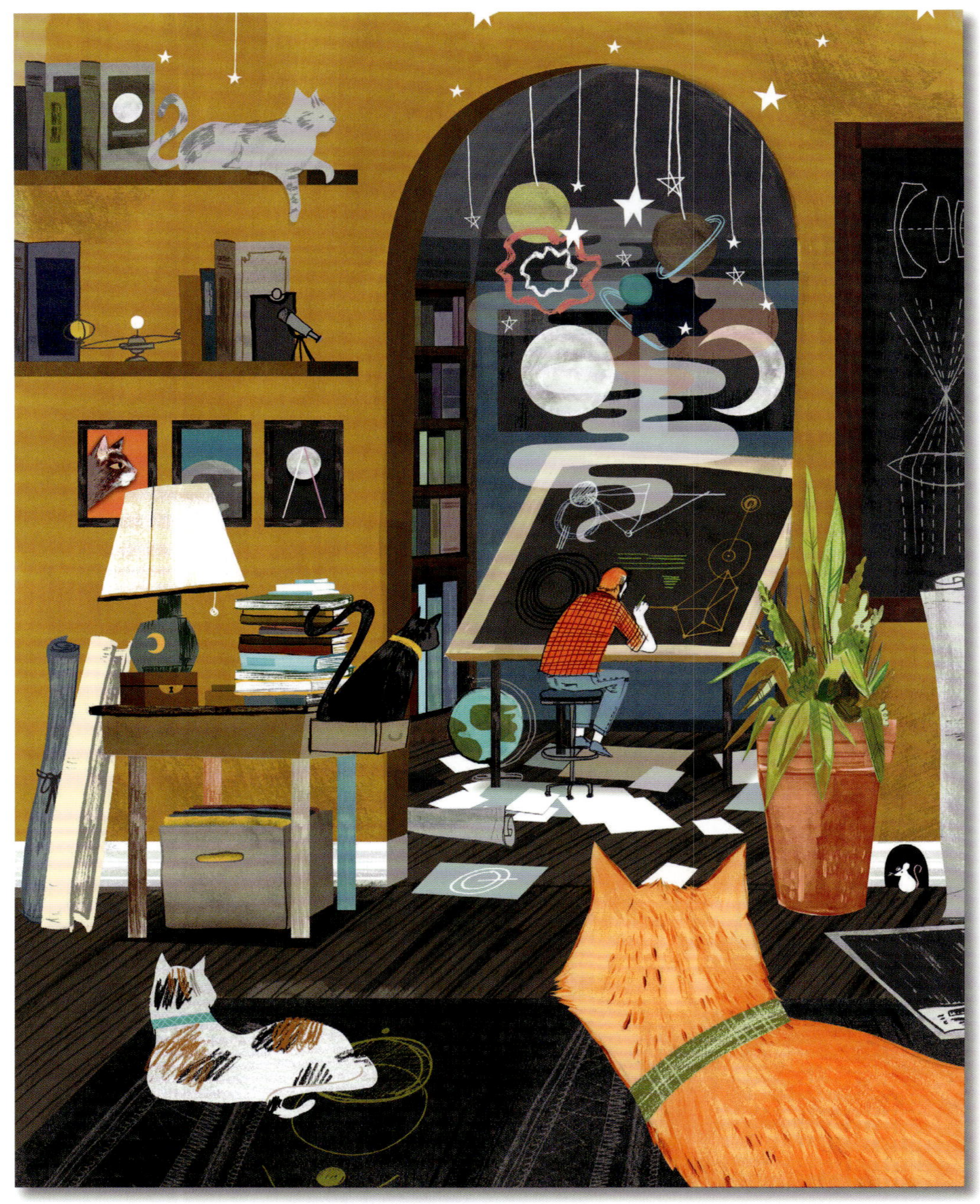

Bill Ferenc

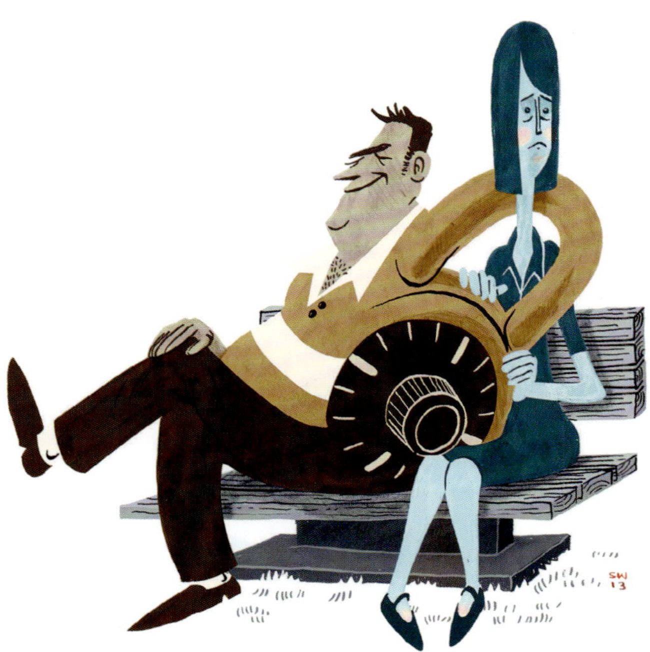

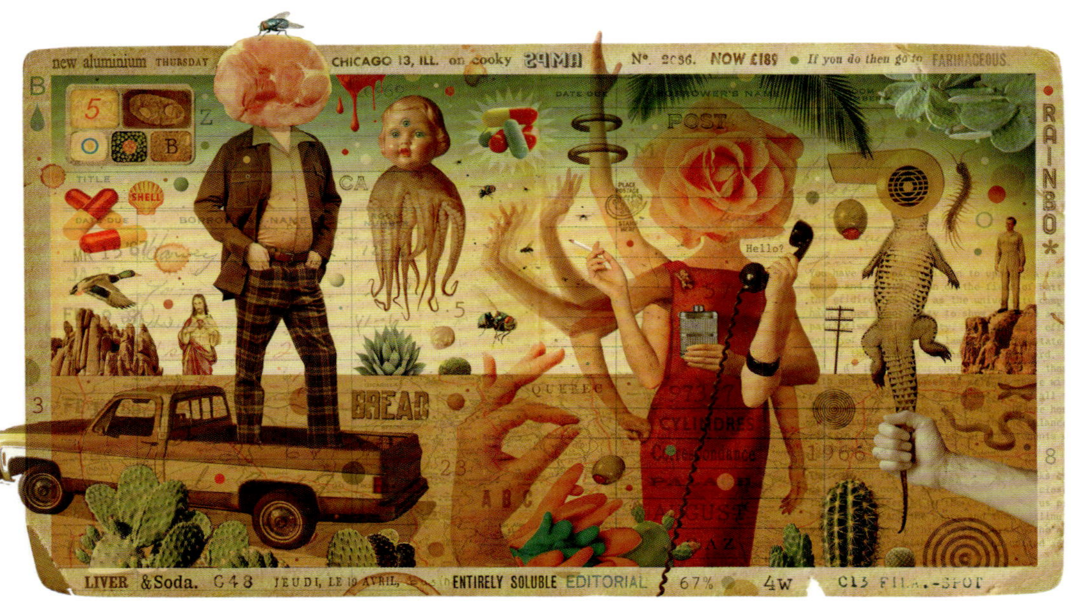

(T) *Sam Washburn* (B) *Michael Waraksa*

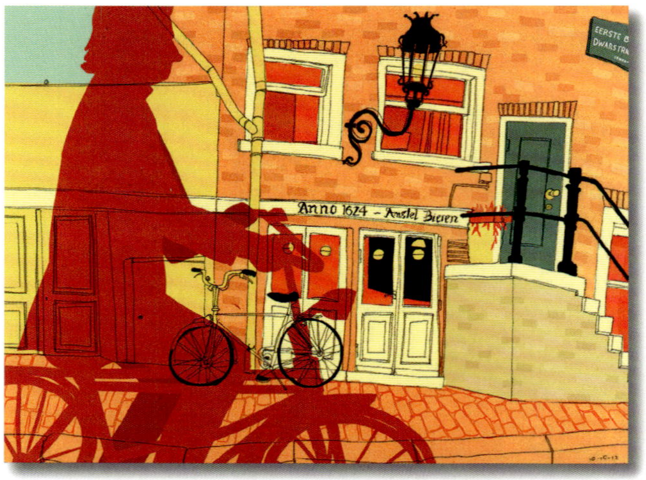

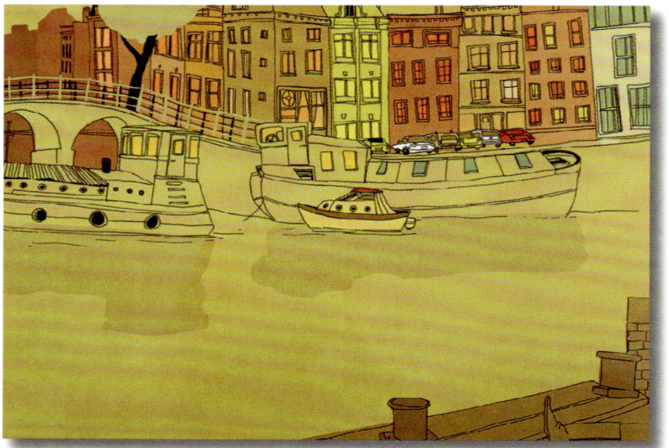

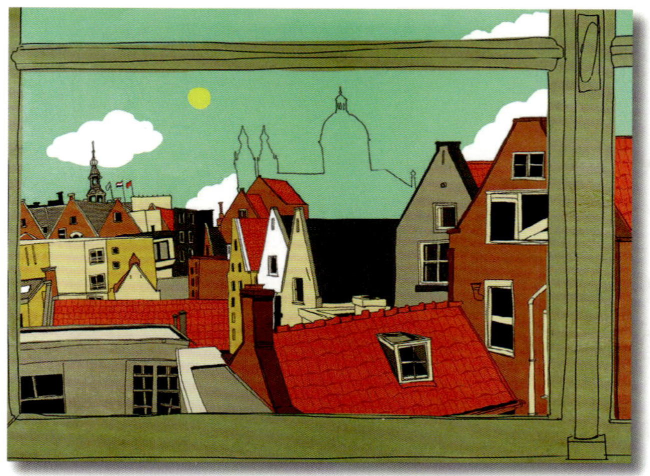

Michael Hirshon

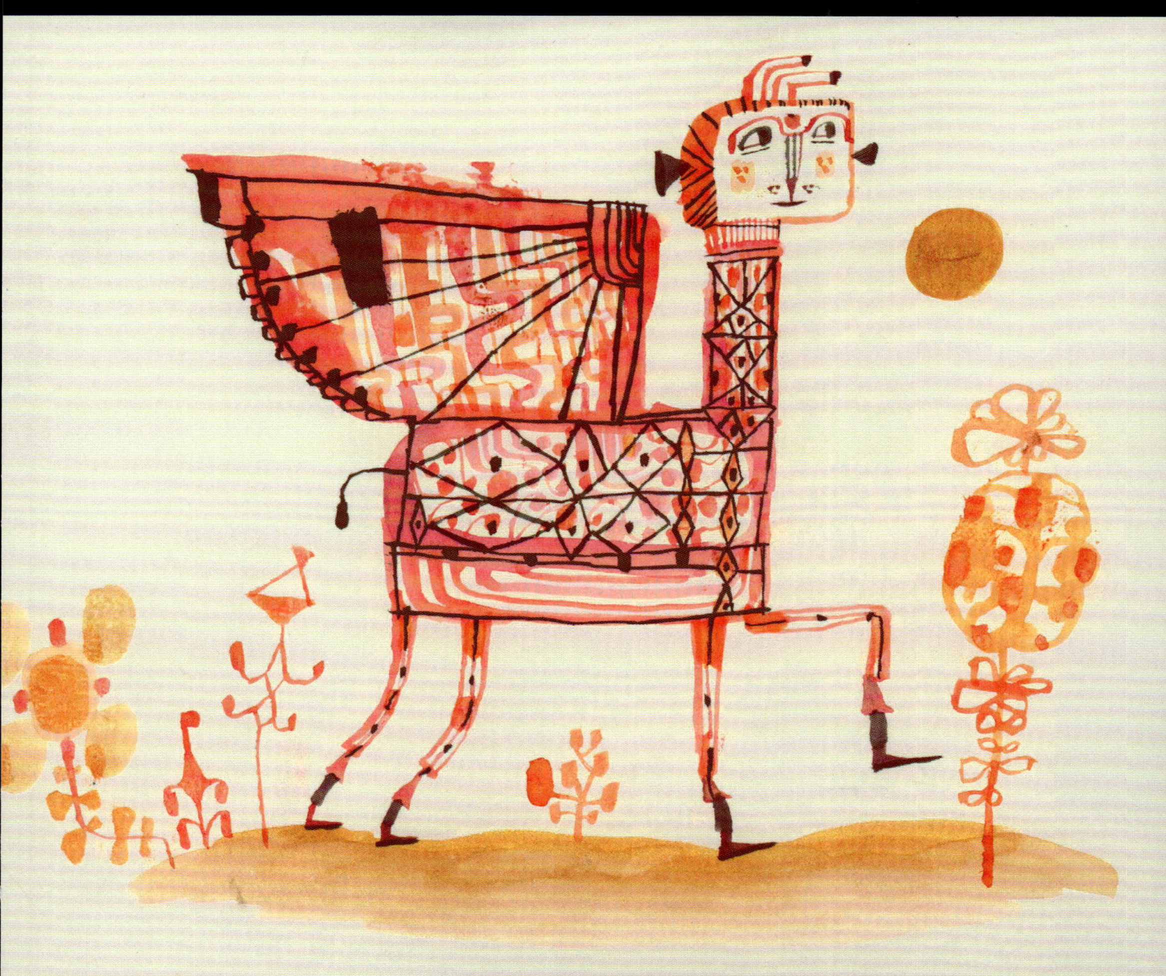

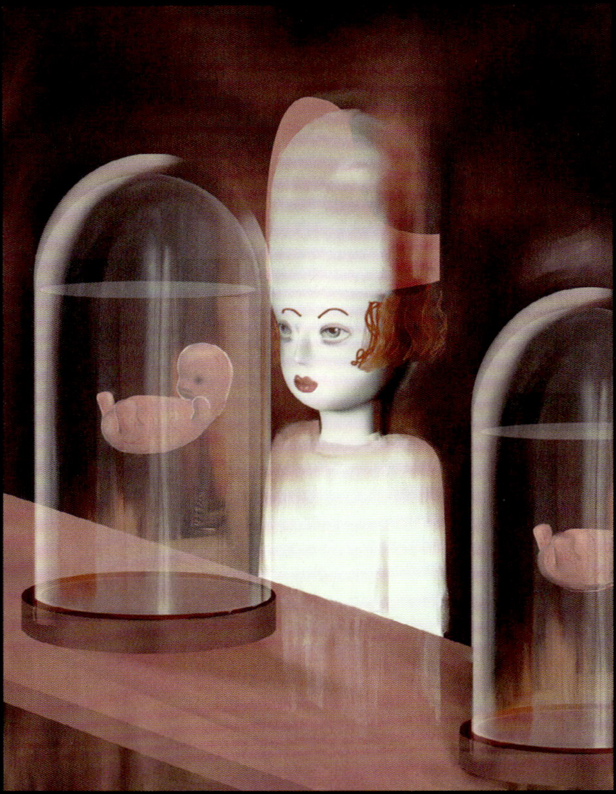

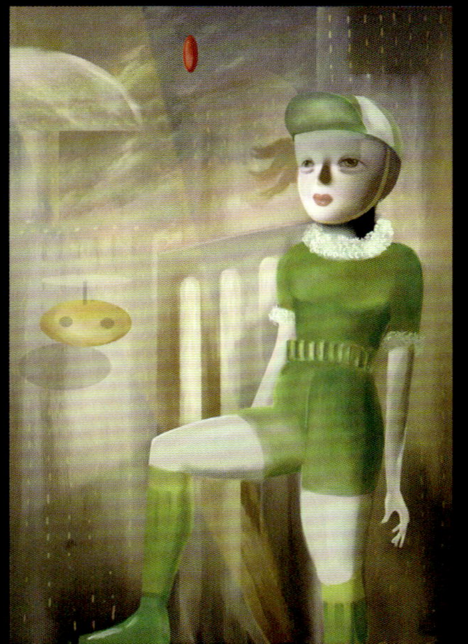

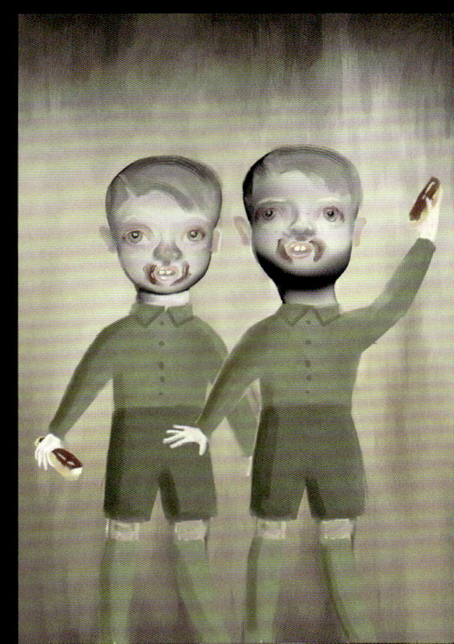

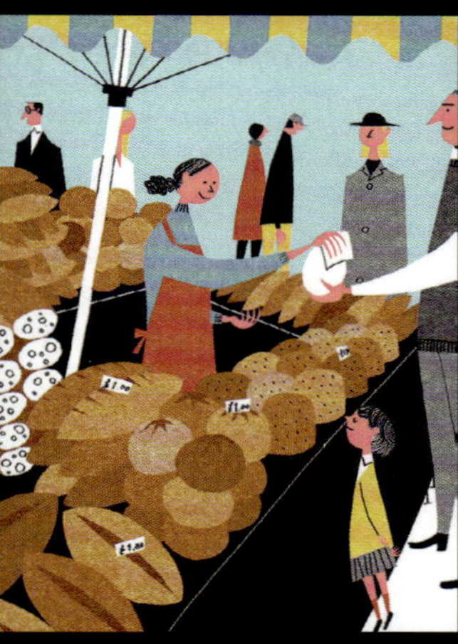

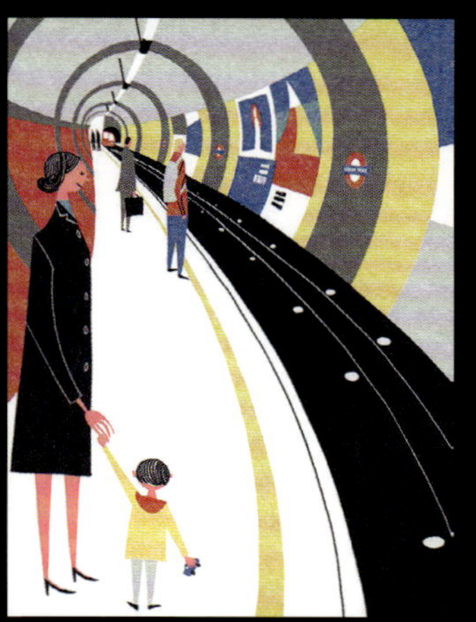

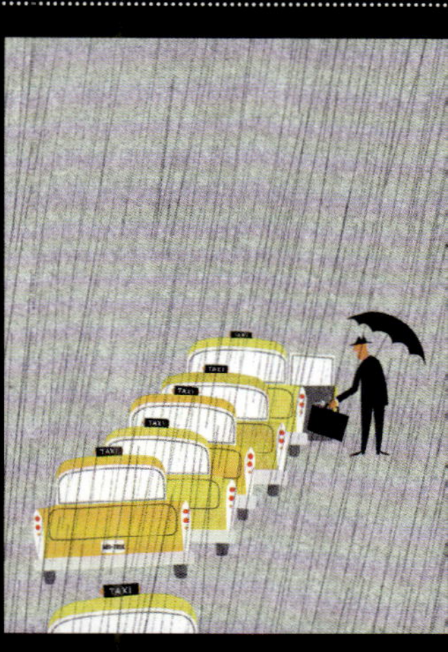

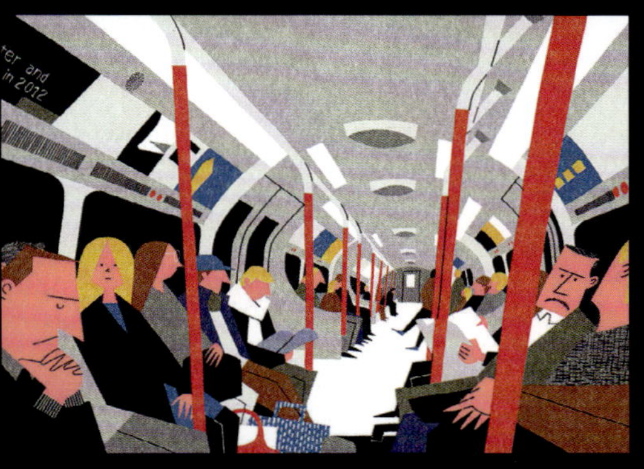

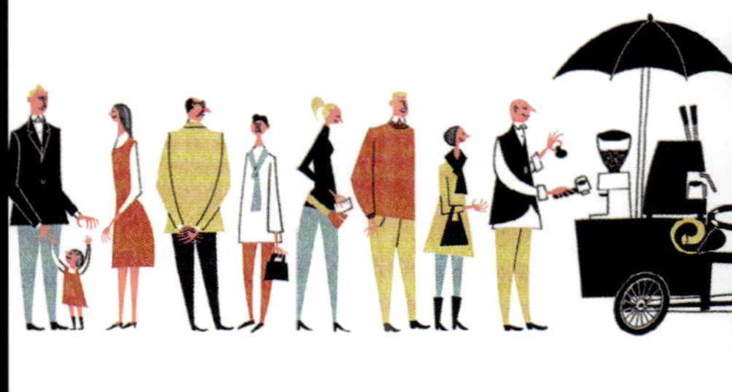

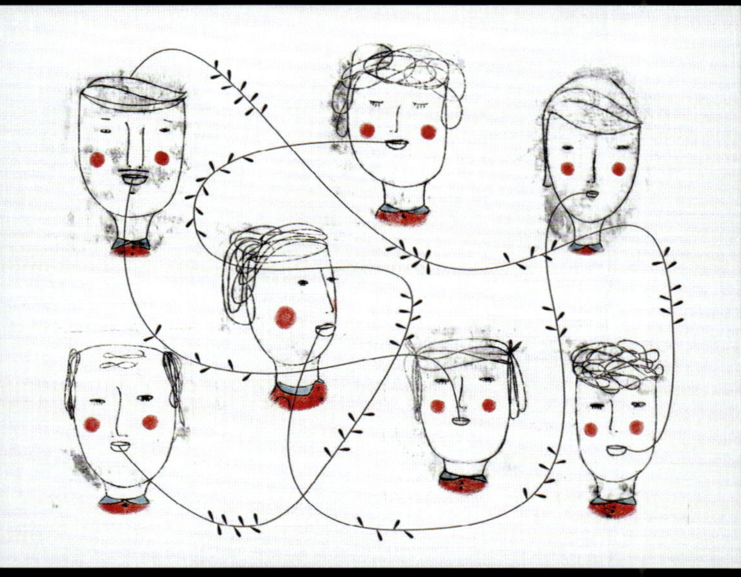

(T) *Ryo Takemasa* (B) *Michela Buttignol*

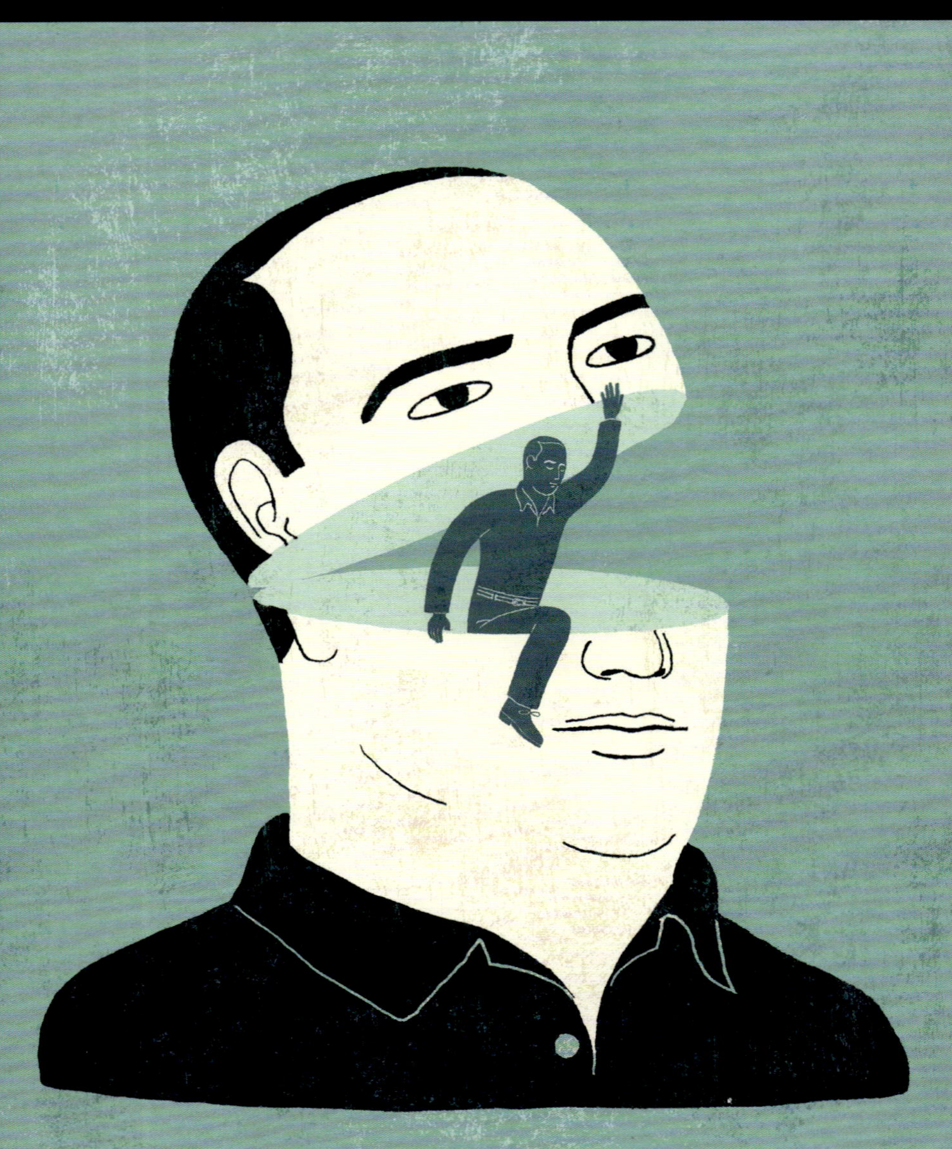

UNPUBLISHED

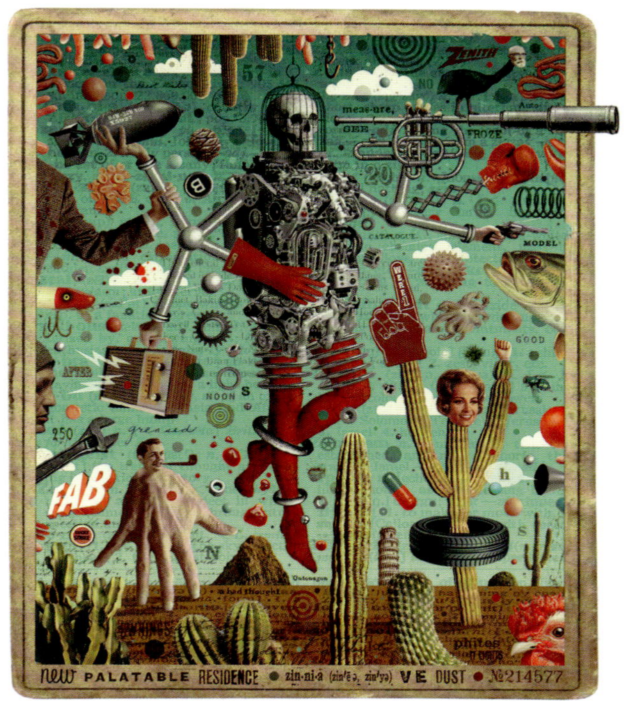

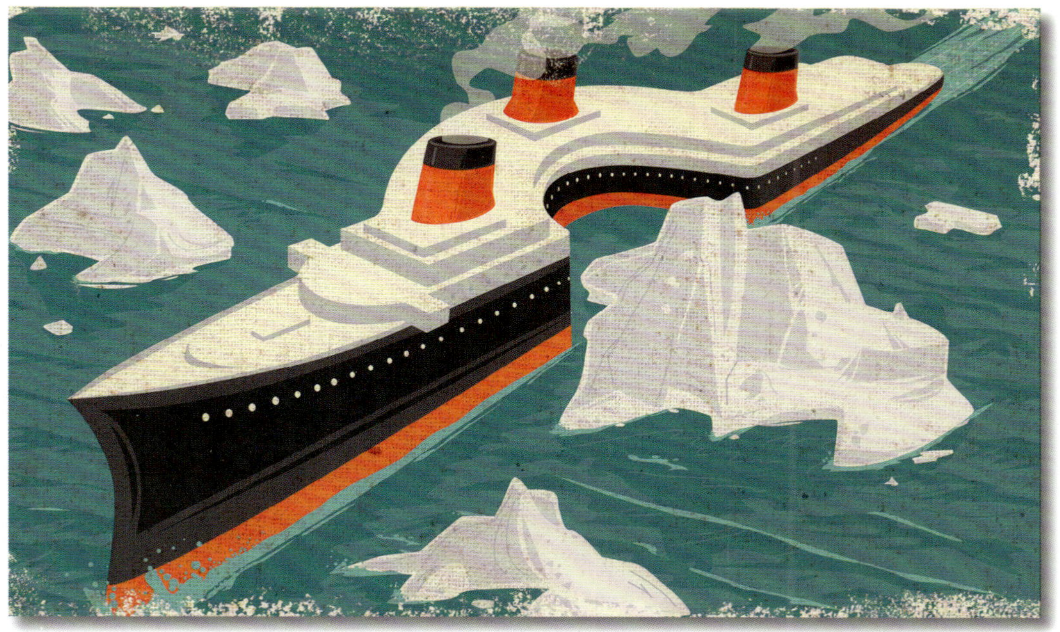

(T) *Michael Waraksa* (B) *Thomas Burns*

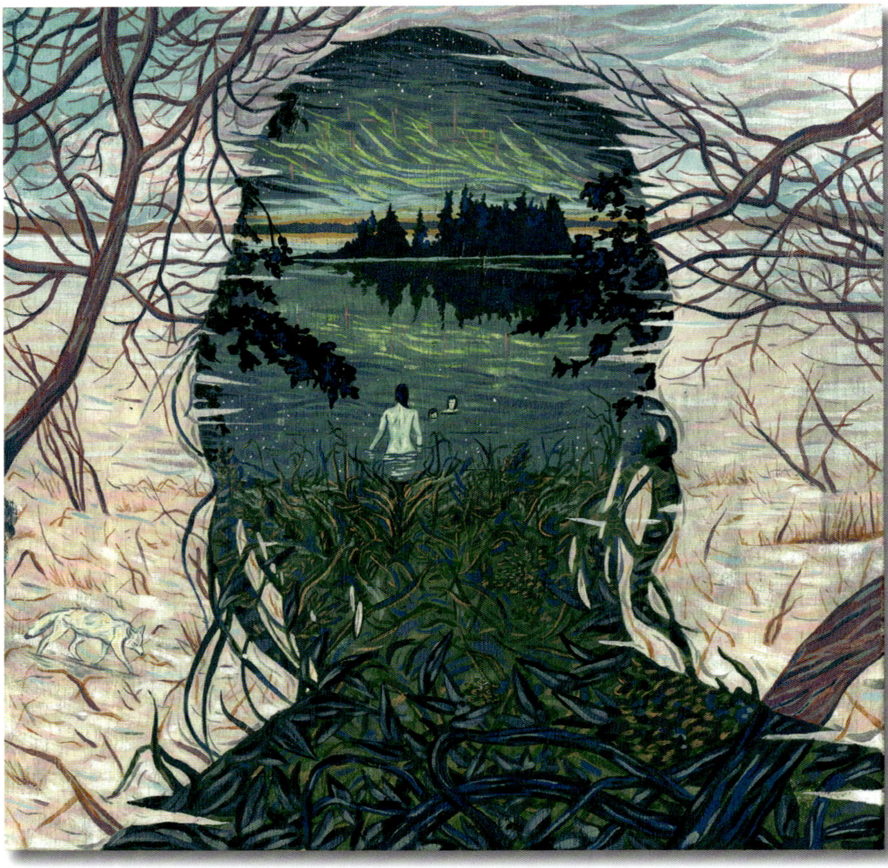

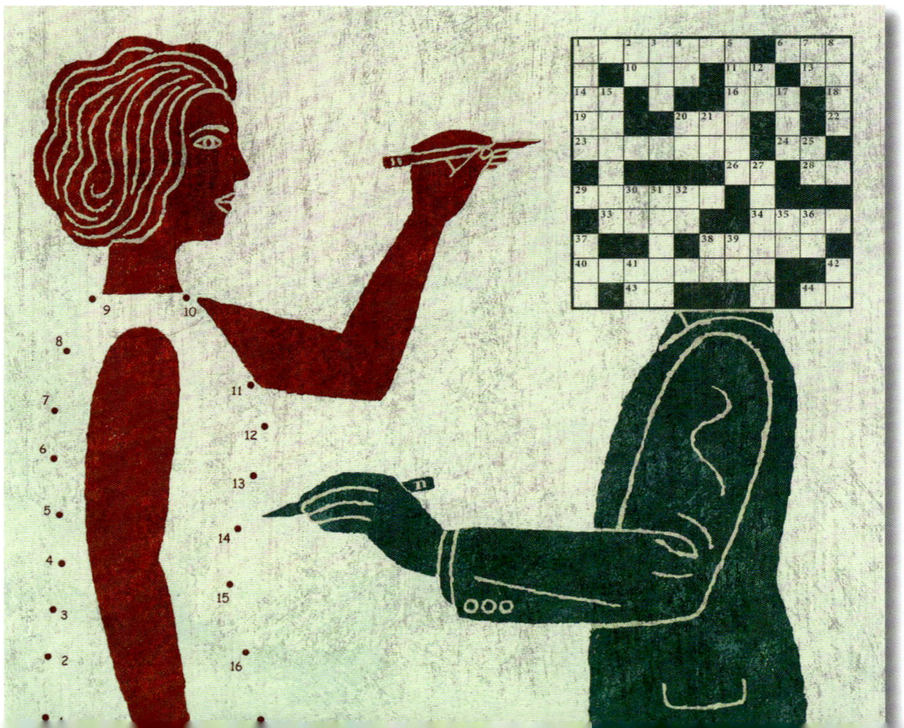

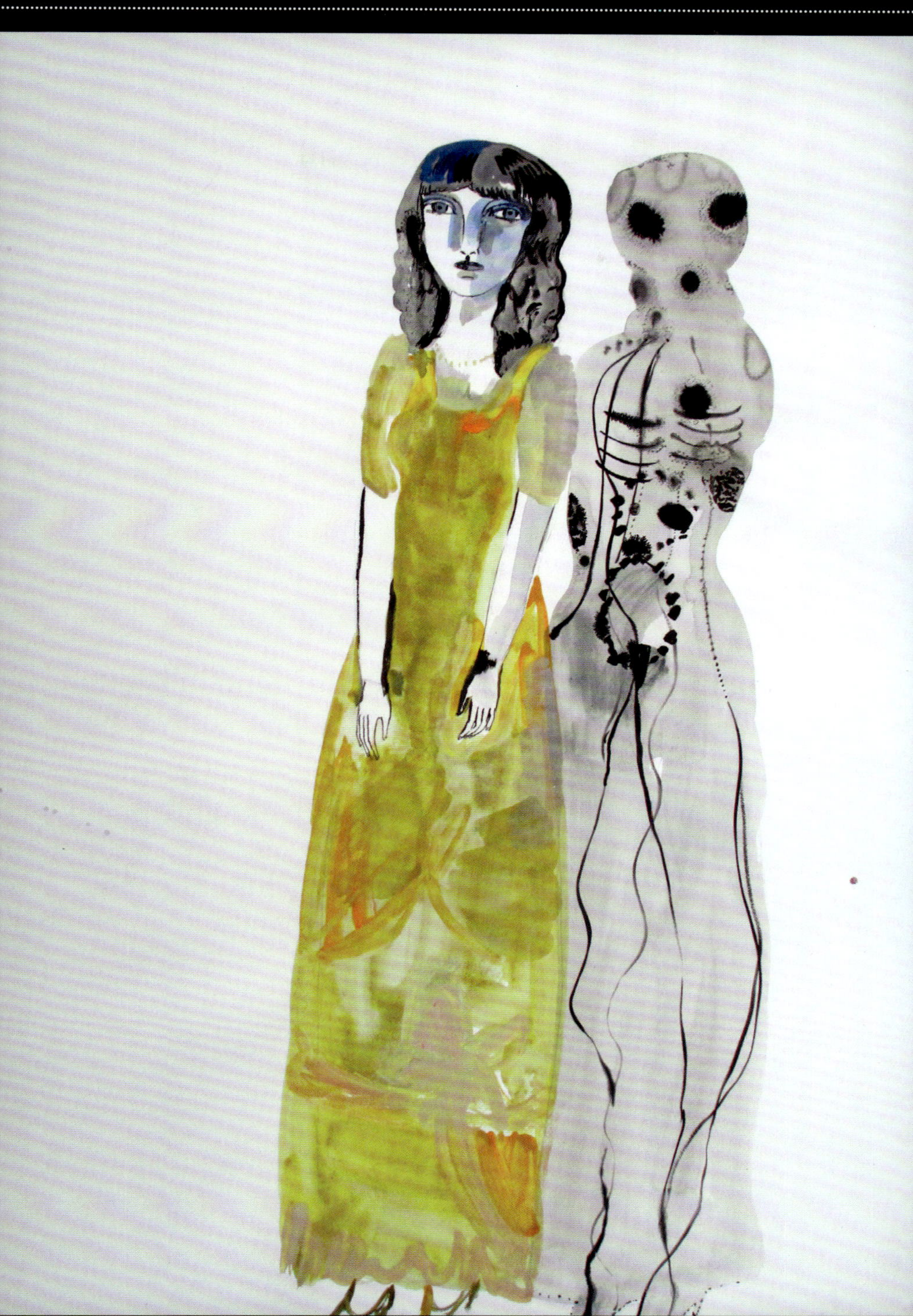

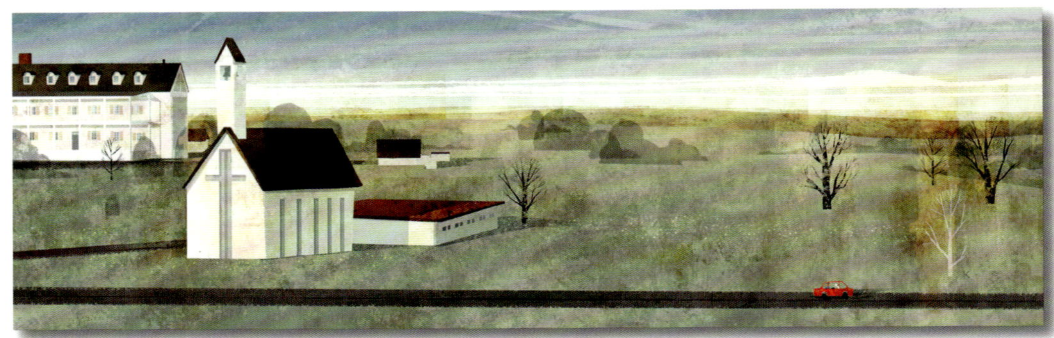

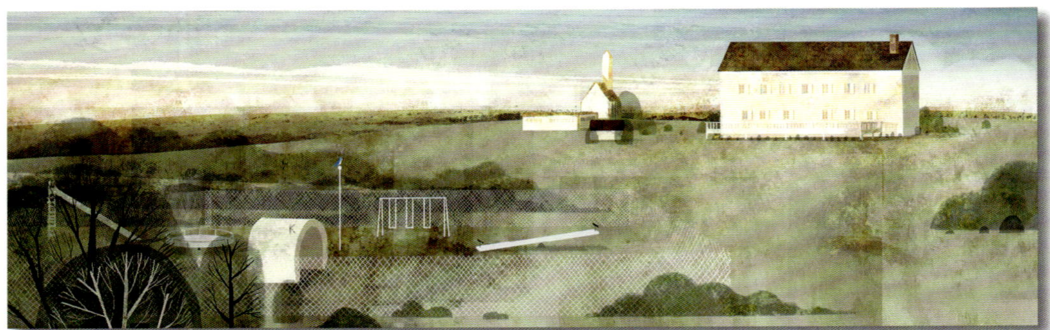

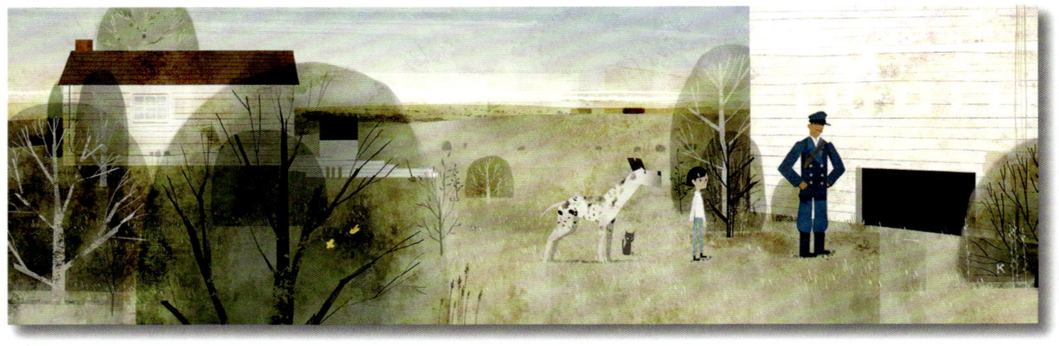

(L) *Kenard Pak* (R) *Natalie Pudalov*

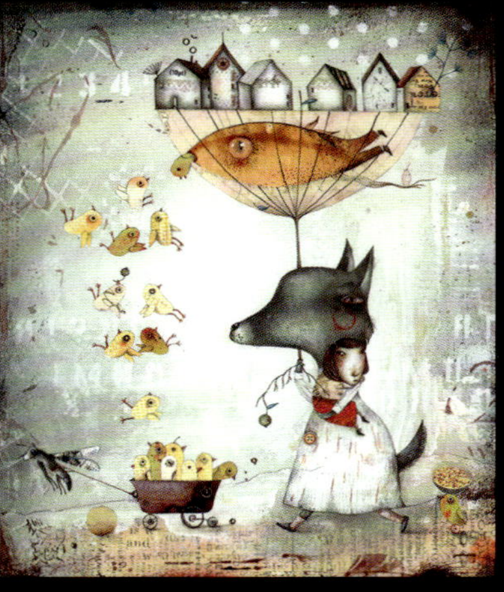

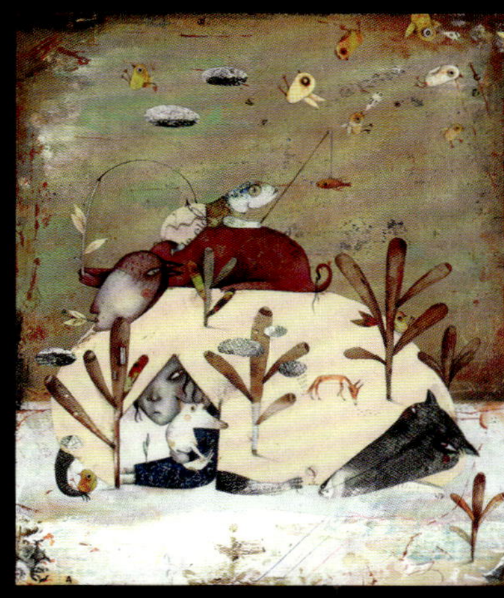

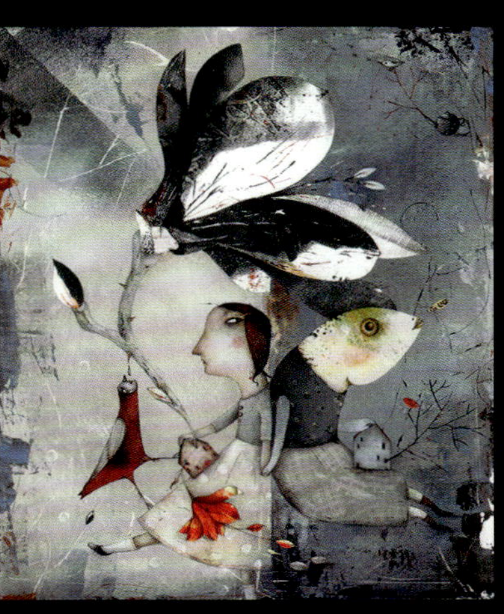

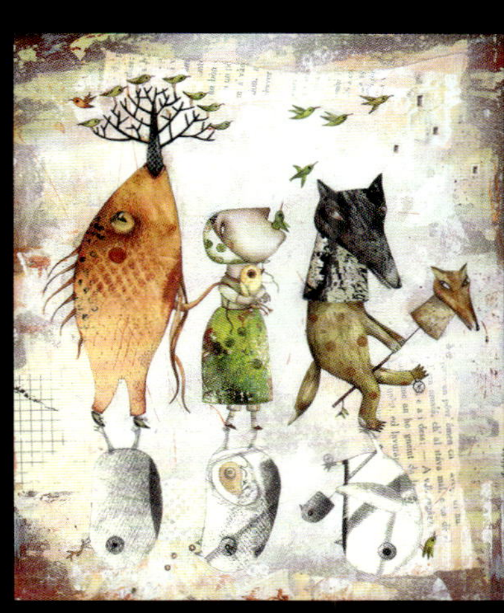

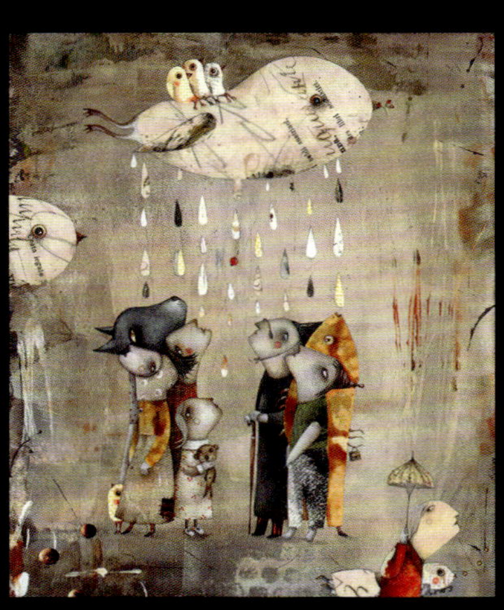

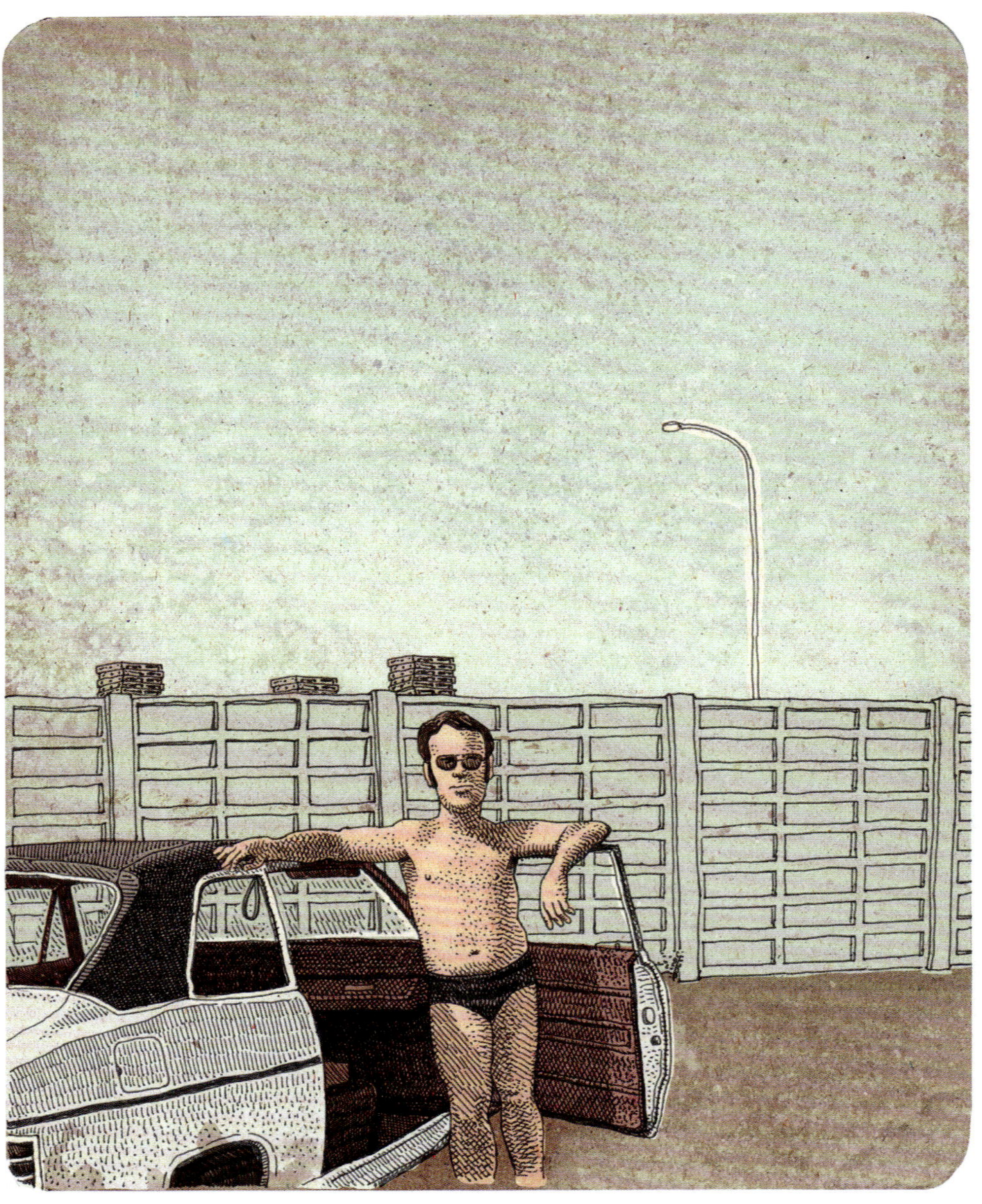

Mario Zucca

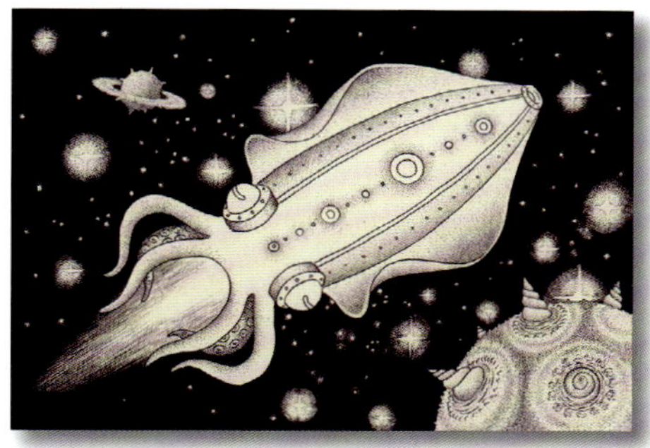

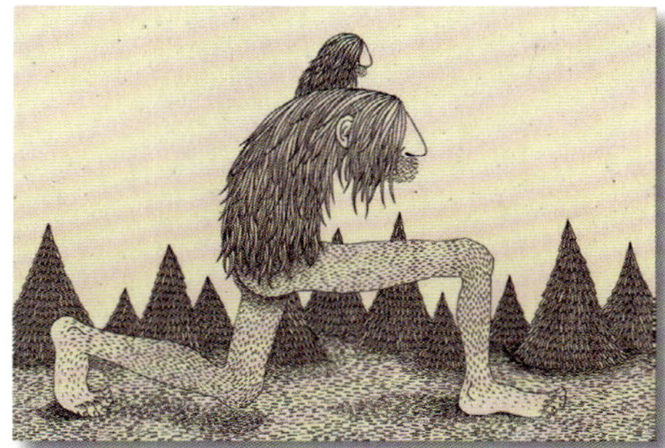

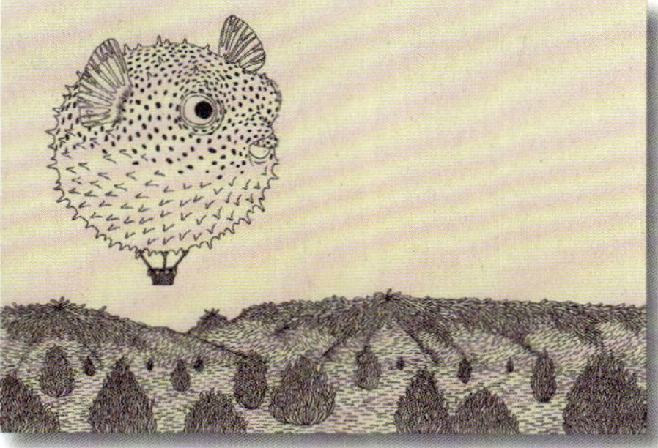

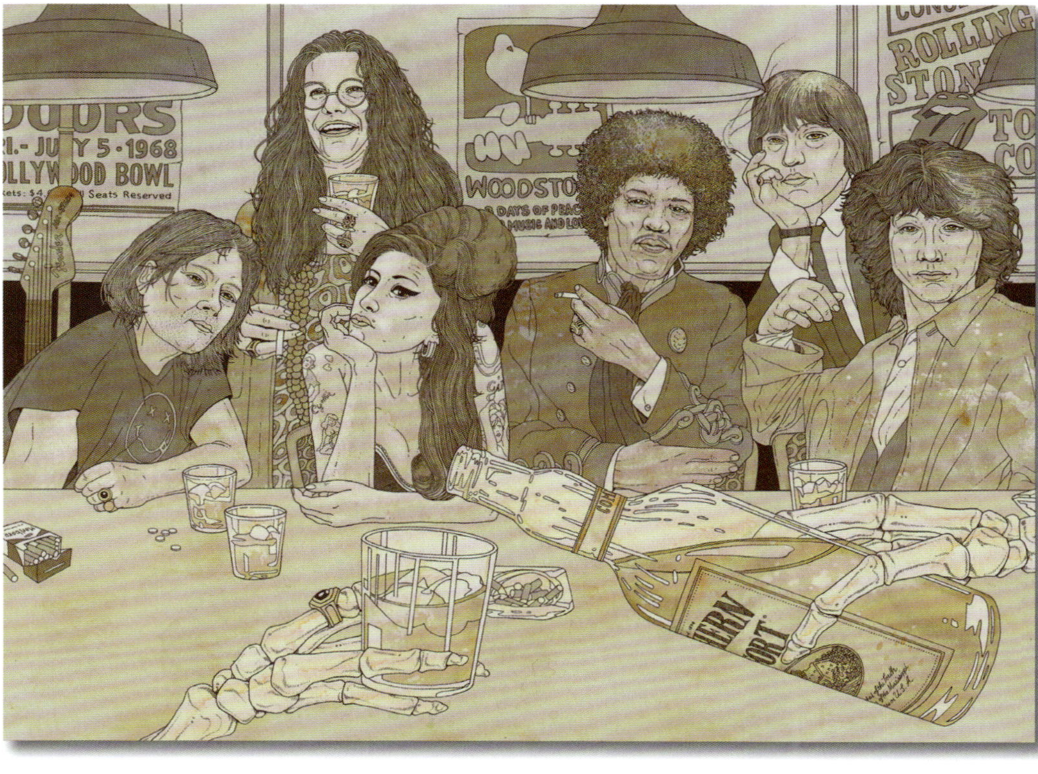

(T) *Veronica Chen* (B) *Dietmar Reinhard*

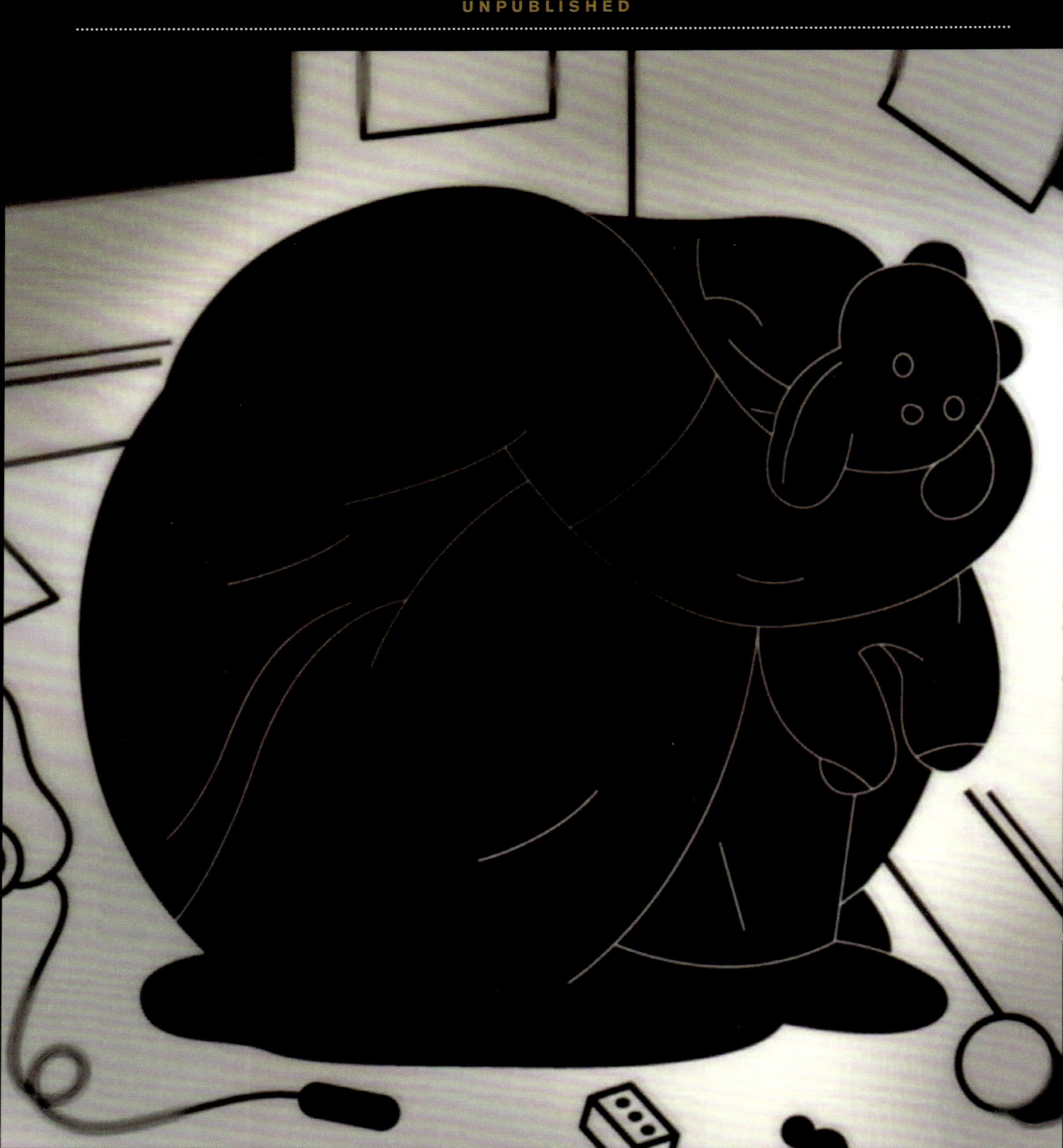

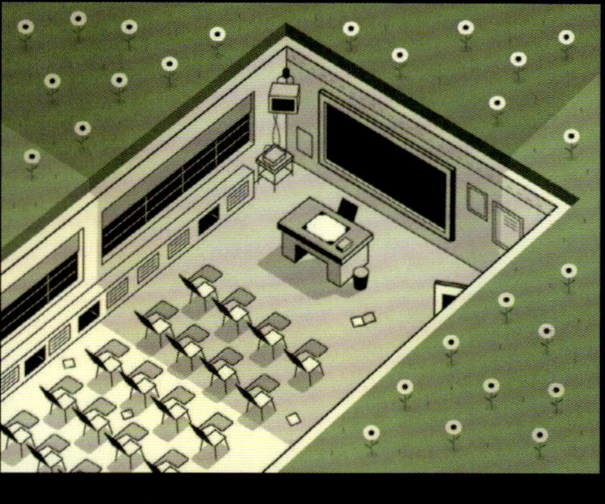

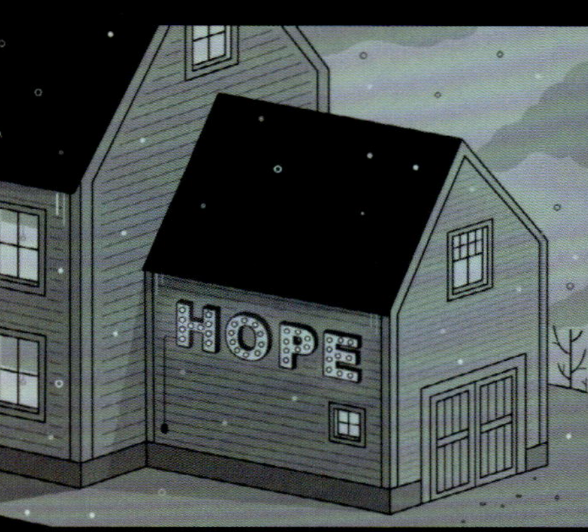
HOPE

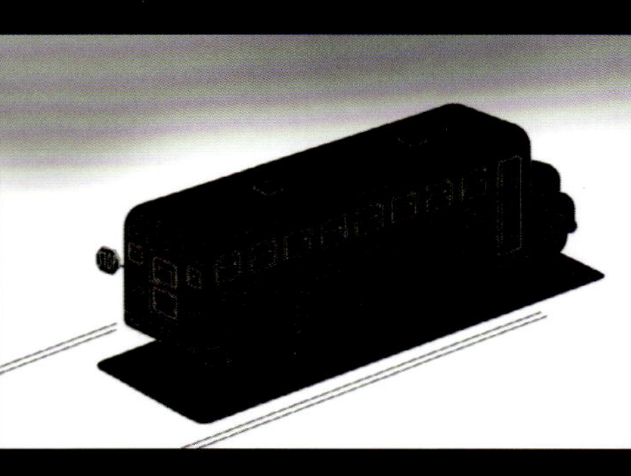

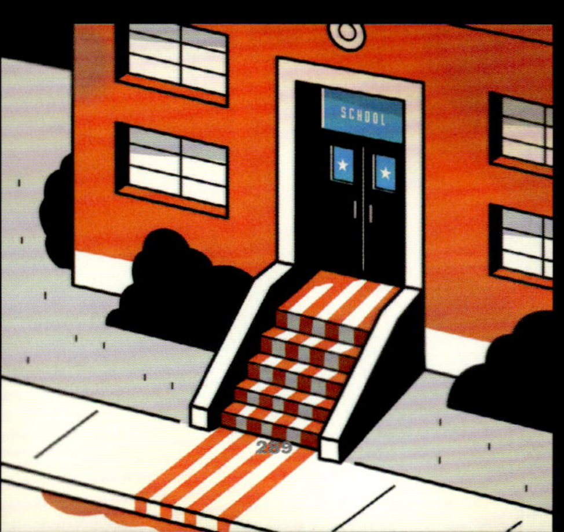
SCHOOL

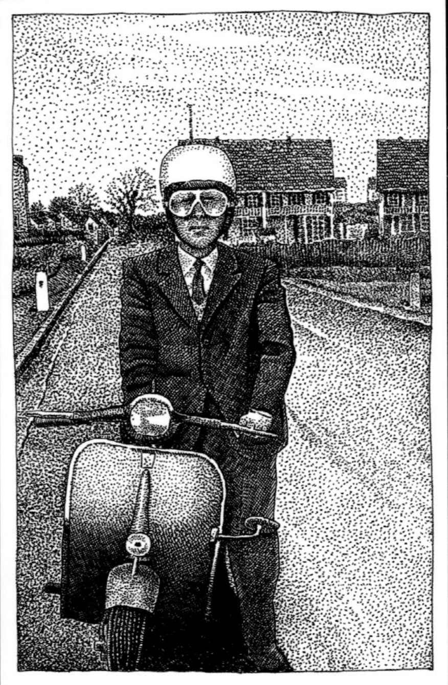

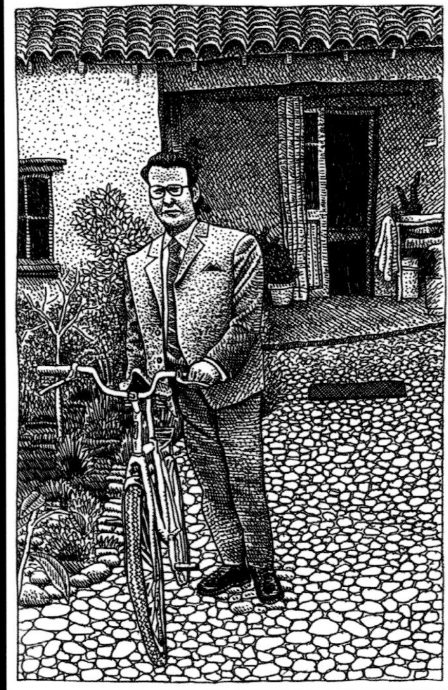

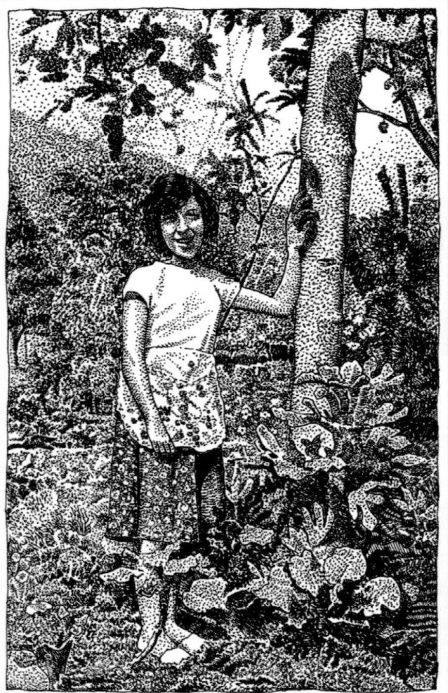

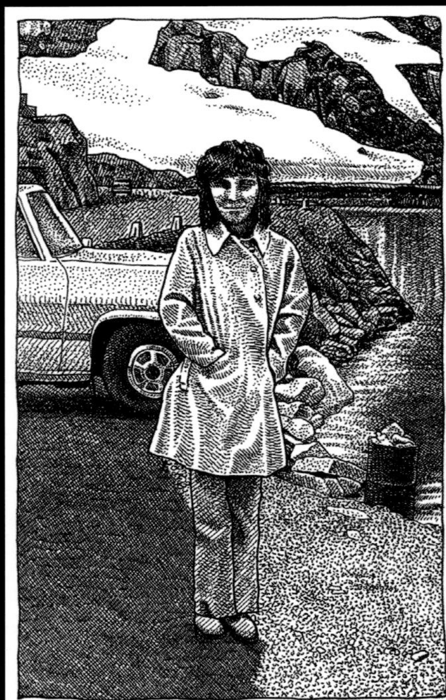

Mario Zucca :=: Davor Bakara

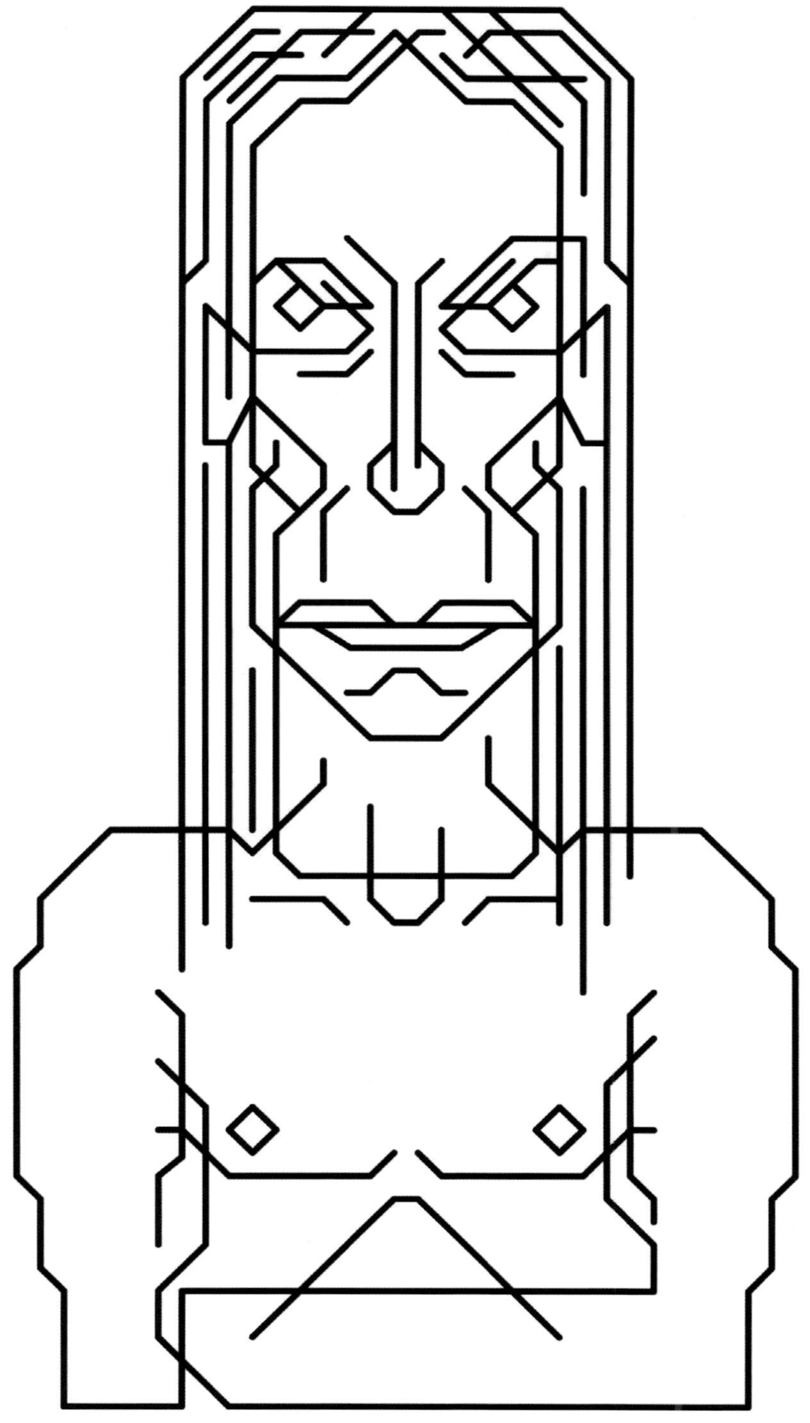

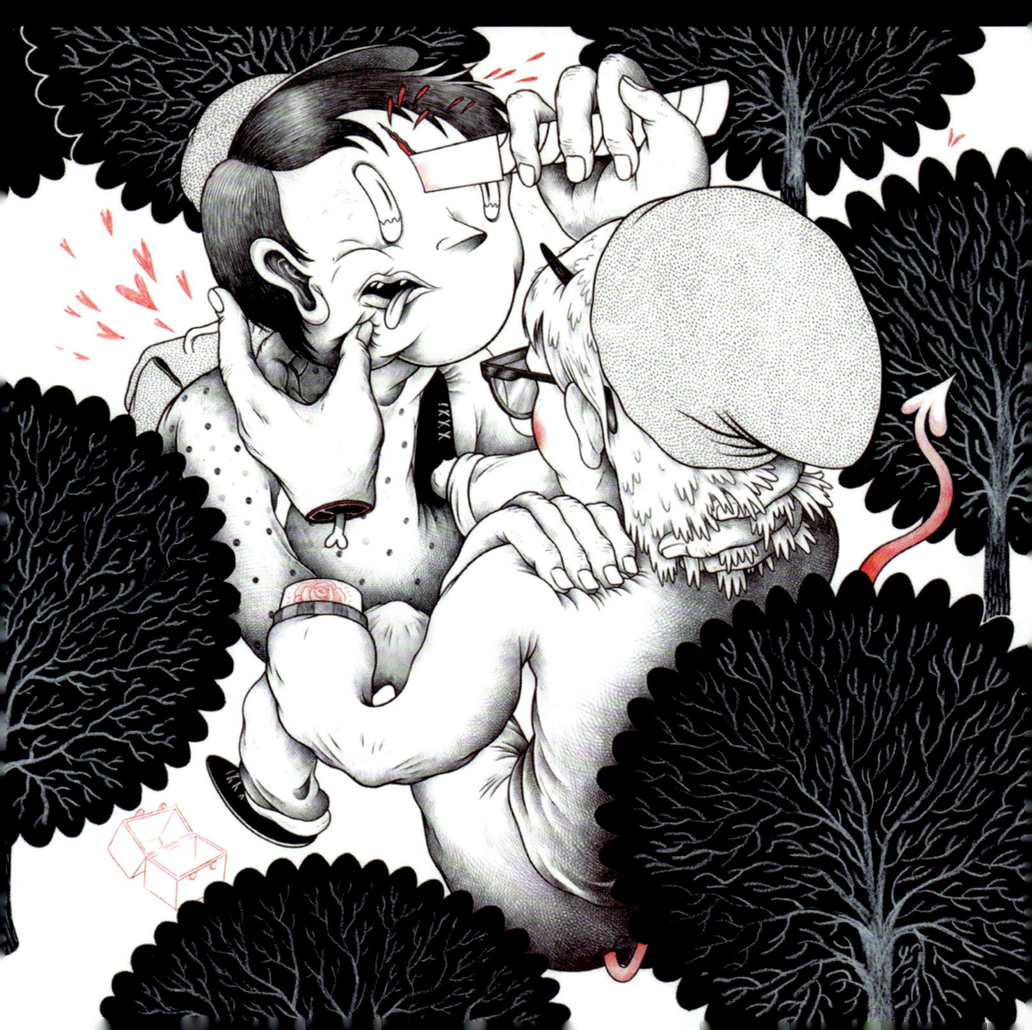

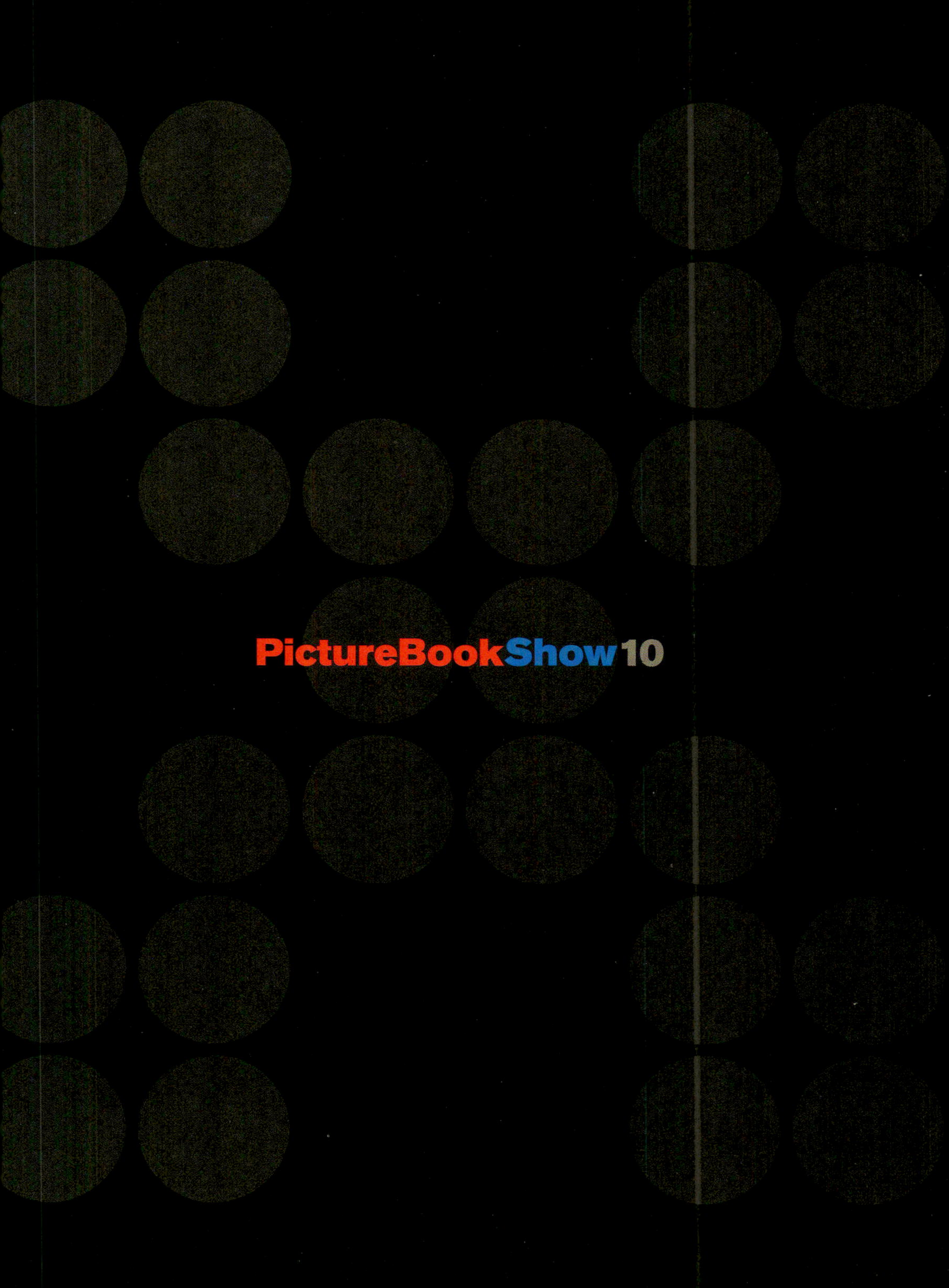

PictureBookShow10

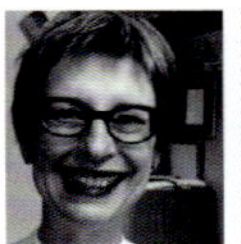

Ann Bobco

Ann is executive art director at Simon & Schuster, where she oversees picture book design for three of its children's imprints: Atheneum, Beach Lane Books and McElderry Books. She designed the Caldecott Honor award-winning, *Olivia*, and has worked closely with Ian Falconer on the six subsequent *Olivia* titles. She has also worked on numerous books with Marla Frazee, including the Caldecott Honor Book, *All the World* and the soon to be published *God Got a Dog* by Cynthia Rylant.

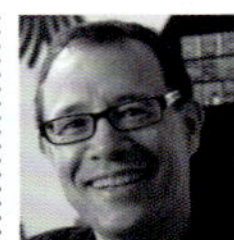

Julien Chung

Julien illustrates and designs for *La Presse+*, a groundbreaking daily news content app in French for the iPad. He also creates illustrations for his own brand, Julien Chung Designs, which licenses his whimsical characters to manufacturers around the world. His animals adorn products ranging from beer glasses to shopping bags, from Christmas ornaments to candy packaging and can be seen in retail shops in Germany, Japan, Korea and the United States. His work in both editorial and licensing has been recognized in international competitions. He resides and works in Montréal

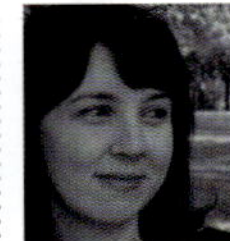

Rachael Cole

Rachael is art director at Schwartz & Wade Books, an imprint of Random House Children's Books. She has taught courses in children's picture book illustration at the School of Visual Arts and has been a thesis advisor for their MFA Illustration as Visual Essay program. Rachael has been a juror on *American Illustration*, Society of Illustrators and the annual Sidewalk Arts Festival at the Savannah College of Art and Design. She has also been a guest speaker at Maryland Institute College of Art, Society of Children's Book Writers and Illustrators and the Children's Book Council.

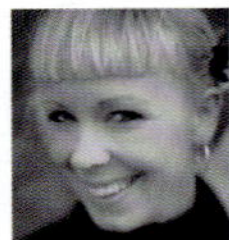

Judith Drews

Judith's work appears in over 30 children's books and also in adult areas of illustration. Her work has been published, exhibited or reviewed around the world and honored by ADC Germany, ADC Europe, Clio Award NY, LIA London, 100 Best Posters, *3x3 Annual* and Stiftung Buchkunst. She was also nominated for the German Design Award. For the past six years Judith is a part of the nominating body for the world's largest children's literature award, ALMA. Judith is based in Berlin.

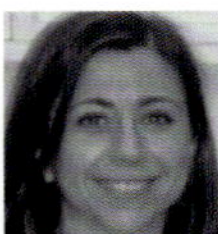

Belén Freijeiro

Belén graduated from the University of Vigo specializing in design and audiovisuals. Her professional activity focusses on the world of children's literature, especially graphic design and visual communication in picture books. She is currently working as an art director in OQO editorial department, supervising picture books in nine different languages. She also teaches a postgraduate course: Illustrated Book and Audiovisual Animation at her alma mater. She was a jury member at Bologna Children's Book Fair and the Gold Blue Book Group Award 2010.

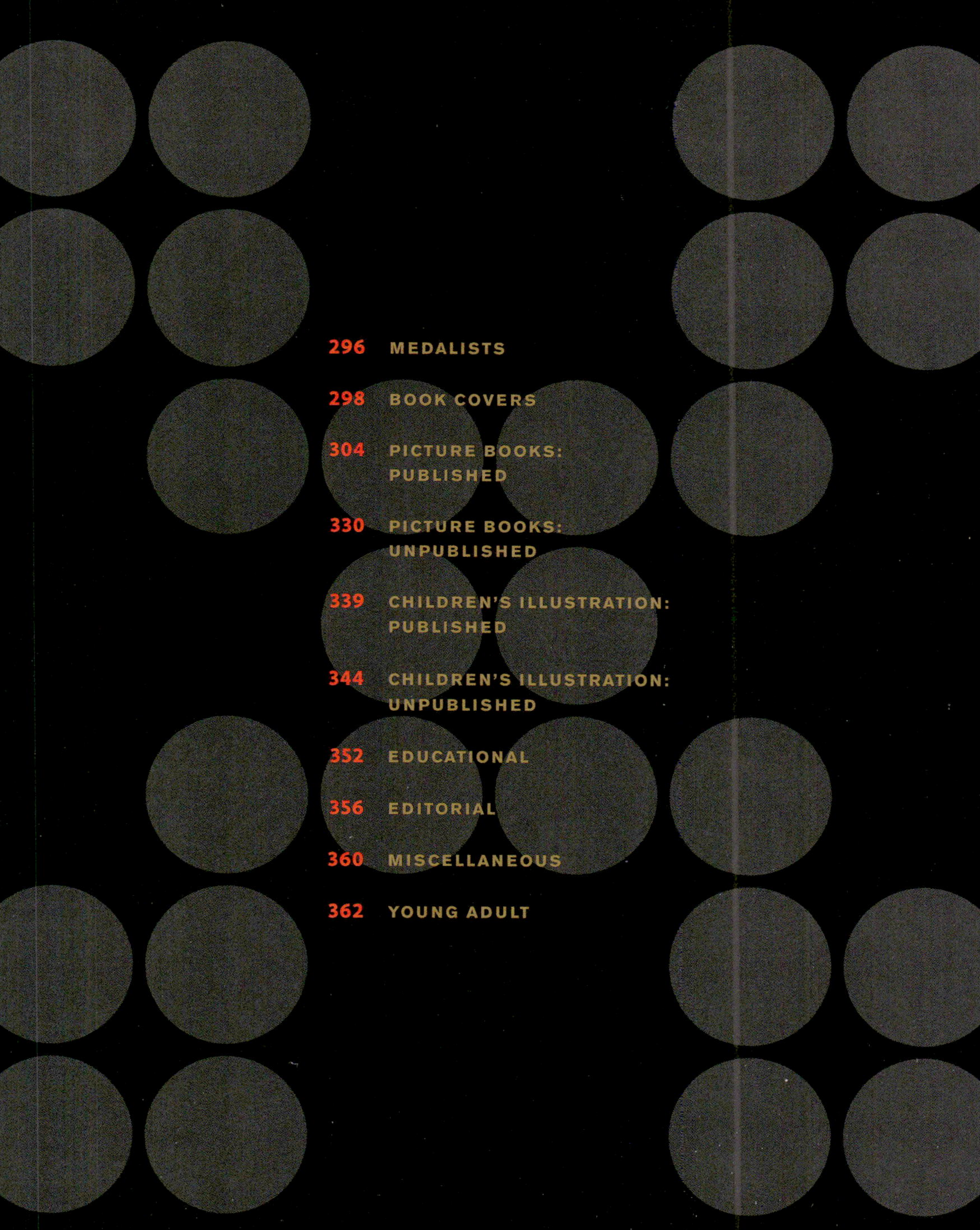

296 MEDALISTS

298 BOOK COVERS

304 PICTURE BOOKS: PUBLISHED

330 PICTURE BOOKS: UNPUBLISHED

339 CHILDREN'S ILLUSTRATION: PUBLISHED

344 CHILDREN'S ILLUSTRATION: UNPUBLISHED

352 EDUCATIONAL

356 EDITORIAL

360 MISCELLANEOUS

362 YOUNG ADULT

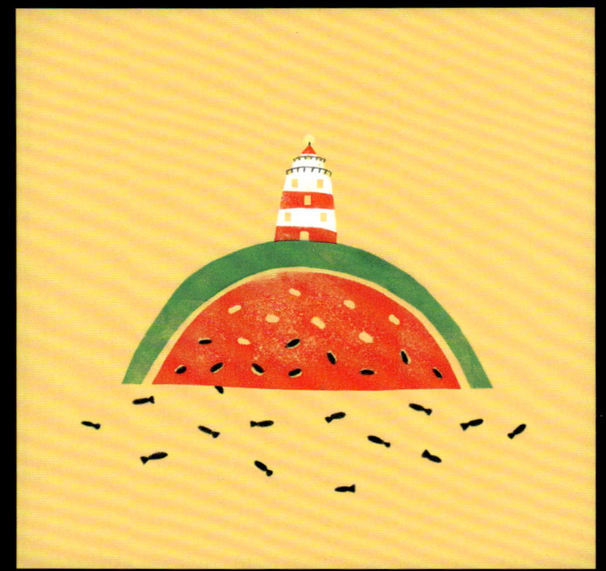

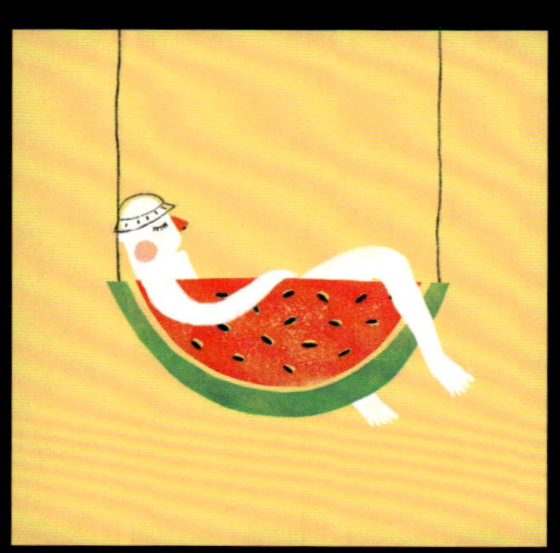

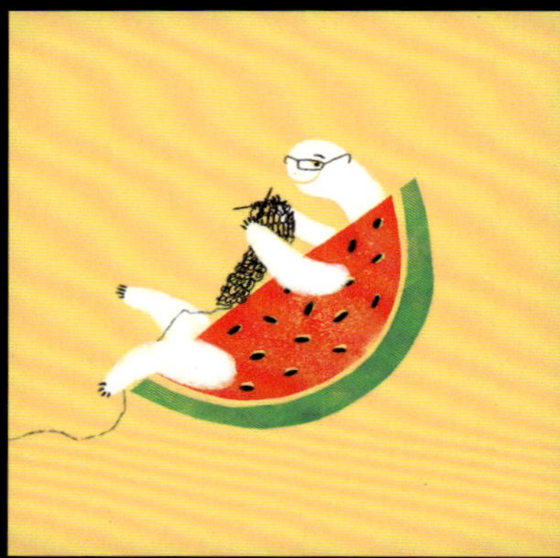

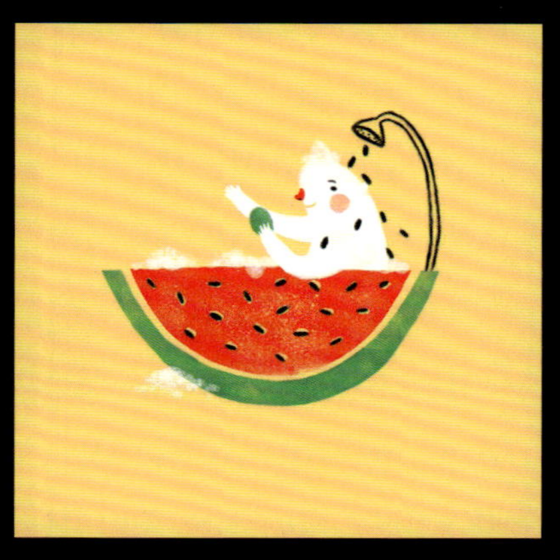

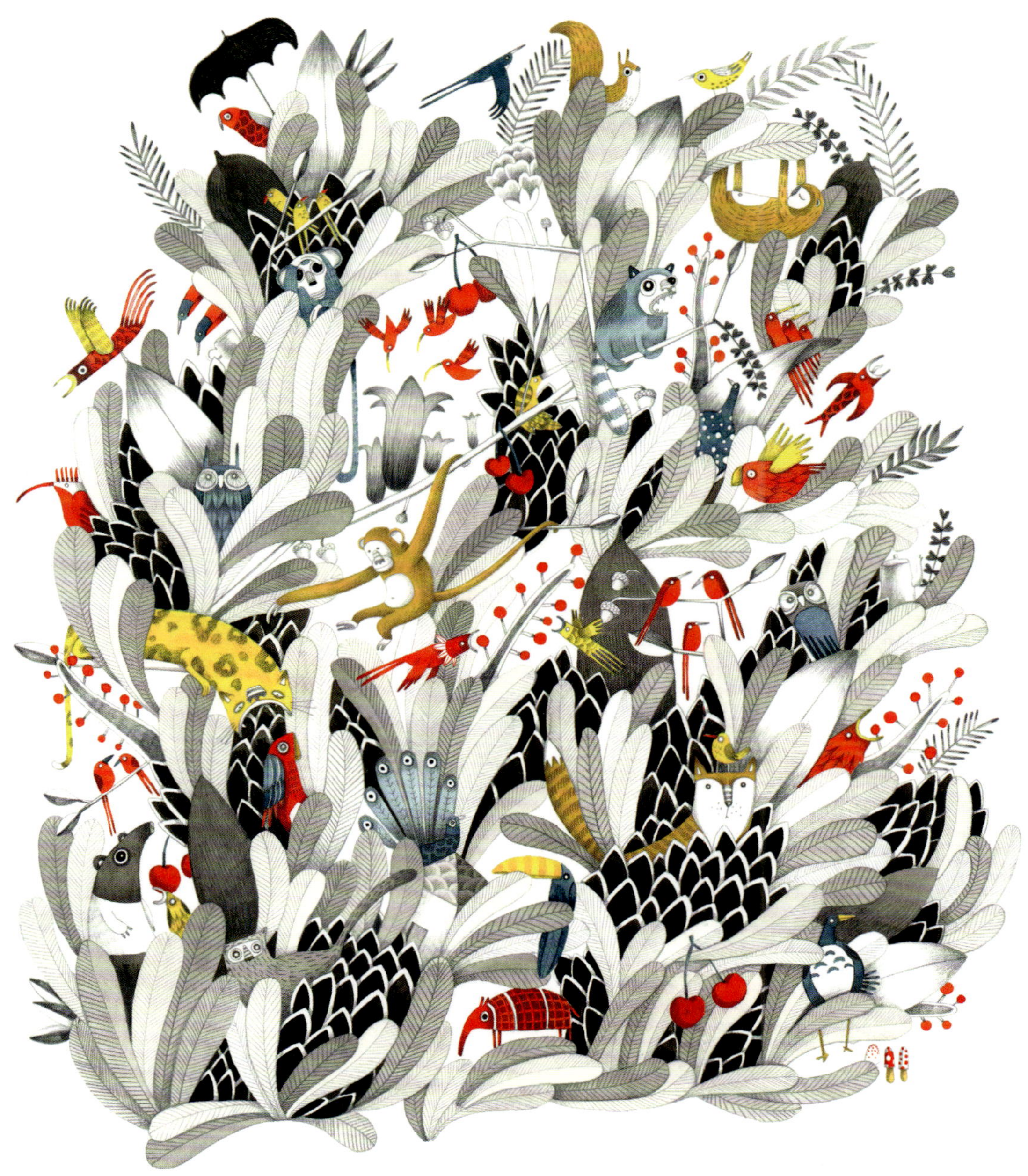

GOLD *Marion Arbona*

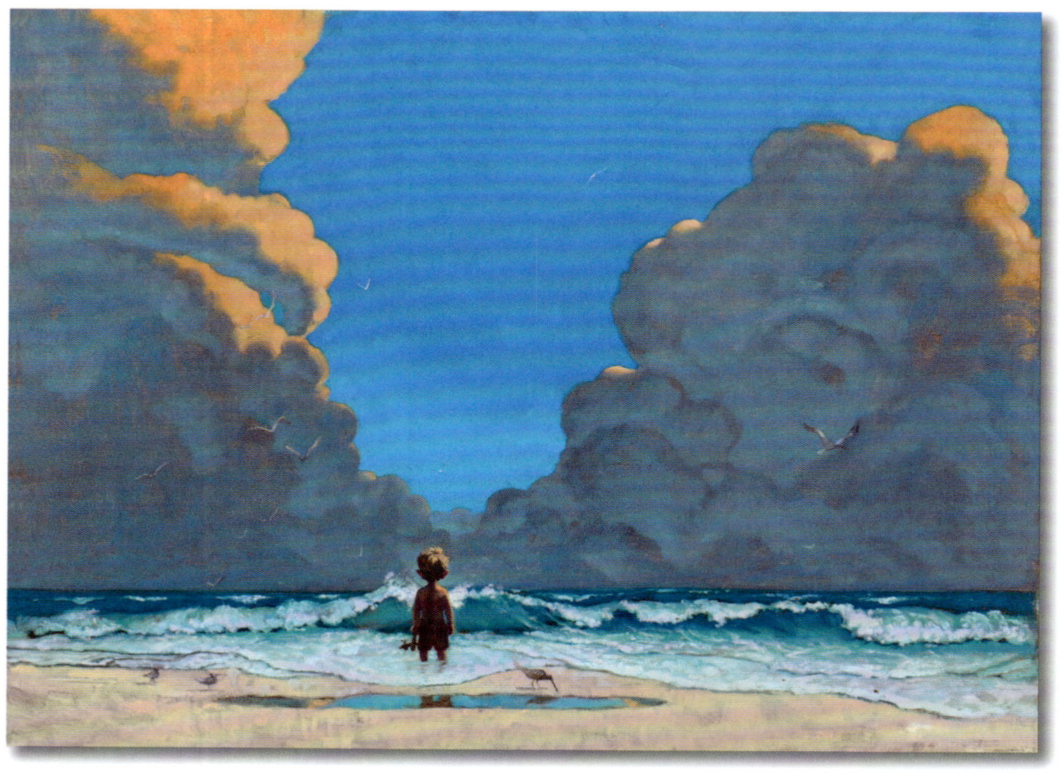

(L) **BRONZE** *T. Lively Fluharty* (R) *Robert Neubecker*

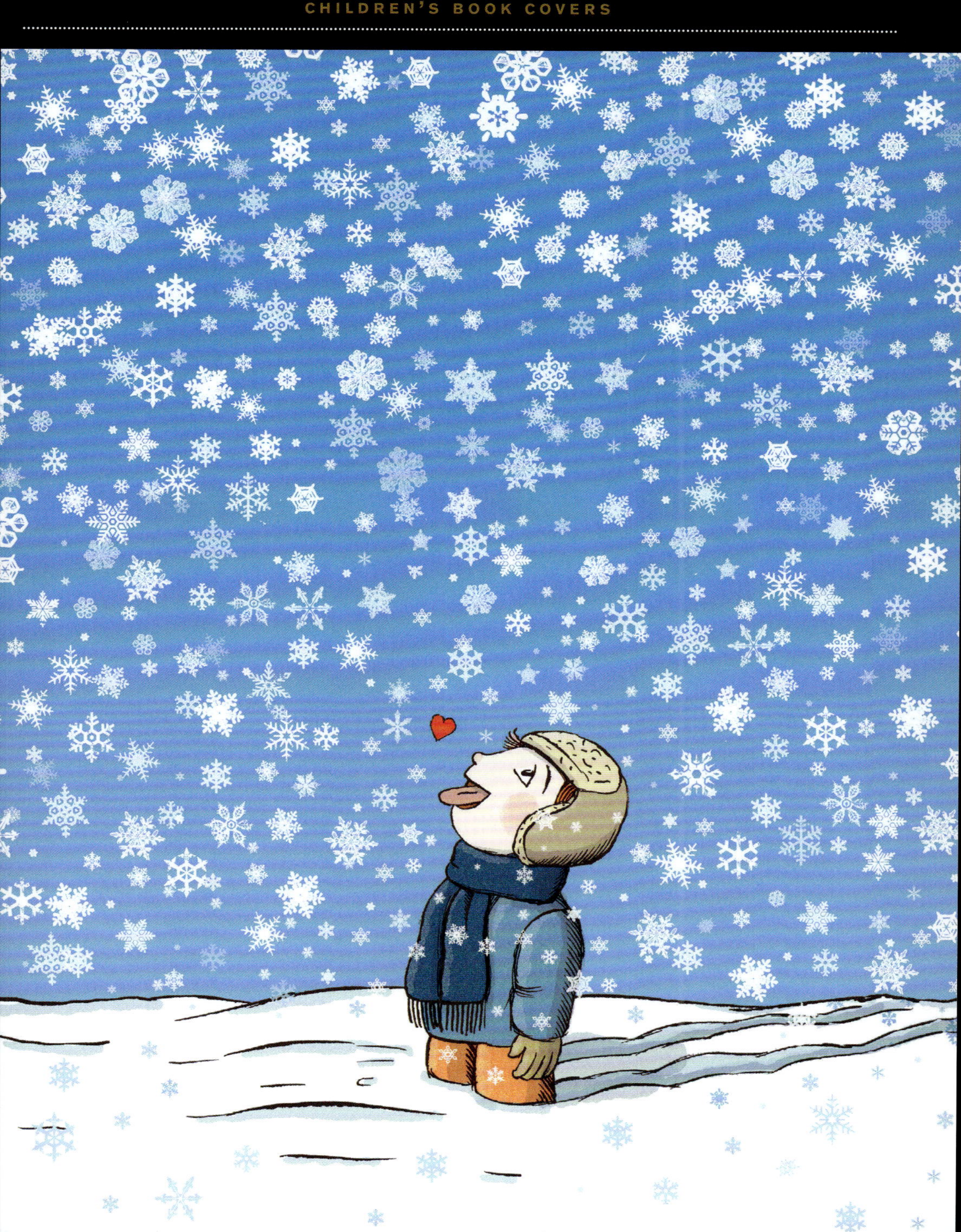

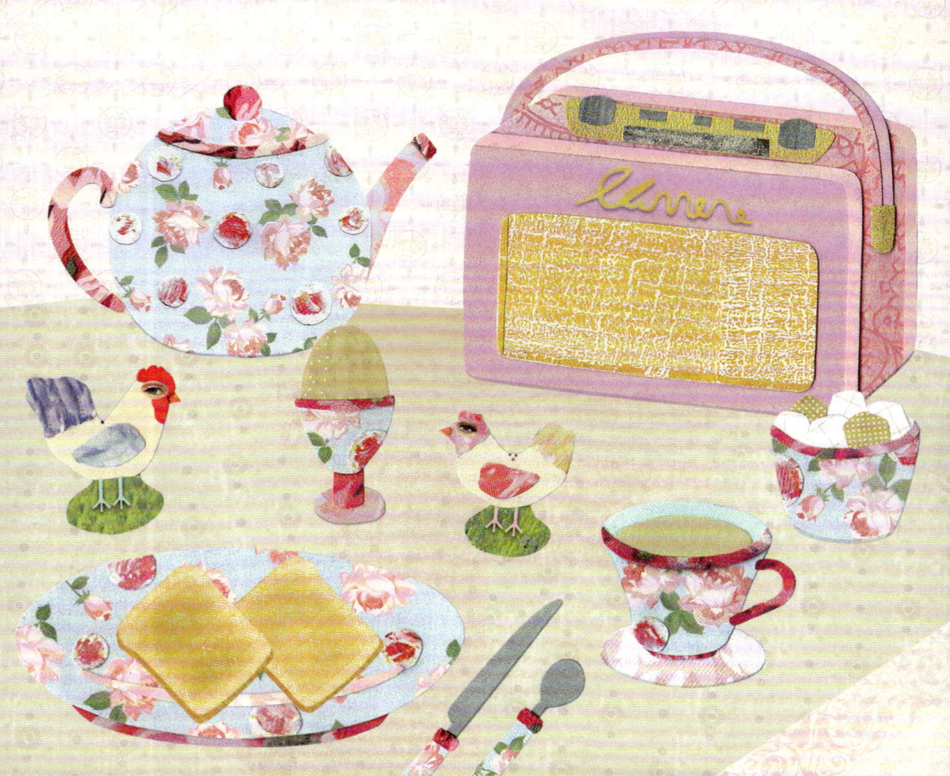

Lianne Harrison

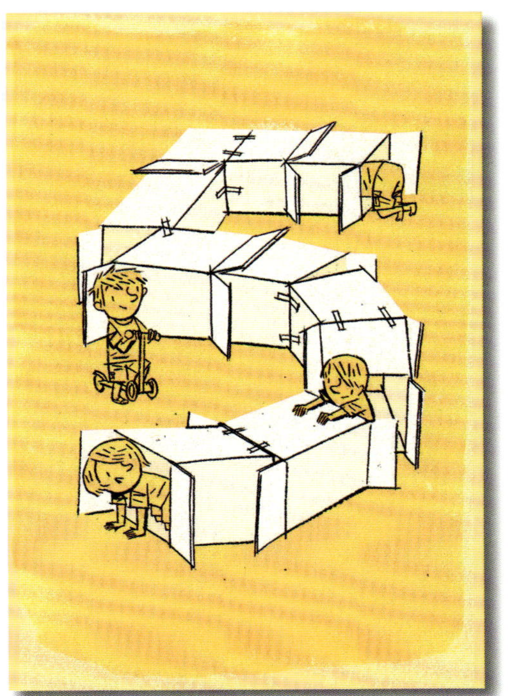
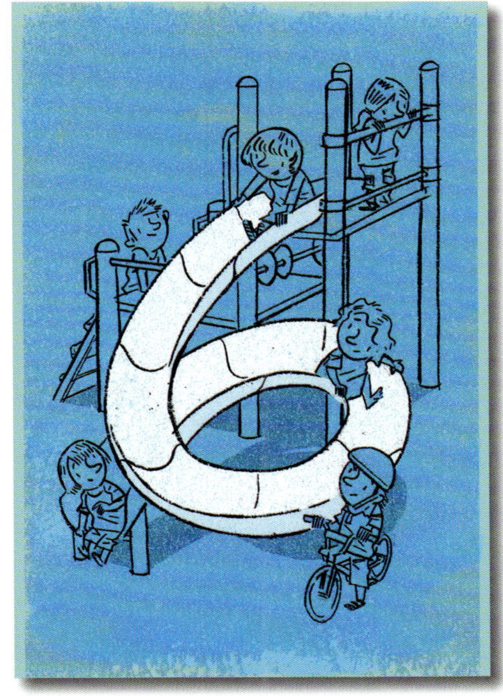
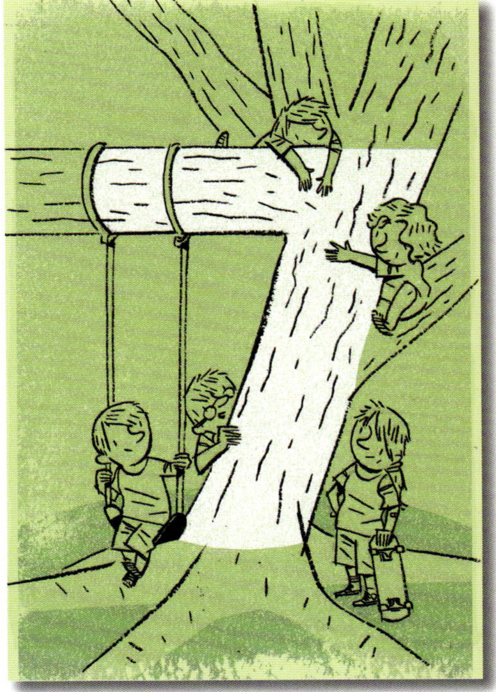
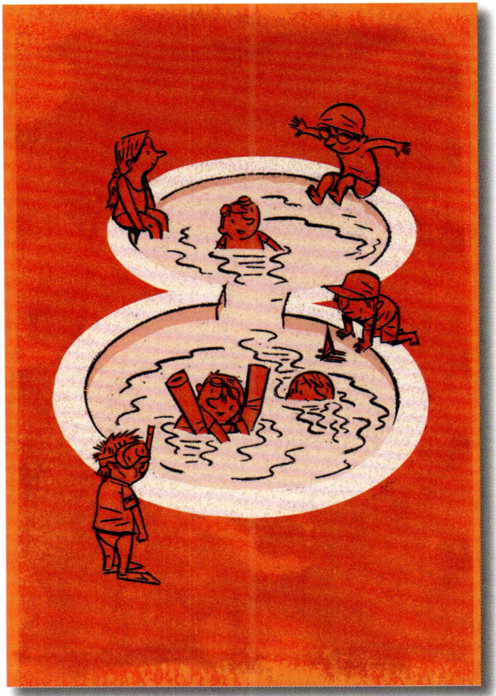

Tom Jellett

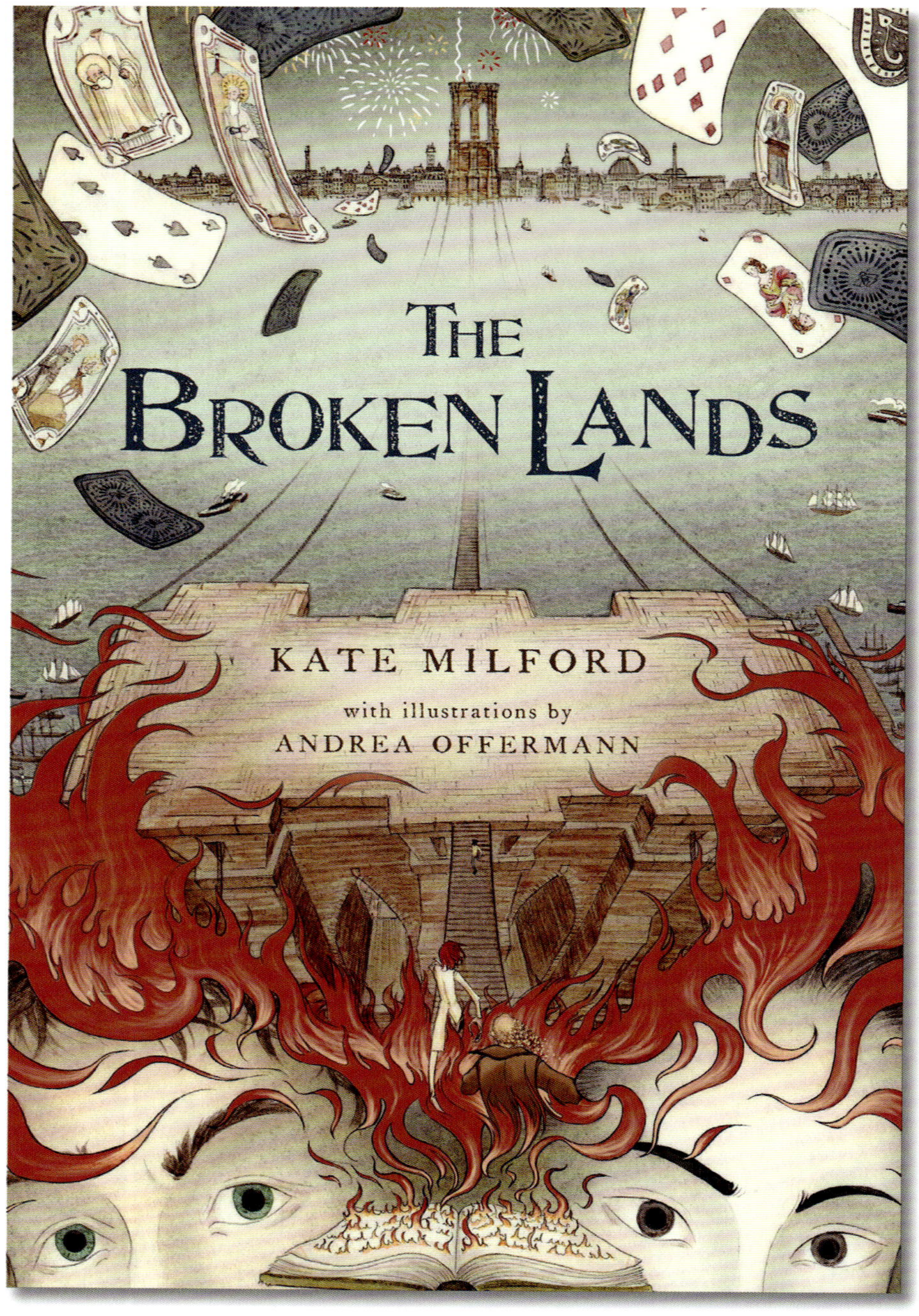

Andrea Offermann

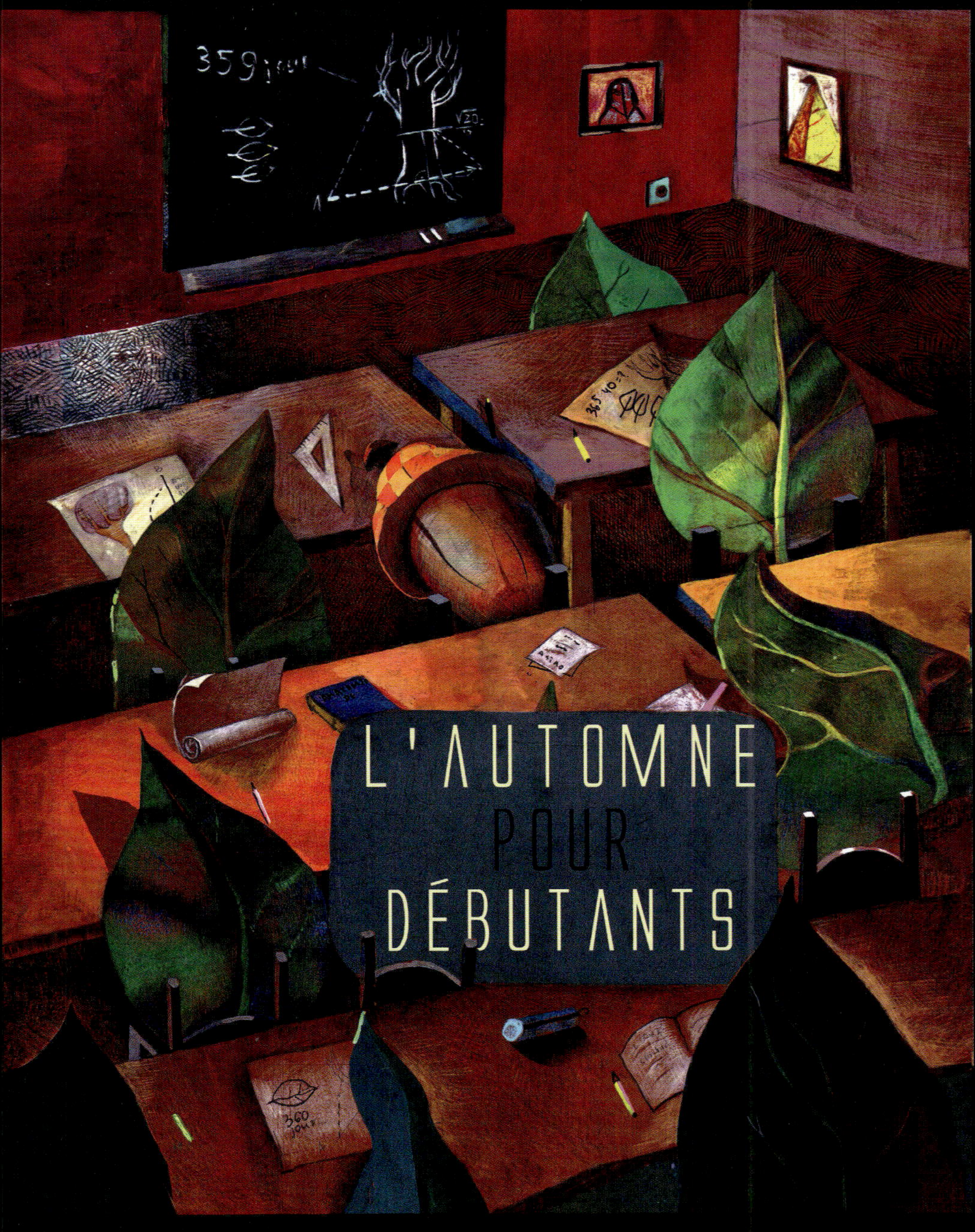

Emma Vakarélova

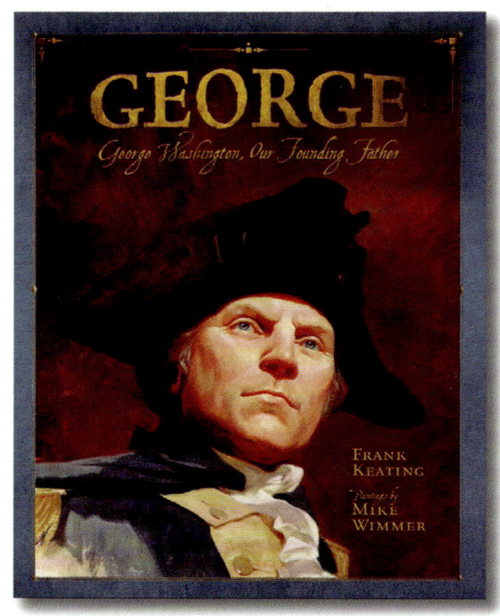

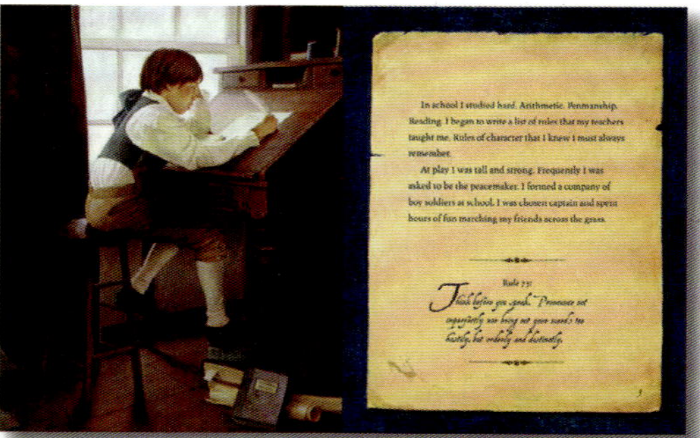

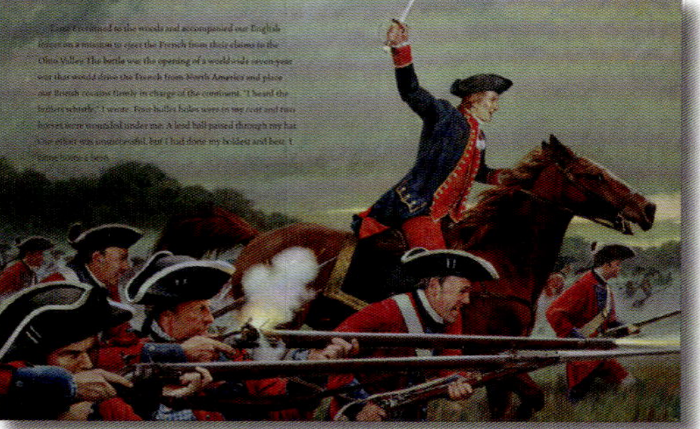

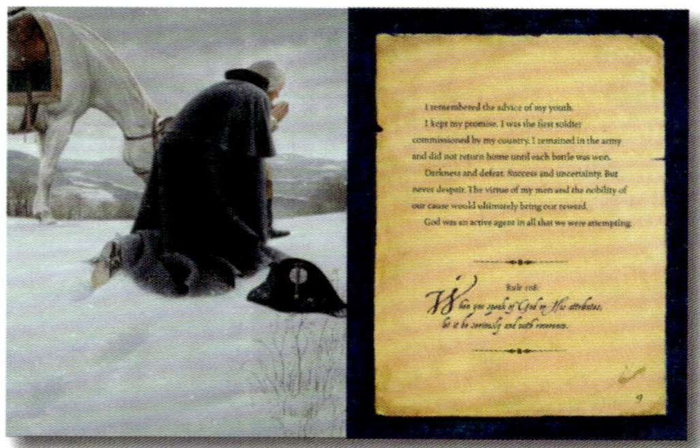

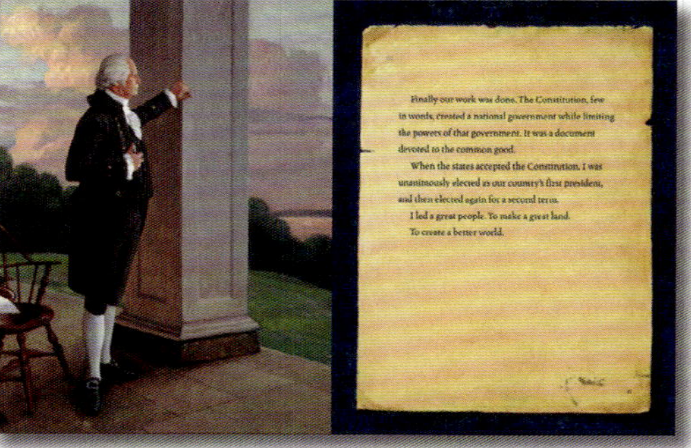

Mike Wimmer

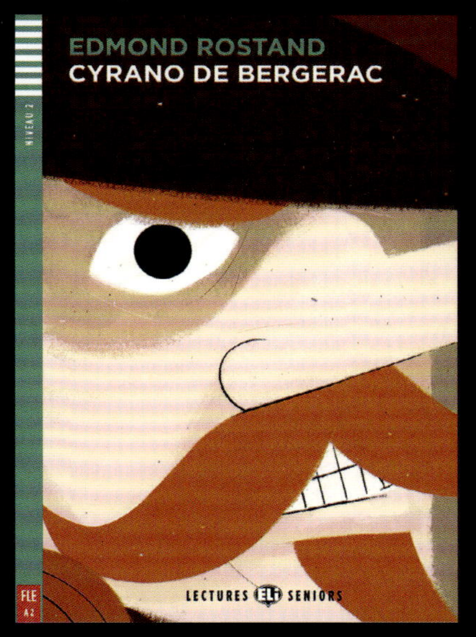

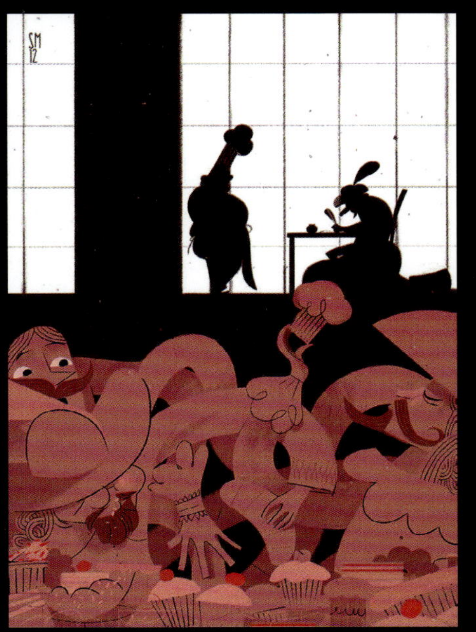

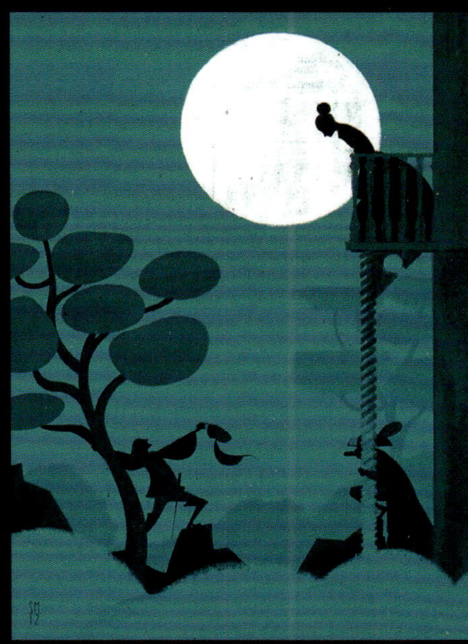

Simone Massoni

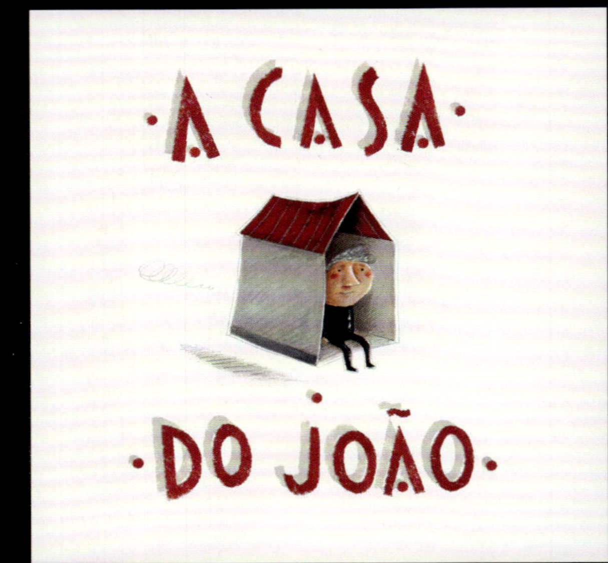
· A CASA ·
· DO JOÃO ·

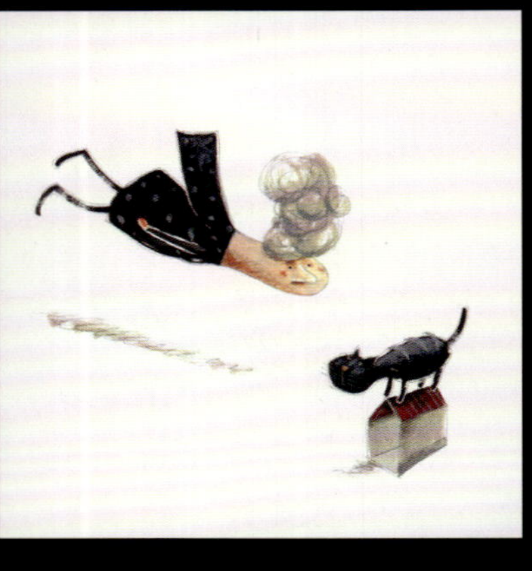

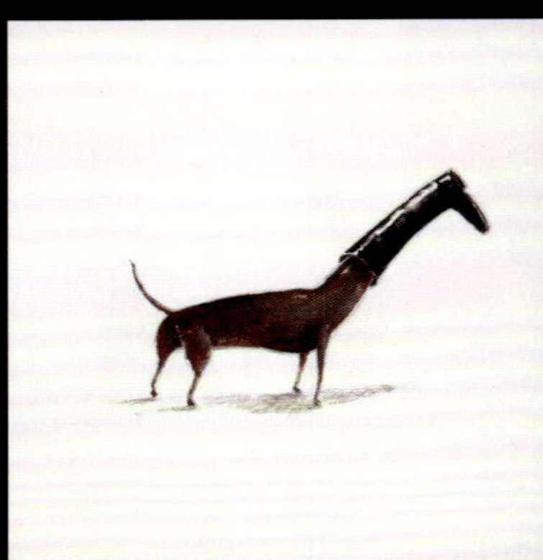

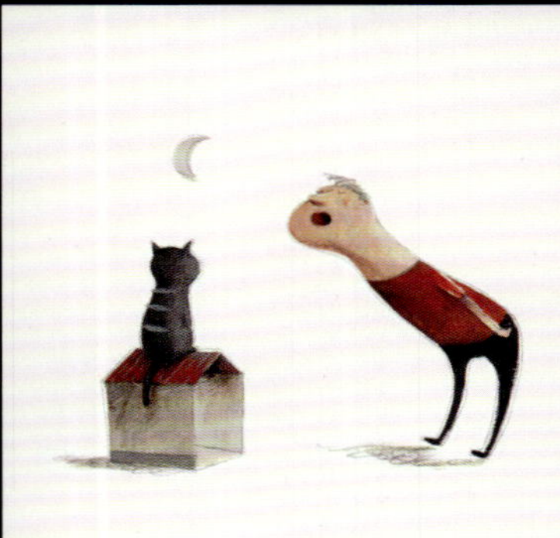

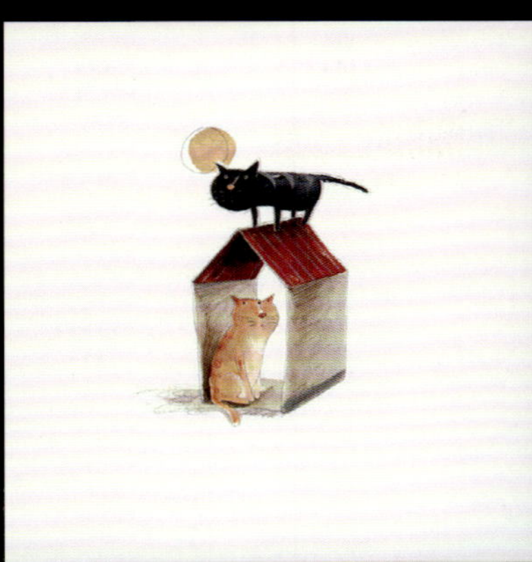

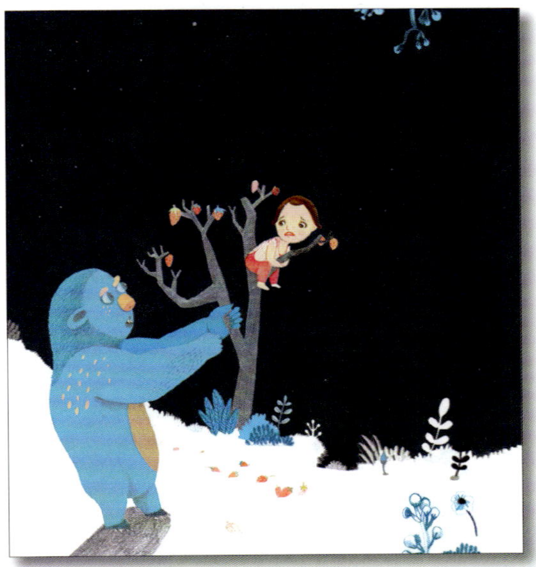

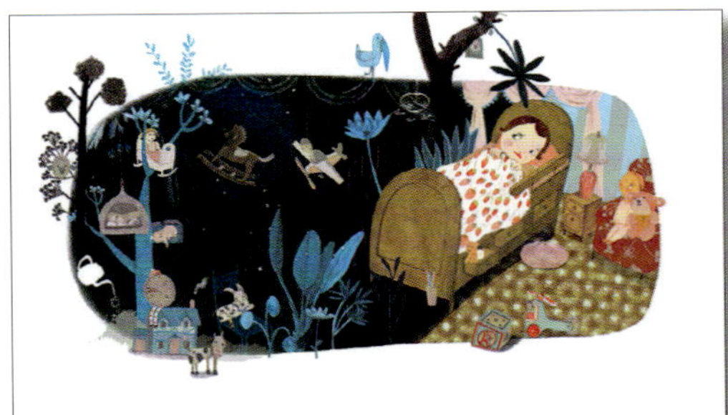

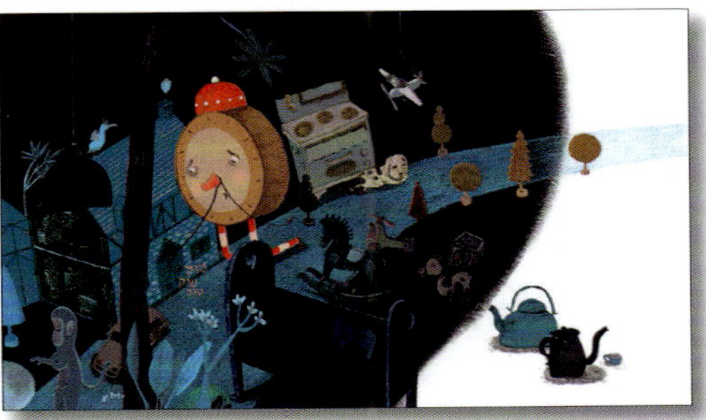

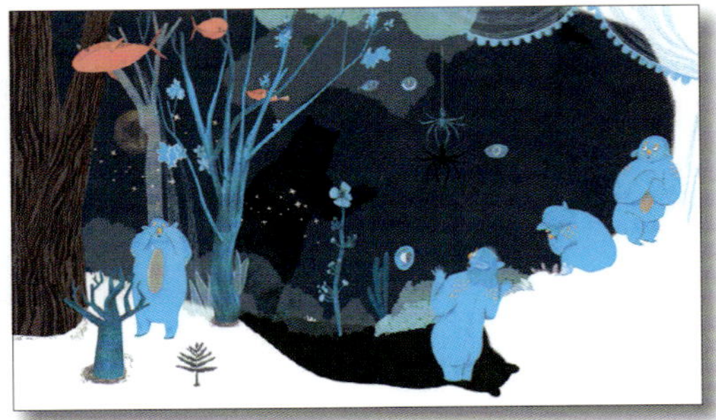

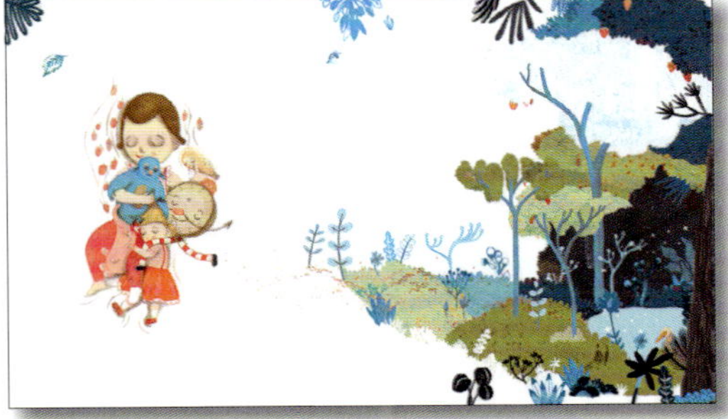

(L) *João Vaz de Carvalho* (R) *Natalie Waksman Shenker*

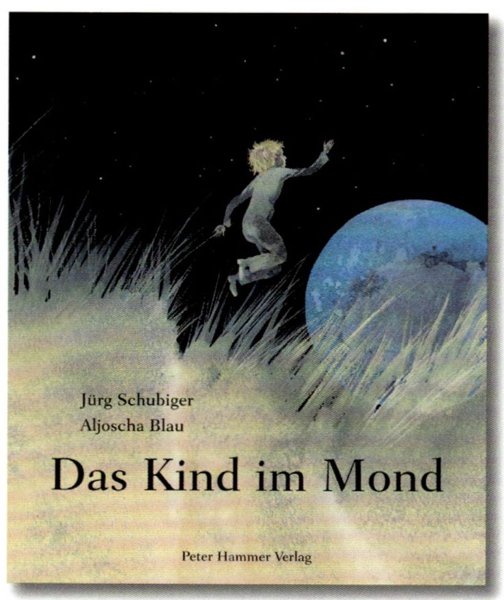

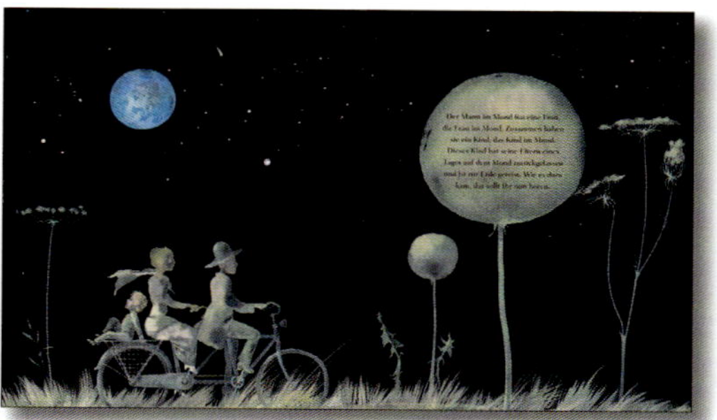

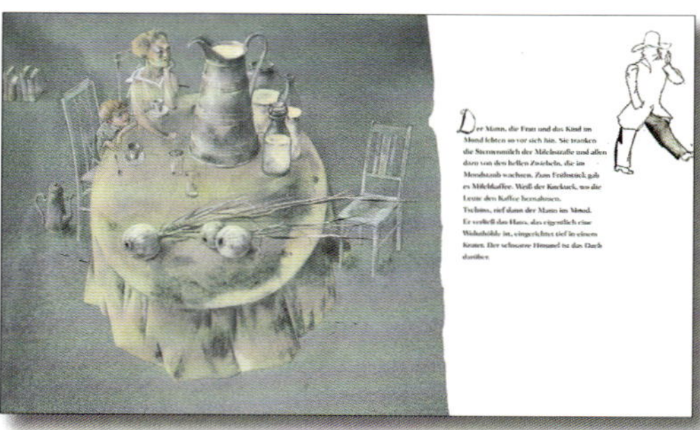

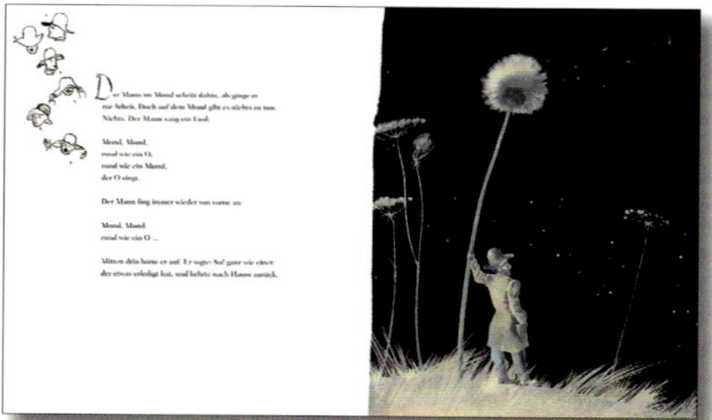

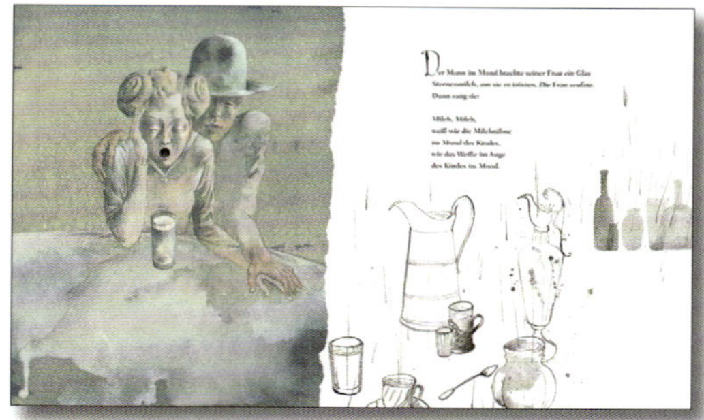

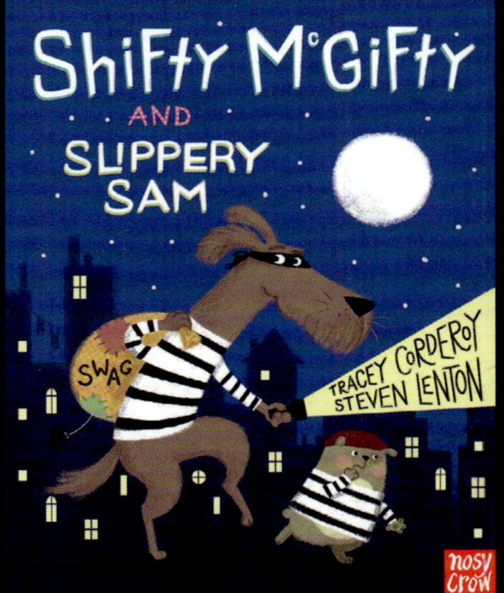

Shifty McGifty
AND
Slippery Sam
SWAG
TRACEY CORDEROY
STEVEN LENTON
nosy crow

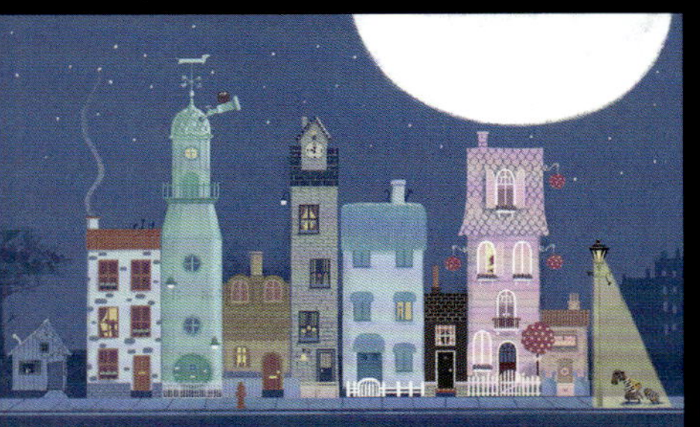

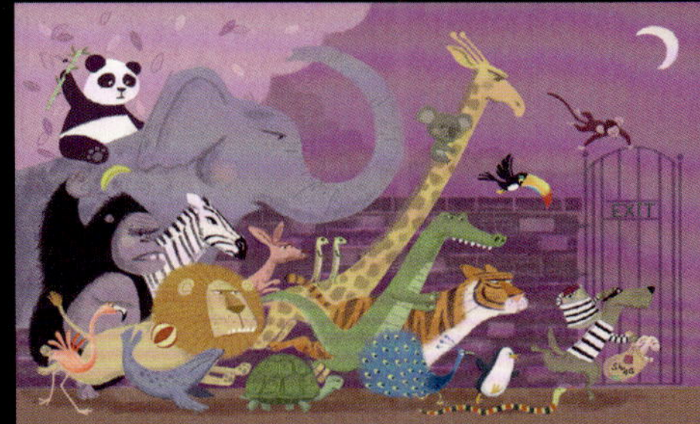

EXIT

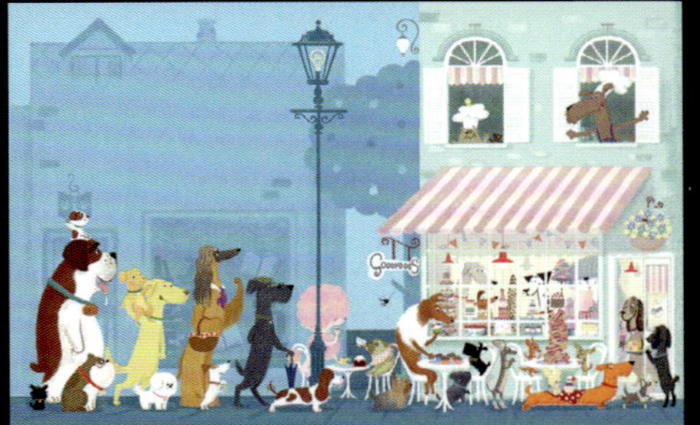

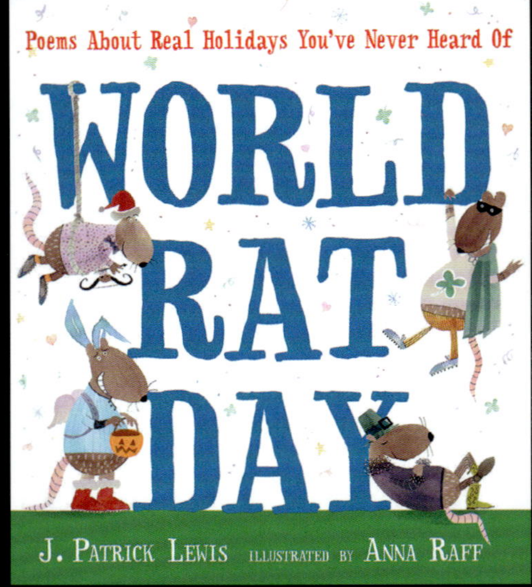
Poems About Real Holidays You've Never Heard Of
WORLD RAT DAY
J. Patrick Lewis   ILLUSTRATED BY Anna Raff

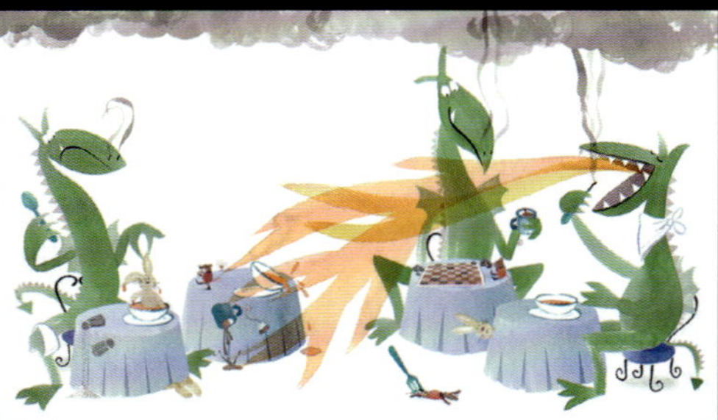

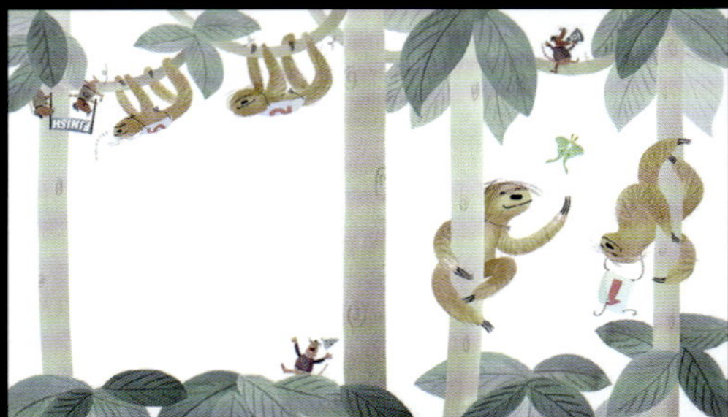

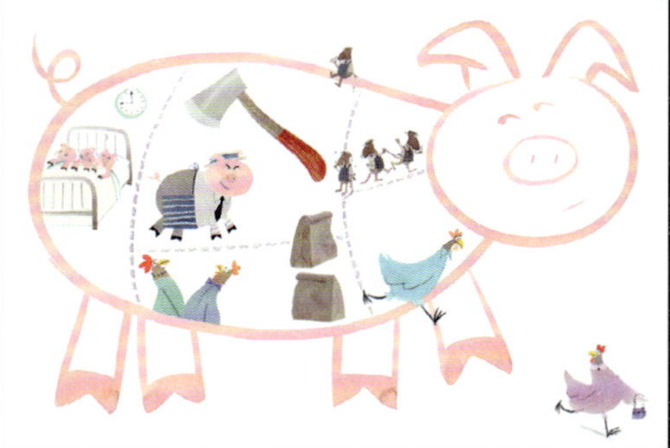

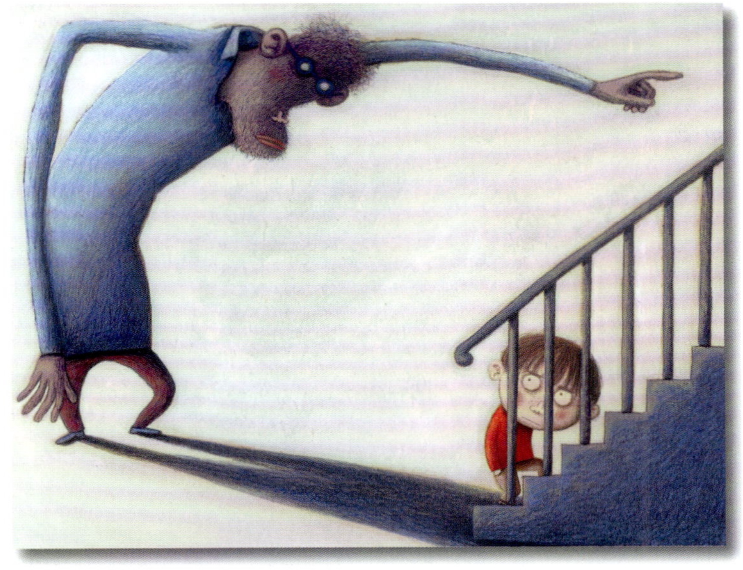

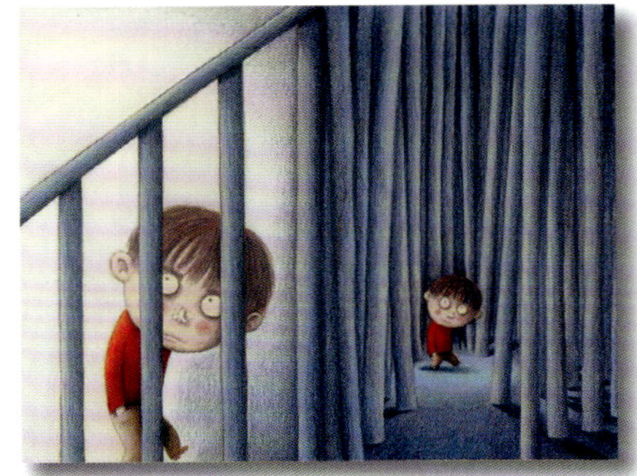

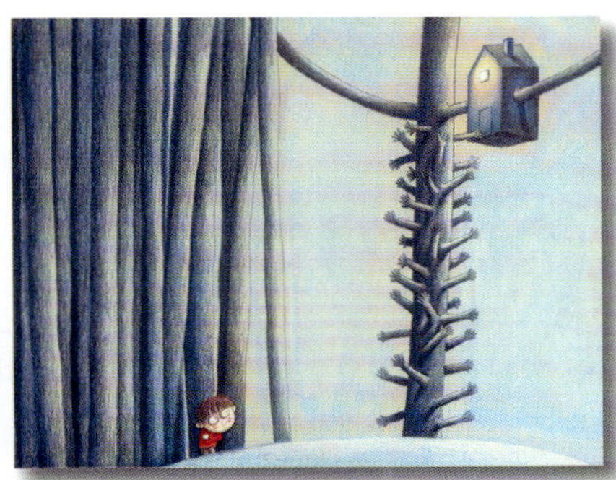

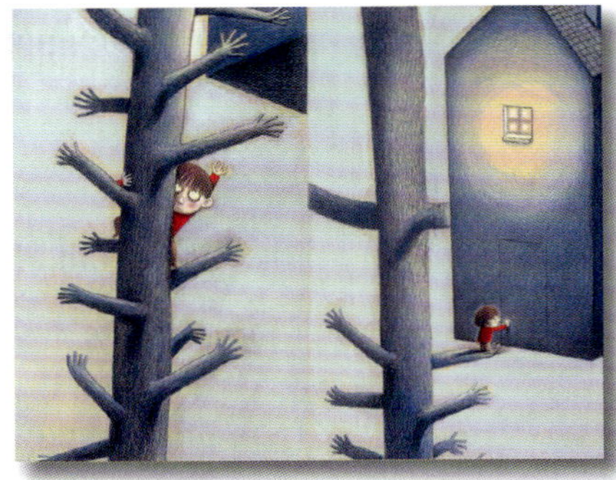

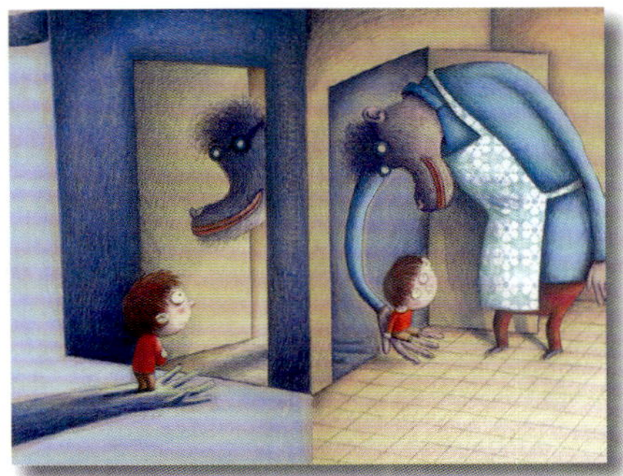

BRONZE *Klaas Verplancke*

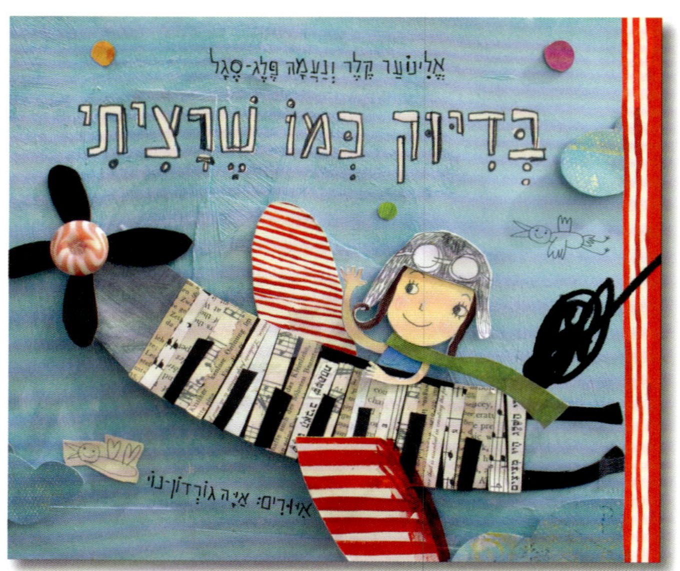

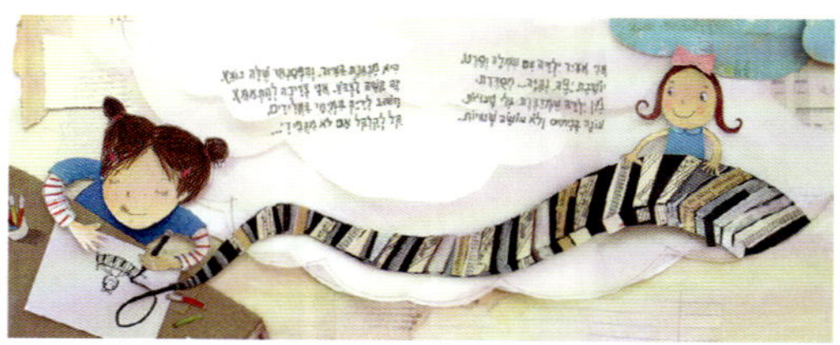

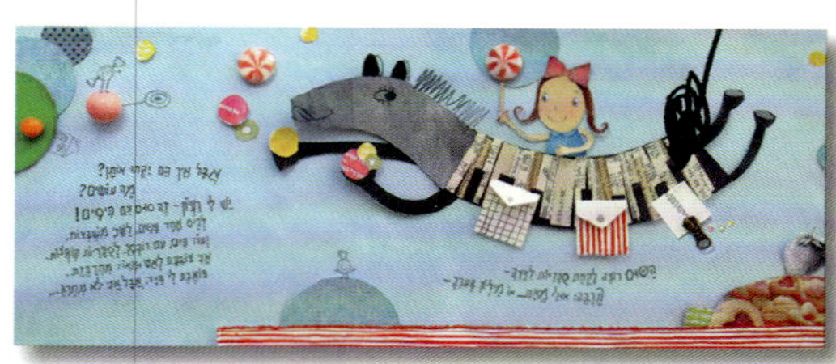

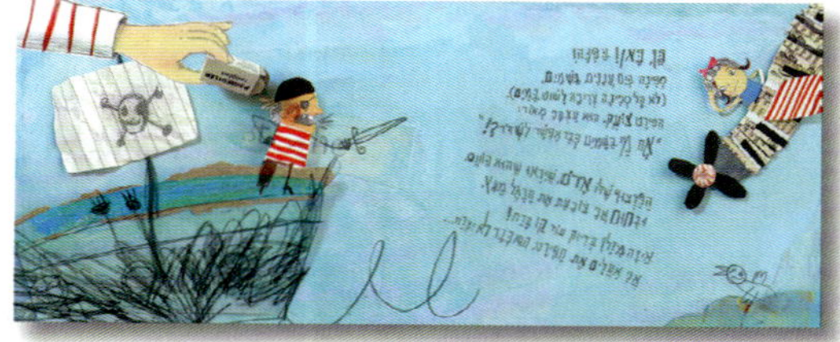

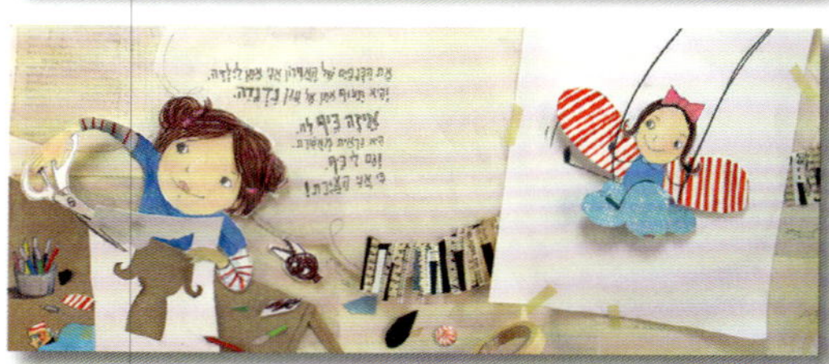

Aya Gordon-Noy

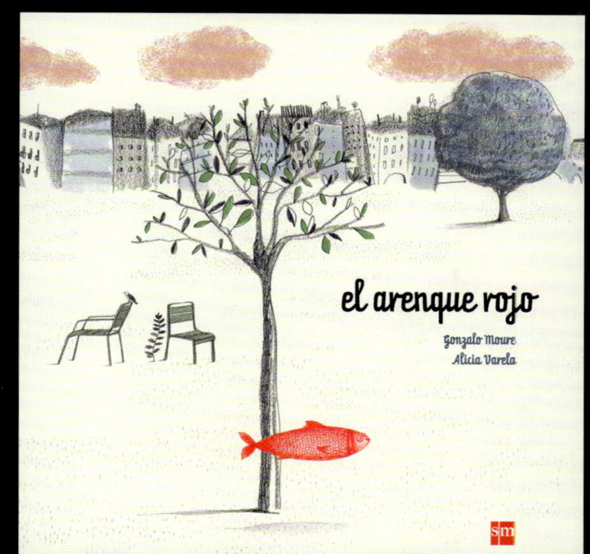
el arenque rojo
Gonzalo Moure
Alicia Varela
sm

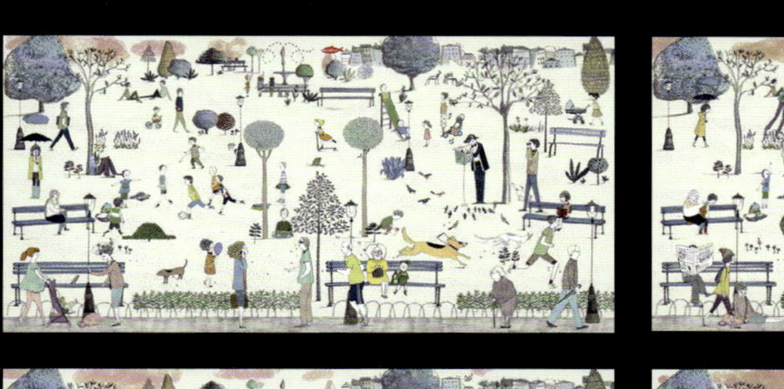

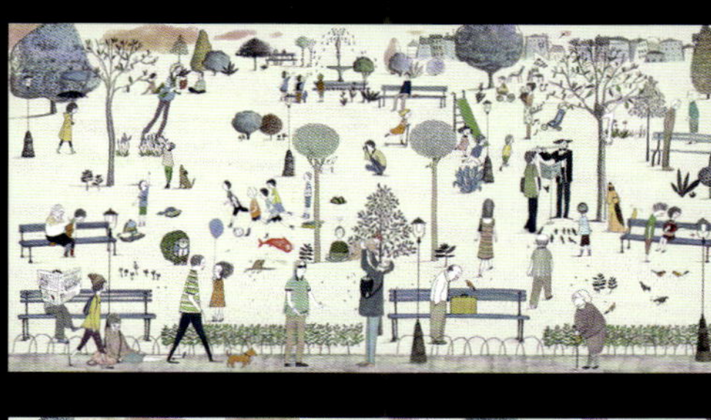

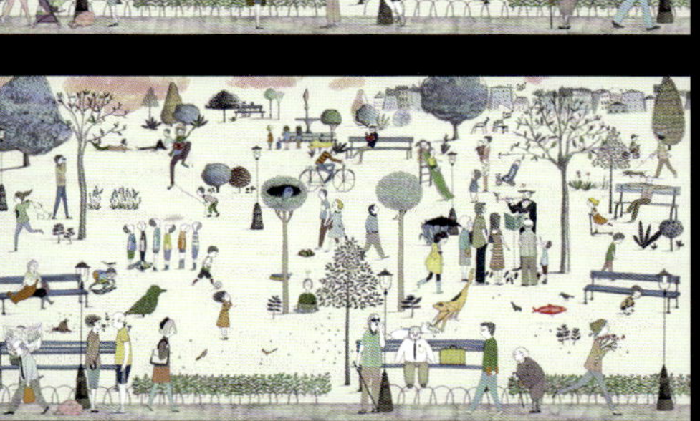

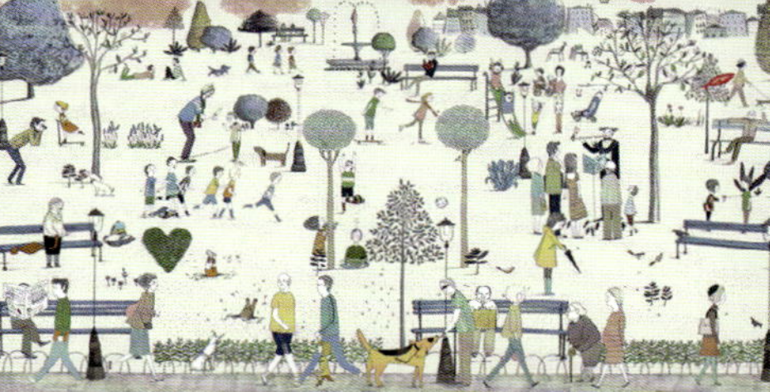

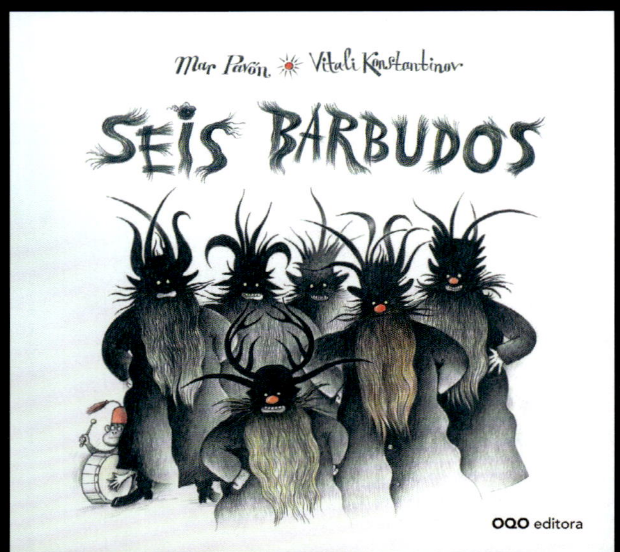
Mar Pavón
Vitali Konstantinov
SEIS BARBUDOS
OQO editora

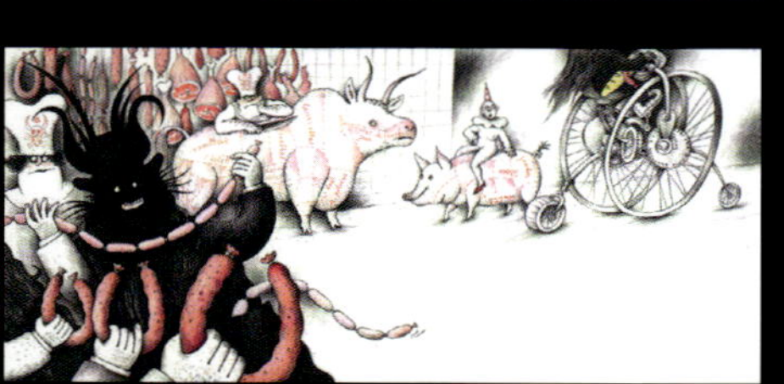

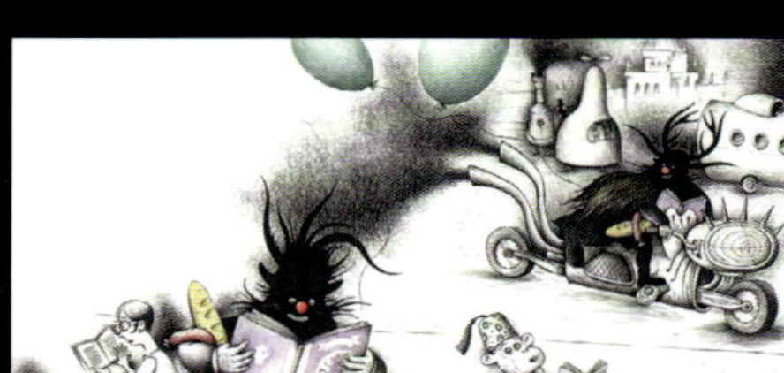

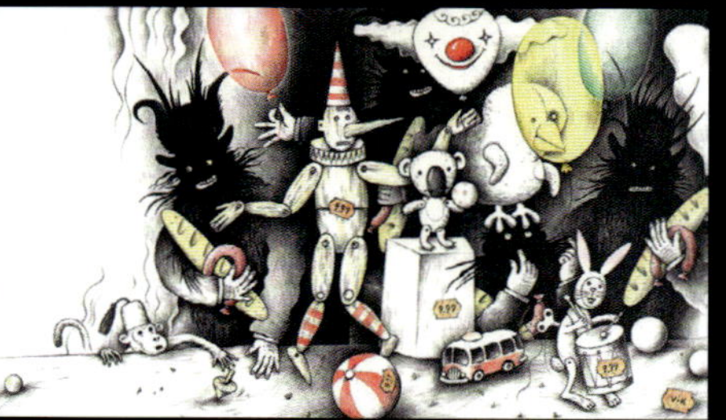

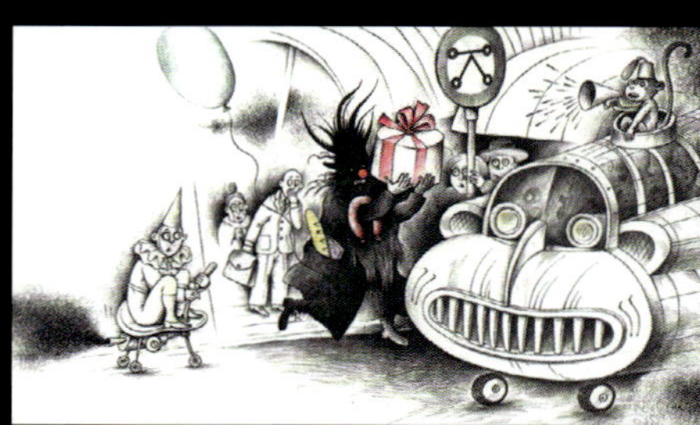

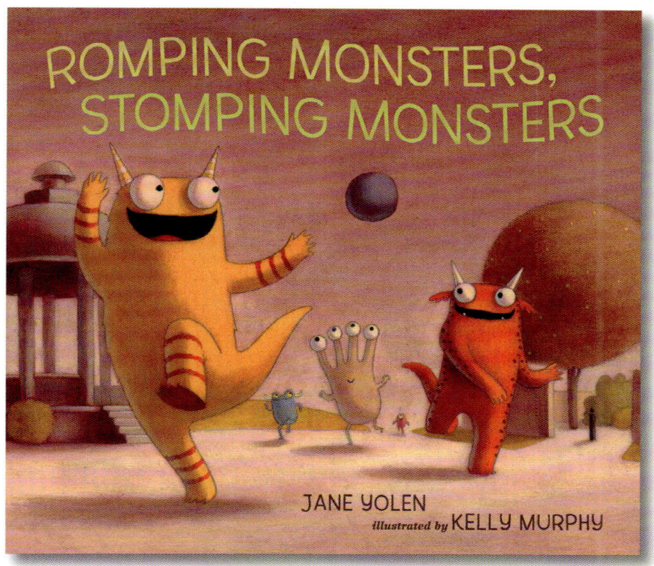

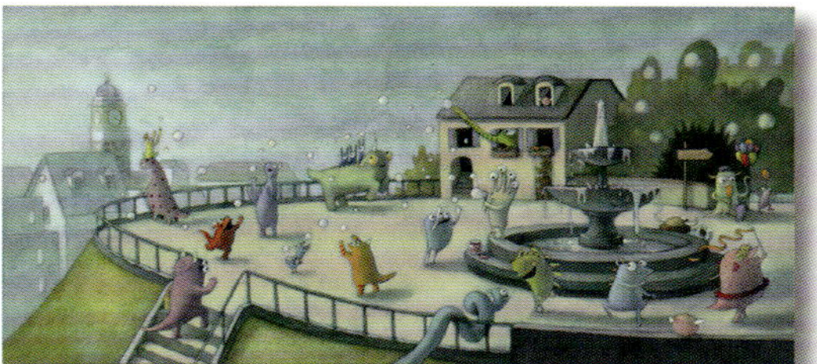

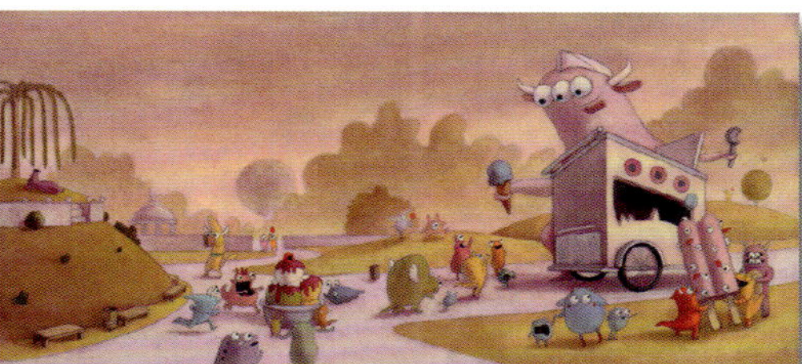

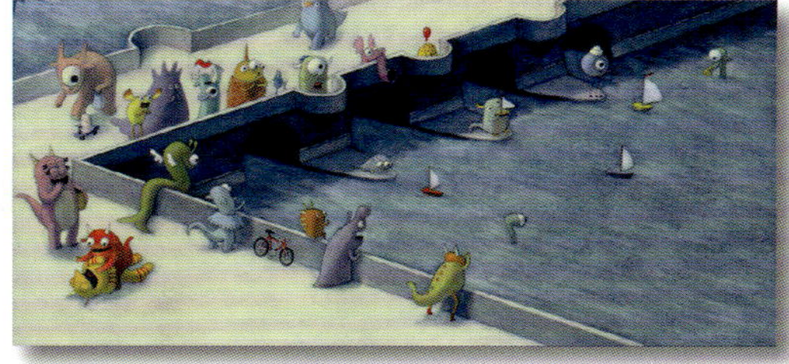

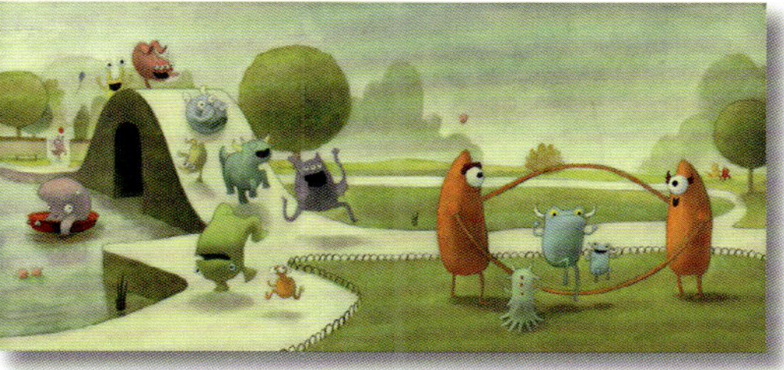

Kelly Murphy

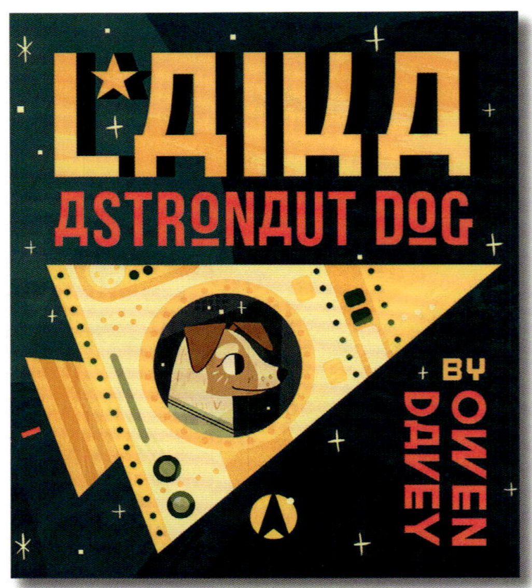

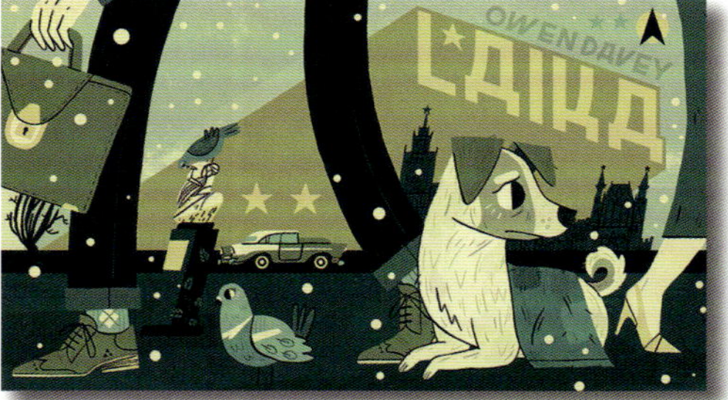

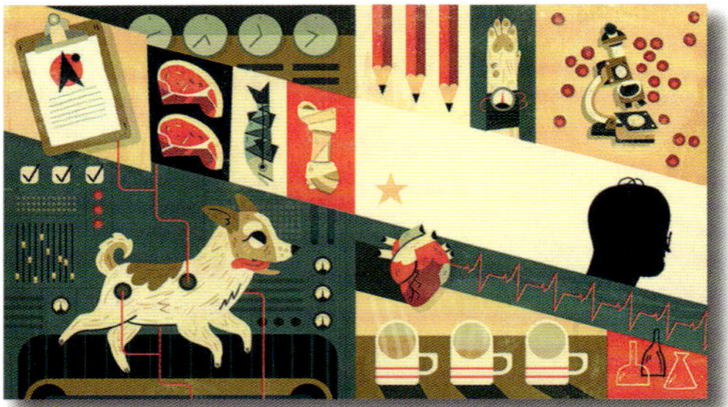

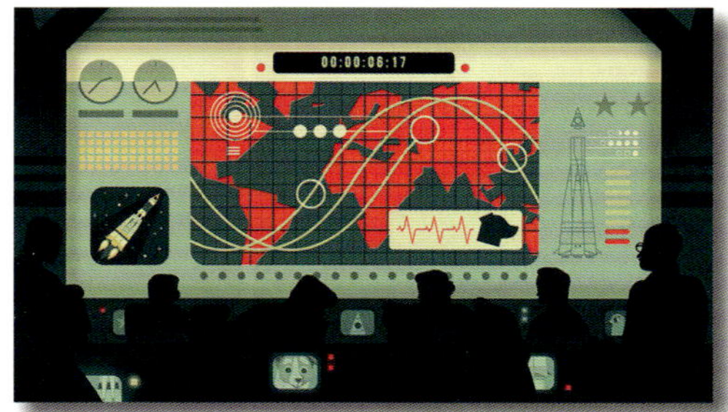

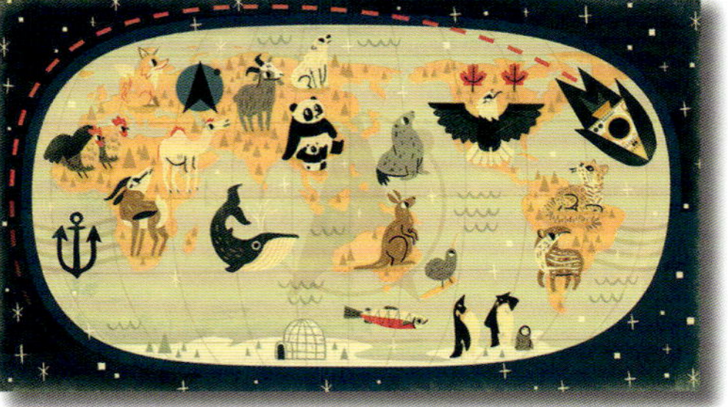

Owen Davey

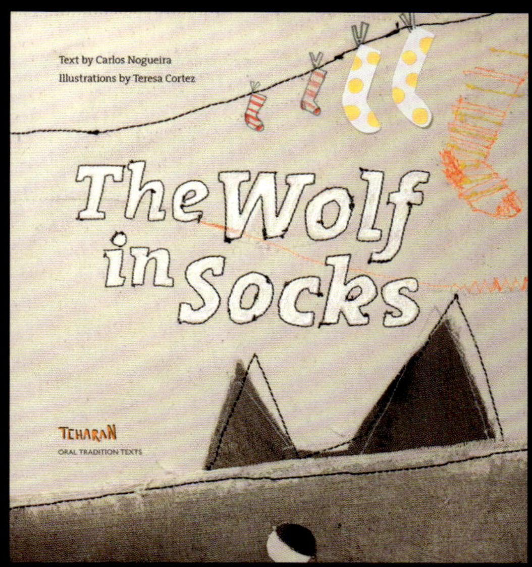

Text by Carlos Nogueira
Illustrations by Teresa Cortez
The Wolf in Socks
TCHARAN
ORAL TRADITION TEXTS

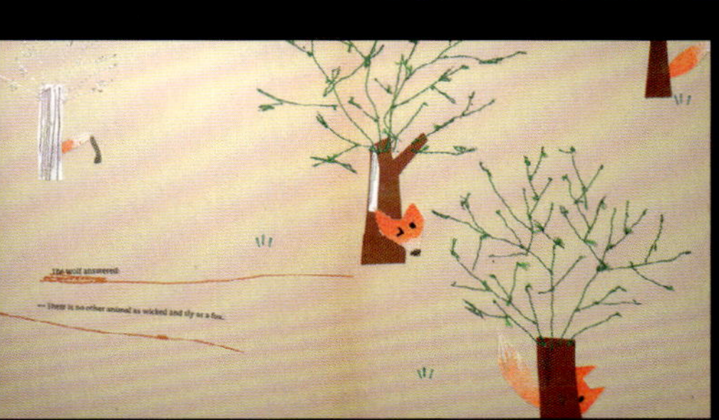

The wolf answered:
— There is no other animal as wicked and sly as a fox.

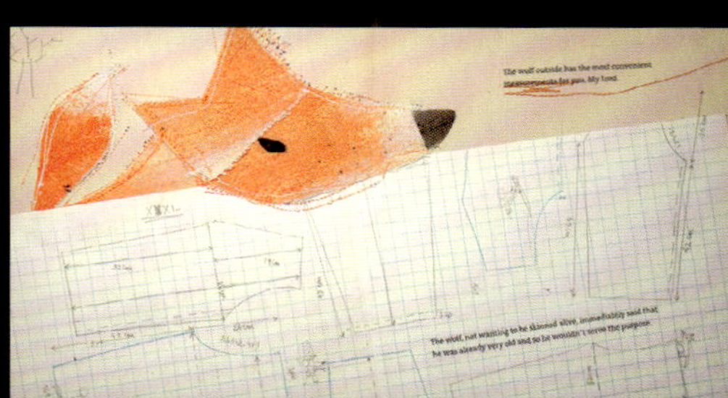

The wolf outside has the most convenient measurements for you, My Lord.
The wolf, not wanting to be skinned alive, immediately said that he was already very old and so he wouldn't serve the purpose.

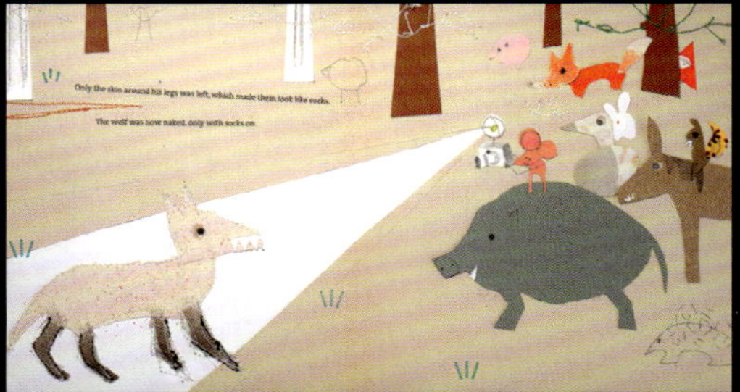

Only the skin around his legs was left, which made them look like socks.
The wolf was now naked, only with socks on.

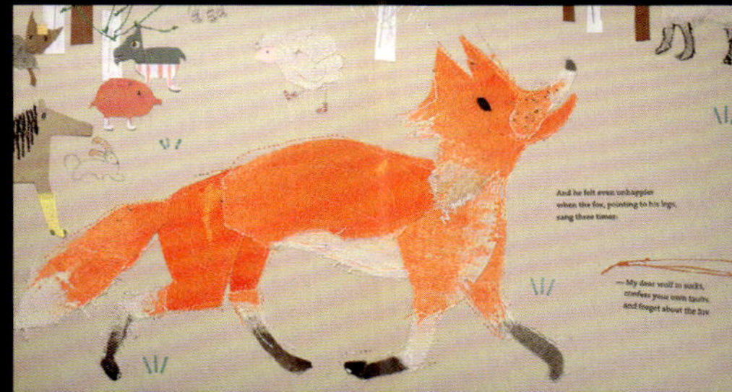

And he felt even unhappier when the fox, pointing to his legs, sang three times:
— My dear wolf in socks, confess your own faults, and forget about the fox.

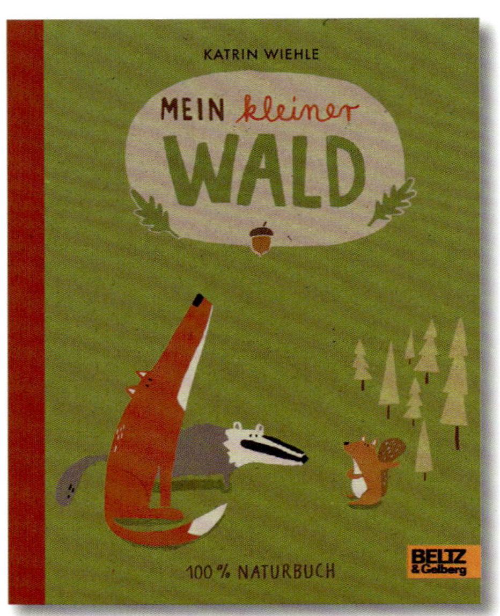

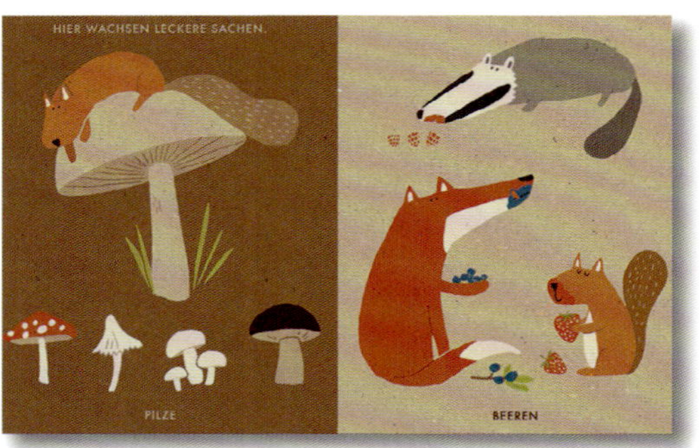

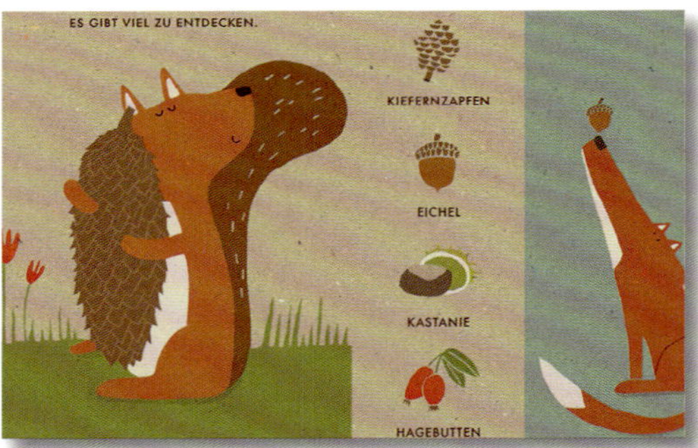

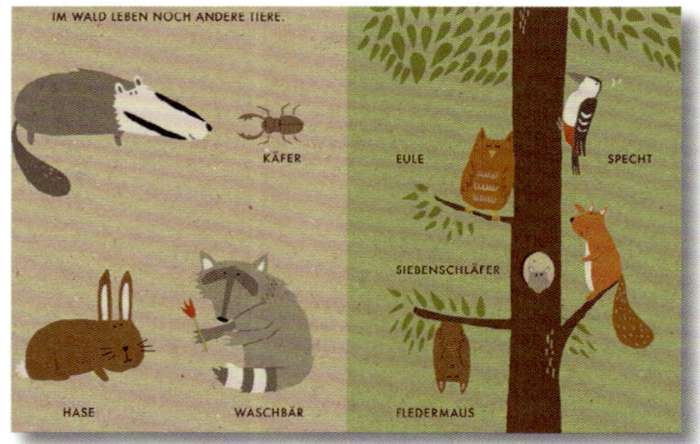

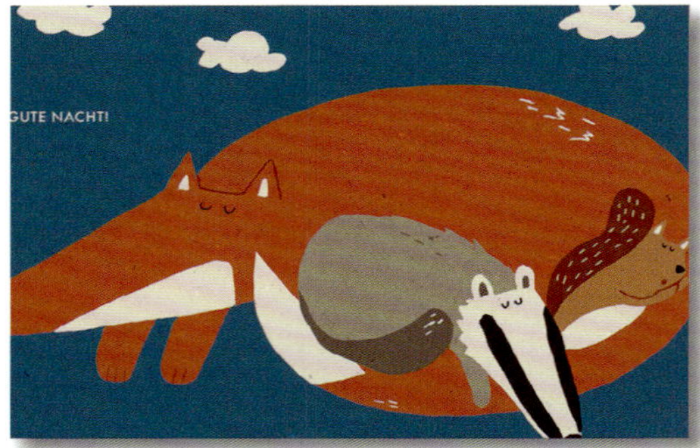

Katrin Wiehle

318

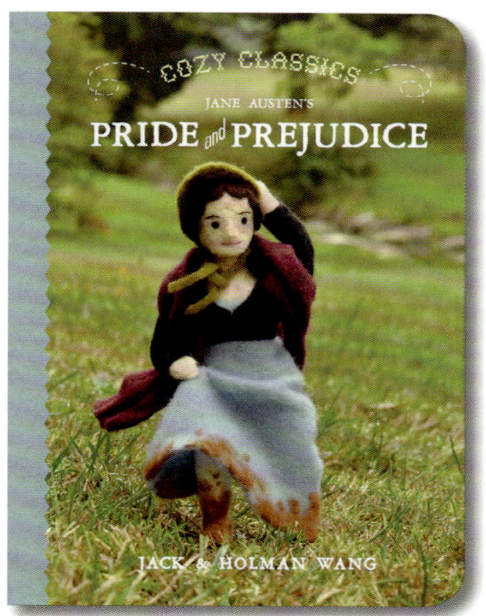

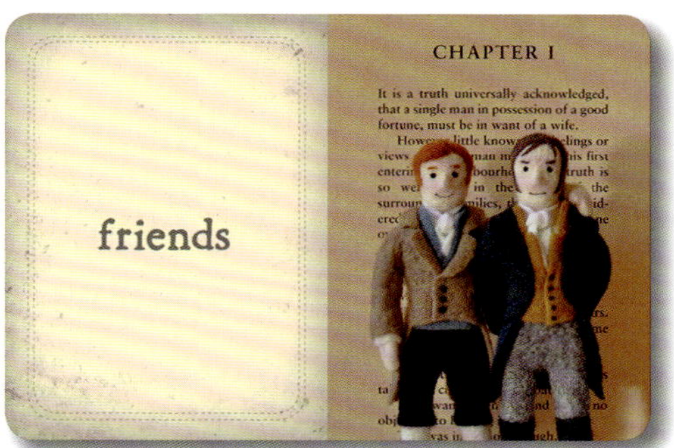

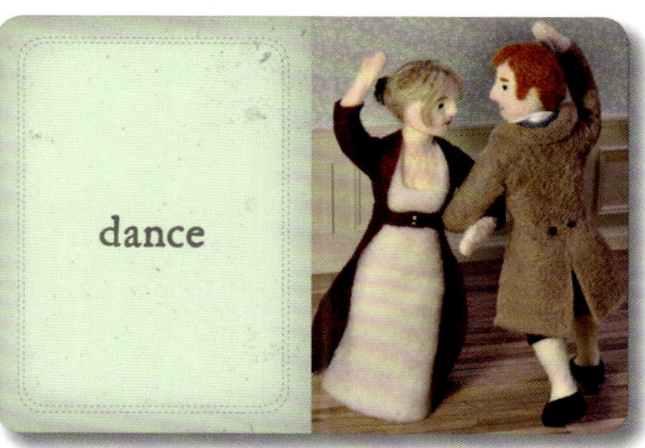

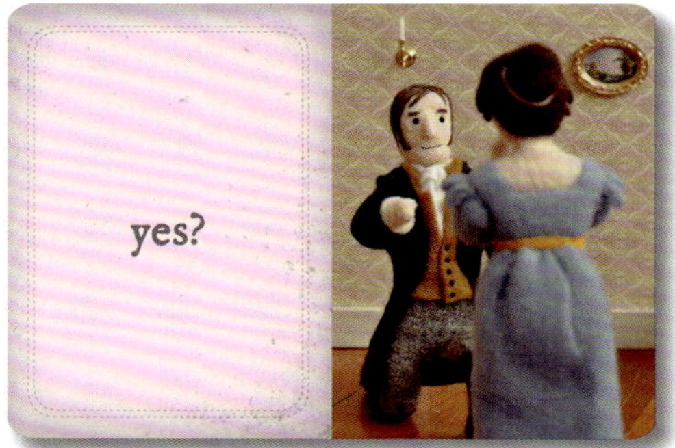

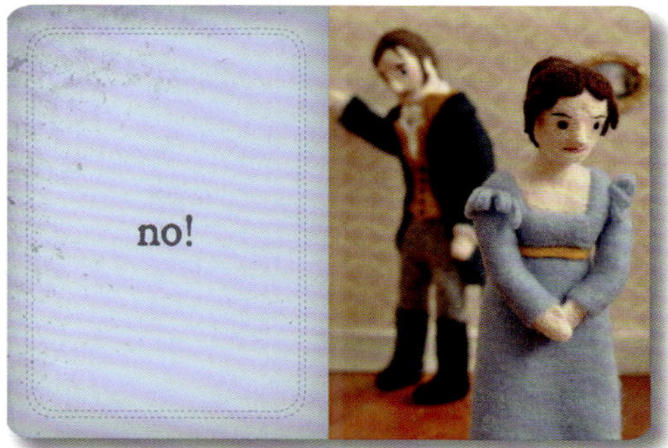

DISTINGUISHED MERIT *Jack Wang and Holman Wang*

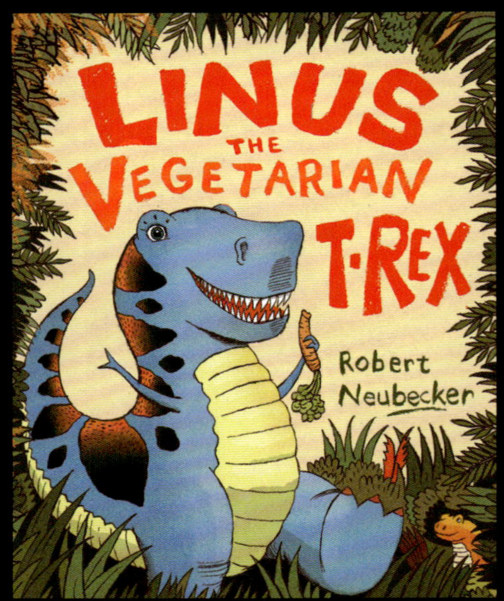

LINUS
THE
VEGETARIAN
T-REX
Robert
Neubecker

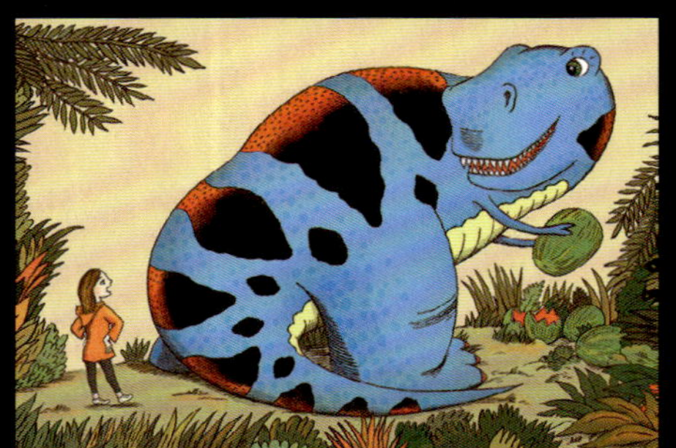

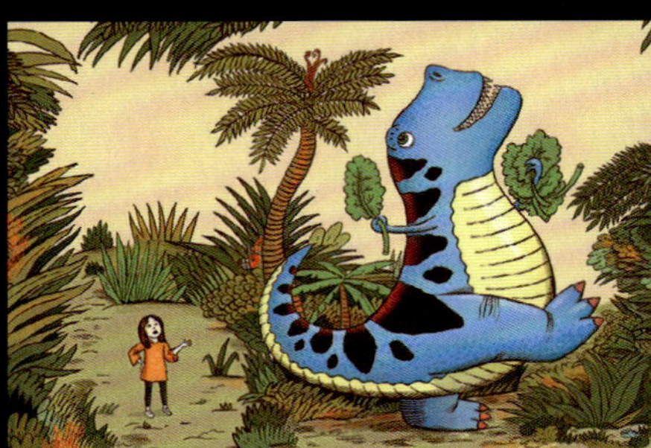

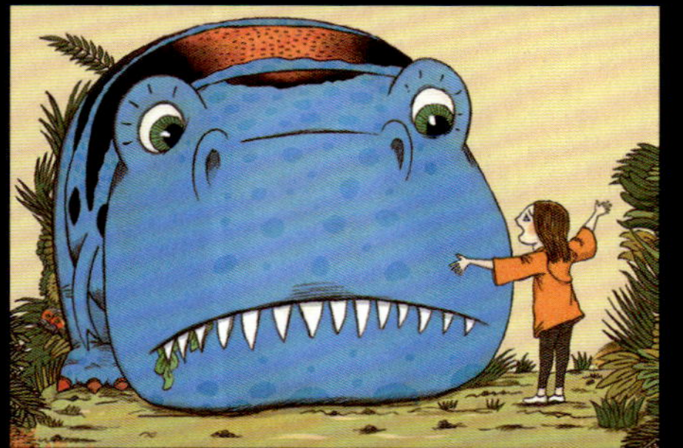

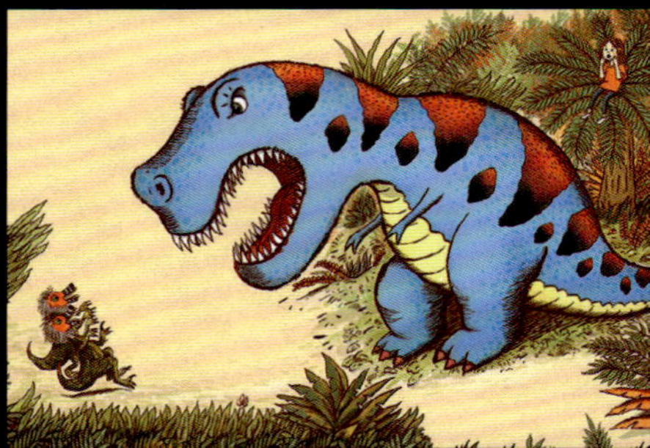

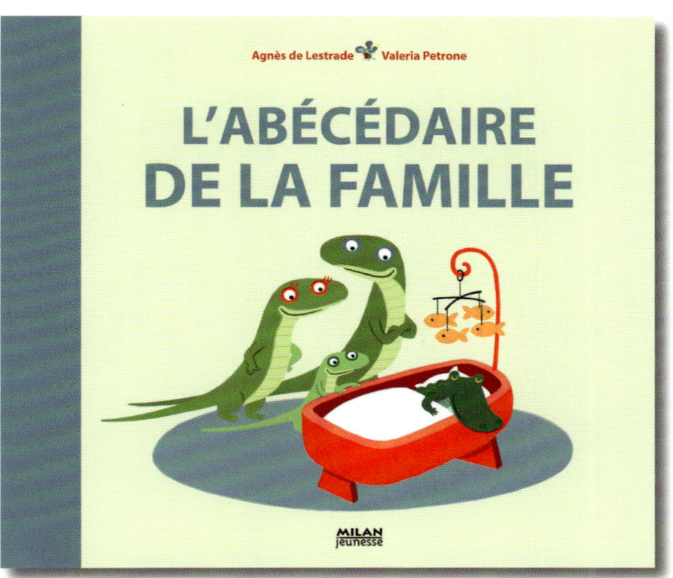

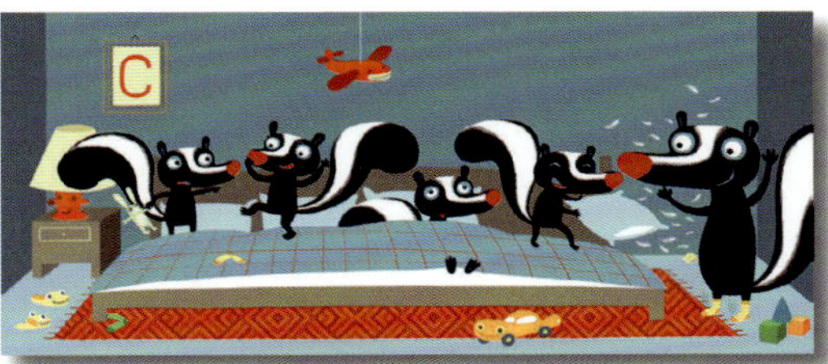
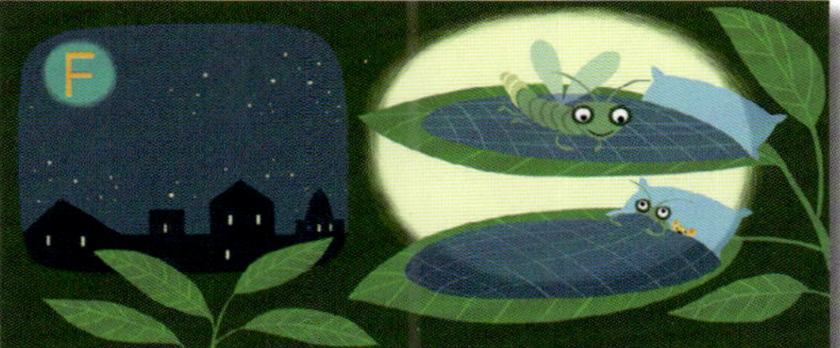
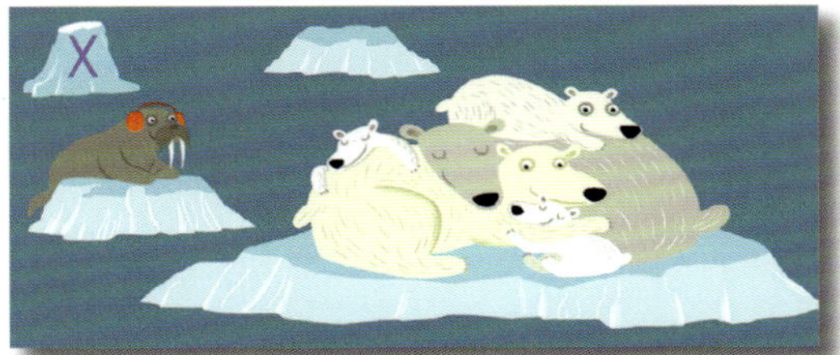
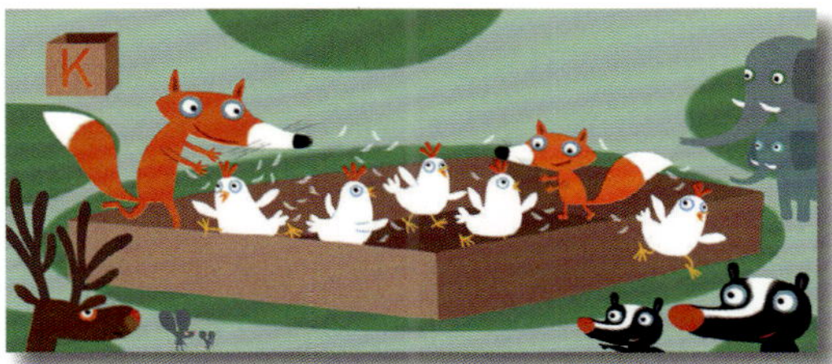
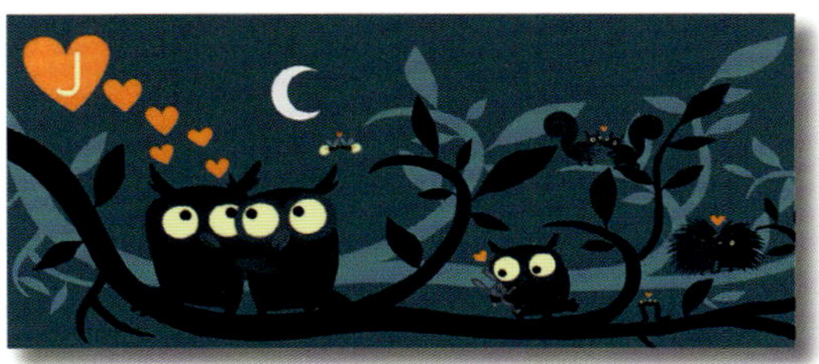

Valeria Petrone

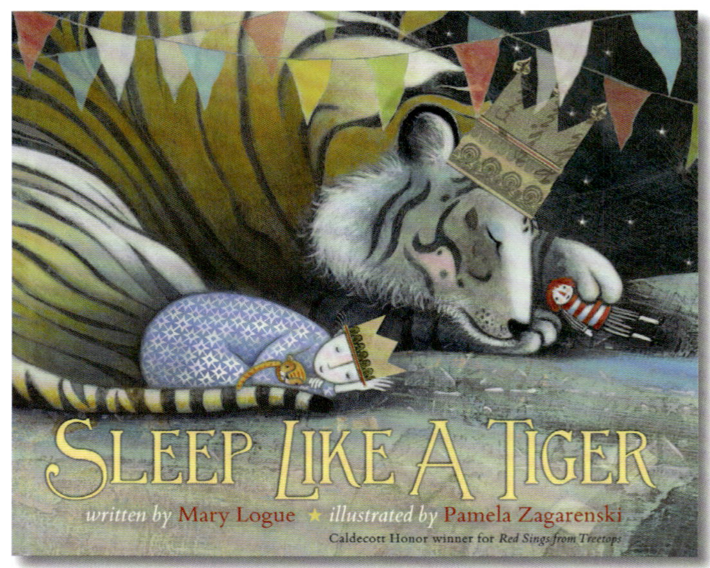

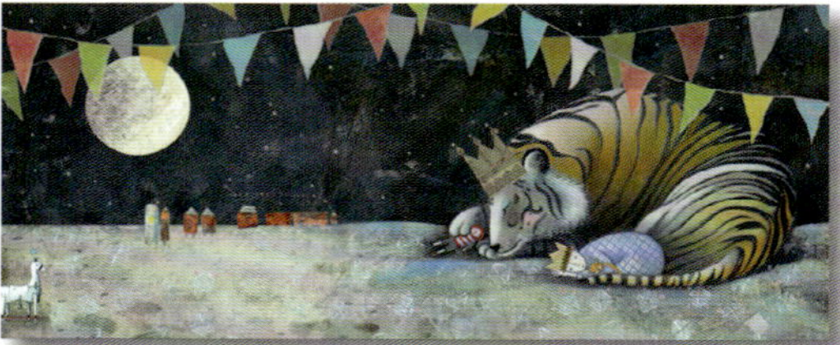

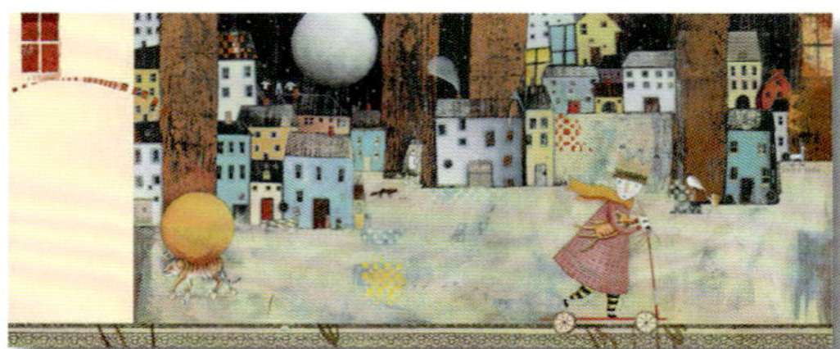

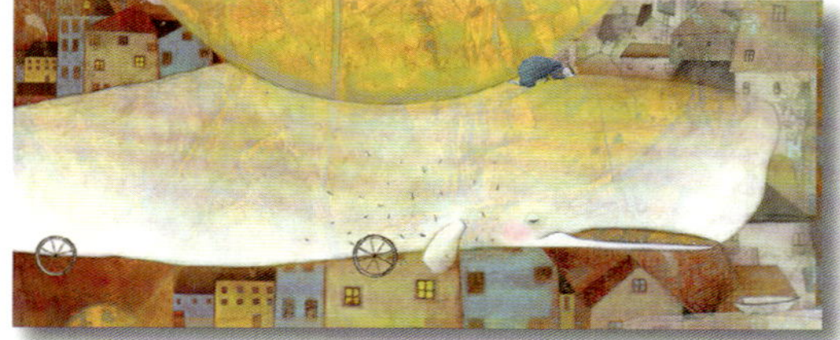

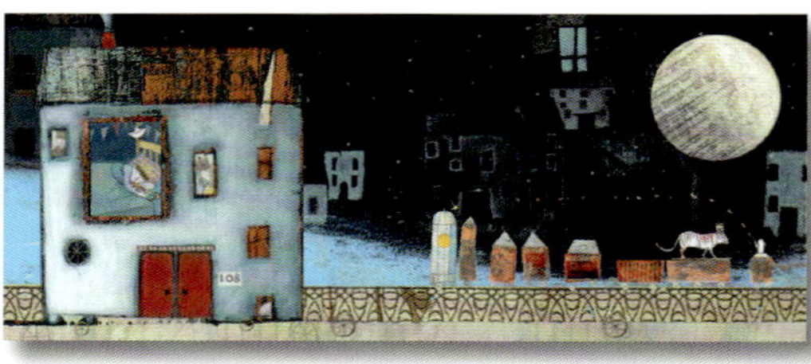

(L) *Pamela Zagarenski* (R) *João Vaz de Carvalho*

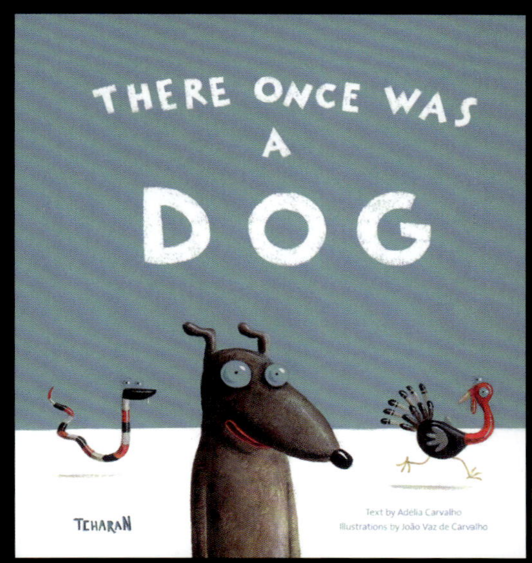
THERE ONCE WAS
A
DOG
TEHARAN
Text by Adélia Carvalho
Illustrations by João Vaz de Carvalho

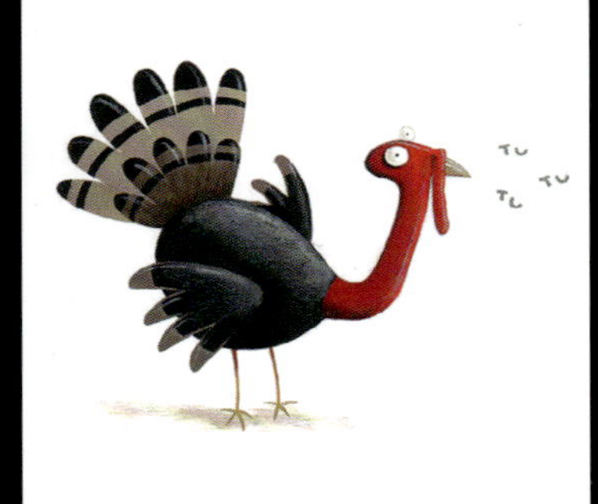

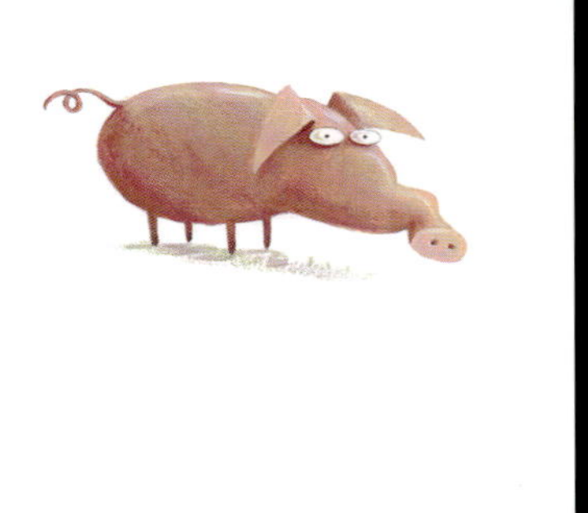

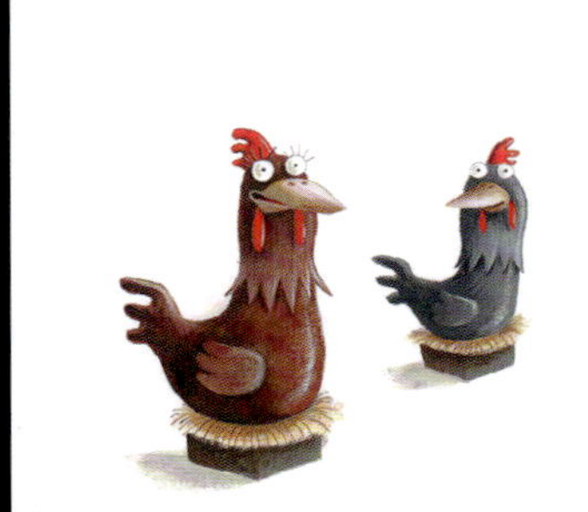

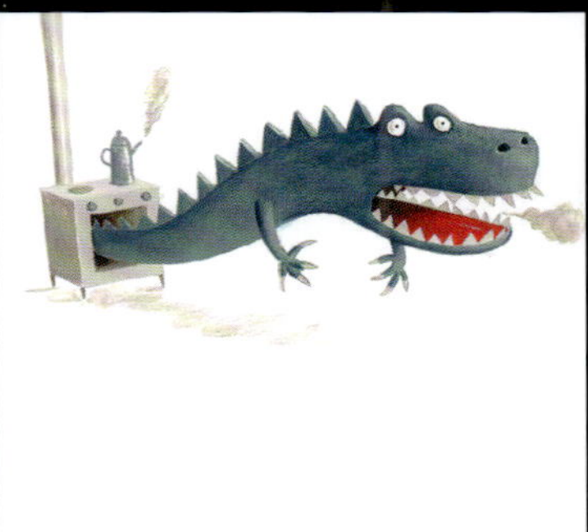

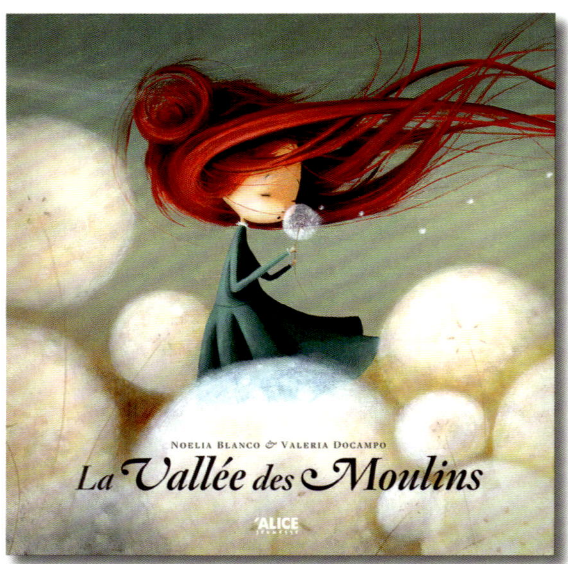

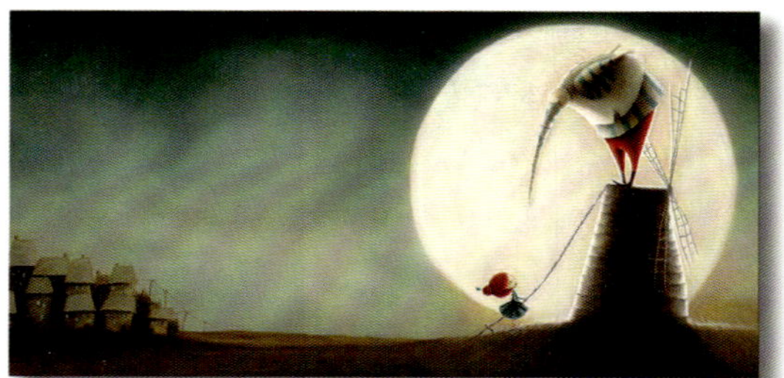

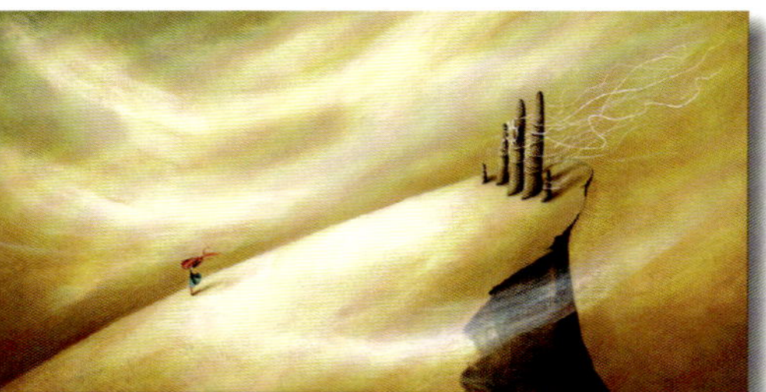

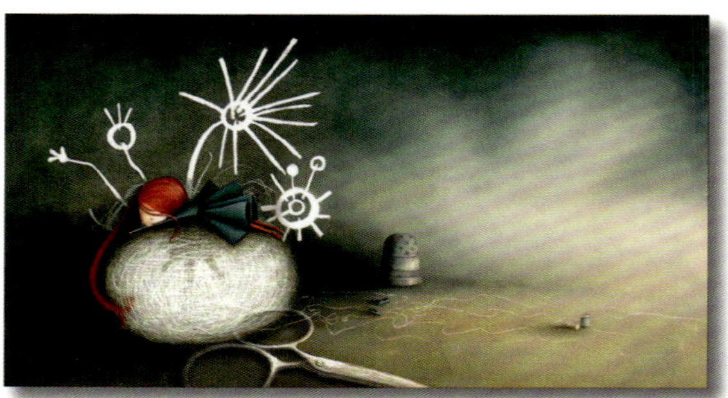

Valeria Docampo

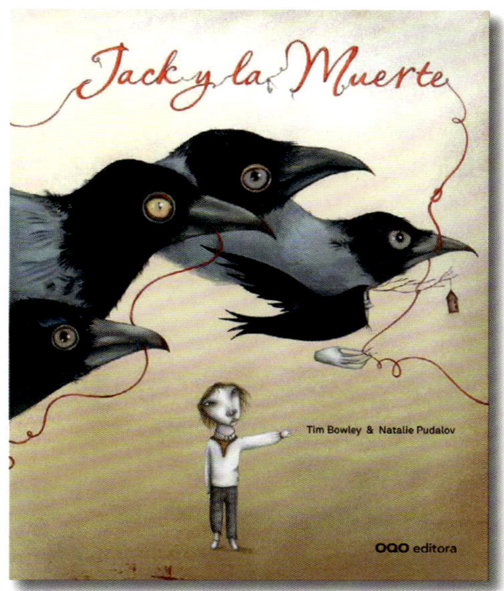

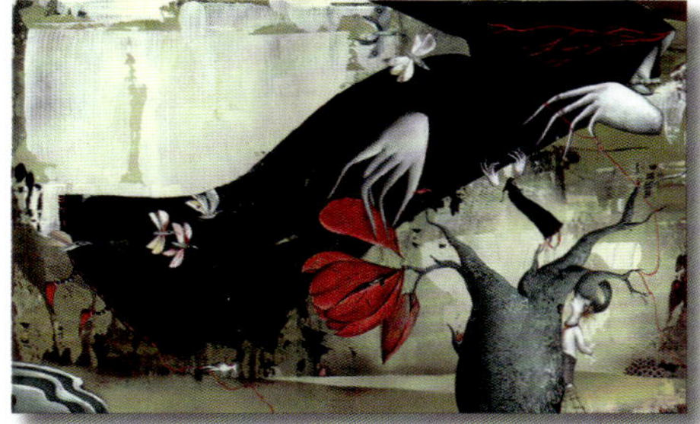

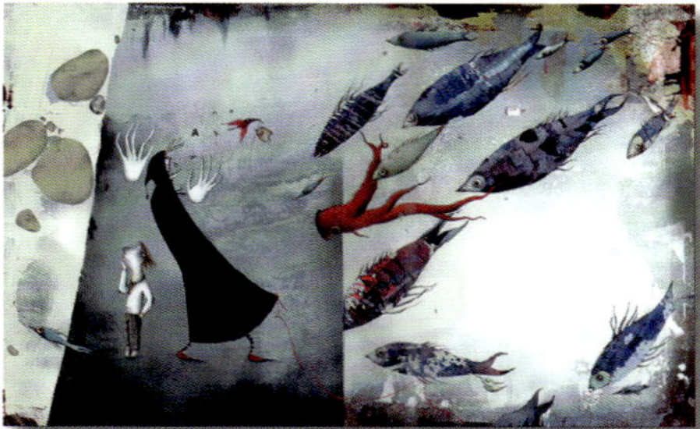

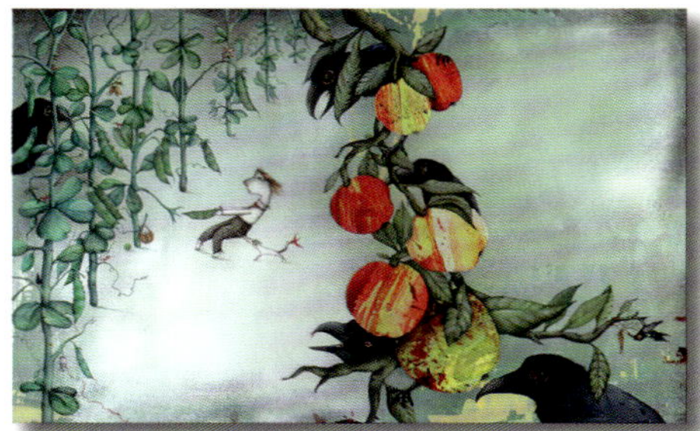

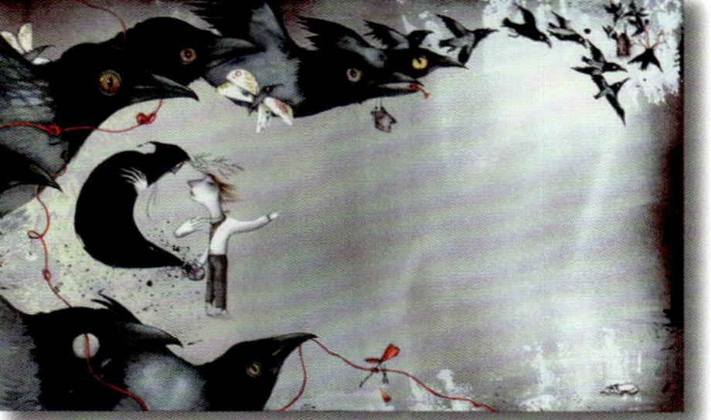

Natalie Pudalov

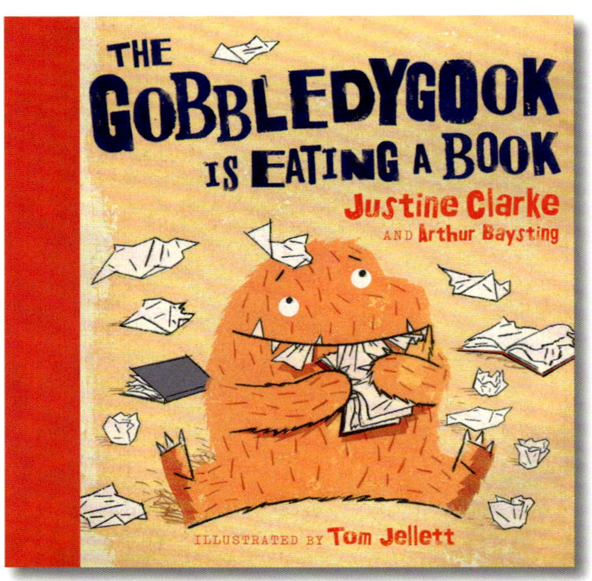

THE GOBBLEDYGOOK IS EATING A BOOK
Justine Clarke
AND Arthur Baysting
ILLUSTRATED BY Tom Jellett

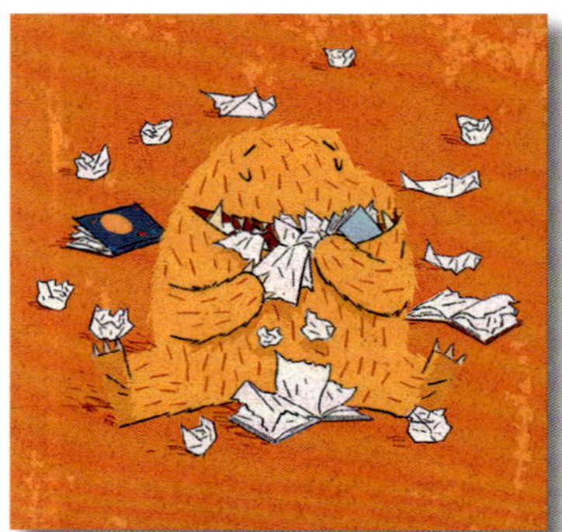

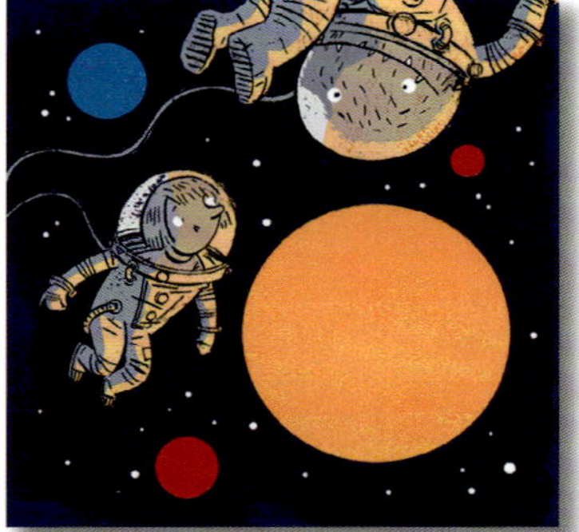

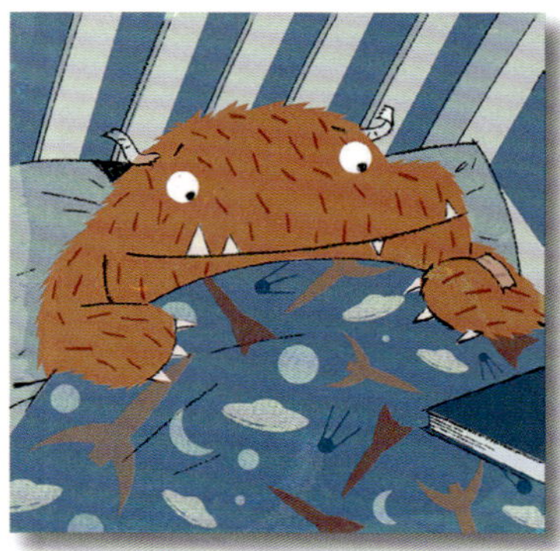

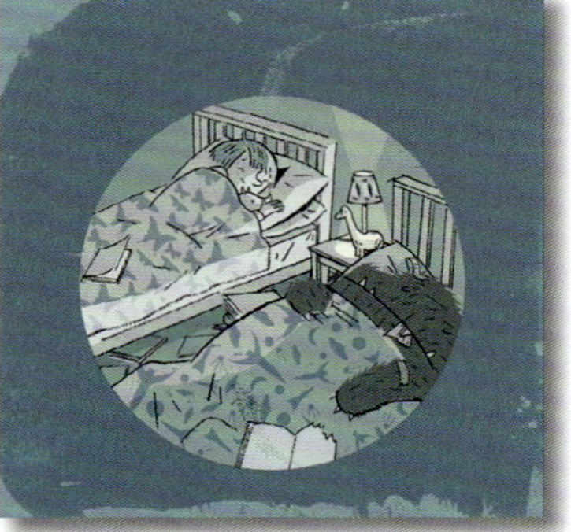

Tom Jellett

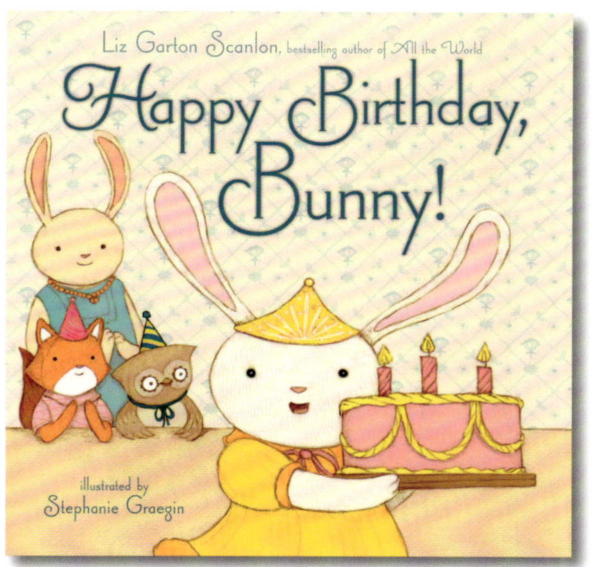

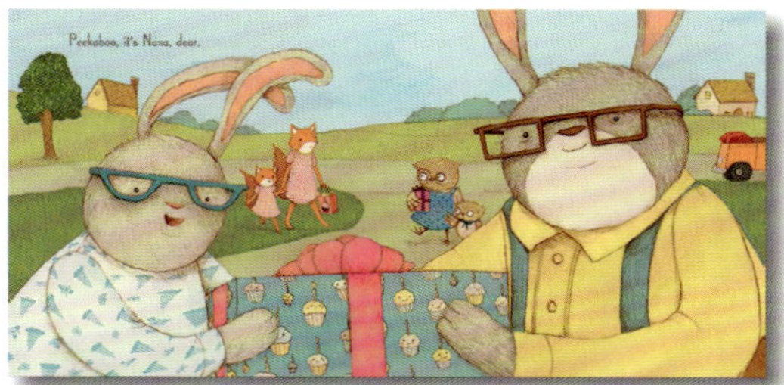

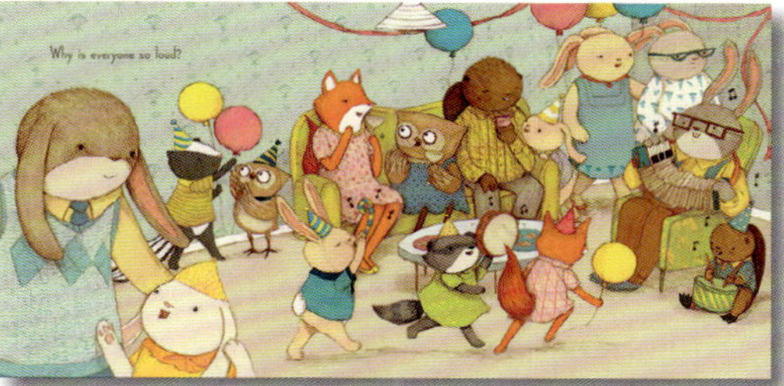

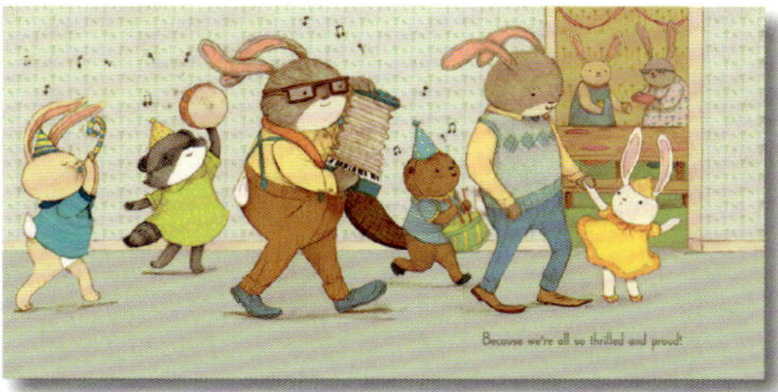

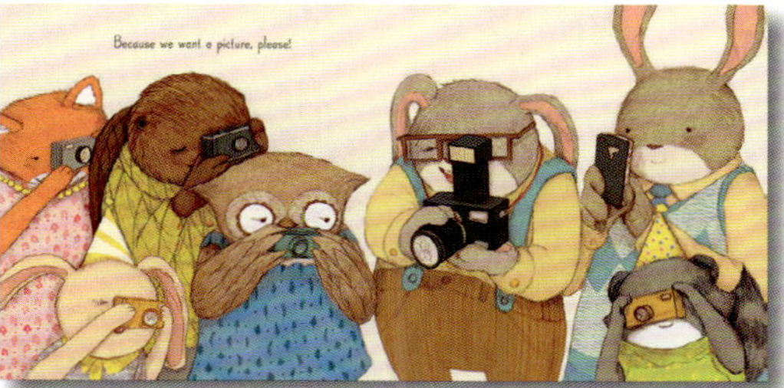

Stephanie Graegin

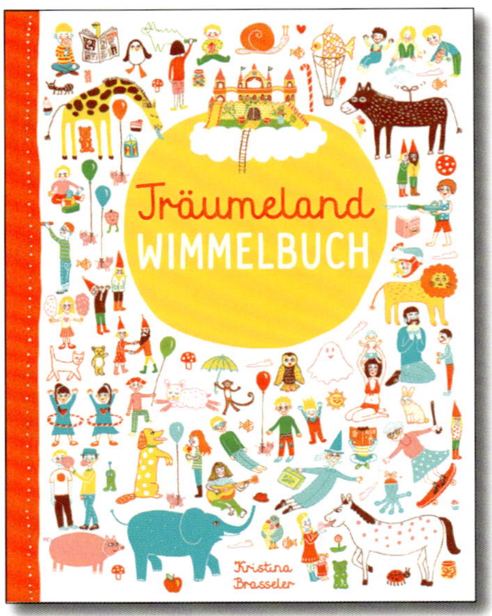

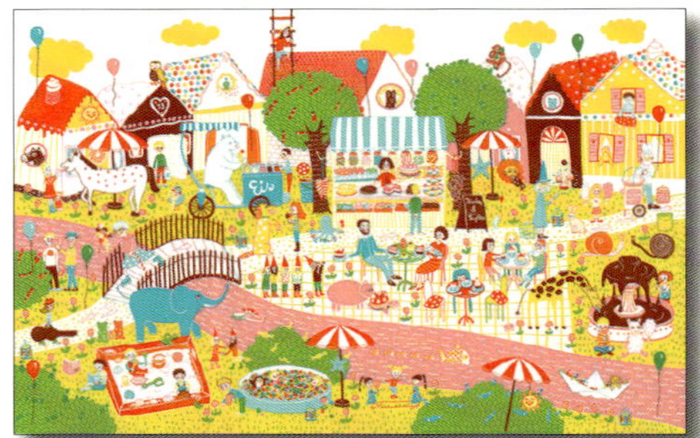

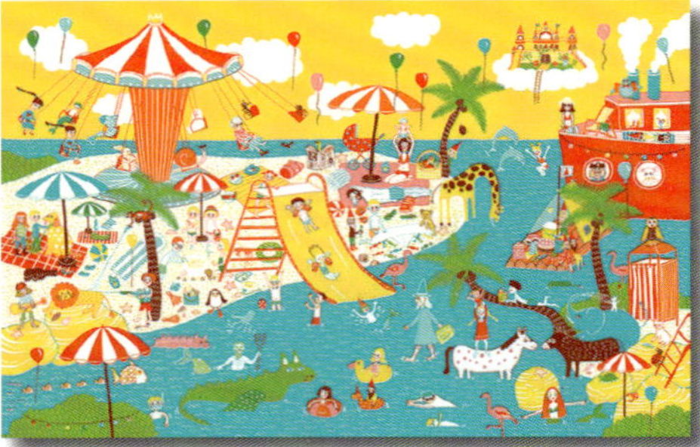

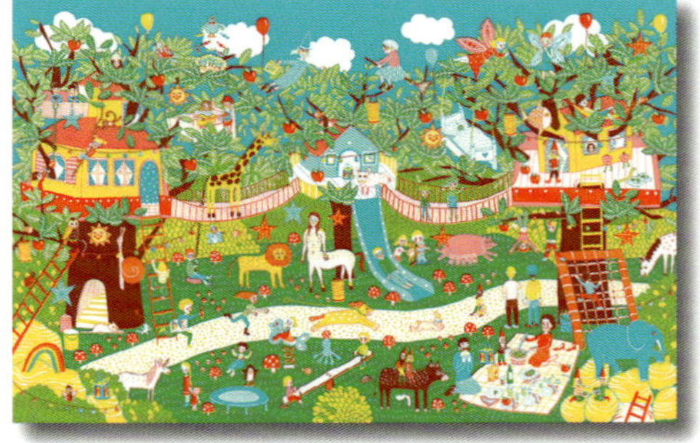

Kristina Brasseler

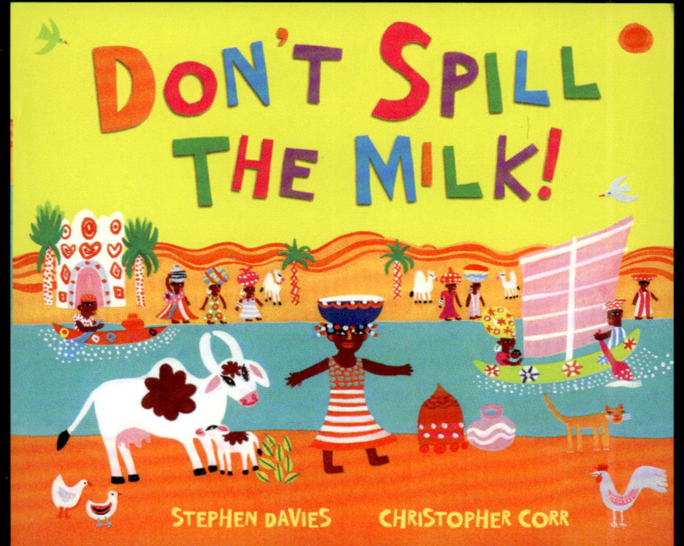
DON'T SPILL THE MILK!
STEPHEN DAVIES   CHRISTOPHER CORR

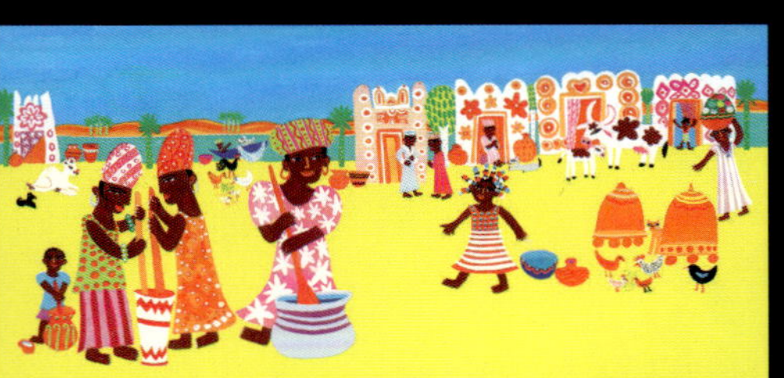

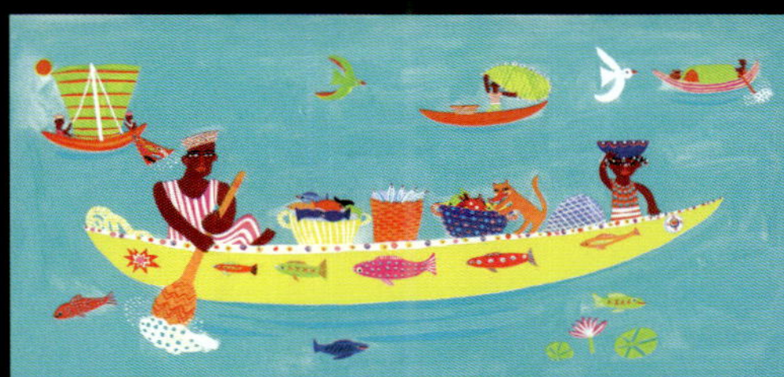

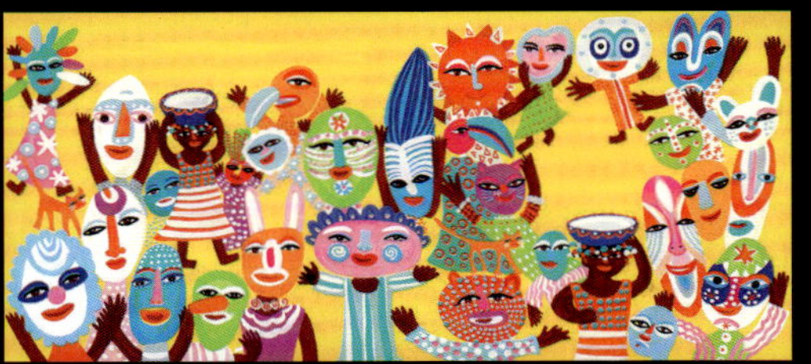

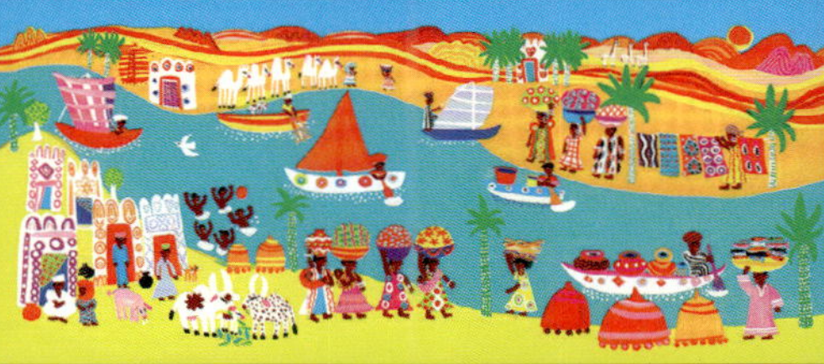

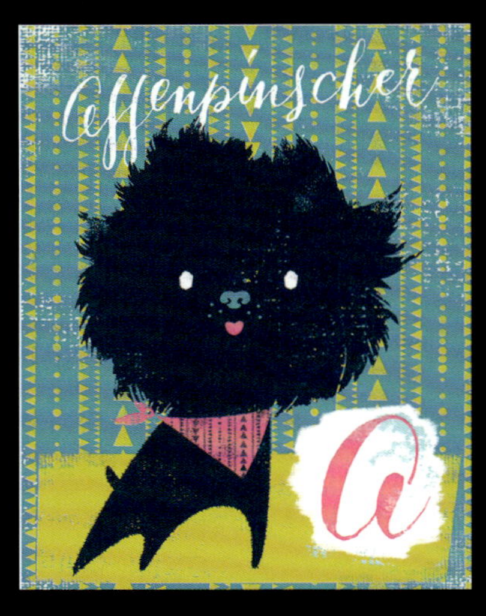
Affenpinscher
a

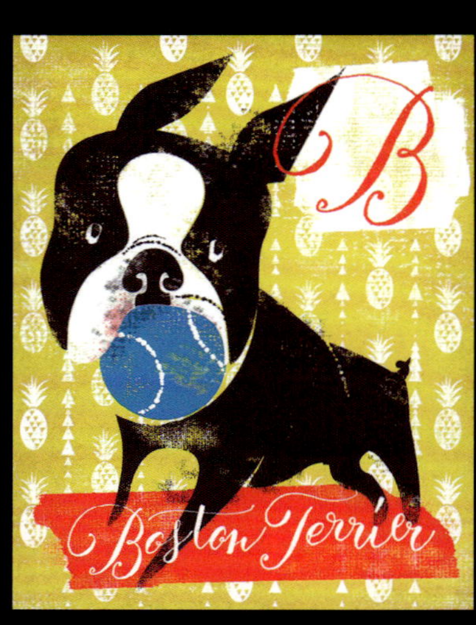
B
Boston Terrier

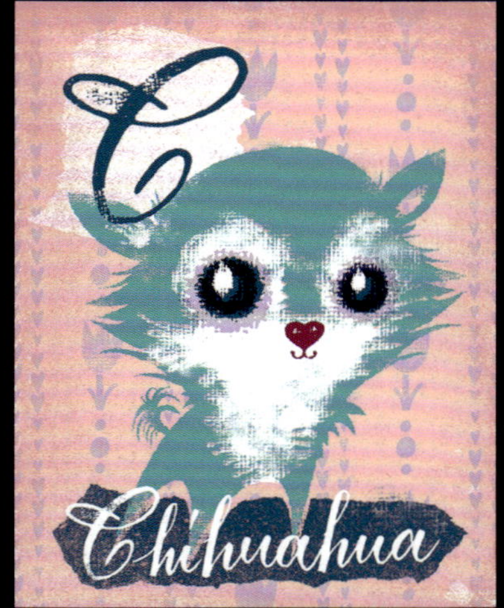
C
Chihuahua

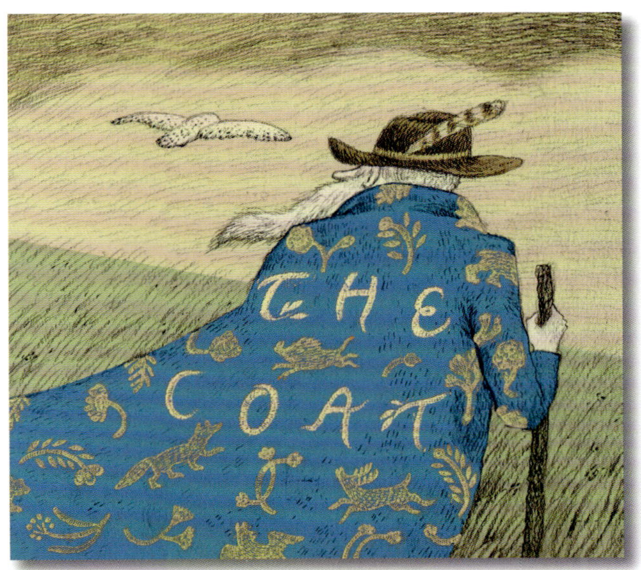

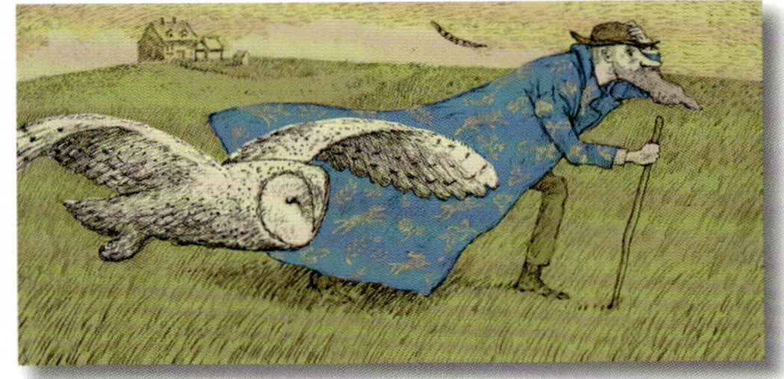

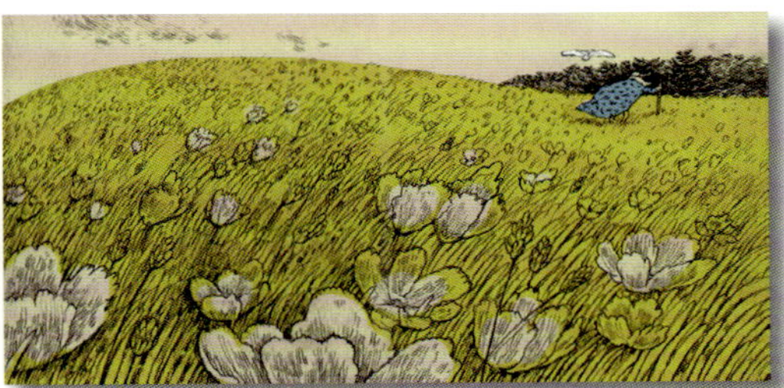

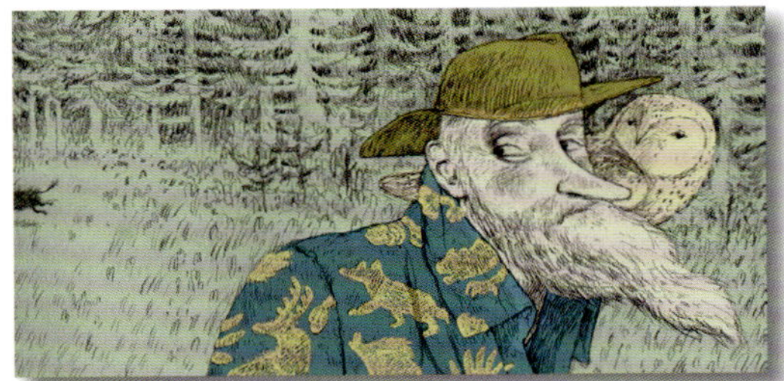

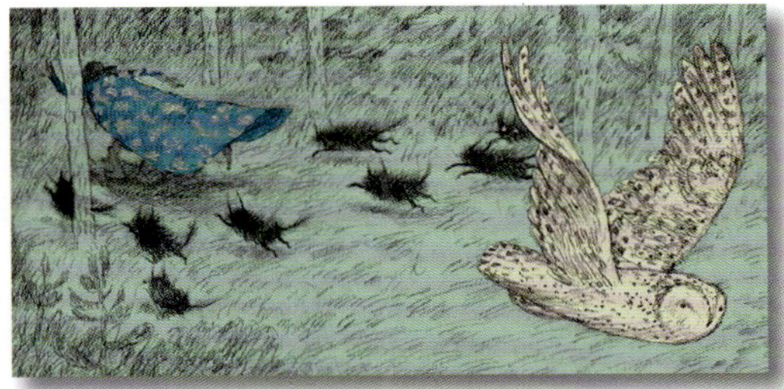

(L) *Debra Ziss* (R) SILVER *Doug Salati*

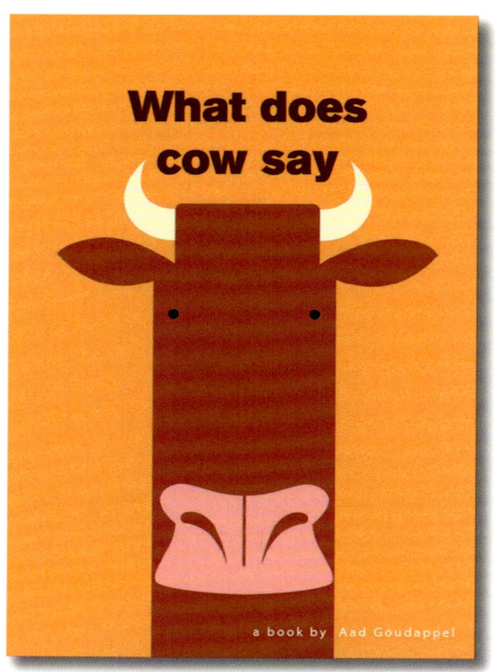
What does
cow say
a book by Aad Goudappel

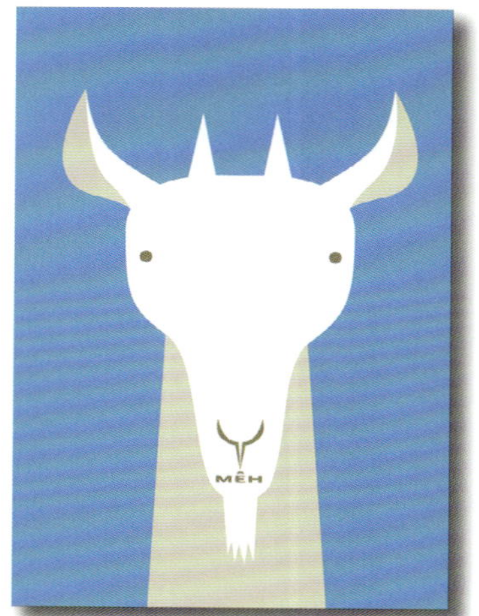
MÉH

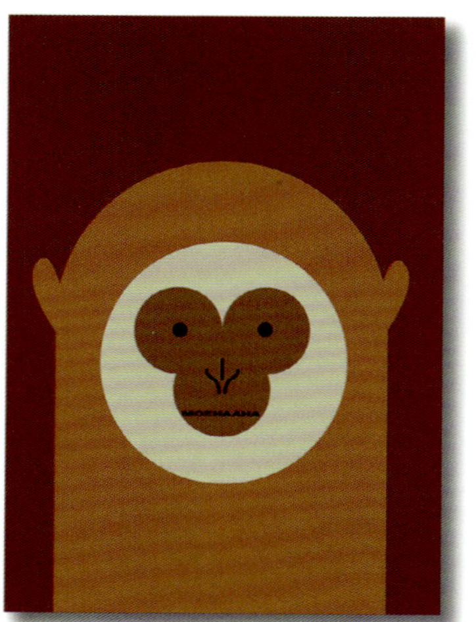
MOEHAANA

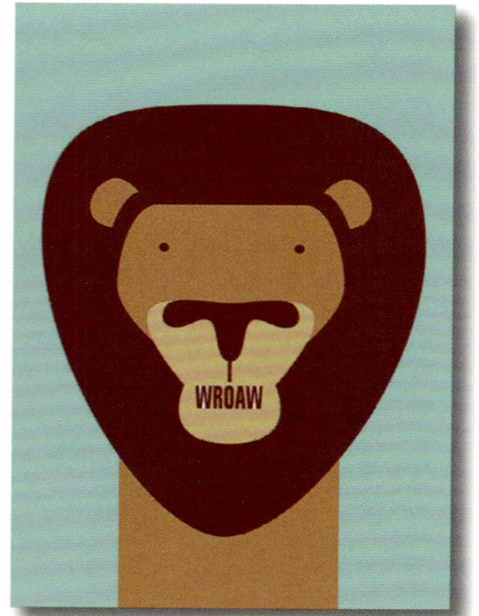
WROAW

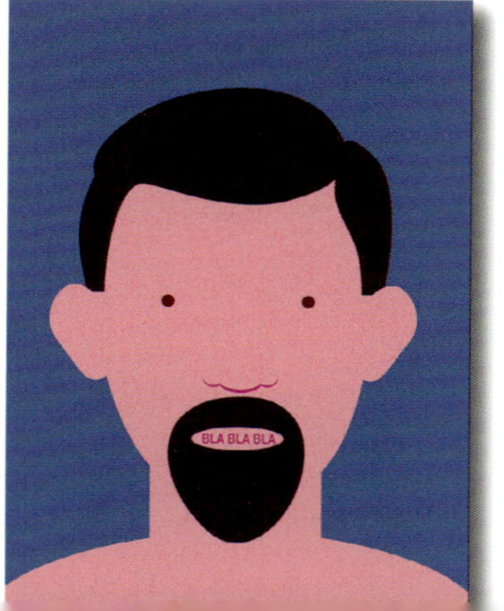
BLA BLA BLA

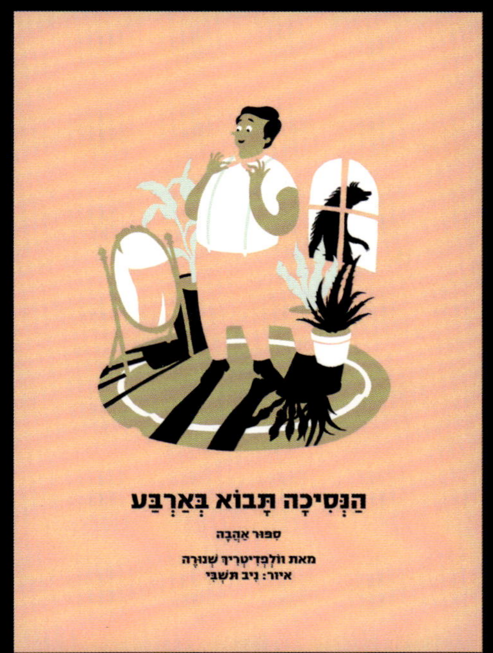
הַנְּסִיכָה תָּבוֹא בְּאַרְבַּע
סִפּוּר אַהֲבָה
מאת וֹולְפְדִיטְרִיךְ שְׁנוּרֶה
איור: נִיב תִּשְׁבִּי

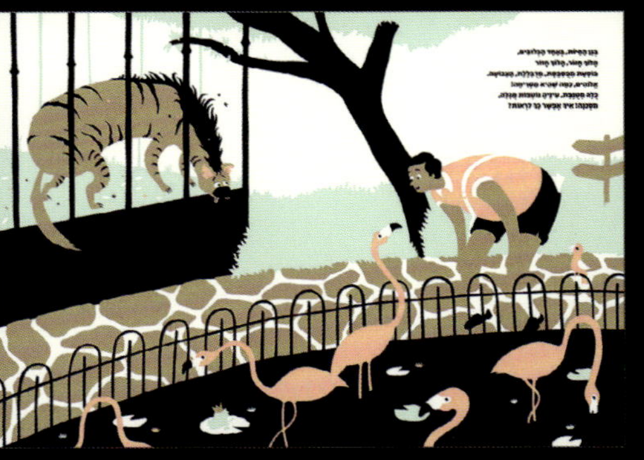

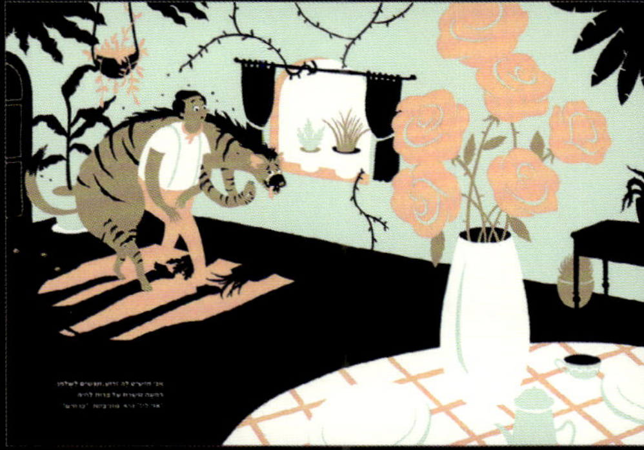

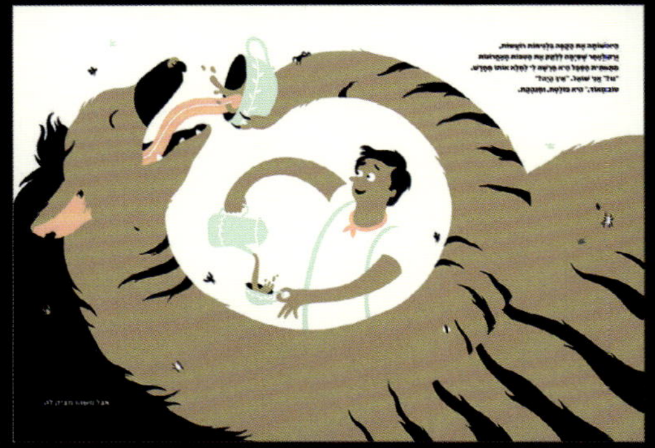

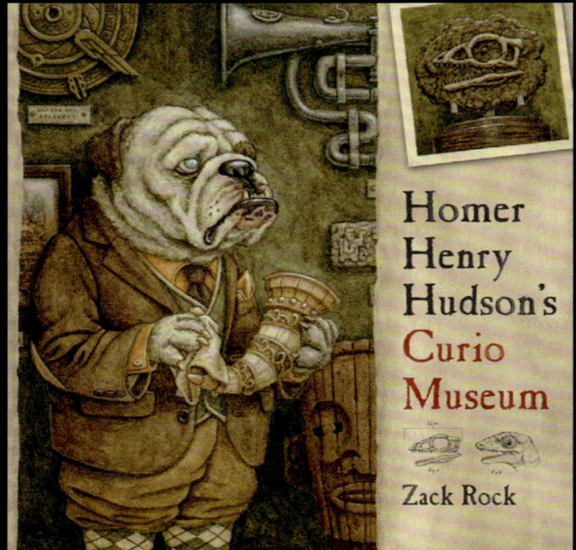
Homer
Henry
Hudson's
Curio
Museum
Zack Rock

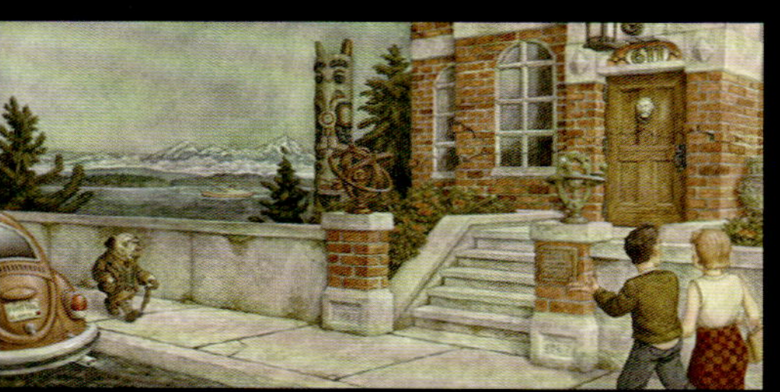

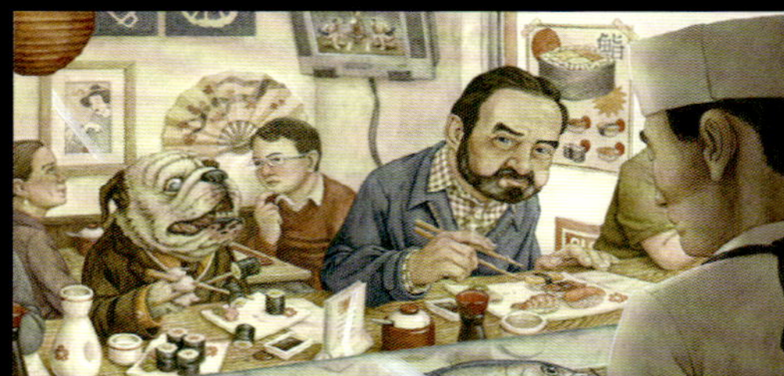

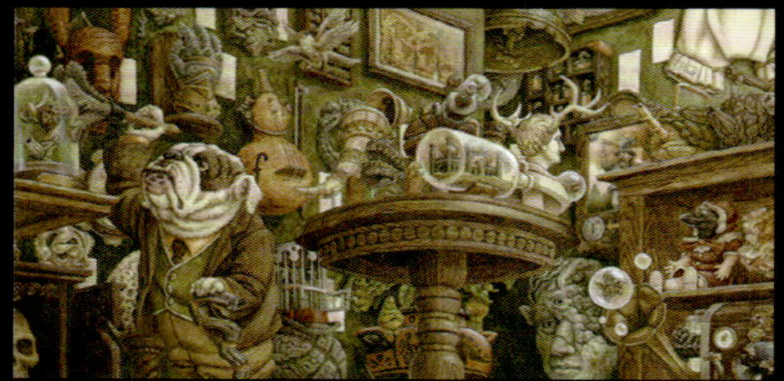

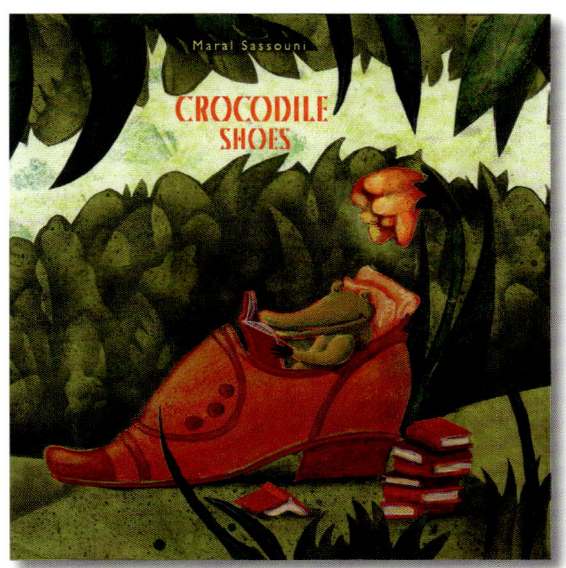

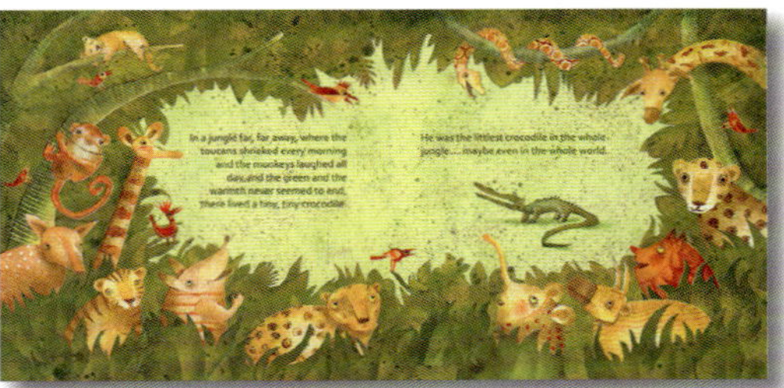

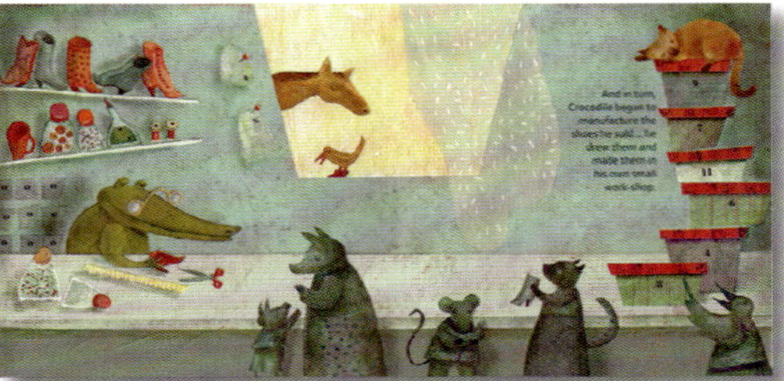

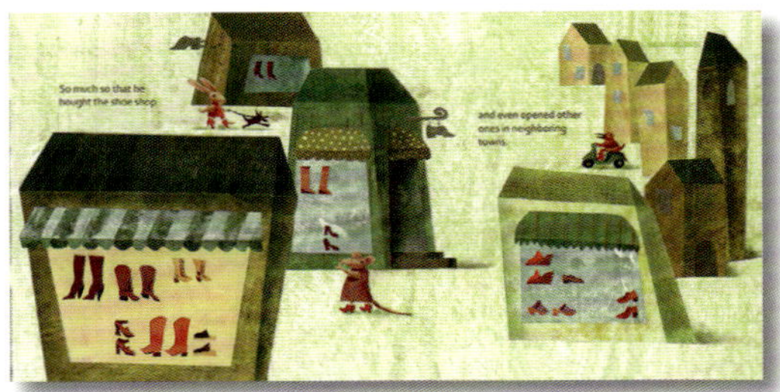

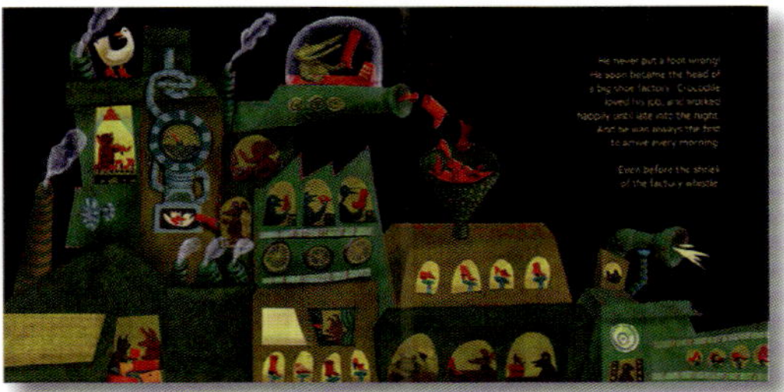

Maral Sassouni

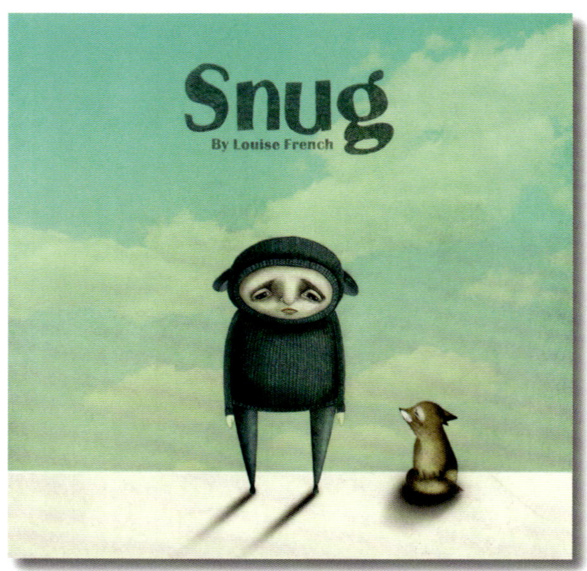

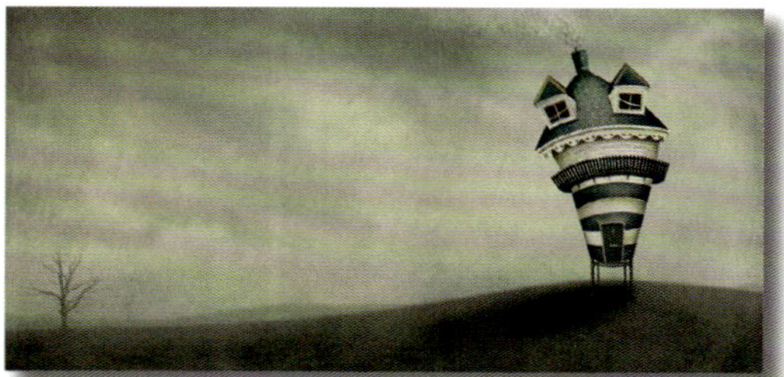

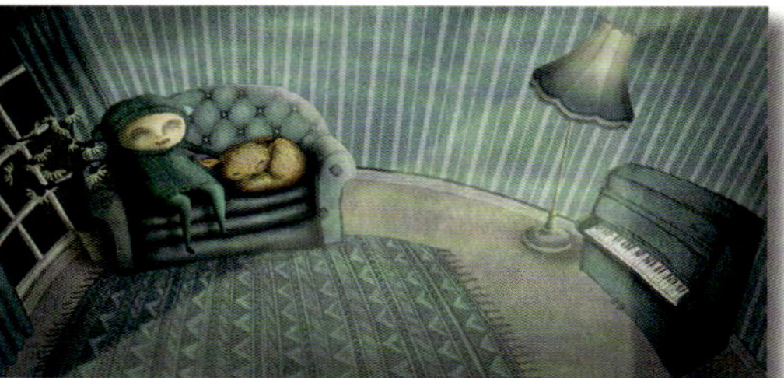

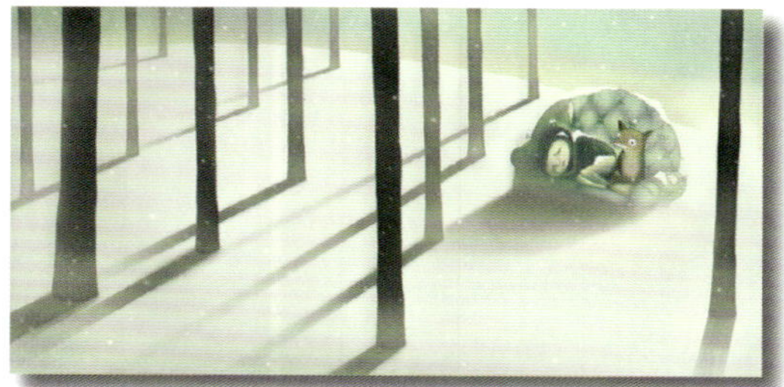

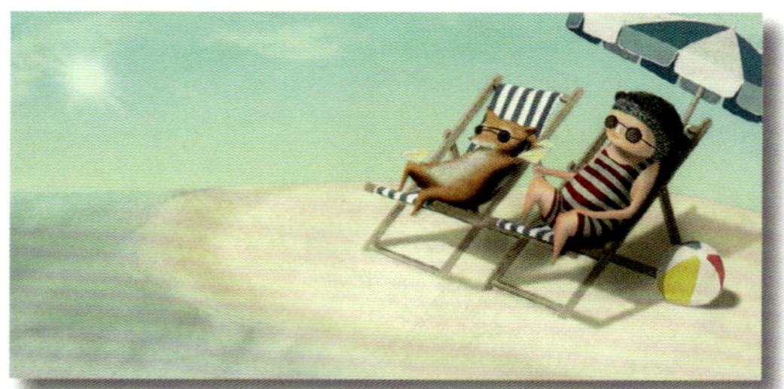

Louise French

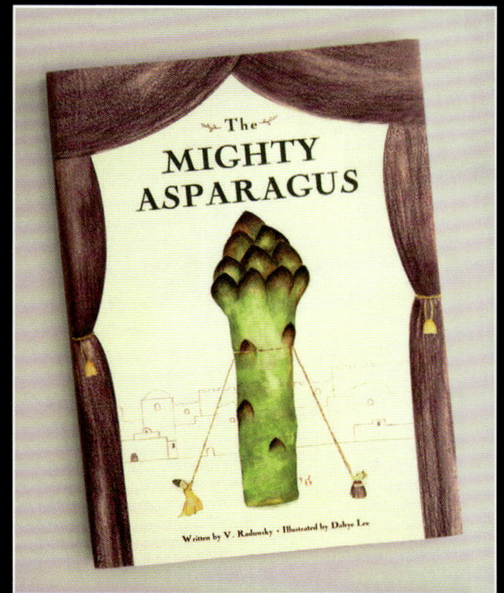
The
MIGHTY
ASPARAGUS
Written by V. Radunsky · Illustrated by Dahye Lee

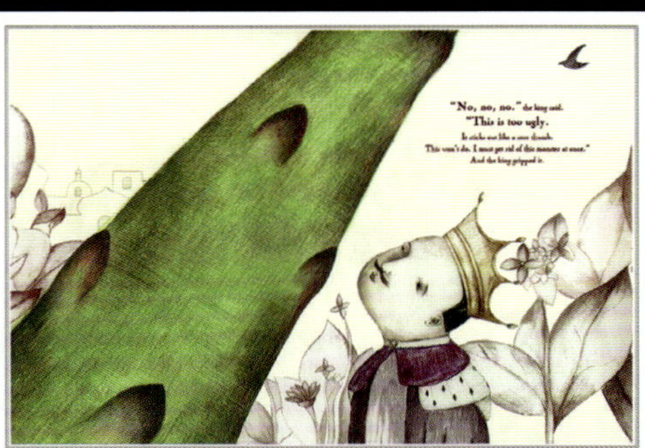

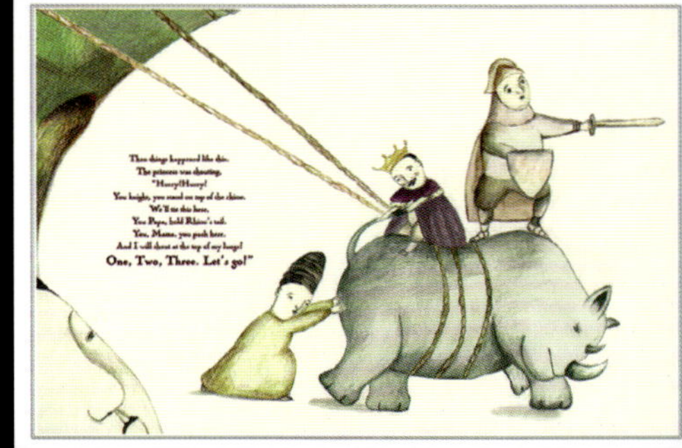

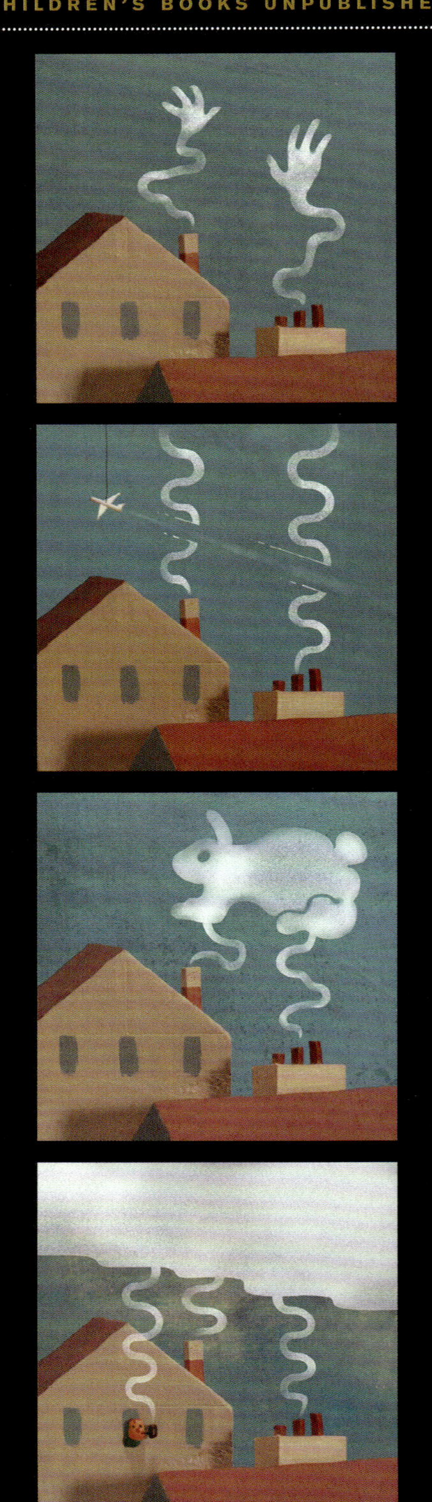

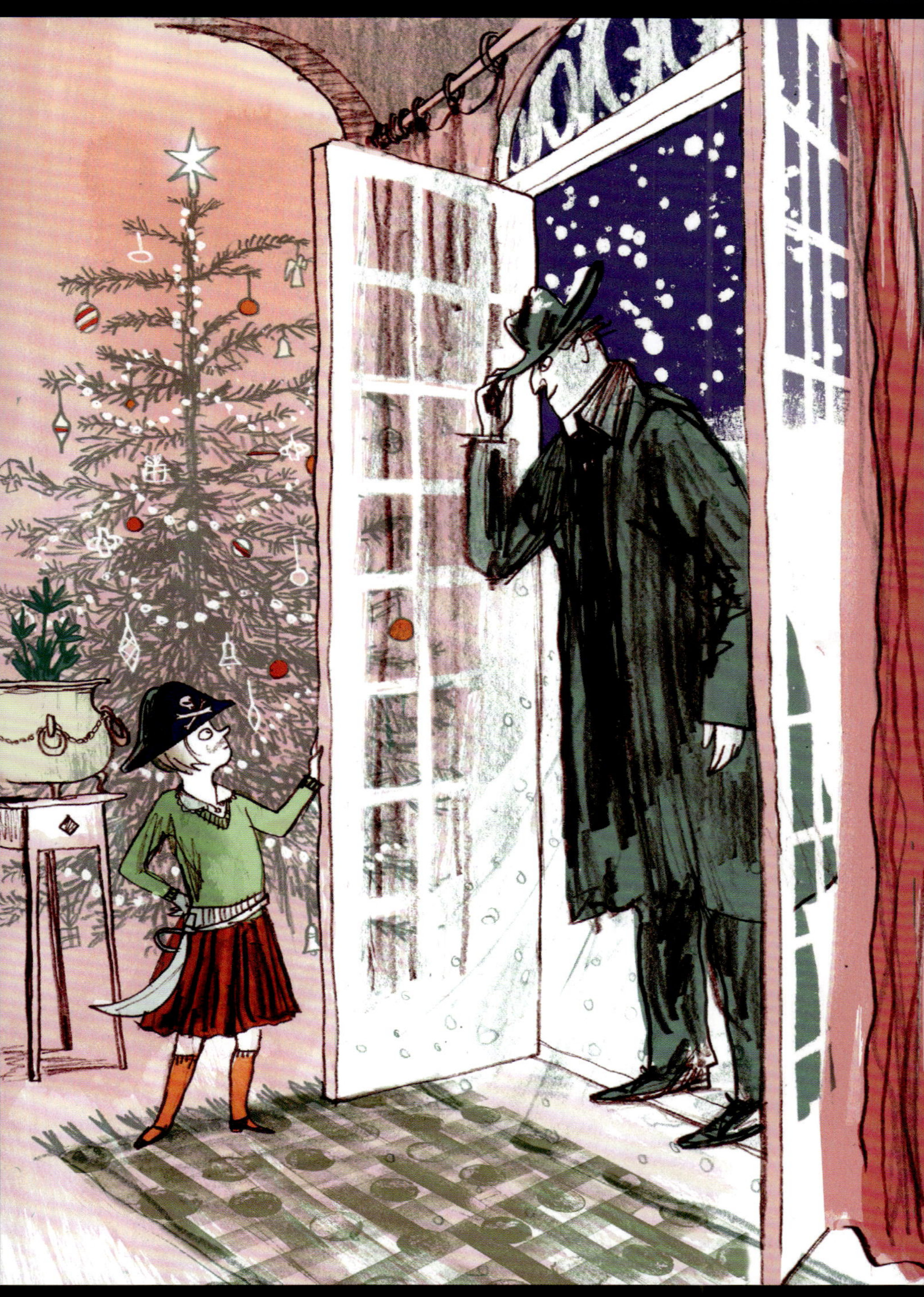

(L) *Hudson Christie* (R) *Sara Ogilvie*

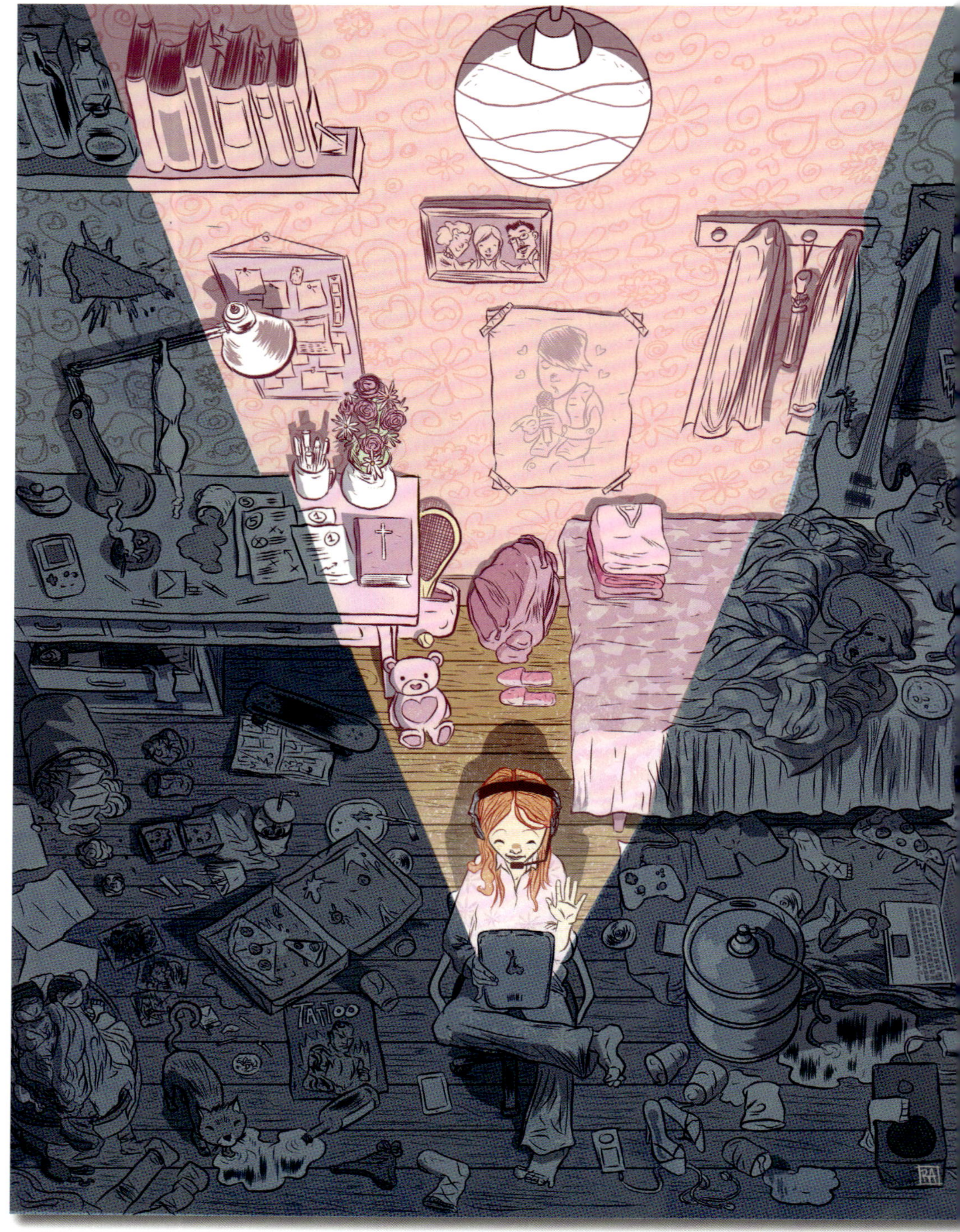

(L) *Rafael Alvarez* (R) *Jamey Christoph*

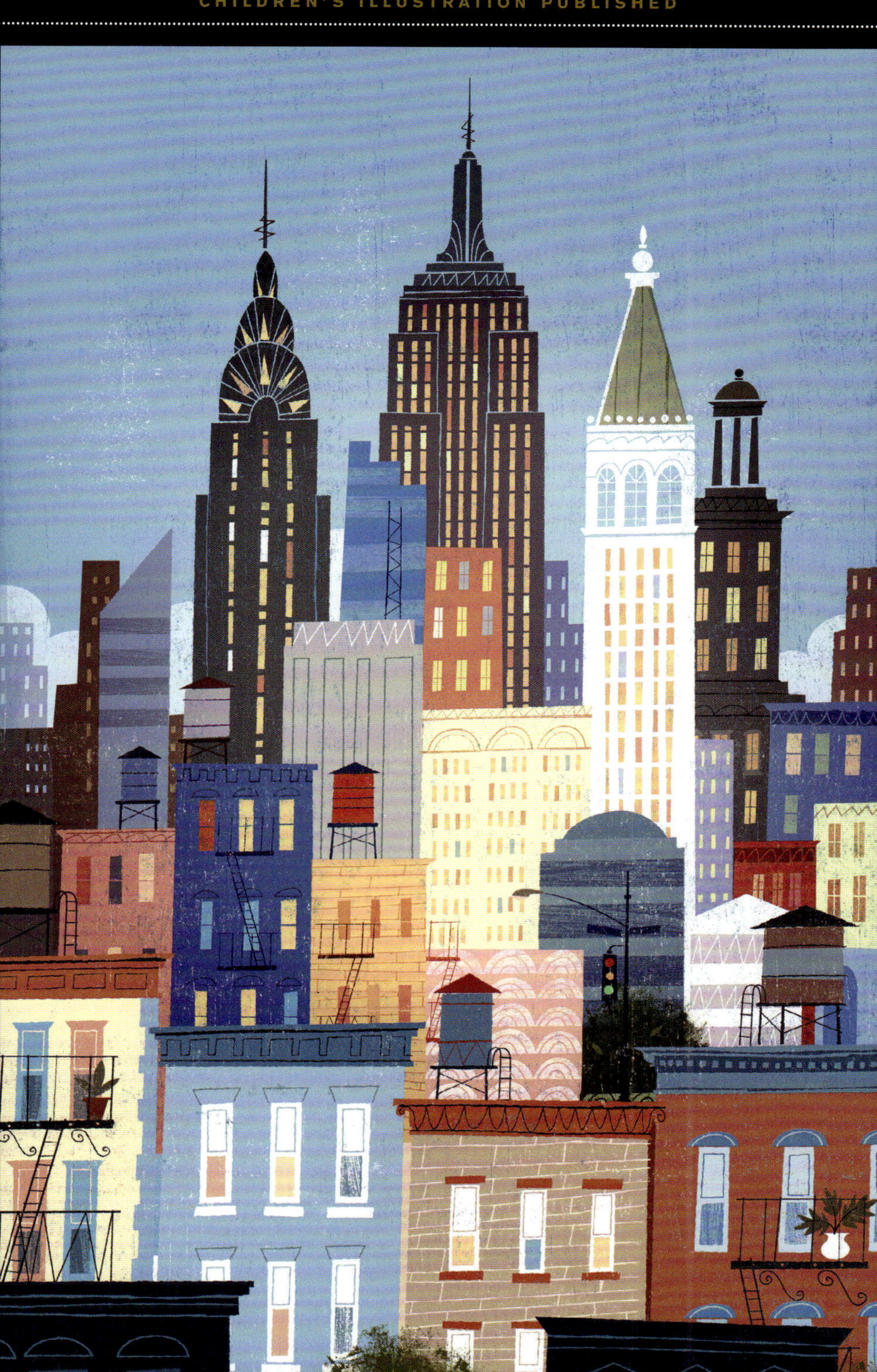

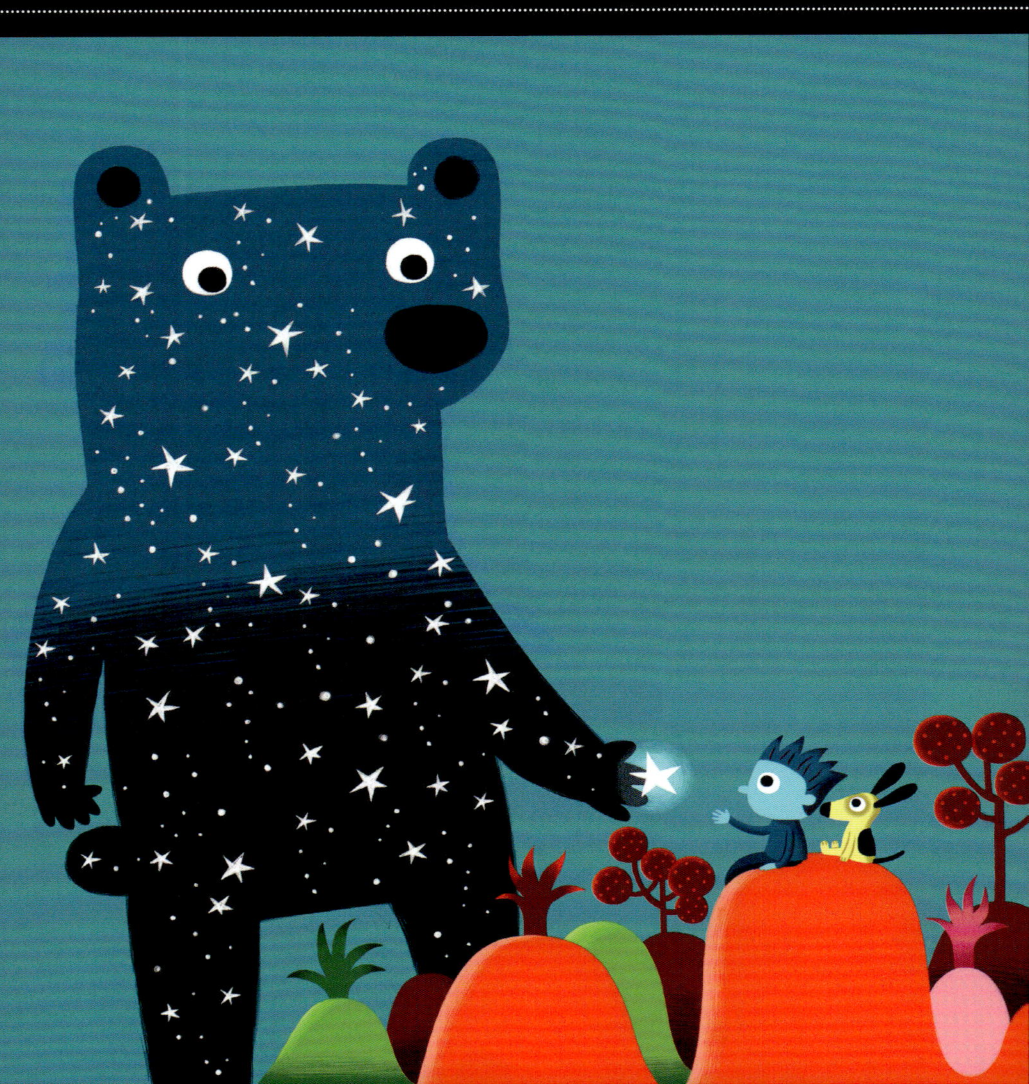

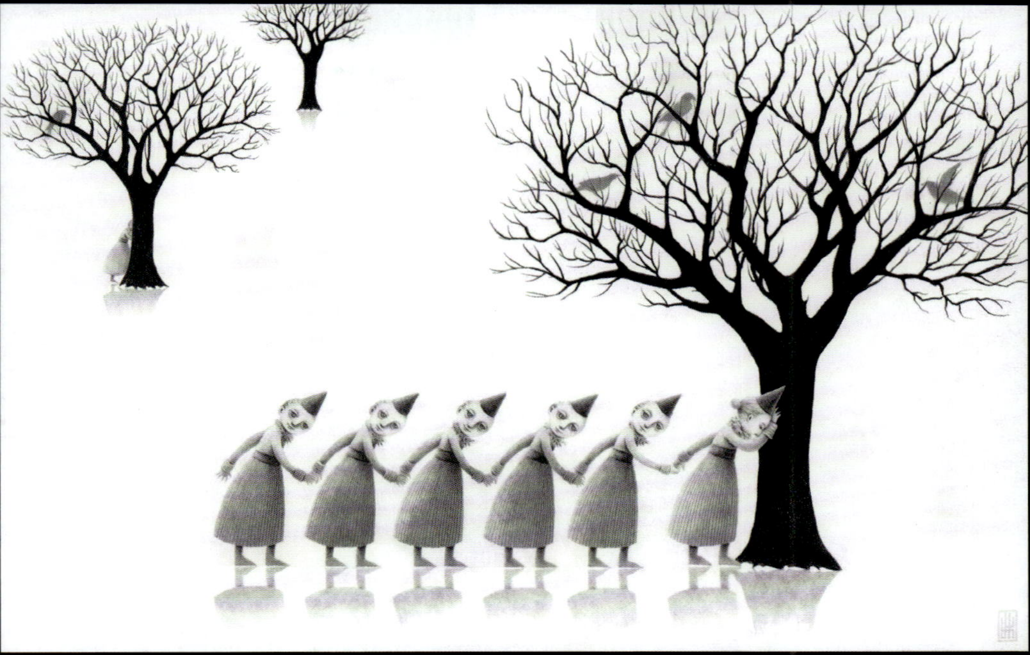

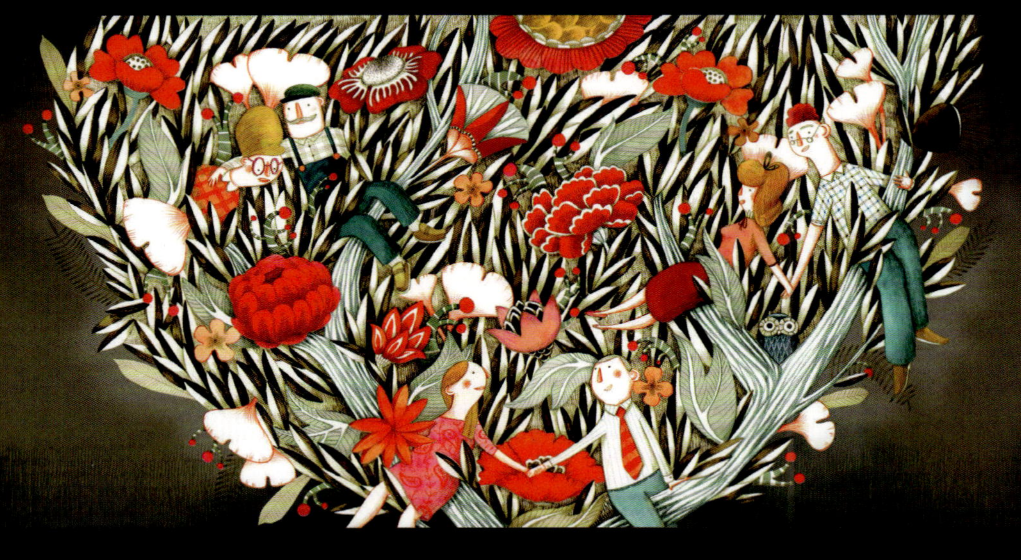

(T) *Yoko Tanaka* (B) DISTINGUISHED MERIT *Marion Arbona*

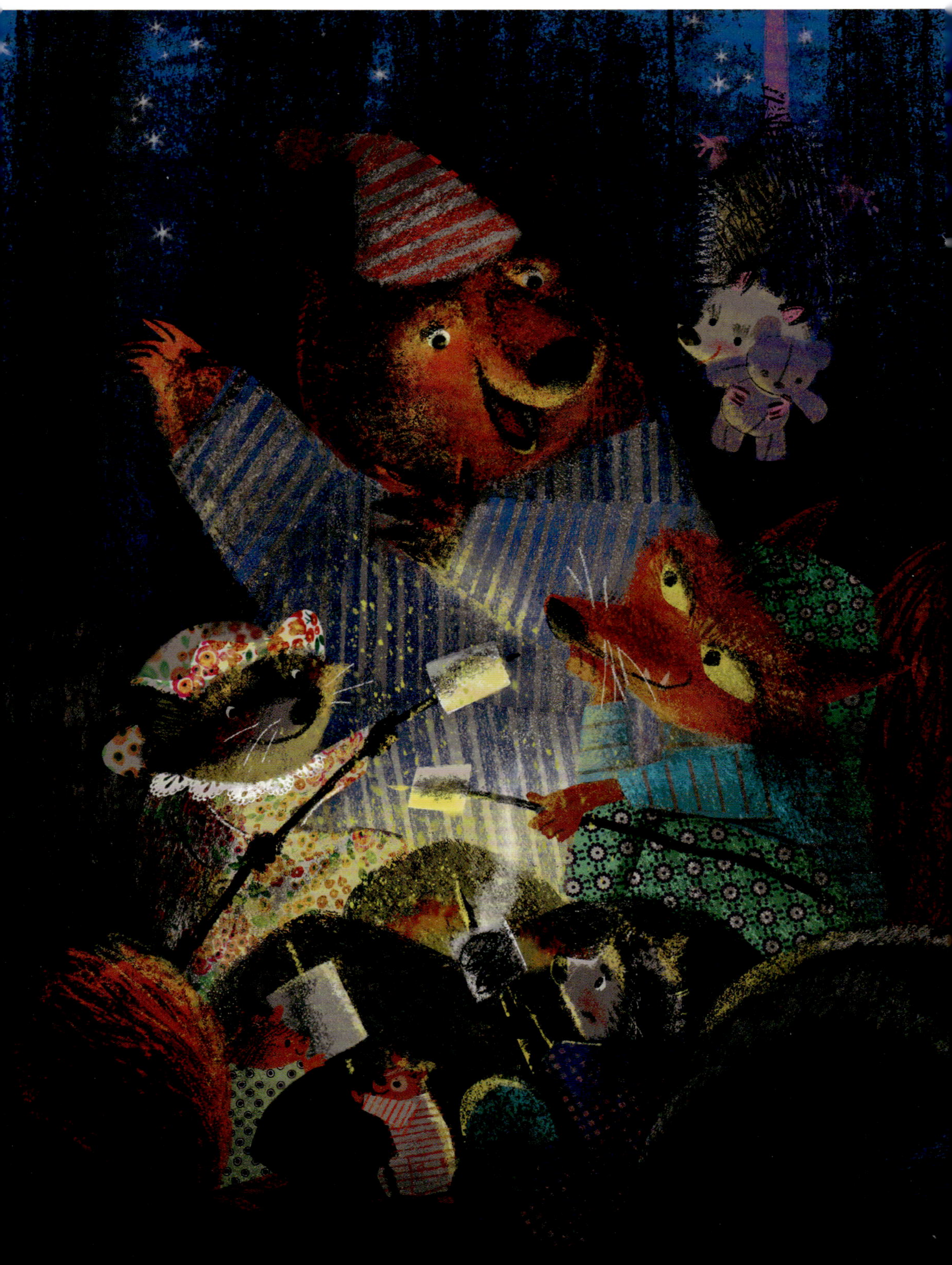

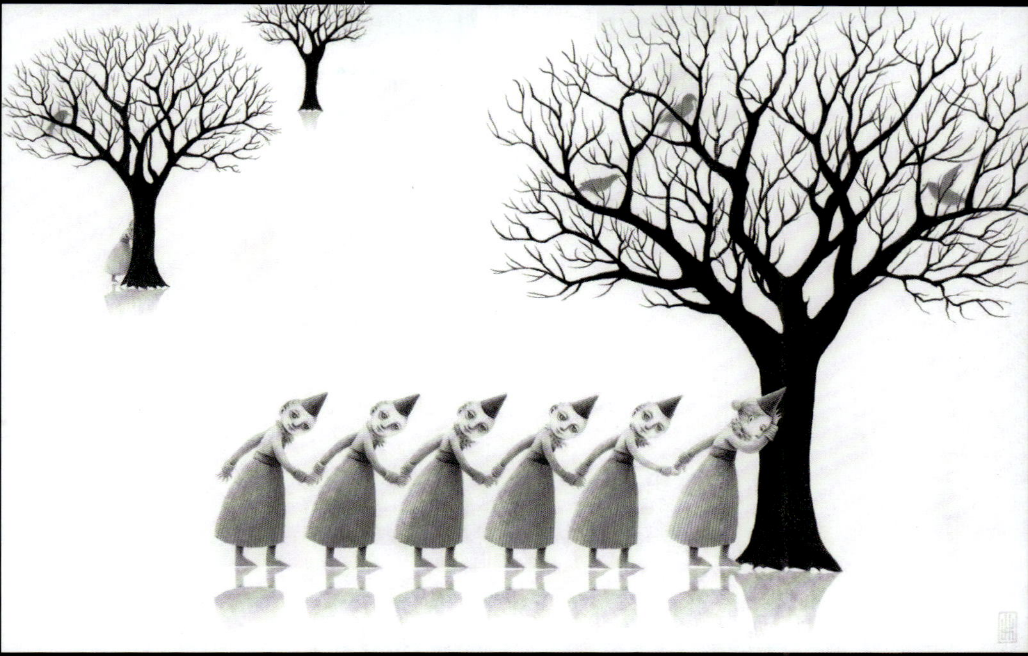

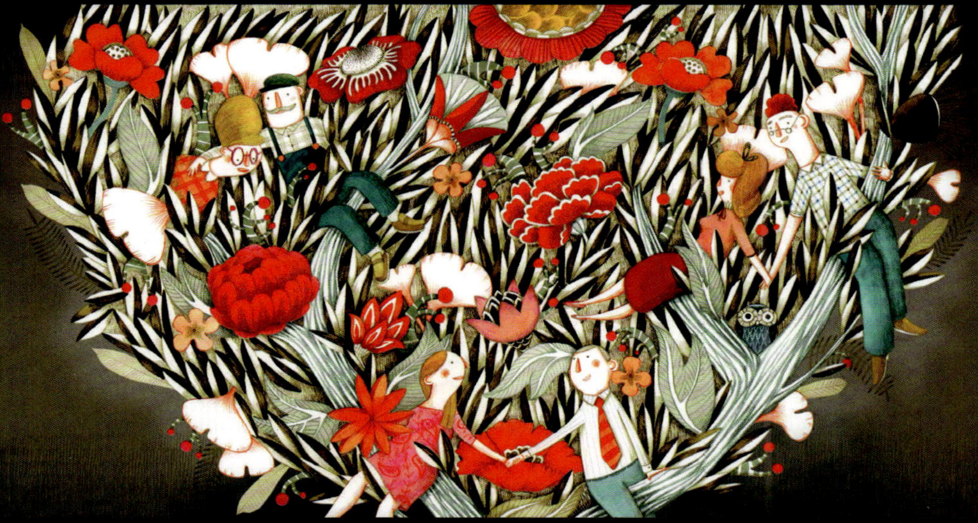

(T) *Yoko Tanaka* (B) DISTINGUISHED MERIT *Marion Arbona*

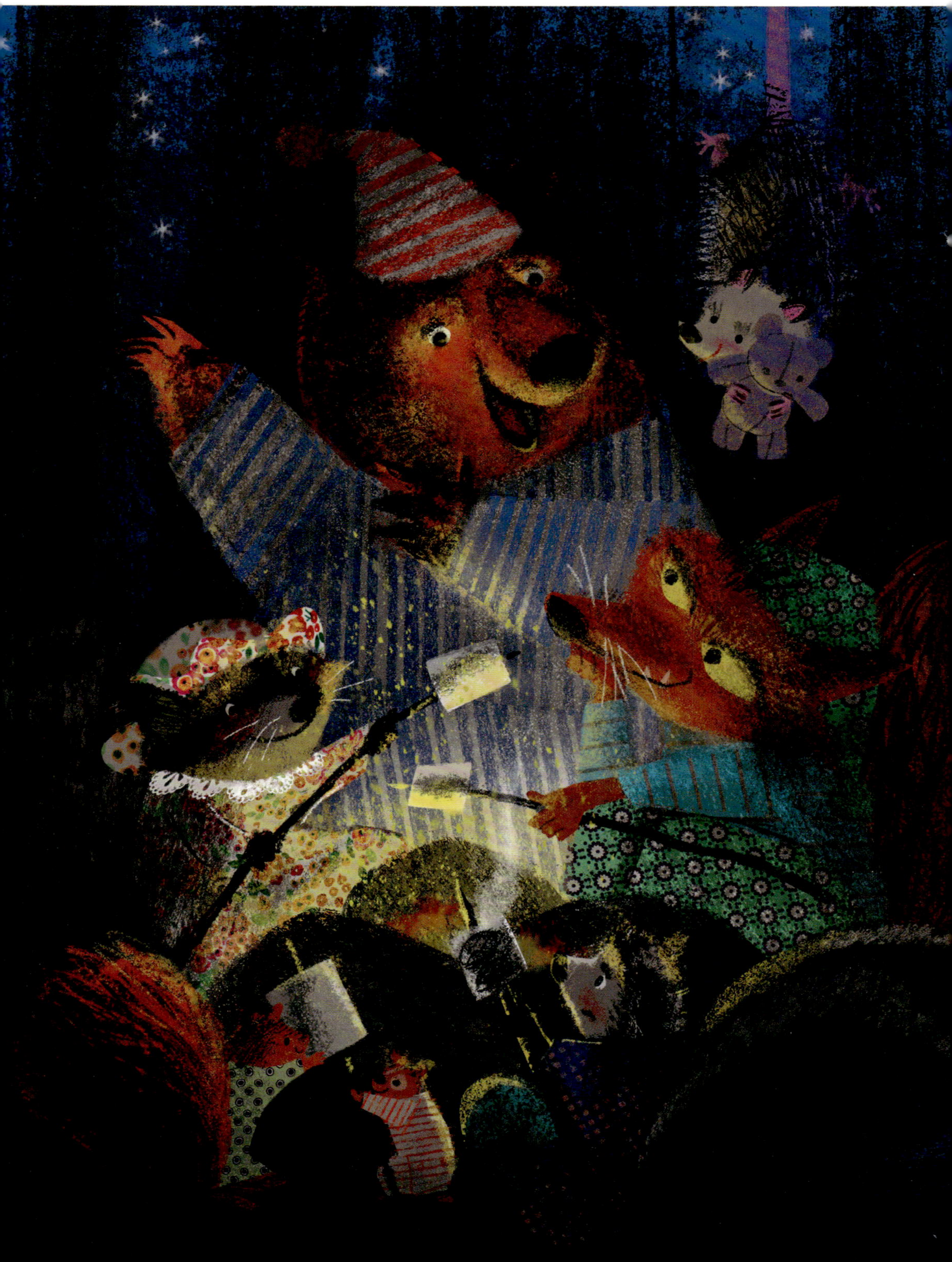

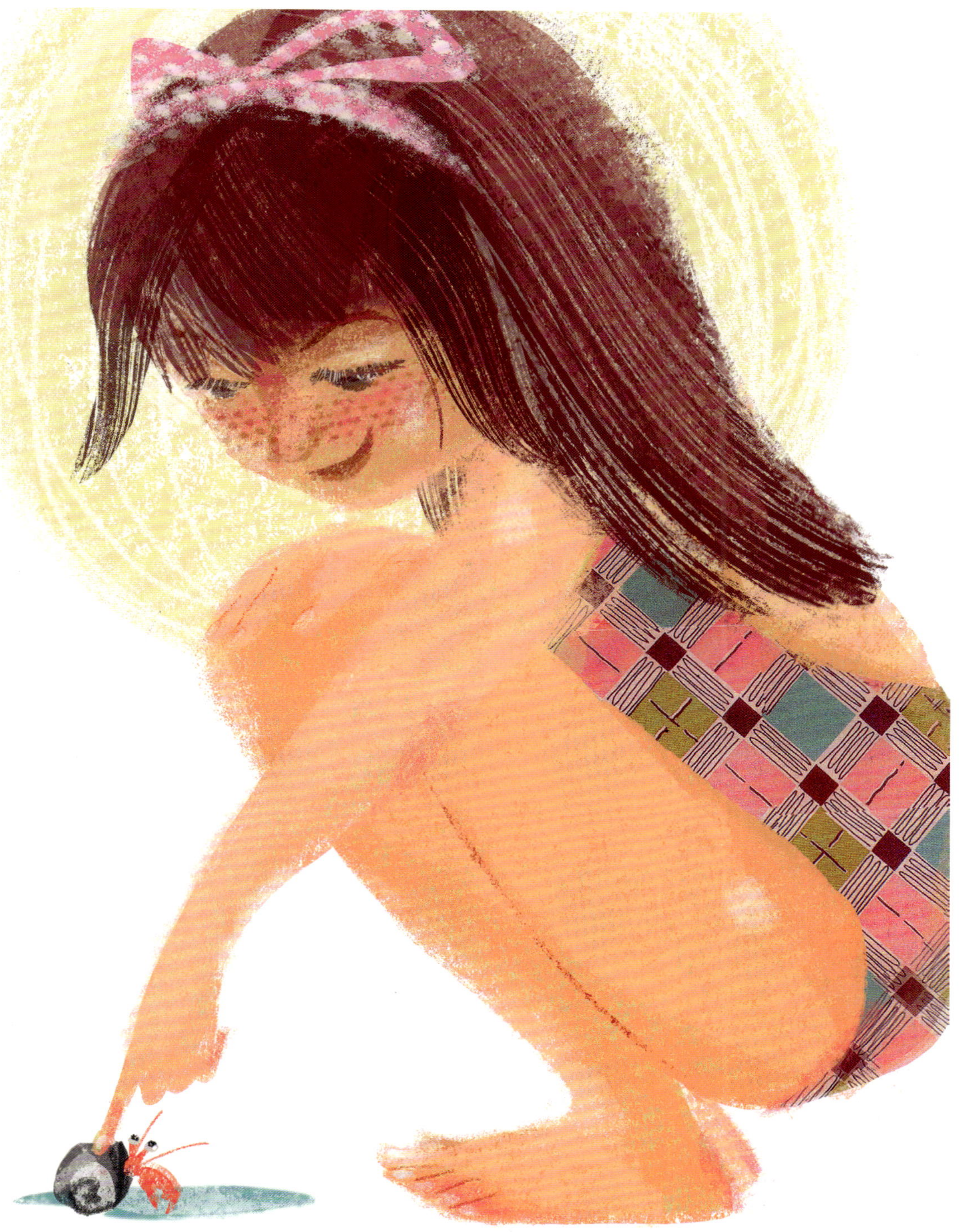

(L) *Susan Gal* (R) *Susan Gal*

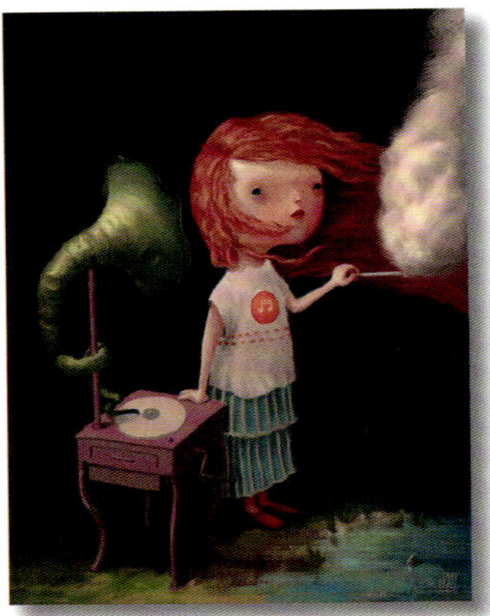
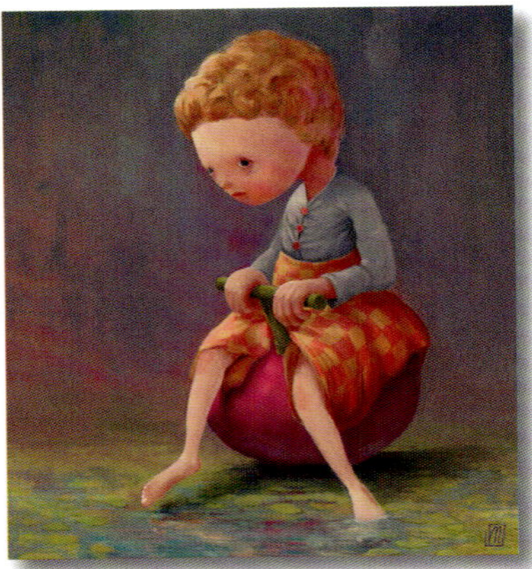
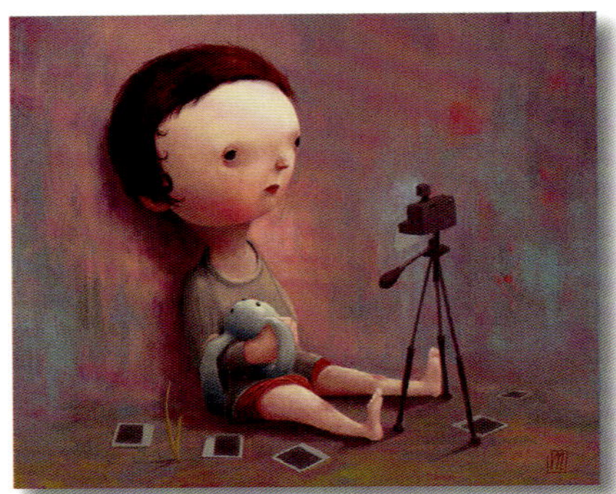
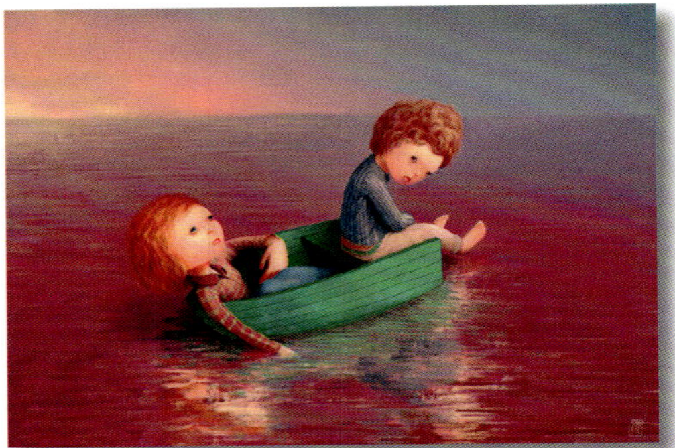
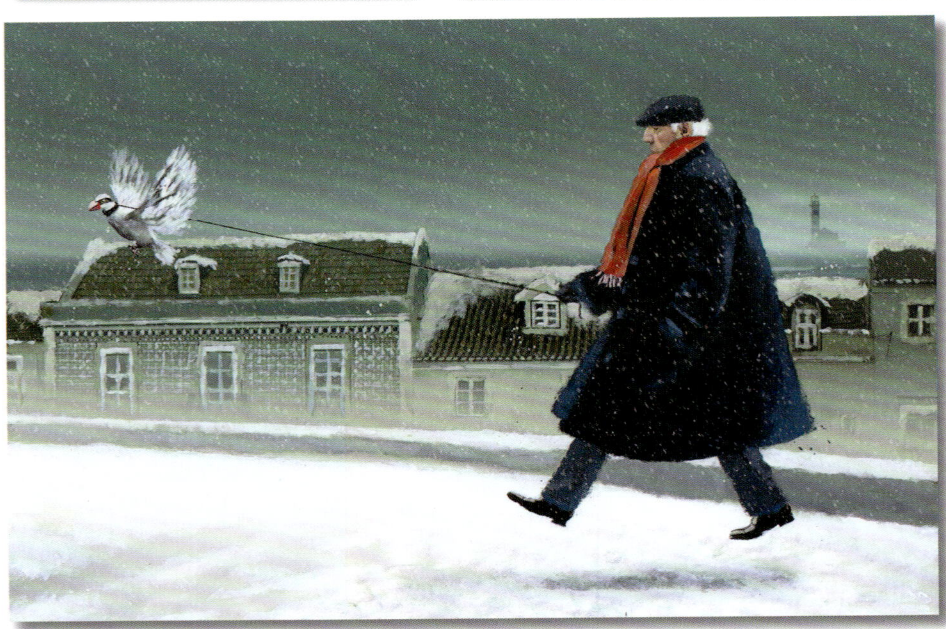

(T) *Marco Piunti* (B) *Francois Thisdale* (R) BRONZE *Nina Cuneo*

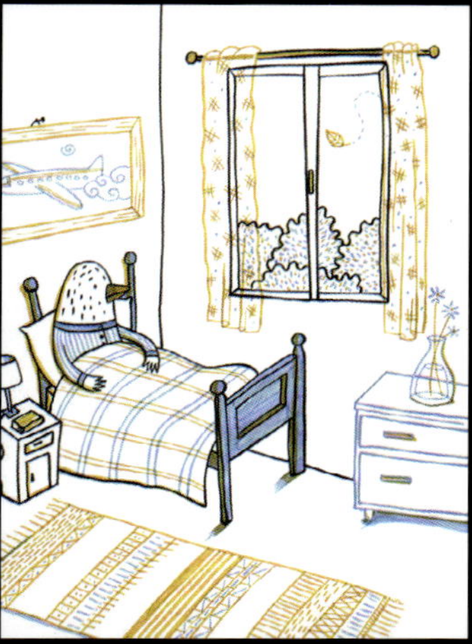

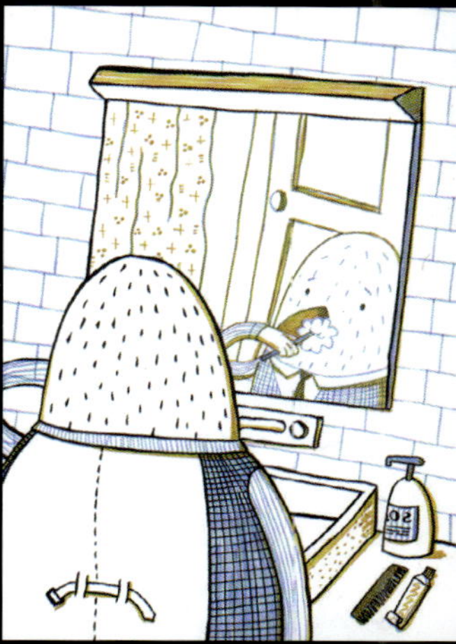

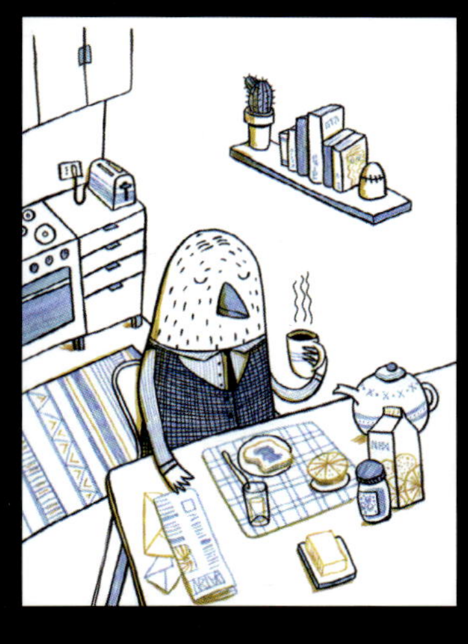

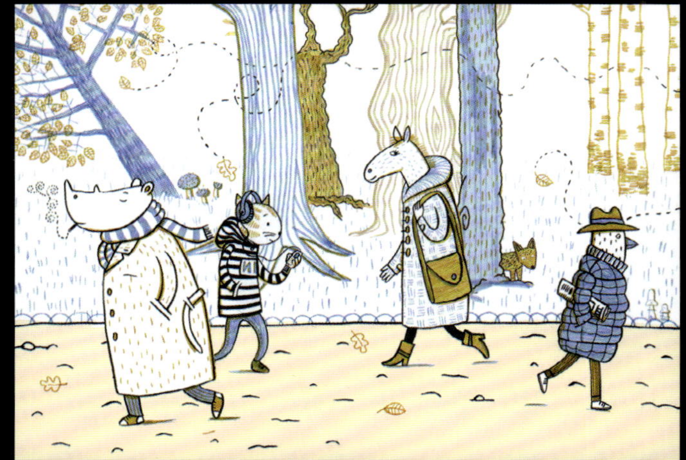

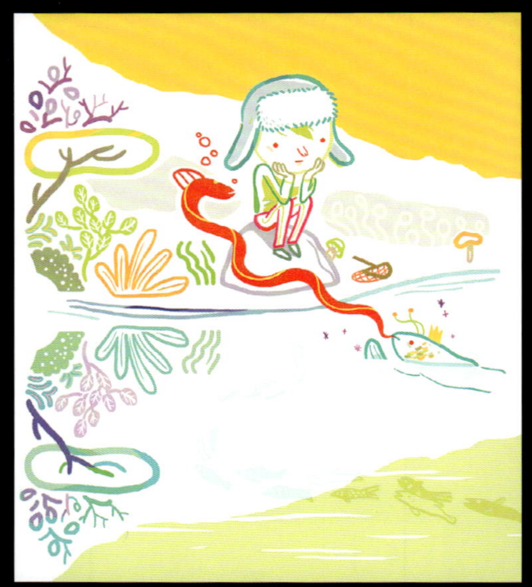

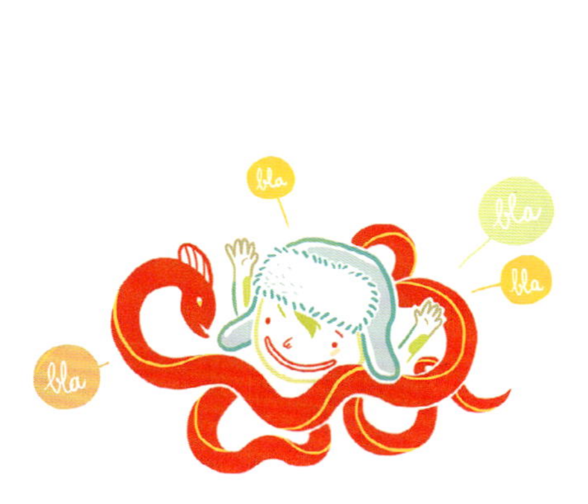

bla
bla
bla
bla

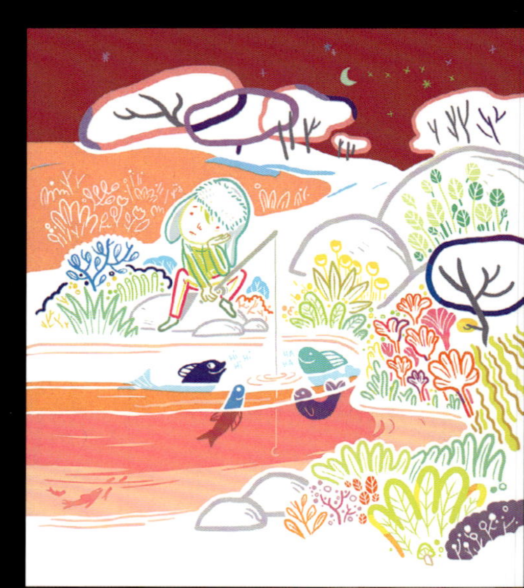

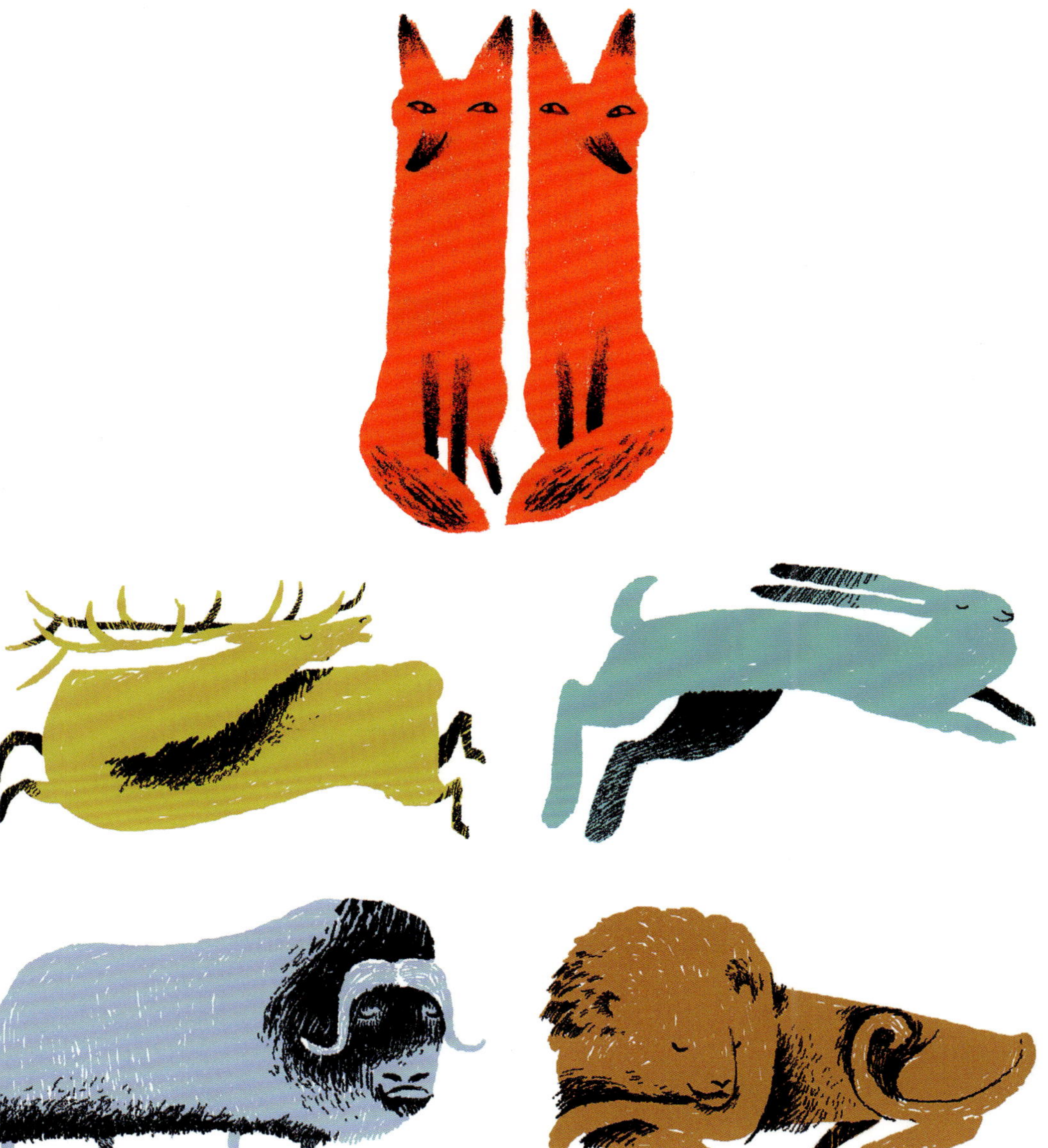

Doug Salati

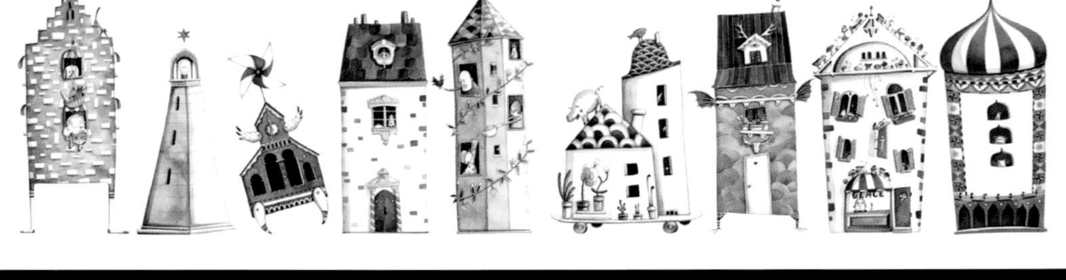

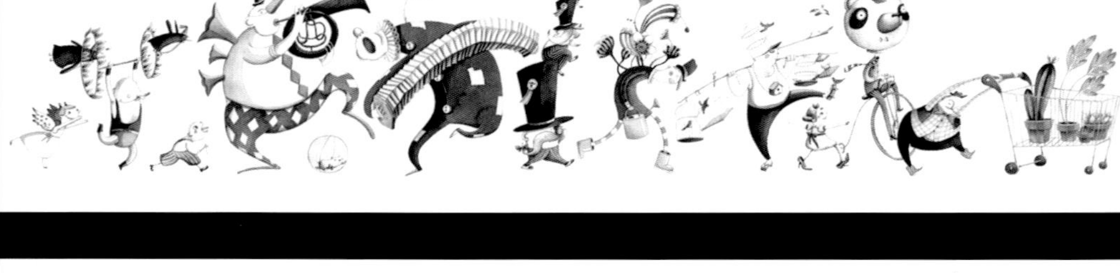

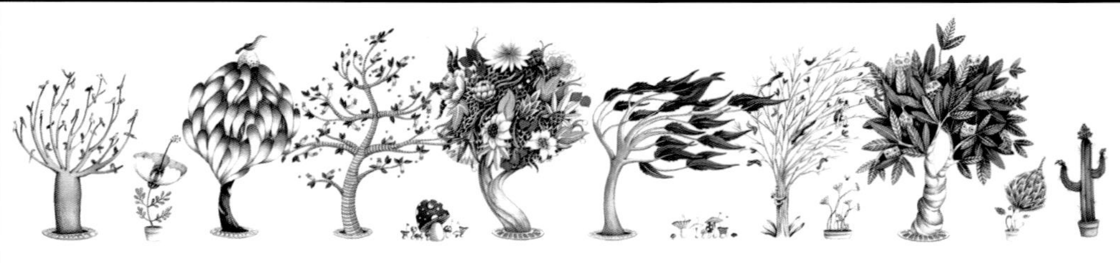

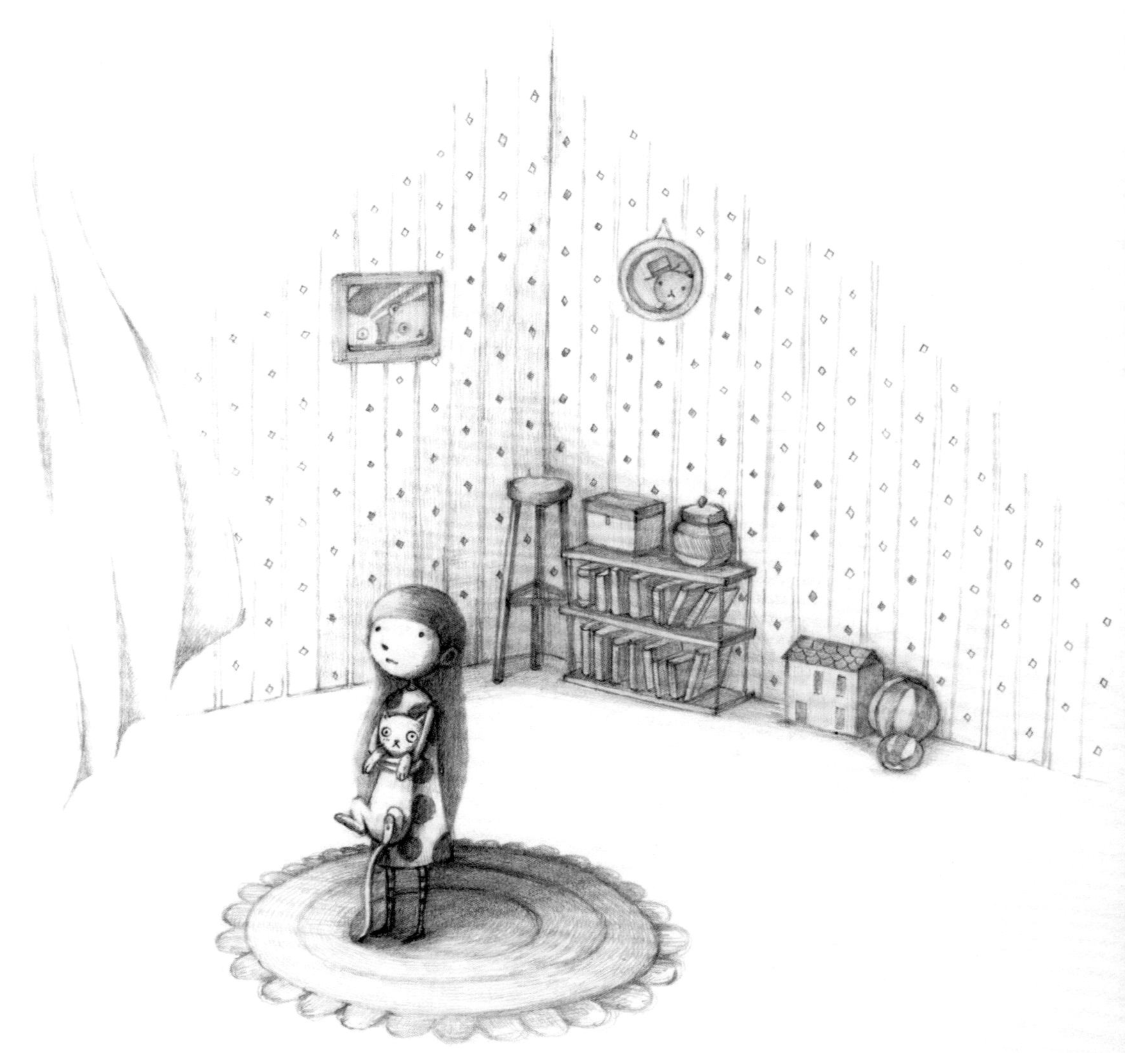

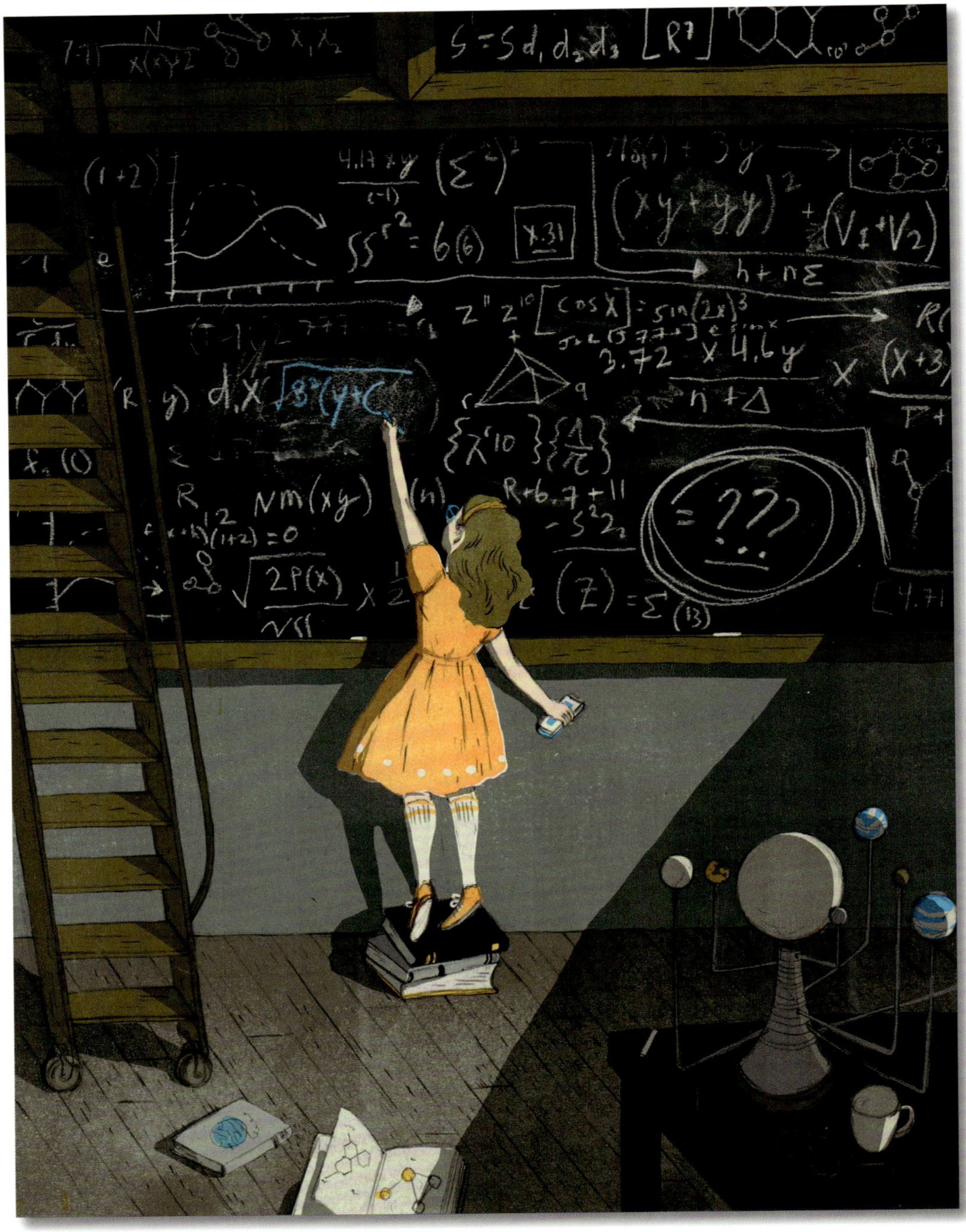

(L) *Byron Eggenschwiler* (R) *Constanze Von Kitzing*

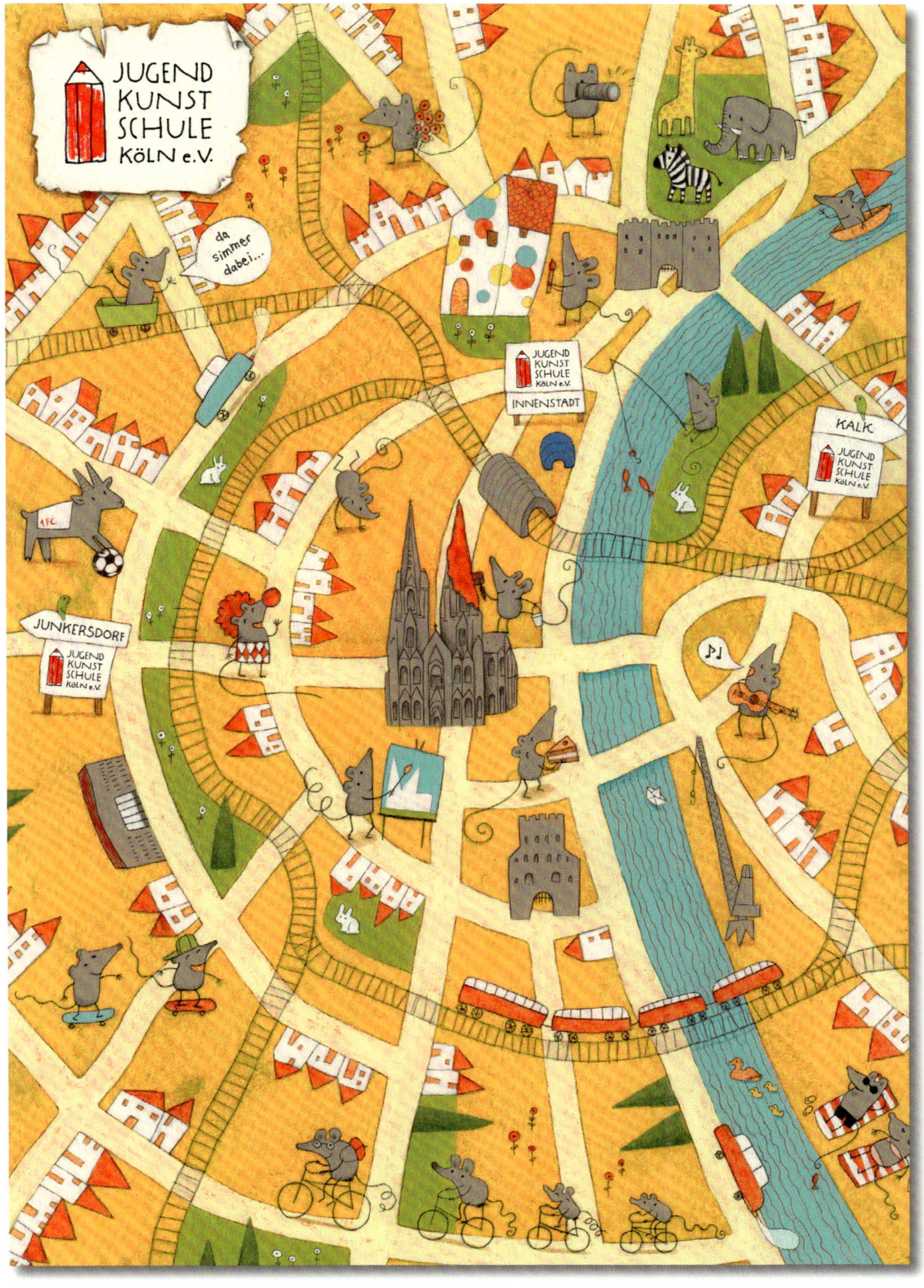
JUGEND
KUNST
SCHULE
KÖLN e.V.
da simmer dabei...
JUGEND
KUNST
SCHULE
KÖLN e.V.
INNENSTADT
KALK
JUGEND
KUNST
SCHULE
KÖLN e.V.
JUNKERSDORF
JUGEND
KUNST
SCHULE
KÖLN e.V.
1.FC

~foRest fRienDs~
by maria carluccio

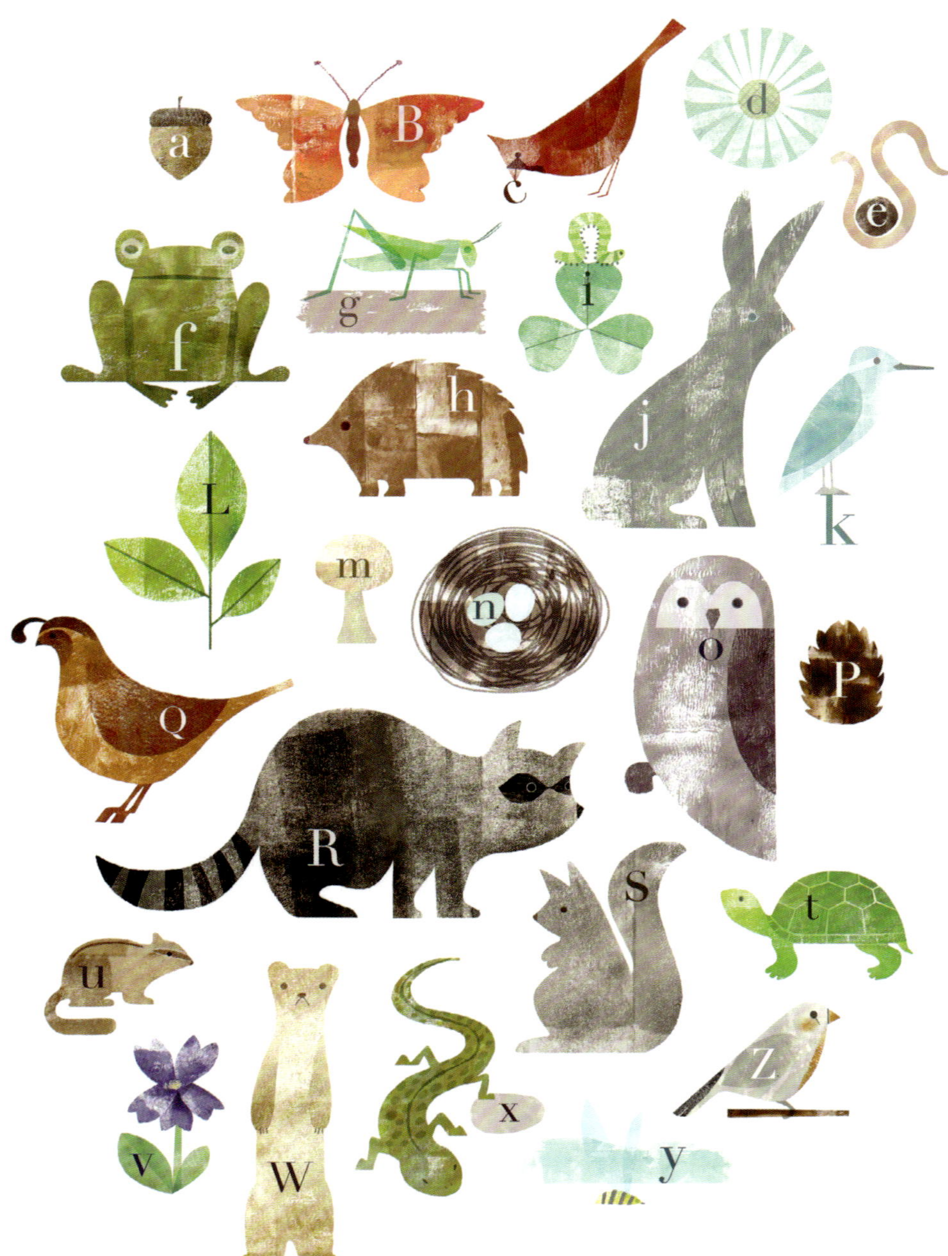

accorn~butterfly~cardinal~daisy~frog~grasshopper~hedgehog~inchworm~jack rabbit~kingfisher~leaf~mushroom~
nest~owl~pinecone~quail~squirrel~turtle~uinata chipmunk~violet~weasel~xantusiilae lizard~yellow jacket~zebra finch.

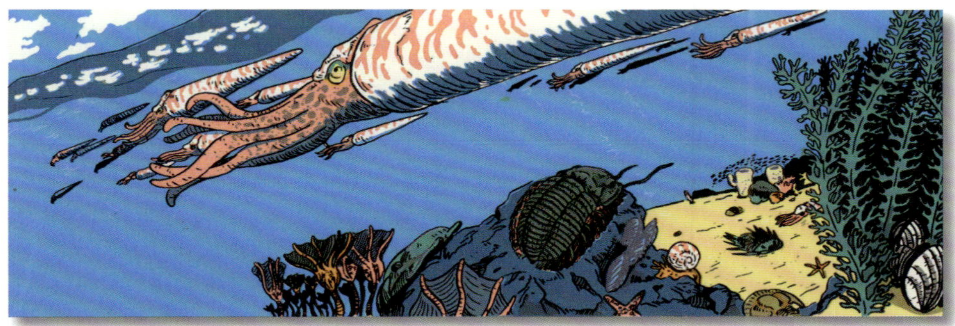

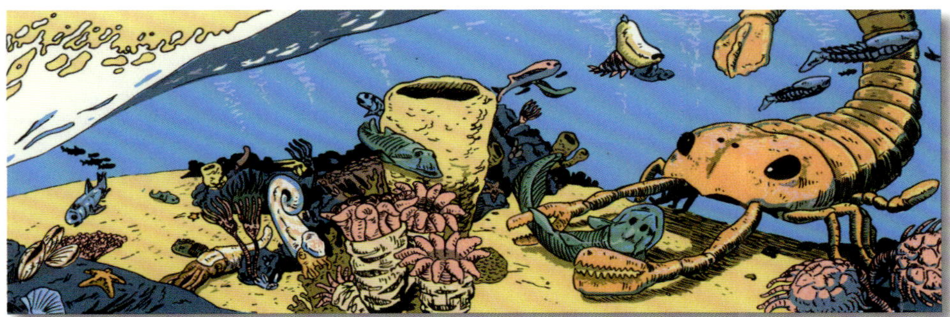

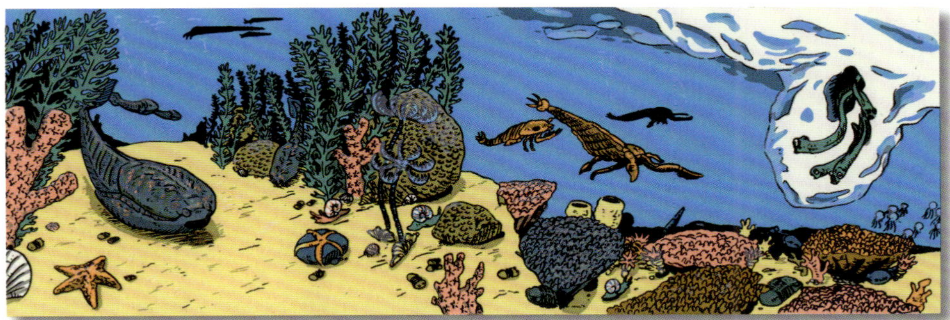

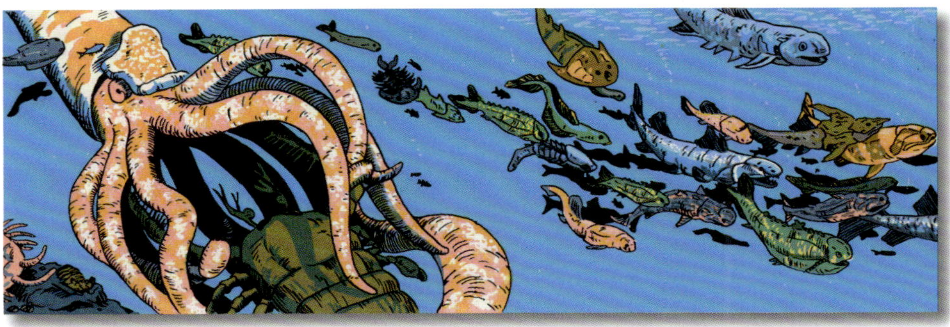

(L) BRONZE *Maria Carluccio* (R) *Estrella Vega*

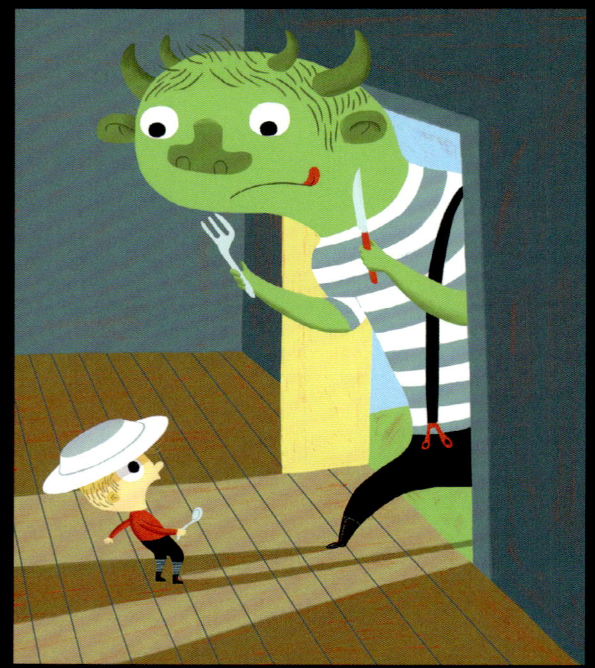

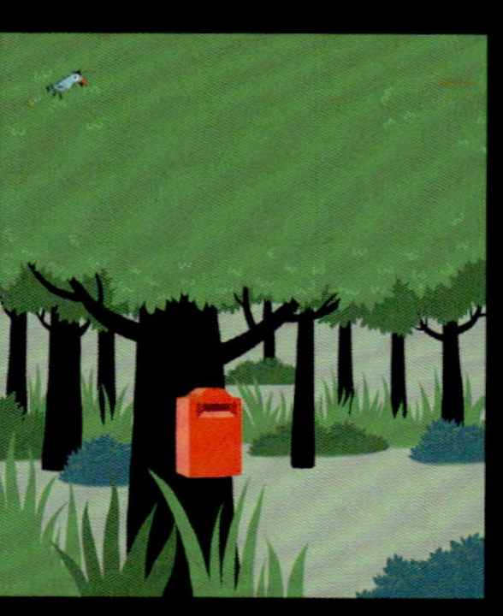

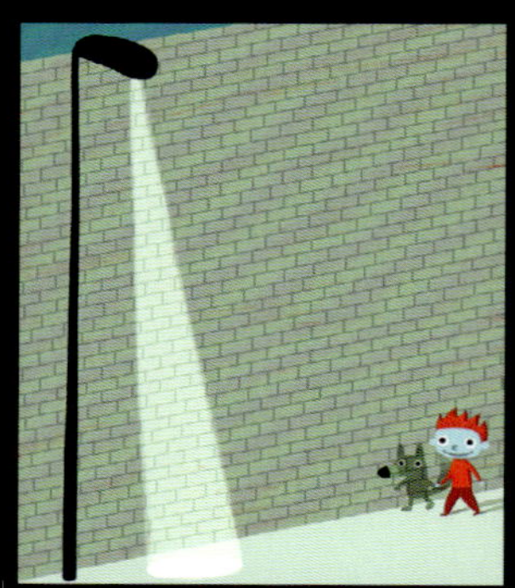

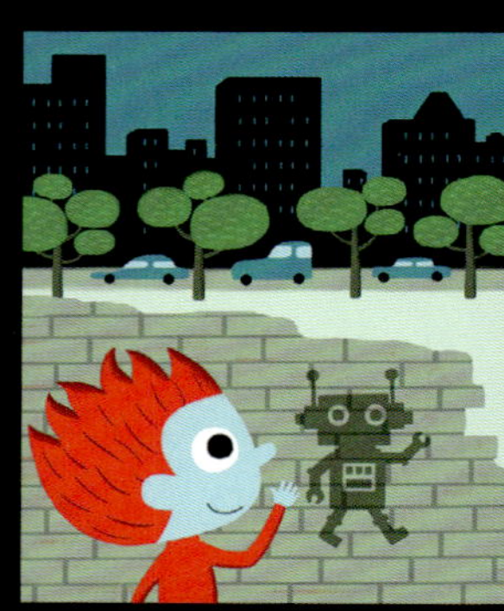

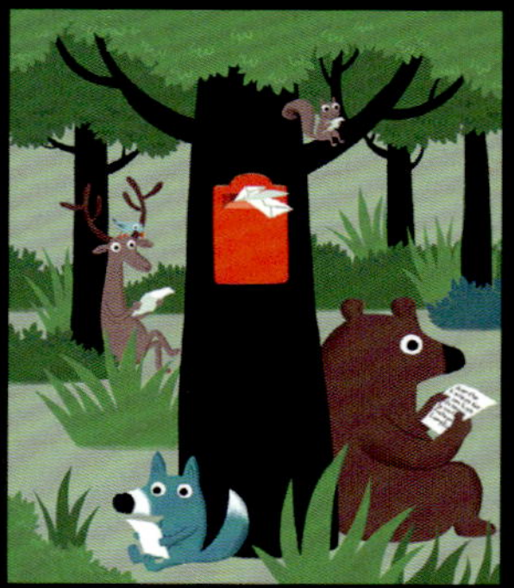

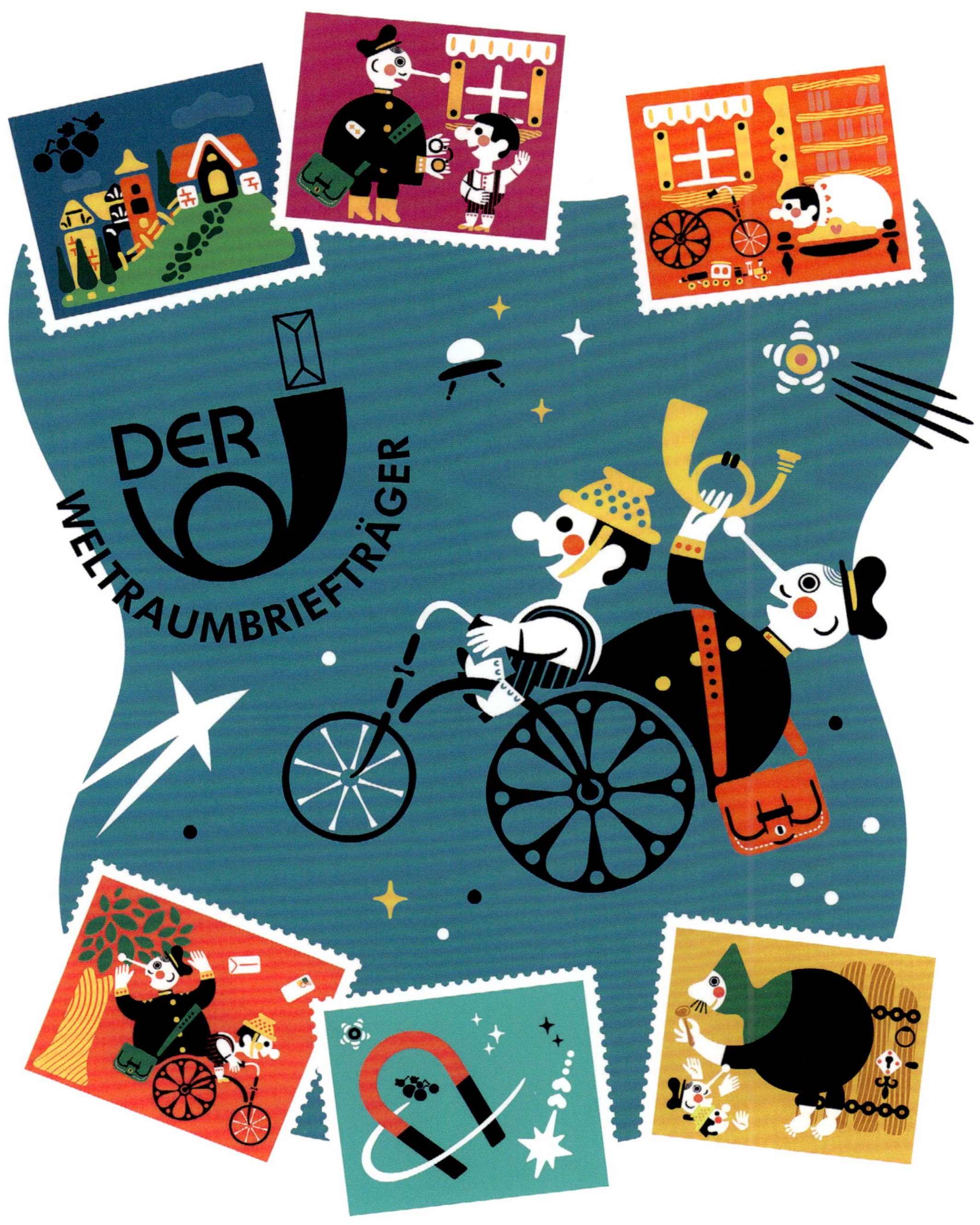

Studio Tipi

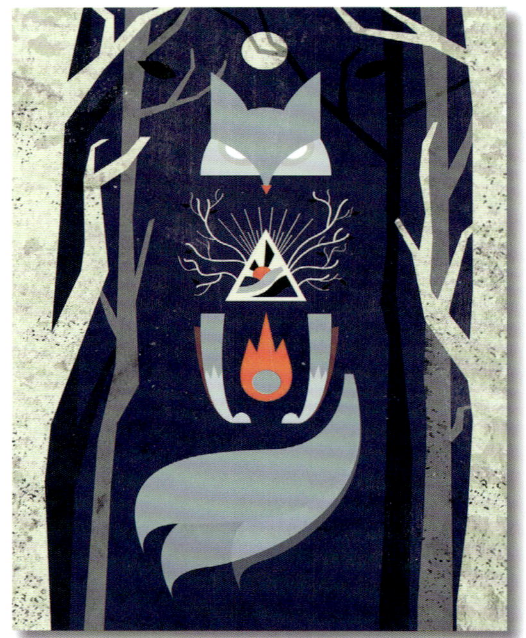
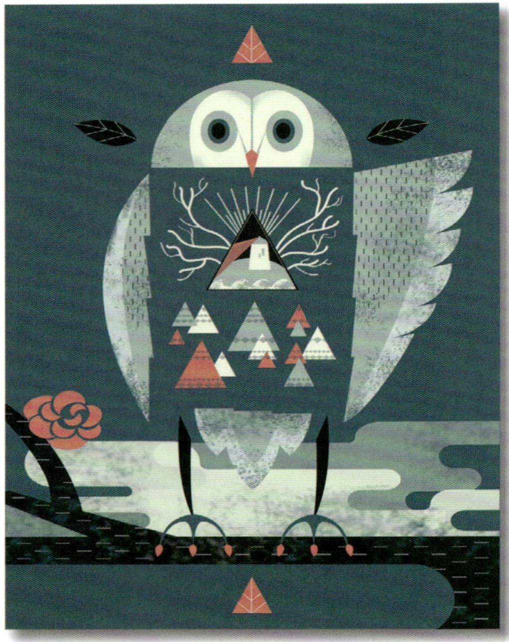
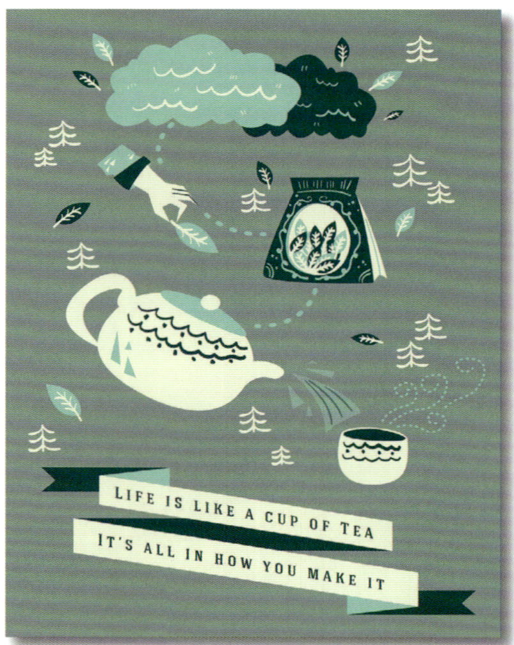

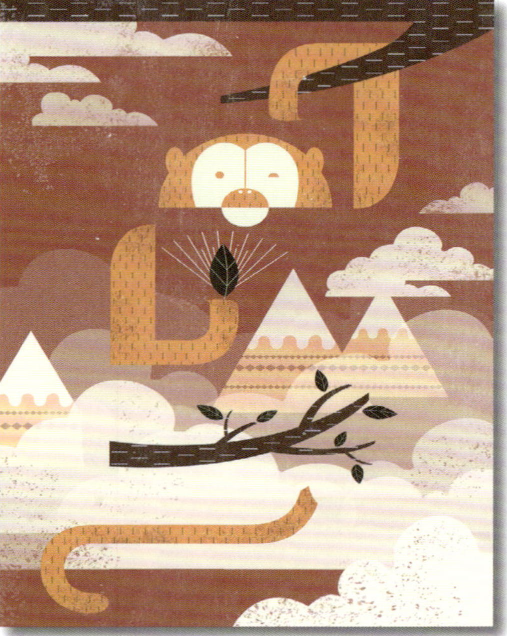

So Yeon Lim

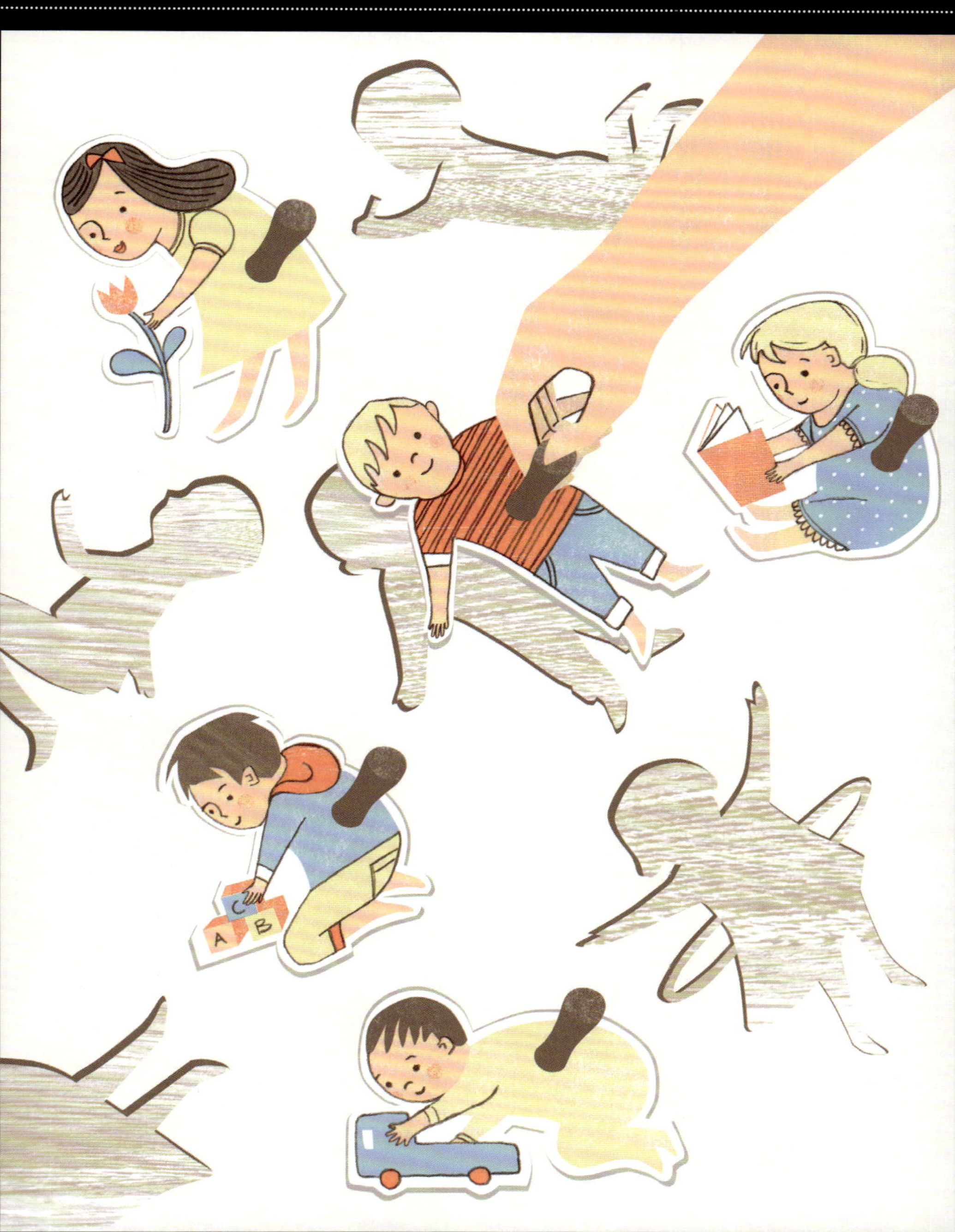

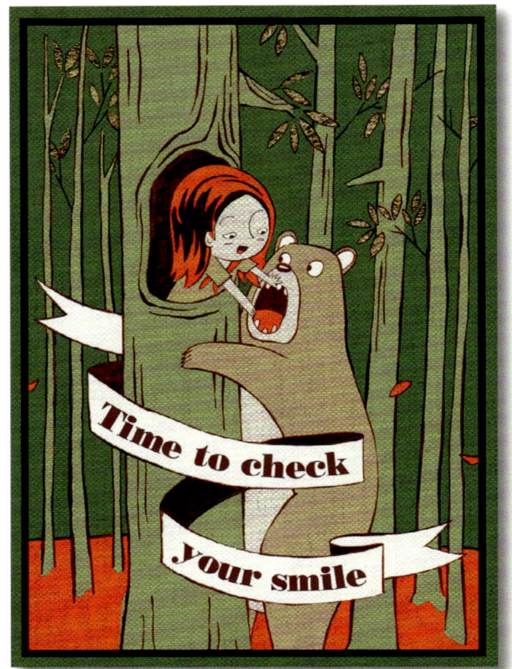

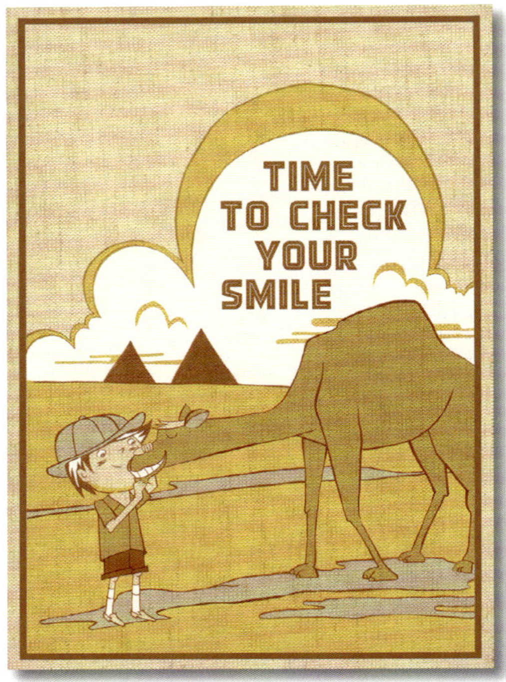

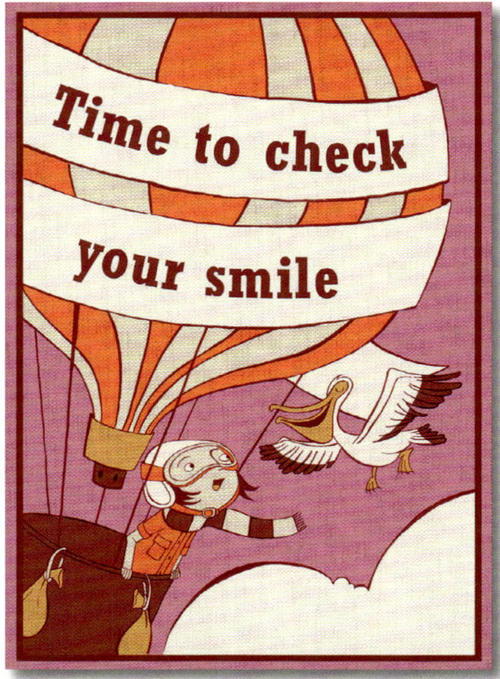

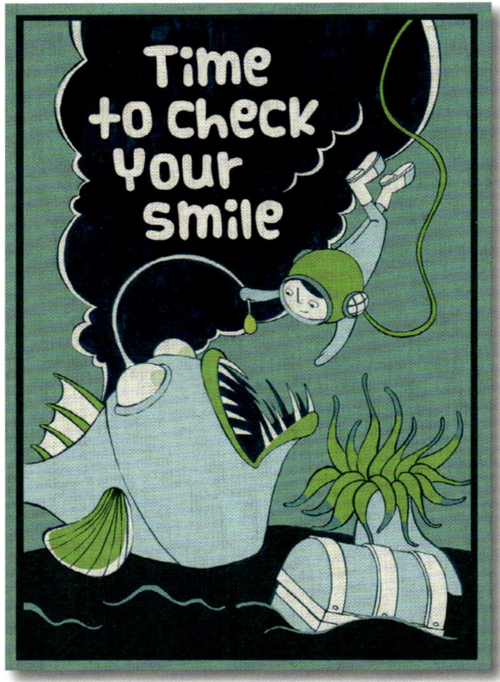

Isabel Roxas

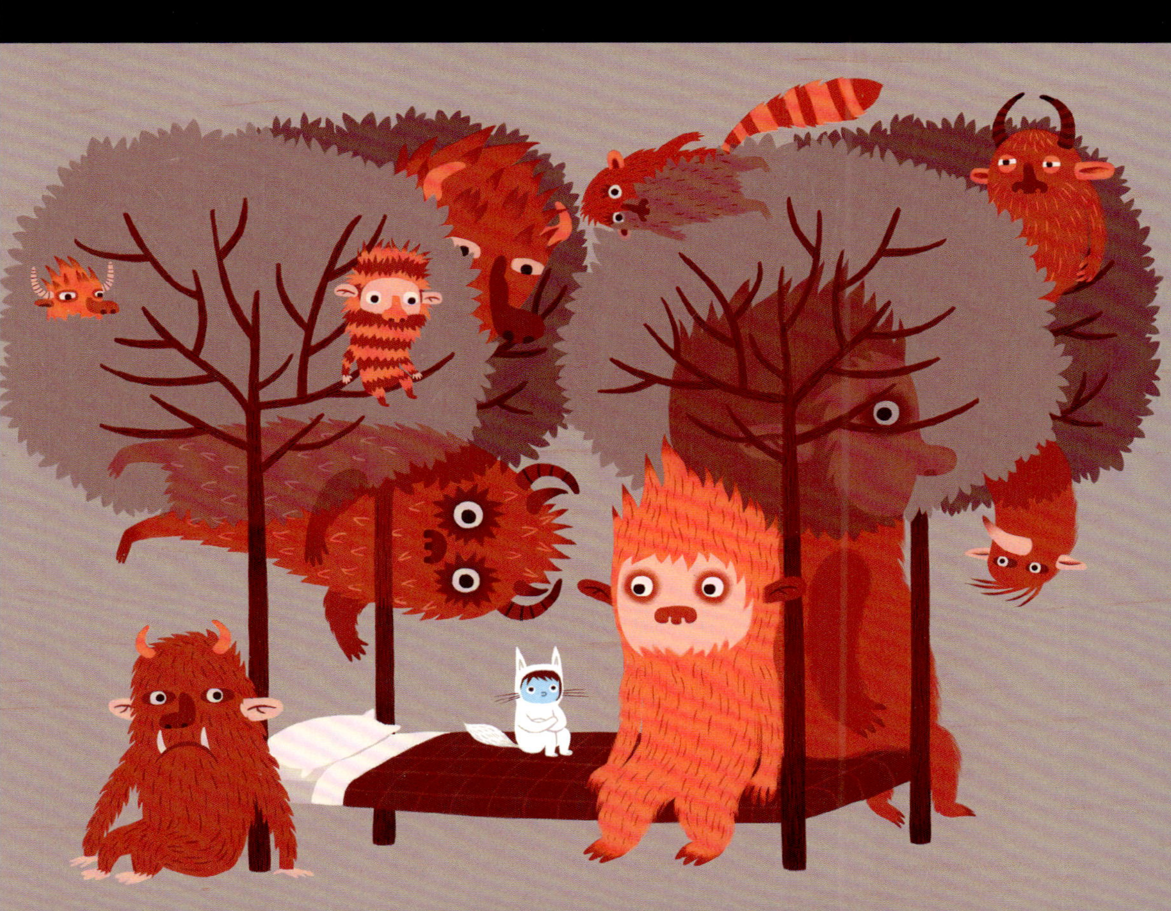

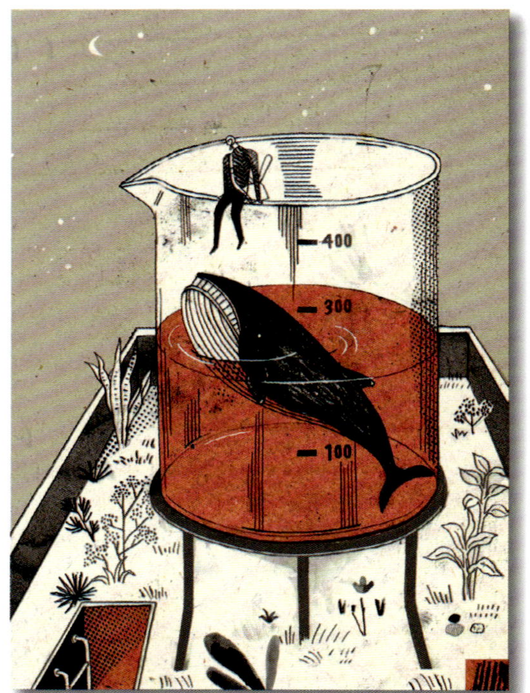

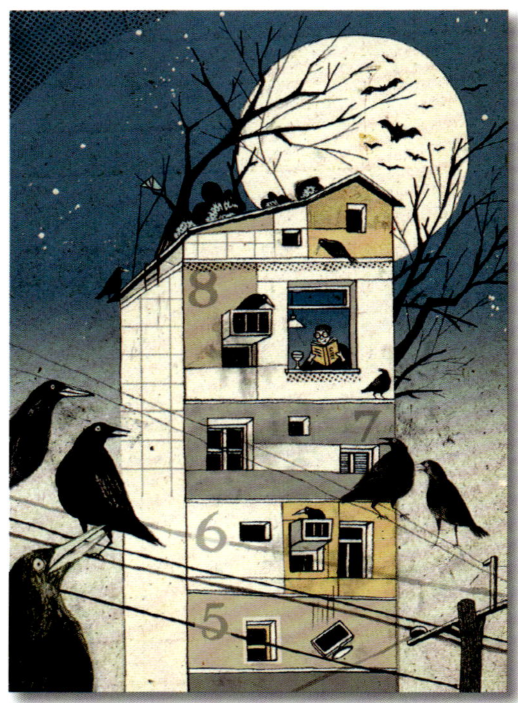

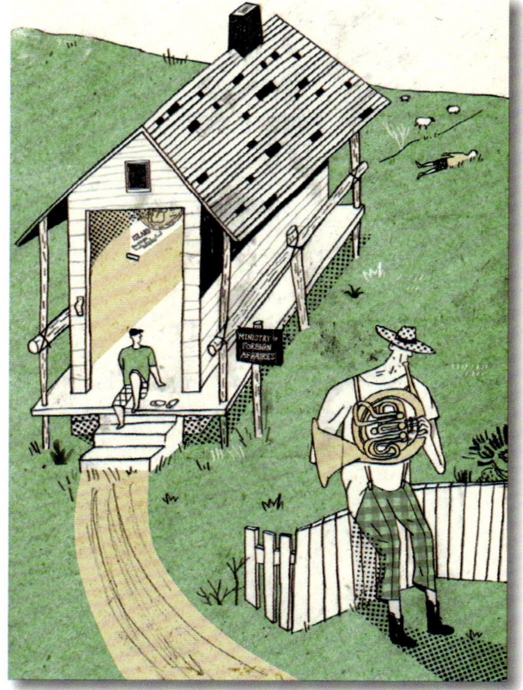

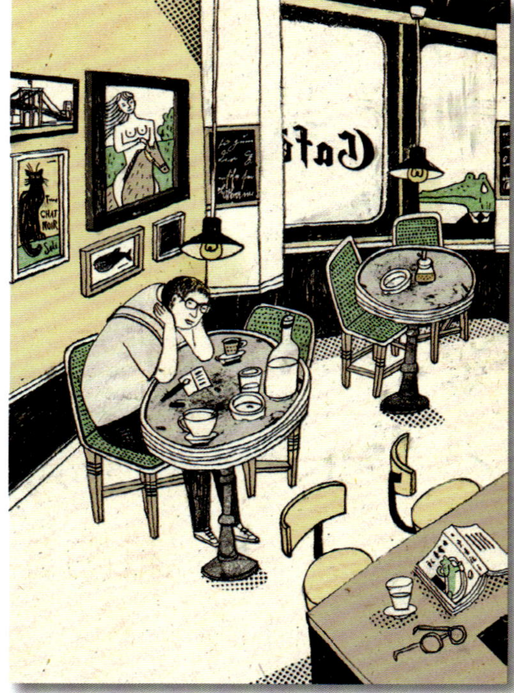

Chia-Chi Yu

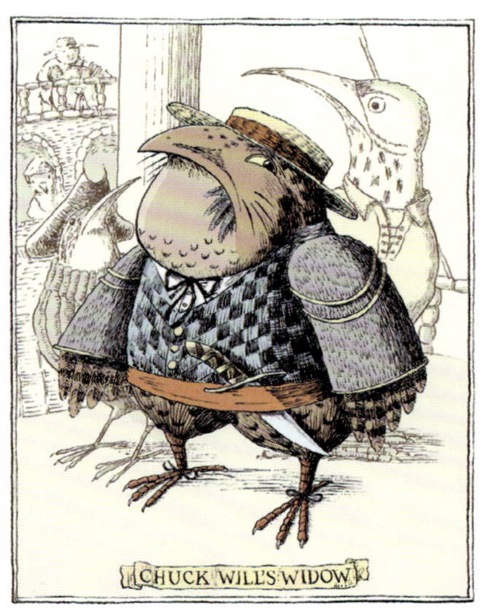
CHUCK WILL'S WIDOW

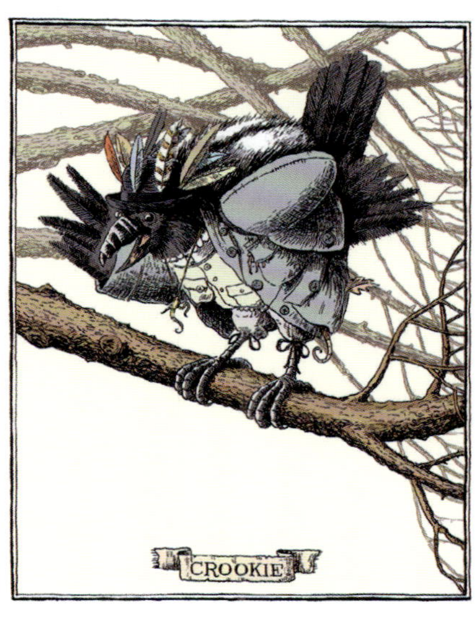
CROOKIE

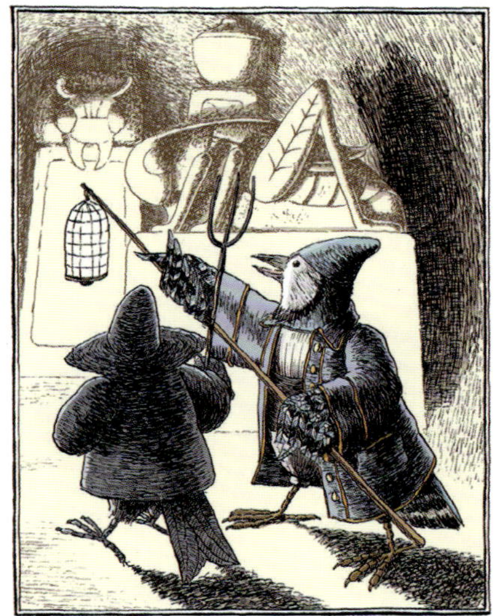

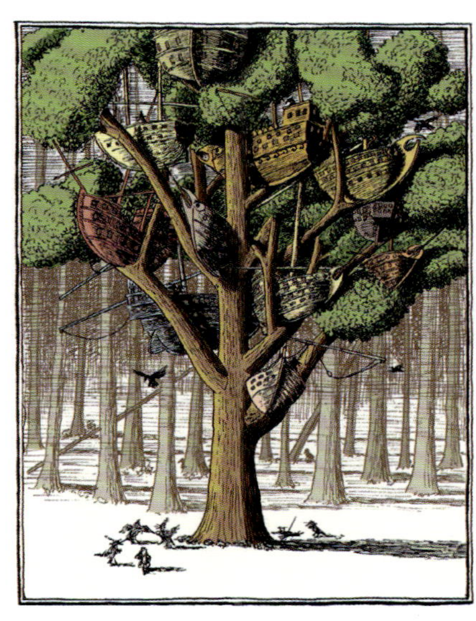

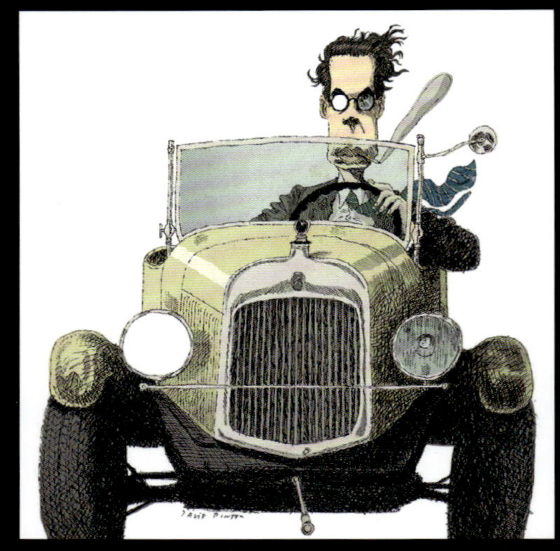

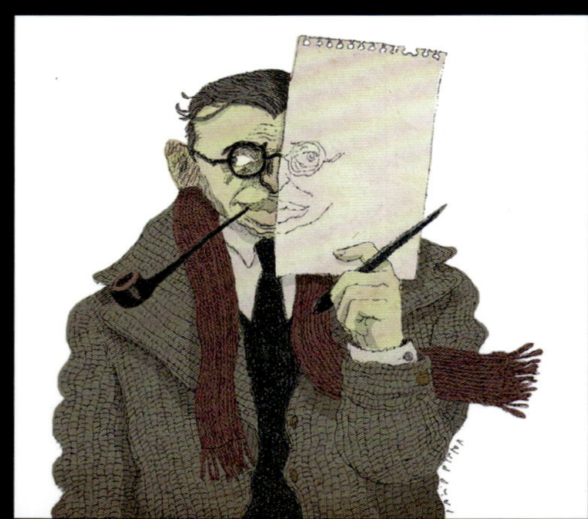

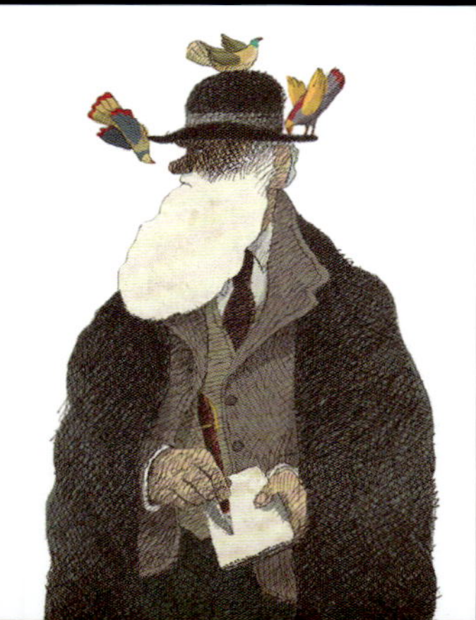

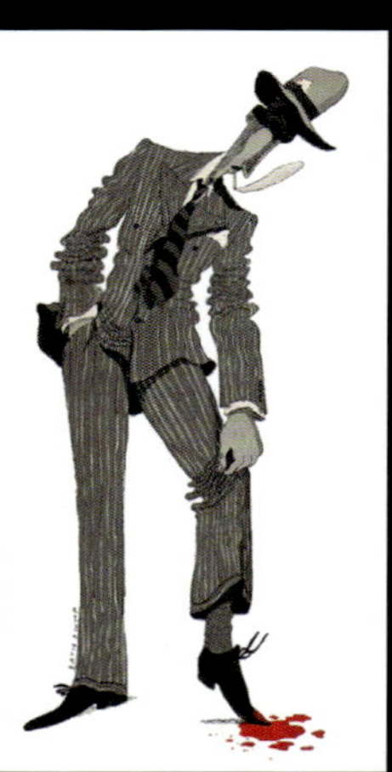

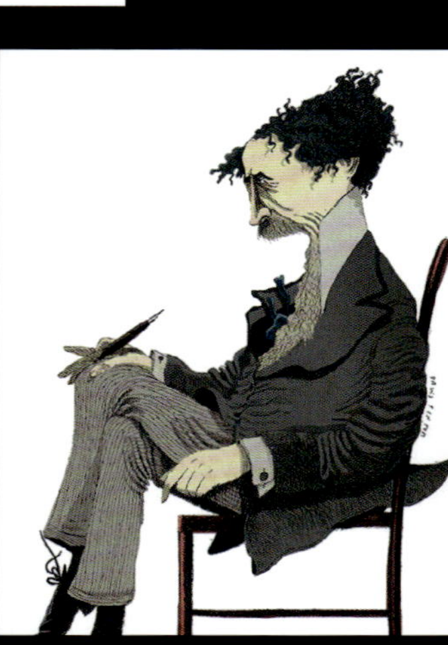

David Pintor

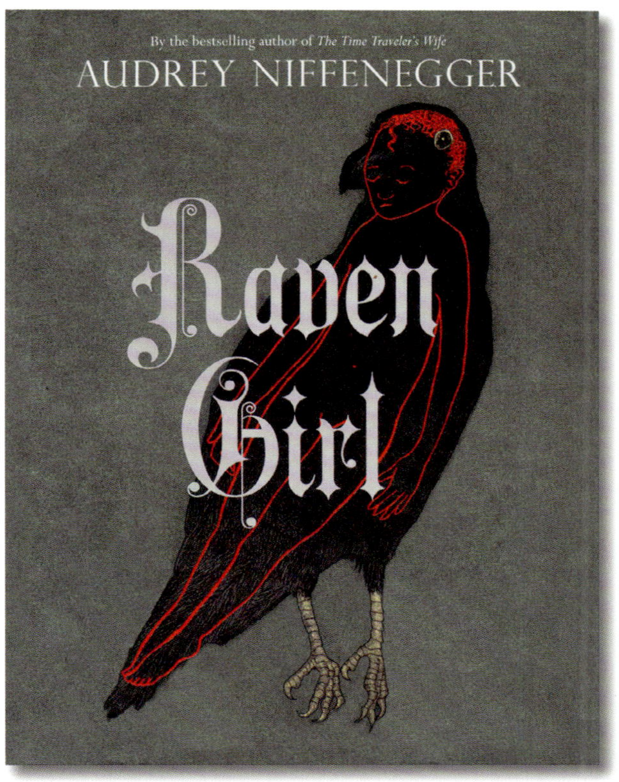

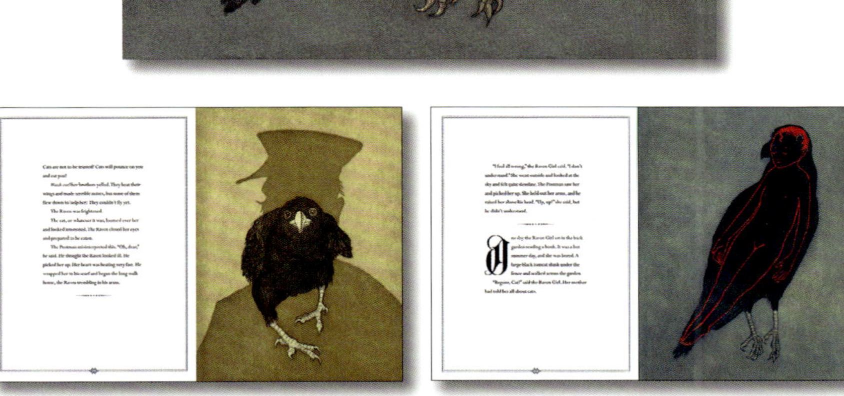

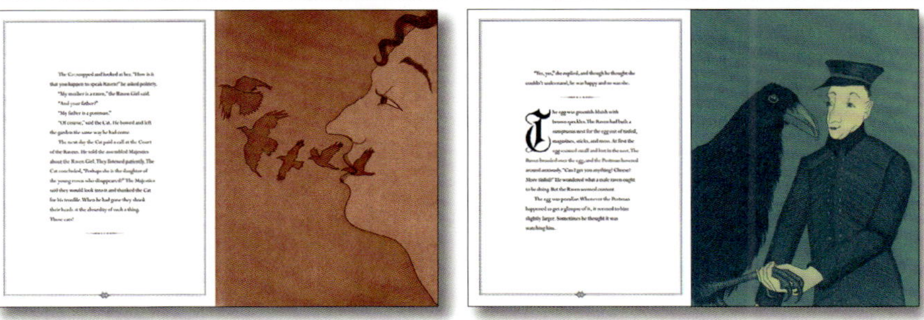

Audrey Niffenegger

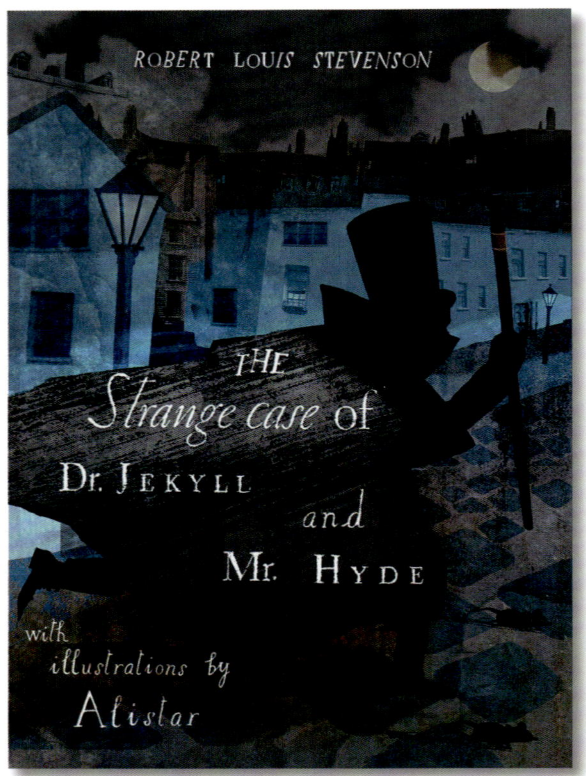

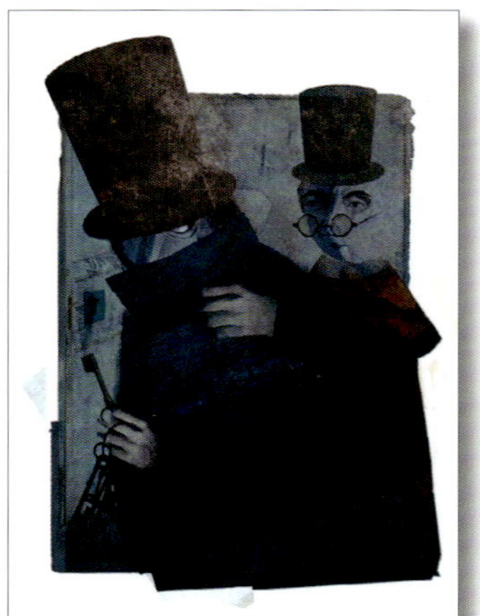 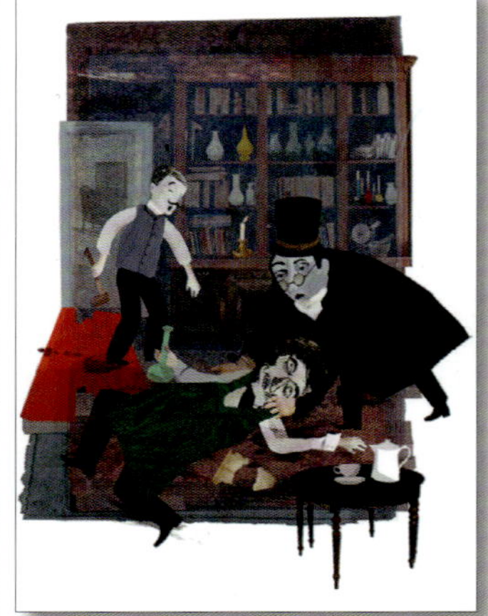 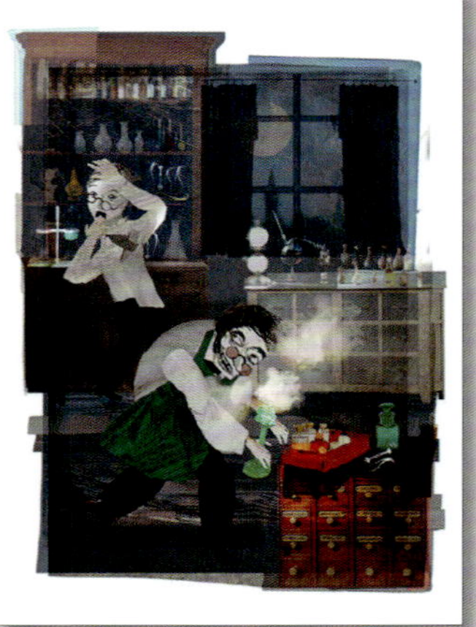

Alistar Khabuliani

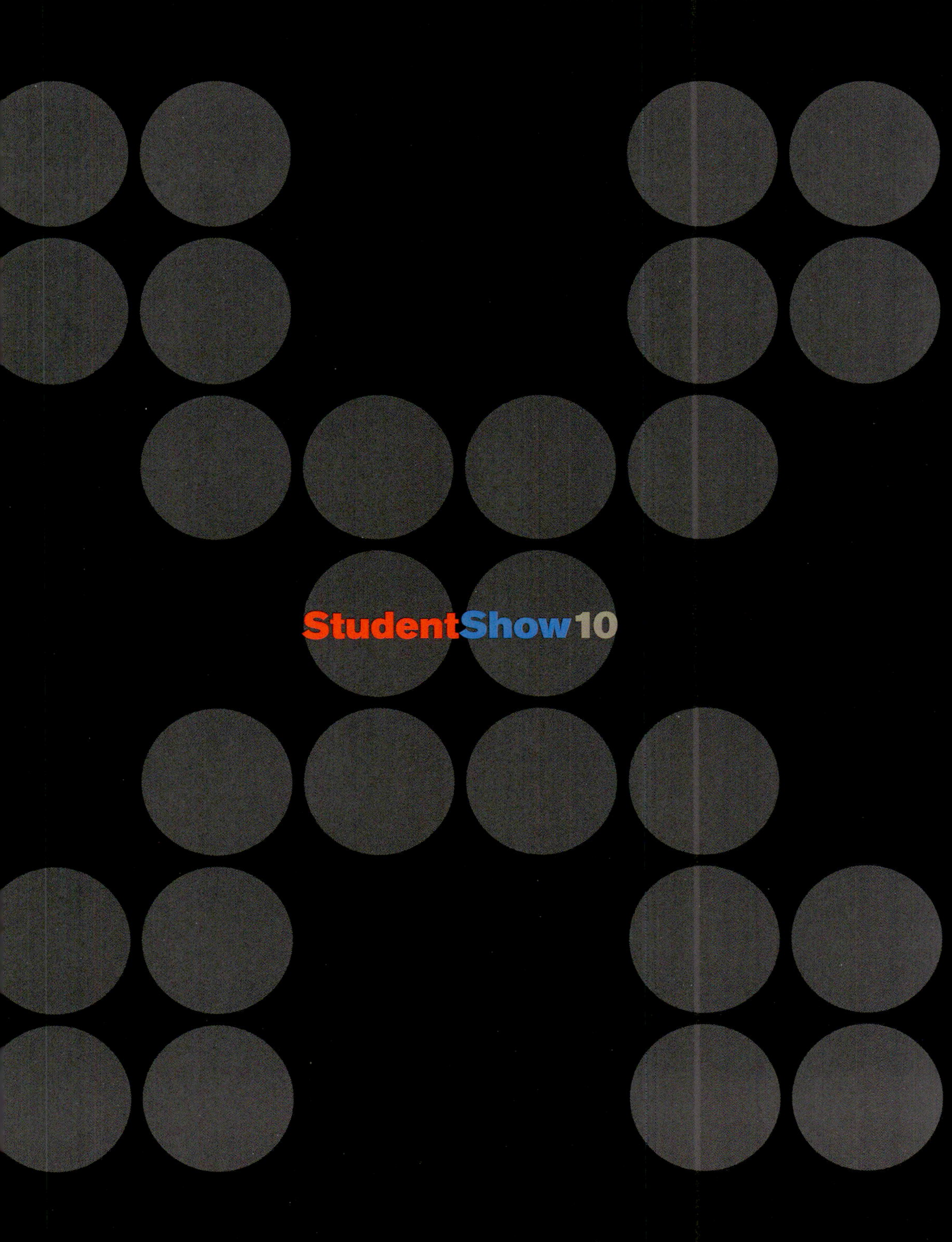
StudentShow 10

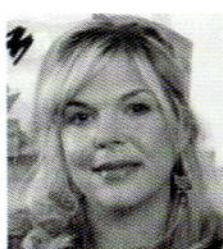

Megan Berkheiser

Megan is an illustrator who lived and worked in New York City for over ten years before moving to Savannah, Georgia. Megan meticulously constructs three-dimensional tabletop sets for her illustrations which she then lights and photographs. Her work can be seen in the editorial, advertising and book markets. Clients include the *New York Times*, *Wall Street Journal*, *Time Magazine*, *Forbes*, *Popular Science*, *Oprah Magazine*, Teleflora, Arbys, United Airlines, Abelson-Taylor Advertising and MTA, Arts for Transit. The Society of Illustrators, *American Illustration*, *3x3 Annual* and The Society of Illustrators Los Angeles have recognized Megan's work. Megan taught illustration at the University of the Arts for ten years, and is currently a professor of illustration at Savannah College of Art and Design.

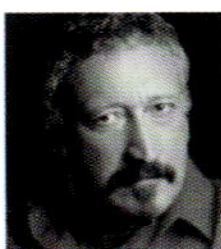

Alan Male

Alan is an illustrator, writer and academic. He directed the illustration course at Falmouth University between 1993 and 2010, leading it to gain an international distinction for excellence. He was promoted to professor, is now director of study for illustration research and is a keynote speaker on the international stage. Alan is the author of *Illustration: A Theoretical and Contextual Perspective*, a textbook published worldwide. His next book, *Illustration: Meeting the Brief* will be published later this year. As an illustrator, Alan has won numerous awards including gold from the Society of Illustrators LA and a Texas Bluebonnet for children's books. He has exhibited internationally and has work in New York State Museum's permanent collection.

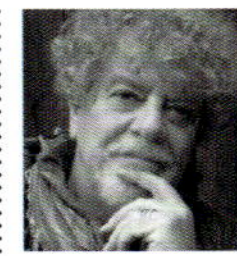

Jean-Christian Knaff

Jean-Christian first studied linguistics at the Université Stendhal in Grenoble, France, where he achieved an MA in English linguistics and Education. As an illustrator, his works have been published in such magazines as *GQ*, *Life*, *Die Zeit*, *New Scientist*, *Cosmopolitan*, ww-*Stern*, *Marie Claire* and *Vogue*. His animation, *The Wild, Wild Circus Company* was nominated for the Nicktoons Animation Festival in the US and is currently aired on the YTV network in Canada. He won the UNICEF award at Annecy International Animation Film Festival in and a gold medal at the New York International Animation Film Festival for the animation made after his book *Manhattan*. His latest published children's books are *Hugo Légo* and *Adam Elefant*.

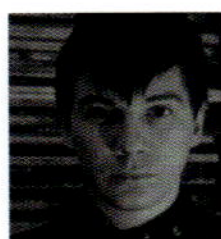

John Malta

John was born in East Cleveland, Ohio and currently lives and works in New York City. John is a recipient of the 2012 Xeric grant for Comic Book Self-Publishers and has exhibited his work in Taiwan, Australia, Vancouver, New York City, Los Angeles, San Francisco, Portland and widely across the Midwest. He has drawn pictures for a myriad companies and publications including the *New York Times*, *Vice Magazine*, *AARP: Life Reimagined*, Dickies Workwear, Lands' End Canvas, *Plansponsor Magazine* and *Surfing Magazine*. Malta designs t-shirts for Blood Is the New Black and edits and self-publishes *Universal Slime*, an annual comics and illustration anthology. His work has been recognized by *3x3 Annual*, *American Illustration* and the Society of Illustrators.

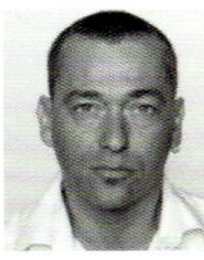

Thilo Rothacker

Thilo is an illustrator based in Stuttgart, Germany. He has studied illustration and design with Heinz Edelmann and works mainly for newspapers and magazines. A partial list of editorial clients includes *Der Spiegel*, the *New York Times*, *le Figaro*, *Frankfurter Allgemeine Zeitung* and *Vanity Fair*. His work has received recognition from the Society of Illustrators, *American Illustration* and *Lürzer's Archive*. He is member of the Art Directors Club of Germany and teaches illustration at the Hochschule Konstanz University of Applied Sciences (HTWG).

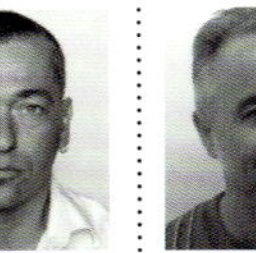

David Sandlin

David's drawings, prints, paintings and installations are in private and public collections worldwide, and his limited-edition artist's books are in the collections of several prominent libraries, including those of the Museum of Modern Art, New York University and Bard College. He has been the recipient of grants from the New York Foundation for the Arts, the Pollock-Krasner Foundation, the Swann Foundation and the Penny McCall Foundation. In 2010, Sandlin was awarded a fellowship at the Cullman Center for Scholars and Writers at the New York Public Library. Sandlin is also well known for his illustration work for the *New Yorker*, the *New York Times*, *Harper's Magazine* and other periodicals. His comics have been published in many anthologies, including *Raw* and *The Best American Comics 2009*, edited by Charles Burns.

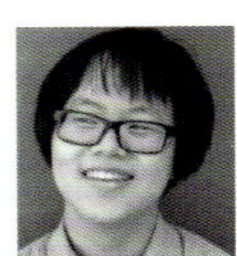

JooHee Yoon

JooHee is an illustrator currently based on the east coast of the United States and enjoys drawing and working with various printmaking techniques. Her illustrations have been published in many magazines and newspapers, including the *New York Times*, the *New Yorker*, the *Globe and Mail* and NPR. She has also exhibited her prints in galleries both in the US and Europe and has won awards from the Society of Illustrators, *Communication Arts*, *American Illustration* and *3x3*.

370, 371   GOLD

372   SILVER

373, 374   BRONZE

377, 398, 404, 405, 417,   DISTINGUISHED MERIT

375   MERIT

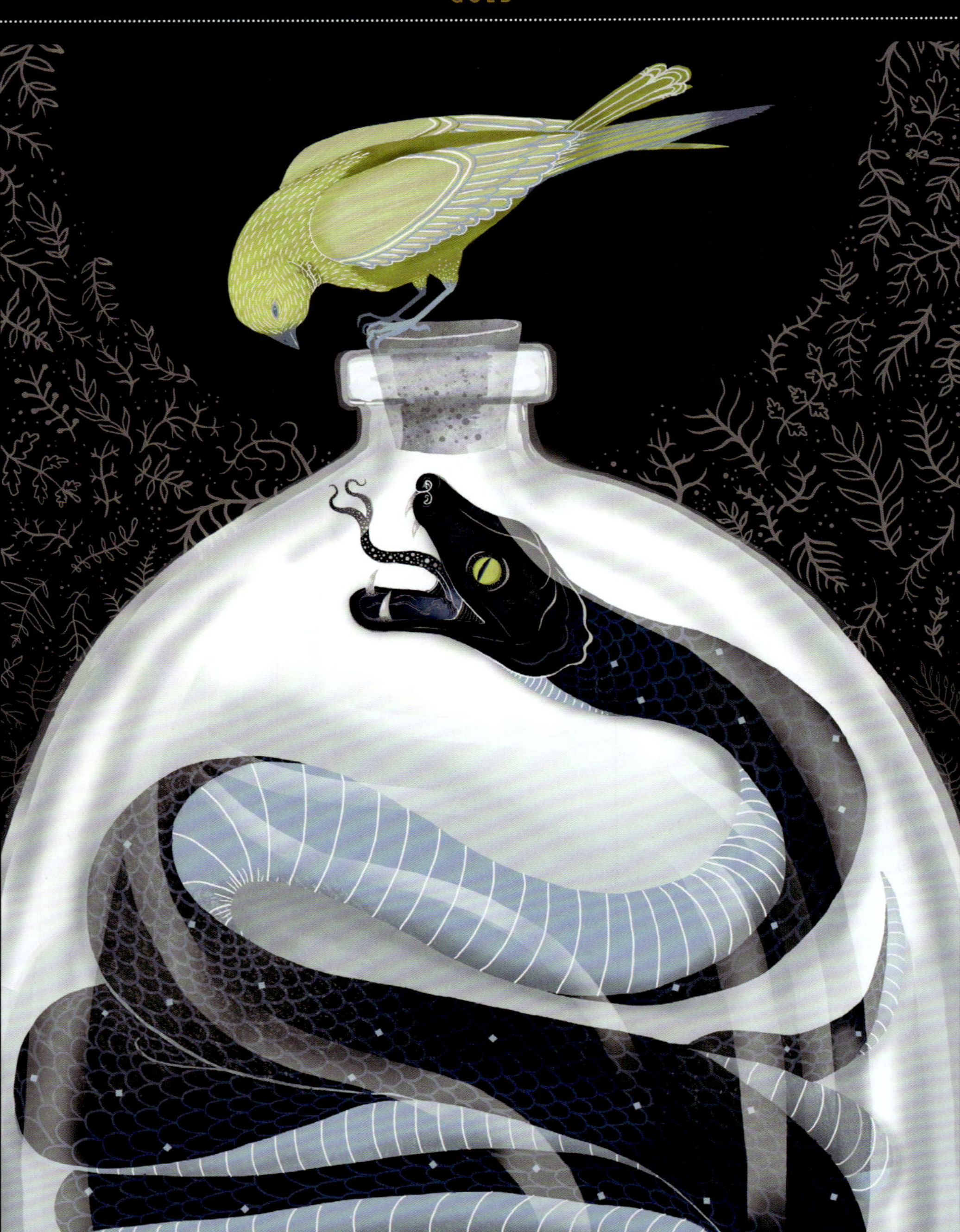

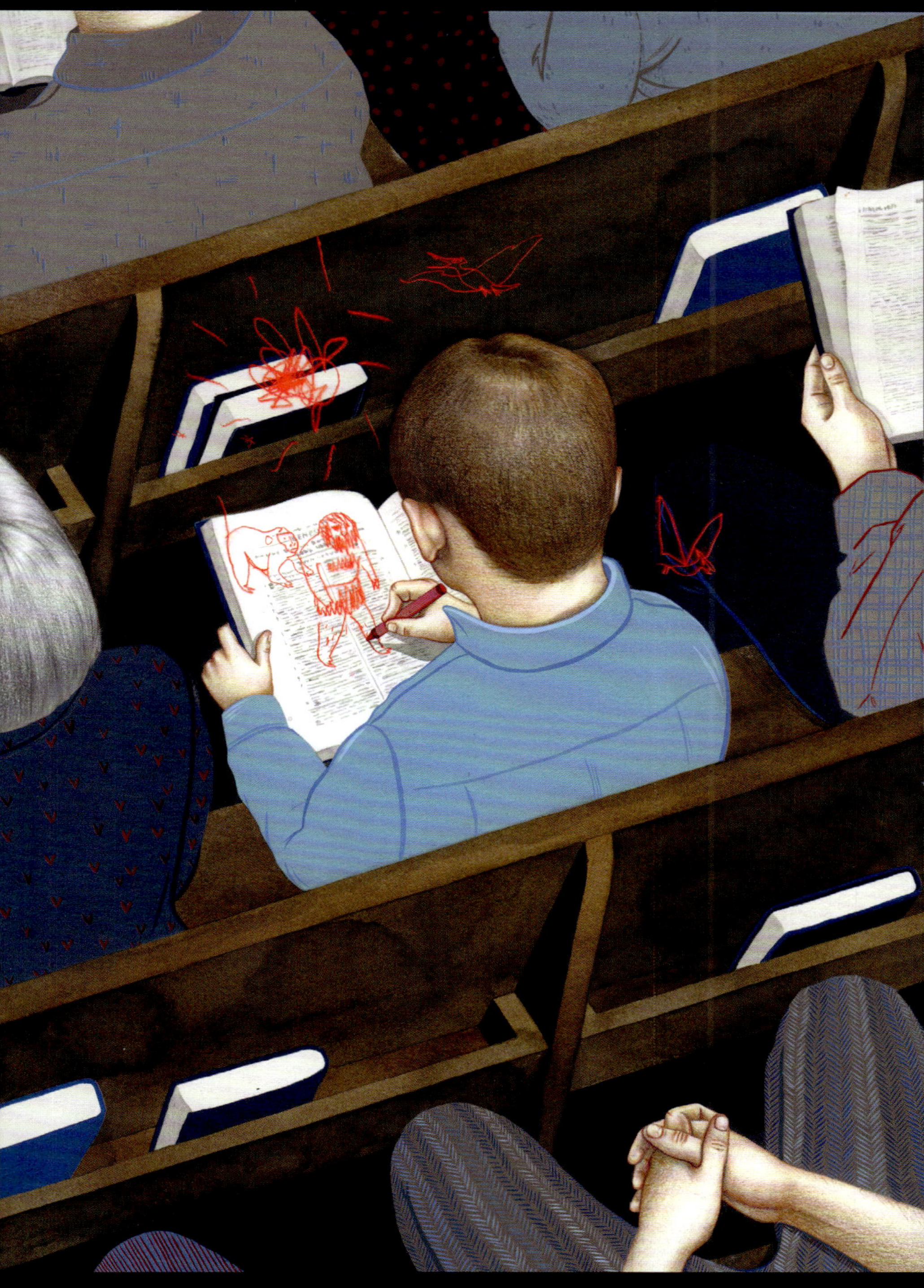

Monica Garwood

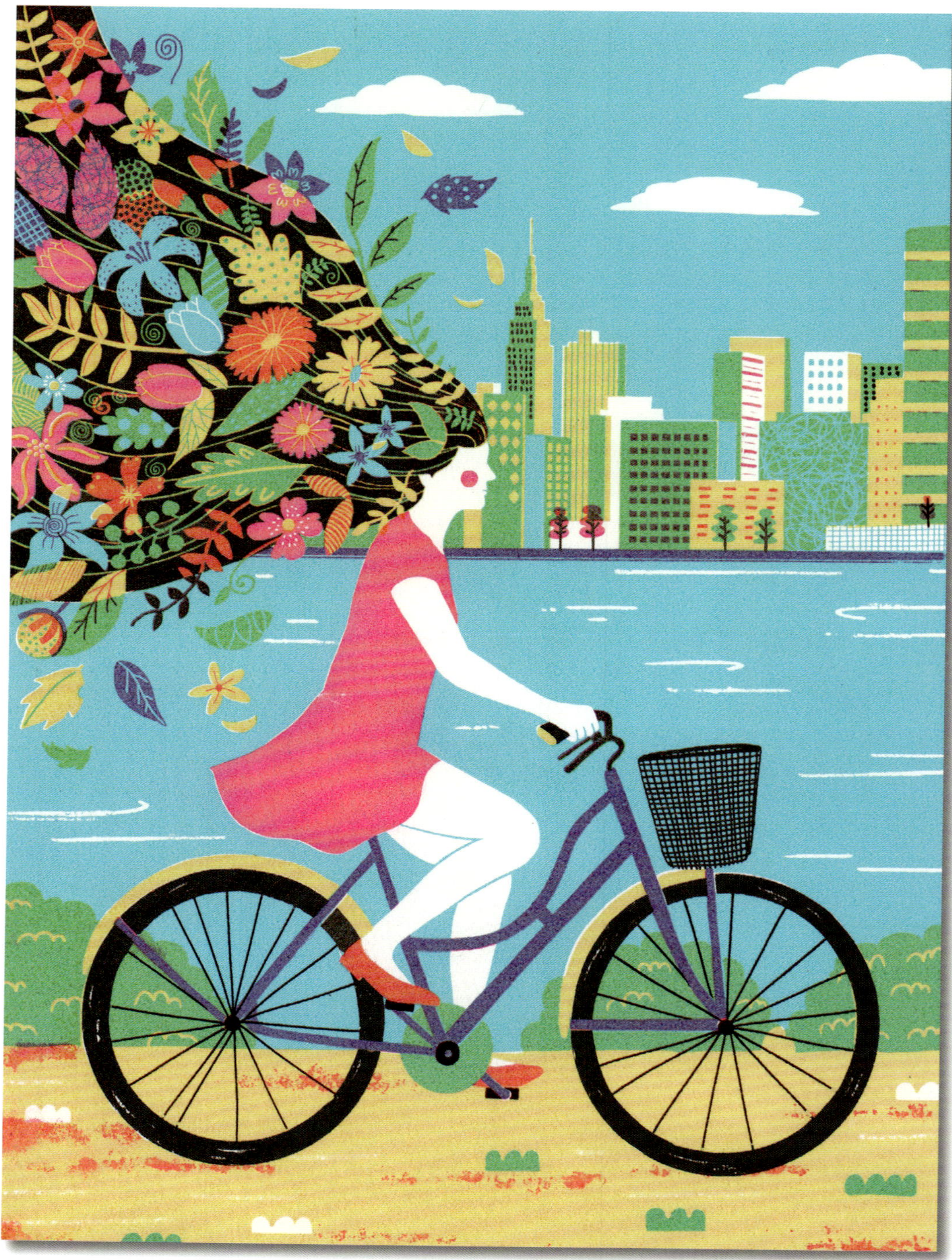

Boyoun Kim

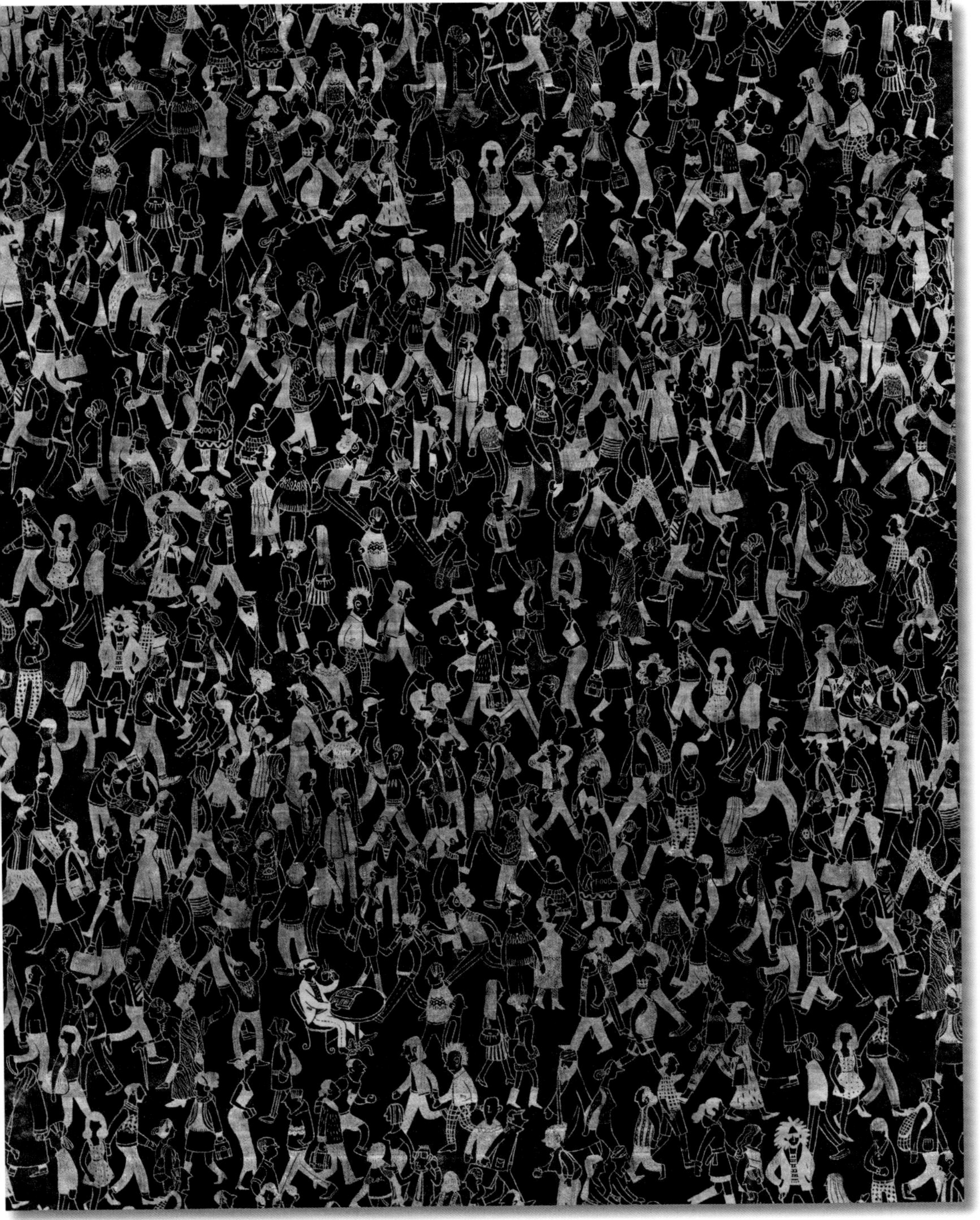

Ping Hua Chou

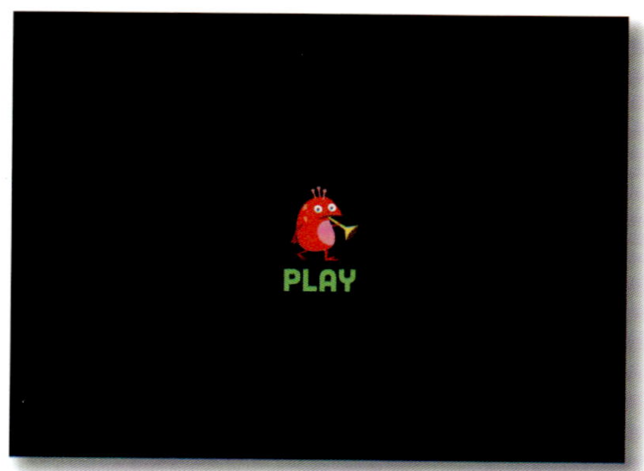

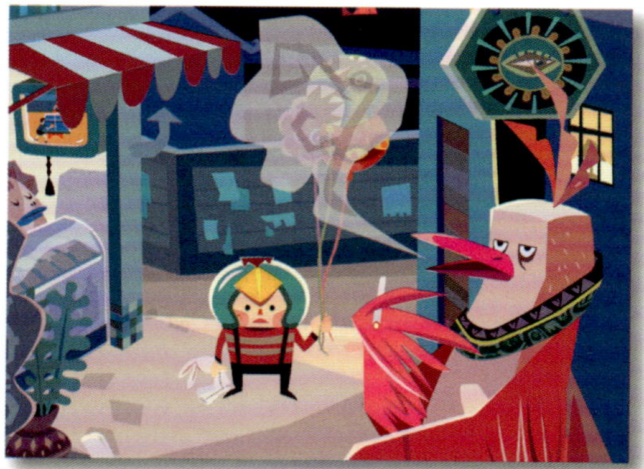

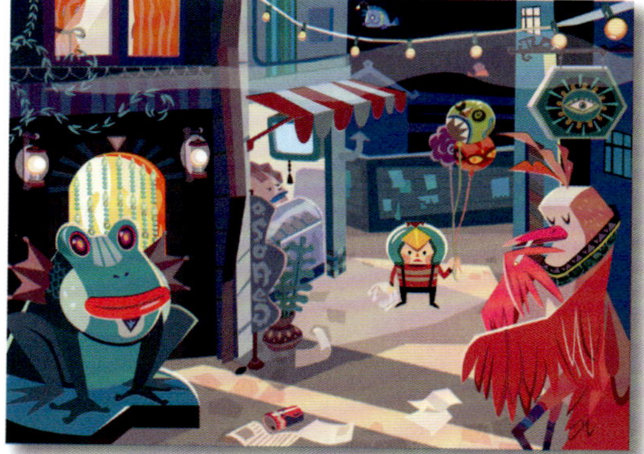

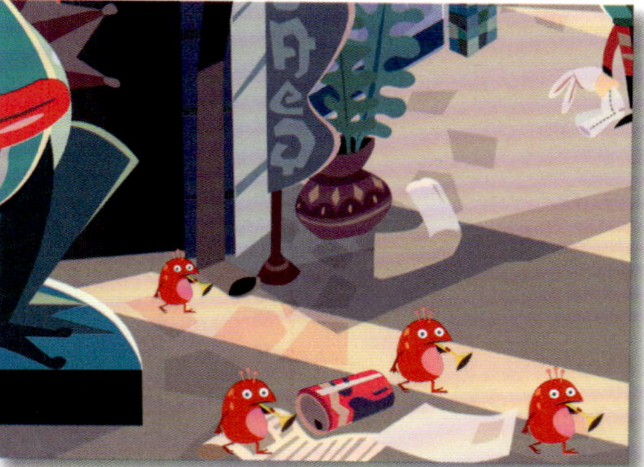

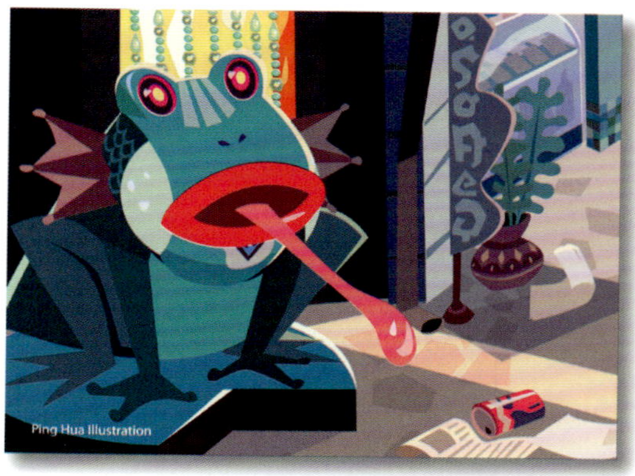

Ping Hua Chou

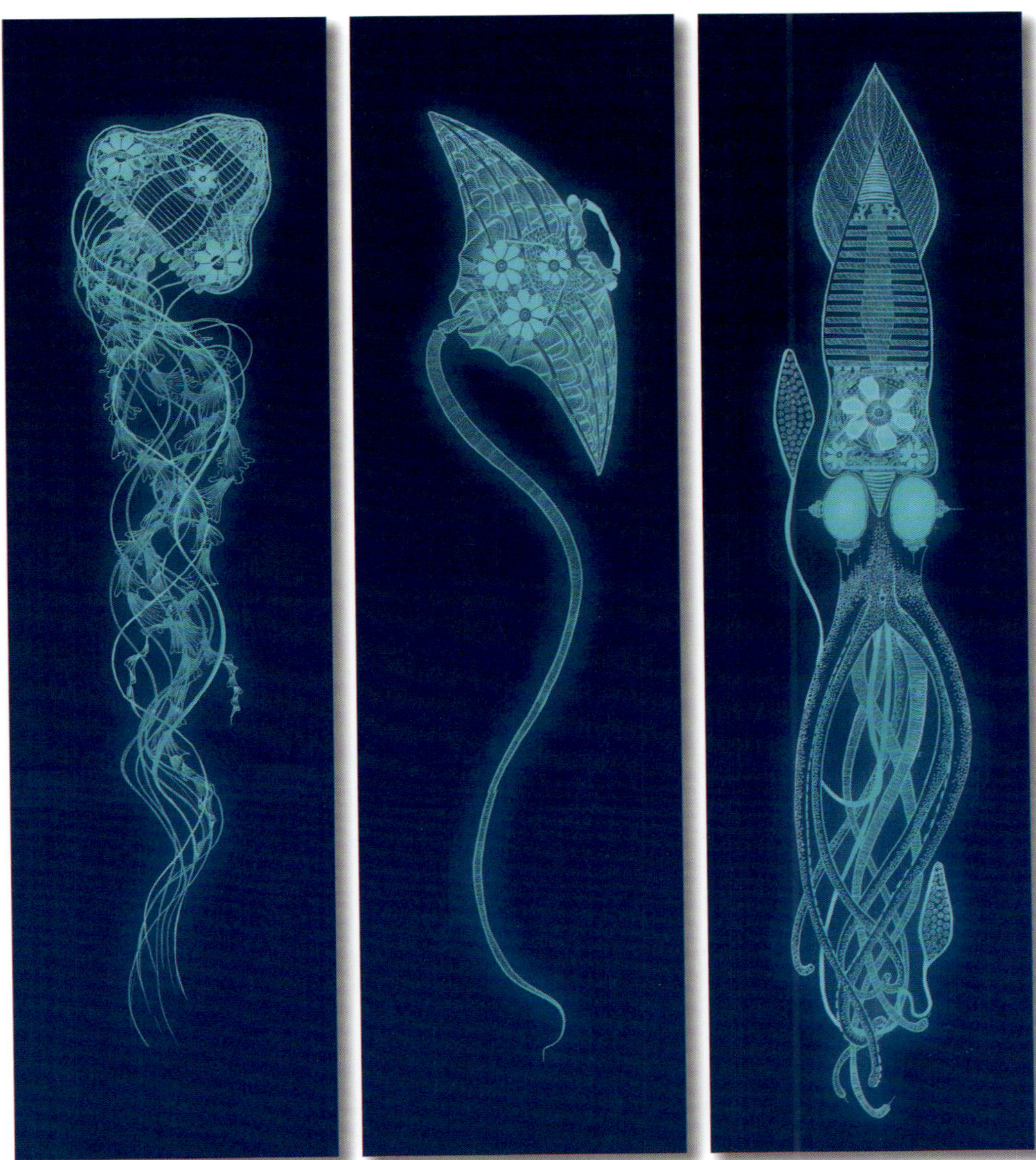

Liisa Aaltio

NED CORK CENTER
BALL
HORNS
Chicago CUBS
ROGER
CRAIG
PITCHER

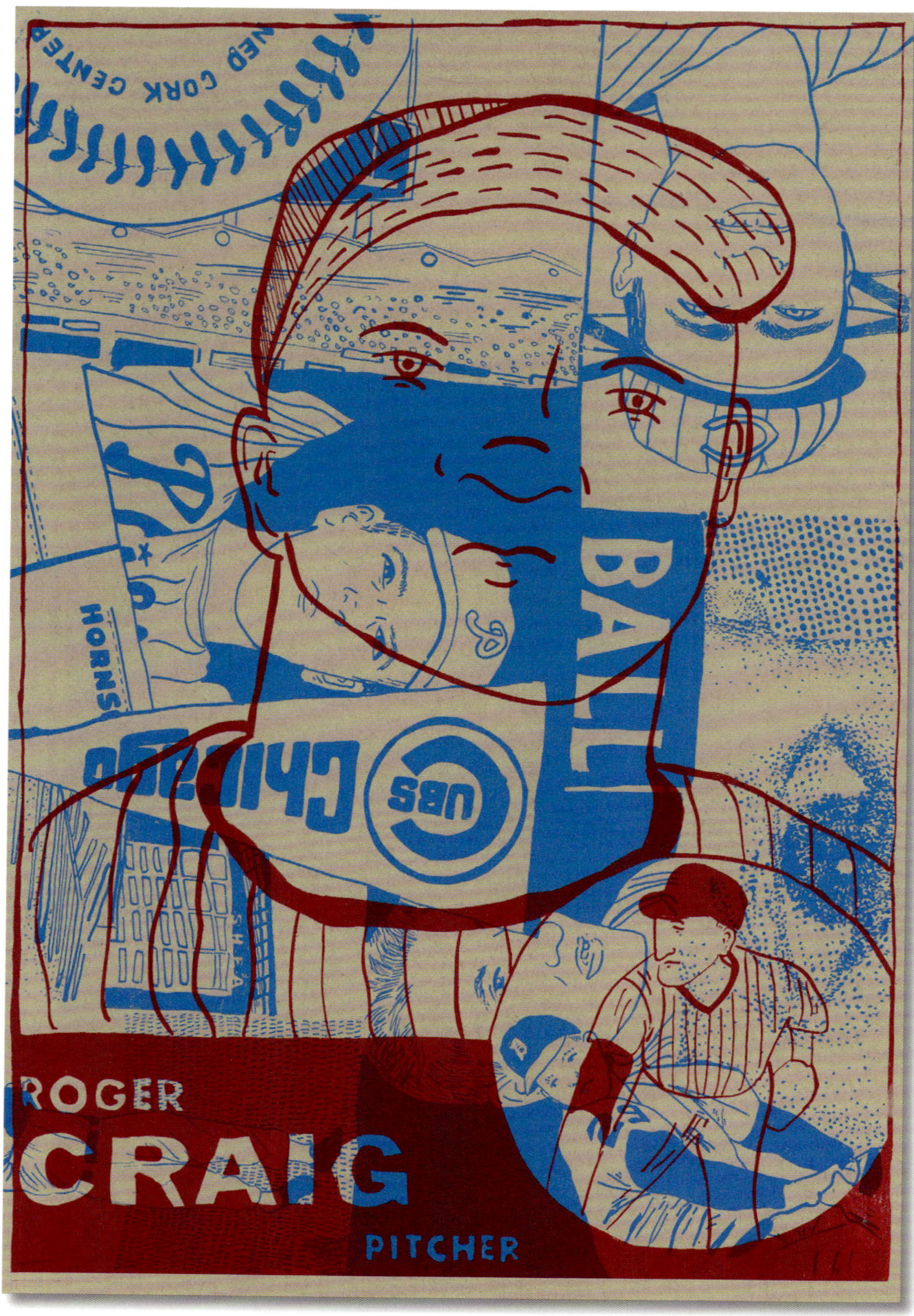

Katie Gross

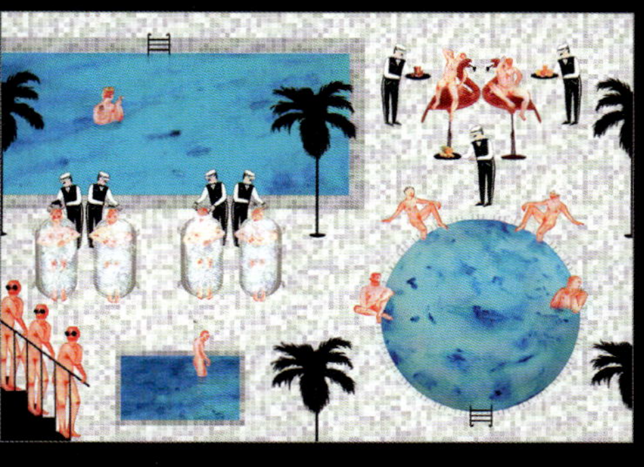
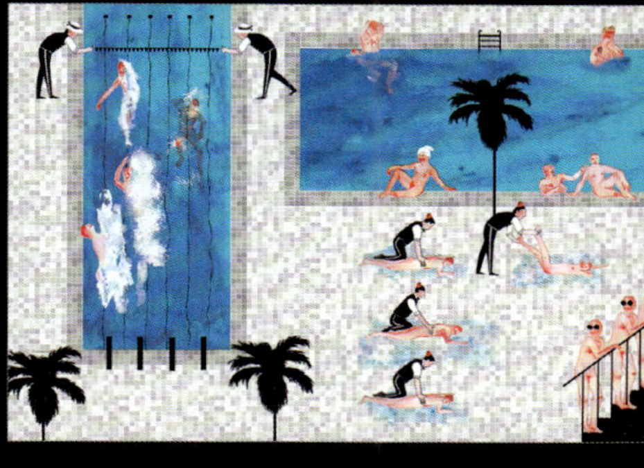
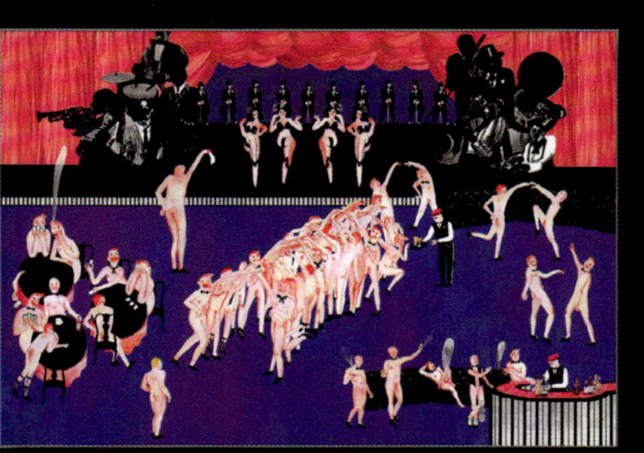
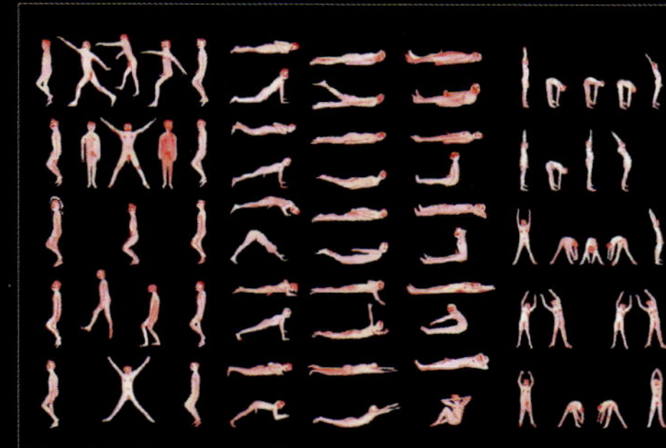

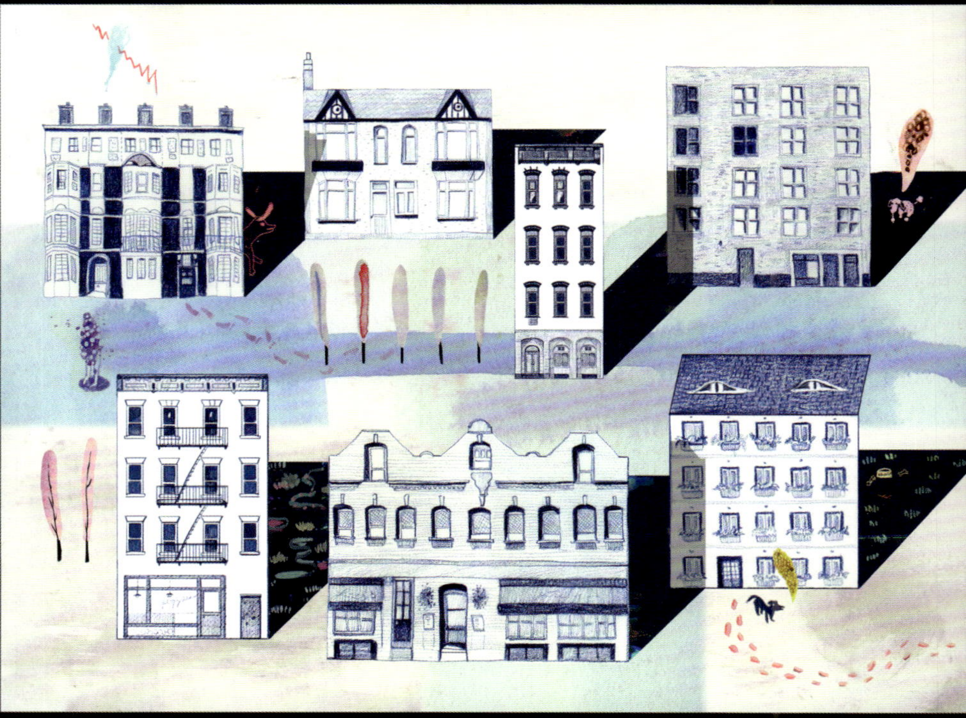

(T) DISTINGUISHED MERIT Tal Granot (B) Boyeon Choi

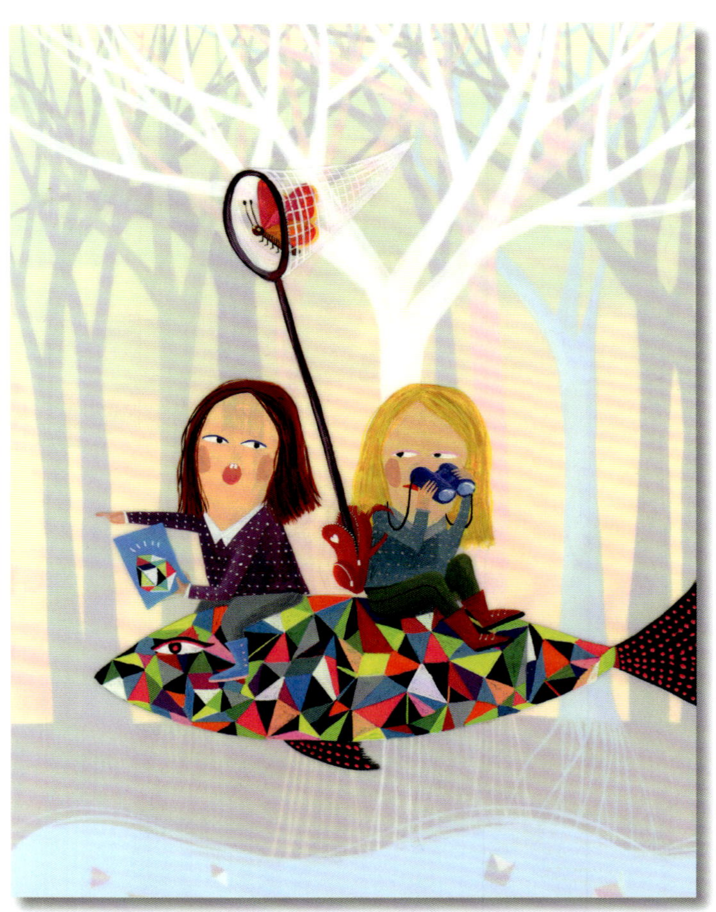

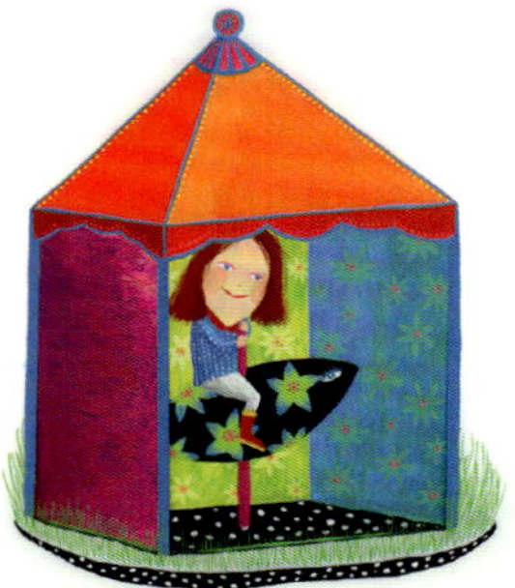
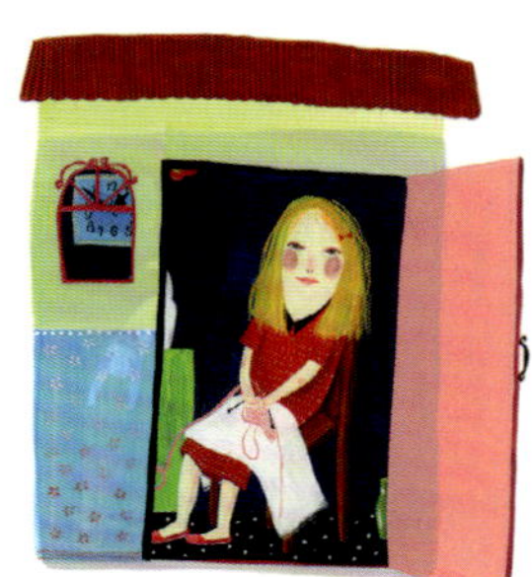
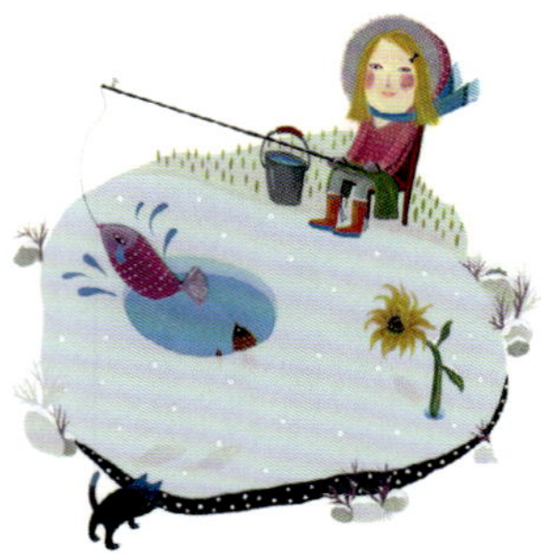

Ayumi Takahashi

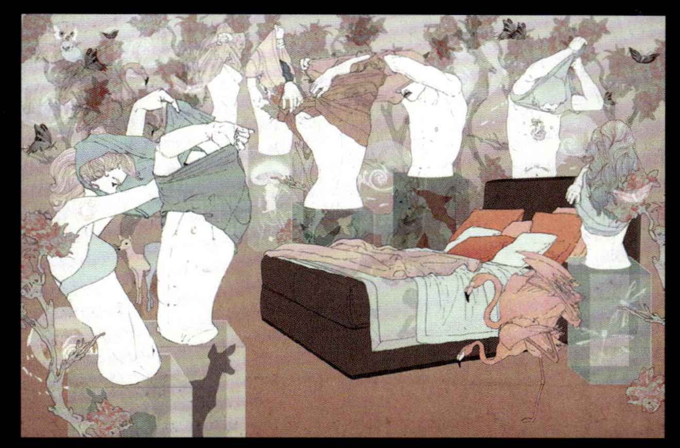

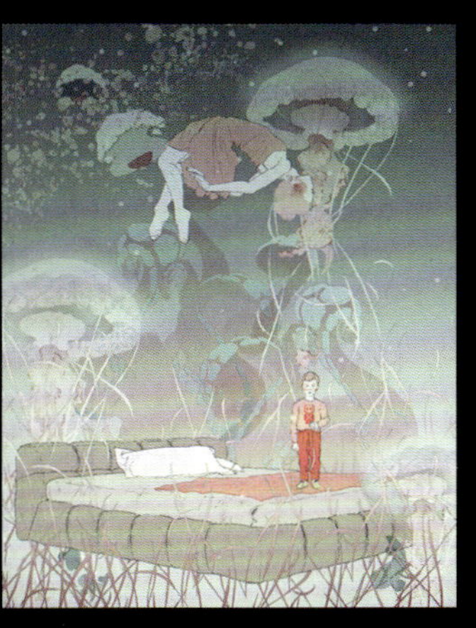

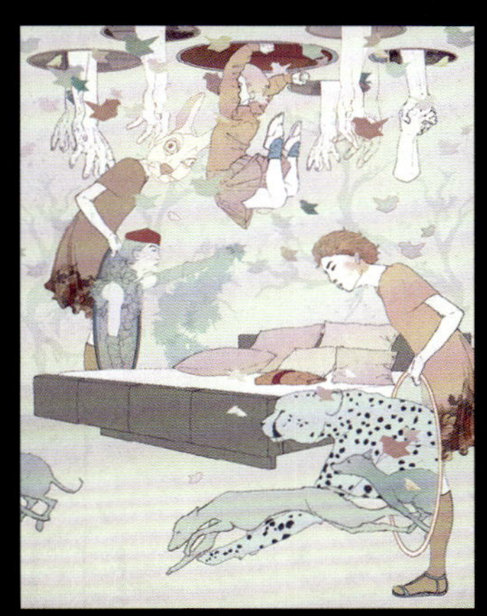

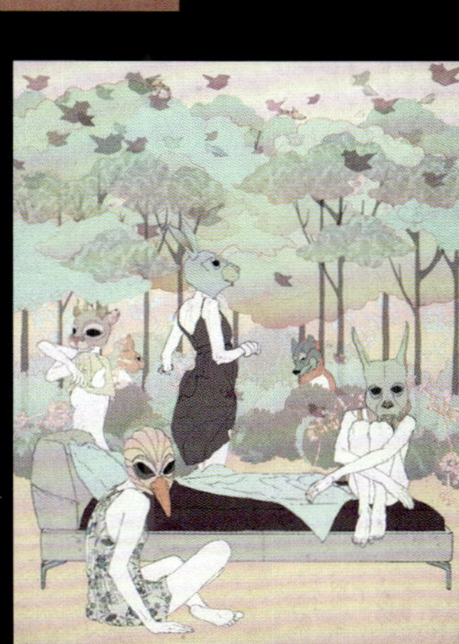

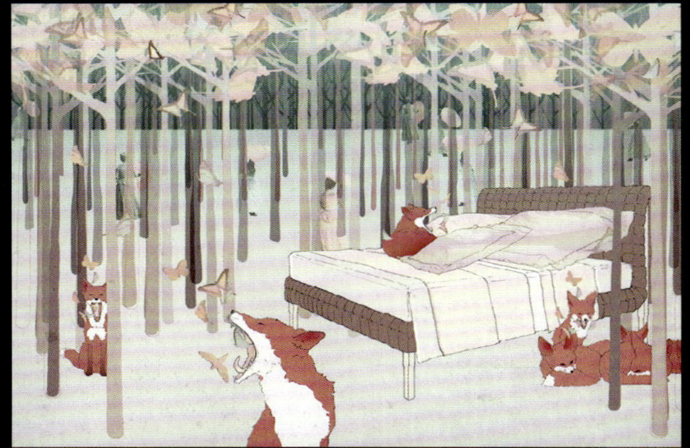

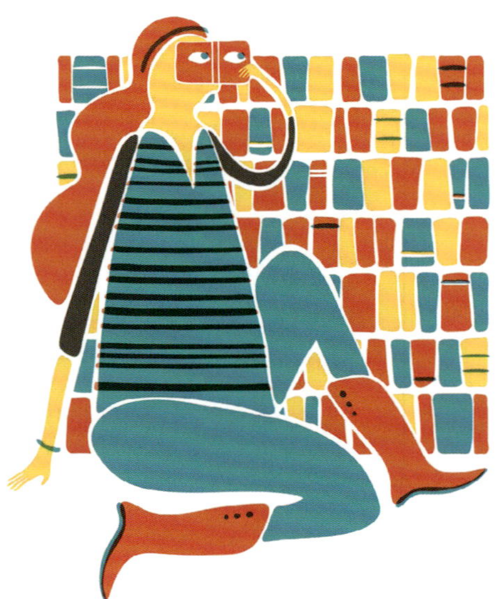

BANNED BOOKS. NEW EYES.
bannedbooksweek.org

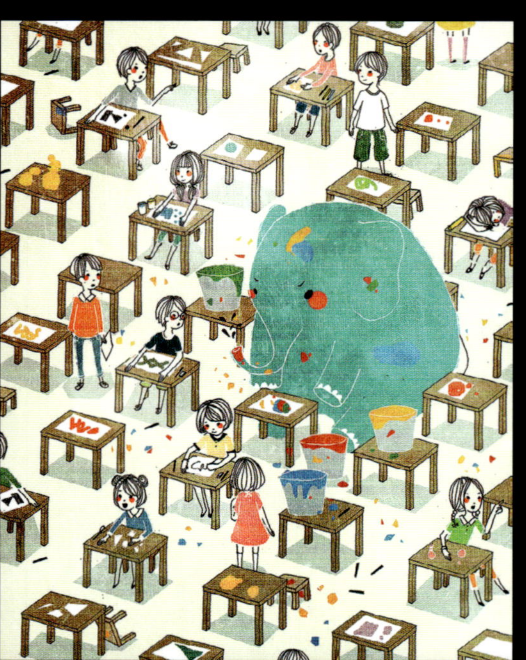

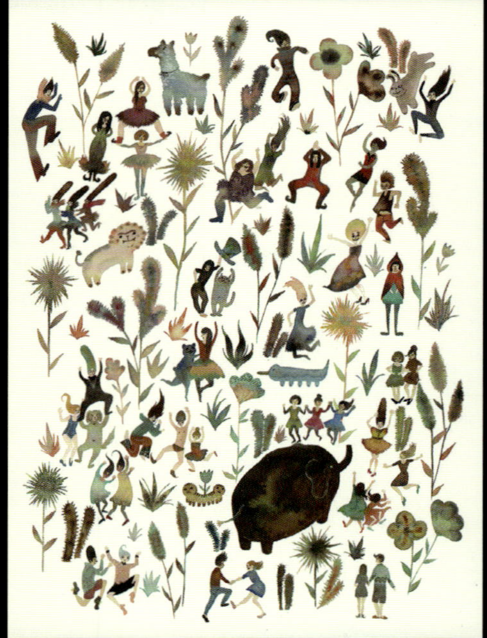

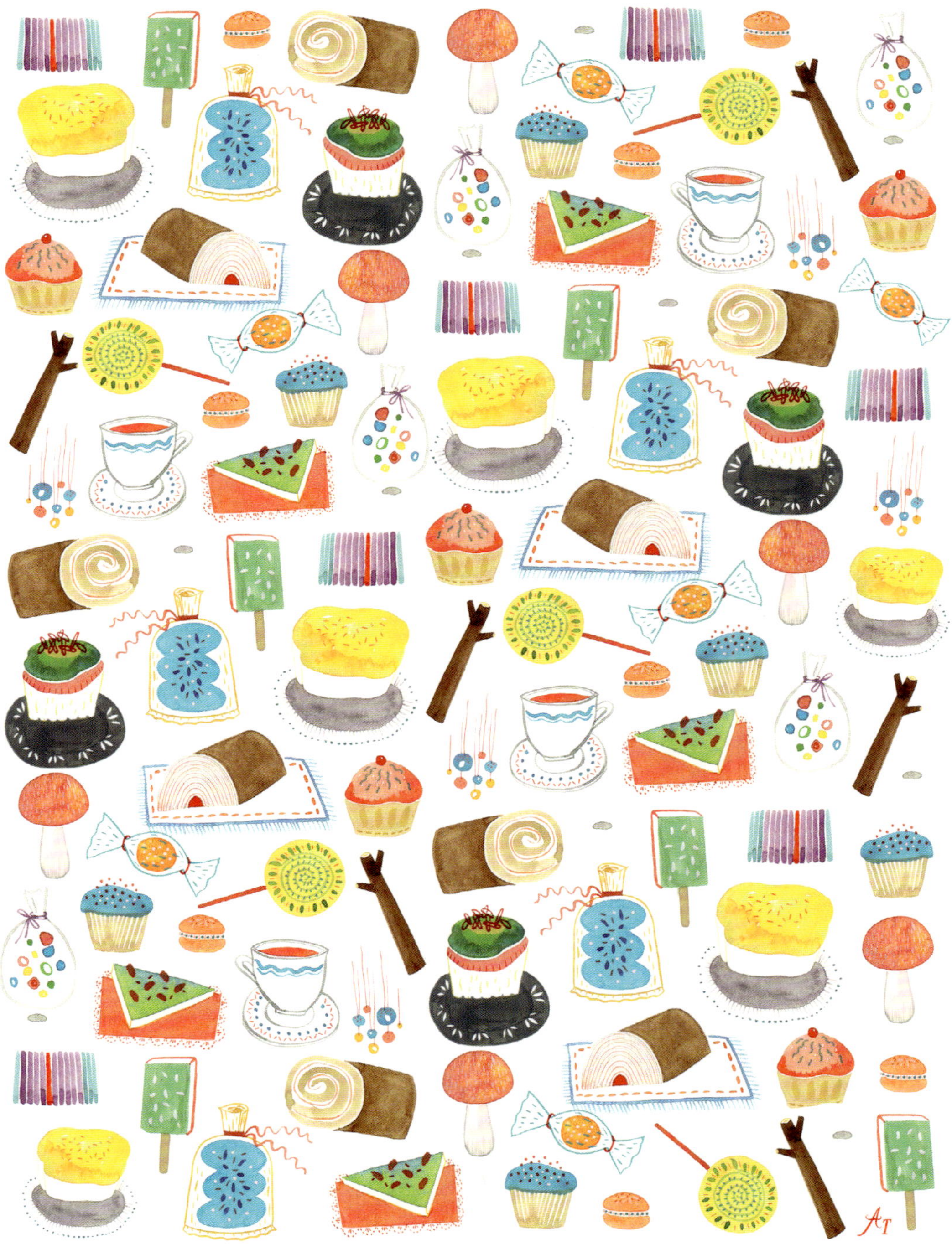

Ayumi Takahashi

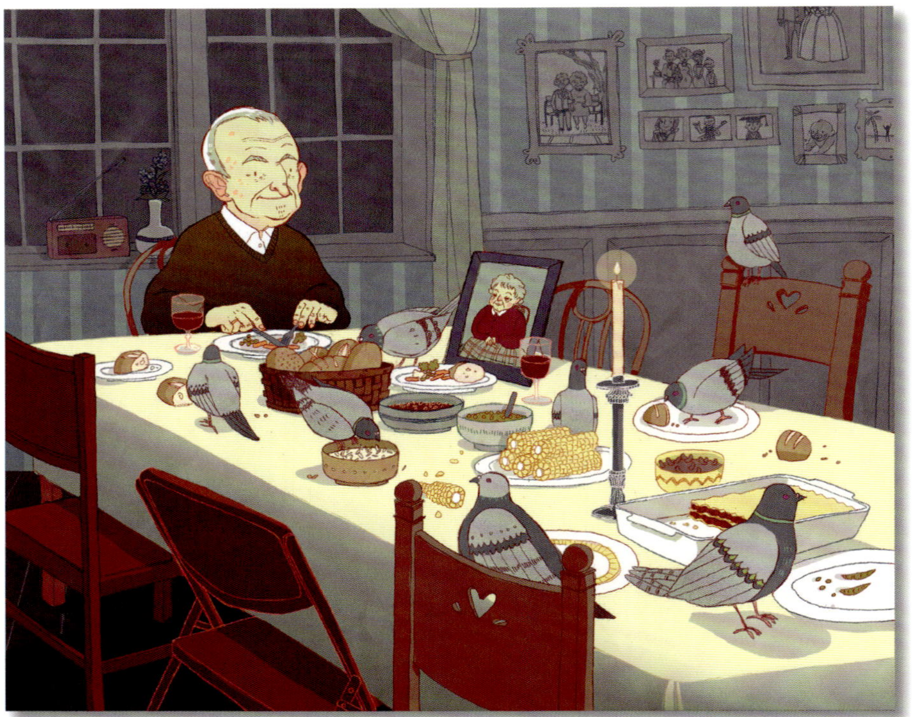

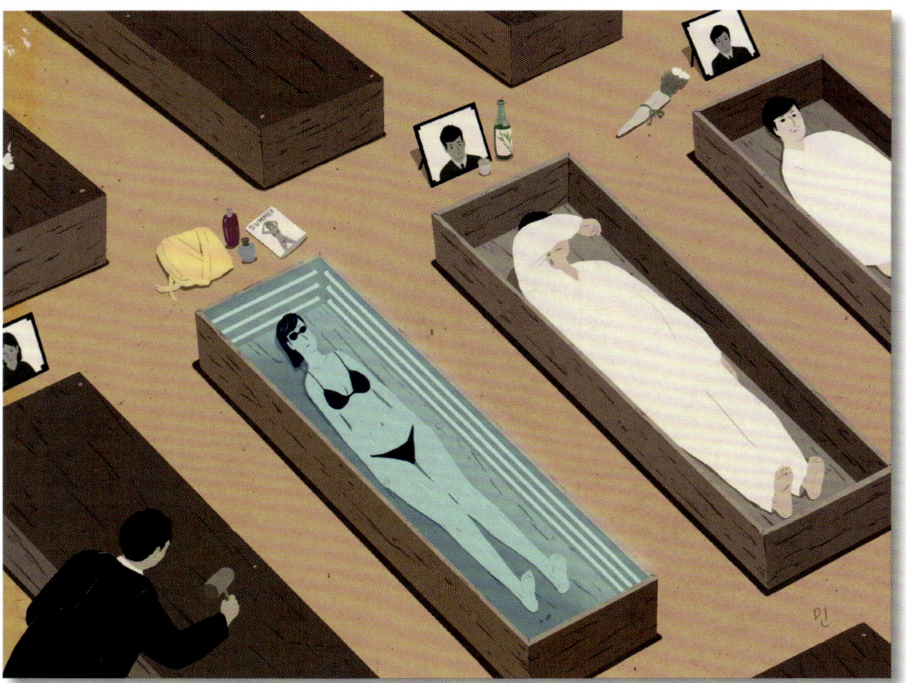

(T) *Deshi Deng* (B) *Min Gyo Chung*

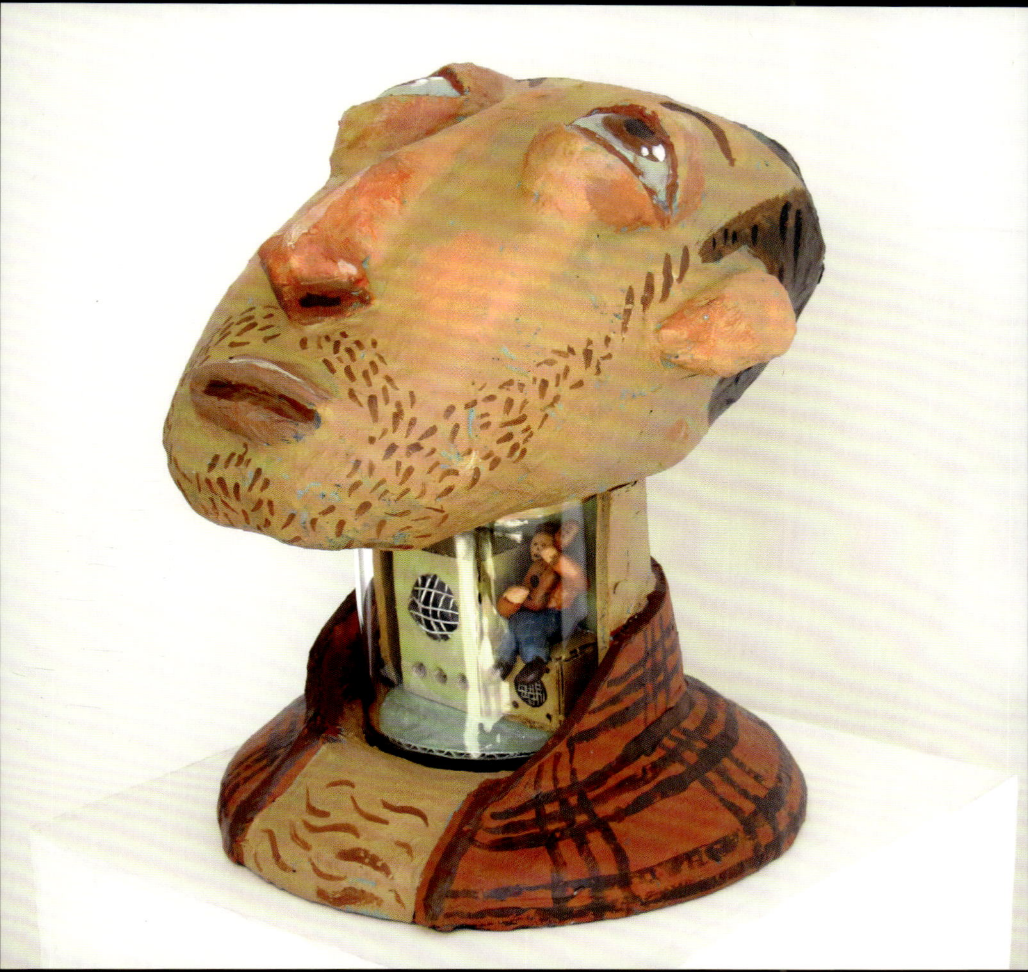

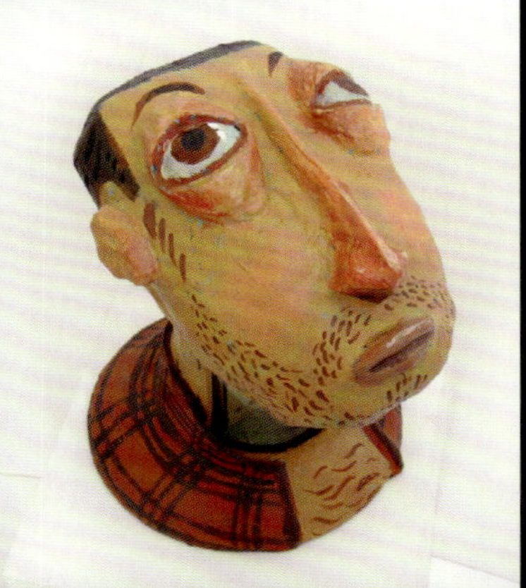

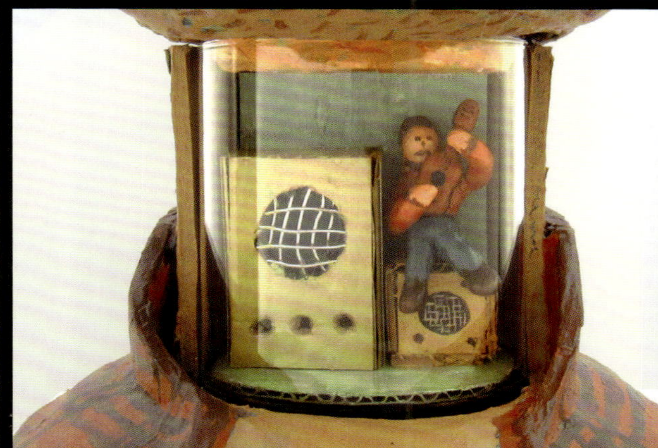

Ryan Cho

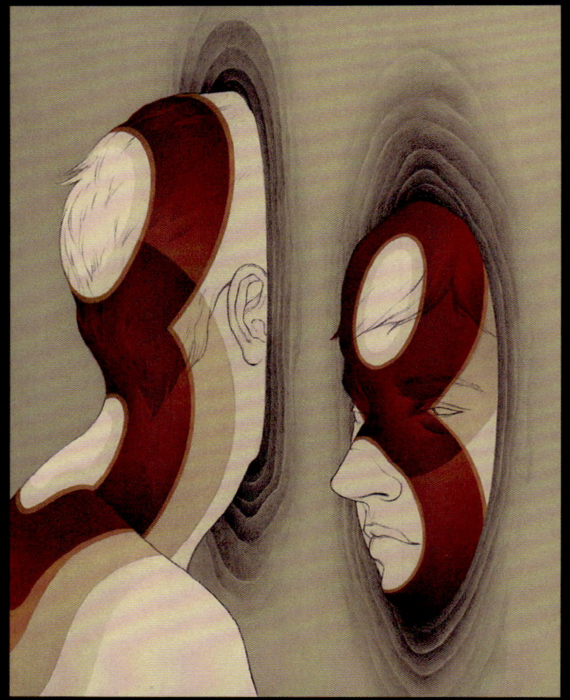

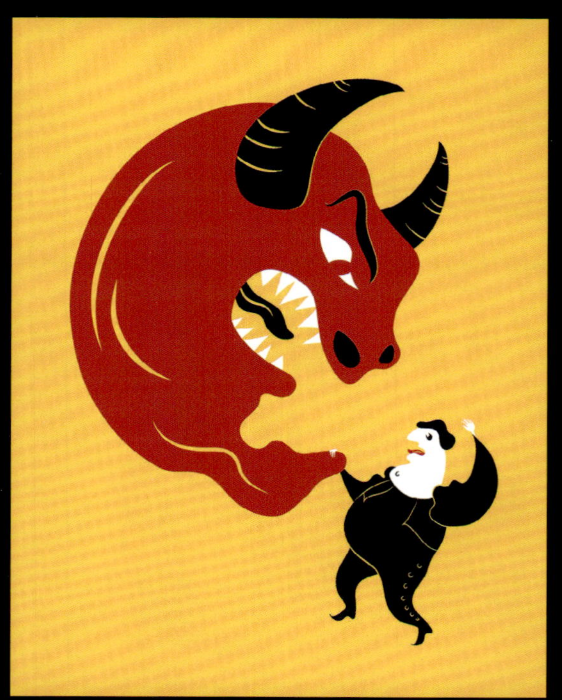

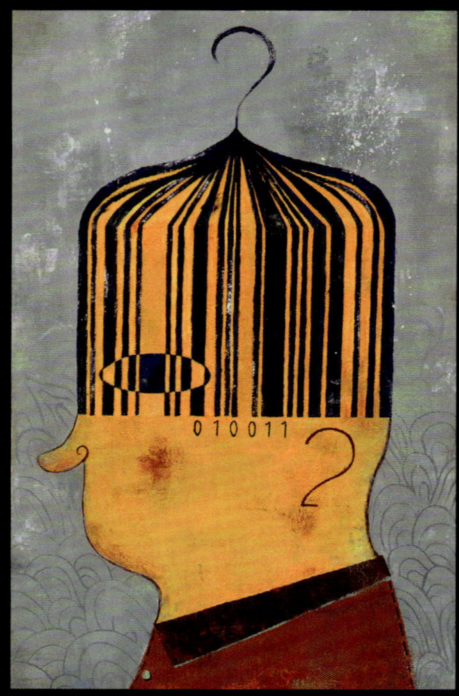

(T) *Ashley Mackenzie* (L) *Reina Castellanos* (R) *Chi Kuan Christina Kong*

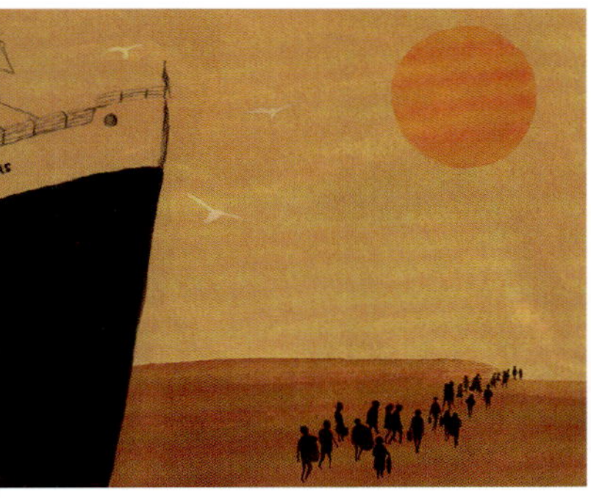

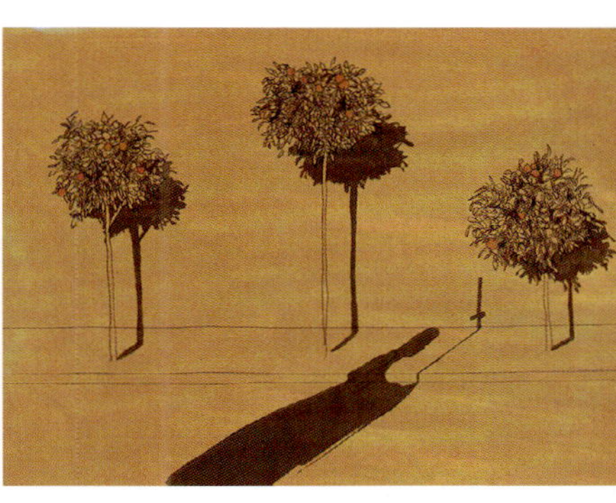

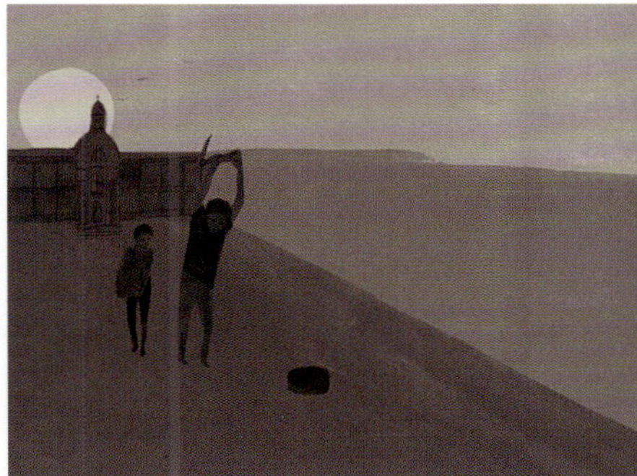
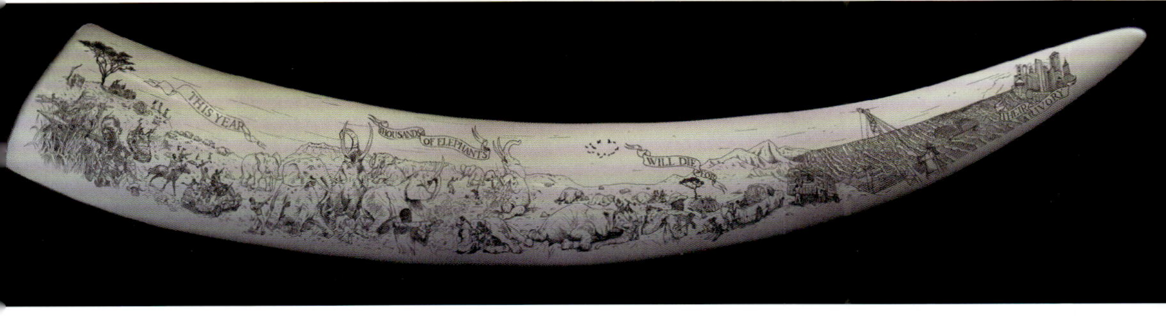

(T) *Trudi Esberger* (B) *Hugh O'Connor*

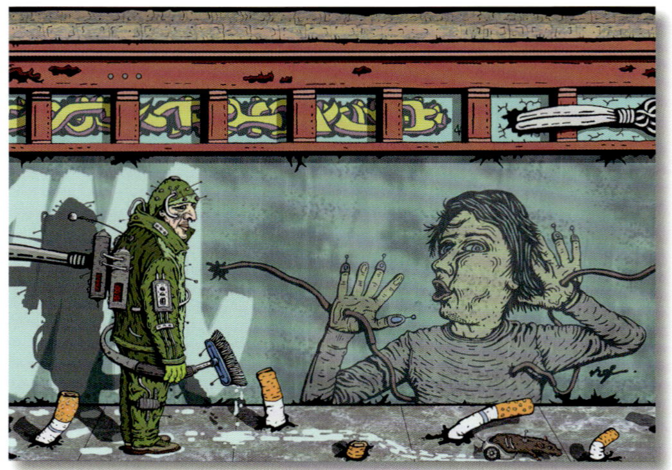

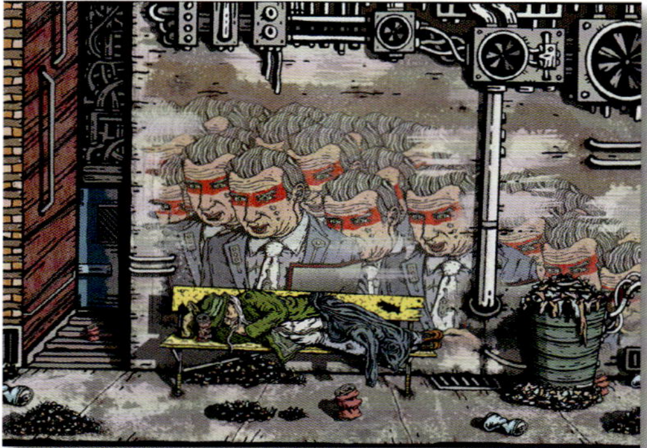

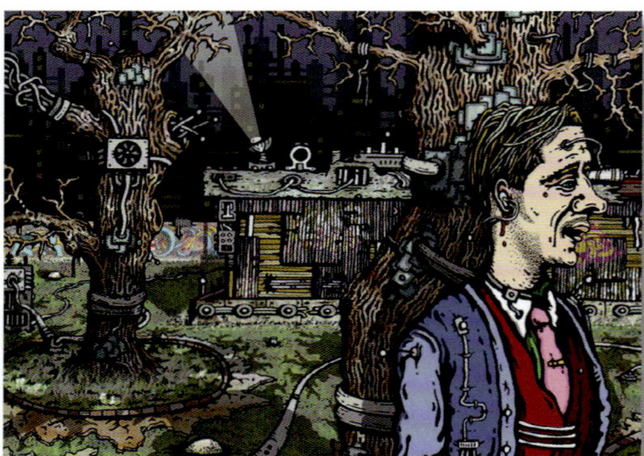

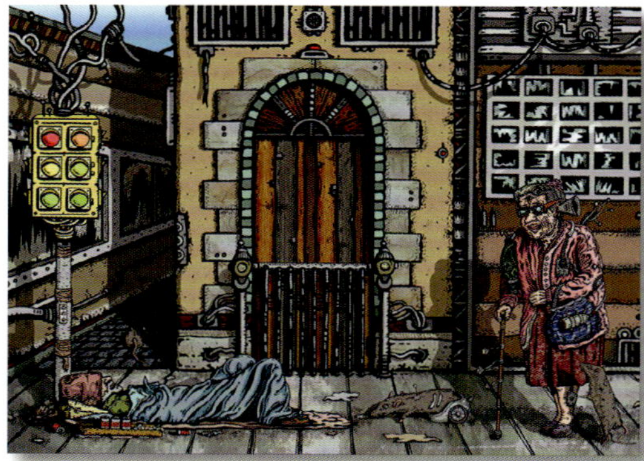

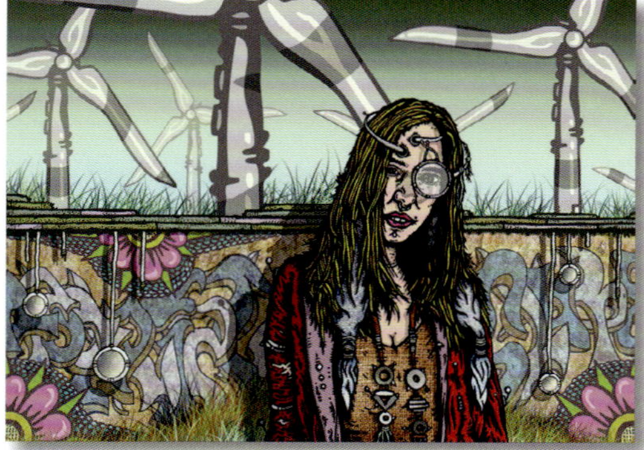

Matthew Denton Burrows

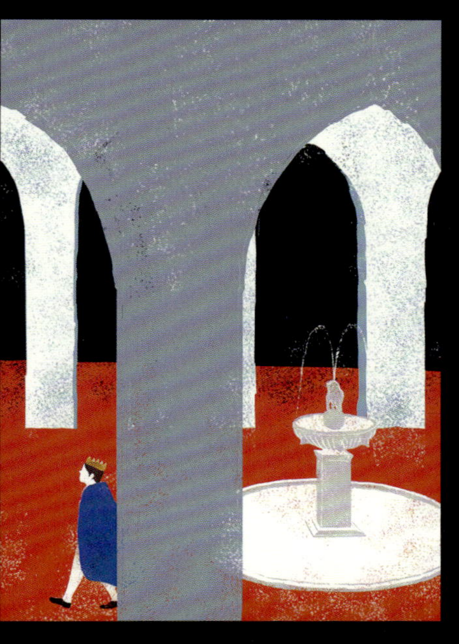

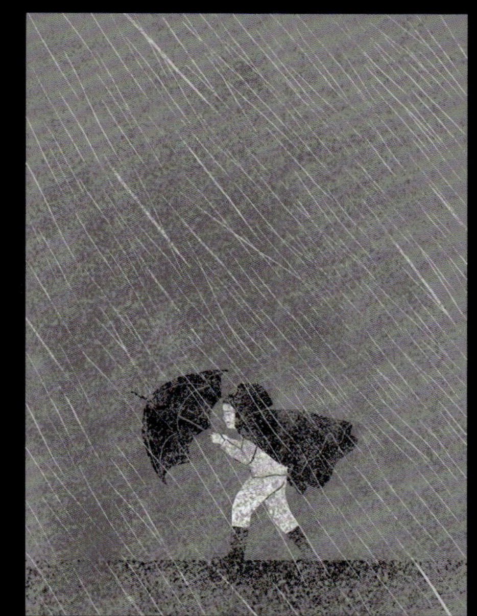

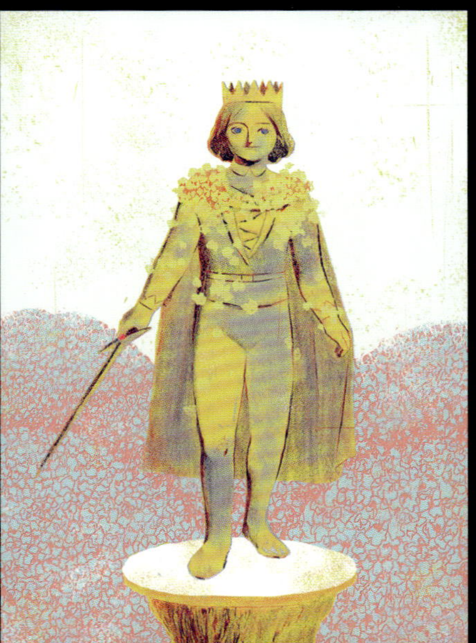

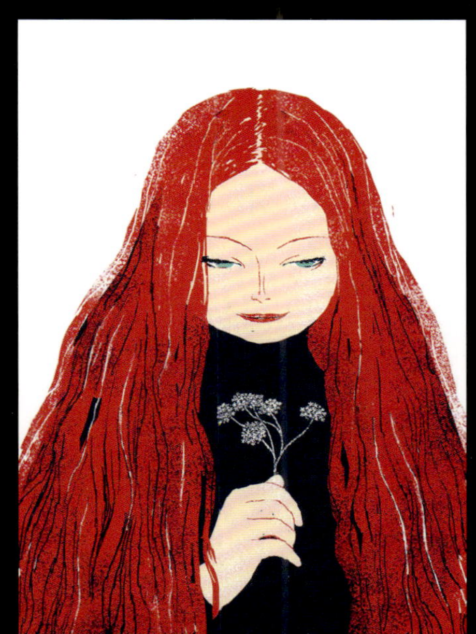

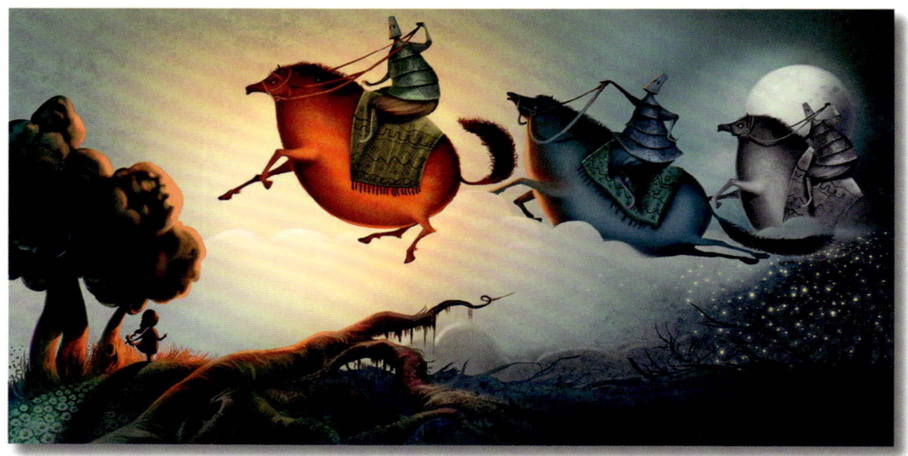

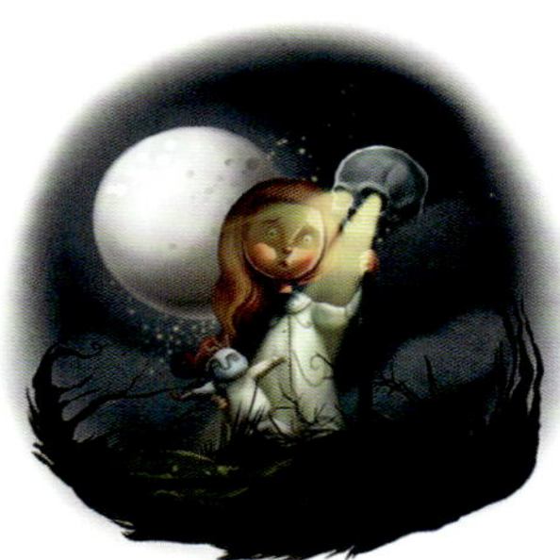

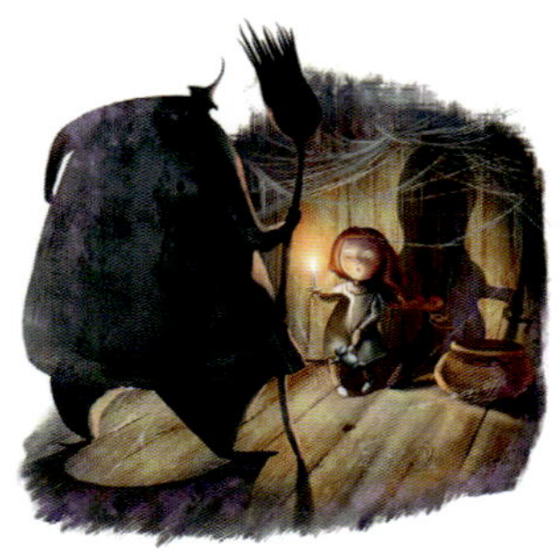

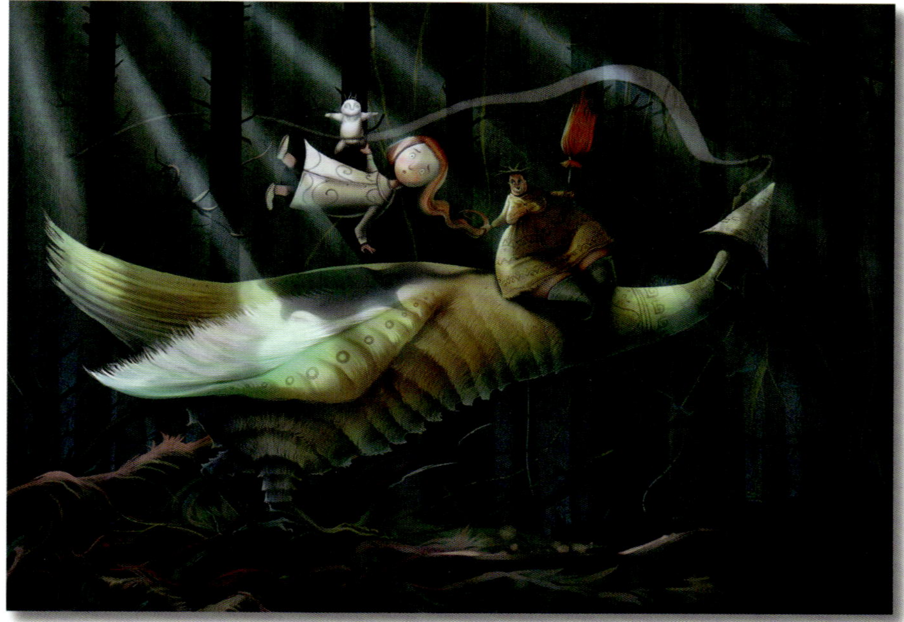

Nuri Keli

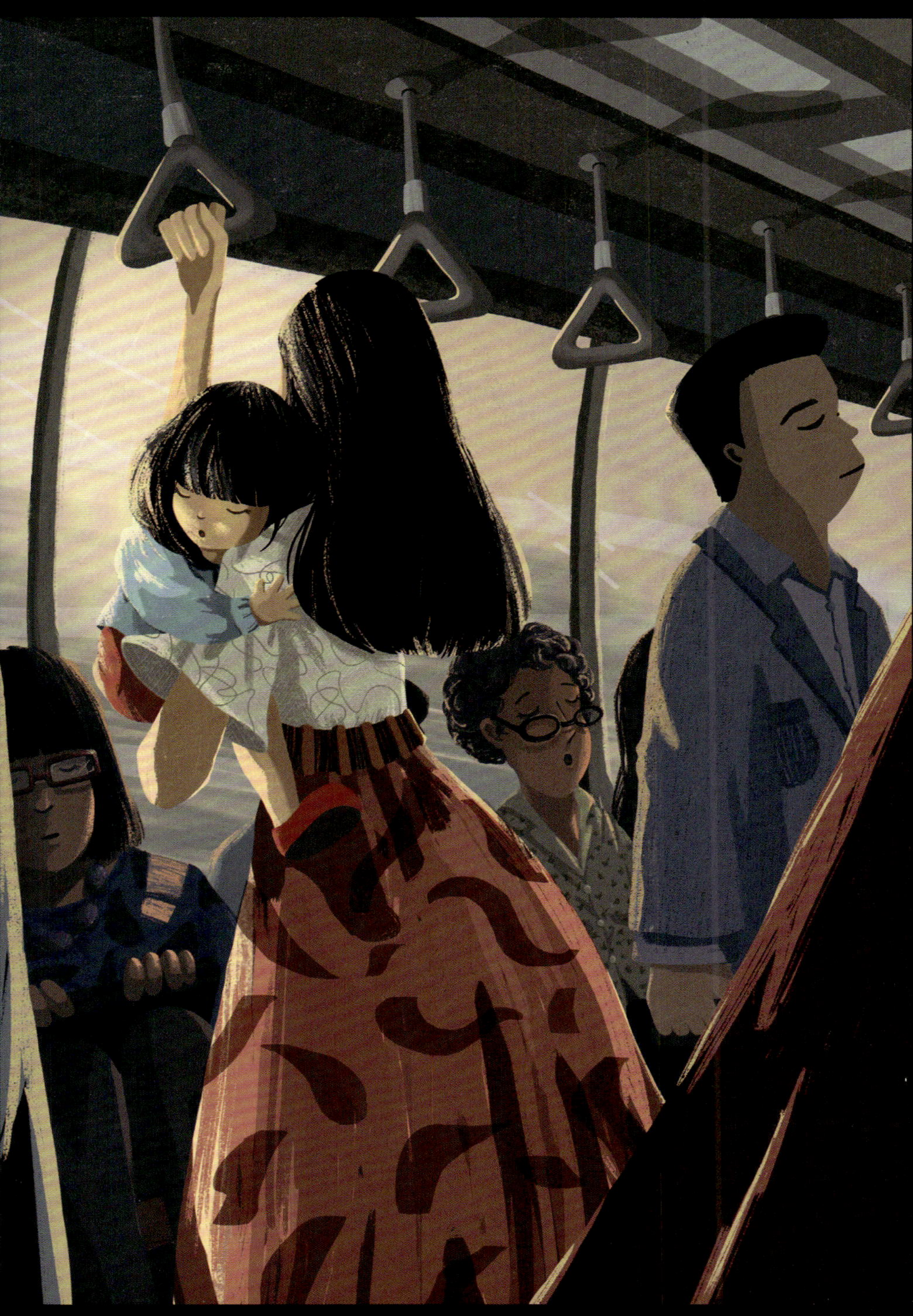

Ziyue Chen

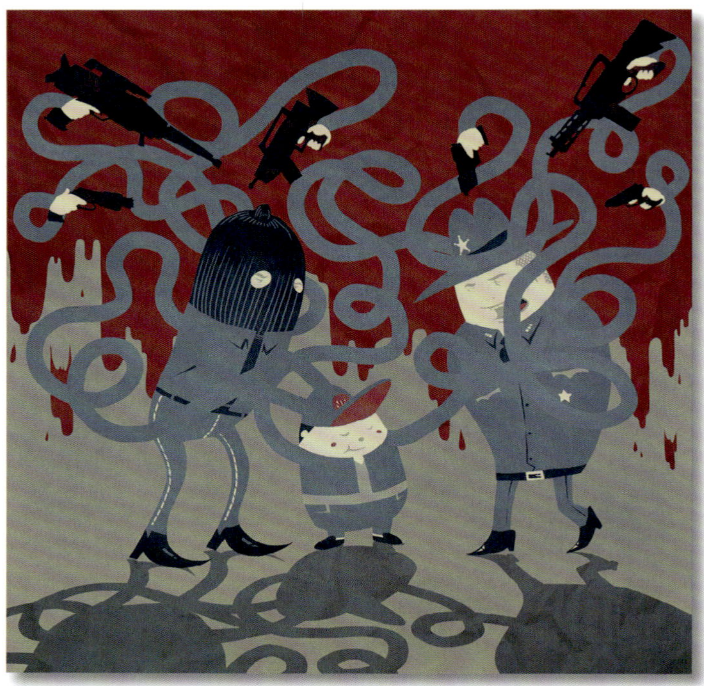

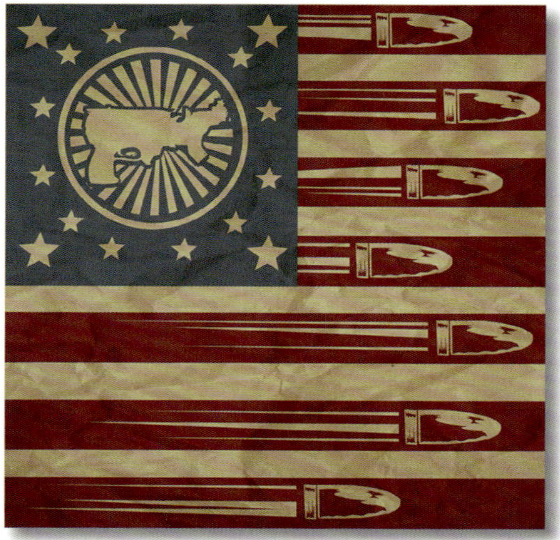

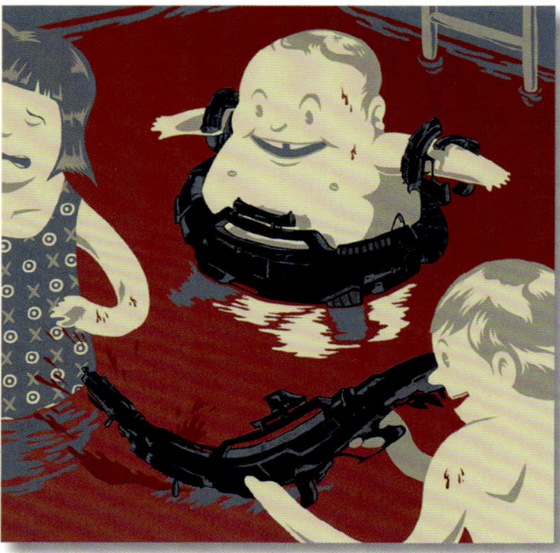

(L) *Nick Nazzaro* (TR) *Matthew Denton Burrows* (BR) *Hye Jin Chung*

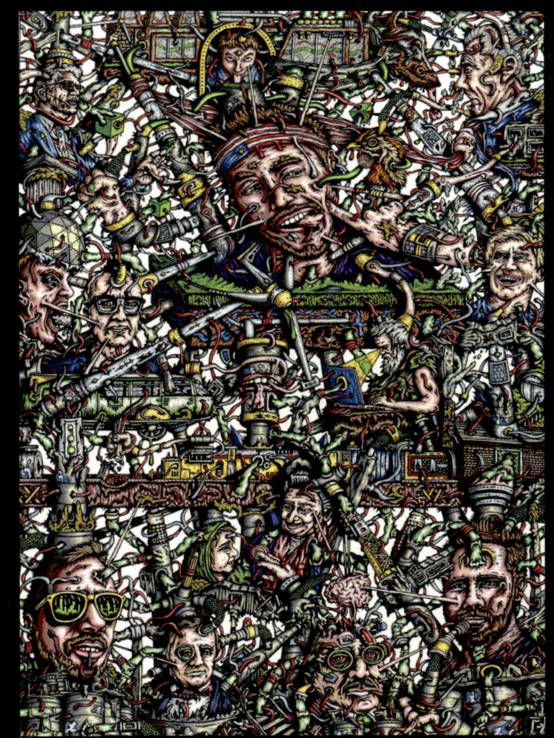

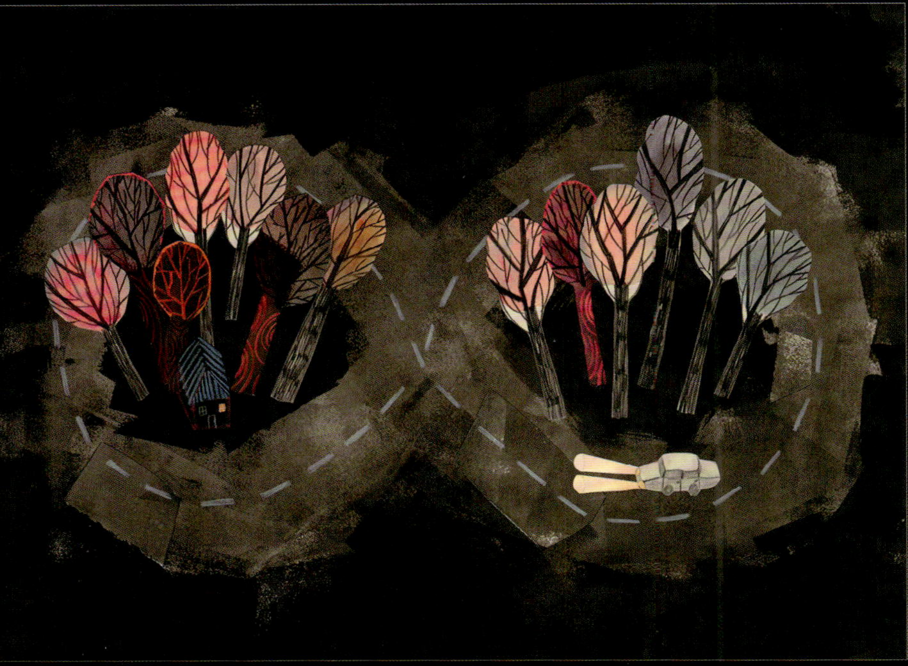

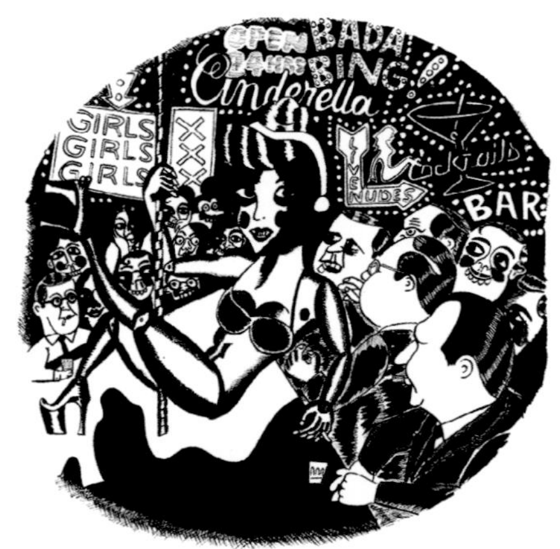

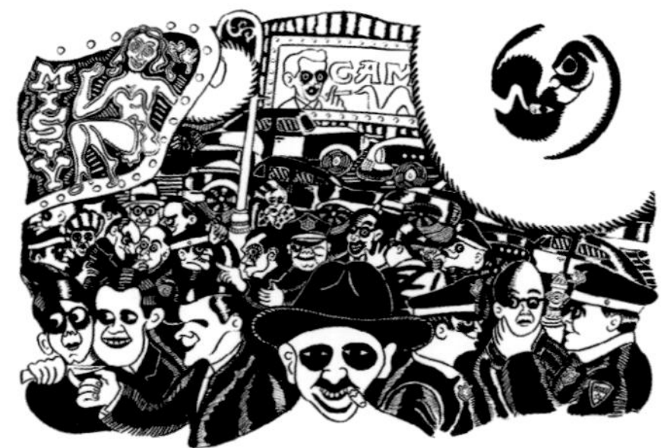

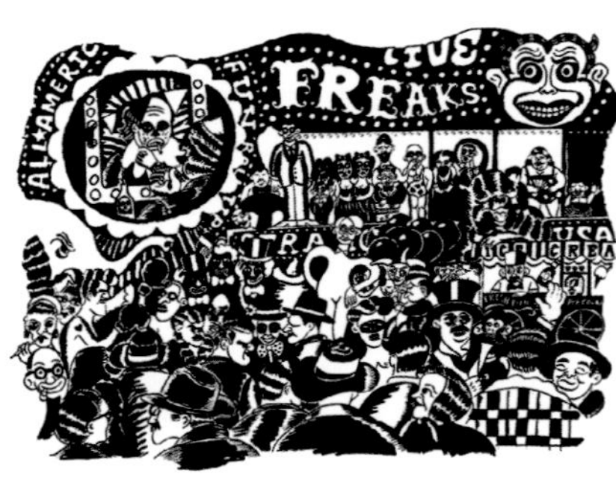

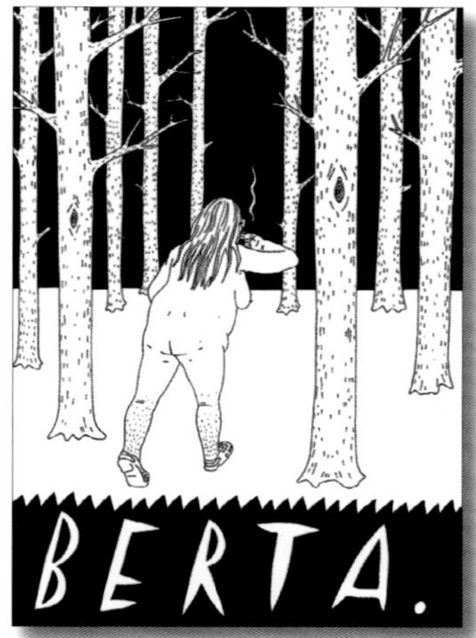

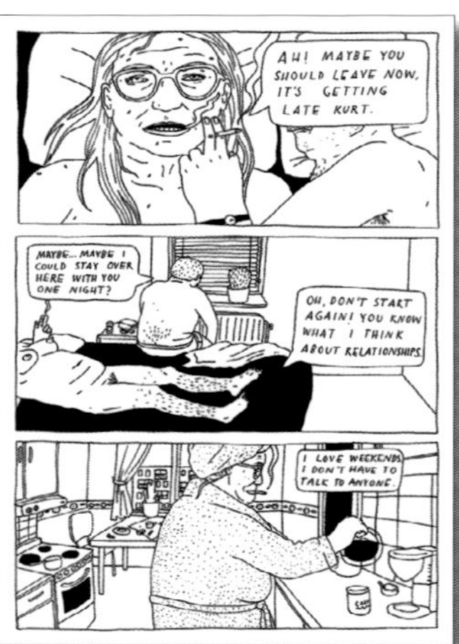

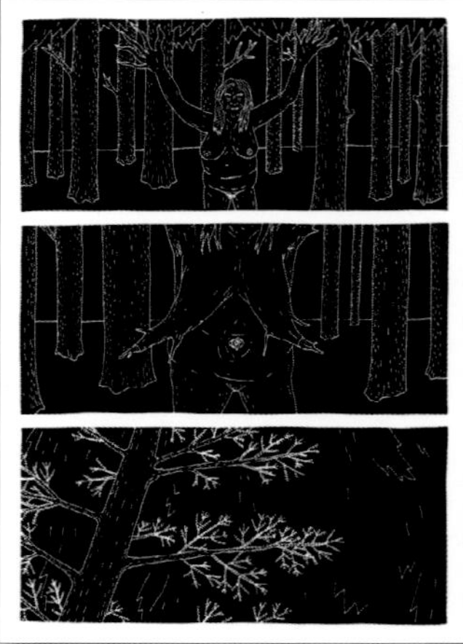

(T) *Jay Lang* (B) *Emma Ahlqvist*

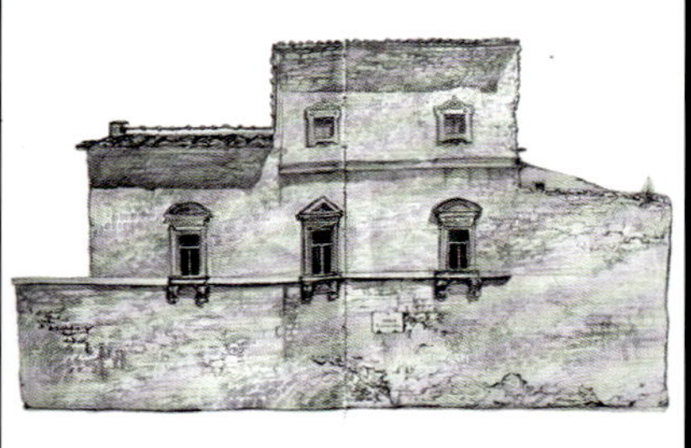

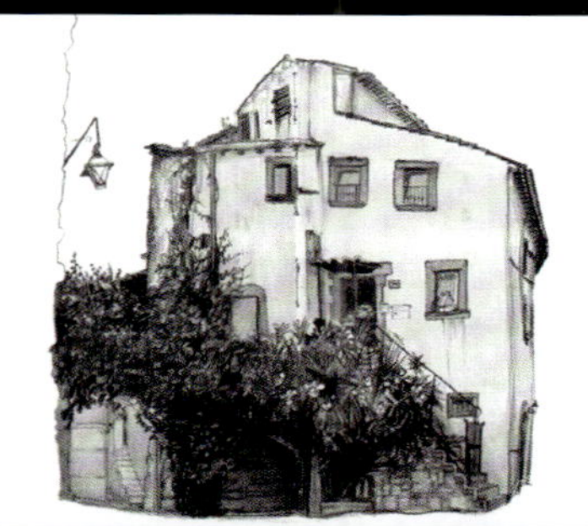

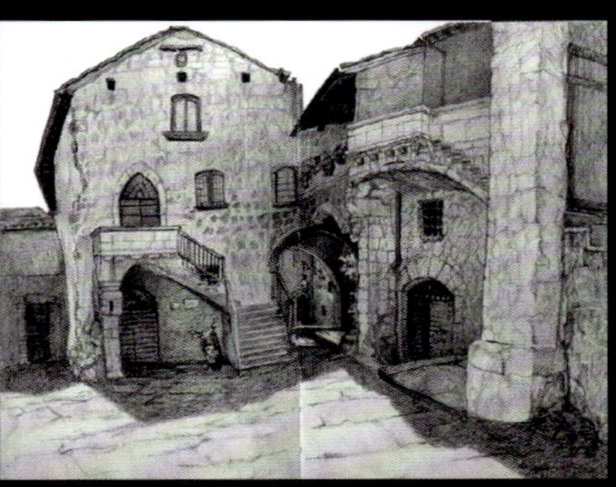

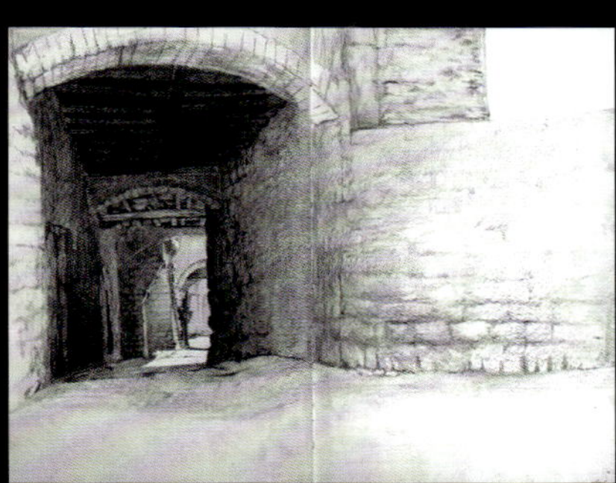

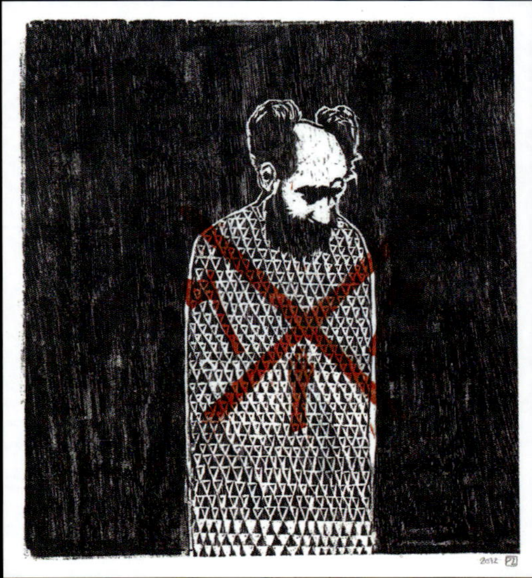

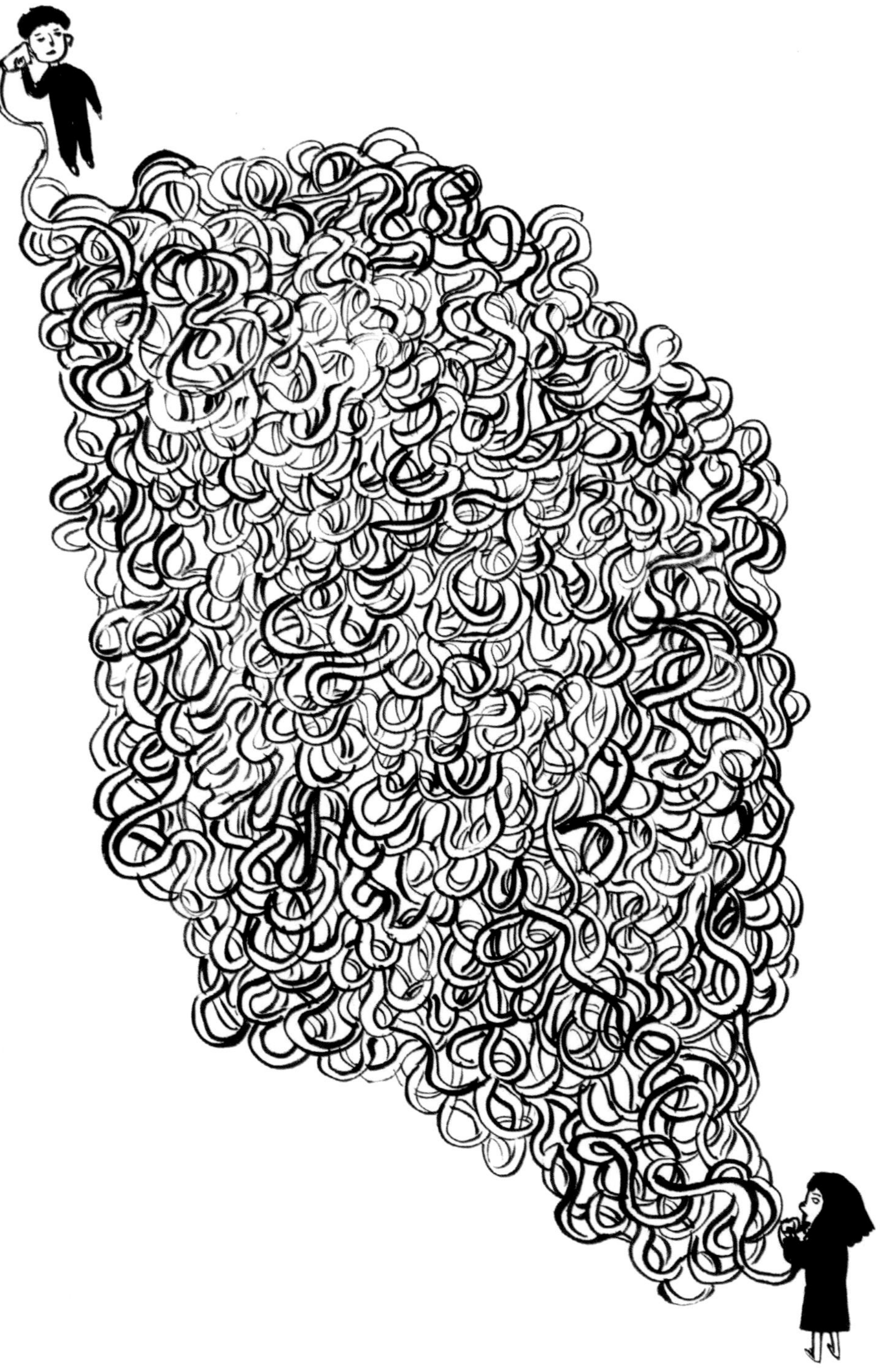

Ji Hyun Yu

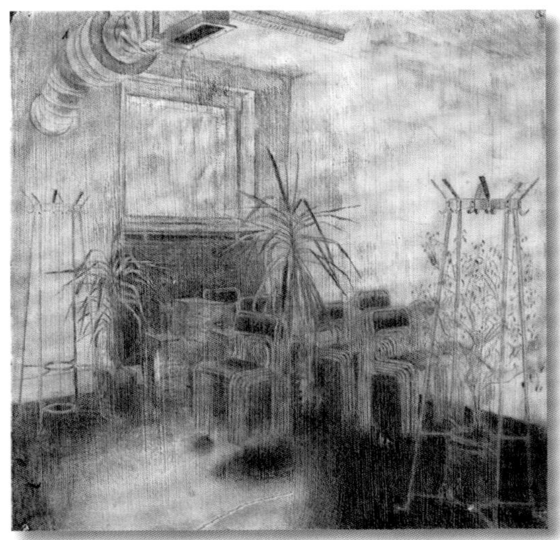
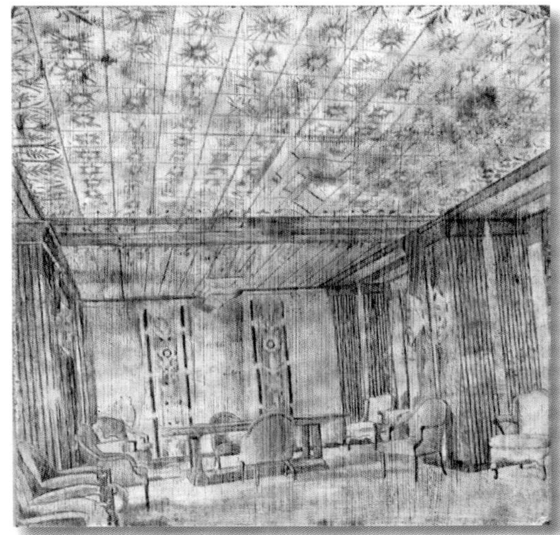
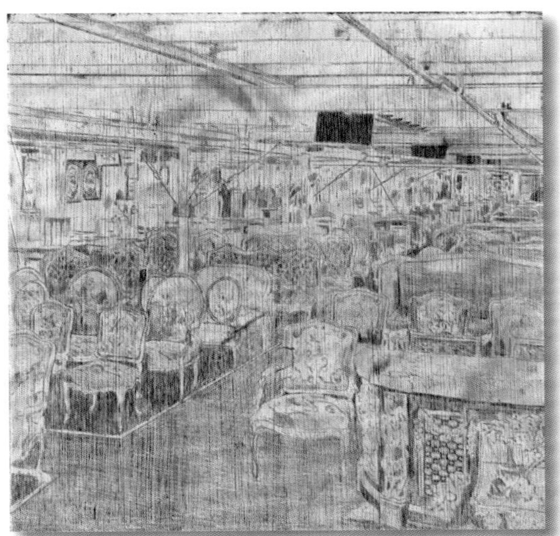
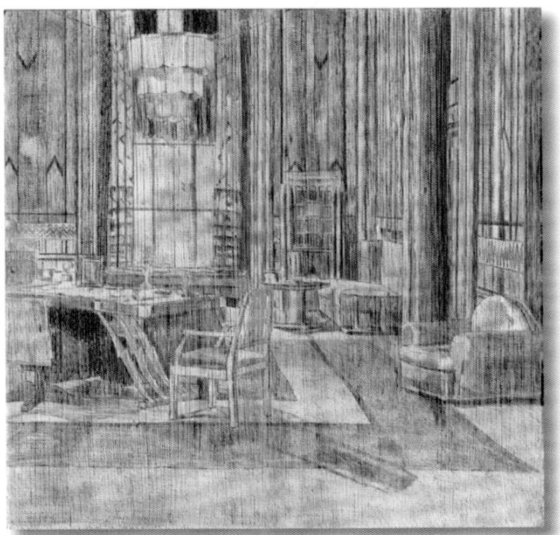

Linnea Gad

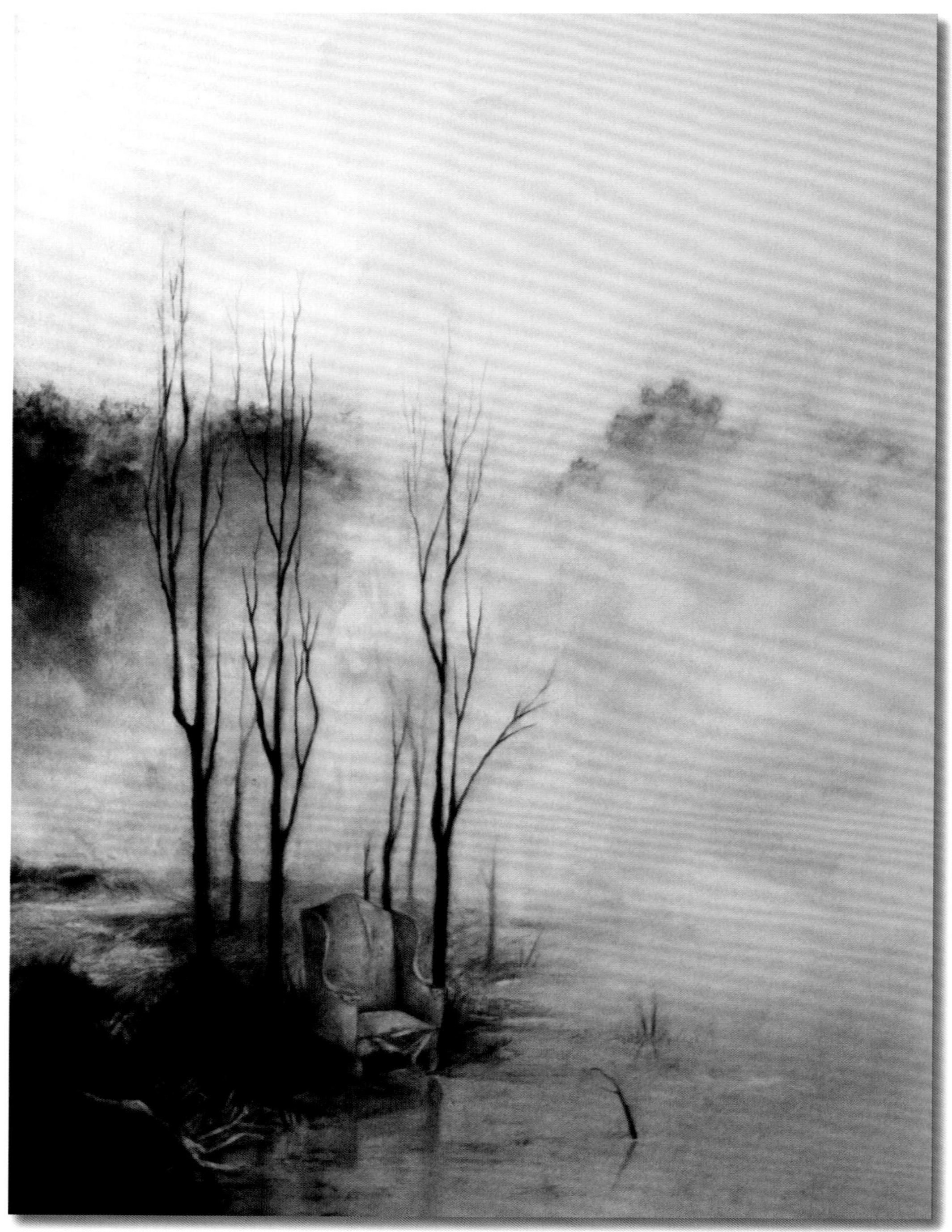

(L) *Kristen Davis* (R) *Evan Mazellan*

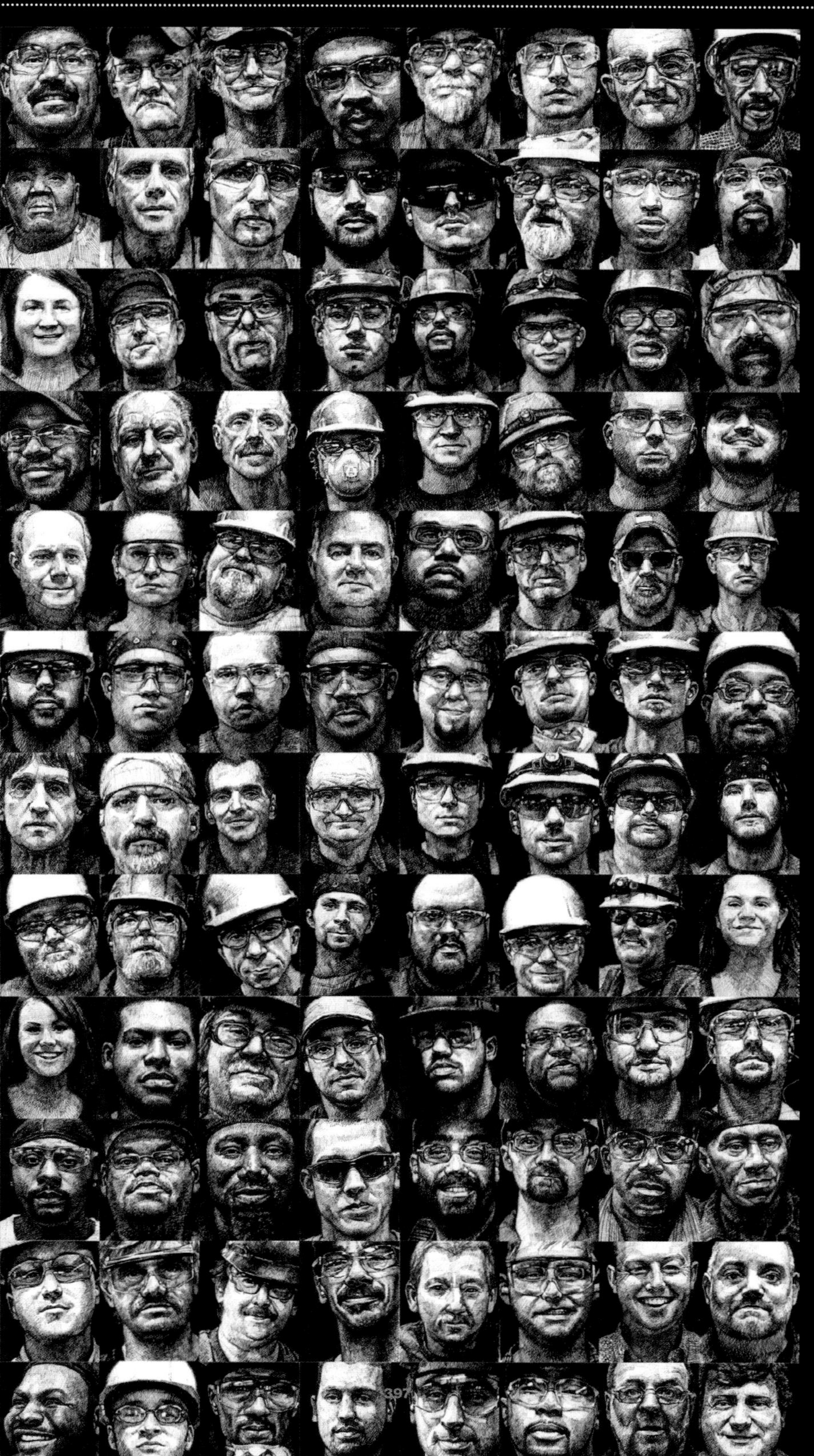

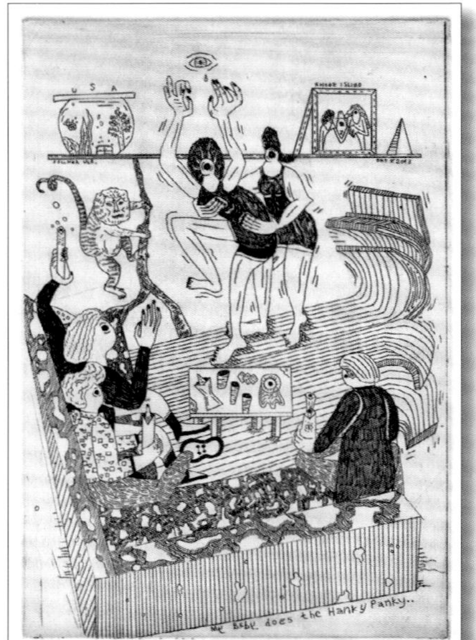
U S A
me baby does the Hanky Panky...

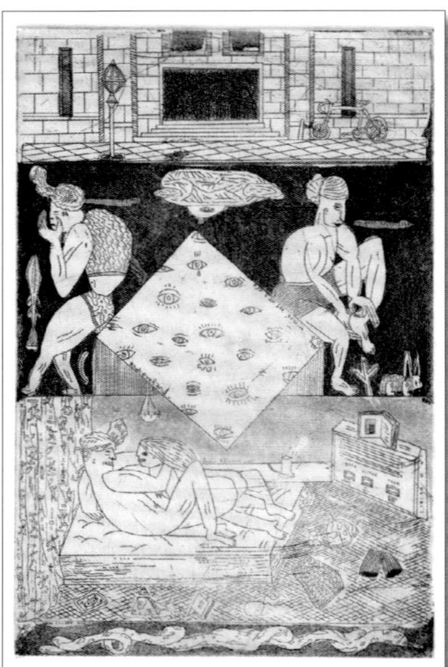

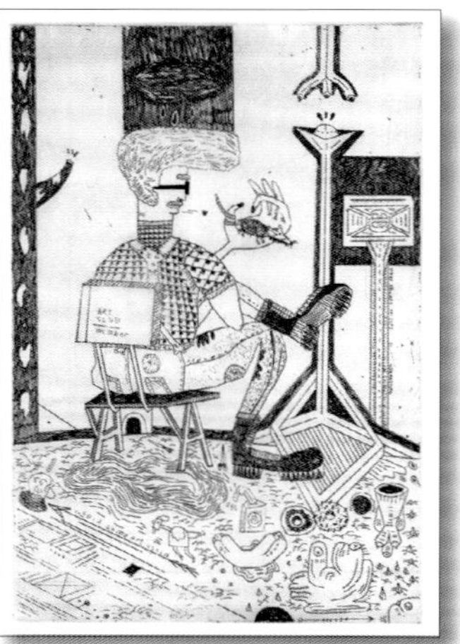

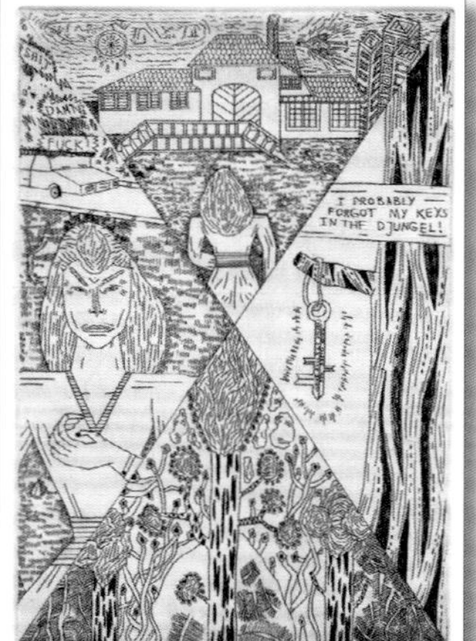
I PROBABLY
FORGOT MY KEYS
IN THE DJUNGEL!

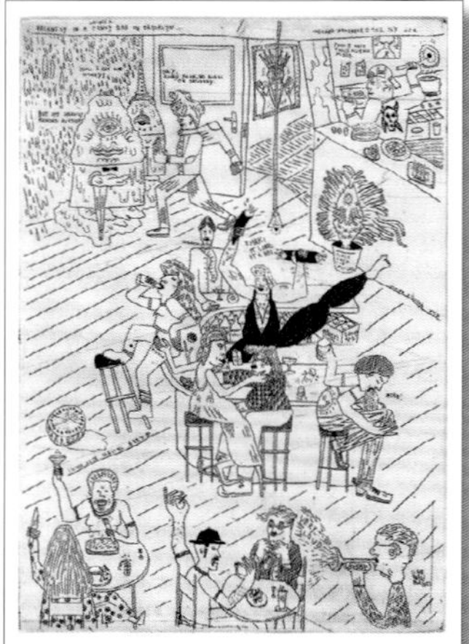

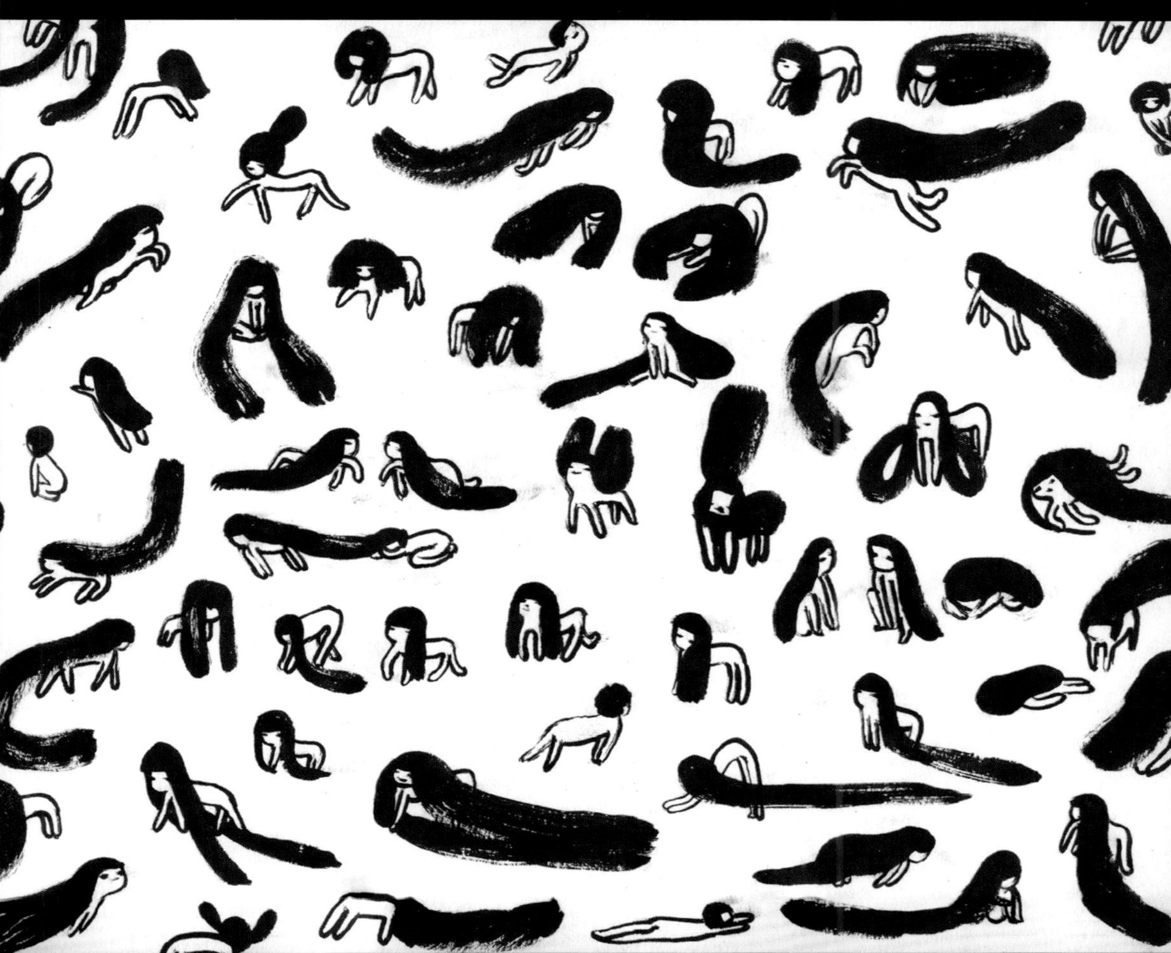

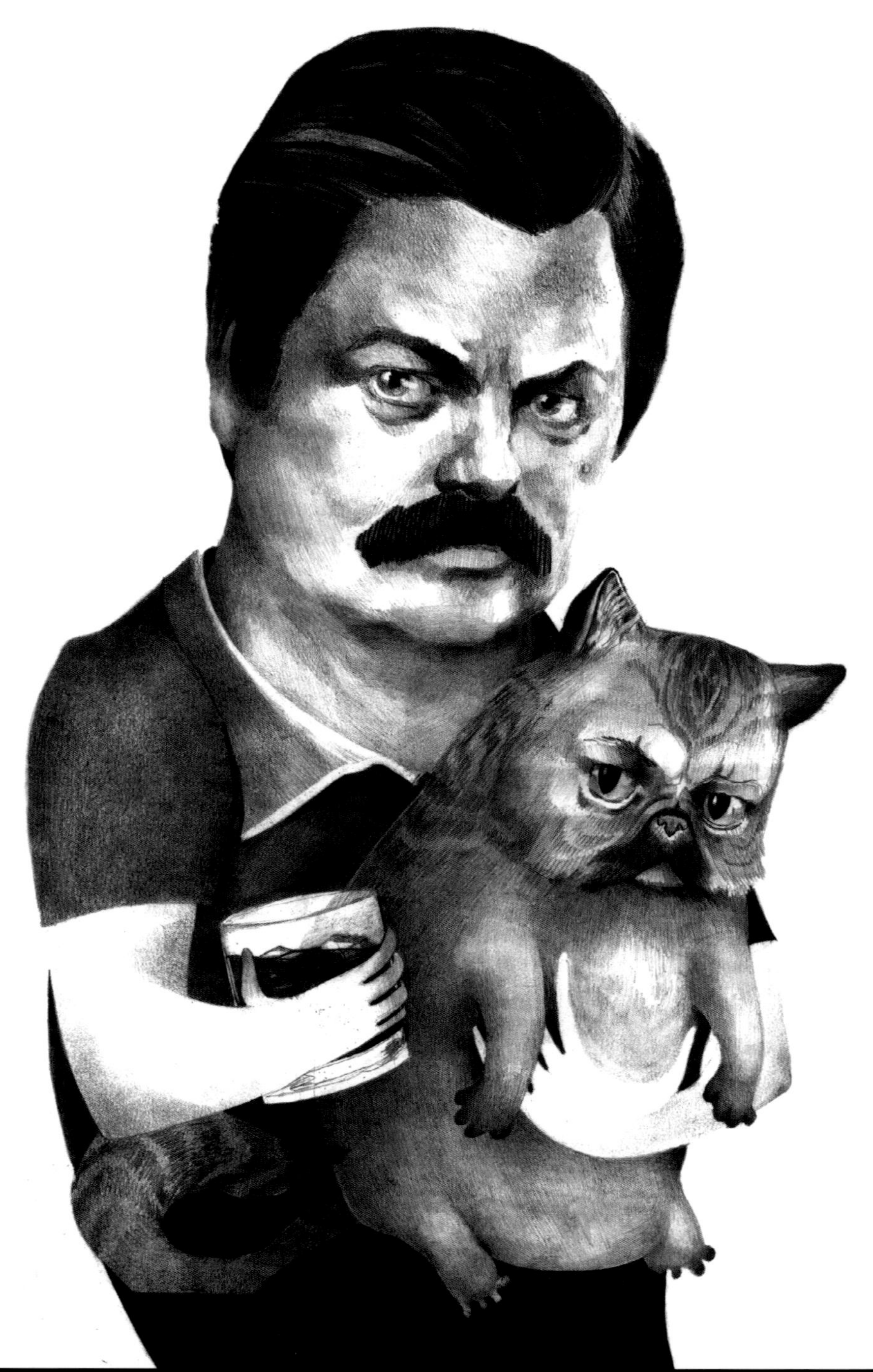

Lauren Hess

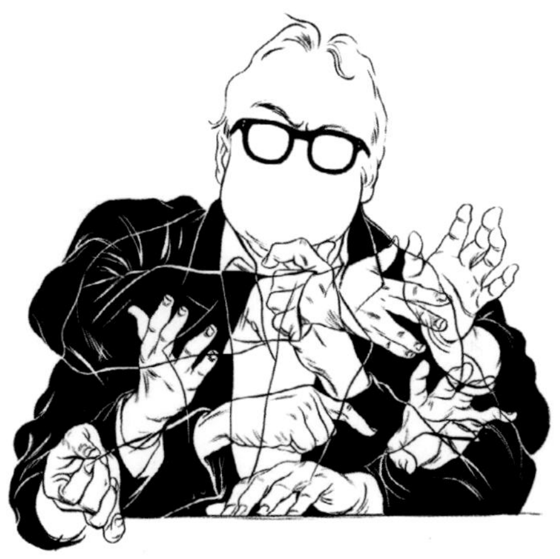

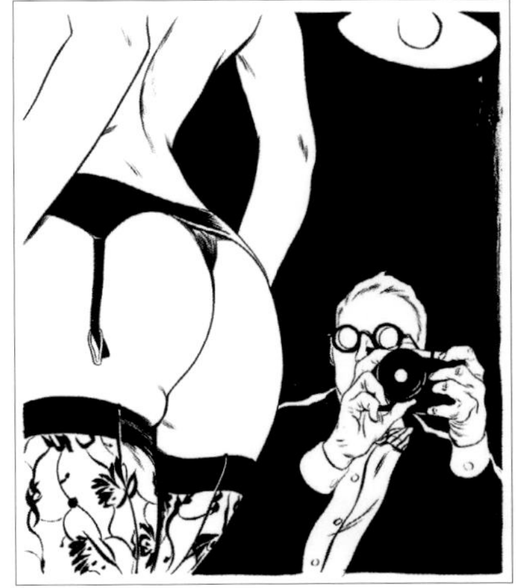

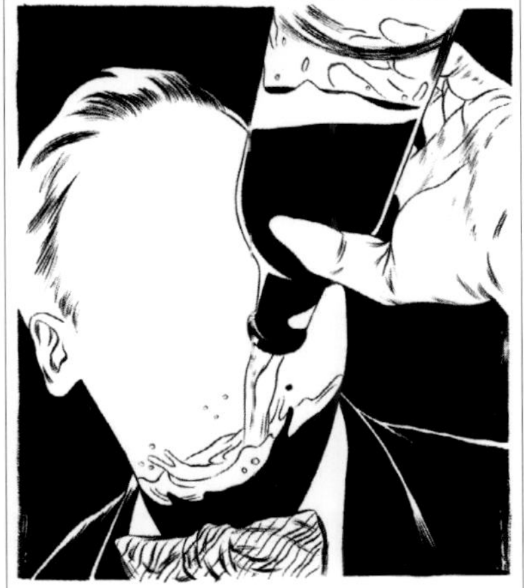

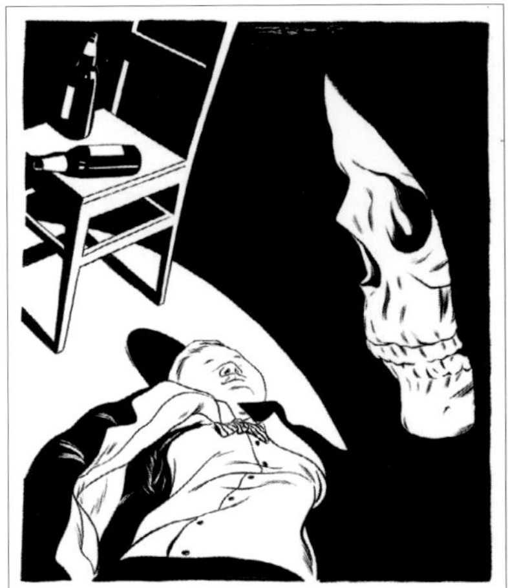

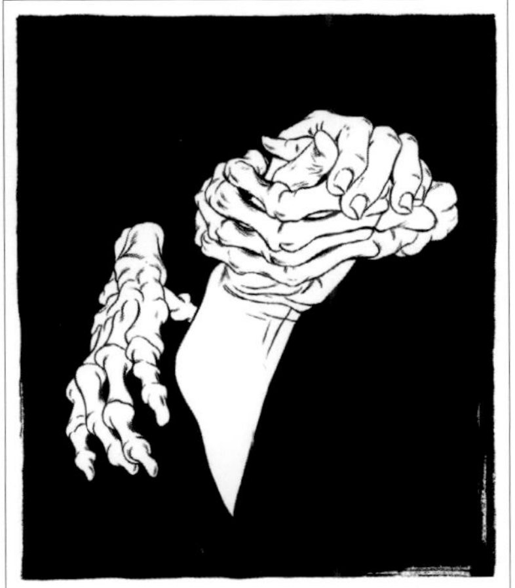

Cun Shi

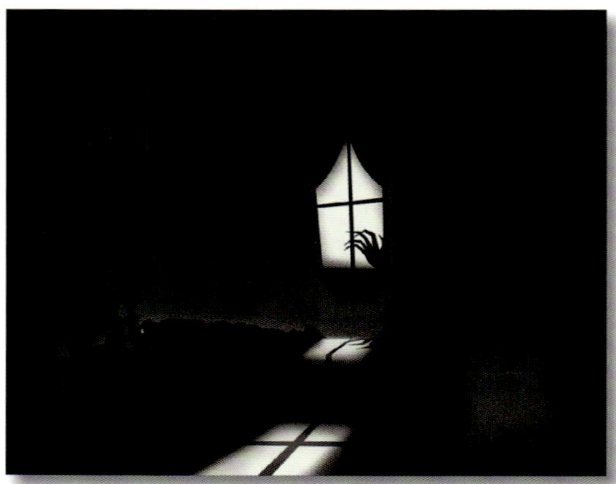

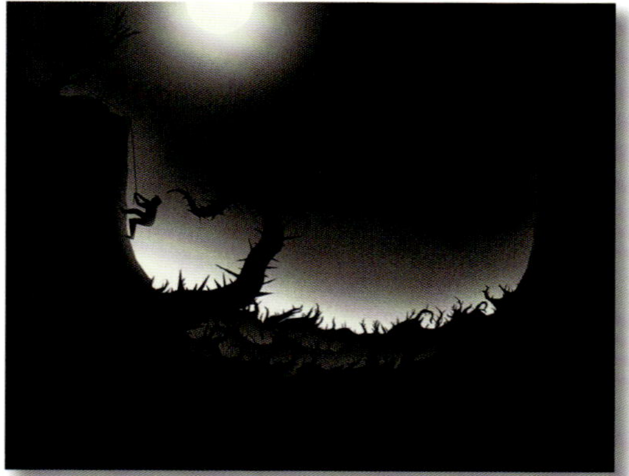

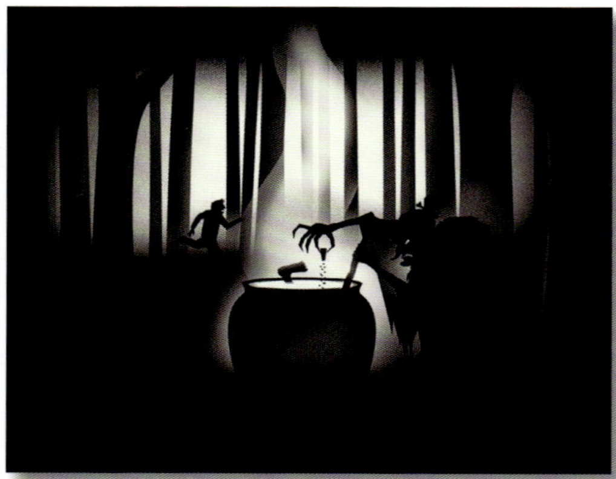

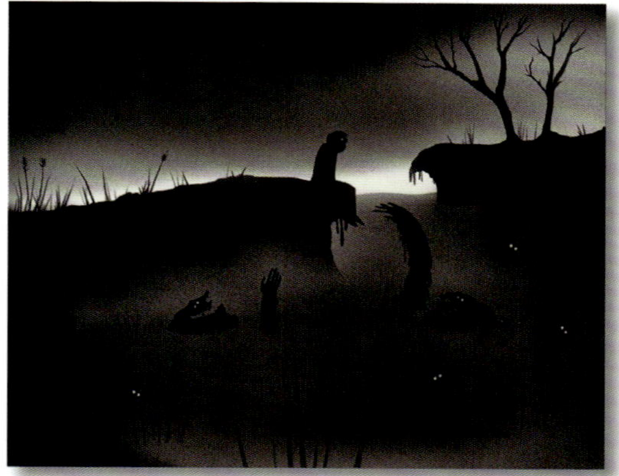

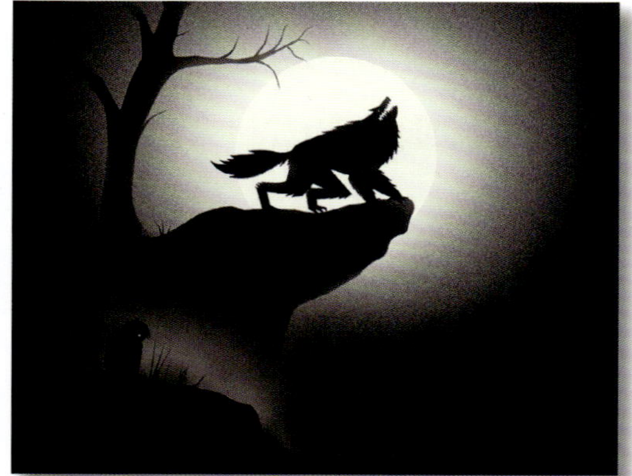

(L) *Caleb Heisey* (R) *Rujun Liu*

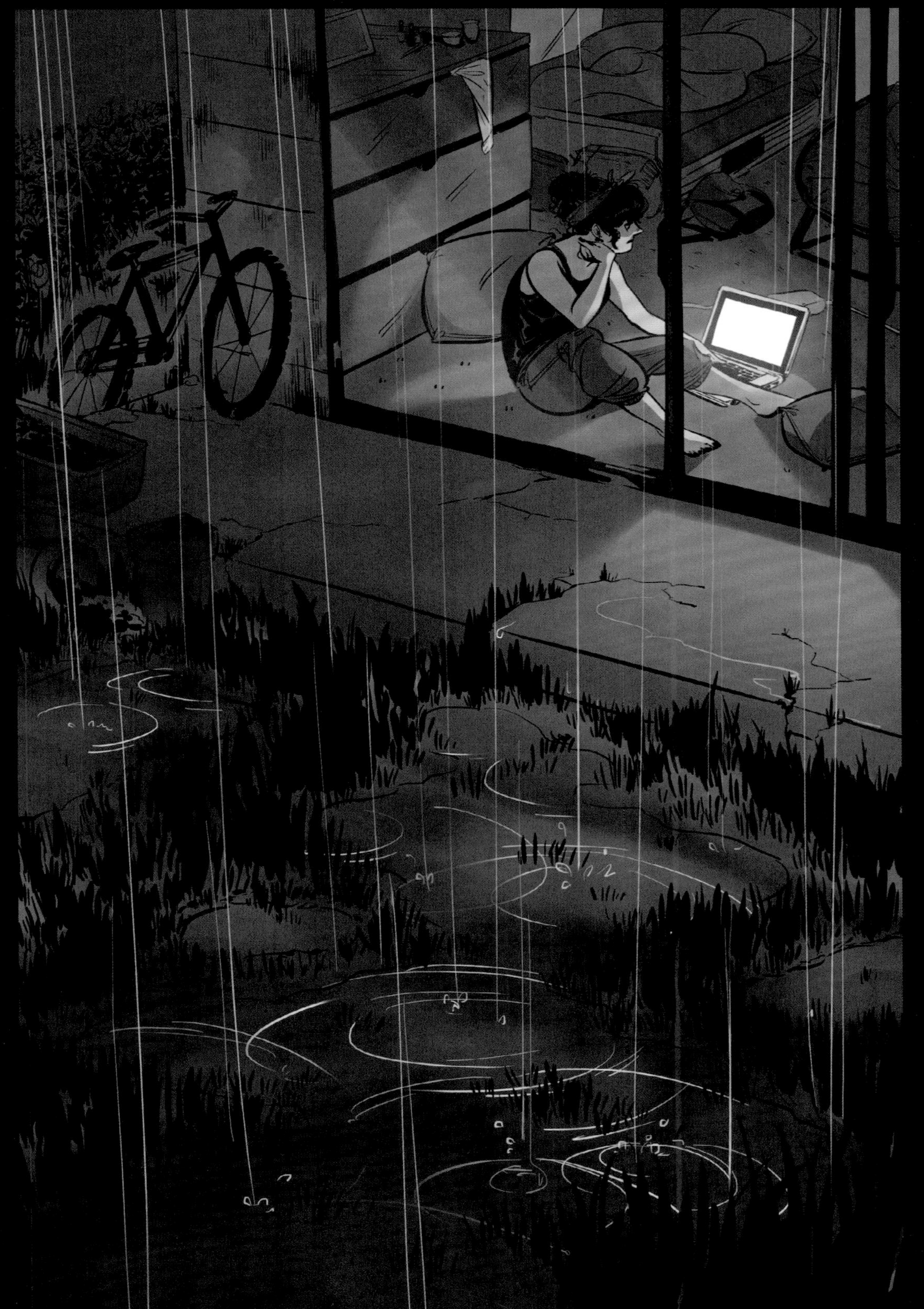

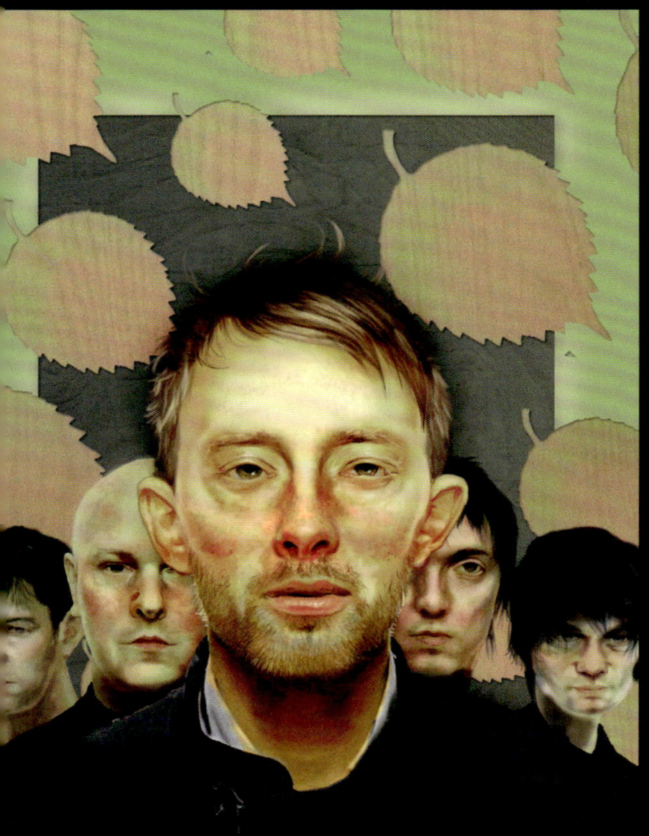

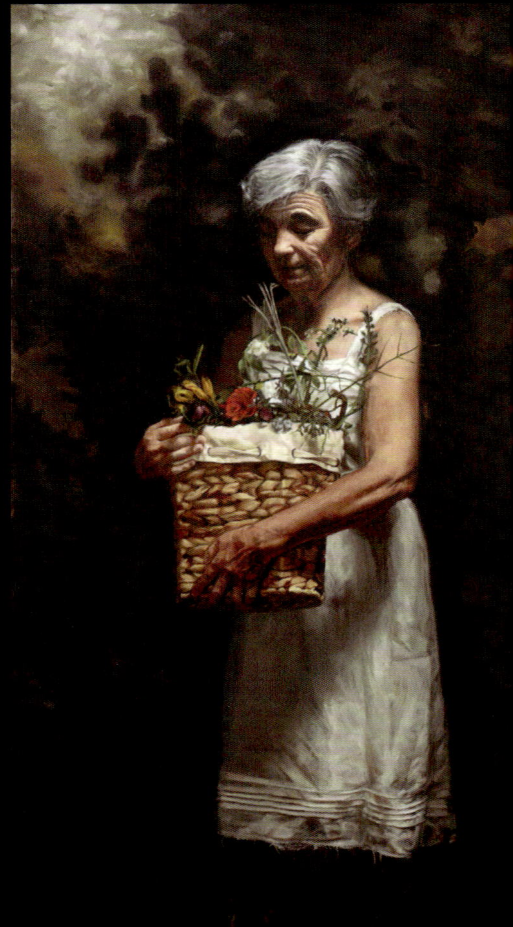

(L) **DISTINGUISHED MERIT** *Kari Brooks* (R) *Jackie Rent*

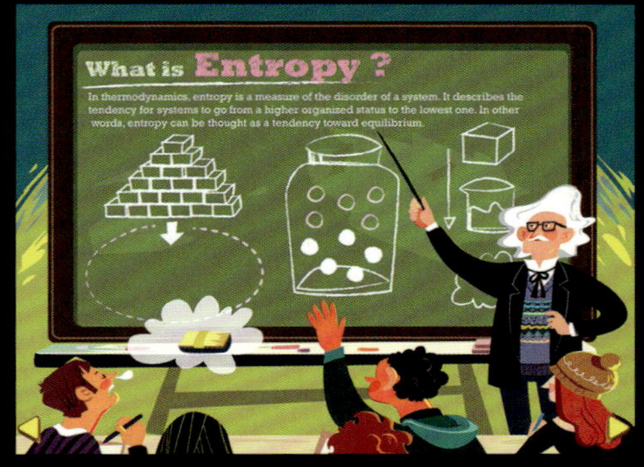
What is Entropy ?
In thermodynamics, entropy is a measure of the disorder of a system. It describes the tendency for systems to go from a higher organized status to the lowest one. In other words, entropy can be thought as a tendency toward equilibrium.

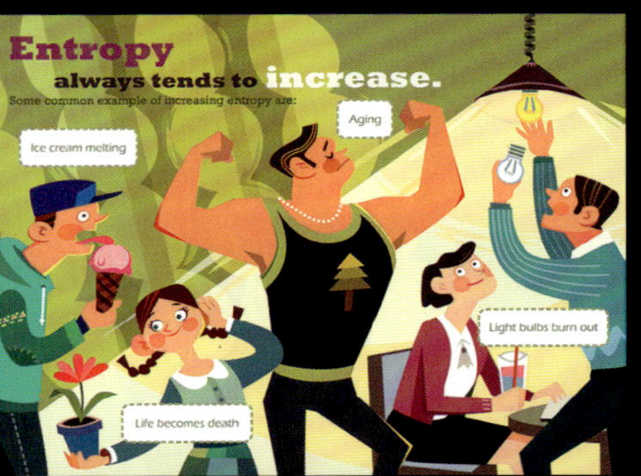
Entropy
always tends to increase.
Some common example of increasing entropy are:
Ice cream melting
Aging
Light bulbs burn out
Life becomes death

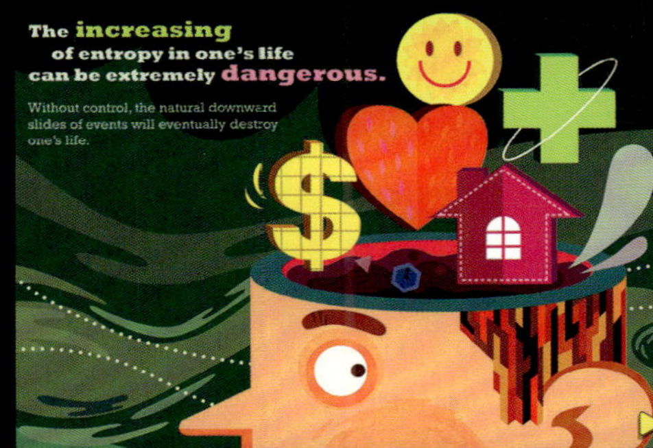
The increasing
of entropy in one's life
can be extremely dangerous.
Without control, the natural downward slides of events will eventually destroy one's life.

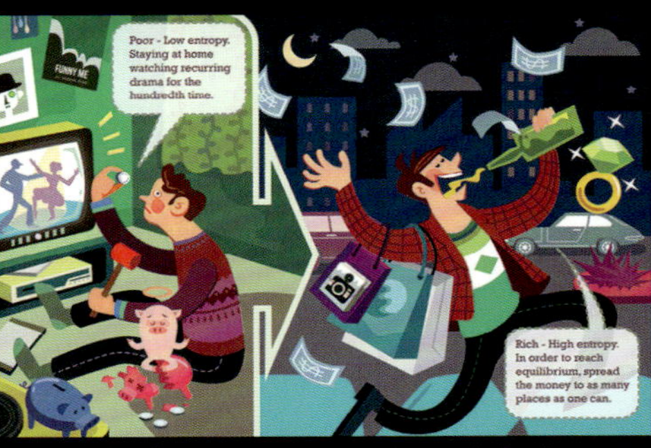
Poor - Low entropy. Staying at home watching recurring drama for the hundredth time.
Rich - High entropy. In order to reach equilibrium, spread the money to as many places as one can.
FUNNY ME
Some behavior can also be explained by the concept of entropy:
Things tend to be disorder. Entropy explains the way people spend money.

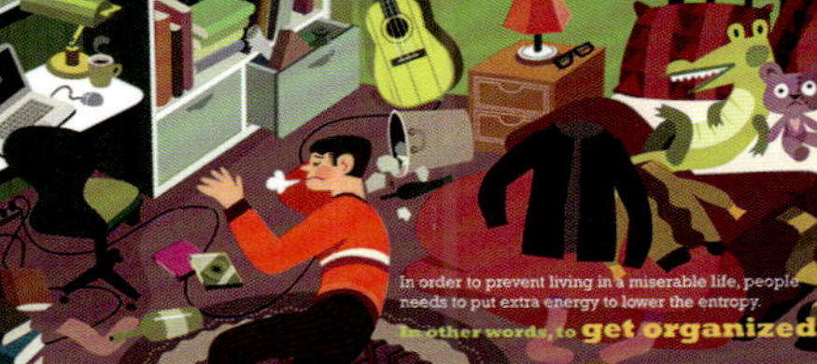
ENTROPY
In order to prevent living in a miserable life, people needs to put extra energy to lower the entropy.
In other words, to get organized!

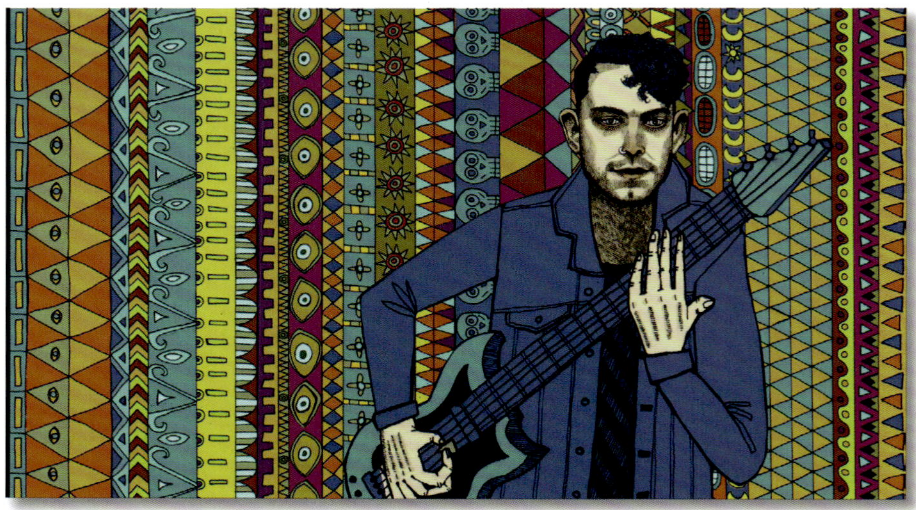

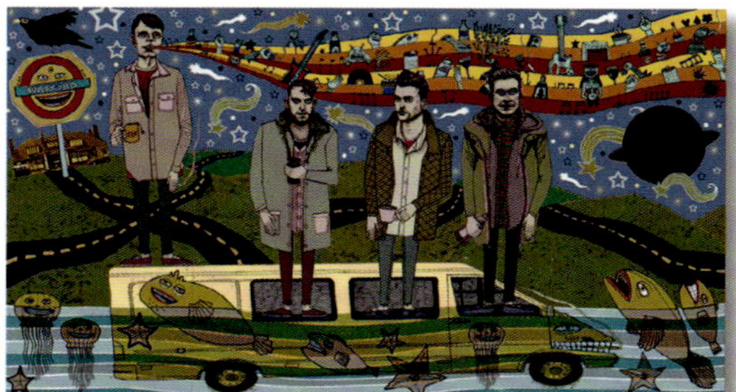

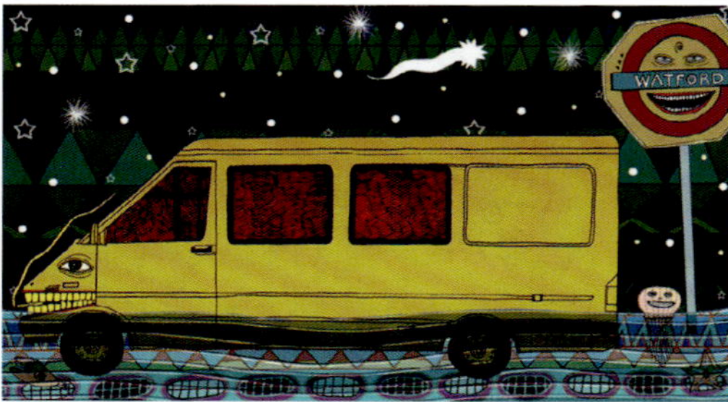

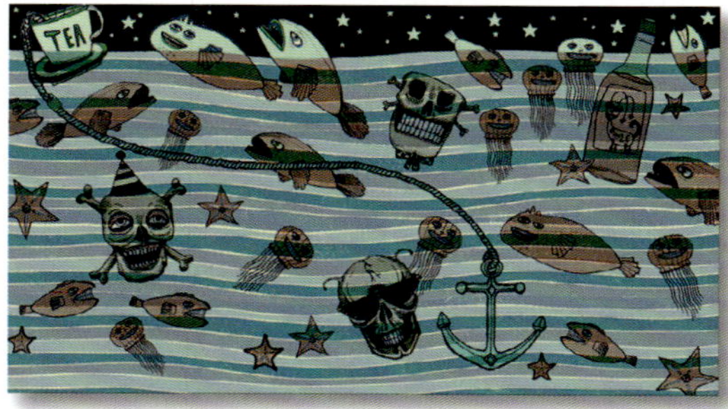

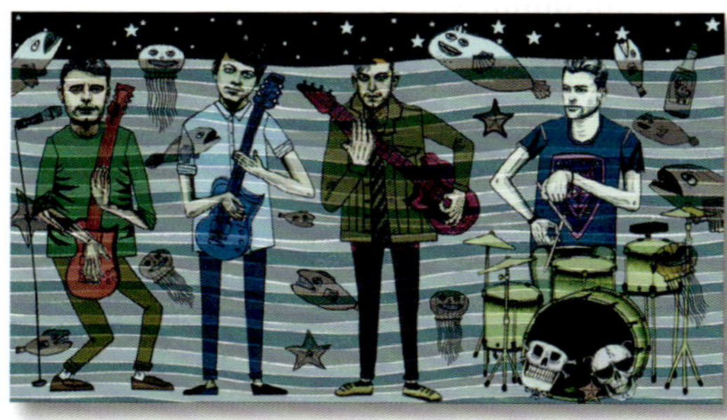

(L) Rebecca Hendin (R) Cyndi Waldron

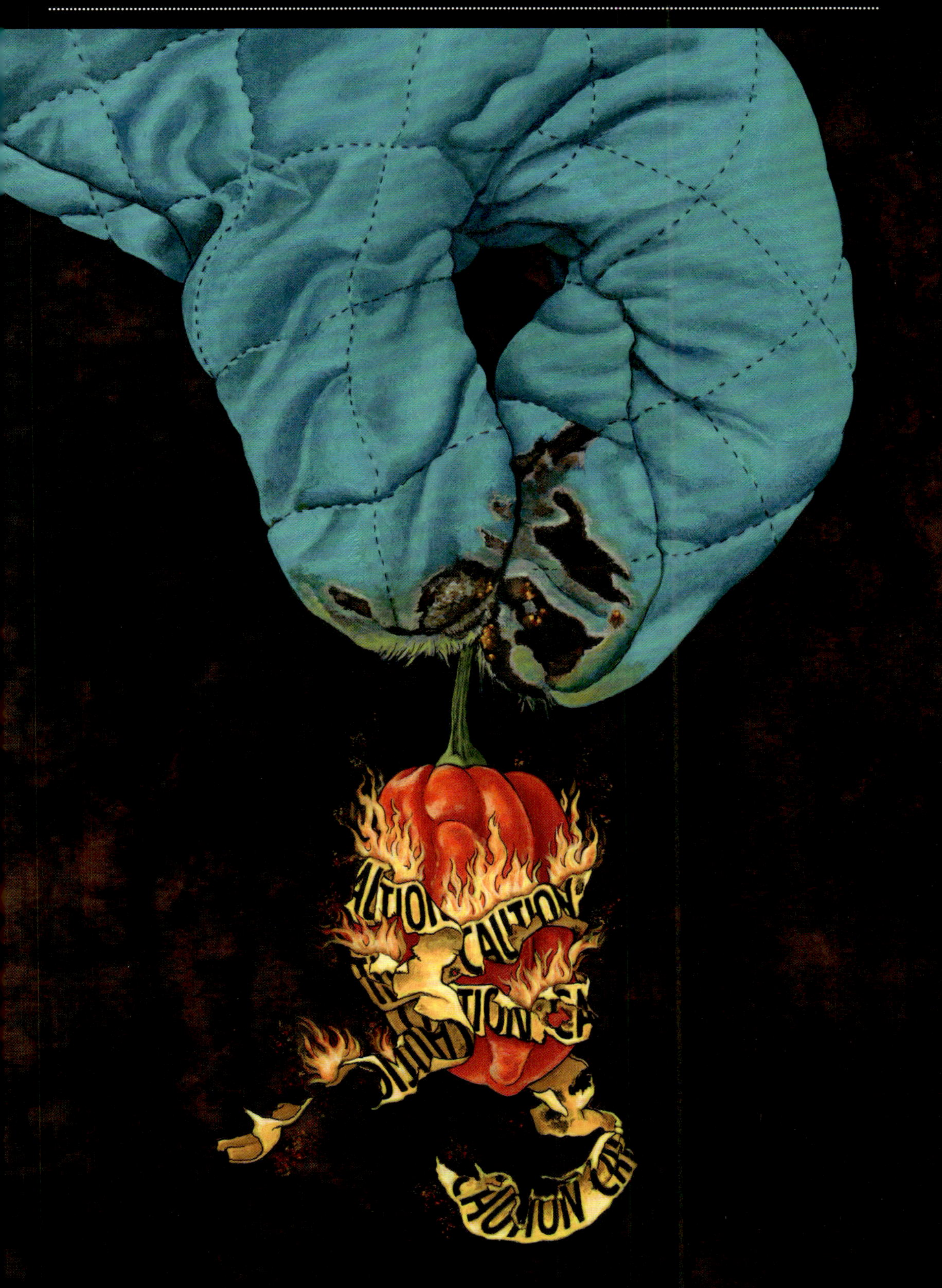

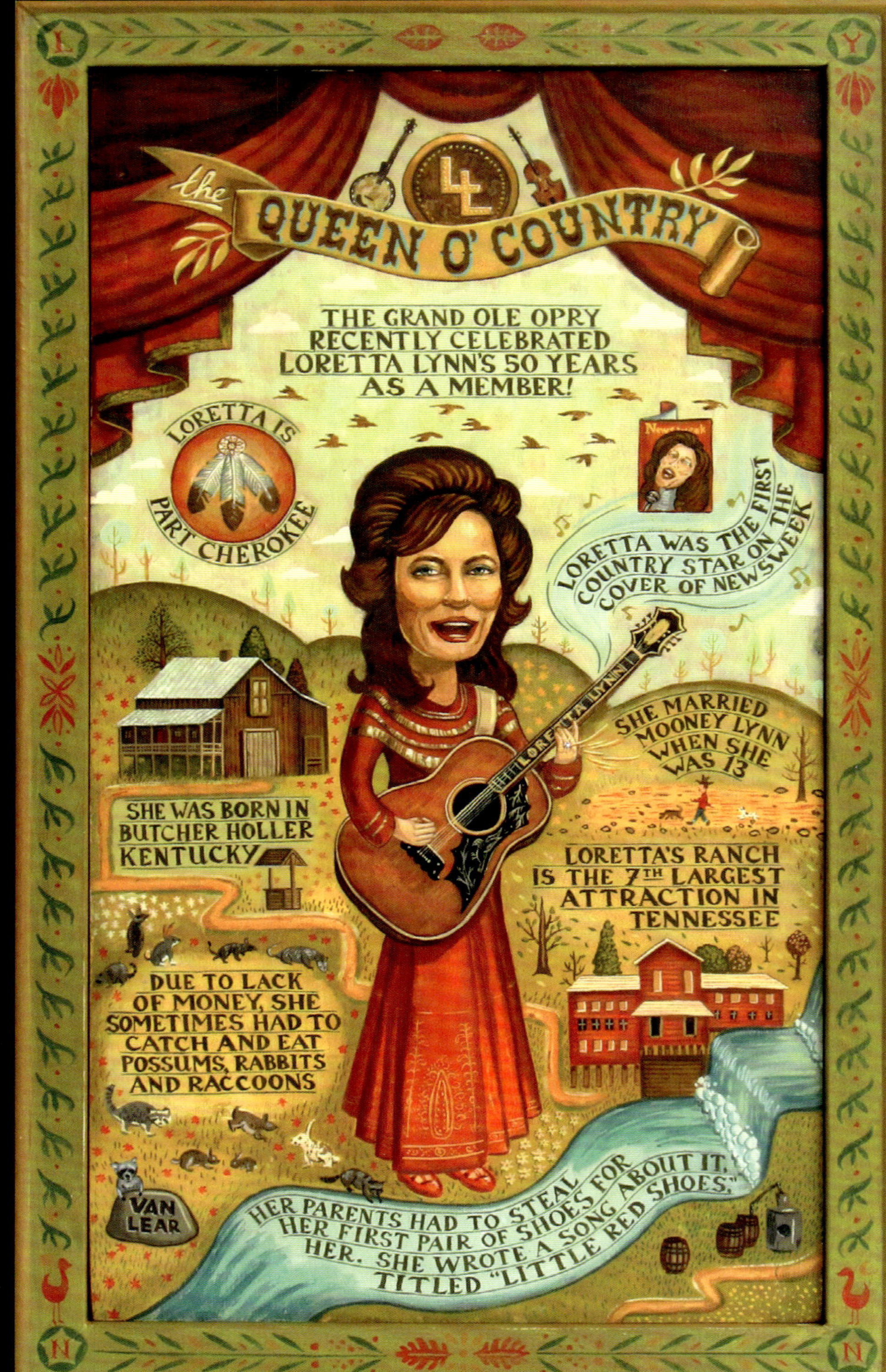
the QUEEN O' COUNTRY
LL
THE GRAND OLE OPRY RECENTLY CELEBRATED LORETTA LYNN'S 50 YEARS AS A MEMBER!
LORETTA IS PART CHEROKEE
LORETTA WAS THE FIRST COUNTRY STAR ON THE COVER OF NEWSWEEK
Newsweek
SHE MARRIED MOONEY LYNN WHEN SHE WAS 13
SHE WAS BORN IN BUTCHER HOLLER KENTUCKY
LORETTA'S RANCH IS THE 7TH LARGEST ATTRACTION IN TENNESSEE
DUE TO LACK OF MONEY, SHE SOMETIMES HAD TO CATCH AND EAT POSSUMS, RABBITS AND RACCOONS
VAN LEAR
HER PARENTS HAD TO STEAL HER FIRST PAIR OF SHOES FOR HER. SHE WROTE A SONG ABOUT IT, TITLED "LITTLE RED SHOES."

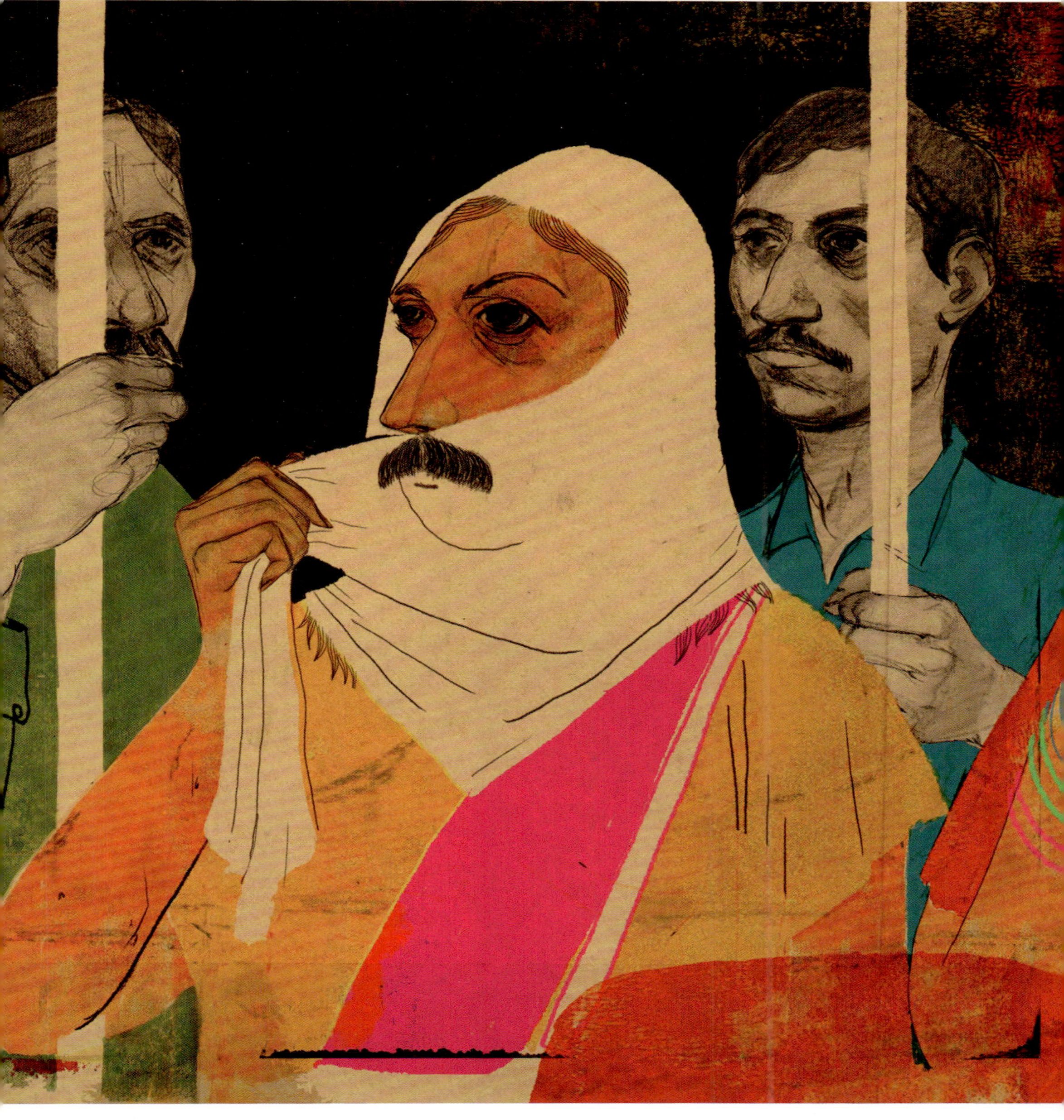

(L) *Ryan Cho* (R) *Pablo Iglesias*

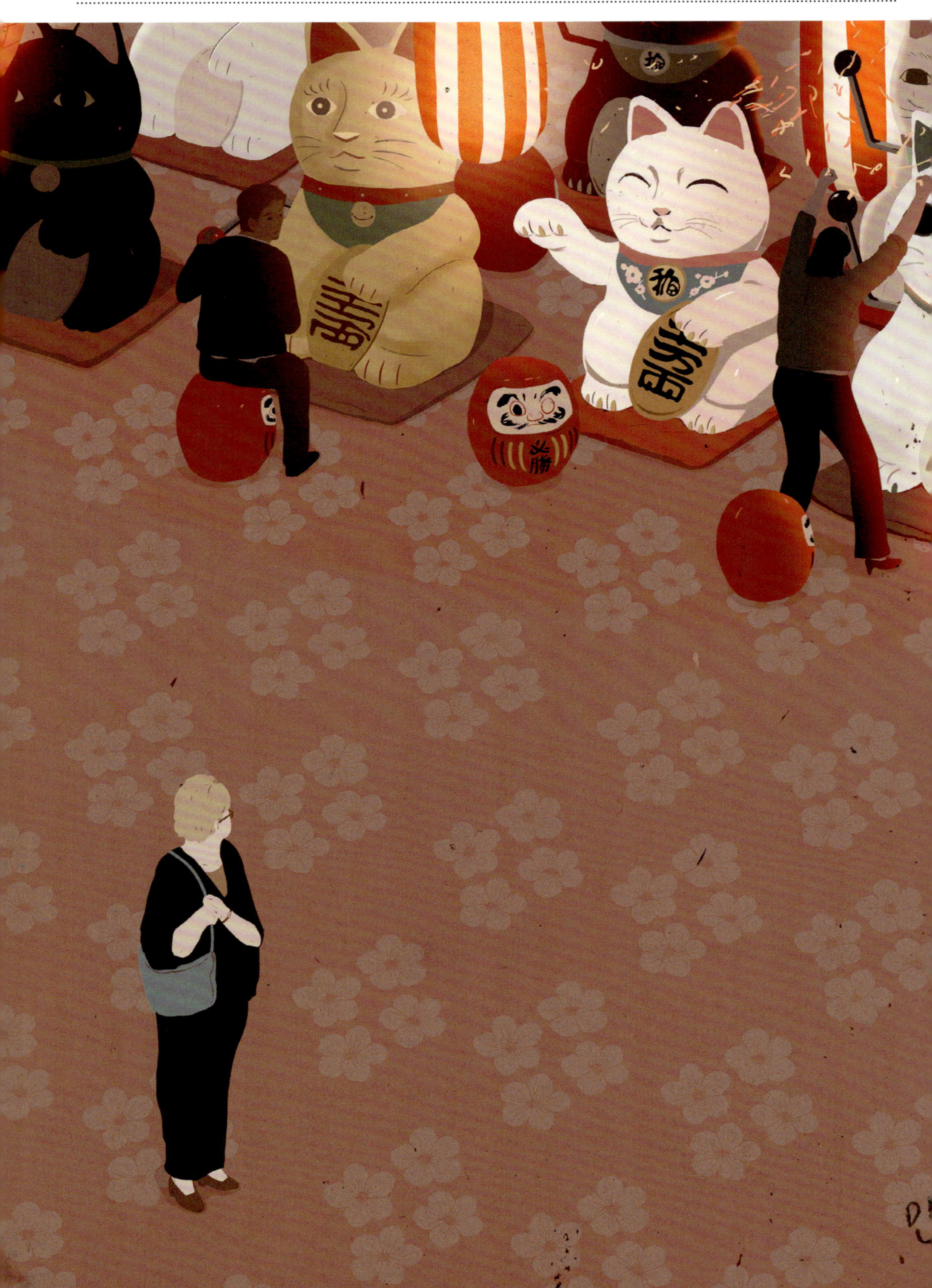

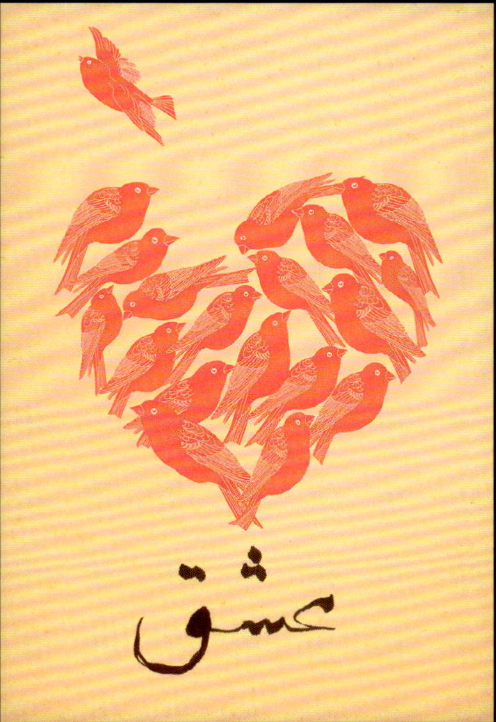

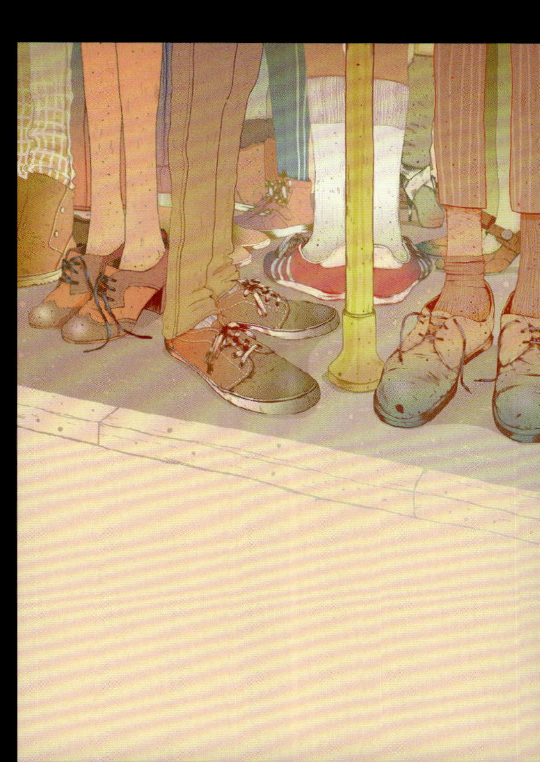

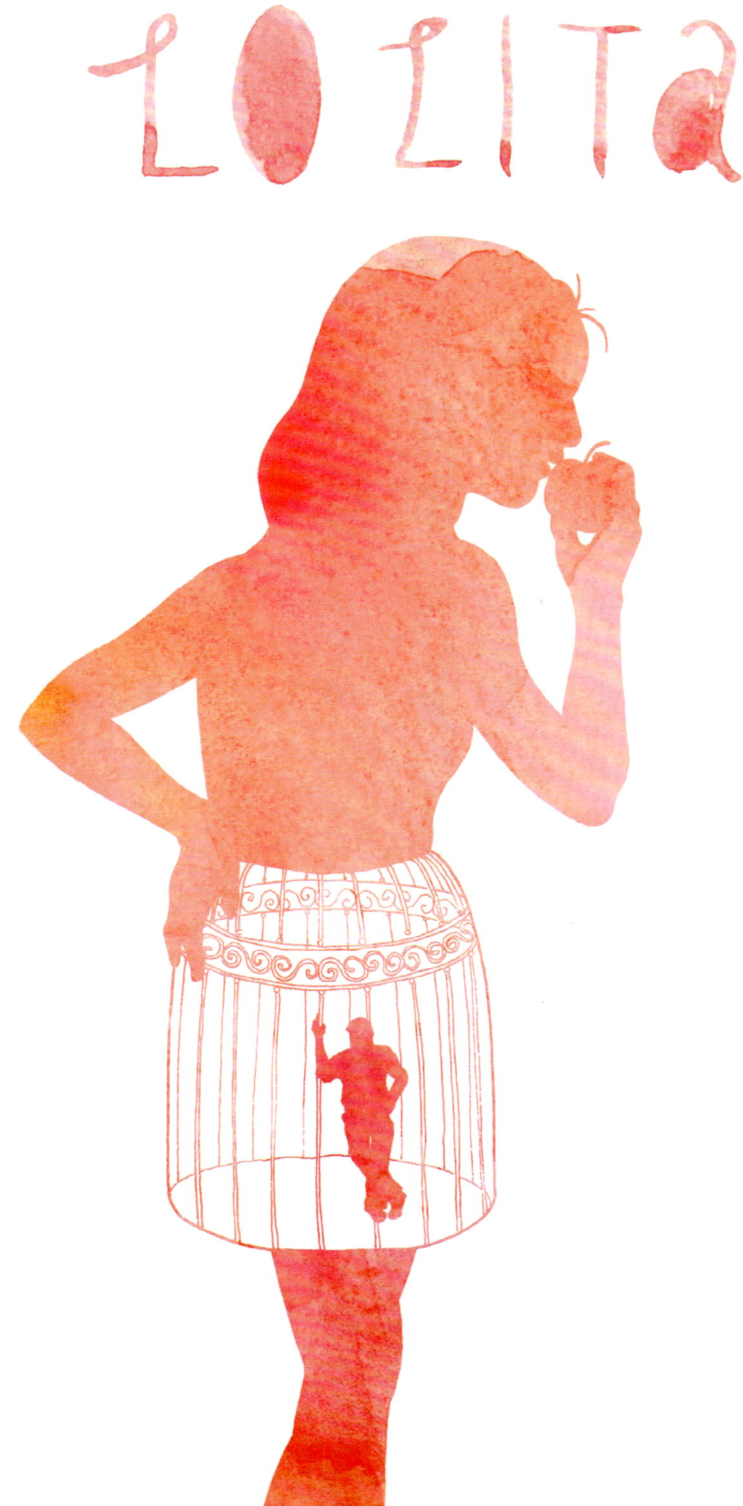

LOLITA

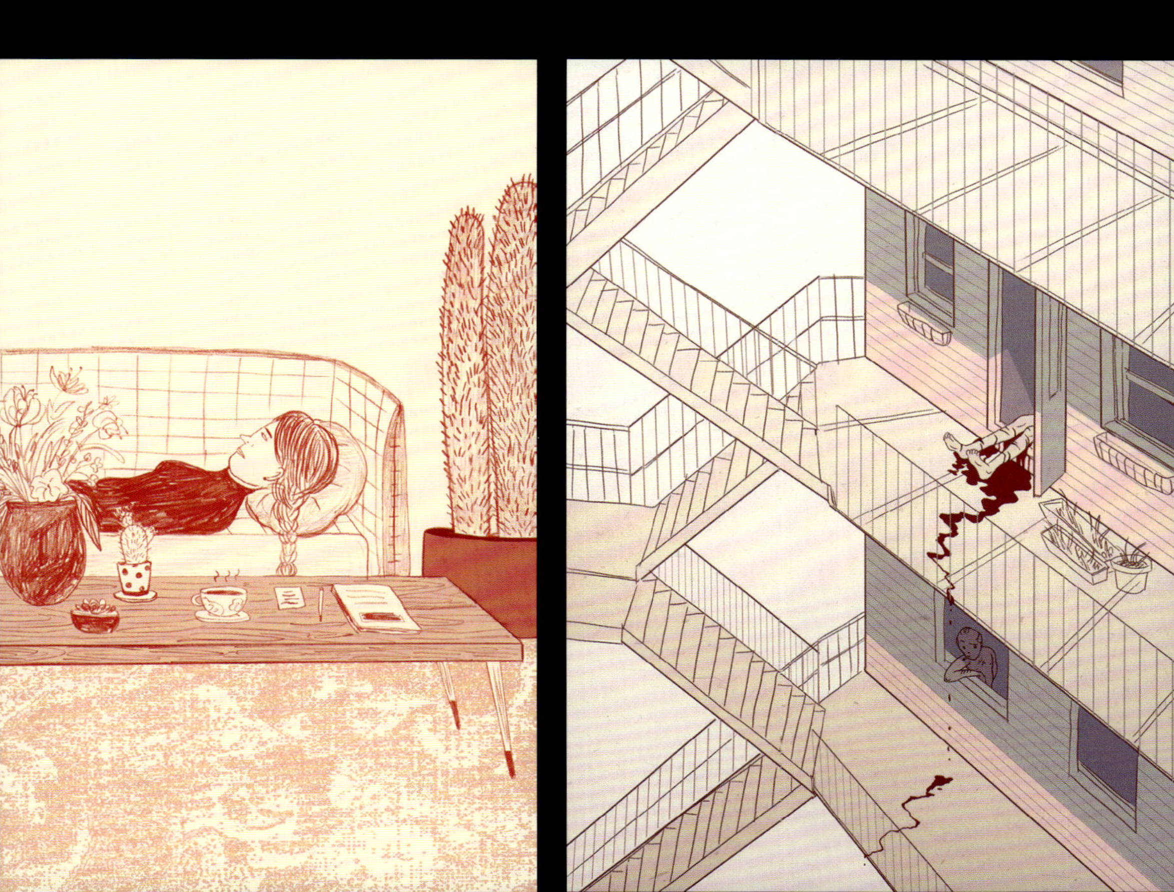

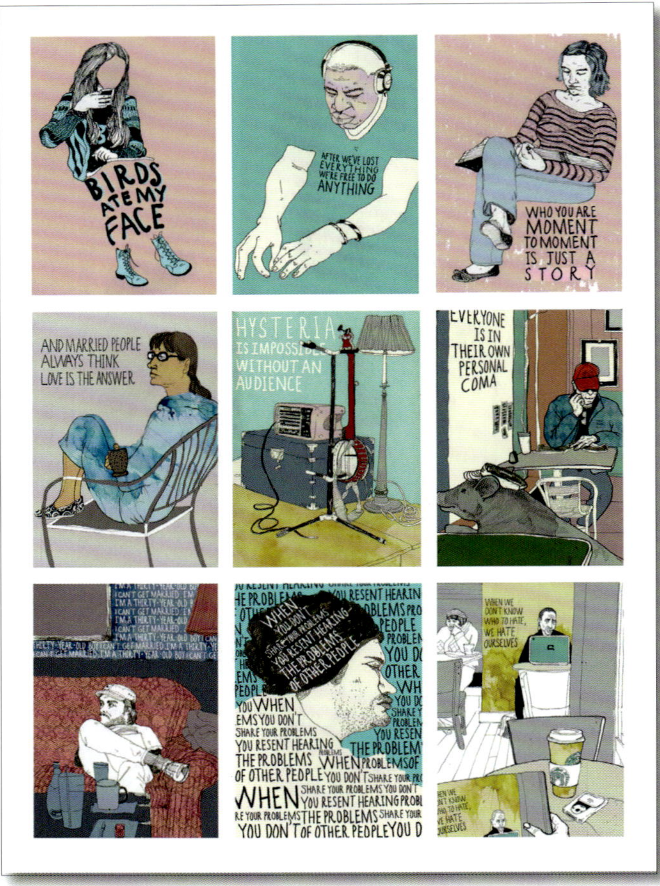

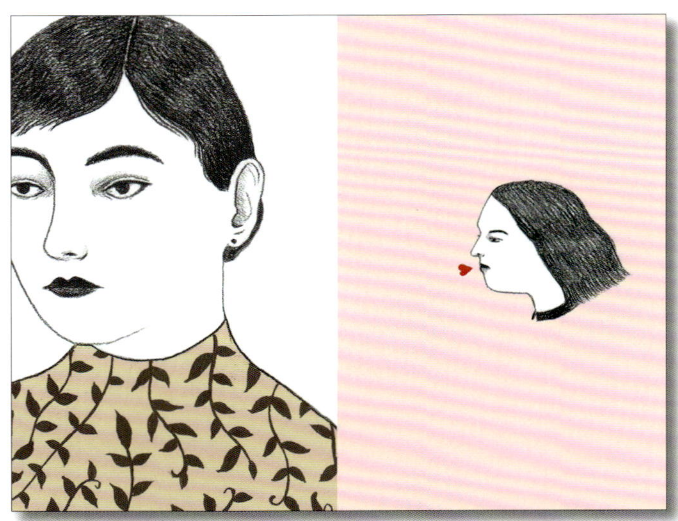

(T) *Nguyen Tran* (B) *Rachel Levit*

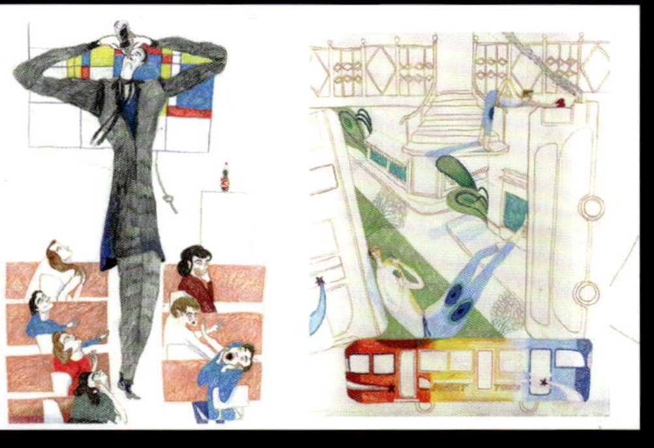

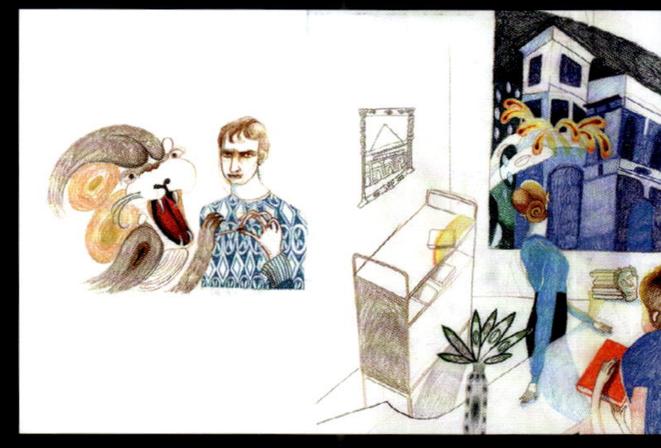

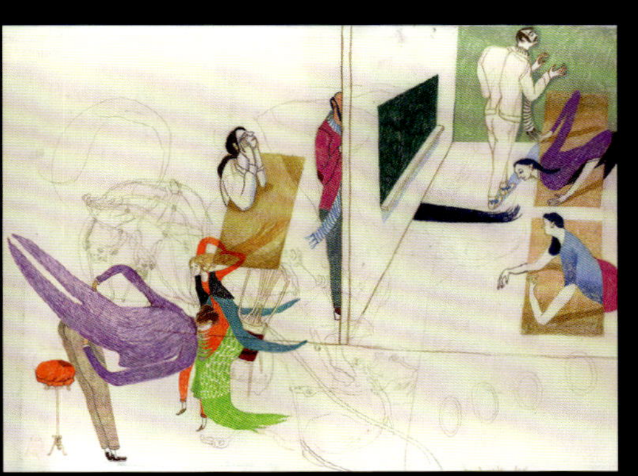

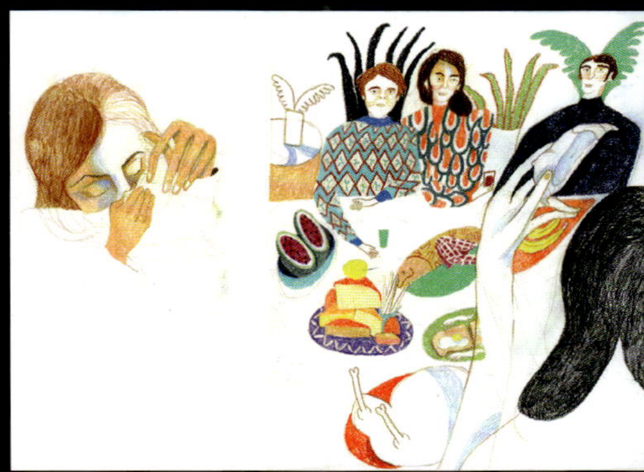

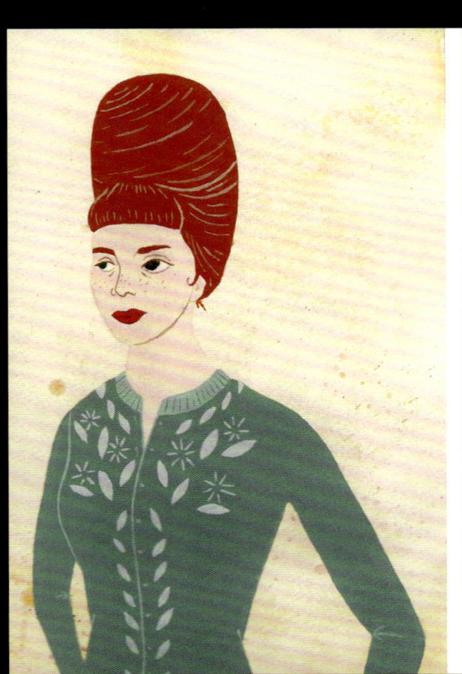

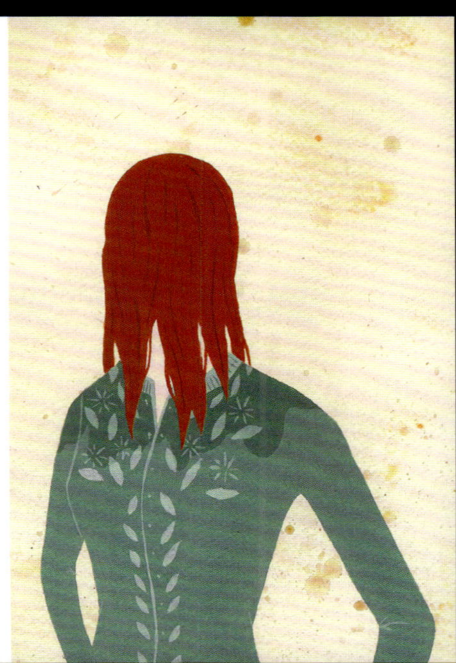

(T) *Keren Katz* (B) *Meghann Stephenson*

Stobbe.

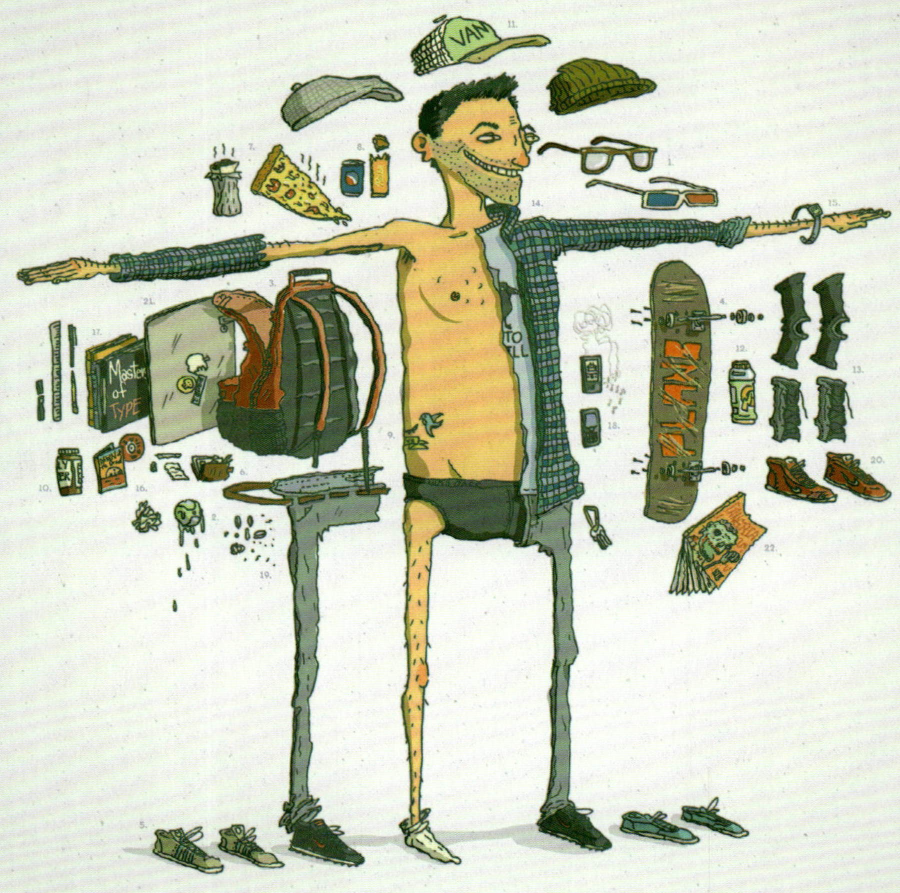

1. Super Spectacles
Pair 1: Not only used for aesthetic reasons, these specs can even enhance the wearers vision back to around 20/20/40.
Pair 2: These super specs, when worn in combination with Pair 1, will allow the viewer to see the world in the THIRD DIMENSION.

2. Soggy Ball(s)
Treasured by the four-legged hair monster, this item is used to distract and/or entertain the great beast.

3. Bottomless Knapsack
This reliable parcel will hold anything and everything one would ever need for real. Also known as a stick trick to the wallet.

4. Exacting Skateboard Setup
A very particular and precise setup, that can only be honed from many, many years of shred slaving.

5. Kicks
Extensive library of shoes for every occasion, and/or whatever.

6. Costanza (style) Wallet
This hand-fed wallet contains anything one would need in any situation. Its ugly equivalent would be Batman's utility belt.

7. Pizza/Burritos
One of his few weaknesses. Much like kryptonite to superman, except delicious.

8. Drug(s) of choice
Two of the most coveted of all ingestibles: Pepsi and Reese's cups. Signs of recent use are sticky aluminum cans and chocolate stains.

9. Tattoos (also see skateboarding)
Each of these badges of honor represents many battles won and lost to just look bad ass.

10. Empty Daily Fiber Pill Bottle
One of the many mysteries that have yet to be solved.

11. Headgear
Much like the shoe library, this collection has been assembled through a very long and rigorous selection process.

12. Three Day Old Gatorade Bottle
A very common sight. Either stowed away in the depths of the bottomless knapsack or quietly boiling in a cup holder (the interior of the car near 3000°).

13. Battlegear
Performance enhancing equipment, that supplements and strengthens appendages weakened from all the years of slashing.

14. Attire
In order from bottom to top:
Signature Plaid Button-up
It's the perfect combination of business and casual.
Graphic Tee
Used to artistically express one's personality through a visual form of communication/fashion.
Skate Denim
Very stylish, yet comfortable. These not only heighten one's outward appearance, but can also increase one's skating ability ten fold.
Designer Briefs
You can never be too sure.
Misc
Belt, socks... check.

15. The Watch
This über cool watch is not only aesthetically pleasing but it's impossible to read.

16. Blue Ray(s)
They can always be found on or near his person. Contact verbs from mild to crazy, resemble blood bath.

17. Design Wizardry
These handy tools are always at close at hand, you never know when you need to summon up a powerful design.

18. Essential Digital(s)
These devices are always at close reach, unless you really need to get a hold of him. Devices consistently remain at 25% battery life (or less).

19. Pocket Treasures
Always a random mix of essentials and the down right mysterious.

20. Skate (Kicks)
They have the amazing ability to shred and only sustain minor damage. Though once the sole has been slightly smashed, they must be retired and replaced with a fresh pair.

21. Dragon Heart (also see MacBook)
If this was to ever become lost or destroyed, he too will go with it... ok wait, never mind. He has an alias at home. It would still hurt though.

22. Splatter Mags
The essential for all mega blast fans. A great way to brush up on your infinite wisdom of the horror film genre. Fake spilling guts, decapitated heads, and splattering brains all in most melting, full colors!

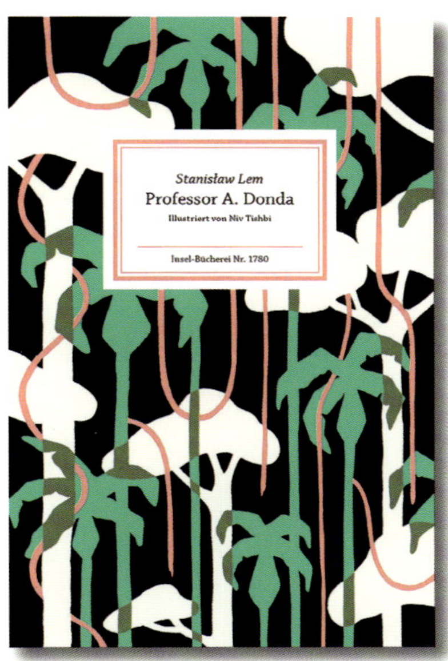

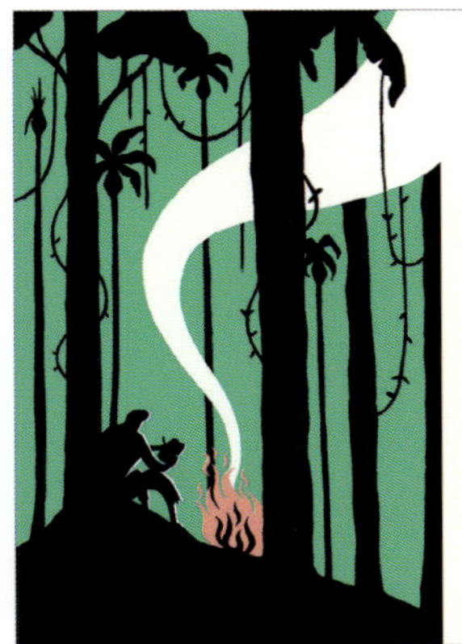

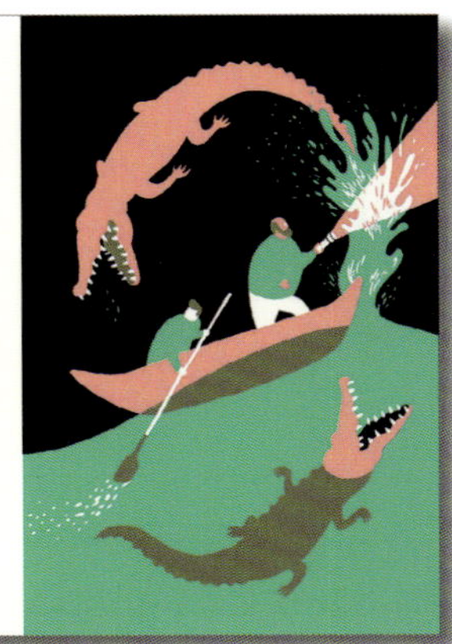

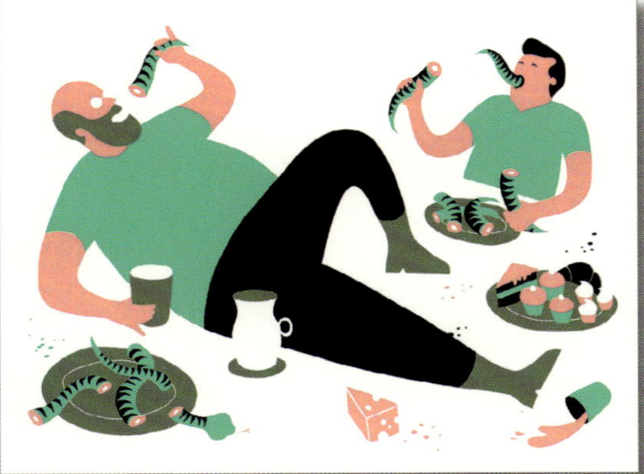

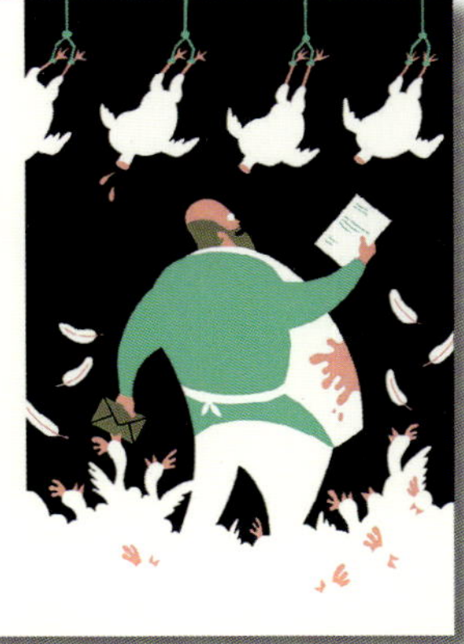

(L) *Jeff Lowry* (R) DISTINGUISHED MERIT *Niv Tishbi*

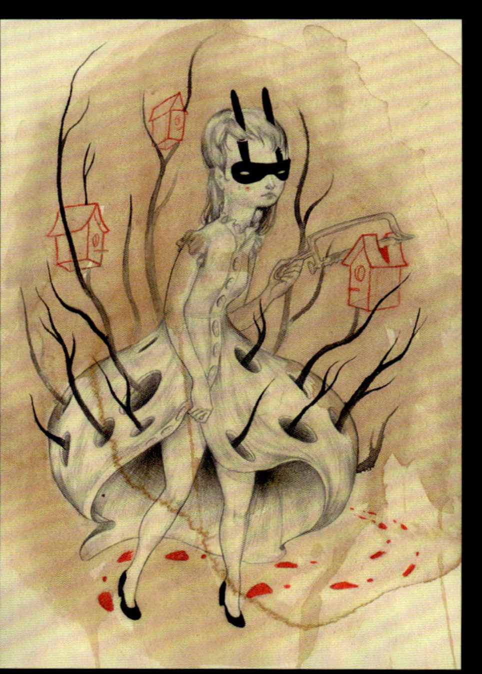
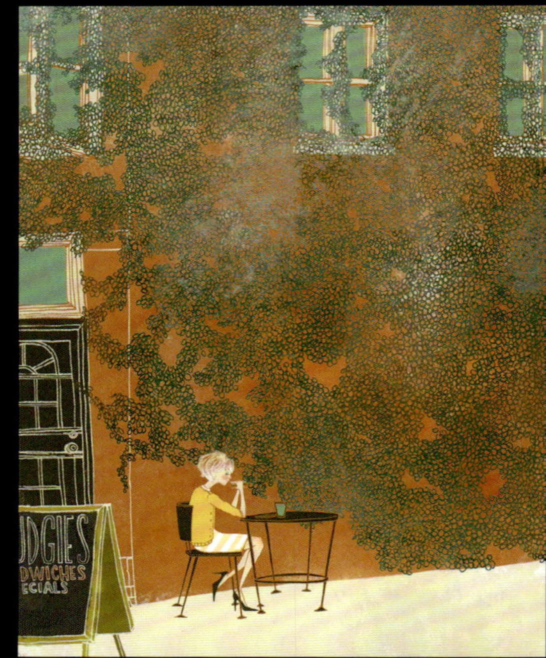

DGIES
DWICHES
ECIALS

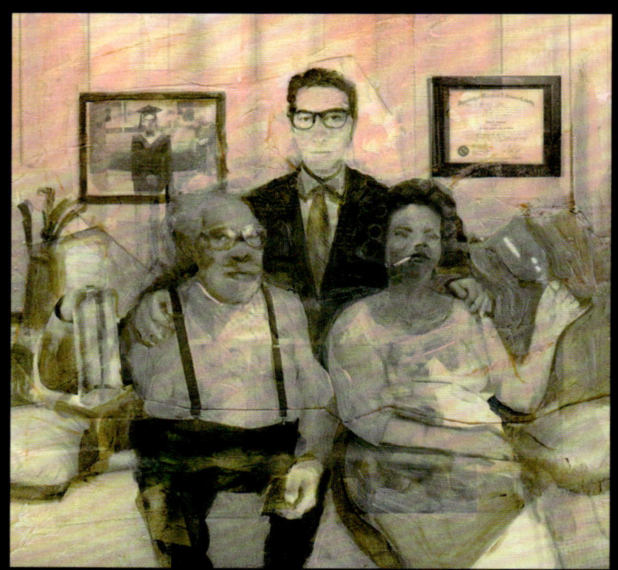

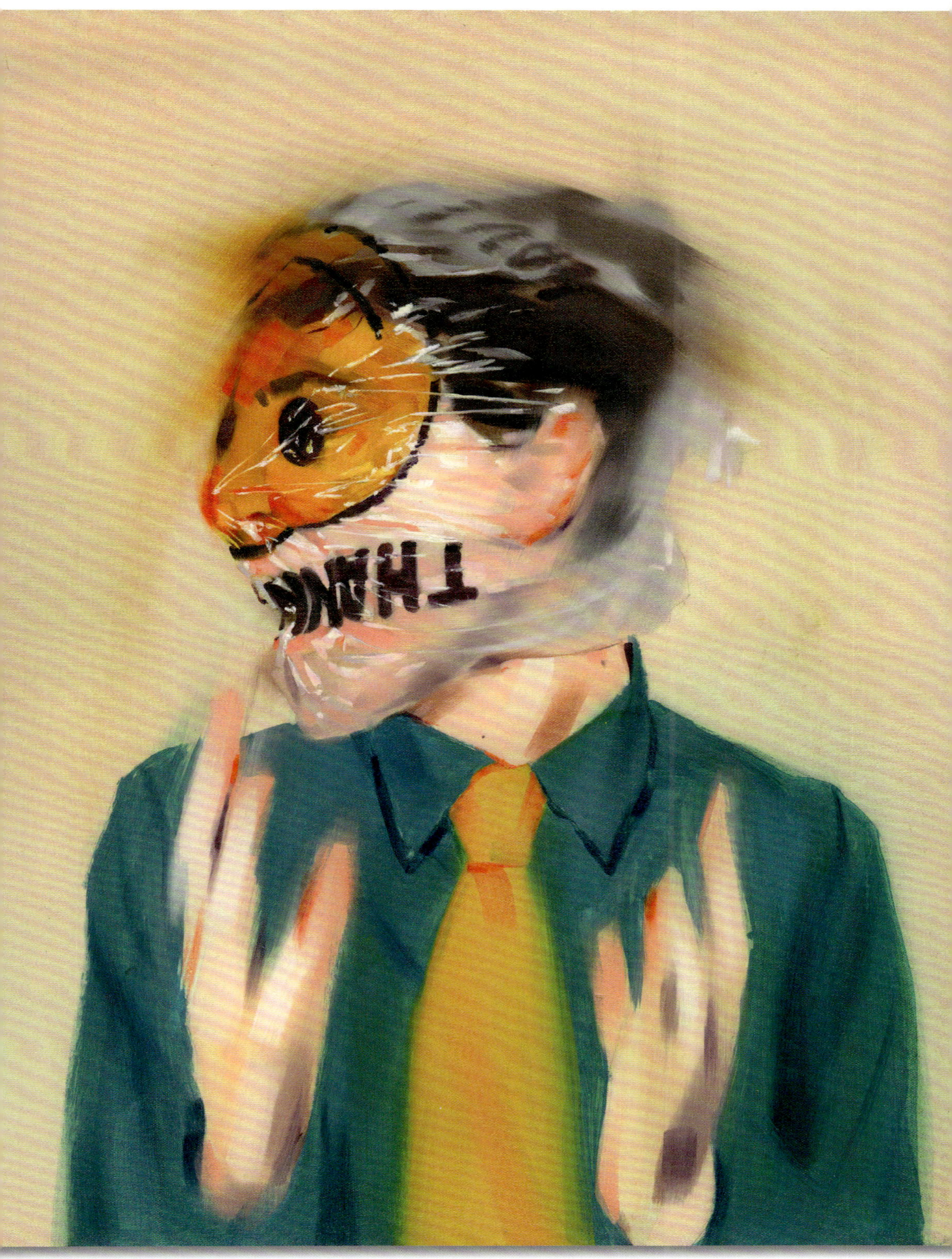

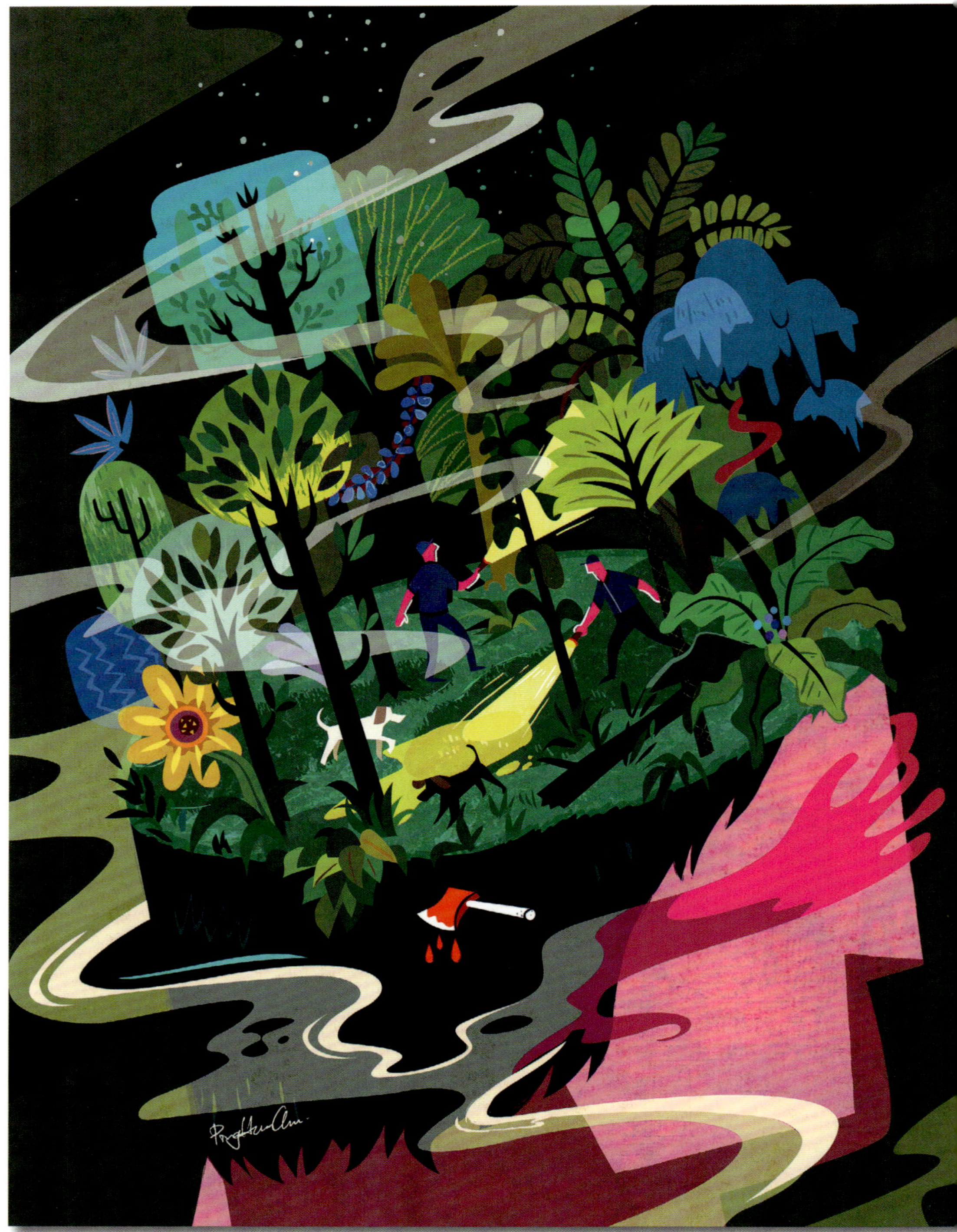

Ping Hua Chou

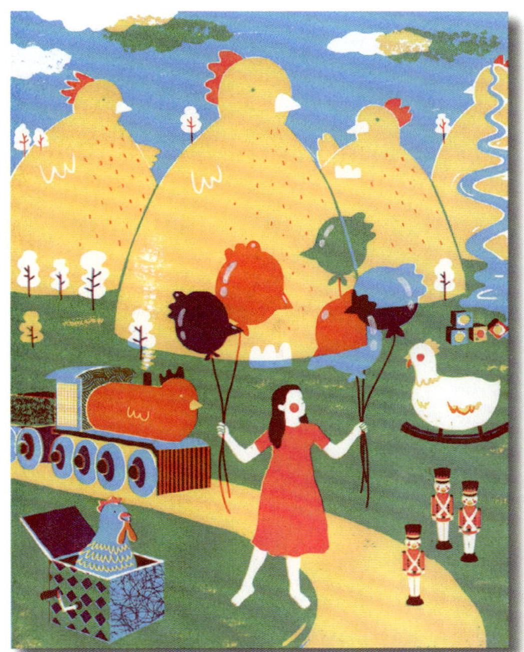
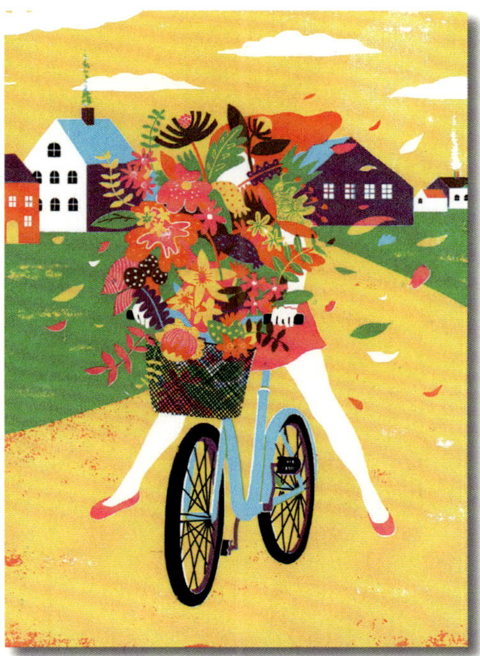

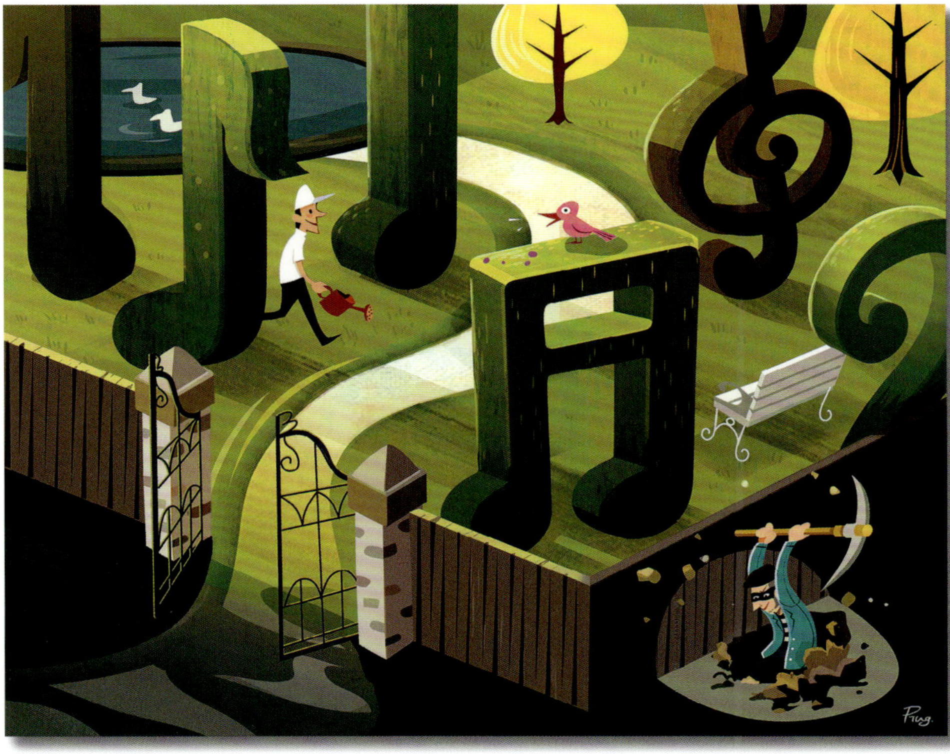

(T) *Boyoun Kim* (B) *Ping Hua Chou*

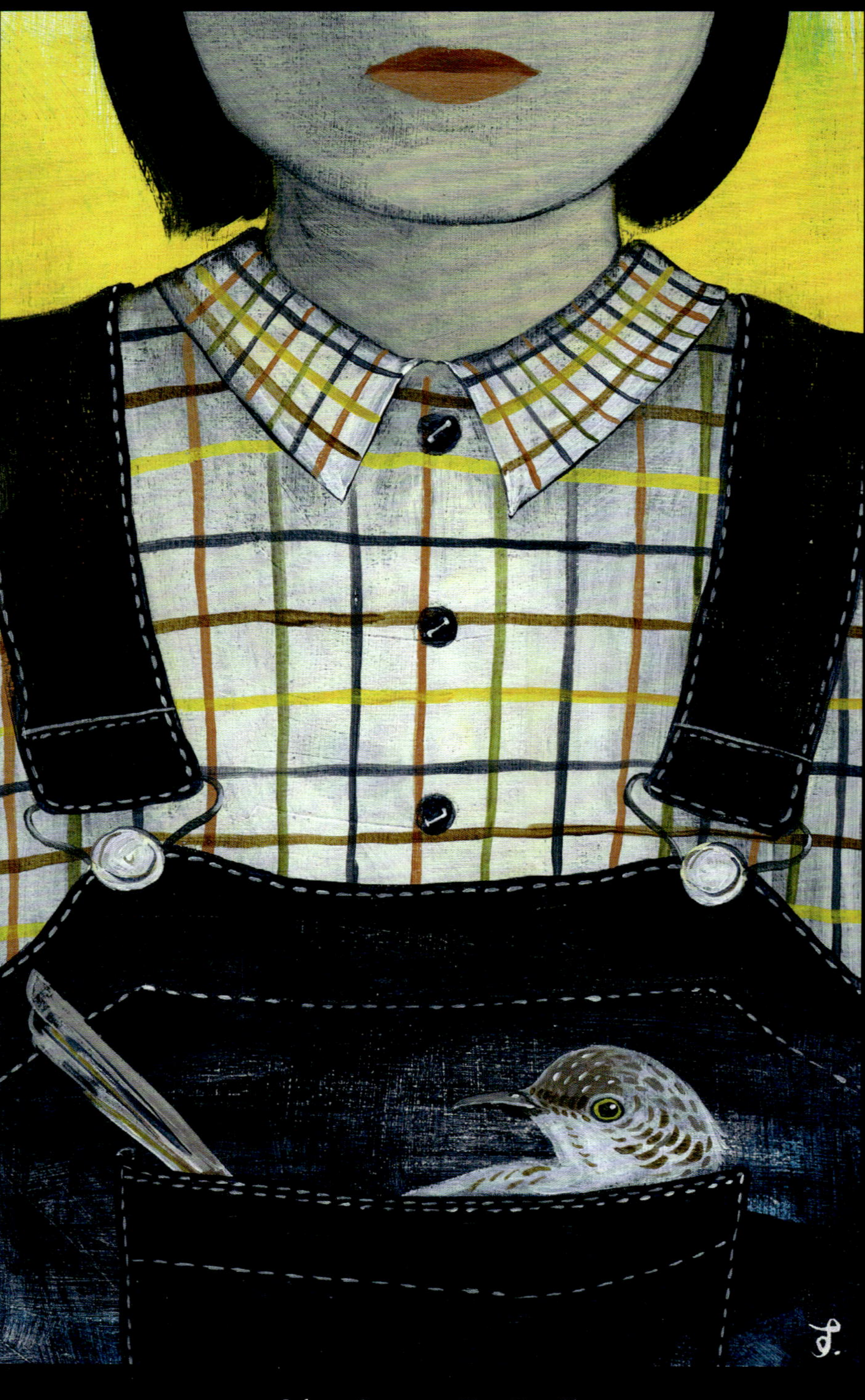

(L) *Suharu Ogawa* (R) *Ping Hua Chou*

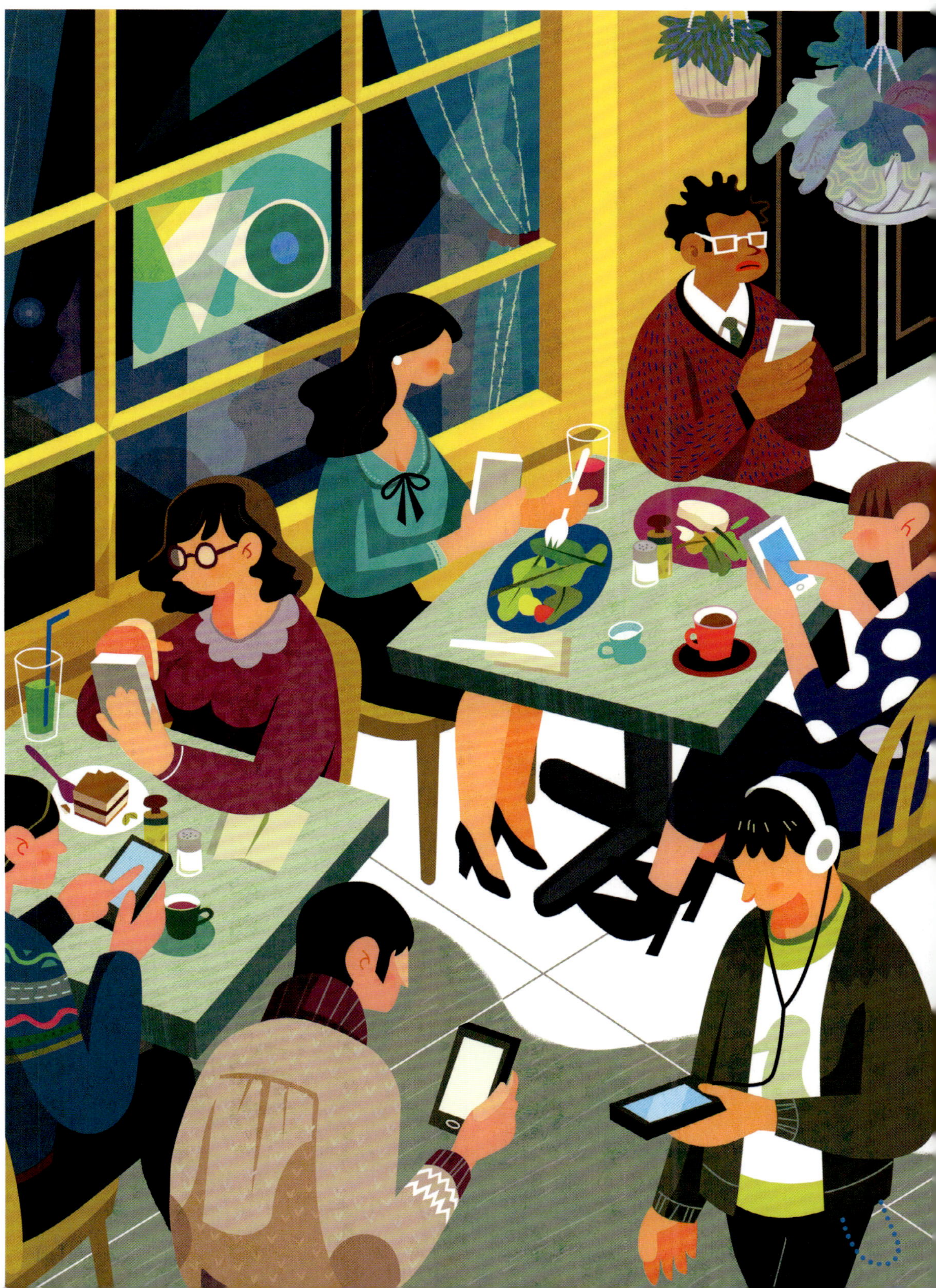

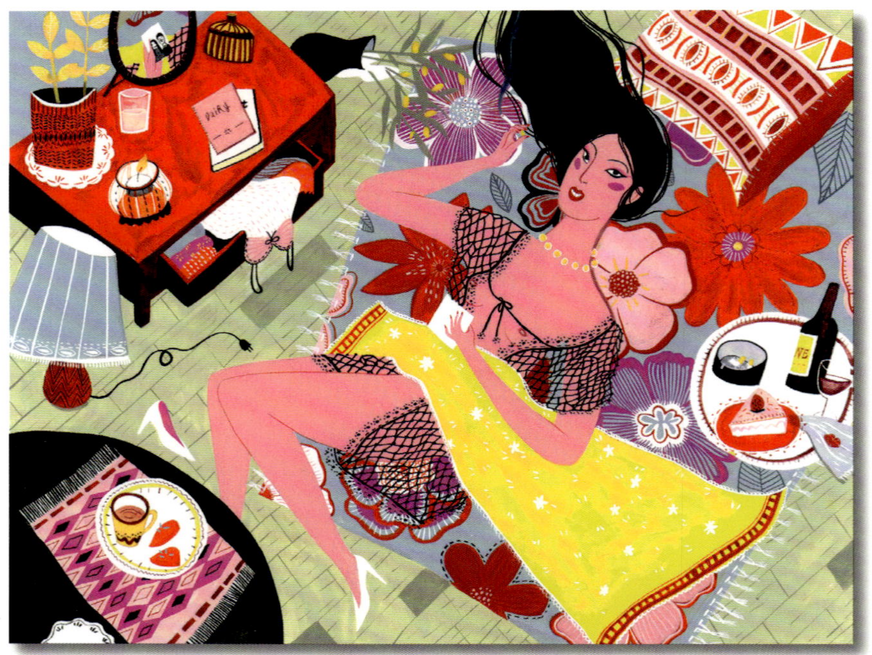

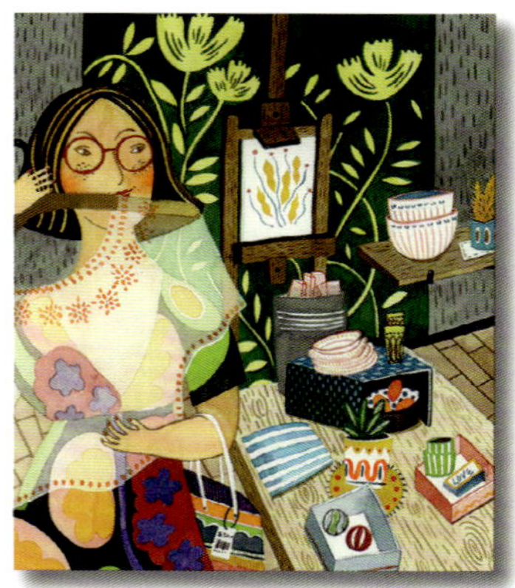

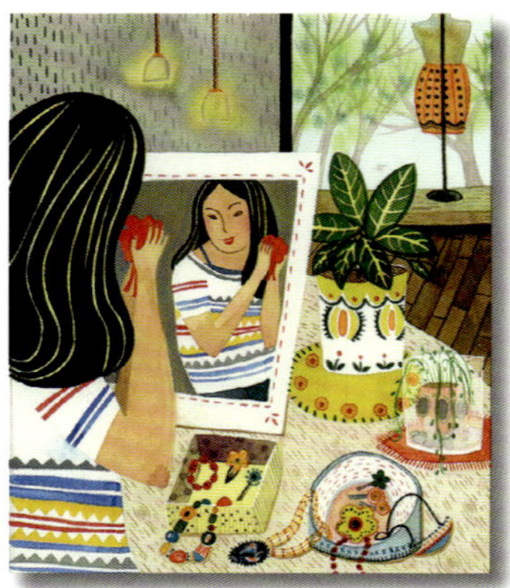

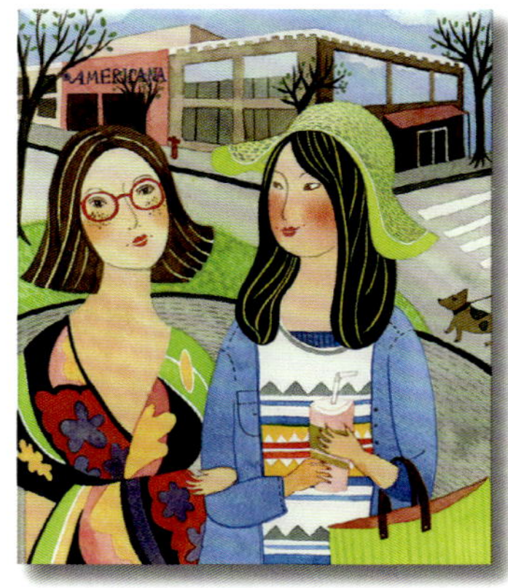

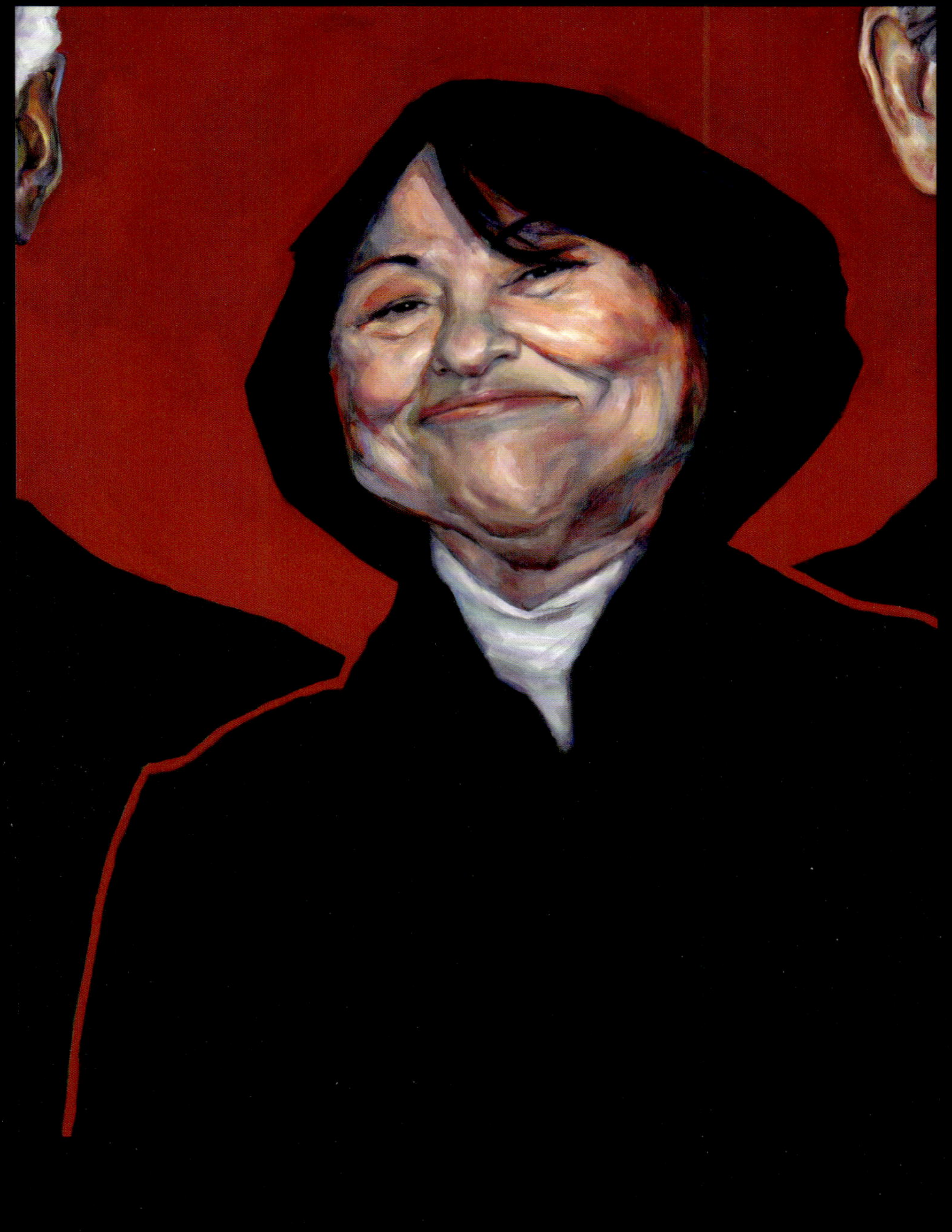

(L) *Ayumi Takahashi* (R) *Lori Klopp*

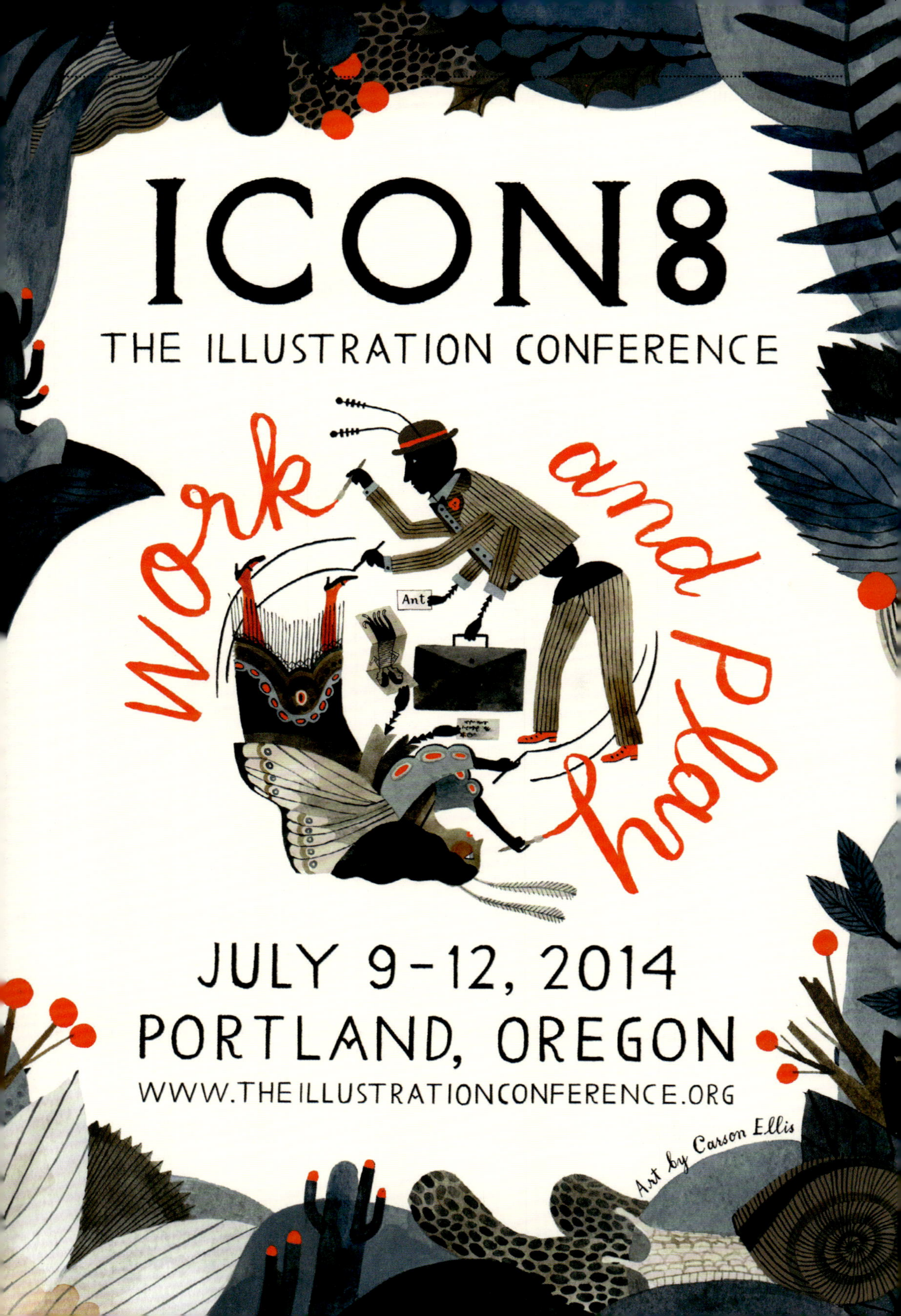

ICON8
THE ILLUSTRATION CONFERENCE
work and play
Ant.
JULY 9-12, 2014
PORTLAND, OREGON
WWW.THEILLUSTRATIONCONFERENCE.ORG
Art by Carson Ellis

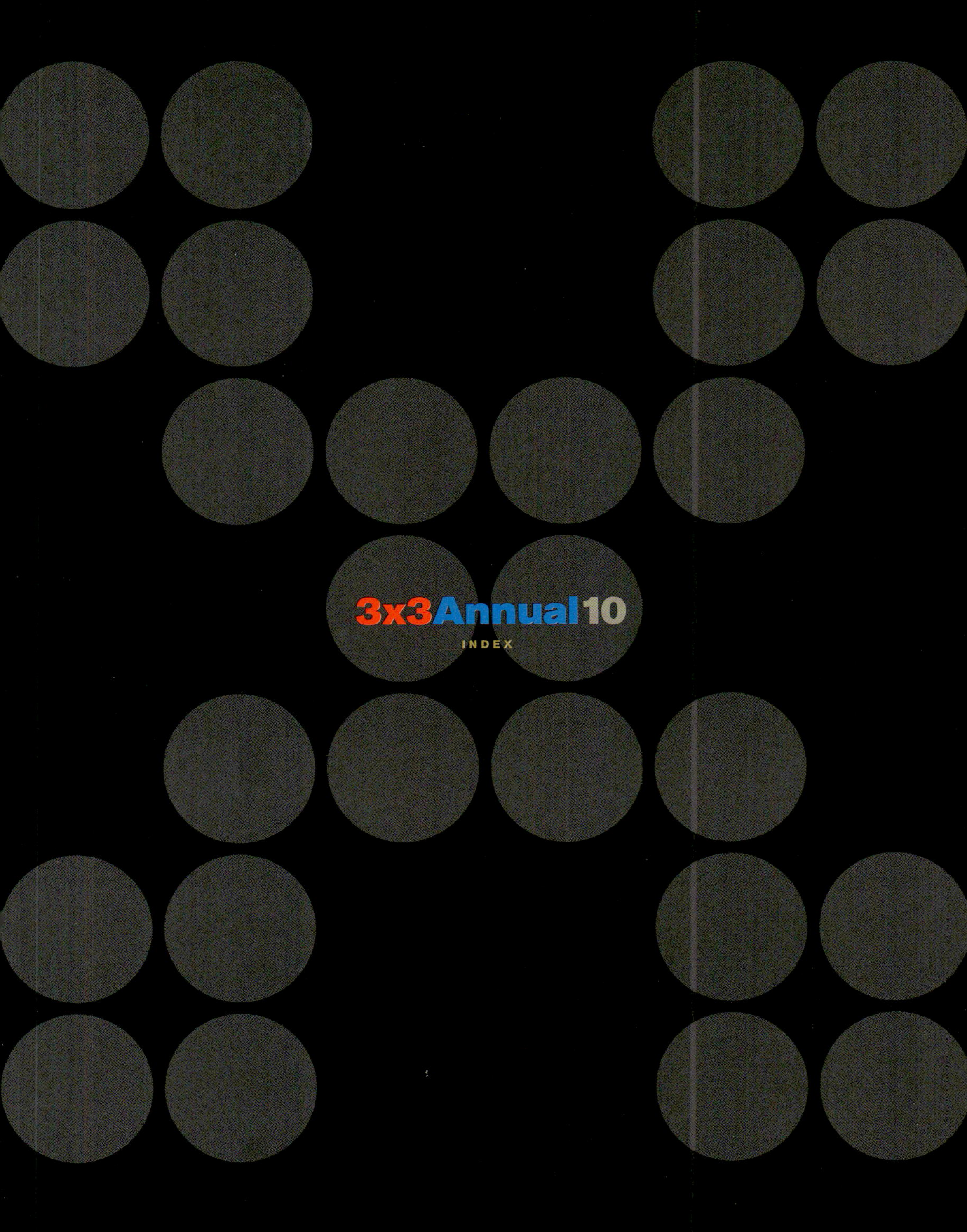
3x3Annual10
INDEX

INDEX

GARY AAGAARD
aagz@msn.com
p 184 CLIENT: James Kirchhausen
GALLERY: Ward-Nasse Gallery, NYC
MEDIA: Oil
DIMENSIONS: 30" × 40"

LIISA AALTIO
liisa.aaltio@gmail.com
p 375 INSTITUTION: OCAD University
INSTRUCTOR: Stephanie Power

MATTIAS ADOLFSSON
mattiasadolfsson@gmail.com
p 95 ART DIRECTOR: Tobias Ryden
AUTHOR: Martin Gelin
PUBLISHER: Dagens Nyheter
MEDIA: Ink and watercolor
DIMENSIONS: 10" × 11.5"
p 169 GALLERY: Gallery Nucleus
MEDIA: Ink and watercolor
DIMENSIONS: 9" × 14.7"

EMMA AHLQVIST
emmsou@hotmail.com
p 392 INSTITUTION: Edinburgh College of Art
INSTRUCTOR: Jonathan Gibbs

MONIKA AICHELE
mail@monikaaichele.com
p 228 DIMENSIONS: 6.9" × 10"

JUSTINAS ALISAUSKAS
jusdiz@gmail.com
p 411 INSTITUTION: Ballyfermot College of
Further Education

RAFAEL ALVAREZ
rafa@alvarezrafa.com
p 340 TITLE: In weiter Ferne, so nah
ART DIRECTOR: Anna Meyer
CLIENT: Suddeutsche Zeitung Magazine

OFRA AMIT
studio@ofra-amit.com
p 183 DIMENSIONS: 7.9" × 8.3"

SCOTT ANDERSON
scott@scottandersonstudio.com
p 68 ART DIRECTOR: Jane Sherman
PUBLISHER: VVM
CLIENT: Seattle Weekly
MEDIA: Digital
DIMENSIONS: 9.75" × 11.25"

MARION ARBONA
marion.arbona@gmail.com
p 297 GOLD
TITLE: Jungle
p 343 DISTINGUISHED MERIT
TITLE: Quelle sacrée chance
AUTHOR: Sandrine Beau
EDITOR: Yves Nadon
PUBLISHER: Les 400 coups
p 350 TITLE: Maisons, arbres, personnages et
animaux

TOHRU PATRICK AWA
patrick_awa@mac.com
p 185 GALLERY: Nucleus
MEDIA: Watercolor, acrylic
DIMENSIONS: 11" × 21.5"

SCOTT BAKAL
info@scottbakal.com
p 194 TITLE: Pollution

DAVOR BAKARA
illustration@davorbakara.com

p 291 TITLE: Iggy Pop
DIMENSIONS: 6" × 10"

ANNA & ELENA BALBUSSO
apiue@balbusso.com
p 59 ART DIRECTORS: Sheri Gee, Raquel Allion
PUBLISHER: The Folio Society
MEDIA: Acrylic, digital
p 38 PUBLISHER: Giunti Progetti Educativi
DIRECTOR: Rita Brugnara
CLIENT: CCBP Consortium for Control of
Organic Products
MEDIA: Acrylic and digital
p 135 ART DIRECTORS: Nicholas Blechman, Rex
Bonomelli
PUBLISHER: The New York Times Book
Review
MEDIA: Acrylic, digital

ANDREW BANNECKER
abannecker@gmail.com
p 190 TITLE: Animism
p 193 TITLE: Cliff House

ISTVAN BANYAI
ibanyai@sbcglobal.net
p 159 ART DIRECTOR: Aviva Michaelov
PUBLISHER: The New York Times/Op-Ed
MEDIA: Pencil, digital
p 244 ART DIRECTOR: Rip Georges
PUBLISHER: LA Times
CLIENT: Los Angeles Times Magazine
MEDIA: Pencil, digital

KAREN BARBOUR
kbarbour@svn.net
p 104 ART DIRECTOR: Aviva Michaelov
PUBLISHER: The New York Times
p 256 DIMENSIONS: 22" × 33"
p 283 TITLE: Ghost
DIMENSIONS: 29.5" × 41"

GABRIELLA BAROUCH
gabriella-777@hotmail.com
p 36 CLIENT: Specialday.dk

JONATHAN BARTLETT
jb@bartlettstudio.com
p 74 DESIGN DIRECTOR: Charles Hively
DESIGN FIRM: HivelyDesigns
CLIENT: 3x3, The Magazineof
Contemporary Illustration

BECK
beckszwm@gmail.com
p 83 PUBLISHER: The Oldie Magazine (UK)
DIMENSIONS: 8.3" × 8.3"
p 88 PUBLISHER: The Oldie Magazine (UK)
DIMENSIONS: 8" × 8"

MELINDA BECK
studio@melindabeck.com
p 79 ART DIRECTOR: Kerri Abrams
CLIENT: The National
MEDIA: Ink, collage, digital
DIMENSIONS: 9" × 11"
p 90 ART DIRECTOR: Abbey Prokell
CLIENT: Real Simple
MEDIA: Ink, collage, digital
p 219 ART DIRECTOR: Melinda Beck
CLIENT: Quicksand
MEDIA: Scratchboard, digital
DIMENSIONS: 16" × 24"
p 220 ART DIRECTOR: Antonia Lui
CLIENT: Chan Can Dance
MEDIA: Ink, collage, digital
DIMENSIONS: 22" × 32"
p 221 ART DIRECTOR: Melinda Beck

CLIENT: Quicksand
MEDIA: Scratchboard, digital
DIMENSIONS: 16" × 24"

WESLEY BEDROSIAN
mail@wesleybedrosian.com
p 258 MEDIA: Digital
p 267 MEDIA: Digita

MAGPIE BELLE
hello@magpiebelle.com
p 175 DESIGNER: Magpie Belle
MEDIA: Drawing, collage

CARIN BERGER
carin@carinberger.com
p 40 TITLE: Stardines
p 42 TITLE: A Perfect Day

JON BERKELEY
jon@holytrousers.com
p 97 ART DIRECTOR: Shelley Walker
DESIGN FIRM: Walker Design &
Communications
CLIENT: Backbone
MEDIA: Digital

BEUGISM
hello@beugism.com
p 148 CLIENT: Motor Sport Magazine
DIMENSIONS: 7.64" × 11.63"

GUY BILLOUT
guy@guybillout.com
p 112 ART DIRECTOR: Bonnie Becker
CLIENT: The Atlantic
DIMENSIONS: 4.3125" × 5.25"
p 118 ART DIRECTOR: Bonnie Becker
CLIENT: The Atlantic
MEDIA: ink on paper, digital
DIMENSIONS: 3.3125" × 4.375"
p 120 ART DIRECTOR: Bonnie Becker
CLIENT: The Atlantic
MEDIA: Ink on paper, digital
DIMENSIONS: 3.875" × 4.8125"

SUE BLANCHARD
sueblanchard@soobee.com
p 208 DESIGNER: Sue Blanchard
PUBLISHER: self-published
MEDIA: Watercolor, ink, digital
DIMENSIONS: 4.5" × 6.24"

ALJOSCHA BLAU
blau.ali@gmx.net
p 308 DISTINGUISHED MERIT
TITLE: The Child in the Moon
ART DIRECTOR: Aljoscha Blau
DESIGNER: Aljoscha Blau
AUTHOR: Jurg Schubiger
PUBLISHER: Monika Bilstein
IMPRINT: Peter Hammer Verlag

PAUL BLOW
info@agoodson.com
p 113 ART DIRECTOR: Kristen Lenz
CLIENT: Washington Post
DIMENSIONS: 12.5" × 21.5"
p 147 DISTINGUISHED MERIT
TITLE: Essen
DESIGN DIRECTOR: Kerstin Leesch
CLIENT: Greenpeace Magazine

JORI BOLTON
jori@joribolton.com
p 139 ART DIRECTOR: Vanessa Solis
CLIENT: Education Week
MEDIA: Gouache, digital
DIMENSIONS: 11" × 6.25"

STEVEN BONNER
steven@stevenbonner.com
p 32 ART DIRECTOR: David Scherer
AD AGENCY: Kempertrautmann
CLIENT: Audi

JENS BONNKE
jb@jensbonnke.com
p 108 ART DIRECTOR: Jens Bonnke
DESIGNER: Jens Bonnke
CLIENT: Büchergilde
p 137 ART DIRECTOR: Brigitte Meyer
CLIENT: NZZ Neue Zürcher Zeitung

FREDDY BOO
boo@freddyboo.com
p 23 DESIGN DIRECTOR: Craig Smith
CLIENTS: Ted Baker, AOI
MEDIA: Digital
DIMENSIONS: 16.5" × 23.5"

KRISTINA BRASSELER
kristinab@gmx.de
p 328 ART DIRECTOR: Kristina Brasseler
AUTHOR: Kristina Brasseler
CLIENT: Wimmelbuchverlag

DAVID M. BRINLEY
dave@davidbrinley.com
p 180 GALLERY: Mezzanine Gallery
MEDIA: Acrylic on cradled masonite
DIMENSIONS: 18" × 24"
p 196 MEDIA: Acrylic on cradled masonite
DIMENSIONS: 18" × 24"
p 196 GALLERY: Mezzanine Gallery
MEDIA: Acrylic on cradled masonite
DIMENSIONS: 18" × 24"

KARI BROOKS
kari@karipaints.com
p 404 DISTINGUISHED MERIT
TITLE: Radiohead: King of Limbs Album
Release
INSTITUTION: SCAD Atlanta
INSTRUCTOR: Rick Lovell

CALEF BROWN
calef@calefbrown.com
p 277 ART DIRECTOR: Calef Brown
MEDIA: Watercolor on paper

NIGEL BUCHANAN
nigel@nigelbuchanan.com
p 138 ART DIRECTOR: Larraine Hall
CLIENT: Law Society Journal
DIMENSIONS: 8.25" × 7.5"
p 164 ART DIRECTOR: Robert Priest
CLIENT: Howler Magazine
DIMENSIONS: 23.6" × 28.3"
p 179 ART DIRECTOR: Nigel Buchanan
DESIGNER: Nigel Buchanan
GALLERY: East Sydney Doctors Gallery
MEDIA: Digital
DIMENSIONS: 12.6" × 23.6"

DANIEL BUENO
bu_eno@yahoo.com.br
p 89 ART DIRECTOR: Vladimir Palibrk
AUTHOR: Andrei Bely
PUBLISHER: Elektrika Pancevo
MEDIA: Digital
DIMENSIONS: 14.2" × 10.2"
p 248 TITLE: Modulos
DESIGN DIRECTORS: Daniel Bueno, Carol
Grespan
PUBLISHER: Unicamp
CLIENT: Pro-Posições magazine

MEDIA: Digital
DIMENSIONS: 7.1" × 9.4"

JUDE BUFFUM
jude@judebuffum.com
p 186 PRODUCTION COMPANY: iam8bit Inc.
CLIENT: Berkley Books (Penguin)
GALLERY: iam8bit Gallery
MEDIA: Giclée prints on canvas
DIMENSIONS: 15.75" × 11.75"

THOMAS BURNS
burnsth1@gmail.com
p 281 ART DIRECTOR: Rick Lovell
MEDIA: Digital
DIMENSIONS: 8.25" × "

MATTHEW DENTON BURROWS
dentonburrows@gmail.com
p 386 INSTITUTION: School of Visual Arts
INSTRUCTOR: Marshall Arisman
p 391 INSTITUTION: School of Visual Arts
INSTRUCTOR: David Sandlin

MICHELA BUTTIGNOL
michelabuttignol@gmail.com
p 279 TITLE: Vines Between Friends

JILL CALDER
jill@jillcalder.com
p 22 ART DIRECTOR: Andy Archer
AD AGENCY: The Leith Agency
CLIENT: First Great Western
MEDIA: Print, digital, online

HARRY CAMPBELL
harry@harrycampbell.net
p 288 BRONZE
TITLE: Newtown Series
ART DIRECTOR: Harry Campbell
MEDIA: Digital

MARIA CARLUCCIO
mariacarluccio@verizon.net
p 354 BRONZE
TITLE: Forest Friends
DESIGNER: Maria Carluccio

ANDRÉ CARRILHO
mail@andrecarrilho.com
p 20 GOLD
TITLE: P.I.I.G.S. vs Pigs
ART DIRECTOR: Paulo Freitas, MAGA
Design
CLIENT: Diário de Notícias
p 33 ART DIRECTOR: André Carrilho
CLIENT: Spam Cartoon
p 84 ART DIRECTOR: Paulo Freitas
CLIENT: Diário de Notícias
p 133 ART DIRECTOR: Josef Reyes
CLIENT: New York Magazine
p 150 DESIGN DIRECTOR: Colin Wilson
ART DIRECTOR: Sarah Morley
CLIENT: The Independent on Sunday
p 153 ART DIRECTOR: Julie Weiss
CLIENT: Vanity Fair
p 153 DESIGN DIRECTOR: Colin Wilson
ART DIRECTOR: Sarah Morley
CLIENT: The Independent on Sunday
p 154 DESIGN DIRECTOR: Colin Wilson
ART DIRECTOR: Sarah Morley
CLIENT: The Independent on Sunday

Q. CASSETTI
q@theluckystone.com
p 237 DESIGNER: Q. Cassetti
CLIENT: Luckystone Partners
MEDIA: Digital
DIMENSIONS: 13" × 19"

p 238 ART DIRECTOR: Q. Cassetti
CLIENT: Luckystone Partners

SOPHIE CASSON
sophiecasson@sympatico.ca
p 121 ART DIRECTOR: Matthew French
CLIENT: The Globe and Mail
DIMENSIONS: 4.5" × 10.7"

JULIEN CASTANIÉ
castanie.julien@gmail.com
p 348 AUTHOR: Julien Castanié

REINA CASTELLANOS
reinacastellanos@gmail.com
p 330 INSTITUTION: Savannah College of Art and
Design
INSTRUCTOR: Eun Lee
p 384 INSTITUTION: Savannah College of Art and
Design
INSTRUCTOR: Eun Lee

JUN CEN
jcen@mica.edu
p 387 INSTITUTION: Maryland Institute College
of Art
INSTRUCTOR: Whitney Sherman

MATTHEW CHASE
matt.chase@swbell.net
p 65 ART DIRECTOR: Ben Olins
DESIGNER: Matt Chase
AUTHOR: Helen Yuet Ling Pang
CLIENT: Herb Lester Associates
MEDIA: Digital
DIMENSIONS: 4.1" × 5.8"

DOUG CHAYKA
doug@dougchayka.com
p 24 ART DIRECTOR: Ivy Sheppard
CLIENT: The South Carolina Broadcasters
MEDIA: Mixed, digital
p 109 ART DIRECTOR: Jason Mark
DESIGNER: Lilli Keinaenen
CLIENT: Earth Island Journal
MEDIA: Digital
p 128 ART DIRECTOR: Ann Chin
CLIENT: Scientific American
MEDIA: Digital

VERONICA CHEN
mail@veronicachen.com
p 287 MEDIA: Ink
DIMENSIONS: 10" × 7"

ZIYUE CHEN
angelinezchen@gmail.com
p 389 INSTITUTION: Ringling College of Art and
Design
INSTRUCTOR: Joe Thiel

NOMI CHI
nomi.illustration@gmail.com
p 418 INSTITUTION: Emily Carr University of Art
and Design
INSTRUCTOR: Durwin Talon

I-HAN CHIANG
noodles0214@gmail.com
p 35 ART DIRECTOR: Chiang I-Han
DESIGNER: Chiang I-Han
ANIMATOR: Chiang I-Han

RYAN CHO
msig2992@yahoo.com
p 383 INSTITUTION: Art Center College of Design
INSTRUCTOR: Jeffrey Decoster
p 408 INSTITUTION: Art Center College of Design
INSTRUCTORS: Paul Rogers, Brian Rea

INDEX

BOYEON CHOI
bo@boyeonchoi.com
p 377 INSTITUTION: School of Visual Arts
INSTRUCTOR: Juliette Borda

PING HUA CHOU
batheney@gmail.com
p 96 TITLE: Cloud Interaction
MEDIA: Digital
DIMENSIONS: 8.5" × 11"
p 373 BRONZE
TITLE: Social White Noise
INSTITUTION: Academy of Art University
p 374 BRONZE
TITLE: Untitled
INSTITUTION: Academy of Art University
INSTRUCTOR: Gordon Silveria
p 405 DISTINGUISHED MERIT
TITLE: Entropy
INSTITUTION: Academy of Art University
INSTRUCTOR: Gordon Silveria
p 420 TITLE: Criminal Evidence in a Pathologized Mind
INSTITUTION: Academy of Art University
INSTRUCTOR: David Ball
MEDIA: Digital
DIMENSIONS: 8.5" × 11"
p 421 TITLE: No Free Freebirds
INSTRUCTOR: David Ball
INSTITUTION: Academy of Art University
p 423 TITLE: Cloud Interaction
INSTITUTION: Academy of Art University

HUDSON CHRISTIE
hudsonedwardchristie@gmail.com
p 338 ART DIRECTOR: Yarek Waszul

JAMEY CHRISTOPH
christoph.jamey@gmail.com
p 341 ART DIRECTOR: Cynthia Matthews von Berg
CLIENT: Galison/Mudpuppy

HYE JIN CHUNG
hey@hyejinchung.com
p 391 INSTITUTION: School of Visual Arts
INSTRUCTOR: David Sandlin

JULIEN CHUNG
julienchung@hotmail.com
p 236 CLIENTS: SCT Inc, Japan, Julien Chung

MIN GYO CHUNG
daniel.mingyo@gmail.com
p 382 INSTITUTION: OCAD University
INSTRUCTOR: Lauchie Reid
p 410 INSTITUTION: OCAD University
INSTRUCTOR: Lauchie Reid

LIVIA CIVES
livciv@gmail.com
p 235 MEDIA: Ink, charcoal pencils, digital
DIMENSIONS: 11.693" × 11.693"

ELLA COHEN
ellakookoo@gmail.com
p 166 SILVER
TITLE: The Homecoming
ART DIRECTOR: Yifat Anzelevich
DESIGN FIRM: Anzelevich Studio
CLIENT: Thesis magazine
MEDIA: Digital
DIMENSIONS: 13" × 9"
p 224 SILVER
TITLE: Welcome to the Dollhouse
PUBLISHER: Paul Paper/Postcards to Alphaville

MEDIA: Digital, silk screen
DIMENSIONS: 8" × 11.3"

JIM COHEN
jim@jimcohenillustration.com
p 242 TITLE: Faces

CHRISTOPHER CORR
chriscorr@yahoo.com
p 45 ART DIRECTOR: Sheri Gee
AUTHOR: Henry Green
PUBLISHER: The Folio Society
DIMENSIONS: 6.25" × 9"
p 329 DESIGN DIRECTOR: Klauss Flugge
ART DIRECTOR: Rona Selby
DESIGNERS: Rebecca Garrill, Kate Grove
AUTHOR: Stephen Davies
EDITOR: Rona Selby
PUBLISHER: Andersen Press

TERESA CORTEZ
info@teresacortez.com
p 317 DESIGN DIRECTOR: Marta Madureira
DESIGNERS: Marta Madureira, Pedro Amado
AUTHOR: Carlos Nogueira
PUBLISHER: Tcharan

ALIJA CRAYCROFT
a@alijacraycroft.com
p 212 ART DIRECTOR: Debra McClutchy
DESIGNER: Alija Craycroft
CLIENT: Oscilloscope Laboratories

MIRKO CRESTA
mirkocresta@gmail.com
p 55 AD AGENCY: EIGA Design
PUBLISHER: NBVD Norman Beckmann Verlag & Design

NINA CUNEO
ninacuneo@gmail.com
p 347 BRONZE
TITLE: Oh No. Not Again.

SYLVIE DAIGNEAULT
sylvie@sylviedaigneault.com
p 250 MEDIA: Colored pencils, colorline paper
DIMENSIONS: 12.5" × 17.5"

TONI DAMKOEHLER
damkoeht@uwgb.edu
p 146 MEDIA: Digital
DIMENSIONS: 10.25" × 15.75"

HUGH D'ANDRADE
hugh@hughillustration.com
p 215 MEDIA: Digital
DIMENSIONS: 12" × 24"

OWEN DAVEY
owen@owendavey.com
p 316 ART DIRECTOR: Mike Jolley
AUTHOR: Owen Davey
PUBLISHER: Templar Publishing

KRISTEN DAVIS
kristen@kdavisillustration.com
p 396 MEDIA: Charcoal on paper
INSTITUTION: Parsons the New School for Design
INSTRUCTOR: Sergio Ruzzier

PIETER DE POORTERE
pdp@telenet.be
p 85 AUTHOR: Pieter De Poortere
PUBLISHER: Glénat, France

DAVID DE RAMÓN
david@davidderamon.com
p 167 DIMENSIONS: 16" × 22"

STEPHANE DEFAGO
stefandefago@gmail.com
p 257 MEDIA: Graphite, digital

NICOLAS DELORT
contact@nicolasdelort.com
p 201 TITLE: Mother's Day
MEDIA: Ink on clayboard
DIMENSIONS: 12" × 24"
p 231 TITLE: Vigil
GALLERY: Galerie Daniel Maghen, Paris
MEDIA: Ink on claybord
DIMENSIONS: 16" × 11"

DESHI DENG
deshi.deng@gmail.com
p 382 TITLE: Untitled
INSTITUTION: Ringling College of Art & Design
INSTRUCTOR: Regan Dunnick

CATHERINE DENVIR
catherine@catherinedenvir.com
p 278 TITLE: New World
AUTHOR: Aldous Huxley

PETER DIAMOND
peter@peterdiamond.ca
p 273 TITLE: Where We're From
DIMENSIONS: 11.6" × 18"

BOJANA DIMITROVSKI
mzavacky@mcmillanagency.com
p 176 BRONZE
TITLE: In the City
ART DIRECTOR: Michael Zavacky
AD AGENCY: McMillan
MEDIA: Digital

VALERIA DOCAMPO
ceciliarebora@yahoo.com.mx
p 324 TITLE: La vallée des moulins
AUTHOR: Noélia Blanco
PUBLISHER: Alice Jeunesse

MAËLLE DOLIVEUX
maelle@maelledoliveux.com
p 41 TITLE: Louise Arner Boyd
AUTHOR: Maëlle Doliveux
MEDIA: Cut paper

PETER DONNELLY
donnellypa@eircom.net
p 232 TITLE: Sea Ways
ART DIRECTOR: Peter Donnelly
MEDIA: Mixed, digital
DIMENSIONS: 11.7" × 1.6"
p 233 TITLE: Southern Comfort
MEDIA: Mixed, digital
DIMENSIONS: 11.7" × 11.2"

ADAM S. DOYLE
mail@adamsdoyle.com
p 195 TITLE: Sing Chronos City Series
GALLERY: Novalis
MEDIA: Oil
DIMENSIONS: 18" × 24"

PATRICK DOYON
doiion@hotmail.com
p 33 DISTINGUISHED MERIT
TITLE: 2012 Animated Film Summit
ART DIRECTOR: Patrick Doyon
ANIMATOR: Patrick Doyon
DIRECTOR: Patrick Doyon
CLIENT: Cinémathèque Québécoise
MEDIA: Pencil on paper

MERITXELL DURAN
meri@meriduran.com

INDEX

p 260 TITLE: Emotional Rescue (A History of Depression)
DESIGNER: Miquel Puig
AD AGENCY: Agencia Bridge
AUTHOR: Jordi Ramis
DIMENSIONS: 30.54" × 38.67"

JEAN-MANUEL DUVIVIER
jmduvivier@skynet.be
p 265 TITLE: Animals in Love
ART DIRECTOR: Jean-Manuel Duvivier
MEDIA: Digital
DIMENSIONS: 30" × 21"

JENSINE ECKWALL
jensineeckwall@gmail.com
p 266 TITLE: I'm An Animal
MEDIA: Watercolor, gouache, digital
DIMENSIONS: 18" × 8"

BYRON EGGENSCHWILER
byron@byronegg.com
p 269 TITLE: The Day of the Triffids
AUTHOR: John Wyndham
p 352 TITLE: Changing the Equation
ART DIRECTOR: Kelly Carter
CLIENT: Delaware Today

TRUDI ESBERGER
trudi@trudiesberger.com
p 385 TITLE: The Lost Children
INSTITUTION: Anglia Ruskin University
INSTRUCTOR: Martin Salisbury

LEO ESPINOSA
leo@studioespinosa.com
p 21 GOLD
TITLE: Cry Me a River: The Rise of the Failure Memoir
ART DIRECTOR: Chris Curry
CLIENT: The New Yorker

SAM FALCONER
sam@samfalconer.co.uk
p 238 TITLE: Memory Palace
MEDIA: Digital

JOÃO FAZENDA
info@joaofazenda.com
p 44 BRONZE
TITLE: Untitled
p 134 TITLE: Untitled

BILL FERENC
bill.ferenc@gmail.com
p 274 TITLE: The Astronomer
DIMENSIONS: 15" × 19"

T. LIVELY FLUHARTY
theflus@integra.net
p 298 BRONZE
TITLE: The Boy and the Ocean
DESIGN DIRECTOR: Josh Dennis
ART DIRECTORS: Josh Dennis, T. Lively
DESIGNER: Josh Dennis
AUTHOR: Max Lucado
PUBLISHER: Goodnews Publishers
CLIENT: Crossway

LOUISE FRENCH
louisefrench1@hotmail.com
p 336 TITLE: Untitled

LINNEA GAD
linneagad@gmail.com
p 395 TITLE: Interior Spaces
MEDIA: Gesso, graphite, and oil on masonite
INSTITUTION: Parsons the New School for Design
INSTRUCTOR: Jordin Isip

SUSAN GAL
susan@galgirlstudio.com
p 344 TITLE: Storytime
p 345 TITLE: Girl & Hermit Crab

MONICA GARWOOD
mgarwood@cca.edu
p 371 GOLD
INSTITUTION: California College of the Arts
INSTRUCTOR: Bob Ciano

CHRIS GASH
theboss@chrisgash.com
p 211 TITLE: Dinner Do's Plates
ART DIRECTORS: Jason Amendolara, Fred Roses
CLIENT: Easy Aces/Fred and Friends
MEDIA: Digital

BEPPE GIACOBBE
b.giacobbe@beppegiacobbe.com
p 138 TITLE: The End of Geography
PUBLISHER: Corriere della Sera
MEDIA: Digital

STEVEN GLANVILLE
stevenglanville@hotmail.com
p 292 TITLE: Slowly, Then All At Once
MEDIA: Ball point pen, Copic marker, china marker
DIMENSIONS: 22" × 22"

CHARLES GLAUBITZ
mrglaubitz@mrglaubitz.com
p 58 TITLE: The World is in Play: Fearless
DESIGN DIRECTOR: Julian Wade
AD AGENCY: 180 Amsterdam
CLIENT: Sony PLaystation
MEDIA: Acrylic on canvas

GOLDEN COSMOS
info@golden-cosmos.com
p 43 DISTINGUISHED MERIT
TITLE: High Times
DESIGNERS: Doris Freigofas, Daniel Dolz
PUBLISHER: Nobrow Press
DIMENSIONS: 53.5" × 9.25"
p 224 TITLE: 12 Hunters
DIMENSIONS: 30.7" × 12.2"

AYA GORDON-NOY
ayagordonoy@gmail.com
p 312 TITLE: Just Like l Wanted
AUTHOR: Elinoar Keller
EDITOR: Yael Gover
PUBLISHER: Kinneret Zmora-Bitan

ALESSANDRO GOTTARDO
conceptualillustration@gmail.com
p 15 GOLD
TITLE: America's Cup: Naples
p 82 TITLE: Snow Country
p 127 TITLE: Calm After the Storm
ART DIRECTOR: SooJin Buzelli
p 132 TITLE: A Farewall To Yarns
DESIGN DIRECTOR: Hannah McCaughey
CLIENT: Outside
p 139 TITLE: Exxon

AAD GOUDAPPEL
aad@aadgoudappel.com
p 17 GOLD
TITLE: Home
ART DIRECTOR: Gijs van den Broek
CLIENT: Heymans
DIMENSIONS: 8.27" × 11.69"
p 36 TITLE: Sustainability
ART DIRECTOR: Gijs van den Broek
CLIENT: Heymans
DIMENSIONS: 8.27" × 11.69"
p 57 TITLE: Intelligent Highways
ART DIRECTOR: Gijs van den Broek
CLIENT: Heijmans
DIMENSIONS: 8.27" × 11.69"
p 60 TITLE: Opera
ART DIRECTOR: Marieke Griffioen
AD AGENCY: EdenSpiekermann
CLIENT: Utrecht City Theatre
p 121 TITLE: Apocalypse
DESIGN DIRECTOR: Eduard van Holst Pellekaan
ART DIRECTOR: Karin Goedhart
CLIENT: Volzin
p 137 TITLE: West Africa
DESIGNER: Colette Korteweg
DESIGN FIRM: ThielenPeters
CLIENT: Management Scope Magazine
DIMENSIONS: 8.27" × 10.87"
p 144 TITLE: Work
ART DIRECTOR: Christiane Weyrauch
CLIENT: Hohe Luft
DIMENSIONS: 8.27" × 11.02"
p 217 BRONZE
TITLE: Ballet
ART DIRECTOR: Marieke Griffioen
AD AGENCY: EdenSpiekermann
CLIENT: Utrecht City Theatre
p 332 TITLE: What Does Cow Say
ART DIRECTOR: Aad Goudappel
AUTHOR: Aad Goudappel

STEPHANIE GRAEGIN
s.graegin@gmail.com
p 327 TITLE: Happy Birthday, Bunny!
ART DIRECTOR: Lauren Rille
AUTHOR: Liz Garton Scanlon
EDITOR: Andrea Welch
PUBLISHER: Simon & Schuster
IMPRINT: Beach Lane

STEPHEN MAURICE GRAHAM
halloleftovers@googlemail.com
p 226 TITLE: Reset Residents
DESIGNER: Stephen Maurice Graham
CLIENT: Reset
MEDIA: Dip Pen, digital
DIMENSIONS: 16.5" × 23.4"

CHRISTIAN GRALINGEN
mundimachinarum@gmx.de
p 163 TITLE: Roboter Portrait
GALLERY: .HBC, Berlin
MEDIA: Collage, digital
DIMENSIONS: 21" × 28"

TAL GRANOT
postmod8@gmail.com
p 377 DISTINGUISHED MERIT
TITLE: Downtown Athletic Club
INSTITUTION: Bezalel Academy for Art and Design
INSTRUCTOR: Gila Kaplan

KAREN GREENBERG
karen@karengreenberg.com
p 249 TITLE: Blue Peacock

LORENZO GRITTI
ella@purplerainillustrators.com
p 126 TITLE: O.G.M.
ART DIRECTOR: Antonella Carnicelli
CLIENT: Terre Di Mezzo Street Magazine

p 253 TITLE: Obsession
p 259 TITLE: Reading Into Her

KATIE GROSS
grosske@newschool.edu
p 376 TITLE: Play Ball Part 1
MEDIA: Silkscreen
INSTITUTION: Parsons the New School for Design
INSTRUCTOR: Scott Nobles

EDDIE GUY
eddie.guy@verizon.net
p 93 TITLE: Guns in Hollywood
DESIGN DIRECTOR: Kory Kennedy
PUBLISHER: Time Inc.
CLIENT: Entertainment Weekly
DIMENSIONS: 10.5" × 11"

OLAF HAJEK
mail@olafhajek.com
p 188 TITLE: Strange Flowers Part 2
CLIENT: Whatiftheworld Gallery
p 191 TITLE: Strange Flowers Part 1
CLIENT: Whatiftheworld Gallery
MEDIA: Acrylic on wood

ASAF HANUKA
assafhan@netvision.net.il
p 86 SILVER
TITLE: The Realist
p 131 DESIGN DIRECTOR: Amir Ziv
ART DIRECTOR: Hagit Antebi
CLIENT: Calcalist Weekend Edition
MEDIA: Digital

LIANNE HARRISON
lianneharrison@myself.com
p 300 TITLE: Bore Da (Good Morning)
AUTHOR: Gwennan Evans
PUBLISHER: Y Lolfa
CLIENT: Welsh Books Council

TAKAHISA HASHIMOTO
contact@takahisahashimoto.com
p 63 TITLE: Woman in Red Blowing a Horn
ART DIRECTOR: Takahisa Hashimoto
PUBLISHER: Adelya Safina
CLIENT: Republique Magazine
p 101 TITLE: Campus of Dreams
ART DIRECTOR: Takahisa Hashimoto
DESIGN FIRM: K-UNITY
CLIENT: Senshu University Extension Center

HEATHER HECKEL
heather.heckel@gmail.com
p 162 TITLE: José
MEDIA: Scratchboard
DIMENSIONS: 5" × 7"

CALEB HEISEY
heiseycb@gmail.com
p 402 TITLE: The Witching Hour
INSTITUTION: Tyler School of Art/Temple University
INSTRUCTOR: Joe Scorsone

REBECCA HENDIN
rebeccahendin@yahoo.com
p 406 INSTITUTION: Central Saint Martins

LARS HENKEL
lars@reflektorium.de
p 102 TITLE: Geo Kosmos
ART DIRECTOR: Jutta Krüger
AUTHORS: Constanze Kindel, Tilman Botzenhardt

CLIENT: GEO magazine
DIMENSIONS: 4.5" × 2.8"

RYAN HESHKA
ryanheshka@telus.net
p 266 TITLE: They Brought Us Here
GALLERY: Roq La Rue Gallery, Seattle
MEDIA: Acrylic and mixed media on paper
DIMENSIONS: 60" × 30"

LAUREN HESS
hesslaurens@gmail.com
p 400 TITLE: Ron
INSTITUTION: Rhode Island School of Design

JODY HEWGILL
jody@jodyhewgill.com
p 27 TITLE: Mary T. & Lizzy K.
ART DIRECTOR: Nicky Lindeman
AD AGENCY: SpotCo
AUTHOR: Tazewell Thompson
CLIENT: Arena Stage
MEDIA: Acrylic on gessoed ragboard
DIMENSIONS: 13" × 17"
p 103 TITLE: Looking Deep
ART DIRECTOR: SooJin Buzelli
PUBLISHER: Assest International
CLIENT: Planadviser
MEDIA: Acrylic on wood panel
DIMENSIONS: 12" × 16"
p 156 TITLE: Shirley MacLaine
ART DIRECTOR: Amanda Bixler
DESIGNER: Brian Sanchez
CLIENT: Saturday Evening Post
MEDIA: Acrylic on gessoed ragboard
DIMENSIONS: 11.5" × 14"

MICHAEL HIRSHON
mike@hirshon.net
p 276 TITLE: My Life in Amsterdam

DAVID HO
ho@davidho.com
p 182 TITLE: The Healer
GALLERY: Pop Gallery Santa Fe
MEDIA: Mixed media
DIMENSIONS: 8" × 10"
p 199 TITLE: The Predator
GALLERY: Pop Gallery Santa Fe
MEDIA: Mixed media
DIMENSIONS: 8" × 10"
p 201 TITLE: Bird Temptation
GALLERY: Pop Gallery Santa Fe
MEDIA: Mixed media
DIMENSIONS: 18" × 24"

OMER HOFFMANN
omer.hoffmann@gmail.com
p 87 TITLE: Meanwhile, In New York
CLIENT: Museum of Cartoon, Israel

BRAD HOLLAND
brad@bradholland.net
p 81 TITLE: Artist on Edge
ART DIRECTOR: Patrick Flynn
DESIGNER: Patrick Flynn
PUBLISHER: MIT Press
CLIENT: The Baffler
MEDIA: Acrylic on Wood
DIMENSIONS: 11" × 14.25"
p 91 TITLE: War
DESIGN DIRECTOR: Frederic Pajak
ART DIRECTOR: Frederic Pajak
DESIGNER: Brad Holland
DESIGN FIRM: Les Cahiers Dessins
CLIENT: Nine Weeks

MEDIA: Pen and ink
DIMENSIONS: 9.25" × 10"

PAUL HOPPE
info@paulhoppe.com
p 239 TITLE: Ruins Girl
MEDIA: Ink on paper, digital
DIMENSIONS: 14" × 18"

DOROTHEA HUBER
post@dorohuber.de
p 198 TITLE: Das Kabinett
MEDIA: Mixed media
DIMENSIONS: 78" × 54"

DAVID HUGHES
david.hughes@intamail.com
p 37 TITLE: A Connecticut Yankee in King Arthur's Court
ART DIRECTOR: Sheri Gee
DESIGNER: Sheri Gee
CLIENT: The Folio Society
DIMENSIONS: 6.25" × 9.5"

STEVEN P HUGHES
stevenhughes@hushart.com
p 141 TITLE: Don't Panic
DESIGN DIRECTOR: Jason Chiu
AUTHOR: Blair Cosgrove
CLIENT: The Globe and Mail
DIMENSIONS: 149" × 182"

ROD HUNT
rod@rodhunt.com
p 25 TITLE: Unleash the Chaos: Lynx Attract From Him + For Her
ART DIRECTOR: Mia Matulic
AD AGENCY: Tullo Marshall Warren
CLIENT: Lynx Deodorant
MEDIA: Digital
p 25 TITLE: Bhartiya City: City of Joy
AD AGENCY: Wieden + Kennedy, New Delhi
CLIENT: Bhartiya City Developers
MEDIA: Digital

IC4DESIGN
info@ic4design.com
p 24 TITLE: Micchan
p 26 TITLE: Mercedes-Benz Türk Campaign
CREATIVE DIRECTOR: Derya Tambay
ART DIRECTOR: Işil Döneray
COPYWRITERS: Işil Döneray, Cengiz Pulgu
AGENCY PRODUCERS: Melis Bircan, Umut Tangör
CLIENT SERVICES MANAGER: Pınar Taşkıran
CLIENT: Mercedes-Benz Türk

PABLO IGLESIAS
iglesias.pab@gmail.com
p 409 TITLE: Safety
INSTITUTION: Sheridan College
INSTRUCTOR: Rick Sealock

JORDIN ISIP
jordin@jordinisip.com
p 106 TITLE: The Anti-Intellectualism of Conservatives
DESIGN DIRECTOR: Ellen Winkler
CLIENT: The Chronicle Review
MEDIA: Ink and digital

TOM JELLETT
tom@tomjellett.com
p 301 TITLE: Stories of 5, 6, 7, 8 Year Olds
DESIGNER: Tom Jellett
AUTHOR: Linsay Knight
PUBLISHER: Random House
CLIENT: Chris Kunz
p 326 TITLE: The Gobbledygook Is Eating a Book

DESIGNERS: Kirby Armstrong, Tom Jellett
AUTHOR: Justine Clarke and Arthur Baysting
PUBLISHER: Penguin Books Australia

MASUKO JO
masuko.jo@gmail.com
p 380 TITLE: Odori
MEDIA: Watercolor, ink, and gouache on paper
INSTITUTION: Parsons the New School for Design
INSTRUCTOR: Jordin Isip

JOHN KACHIK
kachikart@comcast.net
p 29 TITLE: The Midwest Road Trip Spread
ART DIRECTOR: Ryan DiDonato
DESIGN FIRM: DesignGoneSmart
CLIENT: Scion Cars
MEDIA: Pen, digital
DIMENSIONS: 21" × 15"

SAM KALDA
sam.kalda@gmail.com
p 78 TITLE: The Great Gatsby
ART DIRECTOR: John Button
CLIENT: Real Reads UK
DIMENSIONS: 6" × 8.5"
p 100 TITLE: From Schoolhouse to Courthouse
ART DIRECTOR: Erich Nagler
CLIENT: The New York Times
DIMENSIONS: 5.5" × 8"

ALEXANDRA KARDINAR
drushba@drushbapankow.de
p 34 TITLE: Nobody's Fool
ART DIRECTOR: Alexandra Kardinar
DESIGNERS: Alexandra Kardinar, Volker Schlecht
AUTHORS: Alexandra Kardinar, Volker Schlecht, Parov Stelar, Cleo Panther
ANIMATORS: Volker Schlecht, additional animation by Maxim Vassiliev
DIRECTORS: Volker Schlecht, Alexandra Kardinar
CLIENT: Parov Stelar

KEREN KATZ
katzkatzkatz@gmail.com
p 415 TITLE: The Professor Who Was Afraid of Speaking While Wearing Buttoned Shirts
INSTITUTION: School of Visual Arts
INSTRUCTORS: David Sandlin, Maira Kalman

EARL KELENY
ekeleny@sbcglobal.net
p 160 TITLE: Al Sharpton
ART DIRECTOR: Earl Keleny
PUBLISHER: Workbook
MEDIA: Acrylics

NURI KELI
nukeli20@student.scad.edu
p 388 INSTITUTION: Savannah College of Art & Design, Atlanta
INSTRUCTOR: Julie Mueller-Brown

ANGELA KEOGHAN
angela@thepicturegarden.co.nz
p 172 TITLE: Wild Goose Chase Series
MEDIA: Mixed media, digital
p 359 TITLE: The Right Fit
ART DIRECTOR: Meredith Baldwin
PUBLISHER: Bauer Media Group
CLIENT: Little Treasures Magazine

ALISTAR KHABULIANI
contact@alistar.us
p 366 TITLE: The Strange Case of Dr. Jekyll & Mr. Hyde
ART DIRECTOR: Marco Mercatali
PUBLISHER: European Language Institute
IMPRINT: 2012

BOYOUN KIM
boyounillo@gmail.com
p 372 SILVER
TITLE: Bicycle
INSTITUTION: School of Visual Arts
INSTRUCTOR: Chris Buzelli
p 421 TITLE: Chicken Land
INSTITUTION: School of Visual Arts
INSTRUCTOR: Chris Buzelli
p 421 TITLE: Spring
INSTITUTION: School of Visual Arts
INSTRUCTORS: Yuko Shimizu, Marcos Chin

GRACE KIM
grace.jkim90@gmail.com
p 56 TITLE: Tree Calendar
DESIGNER: Grace Kim
MEDIA: Digital
DIMENSIONS: 4" × 12"

EDWARD KINSELLA III
edwardkinsellaiii@yahoo.com
p 98 TITLE: Lincoln's Hazardous Journey
ART DIRECTOR: Maria G. Keehan
CLIENT: Smithsonian Magazine
MEDIA: Mixed media
p 157 TITLE: Tom Wolfe
ART DIRECTOR: Eileen O'Donnell
CLIENT: The Wall Street Journal
MEDIA: Ink, gouache
DIMENSIONS: 13" × 16"
p 200 TITLE: Mountain Top
GALLERY: Ghostprint Gallery
MEDIA: Ink, gouache

KAREN KLASSEN
info@karenklassen.com
p 268 TITLE: Artist Portraits
MEDIA: Digital

LORI KLOPP
lori@loriklopp.com
p 425 TITLE: Sonia Sotomayor Portrait
INSTITUTION: Syracuse University
INSTRUCTOR: John Thompson

CHI KUAN CHRISTINA KONG
tissue.ck@gmail.com
p 384 TITLE: Barcode
INSTITUTION: OCAD University

VITALI KONSTANTINOV
vitali@pittore.de
p 314 TITLE: Seis Barbudos
ART DIRECTOR: Belen Freijeiro
PUBLISHER: OQO ecitora

GRACIA LAM
gracia@gracialam.com
p 117 TITLE: Untitled
CLIENT: The Washington Post

JAY LANG
jay.lang@hotmail.co.uk
p 392 TITLE: Desolation Row Series
INSTITUTION: Camberwell College of Arts

JOHN LANG
john@johnlangart.com
p 71 TITLE: The Year in Closed Government
ART DIRECTOR: Corey Johnson

CLIENT: Santa Fe Reporter
MEDIA: Digital

TINA LE
ole@ecuad.ca
p 330 TITLE: Ellie
INSTITUTION: Emily Carr University of Art and Design
INSTRUCTOR: Jaime Anderson

DELPHINE LEBOURGEOIS
contact@delphinelebour-geois.com
p 183 TITLE: Untitled

DAHYE LEE
sweetldh@gmail.com
p 337 TITLE: The Mighty Asparagus
ART DIRECTOR: Paul Kepple
DESIGNER: Dahye Lee
AUTHOR: V. Radunsky

YANN LEGENDRE
yannlegendre@mac.com
p 19 GOLD
TITLE: Flesh Empire
PUBLISHER: Inculte Publishing
DIMENSIONS: 12" × 16.5"
p 161 TITLE: The Bearded Man
ART DIRECTOR: Elena Proskurova
CLIENT: The Wall Street Journal Europe
DIMENSIONS: 10" × 12"
p 218 TITLE: Poster Series
DESIGN DIRECTOR: Gabe Usadel
CLIENT: Steppenwolf Theater
DIMENSIONS: 27" × 37"
p 246 TITLE: Fresh Ink Collection
DESIGN DIRECTOR: Marta Calle
PUBLISHER: CB2
CLIENT: Crate & Barrel
DIMENSIONS: 78" × 75"

PATRICK LEGER
patricklegerart@hotmail.com
p 52 TITLE: The Postman Always Rings Twice
ART DIRECTOR: Raquel Leis Allion
DESIGNER: Raquel Leis Allion
AUTHOR: James M. Cain
PUBLISHER: The Folio Society
DIMENSIONS: 5.75" × 9"

STEVEN LENTON
steve_lenton@yahoo.co.uk
p 309 TITLE: Shift McGift and Slippery Sam

CONEY LEUNG
yleung@inside.artcenter.edu
p 412 TITLE: Lolita
INSTITUTION: Art Center College of Design
INSTRUCTOR: Steve Turk

RACHEL LEVIT
rachellevitruiz@gmail.com
p 414 TITLE: Sad Girls
MEDIA: Graphite, digital
INSTITUTION: Parsons the New School for Design
INSTRUCTOR: Jordin Isip

SEAN LEWIS
seanislewis@gmail.com
p 282 TITLE: Elk Island

SO YEON LIM
slim.1@go.ccad.edu
p 358 TITLE: Stories Behind Tea

RUJUN LIU
rliu01@risd.edu
p 403 TITLE: Tuesday Night
INSTITUTION: Rhode Island School of

Design
INSTRUCTOR: Kelly Murphy

ANDRÉ DA LOBA
andre@andredaloba.com
p 16   GOLD
TITLE: On Thoughts
ART DIRECTORS: André da Loba, Gémeo
Luís
ANIMATOR: André da Loba
DIRECTOR: Gémeo Luís
CLIENT: Edições Eterogémeas
MEDIA: Linoleum print, stop motion

JEFF LOWRY
jlowry13@email.arizona.edu
p 416   TITLE: Portrait of a Friend
INSTITUTION: The University of Arizona
INSTRUCTOR: David Christiana

MIKE LOWERY
mike@argyleacademy.com
p 70   TITLE: A Few of the Things On My Desk
p 173   TITLE: A Few of My Favorite Places in
Atlanta
p 235   TITLE: Common Birds of North America

GÉMEO LUÍS
eterogemeas@netcabo.pt
p 264   TITLE: Meetings

ELISA MACELLARI
elisamacellari@gmail.com
p 260   TITLE: Falling in a Black Hole
AUTHOR: Elisa Macellari

ASHLEY MACKENZIE
ashmackenzie@gmail.com
p 384   TITLE: 88
INSTITUTION: OCAD University
INSTRUCTOR: Thom Sevalrud

MÁGOZ
magoz@magoz.info
p 115   TITLE: Mental Illness
ART DIRECTOR: Kevin Goodbar
CLIENT: Austin Monthly
MEDIA: Digital
DIMENSIONS: 5" × 6"
p 121   TITLE: Sea Activities in the Winter
ART DIRECTOR: Albert Bernat
CLIENT: Descobrir
MEDIA: Digital
DIMENSIONS: 6.89" × 4.53"

DIEGO MALLO
diego@diegomallo.com
p 106   TITLE: Ear Candy
CLIENT: Ammo Magazine

MASHA MANAPOV
mashka.man@gmail.com
p 82   TITLE: March Eighth
CLIENT: Haaretz Newspaper
MEDIA: Mixed technique
DIMENSIONS: 34.5" × 24.5"

SIMONE MASSONI
sto@sketchthisout.com
p 240   TITLE: Into Me ½
ART DIRECTOR: Simone Massoni
MEDIA: Digital
p 305   TITLE: Cyrano de Bergerac
ART DIRECTOR: Daniele Garbuglia
CLIENT: Eli Readers

BILL MAYER
bill@thebillmayer.com
p 54   TITLE: Devil Frog
ART DIRECTOR: Jim Burke

CLIENT: Dellas Graphics
MEDIA: Mixed Media
p 125   SILVER
TITLE: Frankencorn
ART DIRECTOR: Carolyn Perot
CLIENT: Mother Jones
MEDIA: Mixed media
p 270   TITLE: Bad Luck
MEDIA: Mixed Media

EVAN MAZELLAN
evan.mazellan@student.indwes.edu
p 397   TITLE: The Atlas Foundry
INSTITUTION: Indiana Wesleyan University
INSTRUCTOR: Ron Mazellan

MIKE MCDONNELL
michael.alexander.mcdonnell@gmail.com
p 262   TITLE: Semblance Diagram
DIMENSIONS: 17" × 11"

ANGELA MCKAY
bytherealmckay@gmail.com
p 26   TITLE: House of Fraser
ART DIRECTOR: Dianne Stone
CLIENT: House of Fraser Department
Stores
MEDIA: Watercolor and pen
DIMENSIONS: 177" × 78.75"

STUART MCLACHLAN
stuartrex@iinet.net.au
p 205   TITLE: Untitled

TARA MCPHERSON
tara@taramcpherson.com
p 28   TITLE: Seasonal Girls
ART DIRECTOR: Sam Calagione
CLIENT: Dogfish Head Brewery
MEDIA: Oil
DIMENSIONS: 20" × 24"

GILES MEAD
gilesomead@hotmail.co.uk
p 271   TITLE: Olympic Legacy
AUTHOR: Giles Mead
MEDIA: Digital
DIMENSIONS: 8" × 11.5"

LUC MELANSON
luc@lucmelanson.com
p 111   TITLE: Habits
ART DIRECTOR: Nicholas Blechman
CLIENT: The New York Times Book
Review
p 119   TITLE: La vie en rose
ART DIRECTOR: Louise Rouleau
CLIENT: Premium magazine
p 125   TITLE: Pornomerta
ART DIRECTOR: Jocelyne Fournel
PUBLISHER: Rogers
CLIENT: L'actualite

AARON MESHON
hello@aaronmeshon.com
p 64   TITLE: 3x3 Issue 19 Cover
DESIGN DIRECTOR: Charles Hively
DESIGN FIRM: HivelyDesigns
CLIENT: 3x3, The Magazine of
Contemporary Illustration

RENÉ MILOT
renemilot@renemilot.com
p 69   TITLE: Lookaway, Lookaway
ART DIRECTOR: Robert Grom
PUBLISHER: St. Martin's Press
MEDIA: Digital
DIMENSIONS: 7" × 10"
p 151   TITLE: Lincoln Goes Hollywood, Inside

ART DIRECTOR: Maria Keehan
CLIENT: Smithsonian
MEDIA: Digital
DIMENSIONS: 9" × 10"
p 152   TITLE: Lincoln Goes Hollywood, Cover
ART DIRECTOR: Maria Keehan
CLIENT: Smithsonian
MEDIA: Digital
DIMENSIONS: 9" × 10"

AHWON MIN
min@minahwon.com
p 197   TITLE: Flower Cage

MEREDITH MIOTKE
mmiotke@collegeforcreativestudies.edu
p 418   TITLE: Mudgies
INSTITUTION: College for Creative Studies
INSTRUCTOR: Don Kilpatrick III

MARI MITSUMI
mari-m@tkc.att.ne.jp
p 53   TITLE: Madapple
ART DIRECTORS: Takayo Yanagawa,
Fragment
AUTHOR: Christina Meldrum
PUBLISHER: Tokyo Sogensha
p 201   TITLE: Blind Moon
GALLERY: Galerie Malle
DIMENSIONS: 300" × 400"

ARMINEH MOGHADASI
amogha20@student.scad.edu
p 411   INSTITUTION: Savannah College of Art &
Design, Atlanta
INSTRUCTOR: Rick Lovell

KELLY MURPHY
kelly@kelmurphy.com
p 315   TITLE: Romping Monsters, Stomping
Monsters
AUTHOR: Jane Yolen
PUBLISHER: Candlewick Press

DAVE MURRAY
dave@davemurrayillustration.com
p 206   TITLE: Tuff Cycle
AD AGENCY: Dutch Uncle
DIRECTOR: Dan Chrichlow
p 240   TITLE: Porsche 550A

LÁSZLÓ NAGY
nagy.laszlo75@gmail.com
p 214   TITLE: Band Gig Posters
DESIGN DIRECTOR: Laszlo Nagy
DESIGNER: Laszlo Nagy
DESIGN FIRM: Inhale
CLIENT: Various Clients
MEDIA: Serigraphy
DIMENSIONS: 12.5" × 17"

SCOTT NASH
zephyrnash@gmail.com
p 363   TITLE: The High Skies Adventures of Blue
Jay the Pirate
DESIGN DIRECTOR: Chris Paul
ART DIRECTOR: Ann Stott
AUTHOR: Scott Nash
EDITOR: Mary Lee Donovan
PUBLISHER: Candlewick Press
PRODUCTION COMPANY: NASHBOX

NICK NAZZARO
thenazzaro@gmail.com
p 390   TITLE: The NRA Way
INSTITUTION: The Art Institute of Boston
INSTRUCTOR: Keith MacLelland

INDEX

KEITH NEGLEY
keith@keithnegley.com
p 140 BRONZE
TITLE: Gun Debate
ART DIRECTOR: Sean Noyce
CLIENT: Newsweek
MEDIA: Mixed media
p 272 BRONZE
TITLE: Guilty Pleasure
MEDIA: Mixed

BARBARA NESSIM
barbara@barbaranessim.com
p 158 TITLE: David Bowie Ziggy Stardust Era
ART DIRECTOR: Andrew Johnson
DESIGN FIRM: East Publishing Limited
PUBLISHER: CultureShock Media
CLIENT: The Victoria & Albert Museum
MEDIA: Pastel
DIMENSIONS: 8.46" × 10"

ROBERT NEUBECKER
robert@neubecker.com
p 171 TITLE: Why We Pair Up With Our
Emotional Opposites
ART DIRECTOR: Ronald Plyman
CLIENT: The Wall Street Journal
p 299 TITLE: Winter is for Snow
ART DIRECTOR: Tanya Hughes
AUTHOR: Robert Neubecker
EDITOR: Rotem Moscovitch
PUBLISHER: Disney
IMPRINT: Hyperion
p 320 TITLE: Linus, the Vegetarian T-Rex
ART DIRECTOR: Lauren Rille
AUTHOR: Robert Neubecker
EDITOR: Andrea Welch
PUBLISHER: Simon & Schuster
IMPRINT: Beach Lane

GREG NEWBOLD
greg@gregnewbold.com
p 97 ART DIRECTOR: Scott Feaster
DESIGNER: Scott Feaster
CLIENT: Boy's Life Magazine

CHRISTOPHER NIELSEN
chris@chrisillo.com
p 31 TITLE: A Beautiful Journey
ART DIRECTOR: Craig Johns
DESIGN FIRM: Thursday Design
CLIENT: K.W.Doggett Fine Papers
p 192 TITLE: Head Strong
GALLERY: East Sydney Doctors Gallery

SHAW NIELSEN
shaw@shawnielsen.com
p 61 TITLE: Law Technology News
ART DIRECTOR: Shane DeLeers
CLIENT: ALM

AUDREY NIFFENEGGER
mbradford@abramsbooks.com
p 365 TITLE: Raven Girl
PUBLISHER: Abrams

BEN O'BRIEN
hello@bentheillustrator.com
p 249 TITLE: Greenlands
DESIGN DIRECTOR: Fiona O'Brien
MEDIA: Panama cotton fabric

JAMES O'BRIEN
info@jamesobrien.us
p 105 TITLE: Slow Burn
ART DIRECTOR: Betsy Hayes
AUTHOR: Julie Flaherty
MEDIA: Ink, gouache, digital

DIMENSIONS: 8.5" × 11"
p 155 TITLE: New Southern Journalism: School
of Hard Knocks
ART DIRECTOR: Walker Beauchamp
CLIENT: The Oxford American Magazine
MEDIA: Ink, gouache, digital
DIMENSIONS: 3.5" × 5"

HUGH O'CONNOR
hughoc99@gmail.com
p 385 TITLE: Blood Ivory 2013
INSTITUTION: Dublin Institute of
Technology
INSTRUCTORS: John Short, Tom Kelly

ANDREA OFFERMANN
andreaoffermann@gmail.com
p 302 TITLE: The Broken Lands
ART DIRECTOR: Lynne Polvino
DESIGNER: Sharismar Rodriguez
AUTHOR: Kate Milford
EDITOR: Lynne Polvino
PUBLISHER: Houghton Mifflin Harcourt
IMPRINT: Clarion Books

SUHARU OGAWA
suharu.o@gmail.com
p 422 TITLE: To Kill A Mockingbird
INSTITUTION: OCAD University
INSTRUCTOR: Jean-Christian Knaff

SARA OGILVIE
sara.ogilvie@btinternet.com
p 339 TITLE: Box of Delights
ART DIRECTOR: Sheri Gee
PUBLISHER: The Folio Society

NATSUKI OTANI
natsuki@natsukiotani.co.uk
p 149 TITLE: Ryo
CLIENT: La Mode Outre
MEDIA: Watercolor, ink, digital
DIMENSIONS: 7.06" × 10"

KENARD PAK
ken@pandagun.com
p 284 TITLE: Illustrator
MEDIA: Watercolor, paper, digital
DIMENSIONS: 10" × 3.18"

HSINPING PAN
hsinping@gmail.com
p 73 BRONZE
TITLE: Bouquet
ART DIRECTOR: Paul Wasserman
AUTHOR: G.B. Stern
PUBLISHER: Eat Drink World
DIMENSIONS: 6" × 9"

CURTIS PARKER
cparker@curtisparker.com
p 29 TITLE: Emeryville Mural
ART DIRECTOR: Jay Jung
CLIENT: Panera Bread
MEDIA: Acrylic on canvas
DIMENSIONS: 40" × 12"

LISA PERRIN
hello@madebyperrin.com
p 370 GOLD
TITLE: Containing Risk
INSTITUTION: Maryland Institute College
of Art
INSTRUCTOR: Kali Ciesmier

VALERIA PETRONE
valeria@valeriapetrone.com
p 122 TITLE: Untitled
p 124 TITLE: The Jane Austen Myth

ART DIRECTOR: Maurizio Varotti
CLIENT: Io Donna Magazine
DIMENSIONS: 9" × 11"
p 129 TITLE: Where Have Real Men Gone?
CLIENT: Io Donna Magazine
p 136 TITLE: Life Written on the Face
ART DIRECTOR: Maurizio Varotti
CLIENT: Io Donna Magazine
DIMENSIONS: 7.8" × 11"
p 321 TITLE: L'Abécédaire de la Famille
p 342 TITLE: Rhyme of the Stars
ART DIRECTOR: Francesca Fornario
CLIENT: Pupù- Pubblico Newspaper
p 356 DISTINGUISHED MERIT
TITLE: The Secret of Witch Sandwich
ART DIRECTOR: Maurizio Varotti
CLIENT: Style Piccoli Magazine
p 356 TITLE: The Mailbox in the Wood
ART DIRECTOR: Maurizio Varotti
AUTHOR: Valerio Millefoglie
CLIENT: Style Piccoli Magazine
p 361 TITLE: My Wild Friends: Tribute to
Maurice Sendak Exhibition
PUBLISHER: Baba Libri

ZARA PICKEN
zara@zaraillustrates.com
p 229 TITLE: The Sea
MEDIA: Digital
DIMENSIONS: 4.1" × 5.8"

DAVID PINTOR
davidpintor1975@yahoo.es
p 364 TITLE: Writers

MARCO PIUNTI
info@marcopiunti.com
p 346 TITLE: Recreation Time

GLORIA PIZZILLI
hello@gloriapizzilli.com
p 234 TITLE: Eva
MEDIA: Digital
DIMENSIONS: 11.82" × 11.82"

EMILIANO PONZI
info@emilianoponzi.com
p 47 TITLE: Inferno
DESIGN DIRECTOR: Pietro Corraini
PUBLISHER: Corraini
MEDIA: Digital
p 75 TITLE: Bukowski Series
ART DIRECTOR: Cristiano Guerri
PUBLISHER: Feltrinelli
MEDIA: Digital
p 77 SILVER
TITLE: Before You Go
ART DIRECTOR: Paul Gonzales
CLIENT: LA Times
MEDIA: Digital
p 122 SILVER
TITLE: Scientific Divulgation
ART DIRECTOR: Angelo Rinaldi
CLIENT: La Repubblica Newspaper
MEDIA: Digital
p 133 TITLE: Unheard Monologues
ART DIRECTOR: Angelo Rinaldi
CLIENT: La Repubblica Newspaper
MEDIA: Digital
p 174 BRONZE
TITLE: Intimate Shaving
ART DIRECTOR: Manuel Birnbacher
CLIENT: Süddeutsche Zeitung Magazin
MEDIA: Digital
p 217 TITLE: Tahrir Square Girl
ART DIRECTOR: Andrea Bozzo

PUBLISHER: Il caffè dei giornalisti
MEDIA: Digital

CHARLIE POWELL
cpowell@cruzio.com
p 234 TITLE: Be Happy
ART DIRECTOR: Charlie Powell
MEDIA: Acrylic on paper
DIMENSIONS: 16" × 11"

IKER AYESTARAN PRADILLA
ilustracion@ikerayestaran.com
p 116 TITLE: The Wished Balance
ART DIRECTOR: Angel Hermoza
AD AGENCY: Shannon Associates
PUBLISHER: El Comercio Newspaper
MEDIA: Mixed media
DIMENSIONS: 9.6" × 7.2"

NATALIE PUDALOV
p2natalie@yahoo.com
p 285 TITLE: Friends
AUTHOR: Natalie Pudalov
DIMENSIONS: 20" × 23"
p 325 TITLE: Jack y la Muerte
AUTHOR: Tim Bowley
PUBLISHER: OQO editora, Spain

PUSHART
meganberkheiser@pushart.com
p 225 DESIGN DIRECTOR: Lydia Bradshaw
ART DIRECTOR: Amy Hausman
DESIGNERS: Megan Berkheiser, Mike
Caldwell
DESIGN FIRM: Pushart
CLIENT: MTA, Arts for Transit
MEDIA: Mixed media
DIMENSIONS: 30" × 37"

ANNA RAFF
anna@annaraff.com
p 310 TITLE: World Rat Day
ART DIRECTOR: Kristen Nobles
DESIGNER: Kristen Nobles
AUTHOR: J. Patrick Lewis
EDITOR: Elizabeth Bicknell
PUBLISHER: Candlewick Press

RAID71
chris@raid71.com
p 14 BEST OF SHOW
TITLE: The Popular Face of New York
DESIGN DIRECTOR: Bottleneck Gallery
DESIGNER: Raid71
GALLERY: Bottleneck Gallery
MEDIA: Digital, screenprinted
DIMENSIONS: 18" × 24"

MONICA RAMOS
monica.t.ramos@gmail.com
p 399 TITLE: Human Hairstyles
MEDIA: Ink on paper
INSTITUTION: Parsons the New School for
Design
INSTRUCTOR: Jordin Isip

PATRICK REGOUT
patreg@skynet.be
p 252 TITLE: Home Fitness

JON REINFURT
jon@reinfurt.com
p 92 TITLE: Just Right
ART DIRECTOR: Cory Canady
CLIENT: Common Ground Magazine
MEDIA: Digital

DIETMAR REINHARD
d.reinhard@strong-ads.com

p 18 GOLD
TITLE: Crime
ART DIRECTOR: Dietmar Reinhard
AUTHOR: Ferdinand von Schirach
p 287 TITLE: Who Serves the Drinks at 27 Club?
ART DIRECTOR: Dietmar Reinhard

BILLY RENKL
billyrenkl@bellsouth.net
p 196 TITLE: Thursday, March 31, 1842 (The
Curls of a Maiden's Hair)
GALLERY: Cumberland Gallery, Nashville
MEDIA: Collage
DIMENSIONS: 10" × 13"
p 198 TITLE: Adaptation
GALLERY: Taylor/Bercier Fine Art, New
Orleans
MEDIA: Collage, mixed media
DIMENSIONS: 8" × 10"

JACKIE RENT
jferrent@risd.edu
p 404 TITLE: Wither
INSTITUTION: Rhode Island School of
Design
INSTRUCTOR: Kelly Murphy

RAMONA RING
r.ring@gmx.net
p 379 INSTITUTION: Georg-Simon-Ohm
Hochschule
INSTRUCTOR: Alexandra Kardinar

ZACK ROCK
zack@zackrock.com
p 334 TITLE: Homer Henry Hudson's Curio
Museum
ART DIRECTOR: Rita Marshall
AUTHOR: Zack Rock
EDITOR: Aaron Frisch
PUBLISHER: The Creative Company

ISABEL ROXAS
studioroxas@gmail.com
p 360 TITLE: Tooth Camp Recall Cards
CLIENT: Tooth Camp

JONNY RUZZO
jonny@jonnyruzzo.com
p 177 TITLE: Fashion Portrait Drawings
p 419 TITLE: Descending
INSTITUTION: School of Visual Arts
INSTRUCTORS: Eric White, Steve Ellis

TAKAYUKI RYUJIN
ryujing@yb3.so-net.ne.jp
p 66 TITLE: 7&i 2012summer

TRACY SABIN
tracy@sabin.com
p 213 TITLE: Fig chutney packaging
DESIGNER: Tracy Sabin
DESIGN FIRM: Sabingrafik Inc.
MEDIA: Digital

DOUG SALATI
doug@dougsalati.com
p 331 SILVER
TITLE: The Coat
ART DIRECTOR: Viktor Koen
p 349 TITLE: Animal Studies

MERAV SALOMON
merav.salomon@gmail.com
p 48 TITLE: Frostbites: Tollen Hefte No. 37
DESIGN DIRECTOR: Sussane Berner
ART DIRECTOR: Armin Abmeier
DESIGNER: Naama Tobias
AUTHOR: Merav Salomon

PUBLISHER: Buchergilde Guttenberg
Verlag, Germany
CLIENT: Tollen Hefte, Germany
MEDIA: Pencil and digital
DIMENSIONS: 265" × 205"

MARAL SASSOUNI
maralissima@gmail.com
p 335 TITLE: Crocodile Shoes
AUTHOR: Maral Sassouni

SHERRY SAUNDERS
sherrysaunders@gmail.com
p 245 TITLE: Untitled

MARGUERITE SAUVAGE
margueritesauvage@gmail.com
p 178 TITLE: Ocre
PUBLISHER: Yume
CLIENT: Yume
MEDIA: Digital
DIMENSIONS: 11.69" × 16.53"

VOLKER SCHLECHT
drushba@drushbapankow.de
p 34 TITLE: Nobody's Fool
DESIGN DIRECTOR: Alexandra Kardinar
ART DIRECTOR: Alexandra Kardinar
DESIGNERS: Alexandra Kardinar, Volker
Schlecht
AUTHORS: Alexandra Kardinar, Volker
Schlecht, Parov Stelar, Cleo Panther
ANIMATORS: Volker Schlecht, additional
animation by Maxim Vassiliev
DIRECTORS: Volker Schlecht, Alexandra
Kardinar
CLIENT: Parov Stelar

LUCINDA SCHREIBER
lucindaschreiber@gmail.com
p 34 SILVER
TITLE: Gotye: What Do You Want
DESIGNER: Lucinda Schreiber
ANIMATORS: Lucinda Schreiber, Ed Jackson
DIRECTOR: Lucinda Schreiber
PRODUCTION COMPANY: Photoplay Films
CLIENT: Gotye
MEDIA: Paper animation, stop motion

EUNHYE SEO
eseo01@risd.edu
p 351 TITLE: A Girl and a Cat

SIMON SHAW
dean@watermarkltd.com
p 29 TITLE: Getting Kiwis Reading
ART DIRECTOR: Tony Haigh
AD AGENCY: Clemenger BBDO
CLIENT: Clemenger BBDO

NATALIE WAKSMAN SHENKER
natilw@yahoo.com
p 307 TITLE: Good Night Monster
DESIGNER: Kobi Franco
AUTHOR: Shira Geffen
EDITOR: Dalit Lev
PUBLISHER: Am Oved Publishers

CUN SHI
cun@cunshiart.com
p 401 TITLE: Mr. Nobody
INSTITUTION: School of Visual Arts
INSTRUCTOR: Viktor Koen

STEVE SIMPSON
mail@stevesimpson.com
p 30 BRONZE
TITLE: Fade Street Social Tapas Menu
Cover

INDEX

DESIGN DIRECTOR: Gary Gleeson
DESIGN FIRM: Neworld Associates
CLIENT: Fade Street Social

p 72 TITLE: Becoming a Sucessful Illustrator
SENIOR EDITOR: Leafy Cummins
AUTHORS: Derek Brazell, Jo Davies
PUBLISHER: Bloomsbury Publishing

p 217 TITLE: When I Die...
GALLERY: Damn Fine Dublin

LASSE SKARBOVIK
lasse@stockholmillustration.com

p 30 TITLE: Upbeat
DESIGN DIRECTOR: Simon Packer
ART DIRECTOR: Simon Packer
DESIGNER: Lasse Skarbovik
DESIGN FIRM: Fold7
CLIENT: Upbeat
MEDIA: Digital

p 60 TITLE: Block Wall
DESIGN DIRECTOR: Lasse Skarbovik
ART DIRECTOR: Asa Walton
DESIGNER: Lasse Skarbovik
DESIGN FIRM: Skarbovik Production
CLIENT: Block116
DIMENSIONS: 29.5" × 14.75"

p 246 TITLE: Together
DESIGN DIRECTOR: Britt-Marie Henriksson
DESIGNER: Lasse Skarbovik
CLIENT: Viskaform
DIMENSIONS: 150" wide

p 247 TITLE: Multicultural
DESIGN DIRECTOR: Britt-Marie Henriksson
DESIGNER: Lasse Skarbovik
PUBLISHER: Viskaform
CLIENT: Viskaform
DIMENSIONS: 40" × 30"

ALENA SKARINA
alenaskarina@gmail.com

p 254 TITLE: Treats
MEDIA: Gouache on paper
DIMENSIONS: 9" × 12"

MARK SMITH
marksmith71uk@gmail.com

p 76 TITLE: When the Non-Compete Is Incomplete
DESIGN DIRECTOR: Monica Bussolati
CLIENT: ACC Docket
MEDIA: Mixed, digital

p 80 TITLE: Johns Hopkins Renovated Privy
ART DIRECTOR: Pamela Li
CLIENT: Johns Hopkins Magazine
MEDIA: Mixed, digital

p 110 TITLE: The Financial Bailout
DESIGN DIRECTOR: Charles Hively
DESIGN FIRM: HivelyDesigns
CLIENT: 3x3, The Magazine of Contemporary Illustration
MEDIA: Mixed/digital

p 114 TITLE: The Way We Used To Live
ART DIRECTOR: Pamela Li
CLIENT: Johns Hopkins Magazine
MEDIA: Mixed, digital

p 127 TITLE: When Helping Goes Bad
ART DIRECTOR: Simone Tieber
DESIGN FIRM: Studio630
CLIENT: Binghamton University
MEDIA: Mixed, digital

p 165 ART DIRECTOR: Meaghan Fitzpatrick
CLIENT: ESPN Magazine
MEDIA: Mixed, digital

p 241 TITLE: The True Power of the Auto-

Workers Union Voice
MEDIA: Mixed, digital

CATARINA SOBRAL
catarina@catarinasobral.com

p 216 TITLE: Tradballs
ART DIRECTOR: Paulo Oliveira
DESIGNER: Paulo Oliveira
DESIGN FIRM: Mine This Is
CLIENT: Tradballs
DIMENSIONS: 11.7" × 16.5"

DORON SOHARI
dsohari@gmail.com

p 296 BEST OF SHOW
TITLE: Watermelon

JAMES STEINBERG
jamessteinberg115@comcast.net

p 280 TITLE: Escapist
MEDIA: Acrylic and digital
DIMENSIONS: 8.5" × 11"

p 282 TITLE: Personals

OTTO STEININGER
ottosteininger@gmail.com

p 261 TITLE: Food Choices at the End of the 21st Century
MEDIA: Digital

p 263 TITLE: The Organ Thief
MEDIA: Digital

ULRIKE STEINKE
u_steinke@web.de

p 50 TITLE: Der Zauberlehrling
PUBLISHER: Mario Früh/Buechergilde Gutenberg
PRODUCTION COMPANY: Koesel, Altusried-Krugzell 2012
DIMENSIONS: 3.75" × 4.9"

MEGHANN STEPHENSON
mfstephenson@yahoo.com

p 415 TITLE: Wet and Dry
MEDIA: Gouache and water-color
INSTITUTION: Parsons the New School for Design
INSTRUCTOR: Sergio Ruzzier

STUDIO TIPI
studio@studiotipi.com

p 67 TITLE: Anorak Animals Issue: Cover
CLIENT: Anorak
MEDIA: Digital
DIMENSIONS: 8.66" × 10.23"

p 181 TITLE: Ten Sikh Gurus
CLIENT: Hastings Illagen Design
MEDIA: Digital, silkscreened on Conventry Rag paper, 290gsm, Vellum Finish
DIMENSIONS: 8" × 16"

p 207 TITLE: Secret Jungle
CLIENT: Lagom Design
MEDIA: Digital
DIMENSIONS: 4.72" × 6.69"

p 209 TITLE: Animals Paris
CLIENT: Lagom Design
MEDIA: Digital
DIMENSIONS: 4.72" × 6.69"

p 357 TITLE: The Space Letter Courier
ART DIRECTOR: Sarah Beckhoff
AUTHOR: Bernhard Wunderlich
CLIENT: Nido Magazine

JANET SUNG
janetsung.art@gmail.com

p 413 TITLE: City Murder
MEDIA: Digital
INSTITUTION: Parsons the New School for

Design
INSTRUCTOR: Guy Billout

STEVEN TABBUTT
stovetabbutt@nyc.rr.com

p 202 TITLE: Kingdom
GALLERY: Yukiko Kawase Gallery
MEDIA: Acrylic and pencil on paper
DIMENSIONS: 12.5" × 19"

AYUMI TAKAHASHI
tayumi102@gmail.com

p 378 TITLE: Wonderland
INSTITUTION: Art Center College of Design
INSTRUCTOR: Adam Ross

p 381 INSTITUTION: Art Center College of Design
INSTRUCTORS: Ann Field, Christine Nasser

p 424 TITLE: Memories
INSTITUTION: Art Center College of Design
INSTRUCTOR: Jeffery Smith

RYO TAKEMASA
ryo-t@parkcity.ne.jp

p 279 TITLE: Everyday Life
DIMENSIONS: 16.5" × 11.7"

YOKO TANAKA
yoko@yokotanaka.com

p 343 TITLE: Before Fukushima
CLIENT: Tiny Pencil

BENOIT TARDIF
illustration@colagene.com

p 62 TITLE: Toutes mes solitudes
ART DIRECTOR: Benoit Tardif
AUTHOR: M-C Lemieux-Couture
PUBLISHER: Les éditions de ta Mère
DIMENSIONS: 5" × 7.75"

p 127 TITLE: The Inconvenience of Being Parisien
ART DIRECTOR: Philippe Lamarre
DESIGN FIRM: Toxa
AUTHOR: Aleksi K. Lepage
CLIENT: Urbania

p 255 TITLE: Tailgate Party
MEDIA: Silkscreen
DIMENSIONS: 12" × 16"

MICHAEL TAYLOR
mt@michaeltaylor.co.za

p 183 TITLE: Amateurs
PRODUCTION COMPANY: L'MAD Collection
MEDIA: Gouache
DIMENSIONS: 20.6" × 21.2"

SÉBASTIEN THIBAULT
sebastienthibaultillustrations@gmail.com

p 130 TITLE: Social Networks
ART DIRECTOR: Marco Verdi
CLIENT: Rolling Stone Italy

p 143 TITLE: Common Fights
ART DIRECTOR: Philippe Lamarre
CLIENT: Urbania

p 259 TITLE: Identity Theft

PAPEE THIRAWAT
papeethirawat@gmail.com

p 223 DISTINGUISHED MERIT
TITLE: Answer Man Poster
ART DIRECTOR: Sam Pitino
DESIGNER: Papee Thirawat
CLIENT: Answer Man
DIMENSIONS: 16" × 20"

FRANÇOIS THISDALE
info@thisdale.com

p 346 TITLE: Mister Rodrigues
AUTHOR: François Thisdale

INDEX

JACOB THOMAS
jthomasillustration@gmail.com
p 123 TITLE: Doping In Sports
ART DIRECTOR: Erich Nagler
CLIENT: The New York Times
MEDIA: Ink, digital

DAN BOB THOMPSON
danbobthompson@gmail.com
p 251 TITLE: Monsters
MEDIA: Mixed media

MICHELLE THOMPSON
info@agoodson.com
p 142 TITLE: Gender
ART DIRECTOR: Simon Kaer
PUBLISHER: Infosoft AS
CLIENT: Plot Magazine
DIMENSIONS: 5.5″ × 3.14″

NIV TISHBI
nivtishbi@gmail.com
p 333 TITLE: The Princess Will Come at 4 o'Clock
AUTHOR: Wolfdietrich Schnurre
p 417 DISTINGUISHED MERIT
INSTITUTION: Universität der Künste Berlin

CAROLINE TOMLINSON
info@carolinetomlinson.com
p 32 TITLE: Love at First Sephora
DESIGN DIRECTOR: Loanne Lam
ART DIRECTOR: Tyler Smart
CLIENT: Sephora

CARLA TORRES
carlisima@carlatorres.com
p 247 BRONZE
TITLE: Kitchen Towels

NGUYEN TRAN
nguyen@leftstudio.com
p 414 TITLE: Type and Image
INSTITUTION: Savannah College of Art and Design
INSTRUCTOR: Allan Drummond

HOUSTON TRUEBLOOD
houston@houstontrueblood.com
p 52 ART DIRECTOR: Adam Johnson
PUBLISHER: HarperCollins Publishers
IMPRINT: William Morrow Paperbacks
MEDIA: Digital
DIMENSIONS: 3.25″ × 2.625″

POL TURGEON
pol@polturgeon.com
p 204 TITLE: Terminus
ART DIRECTOR: Charmaine Leblanc
CLIENT: Danse-Cité/Red Rabbit
GALLERY: Atelier Jean-Brillant
MEDIA: Mixed media
p 213 TITLE: Frontenac Noir
ART DIRECTOR: André Cellard
DESIGNER: Pol Turgeon
CLIENT: Domaine des Météores
MEDIA: Mixed media

EMMA VAKARÉLOVA
besvo6@yahoo.com
p 303 TITLE: Autumn for Beginners

ALICIA VARELA
alicia@aliciavarela.es
p 313 TITLE: El arenque rojo (The Red Herring)
DESIGN DIRECTOR: Elsa Aguiar
DESIGNER: Lara Peces

AUTHOR: Gonzalo Moure
PUBLISHER: Ediciones SM

JOÃO VAZ DE CARVALHO
jvazcarvalho@sapo.pt
p 306 TITLE: A Casa do João
DESIGN DIRECTOR: Anabela Dias
AUTHOR: João Manuel Ribeiro
EDITOR: João Manuel Ribeiro
PUBLISHER: Trinta por uma linha
p 323 TITLE: Era uma vez um cao
DESIGN DIRECTOR: Marta Madureira
AUTHOR: Carvalho
EDITOR: Carvalho
PUBLISHER: Tcharan

ESTRELLA VEGA
ashram12@yahoo.com
p 355 TITLE: The Ordovician and the Silurian

GARY VENN
gvenn.illustration@gmail.com
p 145 TITLE: Menorca Map
ART DIRECTOR: Suzanne Pronk
CLIENT: Jamie Oliver Magazine (NL)
MEDIA: Mixed media
DIMENSIONS: 7.16″ × 6.85″

KLAAS VERPLANCKE
mail@klaas.be
p 311 BRONZE
TITLE: Applesauce
ART DIRECTOR: Klaas Verplancke
DESIGNER: Kris Demey
AUTHOR: Klaas Verplancke
PUBLISHER: De Eenhoorn (B)/ Groundwood (CA)

CONSTANZE VON KITZING
info@constanzevonkitzing.de
p 353 TITLE: Map of Cologne
CLIENT: Art School for Kids Cologne

CYNDI WALDRON
waldron.cyndi@gmail.com
p 407 TITLE: Hot
INSTITUTION: Utah Valley University
INSTRUCTOR: Richard Hull

FRANZISKA WALTHER
franz@franzandfriends.com
p 51 TITLE: Der Zeitsparer. Grotesken von Ignaz Wrobel
ART DIRECTOR: Franziska Walther
DESIGN FIRM: Franziska Walther, Sehen ist Gold
PUBLISHER: Kunstanstifter Verlag, Mannheim, Germany
DIMENSIONS: 4.75″ × 7.5″

HOLMAN WANG
wang.holman@gmail.com
p 319 DISTINGUISHED MERIT
TITLE: Cozy Classics Jane Austen's Pride and Prejudice
ART DIRECTOR: Dimiter Savoff
DESIGNER: Sara Gillingham
AUTHOR: Jack and Holman Wang
PUBLISHER: Simply Read Books

JACK WANG
jackwang107@gmail.com
p 319 DISTINGUISHED MERIT
TITLE: Cozy Classics Jane Austen's Pride and Prejudice
ART DIRECTOR: Dimiter Savoff
DESIGNER: Sara Gillingham
AUTHORS: Jack and Holman Wang
PUBLISHER: Simply Read Books

MICHAEL WARAKSA
michaelwaraksa@att.net
p 275 TITLE: New Aluminium Thursday
MEDIA: Collage, digital
p 281 TITLE: Good Afternoon
MEDIA: Collage, digital

SAM WASHBURN
mail@washburnillustration.com
p 275 TITLE: Locked In
MEDIA: Mixed media, digital
DIMENSIONS: 10″ × 8.8″

TIM WEIFFENBACH
tim@illustration-tw.com
p 139 TITLE: Eurocrisis
ART DIRECTOR: Eva Dahme, Bjorn Meier
PUBLISHER: FOCUS Magazine Verlag Gmbh
MEDIA: Digital
DIMENSIONS: 6.7″ × 10″

ALICE WELLINGER
alice.wellinger@vol.at
p 187 TITLE: Tattoed Woman
MEDIA: Acrylic on board
p 203 TITLE: Torso
MEDIA: Acrylic on board

BECK WHEELER
dean@watermarkltd.com
p 210 DISTINGUISHED MERIT
TITLE: Karma Cola
DESIGN DIRECTOR: Heath Lowe
DESIGNER: Emma Kaniuk
AD AGENCY: Special Group
CLIENT: All Good Organics

LEE WHITE
l.white@leewhiteillustration.com
p 230 TITLE: Country Christmas
MEDIA: Watercolor, digital

KATRIN WIEHLE
post@katrinwiehle.de
p 318 TITLE: Mein Kleiner Wald
PUBLISHER: Beltz and Gelberg

CARL WIENS
wiens@kos.net
p 94 TITLE: Temporal Shift
ART DIRECTOR: Liette Savard
CLIENT: Readers Digest Canada
p 142 TITLE: Schools and Gun Violence
ART DIRECTOR: Nicole Roegner
CLIENT: Phoenix Magazine

LIZ WIKSTROM
lizwikstrom@gmail.com
p 393 TITLE: Viterbo, Italy Sketchbook
INSTITUTION: Rhode Island School of Design
INSTRUCTORS: Fed Lynch, Kelly Murphy

MIKE WIMMER
mike@mikewimmer.com
p 304 TITLE: George: George Washington, Our Founding Father
ART DIRECTOR: Chloe Foglia
AUTHOR: Frank Keating
EDITOR: Paula Wiseman
PUBLISHER: Simon & Schuster
IMPRINT: Paula Wiseman Books

ANDREW R. WRIGHT
andrew@andrewrwright.com
p 99 TITLE: Dragons of Komodo
ART DIRECTOR: Cindy Tiberi
CLIENT: Alfred Hitchcock Mystery

Magazine
MEDIA: Linoleum block print on Stonehenge Kraft Paper
DIMENSIONS: 9.75" × 10.5"

p 168 TITLE: Gratitude
ART DIRECTOR: Sean Johnston
CLIENT: Field & Stream
MEDIA: Linoleum block print on Rives BFK
DIMENSIONS: 10.5" × 13.5"

p 170 TITLE: Hunter/Gatherer
ART DIRECTOR: Michael Kiser
CLIENT: Good Beer Hunting
MEDIA: Linoleum block print on Stonehenge Kraft Paper
DIMENSIONS: 18" × 24"

p 233 TITLE: Luumbal
MEDIA: Linoleum block print on Stonehenge Kraft Paper
DIMENSIONS: 14" × 14"

STEPHANIE WUNDERLICH
info@wunderlich-illustration.de

p 46 TITLE: Reineke Fuchs
ART DIRECTOR: Stephanie Wunderlich
DESIGNER: Stephanie Wunderlich
AUTHOR: Johann Wolfgang von Goethe
PUBLISHER: Spring Magazine
CLIENT: Spring Magazine
MEDIA: Papercut
DIMENSIONS: 7.8" × 9.4"

JAMES YANG
james@jamesyang.com

p 107 TITLE: Acceptance of Transgender People
ART DIRECTOR: Tim Luddy
CLIENT: Mother Jones Magazine
MEDIA: Digital
DIMENSIONS: 8" × 8"

p 211 TITLE: Lamp Series
DESIGN DIRECTOR: Al Quattrochi
DESIGNER: Lamp in a Box Inc
DESIGN FIRM: Tornado Design
MEDIA: Digital
DIMENSIONS: 10" × 20"

CHIA-CHI YU
mongrosbebe@gmail.com

p 362 TITLE: Knock the Whale Out
DESIGN FIRM: Our Studio
AUTHOR: Guan-Han Bao
PUBLISHER: Chiuko Publishing

JI HYUN YU
hellohowdyhiya@gmail.com

p 394 INSTITUTION: University of Applied Sciences Mainz, Germany
INSTRUCTOR: Monika Aichele

p 413 INSTITUTION: University of Applied Sciences Mainz, Germany
INSTRUCTOR: Monika Aichele

YEJI YUN
seeouterspace@gmail.com

p 227 DESIGN DIRECTOR: Beck Jean
DESIGNER: Beck Jean
DESIGN FIRM: Log
CLIENT: Jarasum Internation Jazz Festival

PAMELA ZAGARENSKI
pamelaz@sacredbee.com

p 322 TITLE: Sleep Like a Tiger
ART DIRECTOR: Sheila Smallwood
AUTHOR: Mary Logue
EDITOR: Ann Rider
PUBLISHER: Houghton Mifflin Harcourt

NATALYA ZAHN
natalya@natalya.com

p 246 TITLE: NOTpuppy Pattern
DESIGNER: Natalya Zahn
SCREEN PRINTER: James Weinberg
MEDIA: Ink
DIMENSIONS: 16" × 24"

MICHAEL ZAVACKY
mzavacky@mcmillanagency.com

p 222 TITLE: You Can't Unsee This Stuff
ART DIRECTOR: Ian Driscoll
DESIGNER: Jared Barter
AD AGENCY: McMillan
CLIENT: OIAF
DIMENSIONS: 12" × 18"

PAWEL ZAWISLAK
dean@watermarkltd.com

p 243 TITLE: Father Christmas
MEDIA: Pencil, digital

ANDREW ZBIHLYJ
andrew@pieceofshow.com

p 163 TITLE: Sharon
DESIGN DIRECTOR: André Mora
ART DIRECTOR: Chris Skiles
CLIENT: Seattle Met

DANIEL ZENDER
daniel@danielzender.com

p 95 TITLE: Rise of the Rats
ART DIRECTOR: Ashford Stamper
CLIENT: The Pitch

p 143 TITLE: Death Penalty
ART DIRECTOR: Wes Bausmith
CLIENT: LA Times
MEDIA: Acrylic

AI ZHANG
azhang20@student.scad.edu

p 418 INSTITUTION: Savannah College of Art & Design, Atlanta
INSTRUCTOR: Rick Lovell

JING ZHANG
jing@mazakii.com

p 166 TITLE: Cities
ART DIRECTOR: Shenghua Chen
PUBLISHER: CNT Media
CLIENT: China National Travel Magazine
DIMENSIONS: 10" × 5.6"

DEBRA ZISS
missziss@gmail.com

p 330 TITLE: Dogs A-Z

ULRIKE ZÖLLNER
hallo@illulrike.com

p 398 DISTINGUISHED MERIT
TITLE: Etchingstories
INSTITUTION: University of Art Berlin

MARIO ZUCCA
mario@mariozucca.com

p 286 TITLE: Dad and His Ford Taunus, 1969
MEDIA: Pen and ink, digital

p 290 TITLE: Old Family Photos
MEDIA: Pen and ink

PEDRO ZYLBERSZTAJN
pedrozylber@gmail.com

p 393 TITLE: Florestão II/Lenha (Woodsman II/ Lumber)
INSTITUTION: PUC-Rio
INSTRUCTOR: Thereza Miranda

LEGEND
Page numbers in *gold* *denote Best of Show, Gold, Silver, Bronze, or Distinguished Merit awards.*

PUBLISHER'S NOTE
Every effort has been made to ensure that the credits and contact information comply with the informamtion provided us. 3x3 is not responsible for missing information or credits.
We apologize for any omissions or spelling errors that may have been carried through from the original submission of materials.

COLOPHON

© Copyright 2013, 2014 Artisanal Media LLC

The 3x3 Illustration Annual is designed by HivelyDesigns 631 Vanderbilt Street Second Floor Brooklyn New York 11218.

The 3x3 Illustration Annual is published by Artisanal Media LLC

Artisanal Media is the parent company of 3x3 and publishes 3x3's magazine, books and directory.

EDITOR
Charles Hively

DESIGN DIRECTOR
Charles Hively

SENIOR DESIGNER
Sarah Munt

SHOW COORDINATOR
Katrina Kopeloff

COVER ILLUSTRATION
René Milot

HONOREE
Geoffrey Grandfield Illustrator : Educator of the Year

SPECIAL THANKS
To our judges who took time out of their day to judge over 2,800 entries. All judging was done digitally and independently. Judges had two weeks to complete the judging process. They did not know the name of the entrant as judging was done by image number. Results were tabulated automatically when voting was complete. There was no quota established for this show, nor any limits on how many pieces an entrant was allowed in the annual.

This is our tenth juried annual; if you're interested in our previous annuals they are available in our online shop at shop.3x3mag.com.

If you're interested in submitting work for our next competition please join our mailing list at 3x3mag.com/about/mailinglist.

ISBN 9780982634622

Printed in Canada by The Prolific Group

The text faces are Calluna, designed by Jos Buivenga, 2009 and Berthold Akzidenz Grotesque, designed by Hermann Berthold, 1898.

The book was printed four-color process on Anthem Plus Matte Text and Cover made by NewPage, USA.